ANTI-SOCIAL BEHAVIOUR
AND DISORDER:
POWERS AND REMEDIES

SECOND EDITION

AUSTRALIA
Law Book Co.
Sydney

CANADA AND USA
Carswell
Toronto

HONG KONG
Sweet & Maxwell Asia

NEW ZEALAND
Brookers
Wellington

SINGAPORE AND MALAYSIA
Sweet & Maxwell Asia
Singapore and Kuala Lumpur

ANTI-SOCIAL BEHAVIOUR AND DISORDER: POWERS AND REMEDIES

SECOND EDITION

By

Scott Collins B.A., LL.B., LL.D.

and

Rebecca Cattermole B.A., Dip Law.

London
Sweet & Maxwell
2006

First Edition 2004
Second Edition 2006

Published in 2006 by
Sweet & Maxwell Limited of
100 Avenue Road, London NW3 3PF

Typeset by Servis Filmsetting Ltd, Manchester
Printed by Athenaeum Press Ltd, Gateshead, Tyne & Wear

No natural forests were destroyed to make this product:
only farmed timber was used and re-planted.

A CIP catalogue record for this book is available
from the British Library.

ISBN 0–421–95000–5
978–0–421–95000–9

DEDICATION

This book is dedicated by the authors to their families.

CONTENTS

3 SOCIAL EXCLUSION—LOCAL AUTHORITIES, EDUCATION AND CHILDREN, MENTAL HEALTH

4 ENVIRONMENTAL CONTROLS AND ANTI-SOCIAL BEHAVIOUR AND DISORDER

5   HOUSING MANAGEMENT

6 ANTI-SOCIAL BEHAVIOUR ORDERS

APPENDICES *Page*

TABLE OF CASES

TABLE OF STATUTES

TABLE OF STATUTORY INSTRUMENTS

TABLE OF EUROPEAN CONVENTIONS

CHAPTER ONE
Introduction

The use of open space in the United Kingdom has undergone major changes **1-001** in the past few years. It has become more politicised in an effort to make it more sanitised. Today, a person taking a walk in any urban area in the United Kingdom will be unwittingly observed by numerous private and public closed-circuit television cameras; pass through various invisible boundaries demarcating special zones; even though she might think she is on public land, depending on whether she is a child or a person whom the authorities believe belongs to a relevant category of person, might be moved on or even arrested; that task may well be carried out by a part-time community police officer or even a private security guard with a panoply of delegated powers of a constable; and depending on what she does on her walk and where she goes, information about what she does may well be shared amongst numerous local and national public and private agencies. In this book, we consider the law relating to anti-social behaviour and disorder in England and Wales. In our first edition, we observed that there was a new, emerging body of law, anti-social behaviour law, which is relatively unique to the United Kingdom. The most obvious example of it remains the anti-social behaviour order (ASBO) but we use the term "anti-social behaviour and disorder" to cover all the pre-existing common law and statutory law about anti-social behaviour and disorder, recent reforms to that law, and the entirely new laws such as the ABOS, all of which have the common aim of regulating conduct in public with the intention of protecting and enhancing communal life. It covers a wide range of areas: from education law (truancy orders, education supervision orders), environmental health (fixed penalties for disorder, graffiti and litter, fly-tipping, tighter controls on licensed premises), public order (fixed penalty notices disorderly behaviour, kerb-crawling, begging, criminal trespass, unlawful assemblies), housing benefit (withholding payments to anti-social applicants), and childrens law (parenting orders, curfew schemes). In this chapter, we attempt to define the term and examine the government's reasons and policies behind the new laws. In an era of falling crime rates and where recent surveys suggest that the public are not particularly preoccupied with anti-social behaviour and disorder, it is important to consider reasons for the recent rapid expansion of the law in this area. We begin by attempting to define the term "anti-social behaviour and disorder".

Defining Anti-Social Behaviour

The first edition of this text was entitled "Anti-social Behaviour: Powers and **1-002** Remedies". We added the word "disorder" to the title for this edition because the terms "disorder" and "anti-social behaviour" are frequently associated with each other in recent legislation and government policy. Even so, they mean slightly different things. The term "anti-social behaviour" first appeared in a legal context in 1942 as a series of lectures by Hermann Mannheim called "Anti-social behaviour: its causes and treatment" in which what might be described today as a "welfarist" solution to the problem of disorder was advocated. In the United States, the terms used by academics tend to be "disorder" and "incivilities"; the term "anti-social behaviour" is not often used there. Burney[1] remarks that the term "disorder" applies collectively to whole communities, while "anti-social behaviour" is something done by individuals who are thereby singled out and blamed for the harm they inflict on communities. "Disorder" also focuses on a standard list of recognisable elements; anti-social behaviour, she writes, has no clear identity but results in the targeting of individuals or groups through pre-determined controls. The closest statutory definition is found in s.1(1) of the Crime and Disorder Act 1998: anti-social behaviour, as a trigger conduct for the making of an ASBO, is behaving in ". . .a manner that caused or was likely to cause harassment, alarm, distress to one or more persons not of the same household as himself." The phrase, "harassment, alarm or distress", also appears in the Public Order Act 1986, an initial indication that the government had in mind low-level crimes and public order offences. This was certainly how the term was normally understood by police officers.[2] See, for example, Bland and Read, in a review of policing strategies concerning anti-social behaviour:[3]

> "It is difficult to define anti-social behaviour. The range of other terms employed to describe the problem highlights this: quality of life issues, minor disorder, incivilities. None of the forces we visited had a formal definition of anti-social behaviour. The officers we spoke to generally took a pragmatic 'common sense' view based in the operational realities they face day-to-day. So, for the police, at a local level, anti-social behaviour is a description of whatever 'minor' problems intrude on the daily life of the community and leads to calls for police service."

However, for the government, the term means more than just minor breaches of the peace and comparatively trivial disturbances to public order.[4] In the first Home Office guidance about the 1998 Act, issued in March 1999, it was said that the term did not refer just to ". . . run of mill disputes between neighbours, petty intolerances or minor one-off acts." On the other hand, according to that guidance, ASBOs should not be overly used to penalise those who are merely different. The guidance then provided examples of anti-social behaviour: violence, threats of violence and other intimidating behaviour directed at neighbours; persistent unruly behaviour by a small group of individuals on an estate; families whose behaviour when challenged leads to abuse, vandalism, and graffiti; persistent abusive behaviour towards the elderly or the disabled; serious and persistent bullying of children in schools; persistent racist or homophobic behaviour; and persistent anti-social behaviour as a result of drugs and alcohol. The general test, it was suggested, was the existence of ". . .a pattern of behaviour which continues for a period of time but cannot be dealt with easily or adequately through the prosecution of those concerned for a single snapshot or criminal event."

1-003   Anti-social behaviour includes criminal behaviour; but not all anti-social behaviour is criminal. It is crucial to note that all of the new government policy

[1] E. Burney *Making People Behave: Anti-social behaviour, Politics and Policy* (Willan Publishing, 2005).
[2] Chorley, 'Hermann Mannheim: A Biographical Appreciation', (1970) *British Journal of Criminology*, 10: 324–48.
[3] *Policing Anti-Social Behaviour*, Police Research Series Paper 123, Home Office (2000).
[4] *Respect and Responsibility—Taking a Stand Against Anti-Social Behaviour*, Home Office, Cm.5778 (2003).

and legislation in this field has emerged at a time of comparative prosperity, lower unemployment, and generally falling crime rates. That the reforms have come at a time of falling crime rates is expressly acknowledged in the Anti-Social Behaviour White Paper which appeared shortly before the Anti-Social Behaviour Act 2003. In that paper, the Home Office was keen to report on the current government"s achievements since taking office in 1997 with regard to crime reduction: burglary had dropped by 39 per cent, vehicle theft by 32 per cent, violent crime by 26 per cent and street crime by 16 per cent; overall crime has fallen in the second half of 2002—robberies fell by 23 per cent, violent crime has levelled off since the falls in the late 1990s, domestic burglary is falling, and vehicle thefts continued to decline with a 17 per cent fall since 2000.[5] Interestingly, in the same quarterly report, it was noted that, despite the overall trend, the majority of the public believe that crime has risen in the last two years. If crime has fallen, especially street crimes, it is interesting to ask why anti-social behaviour laws are so necessary. It is said in the 2003 Anti-Social Behaviour White Paper, that what really matters is not whether or not crime has fallen but what people think about crime. Admitting that the crime rates have fallen, the Home Office nonetheless see a wider role for anti-social behaviour laws:[6]

"But the fear of crime has not fallen to the same extent. And it is fear of crime—rather than actually being a victim—that can so often limit people's lives, making them feel afraid of going out or even afraid in their own homes . . . Whilst the media coverage of disturbing crimes can fuel the fear of crime, the real experience of anti-social behaviour and disorder makes many more even more afraid of crime."

In the 2003 Anti-Social Behaviour White Paper, anti-social behaviour is seen as an urgent national problem which can only be resolved by public bodies marshalling their forces and resources in partnerships: **1-004**

"All of these are issues which concern everyone in the community. They cannot be written off as generational issues—they impact on the quality of life of young and old alike and they require a response which puts partnership into action. Just as the problems of anti-social behaviour are multifarious, the solution too must operate equally effectively on many levels. While an energetic and constructive police response is essential, it must be supplemented by engagement from a wide variety of partners."

Consider also the strident remarks of the Minister for Crime Reduction in the foreword to the guidance:

"Of the problems which most affect neighbourhoods up and down the country, anti-social behaviour—covering as it does a whole complex of thoughtless, inconsiderate or malicious activity—has perhaps the greatest potential to blight the quality of community life. Every week I hear of aggressive or loutish behaviour which can cause something close to despair among people who are forced to put up with it. Anti-social behaviour is never victimless and too often the victims are the elderly, the minorities, the poor and vulnerable. But as a society we can fight back. And you, the practitioners to whom this guidance is primarily addressed, are the people who can lead that fight back."

---

[5] See also the Home Office, Crime in England and Wales, Quarterly Update to December 2002, HOSB 5/03.
[6] *Respect and Responsibility—Taking a Stand Against Anti-Social Behaviour*, Home Office Cm. 5778 (2003) ("White Paper") pp. 13–14.

The 2003 Anti-Social Behaviour White Paper makes the obvious statement that anti-social behaviour means different things to different people:[7]

"The common element in all anti-social behaviour is that it represents a lack of respect or consideration for other people. It shows a selfish inability or unwillingness to recognise when one's individual behaviour is offensive to others and a refusal to take responsibility for it. More fundamentally, it shows a failure to understand that one person's rights are based on the responsibilities we have towards others and towards our families and communities".

As indicated by the White Paper's title, "Respect and Responsibility", anti-social behaviour is conduct which arises when someone acts in a way which does not show respect and responsibility with respect to others:[8]

"We must ensure that the rights we share are matched by the responsibilities we owe to each other. As individuals we are responsible for our own actions and we should not behave in a way that intimidates or harasses others."

Hence, what is now covered by the term is now even wider than low-level street offences: it is any kind of behaviour which in the opinion of the relevant enforcement agency officer unreasonably offends or is likely to offend members of the community. It is more than just preventing breaches of public order; the aim is to compel irresponsible people to become responsible in the interests of the community at large.

1-005 The same theme of encouraging or enforcing respect and responsibility for the benefit of the community is also expressed in the Home Office Anti-Social Behaviour Action Plan, "Together", published in October 2003, while the Anti-Social Behaviour Act 2003 was still in committee. The Home Secretary said:

"Our approach is based on a fundamental understanding that the rights we exercise as individuals are based on responsibility towards our families and to the community. It is the foundation of a truly civil society that we respect the public spaces we share, the property of our neighbours, and the right of people in our communities to live free from fear and harassment."

Decrying what the Home Secretary in a speech at a conference on anti-social behaviour held at around the same time as the alternative "namby-pamby 60s understanding", the government's approach, he said in the "Together" document is ". . .to put the community first, by shifting the balance from the minority that spread fear and distress to the majority that want to win back their communities for themselves and for their children." The fundamental aim is not to reduce crime and disorder (which is falling anyway) but ". . .to support civic renewal; to strengthen communities, revitalise our democracy and provide opportunity and security for all." Therefore, anti-social behaviour is any activity which is "irresponsible" or "disrespectful" to the community which has the effect of undermining a community's morale, or to undermine a community's integrity. The Home Secretary, speaking in a Standing Committee debate on the Crime and Disorder bill in 1998, said that the "essence" of what the government was attempting in introducing ASBOs was to provide ". . .protection in circumstances where it is not possible to get a

---

[7] White Paper, p.17.
[8] *ibid.*, p.18.

conviction on the basis of the criminal standard of proof."[9] In effect, remarks like that meant, according to some writers, the use of the judicial system and the civil law as an instrument of social control, to enhance it so as to compel "irresponsible" members of the community to act responsibly, regardless of the criminality, if any, of their conduct and the causes of it, so as to promote the integrity of the community.[10]

As Millie and others point out, the lack of conceptual clarity in the defin-   **1-006**
ition of anti-social behaviour and disorder is more than just an academic indulgence.[11] Some anti-social behaviour remedies such as the ASBO are powerful curbs on the freedoms on whom they are imposed so it is important to be clear about the limits to the use of such powers. Secondly, tackling anti-social behaviour and disorder requires strategic thinking and partnerships and that means that the relevant agencies must be clear about the problems they are addressing and the aims they are seeking to achieve. In evidence before the House of Commons Home Affairs Committee on Anti-Social Behaviour, several organisations have criticised the breadth of the definitions. There were four main issues, centering around effectiveness, performance management, jurisprudence and consistency. First, the breadth of the definitions is seen as hindering an effective policy response. See the Crime and Society Foundation:

"If the objective is to impact on activities legitimately concerning the public, it is important to be able to disaggregate different types of behaviours and to specify and measure what is of concern in order to design and evaluate effective policy responses. It is the Foundation's contention that current anti-social behaviour legislation and policy makes difficult such an approach. Problems of definition lead to problems of solution. In the view of the Foundation the combination of a definition based on subjective criteria and an attempt to encompass a wide range of behaviours under one term leads to inappropriate, expensive and sometimes draconian policy responses."

Shelter also argued that "it was imperative that responses draw distinctions between different types of behaviour and recognise the causes of that behaviour. Measures can then be taken which are not only proportionate, but also effective in tackling it." Secondly, it was argued that the wide definition hindered performance management. Hull City Council argued that "a lack of clarity around the definition and measurement of anti-social behaviour does not help" with effective performance management arrangements, and Salford City Council also highlighted this area as problematic. The Home Office acknowledged this problem of measurement; however, it argued that the benefits of the wide definition were more important. Thirdly, several organisations have focused on the jurisprudential or human rights implications of using a broad legal definition. For instance, the Law Society argued that without "a clear standard for enforcers, policy-makers and the public to measure behaviour against . . . it will become increasingly difficult to justify legally any further interference with human rights". Liberty suggested that "in a democracy, if prohibitions and punitive sanctions are to be employed, a greater degree of clarity is required". According to Justice, "the very wide definition of what can constitute anti-social behaviour is of great concern because perfectly lawful activities can become criminalised through the use of an ASBO". In addition, several organisations criticised the fact that the definition of anti-social behaviour was wide enough to include

---

[9] Minister of State for the Home Office, April 30, 1998.
[10] Cracknell, "Anti-Social Behaviour Orders" (2000) 22(1) *J. Soc. Wel. & Fam. L.* at pp.108–115.
[11–12] Millie, Jacobson, McDonald and Hough, *Anti-Social Behaviour Strategies: Finding a Balance* (Joseph Rowntree Foundation, 2005).

behaviour that is already a criminal offence, arguing that this could lead to a twin-track approach by which criminal offences were effectively prosecuted according to a civil standard of proof, albeit that the standard of proof in ASBO cases is actually indistinguishable from the criminal standard. Fourthly, it was been argued that the wide definition of anti-social behaviour has led to inconsistency, with the potential for discrimination and for the unjustified targeting of particular groups. The Children's Society argued that "many children and young people are telling us that they do not understand the term, but they feel that it is targeted towards them". It pointed to research indicating that young persons between 9 and 13 were unsure as to what behaviour they should avoid in order to escape having measures used against them. Several organisations have, more specifically, objected to the term "anti-social" being applied to children who are "merely hanging about in the street". Crisis objected to the equating of begging as anti-social, arguing that "although the act of begging may be deemed anti-social, it is a problem that is best understood and dealt with as a manifestation of social exclusion".

1-007   On the other hand, several councils such as Manchester City Council, preferred a loose definition of the term:

> "I think the definition to secure an anti-social behaviour order, which is that someone has to be acting in a manner "likely to cause harassment, alarm or distress", will go before the magistrates who are familiar with that term from public order offences that come before them every day, and the "conduct capable of causing nuisance or annoyance" to get an injunction in the county court, where there is a lesser burden of proof, is one that county court judges are very familiar with. I think that umbrella, as I have said, covers everything. I do not think there is an incompatibility."

However, it is unlikely that a magistrate, in Manchester or elsewhere, would convict a child suffering from Tourettes syndrome for swearing or an autistic child for "staring over the fence" for a public order act offence; yet, as we discuss below, such children have been made subject to ASBOs, indicating that there may be more complex legal problems associated with ASBOs.[13] It was also said to be flexible as the definition was something that had to be worked out at the local level. The House of Commons Home Affairs Committee on Anti-Social Behaviour concluded that the definition was perfectly clear and worked well. However, in the committee's view, anti-social behaviour is something that must be defined in detail at the local level. Crime and Disorder Partnerships, under s. 6 of the Crime and Disorder Act 1998, have a duty to formulate and implement a strategy for reducing crime and disorder in their area every three years.[14] Before doing so, they must carry out and audit, and it was said that it was this process that produced a local definition of the problems of anti-social behaviour:

> "Every area has a natural ecology of crime and anti-social behaviour which means that what disturbs people, what they tolerate and what they complain about differs from one neighbourhood to another."[15]

1-008   We adopt the definition offered by Millie and others.[16] It is behaviour which causes harassment, alarm and distress to individuals not of the same

---

[13] See para.1-060 and para.6-159.
[14] See para.1.24 and para.3.46.
[15] Chair of the Youth Justice Board, evidence before House of Commons Home Affairs Committee Anti-Social Behaviour 2004/05.
[16-17] See also paras 6-006, 6-007.

household, such that it requires interventions from the relevant authorities; but criminal prosecution and punishment may be inappropriate because the individual components of the behaviour are not prohibited by the criminal law or, in isolation, constitute relatively minor offences.

The History of Anti-Social Behaviour and Disorder

Although many of the legal mechanisms designed to deal with anti-social behaviour and disorder are new, that does not mean that anti-social behaviour and disorder is a new social phenomenon, requiring these new solutions. Rather, it seems to be the case that anti-social behaviour has always been a social problem and what varies over the time is the extent to which it occupies public debate. Burney[18] begins her history of the control of anti-social behaviour and disorder with the common law breach of the peace. The justices' power to keep the King's peace emerged during the unsettled fourteenth century and was primarily directed at whole communities, but it had become a power directed at individuals during the Elizabethan period. During the sixteenth century people who disturbed the peace were "scolds" (and, more often than not, women) and usually before ecclesiastical courts since punishment involved the impugning of the moral character of the accused. The conduct that amounted to a breach of the peace included keeping a bawdy house, bad language, rowdy drunken behaviour, and defamatory remarks. Parish constables could enforce rules of good behaviour but private individuals had to instigate legal proceedings to deal with breaches of it. These were predominantly rural communities where strangers were obvious and not necessarily welcome so they attracted particular attention. The vagrant emerged during the sixteenth century as the archetype criminal and instrument of disorder. Hence, the introduction of Poor Laws, where they would be sent back to their parish of origin. By the eighteenth and nineteenth centuries (where the problem of vagrancy arose again owing to major socio-economic changes—hence the Vagrancy Act 1823 and the Town Clauses Act 1847), disorderly behaviour had became a moral problem. Numerous societies for the reformation of manners had emerged in which citizens were encouraged to monitor drunkenness, rowdy behaviour and poor Sunday observance. Burney and others argue that these efforts were overwhelmed by the scale of the problem caused by increasing urbanisation of the industrial revolution. Peel's police force was established in 1829 where the preservation of "public tranquillity" was given a greater importance than the detection of criminals. Vagrants, the homeless, prostitutes and drunks were subject to police attention throughout the nineteenth century in waves, attributable to economic conditions as well as the complaints or rate-payers associations and anti-vice societies. Rescuing "fallen women" was a particularly middle-class preoccupation in the Victorian era. Numbers of arrests of women for prostitution fell sharply in 1880, largely owing to a change in police arrest practices; similarly, drunkenness accounted for around one-third of arrests in London but fell away following the introduction of licensing laws. There were also fears during the Victorian era, similar to those of today, of bad behaviour of children and young people. Civilising the urban working-class became a priority for Victorian social entrepreneurs through missions and charities, parks and libraries. Byelaws were a common way of controlling behaviour in public places. Pearson considers the way in which the "street-corner" youth was transformed in the popular Victorian mind into "hooligans".[19] Working class youth were divided into "roughs" and "respectables" and the latter were more likely to become involved in the clubs

1-009

---

[18] E. Burney, *Making People Behave: Anti-social behaviour, Politics and Policy*.
[19] G. Pearson, *Hooligan: A History of Respectable Fears* (MacMillan, 1983).

and sporting societies of the late nineteenth century. Better housing and slum clearance in the early twentieth century was partly intended to reduce crime: Burney[20] remarks that the municipal housing drive of the 1920s and 1930s was aimed to set a standard of decency, in support of which disreputable families were excluded: she concludes that from the mid-nineteenth century statutory nuisance controls proliferated with concerns about health and environmental matters. Public order law, developed over time since the Middle Ages, was based on the idea that public conduct must not be so provocative as to arouse an angry reaction. It was not until 1986, in recognition that bystanders might be upset or frightened but not provoked to violence, that the test for low-level public order offences became that of causing "harassment, alarm and distress."

1-010   Accordingly, anti-social behaviour and disorder is not new. What is interesting about the history of the control of it is the cyclical or periodic way in which it appears a public preoccupation. Consider, for example, Cohen's analysis of the "moral panic" in reaction to working-class youth movements of the late twentieth century. A condition, episode, person or group of persons, he writes, emerges to become defined as a threat to social values and interests and its nature is presented in a stylised and stereotypical fashion by the mass media; the moral barricades, he says, are manned by editors, bishops, politicians and other right-thinking people; socially accredited experts pronounce their diagnoses and solutions; ways of coping are evolved or more often resorted to, the condition then disappears, submerges or deteriorates and becomes more visible:

> "Sometimes the panic is quite novel and at other times it is something that which has been in existence long enough but suddenly appears in the limelight. Sometimes the panic passes over and is forgotten, except in folklore and collective memory; at other times it has more serious and long-lasting repercussions and might produce such changes as those in legal and social policy or even in the way society conceives itself."[21]

A successful moral panic requires a suitable enemy, a soft target with little power, easily denounced; and a suitable victim, someone with whom the public can identify. A recent example offered by Cohen is the reaction to the terrible tragedy of James Bulger in which two ten year old boys led a two year old boy away from a shopping centre to a railway line and then battered him to death. The actual number of children who kill, he notes, is minute and has never increased. It was precisely the horror and rarity of the event and its content that made it compelling enough to be a potent symbol for everything that had gone wrong in the United Kingdom at the time: a new breed of violent children, absent fathers, feckless mothers, dysfunctional underclass families, anomic bystanders. The Sun called for "a crusade for a sick society". Tony Blair, then shadow Home Secretary, called it "the hammer blow to our conscience" (and it was about this time that he developed and used the slogan "tough on crime, tough on the causes of crime"). "The hammer blow to our conscience" was adopted as a headline by the Independent. According to the Economist, it was an event which caused the country "to examine the dark corners of its soul."[22] At the same time, a trial judge made a throwaway remark about exposure to violent videos and it was suggested by the Daily Mail that the last video rented by one of the boy's father was *Child's Play 3* and that the two boys "may" have watched it. The Sun staged a public burning of horror videos; another national chain of video stores burned their copies of *Child's*

---

[20] Burney, *Making People Behave: Anti-social behaviour, Politics and Policy*, at p.51.
[21] S. Cohen *Folk Devils and Moral Panics* (2nd ed., Routledge, 2002).
[22] Although Archbishop Carey warned of the dangers of lapsing into a moral panic.

Play. It later emerged that no-one in either child's family had rented the video or hired it or anything like it. As some have observed, the whole tragedy was a turning point in the history of juvenile justice in the United Kingdom, from "soft welfarism" to a more punitive system.[23] Others recent moral panics and folk devils, according to Cohen, include asylum-seekers, single mothers, welfare cheats, child abusers and paedophiles.[24] All of them very real problems but all of them, Cohen argues, exaggerated in terms of their extent and or significance, especially when compared to other social problems; and all of them generating violent or dramatic reactions from the members of the public led by the press, sometimes prompting lasting legal changes.

Following an exhaustive analysis of the history of public perceptions of   **1-011** crime and disorder in respect of working-class urban males, Pearson, taking a much longer historical view, has as his central thesis the notion that "contemporary" fears about the "rising tide" of crime, disorder and lawlessness are a regular theme throughout modern British history and are invariably associated with a nostalgic regret for a mythical "Golden Age" of security and order, usually in the recent past:[25]

> "Without a shadow of doubt, each era has been sure of the truthfulness of its claim that things were getting steadily worse and equally confident of the tranquillity of the past . . . Each era has also understood itself as standing at a point of radical discontinuity with the past. But when we reconnect these bursts of discontent into a continuing history of deterioration, must not the credibility snap? . . . If we listen to the documentation of history, rather than the pulse of our contemporary anxieties, is it not a little fanciful to believe that Britain's well-policed streets in the 1980s are more perilous than Henry Fielding's disorderly London, Engel's fiery Manchester or the turbulent street-life of the original Hooligans?"

In fact, there is nothing staggering, Pearson says, about the observation that crime and disorder are not new; what is surprising is the continual reappearance of these ancient preoccupations as if they were new and unrivalled in scale that renders it necessary to re-state the obvious. Moral panics about rowdy behaviour as a recent problem, a sign of general moral and social collapse and decay, is a myth which only interferes with rational responses to an ancient problem:[26]

> "When the cobwebs of the historical myth are cleared away, then we can begin to see that the real and enduring problem that faces us is not moral decay or declining parental responsibility or undutiful working mothers or any other symptom of spiritual degeneration amongst British people. Rather, it is a material problem. The inescapable reality of the social reproduction of an underclass of the most poor and dispossessed is the material foundation of these hooligan communities . . . it is a way of saying, quite simply, that it is those crimes that are associated with the materially disadvantaged underclass which have provided the continuing thread within this history of respectable fears."

[23] In the Stephen Lawrence case, an equally horrific tragedy, no such panic eventually emerged, even despite the conclusions of the McPherson Report.

[24] For example, the News of the World campaigning for a naming and shaming law of paedophiles, allowing people access to information on the identities and addresses of paedophiles in their areas (the Sarah law) but which lead to a mob attacking the home of a paediatrician who was forced to flee: *Guardian*, August 20, 2000.

[25] Pearson, *Hooligan: A History of Respectable Fears*, pp.209–219.

[26] *ibid*., p.236.

1-012 Neither Cohen not Pearson deny the reality of the problems of anti-social behaviour and disorder. Nor is it suggested that the government's programme with respect to anti-social behaviour and disorder is a mere moral panic. However, it is useful, when attempting to define what is meant by the term anti-social behaviour and disorder, to see it in an historical context. As we discuss below, there is no question in our opinion that these new measures are intended to deal with very real problems. What is new is the way this government has decided to deal with it and at this time, and why it is continually developing new policy, measures and strategies about it and over such a short period of time. Pearson urges policy makers to adopt "historical realism"; that is, they must find some way of holding onto the realities and specificities of public disorder and the anxieties that surround it while throwing out the claim of novelty. Even though he was writing largely with the social and economic circumstances of the 1970s in mind, he concludes that what is required is not more penal legislation but a greater emphasis on policies dealing with what we would now call social exclusion:[27]

> "This has been a history of myth and tradition in which there are no historical bolt-holes in which to hide from the difficulties of the present or to clothe ourselves in the achievements of the past. It is a story of failure. A failure in the development of British society to win the consent of substantial proportions of its people and to find a secure and trusting place in the social fabric for its youth, no less than a failure of rational thought to dispel the illusions of the past. And although we should not over-estimate the problem of crime and hooliganism in British society . . . nevertheless, the continuing presence of the hooligan in our midst serves to remind us of the incapacities of our accustomed habits of thought and practice."

However, the government, motivated by a real and genuine desire to deal with social deprivation and its consequences, has adopted a strategy of kind which contains some aspects of historical realism of the kind advocated by Pearson but also contains strong punitive elements: a third way, between the "namby-pamby" big government solutions of the 1960s, as a former Home Secretary once described it, and the laissez-faire punitive style of the 1980s. In order to understand government policy, it is useful to consider the problems caused by anti-social behaviour and disorder.

The Problem of Anti-Social Behaviour and Disorder

1-013 As we observed earlier, there is no question that the sorts of problems to which the new anti-social behaviours laws are directed are substantial. An attempt to measure the extent of anti-social behaviour took place on September 10 2003 when the Government's Anti-Social Behaviour Unit undertook what it described as the first ever national day count of reports of anti-social behaviour in England and Wales. Over a 24 hour period, there were 66,107 reports of anti-social behaviour. There was no definition of anti-social behaviour but there were four main areas: the statistics show that they measured street drinking, prostitution, vehicle nuisance and abandoned vehicles, noise, "rowdy behaviour", hoax calls, "animal problems", "intimidation etc.", criminal damage and litter. In 1998, there were 59,290 defendants charged with criminal damage offences, 66,747 with public order offences and 1,931 for intimidating or harming witnesses and jurors.[28] Bradford City Council calculated

---

[27] Pearson, *op.cit.*, pp. 241–242.
[28] Social Exclusion Unit, *National Strategy for Neighbourhood Renewal: a framework for consultation* Report of Policy Action Team 8: Anti-social Behaviour, (2000).

that the cost of vandalism to local authority property was about £900,000 in 1998-99 and that they spent £114,000 repairing properties after a burglary.[29] Leeds City Council estimated the costs of anti-social behaviour to be about £3 million to £5 million each year.[30] Salford Housing Department estimated that anti-social behaviour by tenants cost it £2 million each year.[31] According to the Social Exclusion Unit, the direct costs to the victim and the criminal justice system of vandalism are £450 per incident or £1.3 billion.[32] A NACRO study estimated that dealing with anti-social behaviour costs local authority housing departments over £100,000 per year.[33] Public services such as libraries and schools, railway companies and sports centres pay substantial costs to repair vandalism and graffiti. They refer to a report by a railway company that the annual cost of repairing vandalism of a stretch of railway track in Middlesex in 1997 was £300,000. According to an Audit Commission report, Safety in Numbers, in 1999, one quarter of crime victims report emotional problems six months after the event, particularly in cases concerning racial harassment and violence.[34]

In 1998, in England and Wales magistrates courts, around 55,000 persons **1-014** (80 per cent of whom were adults) were charged with criminal damage, 67,000 for public order offences and around 2,000 for intimidation or harming witnesses and jurors.[35] The British Crime Survey in 1998 found that over half of people from the Caribbean and South Asian community were not reporting racist harassment, and the London Research Centre noted that 43 per cent of racist incidents were unreported.[36] Yet, a 1997 survey found that 13 per cent of people from an ethnic minority were victimised more than once a year. Similarly, 34 per cent of men and 24 per cent of women, in a 1996 survey, said that they had experienced violence because of their sexuality and 32 per cent said that they had been harassed because of it.[38] Further, calls to police for "disorder offences" increased by 19 per cent in 1995–96 and 1997–98.[39] Around 250,000 neighbour disputes were reported each year to local authorities in England and Wales.[40] In 1996–97, 59 per cent of possession proceedings commenced on the grounds of nuisance and annoyance resulted in eviction.[41] There was an increase of 127 per cent in the number of possession actions on anti-social behaviour grounds per 1000 tenancies in the same period[42] (although this may also be due in part to changes to the Housing Acts 1985 and 1988, introduced by the Housing Act 1996). In 1997 the Chartered

---

[29] Social Exclusion Unit, *National Strategy for Neighbourhood Renewal*.

[30] Allen and Sprigings, *Managing Risk Together* (1999).

[31] Audit Commission, *Safety in Numbers* (1997).

[32] Social Exclusion Unit, *National Strategy for Neighbourhood Renewal*.

[33] NACRO, *Nuisance and Anti-Social Behaviour—A report of a Survey of Local Authority Housing Departments*, (January, 1998).

[34] M. Fitzgerald and C. Hale, *Ethnic Minorities, Victimisation and Racial Harassment*, (1996) Research Findings No 39, Home Office Research and Statistics Directorate.

[35] *Home Office Analysis of Defendants Proceeded Against in Magistrates Courts* cited on p.20, Social Exclusion Unit, *National Strategy for Neighbourhood Renewal*.

[36-37] London Housing Survey 1992, *Harassment in London*.

[38] A. Mason and A. Palmer, *Queer Bashing A National Survey of Hate Crimes Against Lesbians and Gay Men* (Stonewall, London, 1996).

[39] Audit Commission, *Safety in Numbers*.

[40] J. Dignan, A. Sorsby and J. Hibbert, *Neighbour Disputes—Comparing the Cost Effectiveness of Mediation and Alternative Approaches* (Centre for Criminological and Legal Research, University of Sheffield, 1996).

[41] J. Nixon, C. Hunter and S. Shayer, *The Use of Legal Remedies by Social Landlords to Deal with Neighbourhood Nuisance* (Centre for Regional Economic and Social Research, Sheffield Hallam University, 1999).

[42] Nixon, *et al*, *The Use of Legal Remedies by Social Landlords to Deal with Neighbourhood Nuisance, op.cit.*

Institute of Environmental Health Officers noted that complaints about neighbours had increased by 56 per cent since 1993.[43] Twenty per cent of the work-time of employees of social landlords was spent on dealing with complaints of anti-social behaviour of neighbours. It is estimated that the legal costs per nuisance case amount to around £10,000.[44] In 1996–97, 59 per cent of possession proceedings on nuisance grounds resulted in an eviction. In deprived areas, it is perceived by local inhabitants as being twice as bad than in other areas[45] and 75 per cent of social landlords consider it to be a medium to large problem.[46] Many social landlords do not have systems to record and monitor complaints.[47] Further, most incidents are not reported to the authorities. Many social landlords do not have systems to record and monitor complaints.[48] Further, most incidents are not reported to the authorities.[49] Around three quarters of social landlords consider it a medium to serious problem.[50] It also has more dramatic effects: for example, there were 17 deaths between 1991 and 1994 resulting directly from neighbourhood noise disputes.[51]

1-015   Also important was the public perception of the problem which is that it is a problem that is on the rise. The British Crime Surveys for 1998 to 2001 included assessments by respondents of the extent to which they felt that the quality of their lives had been adversely affected: in 2001, 59 per cent felt it had a minimal impact, 35 per cent a moderate impact, and 6 per cent a substantial impact. The 2001 survey reported that levels of concern about crime were highest in areas where "physical disorder" (i.e. the interviewer's perception of the level of vandalism, graffiti, litter and rubbish) was common. Those living in inner city areas and council estates with high levels of disorder were especially concerned about crime. The more deprived the area, the greater the perception of an anti-social behaviour problem. We consider more recent BCA surveys about anti-social behaviour and disorder below at paras 1-033 to 1-034.

1-016   That anti-social behaviour occurs or is perceived to occur more frequently or persistently in more deprived areas is a common-sense observation that is borne out statistically. Metropolitan authorities were eight times more likely to say that they had a big or very big problem concerning anti-social behaviour than the national average and it was especially high with regard to authorities in West Midlands, the North West and Yorkshire and Humberside.[52] According to a 1993 study, housing allocation policies can lead to concentrations of rehoused deprived families in particular streets and areas and that it was these areas that were said to show the highest levels of problems caused by anti-social behaviour.[53] In the British Crime Survey in 1998, there was said to be a co-relation between the physical disorder (graffiti, vandalism and litter) in an area and the level of victimisation of burglary, vehicle theft and violence: the level of

[43] Audit Commission, *Safety in Numbers*.
[44] Nixon, *et al*, *The Use of Legal Remedies by Social Landlords to Deal with Neighbourhood Nuisance op.cit.*
[45] DETR, *Analysis of the Survey of English Housing 1999–97* (1999).
[46] Nixon, *et al*, *The Use of Legal Remedies by Social Landlords to Deal with Neighbourhood Nuisance op.cit.*
[47] Nixon, *et al*, *op.cit.*
[48] Nixon, *et al*, *op.cit.*
[49] 1998 British Crime Survey.
[50] Nixon, *et al*, *The Use of Legal Remedies by Social Landlords to Deal with Neighbourhood Nuisance, op.cit.*
[51] Dignan, *et al*, *Neighbourhood Disputes—Comparing the Cost Effectiveness of Mediation and Alternative Approaches op.cit.*
[52] Nixon, *et al*, *The Use of Legal Remedies by Social Landlords to Deal with Neighbourhood Nuisance, op.cit.*
[53] D. Page, *Building for Communities: A Study of New Housing Association Estates* (Joseph Rowntree Foundation, York, 1993).

victimisation in areas of high disorder was two and a half times higher for domestic burglary and almost two times higher for violence. Around three quarters of social landlords now consider it a medium to serious problem.[54]

A Policy Action Team report (PAT 8) noted that a link between high levels **1-017** of disorder and anti-social behaviour leading to more serious crime was yet to be established. All the same, they concluded, anti-social behaviour had a significant role in destroying communities, forcing groups and individuals to leave the area, especially in deprived neighbourhoods where anti-social behaviour can rapidly push neighbourhoods into decline. For example, in deprived neighbourhoods there are many vacant houses and large numbers of persons renting so that anti-social behaviour, and the movement away from such areas, can "decimate" a community within months. An earlier PAT report, *Unpopular Housing*, observed that in areas of low housing demand, the two main reasons people wanted to leave the area were crime and anti-social behaviour, and that anti-social behaviour complaints forced tenants to abandon their tenancies. One landlord, they said, reported to them that in up to 50 per cent of anti-social behaviour cases, victims moved away. They also found that anti-social behaviour destroyed the trust between residents and service providers with many residents concluding that these public services were incompetent or indifferent. Deprived communities, they said, were areas where crime was least likely to be reported.

A 1997 report identified the following as increasing the likelihood of crim- **1-018** inal behaviour in a community: low income, parental criminality and poor parental supervision, truancy and low achievement at school, peer involvement or encouragement, lack of skills or training and unemployment, availability of drugs, community disorganisation and homelessness.[55] Those suffering from a mental illness were both perpetrators, as well as victims, in 30 per cent of cases in a Leeds survey.[56] Alcohol also plays a part: in 44 per cent of all violent incidents, the perpetrator was described by the victim as being drunk; and 70 per cent of stabbings and beatings are associated with alcohol.

Government Policy—Social Exclusion and Anti-Social Behaviour and Disorder

Crime rates are falling and the incidence of anti-social behaviour, though a real **1-019** problem, is more or less the same. As we will show below, anti-social behaviour and disorder does not seem to pre-occupy or distress the vast majority of the population to a very great extent at all. Hence, the new anti-social behaviour and disorder laws cannot have been introduced to deal directly with crime, nor even to deal with public perceptions about the problem of anti-social behaviour. Matthews and Pitts[57] survey government policy with respect to crime and disorder prevention over the last 30 or so years. In the 1970s, the Home Office strategy focused on developing situational crime prevention policies by seeking to provide a response to crime which was both cost effective and politically and socially acceptable. By the mid-1980s, problems of displacement and of "designing out" a range of serious crimes, including rape, domestic violence and racist attacks, indicated the limits of the situational perspective and encouraged the promotion of social prevention measures in the form of strengthening neighbourhoods by encouraging citizen involvement and fostering informal controls. By the mid-1990s, the promise of developing more effective social crime prevention measures was called into question by the

---

[54] Nixon, *et al, op.cit.*
[55] J. Bright, *Turning the Tide: Crime, Community and Prevention* (Demos Papers, 1997).
[56] Allen and Springings, *Managing Risk Together* (Salford Housing and Urban Studies Unit, 1999).
[57] R. Mathews and J. Pitts, *Crime, Disorder and Community Safety* (2001).

observation that crime control strategies were most difficult to mobilise in the neediest areas and that dealing with crime in high-risk areas required a different type of approach. It was increasingly felt within British policy circles that the problem of crime required a more comprehensive and better co-ordinated response while retaining a local focus. A series of inter-agency ini-tiatives were established during the 1980s to address the issue of crime, and a number of agencies have become increasingly involved in the prevention and reduction of different forms of crime. The logic of these developments was endorsed and extended by the Morgan Report, the main recommendation of which was that the responsibility for crime prevention and community safety should be devolved to local authorities, was implemented by an incoming Labour government. The subsequent passing of the Crime and Disorder Act 1998 deliberately linked crime control with disorder and saw both as part of a more comprehensive community safety strategy. The shift from crime preven-tion to community safety extended the terms of reference and made everything from crime and incivilities to environmental issues part of a more comprehen-sive agenda. Crime had increasingly became fused with disorder and both became enveloped within the more general notion of community safety; crime had not become normalised but was instead absorbed within a more complex set of overarching relations. From this "get tough" crime control perspective, the claim was that there are a relatively small number of offenders, victims, groups, neighbourhoods ("hot spots") who were "responsible" for a dispro-portionate amount of crime and victimisation. However, as the issue of crime became further integrated into the wider matrix of community safety, the focus necessarily shifted to aggregate problem populations—the underclass, the mar-ginalised and the socially excluded. Consequently, a hybrid discourse, they write, emerged which identified the problem as a limited number of deviant individuals, yet regarded whole sections of the population as "a problem" of social control. Whereas the war against crime was seen as something which could be "won" and criminals reformed or deterred, the terms "underclass" and the "socially excluded" came close to suggesting a permanent condition which has to be managed rather than eliminated. We suggested earlier that the moral panic about anti-social behaviour is periodic and associated largely with social changes caused by fundamental macro-economic changes. It is our thesis that the current government's response to the problem of anti-social behaviour is a unique attempt of a reform-minded government to respond meaningfully to the problems of social exclusion caused by rapid and sudden socio-economic change over the last 40 or so years, but without making any fundamental changes to the new socio-economic order. First, we will consider government policy in the areas of social exclusion, neighbourhood renewal and anti-social behaviour and disorder.

The Prime Minister's Southwark Speech

1-020   "The Third Way" and "tough on crime, tough on the causes of crime" may well be the two effective sound-bites in British political history, but they aptly encapsulate the current government's aspirations with respect to the control of crime, disorder and anti-social behaviour. Senior Labour Party figures had been making statements about the enforcement of responsibility as social policy since 1993: see, for example, Tony Blair's comments on the Bulger case above. The Labour Party issued a paper, "Quiet Life, Touch Action on Criminal Neighbours" in 1995: the criminal courts, it was asserted, were not capable of helping the victims of nuisance neighbours and witnesses are too frightened to cooperate so a new "community safety order" was proposed, like an injunction but with criminal consequences fore breach—today's anti-social behaviour order. The Prime Minister's first speech was delivered in at the

Aylesbury Estate in Southwark on June 2, 1997. The venue was a deliberate choice. In that speech, he outlined the government's programme to deal with social exclusion. It was necessary, he said, to take steps to deal with not just poverty and deprivation but also "fatalism, the dead weight of low expect-ations, the crushing belief that things cannot get better". That required, he said, a radical shift in our values and attitudes. As a society, we must aim to:

> ". . . re-create the bonds of civic society and community in a way compat-ible with the far more individualistic nature of modern, economic, social and cultural life. . . The basis of this modern civic society is an ethic of mutual responsibility or duty, something for something, a society where we play by the rules. You only take out if you put in."

This meant reforming welfare so that government helped people to help them-selves and provide for those who cannot, rather than trying to do it through government; attacking educational failure, enforcing a new code of laws that would crack down on crime and other antisocial behaviour, attacking dis-crimination in all its forms and promoting urban regeneration. The focus of government action would be to shift resources from cure to prevention. It also meant that government, through its various national and local agencies, had to learn to co-ordinate and develop more coherent strategies.

The government defines "social exclusion" as ". . .a shorthand term for   **1-021** what can happen when people or areas suffer from a combination of linked problems such as unemployment, poor skills, low incomes, unfair discrimina-tion, poor housing, high crime, bad health and family breakdown."[58] The three main national agencies with responsibility for dealing with social exclu-sion are the Social Exclusion Unit, (established in 1997, initially part of the Cabinet Office and now the Office of the Deputy Prime Minister), the Neighbourhood Renewal Unit, and, latterly, the Anti-Social Behaviour Unit. The aim of the Social Exclusion Unit was to look closely at improving facil-ities, opportunities and family services in particularly deprived areas. The gov-ernment sees its role in dealing with social exclusion as largely facilitative. Aside from specific economic initiatives such as the New Deal, Working Tax Credits and so on, the main role of government is to develop strategies, poli-cies and guidance for, and to allocate finance to, local agencies, and largely those of local government—"community based strategies approaches to deliver the strategy."[59] A key aim of neighbourhood renewal was the alloca-tion of resources for rolling programmes, designed to tackle deprivation through national and local agencies, which would be "joined-up" into multi-agency partnerships working at all levels working together with a more client-centred approach to designing and delivering services.

The first main project of the Social Exclusion Unit ("SEU") was to report   **1-022** on "how to develop integrated and sustainable approaches to the problems of the worst housing estates, including crime, drugs, unemployment, community breakdown and bad schools". The SEU published a report in September 1998, setting out the need for a "National Strategy for Neighbourhood Renewal" involving national and local government agencies. The goals included bridg-ing the gap between the most deprived neighbourhoods and the rest of England; and in all the poorest neighbourhoods, to achieve lower long-term unemployment, crime, better health, and better qualifications. The report pro-posed that one of the building blocks of the National Strategy should be 18

---

[58] Social Exclusion Unit, *Tackling Social Exclusion: Taking Stock and Looking to the Future* (March 2004).
[59] Social Exclusion Unit, *Tackling Social Exclusion: Taking Stock and Looking to the Future*, p.14. See also National Strategy for Neighbourhood Renewal; Local Strategic Partnerships.

cross-cutting Policy Action Teams ("PATs"), set up to take forward an intensive programme of policy development. It lead to, inter alia, the 2001 Neighbourhood Renewal Plan. In that plan, it was considered essential to co-ordinate services around the needs of each neighbourhood so that someone would take responsibility for change. The main government method for co-ordinating service delivery would be Local Strategic Partnerships ("LSPs"), defined as a single body that brings together at local level the different parts of the public sector as well as private, voluntary and community sectors so that different initiatives and services support, rather than contradict, each other. The key element to the delivery of government strategy, LSPs would bring together local authorities and other public services as well as residents and the private, voluntary and community sector organisations. Through the LSP, partners, such as the local education authority, health authorities and police, are expected to find ways to be more responsive to what communities want, rationalise activity to cut down on bureaucracy and waste, jointly fund a new service, or introduce new ways of working such as sharing information, premises or even budgets. LSPs would also be able to set local targets for improving outcomes in deprived neighbourhoods. They would provide a means to allow partners to link existing local partnerships and plans, bringing strategic functions together.

1-023 The Neighbourhood Renewal Unit ("NRU") was created ". . .to spearhead change across and outside Government, and make sure the Government delivers on its commitments" and which would report to the Minister for Local Government, Regeneration and the Regions, and a Cabinet-level committee chaired by the Deputy Prime Minister. Neighbourhood Renewal Teams in the regions would oversee local renewal strategies, and administer funding and "join up" Government policy. The NRU was expected to create a knowledge management system to share evidence of what works, and ensure that people working on the ground have the necessary skills and training. It would publish proposals about a learning and development strategy for all those involved in neighbourhood renewal including social entrepreneurs and community activists. At regional level, the Unit will work closely with Neighbourhood Renewal Teams in Government Offices for the Regions. Those teams would "interface" with LSPs, as well as joining up regional activity, working closely with Regional Development Agencies and other regional players.

1-024 Government policy is that anti-social behaviour is both a cause and symptom of social exclusion:[60]

"Anti-social behaviour is often fuelled by wider problems of social exclusion and deprivation such as poverty, unemployment, family breakdown, truancy and school exclusions, drug dependency and community disorganisation."

Specifically, it is considered to lead to neighbour decline with people moving away from deprived areas and tenants abandoning housing; it can cause actual fatalities; it creates high levels of fear of crime which can seriously damage quality of life and vulnerable people are most affected by the fear of crime; the effects of victimisation can continue for a long time afterwards with almost one-quarter of crime victims still reporting emotional problems six months after the event, particularly in cases of racial harassment or violence; and incurs large costs to a wide range of people including individuals, schools, local authorities' housing departments and other social landlords. Traditional efforts to deal with anti-social behaviour, according to the government, suffered from lack of a clear policy and information about it and also a lack of clear responsibility to deal with it. Now, dealing with anti-social behaviour

---

[60] The Policy Action Team 8: Anti-Social Behaviour Report (2000).

should be a high priority and a prerequisite for the success of the overall National Strategy for Neighbourhood Renewal. Central government therefore needed to support local government, and one of the ways in which this would be achieved would be through the establishment of Crime and Disorder Partnerships, acting with relevant central government departments such as the Home Office and the DETR. Secondly, there needed to be more effective enforcement, using current powers, to deliver rapid responses by promoting early intervention through spreading good practice and encouraging the development of mediation services, use of warnings, tenancy clauses on anti-social behaviour, a multi-agency case-conference approach and encouraging local authorities to establish specialist teams which engage people from a range of agencies to focus on combating anti-social behaviour, tackling the "hard core" through setting clear expectations of behaviour and taking tough enforcement and penal measures. There would also be rigorous enforcement action using ASBOs and injunctions, with effective action through the criminal courts and evicting where necessary. Hence, the Government sees it response to anti-social behaviour as a "twin track" approach:[61]

> ". . .providing help and support to the individuals and communities and using the full range of powers to ensure acceptable standards of behaviour are upheld. The Government rejects the view that tackling anti-social behaviour is a choice between prevention and enforcement: a successful response involves both. Work to tackle anti-social behaviour should be seen in the wider context of investment in health, education and regeneration and in the reform of public services."

"Respect and Responsibility"

Burney argues that the government was unhappy with the lack of enthusiasm amongst local authorities for the ASBO who saw them as a last measure or too unwieldy.[62] The then Home Secretary declared his intention to streamline the procedure and allow other agencies to apply for them. Things tended to move along a much greater pace in 2003. The Anti-Social Behaviour Unit was established in January 2003. In March 2003, the government published the White Paper on ant-social behaviour entitled "Respect and Responsibility—Taking a Stand Against Anti-Social Behaviour" and then the Anti-Social Behaviour Act 2003. The White Paper declared:

1-025

> "Every society has to have rules and standards of behaviour. Those rules and standards have to be enforced. People who behave anti-socially should not be allowed to get away with it any longer and we believe that it is time for the community to take a stand."

The role of government is to take action where none is being taken, to replicate best practice and "to shift the culture away from protecting the rights of the perpetrator towards protecting the rights of decent people." As noted above, the paper refers to the fear of crime and "the broken window theory". The 2003 Act introduced significant amendments to the ASBO procedure, parenting contracts and orders. Other acts such as the Criminal Justice Act 2003 contained provisions to deal with begging, littering, fixed penalty notices for disorder, and the creation of part-time beat police constables.

---

[61] House of Commons Home Affairs Committee, Fifth Report, Cm. 6588, (2004–05) Anti-Social Behaviour at para.22.
[62] *ibid.*, para 32–33.

"Together" Action Plan

1-026　On October 14, 2003, the Government launched the Anti-Social Behaviour Action plan and the "Together" plan with a series of road shows and the establishment of an anti-social behaviour "Action Line" and anti-social behaviour "Academy" of practitioners. The Prime Minister said the following:

> "I want to make one very simple point in this speech. To the police, housing officers, local authorities—we've listened, we've given you the powers and its time to use them. You've got new powers to deal with nuisance neighbours—use them. You've got new powers to deal with abandoned cars—use them. You've got new powers to give fixed penalty fines for anti-social behaviour without going the court process—use them."

According to Burney,[63] a member of the audience suggested that social exclusion was more important than enforcement; the Prime Minister replied that Connexions, Sure State and welfare-to-work programmes dealt with that. However, the then Home Secretary replied that any local official or police officer who did not use these powers should be sacked. It was described as a campaign across England and Wales:

> ". . .that stakes a stand against anti-social behaviour and puts the needs of the local community first. . . At the heart of this agenda is a desire not just to reduce crime and disorder, but to support 'civil renewal'—to strengthen communities, revitalise our democracy and provide opportunity and security for all."

Tackling anti-social behaviour is described as a new discipline which "cuts across housing, education, social services, transport and environmental services, town centre management, the criminal justice system and policing." As part of the programme, fifty communities across the country have been designated as "Together Action Areas" to get extra help to tackle anti-social behaviour. In these neighbourhoods local authorities, the police and local people will focus efforts to tackle, not tolerate, anti-social behaviour head on. These policies were intended to set out what practical help the Government is giving to councils and other local agencies to tackle anti-social behaviour and disorder:[64]

> "We know that dealing with anti-social behaviour is not always easy. It's a new discipline that cuts across different responsibilities; it is an issue that concerns many local people and there is an increasing range of powers available to practitioners. In some parts of the country efforts to tackle the problem are working well, other areas have more to learn—but everywhere there is much more that can be done. The Government is committed to helping frontline practitioners and organisations meet this challenge."[65]

The criminal justice system is seen as too slow and anti-social behaviour demands swift and immediate action. In the Prime Minister's speech at the launch of the campaign:

> "First, anti-social behaviour is for many the number one item of concern right on their doorstep—the graffiti, vandalism, dumped cars, drug dealers

---

[63] *ibid.*, para 38.
[64] Home Office *Working Together: Tackling and Not Tolerating Anti-Social Behaviour* (2004).
[65] See also, Home Office, *Together: One Year On* (2004) and *Working Together: Tackling and Not Tolerating Anti-Social Behaviour.*

in the street, abuse from truanting school-age children. Secondly, though many of these things are a criminal offence, it is next to impossible for the police to prosecute without protracted court processes, bureaucracy and hassle when conviction will result in a minor sentence."

Home Office Five Year Plan

In July 2004 the Home Office published its strategic plan for the next five   **1-027**
years. The plan recognises the roles that councils play both to address crime and disorder in their communities and the need to tackle crime and its causes. However, it was vital that in its vision to tackling crime and disorder that the Home Office supported councils and their partners in finding the right balance between enforcement, which was important, and prevention, which would provide a sustainable solution to many of the issues it addresses. The recently published ODPM local area agreements noted that the new safer and stronger communities fund, as outlined within the Home Office five year strategy, would be administered through a "mini" local area agreement ("LAA").

Respect Action Plan

In December 2005, it was announced that the anticipated "Respect Bill" had   **1-028**
been shelved due to lack of consensus across Whitehall, and had instead been downgraded to a "Home Office action plan". Similar comments appear in the Respect Action Plan, released in January 2006:

"In this plan, to truly tackle disadvantage and build a dynamic, prosperous and socially just society, we must offer the support and challenge needed to tackle anti-social behaviour, and its causes, and ensure that we all pass on decent values and standards of behaviour to our children. Where people feel confident, safe and supported, they will be able to come together with others in their neighbourhood to build trust, share values and agree what is acceptable behaviour."

Current measures such as ASBOs, truancy orders and so on are said to have the effect of promoting respect and reducing anti-social behaviour. In this plan the government intended to focus more explicitly on the causes of anti-social behaviour, recognising that children learn behaviour from the adults around them, and particularly from their parents and teachers. It was important, therefore, that government agencies intervened earlier in families, homes and schools to prevent children and young people who were showing signs of problems from getting any worse, as well as programmes aimed at involving young people in cultural, sporting and community activities. Granting that anti-social behaviour was not solely a youth issue, it was also proposed that the government address anti-social adults and families, as well as anti-social young people, by building on strong enforcement measures.

"The National Community Safety Plan 2006–2009"

The National Community Safety Plan has five components: **1-029**

(1) making communities stronger to encourage and empower citizens to play their part in building active, cohesive and sustainable communities and to be able to exert pressure for improved performance and greater accountability in local services; propose a new power to enable local people to secure a response from the police and their partners to a

community safety issue that they believe has not been adequately addressed;[66]

(2) further reducing crime and anti-social behaviour; as part of the new "Respect" agenda, ensure that communities are supported and encouraged to stand up for acceptable standards of behaviour, challenge bad behaviour and know what they can expect from local services; and a new service to deal with non-emergency police and anti-social behaviour issues in a "first wave" of areas in 2006;

(3) creating safer environments;

(4) protecting the public and building public confidence; and

(5) improving people's lives so they are less likely to offend.

The last objective involves the following:

"But unless we can deal with the drug and alcohol misuse which so often leads to criminal activity, and improve housing outcomes and employment opportunities for ex-offenders, we will not be able to break the vicious circle of re-offending. We must work together to educate people against the danger of drug and alcohol misuse, enforce the law to protect the vulnerable, and treat those who do misuse drugs through intervention programmes. We must also intervene early to deter youngsters from starting to engage in anti-social behaviour or criminal activity, and we must regenerate those neighbourhoods associated with the social exclusion which so frequently poses a threat to community safety."

Proposed measures include the dealing with re-offending by implementation of end-to-end offender management in the National Offender Management Service and the Reducing Re-offending Strategy, with the aim of reducing re-offending by 5 per cent by 2008 and 10 per cent by the end of the decade; reducing the proportion of young people not in education, employment or training; implementing actions arising from the Green Paper on youth; increase activities for young people and their take-up; reduce drug use by young people, particularly the most vulnerable, and reduce the harms caused by alcohol misuse.

The Third Way

1-030 It would be wrong to see the government's commitment to combating social deprivation and promoting social inclusion as flowing from traditional ideas about social justice and welfarism. Several analysts have argued that social justice is not at all the fundamental principle behind the government's social exclusion policies.[67] That much can be inferred from the Prime Minister's first speech in Southwark and his comments about the fundamental role of government in the 1990s and beyond:

"The 1960s were the decade of 'anything goes'. The 1980s were a time of 'who cares?'. The next decade will be defined by a simple idea; 'we are all in this together.' It will be about how to recreate the bonds of civic society and

---

[66] The "Community Call for Action" see para 3.38.
[67] B. Jordan, *The New Politics of Welfare: Social Justice in a Global Context* (Sage Publications Ltd, 1998); R. Levitas, *The Inclusive Society? Social Exclusion and New Labour* (Macmillan, 1998), D. Byrne, *Social Exclusion* (Open University Press, 1999). See Gray, "The Politics of Risk", *Criminology* 938.

community in a way compatible with the far more individualistic nature of modern, economic, social and cultural life. . . . In the 1960s people thought government was always the solution. In the 1980s people said government was the problem. In the 1990s, we know that we cannot solve the problems of the workless class without government, but that government itself must change if it is to be part of the solution not the problem."

Although the government accepts that fundamental socio-economic changes of the last 40 or so years were a main cause of social exclusion, its eradication was decidedly not going to be achieved by "namby-pamby 60s-style" re-distribution of socio-economic resources or measures aimed at removing endemic, structural inequalities generated by advanced liberal economic strategies. Instead, the emphasis would be on increasing equality of opportunity so as to allow those at risk to participate in social, economic and political rights associated with citizenship. Taking into account the penal and enforcement elements of the social exclusion policy, analysts have identified a moral agenda in which those offenders in social deprived areas who suffer from "moral deficits" because of it are to be compelled to make responsible choices to take advantage of those opportunities. They would be forced to show respect or face punishment; moral engineering rather than social engineering.

The Underlying Principles of the Anti-Social Behaviour Policy

In this section, we consider what several writers have identified as the main **1-031** principles underlying the government's anti-social behaviour and disorder strategy. In some cases, they are expressly incorporated into government policy; in others, the new laws and policies are aspects of wider trends in the criminal justice system and policing and enforcement styles. These principles are the "broken window theory", communitarianism, restorative justice, the "new penology" and the "new policing". They are all largely recent, American in origin, and, generally speaking, tend to sit more comfortably with neo-conservative rather than welfarist political and economic philosophies.

Broken Windows and Zero Tolerance

Anti-social behaviour and disorder, according to the government, could not **1-032** be a cause of crime. In fact, crime rates have fallen. What matters, for the government, is not crime so much as the fear of it. There is a clear co-relation between fear of crime and perceptions of incivilities. Over the past few decades, a number of studies have reported correlations between fear, perceptions of disorder and social disorganisation. Taylor, for example, argues that incivility indicators are the social and physical conditions in a neighbourhood that are viewed as troublesome and potentially threatening by its residents and users of its public spaces.[68] People assess the threat of victimisation from information communicated through interpersonal relationships and the media and the interpretation of symbols of crime in their immediate surroundings. The presence of incivility indicators are seen by residents as signs that the authorities have lost control over the community and may no longer be able to preserve order.[69] They may also symbolise the loss or erosion of

---

[68] L.R. Taylor, "The Incivilities Theses: Theory Measurement and Policy", in R. Langworthy, *Measuring What Matters* (Washington D.C., National Institute of Justice/Office of Community Oriented Policing Services, 1999); see Jackson, "Experience and Expression: Social and Cultural Significance in the Fear of Crime" 44 Brit. J. Criminol. 946.

[69] See Biderman, Johnson, McIntyre and Weir (1967), cited in Jackson (2004).

standards and values and a loss of social control in an area. It is the density and quality of formal and informal social networks that are at the heart of social control; therefore, disorder suggests a loss of social control and therefore also a perception of deteriorating social networks. Many of the assertions have not been empirically demonstrated. Jackson surveyed 6,000 randomly drawn residents of seven sets of towns and villages within the Tynedale District.[70] What intrigued him about this area was that an earlier survey found that although this area had a significantly low crime rate, 80 per cent of residents surveyed said that safety and security were the issues that mattered most to them. Jackson found that to those surveyed physical disorder was the biggest sign of lack of a social control. Perceptions of problems increased as respondents were more authoritarian and concerned about long-term change in their communities. Women tended to be more worried in terms of intensity but not in terms of frequency; the older the respondent, the more worried both in terms of both intensity and frequency. The frequency of worry about personal crime was shaped by subjective appraisals of the threat of victimization. Inferences about the chances of victimisation were shaped by beliefs about the incidence of crime. Some respondents perceived environmental disorder as indicating loss of social control, particularly amongst those who held authoritarian views about law and order.

1-033   It is surprising that the government has developed so many new national policies and measures to deal with anti-social behaviour and disorder when it is not at all related to crime or crime reduction, and, as recent surveys show, the majority of the public do not consider anti-social behaviour and disorder a particularly serious problem. The British Crime Survey 2003–04 reported that 61 per cent of respondents did not consider anti-social behaviour to be a big problem. In 2002/2003, only 21 per cent of respondents said that anti-social behaviour was a fairly big or big problem in their area; but only 16 per cent said this in 2003–04.[71] Since 1996 the proportion of people in the British Crime Survey reporting vandalism, graffiti and other acts of property damage as a "very" or "fairly" big problem has increased from 24 per cent to 28 per cent in 2003–04; the proportion in the British Crime Survey citing rubbish and litter as a problem in their area rose from 26 per cent to 29 per cent over the same period, peaking in 2002–03 at 33 per cent. Those in inner city areas—31 per cent—were more likely to perceive high levels of anti-social behaviour; the average was 16 per cent. Twenty-five per cent of Londoners perceived levels of disorder in their areas to be high. The top five instances of anti-social behaviour were: speeding traffic, cars parked inconveniently, fireworks, rubbish or litter, and "teenagers hanging around". Twenty-nine percent of respondents saw litter as a very or fairly big problem; 28 per cent said the same thing of vandalism and graffiti; 27 per cent mentioned teenagers hanging around. Only 9 per cent considered nuisance neighbours to be a very or fairly big problem in their areas (10 per cent in 2002/03). The number of people perceiving drunk and disorderly behaviour to be a big problem in their local area fell from 23 per cent in 2002/03 to 19 per cent in 2003/04.

1-034   One in five respondents to an Office for National Statistics found the classic "young people hanging about" to have a fairly big effect or big effect on their lives; it was also the most common response in the BCS survey after speeding traffic. Adults in the ONS survey under the age of 45 were more concerned about youth anti-social behaviour than those above 45. When asked about methods for dealing with anti-social behaviour, more respondents preferred preventative action to deal with causes than tough action against perpetrators

---

[70] Jackson, *ibid.*

[71] Finney and Toofail, "Levels and Trends" in Dodd *et al* ed, *Crime in England and Wales 2003/2004*, (Home Office).

(only 20 per cent preferred the latter). Millie and others carried out case-studies in three different areas to learn more about the local experience of anti-social behaviour. These were neighbourhoods where there were high levels of anti-social behaviour and disorder. The cause of anti-social behaviour tended to be associated with young people. There were three main themes: social and moral decline,[72] disengaged youth and families, and also a reflection of what was seen as a universal feature of being young people to get into trouble. The top three incidences of anti-social behaviour were vandalism and graffiti, young people hanging about, and drunkenness.

However, one of main problem with anti-social behaviour and disorder for the government is that it causes crime. This is the "broken window theory", under which if a broken window in a building is left unrepaired, the other windows will soon be broken and, extrapolating to a community as a whole, it is asserted that if minor public order and criminal offences are tolerated, then public order throughout the community is undermined and increased frequency of more serious criminal behaviour is inevitable. Occasional acts of minor criminal and public order offences are said to send out a signal, not so much to people interested in committing crimes but to members of a community as a whole, that "no-one cares". It is this perception by members of the community which leads to the breakdown of wider community controls. According to Wilson and Kelling's seminal article,[73] such a breakdown will not ordinarily lead to a rise in more serious crime; rather, there is a change in the life of the community which affects residents' perceptions of crime. An increasing level of disorder will lead people to assume that crime is rising. They will then become more insecure and change their behaviour—for example, by using the streets less often and avoiding contact with others. This weakens community bonds and increases individual isolation. Such an area then becomes more vulnerable to crime. Therefore, if public authorities take action against anti-social behaviour, regardless of how effective the measure may in fact be, members of the community will behave as though crime and disorder are not on the rise, community bonds will not be weakened and so the area will not become vulnerable to crime. The White Paper expressly adopts the "broken window" theory:[74]

1-035

"If a window is broken or a wall is covered in graffiti it can contribute to an environment in which crime takes hold, particularly if intervention is not prompt and effective. An abandoned car, left for days, soon becomes a burnt-out car: it is not long before more damage and vandalism takes place. Environmental decline, anti-social behaviour and crime go hand in hand to create a sense of helplessness that nothing can be done."

Skogan[75] analysed 40 residential neighbourhoods combined from five different studies in six American cities and concluded that while poverty, instability and the racial composition of neighbourhoods were strongly linked to crime, disorder also had a major role to play in stimulating urban decline. It undermined neighbourhood satisfaction and provoked migration out of the

[72] "For instance, Barnardo's stated that many people would agree with the statement that 'the morals of the children are ten times worse than formerly'—but they pointed out that this statement had in fact been made by Lord Ashley in the House of Commons in 1823." House of Commons Home Affairs Committee, Fifth Report, Cm. 6588 (2004–05) Anti–Social Behaviour Volume I, March 22, 2005, para.10.

[73] "Broken Windows: The Police and Neighbourhood Safety" *Atlantic Monthly*, March 29, 1982, Vol. 249, No. 3; 29–38.

[74] White Paper 2003, p.14.

[75] W. Skogan, *Disorder and Decline: Crime and the Spiral of Decay in American Neighbourhoods* (Free Press, New York, 1990).

1-036

area. He suggested that his findings are consistent with arguments by Wilson and Kelling and that direct action against disorder was a suitable way to tackle crime problems and to help urban neighbourhoods avoid the spiral of decline.

Wilson and Kelling's 1981 article is considered to be extremely influential in the US and in the UK. The broken window theory and zero tolerance are closely related. Young[76] and Wright[77] both discuss the way in which zero tolerance policy and broken window theory were introduced into modern government thinking about public order. In New York in the early 1990s, Police Commissioner Bratton and Mayor Giuliani developed a crime and policing strategy which was later said to have incorporated the theory. The new police strategy was called "zero tolerance". Bratton explains the theory in his paper entitled "Crime is Down in New York City: Blame the Police".[78] Bratton said that he focused police action on subway fare evaders and homeless people who lived in the subways of New York. Soon, the subways were declared crime free and reclaimed for the benefit of the citizens. Other offenders targeted were jaywalkers, the squeegee men, panhandlers, drunks, noisy teenagers and streetwalkers. Aggressive policing included searches, sweeps and arrests of individuals found loitering in streets even though they had not committed any crime under the law. More importantly, Commissioner Bratton modernised the New York City Police Department in ways that were perhaps very necessary but had little to do with zero tolerance policing. He flattened hierarchies and empowered the captains of precincts; police officers were assessed for promotion by the numbers of arrests they made; the police force was expanded from 27,000 in 1993 to 41,000 in 2001; officers had greater access to computers; there was compilation of crime statistics and sharing of data, which made police deployments to crime-affected areas more effective; based on this data, officers were set clear goals and targets; police precinct commanders were directly accountable for levels of crime in their areas; and there was more contact between local communities and other public agencies.

1-037

It is not at all controversial that crime rates in New York City declined across the board through the 1990s and it was largely seen by many as a direct result of the application of broken windows/zero policing policies. Conservative think-tanks such as the influential Manhattan Institute, together with the Giuliani group, propagated the policing philosophy to Latin America for curbing urban crimes. In 1998, police officials from around 150 countries visited the NYPD to learn about the innovative techniques of crime control.[79] The former Home Secretary, Jack Straw, announced in September 1997, in the first speech at a party conference since the Labour Party had come to power, that he wanted ". . .zero tolerance of crime and disorder in our neighbourhoods".

1-038

Sampson and Raudenbush argue that public disorder is not causally linked to crime. Their research, they believe, shows that perceptions of a neighbourhood are not so much determined by things like graffiti as they are by race. On a random basis, 15,141 streets of Chicago were selected for analysis. In their study, they counted the physical signs of decay. They found that disorder and predatory crime were moderately correlated, but that, when antecedent neighbourhood characteristics (such as neighbourhood trust and poverty) are taken into account, the connection between disorder and crime vanished in four out of five tests. They then compared this data with interviews of residents about how disordered they believed their neighbourhoods to be. They concluded that

[76] J. Young, *The Exclusive Society* (Sage Publications Ltd, 1999).
[77] Skogan, *Disorder and Decline*.
[78] W. Bratton, "Crime Is Down in New York City: Blame the Police", in N. Dennis (ed), *Zero Tolerance: Policing a Free Society* (Institute of Economic Affairs, London, 1998).
[79] C.R. Sridhar, "Broken Windows and Zero Tolerance Policing Urban Crimes" *Economic and Political Weekly* (2006).

the actual level of physical disorder was not the most important factor in making people think their neighbourhood was disordered. It was the number of black, and to a lesser extent Latino, neighbours. Latino residents exhibited the same racial bias. Sampson and Raudenbush attribute these responses to what some social theorists have called "implicit bias", a tendency of both whites and minorities to subconsciously associate minorities with undesirable traits like criminality. If race, rather than the reality of a neighbourhood's condition, is what really shapes perceptions of disorder, it may not make any difference whether someone addresses the so-called broken windows. Sampson and Raudenbush conclude that ". . .attacking public order through tough police tactics may thus be a politically popular but perhaps analytically weak strategy to reduce crime".[80] See Harcourt,[81] who considered Skogan's data and found that Skogan failed to report that in four out of the five measures of crime that he used (burglary, physical assault, rape and purse snatching/pocket-picking), there was not a statistically significant relationship between disorder and crime. He only mentioned the one where there was a statistically significant relationship—robbery victimisation and disorder, and, even then, that relationship was questionable. Five out of the 40 neighbourhoods exerted great influence over the findings and when these were taken out of the analysis, the connection between disorder to robbery disappears.

See also Taylor[82] who, in 1981 and then in 1994, surveyed neighbour-   **1-039**
hoods in Baltimore with a view to measuring the relation between incivilities, crime, and fear of crime. Physical conditions had deteriorated significantly on the street blocks assessed in 1981 and 1994. Graffiti and abandoned houses occurred more frequently. Despite the worsening physical conditions, residents did not report that local physical or social problems in the neighbourhood were significantly worse. Incivilities increased over time in neighbourhoods where housing prices were lower and there were fewer black residents. Lower initial stability also contributed to later increases in graffiti. Neighbourhood status at the beginning of the period showed a powerful influence on changes in neighbourhood crime. Overall, crimes, including one property crime, declined faster, or increased more slowly, in neighbourhoods with higher initial house values. Neither residents' reports of incivilities in 1982, nor incivilities assessed in 1981, contributed consistently, independently, and substantially to changes in fear of crime in the neighbourhoods between 1982 and 1994. The changes over time in outcomes, such as fear and moving intentions, were produced by earlier, more fundamental features of the neighbourhood fabric. At the same time, results showed that those residents who viewed their neighbourhood as more problem ridden than their neighbours did were more fearful and less committed than their neighbours. High levels of incivilities might cause later increases in crime, but effects were not as consistent as expected. Earlier deterioration did not cause a neighbourhood to "go downhill" faster. Incivilities made no independent impact on changes in house value, home-ownership, or educational levels; however, they did shape later changes in poverty and vacancy rates. Fear of crime differences were greater between individuals than between neighbourhoods. It was the individual variations, such as gender and age, that lay behind concerns about safety and community disorder. In the majority of cases, fear of crime arose because of

---

[80] Robert J Sampson and Stephen W Raudenbush, "Systematic Social Observation of Public Places: A New Look at Disorder in Urban Neighbourhoods", *American Journal of Sociology*, (2000) 105, pp.637, 638.
[81] B. Harcourt, *Illusion of Order: The False Promise of Broken Windows Policing* (Harvard University Press, 2001).
[82] R. Taylor, *Breaking away from Broken Windows: Baltimore Neighbourhoods and the Nationwide Fight Against Crime, Grime, Fear and Decline* (Westview Press, 2001).

differences between residents responding to the same environmental conditions: some people were afraid because they perceived a lot of problems around them and this was not something that would be affected by broken windows. Taylor,[83] in a different study, selected a sample of 24 small commercial centres in St. Paul, Minnesota, and interviewed merchants and local residents about their perceptions of the incivilities in their area. He found that incivilities were secondary in influencing people's fear of crime. Rather, a person's perceived incivilities and the differences between victimisation within neighbourhoods were more significant factors. Taylor suggests that the focus should be less about trying to bring down actual incivilities, but more on increasing communication and trust between residents in close proximity to each other, which, in turn, will bring down the perceived incivilities. Neighbourhood fabric, and alterations in that fabric, have strong impacts on later decline and very moderate impacts on later crime changes. Direct efforts to enhance neighbourhood stability, maintain house prices and improve local economic development are productive to change crime levels. For those concerned about reducing residents' fear and enhancing commitment to the locale, these results point toward the need for a "direct marketing" approach: he means that efforts should be made to find those individuals who were more fearful and less committed than their neighbours and work with them. For community policing, Taylor concludes that his results argue against according crime reduction or zero tolerance policies a privileged status, relative to other community policing initiatives. Other community policing or problem-oriented policing tools, as well as resources devoted to traditional enforcement, should not be set aside a priori in favour of crime reduction or zero tolerance. Efforts to stabilise neighbourhoods that address disorder, he argues, will prove most useful if carried out within a context recognising the structural sources of neighbourhood changes. Neighbourhood status and low crime are more important than "broken windows" in a neighbourhood for long-term stability and low fear.

1-040   Policing policies introduced under zero tolerance were attacked for being "discriminatory initiatives which target and criminalised economically-excluded groups living on the streets."[84] In a study conducted in 1999 by the New York Attorney-General Eliot Spitzer, with the help of Columbia University's Centre for Violence Research and Prevention, in aggregate across all crime categories and precincts citywide, blacks were stopped by police 23 per cent more often in comparison to the crime rate than whites. Hispanics were stopped 39 per cent more often than whites. The racially discriminatory pattern was evident from the statistics available for the US as a whole and for New York City, which showed that adults arrested for misdemeanours were disproportionately African-American in relation to their representation in the community.[85] The New South Wales Council for Civil Liberties has recorded that zero tolerance policing has been racially discriminatory to Arabic-speaking people.[86] Of course, in the UK, note the controversial "sus" laws and the results of the MacPherson Inquiry into the death of Stephen Lawrence.[87]

1-041   Further, aside from alienating minorities, zero tolerance is not a particularly effective policy. For example, crime in New York was not dramatically reduced

[83] P. Lab, *Crime Prevention at a Crossroads* (Anderson, 1997).

[84] Burke, "The Regulation of Begging and Vagrancy: A Critical Discussion", (2000) 2(2) *Crime Prevention and Community Safety.*

[85] E. Spitzer, *The New York City Police Department's 'Stop and Frisk' Practices: A Report to the People of the State of New York,* Office of the Attorney General, Civil Rights Bureau, (1999) at pp.89, 123.

[86] Michael Hartley Kennedy, "Zero Policing and Arabic-speaking Young People", New South Wales Council for Civil Liberties, (2001).

[87] See para.2-004 and the new stop powers.

during the period because of the policy. First, it had fallen over the same period in other major cities with more traditional policing styles. New York has not achieved a greater crime reduction than that of all other US cities. In fact, the three cyclical measures reveal that New York City's decline was either equal to or below that of several other large cities, including San Francisco, San Jose, Cleveland, San Diego, Washington, St Louis and Houston. These other cities employ a variety of policing strategies.[88] Nor was it ever fully implemented in New York City in any case; Commissioner Bratton certainly introduced classic zero tolerance measures but he also introduced a much more significant modernisation programme associated with a shift of resources so that public order crimes received further attention. Young describes how, in July 1997, he attended a seminar at the Institute for Economic Affairs about zero tolerance.[89] The former Police Commissioner Bratton disappointed the audience in distancing himself from the concept of zero tolerance. He said that action should be taken against a broad spectrum of crime but not solely by way of the imposition of police control. Policing was only a holding operation until social changes would engender a more stable society. That in itself is a fair description of what Wright[90] considers to be an alternative policing/public order theory, the problem-oriented approach (or order-maintenance) which he says was subject to experimentation in parts of the United Kingdom in the 1980s and early 1990s, such as in Leicester. Under this theory, policing means identifying and solving underlying problems within communities. According to the Chief Constable of Thames Valley, zero tolerance is concerned only with solutions and deals with anti-social behaviour through aggressive and uncompromising law enforcement; order-maintenance policing, on the other hand, requires a wider range of tactics and the involvement of other agencies and attempts to treat the underlying causes of the behaviour.[91] It is not simply a matter of responding to individual incidents; such incidents are only symptoms of a deeper problem. A balance must be struck between maintaining order and providing protection for persons liable to create public order problems. Wright argues that a number of factors have hampered this approach, including the lack of reliable data and lack of resources.

Others such as Shapiro[92] are more cynical. The popularity of "quick fixes"   **1-042**
such as broken window theory and zero tolerance is more to do with the populist politics than effectiveness:

"Zero tolerance policing unquestionably makes for effective campaign rhetoric and the original Wilson and Kelling broken window hypothesis is an easy sell to any society frightened by seemingly uncontrollable crime. On its deepest level it is not about crime at all but a vision of a social order disintegrating under glassy-eyed liberal neglect."

It also reflects a vision of city life by socially conservative politicians which is more about urban aesthetics and sanitised public spaces than reducing crime. As Harcourt puts it:

"It is, in effect, a type of 'aesthetic policing' that fosters a sterile, Disneyland, consumerist, commercial aesthetic. It reflects a desire to

---

[88] A. Joanes "Does New York City Police Department Deserve Credit for the Decline in New York City's Homicide Rates?" *Columbia Journal of Law and Social Problems*, Vol 33, No 3, Spring (2000).
[89] Young, *op.cit.*, p.124.
[90] Wright, *op.cit.*, p.112.
[91] Pollard, "Zero Tolerance: Short-Term Fix; Long-Term Liability", in Dennis, *Zero Tolerance: Policing a Free Society* (1997).
[92] *Zero Tolerance Gospel*, in Young, *op.cit.*, (1999).

transform NYC into Singapore, or worse, a shopping mall. The truth is, however, that when we lose the dirt, grit, and street life of major American cities, we may also threaten their vitality, creativity, and character."[93]

Communitarianism

1-043   As we have discussed above, government policy in this area is about protecting and promoting communities. Part of the way this is to happen is through enhancing the role of the local agencies; but also by involving local people in dealing with anti-social behaviour. Hence, Taking a Stand Awards, the neighbourhood warden scheme, Community Support Officers in the police force, and the new Community Justice Centres. Burke and Morrill,[94] and Ramsey[95] argue that communitarianism lies behind New Labour social policy, particularly with regard to ASBOs. Burke and Morrill write:

> "ASBOs were introduced by a New Labour government strongly influenced by the communitarian agenda and its dominant theme that autonomous selves do not live in isolation but are shaped by the values and culture of communities. From this perspective, it has become necessary to take measures to protect and enhance the community against the interests of normless, self-centred atomistic, invariably anti-social individuals."

1-044   Modern communitarianism began as a reaction in academic circles to John Rawls' *A Theory of Justice*. Drawing primarily upon Aristotle and Hegel, political philosophers such as Macintyre, Sandel and Walzer disputed the liberal assumption that the principal task of government is to secure and distribute fairly the liberties and economic resources individuals need to lead freely chosen lives.[96] Whereas Rawls presented his theory of justice as universally true, communitarians argue that the standards of justice must be found in forms of life and traditions of particular societies and hence can vary from context to context. Justice is relative; it is what members of the community think it is (or more precisely, what a judge or administrator might think the community thinks it is). Communitarians claim that moral and political judgments depend on the language of reasons and the interpretive framework within which members of a community view their world and not on abstract principles. For communitarians, traditional liberal institutions and practices are unable to deal with, or have even caused, such modern phenomena as alienation from the political process, unbridled greed, loneliness, urban crime, and high divorce rates. A second wave of 1990s communitarians such as Etzioni and Galston blamed both the left and the right for these problems: the political left, for supporting welfare rights which were economically unsustainable in an era of slow growth and aging populations, and for shifting power away from local communities and democratic institutions and towards centralized bureaucratic structures better equipped to administer the fair and equal distribution of benefits; and the right, for promoting the invisible hand of unregulated free-market capitalism which, they argued, undermined the family, disrupted local communities, and corrupted the political process. There is, they argued, another (third?) way: in order to protect communities, they advocated policies which promote social responsibility rather than, and

---

[93] B. Harcourt, "Policing Disorder: Can We Reduce Serious Crimes by Punishing Petty Offences", *Boston Review*, April–May (2002). Quoted by Sridhar, above.

[94] "Anti-Social Behaviour Orders: An Infringement of the Human Rights Act 1998?", *Nottingham Law Journal* (2002) 11(2) 1.

[95] "What is Anti-Social Behaviour" *Crim. L.R.* (2004) 908–925.

[96] D. Bell, *Stanford Encyclopaedia of Philosophy*.

even at the expense of, individual rights. They see society as ". . . a community whose primary bond is a shared understanding, both of the good for man and the good of the community."[97] They want to replace the "politics of rights" with "the politics of the common good."[98]

Communitarianism has its critics. Appeals to the "common good" have had   **1-045** some unfortunate historical antecedents in the twentieth century. First, it is not exactly clear what community or communities they are referring to and there is an argument that, in complex modern, pluralistic societies, it is impossible to find a discrete, self-contained community with sufficient integrity to have "shared values"; an individual can belong to many different communities and the boundaries between one community and another are blurred and vague. Secondly, what should policy-makers do as regards values in a community which are entrenched but illiberal, such as anti-semitism or homophobia? Some argue that a set of fundamental basic rights should provide sufficient protection for minorities, but this tends to undermine the logical consistency of the entire theory. Thirdly, it has been attacked for having no real interest in, and even a naive view about, the power relations between members of a community and between communities themselves; if a value is entrenched in a community, however that community might be defined, then that may simply be so because it is the value of the most politically and economically powerful leaders of that community. Finally, there is the problem of members who refuse to abide by "shared" values and how they should be compelled to comply with them. See these remarks of Baumann in Liquid Modernity:[99]

> "There is commotion around the need of community mainly because it is less and less clear whether the realities which the portraits of 'community' claim to represent are much in evidence, and if such realities can be found, will their life-expectancy allow them to be treated with the kind of respect which realities command. The valiant defence of community . . . would hardly have happened had it not been for the fact that the harness by which collectivities tie their members to a joint history, custom, language or schooling is getting more threadbare by the year. In the liquid stage of modernity, only zipped harnesses are supplied, and their selling point is the facility with which they can be put on in the morning and taken off in the evening (or vice versa). Communities come in many colours and sizes, but if plotted on the Weberian axis stretching from 'light cloak' to 'iron cage', they all come remarkably close to the first pole."

The reality is, for some writers, that there are no communities anymore. The rise of communitarianism as an underlying principle of the contemporary justice system can be explained as a result of dramatic socio-economic changes of the last 40 or so years. According to Hobsbawm,[1] for example, there was a "Golden Age" prior to the end of the 1970s which was characterised by full employment, rising affluence, and the entry of women into public and working life. Major socio-economic changes were collectively "a juggernaut sweeping all solid institutions aside", as Giddens put it; and Young and others describe a dramatic change from a world of material and ontological security from cradle to grave to one of precariousness and uncertainty.

---

[97] Gutmann, "Communitarian Critics of Liberalism", *Philosophy and Public Affairs*, (1985) 14, 308–22.

[98] Sandel, "The Procedural Republic," *Political Theory*, (1984) 12, 91–112.

[99] Page 169; quoted in Young, "The Maintenance of Order Amongst Lightly Engaged Strangers" (1999) British Criminology Conference, Liverpool.

[1] E. Hobsbawm, *The Age of Extremes* (Penguin, 1994).

Where social commentators of the fifties and sixties berated the complacency of a comfortable "never had it so good" generation, those of today talk of a risk society where social change becomes the central dynamo of existence and where anything might happen.[2] Employment became less secure; There was a change in leisure style from mass consumption to one where, as Young says, choice and preference was elevated to a major ideal and where the constant stress on immediacy, hedonism and self-actualisation has had a profound effect on late modern sensibilities; and perhaps crucially, but also individualistic and even meritocratic. Such a process is combined with a decline in the forces of informal social control, as communities are disintegrated by social mobility of them and left to decay as capital finds more profitable areas to invest and develop. At the same time, families are stressed and fragmented by the decline in communities systems of support, the reduction of state support and the more diverse pressures of work. Thus, as the pressures which lead to crime increase, the forces which attempt to control it decrease. See Morris:[3]

> ". . .the evidence suggests that both the predominant types of crime and increased lawlessness of the last decade are best understood in terms of long-term changes in British society that have been taking place for almost twenty years. . .It is the virtual disappearance of a range of auxiliary agents of social control from park rangers to bus conductors and school attendance officers which have left the police over-exposed and inadequately resourced to deal with the problem of crime. . .increasing resort to incarceration solutions to social problems is equally lacking in effect but ruinously expensive."

1-046   Young argues that the cultural revolution of the 1970s and the economic crises and re-structuring of the 1980s turned a society which was largely inclusive to one which was largely exclusive:[4]

> "That is, from a society whose accent was on assimilation and incorporation to one that separates and excludes. This erosion of the inclusive world of the modernist period. . .involved processes of disaggregation of the sphere of the community (the rise of the individual) and the sphere of work (transformation of labour markets). Both processes are the result of market forces and their transformation by the human actors involved."

Vast sections of the population, Young argues, were now excluded by market forces from the primary labour market and this created a culture of individualism, at the expense of "traditional" institutions of social control such as the family. The inclusive society demanded uniformity and homogeneity, concealed differences between different classes and ethnic groups and sought to assimilate deviance and disorder; the exclusive society involves greater risks and uncertainty and responds to deviance by separation and exclusion. In the exclusive society, the criminal justice system becomes, in the absence of any other effective systems of social control, more and more a part of the average person's everyday life.

Public Safety as a "Human Right"

1-047   In an open letter to the Home Secretary in May 2006, the Prime Minister expressed his desire to see remedies outlined in his Respect Action Plan be

---

[2] Young, *op.cit.*; A. Giddens, *Modernity and Self-Identity* (Stanford University Press, 1991).
[3] In Kavanagh and Seldon (eds), *The Major Effect*, (Macmillan, 1997) pp.314–316.
[4] Young, *op.cit.*, at pp.6–7.

further strengthened and also made faster. He also asked the Home Secretary to consider whether primary legislation was needed to address the issue of Court rulings which over-rule the Government in a way that is inconsistent with other EU countries interpretation of the European Convention on Human Rights. Meanwhile, newspaper reports claimed that the Prime Minister is considering amending the Human Rights Act to require a "balance between the rights of the individual and the rights of the community to basic security."[5] Similar remarks were made by Lord Falconer in a radio interview at about the same time.[6] It may be that the government has in mind something like a human right to security and safety. Such a right does not exist in international law and it is dangerous to consider human security a human right. The UNDP in 1994 first used the term "human security" and it has since been adopted by several governments as part of their foreign affairs policy. Although some proponents of the concept of human security use human rights language, it is not a human right. Oberleitner argues human rights are first and foremost a normative framework, while human security is fundamentally political; human rights give entitlements and impose obligation; human security relies on feasibility and choice.[7] Human security may dilute the legal character of human rights; it allows choice between rights on the grounds of their value to security and even allows governments to defy human rights obligations under the pretext of guaranteeing human security instead. It may be that the government has something simpler in mind; that courts will be required to give some kind of priority to public safety, for example, by balancing human rights against the need to protect the public. Dworkin, writing in response to the government's new plans to amend the Human Rights Act 1998:

"The balancing metaphor is dangerous because it suggests no principled basis for deciding how much torture we should facilitate, or for how many years we should jail people without trial. It leaves that decision up to politicians who are anxious to pander to the tabloids. The metaphor is deeply misleading because it assumes that we should decide which human rights to recognise through a kind of cost-benefit analysis, the way we might decide what speed limits to adopt. It suggests that the test should be benefit to the British public, as Blair declared in his 'Let's talk' speech, when he said that 'the demands of the majority of the law-abiding community have to take precedence'. This amazing statement undermines the whole point of recognising human rights; it is tantamount to declaring that there are no such things."

Dworkin argues that most political decisions require a cost-benefit balancing in which disadvantages to some are outweighed by the overall benefit to the community. Building a new airport is bound to disadvantage some people, but the damage is justified if it is the best choice for the nation. However, some injuries to individuals are so grave that they cannot be justified by declaring that that is what the public wants. A civilised society recognises rights precisely to protect individuals from these grave harms. While, for example, it might well be in the public interest to lock up people who the police think dangerous even though they have committed no crime, or to censor people whose opinions are offensive or unwelcome, or to torture people who we believe have information

---

[5] Sunday May 14, 2006, *The Observer*; while the opposition leader told the *Sun* that he would scrap the 1998 Act entirely.
[6] BBC, May 14, 2006
[7] "Porcupines in Love: The Intricate Convergence of Human Rights and Human Security" (2005) 6 EHRLR 588.

about impending crimes, we do not do that, at least in ordinary legal practice, because we insist that people have a right to a fair trial and free speech and not to be tortured. These rights are insisted upon even though the majority would be safer and more comfortable if they were ignored. For example, the House of Lords in *McCann*, in holding that ASBOs were not a penalty, Lord Hutton adopted a broad balancing approach:[8]

> "I consider that the striking of a fair balance between the demands of the general interest of the community (the community in this case being represented by the weak and vulnerable people who claim that they are the victims of anti-social behaviour which violates their rights) and the requirements of the protection of the defendant's rights requires the scales to come down in favour of the protection of the community and of permitted the use of hearsay evidence in applications for anti-social behaviour orders."

Ashworth argues that this is not the appropriate way to determine issues of the application of human rights.[9] Human rights are not to be "weighed" against the public interest and then discarded. It is the same error made by the Privy Council in *Brown v Stott*,[10] where it is assumed that human rights can be "trumped" by public interest considerations. The Articles of the Convention themselves allow for public interest considerations where appropriate (such as Arts 8 to 11) but it is wrong to assume that such an approach is permissible with respect to Art.6.

The End of Penal Welfarism and the Culture of Control

1-048   Young[11] quotes Hofman who suggested that worthy social democratic critiques of society, which linked crime and punitiveness to lack of stable employment, community and family life, are based on "nostalgic assumptions" that it is possible to bring these entities of the 1960s back into existence by an act of political will. The major socio-economic changes of the last 40 or so years, discussed by Young and others, have caused substantial and permanent changes in criminal justice policy. Feeley and Simon[12] argue that in the UK and the US a "systems analysis" approach to danger management has come to dominate criminal justice to the point where it is now more of a waste management system rather than a retributive or rehabilitative system. A dangerous class of criminal is identified with the underclass generally so that the ultimate operational goal is ". . . the herding of a specific population that cannot be desegregated and transformed but only maintained in a waste-management function." As Lynch summarises it, any investment in this class would be futile and so the waste management model entails security from this class at a minimal cost.[13] Toxic waste containment sites are what Simon calls "underclass communities", where those under the control of community corrections would be required to live and front-line crime control professionals

---

[8] [2003] 1 A.C. 787, at [113].
[9] "Social Control and Anti-Social Behaviour: The Subversion of Human Rights" (2004) LQR 120.
[10] [2003] 1 A.C. 681; see A. Ashworth *Human Rights, Serious Crime and Criminal Procedure* (Sweet Maxwell, 2002).
[11] Young "The Maintenance of Order Amongst Lightly Engaged Strangers" British Criminology Conference, Liverpool (1999).
[12] "The New Penology: Notes on the Emerging Strategy of Corrections and its Implications" (1992) 30 *Criminology* 449–474.
[13] M. Lynch, "Waste Managers? The New Penology, Crime Fighting and Parole Agent Identity" *Law and Society Review*.

merely manage them with little real involvement.[14] The new penology is said to have three elements: risk and probability are applied to the criminal population rather than moralistic judgments about individuals; there is identification and management of criminals rather than punishment or rehabilitation; and the increasing use of actuarial and management tools for classifying and controlling aggregate risk. Whereas in the past the focus was retrospective and on individuals, it is now on the future and on aggregates of individuals. The criminal, under what is called "penal welfarism" was once seen as someone who could be reformed and/or punished and so the reasons for their criminal behaviour were worthy of attention; in the new penology model, as there is no real interest in the individual criminal and so no inquiry as to the reason for the criminal behaviour, attention shifts to how to deal with efficiently and manage the risk of reoffending. The aim of the new penology is essentially actuarial:

> "It is concerned with techniques for identifying, classifying and managing groups assorted by different levels of dangerousness. It takes crime for granted. It accepts deviance as normal. It is sceptical that liberal interventionist crime control techniques do or can make a difference."

See also Garland and the "culture of control": the penal welfarism of the 20th century in the UK and the US was based on a notion of the comparative stability of the post war welfare state and on the associated ideal that the individuals in their social circumstances could be reformed by government intervention. The collapse of penal welfarism, Garland writes, was sudden, radical and unforeseen. He says that, during the 1970s, like a stock market crash, "in the course of a few years, the orthodoxies of rehabilitative faith collapsed in virtually all developed countries." The main reason for the loss of faith, he argues, was the lack of empirical evidence for the effectiveness of the rehabilitative programmes in addition to large-scale socio-economic changes of the kind discussed by Young. The cultural effect of the macro-economic changes were the free-market, neo-liberalism and social conservatism which manifested themselves as proposals to roll back the state at the same time as creating stronger and more authoritarian state agencies. Governments, faced with perceptions of their own failure to control crime, dealt with the problem by what he called "adaptive responses": the withdrawal of police from the community, contracting out police functions, the increased focus on victims, and policies aimed at promoting community involvement in justice, underlying all of which was a philosophy that crime was normal. He uses the phrase, "the new criminologies of everyday life", to describe this style of "new penology" where crime is seen to be more about opportunity of lifestyle, a normal commonplace fact of social life. The aim of correction of the individual is supplanted by "supply side criminology"—reduction of opportunities for crime by target-hardening, increased surveillance and general prevention. Criminals are no longer seen as psychologically or socially defective individuals but rational beings that, as Zedner[15] puts it, can be priced out of criminal activity through the manipulation of incentives and disincentives.   **1-049**

There was also a second set of responses, based on coercive control of offenders, "the myth of the sovereign state": the myth that the state can control crime after all. Garland argues that the state, accepting on the one hand its impotence in the face of rising crime, goes to trouble to express anger   **1-050**

---

[14] J. Simon, *Poor Discipline: Parole and the Social Control of the Underclass, 1890–1990* (Chicago, University of Chicago Press, 1993).

[15] "Policing before and after the Police: The Historical Antecedents of Contemporary Crime Control", (2006) 46 Brit. J. Criminol. 78.

at crime (or "acts out", in the Freudian sense of the phrase, crime control), rather than actually controlling it:

". . .an emerging distinction between the punishment of criminals which remains the business of the state (and becomes once again a significant symbol of state power) and the control of crime which is increasingly deemed to be 'beyond the state' in significant respects. And as its control capacity comes to be viewed as limited and contingent, the state's power to punish takes on a renewed political salience and priority."

The two responses have contradictory ideas about criminal behaviour. In the adaptive response, the criminal is the rational calculating offender; whereas, in "the sovereign state" response, the criminal is the excluded, irrational and irredeemable outsider. So, the state, while it no longer sees itself as the sole provider of security, must nonetheless pursue policies of punitive segregation and even mass imprisonment. All the same, the two responses go hand-in-hand:

"The new infrastructure is strongly oriented towards a set of objectives and priorities—prevention, security, harm reduction, loss-reduction, fear-reduction—that are quite different from the traditional goals of prosecution, punishment and "criminal justice". So while the most prominent measures of crime control are increasingly oriented towards punitive segregation and expressive justice, there is, at the same time, a new commitment, especially at the local level, to a quite different strategy that one might call preventative partnerships. Today's most visible crime control strategies may work by expulsion and exclusion but they are accompanied by patient, ongoing low-key efforts to build up the internal controls of neighbourhoods and to encourage communities to police themselves."

1-051 Zedner is critical of Garland's reliance on rising crimes as a significant explanation for the replacement of penal welfarism by the culture of control. While crime rates rose during the mid-1980s, they stabilised or fell in all common law jurisdictions the last ten years or so later and have fallen further since then. She contends that it is precisely the ability of governments to claim success in securing the decline that licences the introduction of zero tolerance and other similar punitive policies. Techniques of crime control are disassociated from crime itself, so that security became an end in itself:

"Indeed the promise of protection, of freedom from anxiety and insecurity are ends whose measurement has little rational relationship to actual risk. The irony, of course, is that the pursuit of security itself generates insecurity by littering the world with visible reminders of risk (for example, burglar alarms, CCTV cameras and security guards). And more ironically still, it could be said that the reduction of risk acts in the longer-term against the interests of those who invest political and financial capital in its pursuit."

Garland's thesis is, she argues, an over-simplification to an extent: he compresses a period of change which was more protracted and more inchoate than he suggests. Other writers, while broadly accepting Garland's analysis, see the end of penal welfarism as simply a product of residual moralistic conservatism associated with the neo-liberalism of the late 1970s to the present.

1-052 Hughes and McLaughlin[16] apply Garland's thesis to the emerging preventative safety sector, composed of local authority community safety teams,

---

[16] "Towards a New Paradigm of Sovereign Power? Community Governance, Preventative Safety, and the Crime and Disorder Reduction Partnerships" The British Criminology conferences: Selected proceedings, vol.6, (2003) Emerging themes in criminology.

community police officers, health and probation and juvenile justice workers. In the past, crime was seen retrospectively and individually; now it is prospective and in aggregate terms: "Put simply, everyone is a potential criminal and victim." The main goal of policing, they argue, is no longer law enforcement and keeping the peace but information brokering within a patchwork of organisations and individuals concerned with the promotion of public security; the dissemination of police intelligence becomes a form of social control so that their main function is one of intelligence collection and distribution to other agencies which may have a more enhanced capacity to take action. Preventative safety partnerships[17] are part of the new principle of community governance, the process by which local neighbourhoods, groups and localities are increasingly involved in local government, along with formal traditional local government bodies. The primary objective is "to spread responsibility for crime control onto agencies, organisations and individuals that operate outside the criminal justice state and to persuade them to act appropriately." The idea of a sovereign state monopoly of social control is a myth and replaced by a Hayekian vision of dispersed, pluralistic, social control by self-governing local communities which rely on local knowledge and resources: "the state's intention is thus to replace 'old' criminal bureau-professional arrangements with multi-tasking partnerships whose performance will be dominated by the need to produce ever more quantifiable outputs and cost-effective outcomes." Based on communitarian ideals, communities are in this model both the site and agent of governance. As observed earlier, communities are unstable and ill-defined entities in a complex, pluralistic society. They are "weakly bounded and leaky systems", contradictory, unruly and beset with divisions and tensions. Further, in the UK, most such partnerships, Hughes and McLaughlin observe, are in fact corporate duopolies, comprised of the police and the local council. Responsibility for developing and implementing strategies still lies with local authority community safety teams, supported by local police. They are largely dominated by operational police concerns about crime and disorder reduction. Additionally, rather than being networks of inter-related agencies drawing from the public, private and voluntary sectors, they are central state, "top-down" projects, cajoled to "tool up" in increasingly coercive ways against the anti-social.

Managerialism and The New Policing

In a seminal 1996 article, Bayley and Shearing[18] declared that: **1-053**

> "Modern democratic countries like the United States, Britain and Canada have reached a watershed in the evolution of their systems of crime control and law enforcement. Future generations will look back on our era as a time when one system of policing ended and another took its place."

They identify two main developments: the pluralisation of policing by ending the monopoly by the public police in favour of a more complex relationship between police and other political mechanisms; and, following a shift in the mandate and legitimacy of the police themselves, the search by the public police for a new identity. Over the past 30 or so years, they argue, the state's monopoly on policing was broken by the creation of a host of private and community-based agencies that prevent crime and deter criminality, catch law-breakers, investigate offences and stop conflict. At the same time, there

---

[17] Such as the Crime and Disorder Reduction partnership: see para.3-044.
[18] D. Bayley, and C. Shearing, "The Future of Policing" (1996) 30(3) *Law and Society Review* pp.585–606.

were doubts in government about the effectiveness of public policing associated with the increasing civilianisation of public policing (the use of special constables and Community Support Officers,[19] accredited private persons[20]), private security firms and decline in visible police patrols. Bayley and Shearing's conclusion is:

> ". . . the pluralizing of policing and the search by the public police for a new role and methodology mean that not only the government's monopoly on policing has been broken in the late 20th century, but the police monopoly on expertise within its own sphere of activity has ended. Policing now belongs to everybody—in activity, in responsibility, in oversight."

An explanation for the change lies in the kind of socio-economic and cultural changes put forward by Young, above. These changes caused dramatic increases in recorded crime figures since 1954, its effect on popular perceptions about the rise of crime and the growing centrality of law and order as a predominant political concern. Reiner, for example, writes that the rise of the police was a paradigm of the modern in that it was predicated on the project of organising society around a central, cohesive notion of order; and changes in social structure and culture rendered this concept of policing increasingly anachronistic.[21] Others, such as O'Malley, argue the decline of public policing was more to do with the rise of neo-liberalism and managerialism.[22] There is also the "mass private property" thesis: there is more privately-owned space concentrated in the hands of fewer corporate interests but which are open to the public to visit, such as shopping malls, sporting complexes and so on. The more privately-owned public space, the more private policing.[23] However, see Jones and Newburn,[24] who argue that the decline of public policing has more to do with the formalisation of social control. There has been a decline in the prevalence of secondary social control agents such as caretakers, bus conductors, and so on who occupy physical space and carry out surveillance functions. Following their decline, the public police could not fill the gaps, lacking sufficient resources, and so the private security industry and other civil agencies expanded to fill them.

1-054   Matthews and Pitts[25] write that a consequence of the political and academic onslaught, which sought to limit the powers of the sovereign state in the 1960s and 1970s, was the development of a decentralisation strategy through new forms of decentralised community control, adopted because they were cheaper and provided a way of reducing state obligation to provide services, and depoliticised the process of crime control by turning public issues into personal problems. At the same time, the depth and intensity of intervention in many cases was increased. As a result of "net widening", it was argued, these interventions were seen as being largely counterproductive since a growing number of minor offenders were drawn into the mainstream criminal justice process, with a predictable proportion ending up in prison at a later date. Therefore, the decentralising strategy resulted in promoting new forms of social exclusion and marginalisation. There was an unwieldy complex of agencies and organisations which traversed the conventional distinctions

---

[19] See para.2-019.
[20] See para.2-024.
[21] "Policing a Post-Modern Society" (1992) 55/6 *Modern Law Review*, pp.761–81.
[22] "Policing, Politics, Post-Modernity" (1997) 6(3) *Social and Legal Studies* pp.363–81.
[23] See Shearing and Stenning (eds) *Private Policing* (Criminal Justice Systems Annuals, Vol.23, 1987).
[24] See "Urban Change and Policing: Mass Private Property Reconsidered", (1999) 7/2 *European Journal on Criminal Policy and Research*, 225–44; see also Kepma, Stenning and Wood "Policing Communal Spaces" (2004) 44 Brit. J. Criminol. 562.
[25] *Crime, Disorder and Community Safety* (2001).

between the public and the private realms and between state and civil society. Even so, privatisation during the 1980s continued to be promoted, particularly in relation to policing, crime prevention, the use of security equipment and the contracting out of prison management. The rapid development of multi-agency partnerships encouraged the involvement of the private sector alongside voluntary and statutory agencies. In the 1990s the decentralising impulse took a slightly different turn following the implementation of the recommendation of the Morgan Report to devolve responsibility for crime control and community safety to local authorities. Emphasis was placed upon multi-agency partnerships and the establishment of community safety strategy groups which were to be responsible for assessing the nature of crime in each locality, developing a community safety strategy and monitoring interventions. During the 1980s, the Thatcher-led Conservative government had tried to limit the powers of local authorities, which were seen as unreliable, but a decade later this policy was reversed by an incoming Labour government and local authorities in conjunction with the local police were given statutory responsibility for crime prevention and community safety.

Part of the process involved the incorporation of New Managerialism into policing and crime and disorder management strategies. The most important examples of the New Managerialism are "the New Public Administration" in the public sector and "shareholder value" in the private sector. The central principle of managerialism is that the differences between such organisations as, for example, a university and a motor-vehicle company, are less important than the similarities, and that the performance of all organisations can be optimised by the application of universal management skills and theory. The optimal policy is to design organisations that respond directly to consumer demand, and to operate such institutions using the generic management techniques applicable to corporations of all kinds. Therefore, it involves organisational restructuring, enhancing incentives, and expansion in the number, power and remuneration of senior managers, with a corresponding downgrading of the role of skilled workers, and particularly of professionals. It is usually, but not always, associated with market-oriented reforms such as economic rationalism and neo-liberalism. Some have observed that managerialism has in fact little to do with traditional free-market ideals about the importance of small firms in competitive markets in which the manager is also the owner and that it is more consistent with the strand of neo-liberalism which takes the corporation, rather than the small owner-managed firm, as the model for all forms of economic and social organisation.

1-055

Matthews and Pitts[26] argue that New Managerialism turns political and moral decisions into administrative and technical ones. In the name of cost-effectiveness, policy options are counted and discounted. Within the performance indicator culture, which is actively fostered by the New Managerialism, only that which is quantifiable is relevant. The fact that many of these performance indicators are uncertain is generally overlooked in the rush to produce figures and meet targets. The reliance, for example, on official crime statistics as a measure of the effectiveness of specific interventions, or the efficiency of the relevant agencies, is extremely dubious. New Labour was quick to appropriate both the language and the principles of the New Managerialism. Its emphasis on the rationality of "what works", "joined-up solutions" and "empowerment" fitted well with New Labour's avowed commitment to rational public policy and the devolution of power to "local people". The adoption of managerialism within criminal justice incorporated, Matthews and Pitts argue, a significant actuarial dimension that

1-056

---

[26] *Crime, Disorder and Community Safety* (2001).

presented policy choices as a function of competing risks which could be assessed on an objective scale, as well as on the basis of cost-effectiveness. Balancing off these two apparently neutral and "scientific" sets of criteria, they say, opened up considerable latitude for interpretation and discretion. The central appeal of the New Managerialism is that it offered a template for the new, more restricted role of government—a "Third Way"—which New Labour believed was necessitated by the unmanageability of the global economy and the privatisation of personal life precipitated by the radical changes in the class structure of Britain over the preceding thirty years. Thus, the Crime and Disorder Act 1998, in handing new responsibilities over to local authorities and local multi-agency partnerships, prescribed the goals they should pursue, the targets they should achieve and the time scales in which they should operate, but not the means for their achievement. "Product support" is provided via a steady flow of "evidence-based" data about "what works" and "pilot studies" of new administrative arrangements and modes of intervention; while "quality control" is vouchsafed by statutory audits. Meanwhile, "action teams", such as the Home Office PATs, comprising senior officials from the relevant ministries, work on inter-ministerial synchronisation and the articulation of central government activity with that of the local authorities and multi-agency partnerships. In the view of the government, the "joined-upness" of solutions to youth crime and community safety consisted in the simultaneous management of those "risk factors" associated with the onset of crime and delinquency, and the application of "evidence-based" technologies for the correction of familial, cognitive or behavioural deficiencies which lead to persistence.

Restorative Justice

1-057   The White Paper, *No More Excuses*,[27] acknowledged what was described as a need ". . . to reshape the criminal justice system in England and Wales to produce more constructive outcomes with young offenders" and referred to the need to build on three concepts: responsibility, restoration and reintegration. Dignan[28] writes that the new orders contained in the Crime and Disorder Act 1998[29] were the result of a change in the political climate based on concepts of restorative justice. He defines the term "restorative justice" as a convenient shorthand expression that is commonly applied to a variety of practices which seek to respond to crime in a more constructive way than is conventionally achieved through the use of punishment. One of the primary aims of most restorative justice approaches, he says, is to engage with offenders to try to bring home the consequences of their actions and an appreciation of the impact they have had on the victims of their offences. A second aim is to encourage and facilitate the provision of appropriate forms of reparation by offenders, towards either their direct victims (provided they are agreeable) or the wider community. A third aim is to seek reconciliation between victim and offender, where this can be achieved and, even in cases where this is not possible, to strive to reintegrate both victims and offenders within the community as a whole following the commission of an offence. The 1998 Act orders, in his view, appear to be consistent with "restorative justice" principals. He concludes that the short term prospects for restorative justice have been transformed, in the space of little over a year, by changes in the political climate following the general election. However, he identifies

---

[27] "No More Excuses—A New Approach to Tackling Youth Crime In England and Wales," Home Office, 1997 HMSO at para.9.21.
[28] "The Crime and Disorder Act and the Prospects of Restorative Justice" (1999) Crim. L.R. 46–60.
[29] See para.3-071.

what he sees as much broader tension, which is still to be resolved, between the criminal justice policies that were inherited by the incoming Labour Government in 1997, with their emphasis on punishment and social exclusion, and the alternative, more socially-inclusive, problem-solving approach, of which glimpses can be discerned in some of the youth justice reforms considered in his article. In the long-term, he says, the philosophy of restorative justice should be part of a broader crime prevention strategy, linked with a fundamental shift in the direction of a wide range of social policies, that are known to have a bearing on the level of crime.

Morris and Gelsthorpe[30] are more critical. They argue that restorative   **1-058** processes will continue to occupy a marginal place in criminal justice until contradictory values and practices of blaming and punishing are given significantly less emphasis, and restorative values and practices are given significantly more emphasis. They see restorative justice as just one theme in a broadly punitive and controlling piece of legislation and are less optimistic than Dignan about the power and potential of restorative justice to fundamentally alter the current youth or criminal justice systems. The tenor of the 1998 Act, they argue, indicates an ideological shift in favour of punishment and crime control rather than away from it. Second, new managerialism is apparent in the Crime and Disorder Act 1998 in its emphasis on inter-agency co-operation and the statutory duty placed on local authorities to consult widely and to formulate and implement an annual youth justice plan setting out how local youth justice services will be provided and funded. The intention is to make the youth justice system more efficient and effective (and probably more economical too). Thirdly, the ideas behind risk assessment and "actuarial" justice, which involve predictions, of behaviour and taking anticipatory action on the basis of these predictions, underlie the introduction in the 1998 Act orders so that the non-criminal and future behaviour of children is effectively criminalised, even if this is not the primary intention of the legislation. Fourthly, the 1998 Act continues the theme of "community" by adding to the existing set of community based penalties. Finally, the 1998 Act introduces elements of restorative justice through conferencing, reparation and action plan orders and giving victims more of a say with respect to the content of certain orders. They conclude that the orders which are part of the "restorative package" introduced in the 1998 Act do not seem then to go very far. Restorative practices, they argue, will develop in an ad hoc fashion at numerous decision points in the youth justice system, but at no point will the key participants in all of this actually be able to take charge:

"Victims will no longer be marginalised in quite the way that they are currently, but their involvement will hardly be significant. Offenders may be coerced into reparation. Nothing in the research literature suggests that this will be likely to prevent reoffending. And there continues to be an emphasis on blaming rather than restorative processes, as in the parenting order. The critical question is whether or not restorative justice in its Crime and Disorder Act 1998 guise is sufficiently new and radical to revitalise youth justice in England and Wales. It seems to us that despite the good intentions and enthusiasm of many politicians, policy-makers and practitioners, the hold of restorative justice will remain tenuous unless the competing and contradictory values running through criminal and youth justice policy in England and Wales in general, and in the Crime and Disorder Act 1998 in particular, concede more space."

[30] "Something Old, Something Borrowed, Something Blue, But Something New? On the Prospects of Restorative Justice in the Crime and Disorder Act 1998" (2000) Crim.L.R. 18.

Conclusion: Human Rights and the Rule of Law

1-059   In this section, we look at ASBOs themselves, the centre-piece of the new anti-social behaviour and disorder programme as an instance of the interplay between the government's objectives in the area of crime and disorder control and wider pre-existing legal principles. ASBOs are "strange legal hybrids" of criminal law and civil procedure.[31] During the passage of the Crime and Disorder Bill through the House of Lords, Lord Goodhart described it as the creation of a "personal criminal law" under which the defendant is punished not for breaking the law but for breaking a law that applies to him personally.[32] Lord Thomas unsuccessfully moved for an amendment that breaches should be punishable not by the criminal law but as civil contempts. See also Ashworth's comment that it would be "a Trojan horse" use of the civil law[33] and remarks in an article in Criminal Justice by six academics that the ASBO system was "a huge transfer to local officials of the power effectively to criminalise conduct by stealth".[34] It would function as an "Undesirable Persons Act":

> "Unfortunately, the government's latest legislative proposal is neither sensible nor carefully targeted. It takes sweepingly defined conduct within its ambit, grants local agencies virtually unlimited discretion to seek highly restrictive orders, jettisons fundamental legal protections for the grant of those orders and authorises potentially draconian and wholly disproportionate penalties for violations of them."

They also maintained that the new regime was contrary to the ECHR:

> "Human rights law will be contravened because:
>
> (a) the orders will be made under the civil law burden of a balance of probabilities rather than under the criminal law burden of proof of beyond reasonable doubt even though the person subject to the order could go to prison (contra Article 6(2)); and,
> (b) there is no right to cross-examine witnesses."

However, it was conclusively determined by the House of Lords in *McCann*[35] that the ASBO was not contrary to Convention law. Specific procedural issues, such as whether or not ASBOs are civil or criminal proceedings under the ECHR and the standard of proof in ASBO cases, are now settled by the *McCann* case. But there is a wider problem, summarised by Lord Goodhart during the course of the 1998 Act through committee stage in Parliament in this way:

> "Human rights are not just the right to behave well. . .People have a right to be bloody-minded; they have a right within reason to make a bit of a nuisance of themselves. . .We want to live in a law-abiding society with a low level of crime. . .and a low level of vandalism and disorder of all kinds. . .but, at the same time, we do not want to live in an authoritarian state."[36]

---

[31] Ashworth, "Social Control and Anti-Social Behaviour: The Subversion of Human Rights" (2004), L.Q.R. 120(Apr), 263–291.

[32] H.L. Deb. vol.585, col 533.

[33] "A Bill to be Tough On Crime" N.L.J., January 9, 1998, 13.

[34] Ashworth, Gardner, Morgan *et al*, "Neighbouring on the Oppressive", (1998) 16 Criminal Justice 1.

[35] [2003] 1 A.C. 787.

[36] HL Report (HMSO, February 3, 1998), Col. 534.

Following an analysis of the way one local authority applied for ASBOs, **1-060** Burke and Morrill[37] are concerned that the balance has already shifted too far in favour of communities at the expense of individual liberty and due process values. ASBOs, they argue, appeared to be most useful when used against those at an early stage in their anti-social or criminal career; and they are best targeted at those who have behaved in some way that has been proven to a criminal standard. The sweeping nature of the anti-social behaviour order provisions could lead to their being applied in situations for which they were clearly not intended. White[38] refers to Home Office research into the use of s.5 of the Public Order Act 1986 which showed that it had become, in some cases, a vehicle for securing respect for the police and anecdotal evidence that other procedures, such as trespassory assembly orders and orders under the Protection from Harassment Act 1997,[39] have been used for purposes other than those for which they were primarily intended. He puts forward the following example.

"Suppose that an area of open land fronts a block of flats, and becomes a well-known venue for recreation by homosexual couples. A number of homosexual couples take to engaging in visible signs of affection for each other in the open space. This is certainly conduct which might be regarded by some as likely to cause distress, giving those terms their ordinary meaning. If the local authority regarded it as inappropriate for the open space to be used as a meeting place for homosexual couples, then it would not appear to be difficult to construct the case for the use of section 1 of the Crime and Disorder Act 1998 in this context. There is a defence that the conduct alleged to be likely to cause distress was reasonable. An order might be granted prohibiting the couple from visiting the open space or kissing in public. Were the provisions to be used in this way, issues under Articles 8, 10 and 11 of the Convention would be raised. Article 8 of the Convention recognises a right, subject to certain limitations, to respect for private life, which has been interpreted to include respect for individual identity and includes a prohibition on unduly repressive measures against homosexuals. Article 10 provides that everyone has the right to freedom of expression, again subject to limitations. The outer limits of expression have not yet been defined, but a prohibition on overtly expressing one's sexuality in a manner permitted for heterosexual couples could, it is submitted, fall within its ambit (though it is more likely to be regarded as an aspect of private life under Article 8). Finally, Article 11 grants a right, subject to limitations, to freedom of peaceful assembly. A prohibition on using a particular open space (or indeed a curfew order) could arguably breach this Convention right. In all these cases—as distinct from the rights granted under Articles 5, 6 and 7—the nature of the limitation would have to be prescribed by law for one of the interests recognised in the limitations contained in the article and be shown to be necessary in a democratic society. This requires showing that there is a pressing social need for regulation and that the interference with the right is the minimum necessary to secure a legitimate general interest."

---

[37] HL Report (HMSO, February 3, 1998), Col.534.
[38] White, "Anti-social Behaviour Orders Under Section 1 of the Crime and Disorder Act 1998" (1999) E.L. Rev 24 Supp Hrs, 55–62. See also R. Leng, R. Taylor, and M. Wasik, *Blackstone's Guide to the Crime and Disorder Act 1998* (1998), N. Padfield, *A Guide to the Crime and Disorder Act 1998* (Butterworths, 1998) and D. Scanlan, *The Crime and Disorder Act 1998: A Guide for Practitioners* (Callow Publishing, 1998).
[39] See para.2-106 for the further details of the end of Mr Haw's campaign.

Another instance might be legitimate and peaceful protests or picketing as in *Westminster City Council v Haw*.[40] Although this was a case involving powers under the Highways Act 1980, it might be argued that protests which are not otherwise unlawful, such as the placing of placards in the windows of a private residence or non-obstructive picketing, might be a real nuisance to some members of the community as assessed by the relevant agencies. If so, then the application might amount to a breach of the defendant's rights of free speech. In the *Haw* case, Gray J. said that it was important that the defendant was exercising his right to freedom of expression, and doing so on a political issue. Interference with that right was permissible where it was to do so in order to protect the rights of others. Gray J. found no pressing social need to interfere with the display of placards so as to protect the right of others to pass and re-pass. Objection may be taken to the defendant's activities on the ground that they constitute an eyesore, but that is a different matter. Therefore, it was held that the obstruction for which the defendant is responsible was not unreasonable. There are some instances which appear to come close to the example mentioned in White above which are difficult to see how they can be justified: cases where ASBOs are imposed on children whose disabilities caused them to behave in difficult ways: Tourettes Syndrome and swearing; autistic children and "staring over the fence" where, in one case, the child, not having committed any criminal offences and was unknown to the local youth offending team; yet the magistrates, aware of his condition, made the order all the same.[41] Or the case of a 14-year-old from Lincolnshire who had ADHD and was given a two year ASBO with multiple conditions, but a package of support put together by a police officer from the Youth Justice Team, which would have dealt with the underlying problems of his behaviour, was declined by the magistrates who preferred the cheaper option of an ASBO. Nor is it easy to see, at first-glance, the utility of ordering an ASBO against a ten year old boy, regardless of his prior conduct.[42] Or how such an order could possibly be made in respect of a woman who tried to kill herself four times, to require her to stay away from railway lines, bridges, and multi-storey car-parks; it is likely that the imposition of an ASBO and all attendant difficulties would have made her circumstances worse, although there is no information in the report as to whether or not any local health services were involved before or after the making of the order.[43] Cases of this kind reveal two main problems with the use of ASBOs. First, they appear to be used in a disproportionate, heavy-handed way; and secondly, they are a quick and easy populist solution for dealing with complex social problems.

1-061   For example, there is the use of ASBOs to deal with prostitution. More precisely, because obtaining an ASBO takes a great deal of preparation, police forces prefer CRASBOs instead (the grant of an ASBO at the point of conviction by a criminal court). In May 2003, the Birmingham Magistrates made an anti-social behaviour order against a street prostitute; she was banned from loitering in the streets anywhere in England and Wales for three years. Fours hours after the making of the order, she was

---

[40] [2002] WL 31050512, October 4, 2002.
[41] Manchester CC withdrew an ASBO against a teenager who suffers from Tourette syndrome. However, local residents complained the boy repeatedly kicked a football against their properties, threw stones and spat at houses, kicked street lamps and threw rubbish down the street. He was part of a group which used abusive and insulting language to elderly residents when challenged about their behaviour. He also used homophobic abuse repeatedly against a resident. The Council withdrew the anti-social behaviour order but said his bad behaviour was not linked to his medical problem. *Manchester Evening News*, December 28, 2005.
[42] *Independent*, February 10, 2005.
[43] *Guardian*, February 26, 2005. For numerous other instances, see NAPO and ASBO Concern's July 2005 Report, ASBOs: An Analysis of the First 6 Years.

alleged to have been seen "walking" the streets of Edgbaston by two police officers. She was subsequently arrested to appear in court for breach of the order.[44] And yet:

(1) if a woman's personal circumstances are so grave that they compel her to become a street prostitute, it is unlikely that an anti-social behaviour order would make any difference to her and so breach is inevitable;

(2) the subject of the order in this case was likely to be only one of many women who would frequent that area. The purpose of the order may have been to "to send a message", but the penalties for street prostitution are relatively minor when compared to the sentences for breach of an anti-social behaviour order: about half of those persons guilty of breaching the order are given custodial sentences;

(3) the order will not stop prostitution in Birmingham. Nor is it likely to stop prostitution in the particular part of Birmingham where this person was found. Generally, in areas where there is a high level of street prostitution, there is said to be competition for space so that when one street prostitute leaves a site, another will take his or her place almost immediately;

(4) further, there may be other more effective strategies. Some of them may focus on individual cases such as drug therapy and counselling. More general responses might include police targeting kerb-crawlers rather than prostitutes, traffic re-organisation, or the establishment of special and regulated zones for street prostitution away from residential areas;

(5) it may mean that women move to areas with which they are less familiar and have less time to check their customers so as to increase the risk of violence towards them. In fact, practice varies from one police authority to the next. In Ladywood, Edgbaston, 21 ASBOs were issued during 2003 to 2005, a local resident street watch group providing the information necessary to secure them. In Coventry, six CRASBOs were issued in 2005; however, before making the application, proposed respondents are initially referred to local support agencies and the application will proceed only if they continue to work on the street.[45] In Bradford CRASBOs are made against kerb-crawlers in certain cases.

As regards the use of ASBOs in the case of children, it is useful to consider the remarks about ASBOs by the Commissioner for Human Rights on his visit to the United Kingdom.[46] While he was surprised by the enthusiasm for the orders amongst legislators and the executive at any rate, he did not consider them at all to be inherently objectionable:[47]   **1-062**

"Well-drafted orders, prohibiting clearly proven and seriously vexatious behaviour, accompanied by appropriate assistance and supervision may well usefully protect citizens from activity that gravely prejudices their welfare, but which falls outside the scope of effective criminal prosecution."

However, he found it difficult to avoid the impression that the ASBO was being touted as a miracle cure for urban nuisance. The police, local authorities and

---

[44] Sager and Jones, "Crime and Disorder Act 1988: Prostitution and the Anti-Social Behaviour Order", (2001) Crim.L.R., Nov, 873–885.
[45] Matthews, *"Policing Prostitution: Ten Years On"* (2005) 45 Brit. J. Criminol. 877.
[46] June 2005, Council of Europe.
[47] At para.111.

other empowered actors, he said, were placed under considerable pressure to apply for ASBOs, both from central government and from inconvenienced members of the local community. This pressure applied equally to magistrates to grant them. Part of the drive to promote ASBOs involved making them as easy as possible to obtain and open to as many applicants as possible. Some form of responsible screening of ASBO applications by a responsible authority seemed to be at least a minimum guarantee against excessive use. Proper evidential requirements and a sensible control of what actually constituted anti-social behaviour was essential as ASBOs could bring their subjects a misplaced step away from the criminal justice system. The ASBO, he said, blurred the boundaries between the civil and criminal justice systems and so great care had to be taken to ensure that the rights to fair trial and liberty were respected. Detention following the breach of an ASBO drawn up in such a way as to make its breach almost inevitable (such as not entering a demarcated zone near one's residence), and which was applied on the basis of hearsay evidence in respect of non-criminal behaviour, would almost certainly, in his view, constitute a violation of Art.5 of the Convention. However, particular concerns arise in respect of the application of ASBOs to children. ASBOs can be served on children as young as 10 in England and Wales and 12 in Scotland:

"It is one thing to intervene in respect of seriously and repetitively troublesome youths, in respect of whom ASBOs may, on occasion, be appropriate. It is another to slap them on youths that are generally up to no good. There is a world of difference between hassle and harassment. It is not because a child is causing inconvenience that he should be brought to the portal of the criminal justice system. Here again, however, I heard numerous complaints of excessive, victimising ASBOs being awarded. The concern is that the excessive use of ASBOs is more likely to exacerbate anti-social behaviour and crime amongst youths than effectively prevent it and this is for two reasons. First, ASBO breaches have resulted in large numbers of children being detained—46 per cent of young people received immediate custody upon conviction for breach, though only 17 per cent were sentenced to custody for breach where no other offence was considered. The chair of the Youth Justice Board has conceded that the rise in the young offender population in custody in 2004 resulted mainly from breaches of anti-social behaviour orders. Given the high reconviction rates for detained juvenile offenders, one wonders, whether the detention of juveniles for non-criminal behaviour will not lead to more serious offending on release. It is to be recalled, in any case, that the detention of children should be a last resort— detaining children for activity that is not itself criminal can scarcely be consistent with this principle. I was pleased to note that children under 16 cannot be detained for breaching ASBOs in Scotland and would strongly encourage the extension of this rule to the rest of the United Kingdom."

1-063 Criminal law is concerned with censuring and punishing wrongs; the purpose of the ASBO is to prevent future wrongs. Criminal liability depends therefore on proof of discrete acts with discrete results, and a specific state of mind. The unlawful act is related to the defendant's capacity to choose, abstracted from its social situation. However, Ramsey[48] remarks that the test for granting an ASBO is concerned with the future relationship between the defendant and the community; it is the future relationship that renders the defendant liable. He describes the ASBO as a prohibition in appearance only; in fact, it imposes a positive obligation to be aware of the potential effect of actions on the feelings of others. Whether or not a person has fulfilled this duty is a question to

[48] "What is Anti-Social Behaviour" (2004) Crim. L. R.908–925.

be determined by the perceptions of those affected by any default, as well as official perceptions of the person's attitude and its context. It becomes an entirely hypothetical analysis of the effect of the defendant's conduct, past or future:

> "While proof of the existence of some behaviour which causes harassment, alarm or distress is necessary, the key elements of the court's findings are matters either not susceptible to proof or proved only as an actuarial fact or probability. The determination is thus entirely evaluative and in practice will consist of the application of the magistrates 'common sense' to the defendant's behaviour and attitude."

The discretion to be exercised by the magistrates has very little to do with the substantive criminal law; it is in effect the exercise of a public law discretion. If the defendant's conduct and the reasons for it are thought by the magistrates to be acting contrary to public policy, as they understand it, they will grant the ASBO; if they are not contrary to public policy, then an application would be unlikely anyway since the relevant authority would have brought it in the first place. That may be in part why less than 1 per cent of ASBO applications are refused. Section 1(1) and IC (in combination with the "reasonableness" exception in s.1(5)) of the 1998 Act are not descriptions of a general legal duty but the criteria for the exercise of a discretionary administrative power:

> "Criminal trials are a paradigmatic form of adjudication. In the lower courts at least, the key issues of liability turn on proofs of evidence and arguments from relatively precise rules articulating generally formulated duties. By contrast, in the absence of a universal duty defined independently of public policy considerations, the magistrate hearing an ASBO application could find herself determining liability to an order by interpreting broad standards in a way that enjoys a limited but significant freedom from precise rules."

The next question is why the government has decided that it is appropriate for courts to exercise that kind of discretion in the first place. Ashworth[49] argues that one of the main aims of the restorative justice movement is to change the focus of criminal justice away from the assumption that it is a matter concerning only the state and the defendant offender, and towards a conception that includes as "stake-holders" the victim and the community too. It is central to the philosophy of restorative justice that the stakeholders should be able to participate in dialogue about the offence. Traditionally, it is common to refer to the "public interest" in preventing or prosecuting crime: when it is decided to make certain conduct a crime rather than simply a civil wrong, this implies that it should not be merely a matter for the victim whether some action is taken against the malefactor; and even that there is a public interest in ensuring that people who commit such wrongs are liable to punishment, not merely to civil suit, that it is the responsibility of the state to ensure that there is order and law-abidance in society, and to establish a system for the administration of criminal justice. Over time, the effective control of crime and the routine protection of citizens from criminal depredations had come to form elements of the promise that the state holds out to its citizens. This serves as the basis of the justification for maintaining a police force, a system of public prosecutions, the courts, and other aspects of the criminal justice system. However, as we have noted above, many writers have identified the delegation of these functions by the state to others, either by moving it down to the level of the local community or by elements of privatisation: increasing decentralisation

1-064

---

[49] "Responsibilities, Rights and Restorative Justice" (2002) 42 Brit. J. Criminol. 578.

and "responsibilisation" in criminal justice for a variety of political reasons; one aspect of the restorative justice movement, too, is a relocation of authority over responses to crime. Ashworth has two arguments in favour of the principle that criminal justice must be administered "in the public interest", and that it should ensure respect for human rights. First, criminal offences are offences against the state, so it is right that the state should ensure that the response is based on general principles duly established and applicable throughout the jurisdiction. Secondly, the state owes it to offenders to exercise its power according to settled principles that uphold citizens' rights to equal respect and equality of treatment. There is, he argues, an important distinction between tribunals responding in a principled manner to relevant factual differences between cases, and responding on the basis of their own views or preferences. The latter is contrary to the rule of law, a breach of the doctrine of separation of powers, one of the implications of which is that questions of how people are to be treated relative to one another always come to the fore at the point of its application. The power exercised by imposing obligations on offenders in response to their offending ought, in principle, to be exercised consistently as between citizens, according to settled standards. The state must, as the primary political authority, retain control over criminal justice and its administration. It must do so for pragmatic reasons concerned with security (and in order to ensure respect for the rule of law and human rights standards). The state ought, out of fairness to the people in respect of whom its coercive powers are being exercised, to insist on "rule of law" principles and so ensure consistency of response to offences. The ASBO is, for Ashworth, an abrogation of the state's traditional role in the criminal justice system in the interests of restorative justice (or, as Ramsey sees it, communitarianism). Ashworth[50] draws attention to the extraordinarily wide range of conduct falling within the statutory definition. Second, subject to the courts, the penalty for breach may be entirely disproportionate. Thirdly, the order contains no provision for support to the person subject to the order, suggesting that repression and exclusion have a greater priority than prevention. The duration of the order, set at a minimum of two years, is too long, particularly for a young person without any real support. The hybrid order is intended to achieve the admissibility of evidence according to civil rules; the assessment of it according to civil standards; the making of a civil order with the potential for overly-wide terms so that the chances of breach are increased rather than decreased; sentencing for breach which takes account of earlier conduct not proven or admitted in a criminal court. Various aspects of the criminal law have come to be seen as obstacles to dealing with certain kinds of behaviour, so rather than create a hybrid, he writes, perhaps a better approach would be consider amending those rules. More importantly, the government has crossed the boundary from avoidance of responsibility to uphold human rights to evasion.[51]

1-065   It is also useful to compare two different approaches to the problem of anti-social behaviour and housing, specifically nuisance possession proceedings. Manchester City Council's neighbour nuisance strategy group was named Housing Team of the Year 2001 by the Local Government Chronicle, and the Chartered Institute of Housing endorsed their approach as good practice for others to follow. It has resulted in nearly 2,000 successful legal actions, 30 anti-social behaviour orders, and the eviction of 238 families (since 1995). While Shelter criticised Manchester's approach as being "over-zealous" and simplistic, the Council is proud of their tough record: ". . . it sends out a strong

---

[50] "Social Control and Anti-Social Behaviour: The Subversion of Human Rights", (2004) L.Q.R. 263–291.
[51] House of Commons Home Affairs Committee, Fifth Report, Cm. 6588 (2004–05) Anti–Social Behaviour, pp.74–76.

message to tenants that we expect them to behave. Its not about punishment; it is about preventing the problem."[52] Even so, there is an argument that not only are nuisance possession proceedings sometimes simplistic and heavy-handed, they are expensive in terms of costs and demands on homelessness services and emergency housing. Perhaps crucially, they simply move the problem along: for example, an anti-social family will move to the private sector in the same area but where the local authority has no say in the their behaviour as tenants. According to Paul Beardmore, director of housing at Rochdale Metropolitan Borough Council, many of the Manchester's evicted families end up in the private sector in their area so that his council ". . .have been on the receiving end of displacement." Shelter recommends what it considers to be a more rounded approach:[53]

> "We all have the right to somewhere decent to live. Unfortunately, the unacceptable behaviour of a few people can ruin the lives of so many of those who live around them. But these proposals will simply create more problems. We need a more balanced solution—one that challenges and prevents anti social behaviour and does not simply exacerbate poverty and make more people homeless."

Hence, its involvement with Rochdale Metropolitan Borough Council in an initiative whereby those made homeless by anti-social behaviour are given support for up to a year if they sign and abide by the terms of a "good-behaviour" contract. The project started in September last year and so far none of the 35 families in the Rochdale area which have received assistance has been evicted and complaints about them have substantially reduced. A similar scheme has operated in Dundee since 1997, set up by NCH Scotland. It costs £345,000 a year to run but is said to save £462,000 each year in legal costs[54]

The Local Government Association supports appropriate enforcement to deal with anti-social behaviour, welcome powers to local government.[55] **1-066** However, it is critical of the lack of a focus on prevention and rehabilitation. Anti-social behaviour cases, the Association argues, are frequently complex, often involving those who lack basic literacy and or access to employment, have substance misuse issues or lack leisure facilities or decent housing. Enforcement alone may lead to further alienation. Prevention, enforcement and rehabilitation are more likely to create safer and stronger communities in the long run. Anti-social behaviour often involves complex issues, which vary from person to person. "Silo" interventions, focussing on just one aspect of this jigsaw puzzle, are doomed to failure. Central government has made available a range of enforcement measures available to authorities and partner organisations to deal with anti-social behaviour, the most effective approach is to focus efforts on prevention and rehabilitation as well as enforcement. While there are resources being invested in preventative work by central government, councils are faced with a range of national initiatives, inter-agency activities and drives on a wide range of issues. They are continually challenged to co-ordinate these diverse initiatives to make use of them within their communities. Joined-up thinking at a national level, including further rationalisation of initiatives and funding streams, would remove this obstacle. The Home Office needs to demonstrate that the prevention and rehabilitation on focus can be driven cross-departmentally, as well as downwards, to local government, currently unable to resource this effectively. Anti-social behaviour work typically involves a wide range of agen-

---

[52] *Guardian*, June 4, 2003.
[53] Shelter press release, May 20, 2003.
[54] ROOF (Jan/Feb, 2002).
[55] "Sustainable solutions to Anti-social behaviour" (2005).

cies, with the local authority at the hub. Associate organisations working in this area include youth offending teams, Connexions, learning and skills councils, and children and young people's strategic partnerships. They must work effectively with CDRPs to deliver preventative and rehabilitative services, alongside enforcement. Not doing so wastes resources and time, and prevents the provision of a "one stop" approach for offenders.

Conclusion

1-067   It is difficult to take issue with laws and policies that are directed at reducing the consequences of social deprivation and anti-social behaviour and disorder, or to make the criminal justice system more democratic and responsive to community concerns. The government's programme can be seen as an attempt at a realistic and pragmatic response to a serious problem, particularly when traditional ways of dealing with it, as commentators have observed, are out-of-date, having been overtaken by major social and economic changes. It is not suggested that the problems caused by the conduct falling under the umbrella of anti-social behaviour and disorder are over-stated. Nor is any devaluation of the legal reforms over the past ten years intended: anyone acting for a local authority a few years ago in respect of a major disorder problem on a housing estate appreciates the usefulness of the new orders and law. Taking a rounded view of the government's programme at a policy level at any rate, anti-social behaviour will not just trigger a punitive response; in many cases, increasingly, it is also an opportunity for government intervention. However, there is a danger that anti-social behaviour powers will be used inefficiently and at the expense of broader, more effective, but also sometimes more expensive and complicated and less politically impressive long-term solutions, and without any due regard to the personal circumstances of the offender or their human rights: the 2003 Anti-Social Behaviour White Paper is very clear: "Effective enforcement is the key".[56] Authorities are encouraged to take the widest possible view of what constitutes anti-social behaviour and problem-oriented approaches are more likely to be discarded as expensive, overly-complicated and even politically out-of-touch. Of concern to any lawyer, whether or not an "airy-fairy libertarian"[57] or a "member of a detached metropolitan elite"[58] or "a woolly-minded Hampstead liberal",[59] there is added risk that courts become just another arm of the executive. There is a role for the new anti-social behaviour powers, but they perhaps should really be seen as only a part of a range of options available to an authority, all aimed at dealing with the problem of anti-social behaviour. Any court dealing with anti-social behaviour should be able to rely on clearer notions of what constitutes relevant anti-social behaviour and disorder. Tolerance of difference, even if it does cause annoyance to some, is the price one may pay for living in a modern, densely-populated liberal democracy. Courts should be positively discouraged from taking any action unless real regard has been paid to the human rights of the individual concerned and that there are no other possible options to deal with the behaviour.

---

[56] White Paper, p.17.
[57] "We could live in a world which is airy fairy, libertarian, where everybody does precisely what they like and we believe the best of everybody and then they destroy us" David Blunkett, November 11, 2001.
[58] Jack Straw, *Times* April 8, 1998.
[59] Jack Straw, on the Criminal Justice Bill, BBC news, January 24, 2000.

CHAPTER TWO
Anti-Social Behaviour Crimes

Introduction

In this chapter, we consider the criminal law relating to anti-social behaviour; **2-001** that is, where the police are the main authority responsible for the control of anti-social behaviour and disorder. As discussed in Chapter One, we argue that that body of law falling under the heading of anti-social behaviour law is based around criminal law concepts. We noted that there is no authoritative definition of the term "anti-social behaviour" but we suggest that, at the very least, it applies to any activity which is "public" in character, generally criminal and at a fairly low level of seriousness, of the kind that might have been once labelled summary or street offences, and which, if not serious, then is a problem because it is persistent or widespread. We observed in Chapter One that one of the criticisms of the new anti-social behaviour laws, particularly the ASBO, is that the term anti-social behaviour and disorder is deliberately vague and covers too a wide a range of conduct. On the other hand, there are good reasons why the concept should be not be comprehensively defined: the range of conduct that it is intended should fall within the scope of anti-social behaviour is almost endless, and courts should be free to determine for themselves when an ASBO is or is not appropriate. However, anti-social behaviour and disorder has a distinct criminal connotation and we believe that one way around the problem of definition is to recall the criminal laws of anti-social behaviour and disorder. Courts are used to dealing with concepts such as harassment and public order and conduct, which others find annoying, is nonetheless justified or reasonable in their ordinary criminal jurisdiction. We suggest that this might be an appropriate basis for the assessment of conduct as anti-social behaviour and disorder generally. Secondly, the concept of anti-social behaviour and disorder, while based on established concepts of the criminal law, has also generated substantial law reform of the criminal law. Some of these reforms and amendments add to or enhance pre-existing anti-social behaviour and disorder crimes; others are completely new offences. In some cases, they contain restrictions on the limits on the rights of citizens to protest or assemble in public and, in some cases, criminalise such protests and assemblies. It might be argued that one effect is to stigmatise public political protest as anti-social behaviour and disorder, something which courts appear anxious to avoid, so that there has emerged a new tension between the need to control anti-social behaviour and the preservation of the right to engage in legitimate public protests. Thirdly, local authorities have powers to deal with anti-social behaviour in their areas (discussed in more detail in chapter Three). They are required to participate in the development of strategies aimed at reducing crime and disorder with police and other authorities. They may also commence civil and criminal proceedings to protect themselves, their property and their employees from anti-social criminal behaviour or the general well-being of their area.

Police Powers

Persons Acting in an Anti-Social Manner—Powers to Require Name and Address

2-002   Section 50 of the Police Reform Act 2002 provides:

> "(1) If a constable in uniform[1] has reason to believe that a person has been acting, or is acting, in an anti-social manner (within the meaning of section 1 of the Crime and Disorder Act 1998), he may require that person to give his name and address to the constable.
> (2) Any person who—
>
> (a) fails to give his name and address when required to do so under subsection (1), or
> (b) gives a false or inaccurate name or address in response to a requirement under that subsection,
>
> is guilty of an offence and shall be liable, on summary conviction, to a fine not exceeding level 3 on the standard scale."

Section 1 of the Crime and Disorder Act 1998 defines "anti-social manner" in this way:

> "(1) (a) that the person has acted, since the commencement date, in an anti-social manner, that is to say, in a manner that caused or was likely to cause harassment, alarm or distress to one or more persons not of the same household as himself; and (b) that such an order is necessary to protect persons in the local government area in which the harassment, alarm or distress[2] was caused or was likely to be caused from further anti-social acts by him."

The term "anti-social manner" is reasonably well defined in this Act, at least in comparison to other acts dealing with anti-social behaviour. It means anything that causes or is likely to cause harassment, alarm or distress to one or more persons not of the same household. It must therefore be the conduct of the same kind as that which is subject to the Protection from Harassment Act 1997. Even so, there is an argument according to some commentators that it is nonetheless sufficiently ambiguous and unclear that visibly different members of the public are likely to be over-targeted by police officers exercising this specific power. The exercise of the power depends on the officer's subjective interpretation of what is anti-social, what is likely to cause another person harassment, alarm or distress. Bowling and Phillips[4] argue that the more unclear the term, the more subjective it is understood and applied, so that discrimination is more likely to occur either as a result of outright racism or stereotyping. They were considering the use by police officers of the "sus laws", the stop and search power contained in s.1 of the Police and Criminal Evidence Act 1978,[5] to target sections of the population, particularly ethnic minorities,

---

[1] It is proposed that Community Support Officers be given similar powers.

[2-3] The same phrase appears in the Protection of Harassment Act 1997 and so, it is submitted, must have broadly the same legal meaning.

[4] "Policing Ethnic Minority Communities", in Newburn, *Handbook of Policing* (Willan Publishing, 2003).

[5] Which requires "a reasonable suspicion" as the commission of certain offences.

leading to a conclusion of the MacPherson Inquiry into the death of Stephen Lawrence that there was an over-representation of minorities in national stop and search figures, indicating at least racist stereotyping.[6] Hence, Omerod and Roberts' comparison between the stop and search laws and this new power:[7]

> "In a retrograde step back to the infamous 'sus' laws, section 50 provides for uniformed police to require the name and address from any person believed to have been acting, or be acting, in an anti-social manner. This is a significant new power because the trigger—anti-social behaviour—is much wider than even the extremely broadly defined offences under the Public Order Act 1986. The potential for abuse by officers repeatedly harassing groups of youths is obvious. There is no direct power of arrest, but failure to comply is an offence (s.50(2)), and that may form the basis of an arrest under s.25 of PACE."

Compare this power to the power to stop and search under ss.44 to 46 of the Terrorism Act 2000. In *R (Gillan) v Commissioner of Police of the Metropolis*,[8] the House of Lords held that an authorisation and confirmation under ss.44 to 46 of the Terrorism Act 2000, allowing police officers to stop and search members of the public at random for articles that could be used in connection with terrorism, had been lawful as a matter of domestic law. The first issue concerned the construction of the expression "expedient" in s.44(3). The claimants suggested that the powers were sweeping and far beyond anything ever permitted by common law powers, a description echoed by the Court of Appeal, and suggested that Parliament could not have intended to sanction police intrusion into the freedom of individuals unless it was necessary that the police have such a power. In rejecting this part of the claimant's argument, Lord Bingham said that examination of the statutory context showed that the authorisation and exercise of the power were very closely regulated: **2-003**

> "There is indeed every indication that Parliament appreciated the significance of the power it was conferring but thought it an appropriate measure to protect the public against the grave risks posed by terrorism, provided the power was subject to effective constraints. The legislation embodies a series of such constraints."

Lord Bingham then enumerated the ten or so constraints on the use of the power in the legislation. Later in his opinion, Lord Bingham discussed the Human Rights Convention requirement of lawfulness. He said at para.34:

> "The lawfulness requirement in the Convention addresses supremely important features of the rule of law. The exercise of power by public officials, as it affects members of the public, must be governed by clear and publicly accessible rules of law. The public must not be vulnerable to interference by public officials acting on a personal whim, caprice, malice, predilection or purpose other than that for which the power was conferred. That is what, in this context, is meant by arbitrariness, which is the antithesis of legality. This is the test which any interference with or derogation from a Convention right must meet if a violation is to be avoided. . . The stop and search regime under review does in my opinion meet that test."

[6] MacPherson of Cluny, The Stephen Lawrence Inquiry, (1999) para.6.45(b).
[7] "The Police Reform Act 2002—Increasing Centralisation, Maintaining Confidence and Contracting out Crime Control" (2003) Crim. L.R. 141–164.
[8] [2006] 2 W.L.R. 537.

Among considerations supporting that conclusion, Lord Bingham said at p.554A:

> "In exercising the power the constable is not free to act arbitrarily, and would be open to civil suit if he does. It is true that he need have no suspicion before stopping and searching a member of the public. This cannot, realistically, be interpreted as a warrant to stop and search people who are obviously not terrorist suspects, which would be futile and time-wasting. It is to ensure that a constable is not deterred from stopping and searching a person whom he does suspect as a potential terrorist by the fear that he could not show reasonable grounds for his suspicion. It is not suggested that the constables in these cases exercised their powers in a discriminatory manner (an impossible contention on the facts), and I prefer to say nothing on the subject of discrimination."

2-004   Importantly, from December 23, 2004, the chief officers of all forces in England and Wales will be able to designate Community Support Officers[9] (CSOs) with powers of detention.[10] CSOs will not have the same levels of training, experience and supervision as permanently employed police officers and so, it might be argued, if there is a risk with regard to the exercise of this power of a propensity for unfair targeting of certain members of the public and most typically on racial or ethnic grounds, it is likely to be even more prevalent when exercised by comparatively less experienced and less well-trained part-time officers. CSOs designated with these powers will be able to require the name and address of a person who they have reason to believe is acting in an anti-social manner. If a person fails to comply with the requirement or gives a name and address which the CSO believes to be false then the officer may detain the person for up to 30 minutes until the arrival of a constable. Alternatively, a person may choose, if asked by a CSO, to accompany the community support officer to a police station. A CSO may use reasonable force to detain a person and to prevent a detained person from making off. It is an offence to fail to give a CSO a name and address when required or to make off during a detention.

Street Bail

2-005   Bail is the release by the police or the court of a person held in legal custody while awaiting trial. Under the Police and Criminal Evidence Act 1984 and the Bail Act 1976, where a person is arrested and taken to a police station, the custody officer has to decide whether there is sufficient evidence to justify a charge at that stage. If there is not sufficient evidence, he must decide whether there probably will be enough once further inquiries have been made. If not, then the person must be released without charge. Otherwise, the police must release him, either on bail or without bail, unless the person has been charged with homicide, rape or certain other offences, there is doubt about his name or address, or there are reasonable grounds for believing detention is necessary (for example to prevent him committing an offence, or because he will fail to appear in court). If police bail is granted, then this must be in accordance with the Bail Act 1976. This provides for penalties for non-appearance in court. In the case of bail granted after the person has been charged, the custody officer can impose conditions on bail as appear necessary to ensure that the person surrenders to custody when required, to ensure that the person does not commit an offence whilst on bail, to ensure that the person does not interfere

---

[9] See below at para.2-019ff.
[10] Under paras 2, 3 and 4 of Sch.4 of the Police Reform Act 2002; Home Office Circular 72/2004.

with witnesses or do anything else to obstruct the course of justice, and for the person's own protection (or for their interests or welfare if they are under 17 years of age). Reasons must be given for conditions. These conditions cannot currently be attached to bail granted during the investigation stages of an offence, or to bail granted before a decision has been taken to charge or to refer a case to the prosecutor.

In September 2002, the Policing Bureaucracy Taskforce proposed the intro-   **2-006**
duction of street bail, "a legally enforceable instruction to a suspect or offender to attend at a police station, court or any other venue where the matters disclosed could be properly resolved at a time more convenient to police, the suspect and indeed victims and witnesses." Section 4 of the Criminal Justice Act 2003 amends ss.30 to 30D of the Police and Criminal Evidence Act 1984 to create this new form of bail, "street bail". Section 30A provides that a constable may release on bail a person who is arrested or taken into custody in the circumstances mentioned in s.30(1). A person may be released on bail at any time before he arrives at a police station. Any police officer therefore has the power to grant bail to a suspect at the scene of the arrest. Once bailed, the suspect is under a duty to return to a specified station at a later date. Before officers grant street bail, they need to be satisfied that they have the correct name and address for the suspect, the suspect will answer bail, they are not a danger to themselves or to the public and understand the street bail process.

The Home Office, in guidance about the new street bail power, accepted   **2-007**
that it was a significant new police power.[11] The reason offered for street bail was to free up officer time. The guidance also contains criteria for granting it. In making the decision, the officer must take into account the impact of the offence, the loss of evidence, the fitness of the suspect, whether they understand the situation and the likelihood of further offences. It would be rare for it to be granted for a serious offence. Hucklesby suggests that the new power has other side-effects:[12] it enables police to keep track of suspects even when there is not enough evidence to charge under the guise of collecting evidence; it also puts suspects under significant pressure as it leaves open the threat of re-arrest. As in the case of the stop and search laws and s.50 of the 2003 Act, above, the lack of specific guidance about the use of street bail increases the likelihood that it may be used to discriminate against certain groups.

Street bail faces further amendments in the Police and Justice Bill. Schedule   **2-008**
4 of the Bill removes the ban on imposing further requirements, and replaces it with very similar provisions to those in the Bail Act 1976 which govern police bail at a police station. Thus, like custody officers, arresting officers (who may not have the same level of experience and training as a custody officer) will be able to attach conditions to bail, but with such restrictions necessary to make sure those arrested surrender to custody when required, do not commit further offences, do not interfere with witnesses, or are necessary for the person's own protection. Under the new s.30CA, a custody officer would be able to vary the conditions attached to street bail on request. Under new s.30CB, a magistrates' court may, on request, vary the conditions of bail if the custody officer has refused to do this or failed to respond within 48 hours of the request. The Act also makes provisions for conditions to be attached to various types of pre-charge bail to which conditions cannot currently be attached, such as bail granted during the investigation stages, or before a decision has been taken to charge or refer a case to the prosecutor.

---

[11] Home Office Criminal Justice Act 2003: Bail Elsewhere than at a Police Station (61/2003).
[12] "Not Necessarily a Trip to the Police Station: the Introduction of Street Bail", (2004) Crim. L.R. 803–813.

Conditional Cautions

2-009   Conditional cautions were created recently by the Criminal Justice Act 2003. A simple caution is a non-statutory disposal in respect of low-level offences. *Blackstone's Guide to the 2003 Act* contains a precise summary of the gives the following summary of the arguments for and against cautioning:[13]

> "Cautioning has a number of real advantages over prosecution: it is very cheap and efficient, it provides a very immediate response to offending, it is not vindictive and may leave the offender feeling fairly dealt with by the criminal justice system. It avoids the uncertainty inherent in litigation. However, the practice is also subject to a number of criticisms. It is a low visibility procedure (compared with court proceedings) and therefore may be subject to abuse; because it does not involve formal adjudication there is a danger that it may be used where offending cannot be proved; police decision-makers may act as judge and jury; it may involve 'net widening' by which individuals who have not committed a crime or do not deserve to be proceeded against are brought into the criminal justice system. It may be seen as an inappropriately lenient 'slap on the wrist' which fails to adequately condemn offending behaviour."

Home Office guidance[14] states that, in deciding whether to dispose of the matter by way of caution, the officer must consider whether there is enough evidence to prove guilt and, if so, whether the offender admitted guilt. The officer should also take into account the public interest and the views of the victim, if any, the nature of the harm suffered, whether or not the offender has made any reparation and whether or not the offender has had any cautions for similar offences. The significance of the caution should be explained to them, that it will be recorded and, if a sexual offence, they will be a registered sex offender and so requires the offender's informed consent. The officer should also obtain the opinion of another officer of the rank of Sergeant or above.

2-010   The 2003 Carter Report on correctional services recommended strengthening the credibility of non-custodial sentences.[15] One of the conclusions was that "there was considerable scope for low risk, low harm adult offenders who plead guilty to be diverted from the formal court process," which would include the introduction of reparation into conditional cautions:

> "Diversion from court is used widely in other European countries. In Germany, between 25 and 30 per cent of offenders are given conditional dismissals as an alternative to prosecution. The decision is the responsibility of the prosecutor. The offender can be asked to pay a fine or make reparation or undertake community service. They do not get a criminal record. If they fail to keep to the conditions they can be taken to court. A similar approach should be used in England and Wales, building on the new statutory conditional cautions in the Criminal Justice Act. The conditional caution would be linked with financial reparation to the victim, an apology, restorative work, victim-offender mediation or community work. If the offender does not comply with a conditional caution they would be prosecuted. To ensure that costs are not excessive it would make sense to complete a short assessment on each offender given a conditional caution."

---

[13] Taylor *et al*, *Blacktone's Guide to The Criminal Justice Act 2003*, (2004) p.25.
[14] Home Office Circular 30/2005.
[15] Managing Offenders Reducing Crime a New Approach, December 11, 2003.

Under s.23, an authorised person[16] may give a conditional caution to a person **2-011** aged 18 or over if each of the five requirements in s.23 is satisfied. Subsection (3) provides that conditions may be attached to the cautions which have either or both of the following objects: facilitating the rehabilitation of the offender and ensuring that he makes reparation for the offence. The five requirements in s.23 are:

— the authorised person has evidence that the offender has committed an offence;

— a relevant prosecutor has decided that there is sufficient evidence to charge the offender with the offence, and that a conditional caution should be given to the offender in respect of the offence;

— the offender admits to the authorised person that he committed the offence;

— the authorised person explains the effect of the conditional caution to the offender and warns him that failure to comply with any of the conditions attached to the caution may result in his being prosecuted for the offence; and

— the offender signs a document which contains details of the offence, an admission by him that he committed the offence, his consent to being given the conditional caution, and the conditions attached to the caution.

Section 24 provides that if the offender fails, without reasonable excuse, to comply with any of the conditions attached to the conditional caution, criminal proceedings may be instituted against the person for the offence in question, who has previously received a simple caution.

In the Respect Action Plan, the government proposed extending the condi- **2-012** tional caution scheme to include conditions requiring unpaid work:

"To tackle crime and improve community safety we need tools which tackle an individual's offending, while also giving clear signals about behaviour that is unacceptable. Conditional cautioning, which is set to be implemented across the country after a successful evaluation, can provide an effective and appropriate summary response to low-level offending, without a potentially lengthy court process. Currently the conditions which can be attached to a conditional caution are limited to direct compensation. While these conditions have given good results for victims and offenders, and local communities have also derived indirect benefit, we want to go further. Conditional cautions could involve the offender undertaking work—to make good the damage they have caused to the local community that has suffered. In this way, offenders would be giving something back to the community to repair the harm they have caused; and more quickly than if they had gone to court. It would also send a visible message that anti-social behaviour is unacceptable and has serious repercussions for the perpetrator."

Section 22(3) of the Criminal Justice Act 2003 currently states that any conditions attached to a caution must have either or both of the following objects of facilitating the rehabilitation of the offender and ensuring that he makes reparation for the offence, but, it adds, Clause 12 of the new Police and Justice Bill adds a third object of punishing the offender so that the possible

---

[16] Constable, an investigating officer, or a person authorised by a relevant prosecutor for the purposes of this section: Criminal Justice Act 2003, s.22(4).

conditions can include financial penalties or a condition that the offender attends at a specified place at specified times. Therefore, there are concerns that criminal offences are disposed of administratively rather than by a court, about which the Magistrates Association has expressed alarm:

> "The Police and Justice Bill contains proposals to extend the use of conditional cautions (brought in by the CJA 2003 and currently being piloted) so that prosecutors would be able to impose conditions that were not just rehabilitative or reparative, as at present, but punitive. The possibilities are a financial penalty—which is to be determined by the prosecutor—or attending at a specified place/time for a set amount of hours, initially a maximum of 20, but with an order making power for the Secretary of State to extend. We are extremely concerned to see these provisions on conditional cautioning in the Bill. We do not consider it in the interests of justice for prosecutors and police to be able to impose punishments as set out in this Bill without a court being involved, and are alarmed that the Secretary of State would be given power to increase these potential penalties in the future. We are talking about community penalties that a court would impose for serious offences, not extremely low level ones. There is a proposed power for the police to arrest someone without warrant and then detain them while a possible breach of a conditional caution is investigated—a draconian power in relation to something that has never been near a court."[17]

Penalty Notices for Disorder

2-013 Fixed notice penalties have been familiar in for certain road traffic offences for many years.[18] They have also been used for certain customs and excise infringements; and local authorities have always had powers to issue fixed penalty notices to those accused of littering and allowing dogs to foul public spaces. The system of on-the-spot fines for anti-social behaviour is a key part of the government's anti-social behaviour programme, aimed at dealing with what it described as "yob culture". In June 2000, the Prime Minister suggested that police should be given the power to impose on-the-spot fines to drunken louts, to deter drunken and anti-social behaviour.[19] The proposal was not wholly supported by the police: Sir John Evans of the Association of Chief Police said the collection of cash by police was not a practical idea.[20] However, in September 2000, the Home Office issued a consultation paper seeking views on a proposal to introduce fixed penalty notices dealing with disorderly behaviour. At the time of the first edition of this text, the scheme was in the course of being piloted in five areas with an overall payment rate of 60 per cent in 21 days.[21] Now, in the two years since, over 170,000 have been issued.[22] In February 2005 it was estimated that about 57,607 penalty notices for disorder (PNDs) were issued during 2004.[23]

2-014 Under s.1 of the Criminal Justice and Police Act 2001, certain offences are liable to an "on-the-spot" penalty as a PND. These include being drunk in a

---

[17] Magistrates' Association Press Release, February 2, 2006 quoted in House of Commons Research Paper 6/11, The Police and Justice Bill, at p.42. To show that you cannot please everybody, the authors also cite the Daily Mail's response where it is seen as a soft option.

[18] Transport Act 1982.

[19] "Blair: fine louts on the spot", June 30, 2000, BBC News.

[20] "Blair backs down on fining 'louts' ", July 3, 2000, BBC News.

[21] White Paper, p.8. According to a Downing Street press release dated November 5, 2002, 133 notices were issued in August 2002 and 277 in September 2002 of which half had paid the fines and ten elected to go to court.

[22] Respect Action Plan.

[23] *Hansard* February 8, 2005, Column 1418.

highway, other public place or licensed premises,[24] throwing stones, etc. at trains or other things on railways,[25] disorderly behaviour while drunk in a public place,[26] using threatening words or behaviour likely to cause alarm, harassment or distress under s.5 of the Public Order Act 1986, and consumption of alcohol in a designated public place under s.12 of the 2001 Act. Under subs.(2), the Secretary of State may by order amend an entry in this table or add or remove an entry.

Under s.2(1), a constable[27] who has reason to believe that a person aged 16 or over has committed a penalty offence may give him a penalty notice in respect of the offence. A notice may also be given at a police station, but only by an authorised constable.[28] Initially 18 years, it was amended by s.87(2) of the Anti-Social Behaviour Act 2003 to 16 years; further, s.87(3) inserts a new subsection, subs.(5), which empowers the Secretary of State to substitute a different age which is not lower than 10; and, if he selects an age below 16, he may make provision for the parent or guardian to be given the penalty notice and to pay the penalty under that notice. Subsection (4) defines "penalty notice" as ". . .a notice offering the opportunity, by paying a penalty in accordance with this Chapter, to discharge any liability to be convicted of the offence to which the notice relates". Section 3 provides that the penalty payable in respect of a penalty offence is such amount as the Secretary of State may specify by order,[29] but the Secretary of State may not specify an amount which is more than a quarter of the amount of the maximum fine for which a person is liable on conviction of the offence. Section 3(1)(1A), inserted by s.39(4) of the Anti-Social Behaviour Act 2003, provides that the Secretary of State may specify different amounts for persons of different ages. Subsection (3) provides that the penalty notice must be in the prescribed form; state the alleged offence; give such particulars of the circumstances alleged to constitute the offence as are necessary to provide reasonable information about it: specify the suspended enforcement period (as to which see s.5) and explain its effect; state the amount of the penalty; state the justices' chief executive to whom, and the address at which, the penalty may be paid; and inform the person to whom it is given of his right to ask to be tried for the alleged offence and explain how that right may be exercised. The fines are currently £50 to £80, although the Government has announced in the *Respect Action Plan* that it intends to increase the £80 fine to £100.

Under s.4, the person charged may ask to be tried for the alleged offence, in which case proceedings may be brought against him. Section 4(3) provides that such a request must be made by a notice given by the person in the manner specified in the penalty notice and before the end of the period of suspended enforcement. The "suspended enforcement period" is, under s.5, the period in which proceedings for the offence to which a penalty notice relates must not

2-015

---

[24] Licensing Act 1872, s.12.

[25] British Transport Commission Act 1949, s.56.

[26] Criminal Justice Act 1967, s.91.

[27] In uniform, under subs.(2).

[28] Under subs.(5), "Authorised constable" means a constable authorised, on behalf of the chief officer of police for the area in which the police station is situated, to give penalty notices.

[29] Under the pilot schemes, wasting police time or giving false report, sending false message (s.43(1)(b), Telecommunications Act 1984); knowingly giving a false alarm to a fire brigade (s.31, Fire Services Act 1947), using threatening words or behaviour likely to cause alarm, harassment or distress under s.5 of the Public Order Act 1986 are fined £80. Other acts such as being drunk in a highway, other public place or licensed premises, trespassing on a railway (s.55, British Transport Commission Act 1949); throwing stones, etc. at trains or other things on railways (s.56, British Transport Commission Act 1949); disorderly behaviour while drunk in a public place (s.91, Criminal Justice Act 1967); and consumption of alcohol in designated public place (s.12, Criminal Justice and Police Act 2001)—attract £40 fines.

be brought and lasts until the end of the period of 21 days, beginning with the date on which the notice was given. If the penalty is paid before the end of the suspended enforcement period, no proceedings may be brought for the offence.[30] However, this does not apply if the person to whom the penalty notice was given has made a request to be tried under s.4. Under subs.4(5), if, by the end of the "suspended enforcement period" (a) the penalty has not been paid, and (b) the person has not made a request to be tried, a sum equal to one and a half times the amount of the penalty may be registered under s.8 for enforcement as a fine. Section 7 provides that if a person to whom a penalty notice is given decides to pay the penalty, he must pay it to the justices' chief executive specified in the notice. Where a fine is not paid, it will be registered under ss.8 and 9 and the court will enforce the figure as a fine so that continued non-payment may lead to imprisonment.

Home Office Guidance

2-016 According to Home Office guidance,[31] the PND scheme is designed to provide the police with an alternative means of disposal for dealing with low-level, anti-social and nuisance offending.[32] A penalty notice may be issued on the street only by a police officer in uniform, or at a police station by an authorised officer. It does not in any way preclude the use of any existing methods of disposal. An officer may consider it appropriate to issue a PND to a suspect even if they have not directly witnessed the offending behaviour, but have reliable witness testimony instead. Interviews and questioning must be consistent with the practice and procedures established by PACE 1984, Code C. Officers should not issue a PND where the nature of the offence is too serious or it involves any aggravating circumstances. A PND will not be appropriate where there has been any injury to any person or any realistic threat or risk of injury to any person. Officers may seek the views of any potential victim before making a decision on the most appropriate course of action. PNDs should not be used where there has been a substantial financial or material loss to the private property of an individual. A penalty notice will not be appropriate for a penalty offence where there are grounds for believing that the terms of the Protection from Harassment Act 1997 might apply. Nor is it appropriate for any offence related to domestic violence. PND disposal may not be appropriate for those who are known to be substance misusers: such people may be more appropriately dealt with by a court which can direct them to suitable substance treatment. PND disposal will not be appropriate where the victim is non-compliant. A PND may not be issued to a person below 16 years of age; where the suspect is uncooperative or non-compliant or unable to understand what is being offered to them. It will not be appropriate where there is any doubt about the suspect's ability to understand English or where no satisfactory address exists for enforcement purposes (such suspects who are non-resident foreign nationals or the suspect is homeless or sleeping rough). Nor will it be appropriate where the suspect is already subject to a custodial sentence, including Home Detention Curfew; a community penalty other than a fine, including ASBOs; or where it is known that the suspect has previous convictions for disorder offences or where it is known that they have been issued with a number of penalty notices for disorder offences in the recent past, or have been cautioned for such offences.

---

[30] Criminal Justice and Police Act 2001, s.5(2).
[31] "Criminal Justice and Disorder Act: Fixed Penalty Notices Police Operational Guidance", 2005.
[32] The Home Office Guidance for CSOs, "Penalty Notices for Disorder: Supplementary Operational Guidance For Community Support Officers", and for "Accredited persons, Penalty Notices for Disorder: Supplementary Operational Guidance", are remarkably thin in comparison.

It is noted in the guidance that suspects issued with PNDs will not receive a criminal record but this does not preclude the retention of information as police intelligence. An entry may be recorded on the PNC which does not constitute a criminal record but is accessible for police information.[33] It will not constitute a criminal record, but will enable DNA, fingerprints and a photograph to be logged against the entry. Logging of recordable offences will also facilitate checks on whether an individual has previously been issued with a PND for a recordable offence, which is said to be of particular importance for PNDs issued to those under 18 years of age. Police are under a duty to protect the confidentiality of sensitive personal information and this should apply to a PND. However, police also have statutory powers to disclose information to a third party, where disclosure would be in the interest of the prevention or detection of crime. For example, the information could be used in the civil context of seeking an ASBO; the fact that a PND has been issued can be disclosed in an ASBO hearing if it contributes to establishing a pattern of behaviour.

2-017

Roberts and Garside[34] argue that, far from being a soft option, PNDs contribute to the creation of a new class of semi-criminal who face being put on the fast-track to arrest, prosecution and punishment in, what is effectively, a justice freezone. It is an obvious incentive to recipients to pay the fine to avoid the risk of acquiring a criminal record in the event of an unsuccessful challenge in court. For an individual on a low-income, an £80 PND is a significant penalty; for a stockbroker it may be equivalent to loose change. Wealthier individuals, they argue, will be in a far stronger position to buy their way out of prosecution than poorer people. It is also unclear what impact PNDs will have on vulnerable children and families who may be unable to pay them, and what the subsequent consequences of non-payment might be. This flat-rate element of the PND could lead to significant injustices. It also runs counter to the government's expressed desire to link the level of fines issued through the full criminal justice process more clearly to income. In addition, PNDs operate outside the traditional realms of criminal justice, thus bypassing key protections afforded to members of the public accused of an offence. As such, PNDs, they argue, erode justice in the name of speedier punishment. In their analysis of the pilot phase, they observed widespread imposition in cases that otherwise would not have led to a criminal justice response. Overall, PNDs enabled the police to extend their policing of minor disorder, and not simply to do more effectively what they already had been doing. This accords with Home Office research.[35] Evidence from the pilot areas also suggests that PNDs had been issued in place of cautions. In practice it would be difficult for children to be clear about what kinds of behaviour are permissible, and what might lead to PNDs. They say that the most concerning aspect of PNDs is the scope they offer to fast-track elected individuals towards arrest, prosecution and punishment:

2-018

"A comment by one police officer to Home Office researchers suggests that in at least some circumstances PNDs may result in an escalation of criminal justice interventions, not a diversion from them: I can see no value in knowingly issuing large numbers of PNDs without using discretion. The rule of thumb I use is, if they haven't responded to having received two PNDs it is time to raise the stakes and take them to court."

[33] Issue of a PND may be used as evidence of bad character under s.101 of the Criminal Justice Act 2003.
[34] "Punishment before Justice? Understanding Penalty Notices for Disorder" *Crime and Society Foundation* (2005).
[35] Spicer and Kilsby, "Penalty notices for disorder: early results from the pilot" Home Office Findings 232.

Individual discretion by police officers and others may well lead to inconsistencies in application at a force and regional level. Also significant is that PNDs build up information on a new class of the semi-criminal. Even though payment of a PND formally implies no admission of guilt, the police can record details of those issued with a PND. The implication here is that the police will view the recipient as guilty of the offence for which a PND is issued. This conflicts with the Home Office claim that payment of a fine implies no admission of guilt and removes the possibility of the creation of a record of criminal conviction and the possibility of its issue being produced as evidence in any subsequent hearing. The creation of such a quasi-criminal record raises an important question about what assumptions might be drawn about the patterns of behaviour of some individuals based on their PND history. The Criminal Justice Act 2003 allows information of this nature to be used to provide proof of "bad character". Facing trial at a later date on an unrelated matter, an individual who paid a PND on the understanding that this implied no admission of guilt could find such a payment being used as evidence of misconduct or a disposition towards misconduct. There are also indications of a move to link PNDs to ASBOs. They note that the policing Bureaucracy Taskforce in 2002, for instance, made recommendations that a history of receiving a PND should be used in ASBO proceedings as confirmed by Home Office guidance.

Community Support Officers, Accredited Members of the Public and Neighbourhood Wardens

2-019   In Chapter One, we summarised the views of some writers that the focus of the criminal justice system has shifted from "penal welfarism" to "the new penology", whereby the objective of the protection of the community appears to take precedence over the individual with the result that the criminal justice system has become more punitive and managerial. This has in turn caused a major change in the nature of policing. The "public" police, it was observed, are no longer the only agencies permitted to engage in policing activities, and police authorities themselves are required to participate in and exercise their functions through multi-agency authorities. The "privatisation" of policing in the United Kingdom has been described as the most profound change in the last 50 years of policing.[36] The changes began in 1993, with the publication of the 1993 White Paper on Police Reform and the Sheehy Inquiry which followed it. Some functions were transferred entirely to the private sector. Under ss.80 to 86 of the Criminal Justice Act 1991, security arrangements for the transporting of prisoners were allocated to private contractors. Individual forces were encouraged through the 1980s and 1990s to contract out management of custody centres, reception duties and post-charge administration. Newburn and Reiner describe the process over the last decade as not quite direct privatisation but "growing civilianisation".[37]

2-020   In *Neighbourhood Policing*, a Home Office policy document,[38] the government re-iterated its commitment to dealing with anti-social behaviour through community-based policing strategies:

"We all want to see crime and anti-social behaviour in our neighbourhoods reduced and our communities made safer. Effective neighbourhood policing is central to achieving this. We believe that people will see real, long-term

---

[36] Reiner and Newburn "From PC Dixon to Dixon PLC: Policing and Policing Powers since 1954" (2004) Crim. L.R. 601–618.
[37] *ibid.*, p.610.
[38] Home Office, March 2005.

benefits as a result—and so will police forces. We are committed to supporting the neighbourhood policing approach set out in this booklet so that people are, and feel, safer in their homes and the areas where they live."

Full-time uniformed officers will have "a skilled, specialist role"; community support officers will be responsible for street policing. Community Safety Accreditation Schemes are also considered to be a crucial part of the strategy:

"Other authority figures who are not employed directly by the police but who work within communities to help improve people's safety and quality of life. Community Safety Accreditation Schemes are important here. They allow chief constables to accredit people in community safety roles—like security guards, park rangers, housing association employees and parking attendants—and give them some limited powers. This is important for forging links, improving communication and delivering effective policing to neighbourhoods."

The creation of "new public auxiliaries", community support officers' (CSOs) and the accreditation of private citizens so as to carry out police functions are the two main features of the civilianisation of the police service. As early as 1994, a committee established by the Police Foundation and the Policy Studies Institute recommended alternative forms of police patrol, condemned at the time by the Labour Party as "policing on the cheap". However, by 2002, CSOs were a key part of the police reform programme of the government, and also of its anti-social behaviour programme. For example, in *Policing a New Century: A Blueprint for Reform*, a Government White Paper it was said:[39]

"Front-line policing can be strengthened by enhancing the role of the police support staff and by giving them new powers which will allow them to take over tasks currently carried out by police officers for example in custody suites. Other support staff (Community Support Officers) will be empowered to carry out basic patrol functions. They will provide a visible presence in the community with powers sufficient to deal with anti-social behaviour and minor disorder."

Accordingly, the Police Reform Act 2002 Act provides for certain police support staff and civilians to be given limited police powers in various circumstances. The intention is to free up police officer time for their core functions by making more effective use of support staff, and to provide additional capacity to combat low level disorder, and thereby help reduce the public's fear of crime.

Roberts argues the police will benefit in a number of ways: by sub- **2-021** contracting routine policing tasks; by satisfying public demand for high-visibility reassurance policing; by not having to pay for these functions to be performed (in fact, they can charge for accreditation); not being liable for unlawful conduct in their performance; by obtaining closer regulation of private security providers and by encouraging private organisations to take greater responsibility for policing their own concerns.[40] Even security guards in public shopping centres could have themselves "accredited" and thereby gain wide powers to deal with low-level criminal behaviour. In effect, it amounts to privatising policing, at least in regard to low-level public order offences. Despite recommendations that the Act should specify that

---

[39] Cm.5326, Home Office, December 2001, p.11.
[40] "The Police Reform Act 2002—Increasing Centralisation, Maintaining Confidence, and Contracting Out Crime Control" (2003) Crim. L.R. 141–164.

accredited people are caught by s.6 of the Human Rights Act 1998, no such provision was enacted. Nevertheless, private employers and their accredited employees will be treated as "public authorities" within s.6(3)(b) of the Crime and Disorder Act 1998. He also argues that the new scheme sends out a message that what matters is simply that a badge-wearer performs the task efficiently and that there is a danger, as with all such private/public initiatives and multi-agency partnerships, of the loss of accountability and responsibility. He queries the wisdom of allowing civilians to exercise such powers with regard to perpetrators who are normally hostile or even violent towards police officers. Further, not all community support officers will be designated with powers on each occasion and so it will be difficult for a private citizen to know if the community support officer has the powers he claims to have.

2-022   The Explanatory Notes to the 2002 Act state that the Act enables chief officers to appoint suitable support staff to roles providing a visible presence in the community, with powers sufficient to deal with minor issues. Such staff would be under the formal direction and control of the chief officer. In fact, under the current legislation, it is entirely a matter for chief constables as to whether or not to have CSOs and what powers they may be able to exercise. Additionally, it is said to be the government's aim to harness the commitment of those already involved in crime reduction activities, such as traffic wardens, neighbourhood and street wardens and security staff, through "an extended police family". The 2002 Act makes provision for community safety accreditation schemes and a railway safety accreditation scheme and, in certain circumstances, the granting of limited powers to accredited members of those schemes. Parts 4 and 5 of the 2003 Act contain provisions which extend certain powers to police support staff. There are two main groups: "designated civilians" directly employed by the police authorities such as CSOs and escort officers; and "accredited persons" who are not so directly employed. The 2002 Act allows chief officers of police to establish community safety accreditation schemes under which certain persons are granted some police powers. They would include neighbourhood wardens, football stewards and the private security sector.

Community Support Officers

2-023   In September 2005, over 6,300 CSOs were working, and all forces had at least some CSOs.[41] The Government is committed to increasing the numbers of CSOs to 24,000 by the end of March 2008.[42] In evidence to the Home Affairs Committee, Her Majesty's Inspectorate of Constabulary, the Association of Chief Police Officers and the Association of Police Authorities all commented that the introduction of CSOs had been very successful, although the Police Federation was sceptical and reported confusion and divided opinion about CSOs amongst police officers.[43] The Committee concluded:

> "It is clear that Community Support Officers have proved popular with the public in their role as high-visibility patrollers. The Government's proposed expansion in CSO numbers was supported by most of our witnesses, though not by the Police Federation which represents uniformed officers. Several witnesses made the point that CSOs are most useful when they work in close liaison with police officers, and that any extension of their powers which reduced their street presence would be counter-productive. We agree with this assessment. We also think it is desirable that individual police forces and

---

[41] Home Office Statistical Bulletin 12/05.
[42] Home Office, Good Practice for Police Authorities and Forces in Obtaining CSO funding, 2006.
[43] Research Paper 6/11, The Police and Justice Bill, House of Commons, at p.33.

police authorities should be given the flexibility to decide for themselves whether they wish to spend extra resources on CSOs or on other personnel or activities. We recommend that the arrangements drawn up by the Home Office for the proposed neighbourhood policing fund should make allowance for such flexibility, allowing local communities to take decisions in the light of local priorities."

Under s.38, chief officers of police may designate to suitably skilled and trained civilians under their direction and control to exercise powers and undertake duties in carrying out specified functions. A chief officer can designate civilians to perform functions in four categories: community support officer; investigating officer; detention officer; and escort officer. Under subs.(1), the chief officer in charge of a force may designate to any person under his operational control and employed by the relevant police authority as an officer of one or more of the descriptions specified in subsection (2): community support officer; investigating officer; detention officer; and escort officer. Under subs.(5), chief officers are able to confer on such employees some of the powers and duties otherwise only available to police constables and others. Subsection (6) limits the powers that can be conferred on designated persons to the relevant Parts of Sch.4 to the Act. Where a power allows for the use of reasonable force when it is exercised by a constable, a person exercising such a power under a designation shall have the same entitlement to use reasonable force, for example when carrying out a search; and where the designation includes the power to force entry to premises, this power will be limited to occasions when the designated person is under the direct supervision of a constable and is accompanied by them—the exception to this requirement is when the purpose of forcing entry is to save life or limb or to prevent serious damage to premises.[44]

2-024

These powers are set out in Pt 1 of Sch.4 to the Act. Paragraph 1 enables a suitably designated person to exercise powers to issue fixed penalty notices in respect of a range of anti-social behaviour and disorder offences under the Criminal Justice and Police Act 2001.[45] These offences are:

2-025

— being drunk in a public highway, other public place or licensed premises;[46]
— throwing fireworks in a thoroughfare;[47]
— knowingly giving a false fire alarm to a fire brigade;[48]
— trespassing on a railway;[49]
— throwing stones, etc. at trains or other things on railways;[50]
— buying or attempting to buy alcohol for consumption in a bar in licensed premises by a person under 18;[51]
— disorderly behaviour while drunk in a public place;[52]
— wasting police time by giving a false report;[53]

[44-45] Police Reform Act 2002, s.38(8), (9).
[46] Licensing Act 1872, s.12.
[47] Explosives Act 1875, s.80.
[48] Fire Service Act 1947, s.31.
[49] British Transport Commission Act 1949, s.55.
[50] British Transport Commission Act 1949, s.56.
[51] Licensing Act 1964, s.169C9(3).
[52] Criminal Justice Act 1967, s.91.
[53] Criminal Law Act 1967, s.52.

— using public telecommunications system for sending message known to be false in order to cause annoyance;[54]

— behaviour likely to cause harassment, alarm or distress;[55]

— consumption of alcohol in designated public place;[56]

— cycling on a footway;[57]

— dog fouling;[58] and

— littering.

2-026   Under paragraph 2, such officers have the power to detain persons in certain narrowly defined circumstances. As noted above, under s.50 of the Anti-Social Behaviour Act 2003, a designated CSO can require the name and address of a person who he believes to have committed an offence to which the designated powers relate and in the police area to which the designation relates. The powers in this paragraph can be used in relation to relevant fixed penalty offences or in respect of offences that appear to have caused alarm, injury or distress to any other person, or the loss of or damage to any other person's property. Conditions may be applied to the application of this paragraph by designation, such as limiting it to those offences witnessed by the community support officer or excluding particular offences or categories of offence. Where para.3 is applied to a CSO officer, so that he enjoys the same s.50 powers as a constable, the CSO is then given the same power of detention as is conferred by para.2 in relation to a person who fails to comply with the requirement or appears to have given a false or inaccurate name or address.

2-027   Under para.5, a CSO is under the same duty as a constable under s.12 of the Criminal Justice and Police Act 2001 to require an individual not to consume alcohol (or what he reasonably believes to be alcohol) in places designated by local authorities, and surrender alcohol in an unsealed container to the CSO. Paragraph 6 confers similar powers on a CSO as those in para.5, except by way of s.1 of the Confiscation of Alcohol (Young Persons) Act 1997. A designated CSO will be able to confiscate alcohol (or what he reasonably believes to be alcohol) in an unsealed container, from someone who is under 18 years of age or from someone who intends to supply it to someone who is under the age of 18 for their consumption. The CSO may then be able to dispose of the alcohol as he considers appropriate. Failure to comply with a community support officer's request is an offence punishable, on summary conviction, by a fine not exceeding level two on the standard scale (currently £500). When para.7 is specified in a CSO's designation, it extends to him the power of a constable or a uniformed park-keeper, under s.7(3) of the Children and Young Persons Act 1933, to seize tobacco or cigarette papers from any person who appears to be under 16 years old whom he finds smoking in any street or public place. The CSO may then dispose of any seized material in such manner as the relevant police authority provides.

2-028   By para.8, a CSO has the same power of a constable under s.17 of the Police and Criminal Evidence Act 1984—entry for the purpose of saving life or limb or preventing serious damage to property. This would, for example, enable a CSO to enter a property where neighbours suspected an elderly occupant had fallen and was unresponsive. Unlike the power to enter premises conferred in para.9, this power does not require a CSO to be accompanied by a constable.

---

[54] Telecommunications Act 1984, s.43(1)(b).
[55] Public Order Act 1986, s.5.
[56] Criminal Justice and Police Act 2001, s.12.
[57] Road Traffic Offenders Act 1988, s.54.
[58] Dogs (Fouling of Land) Act 1996, s.4.

Under para.9, a CSO has the powers of a constable under s.59 of this Act regarding vehicles used in a manner causing alarm, distress or annoyance. However, the new powers, in so far as they include power to enter premises, are only exercisable when in the company of, and under the supervision of, a constable. Paragraph 10 extends any powers conferred on designated persons for the removal of abandoned vehicles by regulations under s.99 of the Road Traffic Regulation Act 1984. Paragraph 11 and 12 extend to CSOs limited powers to stop vehicles and direct traffic. They also have the powers of a constable under the Terrorism Act 2000 para.13; the purpose of extending such powers to a designated CSO is to enable them to provide valuable support to constables in times of terrorist threat, and to give chief officers the discretion to deploy constables for duties that require their full expertise and powers in such times.

Standardisation and Extension of CSO Powers
The government is satisfied that the CSO system is working well. In August 2005, the Home Office published a consultation paper[59] and noted that there were still some "significant" drawbacks:

2-029

"The public currently have no way of knowing what the powers of CSOs are from one force to the next. This is confusing and disorientating, and leads many members of the public to think that CSOs have no powers at all. Also, it means that in some forces CSOs do not have sufficient powers to play a full part in neighbourhood policing and have a role more similar to that of wardens. For these reasons we think that it is sensible to standardise the powers designated to CSOs and we intend to legislate for a set of standard powers at the earliest opportunity."

In January 2006, the Home Office announced "a robust set of standard powers for CSOs is to be introduced to help tackle low level crime and anti-social behaviour". Currently, powers available to CSOs varied from force to force and there was a fear that the public would misunderstand their role and in some cases prevent CSOs from playing a full part in neighbourhood policing. The proposed "standard set" is intended to ensure that CSOs in all areas have the powers necessary to deal with issues they are likely to encounter on the street, while leaving the designation of a number of powers to the discretion of Chief Officers. While the Association of Chief Police Officers was in favour of standardisation, the Police Federation was not:

2-030

"We are disappointed that rather than using the Bill to standardise CSO powers across the country, this clause will allow different forces to designate different powers to different CSOs. CSOs were sold as the eyes and ears of the service yet it is clear that some will have the power to use reasonable force, despite their lack of training and despite Ministerial reassurances to the contrary during the passage of the Police Reform Act (2002). Anecdotal evidence from front-line officers also suggests that many people are confused as to the difference between "police officers" and "police community support officers". We therefore support the Home Affairs Committee's recommendation that the partial powers of CSOs and accredited community safety organisations should be reflected in different uniforms. We also believe uniforms should reflect the nomenclature used in the Police Reform Act i.e. Community Support Officer, not the more confusing Police Community Support Officer. Paragraph 17 of Schedule 2 is, to all intents

---

[59] Home Office, Standard Powers for Community Support Offices and a Framework for the Future Development of Powers, August 2005.

and purposes, the introduction of mutual assistance for CSOs (and other persons employed by a police force). We believe that this too would be hindered if CSOs in different forces had different powers."

New Powers under the Serious Organised Crime and Police Act 2005 for CSOs

2-031 Meanwhile, new designated powers were made available to CSOs in the 2005 Act. These include:

— the power to require name and address of a person whom a CSO has reason to believe has committed "a relevant offence". Relevant offences are defined under subpara.2(6) of Sch.4 of the Police Reform Act 2002, as relevant fixed penalty offences under para.1 of Sch.4, an offence under s.32(2) of the Anti-Social Behaviour Act 2003 (failure to follow an instruction to disperse) or an offence that causes injury, alarm or distress to another person or loss of or damage to another person's property. Paragraph 1A enables chief constables to designate the power to require name and address without also designating the power of detention;[60]

— breaches of byelaws: the Serious Organised Crime and Police Act 2005 provides that offences committed under relevant byelaws are relevant offences under para.2(6) of Sch.4 of the Police Reform Act 2002. A relevant byelaw is a byelaw from a list of byelaws that has been agreed between a chief constable and a relevant byelaw-making body. As well as being able to require name and address for breach of a byelaw, CSOs can also enforce a byelaw by removing a person from a place if a constable would also have the power to enforce a byelaw in that way;[61]

— control of begging: the Serious Organised Crime and Police Act 2005 makes offences under ss.3 and 4 of the Vagrancy Act 1824 into relevant offences. It also gives CSOs a power to detain a person who they have required to stop committing an offence under ss.3 and 4 of the Vagrancy Act and who has failed to comply with the requirement;[62]

— licensing offences: the *Serious Organised Crime and Police Act 2005* establishes a set of relevant licensing offences. These offences are: sale of alcohol to a person who is drunk, obtaining alcohol for a person who is drunk, sale of alcohol to children, purchase of alcohol by or on behalf of children, consumption of alcohol by children and sending a child to obtain alcohol. Where these offences apply specifically to clubs they are not relevant licensing offences. CSOs may require name and address, but may not detain for those relevant licensing offences that are most likely to be committed by license holders;[63]

— a limited power to enter licensed premises. The 2005 Act allows CSOs to be designated with a power to enter licensed premises, under s.180 of the Licensing Act 2003 for the purposes of investigating relevant licensing offences. They may not enter clubs and must enter all premises with

[60] Inserted by para.2 of Sch.8 to the Serious Organised Crime and Police Act 2005.
[61] Paragraphs 1A(3), 2(3A), 2(6)(ad), 2(6B), 2(6C), 2(6D), 2(6E), 2(6F) of Sch.4 to the Police Reform Act 2002 (see paras.2, 3(4), 3(7) and 3(8) of Sch.8 to the Serious Organised Crime and Police Act 2005).
[62] Paragraphs 2(6)(ac) and 2(3B) of Sch.4 to the Police Reform Act 2002 (see paras.3(4), 3(5), 3(6) and 3(7) of Sch.8 to the Serious Organised Crime and Police Act 2005).
[63] Paragraph 2(6A) of Sch.4 to the Police Reform Act 2002 (see paras.3(3) and 3(8) of Sch.8 to the Serious Organised Crime and Police Act 2005).

a constable, unless the premises are licensed for the sale of alcohol off the premises;[64]

— the power to search detained persons for dangerous items or items that could be used to assist escape. The Serious Organised Crime and Police Act 2005 allows CSOs to be designated with the same powers as a constable, under s.32 of PACE 1984, to search detained persons for anything that could be used to cause physical injury or to assist escape. A CSO must retain any item seized until the arrival of a police officer and comply with their instructions on what to do with the item;[65]

— power to require name and address for road traffic offences. The 2005 Act allows CSOs to be designated with the power to require the name and address of a driver or pedestrian who fails to follow the directions of a community support officer or police officer;[66]

— the power to use reasonable force to transfer control of detained persons. Paragraph 2(4A) of Sch.4 to the Police Reform Act 2002 places a duty on CSOs to remain with a police officer when transferring a detained person to his or her custody until the police officer has the person under control. Paragraph 2(4B) places a CSO accompanying a detained person to a police station under a duty to remain at the police station until the detained person is under control. If a CSO is designated with para.4ZB of Sch.4 then he or she may use reasonable force in complying with duties under 2(4A) and 2(4B). If a CSO is designated with para.4ZA then he or she may use reasonable force when exercising powers;[67]

— the power to search for alcohol and tobacco. Where a person has failed to comply with a requirement under para.5 or 6 or has failed to allow a CSO to seize tobacco under para.7 of Sch.4 to the Police Reform Act 2002, and a CSO reasonably believes that the person is in possession of alcohol or tobacco, then a CSO may search them for it and dispose of anything found. It is an offence to fail to consent to be searched and CSOs can require name and address for this offence. As specified in para.3(10) of Sch.8 to the Serious Organised Crime and Police Act 2005 a CSO may only detain a person for failure to give an adequate name and address if he or she has been designated with powers under para.2 of Sch.4 to the 2002 Act.[68]

Accreditation Schemes

Under s.40 of the 2002 Act, a chief officer of police may establish and main- **2-032** tain a scheme that accredits suitably skilled and trained non-police employees with powers to undertake specified functions in the support of the police. For example, a chief officer may accredit street wardens employed by the local authority with powers to address some anti-social behaviour offences. Persons

[64] Paragraph 8A of Sch.4 to the Police Reform Act 2002 (inserted by para.9 of Sch.8 to the Serious Organised Crime and Police Act 2005).
[65] Paragraph 2A of Sch.4 to the Police Reform Act 2002 (inserted by para.4 of Sch.8 to the Serious Organised Crime and Police Act 2005).
[66] Paragraph 3A of Sch.4 to the Police Reform Act 2002 (inserted by para.6 of Sch.8 to the Serious Organised Crime and Police Act 2005).
[67] Paragraphs 2(4A), 2(4B), 4ZA and 4ZB of Sch.4 to the Police Reform Act 2002 (see paras 2, 3 and 4 of Sch.9 to the Serious Organised Crime and Police Act 2005).
[68] Paragraphs 7B and 7C of Sch.4 to the Police Reform Act 2002 (inserted by para.8 of Sch.8 to the Serious Organised Crime and Police Act 2005).

who have undertaken such schemes may be accredited under s.41. They have powers set out in Sch.5 to the 2002 Act. The list of powers is more limited than those that can be conferred on CSOs under Pt 1 of Sch.4. Accredited persons can issue fixed penalty notices for offences of cycling on a footway (s.54 of the Road Traffic Offenders Act 1988 in respect of s.72 of the Highway Act 1835); dog fouling (s.4 of the Dogs (Fouling of Land) Act 1996) and litter (s.88 of the Environmental Protection Act 1990), but cannot issue fixed penalty notices under the Criminal Justice and Police Act 2001.

2-033　　Under paras 2 and 3 of Sch.5, accredited persons can have conferred on them the power to require the name and address of a person acting in an anti-social manner, as in the case of CSOs under paras 2 and 3 of Sch.4. However, unlike CSOs, accredited persons cannot have conferred on them the power to detain an individual who does not comply with this request. Nor can accredited persons use reasonable force when exercising their powers (in contrast to CSOs under para.4 of Sch.4). By paras 4, 5 and 6, accredited persons can have conferred on them the same powers regarding alcohol consumption in designated places, confiscation of alcohol and confiscation of tobacco as CSOs under paras 5, 6 and 7 of Sch.4. Again as in the case of CSOs, accredited persons can have conferred on them any powers conferred on designated persons for the removal of abandoned vehicles by regs under s.99 of the Road Traffic Regulation Act 1984. Paragraphs 8 and 9 confer on accredited persons the same powers regarding stopping vehicles for testing, and the escorting of abnormal loads, as CSOs under paras 11 and 12 of Sch.4. However, accredited persons are not permitted to enter or search any premises for the purposes of saving life or limb or preventing serious damage to property (as suitably designated CSOs can under para.8 of Sch.4). Accredited persons do not have any of the powers to seize vehicles used to cause alarm, etc. (para.9 of Sch.4). Section 42(1) requires that designated or accredited persons must show that person his designation or accreditation if asked to do so. Under subs.(2), persons designated or accredited by a chief officer of police can only exercise powers if they are wearing a uniform endorsed by the chief officer and identified or described in their designation or accreditation. Accredited persons must also wear a badge in a form to be decided by the Secretary of State.

2-034　　Section 33 of the Anti-Social Behaviour Act 2003 amends Sch.4 to the 2002 Act by adding, as para.2 of the schedule, as 2(aa), so as to include offences under s.32(2) of the 2003 Act. Further, para.4 now includes two new paras, 4A and 4B, which provide them with powers to disperse groups and remove young persons to their place of residence. Paragraph 4A provides that if a designation applies this paragraph to any person, that person shall, within the relevant police area, have the powers which, by virtue of an authorisation under s.30 of the 2003 Act, are conferred on a constable in uniform by s.30(3) to (6) of that Act. Section 41 of the 2003 Act also adds other such powers to Sch.4. Under the new para.11, they shall have the power, where a designation applies, as a constable in uniform to stop a cycle. Further, Sch.5 to the Police Reform Act 2002 is amended, as regards accredited persons, so that they may also have the powers of a constable in uniform to give a fixed penalty notice under Pt 1 of the Criminal Justice and Police Act 2001.

Neighbourhood Wardens

2-035　　Neighbourhood wardens feature regularly in government policy on social exclusion and neighbourhood renewal and national policing strategy.[69]

---

[69] E.g. National Strategy for Neighbourhood Renewal 2001; A New Commitment to Neighbourhood Renewal: National Strategy Action 2003 See also Crime Reduction Toolkit, Home Office; Home Officer Policy Action Teams 6 and 8.

They are said to have "a vital role in neighbourhoods, particularly in deprived areas . . . the first point of contact for local people on issues of local concern—like littering and graffiti." A warden is any person who provides some kind of official or semi-official presence in a residential area, with the primary aim of improving the quality of life. Wardens are generally appointed and managed by a scheme ideally with the support of local residents and key local agencies. Depending on the nature of the local neighbourhood warden scheme, the functions of a neighbourhood warden can include one or more of the following: security patrol; environmental improvements; tenant liaison/information source; looking after void properties; information source for the police or local authority; visits to vulnerable tenants, victims of crime, and intimidated witnesses; professional witness services; responding to minor incidents of anti-social behaviour and low-level neighbourhood disputes; looking after community services; and community development. There are four main types of scheme: patrol, in which crime prevention and a reduction in anti-social behaviour is their primary objective; concierge, in which a person is employed to provide a reception service in a building or group of buildings; caretaker/supercaretaker; and neighbourhood support worker, a person whose role is to promote local organisations, such as residents' associations, youth groups and carers' support groups, to help organise activities for local residents, and to enhance links between residents and local agencies.[70]

Community Justice Centres

The 2003 White Paper referred to the establishment of pilot Community Justice Centres, the main aim of which was described in these terms:[71]   2-036

"The pilots would be able to deal with all low-level disorder offences, housing related matters, especially those relevant to tackling anti-social behaviour. Those who adjudicate would receive special training. The aim would be to facilitate better liaison and communication with the courts, thereby reducing delays in the listing of cases and producing more consistent breach sentencing due to increased awareness of local issues and the impact of anti-social behaviour."

The first centre was opened in Warwickshire in March 2005. A similar Centre was opened in Liverpool in October 2005 (although operational since December 2004). They house in one place the police, the CPS, a magistrates' court, a family court, the Probation Service, the Youth Offending Team, and the Victim and Witness Support. The aim is to bring a number of services under the one roof, such as a courtroom and support and advice services for victims of crime, offenders and the community. The judges of the court will monitor treatment programmes and community punishments, ensuring that the views of people in north Liverpool are reflected in those punishments. Courts in such centres are required to deal with low-level anti-social behaviour and disorder criminal matters. Sentencing is intended to focus on offenders making amends to the community and, according to the Constitutional Affairs Minister, where required, offenders receive the support they need to tackle the issues that may have contributed to them committing a crime.[72]

[70] PAT Report.
[71] At p.80.
[72] Press release, October 20, 2005: *www.cjsonline.gov.uk/the_cjs/whats_new/news-3233.html*

Breaches of Public Order

Breach of the Peace

2-037   All anti-social behaviour and disorder involves a disturbance of some kind to
          the peace, if only because breaches of the peace have a public quality about
          them.[73] Any citizen may take reasonable steps to prevent actual or reasonably
          apprehended breaches of the peace and, "in the case of a citizen who is also a
          constable, it is a duty of imperfect obligation";[74] a police constable (or any
          other person) may make an arrest where a breach of the peace has been com-
          mitted, is committed, or where there is a reasonable cause to believe that such
          a breach will be committed or repeated. In *Howell*, it was held that there was a
          power of arrest whenever a breach of the peace is committed, or where the
          arrestor reasonably believes that such a breach will be committed in the "imme-
          diate future", or where a breach has been committed and it is reasonably
          believed that a renewal of it has been threatened. A person may be detained as
          long as it is reasonable to prevent the breach of the peace or its re-occurrence:
          see, for example, *Austin v Commissioner of Police*, where it was held that, in the
          circumstances of that case, it was reasonable for a crowd of protesters and
          others in the area of Oxford Street to be detained within a cordon for more
          than seven hours.[75] However, the power to arrest and detain in those circum-
          stances must be exercised proportionately. In *Laporte v Chief Constable of
          Gloucester*,[76] a bus was carrying "Wombles", protestors travelling to an air base
          near Cirencester, so that the passengers could participate in a demonstration
          that had been authorised under s.12 and 14 of the Public Order Act 1986. The
          police stopped the bus about five kilometres from the protest. Police officers
          directed them to remove their costumes. Officers found on the coach protective
          clothing, spray paint, two pairs of scissors, a smoke bomb and five shields. The
          Chief Constable concluded that the coach passengers were heading for the air
          base and likely to cause a breach of the peace and so they were escorted back
          to London. The Court of Appeal held that temporary detention at a lay-by was
          lawful, justified by the imminence at that place of the threat of a breach of the
          peace. However, the detention of the passengers back to London was not jus-
          tified as it was disproportionate, although it would have been lawful to order
          them not to proceed to the air base and to leave the area.

2-038   There must be actual or apprehended violence before the constable (or
          private citizen) can take action. In *Howell*,[77] it was said that ". . .a breach of
          the peace occurs when, by unlawful violence, harm is done to a person, or in
          his presence his property, or a person fears on reasonable grounds that unlaw-
          ful violence is likely to cause such harm is imminent." Hence, a non-violent
          disturbance is not a breach of the peace, no matter how noisy or inconvenient
          it may be;[78] nor does mere trespass amount to a breach of the peace.[79] Nor,
          contrary to obiter comments of Lord Denning M.R. in *Chief Constable of
          Devon and Cornwall, Ex p Central Electricity Generating Board*, is there a
          breach of the peace in the mere obstruction or prevention of a person carry-
          ing out his work. In *Bibby v Chief Constable of Essex*,[80] for example, a bailiff

---

[73] Section 40 of the Public Order Act 1986 provides: "Nothing in this Act affects the common law
     powers in England and Wales to deal with or prevent a breach of the peace" preserving the
     common law. See Williams, "Arrest for Breach of the Peace" (1954) Crim. L.R. 578.
[74] *Albert v Lavin* [1982] A.C. 546.
[75] [2005] EWHC 480.
[76] [2005] *All* E.R. 473.
[77] [1982] Q.B. 416.
[78] *ibid.*
[79] *R. v Chief Constable for Devon, Ex p. Central Electricity Generating Board* [1982] Q.B. 458.
[80] (2000) 164 J.P. 297.

sought to take possession at the defendant's store. There was an argument and the police officer asked the bailiff to leave. He refused to do so and so he was arrested. The Court of Appeal held that there must be a sufficiently real and present threat to the peace to justify the extreme step of depriving a citizen of his liberty. The threat must be coming from the person to be arrested. His conduct must interfere with the rights of others. The consequence of the conduct must be violence from a third party and that violence must be unreasonable. The conduct of the person arrested must also be unreasonable.

In *Hawkes v DPP*,[81] the appellant appealed by way of case stated against   **2-039**
her conviction of assaulting a police officer in the execution of his duty. The police had gone to her address to arrest her son. After the arrest, she followed her son into a police car and refused to get out. She was warned but became verbally abusive; she only got out of the car when a second police car arrived. She then started to walk towards her house but a police officer took hold of her arms. She bit the police officer on the arm. The case against her was that the police officer had arrested her for a breach of the peace and that the assault had occurred in the execution of that duty. The appellant argued that the prosecution case had been that she had actually committed a breach of the peace whilst she had been sitting in the police car and was therefore a case of a threatened breach. As such, there was a requirement to establish some sort of violent conduct, but, on the facts, whilst she had exhibited an aggressive manner, she had not been violent. Therefore, the assault of the police officer had occurred when he had been exercising his powers unlawfully and the conviction could not stand. The court held, allowing the appeal, that the appellant had exhibited nothing more than an aggressive manner. While her conduct may have given rise to an imminent threat of violence, there was no evidence to suggest that her conduct involved any violence so as to justify the conclusion that she had actually committed a breach of the peace in the presence of a police officer. Accordingly, her arrest for breach of the peace had been unlawful and had in fact taken place when the police officer had been exercising his powers unlawfully, with the ultimate effect that the conviction for assaulting a police officer in the execution of his duty could not stand.

See also *Steel v UK*,[82] one of the applicant defendants was arrested whilst   **2-040**
attending a demonstration about a grouse shoot after she walked in front of a member of the shoot in order to prevent him from firing. She was charged with causing a breach of the peace and detained by the police for 44 hours before being brought before a court. The finding that she had committed a breach of the peace was upheld on appeal. The defendant then refused to agree to be bound over to keep the peace and was committed to prison for 28 days. The court also heard a related appeal in which the other applicant defendant was arrested at a conference centre as she handed out leaflets and displayed banners protesting against the sale of arms. She was detained for seven hours by the police, but proceedings against her were dropped when the prosecution decided not to offer any evidence. Both defendants applied to the European Court of Human Rights, arguing that their arrests and detentions had not been "prescribed by law" as required by Art.5(1) of the Convention and had constituted a disproportionate interference with their right to freedom of expression, in violation of Art.10. The Court held that, in order for their arrest and detention to be "lawful" under Art.5(1)(c), there had to be full compliance with domestic law and the relevant law had to be formulated with sufficient precision. This latter requirement was met and there had been compliance with the law in Steel's case as the police had been entitled to fear that her conduct, if allowed to continue, might provoke others to

---

[81] *Times*, Nov 29, 2005.
[82] (1998) 28 E.H.R.R. 603.

violence. However, the other applicant defendant's conduct had been wholly peaceful and had not warranted a fear that a breach of the peace was likely to occur. Accordingly, there had been a violation of Art.5(1). As to Steel's committal to prison for refusing to be bound over, this was not a breach of Art.5(1)(b), since the law was formulated precisely enough for her to foresee the consequences of her actions and the binding over order showed sufficiently clearly what was required to comply with it, and whilst the measures taken against her constituted a serious interference with her right to freedom of expression, those measures were not disproportionate, given the nature of her behaviour and the likelihood that she would persist in it. However, it followed from the finding that the other applicant defendant's arrest and detention breached Art.5(1), that the interference with her freedom of expression had not been "prescribed by law" under Art.10(2), and the measures taken against her were disproportionate.

2-041   On the other hand, see *Austin v Commissioner of Police of the Metropolis*.[83] The claimants claimed damages for false imprisonment and breach of their rights under the Human Rights Act 1998 against the Commissioner of Police. In response to a surprise political procession, the police had detained thousands of people in a cordon for several hours in order to prevent a breakdown in law and order. The police had intended to carry out a controlled release of the detained crowd but that was delayed due to the violent behaviour of other groups that had converged in the area making a group release unsafe. Some individuals were released but the claimants' requests for their individual release were refused. It was accepted that the claimants had not themselves been threatening a breach of the peace but others in the group had been doing so. The claimants submitted that they were deprived of their liberty contrary to Art.5, alternatively that any justification for the initial imposition of the cordon had to be shown to have continued until each claimant was released and the defence of necessity was not available. The commissioner submitted that the detention was lawful pursuant to the common law duty to maintain the peace. It was a mere restriction on freedom of movement, which did not engage Art.5(1), alternatively that the exception in Art.5(1)(c) applied. It was also necessary, pursuant to the legitimate aim of protecting public safety, and was proportionate. The court held, giving judgment for the defendant, that necessity could be a factor which, amongst others, might lead to a conclusion that Art.5 did not apply, applied.[84] If the detention was prior to arrest, when arrest was not yet decided upon or not yet practicable, a conditional intention to arrest and bring the person concerned before a judge might suffice, in principle, to fall within the exception under Art.5(1)(c). The test for deciding whether a measure short of arrest could be lawfully taken against a given individual was reasonable suspicion that that individual was presenting the relevant threat. The court noted that the burden of proof was on the claimant to show that the exercise of discretion to detain was unreasonable.[85] The court should accord a high degree of respect for the police officer's appreciation of the risks of what members of the crowd might do if not contained. At the same time the court should subject to very close scrutiny the practical effect that derogating measures had on individual human rights, the importance of the rights affected, and the robustness of any safeguards intended to minimise the impact of the derogating measures on individual human rights. On the facts, their detention was a deprivation of liberty within Art.5(1), but was justified under Art.5(1)(c), as the detention was imposed with the conditional purpose of arresting those whom it would be lawful and practicable to arrest

---

[83] *Times*, April 14, 2005.
[84] *Guenat v Switzerland* (No.24722/94) (1995) 810A D.R. 130.
[85] *Al-Fayed v Commissioner of Police of the Metropolis (No.3)* [2004] EWCA Civ 1579.

and take before a judge, and to prevent such persons from committing violent offences. It was reasonable for the police to consider that all persons in the cordon, including the claimants, were demonstrators and about to commit a breach of the peace, and to continue in that belief after they had requested their individual releases. The police had reasonably believed that the facts necessary to fulfil ss.12(1) and 14(1) of the Public Order Act 1986 were present and it was immaterial that none of the officers had those sections in mind at the time. A direction to disperse under s.14 of the Act could include a direction to disperse by a specified route and to stay in a specified place for as long as necessary to enable the dispersal to take place safely and without disorder. The applicants had been falsely imprisoned but it had been necessary for the protection of everyone to detain the crowd until dispersal could be arranged safely. The need to contain the procession had not arisen out of any negligence by the police.

If there is no unlawful violence or threat of it, then there is no breach of the peace. However, where there is violence, it is irrelevant whether or not the violence was unlawful. It becomes then a question of determining who is responsible for causing it and whether or not the violence emanates from the activity of the defendant, rather than the police or some other public officer acting in the course of the duties. In *Marsh v Arscott*, the police were asked to leave private premises and thereafter they had no power to remain; they refused to leave and a struggle occurred between the defendant and the police. The defendant was arrested. The court said:[86]   **2-042**

> ". . .the police officers having been told to leave, were acting unlawfully in remaining. If the defendant was using no more force than was reasonably necessary to evict them, he was acting lawfully and in arresting him the police were acting unlawfully. This violent incident amounted to a breach of the peace but it was one for which the police officers were responsible and not the defendant himself. . .Suppose that the defendant's threats and use of force towards the police had been unlawful, once again there would have been a breach of the peace. In this event, the defendant would have been responsible for breaching the peace. Thus, regardless of who was acting lawfully and who was acting unlawfully there was at the time of the incident a breach of the peace."

In *Joyce v Hertfordshire Constabulary*,[87] it was held that a police officer could intervene in a struggle between the appellant and another officer but he need not be sure that there had been a lawful arrest. Therefore, the common law power to remove passive demonstrators as trespassers with reasonable force by the landowner may in fact be a breach of the peace justifying the intervention of police officers. On the other hand, the removal of the demonstrators under those circumstances by the police (rather than the landowner) may be lawful if the officers have a reasonable apprehension of the likelihood of violence.

Further, there must be "a real and imminent risk" of a breach of the peace.[88]   **2-043**
Whether a breach is reasonably apprehended as imminent is a question of fact in each case, but there must be something to ground the constable's belief. The test is objective but without the benefit of hindsight. Following the implementation of the Human Rights Act 1998, while courts will assess the reasonableness from the point of view of what the officer knew at the time, they appear to be more willing to scrutinise the basis of the arrest even where they are satisfied that

[86] (1982) 75 Cr. App. 211.
[87] (1985) 80 Cr. App. R. 298.
[88] *R. v Chief Constable of Devon and Cornwall, Ex p. Central Electricity Generating Board* [1982] Q.B. 458; *McLeod v Commissioner of Police for the Metropolis* [1994] 4 All E.R. 553.

the officer was acting honestly, per *Austin*, above.[89] In *Foulkes v Chief Constable of Merseyside*,[90] the claimant called the police after being locked out of his home as a consequence of a family argument. The police officers who attended the scene ascertained that the claimant's family did not want him to return to the house and tried to persuade him to leave for a while, warning him that he might be arrested to prevent a breach of the peace. He insisted that he wanted to return to the house and, when he refused to go away, he was arrested and subsequently detained. The officer who arrested him stated that he believed that violence would have occurred had the claimant returned to the house. The claimant's claim for damages for wrongful arrest and false imprisonment was dismissed and he appealed. The Court of Appeal, allowing the appeal, held that a police officer's common law power to make an arrest on the basis of an apprehended breach of the peace should only be exercised exceptionally. Although the arresting officer had acted with the best of motives and in the genuine belief that by arresting the claimant, a breach of the peace would be prevented, there was not a sufficiently serious and imminent threat to the peace to provide reasonable grounds for arresting someone who was not acting unlawfully.

2-044   See also *Wragg v DPP*.[91] The appellant appealed against the dismissal of his appeal against his conviction for assaulting a police officer acting in the execution of his duty. Police officers had attended a residential property following a heated argument between the appellant and his partner. His partner and her children told the officers that they believed that if the appellant remained at the premises, she might be subjected to violence by the appellant. The officers had spoken to the appellant but he ignored them. Despite warnings, he refused to leave the premises and he was arrested in order to prevent a breach of the peace. There followed a struggle occurred between the appellant and the arresting officers which resulted in injury to the officers. The appellant submitted that the police's conclusion that there was reason to believe that there was a risk of imminent or immediate violence could not be supported on the evidence. It was held, dismissing the appeal, that the officers had to assess whether or not in leaving the appellant in the house that night there was a risk that his partner would be subjected to violence by him. There were matters that were for the police, and the court had to consider, when looking at the matter objectively. For example, the appellant had been drinking and it was reasonable for the officers to take into account his partner's fear of violence and the statements of her children. The officers were entitled to take into account the facts that the appellant had failed to respond to their requests to address the situation and had attempted in their opinion to intimidate them. Accordingly, it had been reasonable in the circumstances of the case for the police to believe that a breach of the peace would be committed in the imminent future if the appellant remained at the premises and consequently he had been lawfully arrested.

2-045   Clearly, the person against whom the action is taken ought to be the person responsible for the disturbance, but a problem arises where there is a "hostile audience": i.e. where persons carrying out a lawful activity attract violence or threats of violence by their nearby critics and opponents. A controversial example might be peaceful protests outside or nearby an animal testing laboratory. The issue for the authorities is whether or not they should restrain the lawful activity. The general view seems to be that, except in exceptional circumstances, the discretion should always favour the lawful activity.[92] The police may enter premises without a warrant where there is a breach of the

[89] *Foulkes v Chief Constable Merseyside Police* [1998] 3 All E.R. 705.
[90] [1998] 3 All E.R. 705.
[91] [2005] EWHC 1389.
[92] *R. v Coventry CC Ex. P. Phoenix Aviation* [1995] 3 All E.R. 37; *Redmond-Bate v DPP* (1999) 163 J.P. 789. See also *Steel*, (1998) 28 E.H.R.R. 603.

peace which is occurring and, if no breach is actually occurring but it is appre-
hended that it is likely to occur, there is also a power to enter and remain.[93]
Subject to the provisions of the Public Order Act 1986, there is also common
law power to break up meetings which are likely to be a breach of the peace.[94]
The power may be used to deal with pickets: a picket may be stopped if the
police form the view that it is likely to lead to a breach of the peace.[95]
Constables also have a common law power to control the highway: in *Moss v
McLachlan*,[96] it was held that a road check, a few miles from a colliery during
the miners' strike of 1984, was reasonable as the police had reason to believe
that striking miners were planning mass pickets and there would be a breach
of peace if they were allowed to continue.[97] Where appropriate, they may seize
property likely to lead to breaches of the peace, such as a loud hailer or placards and banners, and eject trespassers.[98] See also the Court of Appeal's judgment in *Laporte,* the facts of which are set out above. The Court of Appeal
held, dismissing the appeal and cross appeal, that it was reasonable for the
police to apprehend a breach of the peace and to decide to prevent the
respondent and her fellow passengers from proceeding to the protest. The
court below had correctly followed *Moss v McLachlan*[99] in determining
whether the preventive actions taken by the police in the instant case were
legitimate. What was sufficiently "imminent" to justify taking action to
prevent a breach of the peace was dependent on all the circumstances. Action
was not to be taken until it was necessary and reasonable to take the action in
the particular circumstances of the case. What preventive action was necessary
and proportionate was to be determined by how close in proximity, both in
place and time, the location of the apprehended breach of the peace was. The
chief superintendent had been correct to take a blanket approach to the possibility of disruption by returning all individuals on the coaches to London.
In view of the attitude adopted generally by the passengers on the coaches it
would not have been possible to identify those who would not cause a breach
of the peace. The need to prevent an apprehended breach of the peace might
require action to be taken which risked affecting a wholly innocent individual.
There was ample evidence to justify the chief superintendent's assessment of
the situation and order the action he did:

> "We regard what is sufficiently "imminent" to justify taking action to
> prevent a breach of the peace as dependent on all the circumstances. As in
> *Moss*, so here, it is important that the Claimant was intending to travel in
> a vehicle if the preventive action had not taken place. The relatively small
> distance involved did not mean that there was no sufficient imminence.
> What preventive action was necessary and proportionate, however, would
> be very much influenced by how close in proximity, both in place and time,
> the location of the apprehended breach of the peace was. The greater the
> distance and the greater the time involved, the more important it is to
> decide whether preventive action is really necessary and, if it is necessary,
> the more restrained the action taken should usually be as there will be
> time for further action if the action initially taken does not deter. It may
> be that as the police thought, arrest at the lay-by would have been a

---

[93] Private and public premises: *McLeod v Commissioner of Police of the Metropolis*, (1994) 4 All
E.R. 553.
[94] *Duncan v Jones* [1936] 1 K.B. 218.
[95] *Piddington v Bates* [1961] 1 W.L.R. 162; *Smith v Reynolds* [1986] Crim L.R. 559.
[96] (1985) 149 J.P. 167.
[97] See also *R. v Chief Constable of Sussex, Ex p International Traders Ferry*, [1992] A.C. 418.
[98] Masks also: Criminal Justice and Public Order Act 1994 s.60.
[99] (1985) 149 J.P. 167.

disproportionate level of action, but this does not necessarily mean that no action was appropriate.

However, the action of escorting the vehicles back to London without allowing any stops was disproportionate and not justifiable at common law. Action could have been taken which was more limited in its impact on the passengers' rights to freedom of action.

Binding Over

2-046   Magistrates have powers under the common law and statute[1] to bind over a person to keep the peace. As a measure of preventative justice, the magistrates may bind over of their own motion where they consider that a person's conduct is such that there might be a breach of the peace in the future, whether by that person or others.[2] The Law Commission condemned binding over some years ago, but no action has been taken at the government level to adopt the proposal. Meanwhile, the law of binding over was criticised by the European Court of Human Rights. In *Hashman and Harrup v UK*, the applicants blew a hunting horn and engaged in noisy activities with the intention of disrupting a hunt. A complaint was made to the magistrates that the applicants should be required to enter into a recognisance, with or without sureties, to keep the peace and be of good behaviour, pursuant to the Justices of the Peace Act 1861. The applicants were bound over to keep the peace and be of good behaviour in the sum of £100 for 12 months. On appeal, the Crown Court found that the applicants had not committed any breach of the peace, and that their conduct had not been likely to occasion a breach of the peace. However, the applicants' behaviour had been a deliberate attempt to interfere with the hunt and to take hounds out of the control of the huntsman. Therefore, their actions were unlawful and had exposed the hounds to danger; further, they were likely to repeat this behaviour. The applicants' actions were *contra bonos mores* (or against the common good) and therefore they should be bound over to keep the peace and be of good behaviour. The applicants' appeals against the decisions were dismissed. Before the European Court, it was held that there had been a violation of Art.10 of the Convention as the binding over of the applicants was an interference with the applicants' right to freedom of expression under Art.10(1) because the proceedings were brought against the applicants as a result of their protesting against hunting by disrupting the hunt. Such a protest constituted an expression of opinion within the meaning of Art.10(1). The interference was not "prescribed by law". Further, the concept of behaviour *contra bonos mores* was insufficiently precise. The definition of *contra bonos mores* as "behaviour which is wrong rather than right in the judgment of the majority of contemporary fellow citizens" was, in the view of the Court, inadequate because it failed to give a clear indication of the conduct which was prohibited.

Public Order Act Offences

Section 1: Riot and Disorder
2-047   The Public Order Act 1986 is a code which rationalises a range of common law and statutory offences. The 1986 Act itself was substantially amended by the Criminal Justice and Public Order Act 1994 and then by the Crime and

---

[1] On complaint, by way of s.115, Magistrates Court Act 1980; otherwise, mainly under Justices of the Peace Act 1861.
[2] *Veater v Glennon* [1981] 1 W.L.R. 567.

Disorder Act 1998. Section 1 of the 1986 Act deals with riot and disorder. The nature and gravity of such an offence would ordinarily mean that it is outside the scope of this text. However, it is the basis of many of the lower level public order offences and so it is useful to consider briefly its main features. Section 1 provides:

"(1) Where 12 or more persons who are present together use or threaten unlawful violence for a common purpose and the conduct of them (taken together) is such as would cause a person of reasonable firmness present at the scene to fear for his personal safety, each of the persons using unlawful violence for the common purpose is guilty of riot.
(2) It is immaterial whether or not the 12 or more use or threaten unlawful violence simultaneously.
(3) The common purpose may be inferred from conduct.
(4) No person of reasonable firmness need actually be, or likely to be, present at the scene."

Given that it is immaterial whether or not the 12 or more use, or threaten to use unlawful violence, and also whether all of the 12 or more intend to use violence or are aware that their conduct may be violence, a person may be guilty of riot even if 12 or more co-rioters are not guilty of riot because of lack of *mens rea*. However, the accused must use, rather than threaten, unlawful violence.[3] Common purpose can be inferred from the conduct of the rioters. Unlawful violence is defined by s.8 of the 1986 Act. It means:

". . .any violent conduct, so that

(a) except in the context of affray, it includes violent conduct towards property as well as violent conduct towards persons, and
(b) it is not restricted to conduct causing or intending to cause injury or damage but includes any other violent conduct (for example, throwing at or towards a person a missile of a kind capable of causing injury which does not hit or falls short)."

Violent Disorder and Affray
Sections 2 (violent disorder) and 3 (affray) of the 1986 Act are in the same **2-048** terms save that, under s.2, it is three or more persons present together rather than 12; and under s.3, it can be a single person. Violent disorder is triable either way although, under the Criminal Practice Direction[4] Mode of Trial, para.51, cases of violent disorder should normally be committed for trial. Cases of affray should be summarily tried unless there is organised violence, use of weapons, substantial damage, racial motivation or an attack on an emergency worker or police officer. Both are class 4 offences. As to the requirement regarding violent disorder of three or more persons, see *Mahroof*,[5] in which it was held that it was possible to convict one named offender even if no other persons are named in the indictment, so long as there is evidence that there were three people involved in the criminal behaviour. As in the case of riot, it is immaterial whether or not three or more people use of threaten to use violence simultaneously. However, in *McGuigan*,[6] the Court of Appeal held that violent disorder required three or more persons for its commission and was not committed unless three or more persons used or threatened unlawful violence; if two persons used

[3] *R. v Jefferson* [1994] 1 All E.R. 270.
[4] [2002] 3 All E.R. 904.
[5] (1989) 88 Cr. App. R. 317.
[6] [1991] Crim. L.R. 719.

or threatened unlawful violence, a third person could not by aiding and abetting render them guilty of violent disorder. Thus, once the third man was acquitted, the appellants could not be guilty of violent disorder. In *Brodie*,[7] the accused was a member of a group stalking a man for a mile on a footpath in the middle of the night to another point where he was murdered by someone carrying a baseball bat. It was held that, under s.2, conduct was capable of amounting to a threat by way of an implied menace.[8] However, merely possessing a weapon may not be sufficient if it is concealed; nor are mere words alone or the making of a threat in an aggressive tone of voice.[9] Setting dogs on police with the words "Go on! Go on!" was sufficient in *Dixon*[10] under s.3.

2-049   For all three offences, the test is whether a person of reasonable firmness present at the scene would be caused to fear for his personal safety; but no such person need actually be present at the scene. It is therefore an objective standard and what matters is whether that hypothetical person, and not merely the person assaulted, would be put in fear. Relevant considerations include whether or not the person assaulted was in fact actually afraid, the place and time of the incident, and whether the violence was limited to those involved.[11] In *I v DPP*,[12] the defendant appealed against the dismissal of his appeal against a conviction for affray, arising out of an incident in which a number of youths had assembled for the purposes of a fight with a rival gang. Unlit petrol bombs had been carried by some individuals although no potential victims had been present at the scene. Upon the arrival of the police, the group had dissipated and the petrol bombs had been thrown away as they dispersed. The House of Lords held, allowing the appeal, that the carrying of petrol bombs could amount to a threat of unlawful violence for the purposes of affray, even where the weapons were not brandished or waved. However, for the purposes of s.3(1) of the 1986 Act, it was necessary for there to be a threat of violence towards another person present at the scene in circumstances which would cause fear to a notional bystander of reasonable firmness. On the facts of this case, it was held that there had not been anyone present who was capable of satisfying that definition. In *Rothwell*,[13] the appellants were convicted of violent disorder, contrary to s.2(1) of the 1986 Act. Two co-accused were acquitted. The four of them had returned to a nightclub where one of the co-accused had been involved in an incident with a doorman. Violence ensued and the police were called. Counsel for the appellants addressed the jury on the basis that what they had done was either self-defence, or reasonable defence of a friend of an attempt to stop the breach of the peace. The recorder directed the jury that those were not defences to the charge. The Court of Appeal, allowing the appeal, held the recorder was wrong: the prosecution had to establish against each appellant that he was using or threatening unlawful violence. Self defence, reasonable defence of another person and actions which are no more than necessary to restore the peace have always been considered legal justification for what would otherwise be assault and provided a defence to the old common law offence of affray. The word "unlawful" is intended to ensure that those concepts remain as defences to the statutory offences under the 1986 Act which replace the offence of affray.

---

[7] [2000] Crim. L.R. 775.
[8] See also *R. v Church* [2000] 4 *Archbold News* 3, CA—another s.2 offence, the defendant running with a group, other members of which were armed and committed assaults.
[9] *R. v Robinson* [1993] Crim. L.R. 581, under s.3.
[10] (1993) WL 965991.
[11] *R. v. Davidson* [1992] Crim. L.R. 31.
[12] [2002] 1 A.C. 285.
[13] [1993] Crim. L.R. 626–627.

Threatening, Abusive and Insulting Conduct
Section 4 of the 1986 Act deals with threatening, abusive or insulting conduct, **2-050**
It provides:

"(1) A person is guilty of an offence if he:

(a) uses towards another person threatening, abusive, or insulting words or behaviour; or

(b) distributes or displays to another person any writing, sign or other visible representation which is threatening, abusive or insulting, with intent to cause that person to believe that immediate unlawful violence will be used against him or another by any person, or to provoke the immediate use of unlawful violence by that person or another, or whereby that person is likely to believe that such violence will be used or it is likely that such violence will be provoked.

(2) An offence under this section may be committed in a public or a private place, except that no offence is committed where the words or behaviour are used, or the writing, sign or other visible representation is distributed or displayed, by a person inside a dwelling and the other person is also inside that or another dwelling.

(3) A constable may arrest without warrant anyone he reasonably suspects is committing an offence under this section."

It is not necessary to show that the other person believed anything; what must be shown is that the defendant had the intention to cause that person to believe that unlawful violence would be used.[14] Further, the defendant must have intended to provoke the immediate use of violence by that person or another; the person against whom the conduct was directed was likely to believe that that such violence would be used; and it is likely that such violence would be provoked.[15] In *DPP v Ramos*,[16] five days after the explosion of a nail bomb in Brixton, the defendant wrote two letters containing racially motivated threats of a bombing campaign to an Asian community organisation. He was charged, under s.4(1)(b) of the 1986 Act, with distributing material which was threatening, abusive or insulting with intent to cause a belief in the recipient that immediate unlawful violence would be used against him. The magistrate determined that there was no case to answer since there was no indication within the letters as to when the threat was to be carried out. He concluded that there was insufficient evidence to substantiate the charge in respect of immediacy of the threat. The DPP appealed by way of case stated and argued that there was in fact clear evidence upon which the magistrate could have inferred that the recipients were likely to fear immediate unlawful violence. The Court of Appeal allowed the appeal. It is the state of mind of the victim, they held, which was crucial, rather than the statistical risk of violence occurring within a short space of time. Coming five days after the Brixton bomb, the letter was sufficient to allow the magistrate to infer that the victim feared immediate unlawful violence in that something could happen at any time. Therefore, there was a case to answer.

The *mens rea* for this offence is defined in s.6(3): **2-051**

"A person is guilty of an offence under section 4 only if he intends his words or behaviour, or the writing, sign of other visible representation, to be threatening, abusive, or insulting or is aware that it may be threatening, abusive or insulting."

---

[14] *Swanston v DPP* (1997) 161 J.P. 203.
[15] *Winn v DPP* (1992) 156 J.P. 881.
[16] [2000] Crim. L.R. 76, CA.

The phrase "uses towards" connotes the physical presence of the person to whom the words are used. The other person must perceive with his own senses the threatening words or behaviour. If the other person did not hear the words, then no offence has been committed, even if the words were communicated to him by a third party. In *Atkin v DPP*,[17] the conviction was quashed because the person outside the dwelling was only aware of the threat because it was relayed to him by a Customs and Excise officer. Even so, it is not essential that the victim is called to prove that he was present and perceived the conduct.[18]

2-052   "Threatening, abusive words or insulting words or behaviour" is not defined in the 1986 Act. However, the term "threatening, abusive or insulting" appeared in preceding legislation, s.5 of the Public Order Act 1936 and s.54(13) of the Metropolitan Police Act 1839, and cases under those provisions have held that the words "threatening, abusive words or insulting words or behaviour" are to be given their normal, everyday meaning.[19] Rude or offensive words may not be necessarily insulting, even where they are annoying.[20] On the other hand, the Divisional Court, as late as 1986, accepted that two men kissing and cuddling each other at a bus stop was insulting conduct under the 1839 Act in *Masterton v Holden*;[21] see also *Parkin v Norman*,[22] where the Divisional Court held that masturbating in a public toilet was capable of being insulting if the stranger was a heterosexual who would be insulted by homosexual acts. A dwelling is defined as "any structure or part of a structure occupied as a person's home or as other living accommodation." A communal landing in council flats is not a dwelling.[23] Under subs.(2), the offence may be committed in a public or private place, except where the words or behaviour are used or the writing, sign or other visible representation is displayed inside a dwelling and the person who is harassed alarmed or distressed is also inside the dwelling. Additionally, the accused has a defence if he has prove that he was inside a dwelling and had no reason to believe that the words, behaviour, sign, etc. would be seen or heard by a person outside that dwelling; and that his conduct was reasonable.

Sections 4A and 5, Causing Harassment, Alarm or Distress

2-053   Section 4A of the 1986 Act is the offence of causing harassment alarm or distress. Under subs.(1), a person is guilty of an offence if, with intent to cause a person harassment, alarm, or distress, he—

"(a) uses threatening, abusive or insulting words or behaviour, or disorderly behaviour; or
(b) displays any writing, sign or visible representation with is threatening, abusive or insulting,

thereby causing that or another person harassment, alarm or distress."
A constable may arrest without warrant any person he reasonably suspects is committing this offence.[24] The term "harassment, alarm or distress" is not defined and so they have their ordinary language meaning. "Harassment" does not connote any element of apprehension about personal safety.[25]

---

[17] (1989) 89 Cr. App. R. 199.
[18] *Swanston v DPP* 161 J.P. 203.
[19] *Brutus v Cozens* [1973] A.C. 854.
[20] *R. v Ambrose* (1973) 57 Cr. App. 538.
[21] [1986] 1 W.L.R. 101.
[22] [1983] Q.B. 92.
[23] *Rukwira v DPP* [1993] Crim. L.R. 882.
[24] Public Order Act 1986, s.4A(4).
[25] *Chambers v DPP* [1995] Crim. L.R. 896.

In *Lodge v DPP*[26] it was sufficient if the other person in question (in this case, a police officer) was caused to feel alarm, distress or harassment for someone else (in this case, a child). There is no reason why a police officer cannot be a person caused harassment, distress or alarm under this section. It is essential that there is a causal link between the conduct of the accused and the other person's harassment, alarm or distress. The link was not broken, for example, where a person heard the noise of the crowd and its cumulative increase which caused alarm but watched the incident on his CCTV.[27] As the editors of *Blackstone* note, the fundamental issue is whether the defendant intended to cause harassment, alarm or distress. In *Rogers v DPP*[28] it was held that it may be inferred where the defendant's conduct is committed in the context of a large crowd, gathered to protest another person's activities, at which a fence was removed and the police line penetrated, even though there was no evidence that the accused knew that the other was present at the scene or could experience the disorderly behaviour. It may also be inferred, although not automatically, from the use of the words, "black bastard" and other similar racist remarks.[29] As under s.4, the offence may be committed in a public or private place but no offence is committed if the conduct is committed by a person inside a dwelling and the person caused alarm by it was inside that or another dwelling.[30] Subsection (3) provides a defence where the accused can prove that he was inside a dwelling and had no reason to believe that the conduct would be observed by any person outside the dwelling, or that his conduct was reasonable.[31]

Section 5 is a lesser version of this offence: **2-054**

"(1) A person is guilty of an offence if he—

(a) uses threatening, abusive, or insulting words or behaviour or disorderly behaviour; or
(b) displays any writing, sign or visible representation which is threatening, abusive or insulting,

within the hearing or sight of a person likely to be caused harassment, alarm or distress thereby."

Under subs.(1), a constable may arrest a person without warrant if:

"(a) he engages in offensive conduct which a constable warns him to stop, and
(b) he engages in further offensive conduct immediately or shortly after the warning."

"Offensive conduct" is defined in subs.(5) as "conduct the constable reasonably suspects to constitute an offence under this section and the conduct mentioned in paragraph (a) and the further conduct need not be of the same nature." In *Vigon v DPP*[32] the Court of Appeal held that that it was open to justices to find that the behaviour of a market trader who installed a partially hidden video camera in a changing area, so that customers trying on swimwear would be filmed, amounted to insulting behaviour likely to cause harassment, alarm or

[26] *Times*, October 26, 1988.
[27] *Rogers v DPP* (unreported July 22, 1999).
[28] Unreported, July 22, 1999.
[29] *DPP v Weeks, Independent*, July 17, 2000.
[30] Public Order Act 1986, s.4A(2).
[31] The burden of proof lies on the accused on the balance of probabilities. However, note *R. v Lambert* [2001] 3. W.L.R. 206: the imposition of a legal burden on the accused may be contrary to the the Human Rights Act 1998.
[32] [1998] Crim. L.R. 289.

distress within the meaning of s.5 of the 1986 Act. The wording of the section was not limited to rowdy behaviour and the action of setting up the camera and switching it on was sufficient to found a conviction. A warning, for example, may be sufficient if it conveys the idea that, unless the conduct ceases, the offender is breaking the law[33] However, it is necessary for someone under this section for an offence to stand to observe the offensive conduct. In *Holloway v DPP*,[34] in which the appellant used a video recorder to film a group of school children and, while doing this, he stood naked in view of the camera whilst the children were in the background some distance away, the district judge found that no one had in fact seen this but also held that anyone seeing him naked would be likely to be caused harassment, alarm or distress, and that he must have been aware of the likely effect of his naked state on others in a public place. The question for the court was whether a person who had not been seen but could have been seen by anybody had committed an offence under s.5. He contended that s.5 required the insulting behaviour to be actually witnessed by somebody. The Court of Appeal allowed the appeal. It was held that s.5 required the insulting words or behaviour to be "within the. . . sight of a person". Those words meant that some person must have actually seen the abusive or insulting words or behaviour. It was not enough that somebody merely might have seen or could possibly have seen that behaviour. If Parliament had intended that an offence under s.5 would have been committed if the offensive behaviour could have seen by somebody, even if not actually seen, then it would have inserted a provision to that effect in s.5. In contrast, a person could be convicted of an offence of affray under s.3 if a notional person would have seen the conduct complained of, but the legislature did not adopt such wording in s.5, indicating that the parliamentary intention was that the two provisions should be construed differently. Furthermore, the view that someone would have committed an offence under s.5(1), if they could have been seen by somebody, entailed a rewriting of the section and there was no reason why it should be rewritten or construed in that way. Secondly, there was no reason, in a proper case, why a charge under s.5 could not be established where the evidence made it clear that the court could properly and safely draw the inference that there were people who had seen or heard the offending behaviour.

2-055   In *Percy v DPP*[35] a conviction under s.5 with regard to the defacement of a United States flag as a form of protest, was quashed as being a disproportionate response to the accused's right to free speech under Art.10 of the Convention. It was contended that s.5 per se was contrary to Art.10, but this was rejected, the court holding that s.5 satisfies the necessary balance under Art.10(2) between the right to freedom of expression and the right of others not to be insulted or distressed.

2-056   There is a defence in subs.(3) where the accused can prove:

"(a) that he had no reason to believe that any person within hearing or sight who was likely to be caused harassment, alarm or distress, or
(b) that he was inside a dwelling and had no reason to believe that the words or behaviour used or the writing, sign of other visible representation displayed, would be heard or seen by a person outside that or any other dwelling, or
(c) that his conduct was reasonable."

In *Norwood v DPP*[36] the appellant defendant displayed a poster in the first-floor window of his flat in a small rural town in Shropshire, containing words

---

[33] *Groom v DPP* [1991] Crim. L.R. 713.
[34] [2004] WL 2355785.
[35] (2002) 166 J.P. 93.
[36] [2003] EWHC 1564 (Admin).

in very large print "Islam out of Britain" and "Protect the British people". It also bore a reproduction of a photograph of one of the twin towers of the World Trade Centre in flames on September 11, 2001, and a Crescent and Star surrounded by a prohibition sign. The poster had been supplied by, and bore the initials of, the British National Party, of which the appellant was the regional organiser for Shropshire. It had been displayed continuously since a date in November 2001 in one window or another of his flat and was clearly visible to passers-by. A member of the public who was offended by the poster reported the matter to the Police. The defendant was convicted and fined under s.5 of the 1986 Act. The trial judge found the poster was abusive and insulting to Islam; it was likely to cause harassment, alarm or distress; its display was not objectively reasonable within s.5(3)(c) of the 1986 Act; and the offence was religiously aggravated in that it was, as provided by s.28(1)(b) of the 1998 Act, motivated (wholly or partly) by hostility towards members of a religious group based on their membership of that group. On appeal, the Divisional Court found that the District Judge was entitled to find that the first limb of the aggravated s.5 offence was made out, namely that the appellant had displayed the poster intending it to be, or being at least aware that it might be, insulting. The words of the poster alone, and even more so when considered alongside the symbols of one of twin towers of the World Trade centre in flames and the crescent and star surrounded by a prohibition sign, were clearly racially directed and racially insulting. The poster was a public expression of attack on all Muslims in this country, urging all who might read it that followers of the Islamic religion here should be removed from it, and warning that their presence here was a threat or a danger to the British people. Similarly, in relation to the second limb of the offence, namely that the display of the poster was within the hearing or sight of a person likely to be caused harassment, alarm or distress, the court found that, regardless of the evidence of the complainant and the two police officers, the terms of the poster and the circumstances and location of its display were, as matter of plain common sense capable of causing harassment, alarm or distress to those passing by who might see it in the defendant's window. The court considered Art.10 and the s.5(3) defence together, as the question whether a defendant's conduct is objectively reasonable in the court's view included consideration of his right to freedom of expression under Art.10 of the Convention. In the absence of a challenge to the compatibility of s.5 with the Convention, Goldring J. held that the mechanics of the Article's operation on a prosecution under it were to be confined to the objective defence of reasonableness in s.5(3). The main issue was whether the defendant's conduct was objectively reasonable, having regard to all the circumstances, including, importantly, those set out in Art.10. This meant a consideration whether to mark as criminal the defendant's conduct in displaying the poster as a necessary restriction of his freedom of expression for the prevention of disorder or crime and/or for the protection of the rights of others:

"The issue was whether the defendant's conduct went beyond legitimate protest and whether the behaviour had not formed part of an open expression of opinion on a matter of public interest, but had become disproportionate and unreasonable. Nevertheless, reasonableness or unreasonableness of an accused's conduct in an objective sense goes to the root of the court's decision whether or not raised as a section 5(3) defence. If the prosecution has proved, as it must to obtain a conviction, that an accused's conduct was insulting and that he intended it to be, or was aware that it might be so, it would in most cases follow that his conduct was objectively unreasonable, especially where, in the aggravated form, the prosecution have proved that his conduct was 'motivated (wholly or partly) by hostility towards members of a religious group based on their membership of that group'. If the prosecution fails to prove either state of mind, then the question of reasonableness does not arise because the offence cannot be proved."

Goldring J. held that the District Judge, in the circumstances of his findings on the two limbs in s.5(1), could not have sensibly found that the appellant's conduct was reasonable so as to enable him to secure an acquittal through the route of s.5(3); and it was therefore held that the District Judge was entitled, on the evidence before him, to conclude, in the light of his findings on the first two limbs of s.5, that the offence had been made out—in effect that the appellant's conduct was unreasonable, having regard to the clear legitimate aim, of which the section was itself a necessary vehicle, to protect the rights of others and/or to prevent crime and disorder.

2-057   The Human Rights Act 1998 requires that the criminal law should not be invoked unless and until it is established that the conduct which is the subject of the charge amounts to such a threat to public disorder as to require the invocation of the criminal, as opposed to the civil, law. Geddis observes that courts, when considering the application of s.5 to the individual dissenter who recklessly expresses views on matters of public interest in an insulting fashion, give greater substantial weight to the public's right to peace of mind so that the rights of individual dissenters to communicate their opinions are interpreted in a "pro-civility" manner.[37] In *Redmond-Bate v DPP* (a decision predating the commencement of the 1998 Act), the appellant appealed by way of case stated against the dismissal of an appeal against conviction of obstructing a police officer in the execution of his duty. She was one of a group of women preachers and had been arrested on the steps of a cathedral by a police officer who feared a breach of the peace due to the reaction of some members of a crowd that had gathered to listen. The court held, allowing the appeal that the principle question for determination was whether the actions of the arresting officer were reasonable in an objective sense. The court had to assess reasonableness using only what the officer saw and perceived to be the case at the relevant time without the benefit of retrospection. Sedley L.J. said:

"Free speech includes not only the inoffensive but the irritating, the contentious, the eccentric, the heretical, the unwelcome and the provocative provided it does not tend to provoke violence. Freedom only to speak inoffensively is not worth having. What Speakers' Corner (where the law applies as fully as anywhere else) demonstrates is the tolerance which is both extended by the law to opinion of every kind and expected by the law in the conduct of those who disagree, even strongly, with what they hear. From the condemnation of Socrates to the persecution of modern writers and journalists, our world has seen too many examples of state control of unofficial ideas. A central purpose of the convention has been to set close limits to any such assumed power. We in this country continue to owe a debt to the jury which in 1670 refused to convict the Quakers William Penn and William Mead for preaching ideas which offended against state orthodoxy . . ."

Therefore, free speech was to be tolerated in many forms and freedom only to make purely inoffensive utterances would be valueless. On the facts of the instant case, there was no basis for suspecting that a breach of the peace was about to be committed by the appellant if she continued to propound her views and therefore no basis for the arrest. In consequence, the officer was not acting in the execution of his duty when he arrested her. The decision of the Crown Court in dismissing the appeal was contrary to logic and to a liberal

[37] "Free Speech Martyrs or Reasonable Threats to Social Peace?" (2004) P.L. 853–874.

tradition of many years' standing in this country. Compare this with *Norwood*,[38] above, where the court found that even though there was no evidence of distress, it was likely to be caused; while, in *Redmond-Bate*, the slogans and posters did in fact cause a breach of the peace, but a Divisional Court held that it was those who responded in that way who should be convicted and not the appellants who expressed their opinions.

Closer to the line was *Hammond v DPP*.[39] The defendant appeal by way of **2-058** case stated against his conviction under the s.5 of the 1986 Act for displaying an insulting sign within the sight of persons likely to be caused harassment, alarm or distress. The appellant, an evangelical Christian, had gone into a town centre on a Saturday afternoon to preach whilst displaying a sign bearing the words "Stop Immorality", "Stop Homosexuality" and "Stop Lesbianism". As on a previous occasion, he had drawn a hostile reaction from members of the public. Several people were insulted or distressed by the sign and he was assaulted. It was contended that the magistrates were wrong to find that the sign was "insulting" within the meaning of s.5(1)(b), and that he was entitled to the defence that his conduct was reasonable pursuant to s.5(3)(c), having regard to the requirements of the Human Rights Act 1998, Sch.1, Pt I, Art.9 and Art.10. In particular, the restriction on his freedom of expression was not necessary and proportionate to the prevention of disorder or crime. The Divisional Court dismissed the appeal. The Court held that it was open to the magistrates to conclude as a matter of fact that the words on the sign were insulting within the meaning of s.5(1)(b) of the 1986 Act. The words appeared to relate homosexuality and lesbianism to immorality, and it was accepted that the appellant, according to his understanding, was exercising his right to free expression of sincere religious views. However, the magistrates had considered all of the questions which they were required to consider under s.5(3)(c), in the light of Art.9 and Art.10, and it was open to them to conclude that his conduct was not reasonable for the reasons they gave, including the pressing need to show tolerance to all sections of society and the fact that the appellant's conduct was provoking violence and disorder and interfered with others' rights.

In *Dehal v CPS*,[40] the appellant appealed by way of case stated against a **2-059** decision of the Crown Court affirming his conviction under s.4 where he had placed a poster on the notice board of a Sikh temple. The court found that part of the poster was abusive and insulting to the president of the temple. It also found that it had been posted with intent to cause harassment, alarm or distress and that it had caused harassment and distress. The questions referred to the court were whether the Crown Court had been right to conclude that his prosecution had been a proportionate response to his conduct, and that he had no defence under the Human Rights Act 1998, Sch.1, Pt I, Art.10. Moses J. said:

> "There has been and could be no challenge to the finding as to the appellant's intention, but that does not help in any way as to the proportionality of the criminal prosecution. Nor does the fact that the notice was not objectively reasonable. The court had earlier, apparently, found that there was no basis for the allegation being made against the Temple. What was needed was not merely a conclusion, namely that the prosecution was a proportionate response, but a careful analysis of the reasons why it was necessary to bring a criminal prosecution at all. In order to justify one of the essential foundations of democratic society the prosecution must demonstrate

---

[38] [2003] Crim. L.R. 888.
[39] [2004] EWHC 69.
[40] [2005] EWHC 2154.

that it is being brought in pursuit of a legitimate aim, namely the protection of society against violence and that a criminal prosecution is the only method necessary to achieve that aim. The court must carefully consider those considerations and set out their findings as to why they have reached their conclusion. So much is well-settled."

The appeal was allowed because no such reasoning was provided in this case. The important factor upon which the Crown Court should have focused, and upon which on its face it appears not to have focused, was the justification for bringing any criminal prosecution at all. However insulting, however unjustified what the appellant said about the President of the Temple, a criminal prosecution was unlawful as a result of s.3 of the Human Rights Act 1998 and Art.10, unless and until it could be established that such a prosecution was necessary in order to prevent public disorder. There is no such finding or any justification whatever given in the case stated. There was no basis found by the Crown Court for concluding that the prosecution was a proportionate response to his conduct. In those circumstances, the appeal had to be allowed and both questions answered in the negative.

Racially Aggravated Public Order Offences

2-060   Under the Crime and Disorder Act 1998, certain of the above offences are aggravated if racially motivated. Section 28 provides:

"(1) An offence is racially or religiously aggravated for the purposes of sections 29 to 32 below if:

(a) at the time of committing the offence or immediately before or after doing so, the offender demonstrates towards the victim of the offence hostility based on the victim's membership (or presumed membership) of a racial or religious group; or

(b) the offence is motivated (wholly or partly) by hostility towards members of a racial or religious group.

(2) In subsection (1)(a) above,

"membership", in relation to a racial or religious group includes association with members of that group;
"presumed" means presumed by the offender.

(3) It is immaterial for the purposes of paragraph (a) or (b) of subsection (1) above whether or not the offender's hostility is also based, to any extent, on any factor not mentioned in that paragraph.

(4) In this section, "racial group" means a group of persons defined by reference to race, colour, nationality (including citizenship) or ethnic or national origins.

(5) In this section, "religious group" means a group of persons defined by reference to religious belief or lack of religious belief."

The offences which may be aggravated racially are offences under the Offences Against the Person Act 1861, ss.20 and 37 and common assault;[41] criminal damage;[42] Public Order Act 1986, ss.4, 4A and 5;[43] and Protection from Harassment Act 1997, ss.2 and 4 (below). In each case, the aggravated form carries a higher form and transforms the offence from one which may be summarily tried to one which is triable either way.

---

[41] Crime and Disorder Act 1998, s.29.
[42] *ibid.*, s.30.
[43] *ibid.*, s.31.

It is not necessary for the accused to belong to a different racial group: the **2-061** words "African" in the insult "African bitch" describes a racial group and it is no defence that the defendant is in the same racial group.[44] The prosecution must show hostility on the part of the defendant, although, in most cases, the racially abusive insults themselves may be enough:[45] in *DPP v Pal*, the words were "white man's arselicker" and "brown Englishman", and an offence was committed even though both parties were Asian. The expressions "jungle bunny", "black bastard" and "wog" were uttered immediately before and at the time of an offence of violent disorder under s.4 of the Public Order Act 1986 and so, as the words were of a racial nature and threatening and abusive towards the victim, the aggravated version of the offence was made out.[46] The victim's perception of the words can be irrelevant in determining racial motivation.

In *DPP v M*,[47] the DPP appealed against a decision that the defendant had **2-062** no case to answer in respect of a charge of racially aggravated criminal damage. The court had held that the words "bloody foreigners", used by the respondent immediately prior to breaking the window of a kebab shop, were not capable, in the circumstances, of being construed as expressing hostility based on the victim's personal membership of a racial group within the meaning of s.28 of the 1998 Act. The DPP contended that the expression used was capable of describing, and had in the circumstances described, a person who fell within the definition of a racial group for the purposes of s.28(4) of the 1998 Act, and that the court had erred in concluding that because there had been "other more salient explanations" for M's behaviour than hostility because of racial group there was no case to answer. The court had failed to consider s.28(3), which provided that where there was hostility because of racial group it was immaterial that the hostility was based to any extent on other factors. The Divisional Court held, allowing the appeal, that the words "bloody foreigners" used immediately before committing the offence were capable of being construed as expressing hostility based on a victim's membership or presumed membership of a racial group within the meaning of s.28(1)(a). Whilst the legislation referred to "a racial group" that did not mean that a purely inclusive definition of those words should be adopted. The size of the group was immaterial and words or actions could be directed to large or small groups irrespective of origin. While the court in the instant case had correctly accepted that in principle the words "bloody foreigners" could fall within s.28(4), in putting the matter in context it had slipped from a consideration of demonstration of hostility under s.28(1)(a), to a consideration of motivation under s.28(1)(b). In ignoring s.28(3), the court had erred in its approach to whether the prosecution had disclosed a case to answer of racial hostility under s.28(1)(a). The court had mistaken the test of guilt and treated two possible motivations for M's conduct, namely, a dispute over food purchased at the shop and hostility based on the victim's racial group, as mutually exclusive rather than capable of being complementary. *DPP v M* was applied in *AH-Gen's Reference (4 of 2004)*. The question as to whether the words "immigrant doctor" was only an allegation of non-Britishness or part of a demonstration by the defendant of hostility to the victim within the terms of s.28(1)(a) because she perceived his non-Britishness to derive from his race, colour, nationality or ethnic or national origins, involved a question of fact for the tribunal.[49] However, the Court of Appeal found that the trial judge had erred in ruling that someone who was an immigrant and therefore non British

---

[44] *R. v White* [2001] 1 W.L.R. 1352.
[45] *DPP v Pal* [2000] Crim. L.R. 756.
[46] *DPP v McFarlane* [2002] All E.R. (D) 78.
[47-48] [2004] 1 W.L.R. 2758.
[49] [2005] 1 W.L.R. 2810.

could not as such be a member of a racial group within s.28(4). It was a matter that should have been left for the jury as one capable of having been a racially aggravated offence.

2-063 See also *Rogers*,[50] in which the appellant appealed against his conviction for using racially aggravated abusive or insulting words or behaviour contrary to s.31(1)(a) of the 1998 Act. He had called three young Spanish women "bloody foreigners" and told them to "go back to your own country". The prosecution argued that he had demonstrated towards the women hostility based on their membership of a racial group. The judge rejected the appellant's submission that foreigners did not constitute a racial group as defined by s.28(4) of the Act, and that a finding of hostility based on membership of a racial group could not be made. The Court of Appeal dismissed the appeal. For an offence to be aggravated under s.28 of the Act the defendant had to first form the view that the victim was a member of a racial group within the definition in s.28(4). Something then had to be said that demonstrated hostility towards the victim based on membership of that group. Hostility demonstrated to foreigners because they were foreign could be just as objectionable as hostility based on a more limited racial characteristic. The very width of the meaning of racial group for the purposes of s.28(4) gave rise to a danger that charges of aggravated offences could be brought where vulgar abuse had included racial epithets that did not indicate hostility to the race in question. Section 28 was designed to address racist behaviour and prosecutors should not bring charges based on its provisions unless satisfied that the facts truly suggested that the offence charged was aggravated by racism.

2-064 The relevant form of hostility can be demonstrated even if the victim is absent as long as it had occurred in the immediate context of the substantive offence. In *Parry v DPP*,[51] the appellant, appealing against the decision of the Crown Court to uphold a decision to convict him of racially aggravated criminal damage, had thrown nail varnish against a neighbour's door. The police had arrived 20 minutes later and questioned him about the incident and it was then that he made comments demonstrating hostility based on the victim's racial group. At trial, he admitted the substantive offence but denied the racially aggravated element. The Crown Court held that it was not necessary for the purposes of s.28(1)(a) of the 1998 Act for hostility to be demonstrated immediately after a substantive offence, but that in any event, in the case before it, the hostility had been immediate. Moreover, the absence of the victim at the time of the comments made no difference to the commission of the offence. On appeal, the appellant argued that the hostility had to be demonstrated in the presence of the victim, that it had to be demonstrated immediately after the substantive offence, and in this case the hostility had not been immediate. The court agreed that hostility could be demonstrated in absence of the victim as long as it had occurred in the immediate context of the main offence. The word "immediately" in the Act qualified both the words "before" and "after" in it and accordingly hostility had to be demonstrated immediately in either case. The effect of the ordinary, plain meaning of the words used was to strike at the immediate context of the substantive offence. However, the appeal was allowed because it had not been open to the court to hold that the hostility had been "immediate" in this case and so its decision and that of the magistrates' court was quashed.

Stirring Up Racial Hatred

2-065 Section 18 of the Public Order Act 1986 creates the offence of stirring up racial hatred. It provides:

---

[50] [2006] 1 W.L.R. 962.
[51] [2004] EWHC 3112.

"(1) A person who uses threatening, abusive or insulting words or behaviour or displays any written material which is threatening, abusive or insulting is guilty of an offence if—

(a) he intends thereby to stir up racial hatred, or
(b) having regard to all the circumstances, racial hatred is likely to be stirred up thereby."

The offence may be triable either way. On indictment, it is a class 4 offence. As in the case of riot, no proceedings may be instituted except by or with the consent of the Attorney-General.[52] Racial hatred is defined in s.17 as "hatred against a group of persons . . . defined by reference to colour, race, nationality (including citizenship) or ethnic or national origins." Note also s.3(1) of the Race Relations Act 1976: "racial group" is defined as meaning "a group of persons defined by reference to colour, race, nationality or ethnic or national origins". In *Mandla v Dowell Lee*,[53] it was held that Sikhs are a racial group according to the following conditions, the first two being essential:

(1) a long shared history of which the group is conscious as distinguishing it from other groups;

(2) a cultural tradition of its own including family and social customs and manners often, but not necessarily, associated with religious observance;

(3) a common geographical origin or descent from a small number of common ancestors;

(4) a common language but not necessarily peculiar to the group;

(5) a common literature peculiar to the group;

(6) a common religion;

(7) being a minority.[54]

However, the terms are to be given a non-technical and everyday meaning. For example, the term "African" describes a racial group, however inaccurately in anthropological terms; but not "South American" or at any rate a racial group known as such in the UK.[55]

The *mens rea* for the offence is defined by s.18(1)(b):   **2-066**

"A person who is not shown to have intended to stir up racial hatred is not guilty of an offence under this section if he did not intend his words or behaviour, or the written material, to be, and was not aware that it might be, threatening, abusive or insulting."

Again, as per s.4 of the 1986 Act, an offence may be committed in a public or private place and the same exception applies as to private dwellings.[56] Under subs.(5), a person is not guilty of an offence if he did not intend his words, behaviour or written material to be or was not aware that it might be threatening, abusive, or insulting. Section 19 creates an offence of publishing, or

---

[52] Public Order Act 1986, s.27(3).
[53] [1983] 2 A.C. 548.
[54] See also *King-Ansell v Police* [1979] 2 N.Z.L.R. 531 with regard to Jews; *Commission for Racial Equality v Dutton* [1989] Q.B. 783 re Gypsies (as opposed to travellers); however, not Rastafarians, separate from the rest of the Afro-Carib community; *Dawkins v Crown Supplies (Property Services Agency) The Times*, February 4, 1993.
[55] *R. v White* [2001] 1 W.L.R. 1352.
[56] Public Order Act 1986, s.18(2).

distributing written material which is threatening or insulting if (a) he intends thereby to stir up racial hatred, or (b) having regard to all the circumstances racial hatred is likely to be stirred up thereby. The offence is triable either way and the Attorney-General's consent is required.[57]

Public Disorder at Sporting Events

2-067   The Sporting Events (Control of Alcohol, etc.) Act 1985 creates certain offences to do with the possession of alcohol at football matches or on a journey to football matches, such as on coaches and trains and other public carriers. Under s.2(1), it is an offence for a person to be in possession of intoxicating liquor or a "relevant article" at any time before, during, and after a designated sporting event.[58] Further, it is an offence to be in possession of alcohol while entering or trying to enter a designated sporting event. A "relevant article" is a container used to carry liquor or an object which may injure a person. Section 2A makes it an offence to carry items the main purpose of which is the emission of a flare, smoke or visible gas or which is a fireworks. Sections 1 and 1A of the 1985 Act provides that it is an offence knowingly to cause or permit intoxicating liquor to be carried in public transport. In addition, a constable may enter any part of a designated sports ground at any time during the relevant period of a designated sporting event to enforce the 1985 Act. He also has a power of arrest. The Football Offences Act 1991 provides that, at designated football matches,[59] and for a period of two hours before, during, and one hour after, such a match, it is an offence to throw missiles at the playing area or any area adjacent to it or any area where spectators are present; engage or take part in indecent or racist chanting; or enter the playing area or any other adjacent area.[60] They are arrestable offences and triable summarily only. The Football Spectators Act 1989 contains new provisions dealing with the banning of certain individuals from matches. Again, they apply only to designated football matches.[61] Under s.14A of the 1989 Act, a banning order under the 1989 Act prohibits a named person from entering premises for the purpose of attending such matches in England and Wales or, if outside England and Wales, to report to a police station. The banning order may be imposed on conviction of certain relevant offences such as the use or threat of the use of violence at or on the way to a match, or alcohol offences, a s.5 of the Public Order Act 1986 offence, or carrying or using an offensive weapon or firearms; or where, in relation to certain offences that are committed away from a ground or not on a journey to a ground, a "declaration of relevance" is made under s.23 of the 1989 Act such that the court is satisfied that the offence is nonetheless related to a football match.

Public Meetings and Assemblies

Unlawful Processions and Trespassory Assemblies

2-068   Under s.11(7) of the Public Order Act 1986 it is an offence for a person organising a public procession to fail to give notice of the procession to the police. A further offence is committed by the organiser if, having given notice, the

---

[57] See also ss.20 to 23 of the 1986 Act which deal with the public performance, broadcasting and possession of materials intended to, or likely to, stir up racial hatred.

[58] As designated by order by the Secretary of State, Sports Grounds and Sporting Events (Designation) Order 1985 (SI 1985/1151).

[59] That is, association football matches or matches designated by order by the Secretary of State: Football (Offences) (Designation of Football Matches) Order 2000 (SI 2000/2329).

[60] Football Offences Act 1991, ss.2–4.

[61] Football Spectators (Prescription) Order 2000 (SI 2000/2126).

procession starts on a different time or day or takes a different route.[62] It is a defence under s.11(8) that the defendant did not know and neither suspected nor had any reason to suspect the failure to comply with s.11; or under s.11(9) that the differences arose from circumstances beyond his control. The police may impose conditions on the procession under s.12 of the 1986 Act. It is an offence for an organiser to knowingly fail to comply with such a condition, for a person to take part in such a procession, or to incite another person to do so.[63] A public procession may be prohibited under s.13 of the 1986 Act. Outside of the City of London or the metropolitan police area the district council, on application from the chief office of police with the approval of the secretary of state, may make a procession prohibition order; in the City of London or the metropolitan police area, it is the relevant commissioner who may make an order with the consent of the secretary of state. It is an offence for a person to organise a public procession which he knows to be prohibited; for a person to take part in such a public procession; or to incite another person to do so.[64] Alternatively, under s.12 of the 1986 Act, the senior officer may impose directions on persons organising or taking part in the procession as appear necessary to him to prevent disorder, damage, disruption, or intimidation, including directions as to the route of the procession; failure to comply with such a direction is an offence. Initially, a relevant public assembly for the purposes of the 1986 Act was an assembly of 20 or more persons in a public place which is wholly or partly open to the air in s.16 of the 1986 Act. However, this was severely amended by s.57 of the Anti-Social Behaviour Act 2003 by reducing the relevant number of persons from 20 down to two.

Section 14 of the 1986 Act empowers a senior police officer to impose conditions upon public assemblies and it is an offence for an organiser to knowingly fail to comply with the conditions, for a person who takes part in such an assembly knowingly to fail to comply with a condition, or for a person to incite another person to commit an offence under this section.[65] In *Broadwith v Chief Constable of Thames Valley*,[66] the defendant was charged with taking part in a public assembly and failing to comply with a condition imposed by a senior police officer contrary to s.14(5), and wilfully obstructing a police constable in the execution of his duty contrary to s.89(2) of the Police Act 1996. The conditions imposed under s.14 of the 1986 Act specified that the assembly would be held at one location, with the demonstrators proceeding to another location, at which another assembly could take place commencing no earlier than 1.30pm. The defendant arrived at the second location at 1.00pm and was informed that the road was closed pursuant to the conditions. He contended that, on a proper interpretation of the written directions which referred to a "further assembly", the prohibition on assembling at the second location prior to 1.30pm applied only to those demonstrators who had been present at the first location, and thus did not apply to him, because he had not been there. He also argued that since he was on his own at the time, he was not taking part in a public assembly. The magistrates found that the directions were expressed in clear, everyday language with no ambiguity in their meaning, and were binding on the defendant, who was taking part in the assembly. The defendant appealed, arguing that it was not open to the magistrates to adopt a broad-brush approach to the directions, and demonstrators were entitled to rely on a literal, narrow interpretation of the notice, since absolute clarity was essential in respect of statutes carrying a penal sanction. The Court of Appeal

2-069

---

[62] Triable summarily only and punishable up to level 3.
[63] Public Order Act 1986, s.12(4) to (6); triable summarily only.
[64] *ibid.*, s.13(7) to (9); summary only.
[65] *ibid.*, s.14(4) to (6); summary only.
[66] [2000] Crim. L.R. 924.

dismissed the appeal and held that the interpretation put on the directions by the magistrates was justified as the notice made it clear that an assembly at the second location would not be permitted until 1.30pm. Furthermore, the defendant was clearly a demonstrator, due to his arrival with his face covered and on a bus carrying other demonstrators, and because of the fact that he had been in conversation with a group of more than 20 people a short distance away, immediately prior to his arrest. Although s.14 of the 1986 Act applied to groups in excess of 20 (at the time), those groups were necessarily comprised of individuals, against whom action might be taken to ensure that the assembly proceeded along permitted lines. The court found that the defendant had arrived with the intention of demonstrating with the group and had deliberately tried to enter the second location which was closed in accordance with the notice.

2-070   In *Austin v Commissioner of Police of the Metropolis*,[67] Tugendhat J. considered the application of ss.12 to 14 of the 1986 Act in the context of a May Day procession of protesters. The claimants were among protesters and others who were held within a containment of cordon from 2.20pm to 9.30pm before being released. The police detained the crowd because there were fears of violence. They had planned to carry out a controlled release of the crowd when it became safe and practical, but it took longer than expected because of the violent behaviour of a minority in the crowd and also the violent behaviour of other groups. The claimants contended that the detention in the cordon was unreasonable and unlawful and sued for false imprisonment. Tugendhat J. said of ss.12 and 14 that they do not require there to be any focus on the intentions of individuals in the procession or assembly. The police officer may give directions to those taking part, whether or not individually they appear to present a threat. The required threat is not of a breach of the peace, but of serious disruption to the life of the community. A direction under s.12 may bring an existing assembly to an end as a "modified form of dispersal power". Further, a direction under s.14 that some or all members disperse can include a direction that they disperse by a specified route and also that they stay in a certain area for as long as necessary for the dispersal to be effected consistently with the object of preventing disruption, damage, disorder or intimidation. The power to impose conditions is not restricted to situations where disorder results from the assembly itself, but may also be used where the disorder comes from other groups. Nor did it undermine the validity of the exercise of the powers that the senior office did not intend to exercise at the time. The powers are intended to be available in an emergency. It may be, for example, that a senior officer mistakenly relies upon common law powers to stop a procession travelling over a bridge when the breach of the peace was not sufficiently imminent at the time to justify the use of the common law power. Such a direction would not be invalid simply because the police officer was mistaken as to the source of his powers.

2-071   Section 14A of the 1986 Act provides that the chief officer of police may apply to the district council for an order prohibiting the holding of all trespassory assemblies in the district or part of it. He may do so if he reasonably believes that it is intended that a trespassory assembly is to be held which may result in serious disruption to the life of the community or significant damage to the land, building or monument which is of historical, archaeological or scientific importance. The order must not last more that four days and must not apply to an area greater than that represented by a circle of five miles radius from the centre. An assembly is not trespassory where the user of the highway is reasonable as the public have the right to use the highway for any reasonable and normal purpose including peaceful assembly, so long as it does not obstruct

[67] [2005] EWHC 480.

the general public's right of passage and it does not amount to a nuisance.[68] A constable may arrest without warrant anyone he reasonably suspects to be committing an offence under s.14B.[69] Further, a constable in uniform has power, which may be exercised in the area in which the order applies, to stop someone he reasonably believes to be on his way to an assembly prohibited by an order under s.14A and direct him not to proceed in the direction of the assembly.[70]

In *DPP v Jones*,[71] the defendant was involved in a peaceful, non-obstructive demonstration on part of the highway near Stonehenge, which was the subject of an order under s.14A(2) of the 1986 Act, and they were arrested and convicted of trespassory assembly under s.14B(2). Their appeal against conviction was allowed by the Crown Court, which upheld their argument that a peaceful and non-obstructive assembly was a reasonable use of the highway and not unlawful. The prosecution successfully appealed by way of case stated and the convictions were restored. The Court of Appeal held that the public's right to use the highway was restricted to passing and re-passing, and any activities ancillary or incidental to that right, and that a public assembly was not incidental to the right of passage. The House of Lords allowed the appeal. A public highway was a public place where any activity which was reasonable, was not a public or private nuisance, and did not obstruct the highway, was not to be considered a trespass. Therefore, a right of peaceful assembly on the public highway was lawful, subject to those restrictions. It would amount to an unrealistic and unjustified restriction on everyday activities to limiting the lawful use of the highway to use which was "incidental or ancillary" to the right of passage. In each case, it was a matter of fact and degree for the magistrates as to whether a particular use was reasonable and did not conflict with the right to pass and trespass.

2-072

Jones was applied in *Scott v Mid-South Essex Justices*,[72] in which the appellant appealed against a decision of the justices not to convict the interested party, K, of an offence of wilfully obstructing the highway without lawful excuse contrary to s.137(1) of the Highways Act 1980. K had operated a fast food outlet from a trailer parked on a highway in an industrial estate. The appellant brought a private prosecution under the Act after the police failed to act. The justices held that the trailer had caused a minor obstruction every night over a period of time and that the obstruction was wilful. However, they considered that in accordance with *DPP v Jones*, it was a matter of fact and degree in each case whether or not a person had a reasonable excuse for an obstruction. As the trailer was parked on an industrial estate and the minimal level of traffic in the area was attracted by the trailer itself, K had a reasonable excuse. The appellant argued that the decision in *Jones* was of a more limited application and it had merely decided that the use of a highway for political or recreational purposes might comprise a reasonable excuse. Any use was required to be consistent with the purposes for which highways were usually used. Therefore, no reasonable court could have found that the circumstances comprised a reasonable excuse where there was a persistent nightly use of the trailer which had caused an obstruction of the highway. The Divisional Court dismissed the appeal. The justices had not erred in holding that K had a reasonable excuse for the wilful obstruction of the highway. The decision in *Jones* had effectively amounted to a change in the law. Circumstances that might have comprised an offence before that decision might no longer comprise an offence. It was a question of fact and degree in each case and, given that a criminal prosecution was involved, justices had to be sure that the user was not

2-073

[68] *DPP v Jones* [1999] 2 A.C. 240.
[69] Public Order Act 1986, s.14B(4).
[70] *ibid.*, s.14C(1) and (2).
[71] [1999] 2 A.C. 240.
[72] [2004] EWHC 1001.

reasonable. Given the absence of traffic in the industrial estate at the time of the obstruction, the absence of any obstruction and that the public could pass and repass the highway with the ease, the justices had been entitled to hold that the user had been reasonable and to acquit K. A different bench might have come to a different conclusion.

Breaking Up Lawful Meetings

2-074   It is also unlawful for a person to break up a public meeting. Section 1(1) of the Public Meetings Act 1908 provides that a person commits an offence who acts in a disorderly manner at a lawful public meeting for the purpose of preventing the transaction of the business for which the meeting was called together.[73] In contrast to s.14A of the 1986 Act, a public meeting may be lawful under this section even if it is an obstruction on the highway.[74] A person commits an offence who fails to declare his name and address when asked to do so by a constable, who reasonably suspects the person of committing an offence under the 1908 Act, if the constable has been requested to asked to do by the chairman of the meeting.[75]

Dispersal of Groups

2-075   The Anti-Social Behaviour Act 2003 Act contains two new powers for police with regard to people engaged in what the police see as anti-social behaviour: to disperse groups of people; and to remove persons under the age of 16 from the area. The dispersal scheme resembles the powers granted to police to remove trespassers under the Public Order Act 1986 and the Criminal Justice and Public Order Act 1994. Some consider that these powers are heavy-handed. For example, Liberty, in its response to the 2003 Anti-Social Behaviour White Paper,[76] said that:

> ". . .the designating of areas with significant levels of anti-social behaviour so as to empower the police to disperse groups of young people would seem to be unnecessary—current law gives police adequate power to deal with potential breaches of the peace. Rather than creating draconian new police powers perhaps it would be better to invest money in creating places where children and young people can congregate and where there are interesting things to do. Where facilities such as youth centres and sports grounds exist, the need for children in gangs is reduced."

See also the Local Government Association:

> "Whilst these proposals may have some value in persistent cases of neigh-bourhood disorder the LGA is mindful that earlier curfew provisions contained in the 1998 Crime and Disorder Act have not been supported or used by local authorities. . .Decisions to invoke the order should only be taken where police commanders and local authorities are convinced that alternative interventions have failed."

Note also the Children's Bureau's comments:

> "Police powers for group dispersal and fast-track child curfews may penalise law-abiding young people with nowhere to go while encouraging

---

[73] Summary only.
[74] *Burden v Rigler* [1911] 1 K.B. 337.
[75] Public Meetings Act 1908, s.1(3).
[76] See House of Commons Research Paper, *The Anti-Social Behaviour Bill*, Number 3/34, April 2003.

the myth that it is groups of young people who are largely responsible for anti-social or criminal behaviour. The measure will also damage relationships between young people and the police."

The Home Office estimates that dispersal powers were authorised in 809 areas in England and Wales between January 1, 2004, when the powers came into force, and June 30, 2005. In total it estimates that 14,375 people had been dispersed from the 293 areas for which data was collected.[77]

Section 30 of the 2003 Act applies where a relevant officer[78] has reasonable grounds for believing that: (a) any members of the public have been intimidated, harassed, alarmed or distressed as a result of the presence or behaviour of groups of two or more persons in public places[79] in any locality in his police area ("the relevant locality"), and (b) that anti-social behaviour is a significant and persistent problem in the relevant locality. Under s.30(2), the relevant officer may give an authorisation that the powers conferred on a constable in uniform by subs.(3) to (6) are to be exercisable for a period specified in the authorisation which does not exceed six months. Subsection (3) provides that, if a constable in uniform has reasonable grounds for believing that the presence or behaviour of a group of two or more persons in any public place in the relevant locality has resulted, or is likely to result, in any members of the public being intimidated, harassed, alarmed or distressed, he may, under subs.(4) may give any of the following directions:

2-076

(1) a direction requiring the persons in the group to disperse (either immediately or by such time as he may specify and in such way as he may specify);

(2) a direction requiring any of those persons whose place of residence is not within the relevant locality to leave the relevant locality or any part of the relevant locality (either immediately or by such time as he may specify and in such way as he may specify); and

(3) a direction prohibiting any of those persons whose place of residence is not within the relevant locality from returning to the relevant locality or any part of the relevant locality for such period (not exceeding 24 hours) from the giving of the direction as he may specify.

However, this is subject to subs.(5). This provides that such a direction may not be given in respect of certain groups of persons. These are persons engaged in conduct which is lawful under s.220 of the Trade Union and Labour Relations (Consolidation) Act 1992; and those who are taking part in a public procession of the kind mentioned in s.11(1) of the Public Order Act 1986, in respect of which written notice has been given in accordance with s.11 of that Act, or such notice is not required to be given as provided by subs.(1) and (2) of that section. Further, subs.(6) provides that if, between the hours of 9pm and 6am, a constable in uniform finds a person in any public place in the relevant locality who he has reasonable grounds for believing is under the age of 16, and is not under the effective control of a parent or a responsible person aged 18 or over, he may remove the person to the person's place of residence unless he has reasonable grounds for believing that the person would, if removed to that place, be likely to suffer significant harm. Where the power under s.30(6) is exercised, any local authority[80] whose area includes the whole

---

[77] "Use of Dispersal Powers", Home Office Research Development Statistics, June 2005.

[78] A police officer of or above the rank of superintendent: Anti-Social Behaviour Act 2003, s.26.

[79] "Public place" mean (a) any highway, and (b) any place to which at the material time the public or any section: Anti-Social Behaviour Act 2003, s.36.

[80] It has the same meaning as under s.11 of the 2003 Act.

or part of the relevant locality must be notified of that fact.[81] The authorisations must be in writing, must be signed by the relevant officer giving it, and must specify the relevant locality, the grounds on which the authorisation is given, and the period during which the powers conferred by s.30(3) to (6) are exercisable. Before the giving of an authorisation, consultation must take place with any local authority whose area includes the whole or part of the relevant locality. Publicity must be given to an authorisation by either or both of the following methods: publishing an authorisation notice in a newspaper circulating in the relevant locality; and or posting an authorisation notice in some conspicuous place or places within the relevant locality.[82] The authorisation may be withdrawn by the relevant officer who gave it, or any other relevant officer whose police area includes the relevant locality and whose rank is the same as or higher than that of the relevant officer.[83] Before the withdrawal of an authorisation, consultation must take place with any local authority whose area includes the whole or part of the relevant locality.[84]

2-077   In *DPP v L*,[85] the DPP appealed preliminary rulings made by magistrates as a result of which no evidence had been offered against the respondents and the charges against them had been dismissed. A police authorisation to disperse groups intent on anti-social behaviour had been issued by a superintendent pursuant to s.30 of the 2003 Act. The authorisation covered six defined zones. A police constable had seen the respondents, non-residents of all six zones, together with four other youths, in one of the zones covered by the authorisation notice. He directed all six youths to leave the area and directed them not to return to any of the six defined zones within twenty four hours. The respondents later returned to the same zone. At trial the magistrates had preferred the respondent's submissions that the officer only had the power to exclude the respondents from the particular zone; the magistrates were not satisfied that a multiplicity of zones was within the definition of "relevant locality" under the 2003 Act. The DPP argued that the officer was entitled to exclude L and N from all six zones, as to require a separate authorisation in respect of each of the six zones would allow those intent upon indulging in anti-social behaviour to move from one zone to another with impunity, and a separate direction would be needed each time such people moved to a new zone. It was also argued that the magistrates had been wrong to reach the conclusion that the officer's reliance on his local knowledge and on the existence of the authorisation was not a sufficient basis upon which to found a reasonable belief that the presence or behaviour of the group had resulted, or was likely to result in, the public being intimidated, harassed, alarmed or distressed under s.30(3) of the 2003 Act. The Divisional Court allowed the appeal. The authorisation was lawful and appropriate. There was nothing in the Act to prevent an authorisation from applying to two or more non contiguous zones, provided that in making an authorisation the maker stood back and asked himself whether the zones taken together could sensibly be said to amount to a locality. The 2003 Act could not be used to establish a large number of zones over a wide area as that would not be a single locality. The kind of behaviour to which the 2003 Act was directed was likely to be concentrated on particular residential estates or town centres. Under s.30(4)(b) of the 2003 Act, the officer had power to disperse those he saw from either the whole of the locality, in other words all zones, or part of it. Secondly, in determining whether he had reasonable grounds for believing under s.30(3) that the presence or

---

[81] Anti-Social Behaviour Act 2003, s.32(4).
[82] *ibid.*, s.31(1) to (5).
[83] *ibid.*, s.31(6).
[84] *ibid.*, s.31(7).
[85] [2005] EWHC 1229.

behaviour of a group had resulted or was likely to result in the public being intimidated, harassed, alarmed or distressed, a police officer could take into account all information available to him, including what he saw and heard, his local knowledge, what he knew about the particular individuals in the group before him and the existence of the authorisation itself. What might be reasonable grounds in a particular case would vary greatly. The authorisation notice, together with the officer's local knowledge, was capable of giving him reasonable grounds for believing what he needed to believe. It was not necessary that there should have been something about the conduct of the group to cause him to fear those things before he was entitled to give notice to them to go and not return.

Recent guidance, released by the Association of Chief Police Officers,[86] provides that following the identification of a location that may benefit from such an authorisation, the authorising officer may consider using a community consultation process where consideration to the suitability of such action can be given from a wider perspective. Some forces have also used specially formed multi-agency panels for this purpose. This approach, it is said, creates secondary benefits in terms of the media perception of the implementation of the authorisation, i.e. being seen as a multi-agency response to anti-social behaviour, rather than a unilateral police response to the issue. Amongst other advice, the NCPE informed officers, under the heading "Publicity for the Authorisation", that the authorisation notice must be in writing, signed by the relevant officer and specify all of the following in clear language; the relevant locality to which it applies and the grounds on which the authorisation was given. **2-078**

In *Singh v Chief Constable of West Midlands*,[87] a repertory theatre company **2-079**
in Birmingham mounted a production which was considered by Sikhs to be offensive to them. There were protests which were peaceful at first at the theatre. However, police were called the next day when there were further protests. The protesters were issued with a dispersal direction under s.30 of the 2003 Act, requiring them to leave the theatre and its vicinity and not to return to it for 24 hours. The claimant refused to comply with it and so he was arrested and cautioned. He challenged the lawfulness of the arrest. He contended that s.30(3) did not extend the power to deal with the dispersal of protests; the whole section had to be read so that it was consistent with fundamental civil liberties. It was not possible to imply a power to disperse protests into the power. The Divisional Court disagreed: while s.30 did not expressly refer to protests, their inclusion is necessarily implied. The applicant also maintained that the use of the power was a wrongful and disproportionate interference with Arts 9, 10 and 11 of the Convention. While the Court agreed that there was an interference with claimant's rights, it was prescribed by law; the officers were pursuing the legitimate aim of preventing crime and disorder, and protecting public safety and also the rights and freedoms of others. Finally, the applicant challenged the use of the Chief Superintendent's authorisation, made a month earlier, because it had been made for a completely different purpose (the control of the behaviour of Christmas revellers) and it was not contemplated at the time that the authorisation would be used to disperse a political protest. The court held it was not unlawful to rely on it. If public disorder was a continuing problem in a town centre, it would be absurd if the police had to procure a separate authorisation to deal with each successive manifestation or source of disorder.

However, in *Sierney*,[88] the applicant successfully appealed against her conviction for defying an order to disperse from the Shiregreen area of Sheffield **2-080**

---

[86] Practice Advice on Pt 4 of the Anti-Social Behaviour Act 2003 (2005).
[87] [2005] EWHC 2840.
[88] [2006] EWHC 716.

on the ground that no reasons were given. She was among a group ordered out because of police concerns that people had previously been "intimated or harassed" in the area. At about 9.15 on the evening, four police officers attended Shiregreen, an area of Sheffield where they found a group of 10 to 15 young people shouting, drinking alcohol from cans and bottles and chasing each other about. One of the officers decided that he had reason to believe that the presence of the group was likely to intimidate, harass, alarm or distress members of the public and required them to disperse in accordance with the authorisation given by a superintendent. This authorisation stated that, having reasonable grounds to believe that members of the public have been intimidated, harassed, alarmed or distressed as a result of the presence or behaviour of groups of two or more persons within the area specified, namely Shiregreen, Sheffield in accordance with an attached map, and that anti-social behaviour is a significant and persistent problem in the aforementioned area, therefore authorised any constable in uniform within that area to exercise the powers conferred under s.30(3) to (6) of the 2003 Act. The authorisation was to be in force from October 22, 2004 until November 14, 2004 inclusive. Some of the young people complied with the constable's direction. Others, including the appellant, failed to do so, despite three warnings. Members of the group were abusive and assaulted the officers at the scene. The appellant remained at the scene as more people gathered. She was arrested. The trial judge ruled the authorisation failed to specify the general nature of the incidents that made it necessary. The Divisional Court held that an authorisation made under the Anti-Social Behaviour Act 2003, to the effect that police powers under the Act were exercisable in a particular area, had to specify in the instrument of authorisation the grounds upon which the authorisation was made in order to comply with s.31(1)(c)(ii) of the Act. Hallett L.J. observed the Act requires the officer to obtain the agreement of the local authority to the proposed authorisation. It must be limited in time and it must be publicised. Thus, a balancing exercise can be conducted by those responsible for local residents and those responsible for law and order between the interests of people, often youngsters, who wish to meet up on the streets and the interests of the rest of the community. If it turns out that an order was no longer necessary or proportionate, the police officer can withdraw it pursuant to s.31(6) of the Act, again with the agreement of the local authority. The only question for the Court was whether the superintendent's failure to provide any explanation of the grounds upon which he came to his conclusion amounts to a failure to comply with the statutory requirements so that the authorisation was invalid. The Court accepted that the Act did not require the relevant officer to go into a considerable amount of detail. However, the clear words of the Act required the relevant officer to state not merely that he had reasonable grounds for believing that members of the public have been intimidated, harassed, alarmed or distressed, and that there was significant and persistent problem in the locality of anti-social behaviour, but to specify what those reasonable grounds are, if only in general terms. Stating a belief is not the same as stating grounds for that belief.

2-081   Under s.32, a direction under s.30(4) may be given orally, and may be given to any person individually or to two or more persons together, and may be withdrawn or varied by the person who gave it. Section 32(2) provides that a person who knowingly contravenes a direction given to him under s.30(4) commits an offence and is liable on summary conviction to a fine not exceeding level 4 on the standard scale, or imprisonment for a term not exceeding three months, or to both. A constable in uniform may arrest without warrant any person he reasonably suspects has committed an offence under this section. Paragraph 1 of Sch.4 to the Police Reform Act 2002 is amended so that community support officers have the power to detain a person who has committed an offence under this section.[89] In giving or withdrawing an authorisation under s.30, a relevant officer must have regard to any code of practice for the time being in force under this section.[90] In exercising the powers conferred by s.30(3) to (6), a constable in uniform or community support officer must have regard to any code of practice for the time being in force under this section.[91] Section 34 provides that the secretary of state may issue a code of practice about the giving or withdrawal of authorisations under s.30 and the exercise of the powers conferred by s.30(3) to (6).

W v Commissioner of Police for the Metropolis and Richmond-upon-Thames LBC
A Home Office Circular on these provisions stated:[92]   **2-082**

"The aim of these powers is to prevent people from feeling frightened and discouraged from using public spaces because they feel threatened by groups of people hanging around. It also aims to protect children and young people from the risks of being unaccompanied on the streets late at night—risks of older peers encouraging them into criminal activities. These new powers will enable police and local authorities to work together to iden- tify particular problem areas that need targeted action to help local com- munities to remove intimidation and anti-social behaviour from their streets. These powers are not intended to be used in isolation, but should form part of an integrated response to tackling crime and disorder in local areas."

In *W v Commissioner of Police for the Metropolis and Richmond-upon-Thames LBC*,[93] W, at the material time 14 years old, applied for judicial review of the authorisation given to the police by the Metropolitan Police Commissioner ("the Commissioner"), with the consent of the local authority to remove persons under the age of 16 from the dispersal areas in Richmond Town Centre and Ashburnham Road, Ham between the second week of June and October 29, 2004 and between December 4, 2004 and January 4, 2005. It was accepted that there was no issue as to the appropriateness of the designation of the dispersal areas: large numbers of people, often fuelled by binge drink- ing, became involved in incidents of low level anti-social behaviour regularly in the area, which created a major issue for the local community. Similarly, in Ham, of the 95 reported acts of disturbance in a public place in Ham in those three months, 31 of them related to that area the subject of the order, and there were also 14 reports of graffiti and 53 entries relating to criminal damage to vehicles.
Brooke L.J. observed,

"It is often forgotten, however, that English common lawyers contributed to the drafting of the ECHR, and the resolution of points of statutory interpretation in cases like this can very often be achieved without any need to refer to Strasbourg law at all. After all, all of us have the right to walk the streets without interference from police constables or CSOs unless they possess common law or statutory powers to stop us. There is no relevant common law power, and s.30(6) of the 2003 Act does not create an express power to use force."

[89] Anti-Social Behaviour Act 2003, s.33(1)(2)
[90] *ibid.*, s.34(5).
[91] *ibid.*, s.34(5).
[92] 4 of 2004.
[93] [2005] EWHC 1586 (Admin).

The issue was whether the power to "remove" a person to his place of residence, if he is believed on reasonable grounds to be under the age of 16 and not under the effective control of a parent or responsible person aged 18 or over, is permissive or coercive. If it was permissive, no question of any wrongful act or any infringement of his Convention rights can arise. In the case of s.30, the exercise of the power was not restricted to cases of emergency. It was exercisable whenever a person who is believed on reasonable grounds to be under 16 years of age is found between the hours of 9pm and 6am in a dispersal area and the criteria set out in s.30(6)(b) are fulfilled. There was no need for the constable (or CSO) to be satisfied that the child would otherwise be likely to suffer significant harm. Parliament intended to create a coercive power. Part 4 of the 2003 Act was intended to give police officers enhanced powers to minimise anti-social behaviour in defined areas:

> "If Parliament were to be taken to have regarded all children found in such areas between the relevant hours as potential sources of anti-social behaviour, a coercive power to remove them might be a natural corollary. However, to attribute such an intention to Parliament would be to assume that it ignored this country's international obligations to treat each child as an autonomous human being. We are not willing to attribute such an intention to Parliament. Furthermore, if the author of the Home Office circular accurately reflects the thinking of his department, that was not the intention of the promoting department, either. The circular identifies the need to protect a child from the undesirable influence and example of older peers. The fulfilment of such a purpose does not necessarily imply the need for a coercive power. If Parliament considered that such a power was needed, it should have said so, and identified the circumstances in which it intended the power to be exercised."

The court also referred to the long standing and clear presumption that Parliament did not intend to authorise tortious conduct except by express provision, and s.30(6) contains no such express provision. Therefore, the power to remove in s.30(6) was permissive, not coercive. It therefore conferred no power on the police or a CSO to interfere with the movements of someone under the age of 16 who was conducting himself lawfully within a dispersal area between the hours of 9pm and 6am. Such a person was just as susceptible as anyone else to being made the subject of a s.30(4) direction. Section 30(6) merely conferred on the police "a very welcome express power" to use police resources to take such a person home if he is willing to be taken home.

2-083   The Association of Chief Police guidance on the dispersal power was amended to take into the remarks made in this judgment. It states that it is ". . .important that this power is used proportionately, reasonably and with discretion to comply with the requirements of the Human Rights Act 1998 in relation to freedom of association." At para.3.1, the authorisation does not give a power to direct people to leave the area simply because they are there per se. There must be evidence of anti-social behaviour taking place for it be used, and it does not provide a power of curfew. Before giving a direction, the officer must have reasonable grounds for believing that the presence or behaviour of a group of two or more persons in any public place within the defined relevant locality has resulted in, or is likely to result in, any member of the public being intimidated, harassed, alarmed or distressed. These standardised set of powers are contained in the Police and Justice Bill.

2-084   Meanwhile, the Court of Appeal[94] reversed the decision. A child in close proximity with anti-social behaviour in an authorised dispersal area at night

[94] [2006] EWCA Civ 458.

may well need protection from the physical and social risks of the behaviour of others. How better to do this than to take the child home? First, the power of the constable under s.30(6) to "remove" the person under 16 to his place of residence carries with it a power to use reasonable force if necessary:

> "It is of course correct, as the Divisional Court said, that all of us have the right to walk the streets without interference from police constables unless they have common law or statutory powers to stop us. There is no relevant common law power. The Divisional Court said that section 30(6) does not create an express power. But that, in our view, begs the question. If 'remove' carries with it the power to use reasonable force if necessary, there is an express power."

The Court then considered other statutory contexts where there was a power to remove. Further, in the context of this section, the word "remove" naturally and compellingly means "take away using reasonable force if necessary". It was not a matter of implication, but of meaning. If the word did not have this meaning, the power would in the context be pointless. The police did not need an express power merely to use their resources to take a child or young person home, if he was willing to be taken home, in the circumstances contemplated by the sub-section. The word "remove" nearly always connoted a use of force. In the context of a power given to constables, the word "remove" connoted the use of reasonable coercion, if necessary. While the section was not drafted to cover explicitly all contingencies which might arise, a child in a designated dispersal area in Richmond, whose place of residence is in Newcastle-upon-Tyne, or a child whose place of residence is locked and unoccupied, may well be in need of police protection under the 1989 Act; as may a child who refused to give his name and address, who may also possibly be obstructing the police in the exercise of their duty. A child's need for protection must surely outweigh any theoretical right to conceal his identity. The Court noted that the power was given, not only to constables, but to community support officers, whose training and other powers are much more limited. Even so, these considerations did not persuade the court to give a limited meaning to the word "remove" which it did not in its context have. As to the scope of s.30, the Court of Appeal denied that had a curfew effect. (Compare this section to the child curfew zone of s.14 and 15 of the Crime and Disorder Act 1998.)[95] Section 30 of the 2003 Act was concerned in the first instance with areas where anti-social behaviour by those over the age of 16 is a significant and persistent problem. Dispersal directions under s.30(4) may of course include directions to those who are under the age of 16, but that is incidental. Section 30(6) would only have a "curfew effect" if it gave an arbitrary power of removal; as if it gave a constable power to remove to his place of residence any unaccompanied child within a designated dispersal area at night whatever the child was doing and whatever the circumstances prevailing in the area. However, the sub-section did not give such an arbitrary power. There were legislative constraints on the powers conferred by s.30 of the 2003 Act. These included the requirement to designate an area (s.30(1)(a)); that anti-social behaviour should be a significant and persistent problem (s.30(1)(b)); that the period was limited to not more than six months (s.30(2)); that the constable had reasonable grounds for believing that the presence or behaviour of a group of two or more persons in a public place had resulted, or was likely to result in, members of the public being intimidated, harassed, alarmed or distressed (s.30(3)); that the constable's first main power was to give dispersal directions (s.30(4)); the limitations in s.30(5); the formal safeguards for authorisation (s.31(1)) and the

---

[95] See para.3-102.

required seniority of the relevant officer (s.36); the requirement for the consent of the local authority (s.31(2)); and the requirement for publicity (s.31(3), (4) and (5)). Specifically for the power in s.30(6), there was the constraint that the constable must have reasonable grounds for believing that a person under the age of 16 was not under the effective control of a parent or a responsible person aged 18 or over; and the requirement that, if the power under s.30(6) was exercised, a relevant local authority must be notified (s.32(4)). A constable exercising the power given by s.30(6) of the 2003 Act was not free to act arbitrarily. He was not free to act for a purpose other than that for which the power was conferred. The power was not a power of arrest. The purpose for which the power was conferred is, in our view, clear and largely uncontentious. It was to protect children under the age of 16 within a designated dispersal area at night from the physical and social risks of anti-social behaviour by others. Another purpose was to prevent children from themselves participating in anti-social behaviour within a designated dispersal area at night. The subsection did not confer an arbitrary power to remove children who were not involved in, nor at risk from exposure to, actual or imminently anticipated anti-social behaviour. It did not confer a power to remove children simply because they were in a designated dispersal area at night:

"Children are, so far as this legislation goes, free to go there without fear of being removed, provided that they do not themselves participate in anti-social behaviour and provided that they avoid others who are behaving anti-socially. Furthermore, the Secretary of State accepts that the discretionary power can only be used if, in the light of its purpose, it is reasonable to do so; and the Commissioner accepts that, to act reasonably, constables must have regard to circumstances such as how young the child is; how late at night it is; whether the child is vulnerable or in distress; the child's explanation for his or her conduct and presence in the area; and the nature of the actual or imminently anticipated anti-social behaviour. It follows that section 30(6) of the 2003 Act does not have a curfew effect such as W apprehended."

Harassment

Protection from Harassment Act 1997

The Common Law: Stalking and Watching and Besetting

2-085 Understanding the legal meaning of harassment under the Protection from Harassment 1997 Act (and also s.1 of the Crime and Disorder Act 1998) begins by looking at what preceded the Act: stalking and watching and besetting. There was no definition of stalking in the English legal system. Finch defines it in these terms:[96]

"It is clear that the behaviour that is common in stalking cases is varied in nature; it may be inherently unpleasant or apparently innocuous, it may be entirely lawful or amount to a substantive criminal offence. Stalking has a nebulous quality that renders the formulation of a precise legal definition somewhat problematic. Disciplines other than the law have not found it difficult to formulate definitions of stalking. For example, stalking has been described as 'a constellation of behaviours involving repeated and persistent attempts to

---

[96] "Stalking: The Perfect Stalking Law—an Evaluation of the Efficacy of the Protection from Harassment Act 1997" (2002) Crim. L.R. 703–719; see also Wells, "Stalking: The Criminal Law Response", (1997) Crim. L.R., 463–470.

impose on another person unwanted communication and/or contact'[97] and as a situation in which "one person causes another a degree of fear or trepidation by behaviour which is on the surface innocent but which, when taken in context, assumes a more threatening significance." [98]

However, she adds that such definitions encapsulate the central characteristics of stalking, but do not readily translate into a workable legal definition. A Home Office paper, "Stalking—The Solutions", which preceded the Protection from Harassment Act 1997, examined "possible new measures to deal with the menace of stalking" and defines stalking as "a series of acts which are intended to, or in fact cause, harassment to another person", although there were comments by the minister made in Parliament[99] that "the Bill covers not only stalkers but disruptive neighbours and those who target people because of the colour of their skin." The Bill was described by the minister as "building on the provisions of section 4(a) of the Public Order Act 1986."[1] The protracted judicial debate in cases such as *Ireland*,[2] which considered whether or not malicious phone calls are bodily harm, while clearly harassment today under the 1997 Act, indicated the difficulties in relying on existing criminal law remedies available to complainants before the 1997 Act.

The 1997 Act drew in part from the old statutory offence of "watching and besetting": see s.7 of the Conspiracy and Protection of Property Act 1875, repealed by Trade Union and Labour Relations (Consolidation) Act 1992. The 1875 Act section provided that an offence was committed by any person:

2-086

". . .who with a view to compel any other person to abstain from doing . . . any act, which such other person has a legal right to do . . . wrongfully and without legal authority. . . watches or besets the house or other place where such other . . . works, or carries on business, or happens to be, or the approach to such house or place.".

In *DPP v Fidler*,[3] the defendants were present outside a licensed clinic housing medical staff whose duties included the procuring of legal abortions. They were part of a group opposed to the procuring of abortions. Another group, of opposing views, were also present. The groups were instructed by the police to stand separately and apart on either side of the clinic. The defendants repeatedly refused to rejoin their own group when requested to do so, asserting their rights to walk where they liked and to speak to whoever they liked, and were arrested and charged under s.5(1)(a) and 6 of the Public Order Act 1986 and watched and beset the premises contrary to s.7 of the Conspiracy and Protection of Property Act 1875. The magistrates found that there was no case to answer in respect of each charge. The DPP appealed on the ground that it was unnecessary to establish that F had "compelled" someone to refrain from a legal act and that watching and besetting "with a view to compulsion" was sufficient. The appeal was dismissed. Nolan LJ:

"A group of people watching and besetting premises may be seeking to achieve a common purpose or object in doing so, such as the prevention of abortions, but the individual members of the group may have different motives for joining it. If that is the right approach then the conclusion for

[97] P. Mullen, M. Pathe, R. Purcell, and G. Stuart, "Study of Stalkers" (1999) 156 *American Journal of Psychiatry*, 1244.
[98] Goode, "Stalking: a Crime of the Nineties?" (1995) 19 *Criminal Law Journal*, 21 at p. 24.
[99] Hansard, December 17, 1997, Vol 781.
[1] See *DPP v Dziurzynski* [2002] EWHC 1380.
[2] [1998] A.C. 147.
[3] [1992] 1 W.L.R. 91.

which Mr Gee contends is that the purpose of the respondents, prima facie at least, was not merely to dissuade others from performing or undergoing abortion but to compel them to abstain, or more simply to prevent them from doing so. In my judgment that contention goes too far. There was no evidence that anyone was either prevented, or likely to be prevented, or intended to be prevented from performing or undergoing an abortion in the strict sense of being rendered unable to do so. The long-suffering police were in control of the situation. It seems plain enough that the purpose of the anti-abortion group in watching and besetting the clinic was to stop abortions from being carried out there, but it is equally plain that the means employed to implement this purpose were confined to verbal abuse and reproach and shocking reminders of the physical implications of abortion. Physical force was neither used nor threatened. The evident purpose of the demonstrators' behaviour was to embarrass and shock and shame those concerned into abstaining from abortion. In my judgment, the justices were right to find that this purpose, thus implemented, was a purpose of dissuasion rather than one of compulsion."

In *R. v Bonsall*,[4] four striking miners, who had taken part in mass picketing at Cresswell Colliery with 500 to 800 other miners, appealed against convictions of offences under the s.5 of the Public Order Act 1936 and s.7 of the Conspiracy and Protection of Property Act 1875. Their appeals were dismissed. The judge expressed the conclusion of the court that persons who chose to gather in such overwhelming numbers and who either were themselves party to certain savage utterances or, by remaining there when they could have drifted away, lent a sharpened edge to the insults hurled and the tenor that their numbers conveyed (their intention being to compel the working miners to stop working, rather than to dissuade them), were each party to being the besetting within the 1875 Act. On the other hand, see *Thomas v National Union of Mineworkers (South Wales Area)*:[5] it was not ultra vires for a union to embark on a course of action which merely involves a risk that a criminal or tortious act might be committed. Members of the National Union of Mineworkers who, during the miners' strike, voted to resume working, were able to get to work only in buses assisted by a police presence, due to the nature of the picketing at their place of work. They sought injunctions to restrain the picketing on a number of grounds, one of which was that secondary picketing was ultra vires as it was bound to involve the tort of nuisance, and be a criminal offence under the Conspiracy and Protection of Property Act 1875. The applications were refused: it would not be ultra vires if the union's act merely involved a risk that a criminal offence or a tort might be committed. The position would be different if the act was bound to involve a criminal act.

The 1997 Act: Fear of Violence

The Protection from Harassment Act 1997 contains two criminal offences. The more serious of the two is that under s.4(1) which provides:

2-087

"A person whose course of conduct causes another to fear on at least two occasions that violence will be used against him is guilty of an offence if he knows or ought to know that his course of conduct will cause the other so to fear on each of these occasions."

---

[4] Crown Court (Derby) October 16, 1984.
[5] [1986] Ch. 20.

This offence is triable either way.[6] On indictment, it is a class 4 offence. "Course of conduct" is defined in s.7(3) simply as involving conduct on at least two occasions. Under subs.(4), conduct can include speech. The further apart the acts alleged to be conduct in time, the less likely it will be regarded as a course of conduct.[7] Violence is not defined; however, see the analogous offences under the Public Order Act 1986: the conduct must cause the victim to fear that violence will be used and not merely that a fear as to what might happen.[8] The *mens rea* is defined in s.4(2): it must be shown that the accused ought to know that the course of conduct will cause another to fear that violence will be used against him on any occasion if a reasonable person in possession of the same information would think the course of conduct would cause the other to fear on that occasion.

There are express defences set out in subs.(3). These are: **2-088**

"(a) his course of conduct was pursued for the purpose of preventing or detecting crime;
(b) it was pursued under any enactment or rule of law or to comply with any condition or requirement imposed by any person under any enactment, or
(c) it was reasonable for the protection of himself or another or the protection of the another's property."

Harassment and "Political" Harassment
The lesser offence is set out in ss.1 and 2 of the 1997 Act, the actual offence of **2-089**
harassment. Section 1 provides:

"(1) A person must not pursue a course of conduct:

(a) which amounts to harassment of another, and
(b) which he knows or ought to know amounts to harassment of the other."

Under this section, violence per se is not relevant; nor is it essential that the activities be unlawful activities in themselves. Harassment does not connote any element of apprehension about personal safety.[9] As we noted earlier, it is of some assistance that the 1997 Act might be considered a modernised version of "watching and besetting" or directed at stalking. However, it inevitably covers a wide range of behaviour: in *Hipgrave v Jones*,[10] Tugendhat J. said:

"Harassment can cover a very wide range of conduct. It may involve actions alone, or words alone (s.7(4)), or both. The actions may be so grave as to amount to criminal offences against public order, or against the person, which cause serious alarm, or they may be little more than boorishness or insensitive behaviour, so long as it is sufficient to cause distress. The words may be, at one extreme, incitements to, or threats of, violence that cause alarm, or at the other, unwelcome text messages sent, for example, to a woman wrongly perceived to be a girlfriend. The conduct may be that of an individual, or of an organisation, including the news media: *Thomas v News Group* [2001] EWCA Civ. 1233; [2002] EMLR 4CA. It may include strip searches (subject to the meaning of 'a course of conduct'): *Home Office v Wainwright* [2001] EWCA Civ 2081, per Buxton LJ at para [62]."

---

[6] Protection from Harassment Act 1997, s.4(4).
[7] *Lau v DPP* [2000] Crim. L.R. 580.
[8] *R. v Henley* [2000] Crim. L.R. 582.
[9] *Chambers v DPP* [1995] Crim. L.R. 896.
[10] [2004] WL 2810934.

Section 2(1) provides that a person who pursues a course of conduct in breach of s.1 is guilty of an offence. The definition of the term "course of conduct" (which itself has been amended—see below) applies here also, save that it need not have the same effect or intent of causing a fear of violence. Again, the further apart the events in time, the less likely they will be considered to be a course of conduct. In *Baron v CPS*,[11] the conduct consisted in part by the delivery of two letters sent four months apart; it was held that this could constitute a relevant course of conduct. So could a number of telephone calls made over a period of five minutes, depending on the nature of the calls.[12] In *Pratt v DPP*,[13] the defendant appealed against his conviction for harassment. There were two incidents, separated by a period of some three months. In the first, he threw water over his estranged wife; and in the second, he chased her through the matrimonial home swearing and questioning her constantly. The justices concluded that the two incidents amounted to a course of conduct for the purposes of s.7, having regard to the background of the marriage breakdown and, in the case of the second incident, a breach of an undertaking not to threaten, harass or pester his wife. The defendant submitted that the time interval and lack of similar facts meant that his behaviour did not amount to a course of conduct within the meaning of the Act. The Court of Appeal held, dismissing the appeal, that the magistrates had been entitled to conclude that the two incidents were sufficiently similar in type and context as to be a course of conduct under the 1997 Act. However, the court added that prosecuting authorities should be cautious in bringing charges for the offence of harassment in circumstances where only a small number of incidents had occurred. The prosecution should ensure not merely that two or more incidents had occurred but that such repetitious behaviour had caused harassment to the other person.

2-090   At one of the scale, sustained and violent bullying by a husband against his wife has been held to be harassment for the purposes of an offence under s.4.[14] Presenting an unwanted gift on one occasion is not harassment but it may form an important part of the background to a case; and if repeated, it may be harassment.[15] The conduct for the purposes of this offence (and that under s.4) must be directed at the complainant and not, for example, at a member of the complainant's family.[16] Publishing articles in newspapers may be harassment but only in very rare circumstances and subject to the law relating to libel and the Human Rights Act 1998.[17] In *Thomas v News Group Newspapers Ltd*[18] the publishers appealed against the dismissal of its application to strike out the claimant's claim for harassment in respect of the publication of a series of newspaper articles. It argued that the claim disclosed no reasonable prospects of success on the ground that the newspaper articles had not constituted the requisite course of conduct for the purposes of the 1997 Act. The claimant argued that the articles had unnecessarily referred to her as "a black clerk" and, further, had suggested that, had it not been for her race, two police officers would not have been subject to disciplinary proceedings over remarks made about a third party in her presence. The Court of Appeal dismissed the appeal. The publication of a series of articles in a newspaper could constitute a course of conduct amounting to harassment for the purposes of s.1 of the 1997 Act. On the facts of this case, it was foreseeable that the articles in

---

[11] June 13, 2000.
[12] *Kelly v DPP* (2002) 166 J.P. 621.
[13] [2001] EWHC 483 (Admin).
[14] *R v Jubb* [2004] EWCA Crim 3401; *R v Patel* [2005] 1 Cr. App. R. 27.
[15] *King v DPP*, *Independent*, July 3, 2000.
[16] *DPP v Dziurzynski* (2002) 166 J.P.L. 545.
[17] *Thomas v News Group Newspapers Ltd*, *The Times*, July 25, 2001.
[18] [2001] EWCA Civ 1233.

question would have been likely to provoke a racist reaction and that as a result, the Claimant would have been caused distress.

In *DPP v Dziurzynski*,[19] the DPP appealed against the dismissal of a charge **2-091** that the defendant, an animal rights protestor, had pursued a course of conduct which amounted to the harassment of the employees of a company, contrary to the s.2 of the 1997 Act. The defendant argued that the intention of the 1997 Act had been to protect individuals rather than groups of people. The Court of Appeal dismissed the DPP's appeal. Parliament had not intended to make harassment directed at a limited company a criminal offence. The legislative history supported the conclusion that "person" did not mean a corporation, and it was significant that the words "him" and "victim" had been used in ss.4 and 5 of the Act respectively. Section 7(2) provides that references to harassing a person include alarming them or causing them distress. In *DPP v Ramsdale*,[20] it was said that the term included molestation, annoyance or worry and "alarm" and "distress" were to be read disjunctively and not conjunctively. In *KD v Chief Constable of Hampshire*,[21] the claimant claimed damages for battery and harassment against the defendant chief constable on the basis that he was vicariously liable for the acts of one of his officers. She claimed that a police officer had invaded her privacy and sexually harassed her. He had interviewed her on several occasions following allegations by her daughter that she had been raped and beaten by her former partner. The statements taken by the officer included details of her sexual conduct that were not relevant to the investigation and which it was alleged had been elicited by the officer to satisfy his prurient interest. The claimant said that the officer had visited her home several times and telephoned her for personal discussions about his or her private life unrelated to the investigation, that he had touched her sexually and made sexual remarks and conducted himself in a manner which amounted to harassment or assault or both. He had denied all the allegations and asserted that the statements contained information volunteered to him by the claimant, and that any telephone calls or visits were proper and reasonable for the purpose of the investigation. He denied touching the claimant at all when giving evidence, but in previous statements he had admitted touching her on the arm in order to reassure her. He had been found guilty of discreditable conduct in the disciplinary proceedings brought against him. The chief constable and the officer submitted that, under s.1(3)(a) of the 1997 Act, which contained an exception for a course of conduct pursued "for the purpose of preventing or detecting crime", the test of a defendant's purpose was purely subjective; accordingly a defendant was to be judged on the basis of whether or not he had an honest belief that the conduct was pursued for that purpose. The officer submitted that the draughtsman had deliberately omitted from the 1997 Act the requirement that any infringement of the right under the Human Rights Act 1998 Sch.1, Pt I, Art.8 should be necessary or proportionate. Tugendhat J. held, giving judgment for the claimant, that, in considering the 1997 Act in relation to events which occurred after the coming into force of the Human Rights Act 1998, the courts would be bound to interpret s.1(3)(a) as being subject to the tests of necessity and proportionality. Further, obtaining information from a woman about her sexual activities for the purposes of criminal proceedings would engage Art.8, and would be subject to the tests of necessity and proportionality. The information supplied to the officer had been in response to his explicit questions, and had not simply been volunteered by the claimant. The visits and the taking of the statements was a course of conduct and plainly

---

[19] [2002] EWHC Civ 1380.
[20] *Independent*, March 19, 2001.
[21] [2005] EWHC 2550.

amounted to harassment. The officer's purpose in obtaining and recording the sexually explicit details in the statements was not to prevent or detect crime. The only purpose was the officer's own gratification. He touched the claimant in the way she had alleged, and as such committed batteries against her and this touching was unacceptable from a police officer on duty. The incidents of touching also formed part of the whole course of conduct which amounted to harassment.

2-092   Section 1(1)(b) defines the *mens rea* for the offence: the accused knows or ought to know that the course of conduct amounts to harassment of the other. See also s.1(2):

> "For the purposes of this section, the person whose course of conduct is in question ought to know that it amounts to harassment of another if a reasonable person in possession of the same information would think the course of conduct amounted to harassment of the other."

Course of conduct is defined by s.7(3) of the 1997 Act. It was recently amended by s.125(7) of the Serious Organised Crime and Police Act 2005 so that it can accommodate the new offence of "political harassment" (which we discuss below). It provides:

> "(3) A "course of conduct" must involve—
>
> (a) in the case of conduct in relation to a single person (see section 1(1)) conduct on at least two occasions in relation to that person, or
> (b) in the case of conduct in relation to two or more persons (see section 1(1A)), conduct on at least one occasion in relation to each of those persons".

Harassment and Public Protest

2-093   It is against this background that the Serious Organised Crime and Police Act 2005 introduced an offence directed at preventing harassment of a largely political in character. There is now a new subs.1(1A), in the 1997 Act. This new subsection provides:

> "(1A) A person must not pursue a course of conduct—
>
> (a) which involves harassment of two or more persons and
> (b) which he knows or ought to know involves harassment of those persons and
> (c) by which he intends to persuade any person (whether or not one of those mentioned above)—
>   (i) not to do something that he is entitled or required to do or
>   (ii) to do something that he is entitled to do".

As the explanatory notes to the section make clear, the aim is to prevent political activity which reaches such a level that it amounts to harassment. What is required is activity that amounts to harassment *with* the intention of persuading someone to do or not do something. It may also be relevant that injunctions and other civil remedies directed at prohibiting the activities of extremist protesters appear to be unwieldy, expensive and out-of-date—and even redundant—by the time the matter has reached court, even on an ex parte basis. There are obvious difficulties in the enforcement of civil remedies on individuals acting through unincorporated protest organisations with sometimes deliberately fluid memberships and lack of records in addition.

2-094   The line between political protest and harassment is now an even finer one. The very purpose of public protest is to persuade someone from doing something. Where that harassment consists of illegal conduct, then it is comparatively straight-forward. As Gross J. commented in *EDO MBM Technology Ltd v Campaign to Smash EDO*,[22] the primary intention of the 1997 Act was to deal with the phenomenon of "stalking". Most of the reported cases on injunctions under the 1997 Act concerned restraints of harassment in "animal rights" and "GM crops" cases. At common law and now, under the HRA and the Convention, Arts 10 and 11, freedom of speech or expression, and freedom of assembly and association, constitute rights which are expected to be safeguarded by the courts. Restrictions on these rights must be convincingly established, justified by compelling reasons, subject to careful scrutiny and proportionate and no more than necessary. However, Arts 10 and 11 contemplate situations, where it is proper to impose restrictions on rights of expression and assembly. In *Burris v Azandi*,[23] concerning threats of violence and harassment by the defendant at the plaintiff's house, the Court of Appeal emphasised the need to protect the interests of those who invoked the court's jurisdiction. It was not a valid objection to the making of an exclusion zone order as a term of the injunction that the conduct to be restrained was not in itself tortious or otherwise unlawful; but such orders should not be made readily or without good reason. Lord Bingham noted that ". . . respect for the freedom of the aggressor should never lead the court to deny necessary protection to the victim." See also *Monsanto v Tilly*.[24] The applicant was licensed to execute research and development in trials of genetically modified (GM) plants and crops. In 1998, the respondents and others founded an "association", whose aim was to campaign against GM research. Whilst the respondent's opinions concerning the perceived public safety of GM crops were genuine, the association used unlawful methods to advance their campaign. The principal method employed was to uproot GM crops in order to gain publicity. The applicant took action against the respondents, seeking injunctions to prohibit trespass on land and interference with its plants, crops and land. Based on the defence that the respondent's actions were justified by necessity to protect third parties and the public, unconditional leave was granted in order to defend against the action for trespass. On appeal, it was held, allowing the appeal, that the respondents could not rely either on the defence of necessity or of public interest. Stuart-Smith L.J. said:

"In a democratic society the object of changing government policy had to be effected by lawful and not unlawful means. Those who suffered infringement of their lawful rights were entitled to the protection of the law. If others deliberately infringed those rights in order to attract publicity to their cause, however sincerely they believed in its correctness, they had to bear the consequences of their lawbreaking. That was fundamental to the rule of law in a civilised and democratic society."

Whilst in exceptional circumstances the respondents could protect those in immediate and serious danger by uprooting the whole crop, in the instant case, only some plants had been damaged and it was clear that the real aim of the campaign had been to attract publicity, which had been further advanced by a public court hearing. Even in circumstances of emergency, trespass was not justified where a public authority was responsible for the protection of public interests.

In *University of Oxford v Broughton*,[25] the applicants applied for the continuation of an injunction against the respondent individuals and organisations. **2-095**

---

[22] [2005] EWHC 837 (QB).
[23] [1995] 1 W.L.R. 1372.
[24] T.L.R., November 30, 1999.
[25] [2004] EWHC 2543 at [80].

The applicants were engaged in the construction of a research laboratory and some of the work to be carried out at the laboratory involved experimentation on live animals. The respondents objected to the experimentation. They had organised demonstrations and some even resorted to criminal activities in a bid to stop the construction. The applicants obtained an injunction to restrain them. The injunction was granted in favour of the "protected persons" and prohibited the respondents from harassing the applicants contrary to the Protection from Harassment Act 1997. The respondents argued that the injunction was flawed as the protected persons were not named. That meant that the respondents were unable to identify the protected persons. Accordingly, there was a risk of accidental infringement and a potential breach of their right to a fair trial. Grigson J. granted the application. He remarked:

"There is a body of opinion which holds that the use of live animals in research is both immoral and unjustified. How large is the number of persons holding that opinion is a matter of conjecture. Those who hold those opinions want to stop research which involves experiments on live animals. They can be described as the Animal Rights Movement. This movement is entirely amorphous. It has no structure only a community of belief. There is no consensus as to the means by which the research involving live animals may be stopped. The Animal Rights Movement includes those who restrict their activities to that which is lawful and, at the other end of the spectrum, those who believe that they are morally justified in committing crime in order to achieve their aims. It includes organisations with a formal structure such as the R.S.P.C.A. and the League against Cruel Sports. Within this 'broad church' are groups whose activities are directed against specific targets, for example, SHAC. Whilst such groups may have founders and organisers, they have no formal membership. Their activities are advertised and those who support their aims are invited to participate. The activities are, as advertised, lawful although, on occasions, these advertised activities may be accompanied by actions which are either tortious (for example trespass) or which are deliberately criminal (for example assault or criminal damage). . . .The right of freedom of expression is not to be exercised in a vacuum created by the assumption that only the views of the animal rights movement are correct. Those who believe that experimentation on live animals is both morally and scientifically justified also have the right of freedom of expression. Further such people and those who, in the broadest sense, work for them have the right to respect for their private and family life, their homes and correspondence under Article 8."

He held that the purpose of the injunction was to prevent harassment as defined by the 1997 Act. The restraint was designed to prevent acts which could, if continued, constitute an offence. It would be pointless if the applicant had to wait for an offence to be committed before they could apply for an injunction. Consequently, there was a power to grant injunctions in wide terms to prevent the harassment of a class of persons. Accordingly, there was no requirement for the protected persons to be named. The anonymity of the protected persons did not make it impossible for the respondents to comply with the injunction. There was no danger of accidental harassment. Given that the respondents had little difficulty in identifying suitable targets for harassment, it followed that they could identify those protected by the injunction. It was clear that the respondents' right to a fair trial under the Human Rights Act 1998 Sch.1, Pt I, art.6(1) had not been infringed. Further, there was ample evidence to suggest that the respondents would continue to harass the applicant if the injunction was not continued. Moreover, if the matter went to trial, it was likely that the applicants would succeed. Accordingly, it was just and convenient to continue the injunction, which was necessary to enable the applicants to go about their lawful business. The restrictions placed upon the respondents were proportionate. The injunction was expanded to include prohibition on photographing the protected persons so as to prevent them from being identified as potential targets.

In *EDO MBM Technology,* the applicant, the managing director of a **2-096** company manufacturing weapons equipment used in Iraq by the armed forces, sought an interim injunction, pending trial or further order, restraining the respondents from harassing him, his staff and others. Two of the respondents were campaign groups which had held demonstrations protesting against the company's activities. Others were campaigners who had been convicted of obstruction of the highway during one of those demonstrations and others still campaigners who had been convicted of aggravated trespass arising out of the same incident. The respondents contended, inter alia, that there was no proper basis for alleging there had been incitement or instigation of violence. In the absence of violence or the threat of violence, the rights to freedom of speech and assembly under the Human Rights Act 1998 Sch.1, Pt I, art.10 and art.11 were not to be restricted. Secondly, the mischief at which the Protection from Harassment Act 1997 was aimed was stalking of individuals, not political protest. There was no good reason for the grant of a civil injunction because the police were able to control any protests using the available means of the criminal law. Gross J. noted that there was understandable concern that an Act passed to combat stalking should not be used to clamp down on rights of protest and expression, valued parts of our democratic tradition. It is also true, however, that there comes a point when protest and expression may cross the line into harassment. It was submitted that the 1997 Act should be read and given effect to compatibly with the Convention; that, absent violence or the threat of violence, freedom of speech and assembly were not to be restricted; that the first instance authorities were to be distinguished on the ground that in those cases there had been a concerted campaign against individuals and the campaigning groups had the avowed intention of, inter alia, employing unlawful means. Furthermore, although the definition of "harassment" in the Act was inclusive rather than exhaustive (see s.7(2), below) that unless the "harassment" did involve alarm and distress, it was difficult to justify restricting freedom of expression and assembly. Gross J. agreed that great care was needed in applying the Act to situations of public protest. The drawing of lines in this area, however, involves an intensely factual inquiry and difficult questions of degree and there were no fixed limits as to its applicability, whether as to categories of cases or inflexible threshold requirements. Therefore, while it must be likely that most restrictions on freedom of expression or assembly would result from a risk of violence or the threat of violence, "harassment" is not confined to acts which place the victim in fear of violence: "the right not to be harassed is not or not only a right not to be placed in fear of violence or subjected to violence." Nor could "harassment" be read as *confined* to conduct which alarms or causes distress, although it would be unlikely that conduct which does not amount to that will be restrained by interim injunction. The avowed intention of an association or individuals whom it is sought to injunct, was essentially a matter of evidence and proof; the fact that individuals or associations express their objectives in more guarded terms cannot confer an immunity from an injunction under the Act, if it is established that their conduct or the apprehension of their conduct otherwise warrants it. Finally, he was not persuaded that the protests in this case can be distinguished, or so readily distinguished, from those in the "animal rights" and "GM crops cases". Gross J. held, granting the application in part, that, whilst most restrictions on freedom of expression or assembly would result from a risk or threat of violence, an injunction to prevent harassment was not limited to acts which placed the victim in fear of violence. In the instant case, there had been a campaign which had included the offences committed by some campaigners and had included, at the least, seriously arguable instances of harassment such as targeting of directors' homes or neighbourhoods, intimidation of employees and criminal damage. Those who suffered infringement of their lawful rights were entitled to the protection of the law. Secondly, there was understandable concern that an Act passed to combat stalking should not be used to clamp down on rights of protest and expression, but there came a point when protest and expression might cross the line into harassment.

Harassment in a Persons Home

2-097   This is also a new offence introduced by s.126 of the Serious Organised Crime and Police Act 2005 into the Criminal Justice and Police Act 2001, and it must be the case that it arose in the same context as that which motivated the amendments to the 1997 Act so as to deal with politically motivated harassment. For example, extremist animal rights activists have in the past identified particular individuals and directed their violence at them, including the homes and members of their families. For example, the Hall family were targeted for six years by activists who aimed to stop them breeding guinea pigs for research. The animal rights activists were jailed for 12 years for conspiracy to blackmail. Bricks were thrown through windows, death threats made to farm workers, pyrotechnics set off outside their homes and hundreds of malicious letters sent. The campaign culminated in the digging up of the grandmother's grave and the theft of her body in October 2004. Section 42A(1) provides that a person commits an offence if they are present outside or in the vicinity of any premises that are used by any individual as his dwelling[26] and he is present there ". . .for the purpose of representing to the resident or another individual (whether or not the one who uses the premises as his dwelling) or of persuading the resident or such another individual" that he should not do something that he is entitled to do or do something that he is not under any obligation to do. Further, the person must intend his presence to amount to harassment of or cause alarm and distress to the resident or knows or ought to know that his presence is likely to result in the harassment of, or cause alarm or distress to the resident. The presence of that person must also amount to harassment or cause alarm or distress to any person who is a resident or present in the dwelling or in another dwelling in the vicinity.

Harassment Directions

2-098   Under s.42(1) of the Criminal Justice and Police Act 2001, a constable may give a direction to any person if:

"(a) that person is present outside or in the vicinity of any premises that are used by any individual ("the resident") as his dwelling;[27]
(b) that constable believes, on reasonable grounds, that that person is present there for the purpose (by his presence or otherwise) of representing to the resident or another individual (whether or not one who uses the premises as his dwelling), or of persuading the resident or such another individual—

(i)   that he should not do something that he is entitled or required to do; or

[26] As defined in Pt 1 of the Public Order Act 1986.
[27] In this section "dwelling" has the same meaning as in Pt 1 of the Public Order Act 1986: Criminal Justice and Police Act 2001, s.42(9).

(ii) that he should do something that he is not under any obligation to do; and

(c) that constable also believes, on reasonable grounds, that the presence of that person (either alone or together with that of any other persons who are also present)—

(i) amounts to, or is likely to result in, the harassment of the resident; or
(ii) is likely to cause alarm or distress to the resident."

A direction under s.42 is deemed to be a direction requiring the person to whom it is given to do all such things as the constable giving it may specify as the things he considers necessary to prevent the harassment of the resident, and/or the causing of any alarm or distress to the resident.[28] The order may be given orally; and where a constable is entitled to give a direction under this section to each of several persons outside, or in the vicinity of, any premises, he may give that direction to those persons by notifying them of his requirements either individually or all together.[29] The requirements that may be imposed by a direction under this section include a requirement to leave the vicinity of the premises in question (either immediately or after a specified period of time).[30] Under subs.(5), a direction under this section may make exceptions to any requirement imposed by the direction, and may make any such exception subject to such conditions as the constable giving the direction thinks fit. Those conditions may include conditions as to the distance from the premises in question at which, or otherwise as to the location where, persons who do not leave their vicinity must remain; and conditions as to the number or identity of the persons who are authorised by the exception to remain in the vicinity of those premises. The power of a constable to give a direction is subject to certain limits. He may not give such a direction under this section when there is a more senior-ranking police officer at the scene; and he has no such power to direct a person to refrain from conduct that is lawful under s.220 of the Trade Union and Labour Relations (Consolidation) Act 1992, the right to peacefully picket a work place.

Any person who knowingly contravenes a direction given to him under this section shall be guilty of an offence and liable, on summary conviction, to imprisonment for a term not exceeding three months or to a fine not exceeding level 4 on the standard scale, or to both.[31] A constable in uniform may arrest without warrant any person he reasonably suspects is committing an offence under this section. Section 127 of the Serious Organised Crime and Police Act 2005 amends s.42(4) in order to provide a power to direct a person to stay away from a person's home. Subsection (4) of s.42 now provides that the requirements that may be imposed by a direction under s.42 include a requirement to leave the vicinity of the premises and to stay away for up to three months. Under a new subsection, subs.(7A), a person who returns to the premises in breach of such a direction is guilty of an offence. **2-099**

Section 241, Trade Union and Labour Relations Act 1992

Section 241 of the Trade Union and Labour Relations Act 1992 provides: **2-100**

"(1) A person commits an offence who, with a view to compelling another person to abstain from doing or to do any act which that person has a legal right to do or abstain from doing, wrongfully and without legal authority—

---

[28] Criminal Justice and Police Act 2001, s.42(2).
[29] *ibid.*, s.42(3).
[30] *ibid.*, s.42(4).
[31] *ibid.*, s.42(7).

(a) uses violence to or intimidates that person or his wife or children, or injures his property,
(b) persistently follows that person about from place to place,
(c) hides any tools, clothes or other property owned or used by that person, or deprives him of or hinders him in the use thereof,
(d) watches or besets the house or other place where that person resides, works, carries on business or happens to be, or the approach to any such house or place, or
(e) follows that person with two or more other persons in a disorderly manner in or through any street or road.

(2) A person guilty of an offence under this section is liable on summary conviction to imprisonment for a term not exceeding six months or a fine not exceeding level 5 on the standard scale, or both.
(3) A constable may arrest without warrant anyone he reasonably suspects is committing an offence under this section."[32]

Although the offence was created by the Trade Union and Labour Relations (Consolidation) Act 1992, it is not limited to trade disputes. The aim is to make criminal that which was already recognised as a civil wrong.[33] Hence, "wrongfully" means "wrong" in the tortious sense.[34] Courts are reluctant to define the term "intimidate" exhaustively; however, it has been held to mean ". . .putting persons in fear by the exhibition of force or violence or the threat of force or violence and there is no limitation restricting the meaning to cases of violence or threats of violence to the person."[35] "Persistently follows" has been held to mean dogging a workman's footsteps.[36] There is no offence where a worker did not let miners of a union have safety lamps because the act was not unlawful at the time.[37] It has been that "watches and besets" means preventing access to and egress from somewhere, such as a sit-in.[38] Lawful picketing is not watching and besetting unless it amounts to a nuisance or some other tort such as obstruction of the highway.[39] The section makes clear that the *mens rea* is not concerned with motive but with purpose, a more objective concept, and which must be to compel and not merely to persuade.[40] However, it is not necessary to show that the compulsion was effective.[41]

Trespassory Offences

Criminal Trespass

2-101 Section 68(1) of the Criminal Justice and Public Order Act 1994 provides that a person commits the summary offence of aggravated trespass:

". . .if he trespasses on land [in the open air] and, in relation, to any lawful activity which persons are engaging in or are about to engage in on that or

---

[32] Subsection (3) has been repealed by the Serious Organised Crime and Police Act 2005, Sch.17, Pt 2.
[33] *Ward Lock & Co Ltd v Operative Printers' Assistants Society* (1906) 22 T.K.R. 327, of the precursor, section 7, Conspiracy and Protection of Property Act 1875.
[34] *Thomas v N.U.M. (South Wales Area)* [1986] Ch. 20.
[35] *R. v Jones* [1974] 59 Cr. App. R. 120.
[36] *Smith v Thomasson* (1890) 62 L.T. 68.
[37] *Fowler v Kibble* [1922] 1 Ch. 487.
[38] *Gatt v Phillip* 1983 J.C. 51.
[39] *News Group Newspapers Ltd v SOGAT 82 (No. 2)* [1987] I.C.R 181.
[40] *DPP v Fidler* [1992] 1 W.L.R. 91.
[41] *Agnew v Munro* (1891) 18 R (J) 22.

adjoining land [in the open air], does anything which is intended by him to have the effect of:

(a) intimidating those persons or any of them so as to deter them or any them engaging in that activity;
(b) of obstructing that activity; or
(c) of disrupting that activity."[42]

Whether an activity is lawful is defined by s.68(2) of the Criminal Justice and Public Order Act 1994: an activity on any occasion on the part of a person or persons on land is "lawful" if he or they may engage in the activity on the land on that occasion without committing an offence or trespassing on the land. There is only such an activity when there is someone present on the land who could be intimidated or not allowed to do what they are entitled to do.[43] Under s.68(1)(c), actual disruption is not necessary and the intention to disrupt is sufficient: for example, running towards a hunt was not evidence of a disruption but it was evidence of the requisite intention to disrupt it.[44] A constable in uniform has a power of arrest without warrant where he reasonably suspects a person of committing an offence under s.68.[45] If a senior police officer present at the scene reasonably believes that a person is committing or intends to commit the offence of aggravated trespass on the land or that two or more persons are trespassing on the land with the common purpose of intimidating persons so as to deter them from engaging in a lawful activity or of obstructing or disrupting a lawful activity, he may direct them to leave the land.[46] If that person fails to leave the land as soon as practicable or he re-enters the land within three months, he commits a summary offence.[47] That person has a defence if he can show he was not trespassing on the land or that he had a reasonable excuse for failing to leave the land as soon as practicable or for re-entering the land.[48] It was held in *Capon v DPP*[49] that the actual commission of an offence of aggravated trespass was not a precondition to a police officer issuing a direction under s.69 of the 1994 Act, and that such a direction was lawful provided that the police officer had a genuine belief that lawful activity would be obstructed if the persons in question remained on the land.

In *DPP v Tilly*,[50] the appellant was convicted of aggravated trespass, contrary to s.68 of the 1994 Act. She had entered a field and damaged a crop forming part of a government sponsored trial of genetically modified organisms. The question for the court was whether the offence of aggravated trespass under s.68 of the 1994 Act was made out where the person engaged in the relevant activity was not physically present on the land at the time of the alleged trespass. The Divisional Court allowed her appeal and held that a person could not commit the offence of aggravated trespass unless the individual engaged in the relevant lawful activity was physically present on the land in question at the time of the alleged trespass. It was not possible to obstruct or disrupt a person from engaging in a lawful activity if that person was absent. Note also *DPP v Barnard*:[51] the defendants, along with others, unlawfully entered a working open cast mine. It was alleged that they had

2-102

---

[42] Criminal Justice and Public Order Act 1994, s.68(1). The words, in square brackets were removed by s.59 of the Anti-Social Behaviour Act 2003.
[43] See *Tilly v DPP* [2002] Crim. L.R. 128.
[44] *Winder v DPP* (1996) 160 J.P. 713.
[45] Criminal Justice and Public Order Act 1994, s.68(4).
[46] *ibid.*, s.69(1).
[47] *ibid.*, s.69(3).
[48] *ibid.*, s.69(4),(5).
[49] *Independent*, March 23, 1998.
[50] [2002] Crim. L.R. 128.
[51] [2000] Crim. L.R. 37.

entered the land with intent to intimidate, obstruct or disrupt those engaged in lawful activity on the land, contrary to s.68 of the 1994 Act. The informations were dismissed on the grounds that there was no evidence of an overt act or an intention to commit an act of aggravated trespass over and above the mere act of trespass. The prosecution appealed by way of case stated. The appeal was dismissed. It was held that for aggravated trespass to be proven, there must be shown some degree of intimidation, obstruction or disruption. Although there might be occasions when unlawful occupation could constitute aggravated trespass, it would need to be distinct from the original trespass; and it also required detailed evidence of the intruder's acts. In this case, the magistrate had been correct to find that the particulars of the allegation in the information showed no more than that the defendants had trespassed.

2-103   In *Jones*,[52] the House of Lords considered the extent to which international law affected the range of s.68 of the 1994 Act. The appellants had been charged with, or convicted of, aggravated trespass or criminal damage arising out of the protests at military bases by way of protest against the war in Iraq. They claimed that they were entitled to rely upon s.3 of the Criminal Justice Act 1967 as they were using reasonable force to prevent the commission of a crime, or that their acts of disruption were not aggravated trespass because the activities of the Crown at the military bases were not lawful within the meaning of s.68 of the 1994 Act, since they were being carried out in pursuance of a crime of aggression under customary international law. The questions for the House of Lords were whether the crime of aggression was capable of being a "crime" within the meaning of s.3 of the 1967 Act and, if so, whether the issue was justiciable in a criminal trial, and whether the crime of aggression was capable of being an "offence" within s.68(2) of the 1994 Act and, if so, whether the issue was justiciable in a criminal trial. The appeals were dismissed. For the purposes of the instant proceedings, the court accepted that customary international law was, without the need for any domestic statute or judicial decision, part of the domestic law of England and Wales, since the Crown did not challenge that proposition. Customary international law recognised a crime of aggression and understood it with sufficient clarity to permit the lawful trial of those accused of the crime. It did not lack the certainty of definition required of a criminal offence. It was at least arguable that war crimes, recognised as such in customary international law, would be triable and punishable under English domestic criminal law. However, war crimes were distinct from the crime of aggression. A crime recognised in customary international law might be assimilated into the domestic criminal law of England and Wales. However, the authorities did not support the proposition that that result followed automatically. The focus of the 1967 Act was entirely domestic. It was very unlikely that Parliament understood "crime" in s.3 as covering crimes recognised in customary international law, but not assimilated into domestic law by any statute or judicial decision. Therefore, "crime" in s.3 did not cover a crime established in customary international law, such as the crime of aggression. It was clear that the crime of aggression was not a crime in the domestic law of England and Wales within the meaning of s.3. The fact that it had not been incorporated by statute was relevant. When it was sought to give domestic effect to crimes established in customary international law, the practice was to legislate. There were no compelling reasons in the instant case for departing from the democratic principle that it was for Parliament, not the executive or judiciary, to determine what types of conduct attracted criminal penalties. The court would be very slow to review the exercise of prerogative powers in relation to the conduct of foreign affairs and the deployment of the armed services, and slow to adjudicate on

---

[52] [2006] UKHL 16.

rights arising out of transactions entered into between sovereign states on the plane of international law. "Offence" in s.68(2) must be understood as meaning an offence under the domestic criminal law of the relevant UK jurisdiction. The crime of aggression was not an "offence" under s.68(2), for the same reasons that it was not a "crime" for the purposes of s.3.

See also *Ayliffe, Swain and Percy v DPP*:[53] the appellants appealed by way of case stated against their convictions arising as a result of separate and independent actions taken by them at military bases by way of protest against the Iraq war. All the appellants had been convicted of aggravated trespass contrary to s.68 of the Criminal Justice and Public Order Act 1994; and some had been convicted of criminal damage. The appellants had originally argued, amongst other matters, that the war against Iraq had been illegal, so that the activities carried out by staff at the bases were unlawful and carried out in pursuit of "an unlawful war of aggression". Further, they had argued that there was a strong possibility that the activities carried on at the bases were unlawful because they amounted to war crimes under ss.51 and 52 of the International Criminal Court Act 2001. In connection with the aggravated trespass offences under s.68 of the 1994 Act, the questions raised concerned the manner in which the judges had dealt with issues, in particular disclosure, which related to the lawfulness of the activities conducted at the different bases. The appeals were dismissed. Relying on *Jones*, above, for the purpose of s.68(2) of the 1994 Act, an act of aggression or crime against peace did not constitute an offence contrary to the law of England and Wales. It had been correct to rule that the activity at the military base was lawful. There had been no requirement to consider the legality of the operations because the arguments raised by the appellants in connection with crimes of peace or crimes of aggression were not justiciable. However, the judge had been wrong to decide that issues of war crimes and reasonable force to prevent a crime were not justiciable. Nevertheless, that did not affect the circumstances of the instant cases. The general allegations made by the appellants in respect of war crimes had not raised any issue which required disclosure by the prosecution or consideration by the judge in connection with the lawfulness of the activities at the bases.

2-104

Trespassing at a Designated Site

The Serious Organised Crime and Police Act 2005 creates the new offence of trespassing on a designated site. A designated site is any site specified or described in an order made by the Secretary of State and designated for the purposes of this section by the order.[54] However, he may only do so in respect of a site that is comprised of Crown land or land belonging to Her Majesty in her private capacity; or "if it appears to the Secretary of State that it is appropriate to designate the site in the interests of national security." It is a defence if the person did not know and had no reasonable cause to suspect that the site was in fact a designated site. Under s.132 of the 2005 Act, any person who organises, takes part in, or carries on, a demonstration in a public area is guilty of an offence if, when the demonstration starts, authorisation for the demonstration has not been given under s.134(2) of the 2005 Act. However, this section does not apply to a procession, a notice of which is required to be given under s.11(1) of the Public Order Act 1986, or for the purposes of ss.12 and 13 of the 1986 Act. Nor does it apply to conduct which is lawful under s.220 of the Trade Union and Labour Relations (Consolidation) Act 1992.[55] Section

2-105

---

[53] [2005] EWHC 684 (Admin).
[54] Serious Organised Crime and Police Act 2005. s.128(1) and (2). For example, as from April 1, 2006, it is a criminal offence to trespass on designated sensitive Ministry of Defence sites.
[55] *ibid.*, s.132(4).

133 requires a person seeking authorisation for a demonstration in the designated area to give written notice to the Commissioner of Police of the Metropolis, not less than six clear days before the day on which the demonstration is to start or if that is not reasonably practicable, not less than 24 hours. Subsections (3), (4) and (5) state what the notice must contain. If a valid notice is received at a police station in time, then the Commissioner must give authorisation,[56] but he may also impose such conditions for the purpose of preventing serious public disorder, serious damage to property, disruption, and hindrance to any person wishing to enter or leave the Palace of Westminster. Under s.134(7), a person who takes part in or organises a demonstration in a designated area commits an offence if he knowingly fails to comply with a condition, or knows or should have known that the demonstration is carried. Additionally, the senior police officer may impose additional conditions on those taking part in or organising a demonstration, or to vary a condition of the authorisation of the demonstration, if he reasonably believes it is necessary to prevent any of the things mentioned above.[57] Section 137 prohibits the use of loudspeakers in a designated area except by the emergency services or in the case of an emergency. Section 138 of the 2005 Act provides that the Secretary of State may by order specify an area as the designated area for the purposes of ss.132 to 137; and, with Parliament House in mind as an obvious designated area, subs.(3) provides that the area shall be no more than one kilometre in a straight line from the point nearest to it in Parliament Square.

2-106   In *Haw v Secretary of State for the Home Department*,[58] the claimant demonstrator applied for judicial review of the refusal of the second defendant Commissioner of Police to confirm that the notice and authorisation regime set out in the 2005 Act did not apply to him. He had maintained a permanent political demonstration in an area close to the Houses of Parliament. That area was, for the purposes of s.132(1), a designated area in which it was a criminal offence for a person to demonstrate if, when the demonstration started, authorisation for the demonstration had not been given by the commissioner. Section 178(10) of the Act conferred on the first defendant Secretary of State power to make such provision as he considered appropriate for "transitory, transitional or saving purposes in connection with the coming into force of any provision" of the Act. By the Serious Organised Crime and Police Act 2005 (Commencement No. 1, Transitional and Transitory Provisions) Order 2005 art.3 and art.4(2), the Secretary of State contended that continuing demonstrations that had commenced before s.132(1) of the Act came into force required notice to, and authorisation from, the commissioner. The claimant wrote to the defendants for confirmation that the notice and authorisation regime set out in the 2005 Act did not apply to him but both refused to give the confirmation sought. He contended that those parts of the Order that required authorisation for a continuing demonstration that had commenced before the Act came into force were ultra vires the Act as they amounted to an amendment for which there was no power under s.178(10) of the Act. The Secretary of State contended that the court should apply a modern purposive approach to the interpretation of the Act. The Divisional Court, granting the application, held that the 2005 Act as enacted did not apply to a continuing demonstration that had commenced before s.132(1) of the Act came into force. The Order extended the application of s.132(1) so as to criminalise conduct that was not so under the Act. As such the alteration made by the Order was in fact an amendment and ultra vires s.178(10) of the Act. It could not be said that Parliament intended the

---

[56] Serious Organised Crime and Police Act 2005, s.134(1),(2).
[57] *ibid.*, s.135.
[58] [2005] EWHC 2061.

Act to catch continuing demonstrations. There was no room for a modern purposive approach as the words of the Act were clear and could be given effect. In addition, penal statutes should be given a statutory construction that was in favour of the liberty of the individual. However, the Court of Appeal completely rejected this approach and found against Mr Haw.[59] Parliament's intention was clear: it was to regulate all demonstrations within the designated area, whenever they began. The court accepted the general principle that a person should not be penalised except under clear law and they were mindful of the importance of the liberty of the individual. However, whether or not there is "clear law" depends in this context upon the true construction of the relevant statute. The court, having reached the conclusion that in the case of the Act, once the intention of Parliament was ascertained from the language used, construed in its context, there was in the relevant sense clear law.

Protecting Animal Research Organisations

The Serious Organised Crime and Police Act 2005 creates somewhat specialised criminal offences in relation to animal research organisations, parliament doubtless with the same considerations in mind as those which motivated the amendments by the 2005 Act to the Protection from Eviction Act 1977. Under s.145, it is an offence if a person with the intention of harming an animal research organisation does what is called "a relevant act", or threatens that he or someone else will do a relevant act, and in such circumstances in which that act or threat is intended or likely to cause a second person (called "B" throughout these provisions) to take "steps". "Relevant act" means an act amounting to a criminal offence, or a tortuous act causing B to suffer loss or damage of any kind.[60] The phrase "steps" is defined in s.145(2). They are: **2-107**

(a) not to perform any contractual obligation owed by B to a third person ("C"), whether or not non-performance amounts to a breach of contract;

(b) to terminate any contract B has with C;

(c) not to enter a contract with C.

"Harm, under subsection (5) means;

(a) to cause the organisation to suffer loss or damage of any kind; or

(b) to prevent or hinder the carrying out by the organisation of any of its activities.[61]

Further, under s.146(1), a person ("A") commits an offence if, intending that B to abstain from something he is entitled to do or to do something he is entitled to abstain from, makes a threat to B that A or someone else will do "a relevant act", and A does this wholly or mainly because B is a person of a kind that is defined in s.146(2). These include employees or officers of an animal research organisation, students of such educational establishments that it is an animal research organisation, a lessor or licensor of premises occupied by such an organisation, a customer, a person with a financial interest in one, and so on. The term "animal research organisation" is defined in s.148 of the 2005 **2-108**

---

[59] [2006] EWCA Civ 532.
[60] Serious Organised Crime and Police Act 2005, s.145(3).
[61] But not anything done in furtherance of a trade dispute: Serious Organised Crime and Police Act 2005, s.145(6).

Act so as to include owners, lessees and licensees of places licensed by s.4 and 5 of the Animals (Scientific Procedures) Act 1986, or a scientific procedure establishment designated as such under s.6 of the 1986 Act, or a breeding or supplying establishment designated under s.7 of the 1986 Act.

Police Directions Regarding Trespassers

2-109   Section 61 of the Criminal Justice and Public Order Act 1994 provides:

> "(1) If the senior police officer present at the scene reasonably believes that two or more persons are trespassing on land are present there with the common purpose of residing there for any period, that reasonable steps have been taken by or on behalf of the occupier to ask them to leave and—
>
> (a) that any of those persons has caused damage to the land or the property on the land or used threatening, abusive or insulting words or behaviour towards the occupier, a member of his family or an employee or agent of his; or
> (b) that those person have between them six or more vehicles on the land,
>
> he may direct those persons or any of them to leave the land and to remove any vehicles or other property they have with them on the land."

Under subs.(4) if a person knowing that a such a direction applies to him, fails to leave the land as soon as reasonably practicable, or having left, again enters that land as a trespasser within three months, he commits a summary offence. Interestingly, under subs.(6), no proceedings may be brought for an offence under this section except by, or with the consent of, the Attorney General. A constable in uniform may arrest any person he reasonably suspects is committing or has committed an offence under s.128 without a warrant.[62]

2-110   In *R (on the application of Fuller) v Chief Constable of Dorset*;[63] the applicant applied for judicial review of a decision to evict her from a travellers' encampment under s.61 of the 1994 Act. The applicant and a number of other travellers arrived at the site owned by the local authority in July 2001. The local authority agreed to let them stay on the site until the end of August under its "toleration" policy. However, on August 14, there was an alleged incident in which police officers were forcibly held at the site and threatened. The local authority informed the travellers that they were to be treated as trespassers and were required to vacate the site at the end of the month. At the same time, the Chief Constable issued a direction under s.61 requiring the travellers to leave the site at the same time. The applicant argued that the s.61 direction was invalid and that the section was incompatible with her rights under the Human Rights Act 1998. The court granted the application in part, holding that the s.61 direction was invalid. A direction under that section could only be issued once a trespasser had been asked to leave a site by the owner and had failed to do so. As the direction had been given at the same time as the local authority's order to leave, the applicant had had no opportunity to comply. In addition, a s.61 notice could only direct immediate vacation of a site. The notice had required vacation in two days' time and was therefore invalid for that reason also. A valid s.61 notice could have been given on August 31 if the applicant had refused on that date to vacate. The section was not incompatible with the applicant's Convention rights. Article 3 did not apply as there was no question of inhuman or degrading treatment or punishment. The power to give a direction under s.61 did not infringe the procedural safeguards of art.6 as a person

---

[62] Serious Organised Crime and Police Act 2005, s.130.
[63] [2003] QB 480.

aggrieved had recourse to the court. Article 8 was not applicable as the "home" established by the applicant was not permanent and had been set up illegally, and she had been aware of its temporary nature. The interference with her art.8 right was therefore justified and there had been no breach of that article. The court also observed that it was doubtful whether a landowner who compelled a trespasser to remove his possessions from his land interfered with the peaceful enjoyment by the trespasser of his possessions within the meaning of Sch.1, Pt II, art.1. In any event, the second paragraph of the article preserved the right of the state to enforce such laws as it deemed necessary to control the use of property in accordance with the general interest; s.61 was such a law.

"Land" is defined restrictively in this part of the 1994 Act: it does not include **2-111** buildings other than agricultural buildings or schedule monuments; nor does it include land forming part of a highway unless it is a footpath, bridleway, or byway.[64] It is a defence that the person was not trespassing on the land or that he had a reasonable excuse for failing to leave as soon as practicably or for re-entering the land. Following the making of the direction, a constable in uniform may arrest without warrant anyone he reasonably suspects of the committing the offence and he may also seize and remove any vehicles.[65]

By s.60 of the Anti-Social Behaviour Act 2003, there is inserted a new **2-112** section, s.62A. It provides that if the senior police officer present at a scene reasonably believes that the conditions in subs.(2) are satisfied in relation to a person and land, he may direct the person (a) to leave the land; and/or (b) to remove any vehicle and other property he has with him on the land. The conditions are:

(1) that the person and one or more others ("the trespassers") are trespassing[66] on the land;

(2) that the trespassers have between them at least one vehicle on the land;

(3) that the trespassers are present on the land with the common purpose of residing there for any period;

(4) if it appears to the officer that the person has one or more caravans in his possession or under his control on the land, that there is a pitch on a relevant caravan site[67] for that caravan[68] or each of those caravans; and,

(5) that the occupier[69] of the land or a person acting on his behalf has asked the police to remove the trespassers from the land. Under s.62A(3), a direction under s.62A(1) may be communicated to the person to whom it applies by any constable at the scene.

A new section, s.62B, inserted by s.61 of the Anti-Social Behaviour Act **2-113** 2003, provides that it is an offence to fail to comply with direction under s.62A. A person commits an offence if he knows that a direction under s.62A(1) has been given which applies to him and he fails to leave the relevant

---

[64] Criminal Justice and Public Order 1994, s.69(1).

[65] *ibid.*, s.61(5).

[66] This is defined in the new s.62D(2) as trespass as against the occupier or an infringement against the commoner's rights.

[67] This means a caravan site which is situated in the area of a local authority within whose area the land is situated: or a registered social landlord: Human Rights Act 1998, s.62A(4).

[68] "Caravan" and "caravan site" have the same meaning as in Pt I of the Caravan Sites and Control of Development Act 1960: Criminal Justice and Public Order Act 1994, s.62A(4).

[69] Defined as, in the case of land to which the public has access, to include the local authority and any commoner and, in any other case, includes the commoners or any of them: *ibid.*, s.62D(3).

land as soon as reasonably practicable, or he enters any land in the area of the relevant local authority[70] as a trespasser before the end of the relevant period with the intention of residing there. Under subs.(2), the relevant period is the period of three months starting with the day on which the direction is given. A person guilty of an offence under this section is liable on summary conviction to imprisonment for a term not exceeding three months or a fine not exceeding level 4 on the standard scale or both.[71] A constable in uniform who reasonably suspects that a person is committing an offence under this section may arrest him without a warrant. By subs.(5), it is a defence for the accused to show:

"(a) that he was not trespassing on the land in respect of which he is alleged to have committed the offence;
(b) that he had a reasonable excuse

(i) for failing to leave the relevant land as soon as reasonably practicable, or
(ii) for entering land in the area of the relevant local authority as a trespasser with the intention of residing there; or

(c) that, at the time the direction was given, he was under the age of 18 years and was residing with his parent or guardian."

2-114   Another new section introduced by s.62 of the 2003 Act, s.62C, deals with another consequence of failing to comply with direction under s.62A—seizure. It provides that. if a direction has been given under s.62A(1) and a constable reasonably suspects that a person to whom the direction applies has, without reasonable excuse, failed to remove any vehicle on the relevant land which appears to the constable to belong to him or to be in his possession or under his control, or entered any land in the area of the relevant local authority as a trespasser with a vehicle before the end of the relevant period with the intention of residing there, the constable may seize and remove the vehicle. Again, the relevant period is the period of three months starting with the day on which the direction is given.

Raves and Parties

2-115   Section 63 of the Criminal Justice and Public Order Act 1994 Act deals with raves. Initially, s.63(1) provided that it applied to:

". . .a gathering of land in the open air of 100 or more persons (whether or not trespassers) at which amplified music is played during the night (with or without intermissions) and is such as, by reasons of its loudness and duration and the time at which it is played, is likely to cause serious distress to the inhabitants of the locality. . ."

However, this subsection was amended by s.58 of the Anti-Social Behaviour Act 2003 so that the figure of 100 persons is reduced to 20. Further, there is now, by virtue of the same section of the 2003 Act, a new subsection. Section

---

[70] Defined by s.62E(3) as a London borough or Common Council of the City of London, a county council, a district council or the Council of the Isles of Scilly, and in Wales, a county council or county borough council. "Relevant local authority" means: (a) if the relevant land is situated in the area of more than one local authority (but is not in the Isles of Scilly), the district council or county borough council within whose area the relevant land is situated; (b) if the relevant land is situated in the Isles of Scilly, the Council of the Isles of Scilly; (c) in any other case, the local authority within whose area the relevant land is situated: s.62E(6).
[71] Criminal Justice and Public Order Act 1994, s.62A(3).

1(1A) of the 1994 Act provides that s.1 now also applies to any kind of gathering on land of 20 or more persons who are trespassing on land, and it would be a gathering of a kind mentioned in subs.(1) if it took place on land in the open air. An offence is committed under s.63(7A) if he knows that a direction under subs.(2) has been given which applies to him and he makes preparations for, or attends a gathering to which, this section applies within the period of 24 hours starting when the direction is given.[72]

Under subs.(6), if a person knowing that a direction has been given which applies to him fails to leave the land as soon as reasonably practicable, or having left again enters the land within the period of seven days beginning with the day on which the direction was given, he commits an offence and is liable on summary conviction to imprisonment for a term not exceeding three months or a fine not exceeding level 4 on the standard scale, or both. In proceedings for an offence under this section it is a defence for the accused to show that he had a reasonable excuse for failing to leave the land as soon as reasonably practicable or, as the case may be, for again entering the land.[73] Section 65(6) of the Anti-Social Behaviour Act 2003 amends this section by adding a new subsection, subs.(7A). This provides that a person commits an offence if he knows that a direction under subs.(2) has been given which applies to him, and he makes preparations for or attends a gathering to which this sections applies within a period of 24 hours starting when the direction was given.[74] A constable in uniform who reasonably suspects that a person is committing an offence under this section may arrest him without a warrant.[75] If a police officer of the rank of superintendent reasonably believes that two or more persons are making preparations for the holding there of a such a gathering; ten or more persons are waiting for such a gathering to begin there; or ten or more persons are attending such a gathering which is in progress, he may give a direction that those person and any other persons who come to prepare or wait for or attend the gathering are to leave the land and remove any vehicles or other property they have with them on the land.[76] The same defence applies. However, there are additional police powers. A constable in uniform has the power to arrest without warrant anyone he reasonably suspects of committing an offence under s.63.[77] They may seize and remove and vehicles and sound equipment.[78] Within five miles of the boundary of the site of the rave, a constable may stop a person whom he reasonably believes to be attending the rave and direct him not to proceed there; breach of the direction is a summary offence.[79] A constable may be authorised to enter land for any purpose under s.64(1) or (2) by a police officer of the superintendent or above without a warrant.[80]

2-116

Unlawful Encampment Directions

Under s.77 (1) of the Criminal Justice and Public Order Act 1994, if it appears to a local authority that persons are for the time being residing in a vehicle or vehicles within that authority's area, on any land forming part of a highway, any other unoccupied land, or any occupied land without the consent of the

2-117

---

[72] Liable on summary conviction to imprisonment for a term of not more than three months or a fine nor more that level 4 on the standard scale: Public Order Act 1986, s.63(7B).
[73] Criminal Justice and Public Order Act 1994, s.62 (7).
[74] Under s.63(7B), a person guilty of the offence is liable on summary conviction to imprisonment for a term not exceeding three months or a fine on level 4 of the standard scale or both.
[75] Criminal Justice and Public Order Act 1994, s.63(8).
[76] *ibid.*, s.63(2).
[77] *ibid.*, s.63(8).
[78] *ibid.*, s.67(4).
[79] *ibid.*, s.65(1) to (3), (5).
[80] *ibid.*, s.64(3).

occupier, the authority may give a direction that those persons and any others with them are to leave the land and remove the vehicles and any other property they have with them on the land. It is an offence under subs.(3) for a person, knowing that a direction under subs.(1) has been given which applies to him, to fail to leave the land as soon as practicable or to remove any vehicle or property from the land; or, having left it, to re-enter it within three months. "Land" means land in the open air.[81] The notice of the direction must be served on the person to whom it applies and while it is necessary to specify the land, it is not necessary to name all the occupants.[82] If it is impracticable to serve it on a person, then it is served if it is fixed in a prominent place to every vehicle on the land.[83] Notice must also be given to the owner and occupier. It is a defence that the accused could not comply with the direction as soon as practicable if it was due to illness, mechanical breakdown, or other immediate emergency.[84]

2-118   Section 78(1) provides for a magistrates removal order. On a complaint made by a local authority, a magistrates' court, if satisfied that persons and vehicles in which they are residing are present on land, within that authority's area, in contravention of a direction under s.77, may make an order requiring the removal of any such vehicle or other property. Such an order may authorise the local authority to take such steps as are reasonable to see that the order is complied with. In *Shropshire County Council v Wynne*,[85] it was held that it was not the function of the magistrates to assess the reasonableness of the local authority's decision to issue the direction: all the court was required to do was see that the relevant formalities had been complied with or to assess any defence based on mechanical failure, illness or other emergency to an offence under s.77(3). The magistrates' order may authorise the authority to take such steps as necessary to ensure that the order is complied with including entering the land and to remove the vehicle or property. The authority must give the owner and occupier of the land 24 hours notice of the application. It is an offence for a person to obstruct wilfully any person in the exercise of the power conferred upon him by an order under s.78.

Public Nuisance Offences

Public Nuisance

2-119   Many forms of nuisance are punishable under statute and usually in the magistrates' courts. They are common-law offences, triable either way.[86] When tried on indictment, they are class 4 offences. The test for nuisance as a crime and as a tort is the same: conduct by the accused which renders the enjoyment of life and property uncomfortable.[87] However, criminal nuisances must be public. Not all of the public need be affected, but it must be shown that the act or omission was sufficiently widespread or indiscriminate as to amount to a public, rather than a private, nuisance. It is sufficient to show that a representative cross-section of the class has been affected or ". . .so widespread in its range or so indiscriminate in its effect that it would not be reasonable to expect one person to take proceedings on his own responsibility to put a stop to it".[88]

---

[81] Criminal Justice and Public Order Act 1994, s.77(6).
[82] *ibid.*, s.77(2).
[83] *ibid.*, s.79(2).
[84] *ibid.*, s.77(5).
[85] [1998] C.O.D. 40.
[86] Magistrates Courts Act 1980, s.17(1), Sch.1.
[87] *White* (1775) 1 Burr 333. In *AH-Gen v. PYA Quarries Ltd.* [1957] 2 Q.B. 169: "materially affects the reasonable comfort and convenience of a class of Her Majesty's subjects." See *R. v Johnson* [1996] 2 C.R. App. R. 434.
[88] *AH-Gen v PYA Quarries Ltd.* [1957] 1 Q.B. 169.

In *Rimmington*,[89] the appellants appealed against a decision refusing their **2-120** appeals against convictions of causing a public nuisance at common law. One of the appellants, R, had sent a large number of separate postal packages containing racist material to individual members of the public based on their perceived ethnicity. He had been charged on indictment of a single count of public nuisance, contrary to common law. The other, G, had posted an envelope containing salt to the address of a friend as a practical joke. The envelope did not reach G's friend, as at a post sorting office some of the salt leaked onto a postal worker's hands. The postal worker raised the alarm believing that the salt was anthrax. The sorting office was evacuated, the second delivery was cancelled and the police were called. R and G submitted that the conduct formerly chargeable as the crime of public nuisance had now become the subject of express statutory provision, that the offence should be charged under the appropriate statutory provision, and that the crime of public nuisance had therefore ceased to have any practical application or legal existence. Further, the crime of causing a public nuisance, as currently interpreted and applied, lacked the certainty and predictability necessary to meet the requirements of the common law itself or the Human Rights Act 1998 Sch.1, Pt I, art.7. The House of Lords, allowing the appeals, held that that the most typical and obvious causes of public nuisance were the subject of express statutory prohibition. Where Parliament had defined the ingredients of an offence, possible defences, a prescribed mode of trial and a maximum penalty, it was ordinarily proper that conduct falling within that definition be prosecuted under the statutory offence and not a common law offence for which the potential penalty was unlimited. Good practice and respect for the primacy of a statute required that conduct falling within the terms of a specific statutory provision should be prosecuted under that provision, unless there was good reason for doing otherwise. Although cases of common law public nuisance were relatively rare, it was not open to the court to conclude that the common law crime of causing a public nuisance no longer existed. Secondly, guiding principles of common law, that no one should be punished under a law unless it was sufficiently clear and certain to enable him to know what conduct was forbidden before he did it, and that no one should be punished for any act that was not clearly and ascertainably punishable when the act was done, were entirely consistent with Art.7. The offence of public nuisance as defined in *Stephens*,[90] was clear, precise, adequately defined and based on a discernible rational principle. In the instant case, R had not caused a common injury to a section of the public, so his conduct lacked the essential ingredient of common nuisance. To permit a conviction of causing a public nuisance to rest on an injury caused to separate individuals, rather than on an injury suffered to the community or a significant section of it as a whole, was to contradict the rationale of the offence, pervert its nature, and change the constituent elements of the offence to the detriment of the accused. R's conviction was quashed. A defendant was responsible for a nuisance which he knew, or ought to have known, would be the consequence of what he did or omitted to do. In G's case it had not been proven that G knew or should reasonably have known that the salt would escape into the sorting office or in the course of the post. G's conviction was therefore quashed. The main issue was what kind of *mens rea* was required. Lord Bingham and Lord Rodger confirmed that it is that the defendant knew or reasonably should have known that the acts done would cause a substantial injury to a significant section of the community. Negligence is therefore sufficient, particularly, as Lord Rodger noted, if the offence is essentially regulatory in nature.

---

[89] [2005] UKHL 63.
[90] (1865–66) L.R. 1 Q.B. 702.

2-121   A person is guilty of a common law public nuisance offence where, without any lawful justification or where he omits to discharge a legal duty, his actions or omissions endanger the life, health, property, morals or comfort of the public or obstructs the public in the exercise or enjoyment of their rights.[91] In *Sykes v Holmes*,[92] the Divisional Court held that trespassing on school premises after school hours and interfering with school property was a nuisance because it was an undue influence with the comfortable and reasonable enjoyment of land, even though there were no other users of the school at that time. A fake bomb threat,[93] the making of obscene phone calls,[94] and rave parties have been held to be public nuisances.[95] A public nuisance is the result of an act or an omission. An example of a public nuisance caused by omission is *AH-Gen v Heatley*,[96] in which the defendant permitted his land to become covered with rubbish even though others were responsible for depositing it there; see also *R. v Watts*,[97] allowing a house near the highway to become ruinous. Leaving unburied a corpse of a person for whom the defendant was bound to provide a "Christian" burial (such as his spouse or child) is an indictable offence at common law if it is shown that he had the ability to provide for such a burial.[98] On the other hand, burning a corpse instead of burying it is not an offence at common law if it is done in such a way that it does not annoy the public.[99] It is also an offence at common law to remove without lawful authority a corpse from a grave.[1]

2-122   In *Johnson*,[2] the accused made hundreds of telephone calls to 13 randomly selected women in South Cumbria over a five year period. It was accepted that this could amount to a public nuisance. The court held that it a matter for the jury as to whether or not there was a sufficient number of persons complaining about the calls to amount to a public nuisance. It was said that it was permissible to consider the cumulative effect of a large number of individual acts directed at a number of individual people. In *Lowrie*,[3] the appellant was sentenced to eight years imprisonment following his guilty plea to 12 counts of public nuisance. L had made a series of hoax phone calls to the emergency services claiming, inter alia, that he was reporting a fire or that he required an ambulance.

2-123   Long user is no defence.[4] Nor is "coming to a nuisance". *Mens rea* is almost irrelevant: the purpose of the act or omission is not material if the result or probable result is to affect the public.[5] All the prosecution need show is that the defendant knew, or ought to have known, that as a result of his acts, a public nuisance would be committed.[6] In *Shorrock*, the defendant had let his field for a weekend to three individuals who used it for a acid house party which caused a disturbance over a wide area.[7] The defendant denied knowledge of the purpose of his licensees. The Court of Appeal held that the

---

[91] *R. v Shorrock* [1994] Q.B. 279.
[92] [1985] Crim. L.R. 791.
[93] *R. v Madden* 61 Cr. App. R. 254; and also an offence under s.51 of the Criminal Law Act 1977.
[94] *R. v Johnson* (A.T.) [1996] Cr. App. R. 434.
[95] See *R. v Shorrock*, [1994] Q.B. 279.
[96] [1897] 1 Ch. 560.
[97] (1703) 1 Salk 357.
[98] *R. v Vann* (1851) 2 Den. 325.
[99] *R. v Price* (1884) 12 QBD 247.
[1] *R. v Sharpe* (1857) Dears & B. 160.
[2] [1996] 2 Cr. App. R. 434.
[3] [2004] EWCA Crim 2325
[4] *Foster v Warblington D.C.* [1906] 1 K.B. 648, at 655.
[5] *R. v Carlisle* (1834) 6 C.&P. 636.
[6] *R. v Shorrock*, [1994] QB 279.
[7] [1994] Q.B. 279.

defendant was guilty of an offence if he knew, or ought to have known, that there was "a real risk" that the consequences of the licence granted by him in respect of the field would be to create the sort of nuisance that in fact occurred. Within the context of the general law of vicarious liability in criminal law, it is no defence for an employer to say that he personally did not supervise works which were performed by his employers or contractors in such a way as to be a public nuisance, even where his express orders had been disobeyed.[8] Additionally, under s.1(1) of the Criminal Law Act 1977, conspiracy to commit a public nuisance is an offence.[9] The general law of statutory author-isation is relevant to the offence. A statute may authorise and legalise acts which would otherwise be a nuisance. That is, a defendant has a complete defence if it is given specifically, or by necessary implication, and the manner in which the act was done follows the authority of the statute and avoids causing a nuisance if it can be avoided with reasonable care.

Outraging Public Decency

It is a common law offence to engage in openly lewd, scandalous behaviour and anything which is said to outrage decency, is offensive, or injurious to public morals by tending to corrupt and deprave the mind and destroy good order. By reason of s.320 of the Criminal Justice Act 2003, the offence of out-raging public decency is now an offence triable either way under para.1A of Sch.1 to the Magistrates' Courts Act 1980. Given the scope of the Obscene Publications Act 1959, there was an issue as to whether or not the offence still existed. In *Gibson and Sylveire*,[10] the defendant sculpted a human head and attached to each ear an earring made from a freeze-dried human foetus and it was displayed in the other defendant's gallery. The Court of Appeal held that the offence still existed despite the 1959 Act; and that "obscene" under the common law offence referred to acts which, while they did not necessarily lead to the corruption of public morals (as required by s.2(4) of the 1959 Act), must be acts which involved an outrage of public morals. There were two types of offence involving obscenity: those involving corruption of public morals; and those which involved an outrage on public decency whether or not public morals were involved. In the 1959 Act, "obscene" meant the former; and the common law offence referred to the latter. However, the *mens rea* requirement was the same as the common law offence of obscene libel: that is, an intent to do something which was in fact obscene, regardless of what the defendant might think the likely effect would be. The prosecution must prove that the act complained of was committed in public where there was a real possibility that members of the public would see it.[11] It must also be proved that the act was of such a lewd, obscene or disgusting character that it is an outrage on public decency so that it is sufficient if the act disgusted or annoyed the persons who saw it or were capable of seeing it.[12] More than one person should have seen the indecency.[13] It is not necessary to prove that the person who saw it was dis-gusted or annoyed. There must be a real possibility that the public might see it.[14] Under the common law version of the offence, police officers are members

2-124

---

[8] *R. v Stephens* (1866) L.R. 1 Q.B. 702. However, see *Chisholm v Doulton* (1889) 22 QBD 736, at 740.

[9] *R v Soul* 70 Cr. App. R. 295: conspiring to assist an inmate to escape from Broadmoor.

[10] [1902] 2 Q.B. 619.

[11] *R. v Walker* [1996] 1 Cr. App. 111.

[12] At common law, it is an indictable offence of outraging public decency to expose the person or engage in or simulate a sexual act. The "person" refers to the penis only; and there must be an intent to insult and annoy.

[13] *Rose v DPP Times*, April 12, 2006.

[14] *R. v Walker* [1996] 1 Cr. App. R .111; *R.v Mayling* [1963] 3 Q.B. 717.

of the public who can be annoyed by the act complained of. The jury may also
infer disgust and annoyance without evidence that anyone was actually dis-
gusted and annoyed.[15]

2-125   The common law offence need not be committed in public; it is enough that
members of the public can see him.[16] It may be committed anywhere where
the public may resort to, whether as of right or not. However, in *Walker
(Steven)*,[17] the defendant was convicted of committing an act outraging
public decency as regards a complainant who was a girl aged 10. The complainant was at the appellant's house visiting her friend, the appellant's daughter. Both little girls were in the sitting-room of the house when the appellant
entered. The complainant went into the kitchen where the appellant initiated
what he described as "a game". He put a tea towel over the little girl's eyes and
said to her, "If anything goes into your mouth, you have to suck it for two
minutes." The appellant told her to open her mouth, but she said, "No." She
took off the towel and went into the living room. The prosecution case was
that he was encouraging her by that means to take his penis into her mouth.
In the event, that did not happen. However, in the living room, the appellant
went to lie on the settee. The complainant and her friend, the appellant's
daughter, were reading aloud. The appellant had said that whichever little girl
read the best would get 20 pence. The complainant's evidence was that she
heard the appellant's zip go down, but he pulled it back up. She said, "No,
Steve." However, he undid his zip again when his daughter was reading or
about to read. The complainant saw that he was "going up and down with his
hands and he had his willy out of his zip. He was moving it up and down for
about half a minute." She ran home crying. There was evidence from her
mother that she was white and shaky, and for a few days afterwards, moody.
She had not been like that before. The appellant's defence was that nothing of
an obscene or sexual nature had occurred. It was alleged in his defence that
the offence was said to have been committed by the defendant in his own
home. On appeal, he argued that the offence of committing an act outraging
public decency could not be committed in or at a place to which the public
have no access, in this case the defendant's private home. The Court of Appeal,
allowing the appeal, held that it was a necessary condition for guilt of the
offence that at least two people must have been able to witness what happened.
In the Court's view, there was a further requirement dictated by the very
purpose for which the offence existed: that reasonable people might venture
out in public without the risk of outrage to certain minimum standards of
decency. That meant that the offence be committed in a place where there
existed a real possibility that members of the general public might witness
what happens. It did not mean that the very spot where the act is done must
itself be a place of public resort. In this case, the requirement in the instant
case was plainly not met.

2-126   See also *Rose v DPP*:[18] the appellant appealed by way of case stated from a
decision finding him guilty of committing an act outraging public decency by
behaving in an indecent manner. At around 1.00am in the morning, his girlfriend performed an act of oral sex upon him in the foyer of a bank. The only
person who saw it was the manager when she perused the CCTV footage of
the foyer days later. The appellant said in his police interview that he and his
girlfriend had simply forgotten about the camera in the excitement of the
moment. He argued that he could not have outraged public decency because
no one saw it at the time it was being committed. The Deputy District Judge

---

[15] *R. v Lunderbach* [1991] Crim. L.R. 784.
[16] *R. v Thallmann* (1863) 9 Cox CC 388; *R. v Wellard* (1884) 9 Cox CC 388.
[17] *The Times*, April 14, 1995.
[18] [2006] EWHC 852 (Admin).

found that the act of oral sex was of such a lewd, obscene and disgusting nature as to constitute an outrage of public decency. He knew or ought to have known about the CCTV camera and that passers-by could have seen him. It was sufficient that the bank manager saw him on CCTV for the offence to be established. The appeal was allowed. The Court of Appeal held that the act of oral sex in public at any rate was indecent. However, the only evidence of anyone seeing this act was of one person seeing it, and, on the authorities that is not a sufficient public element for the offence to be established. Further, the viewing privately of a private recording of an act which had not previously been seen by any person is insufficient to constitute the offence because the offence is committed when it is committed.

Prostitution Offences

Matthews observes that a gradual reduction in the use of police resources directed at controlling prostitution in favour of broader and more generalised multi-agency strategies in which the police play a major role.[19] As these multi-agencies have become more extensive and influential, the policy have been able to limit their responsibility for policing prostitution. At the same time, the focus increasingly turned towards the client and the kerb-crawler. The shift has seen a substantial reduction in the numbers of women arrested and convicted for prostitution: for example, between 1994 and 2004 in Bradford there was a fall from 250 to 90, and in Cardiff from 150 to 30.   **2-127**

The government considers prostitution a form of anti-social behaviour as it causes distress and nuisance to local residents. They refer to problems caused by discarded condoms and needles, traffic problems and telephone boxes defaced by advertisements.[20] A number of police and local authorities have successfully applied for ASBOs against street prostitutes (but there have been no such orders or applications against their customers).[21] The Home Office 2004 Consultation Paper, *Paying the Price*,[22] is an attempt to develop what the government calls a realistic and coherent strategy to deal with prostitution to address issues of prevention, protection and support, and justice. A Co-ordinated Prostitution Strategy was released in January 2006. The key objectives of the strategy are: **2-128**

". . .to challenge the view that street prostitution is inevitable; achieve an overall reduction in street prostitution; improve the safety and quality of life of communities affected including those directly involved in street sex markets; and to reduce all forms of commercial sexual exploitation."

Changing attitudes is a key element of the strategy:

"It is crucial that we move away from a general perception that prostitution is the 'oldest profession' and has to be accepted. Street prostitution is not an activity that we can tolerate in our towns and cities. Nor can we tolerate any form of commercial sexual exploitation, whether it takes place on the street, behind the doors of a massage parlour or in a private residence."

The key points of the strategy are: tackling demand—responding to community concerns by deterring those who create the demand and removing the opportunity for street prostitution to take place; developing routes out—proactively

[19] "Policing Prostution: Ten Years On" (2004) 45 *Brit. J. Criminol.* 877.
[20] White Paper, p. 48.
[21] See paras. 2–129ff below.
[22] July, 2004.

engaging with those involved in prostitution to provide a range of support and advocacy services to help them leave prostitution; ensuring justice—bringing to justice those who exploit individuals through prostitution, and those who commit violent and sexual offences against those involved in prostitution; tackling off street prostitution—targeting commercial sexual exploitation, in particular where victims are young or have been trafficked. The way in which these objectives are to be achieved is through multi-agency partnerships.

Soliciting

2-129   Section 1 of the Street Offences Act 1959 provides that it is an offence for a common prostitute to loiter or solicit in a street or public place for the purpose of prostitution. Under subs.(3), a constable may arrest without warrant anyone he finds in a street or public place and suspects with reasonable cause to be committing an offence under this section. The term "street" is defined to include any bridge, road, lane, footway, subway, square, alley or passage, whether it is a thoroughfare or not, which is open to the public, as well as the doorways and entrances of premises abutting on such a street, and any ground adjoining and open to a street.[23] The offence is triable summarily only. "Soliciting" means any conduct by a woman (but not by a man) which invites or importunes another to engage in an act of prostitution.[24] The woman need not actually be in a street or a public place if she is nonetheless seen soliciting from the street and public place. Hence, a woman in a bay window of a house under a red light in a low-cut top and mini-skirt and receiving men for the purposes of prostitution may be soliciting.[25] "Loitering" means lingering without an intent to move on, on foot or in a vehicle.[26] As to "public place", it is irrelevant that the public must pay to enter or that the owner reserves the right to refuse admission. On the other hand, if entry is restricted to a certain class of the public it may not be a public place.[27] Prostitution does not mean that the woman offer herself for full sexual intercourse or even to be genuine in her offer; rather, it is the making of the offer which is offensive to the law.[28]

Kerb-Crawling

2-130   Under s.1 of the Sexual Offences Act 1985, a man[29] commits an offence if he solicits a woman for the purposes of prostitution from a motor vehicle while it is in a street or public place; or in a street or public place while in the immediate vicinity of a motor vehicle that he has just got out of or off; and persistently or in such a manner or in such circumstances as to be likely to cause annoyance to the woman or any of the women) solicited or nuisance to other persons in the neighbourhood. Further, under s.2 of the 1985 Act, a man commits an offence if in a street or public place he persistently solicits a woman or different women for the purposes of prostitution. Both offences are summary only. Section 4 provides that references to a man soliciting a woman for the purpose of prostitution are references to his soliciting her for the purpose of obtaining her services as a prostitute. "Street" has the same meaning as under the Street Offences Act 1959.[30] It is not necessary to show that there were persons present to witness the incident. All that is required is a likelihood of nuisance to other persons in the neighbourhood. The

[23] Street Offences Act 1959, s.1(4).
[24] *DPP v Bull* [1995] Q.B. 88.
[25] *Behrendt v Burridge* [1977] 1 W.L.R. 29; *Smith v Hughes* [1960] 1 W.L.R. 830.
[26] *Williamson v Wright* (1924) J.C. 57; *Bridge v Campbell* (1947) 177 L.T. 444.
[27] *Glynn v Simmonds* [1952] 2 All E.R. 47.
[28] *R. v McFarlane* [1994] Q.B. 419.
[29] Under s.4(4) of the Sexual Offences Act 1985 Act, s.6 of the Interpretation Act 1978 does not apply, so that "man" is not to be interpreted as importing the feminine gender as well.
[30] Sexual Offences Act 1985, s.4(4).

magistrates may use their local knowledge of the area including the degree to which it is used by prostitutes.[31] By s.71 of the Criminal Justice and Police Act, the offence is an arrestable offence. The offence under s.2 of persistent soliciting means proving more than one act of soliciting. Two invitations to the same person may amount to persistence.[32]

It was proposed in the Anti-Social Behaviour White Paper that those con- **2-131** victed of kerb-crawling, under the new conditional caution system in the Police and Justice Bill, will be required as a condition of their cautioning "to face up to the consequences of their behaviour", presumably by way of attending courses about the causes and effects of prostitution. Further, under the Powers of Criminal Courts (Sentencing Act) 2000, courts may be permitted as an additional sentence, to take away the driving licences of defendants on conviction.[33]

Brothels and Disorderly Houses
Under s.33 of the Sexual Offences Act 1956, it is an offence for a person to **2-132** keep, manage, act or assist in the management of, a brothel. Section 34 provides that it is an offence for a landlord of any premises or his agent to let the whole or part of the premises knowing that they would be used, in whole or part, as a brothel, or where they are being used as a brothel, to be wilfully a party to that use continuing. It is also an offence for a tenant or occupier or person in charge of any premises to permit knowingly the whole or part of the premises to be used as a brothel.[34] Finally, under s.36, it is an offence for the tenant or occupier of any premises knowingly to permit the whole or part of the premises to be used for the purposes of habitual prostitution. All the offences are triable summarily only. A brothel is a place where people may resort to for the purposes of unlawful sexual intercourse and is used by more than one woman for the purposes of prostitution.[35] It is not necessary for there to be full sexual intercourse: hence, a massage parlour where masturbation only takes place regularly by more than one woman may be a brothel.[36] However, premises may be a brothel even though on any one day only one prostitute was present. It is not necessary to show nuisance.

A woman who uses premises exclusively for herself and her own prostitu- **2-133** tion is not keeping a brothel. A landlord who lets flats which are used as a brothel is not necessarily keeping a disorderly house; and he is not liable simply because he does not try to evict his tenants.[37] A person who acts in a menial capacity such as a receptionist and other light administrative duties in a brothel may be assisting in the management of a brothel even if she is primarily a prostitute rather than a manager.[38] Compare this with a person who simply cleans the premises and does not admit or deny admission to others: they are not so liable.[39] Keeping a disorderly house is a common law offence. A brothel is a disorderly house but so also are common betting houses and disorderly places of amusement: in fact, any premises in which there are activities going on in them which attract numbers of disorderly persons is a disorderly house.[40] As a general rule, a disorderly house are premises which are outside of ordinary morality and where activities go on which violate law and good order. The basic elements are: the premises are open, of bad repute,

---

[31] *Paul v DPP* (1990) 90 Cr. App. 173.
[32] *Darroch v DPP* (1990) 91 Cr. App. R. 78.
[33] White Paper, p.48.
[34] Sexual Offences Act 1956, s.35.
[35] *Winter v Woolfe* [1931] 1 K.B. 549.
[36] *Stevens v Christy* (1987) 85 Cr. App. R. 249.
[37] *R. v Stannard* (1863) 9 Cox CC 405; *R. v Barett* (1862) 9 Cox CC 255.
[38] *DPP v Curley* [1991] C.O.D. 186.
[39] *Abbott v Smith* [1965] 2 Q.B. 662n.
[40] *R. v Rogier* (1823) 1 B&C 272.

and conducted so as to violate the law and good order.[41] The offence is not predicated on nuisance so it is not necessary for any indecency or disorderly conduct to be seen from outside of the house.[42] There must also be persistent use.[43] While the premises need not be open to the public at large, there must be an element of openness about it.[44] Nor is it required that criminal offences be committed by visitors. Indecent performances are sufficient or some activity which outrages public decency, tends to deprave or corrupt, or otherwise injures the public interest.[45] See also s.8 of the Disorderly Houses Act 1751:

". . .any person who shall appear, act or behave him or herself as master or mistress or as the person having the care, government or management of any bawdy-house[46] or other disorderly house shall be deemed and taken to be the keeper thereof and shall be liable to be prosecuted and punished as such, notwithstanding he or she shall not be the real owner or keeper thereof".

2-134 Under s.30 of the Sexual Offences Act 1956, it is an offence for a man knowingly to live wholly or in part on the earnings of prostitution. That includes a man who lives with or is habitually in the company of a prostitute or who exercises control, direction or influence over a prostitute's movements in a way which shows that he is aiding, abetting or compelling her prostitution with others. See also s.5 of the Sexual Offences Act 1967: it provides that it is an offence for a man or woman knowingly to live wholly or in part on the earnings of prostitution on another man. Both offences are triable either way. For the s.30 offence, the woman must be a prostitute, but not necessarily a common prostitute. It is not an offence merely to let premises to a prostitute. However, whether the letting amounts to living off the earnings of a prostitute depends on whether the relationship between the prostitute and landlord is a "joint venture" or "parasitic".[47] That kind of relationship can be indicated by a high rent or if the landlord adapts the premises for the purpose of prostitution. Factors such as location, layout method of payment and so on are relevant.

"Carding"—Placing Advertisements relating to Prostitution
2-135 Sections 46 and 47 of the Criminal Justice and Police Act 2001 provide that a person commits an offence if he places on, or in the immediate vicinity of, a public telephone[48] an advertisement relating to prostitution, and he does so with the intention that the advertisement should come to the attention of any other person or persons. Under s.47(2), for the purposes of this section, an advertisement is one relating to prostitution if advertises the services of a prostitute, whether male or female or indicates that premises are premises at which prostitution services are offered. In any proceedings for an offence under this section, any advertisement which a reasonable person would consider to be an advertisement relating to prostitution shall be presumed to be such an advertisement, unless it is shown not to be. A person guilty of an offence under this section is liable on summary conviction to imprisonment for a term not exceeding six months or to a fine not exceeding level 5 on the standard scale, or both.

[41] *R . v Tan* [1983] Q.B. 1053.
[42] *R. v Brady* [1964] 3 All E.R. 616; *R. v Rice* (1866) LR 1 C.C.R. 21.
[43] *Moores v DPP* [1992] Q.B. 125.
[44] *R. v Berg* (1928) 20 Cr. App. R. 38.
[45] *R v Quinn* [1962] 2 Q.B. 245.
[46] i.e., a brothel.
[47] *R. v Stewart* (1986) 83 C.R. App. R. 327; *Shaw v DPP* [1962] A.C. 220.
[48] "Public telephone" means (a) any telephone which is located in a public place and made available for use by the public, or a section of the public, and (b) where such a telephone is located

Town Police Clauses Act 1847

The 1847 Act applies to ". . .such towns or districts in England or Ireland as   **2-136**
shall be comprised in any Act of Parliament hereafter to be passed which shall
declare that this Act shall be incorporated therewith." Section 28 provides that
a person who commits any of a long and seemingly random list of offences in
a street "to the obstruction, annoyance, or danger of the residents or passengers" shall be liable to a fine not exceeding level 3. The offences include:
suffering to be a large any unmuzzled ferocious dog or sets such a dog or
animal on any other person or animal; the slaughter or dressing of cattle; the
riding or driving "furiously" of any horse or carriage or cattle; causing any
public carriage, sledge, truck or barrow to stand longer than necessary for the
loading and unloading of goods or the setting down of passengers; leaving
furniture, goods, wares, or merchandise on the footway; placing a line or cord
or pole across any street; wilfully and indecently exposing his person;[49] publicly offering for sale or distribution any profane publication or singing any
profane or obscene song or using profane or obscene language; wilfully or
wantonly disturbing residents by pulling or ringing any door bell; flying a kite;
throwing or laying down stones, coals, slates, shells, bricks, timber or iron;
throwing things from the roof or any part of a house. Section 35 of the 1847
Act provides that ". . .any person keeping a house, shop, room. . .or other
place of public resort for the sale of refreshments of any kind who knowingly
suffers common prostitutes or reputed thieves to assemble at and continue in
his premises" shall be liable to a penalty not exceeding level 1. Similarly,
anyone who ". . .uses or acts in the management of any house, room, pit, or
other place, for the purpose of fighting, baiting, or worrying any animals shall
be liable to a penalty" not exceeding level 4.

Vagrancy and Begging

The Government in the Anti-Social Behaviour White Paper believes that   **2-137**
no-one in the United Kingdom should beg. The reality, they say, is that the
majority of people who beg are doing so to sustain a drug habit and are often
caught up in crime and anti-social behaviour:

> "The public can feel intimidated by people begging at cash points, or
> outside shops or by asking them for money. It is necessary to tackle the
> nuisance and intimidation caused to those going about their lawful busi-
> ness by people who beg persistently. We need to ensure that we address the
> problem of begging and its underlying causes. If we help people who
> beg because of drug use to access effective and appropriate treatment, we
> help not only them, but also communities and those intimidated by
> begging."

Similar comments are made in the *Together Action Plan*:

> "It is important to adopt an approach that ensures local agencies take action
> to tackle begging, by using the full range of enforcement powers available,
> backed-up by access to drug treatment. An arrest can provide an opportun-
> ity for an individual to engage with the arrest referral scheme and voluntar-
> ily accept a referral to appropriate treatment. All custody suites across the
> country now have voluntary arrest referral schemes that offer opportunities

---

in or on, or attached to, a kiosk, booth, acoustic hood, shelter or other structure, that structure: Criminal Justice and Police Act 2001, s.47(5).
[49] Unlike the common law offence, police officers keeping watch on a public lavatory are not passenger or residents: *DPP v Cheesman* [1991] 2 W.L.R. 1105.

to access effective treatment and support. We need to ensure that we address the problem of begging and its underlying causes. If we help people who beg because of drug use to access effective and appropriate treatment, we help not only them, but also communities and those intimidated by begging."

The government's Anti-Social Behaviour Unit proposes to the 30 Criminal Justice Interventions Programme areas help and support in tackling begging and other problem street culture; establish "trailblazers in Brighton, Bristol, Leeds, the London borough of Camden and the City of Westminster, which will audit and profile the people begging in their areas and take action to meet local targets for significant reductions in the number of beggars"; and make begging a recordable offence (see below) to ensure courts can access the new community penalties in the Criminal Justice Act 2003 for a range of persistent offences including drug, alcohol or mental health treatment.[50]

Vagrants

2-138   It is necessary to consider the current law relating to begging and vagrancy. Section 3 of the Vagrancy Act 1824 provides:

"Every person wandering abroad or placing himself or herself in any public place, street, highway, court or passage, to beg or gather alms, or causing or procuring or encouraging any child or children to do so, shall be deemed an idle and disorderly person. . .and it shall be lawful for any justice of the peace to commit such offender to the house of correction for any time not exceeding one calendar month."

The Serious Organised Crime and Police Act 2005 makes offences under ss.3 and 4 of the Vagrancy Act 1824 into "relevant offences" for the purposes of the Police Reform Act 2002 so that CSOs may be designated to have powers of arrest in respect of them. It also gives CSOs a power to detain a person who they have required to stop committing an offence under ss.3 and 4 of the Vagrancy Act and who has failed to comply with the requirement. Both offences were made recordable offences by the National Police (Recordable Offences) Regulations 2000 and 2003. The relationship between drug use and begging is illustrated by the Criminal Justice and Court Services (Amendment) Order 2004: as from July 2004, they are one of 11 offences which can lead to drug testing requirements being included in conditions of release on licence, or specified in a notice of supervision, on probation.

2-139   Under s.4 of the Children and Young Persons Act 1933, it is an offence for any person who causes or procures a child or young person under the age of 16 and who has responsibility for that child or young person to allow him to be in any street, premises or place for the purpose of begging or receiving alms or inducing the giving of alms, whether or not there is any pretence of singing, playing or performing, offering anything for sale or otherwise.[51] If any person while singing, playing, performing, offering anything for sale or otherwise in a street or public place[52] has with them a child who has been lent or hired out to him, the child is deemed to be in that place for purpose of the giving of alms.[53] If a person having responsibility for a child or young person is charged with an offence under these provisions, and it is proved that the child or young

---

[50] *www.together.gov.uk/article.asp?c=270&displayCat=no&aid=1077.*
[51] Summary conviction a fine up to level 2 on the standard scale or imprisonment up to three months or both.
[51] Any public park, garden, sea beach, railway station and any public ground: Children and Young Persons Act 1933, s.107(1).
[53] Children and Young Persons Act 1933, s.4(3).

person was in any street, premises or place for the purpose of begging or receiving of alms or inducing the giving of alms and that the person charged allowed him to be there, they are presumed to have allowed him to be there for that purpose unless the contrary is proved.[54]

Rogues and Vagabonds

Section 4 deals with the deeming of certain persons as "rogues and vagabonds".[55] These persons are: **2-140**

(1) "every person committing any of the offences herein before mentioned after having been convicted as an idle and disorderly person";

(2) "every person wandering abroad and lodging in any barn or outhouse or in any deserted or unoccupied building or in the open air or under a tent or in a cart or wagon. . .and not giving a good account of himself or herself";[56]

(3) "every person wilfully, openly, lewdly and obscenely exposing his person with intent to insult any female";[57]

(4) "every person wandering abroad and endeavouring by the exposure of wounds or deformities to obtain or gather alms";

(5) "every person found in any dwelling house, warehouse, coach-house, stable, or outhouse or any yard, garden or area, for any unlawful purpose"; and

(6) "every person apprehended as an idle and disorderly person and violently resisting any constable or other peace officer and subsequently convicted of the offence".

The section also provides that it shall be lawful for any justice of the peace "to commit such offender to the house of correction for any time not exceeding three months".

In *Gray v Chief Constable of Greater Manchester*,[58] the defendant was a professional busker and stood in a busy public passageway singing and playing a guitar and passer-by threw coins into his open guitar-case. The Court of Appeal allowed his appeal against conviction of placing himself in a public place to beg or gather alms contrary to the s.3 of the 1824 Act on the grounds that although he had been soliciting payment, he had not been "begging or gathering alms", as he was offering something in return for the money, and the mischief to which the 1824 Act was directed was conduct which forced a passer-by to deal with the offender's activities. "Enclosed area" was considered in *Talbot v Oxford City Magistrates Court*: the defendant was apprehended in an office within a university building and convicted of an offence contrary to s.4 of the Vagrancy Act 1824. The defendant appealed by way of case stated against the conviction contending that an office did not fall within the ambit of an "enclosed area" as defined by s.4, and that the words had to be taken in context with the rest of the section which referred to the outdoors and buildings other than office buildings. The Court of Appeal, allowing the appeal and **2-141**

---

[54] Children and Young Persons Act 1933, s.4(2).

[55] Sections 34(3)(b) and 121(5) of the Magistrates Court Act 1980 and s.70(1) of the Criminal Justice Act 1982 apply as under s.3.

[56] However, see s.1 of the Vagrancy Act 1935: a person is not so liable if they have made reasonable attempts to find accommodation.

[57] Unlike the common law offence, there is no requirement that the exposure should take place in public.

[58] [1983] WL 215709.

quashing the conviction, held that a room within a building did not constitute an enclosed area for the purposes of s.4.[59]

Incorrigible Rogues

2-142 Section 5 takes things further. Persons who are deemed to be rogues and vagabonds who commit further offences under this act may be deemed to be "incorrigible rogues" and committed to the Crown Court. Under s.10, the Crown Court may sentence the offender to be imprisoned for any period up to a year.[60] The Crown Court must satisfy itself that the offender has in fact been convicted as an incorrigible rogue by reference to the record. However, it should also examine the circumstances of the conviction. An appeal against conviction lies to the Crown Court under s.14 of the 1824 Act and s.108 of the Magistrates Court Act 1980. There is no appeal against the conviction to the Court of Appeal. Section 10(1) of the Criminal Justice Act 1968 gives a right to appeal against the crown court's sentence and the Court of Appeal can consider the circumstances afresh. In *Jackson*,[61] the Court of Appeal held that the 1824 Act is not applicable to modern machinery of the criminal justice system. Further, in reality, few beggars and vagrants are arrested much less convicted. Even so, the Anti-Social Behaviour White Paper considers begging to be anti-social behaviour because it is a nuisance to the public.[62] It is proposed that begging will be made a recordable offence so as to enable police forces to fingerprint offenders so as to encourage appropriate sentencing and to keep track of persistent offenders.

Byelaws

2-143 Most anti-social behaviour can fall within byelaws of a local authority. See *Local Authority Byelaws in England: A Discussion Paper*:[63]

> "Empowering local people to influence decisions which affect their local area is a high priority for the Government. Local communities should be able to tackle issues relating to public spaces which contribute to poor quality environments or unnecessarily prevent positive uses of public spaces. We recognise that in some circumstances local byelaws might be a useful way of dealing with such issues. But for this to be successful the byelaw-making process needs to be straightforward and, once made, byelaws must be able to be effectively enforced."

A byelaw is a law which is made by a local authority under a statutory power and confirmed by the Secretary of State to take effect in a specific area of the local authority. There is a general power under s.235 of the Local Government Act 1972 whereby district councils and London boroughs may make byelaws for good rule and government and for the suppression of nuisances. There are more specific statutory powers: public walks and pleasure grounds;[64] open spaces; burial grounds;[65] use of the seashore and promenades, including bait-digging, fishing, horse-riding, and interference with life-saving equipment;[66]

---

[59] See also *Knott v Blackburn* [1944] K.B. 77.
[60] See *R. v Walters* [1969] 1 Q.B. 255; *R. v Holding* 25 CR App 28; *R. v Long* 25 Cr App 31; *R. v Graves* [1976] Crim. L.R. 697.
[61] [1974] Q.B. 517.
[62] White Paper, para.3.40.
[63] Office of the Deputy Prime Minister, March 2006, p.5.
[64] Public Health Act 1875, s.164.
[65] Open Spaces Act 1906, ss.12, 15.
[66] Public Health Acts Amendment Act 1907, ss.82, 83.

public bathing;[67] markets, including operating hours, maintaining cleanliness, preventing obstruction, use of water taps and prevention of fires;[68] amusement premises; pleasure fairs; hairdressers and barbers.[69] The Secretary of State has published a model code which contains clauses about activities as diverse as music near houses, churches and hospitals, indecent language; fighting; nuisances contrary to public decency; and cycling on footpaths. Byelaws made under s.235 of the 1972 Act must be made under the seal of the authority and then submitted to the Secretary of State for the Home Office for confirmation. The authority must publish their intention to seek to have the byelaw confirmed so that it may be inspected by members of the public. The Secretary of State may reject or confirm the byelaw and, if the latter, may fix a date as from when the byelaw shall take effect.[70]

Other agencies and bodies, national and local, may make byelaws. The **2-144** Department for Environment, Food and Rural Affairs has responsibility for byelaws on countryside recreation, for local nature reserves and to address dog fouling, although these byelaws are being replaced by dog control orders. The Department for Transport has policy responsibility for byelaws relating to railways and other guided transport systems, ports and harbours, airports, bridges and tunnels, walkways and taxis. There is a national set of byelaws in operation for the rail network. These may be enforced by any rail operator defined in the byelaws. Section 46 of the Railways Act 2005 has transferred the powers to make byelaws to the railway operators, and these are subject to confirmation by the Secretary of State. In view of the special national considerations which apply to railway byelaws the Secretary of State for Transport is responsible for confirming byelaws made under s.35 of the Highways Act 1980 by a local highway authority or a district council to regulate matters such as: the conduct of persons using a walkway; the times at which a walkway may be closed to the public; and the placing or retention of anything (including any structure or projection) in, on or over a walkway. Airport byelaws are made under the Airports Act 1986 Pt VI, ss.63, 64 and Sch.3. Some 40 or so airports in England, Wales and Scotland currently have byelaws confirmed under s.63(5) of the Airports Act 1986, allowing the airport operator to regulate the use and operation of the airport and the conduct of persons while within the airport. They cover such matters as lost property, regulation of advertising, regulation of vehicular traffic in areas where road traffic enactments do not apply, including car parking and areas where taxis may ply for hire. They may also be used to regulate behaviour, preserve order and restrict or prohibit access to any part of the airport. The Secretary of State for Transport has responsibility for confirming byelaws made by a local authority under s.68 of the Town Police Clauses Act 1847, as incorporated with the Public Health Act 1875, to regulate hackney carriages and the conduct of their drivers and proprietors. The Secretary of State confirms byelaws made by local authorities under s.6 of the Town Police Clauses Act 1889, as incorporated with the Public Health Act 1875 in relation to horse drawn omnibuses. Under para.26 of Sch.11 to the Greater London Authority Act 1999, Transport for London has powers to make byelaws for any of its railways. Byelaws, made under previous legislation, already exist for London Underground and the Docklands Light Railway. Separate byelaws also exist for the Croydon Tramlink, made under s.46 of the Croydon Tramlink Act 1994. The Department for Culture, Media and Sport has responsibility for byelaws relating to public libraries under the Public

---

[67] Public Health Act 1936, s.231.
[68] Food Act 1984, s.60.
[69] Public Health Act 1961, ss.75,77, as amended by s.22 of the Local Government (Miscellaneous Provisions) Act 1976.
[70] Local Government Act 1972, s.236.

Libraries and Museums Act 1964. These byelaws define acceptable behaviour inside libraries and museums. The requirements that need to be followed are set out in s.236 of the Local Government Act 1972. Control of Trafalgar Square and Parliament Square was handed over from the Department for Culture, Media and Sport to the Greater London Authority (GLA) on October 1, 2000. However, any byelaws made by the GLA under s.385 of the Greater London Authority Act 1999, relating to either Trafalgar Square or Parliament Square Gardens, must currently be confirmed by the Secretary of State for Culture, Media and Sport. The Home Office has responsibility for byelaws relating to the consumption of alcohol in public places. However, legislation under the Criminal Justice and Police Act 2001 is replacing byelaws with powers which do not require the approval of the Secretary of State. Byelaws related to drinking in public will therefore cease to have effect from September 1, 2006. The Department of Health has policy responsibility for byelaws relating to the practice of acupuncture and businesses providing tattooing, semi-permanent skin colouring, cosmetic piercing and electrolysis under Pt VIII of the Local Government (Miscellaneous Provisions) Act 1982. There are a number of byelaw-making powers related to local light railways and tramways. Examples of relevant legislation are s.59 of the Leeds Supertram Act 1993, s.46 of the Croydon Tramlink Act 1994, para.26 of Sch.11 to the Greater London Authority Act 1999 and s.62 of the Greater Nottingham Light Rapid Transit Act 1994. Byelaw-making powers are also included in a number of local acts and Transport and Works Act Orders.

2-145   Byelaws are said to have the force and effect of law. However, there is an importance difference in that courts have the jurisdiction to quash byelaws. The basic rule is that the byelaw must be reasonable, certain, consistent with the general law and intra vires the authority which made it.[71] "Unreasonable" is a reference to *Wednesbury* unreasonableness.[72] On the assumption that Parliament cannot be taken to have authorised the making of unintelligible delegated legislation, where the byelaw is challenged directly on the ground of uncertainty, the test is whether the byelaw can be given no meaning or no sensible and ascertainable meaning and not merely ambiguous or leading to uncertain results.[73] However, where a defendant in a criminal prosecution makes such a challenge, then, in accordance with Art.7(1) of the European Convention of Human Rights and general rules about criminal provisions, the test should be whether it contains adequate information as to the duties of those who are to obey it.[74]

2-146   A byelaw may also be void if inconsistent with the general law or if it deals with a subject that has already been covered by a statute.[75] A byelaw cannot allow what is not otherwise permitted; nor can it forbid what a statute expressly or impliedly allows.[76] A byelaw may also be quashed if it is repugnant to a basic common law principle.[77] Byelaws made under the Local Government Act 1972 may provide for fines on summary conviction up to level 2.[78] If a continuing offence, the byelaw may provide for a further fine for each day that the offence continues. Any person may commence proceedings

---

[71] That is, the ultra vires doctrine of judicial review; see *Secretary of State for Defence v Percy* [1999] 1 All E.R. 732.

[72] *Kruse v Johnson* [1898] 2 Q.B. 91; *Cinnamond v British Airports Authority* [1980] 1 W.L.R. 582.

[73] *Percy v Hall* [1997] Q.B. 924; *Fawcett Properties Ltd v Buckingham County Council* [1961] A.C. 636.

[74] As in *Kruse v Johnson* [1898] 2 Q.B. 91; see also *Percy v Hall*, [1997], at QB 924 pp. 941 and 950.

[75] *Morrissey v Galer* [1955] 1 W.L.R. 110.

[76] See *Powell v May* [1946] K.B. 330.

[77] *Nicholls v Tavistock U.D.C.* [1923] 2 Ch 18; *London Passenger Transport Board v Sumner* (1935) 99 J.P. 387.

[78] Local Government Act 1972 Act, s.237; fixed at level 2 by the Criminal Law Act 1977, s.31(2)(a).

for a breach of a byelaw unless stated otherwise.[79] A local authority (and any other person) may apply for an injunction to restrain a threatened breach of a byelaw.[80] It is a defence in any such proceedings that the byelaw is invalid. However, in *DPP v Hutchinson*, it was held that even though the byelaw was ultra vires the enabling act, the defendants were liable to be convicted if the conduct breached the byelaw if it had been properly drawn up.[81]

In *Boddington v British Transport*, the defendant appealed against the dismissal of his appeal by way of case stated against his conviction of smoking a cigarette in a railway carriage where smoking was prohibited, contrary to Byelaw 20 of the British Railways Board's byelaws 1965, made under s.67 of the Transport Act 1962. His defence was that Network South Central's decision to post notices banning smoking in all carriages of its trains was ultra vires its powers to bring byelaw 20 into force. The court had held that it was not open to the defendant to raise that public law defence in the criminal proceedings brought against him. The House of Lords, dismissing the appeal, held that a defendant in criminal proceedings was entitled to contend that subordinate legislation, or an administrative act made under it, was ultra vires, and for those purposes it made no difference whether the error of law alleged was patent or substantive, or latent or procedural. If the defendant managed to rebut the presumption in favour of the lawfulness of the subordinate legislation or administrative act, the legislation or act had no legal effect at all and could not found a prosecution. In certain cases, parliament might prohibit the bringing of public law challenges in that manner by statute, but, in construing legislation, there was a strong presumption that Parliament did not intend to inhibit such challenges. In this case, there was nothing in the byelaws or the Act to rebut the presumption that the defendant was entitled to defend himself against a criminal charge on the basis of the validity of the decision to put no smoking notices in every carriage. However, in the circumstances, the way the byelaw had been brought into force was not ultra vires.

2-147

Byelaws are currently enforced through the Magistrates Courts, with fines ranging from £200 to £2,500. Enforcement by this means can be a time consuming and resource intensive process. It is also out of keeping with current anti-social behaviour and environmental initiatives, such as the control orders referred to in this paper which provide for fixed penalty notices leading to on-the-spot fines enforced by the local authority. The Deputy Prime Minister said that legislation which would allow byelaws to be enforced through an alternative means, such as fixed penalty notices, would significantly improve the enforcement of byelaws. ODPM guidance to local authorities advises that the following activities are relatively trivial nuisances and so are not normally considered to warrant criminal sanction. Therefore, the First Secretary of State would not normally be prepared to confirm byelaws on these matters: filming, video-recording, taking of photographs, glue sniffing, loitering, persistent canvassing and leaflet distributing, pigeon feeding, and spitting.[82] There are a number of transport byelaws, confirmed by the Secretary of State for Transport, which do regulate some of these activities. Furthermore, amended Trafalgar Square and Parliament Square Gardens Byelaws made in 2002, and confirmed by the Secretary of State for Culture, Media and Sport, banned the feeding of pigeons because this was causing significant environmental and other problems in an important tourism location. Strong views were said to have been expressed both for and against the introduction of these particular byelaws.

2-148

---

[79] *R. v Stewart* [1896] 1 Q.B. 300.
[80] *Burnley BC v England* (1977) 76 L.G.R. 393.
[81] [1990] 1 A.C. 783.
[82] ODPM Consultation paper, p.17.

CHAPTER THREE
Social Exclusion—Local Authorities, Education and Children, Mental Health

3-001   *"The precocity of youth in London is perfectly astounding. The drinking, the smoking, the blasphemy, indecency and immorality that does not ever cause a blush is incredible and charity schools and the spread of education do not seem to have done much to spread this scourge."* Henry Mayhew, 1851.

3-002   If, in Chapter Two, we considered the punitive aspects of the law of anti-social behaviour and disorder, in this chapter we consider what might be called "interventionist" anti-social behaviour and disorder functions. To an extent, the government tempers the rigour of its anti-social behaviour and disorder programme with interventionist measures. Anti-social behaviour may trigger a punitive measure but also intervention—but largely in respect of children. In Chapter Two we dealt with those controls of criminal character where police authorities were generally the main enforcement agency. However, as we stated in Chapter One, anti-social behaviour and disorder involves more than purely criminal behaviour and traditional methods of controlling or penalising it. We referred in Chapter One to government policy to eradicate social exclusion so as to renew local communities. These policies and strategies are generally required to be implemented through local agencies which include local authorities. Local authorities have been given new powers and functions to deal with anti-social behaviour in key areas, such as children and young people, education, the environment and the provision of housing (the last two areas are to be considered in later chapters). They are required to develop and implement their own area-wide programmes to control and reduce crime and anti-social behaviour in consultation with other local agencies, under the guidance of relevant government departments. In some cases, local authorities may be able to exercise these new functions in their own right; in others, they can only do so in partnership with other local agencies. Additionally, bearing in mind the government's view as to the relationship between social exclusion and anti-social behaviour, there are new measures, some punitive and some interventionist (and some a mixture of both) in key areas such as children and education.

Local Authorities and Other Agencies

3-003   In this section, we consider the basic rules as to how local authorities may exercise their functions to deal with anti-social behaviour and disorder in their areas. We then look at how they may exercise general specific functions and powers in respect of criminal and civil proceedings, the traditional means by which local authorities may deal with anti-social behaviour to protect themselves, their own property and employees and the inhabitants of their areas.

The Ultra Vires Doctrine

In one sense, the government had no choice but to implement and conduct its **3-004** social exclusion and anti-social behaviour strategies through local agencies and authorities. The constitutional model in the UK is that central government develops policy and legislation, local authorities execute them. However, along with police authorities, local authorities, whether in multi-agency partnerships or not, still remain the lead agency in dealing with anti-social behaviour in their areas. Therefore, it is important to understand a local authority's powers and functions. Local authorities have a unique constitutional role in modern government. They are creatures of statute and may only exercise the powers that are expressly conferred on them or which are reasonably ancillary or incidental to those specific powers. Yet, they have also conferred on them by statute quite general powers. They are public bodies exercising statutory functions so they are subject to public law rules such as procedural fairness and *Wednesbury* reasonableness; yet they are substantial private landowners, property owners and contractors, as well as major employers with private law rights they are entitled to, and even, obliged to protect and secure.

For the purposes of this chapter, the term local authority refers to county, **3-005** district, London borough councils and metropolitan councils and parish councils, and in Wales and county and county borough councils. Joint authorities and certain residuary bodies may also be local authorities for specific purposes. All local authorities are corporate bodies. Local authorities do not have untrammelled general powers to act how they see fit. A private legal person may do as they wish so long as they act within the law; corporate bodies, including local authorities, under the ultra vires doctrine, can only exercise those powers which are granted to them by a statute or may be derived by implication from the statute.[1] Hence, s.111 of the Local Government Act 1972 provides that they may do anything which is calculated to facilitate their statutory functions or is conducive or incidental to the discharge of any of their functions. The rule tends to be strictly enforced by the courts.[2] In spite of, or perhaps because of, the rigour of the ultra vires doctrine, local authorities have been given wide powers by statute which enable them to act for the general good of their areas. Under ss.120 and 124 of the 1972 Act, they may purchase land for the benefit, improvement or development of their areas; see also s.2 of the Local Authorities (Land) Act 1963 which provides for a power to erect or construct buildings or carry out works for the benefit or improvement of their areas. Section 137 of the 1972 Act provides that an amount to a prescribed limit[3] may be spent for the benefit of an area or part of it or for the inhabitants (although the power is restricted in practical terms by capping of total expenditure). They may also spend money on gifts donated for the benefit of inhabitants of the area under s.139.

By far the most significant statutory inroad into the ultra vires doctrine is **3-006** s.2 of the Local Government Act 2000. Under s.2(1), a local authority has the power to do anything which they consider likely to achieve the promotion or improvement of the economic well-being of its area, the social well-being of their area, or the environmental well-being of their area, and for the whole or any part of their area or all or any persons resident or present in their areas. In doing so, a local authority is required by s.2(8) to have regard to their s.4

---

[1] *Att-Gen v Great Eastern Railway Co.* (1880) 5 App. Cas 473, at 478.
[2] See, for example, *Credit Suisse v Waltham Forest LBC* [1997] Q.B. 362; *Credit Suisse v Allerdale D.C.* [1995] 1 Lloyd's L.R. 315.
[3] Between £1.90 and £3.50 depending on the authority, multiplied by the population of the area: s.137 (4AA) (4AB) of the Local Government Act 1972 and the Local Authority (Discretionary Expenditure Limits) Order 1993 (SI 1993/414).

"community strategy". Under s.2, the power includes incurring expenditure, giving financial assistance to any person, entering into arrangements or agreements with any person, co-operating with or facilitating or co-ordinating the activities of any person, or providing staff, goods, services or accommodation to any person. They may also do anything in relation to, or for the benefit of, any person or area situated outside their area if they consider that it is likely to achieve any one or more of the objects set out in s.2(1). Subject to *Wednesbury* reasonableness, it is for the authority to decide whether any action promotes well-being. There are certain restrictions, set out in s.3. These are that they may not do anything they are unable to do by virtue of any prohibition, limitation or restriction of their powers contained in any other enactment;[4] nor are they permitted to raise money. They must also have regard to Secretary of State guidance. The scope of the power was considered judicially in *R. (on the application of J) v Enfield LBC*,[5] and *R. (on the Application of W) v Lambeth LBC*.[6] Both cases dealt with the provision of accommodation and other assistance to persons not otherwise obviously entitled to it under the Housing Act 1996, the Children Act 1989 and the National Assistance Act 1948. It was held that there was a power to provide financial and other assistance under s.2 of the 2000 Act to such persons as s.2(4)(b) expressly dealt with financial assistance and, in the circumstances, it would promote the social well-being of the area by benefiting the applicants as persons who resided there. The section might also be relied upon by a council to implement a "name and shame" publicity campaign within their area in respect of individuals, even children, found guilty of anti-social behaviour.[7]

Powers to Deal with Anti-Social Behaviour—Court Proceedings

3-007   The traditional civil remedies to deal with anti-social behaviour are damages or an injunction and, in the case of anti-social behaviour on land, possession proceedings. Ordinarily, the victim of the anti-social behaviour is the only person with standing to bring proceedings. However, there are some situations where another person may set down proceedings for another person's benefit: a registered social landlord, for example, may apply for an injunction on behalf of a tenant where it can be shown that another tenant is in breach of the terms of his tenancy condition by causing a nuisance. As a corporate body, a local authority has the right to take proceedings in their own name with regard to their own private law rights as though they were any other legal person without having to rely upon a statutory power.[8] In *Attorney General v Logan*, for example, the local authority had statutory powers to take steps as regards a public nuisance, in addition to common law rights as an owner of real property affected by the nuisance. However, unlike a private legal person, even where the authority is acting in reliance upon their rights as a landowner, their decisions to take legal action must be reasonable in the *Wednesbury* sense and they must be careful not to overlook increasingly important human rights considerations of access to urban land.[9] However, at common law, in the absence of statutory authority, they are bound by the same rules as private individuals in public interest cases

---

[4] DETR, "Power to Promote or Improve Economic, Social or Environmental Well-being: Guidance to Local Authorities from the DETR", March 2001.
[5] [2002] EWHC 432.
[6] [2002] EWCA 613.
[7] See Kennedy L.J. in *R v Metropolitan Police Commssioner, London or Ors, Ex p. Stanley, Marshall and Kelly*. [2005] H.L.R. 8, [2004] WL 2246293.
[8] *Att-Gen v Logan* [1891] 2 Q.B. 100; *CIN Properties v Rawlins* [1995] 39 E.G. 148.
[9] Gray and Gray, "Civil Rights and Civil Wrongs and Quasi-Public Space" (1999) EHRLR 1 46–102.

such as those for a public nuisance which can only proceed with the consent of the Attorney-General.[10] Hence, s.222 of the 1972 Act gives authorities a general power to set down any kind of case, whether or not it has a public interest element, without seeking to involve the Attorney-General. It provides that local authorities may set down civil proceedings in their own name in order "to protect or promote the interests of the residents of their area where they consider it expedient for the promotion or protection of the interests of the inhabitants of their area"; they may also prosecute or defend or appear in any legal proceedings and make representations in their own name in any public inquiry. The authority must not take such any steps without considering whether "it is expedient for the promotion or protection of the interests of the inhabitants of their area" and there is a rebuttable presumption that they have done so.[11]

While expediency is a matter for the authority and not the court, any exercise of this power by a local authority may be subject to judicial review if there is a failure to consider the interests of the inhabitants or if the authority took into account irrational considerations or failed to consider relevant ones. In *Barking and Dagenham LBC v Jones*,[12] for example, it was held that the council were entitled to set down that proceedings for an injunction to restrain repeated breaches of consumer protection legislation, even though there was little in the way of evidence of complaints from customers in the council's area. However, the council had reasonably considered certain relevant matters such as that local businesses were at risk; only the council had the necessary powers of entry, search and seizure to deal with the respondent's activities effectively and promptly; the respondents' activities might give the borough a bad name; and the continual investigation by the authority of the respondent firm's behaviour was diverting the authority's time and money. It was also suggested in the *B&Q* case that, even if proceedings for an injunction were issued without thought of the limits of s.222, that decision can be ratified subsequently. That there is a prospect of judicial review proceedings should not necessarily delay the determination of the application for an injunction: in *R. v South Somerset DC Ex p. DJB (Group) Ltd*, it was noted that there was no reason why both applications could be heard at the same time by a Chancery judge.[13]   **3-008**

Most of the caselaw on s.222 concerns injunctions in aid of other legal proceedings. A clear breach of statute is not always enough for an authority to have the power to apply for an injunction.[14] In the *B&Q* case it was suggested that, at least regarding breaches of criminal law, the authority should at least try criminal proceedings before making the application for an injunction. The council in the circumstances of that case were held to be entitled to take the view that the maximum fine would not necessarily deter offenders. The fine would be far less than the profits which would be made from illegal Sunday trading; and the continued trading might encourage other traders to trade unlawfully or create resentment amongst law-abiding traders. In *Runnymede BC v Ball*,[15] the authority applied for an injunction to restrain an unlawful Gypsy caravan site (prior to the implementation of s.187B of the Town and Country Planning Act 1990) in contravention of planning law and despite measures such as enforcement and   **3-009**

[10] Except where a private right of the authority was interfered with at the same time as a public right or where authority suffered some damage from the interference with the public right: *Boyce v Paddington BC* [1903] 1 Ch. 109.
[11] *Stoke-on-Trent CC v B&Q (Retail) Ltd* [1984] Ch. 1; see *R. v Richards* (Unreported, July 28, 1998) as regards criminal proceedings.
[12] Unreported, July 30, 1999.
[13] *The Times*, April 26, 1989.
[14] *Stafford BC v Elkenford* (1977) 75 LGR 337.
[15] [1986] 1 W.L.R. 353.

stop notices. The authority had not set down criminal proceedings and it was accepted that the penalties on conviction have been substantial. However, it was held that the proceedings were proper and reasonable as, had the authority waited for criminal proceedings, the site would have been well-established and there were reasons to doubt whether any financial penalty would ever have been paid in any event. Further, the site was on Green Belt land and the court accepted that this was a matter of public importance. In *Wychavon DC v Midland Enterprises (Special Events) Ltd*, another application for an injunction to restrain the deliberate flouting of Sunday trading laws, it was held that the test is simply whether or not there was sufficient evidence to conclude that, unless an injunction was granted, the defendant would continue to break the law.[16] However, note Lord Templeman's qualifications on this rule in the *B&Q* case:

". . . a local authority should be reluctant to seek and the court should be reluctant to grant an injunction which if disobeyed may involve the infringer in sanctions far more onerous than the penalty imposed for the offence.[17] In *Gouriet v. Union of Post Office Workers* [1978] AC 435, Lord Wilberforce said at page 482 that the right to invoke the assistance of civil courts in aid of the criminal law is 'an exceptional power confined in practice to cases where an offence is frequently repeated in disregard of a usually inadequate penalty. . .or to a case of emergency.' In my view, there must also be certainly something more than infringement before the assistance of civil proceedings can be invoked and accorded for the protection and promotion of the interests of the inhabitants of the area."

3-010   In *Guildford BC v Hein*,[18] the appellant appealed against the grant of an injunction to the respondent local authority, by virtue of s.222 of the 1972 Act, that restrained her from keeping any more than three dogs of the same gender at her property at any one time, and a declaration which imposed instructions on the appellant to the delivery up to other persons of dogs removed from her and in the possession of the local authority. She had kept dogs on her land for some 30 years and, during that time, been convicted of a number of offences of cruelty to dogs and of unlawfully keeping a breeding establishment for dogs. In 1996, she was disqualified for seven years from having custody of dogs and was ordered to deliver up to the local authority the dogs in her custody at that time. During 2001, pursuant to a further order, 26 more dogs were removed from her custody. The local authority had sought an injunction preventing the return of the dogs to the appellant upon the expiry of the disqualification order and a declaration that it was entitled to sell or dispose of the dogs in its possession. The local authority appealed against the decision not to award it damages relating to the expense of caring for the dogs while in its custody. The Court of Appeal held, allowing the appeals in part, that the local authority had no statutory or common law right, nor the benefit of a court order, enabling it to retain possession of the dogs when the bailment created by the order came to an end. It was obliged to return the dogs to the appellant unless it was able to show that redelivering them to the appellant would be aiding and abetting a criminal offence. If the dogs had been returned to the appellant, they would have been at serious risk of unnecessary suffering and there was a serious possibility that the appellant would have again committed the offence which had caused the disqualification. Section 222 of the 1972 Act gave a local authority the power to institute and maintain proceedings to enforce obedience to the

[16] See (1987) 86 L.G.R. 83, at 89; *City of London Corp. v Bovis Construction Ltd.* (1988) 86 L.G.R. 660.
[17] A remark that might also apply to ASBO proceedings.
[18] [2005] EWCA Civ 979.

criminal law within its district. It was not necessary for a local authority to establish that there had been a deliberate and flagrant flouting of the criminal law. The question to be asked was whether, in the circumstances, criminal proceedings were likely to prove ineffective in achieving the public interest purposes for which the legislation in question had been enacted. This was an exceptional case; there was something more than the risk of a mere infringement of the criminal law. The grant of the injunction was upheld. The declaration granted by the judge could not stand. The court had sought to grant relief, not in aid of the criminal law by preventing unlawful breeding and cruelty to the dogs, but to make good a gap in the law. Whilst the court could sympathise with the local authority's claim for damages to cover the expenses of caring for the dogs whilst they had been in its custody, there was no legal basis upon which the local authority was entitled to them.

Unlike the Crown, a local authority may be required to give a cross-undertaking in damages. In *Rochdale BC v Anders*[19] a Sunday trading case, the injunction was refused as the council were not willing to give such a cross-undertaking. However, in *Kirklees BC v Wickes Building Supplies*,[20] the House of Lords held that there was a discretion as to whether to require the cross-undertaking and it was not likely to be insisted upon when the authority was acting as a law enforcement authority.[21] On the other hand, in *Waltham Forest LBC v Scott Markets*,[22] yet another Sunday market trading case, the council were ordered to give such an undertaking as their case was a weak case, there was no particular urgency and no evidence that the illegal market was causing any trouble. As to costs, it is not necessarily the case that, even if the authority are unsuccessful, they should be required to pay the respondent's costs. In *Bradford MBC v Booth*,[23] it was held that courts should consider both the financial prejudice to the complainant of not receiving his costs and the need to encourage public authorities to make and stand by honest and reasonable public decisions, without fear of financial prejudice should the decision be unchallenged. In *Uttlesford DC v Sanders*,[24] the local authority applied for an injunction under s.187B of the Town and Country Planning Act 1990 to restrain the respondent from providing an airport parking service in breach of conditions attached to planning permission. The respondent ran a car valeting business from a site in the vicinity of Stansted Airport. The local authority had adopted a planning policy prohibiting airport related car parking outside designated areas. The site occupied by the respondent was not within a designated area. The previous occupier of the site had run a garage business in accordance with a planning permission granted by the local authority. That permission was subject to conditions that prevented the site being used for car parking. The respondent provided a service whereby customers could leave their cars at the site for a period of time, during which they would be valeted. The cost of the valet, which included a return journey to the airport, varied depending on the length of time for which the car was to be left. The respondent argued that a distinction should be drawn between parking with motoring services, such as those he provided, and parking without such services; and that the local authority should provide an undertaking in damages as an injunction would cause him dramatically high losses by completely halting a very large proportion of his business. The court granted the application on the ground that the respondent's real business activity was the provision of airport

3-011

---

[19] [1988] 3 All E.R. 490.
[20] [1993] A.C. 227.
[21] See also *Securities and Investment Board v Lloyd-Wright* [1993] 4 All E.R. 210.
[22] [1988] C.M.L.R. 773.
[23] (2001) 3 LGLR 8.
[24] [2005] WL 2290363.

car parking, with the provision of valeting services being strictly ancillary. He was therefore in breach of the conditions attached to the planning permission granted to the previous site owner. It was appropriate to grant an injunction: there had been a flagrant and considered breach of planning control motivated by commercial gain. The court was not obliged to seek an undertaking in damages from the local authority, and ought not to consider it appropriate to do so where the local authority was carrying out its statutory duties under planning control. However, the fact that the court was not obliged to seek such an undertaking was something that had to be considered when deciding whether it was appropriate to grant the injunction.

3-012   Authorities now routinely apply for injunctions to restrain nuisance and anti-social behaviour of their tenants, usually in reliance upon their housing management powers under the Housing Act 1985, or as ordinary landlords or property-owners (in addition to injunctions under s.152 of the Housing Act 1996). However, recent cases suggest that there seems to be no reason why they cannot rely upon ss.111 and 222 of the 1972 Act (and s.2 of the 2000 Act) to obtain much wider orders in respect of local authority inhabitants generally. In *Nottingham CC v Zain*,[25] the authority believed that the defendant was involved with drug dealing on one of their estates. Relying upon s.222, they obtained an interim injunction restraining the defendant from entering the estate on the ground that his activities were a public nuisance. The injunction was subsequently discharged by a different judge because, although s.222 empowered the authority to institute civil proceedings where they considered it necessary or expedient for the promotion or protection of the interests of inhabitants, it did not authorise an authority to bring such proceedings unless they had a specific statutory duty to protect the interest of the local inhabitants. The Court of Appeal allowed the local authority's appeal. First, the authority were a highway authority regarding the estate under s.130 of the Highways Act 1980 and were required to protect the rights of the public to the use and enjoyment of the highway, which were interfered with by the defendant. Secondly, s.222 of the 1972 Act empowered the authority to take steps to end all kinds of public nuisance in their area, so long as they were steps considered to be expedient for the promotion and protection of the interests of inhabitants, regardless of whether the authority was under a statutory duty to put a stop to the nuisance. Keene L.J. added that where the authority seeks an injunction in its own name to restrain an activity which is a breach of the criminal law, but not a public nuisance, they may have to demonstrate that they have some particular responsibility for enforcement of that branch of the law. The interesting question put in the course of Schiemann L.J.'s judgment in the *Zain* case was whether or not the authority could use their powers to obtain an injunction against someone suspected of being a burglar or rapist to prevent him from entering their area:

> "One could see that it would be arguable that this protected the interests of inhabitants of their area. It is arguable that the Attorney General could in principle apply for such an injunction. It is arguable that section 222 enables a local authority to do anything of this kind that the Attorney General could do. However, as at present advised, I am by no means persuaded that a local authority is empowered to seek such an injunction."[26]

On the other hand, Grace writes that the power to apply for precisely such an injunction may be grounded in s.2 of the 2000 Act, thereby effectively extending the reach of s.222 so that the two powers combined amount to a very broad, general power to bring any proceedings, criminal or civil, of any kind

---

[25] [2002] 1 W.L.R. 607; [2003] H.L.R. 16.
[26] *Zain* at 613.

at all, so long as it can be shown that to do so would be in the interests of the inhabitants in their area in some way.[27]

However, the ultra vires doctrine are natural limits to the local authority's **3-013** power under s.222 of the 1972 Act and s.2 of the 2000 Act to act, even in the face of persistent breaches of criminal law. In *Worcestershire CC v Tongue*,[28] the local authority appealed against a decision that the court did not have jurisdiction to grant an injunction permitting the local authority to go onto land belonging to the respondent in order to remove cattle kept there. He had been convicted of offences of cruelty to his cattle and had been disqualified by the magistrates' court from having custody of cattle for the rest of his life. He had also breached the orders and had been sentenced accordingly, but continued to keep cattle. The local authority sought an injunction authorising them to remove the cattle from the respondent's care, contending that it was responsible for maintaining the welfare of animals in the region and that the respondent had continued to keep livestock in breach of the disqualification orders. The Court of Appeal dismissed the appeal. The order sought asked the civil court to go well beyond what the criminal court could have been asked to do under ss.2 and 3 of the Protection of Animals (Amendment) Act 2000 without a further charge of cruelty being made. The local authority was pointing to deficiencies in the criminal law and asking the civil court to make an order to overcome them. Though the local authority had functions in the area of animal welfare, those functions did not go so far as to cover the injunction sought, and s.222 did not confer on the court the jurisdiction to grant it. Nor did the local authority have sufficient interest in the subject matter of the order such as would enable the court to have jurisdiction to grant the relief claimed. At para.32:

"An injunction restraining continuation of the breach is one thing. It is quite another to grant an order to remove cattle belonging to others from land belonging to others and to seek ancillary orders such as one requiring the owners to permit the Council entry on their land and to deal with cattle as the Council thinks appropriate. What confers on the Council such rights, when Parliament has allowed the criminal court to give the prosecutor many rights but not those sought in the present circumstances? Whilst accepting that a local authority has functions in the area of animal welfare, I do not accept that the functions, which are spelt out by statute, go as far as to cover what the Council now seeks from the court."

Court Proceedings on Behalf of Employees

As the public face of a local authority, officers and agents in the course of their **3-014** everyday employment are frequently subject to acts of harassment, nuisance and annoyance and even violence. Were the officer to take legal action, he would be entitled to damages and or an injunction. Where this kind of intimidation or harassment takes place on or near property owned by the authority, then the authority may be able to rely upon their private law rights as a landowner. However, it may be that the officer must suffer this kind of conduct elsewhere because of his employment, such as at his home or in some public place which is not owned by the authority. It is unlikely that officers could afford the expense of litigation, particularly against a legally-aided defendant. It is in the authority's interest to ensure that staff work in a safe and secure environment. Therefore, authorities may wish to set down proceedings for, or on behalf of, their officers. A relevant power is s.111(1) of the 1972 Act which provides:

"Without prejudice to any powers exercisable apart from this section but subject to the provisions of this Act and any other enactment passed before

---

[27] Grace, "A Missed Opportunity or Two" (2001) *Journal of Local Government Law* 4 at p.121–122.
[28] [2004] Ch. 236.

or after this Act, a local authority shall have power to do any thing (whether or not involving the expenditure borrowing or lending of money or the acquisition or disposal of any property or rights) which is calculated to facilitate or is conducive or incidental to the discharge of any of their functions."

Section 112(1) provides:

"Without prejudice to section 111 above but subject to the provisions of this Act, a local authority shall appoint such officers as they think necessary for the proper discharge by the authority of such of their or another authority's functions as fall to be discharged by them."

3-015   These provisions were considered in *R. v Broadland DC Ex p. Lashley*, in which it was held that maintaining an efficient administration and the preservation of good relations with employees were themselves functions of a local authority.[29] If, in order to promote the purposes of s.111, the authority wishes to act on behalf of a member of staff who, as a result of their work, is the object of anti-social behaviour, the authority may either offer to indemnify the officer the legal costs of the proceedings,[30] or set down proceedings in their own name. In *R v Comninos Ex p. Bedford BC*,[31] the auditor appointed by the Audit Commission to audit the accounts of the council sought a judicial review of the council's decision to fund libel proceedings, brought by three of its officers against a local newspaper, and to indemnify them against any costs liabilities arising from their claims. The council had resolved to take such action in order to protect the officers from personal attacks through the press and other media. The funding agreement was entered into in June 2000, from which date the auditor had been kept informed of all relevant developments. Proceedings were not issued by the auditor until July 2002. The auditor argued that while a local authority had the power, under s.111(1) of the 1972 Act, to give an officer an indemnity in respect of "defensive" proceedings; it had no such power in the case of "offensive" proceedings and, if local authorities were allowed to fund libel proceedings issued by officers, the rule whereby local authorities were precluded from suing for defamation could easily be circumvented.[32] Sullivan J. held that the delay in the bringing of proceedings had been extreme and that the local authority had the power under s.111 to fund libel proceedings brought by its officers and to indemnify those officers against costs incurred. There was nothing in the authorities cited to the court, nor any reason in principle, to justify a distinction being made between "defensive" and "offensive" proceedings. Furthermore, the rule preventing local authorities from suing for defamation did not apply as the Council had not acted to protect its own reputation and, in seeking to protect its officers from personal attacks, had acted for a proper purpose.

Powers of Arrest and Section 222

3-016   Section 91 of the Anti-Social Behaviour Act 2003, added at a late stage during the course of the Act through Parliament, attaches a power of arrest similar to that found under ss.152 and 153 of the Housing Act 1996. It provides that this section applies to proceedings in which a local authority is a party by virtue of s.222. Under subs.(2), if the court grants an injunction which pro-

---

[29] *R.v Broadland DC, ex p. Lashley* [2000] L.G.R. 708 and [2001] L.G.R. 264.
[30] See, for example, *Burgoine v Waltham Forest LBC* [1996] 95 L.G.R. 520; *R. v DPP Ex p. Duckenfield* [2000] 1 W.L.R. 55, and *R. v Westminster CC, Ex p. UMPO* [2000] L.G.R. 611.
[31] [2003] EWHC 121 (Admin).
[32] *Derbyshire County Council v Times Newspapers Ltd* [1993] A.C. 534.

hibits conduct which is capable of causing nuisance or annoyance to a person it may, if subs.(3) below applies, attach a power of arrest to any provision of the injunction. Subsection (3) applies if the local authority applies to the court to attach the power of arrest and the court thinks that either "(a) the conduct mentioned in subsection (2) consists of or includes the use or threatened use of violence, or (b) there is a significant risk of harm to the person mentioned in that subsection." "Harm" is defined in subs.(4) to includes serious ill-treatment or abuse (whether physical or not). The aim is the same as of ss.152 and 153 of the Housing Act 1996: to speed up the committal process where certain conditions are satisfied. The existence of this new power of arrest tends to support Grace's comment, summarised in para.3-012, above. This was that, in contrast to Shiemann L.J.'s obiter remarks in the *Zain* case, the combination of s.2 of the 2000 Act, the well-being power, and s.222 are wide enough to allow an authority to set down proceedings for an injunction for nearly any public purpose they wish—for example, to restrain a suspected rapist from entering their area—well outside of the usual range of objectives of interest to local authorities. It is difficult to think of instances of cases which might fall within s.222 and not some more specific statutory power such as under the Housing Acts 1985 and 1996, and involve the threat of violence.

The lack of utility in obtaining an injunction with a power of arrest was considered in *G v Harrow LBC*,[33] in which G, a fourteen year old, appealed against the granting of an interlocutory injunction pursuant to s.152 of the Housing Act 1996 to which a power of arrest pursuant to s.152(6) was attached. The local authority applied for the injunction after receiving numerous complaints about G. The appellant submitted that, since committal to prison and sequestration of goods as means of enforcement were unavailable because he was a minor, the court should not have granted the injunction. The authority argued that the injunction could be indirectly enforced by reason of the relationship between the injunction and outstanding possession proceedings in respect of the council flat in which he and his family resided. The court allowed the appeal. There was nothing to indicate that the question of enforcing the injunction was ever fully considered. The terms of the penal notice with its reference to imprisonment appeared to confirm that the problems of enforcement against a minor were never properly addressed. The judge would have been aware that G would have no source of income and no goods which could be sequestrated. Given that an injunction was intended to regulate the conduct of the individual to whom it was addressed by the direct enforcement of the injunction against that individual, in the absence of such direct means of enforcement it was not appropriate to rely on threats or fears of indirect consequences in related proceedings. Accordingly, the injunction could not be properly or effectively enforced and should not have been granted. At para.29:

3-017

"Anti-social behaviour is a continuing problem in society and can blight the quiet enjoyment of life of those affected by it. Local authorities, amongst others, are charged with tackling such behaviour and in deciding which steps to take and which remedies to seek, they should carefully consider, in the light of the circumstances of each individual case, whether a civil injunction would be a more efficacious remedy than an ASBO or vice versa and whether there exist circumstances in any particular case which would justify seeking both orders. Amongst the considerations which will no doubt play a part in this decision making process are the speed with which the remedy can be obtained, the scope of the order which may be sought and the speed and effectiveness of enforcement proceedings. It may be that the criminal

[33] [2004] EWHC 17.

sanctions which can attend proof of breach of an ASBO will be a relevant consideration in this context especially where the subject of the order is, as is so often the case, a minor. When, however, for whatever reason it is thought necessary to seek a civil injunction against a minor, the applying authority should, in particular in applications without notice, be in a position to place before the judge evidence as to the personal circumstances of the minor which would make enforcement by way of fine or sequestration of assets an effective sanction for breach."

3-018   In the Respect Action Plan the government claimed that that these injunctions "have been successfully used to break up major drug activity and the disorder associated with it."[34] However, a problem identified with s.222 was that it made no provision for what happens when a person is arrested:

> "Currently, when these injunctions are breached, there can be a delay before a court hearing. We will legislate so that those suspected of breaching an injunction can be brought before the courts within 24 hours of arrest. This will ensure swift action to bring perpetrators to justice and a person suspected of a breach can be held in custody until the hearing if necessary."

Clause 20 of the Police and Justice Bill will replace s.91 of the 2003 Act with a new provision. The purpose of the amendment is explained in the draft Partial Regulatory Impact Assessment:

> "To do nothing would mean that injunctions issued pursuant to s222 of the Local Government Act 1972, may be considered not be as effective as injunctions issued pursuant to s153 of the Housing Act 1996. This may therefore result in practitioners not having as much confidence in what is a potentially a very effective tool. Naturally communities want to know that these measures have "teeth", and that a suspected breach will result in immediate action. Where an arrest is made and the subject is not brought before the courts as soon as possible, this could give rise to a sense that the power of arrest is inadequate as a result of failure to ensure breaches are dealt with quickly and visibly."

The power to attach a power of arrest to a s.222 injunction will remain unchanged, but cl.20 and Sch.7 to the Bill will add a new provision concerning what happens thereafter. Under subs.(4), where a power of arrest is attached to an injunction, if the person subject to the injunction is suspected of breaching it he may be arrested without warrant. The arresting officer, under subs.(5), will have to inform the local authority forthwith. The person arrested will have to be brought before the court within 24 hours under subs.(6). If not dealt with immediately the court will have to remand him/her on bail or in custody. Paragraph 4(1) of Sch.7 provides that a person may not be remanded in custody or on bail for a period of more than eight days at a time, except with the consent of all parties in a case where the person arrested is remanded on bail or where the case is adjourned to allow for a medical examination.

Procedural Issues and Injunctions
3-019   It is useful to consider the practical difficulties in many cases facing a local authority applying for an injunction to deal with anti-social behaviour. The cost of legal proceedings of this kind is obvious. However, the procedural

---

[34] Home Office, draft Partial Regulatory Impact Assessment.

machinery involved in setting down an application and obtaining the order, even under the new Civil Procedural Rules (CPR), may be convoluted and unwieldy, and ultimately so ineffective in terms of delay and enforcement that it is pointless. For example, an injunction against violent or extremist protesters is generally unenforceable if the names of the protesters are not known.[35] There is a procedure under CPR Pt 55 available to a local authority: where the names of some or all of the trespassers are not known, "persons unknown" may be listed along with any known defendants in the claim from. Service is effected by placing notices on conspicuous parts of the land and, if practicable, through delivery of an envelope marked "to the occupier". The order for possession under CPR Pt 55 takes effect *in rem* to apply to all persons trespassing on the land; the traditional position was that an injunction could only be obtained against named persons. Although it may well be a convenient way around the usual injunction rules, it may not be available where, for example, the activity is not being performed with regard to any particular land. It is a useful remedy where the protest is organised by a specific organisation, having a legal status against which the injunction can be enforced; but not where the group is an unincorporated association. However, it might be possible to proceed against the executive or management of the association personally, but that means proving that they had direction or control over the activities of the protesters. Alternatively, there is the representative procedure of CPR Pt 19.6 which gives the court a wide discretion, "where more than one person has the same interest in a claim", to allow proceedings to continue against any one or more of them as representing all or as representing some of them. The order is binding on all the persons represented, but may not be enforced against any person not a party to the proceedings without leave of the court. The procedure was used in the case of *M Michaels (Furriers) Ltd v Askew*,[36] where the plaintiff's premises were picketed and damaged by those opposed to the fur trade. One of the named defendants was Animal Aid, an unincorporated national association, which was sued as representing all its members. The court held that this was a proper use of the representative procedure, since there was an arguable case that unidentifiable persons who were members of the organisation were involved in the picketing, or in counselling or procuring it. In those circumstances, the rule allowed the court to do justice in the particular case. On the other hand, in *UK Nirex Ltd v Barton*[37] Henry J. held that it was not appropriate to allow a representative action against all members of a group, known as Lincolnshire and Northamptonshire Against Nuclear Dumping, because of the divergence of interests between those persons: some would be law-abiding, others not. See also *Huntingdon Life Sciences v Curtin*:[38] animal rights protesters picketed the company's sites and directors' houses, entry was obstructed, violence threatened, criminal damage was caused and visitors were videoed. The company sought an ex parte injunction under the Protection from Harassment Act 1997, which was refused at first instance, but granted on appeal in narrow terms so as not to deprive anyone of their legal rights. The court ordered substituted service by fixing notices in appropriate places so that any demonstrator could see what kind of activities were and were not prohibited.

As Tromans and Thomann note,[39] the real problem with representative **3-020** actions is not so much in obtaining the injunction, as in policing it. Contempt proceedings will not run against a party, even if technically covered by the terms of the order, unless it can be proved that he or she actually knew of its

---

[35] Tromans and Thomann "Environmental Protest and the Law" (2003) J.P.L. 1367.
[36] (1983) 127 Sol. J. 597.
[37] *The Times*, October 14, 1986.
[38] [1998] Env.L.R. D9.
[39] Tromans and Thomann *op.cit.*

terms before the breach. There are also service difficulties: the normal practice is to serve personally a copy of the order on the persons involved, endorsed with a penal notice spelling out the consequences of non-compliance. However, the fact that a court may have allowed substituted service of the order, by a general notice or otherwise, will not necessarily carry weight with the court which enforces against breaches of the order. However, in *Bloomsbury Publishing Group v News Group Newspapers Ltd*,[40] Morritt V.C. held that under the CPR there was no requirement that a defendant had to be named. The case concerned an injunction sought by the publishers of Harry Potter against defendants described as "the person or persons who have offered the publishers of the Sun, the Daily Mail and the Daily Mirror newspapers a copy of the book 'Harry Potter and the Order of the Phoenix' . . ." Morritt V.C. held in granting the injunction that the failure to give the name of the defendant could not invalidate the proceedings, provided the description used was sufficiently certain to identify those who were involved and those who were not. Tromans and Thomann refer to another decision of Morritt V.C., *Hampshire Waste Services Ltd v Three Others and Persons Unknown*,[41] in which Hampshire Waste Services applied for an interlocutory injunction against "Persons intending to trespass and/or trespassing upon incinerator sites" at six named locations operated by the company. This was to take place on a planned "Global Day of Action Against Incinerators", publicised on the internet. Previous such Days had been marked by environmental protests, which had resulted in incinerators having to be shut down at great cost to the operators. The injunction was granted, but not in the terms sought, as the words "trespass" and "intending to trespass" were objectionable, since they were dependent on a legal conclusion as to whether the tort of trespass was involved, and on the subjective intention of the persons described. The injunction was granted against "persons entering or remaining without the consent of the claimants. . . on any of the [named] incinerator sites. . . in connection with the Global Day of Action Against Incinerators (or similarly described event) on or around July 14, 2003". The judge allowed a substituted form of service by fixing the relevant documents in conspicuous places around the perimeters of the sites. The Vice-Chancellor expressed serious doubts as to whether the injunction would be effective as a deterrent, and whether it would add anything to the criminal law and any remedy in damages for trespass. However, he held that the court should not, if it saw a clear case for the grant of an interlocutory injunction, withhold it on the grounds of any perceived difficulty in enforcement.

Possession Proceedings
3-021   Aside from possession proceedings regarding their tenants, local authorities may be able to rely upon possession proceedings to deal with anti-social behaviour activity if it takes place on their own land. The CPR has been expressly amended for that purpose. Accelerated possession proceedings are a useful method by which a local authority can rid itself of troublesome protestors.[42] Title to land might be voidable for some kind of failure to comply with a public law requirement, such as failing to carry out an environmental assessment; but this did not affect capacity to bring summary possession proceedings.[43]
3-022   The CPR Pt 55, s.1 concerns possession claims, that is, all claims for the recovery of land, including relief from forfeiture. All claims for possession, whether

[40] [2003] EWHC 1205.
[41] Ch D, Sir Andrew Morritt V-C, LTL 8/7/2003 (Extempore) Unreported elsewhere.
[42] See Tromans and Thomann, *op.cit.*
[43] The Newbury bypass cases: *Secretary of State for Transport v Haughian* [1997] Env. L.R. 59; *Secretary of State for Transport v Fillingham* [1997] Env. L.R. 73; *Bromley LBC v Susannah* [1999] Env. L.R. D13.

of residential or commercial property, must generally be issued in the county court for the district in which the land is situated.[44] If the claimant starts in the wrong county court the judge will order that the claim may be transferred to the county court in which it ought to have been started, continue in the county court in which it has been started, or be struck out.[45] It will sometimes be possible to issue in the High Court but only in "exceptional circumstances".[46] The value of the property and the amount of any financial claim may be relevant circumstances, but "these factors alone will not normally justify starting the claim in the High Court". Otherwise, a claim wrongly started in the High Court will normally be struck out or transferred to the county court by the court on its own initiative. This is likely to result in delay and the court will normally disallow the costs of starting the claim in the High Court and of any transfer.[48]

Proceedings are started with a claim form, for use in all possession claims **3-023** (other than accelerated possession) and particulars of claim. In most possession claims, the hearing date will be not less than 28 days from the date of issue of the claim form; it may be possible to have this period varied under r.3.1(2)(a)(b) in urgent cases. The standard period between the issue of the claim form and the hearing will be not more than eight weeks.[49] The Practice Direction[50] states that particular consideration should be given to the exercise of the power to shorten time periods if the defendant, or a person for whom the defendant is responsible, has assaulted or threatened to assault the claimant, a member of the claimant's staff or another resident in the locality; there are reasonable grounds for fearing such an assault; or the defendant or a person, for whom the defendant is responsible, has caused serious damage or threatened to cause serious damage to the property or to the home or property of another resident in the locality. The claim form has a section relating to "anti-social behaviour" in which the claimant can indicate that he is relying upon "actual or threatened assault" or "actual or threatened serious damage to the property". If the claimant does wish to rely upon such behaviour and wishes the court to deal with the claim quickly, a witness statement setting out any necessary additional material not shown on the particulars of claim be filed and served with the claim form.

The defendant must be served with the claim form and the particulars of **3-024** claim not less than 21 days before the hearing date.[51] However, the court may extend or shorten the time for compliance under CPR r.3.1(2)(a)(b). The normal rules of service in Pt 6 will generally apply to standard claims. However, where the claimant serves the claim form and particulars of claim, he must produce a certificate of service of those documents at the hearing.[52] There is no requirement on the defendant to file an acknowledgement of service. However, he must file a defence. If he fails to do so within 14 days of service of the particulars of claim he may take part in the hearing, but his failure to do so may be taken into account when deciding what order to make about costs.[53] It is not possible for the claimant to obtain judgment in default.[54] The defence filed must be in the form set out in the relevant practice direction.[55] If the defendant wishes

---

[44] CPR 55.3(1).
[45] CPR 30.2(3).
[46-47] PD 55, 1.1.
[48] PD 55, 1.2.
[49] CPR 55.5(3).
[50] CPR 55.5(3).
[51] CPR 55.5(3).
[52] Rule 6.14(2)(a)—filing of a certificate within seven days does not apply: CPR 55.8(6).
[53] CPR 55.7(3).
[54] CPR 55.7(4)
[55] CPR 55.3(5), the revised form N11.

to put in written evidence, in addition to matters set out in his defence (the N11 form), he must serve the witness statements at least two days prior to the hearing. Where the claim is an appropriate one for shortening the time between issue and the hearing of the claim, but the case cannot be determined at the first hearing, "the court will consider what steps are needed to finally determine the case as quickly as reasonably practicable" under PD 55, para.3.3.

3-025   At the initial hearing, or at any adjournment of that hearing, the court may decide the claim or give case management directions.[56] Where the claim is "genuinely disputed on grounds which appear to be substantial" case management directions will include the allocation of the claim to a track or directions to enable it to be allocated.[57] It should be noted that the court may give case management directions in relation to a claim without allocating to a specific track. If the case is allocated to the fast track or the multi-track or if the court so orders the normal rules about evidence in Pt 32 will apply.[58] However, in any other case it will be possible to prove the case by written evidence. Rule 55.8(3) expressly provides that any fact that needs to be proved by the evidence of witnesses at a hearing (or adjourned hearing) may be proved by evidence in writing. The general criteria for allocation set out in CPR, r.26.8 are not strictly appropriate to possession claims. Rule 55.9e provides that the matters to which regard should be had include: the matters set out in r.26.8 as modified by the relevant practice direction; the amount of the arrears in a rent case; the importance to the defendant of retaining possession; the importance of vacant possession to the claimant. In most instances the case will probably be allocated to the fast track. Under CPR r.32.1, courts have powers to limit the scope of cases, such as limiting the evidence and cross-examination so that it should be able to hear the bulk of defended claims within one day. It will only be possible to allocate the case to the small claims track if the parties agree, in which case special provisions will apply in relation to costs, allowing recovery under a modified form of the fast track rules unless all parties want the small claims costs rules to apply. If the parties do agree otherwise the court may, when it allocates the claim, order that r.27.14 applies.

3-026   It is possible for a claimant to apply for summary judgment in possession claims but not where the claim is in respect of residential premises "against a tenant or person holding over after the end of his tenancy, whose occupancy is protected within the meaning of the Rent Act 1977 or the Housing Act 1988".[59] The county courts have always been in the practice of assessing costs at the end of short possession claims but the sums received have been small. PD 44, para.4.4(1)(b) states that the general rule is that the court will make a summary assessment of cost at the conclusion of any hearing which has lasted less than one day". Paragraph 4.5 of PD 44 requires that a written statement of costs should be prepared in Form 1 of the schedule of costs forms. The requirement to provide a detailed statement has had some effect on costs orders made in that higher sums are awarded more frequently than before. A landlord was only entitled to fixed costs where judgment was given for possession of land suspended on payment of arrears of rent in addition to current rent, and there was no defence filed "unless the court otherwise orders".[60] This provision has been retained notwithstanding the introduction of Pt 55. As from March 25, 2002 this rule was extended to all orders for possession where "one of the grounds for possession is arrears of rent (whether or not the order

---

[56] CPR 55.8(1).
[57] CPR 55.8(1)(2).
[58] CPR 55.8(1).
[59] CPR 24.3(2)(a).
[60] CCR Ord 38, App.B, Pt II, retained per Sch.2 to the CPR.

for possession is suspended on terms) and the defendant has neither delivered a defence, admission or counterclaim, nor otherwise denied liability".[61]

Criminal Proceedings by Local Authorities

Section 222 of the 1972 Act also expressly empowers local authorities to defend and prosecute criminal proceedings. In all criminal proceedings, the prosecutor is the person who commences the prosecution process. If the prosecution is commenced by the laying of information before a magistrate, the prosecutor is the person who signs the information or authorises another person to lay it on his behalf.[62] In the case of an oral information, the prosecutor is the person who goes before the magistrates or the magistrates' clerk to make the allegation. Alternatively, the prosecution may be commenced by the police charging the accused at the police station, in which case the prosecutor is the police officer who signs the charge sheet. Where proceedings are commenced by a charge, the prosecutor is in fact the custody sergeant who accepts the charge, and the prosecution is brought by the police force (more precisely, brought by the DPP through the CPS). Where the charge is signed by someone else, then that person will not have standing in any subsequent proceedings (unless authorised to do so by the DPP under s.5 of the Prosecution of Offences Act 1985) and the charges are likely to be dismissed. That does not mean that simply because the police arrested and charged an individual that the prosecution must always be brought by the police. In *Stafford Justices Ex p. Customs and Excise Commissioners*,[63] it was held that a person such as a customs officer who has investigated an offence and arrested a suspect does not, by taking him to a police station to be charged by the custody officer, surrender prosecution of the proceedings. See also *Croydon Justices Ex p Holmburg*:[64] the defendant was alleged to have committed trademark offences. Investigations were carried out by trading standards officers who sought assistance from the local police in surveillance operations and when entry to the defendant's premises was effected. The police arrested the defendant and interviews took place under police procedure by a police officer with a trading standards officer present. The trading standards officers decided to charge the defendant. At his trial, the defendant argued that the only competent prosecutor was the DPP and not the local authority. The justices rejected that submission and, on the defendant's judicial review application, it was held that the question was whether the proceedings had been instituted on behalf of a police force and that was a question of fact. The seeking of police assistance does not of itself turn proceedings into police proceedings. Only rarely would proceedings following a weights and measures investigation resulting in a charge by a local authority be police proceedings.

The vast majority of prosecutions are carried out by the Director of Public Prosecutions under s.3 of the Prosecution of Offenders Act 1985 on behalf of police forces. However, s.6(1) of the 1985 Act provides that nothing in the 1985 Act shall preclude any person from instituting criminal proceedings, subject to the DPP's discretion to take over the conduct of criminal proceedings in any case where it appears to him to be appropriate to do so under s.6(2). It is therefore possible for the DPP to take over a prosecution commenced by another person and discontinue it. In *Duckenfield*,[65] the Divisional Court approved of the DPP's policy that it would only intervene in a private prosecution to stop it when there was clearly no case to answer, and will not otherwise intervene

3-027

3-028

---

[61] Civil Procedure (Amendment No 5) Rules 2001 (SI 2001/4015), para.42.
[62] Magistrates Courts Rules 1981 SI 1981/552, r.4(1).
[63] [1991] 2 Q.B. 339.
[64] (1993) 157 J.P.N. 202.
[65] [2001] 1 W.L.R. 55.

to stop a private prosecution where there is sufficient evidence to support it. Nor does the fact that the public prosecuting authorities have commenced proceedings for a minor offence prevent a private prosecution for a more serious one.[66] Where the accused has been committed for trial in a proceedings conducted by a private prosecutor, the police may be compelled to produce all relevant statements and documents through an application for a witness summons under the Criminal Procedure (Attendance of Witnesses) Act 1965. Where proceedings have not yet begun, although contemplated, neither the police nor the CPS nor any other person are obliged to disclose any material at all.[67]

3-029   If any person may commence a prosecution, then, prima facie, that includes local authorities. This is qualified to an extent by the unusual constitutional role of local authorities. Decisions to institute prosecutions must be reasonable in the usual public law sense. Otherwise, there seem to be few other limits to the authority's powers. In *R v Jarrett and Steward*,[68] the defendants were convicted of conspiracy to defraud, one of the defendants having earlier pleaded guilty to five counts of applying a false trade description under the Trade Descriptions Act 1968. The conspiracy was said to be between the two appellants to defraud purchasers of second-hand cars by altering the odometer readings. The prosecution was brought by the local authority. On appeal, the defendants argued that in bringing the prosecution, the local authority was acting under their capacity as a weights and measures authority and therefore they had no power under the 1968 Act to charge conspiracy because a prosecution was outside the powers granted by that Act and the Weights and Measures Act 1985. The Court of Appeal dismissed the appeal and held that the authority was empowered by s.222 of the 1972 Act to bring a prosecution for conspiracy. The authority could prosecute any legal proceedings if they considered the matter fell within the very wide terms of s.222. In *Middlesbrough BC v Safeer*,[69] the council charged the defendants with using a motor vehicle on a road without there being in force a policy of insurance relating to the use of that vehicle, contrary to the provisions of s.143 of the Road Traffic Act 1988. The justices convicted the defendants and, in their appeal to the Crown Court, the defendants successfully argued that the council had no power to bring the prosecutions under that section. The Crown Court, allowing the appeal, found that s.4 of the Road Traffic Offenders Act 1988, which permitted local authorities to institute proceedings for offences under ss.15A, 17 or 18 of the Road Traffic Act 1988 and various other offences including dogs on roads, contained a complete list of offences in respect of which a local authority might institute proceedings, and that the Council could not rely on s.222 of the Local Government Act 1972 to bring criminal proceedings for a breach of s.143. The Council appealed by way of case stated. On appeal, the respondents submitted, inter alia, (i) that there was a substantial and relevant difference between the use of the words "may institute proceedings for an offence" in s.4 of the Road Traffic Offenders Act 1988 and having "power to prosecute" in s.222, in that the word "prosecute" meant that it was not possible for a local authority to institute proceedings because the word "prosecute" only authorised procedures that occurred after proceedings had been instituted; and (ii) that because the 1988 Act was described in its preamble as a consolidating Act, it contained a comprehensive code and set out exclusively all the powers that might be given in relation to those matters and therefore could not include the power to prosecute under s.143. The Court of

---

[66] *Bow Street Stipendiary Magistrate Ex p. South Coast Shipping Co.* [1993] Q.B. 645.
[67] *DPP Ex p. Hallas* (1988) 87 Cr. App. R. 340.
[68] [1997] Crim. L.R. 517.
[69] [2002] 1 Cr. App. R. 23.

Appeal, allowing the appeal, held that, as a matter of statutory construction, s.222 of the 1972 Act was sufficient to empower a local authority to institute criminal proceedings where they considered it expedient for the promotion of the protection of the interests of its inhabitants. The use of the word "prosecute" meant that a local authority was entitled to take all steps necessary to institute and pursue a prosecution and did not exclude the institution of proceedings. Nor was there anything in the 1988 Act which laid down that the power to prosecute was to be used solely or exclusively for the purposes set out in it. However, the fact that a local authority had to be satisfied that a prosecution was in the interests of the inhabitants before a prosecution could be brought under s.222 meant that a higher threshold was to be applied under that section than was necessary under s.4 which did not include that restraint. It followed that the Council had the right to prosecute the respondents for offences of having no insurance.

There are also geographical limits to a local authority's power to prosecute. **3-030** In *Brighton and Hove CC v Woolworths Plc*,[70] the local authority appealed against the dismissal of informations they had laid against Woolworths in which it was alleged that the company had failed to comply with essential safety requirements contrary to the Toy (Safety) Regulations 1995 and s.12(1) of the Consumer Protection Act 1987 by selling, in certain branches of its store, scooters which were unsafe and the subject of an order for suspension from sale. The council issued a notice under s.14 of the 1987 Act for the suspension of sales of the scooter which had been delivered to Woolworth's offices. There were then further breaches of the suspension in Woolworth's stores in other areas. The council then purported to prosecute on behalf of the enforcement authorities for those areas. The magistrates found that there was no express provision for a suspension notice to have effect outside the area of the enforcement authority by which it was served, and that there was no admissible proof that the local authority had had delegated authority to prosecute. The council argued that it was not necessary to show that the informations were prosecuted under powers delegated by other local authorities, and the council local authorities for the areas concerned had not had the power to prosecute because they did not issue the suspension notice. The issues were whether, on the proper construction of s.14 of the 1987 Act, a suspension notice served by an enforcement authority pursuant to that section had effect outside its area; and whether the serving enforcement authority had power to prosecute an alleged breach of notice committed outside its area in the absence of proper delegated authority. The Divisional Court held, dismissing the appeal, that a suspension notice issued pursuant to s.14 of the 1987 Act was valid outside of the weights and measures area from which it had been issued. However, the authority had no power to prosecute a breach of the notice committed outside its area in the absence of properly delegated authority to do so. Section 14(1) of the 1987 Act did not limit the power of the enforcement authority, or the weights and measures authority, to issue a suspension notice with countrywide effect. The scope of the power found in s.14 of the 1987 Act was to be found in s.14 alone; and s.27 of the 1987 Act identified the bodies on which powers were conferred. In this case, the local authorities of the areas affected had the power to prosecute for breaches of the suspension notice in their area, but the council did not have such a power.

Where a local authority prosecutes an offence, the Crown Prosecutors' Code **3-031** applies. Issued by the Director of Public Prosecutions under s.10 of the Prosecution of Offences Act 1985, it sets out the basic principles Crown Prosecutors are required to follow in the course of conducting a prosecution. Decisions to prosecute by the CPS, where it is alleged that the terms of the

[70] [2002] EWHC 2565.

Code are not applied, are liable to challenge by way of judicial review or abuse of process.[71] Although it is said to be a code for crown prosecutors, it is regarded as applicable to other prosecutors, such as Customs and Excise and local authorities, and with the same consequences if it is not applied. In *R. v London Buses Services Ltd Ex p. H*,[72] it was held that it was something that even private prosecutors such as a bus company should take into account. The purpose of the Code is ". . .to ensure that prosecutors make fair and consistent decisions about prosecutions."[73] Prosecutors must be fair, independent and objective. It recommends that police should seek the opinion of the CPS when making the decision to prosecute;[74] and so local authorities should also consult their lawyers. It contains the two-stage test:[75]

(1) *the evidential test:* if the case does not pass this test it must not go ahead. Prosecutor must be satisfied that there is a ". . .realistic prospect of conviction". An objective test, the authority must consider whether the evidence can be used in court or whether it is reliable;

(2) *the public interest test:* if the evidential test is passed, the prosecutor must consider whether it is in the public interest; essentially, a balancing exercise, weighing the seriousness of the offence, the circumstances of the offender, the effect on the victim, whether the court is likely to award a nominal penalty, delay between the offence and the charge or the hearing. At para.6.7, prosecutors are required to pay particular regard to the interests of the victim. If a prosecution is not in the public interest, prosecutors should look to alternatives such as a caution.

3-032   Charges should be as simple and clear as possible. In particular, there should be no more charges than necessary. It is wrong, for example, to overload an indictment simply to pressure the accused into pleading guilty; nor should prosecutors go ahead with a serious charge merely to persuade the offender to plead guilty to a lesser one.[76] Where the defendant wants to plead guilty to some but not all charges, prosecutors should not accept a guilty plea merely because it is convenient; they should only accept pleas if they think the court is able to pass a sentence that matches the seriousness of the offence.[77]

RIPA

3-033   As an investigating and prosecuting authority, the Regulation of Investigatory Powers Act 2000 applies. Under the 2000 Act, any inspection or surveillance that is likely to result in obtaining private information about an individual is likely to require prior authorisation.[78] There are three main types of surveillance under s.26 of the 2000 Act: "directed surveillance", "intrusive surveillance" and "conduct and use of human intelligence sources". In reality, for local authorities, only directed surveillance is relevant, the other two being very difficult to justify or simply not practical. "Directed surveillance" is defined in s.26 as covert surveillance undertaken in relation to a specific investigation or specific

---

[71] *R. v DPP Ex p. Manning* [2001] Q.B. 330.
[72] [2002] EWHC 224.
[73] Crown Prosecutors Code, para.1.1.
[74] *ibid.*, para.3.2.
[75] *ibid.*, para.4.
[76] *ibid.*, para.7.1.
[77] *ibid.*, para.9.
[78] See Mason, "Human Rights, Privacy and Local Authority Investigations: Learning to Live with the Regulation of Investigatory Powers Act 2000" *J.L.G.L.* (2002) 84; Ferguson and Wadham, "Privacy and Surveillance: A Review of the Regulation of the Investigation of Investigatory Powers Act 2000" E.H.L.R. (2003) 101–108.

operation which is likely to result in the obtaining of private information about a person, whether or not specifically identified for the purposes of the investigation or operation; and otherwise than by way of an immediate response to events or circumstances, the nature of which is such that it would not be reasonably practicable for an authorisation under this part to be sought for the carrying out of surveillance. Under s.26(9) of the 2000 Act, surveillance is covert where it is carried out in a manner calculated to ensure that the persons subjected to it are unaware that it is taking place. That would exclude, for example, routine food safety inspections in the presence of the addressee. The phrase, "otherwise than by way of an immediate response to events or circumstances", means that if the surveillance is carried out by way of an immediate response to suspicious circumstances while on site, the 2000 Act does not apply. However, if the relevant investigatory officer were to go back to the office and then return to the scene to investigate the complaint further, this then is directed surveillance, for which proper authorisation must be obtained.

Under ss.28 and 29 of the 2000 Act, the surveillance must meet certain criteria before it may be authorised. These are: it is in the interests of national security; to prevent or detect crime or preventing disorder; it is in the interests of economic well-being of the UK; interests of public safety; protecting public health; and assessing or collecting any tax duty levy or other imposition payable to a government department. Before directed surveillance or the use and conduct of a human intelligence can be legally undertaken under the Act an authorisation is required from an authorised officer. The Regulation of Investigatory Powers (Directed Surveillance and Covert Human Intelligence Sources) Order 2003 sets out the designated officers, prescribed by offices, ranks or positions, in public authorities who are entitled to authorise directed surveillance under s.28 of the Act, and the use and conduct of human sources under s.29 of the Act. Individuals holding more senior offices, ranks or positions to those listed may also grant authorisations under the Act. Under the Order, only an assistant chief officer or the officer responsible for the management of an investigation may authorise directed surveillance pursuant to s.30 of the Act. Further, the authorisation must be in writing. An Authorised Officer can only grant an authorisation where he considers it both necessary and proportionate. The Order limits the granting of authorisations for local authorities[79] to the purpose of preventing or detecting crime or of preventing disorder. The explanatory memorandum to the Order states that the Order seeks to correct an error in relation to the entries for local authorities to the grounds on which they can authorise activity under the Act. Local authorities had inadvertently been given protecting public safety and protecting public health as grounds for authorising activity while not needing them. This restriction, by virtue of the 2003 Order, has the effect of now restricting the undertaking of directed surveillance and the use of human sources in the specific areas of planning enforcement public nuisance, the Environmental Protection Act 1990, and to investigations in relation to breaches of statutory notices and orders which may result in proceedings by way of a criminal prosecutions and conviction for a crime. The main reason is that, in the opinion of the Home Office, prior to the issue of a statutory notice, only overt surveillance should be undertaken and it should be a sufficient means by which an authority can gather enough evidence of any transgression that falls short of criminal conduct. What are the consequences for non-compliance with the 2000 Act? Unlike the fruits of an unlawful interception pursuant to s.17 of the 2000 Act, evidence obtained by unauthorised surveillance, even intrusive surveillance, remains prima facie

3-034

---

[79] County, District and London Borough Councils (and the Common Council of the City of London in its capacity as a local authority, the Council of the Isles of Scilly, and any County Council or County Borough Council in Wales).

admissible. On the other hand, such evidence obtained, for example, by way of entrapment, may be grounds for a submission that proceedings should be stayed as an abuse of process. Alternatively, it might be something which might be excluded in the exercise of the judge's power under s.78 of PACE.[80]

Delegation

3-035   Any decision taken by an officer of a local authority must also be authorised by the local authority in one of four ways:

>   (1) by a committee or sub-committee resolution of the local authority authorising the officer to act;
>
>   (2) to delegated authority from a committee, under which the authority's standing orders might provide that a particular chief officer has the power to decide whether or not to institute legal proceedings, such as the chief environmental health officer as regards decisions to commence prosecutions under food safety laws in consultation with the legal department. If the officer is acting under delegated powers, it is important to ensure that the standing order giving effect to the resolution and the resolution itself are drafted properly and consistently;
>
>   (3) it may be delegated to an officer in consultation with the chair of the committee and vice-chair of the committee; or
>
>   (4) the authorisation may come from a superior officer. As the decision to set down proceedings is a judicial decision, as opposed to an administrative one, the officer must not only be authorised but he is to make a judicial decision which cannot be delegated if the statute specifically names a particular person or office as the relevant officer.[81] The only time when an officer can delegate such a judicial function is if he has the requisite committee authority to delegate that function.[82] Standing orders may give officers the power to authorise subordinates and there is no duty to evidence a decision to prosecute in writing.[83]

3-036   The reasons why a power of delegation may be spelt out of legislation conferring functions on a public official in virtue of his or her office were described by Lord Greene M.R. in *Carltona Ltd v Commissioners of Works*.[84] In that case, a power to requisition property was given by the Defence Regulations to any "competent authority", an expression which included the Commissioners of Works. By statute, the post of First Commissioner of Works was held by the Minister of Works. The Minister's power had been exercised in the case before the court by an assistant secretary. Lord Greene considered that there was no substance in the argument that the decision was therefore not, as in law it had to be, the decision of the First Commissioner:

> "In the administration of government in this country the functions which are given to ministers . . . are functions so multifarious that no minister could ever attend to them. To take the example of the present case no doubt

[80] *R. v P. The Times*, May 23, 2000; *R v DPP Ex p. Kebilene* [1999] 3 W.L.R. 972; *R. v Preston (Stephen)* [1994] 2 A.C. 130; *Malone v United Kingdom* (A/82) (1985) 7 E.H.R.R. 14; *R. v Aujla (Ajit Singh)* [1998] 2 Cr. App. R. 16; *Khan v United Kingdom* 8 B.H.R.C.
[81] For example, The Health and Safety At Work Act 1974. *R v Gateshead Ex p Tesco Stores* [1981] 1 All E.R. 1027; *Re Prince Blucher* [1931] 2 Ch. 70.
[82] *Hilliers v Sefton MBC* unreported, November 29, 1996.
[83] If the authorised person has taken a judicial decision to prosecute, a rubber stamp of his signature is enough: *R. v Brentford Justices, Ex p. Catlin* [1975] 2 All E.R. 201.
[84] [1943] 2 All E.R. 560; see also *Chief Constable of the West Midlands Police v Birmingham Justices, P* [2002] EWHC 1087 (Admin) re powers of Chief Constables and ASBOs.

there have been thousands of requisitions in this country by individual ministries. It cannot be supposed that this regulation meant that, in each case, the minister in person should direct his mind to the matter. The duties imposed on ministers and the powers given to ministers are normally exercised under the authority of the ministers by responsible officials of the department. Public business could not be carried on if that were not the case. Constitutionally, a decision of such an official is, of course, the decision of the minister. The minister is responsible. It is he who must answer before Parliament for anything that his officials have done under his authority, and, if for an important matter he selected an official of such junior standing that he could not be expected competently to perform the work, the minister would have to answer to Parliament."

Sedley L.J. remarks that, although the *Carltona* case is frequently cited as a source of the "alter ego" doctrine, it can be seen that Lord Greene's reasoning is in fact predicated on the proposition that the departmental head is responsible for things done under his authority. The relevance of the alter ego doctrine is that Crown servants were at that time taken in law to hold their positions by grace and not by contract, so that the minister was first among equals, not an employer with servants or a principal with agents. His implied power to delegate functions depended, therefore, on two things: the conferment of a power in terms which implicitly permitted their delegation and the existence of persons to whom he could delegate them without parting with ultimate responsibility.[85] It may be sometimes possible to imply a delegation. In *Nelms v Roe*,[86] the information against a driver had been signed on behalf of the Metropolitan Police Commissioner, in whom the statutory power vested, by a police inspector on the authority of his superintendent. There had been no express delegation of power to either. The Divisional Court held that there was an implied delegation and sub-delegation of authority, preferring this route to the *Carltona* route which had also been argued. Lord Parker C.J. said:

"In the present case Mr Farquharson urged that exactly the same principles ought to be applied to the Commissioner of Metropolitan Police as apply in the case of Ministers. It has always been a principle in this country that, a Minister being responsible to Parliament for the acts of officers of his department and having to act through others, an act done by the proper officer of his department is the act of the Minister; the proper responsible officials are the alter ago of the minister. And accordingly no question of delegation arises. That principle is very well known; the case which is always quoted in connection with that is Carltona v. Works Commissioners… I feel grave difficulties in extending that well-known principle to a case such as this, to the Commissioner of the Metropolitan Police. It is not, I think sufficient to say that it is a principle which it applicable when ever it is difficult or impractical for a person to act for himself, in other words when ever he has to act through others the principle applies. I see grave difficulties in going that far, and, as it seems to me, superintendent Williams was, by reason of his position, not the alter ego of the Commissioner but merely had implied delegated authority, by reason of his position, from the Commissioner."

Lord Parker went on to deal with and to reject the consequent argument, that the further delegation from superintendent to inspector was contrary to legal principle, holding that the commissioner had impliedly delegated not only the

[85] *Chief Constable of the West Midlands Police v. Birmingham Justices, P* [2002] EWHC 1087.
[86] [1970] 1 W.L.R. 4.

power but a power to delegate it. The *Carltona* principle may also be subject to two qualifications. One is that some functions are such that they cannot, consistently with the statutory purpose, be delegated at all.[87] The other is that delegation has to be to somebody suitable. As *Carltona* demonstrates, who is suitable is primarily for the office-holder to decide.

3-037   There are functions imposed upon individuals in virtue of their office which may not be delegable at all: for example the function of a health and safety inspector under s.38 of the Health and Safety at Work Act 1974. In *R (WH Smith Ltd) v Croydon Justices*,[88] Elias J. said at para.15:

> ". . .where the power to take certain steps is given to an officer appointed pursuant to statute then it is only going to be in a very exceptional case that the courts will imply a power to delegate in the absence of any express provision."

He cited in support a passage from De Smith, Woolf and Jowell, *Judicial Review of Administrative Action*:[89]

> "Where the exercise of a discretionary power is entrusted to a named officer—e.g. a chief officer of police, a medical officer of health or an inspector—another officer cannot exercise his powers in his stead unless express statutory provision has been made for the appointment of a deputy or unless in the circumstances the administrative convenience of allowing a deputy or other subordinate to act as an authorised agent very clearly outweighs the desirability of maintaining the principle that the officer designated by statute should act personally."

3-038   The consequences of deciding to commence proceedings without proper authorisation are grave. In the *WH Smith* case the applicant sought judicial review of the justices' decision that informations issued by the local authority for their prosecution for breaches of health and safety legislation were valid. It submitted that the charges could not be tried because, although the local authority in instituting the proceedings had acted upon instructions from the health and safety inspector, the commencement of legal action was reserved to the inspector alone by virtue of s.38 of the Health and Safety at Work etc. Act 1974. It was held, granting the application and quashing the decision, that the inspector had neither the express nor the implied authority to delegate the power conferred upon him by s.38, and so therefore the justices had no power to hear the charges.

3-039   At common law, confidential information cannot be used for another purpose without the express consent of the individual concerned. Most personal information provided to a local authority for a specific purpose will give rise to a duty of confidentiality. There are a number of exceptions. It may be disclosed if it is in the public interest.[90] Note also the Human Rights Act 1988: under Art.8(1) of the Convention, respect for private and family life, most disclosures of personal information will amount to a breach and must therefore be justified under Art.8(2). In *R. (on the application of Robertson) v Wakefield MDC*,[91] the applicant sought judicial review of the refusal of an electoral registration officer, to grant his request to have his name and address removed

---

[87] *See R v Chief Constable of Greater Manchester Exp. Lainton*, CA, unreported, March 28, 2000 para.28.
[88] Unreported, November 6, 2000.
[89] De Smith, Woolf and Jowell *Judical Review of Administrative Action* (5th edn, Sweet & Maxwell, 1999), p.66.
[90] *AH-Gen v Guardian Newspapers (No.2)* [1990] 1 A.C. 109.
[91] [2002] Q.B. 1052.

from copies of the electoral register supplied to commercial organisations. Under the Representation of the People Regulations 1986 the officer was obliged to supply copies of the register to any person who paid the prescribed fee. The applicant wrote to the registration officer to say that he did not intend to complete the application form for inclusion on the ground that he objected to the practice of selling copies to commercial interests. The applicant argued that the 1986 Regulations did not allow for "the data subject's right to object" as provided by the Data Protection Directive 95/46 Art.14(b); and that his right to family and private life under Art.8 of the Convention had been infringed. The application was allowed. Maurice Kay J. held that Art.14(b) of the Directive had been successfully implemented into national law by s.11 of the Data Protection Act 1998. However, the right to object under s.11 had not been transposed into the 1986 Regulations, so that the registration officer had administered the register unlawfully. Secondly, the disclosure of personal details exposed electors to invasive marketing strategies so that, prima facie, Art.8 had been engaged. In particular, the failure to afford electors a right of objection was disproportionate to the legitimate economic aim of maintaining a commercially available register.

A particular problem concerns the exchange of information between authorities, especially personal or confidential information. The police may provide any such information where the common law duty to detect and prevent crime is activated. Other authorities are not subject to any such duty. Hence, s.115 of the Crime and Disorder Act 1998 provides that any person (including other authorities or any person acting on their behalf) can lawfully disclose information, where necessary or expedient for the purposes of any provision of the 1998 Act, to a chief officer of a police, a police authority, a local authority, probation service or health authority. Note also s.17 of the 1998 Act. The Guidance suggests that this section can authorise the disclosure of information in civil proceedings. For example, it might cover the sharing of information about the criminal history of a tenant in eviction proceedings under the Housing Act 1985 on the ground of anti-social or criminal behaviour, which could be considered a measure to reduce crime in the area. While the police may rely upon their common law duty, s.115 imposes a mere power. Therefore, authorities may still be bound by common law duties of confidence or statutes controlling the disclosure of information such as the Data Protection Act 1998. **3-040**

Under the common law rule, confidential information may be disclosed if it is in the public interest.[92] An instance is *Woolgar v Chief Constable of Sussex*[93], in which the applicant, a nurse, appealed against the refusal of an injunction restraining the chief constable from disclosing the contents of a police interview under caution to the United Kingdom Central Council for Nursing Midwifery and Health Visiting (the UKCC). Following a patient's death, she was interviewed by the police over alleged drug misuse, but the information obtained was insufficient to sustain criminal proceedings. The UKCC had launched its own investigation, following a referral by the local health authority, and made a request for information to the police. This was resisted by the Royal College of Nursing on the applicant's behalf. The applicant argued that she was reasonably entitled to assume that her comments in the interview would be treated as confidential, unless later used to found criminal charges, and that her reasonable belief was reinforced by the wording of the caution. Further, the preservation of confidentiality was essential to secure the ongoing supply of information to the police and provide confidence that such information would not be used for other purposes. The Court of Appeal dismissed **3-041**

---

[92] *Campbell v Frisbee* [2002] E.M.L.R. 31; *Campbell v MGN Ltd* [2003] 1 All E.R. 224.
[93] [2000] 1 W.L.R. 25.

the appeal. Comments made in police interviews were confidential and remained so even if not used in criminal proceedings.[94] However, disclosure to a regulatory body could be justified in the absence of consent, if it was justified by the public interest in the proper functioning of the regulatory body. Even so, confidentiality attached to such material would be preserved where a regulatory body operating in the field of public health and safety sought disclosure of material relevant to its own internal investigation. Disclosure in the instant case was further justified under Art.8 of the European Convention on Human Rights. The Court held that the police could disclose material even without a request for disclosure from a regulatory body, if they felt it was necessary, but, in every case, the competing viewpoints should be weighed carefully. It was desirable, unless impracticable, that, where the police were minded to disclose, they should inform the individual affected, in order that an application to the court could be made if required.

The Multi-Agency Approach

3-042   In Chapter One, we observed that the multi-agency approach is a key part of the government's anti-social behaviour and disorder policy. We discussed in Chapter One and Two major changes observed by numerous commentators in policing and criminal justice in the United Kingdom over the past decade, in the shift away from "penal welfarism" to a system which is more punitive, but also more managerial and restorative. An aspect of that change, according to some writers, was the proliferation of "preventative safety partnerships". It is a development that straddles both Conservative and Labour party administrations in the late 1980s and 1990s. Home Officer Circular 8/1984 laid down the principle that crime prevention should be a significant and integral goal of local and national public policy. It stressed the need for a co-ordinated approach and joint strategies involving partnership. Then, in the Morgan Report[95], the concept of "community safety" was introduced, and that crime reduction should be "holistic", covering both situational and social approaches. It noted that crime reduction was a peripheral issue for major agencies and a core activity of none of them and so advocated the development of multi-agency crime prevention co-ordinated by local authorities. The Safer Cities was launched in March 1988 by the Home Office as its contribution to the Action for Cities Programme: a local steering committee with representatives from local government, police, probation, voluntary bodies and commerce was established in each project area; project co-ordinators were tasked with undertaking a crime audit and developing a three-year strategy and annual action plans. In 1992, 40 new schemes were established, each running for three years. Following the introduction of the Crime and Disorder Act 1998, the consultation document *Getting to Grips with Crime: A New Framework for Local Action* set out the government's intention to provide a new legislative framework to maximise the contribution of all the key partners to crime prevention and community safety and one which, it was intended, would give local people an opportunity to contribute to the process. The document acknowledged the importance of the Morgan Report and its assertion of the need for broadly based multi-agency approaches to crime prevention, and the need to involve voluntary and business sectors as partners. It noted that one of the biggest barriers to progress was the lack of a statutory role for local authorities. Crime prevention strategies should be targeted on a manageable geographic and demographic area to provide a recognisable commu-

[94] *Taylor v Director of the Serious Fraud Office* [1999] 2 A.C. 177.
[95] "Safer Communities: the Local Delivery of Crime Prevention through the Partnership Approach" Home Office Standing Conference on Crime Prevention August 1991.

nity upon whose needs they could focus. There were no cost implications for this proposed legislation:

"It costs nothing to make crime one of the factors which is routinely considered when, say, new policies for the delivery of social services are planned, or new housing estates are built . . . The proposals set out in this paper are not about requiring local government to deliver a major new service, or to take on substantial new burdens. Their aim is to give the vital work of preventing and reducing crime a new focus across a very wide range of local services, including . . . those provided by local authorities. It is a matter of putting crime and disorder considerations at the heart of decision making, where they have always belonged."

Local authorities are required to develop and implement strategies on their own and also in partnership with other local agencies. The main multi-agency partnership in the area of urban renewal at the local level is the Local Strategic Partnership (the LSP). Part of the LSP's strategic function is to consider anti-social behaviour in their areas and how to deal with it. More particularly, local authorities are required to enter into Crime and Disorder Reduction Partnerships (CDRPs) with other local agencies with an interest or role in controlling anti-social behaviour and in which local authorities and police authorities are likely to take the leading role. There are also several comparatively new local agencies, particularly those dealing with children and young people, having their own independent functions but also having a role in the development and implementation of local and regional strategy. **3-043**

Local Strategic Partnerships
Section 4 of the Local Government Act 2000 provides that every local authority shall prepare a "Community Strategy for promoting or improving the economic, social and environmental well-being of their area and contributing to the achievement of sustainable development in the United Kingdom." Statutory guidance on Community Strategies, to which local authorities must have regard in discharge this duty, is that these strategies are to be produced in partnership with all local delivery agencies and their communities. The 2000 guidance also announced the creation of Local Strategic Partnerships (LSPs), underlying an expectation on local authorities to seek the participation of local stakeholders in this process, through the relevant LSP where possible. The LSP has a formal role in agreeing to the expenditure of the neighbourhood renewal fund, and LSPs in receipt of NRF must also produce a Local Neighbourhood Renewal Strategy, often as part of the Community Strategy, setting out how they will narrow the gap between the most deprived neighbourhoods and others. Those LSP's pooling funding within their Local Area Agreement must include six mandatory neighbourhood renewal outcomes within the agreement. These outcomes cover the six key neighbourhood renewal themes (crime, education, health, housing, liveability and unemployment). Two main styles have been adopted by LSPs: advisory and commissioning.[96] Advisory LSPs typically have a large membership working to build consensus and acting to co-ordinate and make recommendations. A commissioning LSP, on the other hand, makes decisions, commissions action and is actively involved in the delivery of the Community Strategy and Neighbourhood Renewal floor targets, a less common model outside the most deprived local areas. **3-044**

[96] "Local Strategic Partnerships: Shaping their future" (2005) Office of the Deputy Prime Minister.

3-045   LSPs were originally envisaged as "a partnership of partnerships":[97]

> "Proliferation of these separate partnerships can lead to fragmentation, duplication and inefficiency. LSPs were established in part to bring some order to this situation by placing themselves at the apex of local partnership arrangements... LSPs will be able to slot any statutory partnerships into their emerging structure."

Departmental guidance in 2005 required LSPs to ensure that partnership arrangements were inclusive, meaning that members from all sectors of the LSP should agree the partnership structure and have adequate opportunity to influence and hold to account members of the executive. It was important that, as far as possible, boards and the core membership of LSPs reflect the diversity of their area. The lead representative from each of the main thematic partnerships, such as the Children's Trust and Crime and Disorder Reduction Partnerships would be expected to be a core member of the board, as would a senior planner.

Crime and Disorder Reduction Partnerships

3-046   Under s.5 of the Crime and Disorder Act 1998, local authorities,[98] the police, health authorities, police and probation committees are required to work together to deal with the problems of crime and disorder in their area, as defined in s.6 of the 1998 Act. Other agencies may be specified by the Secretary of State under s.5 of the 1998 Act. Section 6 of the 1998 Act provides that the above authorities shall "...formulate and implement, for each relevant period, a strategy for the reduction of crime and disorder in the area". Before doing so, they must first carry out a review of "the levels and patterns of crime and disorder in the area (taking due account of the knowledge and experience of persons in the area)"; prepare an analysis of the results of that review; publish in the area a report of that analysis; and obtain the views on that report from persons or groups in the area.[99] The strategy must include the objectives to be pursued by the authorities and other co-operating persons or bodies and the long-term and short-term performance targets for measuring the extent to which these objectives have been achieved.[1] Having formulated the strategy, the authorities are to publish in the one document the review and reports about crime and disorder, and the strategy, including the objectives and performance targets.[2] While there is a duty to review the strategy and monitor its effectiveness, the relevant period is for three years.[3]

3-047   There are more than 370 such partnerships in England and Wales. Guidance issued by the Home Office about crime and disorder plans recommended the involvement of senior officers and managers such as the chief executive of the local authority. In areas where there is a two tier system of local government, county councils were to work on an equal basis with district councils, but it is suggested that the strategies themselves should be focused on the district level area. The police plan and the crime and disorder strategy should be consistent and supplementary with regard to each other. The strategies are to be based on the findings of the local crime and disorder audit and should address issues that

---

[97] Local Government White Paper 2001 'Strong Local Leadership—Quality Public Services'.
[98] Local authority has the same meaning as under s.270(1) of the Local Government Act 1972. Further, the council for each local government area and where the area is a district and the council is not a unitary authority, the council for the county that includes the district: Crime and Disorder Act 1998, s.5(3).
[99] Crime and Disorder Act 1998, s.6(2).
[1] *ibid.*, s.6(4).
[2] *ibid.*, s.6(5).
[3] *ibid.*, s.6(7)(a).

are important to inhabitants from one area to another. However, the guidance recommends that authorities consider racial crime and witness intimidation, and repeat victimisation, including domestic violence. It is predicted that youth crime is likely to be an issue in virtually every local crime and disorder strategy and would be a major part of any strategy. For example, the strategy may require action regarding truancy and school exclusions as well the provision of facilities for young people; it is therefore expected that the authorities will rely heavily on youth offending teams. The authorities should also consult with Neighbourhood Watch groups, tenants associations and other voluntary and community groups, local business groups and groups representing local minorities. The audit should analyse the patterns of crime and disorder in the area in the form of an initial examination of the main patterns, followed by more detailed data collection and analysis. It should present information on the levels and patterns of crime and disorder, on the nature of offenders, crime settings, the impact of crime and the characteristics of victims. The purpose of the audit is to help set strategic priorities in the sense that it should be more than a description of the problems, but consist of judgments about which problems are particularly deserving of action. Much depends on the nature of the authority's area: the larger the area covered by the strategy, the more general are the objectives since larger areas are more likely to have more entrenched problems with crime and disorder. It is suggested that tackling fear of crime and repeat victimisation would be primary strategic objectives in most strategies.

In 2004, the government undertook to conduct a review of CDRPs:[4]   **3-048**

"There are now 354 Crime and Disorder Reduction Partnerships in England and 22 Community Safety Partnerships in Wales. Some work well, implementing robust multi-agency strategies shaped by the needs and concerns of local people, contributing to sustained reductions in crime and tangible improvements in local quality of life. However, some CDRPs are demonstrably less effective than others. For example, partnerships sometimes struggle to maintain a full contribution from key agencies. Lack of clarity about roles and responsibilities and blurred lines of accountability can lead to some agencies abrogating their responsibility for crime reduction. Furthermore, under present arrangements, CDRPs are neither fully visible nor properly accountable to the communities they serve, nor are they firmly embedded in the local democratic framework. These issues lie at the heart of the Government's reform programme. The Government's overriding aim is to make CDRPs the most effective possible vehicle for tackling crime, anti-social behaviour and substance misuse their communities. In support of this, we intend to review formally the partnership provisions of the Crime and Disorder Act 1998 (as amended by the Police Reform Act 2002). The review will consider which aspects of existing legislation are most effective and which have been less successful and why. It will recommend legislative and other changes to enable local agencies to work together more effectively with local people to combat crime, anti-social behaviour and drug misuse in their communities."

The results of review were published in 2006.[5] These were the main recom-   **3-049**
mendations:

(1) splitting the strategic and the operational decision making responsibilities of CDRPs, so that the CDRPs at district level would be able to concentrate on delivery;

---

[4] *Building Communities, Beating Crime: A Better Policing Service for the 21st Century* Cm.6360 (2004), p.158.
[5] Home Office, "Review of the partnership provisions of the Crime and Disorder Act 1998— Report of findings", January 2006.

(2) encouraging mergers of CDRPs, as "too often, smaller CDRPs lack the critical mass and infrastructure they need";

(3) increasing the number of merged CDRPs would facilitate "greater coterminosity across agency boundaries";

(4) changing the requirement for CDRPs to produce three yearly audits of crime and disorder in their area, and instead asking them to undertake regular strategic assessments, on at least a six monthly basis, to produce rolling community safety plans;

(5) giving agencies in the partnerships a duty rather than a power to share depersonalised information;

(6) requiring CDRPs to produce regular reports to their communities;

(7) dispensing with the requirement to produce an annual report for the Home Secretary;

(8) ensuring that local authority cabinet members with the community safety portfolio should sit on the Local Strategic Partnership with strategic responsibility for the CDRPs in the area;

(9) extending the powers of local authority Overview and Scrutiny Committees to encompass the work of CDRPs/CSPs.

3-050   Schedule 6 of the Police and Justice Bill amends the Crime and Disorder Act 1998 to allow the Secretary of State to change the list of "responsible authorities" with regard to CDRPs by order. It also extends the scope of the strategies which CDRPs must formulate so as to include anti-social behaviour, behaviour which otherwise adversely affects the local environment, and combating alcohol and other substances as well as drugs. Paragraph 5 of Sch.6 places "relevant authorities" under a duty to share depersonalised data for the purposes of reducing crime and disorder. Clause 15 would insert a new s.21A into the Local Government Act 2000 to extend the remit of local authority overview and scrutiny committees to ensure that they review and scrutinise or make reports or recommendations on CDRPs. It also introduces the notion of "the community call for action".

"Community Call for Action"
3-051   In the 2004 White Paper, where there was a particular problem with crime or anti-social behaviour which was not being adequately dealt with, there should be a trigger for local action:[6]

> "Communities rely on the police and their partners to use the powers that only they have available to them to keep their communities safe. They need to be given a guarantee that when faced with a problem that requires the use of those powers, action will be taken on their behalf. The Government does not want to see local communities being left to fend for themselves because they have not been able to get a response from local agencies. Neither do we want the police or local authorities to be left to deal with recurring problems because they cannot get one or more of their partners to take action to resolve them. The Government therefore proposes introducing a specific mechanism to trigger such action. The Government considers that one option could be to strengthen the role of local councillors in this respect by giving them the right to trigger action on the part of police and other relevant agencies when they are presented with acute or persistent problems of

---

[6] *Building Communities, Beating Crime: A Better Policing Service for the 21st Century* Cm.6360 (2004), pp.70–1.

crime or anti-social behaviour to which local communities have been unable to get an effective response. This would not be about individual complaints—nor could it be triggered by individuals—but rather by community groups, after persistent efforts to secure action have come to nothing. This power would give elected representatives greater ability to obtain a solution for their communities. This new power would give communities a greater guarantee that they will be properly protected. But we recognise that it will be vital to put in place sufficient safeguards to prevent malicious or vexatious use of the power or its misuse by groups with extremist views. Councillors would have to demonstrate that the case met certain conditions before they were able to invoke the trigger power. Agencies would be able to decline requests under certain circumstances if, for example, they were frivolous, vexatious or would involve a disproportionate burden on agencies. We are proposing that this should be an avenue of last resort rather than a mainstream way of doing business."

See also the Respect Action Plan: **3-052**

"In the police reform White Paper, Building Communities, Beating Crime, we committed to introducing a power that will give local communities a formal way to request and ensure that action is taken by the police, local authorities and others in response to persistent anti-social behaviour or community safety problems. Or if that action is not taken—they will know why not publicly. We will place a duty on district level ward councillors to consider issues, and respond within a prescribed timescale. The majority of problems should be resolved at this stage. However, for particularly difficult problems the councillor will have a new power to refer them to the scrutiny committee of the local authority. The committee would have a duty to consider any referred issue and respond within a prescribed timescale. We will also place a duty on responsible authorities, co-operating bodies and registered social landlords to respond to the committee's report again within a prescribed timescale. At every stage local agencies will have to make public the action they will take or the reason they will not take action."

Clause 15 of the Police and Justice Bill inserts a new s.21A into the Local Government Act 2000. Under subs.(4) councillors are under a duty to respond to a call for action from anybody living or working in the area which they represent, on a crime and disorder (including anti-social behaviour and behaviour adversely affecting the environment) or substance misuse matter in that area. The ward councillor's response must indicate what (if any) action he or she proposes to take to resolve the matter. The ward councillor may refer any such matter to the scrutiny committee of the council for consideration. The ward councillor will do this when reasonable steps to resolve the problem through more informal means have been taken but have failed. If the councillor does not take the matter forward, then the person raising the matter may refer it to the local authority executive for consideration. The council executive, under subs.(5), must consider any matter referred to them, and they may refer it to the overview and scrutiny committee. That committee is required by subs.(6) to consider a crime and disorder matter referred to them by a ward councillor or the council executive, and the committee may then make a report or recommendations to the council executive or local authority; and a copy of the report must be sent to such of the responsible authorities and co-operating bodies of the CSP as it considers appropriate. These authorities and co-operating bodies which receive a copy of the report or recommendations are, under subs.(8), under a duty to consider the report or recommendations and respond to the committee indicating what (if any) action they will take.   **3-053**

3-054   According to the Regulatory Impact Assessment, responses to this proposal in the White Paper were mixed, with the Association of Chief Police Officers expressing particular concerns. Police respondents were concerned that the mechanism should not result in the adverse skewing of police activity or provide a resort for those who can shout the loudest. The APA agreed with the proposal that ward councillors should be the way to initiate the trigger. They were clear that the mechanism should result in action being taken by other partners and not simply the police. The APA favoured a moderation of the operation of the mechanism by a joint scrutiny body of local and police authority representatives. The LGA felt that there may be some value in the concept of such a mechanism, but that the practicalities needed careful consideration if it was not, in practice, to undermine partnership working. ACPO had serious concerns over the proposals, especially the possible infringement on the operational responsibility of the police service.

Local Criminal Justice Boards

3-055   There are 42 Local Criminal Justice Boards (LCJBs) in England and Wales, based on police force and criminal justice areas. Membership comprises chief officers of police, CPS, the Court Service, Youth Offending Teams, prisons officers and probation officers. LCJBs have been in place in each of the 42 criminal justice areas in England and Wales since April 1, 2003. They have replaced Area Criminal Justice Strategy Committees, Trail Issues Groups, Chief Officers' Groups and any existing Criminal Justice Boards. Local Criminal Justice Boards are responsible for local delivery of Criminal Justice Service Objectives, improvement in the delivery of justice, the service provided to victims and witnesses and securing public confidence. They are accountable to the National Criminal Justice Board, with whom they also agree local targets. In 2003/04 their priority targets were: narrowing the justice gap (bringing more offences to justice); tackling persistent offenders; improving the level of confidence in the CJS; and "The Street Crime Initiative". The Government has kept the membership of LCJBs deliberately narrow in order to focus attention on delivery, with only those holding key responsibility for the delivery of CJS targets included.

3-056   Government guidance urges CDRPs and the LCJBs to work together.[7] There are overlaps between the two agendas and so it was noted that they could reinforce each other's work. Key areas of common interest were: tackling prolific and other priority offenders, engaging communities; reducing domestic violence; and reducing re-offending. When engaging communities, CDRPs and LCJBs should seek to promote each others' work wherever possible. For example, CDRPs can help to inform communities of the work the LCJB is doing to reform the CJS, and in particular pass on to communities information on how issues of local concern are being dealt with by the CJS. In return, the LCJB can help raise awareness of CDRPs' priorities for action on local issues within the CJS. CDRPs, with their access to local partners, could help the LCJB identify and tap into key local communities. CDRPs could also allow the LCJB to add CJS-specific questions to questionnaires and other community engagement processes, focus groups and so on. The LCJB can provide access to CJS-wide media and can work to communicate key community safety/fear of crime issues through their local media links. The LCJB could add value by rationalising approaches to certain communities across the CJS area, e.g. information for Lesbian, Gay, Bisexual & Transgender communities. There was also the potential for a joint approach in relation to unpaid work. Under the Community Payback initiative over five million hours of unpaid work have been undertaken by offenders. CDRPs and LCJBs could

---

[7] "CDRPs and LCJBs: How to Work Together" Home Office, November 2005.

play an important role in enabling more local people to have a say in the type of work undertaken and in making this agenda more visible.

Youth Justice Agencies

The inquiry by Lord Laming, in January 2003, into the death Victoria Climbié **3-057** made 108 recommendations, addressing both central and local government, as well as the provision of public services. This was followed by a Green Paper, *Every Child Matters*, and the policy documents *Every Child Matters—Next Step* and *Keeping Children Safe*. The Green Paper observed that "Children's needs are complex and rarely fit neatly within one set of organisational boundaries", and highlighted that the main problem was the fragmentation of responsibilities for children among different agencies. The Government said that it ". . .wants to move to a system where the key services and budgets for children and young people are placed within a single organisational focus locally".[8] This would be done by way of Children's Trusts, the primary purpose of which would be to secure integrated commissioning leading to more integrated service delivery and better outcomes for children and young people". These trusts would be formed through the pooling of budgets and resources across the Local Education Authority, children's social services, Connexions, certain health services, and where agreed locally, Youth Offending Teams (YOTs).

A Children's Trust would not necessitate structural change or staff transfers. **3-058** Rather, they would be based on local government but engage a wide range of partners, including voluntary and community sector organisations, and determine how best to spend pooled budgets to secure the most effective integrated delivery of services, based on the overall vision agreed by all partners in the local area. The Children's Trust may also commission services on behalf of the Local Safeguarding Children Board. The Government said in the Green Paper that it was recommending that most areas should have a Children's Trust by 2006 "so that there is a strong foundation of learning in place to allow all areas to have one by 2008", adding that this would not be a matter for legislation.[9]

Hence, s.10 of the Children Act 2004 places a duty on all local authorities **3-059** in England to make arrangements to promote co-operation between the authority, the "relevant partners", and other locally determined partners, to improve the wellbeing of children in the authority's area. The arrangements must cover all children and young people under the age of 18, while s.10(9) extends the potential for the inclusion of all 18 and 19 year olds, young people aged 20 and over leaving care, and young people up to the age of 25 with learning difficulties. Taken together, these provisions ensure that the local authority can include all agencies that provide services to children and young people. The "relevant partners" must co-operate with the local authority in making arrangements to improve children's wellbeing. This duty requires them to work together with the local authority at every level in making the arrangements. The relevant partners are as follows: the district council in two tier authorities; the police authority and the chief officer of police for a police area any part of which falls within the area of the local authority; a local probation board for an area, any part of which falls within the area of the local authority; and the youth offending team (YOT). In order to deliver the outcomes for children and young people, they and local authorities with responsibility for establishing them, with the co-operation of other partners, will need to continue to discharge their statutory functions under ss.38–40 of the Crime and Disorder Act 1998, including services to the Courts, dealing with offenders and submitting Youth Justice Plans.

[8] *Every Child Matters* Cm.5860 (2003) 69–70, para.5.7.
[9] *Every Child Matters Next Steps* (2004), 18, para.2.25.

3-060   Under s.10, the local authority and the relevant partners have the power to establish and maintain a pooled fund and pool other resources for the purpose of the co-operation arrangements. Other resources are defined as staff, goods, services, accommodation or other non-pecuniary resources. Section 10(1)(c) states that other agencies that exercise functions, or are engaged in activities, in relation to children and young people should also be involved. These might include: children and young people themselves; voluntary and community sector agencies; agencies with responsibility for delivering other front-line statutory services to children, young people and their families, providers of health services (including NHS Trusts and General Practitioners), and, where appropriate, the immigration services; childcare, culture, sport and play organisations; families, carers and communities. The Act also specifically requires authorities to "have regard to" the importance of parents and other persons caring for children when making arrangements under s.10. As the universal service provider that maintains contact with most children five days a week throughout most of the year, schools are central to the drive to improve all five outcomes for children and young people. They should therefore be appropriately involved in the local children's trust co-operation arrangements.

3-061   The Children Act 2004 requires local authorities to establish and operate Local Safeguarding Children's Boards (LSCBs) as the statutory successors to Area Child Protection Committees. The work of LSCBs fits within the wider context of the children's trust, and whilst it contributes to the overall goal of improving the wellbeing (i.e. the five outcomes) of all children, it has a particular focus on aspects of the "staying safe" outcome. Whereas the children's trust has a wider role in planning and delivery of services, LSCBs are not front-line delivery organisations: their objectives are about co-ordinating and ensuring the effectiveness of what their member organisations do individually and together to safeguard and promote the welfare of children in the local authority area. They are expected to contribute to broader children's trust delivery and commissioning arrangements, for example through the Children and Young People's Plan. The role and functions of LSCBs are set out in *Working Together to Safeguard Children*:[10] a guide to interagency working to safeguard and promote the welfare of children.

3-062   Connexions brings together all the services and support young people need during their teenage years, offering differentiated and integrated support to young people through Personal Advisers (PAs). For some young people this may be just for careers advice, for others it may involve more in-depth support to help identify barriers to learning and find solutions brokering access to more specialist support, e.g. drug abuse, sexual health and homelessness. PAs work in a range of settings including schools, colleges, one-stop shop community centres and on an out-reach basis. Connexions is a national strategy delivered through a range of local partnership arrangements based either on local authority boundaries or Learning and Skills Council (LSC) boundaries. Funding is through a grant from the Secretary of State for Education and Skills.

3-063   Local Education Authorities (the statutory sector) work with a range of organisations to provide what is known as the "Youth Service". The priority age group for the Youth Service is 13–19 year olds, but the target age group may extend to 11–25 year olds in some cases. Provision is usually in the form of youth clubs, projects, information and advice and counselling services, outdoor activities, community and study support centres, or through "detached" or outreach work aimed at working with young people on their own territory, and often focused on those at risk from alcohol or drug

---

[10] 2005 and 2006.

misuse, or drifting into crime. There is an increasing emphasis on youth workers working with disadvantaged, "at risk" and socially excluded young people. The Youth Service is expected to make a vital contribution in ensuring the success of the Connexions Service, particularly in relation to the identification of young people at risk, often including the most vulnerable and disaffected. Youth workers may be best placed to act as a young person's PA. They also have specialist knowledge, extensive expertise and experience, often of working with the hardest to help young people. The Youth Service is also required to work closely in the Connexions Partnership and local management committees to assist in the making of youth service plans.[11]

Youth Offending Teams   **3-064**
   Section 37 of the Crime and Disorder Act 1998 provides:

"(1) It shall be the principal aim of the youth justice system to prevent offending by children and young persons."

Under s.38, it is the duty of each local authority,[12] acting in co-operation with the police authority and every probation committee or health authority to secure that, to such extent as is appropriate for their area, all youth justice services are available there. It shall be the duty of the police authority. "Youth justice services" means any of the following: the provision of persons to act as appropriate adults to safeguard the interests of children and young persons detained or questioned by police officers; the assessment of children and young persons, and the provision for them of rehabilitation programmes; the provision of support for children and young persons remanded or committed on bail while awaiting trial or sentence; the placement in local authority accommodation of children and young persons remanded or committed to such accommodation under s.23 of the Children and Young Persons Act 1969; the provision of reports or other information required by courts in criminal proceedings against children and young persons; the provision of persons to act as responsible officers in relation to parenting orders, child safety orders, reparation orders and action plan orders; the supervision of young persons sentenced to a probation order, a community service order or a combination order; the supervision of children and young persons sentenced to a detention and training order or a supervision order; the post-release supervision of children and young persons under s.37(4A) or 65 of the 1991 Act or s.31 of the Crime (Sentences) Act 1997. Local authorities, under s.40, are also required, after consultation with the relevant persons and bodies, to formulate and implement for each year a plan (a "youth justice plan") setting out how youth justice services in their area are to be provided and funded; and how the youth offending team or teams established by them are to be composed and funded, how they are to operate, and what functions they are to carry out.[13]

Section 41 establishes the Youth Justice Board. The Board shall consist of   **3-065**
10, 11 or 12 members appointed by the Secretary of State. The members of the Board shall include persons who appear to the Secretary of State to have extensive recent experience of the youth justice system. The Board has these functions, namely: to monitor the operation of the youth justice system and the provision of youth justice services; to advise the Secretary of State on

---

[11] "Working Together: Connexions and the Statutory Youth Service" (April, 2002).
[12] Crime and Disorder Act 1998, s.42: local authority" means (a) in relation to England, a county council, a district council whose district does not form part of an area that has a county council, a London borough council or the Common Council of the City of London; (b) in relation to Wales, a county council or a county borough council.

the operation of that system and the provision of such services, how the principal aim of that system might most effectively be pursued, the content of any national standards he may see fit to set with respect to the provision of such services, or the accommodation in which children and young persons are kept in custody, and the steps that might be taken to prevent offending by children and young persons; to monitor the extent to which that aim is being achieved and any such standards met; to obtain information from relevant authorities and to publish it. They are also required to make known and to promote good practice in the operation of the youth justice system and the provision of youth justice services, the prevention of offending by children and young persons; and working with children and young persons who are, or are at risk of becoming, offenders. It shall also make grants, with the approval of the Secretary of State, to local authorities or other bodies for them to develop such practice, or to commission research in connection with such practice.

3-066   Local authorities are under a duty to establish youth offending teams for their area. A YOT shall include at least one of the following: a probation officer; a social worker of a local authority social services department; a police officer; a person nominated by a health authority any part of whose area lies within the local authority's area; and a person nominated by the chief education officer appointed by the local authority and any other person as the local authority thinks appropriate after consulting the persons and bodies in s.38(2) of the 1998 Act.[14] The YOTs roles are: (a) to co-ordinate the provision of youth justice services for all those in the authority's area who need them; and (b) to carry out such functions as are assigned to the team or teams in the youth justice plan formulated by the authority in the youth justice plan. In more concrete terms, the functions of the YOT is to carry out specific statutory functions imposed on them, particularly in respect of managing young offenders; and also to connect with services such as education and health, and direct the young people under their supervision to help in addressing their offending behaviour.

Children

National Policy

3-067   In this part, we focus on old and new measures which are directed towards children guilty of criminal offences and anti-social behaviour. The Home Affairs Committee summarised the relationship between anti-social behaviour of children and young persons and social exclusion in these terms:

> "Whilst there have been differences amongst organisations in terms of where to put the emphasis, the clear themes to have emerged from our inquiry are that the young perpetrators of anti-social behaviour often:
> — suffer from serious disadvantages and social exclusion and
> — have significant support needs, but
> — frequently also have a disregard for the effects of their actions, and
> — are likely to progress to more serious criminal activity in the absence of appropriate intervention."[15]

---

[13] Criminal Justice Act 1991, s.40(2): in subs.(1) above "the relevant persons and bodies" means the persons and bodies mentioned in s.38(2) above and, where the local authority is a county council, any district councils whose districts form part of its area.
[14] Crime and Disorder Act 1998, s.39.

It is sufficient to say that the association between social deprivation and children and young people within the criminal justice system is compelling. In the 2003 Green Paper *Every Child Matters*, anti-social behaviour can lead to more serious criminal activity. It extends into adult life: according to a report of Her Majesty's Chief Inspector of Prisons,[16] more than a third of young adult offenders were in local authority care and half of them have no educational qualifications, many were functionally illiterate and a substantial minority were homeless immediately prior to imprisonment. The government, in the Anti-Social Behaviour White Paper, sees strong families as the key to strong communities:[17]

"These are communities where people know their neighbours and can call on them in good times and in bad. These are neighbourhoods that are safe, where parents take responsibility for their children's well-being and behaviour, where parents are confident in bringing up their children and know there are good schools and good services."

Dysfunctional families, on the other hand, can create havoc on an estate or inner city neighbourhood. In the government's view, the past approach, characterised as refraining from making demands in order not to be judgmental, alienates the victims of these families and fails children by not asserting their need for discipline by their parents.[18] In every neighbourhood, it is contended, there are a small number of families who are at the root of it and yet refuse to take help. Hence, where support and negotiation fail, the broad policy is that there should be powers to take swift action to ensure compliance and to protect the broader community.[19] At the same time, government policy is also aimed at ensuring children make a positive contribution to the community and to society. Steering children away from anti-social or offending behaviour was one of the five key outcomes that are said to matter for children in the government's green paper, *Every Child Matters*.[20] Measures to deal with anti-social behaviour in children and young people involve punishment if only to encourage a sense of responsibility but also intervention:

"When children and young people engage in anti-social behaviour or commit offences, we need to ensure that they to face up to their actions and redress the harm they have caused. We also need to ensure that the system tackles the underlying causes of such behaviour."

Further principles were outlined in the accompanying paper of youth justice.[21] The basic approach is defined in these terms:[22]

"When children and young people do become involved in crime we would continue to operate a distinct youth justice system broadly on present lines, with a clear and visible response to offending behaviour from age 10 upwards. This is the right way to maintain and indeed improve public confidence in our response to youth crime, given the evidence on reconvic-

[15] Home Affairs Committee *Anti-Social Behaviour* (Cm6588) Fifth Report, 2004–05, para.87.
[16] Home Office 1997.
[17] *Respect and Responsibility—Taking a stand against Anti-Social Behaviour* Cm.5778 (2003) p.21.
[18] *ibid.*, p.23.
[19] *ibid.*, p.34.
[20] *Every Child Matters* Cm.5860 (2003).
[21] *Youth Justice—The Next Steps*, (September, 2003).
[22] *ibid.*, para.3.

tions, that this Government's First Parliament youth justice reforms are moving us in the right direction. Our changes would build on this good foundation by making the system more flexible and effective, drawing on some of the wider risk reduction approaches as well as the simplified sentencing approach we are introducing for adults and (through the wider Green Paper work) seeking to establish closer working with other services dealing with children and young people."

3-068   The Home Office identified six "key objectives" of the new youth justice system: tackling delays, creating a sense of responsibility in young offenders, intervention to deal with the risk factors associated with re-offending, encouraging reparation to victims, and reinforcing parental responsibility.[23] In the same paper, they identify six "key themes" to achieving these objectives: partnership and multi-agencies, early intervention, reparation, parenting, more effective custodial sentences, and a national framework. Partnership and multi-agencies involve the new YOTs, in addition to the local social services authority, the police, education authorities, and probation. In *Youth Justice—The Next Steps* the main themes of the youth justice system were identified as:

"...further development of pre-court interventions in a way that reassures communities; clarifying the purposes of sentencing juveniles; completing the process of broadening interventions with parents which we are taking forward in this Session's legislation; improving young defendants' and their families' understanding of trials and trial preparation; managing young remandees in ways which help to prevent the guilty re-offending, including appropriate use of better community supervision; rationalising juvenile sentences to produce a structure which is simpler to understand, more coherent and offers maximum flexibility of interventions; establishing community intensive supervision and surveillance as the main response to repeat and more serious offending while still having custody available; introducing more graduated progression for individuals between secure, open and community facilities; and improving youth justice staff skills and organisation."

Criminal and Civil Capacity of Children in Court Proceedings

3-069   The old common law rule is that a child does not have capacity to consent to or carry out legally effective acts. Now, subject to specific rules as to capacity in certain cases usually prescribed in statute, it is a question of fact whether a child has sufficient understanding to be capable of making up its own decisions. A child will be liable for its own torts if it is capable of distinguishing between right and wrong; a parent is not prima facie liable for torts committed by his child. If the child injures others using some dangerous thing, the parent or any other person in charge of the child may be liable if they had control over it, or they were negligent in allowing the child to use it if it was known to be dangerous, or they did not exercise sufficient control over the child.[24] In civil proceedings, a child must have a litigation friend to conduct them on his behalf (unless the court orders otherwise).[25] The child may make the application; or the court may make the appointment if it is of the opinion that it is desirable for a litigation friend to act for the child.

[23] "Crime and Disorder Act 1998—Implementing the Act, Delivering the Aim" Conference, November 4, 1998.
[24] *North v Wood* [1914] 1 K.B. 629; *Dixon v Bell* (1816) 5 M. & S. 198.
[25] CPR 21.2.

Where a claimant wishes to take a step in proceedings against a child who does not have a litigation friend, he must apply to the court for an order appointing a litigation friend. The litigation friend is not a party and is an officer of the court appointed to look after the child's interests.[26] Except where a court has made on order permitting a child to conduct proceedings without a litigation friend, a person may not, without the permission of the court, make an application against a child before proceedings have started, or take any steps whatsoever in the proceedings except the issue and service of a claim form. Any steps taken before a child has a litigation friend have no effect. Where a claim is made by, or on behalf of, a child or against a child, no settlement, compromise or payment and no acceptance of money paid into court is valid without the court's approval;[27] the court must also approve settlements relating to appeals and applications.[28] The court cannot compel a compromise and will not sanction one against the opinion of the litigation friend.[29] An injunction may be granted against a child, but not an order for specific performance; and a court will not order specific performance at the suit of a child.[30] A claimant who is a child is bound by a judgment or order to the same extent as an adult. A judgment against a child who is a defendant is binding in the same way, except that if it was obtained without the appointment or approval of the litigation friend, it will be set aside.[31] A child claimant is not personally liable for costs of legal proceedings. Subject to the court's discretion, a successful defendant may be able to recover costs from the litigation friend;[32] and the litigation friend may be able to recover costs from the child's property.[33] A child defendant has not usually been ordered to pay costs except for fraud.[34] A litigation friend is not liable to pay the costs of an unsuccessful defence unless he is guilty of gross misconduct.[35]

In criminal proceedings, every court dealing with a child[36] or young person, as an offender or otherwise, is required to have regard to their welfare; and, where appropriate, take steps for removing the child from undesirable surroundings and ensure that the child receives proper provision for his education and training.[37] It is now conclusively presumed that no child under the age of 10 years can be guilty of a criminal offence; s.34 of the Crime and Disorder Act 1998 abolished the rule, this presumption applied to child between the ages of 10 and 14.

3-070

History of the Juvenile Criminal Justice System and Restorative Justice

Government responses to children and young people who break the law have vacillated in England and Wales, as in other countries, between a welfare approach and a more repressive approach emphasising punishment. Some writers have identified in other European countries a more lasting commitment to welfarism and to maintaining a separation of young people

3-071

---

[26] *Sinclair v Sinclair* (1845) 13 M. & W. 640.
[27] CPR 21.10(1).
[28] PD 52.
[29] *Re Birchall, Wilson v Birchall* (1880) 16 ChD 41.
[30] *Lumley v Ravenscroft* [1895] 1 Q.B. 683; *Flight v Bolland* (1828) 4 Russ 298.
[31] *Henry v Archibald* (1871) IR 5 Eq 559.
[32] *Slaughter v Talbot* (1739) Willes 190, *Flight v Bolland, ibid.*
[33] CPR 21.43(3); PD 21, 2.3(2)(e).
[34] *Woolf v Woolf* [1899] 1 Ch. 343.
[35] *Morgan v Morgan* (1865) 11 Jur NS 233; *Rutter v Rutter* [1921] P 136, 141–142.
[36] For the purposes of the Children and Young Persons Act 1933, a young person is a person aged 14 and under 17 years: s.31(2).
[37] Children and Young Persons Act 1933, s.44(1).

from the adult system; policy in England and Wales, on the other hand, emulating policy shifts in the USA, has moved towards a "dramatic repenalization of youth offending".[38] Compared to its European neighbours, and other parts of the UK, it has traditionally adopted a more punitive and less welfare-oriented approach to youth justice.[39] Since the Second World War there have been a significant number of shifts in government policy towards young offenders, often with policy swinging between an emphasis upon "care/welfare" and "control/punishment", as the political mood has changed.

3-072   As Baroness Hale in *R v Durham Constabulary, Ex p. R*[40] observed, both national and international law recognise that the criminal justice system is part of the process of bringing up children to be decent law-abiding members of the community. The straightforward retributive response, which is proper in the case of an adult offender, is modified to meet the needs of the individual child. For example, r.5 of the Beijing Rules 1985:[41]

> "The juvenile justice system shall emphasise the well-being of the juvenile and shall ensure that any reaction to juvenile offenders shall always be in proportion to the circumstances of both the offenders and the offence."

Under the rules, the first objective of juvenile justice is the promotion of the well-being of the juvenile, whether or not they are dealt with in family courts or the criminal justice system. The second objective is proportionalilty, which aims to limit what otherwise might be the excessive interventions motivated by the welfare principle. While the Beijing Rules are not binding on member states, they are reflected in the UN Convention of the Rights of the Child 1989, Art.3.1:

> "In all actions concerning children, whether undertaken by public or private social welfare institutions, courts of law, administrative authorities or legislative bodies, the best interests of the child shall be a primary consideration."

Note also Art.37 in which arrest, detention are imprisonment are said to be measures of last resort in the case of a child, and no child shall be separated from adults unless it is considered in the child's best interests to do so. Article 40 requires states, in the case of a child accused of infringing the criminal law, to take into account the child's age and the desirability or promoting the child's re-integration into society. Article 40.3 encourages measures for dealing with children accused of criminal offences without resort to judicial proceedings, and Art.40.4 encourages educational and welfare based community disposals to ensure the child is dealt with in a manner appropriate to their well-being and proportionate to their circumstances and the offence.

3-073   Newburn identifies three distinct phases in the history of government response to offending by children and young people.[42] In the 1960s, the dominant assumption was that punitive sanctions were ineffective, but that other social and welfare interventions could produce positive effects. Initially, the

---

[38] See Ros Burnett, Catherine Appleton "Joined-Up Services to Tackle Youth Crime" (2002) 44 Brit. J. Criminol. 34; Muncie J, "Policy Transfers and What Works: Some Reflections on Comparative Youth Justice," *Youth Justice*, 1/3: 27–35.

[39] Crawford and Newborn, "Recent developments in restorative justice for Young People in England and Wales" (2002), 42 Brit. J. Criminol. 476.

[40] [2005] WL 607489.

[41] United Nations Minimum Standard Rules for the Administration of Juvenile Justice (1985).

[42] Newburn "Youth Crime and Justice" in M. Maguire, R. Morgan and R. Reiner, eds., *The Oxford Handbook of Criminology*, (Oxford University Press, 1997), pp.613–60.

Children and Young Persons Act 1933 was the primary statute in regard to the magistrates juvenile court in criminal and care and protection proceedings aged 8 to 16; the Criminal Justice Act 1948 introduced the concept of the "short, sharp, shock" of detention centre orders as a trade-off for the abolition of flogging as a sentence.[43] Section 34 of the Crime and Disorder Act 1998 abolished the rebuttable presumption that a child between the ages of 10 and 14 years is incapable of committing an offence. At 10 years, the age of criminal responsibility in England and Wales is the second lowest in Europe (lower still, at eight years, in Scotland).[44] In *R v Durham Constabulary, Ex p. R*,[45] Lord Bingham observed that the comparatively low age of criminal responsibility in the UK made it possible to prosecute young offenders who have not entered their teens, but it has long been recognised as undesirable in many cases for young offenders to be drawn into the process of the criminal courts unless it was really necessary. At para.2:

> "So informal procedures grew to deal with cases which were not so serious as to leave no realistic alternative to prosecution. There were always of course some cases which, although disclosing a breach of the criminal law, were so trivial as to be properly ignored or dealt with by informal and unrecorded advice of admonition. But there were other cases which were too serious to be dealt with in that way but not so serious as necessarily to call for prosecution."

During the 1960s, the main aim of child welfare oriented policy-makers was to decriminalise responses to juvenile offenders. Ball cites as the rationale at the time for encouraging the use of cautions a comment in a 1960 Home Office Committee Report:

> "Since a conviction may have serious consequences for a young person's career, there is a natural reluctance to prosecute... A caution spares offenders the stigma of a court appearance and may preserve whatever deterrent effect is presented by the threat of prosecution. A caution may be given in the hope that if a juvenile is not immediately treated as a delinquent then there is less chance of his behaving like one in the future."

Reforms were planned by the Labour Government in the 1960s, based on the Scottish children's hearing system under the Social Work (Scotland) Act 1968,[46] which diverted children away from the criminal justice system into a specialist child care system. See also the Children and Young Persons Act 1969 which, as originally designed, would have replaced the prosecution of children under the age of 14 with care proceedings, where only welfare disposals were possible, and also restricted the prosecution of young persons of 14 but under 17. Following the change of government in 1970, the reforms were never implemented fully, but the 1969 Act as implemented favoured supervision over punitive measures and care orders, administered by local social services authorities rather than probation and prison services.

From the mid-1970s until the early 1990s, there was a growing view that **3-074** state intervention per se was ineffective and costly. This pragmatic view persisted, Newburn argues, despite periodic punitive mood swings which saw the

---

[43] See Ball, "Youth Justice? Half a Century of Responses to Youth Offending" (2004) Crim. L.R. pp.167–180.

[44] 14 in Germany, 16 in Spain, 18 in Belgium.

[45] [2005] WL 607489.

[46] Described by Baroness Hale as the high watermark of the welfare based system in *Ex p. R*, at para.30.

reassertion of the disciplinary hard edge of Conservative "law and order", such as the ultimately unsuccessful introduction of the "short, sharp, shock" initiative in the early 1980s. Increased responsibilities for local authority social workers existed alongside traditional judicial procedures. Throughout the 1970s, the use of custodial sentences and care orders, including removal from home, increased relentlessly. However, in 1979, the incoming Conservative government through the Criminal Justice Acts 1982 and 1988 replaced indeterminate Borstal training with fixed term sentences, training for young adult and juvenile offenders and the encouragement of the use of the caution directed at controlling the use of custody resulted in a drop of about 20 per cent in juvenile custody rates between 1981 and 1988. In 1979, there were 7,700 children in custody and 1,600 in 1991; 85 per cent of those cautioned in the late 1980s were not convicted for a further standard list of offences within two years; whereas the earlier a male offender has his first court appearance, the more liable he is to re-offend. The Children Act 1989 removed magistrates' child care and protection from the juvenile court to the family courts.[47] Home Office guidance throughout the period had three essential conditions to be met before a young offender could be cautioned: there had to be enough evidence to support a prosecution; the young offender had to admit the offence; and the parent or guardian had to give informed consent to the giving of a caution. Pratt writes that the debate about justice and welfare was something of a "sideshow" in this period, and that a new form of penological discourse and practice was emerging in juvenile justice: namely "corporatism".[48] Efficient and effective "management" of the offending population was now to the fore, legitimated by the rediscovery that "something works"; that "something" being the infliction of a "just measure of (community-based) pain". The emergent managerialist and actuarialist discourses of the late 1980s were joined in the early 1990s by the embracing of "populist punitiveness" by politicians on both sides of the House of Commons.

3-075   As Ball argues, the moral panic surrounding the murder of Jamie Bulger by two ten year olds in 1993, along with increased media interest at the time in youth offending, prompted more punitive measures, such as Home Secretary guidance in 1994 which removed acknowledgement of the vulnerability of young people and discouraged the use of more than one caution for young offenders, despite Home Office research that only 8 per cent of a sample of offenders cautioned in 1991 had more than two cautions. Accordingly, there followed a rapid rise in court appearances and in the use of custody for young offenders. Since then there has been a discernable erosion of the principle of preferential treatment of young offenders. Instead of perceiving a child offender as lacking the competence to think their actions through and being capable of outgrowing their troublesome behaviour, children are now treated as fully competent, aware of the repercussions of their actions and mature enough to accept responsibility for them in the form of appropriate punishment.[49] Bottoms argues that there are reasons for the attractiveness of this new "disciplinary common sense":[50] it is popular because of the belief that increased punitiveness may be effective in reducing crime through general deterrence and incapacitation; secondly, because it is hoped that it will help foster a sense of moral consensus around issues where currently dissension or moral pluralism exists; and thirdly, because politicians believe that it will be a

---

[47] Home Office Office Statistical Bulletin 20/92, and 14/95.
[48] "Corporatism: The Third Model of Juvenile Justice", Brit. J. Criminol. (1989) 29/3: p.236–54.
[49] Ball, citing Fionda, "Youth Justice", in Foonda (ed) *Legal Concepts of Childhood* (Hart Publishing, 2001), at p.77.
[50] "The Philosophy and Politics of Punishment and Sentencing", in C. Clarkson and R. Morgan, (eds.) *The Politics of Sentencing Reform* (Clarendon Press, 1995) pp.17–49.

vote-winner. It was under these circumstances, and against a backdrop of successive electoral failures, that New Labour sought to redefine itself in the law and order landscape. In opposition, New Labour drew on the managerialism of the justice model, and added its own blend of communitarianism and populism.[51]

Further reform proposals followed the election of the Labour Government in 1997: the 1997 White Paper, tellingly entitled *No More Excuses*, lead to the enactment of the Crime and Disorder Act 1998 and the Youth Justice and Criminal Evidence Act 1999. These reforms included: the aim of prevention as the main aim of the youth justice system, the establishment of youth justice boards and youth offending teams, the replacement of reprimands and warnings for cautions, and the creation of referral orders. There were two problems identified with the caution system: contrary to the Home Office own figures (as noted above), there was a perception that a significant number of offenders were cautioned several times; secondly, and more significantly, there was an opportunity, which was not taken, to intervene constructively to address the offender's personal circumstances and so obviate the risk of repeat offending. The welfare-based proposals of the 1969 Act had been replaced by a much more specifically punitive range of sentencing criteria and disposals, including custodial sentences the use of which, as Baroness Hale noted in *Ex p. R*, had "rocketed" in recent years.[52] She notes the report of the Joint Committee on Human Rights to the UN Convention on the Rights of the Child 2002–2003 in which it is noted that on January 31, 2002, there were nearly 3,000 children under 18 in custody on England and Wales, twice as many as ten years ago, and during a period when recorded offending by children had been in decline. In line with the European average during the early 1990s, the numbers of juvenile and young offenders increased significantly between 1995 and 1997, since when they have remained largely stable. Thus, the number of 15 to 17 years olds detained (in prisons) on June 30, 1995 was 1,675, rising to 2,479 on the same date in 1997. On December 31, 2004 the corresponding figure stood at 2,169. An equivalent pattern obtains for young offenders (between the ages of 18 and 20); on June 30, 1995, 5,872 were detained, rising to 7,684 on the same date in 1997, and standing at 8,073 on the last day of last year.[53] Yet, at the same time, the new system was linked to constructive intervention, through referral to the youth offending team and might involve a conference enabling the offender to understand his offence and to make amends. However, even diversionary schemes should be implemented consistently with a child's human rights and legal safeguards. Hence, Baroness Hale:

3-076

"The rigidity of the scheme undermines the emphasis given to diverting children away from the criminal justice system, propels them onto it and on a higher rung of the ladder earlier than they would have previously have arrived there and seriously risks offending the principle that intervention must be proportionate both to the circumstances of the offender and the offence."

The Council for Europe Human Rights Commissioner, in his 2005 report, considered the two themes of the juvenile criminal justice system and also the anti-social behaviour in respect of children, penal enforcement and interventionism as "a curious contradiction in policy", which he said

3-077

[51] "Tackling Youth Crime and Reforming. Youth Justice: The Origins and Nature of "New Labour" Policy", *Policy Studies* (1998) 19(3/4): pp.199–211.

[52] White Paper *No more excuses*, para.38.

[53] Report by Mr Alvaro Gil-Robles, Commissioner for Human Rights, on his visit to the United Kingdom, June 8, 2005, para.86.

reflected a broader disparity between the reality of juvenile crime and the perception of it:

> "Whilst the British Crime Survey suggests that youth crime has marginally decreased over the last few years this is not the general public perception—in a recent survey, 75% of interviewees believed it rather to have worsened. I was struck, moreover, by the insistence with which MPs, of all parties, informed me of the concerns in their constituencies over crime and anti-social behaviour. The frequency with which such complaints were raised during constituency meetings led almost all I spoke to stress the need to strike an appropriate balance between individual and collective rights in order to protect the quality of life of the community—the implication being, of course, that the former had for too long been privileged at the expense of the latter."

His overall impression was that more effort might be expended on explaining the successes of positive reforms and presenting an accurate picture of juvenile crime, rather than concocting new measures, which may well inspire confidence through empowering local communities to act themselves, but which would appear neither necessary nor appropriate. The high levels of youth detention would appear to suggest a lack of suitable alternatives, he said, but, as he noted, a wide range of alternatives already exists. He believed that magistrates and judges do not yet have sufficient confidence in these alternatives and, at the same time, the judiciary faced considerable pressure from a public opinion generally in favour of strict custodial sentences.[54]

3-078   The Home Affairs Committee in its report on anti-social behaviour approved of the following remarks put to them in evidence from Centrepoint:

> "People who commit anti-social behaviour are often among the most vulnerable in society and can have complex mental health needs or drug and alcohol addiction. Young people who behave in an anti-social way are often making the difficult transition into independent adulthood, in many cases from a background including care, homelessness or time in a young offender's institution and just like older perpetrators of anti-social behaviour they need support to address and manage behaviour."[55]

The committee also considered remarks by a police officer:

> "I have done 400 acceptable behaviour contracts. Not one of those young people were actually doing anti-social behaviour because they wanted to do it. A lot of them did not know it was anti-social behaviour; we had to re-educate them. In the lives of those 400 people, 10% were known to the youth justice system and were going through the courts and getting the support that they would be offered but 69% were known to child protection due to drugs, drink, mental health issues, tenancy issues, domestic issues in the family, lack of parental guidance or peer group pressure. All these issues were underlying the consequences of the bad behaviour."[56]

The committee also noted comments that it was important not to group all young people together: children who annoy residents by playing football in the

---

[54] He commented: "I was even informed by a member of the judiciary of the publication in the press of the names and photos of judges considered by editorial staff to have been too lenient in their sentencing."
[55] Home Office Committee Report, para.88.
[56] *ibid.*, para.89.

street do not have the same characteristics as those who terrorise local neighbourhoods. A member of the Family Welfare Association and JUSTICE, the committee said, expressed concerns that overly sensitive people may object to children playing in the common area of an estate or on a street; many children were unlikely to be any worse than similar children a generation ago and that what has changed are the communities around them. Nonetheless, the committee concluded:

> "...Activities such as playing football in the street are not necessarily harmless: persistent use of a garden gate, house wall or car or other inappropriate locations as goalposts—perhaps accompanied by abuse or threats when challenged—can amount to intolerable behaviour which should not be dismissed by the authorities."

The committee noted that there had been a dramatic change from what it called "welfare" to "justice" as the fundamental principle of the juvenile justice system. This translated in moderns into "intervention" and "enforcement". They heard evidence from numerous organisations which argued that the current system was too punitive and that the causes of anti-social behaviour were being neglected. Consider for example in *Ex p. R*, the members' disappointment at the failure of the YOT to work with the child in ways which might have helped him to see why his conduct was unacceptable and to engage with girls in a more sensible and ultimately more successful way.[57] The committee also noted arguments that enforcement powers should be used only as a last resort from Barnardo, the Association of Directors of Social Services and the NCH. However, the committee rejected these criticisms as they were based, in the committee's view, on a false assumption that there was a distinction after all between prevention and enforcement. Enforcement, the committee, concluded, had "a crucial preventative role in itself and that needs to be recognised and which needs to be seen as the responsibility of everyone."[58] **3-079**

Children and the Criminal Justice System

"Restorative Justice" and the New Orders of the 1998 Act
The White Paper, *No More Excuses*, acknowledged what was described as a **3-080**
need "...to reshape the criminal justice system in England and Wales to produce more constructive outcomes with young offenders" and referred to the need to build on three concepts: responsibility, restoration and reintegration. Restorative principles were endorsed in the 2002 White Paper, *Justice for All*:[59]

> "We must actively encourage offenders to make amends for the crime they have committed...Restorative justice schemes have the potential to offer constructive, community-based responses to crime. They bring together all parties...with a stake in a specific offence to resolve how to deal with the aftermath of the offence and any implications for the future..."

See also the 2003 consultation document, *Restorative Justice: the Government's Strategy* where the main aim of the criminal justice system is "...to maximise the use of restorative justice, where we know it works well, to meet victims' needs and to reduce re-offending."[60] The Home Office envisions restorative justice assuming a central role, not just in criminal justice, but in

---

[57] Home Office Committee Report, para.43.
[58] *ibid.*, para.102.
[59] *Justice for All*, Cm.5563 (2002)paras 5.8 and 7.32.
[60] Para.5.1: *www.homeoffice.gov.uk/justice/victims/restorative/index.html*.

conflict-resolution across society, helping to build, in the words of the former Home Secretary David Blunkett, "a society where everyone recognises their responsibility for the problems we all face, and one in which individuals and communities get involved in building solutions." Restorative justice programmes have been part of the adult criminal justice system in some areas of the UK since the mid-1980s. For adult offenders, one of the statutory purposes of sentencing set out in s.142 of the Criminal Justice Act 2003 is the "making of reparation by offenders to persons affected by their offences." These programmes usually take place through the Probation service or through independent mediation services. However, it has not been a recognised part of the statutory services until recently. The courts have discussed the principle of restorative justice and its impact on sentencing. In *Collins*,[61] the defendant appealed against a total sentence of seven years' imprisonment, comprising three years and six months for unlawful wounding, and three years and six months for robbery. The offence of unlawful wounding occurred when he repeatedly stabbed his former partner with a knife, causing severe injuries to her upper body and arms. The robbery consisted of the defendant grabbing hold of a woman's handbag and forcing her to release it. The Court of Appeal held, allowing the appeal, that the total sentence of seven years' imprisonment was excessive, especially considering the defendant's plea of guilty and the fact that he had successfully participated in a restorative justice programme. Accordingly, a term of one year and six months was substituted for the sentence of three years and six months imposed on the defendant for the robbery, bringing his total sentence to five years' imprisonment. The appellant undertook to take part in the restorative justice programme. The Court described this as a comparatively recent programme designed to ensure effective sentencing for the better protection of the public. They said that they saw clear evidence in the way that that programme was carried out to show that it was going at least some way to achieving its purpose and was to be encouraged. To this appellant's credit, the Court said, he took part in the programme. It was by no means a soft option: the appellant was required to agree to attend a conference at which not only the school teacher and members of her family attended, but also members of the appellant's own family. The victim was there with five other members of her family and the appellant was there with two other members of his. As a result of that conference, face to face with his victim, the appellant was required to write a letter of apology to her. The Court commented on the letter and other letters that he wrote to her and also, to the complainant's great credit, the merciful letter that she wrote hoping that things would go well in the future. Further, he was required to deal with the drugs problem that, to some extent, had led to these serious offences. He agreed to attend Narcotics Anonymous on a regular basis and applied for a change of prison where a drug treatment programme was available. Importantly, he was also required to write to a liaison police officer every three months to report upon his progress. The Court held that this was a powerful feature of the sentence. The judge referred to the fact that the appellant had written to the victim, but the Court of Appeal also found that it was to the credit of the appellant that he took part in that programme and that this was a factor properly to be taken into account. While the Court did not interfere with his sentence for unlawful wounding, he reduced the sentence as regards the robbery from three and a half years to one and half years, making a total of five years in all.

3-081   See also *O'Brien*.[62] The appellant appealed against a sentence of two-and-a-half years' imprisonment following a plea of guilty and committal from the magistrates' court, six months for theft and two years' imprisonment

[61] [2003] WL 1610401.
[62] [2004] WL 3054263.

consecutive for burglary. In the first offence, the appellant, needing money for his drug addiction, visited his elderly mother's house in December 2003 and stole perfume, a table lamp and a portable television. His mother, a stroke victim, contacted the police after he had denied the theft and told her he would get the television back the next day. He was granted bail, but shortly after committed a serious burglary. He entered a home in London in the early hours of January 2004 when the occupant was upstairs. She came downstairs and saw the appellant going through a chest of drawers and holding a velvet bag. Notwithstanding that she confronted him, the appellant stole that bag which contained a pair of binoculars of sentimental value. He was clearly intent on taking more because stacked by the front door was silverware. He did not use any violence, but it must have been very frightening to the victim. The Court of Appeal noted "the victim, a thoroughly distinguished member of society, has thereafter exhibited considerable compassion to the appellant, compassion that on one view he did not deserve." In many ways, the Court said, there was much about him that was routine, particularly with regard to this kind of offence: he was in his 30s, had a bad record for dishonesty, including burglary, and stole to support his addiction. Moses J. observed:

"However, there is one feature of this case that is of significance and upon which the appeal is founded. The appellant agreed to enter into a Restorative Justice Conference and signed an Outcome Agreement. The conference required the co-operation of the victim. To her immense credit she agreed to go and confront the appellant. At that conference the appellant apologised. He accepted that what had happened was serious and that he intended to steer clear of drugs and keep out of trouble in the future. He therefore agreed to undertake drugs rehabilitation in prison, employment training and to write to the victim. . . The importance of the Restorative Justice Programme has been stressed in the courts. It is a significant matter when victim and offender agree to meet if the outcome is a settled and clear intention to keep clear from crime in the future and to acknowledge the effect on the victim and the seriousness of the past offence. This court in R v Collins[63] stressed the need for courts to bear in mind, when sentencing, the significance of such a programme which was described by this court as being by no means a soft option. Serious though these offences were, we take the view that the judge failed to give sufficient credit for the fact that the appellant had agreed to attend a Restorative Justice Conference which had, as it appeared then certainly, a sensible and possibly optimistic outcome. . . Accordingly the sentence was reduced to six months' imprisonment and two years' imprisonment shall no longer run consecutively, but run concurrently, making a total sentence of two years' imprisonment."

There are several orders in the Crime and Disorder Act 1998 which are said to be based on restorative justice principles. Dignan[64] defines the term "restorative justice" as a convenient shorthand expression that is commonly applied to a variety of practices which seek to respond to crime in a more constructive way than is conventionally achieved through the use of punishment. Marshall defines it as ". . .a process whereby parties with a stake in a specific offence collectively resolve how to deal with the aftermath of the offence and its implications for the future".[65] As Edwards points out, it is not a definition

3-082

---

[63] [2003] EWCA Crim 1687.
[64] "The Crime and Disorder Act and the Prospects for Restorative Justice" (1999) Crim. L.R. Jan, 48–60.
[65] *Restorative Justice: An Overview* (Home Office Research Development & Statistics Directorate, London, 1999).

which is universally accepted: the term covers a range of policies and practices which is too large and unspecific to have a clear answer and is more of an umbrella term encompassing different penal and criminological ideas.[66] There is no single coherent version of the restorative paradigm, as restorative justice consists of several primary objectives.

3-083   According to Dignan,[67] one of the primary aims of most restorative justice approaches is to engage with offenders to try to bring home the consequences of their actions and an appreciation of the impact they have had on the victims of their offences. A second aim is to encourage and facilitate the provision of appropriate forms of reparation by offenders towards either their direct victims (provided they are agreeable) or the wider community. A third aim is to seek reconciliation between victim and offender where this can be achieved and, even in cases where this is not possible, to strive to reintegrate both victims and offenders within the community as a whole following the commission of an offence. The 1998 Act orders, in his view, appear to be consistent with "restorative justice" principals. He concludes that the short term prospects for restorative justice have been transformed in the space of little over a year by changes in the political climate following the general election. However, he identifies what he sees as much broader tension, which is still to be resolved, between the criminal justice policies that were inherited by the incoming Labour Government in 1997, with their emphasis on punishment and social exclusion, and the alternative, more socially-inclusive, problem-solving approach of which glimpses can be discerned in some of the youth justice reforms considered in his article. In the long-term, he says, the philosophy of restorative justice should be part of a broader crime prevention strategy linked with a fundamental shift in the direction of a wide range of social policies that are known to have a bearing on the level of crime.

3-084   We discussed, in Chapter One, academic opinion of the fundament changes in the criminal justice system described as "the new penology". The individual, his guilt and the social explanations for his offending, is replaced by the management of criminal behaviour and situations through the use of actuarial techniques. The offender is seen as a rational, responsible decision maker, who responds to situational opportunities to engage in crime; and crime can thus be "designed out" through the probabilistic identification of "high"- and "low" risk offenders and situations, and the setting in place of appropriate regulatory devices. Rehabilitation is replaced by an analysis of the individual risks of reoffending by changing deficits in their attitudes, beliefs and behaviour so that they can meet their own needs and manage their own risks of reoffending. Notions of social justice which challenge the socio-economic constraints that often structure offenders' choices and decision to desist from crime hold little appeal to penal regimes which focus on actuarial risk. Gelsthorpe and Morris[68] restorative processes will continue to occupy a marginal place in criminal justice until contradictory values and practices of blaming and punishing are given significantly less emphasis and restorative values and practices are given significantly more emphasis. They see restorative justice as just one theme in a broadly punitive and controlling piece of legislation and are less optimistic than Dignan and others about the power and potential of restorative justice to alter fundamentally the current youth or

---

[66] A. Ashworth, "Is Restorative Justice the Way Forward for Criminal Justice?" in McLaughlin et al., *Restorative Justice: Critical Issues* (Sage, London, 2003) at p.1.64.
[67] Dignan "Youth Justice Pilots Evaluation: Interim Report on Reparative Work and Youth Offending Teams" (2000).
[68] A. Morris, L. Gelsthorpe "Something Old, Something Borrowed, Something Blue But Something New? A comment on the prospects for restorative justice under the Crime and Disorder Act 1998" Crim. L.R. (2000) pp.18–30.

criminal justice systems for a number of reasons. The tenor of the Crime and Disorder Act 1998, they argue, indicates an ideological shift in favour of punishment and crime control rather than away from it. They point to a continued emphasis in the 1998 Act on proportionality, whereby the reparation requirements which sentencers will specify in the order "shall be such as in the opinion of the court are commensurate with the seriousness of the offence" under s.67 of the 1998 Act. Secondly, managerialism is apparent in the Crime and Disorder Act 1998 in its emphasis on inter-agency co-operation and the statutory duty placed on local authorities to consult widely and to formulate and implement an annual youth justice plan setting out how local youth justice services will be provided and funded. The intention is to make the youth justice system more efficient and effective (and probably more economical too). Thirdly, the ideas behind risk assessment and "actuarial" justice which involve predictions of behaviour, and taking anticipatory action on the basis of these predictions, seem to underlie the introduction in the 1998 Act orders so that the non-criminal and future behaviour of children is effectively criminalised, even if this is not the primary intention of the legislation. Finally, the 1998 Act continues the theme of "community" by adding to the existing set of community based penalties. Finally, the 1998 Act introduces elements of restorative justice through conferencing, reparation and action plan orders and giving victims more of a say with respect to the content of certain orders. They conclude that the orders which are part of the "restorative package" introduced in the 1998 Act do not seem to go very far. Restorative practices, they argue, will develop in an ad hoc fashion at numerous decision points in the youth justice system, but at no point will the key participants in all of this actually be able to take charge:

"Victims will no longer be marginalised in quite the way that they are currently, but their involvement will hardly be significant. Offenders may be coerced into reparation. Nothing in the research literature suggests that this will be likely to prevent reoffending. And there continues to be an emphasis on blaming rather than restorative processes, as in the parenting order. The critical question is whether or not restorative justice in its Crime and Disorder Act 1998 guise is sufficiently new and radical to revitalise youth justice in England and Wales. It seems to us that despite the good intentions and enthusiasm of many politicians, policy-makers and practitioners, the hold of restorative justice will remain tenuous unless the competing and contradictory values running through criminal and youth justice policy in England and Wales in general, and in the Crime and Disorder Act 1998 in particular, concede more space."

Some writers are concerned with the impact of restorative justice on the state's role as to maintain a system for the administration of justice and to ensure that proper standards of procedural protection are applied. Ashworth[69] argues that it should remain the responsibility of the state towards its citizens to ensure that justice is administered by independent and impartial tribunals, and that there are proportionality limits which should not only constrain the measures agreed at restorative justice conferences, etc. but also ensure some similarity in the treatment of equally situated offenders. If the state does delegate certain spheres of criminal justice to some form of community-based conference, the importance of insisting on the protection of basic rights for defendants is not diminished. While many of the reforms are welcome, there must be a proper and thorough analysis of restorative justice

3-085

[69] A. Ashworth "Responsibilities, Rights and Restorative Justice" (2002) 42 Brit. J. Criminol. 578 at pp.590–591.

innovations. He suggests that restorative justice processes for offenders who might otherwise go to court should (a) be led by an independent and impartial person; (b) be required to submit its decisions for court approval; (c) allow the participation of the victim, the offender, and their families or significant others; (d) make provision for access to legal advice before and after any restorative justice processes, at a minimum; (e) focus on apology and on the appropriate reparation and/or compensation for the offence; and (f) be required to respect relevant principles, such as not imposing on the offender a financial burden that is not means-related. If, contrary to the argument here, a restorative justice conference is permitted to make proposals for community restoration, or other responses going beyond reparation to the individual victim(s), there should be clear and circumscribed proportionality limits for those measures.

3-086   Gray argues that the significance attached to the management of risk, through the responsibilisation of offenders, is evident in the Crime and Disorder Act 1998, which sets out a new framework for the governance of youth crime. Under the 1998 Act, the youth justice system is guided by the primary aim of preventing criminality among young people by addressing the risk factors associated with offending. There has been a blurring of needs with risks; the concept of risk is understood in terms of individual shortcomings in young offenders' attitudes, behaviour and cognitive skills arising from faulty moral training in the family or school, or through contact with delinquent peers. Deficiencies in family upbringing, peer contact and the school environment are framed as calculable risks which can be managed through preventative intervention in childhood, such as the child safety and the parenting orders.[70] Once the young person reaches the age of criminal responsibility, deficient moral reasoning is to be confronted through cognitively based offending behaviour programmes such as the action plan, reparation orders, or supervision orders. Overall, the 1998 Act focuses on "responsibilising" young offenders by addressing the risks posed by deficiencies in their moral upbringing. However, Gray argues that the ethos of restorative justice combines key elements from both the new culture of crime control and penal welfarism. The principle of holding young offenders responsible for their offending sits well with the moral agenda of advanced liberal penalty, while the appearance of restorative and reiterative principles could be interpreted as evidencing "a re-enchantment" with the traditional rehabilitative concerns of penal welfarism. However, there may be something far more old-fashioned at issue:

"Far from seeking to heal relations between offenders, victims and communities, as is intimated in the literature, the principle of restoration has been translated in recent youth justice practice as yet another way to hold young offenders responsible for their actions. Predictably, reintegration or social inclusion in restorative youth justice practice has not been pursued as part of a wider social justice agenda, which either provides young offenders with adequate social support or reduces inequalities. Instead, it carries the same moralizing connotations that underlie other inclusionary policy measures developed by New Labour. . .there is an assumption that it is the responsibility of young offenders to take advantage of these programmes in order to successfully negotiate their own social risks and so attain integration or inclusion, particularly once shortcomings in their moral reasoning have been corrected through participation in restorative interventions."

[70] Gray, at 939, citing Hannah-Moffat "Moral Agent or Actuarial Subject: Risk and Canadian Women's Imprisonment" (1999) *Theoretical Criminology*. 3:71–94.

Duties Regarding Children in Need

If any person 16 years or above, with responsibility for any child or young **3-087** person under that age, wilfully assaults, ill-treats, neglects, abandons or exposes the child, or causes or procures him to be assaulted, ill-treated, neglected, abandoned or exposed in a manner likely to cause him unnecessary suffering or injury to health, they have committed an offence under s.1(3) of the Children and Young Persons Act 1933.[71] Under s.1(2), that applies also in the particular case of a parent or other person legally liable to maintain a child or young person (including the legal guardian of a child or young person) who has neglected him in a manner likely to cause injury to his health if he has failed to provide adequate food or clothing, medical aid or lodging.

If any person gives, or causes to be given, to any child under the age of five **3-088** intoxicating liquor, except by order of a medical practitioner or in the case of sickness or apprehended sickness, or some other urgent cause, he is guilty of an offence.[72] The holders of a justice's licence must not allow and no person may cause or procure or attempt to cause or procure any person under the age of 14 to be in licensed premises during the permitted hour.[73] It is an offence for the licence holder or his servant to sell intoxicating liquor to a person under 18, or knowingly to allow a person under 18 to consume intoxicating liquor, or for the licence holder knowingly to allow any person to sell intoxicating liquor to any person under the age of 18.[74] It is also an offence to supply to or for persons under the age of 18 certain substances which may cause intoxication if inhaled.[75] A person found drunk in any highway or other public place, whether a building or not, or on any licensed premises, while having a child apparently under the age of seven years, may be arrested, and if the child is under seven years, is liable on summary conviction to a fine not exceeding level 2 or imprisonment for one month.[76] It is an offence for a person to supply or offer to supply a substance, other than a controlled drug, to a person under the age of 18 years, whom he knows or has reasonable cause to believe to be under the age of 18 or to a person who is acting on behalf of a person under that age, and whom he knows or has reasonable cause to believe to be acting, if he knows or has reasonable cause to believe that the substance is, or its fumes are, likely to be inhaled by a person under the age of 18 for the purpose of causing intoxication.[77]

A person who sells to a person under the age of 16 years any tobacco or cig- **3-089** arette papers, whether for his own use or not, is guilty of an offence under section 7(5) the Children and Young Persons Act 1933. It is a defence to prove that he took all reasonable precautions and exercised due diligence. It is the duty of any constable or park-keeper in uniform to seize any tobacco or cigarette papers in the possession of any person under the age of 16 years whom he finds smoking in any street or public place. Any person carrying on a retail business who sells cigarettes to any person, other than in pre-packed quantities of ten or more in their original package, commits an offence.[78] Any person who carries on a retail business and does not display a notice in the required form as to the illegality of selling cigarettes to a person under the age of 16 years commits an offence.[79] Local authorities are under a duty to consider, at least once a year, the

---

[71] See *R v Sheppard* [1981] A.C. 394.
[72] Level 1, standard scale. Children and Young Persons Act 1933, s.5.
[73] Level 1, standard scale. Licensing Act 1968, ss.20, 168.
[74] Licensing Act 1968, s.169.
[75] Intoxicating Substance (Supply) Act 1985, s.1.
[76] Licensing Act 1968, s.8.
[77] Intoxicating Substances (Supply) Act 1985 s.1(1); level 5 fine, imprisonment up to six months.
[78] Children and Young Persons (Protection from Tobacco) Act 1991, s.3.
[79] *ibid.*, s.4; or any machine: s.4.

extent to which it is appropriate for it to carry out in its area a programme of enforcement action relating to these provisions and to carry it out.[80]

3-090   Where there is provided in any building other than a dwelling an entertainment for children, or at which children are like to be the majority of persons attending, then if the number of children exceeds 100, it is the duty of the person providing the entertainment to station and keep stationed wherever necessary sufficient properly instructed adult attendants to prevent more children, or other persons, being admitted to the building than can be properly admitted to it, and to control the movement of children and others inside and when entering and leaving and to take other measures for their safety.[81] Where the occupier of a building permits, for hire or reward, the building to be used for the purpose of an entertainment, he must take all reasonable steps to secure the observance of these provisions.[82] A constable or authorised officer of the licensing authority may enter any building in which he believes that such an entertainment is being held or about to be held, to see whether the provisions are being carried out. Persons failing to fulfil these provisions are liable to a fine not exceeding level 3 on the standard scale and, if the building is licensed, the licence may be revoked. Licensing authorities may also impose conditions and restrictions on the admission of children to film exhibitions involving the showing of works designated as unsuitable for children and to control the holding of film exhibitions organised mainly for children.[83]

Local Authority Duties and Powers

3-091   Section 17 of the Children Act 1989 provides that it is the general duty of every local authority[84] to safeguard and promote the welfare of children in their area who are in need. The duty is discharged by the provision of a variety of services appropriate to the children's needs. A child is in need if he is unlikely to achieve or maintain, or have the opportunity of achieving or maintaining, a reasonable standard of health or development without the provision for him of services by a local authority under Pt III of the 1989 Act; or if his health and development is likely to be significantly impaired or further impaired without that provision; or he is disabled. The local authority are entitled to take into account available resources before committing themselves to the provision of services.[85] However, where there is a specific duty, lack of resources will not justify a failure to perform the duty.[86] They owe a duty of care to children in the provision or lack of provision of services with regard to operational decisions as opposed to policy decisions.[87] Local authorities must also take reasonable steps to identify the extent to which there are children in need in their area.[88] They must publish information about their services provided under s.17 and take reasonable steps to ensure that those who might benefit from these services are aware of them.[89] They are also under a duty to promote the upbringing of children in need by

[80] Children and Young Persons (Protection from Tobacco) Act 1991, s.5
[81] Children and Young Persons Act 1933, s.12(1).
[82] *ibid.*, s.12(1).
[83] Cinemas Act 1985, s.13.
[84] Children Act 1989. s.105: "local authority" means, in relation to England and Wales, the council of a county, a metropolitan district, a London Borough or the Common Council of the City of London and, in relation to Scotland, a local authority within the meaning of s.1(2) of the Social Work (Scotland) Act 1968.
[85] *R. v Gloucestershire CC, Ex p. Barry* [1997] A.C. 584.
[86] *R. v East Sussex CC, Ex p. Tandy* [1998] A.C. 714.
[87] *Barrett v Enfield LBC* [1999] 3 All E.R. 193.
[88] Children Act 1989, Sch.2. para.1(1).
[89] *ibid.*, Sch.2. para.1(2).

their families so long as this does not conflict with other duties under the 1989 Act.[90]

Specific services which the local authority may provide, as it considers **3-092** appropriate, for children living with their families include advice, guidance and counselling; occupational, social, cultural or recreational activities; home help; assistance with travel to receive a 1989 Act service.[91] They must take such steps as reasonably practicable to enable any child within their area in need, and who is living apart from their family, to promote contact with the family.[92] Any service provided by a local authority in the exercise of their functions may be provided for a family of a child in need or any member of that family provided it is with a view to safeguarding or promoting the child's welfare.[93] They must provide day care and or after school care for children in need[94] and may do so regarding children aged five or under whether or not they are in need.[95] They must provide accommodation for any child in need in their area who appears to them to require it as a result of there being no person with parental responsibility for him or because they are lost or abandoned or the person looking after them is prevented from returning to look after them.[96]

They are also required to provide accommodation for children they are **3-093** looking after.[97] They have a general duty regarding any child they are looking after to safeguard and promote his welfare and make use of such services as appear to be reasonable.[98] In addition to providing accommodation they must also maintain him in other respects.[99] A child is "looked after" if he is in the local authority's care, or provided with accommodation by the authority, in the exercise of any social services functions under the Local Authority Social Services Act 1970.[1] They must also make arrangements to enable such a child to live with parents unless that would not be reasonably practicable or not consistent with his welfare.[2] They must also ensure, so far as it is reasonably practicable and consistent with his welfare, that the child's accommodation while he is being looked after is near his home or with a sibling.[3] The authority may also advise, assist, and befriend such children with a view to promoting their welfare.[4] If it appears to the local authority that it is necessary, for the protection of members of the public from serious injury, to exercise their powers with respect to a child, whom they are looking after in a manner which may not be consistent with their general duties towards such a child, they may do so.[5] The Secretary of State, in order to protect members of the public from serious injury, may give directions to a local authority as to the exercise of their powers with respect to such a child.[6]

Under Pt V of the Children Act 1989, a local authority is required to inves- **3-094** tigate where they have reasonable cause to suspect that a child[7] is suffering

---

[90] Children Act 1989, s.17(1).
[91] *ibid.*, s.17(2); sch.2, para.8.
[92] *ibid.*, s.17(2), Sch.2, para.10.
[93] *ibid.*, s.17(3).
[94] *ibid.*, s.18(5).
[95] *ibid.*, s.18(6).
[96] *ibid.*, s.20(1).
[97] *ibid.*, s.23(1).
[98] *ibid.*, s.22(3).
[99] *ibid.*, s.23(1).
[1] *ibid.*, s.22(1).
[2] *ibid.*, s.23(5).
[3] *ibid.*, s.23(7).
[4] *ibid.*, s.24; see also Care Standards Act 2000.
[5] Children Act 1989, s.22(6).
[6] *ibid.*, s.22(8).
[7] *ibid.*, s.105, a person under the age of 18.

significant harm.[8] An authority should also investigate when they are informed that a child has contravened a curfew notice ban under the Crime and Disorder Act 1998[9] or if the child is in police protection (see below). They may also investigate where a question arises in family proceedings with respect to the welfare of the child and the court believes that a care order or supervision order might be appropriate;[10] or the court discharges an education supervision order and directs the authority to carry out an investigation;[11] or the LEA notifies the local authority that a child subject to an education supervision order is failing to comply with it.[12] The authority or someone acting on their behalf must have access to the child unless they believe they have already sufficient information.[13] If they are refused access, the authority must apply for an emergency protection order or a child assessment order or supervision order.[14] They may call on any local authority, LEA, housing authority, health authority, or primary care trust for assistance and those authorities must do so, especially as regards information and advice, unless it is unreasonable to do so. Under s.6 of the Disabled Children Act 2000, a person with parental responsibility for a disabled child, and who provides a substantial amount of care on a regular basis for that child, may ask a local authority to carry out an assessment of his ability to provide care for the child and the local authority must carry out such an assessment if they are satisfied that the child and his family are persons for whom it may provide services.

3-095   If attempts to have a child examined or assessed voluntarily have been unsuccessful, they may apply to court for a child assessment order under which a child may be required to be produced and made available for assessment.[15] The order is for the assessment of the state of the child's health or development or the way the child has been treated.[16] The court may also make an emergency protection order on the application of any person authorising the removal of the child or preventing the child from being removed for a period.[17] In determining any application under Pt V, the court is required to have regard to the "welfare principle" as defined in s.1 of the 1989 Act, the presumption against the making of an order,[18] and that delay tends to prejudice the child.[19]

3-096   The police have powers to take a child into "police protection". Where a constable has reasonable cause to believe that a child would otherwise be likely to suffer significant harm, he may remove the child to suitable accommodation and keep him there, or take such steps as are reasonable to ensure that the child's removal from any hospital or other place in which he is then being accommodated is prevented.[20] As soon as is reasonably practicable after taking a child into police protection, the constable concerned must secure that

---

[8] "Harm" means ill-treatment, impairment of health or development: Children Act 1989, s.39. Significant is defined in s.9 in this way: where the question of whether harm suffered by a child is significant turns on the child's health or development, his health or development shall be compared with that which could reasonably be expected of a similar child. See also Dept of Health "The Children Act 1989 Guidance and Regulations" Vol 1 Court Orders (1991).

[9] Children Act 1989 s.47(1)(a), added by ss.15(4), 119 and Sch.8 of the Crime and Disorder Act 1998.

[10] *ibid.*, s.37(1).

[11] *ibid.*, s.36.

[12] *ibid.*, Sch.3 Pt III, para.19(2).

[13] *ibid.*, s.47(4).

[14] *ibid.*, s.47(6).

[15] Children Act 1989, s.43.

[16] *ibid.*, s.43(1)(b).

[17] *ibid.*, s.46.

[18] *ibid.*, s.1(5).

[19] *ibid.*, s.1(2).

[20] Children Act, s.46.

the case is considered by a designated officer.[21] The designated officer must release the child from police protection unless he considered that there is still reasonable cause for believing that the child would be likely to suffer significant harm if released. While the child is in police protection, the designated officer may apply on behalf of the child to the appropriate authority[22] for an emergency order to be made, but the application may still be made whether or not that authority knows of it or even agrees to it being made.[23] Under s.43(b) of the 1989 Act, the constable must, as soon as reasonably practicable, inform the local authority, and/or the authority, in which the child is ordinarily resident, of what has happened. When the local authority is informed, they must make such inquiries as are necessary to enable it to decide what action to take to safeguard or promote the child's welfare.[24] No child may be kept in police protection for more than 72 hours.[25] The constable also has powers of entry and search.[26]

On the application of any local authority or authorised person, the court may make a care order, placing the child with respect to whom the application is made in the care of a designated local authority (care order); or putting him under the supervision of a designated local authority or of a probation officer (supervision order).[27] A court may only make a care order or supervision order if it is satisfied that the child concerned is suffering, or is likely to suffer, significant harm; and that the harm, or likelihood of harm, is attributable to the care given to the child, or likely to be given to him if the order were not made, not being what it would be reasonable to expect a parent to give to him; or the child's being beyond parental control. The application under this section may be made on its own or in any other family proceedings. Under a care order, the authority must receive the child into its care. The authority has parental responsibility for the child. They also have the power to determine the extent to which the parent may have contact with the child, but allow the child reasonable contact with the parents unless the court order stipulates otherwise.[28] The order lasts until the child is 18. A supervision order merely places the child under the supervision of the authority.[29] The authority is then obliged to "advise, assist and befriend" the child, to take such steps as are reasonably necessary to give effect to the order. The order may contain details such as to where the child shall live, what activities, if any, the child must participate in and medical evaluations.

3-097

On the application of a local education authority, the court may also make education supervision orders.[30] The court must be satisfied that the child (of compulsory school age) is not being properly educated. It has effect for only one year. It is the duty of the supervising authority to advise, assist and befriend the child and give directions to the supervised child and his parents so that the child is properly educated. If a parent persistently fails to comply with the directions made under the order, they are guilty of an offence.[31] If the child fails to comply with any directions, the authority must notify the appropriate authority which must then investigate the child's circumstances.

3-098

---

[21] Children Act 1989, s.46(3)(3): the officer designated by the chief officer of the police area concerned.
[22] The local authority in which the child is ordinarily resident: Children Act 1989, s.46(3)(b).
[23] Children Act 1989, s.46(8).
[24] *ibid.*, s.47.
[25] *ibid.*, s.46(6).
[26] *ibid.*, s.47.
[27] *ibid.*, s.31.
[28] *ibid.*, s.38.
[29] *ibid.*, s.35.
[30] *ibid.*, s.36.
[31] *ibid.*, s.36(10), Sch.3, para.18(2).

Child Safety Orders

3-099   The government believes that ". . .early intervention when a child begins to behave anti-socially or disruptively in a way which puts him or her at risk of offending is more effective than waiting until that child is old enough to be dealt with by the youth justice system."[32] This principle is predicated on research which indicates that it is the quality of relationships within families and the effectiveness of parental supervision are "crucial influences" on whether children are likely to re-offend.[33] The child safety order is intended to supplement welfare provisions of the Children Act 1989. Section 11(1) of the Crime and Disorder Act 1998 provides that a magistrates' court, on the application of a local authority,[34] may make a child safety order where the court is satisfied that one or more of the conditions specified in subs.(3)—set out below—are fulfilled with respect to a child under the age of 10. The court may order that the child be under the supervision of the responsible officer[35] and that he must comply with such requirements as are so specified; further, under subs.(5), these requirements must take into account that which the court considers desirable in the interests of securing that the child receives appropriate care, protection and support and is subject to proper control; or preventing any repetition of the kind of behaviour which led to the child safety order being made.[36] Under subs.(2), a court shall not make a child safety order unless it has been notified by the Secretary of State that arrangements for implementing such orders are available in the area in which it appears that the child resides, or will reside, and the notice has not been withdrawn. The threshold conditions in subs.(3) are:

(1) that the child has committed an act which, if he had been aged 10 or over, would have constituted an offence;

(2) that a child safety order is necessary for the purpose of preventing the commission by the child of such an act as is mentioned in para.(a) above;

(3) that the child has contravened a ban imposed by a curfew notice; and

(4) that the child has acted in a manner that caused or was likely to cause harassment, alarm or distress to one or more persons not of the same household as himself.

The maximum period permitted for the order is three months or, where the court is satisfied that the circumstances of the case are exceptional, 12 months.[37] Proceedings under this section or s.12 below shall be family proceedings for the purposes of the 1989 Act or s.65 of the Magistrates' Courts Act 1980 (the 1980 Act); and the standard of proof applicable to such proceedings shall be that applicable to civil proceedings.[38] Section 12 of the 1998

---

[32] Home Office, 2000, Crime and Disorder Act Guidance Document: Child Safety Order, para.2.1.
[33] *ibid.*, para.2.2, see also Graham and Bowling, Young People and Crime, (1995) Home Office Research Study 145.
[34] "Local authority" has the same meaning as under the Children Act 1989: Crime and Disorder Act 1998, s.11(7).
[35] "Responsible officer", in relation to a child safety order, means one of the following who is specified in the order: a social worker of a local authority social services department; and a member of a youth offending team: Crime and Disorder Act 1998, s.11(8).
[36] Requirements included in a child safety order shall, as far as practicable, be such as to avoid: (a) any conflict with the parent's religious beliefs; and (b) any interference with the times, if any, at which the child normally attends school: Crime and Disorder Act 1998, s.12(3).
[37] Crime and Disorder Act 1998, s.11(4).
[38] *ibid.*, s.11(6).

Act requires that, before making a child safety order, a magistrates' court shall obtain and consider information about the child's family circumstances and the likely effect of the order on those circumstances; and the court must explain to the parent or guardian of the child in ordinary language the effect of the order and of the requirements proposed to be included in it; and the consequences which may follow (under subs.(6) below) if the child fails to comply with any of those requirements; and that the court has power (under subs.(4) below) to review the order on the application either of the parent or guardian or of the responsible officer. Section 12(4) provides that, if, while a child safety order is in force in respect of a child, it appears to the court which made it, on the application of the responsible officer or a parent or guardian of the child, that it is appropriate to make an order under this subsection, the court may make an order discharging the child safety order or varying it. If such an application is dismissed, then no further application for its discharge shall be made under that subsection by any person except with the consent of the court which made the order.[39] Under s.11(4) of the 1998 Act, the normal maximum duration of such an order will be three months and, in exceptional circumstances, for up to 12 months.

Section 12(6) of the 1998 Act deals with the consequences of the child failing to comply with the terms of the order: where a child safety order is in force and it is proved to the satisfaction of the court which made it, or another magistrates' court acting for the same petty sessions area, on the application of the responsible officer, that the child has failed to comply with any requirement included in the order, the court may discharge the order and make in respect of him a care order under subs.(1)(a) of s.31 of the 1989 Act;[40] or it may make an order varying the order by cancelling any provision included in it or by inserting in it (either in addition to or in substitution for any of its provisions) any provision that could have been included in the order if the court had then had power to make it and were exercising the power. An appeal against the making of a child safety order lies to the High Court. On such an appeal, the court may make such orders as may be necessary to give effect to its determination of the appeal; and may also make such incidental or consequential orders as appear to it to be just. Any order of the court on an appeal under this section (other than one directing that an application be re-heard by a magistrates' court) shall, for the purposes of subs.(4) to (6) of s.12 above, be treated as if it were an order of the magistrates' court from which the appeal was brought and not an order of the High Court.[41] **3-100**

Government guidance is that the responsible officer should prepare a plan to support the order before it is made, meet with the child and family after the order and aim to work with the child's parents or guardian; this requires a "multi-agency" approach between those bodies with powers regarding child welfare and, in effect, this is likely to be the local YOT, and all child safety orders are to be implemented in accordance with a local authority's annual youth justice plan as required by s.40 of the Act.[42] If the responsible officer convinces the court that the child has failed to comply with any requirement included in the order, the court may discharge the child safety order and make a care order and variation of the original order. The maximum length of the order is three months except in exceptional circumstances when it may be extended to 12 months. **3-101**

---

[39] Crime and Disorder Act 1998, s.12(5).
[40] This applies whether or not the court is satisfied that the conditions mentioned in s.31(2) of the 1989 Act are fulfilled: Crime and Disorder Act 1998, s.12(7).
[41] Crime and Disorder Act 1998, s.13.
[42] Para.2.4.

Child Curfews Zones

3-102   According to Home Office Guidance on the Crime and Disorder Act 1998, the government believes that early intervention before habits become ingrained, and before a child has started to identify himself or herself as an offender, will often be more effective than waiting until that child is old enough to end up in the criminal justice system. Hence, a new approach was required. They cite research carried out in 1995 which shows[43] that the quality of relationships within families, the degree of parental supervision, peer group pressure and the way in which children use their leisure time, can be crucial in determining whether or not children are likely to offend. Early targeted intervention with children who are particularly at risk of drifting into crime can help prevent later offending. The Crime and Disorder Act 1998 provides two new powers to enable local authorities and the police to intervene effectively with such children. One is the child safety order, aimed at individual children under 16.[44] The second is the power for local authorities to use local child curfews to address particular problems of unsupervised children under the age of 10 out on the streets late at night. (Compare this to the mere power to remove under s.30(6) of the Anti-Social Behaviour Act 2003 and *W v Commissioner of Police for the Metropolis and the London Borough of Richmond-upon-Thames*.[45]) Government policy is that, for a number of obvious reasons, children under the age of 10 should not be out late at night unsupervised: they may be placed at risk and may create problems for the local community because such children, particularly when gathered in large groups, can become involved in anti-social or potentially criminal behaviour. The new child curfew powers are set out in s.14 of the 1998 Act. Under s.14(1), a local authority[46] (or a chief office or police)[47] may make a scheme (a "local child curfew scheme") for enabling the authority to give a notice imposing, for a specified period not exceeding 90 days, a ban to which subs.(2) below applies. Subsection (2) applies to a ban on children of specified ages (under 10) being in a public place[48] within a specified area during certain hours between 9pm and 6am and otherwise than under the effective control of a parent or a responsible person aged 18 or over. Under s.14(2) of the 1998 Act, the local child curfew notice may apply no earlier than 9pm and no later than 6am. The actual extent of the hours of operations within those limits is a matter for local determination. So, for example, if a local child curfew scheme was to operate during summer months an authority may decide not to begin the local child curfew before 10pm. The local child curfew notice can apply to any children under the age of 10 as determined by the local authority. The notice may, therefore, be restricted to particular ages of children under 10. There is added flexibility in the arrangements in that, under s.14(6), a local child curfew notice may apply different limits to different age groups of children. The local authority might, for example, want to set a later hour for the older children, the eight and nine year olds. Under s.14(3), before making a local child curfew scheme, a local authority shall consult every chief officer of police, any part of whose police area lies within its area; and such other persons or bodies as it considers

---

[43]   Graham and Bowling *Young People and Crime*, (1995). Home Office Research Study 145.
[44]   Initially under 10 years of age; amended by s.48 of the Criminal Justice and Police Act 2001.
[45]   [2006] EWCA Civ 458; see para.2-085.
[46]   "Local authority" means (a) in relation to England, the council of a district or London borough, the Common Council of the City of London, the Council of the Isle of Wight and the Council of the Isles of Scilly; (b) in relation to Wales, the council of a county or county borough: Crime and Disorder Act 1998, s.14(8).
[47]   Following an amendment by way of s.49 of the Criminal Justice and Police Act 2001.
[48]   "Public place" has the same meaning as in Pt II of the Public Order Act 1986: Crime and Disorder Act 1998, s.14(8).

appropriate. Section 49 of the Criminal Justice and Police Act 2001 amends s.14 by way of adding a new subs.(3A). Subsection (3A) provides that before a chief officer of police makes a child curfew scheme, a chief officer of police shall consult every local authority any part of whose area lies within the area to be specified; and such other persons or bodies as he considers appropriate.

Home Office guidance is that local child curfew schemes are designed to be **3-103** part of an integrated response to reducing crime and disorder in local areas. Therefore, in drawing up proposals for a local child curfew scheme the local authority should bear in mind the effect that such a local child curfew scheme will have, not only on the area specifically affected by the proposals, but the community in general. The Home Office recommends that the proposed scheme should also be consistent with the local crime and disorder reduction strategy produced under s.6 of the Crime and Disorder Act 1998, the local policing plans and the work of youth offending teams in dealing with local youth crime problems, as set out in the youth justice plan under s.40 of the 1998 Act. Under the section, they may also consult other such persons or bodies as the local authority considers appropriate. The Home Office Guidance suggests that the latter group may include the local authority social services and education, the local YOT, health authority, the probation service, local youth service and voluntary organisations with an interest in children's issues and community safety and other individuals or groups who have a useful contribution to make, and local authorities will have to decide, in the light of their local knowledge, who they should consult at this stage. A local child curfew scheme shall be made under the common seal of the local authority and shall not have effect until it is confirmed by the Secretary of State.[49] Having been confirmed, the notice shall be published by posting it in some conspicuous place or places within the specified area; and in such other manner, if any, as appears to the local authority to be desirable for giving publicity to the notice.[50] The local authority may well decide to use local news media such as newspapers and radio or arrange for the distribution of handbills or mail drops.

Under s.15, where a constable has reasonable cause to believe that a child is **3-104** in contravention of a ban imposed by a curfew notice, then, under subs.(2) and (3), the constable shall, as soon as practicable, inform the local authority for the area that the child has contravened the ban; and he may remove the child to the child's place of residence unless he has reasonable cause to believe that the child would, if removed to that place, be likely to suffer significant harm. Primary responsibility for enforcing the local child curfew will be a matter for the police and will be carried out as part of normal operational policing duties. Children found in breach of a local child curfew will in most cases come to the attention of the police first. However, it is recommended that there should be close consultation with the local social service departments, in particular given the responsibilities being placed on the social services department under s.15(4) of the 1998 Act.

A major issue is how to deal appropriately and sensitively with children **3-105** found in breach of a local child curfew. The police, according to the guidance, are used to dealing sensitively with young children who are at risk as part of their existing duties. Section 15 of the 1998 Act provides that a police officer shall remove a child to the child's place of residence where he or she has reasonable cause to believe that the child is in breach of a curfew notice, unless he or she has reasonable cause to believe that the child would, if left there, be likely to suffer significant harm. To ensure that there is a measure of

[49] Crime and Disorder Act 1998, s.14(5), (6).
[50] *ibid.*, s.14(7).

consistency with the powers under s.14, in relation to supervision of a child by a parent or responsible person aged 18 or over, the police officer will need to ensure that the child is returned into the custody of a parent or a responsible person who is aged 18 or over.

3-106   It is observed in the guidance that it would be reasonable to assume that if there is no parent or responsible person aged 18 or over at the child's normal place of residence then the child, if left alone, may be at risk of suffering significant harm; or the circumstances of the child's home may be such that, even though he is not alone, he may still be at risk of significant harm. If so, the police officer may then use powers either under s.15(3) of the 1998 Act or under s.46 of the Children Act 1989, and take the child temporarily to a police station, or to other accommodation with the prior agreement of the social services department. According to Home Office guidance on the curfew powers, it is necessary to ensure that there is effective liaison between the police and the social services department to determine what is the most suitable accommodation for children found in breach of a local child curfew: one of the features that the Home Secretary will look for in considering a local child curfew scheme will be evidence that the local authority has in place mechanisms to deal effectively with children found in breach who it is not safe to return to their home. Whether the police use powers in the 1998 Act or under s.46 of the 1989 Act, police station accommodation will be inappropriate in these circumstances and appropriate arrangements need to be in place to deal with such children so that they are placed in suitable temporary accommodation.

3-107   Social services are expected to play an important role in the successful operation of a curfew notice. The local authority should ensure that effective liaison and dialogue exists between the police and social services department, particularly on the need for the social services department to support the process. The police will look to them to receive children found in breach of a curfew who cannot be returned to their homes. In those cases where the social services are not already involved, they will be required to be informed as soon as practicable that a child within their area has been taken into police protection under s.15(2) of the 1998 Act. Once the social services department has been informed that a child in their area has been found in breach of a local child curfew they will be required to investigate the circumstances behind the breach. As a mandatory statutory requirement, the social services department must carry out its investigation as soon as practicable and, in any event, within 48 hours of being informed by the police. This is likely to involve a visit to the family to establish why the child has been found in breach of a local child curfew. The social services department has available to it a number of options, including their existing powers under the 1989 Act and the newer power to apply to the courts to impose child safety orders, such as a child safety order under s.11 of the 1998 Act.

3-108   Each local child curfew notice can last up to 90 days.[51] These days run consecutively. Within that time period a local authority may apply the local child curfew notice on any day according to the specifications of the local child curfew notice as to whom the local child curfew notice shall apply, the area and times as to which it is to apply. For example, the authority (or chief officer of police) may decide not to apply the notice each day, but only at weekends. During this period, the authority may consider that it would be appropriate to apply the local child curfew beyond the initial 90 days. Once the initial period of 90 days has expired a local authority may seek an extension of a local child curfew notice under the scheme without making a further application to the Home Secretary. However, there are certain con-

---

[51] Crime and Disorder Act 1998, s.14(1).

ditions which apply. The continuation of a local child curfew notice must relate to the local child curfew scheme which was confirmed. The initial application to the Home Secretary seeking confirmation of the local child curfew scheme must include details, not only of the consultation arrangements with those in the area affected by the local child curfew notice, but an undertaking to consult those affected by the continuation of the local child curfew notice in that area.

The Police and the Criminal Courts—New Sentencing Orders

Police Arrest and Detention
Where a child or young person is in police detention, steps must be taken to ascertain the identity of a person responsible for his welfare.[52] That person must be informed, unless it is not practicable to do so, that the child or young person has been arrested, why he has been arrested and where he is being detained. The custody officer must, as soon as practicable, inform the appropriate adult of the grounds of the detention and ask them to attend to see the child.[53] The term "appropriate adult" means the parent or guardian, or, if the child is in care, the care authority; a social worker; or if there are no persons available falling within those categories, an adult aged 18 or over who is not a police officer or employed by the police service.[54] The appropriate adult must be allowed to see the custody record and witness the juvenile being advised of his rights under the Code of Practice.[55] The juvenile must not be interviewed or asked to provide a statement in the absence of the appropriate adult; when the adult is present during the interview, he must be informed that he is not expected to act as an observer and also that his presence is required to advise the juvenile and to see that the interview is conducted fairly and to facilitate communication with the juvenile.[56] A juvenile must not be placed in a police cell unless there is no other secure accommodation available and the custody officer considers that that a cell provides more comfortable accommodation that any other secure accommodation in the station.[57]

3-109

Alternatives to Charging—Final Warning Scheme
By s.65(8) of the 1998 Act, a constable can no longer caution a child or young person. Instead, where a constable has evidence that a child or young person ("the offender") has committed an offence and the constable considers that the evidence is such that, if the offender were prosecuted for the offence, there would be a realistic prospect of his being convicted, and the offender admits to the constable that he committed the offence, then, provided also that the offender has not previously been convicted of an offence and the constable is satisfied that it would not be in the public interest for the offender to be prosecuted, the constable may *reprimand* the offender, unless the offender has previously been reprimanded or warned. In addition, or alternatively, the constable may *warn* the offender—if the offender has not previously been warned—or where the offender has previously been warned, the offence was committed more than two years after the date of the previous warning—and the constable considers the offence to be not so serious as to require a charge

3-110

[52] Children and Young Persons Act 1933, s.34(2).
[53] Code C: Code of Practice for the Detention, Treatment and Questioning of Persons by Police Officers, para.3.0.
[54] Code C: para.1.7.
[55] Code C: paras 3.1 to 3.5A.
[56] Code C: para.11.
[57] Code C, para.8.8: nor should they share a cell with an adult—para.8.8.

to be brought. However, no person may be warned more than once. Where the offender has not been previously reprimanded, the constable shall warn, rather than reprimand, the offender if he considers the offence to be so serious as to require a warning. Such a warning shall be given at a police station and, where the offender is under the age of 17, in the presence of an appropriate adult;[58] and the constable must explain to the offender and, where he is under that age, the appropriate adult, in ordinary language in the case of a *reprimand*, the effect of subs.(5)(a) of s.66 below; and in the case of a *warning*, the effect of subss.(1), (2), (4) and (5)(b) and (c) of that section, and any guidance issued under subs.(3) of that section.

3-111   Having issued such a warning, then, under s.66, the constable shall as soon as practicable refer the person to a YOT. The YOT must assess any person referred to them and, unless they consider it inappropriate to do so, shall arrange for him to participate in a rehabilitation programme. Where a person who has been warned under s.65 above is convicted of an offence committed within two years of the warning, the court, by or before which he is so convicted, shall not make an order under subs.(1)(b) (conditional discharge) of s.1A of the Criminal Courts Act 1973 in respect of the offence, unless it is of the opinion that there are exceptional circumstances relating to the offence or the offender which justify its doing so; and where it does so, shall state in open court that it is of that opinion and why it is.[59] Any reprimand of a person under s.65 above, any warning of a person under that section and any report on a failure by a person to participate in a rehabilitation programme arranged for him, may be cited in criminal proceedings in the same circumstances as a conviction of the person may be cited.[60]

3-112   Government guidance states that the aim of the final warning system is to replace "repetitive" but ineffective cautions and goes much further.[61] The police have responsibility for making decisions on disposals under the final warning scheme, but may ask the YOT to help by carrying out a prior assessment of the young offender. The YOT is responsible for ensuring that effective interventions are delivered in support of final warnings. Where there is doubt about whether a prosecution should be brought, it may also be useful to seek the opinion of the Crown Prosecution Service at an early stage. As well as advising on points of law and the sufficiency of the evidence, they may also be able to give guidance on public interest considerations. There is only strictly limited discretion for the police to take informal action, such as "firm advice" to a young person and his or her parents. Informal action should be taken only in exceptional circumstances where the police consider that it will be sufficient to prevent future offending. This will almost always be in cases of anti-social behaviour where the behaviour falls short of being "criminal" or for very minor non-recordable offences. To ensure that the final warning scheme has a real impact on offending behaviour, any informal action should be confined to such circumstances. For a first offence, the juvenile should receive a reprimand; for a second, a final warning; and for the third, a charge. Unlike adult cautions, the young person does not "consent" to the reprimand or final

[58] In this section "appropriate adult", in relation to a child or young person, means: (a) his parent or guardian or, if he is in the care of a local authority or voluntary organisation, a person representing that authority or organisation; (b) a social worker of a local authority social services department; (c) if no person falling within paragraph (a) or (b) above is available, any responsible person aged 18 or over who is not a police officer or a person employed by the police: Crime and Disorder Act 1998, s.65(7).
[59] Crime and Disorder Act 1998, s.66(4).
[60] *ibid.*, s.66.
[61] Home Office/Youth Justice Board, "Final Warning Scheme—Guidance for the Police and Youth Offending Teams" (November, 2002).

warning. Under the legislation, it is a matter for the police to decide the appropriate disposal in accordance with the statutory criteria. Young people and their parents/carers or other appropriate adults should have access to information about the options available, including the final warning scheme, so that they can make an informed decision before the question as to whether they admit the offence is put to them. The police should ensure that victims are informed of developments in the case. This function may be performed by the YOT, police officer or victim worker according to the local protocol. Victims should have the opportunity to give fully informed consent to any involvement in the final warning process. Their involvement can be increased if they receive advanced notification that the youth offending team will be in contact with victims of the offence unless they request otherwise. Victims should be given the name and contact details of a YOT worker to ask for further information or talk through any concerns. Police and YOTs should ensure that victims are enabled to make informed choices about whether they wish to be involved in the final warning scheme and if so in what way. If victims are involved in a way that is appropriate for them, this can be helpful to their recovery after crime.

All reprimands and final warnings must be given orally, and supple- **3-113** mented with written information clearly explaining the effect of the reprimand/warning. In giving a reprimand the officer should specify the offence that has led to it and make clear that: the reprimand is a serious matter; any further offending will result in a final warning or prosecution in all but the most exceptional circumstances; a record of the reprimand will be kept by the police until the offender is 18 years old, or for five years, whichever is longer; the young person's reprimand may be cited in any future criminal proceedings; if the offence is one covered by the Sex Offenders Act 1997, the young person is required to register with the police for inclusion on the sex offenders register. In giving a final warning the officer should specify the offence that has led to it and make clear that: the final warning is a serious matter; any further offending will result in prosecution in all but the most exceptional circumstances; a record of the final warning will be kept by the police until the offender is 18 years old, or for five years, whichever is longer; the final warning may be cited in any future criminal proceedings; if the young person is convicted of a further offence within two years of getting the warning, the option of conditional discharge will only be open to the courts in exceptional circumstances; the young person can expect a more serious sentence; if the offence is one covered by the Sex Offenders Act 1997, the young person is required to register with the police for inclusion on the sex offenders register; the final warning will be followed up by the local youth offending team; that the YOT will assess the young person and, unless they consider it inappropriate, devise an intervention programme designed to tackle the reasons for the offending behaviour, prevent any re-offending and repair some of the harm done; and unreasonable non-compliance with the intervention programme will be recorded and could be cited in any future criminal proceedings.

In *R (on the application of U) v Commissioner of Police of the Metropolis*,[62] **3-114** the claimants, who were both aged 15 at the relevant time, were suspected of having committed indecent assaults. The police decided to apply the Final Warning Scheme. Home Office Guidance at the time provided that a reprimand or warning could only be given if the young person made a clear and reliable admission to all the elements of the offence, having been made aware of the consequences of such an admission. In the case of offences covered by the Sex Offenders Act 1997, the young person had to be told that he would be required to register with the police for inclusion in the Sex Offenders Register. The claimants in the present cases were not made aware at any time of that

---

[62] [2003] 1 Cr. App. R. 29.

particular requirement. They applied for judicial review submitting that no final warning should have been given without their express informed consent. They argued that the Act and the guidance given by the Home Office in relation to the Scheme did not comply with, inter alia, Art.6 of the European Convention on Human Rights. The Court of Appeal allowed the applications, and held that informed consent was required before the procedure of giving final warnings could comply with Art.6 of the Convention. That meant that the claimants were entitled to a fair trial of the allegations made against them attended by all the guarantees which were required by the Convention. Although the decision was taken not to prosecute, the claimants were required to subject themselves to a procedure that had the effect of publicly pronouncing their guilt of the offence of indecent assault. Therefore, they had been denied a right to a trial of the charges against them, and had been declared guilty by an administrative process. The system of cautions could only conform to the Convention if its procedures could properly be said to amount to a waiver to have one's case dealt with by a court. That would require the informed consent by the offender to the procedure being adopted. Nevertheless, that did not mean that the Scheme itself was unlawful in the sense that the Act did not conform to the Convention. There was nothing in the Act that required the police to proceed without the consent of the offender. The vice lay with the guidance, and the practice adopted pursuant to that guidance. The appropriate practice had to ensure that, before a reprimand or final warning was administered, the offender and his or her parent, carer or other appropriate adult should be told of the consequences and asked whether or not they consented to that course being taken. The House of Lords,[63] allowing an appeal, noted that it was accepted by the parties that in the period of time before the police became satisfied that it would not be in the public interest to prosecute him, the child was facing a criminal charge, and so Sch.1, Pt I, Art.6 was engaged. However, any criminal charge had ceased to exist when a firm decision had been made not to prosecute him. At para.12, Lord Bingham noted:

> "For good and understandable reasons, the protection given to criminal defendants by article 6 covers not only the trial itself but extends back to the preparatory and preliminary processes preceding trial and forwards to sentence and appeal. But the primary focus is on the right itself, because that is the stage at which guilt is decided with the possibility of condemnation and punishment. I find it had to see how a criminal charge can be held to endure once a decision has been made that rules out the possibility of any trial or condemnation or punishment."

Therefore, the decision not to prosecute ruled out the possibility of any trial or punishment. Determination of a criminal charge had to expose the offender to the possibility of punishment, and a process which could only culminate in measures of a preventative, curative or rehabilitative kind would not ordinarily be the determination of a criminal charge. The obligation to register under the 1997 Act was not a penalty within the meaning of Sch.1, Pt I, Art.7. Further, in deciding whether a warning ought to be given under s.65 of the 1998 Act, it was no part of a police officer's duty to adjudicate on or to determine whether or not the offender was guilty. Had Parliament envisaged the exercise of such a function it would not have entrusted it to a police officer. Neither the warning given to the child, nor the decision to warn him, following a firm decision that it was not in the public interest to prosecute him and in circumstances where he was exposed to no possibility of punishment but

[63] [2005] 1 W.L.R. 1184.

was the subject of measures designed to promote his welfare, did not involve the determination of a criminal charge against him. Had they done so, there would have been no valid waiver by him of his right to a fair trial, but as it was, his Art.6 rights were not engaged. The appeal had proceeded on the basis of the parties' acceptance that the child had been facing a criminal charge until such time as the police decided that it would not be in the public interest to prosecute him. However, the child had not been charged nor had he been served with any criminal process. A person would normally only become subject to a criminal charge from the time when he was formally charged or served with a summons, and arrest would not ordinarily mark the beginning of that period. Even so, several members of the House of Lords expressed misgivings about the scheme, particularly as regards the failure to tell the child and his parent the full consequences of the warning, including the sex offender registration requirement, about which both felt an understandable grievance. Any educational benefit to be gained from diversion, as Baroness Hale noted, is severely jeopardised if the offender feels unjustly treated; nor was it reasonable that no further steps at all were taken by the youth offending team to work with the child in ways in which might have helped him see why his conduct was unacceptable. However, in the circumstances of this case, it did not mean that there was a breach of his Convention rights.

Puech and Evans[64] suggest that the majority of juveniles will continue to be **3-115** dealt with by the police rather than the courts and therefore by an "administrative" rather than "judicial" process. They refer to Pitts' remarks that the 1998 Act effectively introduces a "three strikes and out" policy.[65] He suggests that a juvenile who re-offends after a warning can expect a community penalty such as a reparation, action plan or referral order and that any further offending is likely to result in a custodial sentence: the logic of juvenile sentencing is that there must not be a ladder leading inevitably to custody and that custody should be reserved for the most serious, violent or sexually dangerous offenders: Puech and Evans refer to criteria for imposing custody on a juvenile contained in s.79 of the Powers of the Criminal Courts (Sentencing) Act 2000 mean that custody cannot be a presumptive sentence at any stage of the tariff. However, they argue, it is widely expected that the provisions of the 1998 Act taken together are likely to result in an increase in custodial sentences. They carried out research into the way youth offending teams were carrying out assessments and developing rehabilitation programmes based on final warnings (as at 2001). They conclude:

"Despite the low visibility of pre-court decision-making it now has even greater significance for the youth justice system. Above all many of the young people and YOT workers in our sample see the warning system as arbitrary, unfair, and disproportionate especially as it may involve compulsory participation in a rehabilitation (change) programme. This is in sharp contrast to the emphasis in the Crime and Disorder Act on proportionality in sentencing and in contrast to the way in which some adult first offenders are dealt with because the existing cautioning system still applies to them. Outcome measures such as re-offence rates may be one measure of effectiveness. Policy makers ignore processes at their peril if their aims are not to be frustrated. It has to be recognised that this is very much an exploratory study. Even so it does suggest that there is a considerable gap between the aspirations and the rhetoric of the Home Office or the Youth Justice Board and what is happening on the ground and this justifies further investigation."

[64] "Reprimands and Warnings: Populist Punitiveness or Restorative Justice" (2001) Crim. L.R. 794–805.
[65] J. Pitts "Dear Jack Straw" (1998) Criminal Justice Matters No. 31.

Detention After Charge

3-116   Where a juvenile is arrested for an offence other than under a warrant and then charged, the custody officer must order his release from detention on bail or without it unless there are reasonable doubts about his real name and address; his capacity to answer bail; if it is imprisonable offence, further offending; injury to others or damage to property; and so on.[66] If the custody office decides to detain the juvenile, a written notice must be given to the appropriate adult. Unless it is not practicable, or it would cause the public further harm, the juvenile (so long as he is above 12 years) will be moved to local authority accommodation if there is no other suitable secure accommodation.[67] A child or young person arrested under a warrant must not be released unless his parent or guardian enters into a recognisance for such amount as the custody officer thinks fit.[68]

3-117   In summary proceedings, where a child or young person is remanded and is committed for trial or sentence, and he is not released on bail, the remand or committal must be to local authority accommodation.[69] It must be that authority which is looking after him, if that applies; the authority in which he resides; or the one in which the offence was committed.[70] The court may remand them with a requirement that they be kept in secure accommodation, after having consulted the local authority, so long as the child is above 12 years or a young person and not a violent offender; and then, only if he is charged with a serious violent of sexual offence or the offence would be punishable by imprisonment if an adult for a term of 14 years or more; or he has a recent history of absconding or committed an offence while on remand.[71] If there is no secure accommodation requirement, and after consultation with the local authority, then the court may require them to comply with conditions as could be imposed under the Bail Act 1976. A court remanding a person to local authority accommodation, may, after consultation with the authority, impose requirements for securing compliance with conditions imposed on that person. Where a person is remanded to local authority accommodation, the court may, on the local authority's application, impose conditions.[72] Local authorities are bound to comply with any security requirement that might be imposed on them.[73] The court may also request the local authority to do so regardless of whether or not the local authority or LEA think it is necessary.[74] If a person aged 17 is remanded into custody, he is remanded to a custody centre, but if there are none available he may be remanded to a prison.[75] Any male person who is aged 15 or 16 who is remanded or committed for trial, and not bailed, must be remanded to local authority accommodation, unless he is remanded to a remand centre or prison.[76] The court must consult a probation officer, a social worker of the local authority social services department or a member of a YOT in order to declare the person who is charged or has been convicted of a serious violent or sexual offence or an offence punishable, were he an adult, with imprisonment for a term of 14 years or more; or has a history of absconding or offending while remanded; and if so, he may be remanded to local authority accommodation and require him to be kept in secure accommodation if it would be undesirable

[66] PACE 1984, s.38.
[67] *ibid.*, s.38B.
[68] Children and Young Persons Act 1969, s.29(1).
[69] *ibid.*, s.23(1).
[70] *ibid.*, s.23(2).
[71] *ibid.*, s.23(4).
[72] *ibid.*, s.23(11).
[73] Criminal Justice Act 1991, s.61(1), as amended by s.120 of the Crime and Disorder Act 1998.
[74] Children and Young Persons Act 1969, s.9(1).
[75] Criminal Justice Act 1948, s.27.
[76] Crime and Disorder Act 1998, s.98(1).

for him to be remanded to a remand centre because of his physical or emotional immaturity or a propensity to harm himself and there is secure accommodation available. Otherwise, it must remand him to a remand centre if there is no propensity for self-harm or if he is not physically and emotionally immature and there a centre available to him; or it must remand him to prison if that is also the case and there is no centre available to him.[77] The authority may apply for particular conditions. The authority is under a duty to secure that it is in a position to comply with the relevant requirements if they apply. A child or young person who has been remanded or committed to local authority accommodation may be arrested without warrant by a constable if he has reasonable grounds for suspecting that the child or young person has broken any conditions attached to that remand. The child must be brought before the court as soon as practicable and in any event within 24 hours of his arrest.[78]

Summary Trials

Where a child or young person is charged with an offence, the court may, and in respect of a child or young person under the age of 16 must, require the parent or guardian to attend court at all times.[79] If he is looked after by a local authority, then it is that authority; otherwise, it is the authority in whose area it appears to the court that he resides or the offence was committed.[80] Where a person under the age of 18 appears before a magistrates' court on an information charging him with an indictable offence, other than homicide, he must be tried summarily unless: (1) the offence is one punishable in the case of an adult with imprisonment for 14 years or more and the court considers that if he is found guilty of the offence it ought to be possible to sentence him accordingly; or (2) he is charged jointly with an adult and the court concludes it is necessary to commit both to trial.[81] If he is found guilty by the magistrates on a summary trial, it may impose a fine not exceeding the prescribed amount, or it may exercise the same powers as it could have exercised if he had been found guilty of an offence for which, but for the restriction as to the imposition of imprisonment for young offenders, he could have been sentenced on indictment for a term not exceeding the maximum term of imprisonment for the offence on conviction on indictment, or six months whichever is the less.[82]

3-118

Youth Courts

If a child or young person is convicted by a court for an offence other than homicide, and it is not a youth court, it may remit the case to a youth court.[83] The offender must be brought before a youth court and the court may deal with him as though he had been tried and convicted in that court. If it does not remit, and the court would be required to refer the offender to a youth offender panel, the court may remit the case. If the court is not required to refer the offender to a youth offender panel, the case may be dealt with by means of an order discharging the offender absolutely or conditionally, a fine, or a recognisance entered into by a parent or guardian to take proper care of him and exercise proper control.[84] A youth court is a court of summary jurisdiction sitting for the purpose of hearing any charge against a child or young person or for any other express statutory purpose. The court must consist of

3-119

---

[77] Children and Young Persons Act 1969, s.23(4).
[78] *ibid.*, s.23A, added by s.23 of the Criminal Justice and Public Order Act 1994.
[79] Children and Young Persons Act 1933, s.34A(1).
[80] Children and Young Persons Act 1969, s.23(2)(b).
[81] Magistrates Court Act 1980, s.24.
[82] *ibid.*, s.24(3).
[83] Powers of Criminal Courts (Sentencing) Act 2000, s.8.
[84] *ibid.*, s.8(8).

a District Judge sitting alone or not more than three justices who must include a man and a woman.[85] There must be one for every petty sessions area. No one may be present during a sitting of the youth court unless they are immediately concerned with a case before the court, or a bona fide representative of the media, although there are complex restrictions as to what can be reported.[86]

Sentencing Options

3-120   Courts have available to them a range of measures with respect to children. There is the common law power to bind over but, additionally, a statutory power to bind over parents and guardians. The power to impose an absolute or conditional charge applies equally to children and to adults but this is subject to the final warning and reprimand scheme. Special sentences that apply only to children and young people are: referral to a youth offender panel, reparation orders and parenting orders. Children may be fined, but this is subject to a statutory ceiling.[87] Guardians and parents made be made to pay fines, compensation and costs.[88] Children and young people may be made subject to community sentencing orders in certain conditions.[89] Action plans, supervision orders, curfew orders and attendance centre orders are special kinds of community orders applicable to children and young people. Certain forms of community orders are available only to offenders aged 16 years and older: rehabilitation orders, drug treatment and testing orders and curfew and community punishment orders for persistent petty offenders. There are only three forms of custodial sentence for offenders under the age of 18: detention and training, detention for serious offenders and detention at Her Majesty's pleasure for murder.

Pre-sentence reports

3-121   Where the court requires it, a youth offending term member, a social worker of a local social services authority or a probation officer must prepare a pre-sentence report. This is a report in writing made with a view to assist the court in determining the most suitable method of dealing with an offender.[90] The court must provide a copy to the offender and his legal representatives and to the prosecutor.[91] A court must obtain and consider such a report if it considers that the offence was so serious that a custodial sentence is the only suitable means of sentencing the offender.[92] It does not invalidate a sentence if the court proceeds without a report; however, it must be obtained and considered by an appellate court.[93]

Binding Over and Discharge

3-122   The court may consider an order binding over or discharging conditionally or absolutely a person convicted of an offence who is under 18, and must consider doing so in respect of a someone under 16 years of age.[94] These powers may only be exercised if the court is satisfied that it would be desirable in the interests of preventing the commission of him of further offences.[95] The court must obtain

---

[85] Youth Courts (Constitution) Rules 1954.
[86] Children and Young Persons Act 1933, s.49, as amended by Youth Justice and Criminal Evidence Act 1999.
[87] Powers of Criminal Courts (Sentencing) Act 2000, ss.16 to 32.
[88] *ibid.*, s.137.
[89] *ibid.*, s.33.
[90] *ibid.*, s.162.
[91] *ibid.*, s.156(2).
[92] *ibid.*, ss.79, 80.
[93] *ibid.*, s.81.
[94] *ibid.*, s.150.
[95] *ibid.*, s.150(1).

the consent of the offender's parent or guardian in order to order that the parent or guardian enter into a recognisance to take proper care of him and exercise proper control over him.[96] If the parent or guardian refuses to consent and the court considers this refusal to be unreasonable, then it may order the parent or guardian to pay a fine.[97] Where the court orders a community sentence, it may include in a recognisance a provision that the parent or guardian ensure that the offender complies with the requirements of the sentence.[98] The recognisance must not be for a period exceeding three years, or where the offender will reach 18 years in a period shorter than three years, for a period exceeding this shorter period.[99] The parent or guardian has rights of appeal to the Crown Court if made by magistrates or the Court of Appeal, if made by the Crown Court.[1]

Referral Orders

Under s.16 of the Powers of Criminal Courts (Sentencing) Act 2000, courts (i.e. a youth court or a magistrates' court) have a power to refer any offenders aged under 18 to youth offender panels—the referral order. Referral orders are now the most used sentence for young offenders;[2] they require offenders to attend community-based youth offender panel meetings at which they are encouraged to face and accept responsibility for their actions, including in some cases meeting their victims. At least one member of the panel must be a member of the youth offending team. It is precondition that the offence nor any connected offence is one for which the sentence is fixed by law. Nor can it do so if the court is proposing to impose a custodial sentence on the offender or make a hospital order (within the meaning of the Mental Health Act 1983) or if it proposes to discharge him absolutely in respect of the offence. It is also subject to other conditions, set out in s.17(1): the offender has pleaded guilty to the offence and to any connected offence; he has never been convicted by or before a court in the United Kingdom of any offence other than the offence and any connected offence; and he has never been bound over in criminal proceedings in England and Wales or Northern Ireland to keep the peace or to be of good behaviour. If these "compulsory referral conditions" are satisfied the court shall sentence the offender for the offence by ordering him to be referred to a youth offender panel. **3-123**

Additionally, under s.16(3) of the 2000 Act, if certain "discretionary referral conditions" exist, the court may sentence the offender for the offence by ordering him to be referred to a youth offender panel. These are set out in s.17(2): the offender is being dealt with by the court for the offence and one or more connected offences; although he pleaded guilty to at least one of these offences, he also pleaded not guilty to at least one of them; he has never been convicted by or before a court in the United Kingdom of any offence other than these offences; and he has never been bound over in criminal proceedings in England and Wales or Northern Ireland to keep the peace or to be of good behaviour. Section 18(1) provides that a referral order shall specify the youth offending team responsible for implementing the order, require the offender to attend each of the meetings of a youth offender panel to be established by the team for the offender and specify the period for which any youth offender contract, taking effect between the offender and the panel under s.23 below, is to have effect (which must not be less than three nor more than 12 months). The **3-124**

---

[96] Powers of Criminal Courts (Sentencing) Act 2000, 150(11). An order under s.150 must not require the parent or guardian to enter into a recognisance for an amount greater than £1000 and their means must be taken into account.

[97] *ibid.*, s.150(2)(b): again, not exceeding £1000.

[98] *ibid.*, s.150(2).

[99] *ibid.*, s.150(4).

[1] *ibid.*, s.150(8).

[2] Edwards, "Restorative Justice and the Court of Appeal" (2006) Crim. L.R. 110–123L.

youth offending team must be a team having the function of implementing referral orders in the area in which it appears to the court that the offender resides or will reside.[3] On making a referral order the court shall explain to the offender in ordinary language, the effect and consequences of the order.

3-125   Under s.19 of the 2000 Act, a court making a referral order may make an order requiring the appropriate person, or, in a case where there are two or more appropriate persons, any one or more of them, to attend the meetings of the youth offender panel.[4] Where an offender is aged under 16 when a court makes a referral order in his case, the court shall exercise its power under this section so as to require at least one appropriate person to attend meetings of the youth offender panel; and if the offender falls within subs.(6) below (i.e. the child is looked after by a local authority), the person or persons so required to attend those meetings shall be or include a representative of the local authority mentioned in that subsection. However, the court shall not under this section make an order requiring a person to attend meetings of the youth offender panel if the court is satisfied that it would be unreasonable to do so, or to an extent which the court is satisfied would be unreasonable.

3-126   Where a referral order has been made in respect of an offender (or two or more associated referral orders have been so made), it is the duty of the youth offending team to establish a youth offender panel for the offender and to arrange for the first meeting of the panel to be held for the purposes of s.23 of the 2000 Act, and subsequently to arrange for the holding of any further meetings of the panel required by virtue of s.25. At each of its meetings a panel shall, however, consist of at least one member appointed by the YOT from among its members; and two members so appointed who are not members of the team. It is the offender's duty to attend meetings with the panel as required by them. If the offender fails to attend any part of such a meeting, then, under s.22 of the 2000 Act, the panel may adjourn the meeting to such time and place as it may specify; or end the meeting and refer the offender back to the appropriate court. One person aged 18 or over chosen by the offender, with the agreement of the panel, shall be entitled to accompany the offender to any meeting of the panel (and it need not be the same person who accompanies him to every meeting). The panel may allow to attend any such meeting any person who appears to the panel to be a victim of, or otherwise affected by, the offence, or any of the offences, in respect of which the offender was referred to the panel; and/or any person who appears to the panel to be someone capable of having a good influence on the offender. Where the panel invite the victim to attend a meeting of the panel, the panel may allow the victim to be accompanied to the meeting by one person chosen by the victim with the agreement of the panel.

3-127   At the first meeting of the youth offender panel established for an offender, the panel shall seek to reach agreement with the offender on a programme of behaviour, the aim (or principal aim) of which is the prevention of re-offending by the offender.[5] The terms of the programme may, in particular, include provision for any of the following:

(1) the offender may be required to make financial or other reparation to any person who appears to the panel to be a victim of, or otherwise affected by, the offence, or any of the offences, for which the offender was referred to the panel;[6]

---

[3] Powers of Criminal Courts (Sentencing) Act 2000, s.18(2).
[4] *ibid.*, s.20.
[5] *ibid.*, s.23(1).
[6] No term which provides for anything to be done to or with any such victim or other affected person as is mentioned in subs.(2)(a) above may be included in the programme without the consent of that person: Crime and Disorder Act 1998, s.23(4).

(2) to attend mediation sessions with any such victim or other person;

(3) to carry out unpaid work or service in, or for, the community;

(4) to be at home at times specified in, or determined under, the programme;

(5) to attend a school or other educational establishment or at a place of work;

(6) to participate in specified activities (such as those designed to address offending behaviour, those offering education or training or those assisting with the rehabilitation of persons dependent on, or having a propensity to misuse, alcohol or drugs);

(7) to present himself to specified persons at times and places specified in, or determined under, the programme;

(8) to stay away from specified places or persons (or both).

However, it may not provide for the electronic monitoring of the offender's whereabouts or for the offender to have imposed on him any physical restriction on his movements.[7] Where a programme is agreed between the offender and the panel, the panel shall cause a written record of the programme to be produced in language capable of being readily understood by, or explained to, the offender; and for signature by him. Once the record has been signed by the offender and a member of the panel on behalf of the panel, the terms of the programme, as set out in the record, take effect as the terms of a "youth offender contract" between the offender and the panel and the panel provide the offender with a copy of it . Under s.25, where it appears to a youth offender panel to be appropriate to do so, the panel may end the first meeting, or any further meeting, without having reached agreement with the offender on a programme of behaviour of the kind mentioned in s.23(1) above, and resume consideration of the offender's case at a further meeting of the panel. If, however, it appears to the panel at the first meeting, or any such further meeting, that there is no prospect of agreement being reached with the offender within a reasonable period after the making of the referral order (or orders), then the panel shall refer the offender back to the appropriate court. Further, if at a meeting of the panel, an agreement is reached with the offender but he does not sign the record, and his failure to do so appears to the panel to be unreasonable, the panel shall end the meeting and refer the offender back to the appropriate court.

During the period of the referral order, the panel is to meet and hold progress meetings about the offender. Under s.26, if at any time after a youth offender contract has taken effect under s.23 above, but before the end of the period for which the contract has effect, the specified team shall, if so requested by the panel, arrange for the holding of a meeting of the panel under this section ("a progress meeting"). The panel may make a request under subs.(1) above if it appears to the panel to be expedient to review the offender's progress in implementing the programme of behaviour contained in the contract, or any other matter arising in connection with the contract. However, the panel must make such a request if the offender has notified the panel that he wishes to seek the panel's agreement to a variation in the terms of the contract; or he wishes the panel to refer him back to the appropriate court with a view to the referral order (or orders) being revoked on account of a significant change in his circumstances (such as his being taken to live abroad) making compliance with any youth offender contract impractical or because it appears to the panel that the offender is in breach of any of the terms of the contract.

3-128

[7] Powers of Criminal Courts (Sentencing) Act 2000, s.23(3).

3-129   At the progress meeting, the panel shall review the offender's progress or any such other matter; discuss with the offender any breach of the terms of the contract which it appears to the panel that he has committed; consider any variation in the terms of the contract sought by the offender or which it appears to the panel to be expedient to make in the light of any such review or discussion; and/or consider whether to accede to any request by the offender that he be referred back to the appropriate court. Where the panel has discussed with the offender a breach of the contract, the panel and the offender may agree that the offender is to continue to be required to comply with the contract without being referred back to the appropriate court; or the panel may decide to end the meeting and refer the offender back to that court. Where a variation in the terms of the contract is agreed between the offender and the panel, the panel provide him with a written record of the variation in language capable of being readily understood by, or explained to, the offender and for signature by him. Any such variation shall take effect once the record has been signed by the offender; and by a member of the panel on behalf of the panel. Where the panel has discussed with the offender such a request to vary the contract, the panel may, if it is satisfied that there is (or is soon to be) such a change in, decide to end the meeting and refer the offender back to the appropriate court.

3-130   Where the compliance period in the case of a youth offender contract is due to expire, the specified team shall arrange for the holding, before the end of that period, of a meeting of the panel ("the final meeting") under s.27 of the 2000 Act. At that final meeting, the panel shall review the extent of the offender's compliance to date with the terms of the contract; and decide, in the light of that review, whether his compliance with those terms has been such as to justify the conclusion that, by the time the compliance period expires, he will have satisfactorily completed the contract; and the panel shall give the offender written confirmation of its decision. Where the panel decides that the offender's compliance with the terms of the contract has been such as to justify that conclusion, the panel's decision shall have the effect of discharging the referral order (or orders) as from the end of the compliance period. Otherwise the panel shall refer the offender back to the appropriate court.

Reparations Orders

3-131   Section 73(1) of the 2000 Act provides that, where a child or young person (i.e. any person aged under 18) is convicted of an offence, other than one for which the sentence is fixed by law, the court by, or before, which he is convicted may make an order—a "reparation order"—requiring him to make reparation specified in the order to a person or persons so specified, or to the community at large; and any person so specified must be a person identified by the court as a victim of the offence or a person otherwise affected by it. "Reparation" means, by s.73(3) of the 2000 Act, reparation for the offence otherwise than by the payment of compensation; and the requirements that may be specified in a reparation order are set out in ss.74(1) to (3) below. The court shall not make a reparation order in respect of the offender if it proposes to pass on him a custodial sentence; or to make in respect of him a community service order, a combination order, a supervision order which includes requirements authorised by Sch.6 to this Act, an action plan order or a referral order. Before making a reparation order, a court shall obtain and consider a written report by a probation officer, a social worker of a local authority social services department or a member of a YOT, indicating the type of work that is suitable for the offender; and the attitude of the victim or victims to the requirements proposed to be included in the order.[8] Before making a reparation order,

[8] Powers of Criminal Courts (Sentencing) Act 2000, s.73(5).

the court shall explain to the offender, in ordinary language, the effect of the order and of the requirements proposed to be included in it; the consequences which may follow (under Sch.8 to this Act) if he fails to comply with any of those requirements; and that the court has power (under that Schedule) to review the order on the application either of the offender or of the responsible officer.

The requirements of the reparation order in s.74 shall not include a require- **3-132** ment to work for more than 24 hours in aggregate or to make reparation to any person without the consent of that person. However, the reparation shall in the opinion of the court be commensurate with the seriousness of the offence, or the combination of the offence and one or more offences associated with it. The terms of the order must, as far as practicable, be such as to avoid any conflict with the offender's religious beliefs or with the requirements of any community order to which he may be subject; and any interference with the times, if any, at which he normally works or attends school or any other educational establishment. Any reparation required by a reparation order shall be made under the supervision of the responsible officer; and shall be made within a period of three months from the date of the making of the order.[9]

By virtue of s.75, Sch.8 to the 2000 Act contains provisions as to the con- **3-133** sequences of failing to comply with the orders and for revoking and amending them. If the local youth court is satisfied, on the application of the responsible officer, that the offender has failed to comply with any requirement included in the order, then it may order the offender to pay a fine of an amount not exceeding £1,000, make a curfew order in respect of him, or make an attendance centre order in respect of him. If the reparation order was made by a magistrates' court, then it may revoke the order and deal with the offender for the offence, in respect of which the order was made, in any way in which he could have been dealt with for that offence by the court which made the order if the order had not been made. If the order was made by the Crown Court, it may commit him in custody or release him on bail until he can be brought or appear before the Crown Court; and the court may deal with him, for the offence in respect of which the order was made, in any way in which it could have dealt with him for that offence if it had not made the order. In dealing with an offender under this paragraph, a court shall take into account the extent to which he has complied with the requirements of the reparation order (or action plan order).

When a child or young person is convicted of an offence, the court may also **3-134** order him to make reparation specified in the order to any person specified in the order or to the community at large.[10] It is not a community sentence order so that the offence itself need not be so serious as to warrant a community sentence. The court must consider a report written by a responsible officer (which is not a pre-sentence report). The person specified in the order must be a victim of the offence or a person affected by it. The victim's role is enhanced regarding such orders. The officer must contact the victim as soon as possible. The court cannot make such an order if it is intending to pass a custodial sentence or to make a community punishment order, supervision order, an action plan order or a referral order. The order cannot require the offender to work for more than 24 hours in all; nor can it do so without the consent of the victim of, or person affected by, the offence.

Action Plan Orders
If the principle aim of the youth justice system is to prevent offending by chil- **3-135** dren and young people, the action plan order is aimed at providing courts with

[9] Powers of Criminal Courts (Sentencing) Act 2000, s.74(8).
[10] *ibid.*, ss.73, 74.

a new type of community sentence designed to provide ". . .a short but intensive and individually tailored response to offending behaviour so that the factors associated with the offending can be addressed as well as the offending itself."[11] Section 69 of the 2000 Act provides that where a child or young person is convicted of an offence, and the court by or before which he is convicted is of the *opinion* (mentioned in subs.(3), below), the court may make an order—"an action plan order"—which requires the offender, for a period of three months beginning with the date of the order, to comply with an action plan; that is to say, a series of requirements with respect to his actions and whereabouts during that period, and which places the offender for that period under the supervision of the responsible officer[12] and requires the offender to comply with any directions given by the responsible officer with a view to the implementation of that plan. The requirements included in the order, and any directions given by the responsible officer, may include requirements authorised by s.70, below. Subsection (3) provides that the *opinion* referred to in subs.(1), above, is that the making of an action plan order is desirable in the interests of securing the rehabilitation of the offender; or preventing the commission by him of further offences. The court shall not make an action plan order in respect of the offender if he is already the subject of such an order or the court proposes to pass on him a custodial sentence or to make in respect of him a probation order, a community service order, a combination order, an attendance centre order, a supervision order or a referral order. Before making an action plan order, the court shall obtain and consider a written report by a probation officer, a social worker of a local authority social services department or a member of a YOT indicating the requirements proposed by that person to be included in the order, the benefits to the offender that the proposed requirements are designed to achieve, and the attitude of a parent or guardian of the offender to the proposed requirements. Where the offender is aged under 16, it shall consider information about the offender's family circumstances and the likely effect of the order on those circumstances. Before making an action plan order, the court shall explain to the offender in ordinary language the effect of the order and of the requirements proposed to be included in it; the consequences which may follow (under Sch.8 to this Act) if he fails to comply with any of those requirements; and that the court has power (under that Schedule) to review the order on the application either of the offender or of the responsible officer.

3-136   Section 70 sets out the requirements which may be included in action plan orders:

(1) to participate in activities specified in the requirements or directions at a time or times so specified;

(2) to present himself to a person or persons specified in the requirements or directions at a place or places and at a time or times so specified;

(3) subject to subs.(2), below, to attend at an attendance centre specified in the requirements or directions for a number of hours so specified;[13]

(4) to stay away from a place or places specified in the requirements or directions;

[11] *The Crime and Disorder Act Guidance Document: Action Plan Order*, Home Office, December 1999.

[12] In this Act "responsible officer", in relation to an offender subject to an action plan order, means one of the following who is specified in the order, namely: (a) a probation officer; (b) a social worker of a local authority social services department; (c) a member of a youth offending team: Powers of Criminal Courts (Sentencing) Act 2000, s.69(4).

[13] Subsection (1)(c) above applies only where the offence committed by the offender is an offence punishable with imprisonment: Powers of Criminal Courts (Sentencing) Act 2000, s.70(2).

(5) to comply with any arrangements for his education specified in the requirements or directions;

(6) to make reparation specified in the requirements or directions to a person or persons so specified or to the community at large; and

(7) to attend any hearing fixed by the court under s.71 below.

Requirements included in an action plan order and directions given by a responsible officer shall, as far as practicable, be such as to avoid any conflict with the offender's religious beliefs or with the requirements of any other community order to which he may be subject; and any interference with the times, if any, at which he normally works or attends school or any other educational establishment.

Immediately after making an action plan order, a court may, under s.71 of **3-137** the 2000 Act, fix a further hearing for a date not more than 21 days after the making of the order; and direct the responsible officer to make, at that hearing, a report as to the effectiveness of the order and the extent to which it has been implemented. At a hearing fixed under this subs.(1), the court is to consider the report and may, on the application of the responsible officer or the offender, amend the order by cancelling any provision included in it or by inserting in it (either in addition to or in substitution for any of its provisions) any provision that the court could originally have included in it. By s.72, Sch.8 to 2000 Act (which makes provision for dealing with failures to comply with action plan orders and reparation orders and for revoking and amending such orders) shall have effect so far as relating to action plan orders.

Parenting Orders

According to a Home Office study, 42 per cent of juveniles with low or **3-138** medium level parental supervision offend, so that improving the quality of the relationship between parent and child is crucial in preventing anti-social behaviour and criminal activity.[14] There are two parts to the parenting order: that the parent or guardian attends guidance and counselling sessions to help them deal with the child; and it may impose requirements on the parent or guardian as to the exercise of control over the child. Section 8 of the Crime and Disorder Act 1998[15] defines a parenting order as an order which requires a parent to comply, for a period not exceeding twelve months, with such requirements as are specified in the order and to attend for a concurrent period (again not exceeding 12 months), such counselling or guidance programmes as may be directed by a responsible officer. Where, in any court proceedings, a child safety order is made in respect of a child, an anti-social behaviour order or sex offender order is made in respect of a child or young person, a child or young person is convicted of an offence or a person is convicted of an offence under s.443 (failure to comply with school attendance order) or s.444 (failure to secure regular attendance at school of registered pupil) of the Education Act 1996, a court may make a parenting order under s.8 if certain conditions are fulfilled in respect of a person who is a parent or guardian of the child or young person or, as the case may be, the person convicted of the offence under s.443 or 444. The relevant condition is that the parenting order would be desirable in the interests of preventing any repetition of the kind of behaviour which led to the child safety order, anti-social behaviour order or sex offender order being made; the commission of any further offence by the child or young person; or the commission of any

[14] Crime and Disorder Act Guidance Document, Home Office, December 1999.
[15] As amended by s.18 of the Anti-Social Behaviour Act 2003.

further offence under s.443 or 444 of the Education Act 1996.[16] The order shall require the parent to comply, for a period not exceeding twelve months, with such requirements as are specified in the order; and to attend, for a concurrent period not exceeding three months and not more than once in any week, such counselling or guidance programme as may be specified in directions given by the responsible officer. By way of an amendment to the 1998 Act by s.18(3) of the Anti-Social Behaviour Act 2003, s.8(7A) is inserted, which provides that a counselling or guidance programme which a parent is required to attend by virtue of subs.(4)(b) above may be or include a residential course, but only if the court is satisfied: (a) that the attendance of the parent at a residential course is likely to be more effective than his attendance at a non-residential course in preventing any such repetition or, as the case may be, the commission of any such further offence, and (b) that any interference with family life which is likely to result from the attendance of the parent at a residential course is proportionate in all the circumstances. The requirements that may be specified are those which the court considers desirable in the interests of preventing any such repetition or, as the case may be, the commission of any such further offence.

3-139 Further, under s.9(1) of the 1998 Act, where a person under the age of 16 is convicted of an offence, the court by or before which he is so convicted, if it is satisfied that the relevant condition is fulfilled, shall make a parenting order; and if it is not so satisfied, shall state in open court that it is not and why it is not. Before making a parenting order a court shall obtain and consider information about the person's family circumstances and the likely effect of the order on those circumstances. It must also explain to the parent in ordinary language the effect of the order and of the requirements proposed to be included in it, the consequences which may follow (under subs.(7) below) if he fails to comply with any of those requirements and that the court has power (under subs.(5) below) to review the order on the application either of the parent or of the responsible officer.

3-140 Once again, requirements specified in, and directions given under, a parenting order shall, as far as practicable, be such as to avoid any conflict with the parent's religious beliefs; and any interference with the times, if any, at which he normally works or attends an educational establishment. Parenting orders may be varied or discharged on the application of the parent, but where an application is dismissed no further application for its discharge shall be made under that subsection by any person, except with the consent of the court which made the order. If, while a parenting order is in force, the parent, without reasonable excuse, fails to comply with any requirement included in the order, or specified in directions given by the responsible officer, he shall be liable on summary conviction to a fine not exceeding level 3 on the standard scale.[17]

3-141 The Anti-Social Behaviour Act 2003 creates parenting contracts and parental orders in the case of anti-social behaviour. Section 25 provides that, where a child or young person has been referred to a YOT, the YOT may enter into a parenting contract with a parent of the child or young person if a member of that team has reason to believe that the child or young person has engaged, or is likely to engage, in criminal conduct[18] or anti-social behaviour.[19]

---

[16] Crime and Disorder Act 1998, s.8(6).
[17] *ibid.*, s.9(7).
[18] "Criminal conduct" means conduct which: (a) constitutes a criminal offence, or (b) in the case of conduct by a person under the age of 10, would constitute a criminal offence if that person were not under that age: Crime and Disorder Act 1998, s.29(1).
[19] "Anti-social behaviour" means behaviour by a person which causes or is likely to cause harassment, alarm or distress to one or more other persons not of the same household as the person: Crime and Disorder Act 1998, s.29(1).

The contract must contain a statement by the parent that he agrees to comply with such requirements as may be specified in the document for such period as may be so specified, and a statement by the YOT that it agrees to provide support to the parent for the purpose of complying with those requirements. It may also contain a requirement to attend a counselling or guidance programme. The purpose of the requirements is to prevent a child or young person from engaging in criminal conduct or anti-social behaviour or further criminal conduct or further anti-social behaviour. The contract must be signed by the parent and signed on behalf of the youth offending team. However, a parenting contract does not create any obligations in respect of whose breach any liability arises in contract or in tort.

Further, under s.26 of the 1998 Act, where a child or young person has been **3-142** referred to a YOT, a member of the YOT may apply to a magistrates' court for a parenting order in respect of a parent of the child or young person. If such an application is made, the court may make a parenting order in respect of a parent of the child or young person if it is satisfied that the child or young person has engaged in criminal conduct or anti-social behaviour, and that making the order would be desirable in the interests of preventing the child or young person from engaging in further criminal conduct or further anti-social behaviour. The order requires the parent to comply, for a period not exceeding twelve months, with such requirements as are specified in the order, and to attend, for a concurrent period not exceeding three months, such counselling or guidance programme as may be specified in directions given by the responsible officer. A counselling or guidance programme which a parent is required to attend may be, or include, a residential course, but only if the court is satisfied that the following two conditions are fulfilled. These are, first, that attendance of the parent at a residential course is likely to be more effective than his attendance at a non-residential course in preventing the child or young person from engaging in further criminal conduct or further anti-social behaviour; and, secondly, that any interference with family life which is likely to result from the attendance of the parent at a residential course is proportionate in all the circumstances. In deciding whether to make a parenting order under s.26, a court must take into account (amongst other things) any refusal by the parent to enter into a parenting contract under s.25 in respect of the child or young person; or if the parent has entered into such a parenting contract, any failure by the parent to comply with the requirements specified in the contract.[20] Before making a parenting order under s.26 of the 1998 Act, in the case of a child or a young person under the age of 16, a court must obtain and consider information about the child or young person's family circumstances and the likely effect of the order on those circumstances. Under s.28 of the 2003 Act, an appeal lies to the Crown Court against the making of a parenting order section under s.26 of the 1998 Act and s.10 of the 1998 Act applies in relation to an appeal under this section as they apply in relation to an appeal under subs.(1)(b) of that section.

Home Office Guidance on Parenting Contracts and Parenting Orders
Government guidance on parenting contracts guidance provides insight into **3-143** the way in which they are supervised and monitored by the relevant authorities and officers.[21] The suitability of a parent or guardian for a parenting order is normally determined by an assessment process carried out by a practitioner from a YOT. If the assessments provide evidence that parents could be supported to positively influence their child's behaviour, and the parents are not willing to engage with support voluntarily, it will usually be appropriate to

[20] Crime and Disorder Act 1998, s.27(1).
[21] *Parenting Contracts & Orders Guidance*, Home Office, 2004.

recommend a parenting order to the court. A judgment about the suitability of a parenting intervention and recommendations are usually made in a pre-sentence report (PSR). The recommendation takes into consideration the potential needs of both the parents or guardians and the child and the likely effectiveness in terms of changing their behaviour. When preparing PSRs in cases where a parenting order is inappropriate due to, for example, domestic violence, abuse or continuing civil disputes, practitioners will need to take into account the level of information the court needs to make a decision. It may be that detailed sensitive information will not be necessary and that a general phrase such as "while family tensions or civil matters are to be resolved" will be sufficient for the purpose. Where the parents are not already known to the YOT in this way, the court will want to provide the opportunity for the youth offender panel to engage parents and young people in agreeing a contract which could include provision of parenting support on a voluntary basis or through a parenting order. If the parents do not attend the panel their case can be referred back to court, and the YOT would provide an assessment. The core requirement of a parenting order is that the parent attends a parenting programme. Details and duration of the programme are specified in directions given by the responsible officer. The programme can last for up to three months. The arrangements should be as flexible as possible, and take account of programme availability and timing. It may be provided by the responsible officer or, for example, the local authority social services department or a local voluntary sector organisation working with parents. The local authority youth justice plan should set out the general arrangements for delivering parenting orders. The court will need to decide the length of the order. This needs to allow sufficient time for: assessing parents; any individual work needed to prepare the parents for the programme; any waiting time before the programme can start; the programme itself; and the time any specific requirements should run. The responsible officer will need to assess what kind of counselling or guidance programme is required, in consultation with the provider. This should cover, for example, who will provide the sessions; whether they should be group, individually or family-based; and whether there are particular cultural and social factors to be considered. During the programme the responsible officer and the programme provider (if different) will need to monitor the parents' progress at suitable intervals. The parent might also find it helpful to be involved in some voluntary follow-up work when the order has been completed, such as attending a parent support group.

3-144   A parenting order can include a residential course, but only if two conditions are met: (a) that the attendance of the parent or guardian at a residential course is likely to be more effective than their attendance at a non-residential course in preventing the child or young person from engaging in a repetition of the behaviour which led to the making of the order; and (b) that any likely interference with family life is proportionate in all the circumstances. A YOT recommending a parenting order with a residential component should provide evidence that these conditions are met. For the court to decide whether any likely interference with family life is proportionate the YOT will need to explain the programme. This need not be continuous; a small number of residential weekends structured within a wider non-residential programme may be suitable. Arrangements for the care of the child (and any siblings and dependants) will be a crucial consideration. Voluntary attendance by the child and siblings may be desirable as intensive family work can be particularly effective. The court may also include in a parenting order specific requirements for the parent to comply with for not more than 12 months. These may be what the court considers desirable to prevent any repetition of the particular behaviour which led to the child safety, anti-social behaviour or sex offender order, or any further offence by the child or young person. Although discretionary, it may be helpful to include further requirements such as for supervision. These requirements would need to be tailored to address the problems which led to the parenting order and should, if possible, be linked to the requirements of any order imposed on the child or young person. They could include requiring the parent to ensure that the child: attends school or other relevant educational activities, such as mentoring in literacy or numeracy or a homework club; attends a programme or course to address relevant problems, such as anger management or drug or alcohol misuse; avoids contact with disruptive and, possibly, older children; avoids unsupervised visits to certain areas such as shopping centres; and is at home during certain hours at night and is effectively supervised.

In *M v Inner London Crown Court*,[22] M, whose daughter had been convicted   **3-145** of an offence of wounding, sought judicial review of the decision of the Crown Court to uphold the imposition by the youth court of a 12 month parenting order under s.8 of the 1998 Act and a compensation order. She argued that parenting orders were incompatible with the Human Rights Act 1998 Sch.1, Pt I, Art.6 and Art.8. As to Art.6, the magistrates should, before making an order, apply the heightened civil standard of proof and in that way be sure that it was appropriate to make the order. As to Art.8, it was submitted that parenting orders were not a proportionate response to the objective that they sought to achieve. It was further contended that the youth court had acted irrationally in making the parenting order in her case. The court granted the application in part, holding that parenting orders did not breach Art.6. The decision as to whether or not an order should be made was an exercise of judgment or evaluation. Nor did parenting orders infringe Art.8. Their objective of addressing the problems caused by juvenile crime was sufficiently important to justify limiting a fundamental right. Furthermore, the means used to impair that right did not exceed what was necessary to accomplish the objective: parenting orders were preventive, numerous safeguards existed, the degree of interference with Art.8(1) was very limited when balanced against the importance of tackling youth crime, and there was compelling evidence that the orders achieved their purpose of preventing reoffending. Further, given that the pre sentence report had stated that M would not be receptive to or suitable for a parenting order and that her daughter's conduct had, the offence apart, been exemplary, the youth court had acted irrationally in making an order in the instant case.

Barnado's, in evidence before the Home Affairs Committee on Anti-Social   **3-146** Behaviour, said that those attending residential courses were predominantly single mothers, a substantial amount experiencing numerous problems including debt, ill-health, housing problems and domestic violence, and a high percentage had been seeking help with their children's behaviour for some time, but almost none had been provided with any assistance. Generally, the courses were considered to be successful. Even so, there were funding problems. The Magistrates Association argued:

"When making an ASBO in respect of young people magistrates are required to make an parenting order if satisfied that this would help prevent repetition of the behaviour. Information is sought from the YOTs when considering this and YOTs are very reluctant to recommend parenting orders. Resources are part of the problem."[23]

The Local Government Association and officers of Youth Offending Services made similar complaints. Between April and December 2004, there

[22] [2003] 1 F.L.R. 994.
[23] Home Office, Fifth Report Session 2004/05 Report, para.155.

were 1162 parenting orders; only 41 parenting orders were applied for by YOTs and 13 by local authorities. The vast majority were made following criminal convictions.[24]

Family Group Conferencing

3-147 Where it is the child's entire family that is involved in anti-social behaviour, informal techniques such as family group conferencing may be more appropriate. According to welfare organisation guidance, family group conferences are a way of giving families the chance to get together to try and make the best plan possible for children. The decision makers at a family group conference are the family members, and not the professionals.[25] A Family Welfare Association officer said that conferencing can be "remarkably effective", although much depends on the family:

"You say to a family 'Let us get you all into one room so that everybody can bring to bear their ideas about the problem' and it is the professionals who are sitting outside waiting anxiously to hear what they will be summoned in to offer. Suddenly they will say "We want to see the social worker" and the social worker will come into the room and the family will say "What we want is respite care, one day a month, could you organise that? We have got a package we think will work if this child can have respite care say over a weekend or if we could all have a holiday together." It is a negotiated contract process. It can be very effective for a group of families who are able to negotiate. It is not particularly useful for families who thrive on conflict, high expressed emotion, and where it is hard to regulate behaviour."

The Association of Directors of Social Services backed interventions such as family group conferencing, arguing that these were preferable to imposing a parenting order.[26]

Further Amendments

3-148 The Prime Minister, in a speech in September 2005, proposed that parenting contracts and parenting orders should be used more widely, and that housing officers and schools should have the power to issue the orders:

"A parenting order can make clear to parents their responsibility to ensure that their child attends school, that the child takes part in literacy or numeracy clubs or that they attend programmes dealing with problems such anger management or alcohol misuse. Parenting orders can also stop children visiting areas such as shopping centres and ensure a child is at home being supervised at night."

The new powers will apply to children at a much earlier stage, he said, not just when they have committed a criminal offence but when they are about to get involved in anti-social behaviour.

3-149 The "Respect Action Plan" set out the plans in more detail:

"ACTION: Legislate to expand the use of parenting orders. Most parents accept help when offered or will take it when they have good information. But where parents are not willing to engage, we will expand the use of

[24] 2004/05 Report, para.156.
[25] Barnado's Family Rights Group, NCH "Family Group Conferences: Principles and Practice Guidance", 2002.
[26] Evidence before the Home Affairs Committee Report on Anti-Social Behaviour 2004–05, paras 158–59.

parenting contracts and orders to secure their engagement. Parenting contracts are voluntary written agreements that are used by a range of agencies to gain the co-operation of parents in relation to the supervision of their child. Parenting orders are court orders and are currently available to local education authorities and youth offending teams. The courts also have powers in certain circumstances to impose parenting orders. They are used to gain compliance from parents and will often contain specific requirements to help curb the antisocial behaviour of children in their care or guardianship and to help them become better parents. We have outlined our intention to extend parenting orders in the following ways:

— A new trigger of 'serious misbehaviour' will be added to the existing trigger of exclusion from school, so that a parenting order can be made before a child is excluded.
— Schools will also be able to seek parenting orders.
— Local authorities will be given new powers to extend the range of agencies that can enter into parenting contracts and orders where anti-social behaviour occurs in the community. This may include community safety officers and housing officers."

See also the Education White Paper, published in October 2005, which stated the Government would legislate to enable school governors to make use of these new powers:[27] **3-150**

"We will legislate to extend the scope of parenting orders and parenting contracts in particular, so that governing bodies can use them to make parents take responsibility for their children's behaviour at school."

Many of these proposals are contained in Cll 16 and 17 of the Police and Justice Bill. New ss.25A and 25B would allow local authorities and registered social landlords to apply for parenting contracts and new ss.26A and 26B would allow them to apply for parenting orders. Clause 18 would allow the Secretary of State to make an order enabling a local authority to contract out the functions of entering into parenting contracts and applying for parenting orders.

Some housing management organisations have expressed caution in the use of such powers. The National Housing Association said: **3-151**

"Housing associations work closely with the police and social services to tackle the effects and causes of anti-social behaviour. However, we believe that the use of parenting orders should be led by experts in the field. Parenting orders should be sought in the most appropriate circumstances, both parents and children should be helped to get the maximum benefit from counselling and guidance services, which in turn must be properly monitored. Housing associations would prefer to work in partnership with professionals, who are properly trained and resourced to do this."

Community Orders

A court may make an order in respect of any person under the age of 18 convicted of an offence by it placing him under the supervision of a local authority,[28] probation board or a member of a YOT ("a supervision order").[29] The **3-152**

---

[27] *Higher Standards, Better Schools for All*, Cm.6677, October 2005.
[28] County council, county borough council, metropolitan district or London borough, Common Council of the City of London: Powers of Criminal Courts (Sentencing) Act 2000, s.67(1).
[29] Powers of Criminal Courts (Sentencing) Act 2000 Act, s.64: "the supervisor" is the relevant local authority, an actual officer of the probation board or member of the youth offending team.

order will contain the name of the area of the local authority area and petty sessions area in which it appears to the court making the order that the offender resides or will reside and provisions appropriate to facilitate the performance by the supervisor of his functions.[30] The supervisor must "advise, assist and befriend" the offender.[31] The order ceases to have effect at the end of three years (unless revoked) or such shorter period as may be specified. A copy of the order is sent to the offender and if under 14, to his parent or guardian, the local authority concerned, the supervisor, and, if the offender is required to reside with an individual or to undergo treatment under the direction of an individual, to that person.[32] A local authority, alone or with other authorities, must make arrangements with such persons as appear to them to be necessary for the provision of facilities with respect to the requirements of the order to be carried out effectively and, in doing so, must consult the probation board.[33] The arrangements must be specified in a scheme. The requirements of the order may include the following: to live at a specified place, to present himself to a specified person within a certain period, and to participate in specified activities. He may also be required to live at a specified place, to make reparation to specified persons or the community at large, to live in specified local authority accommodation, to be treated for a mental condition, and, if he is school age, to comply with arrangements for his education.[34] Breach of the supervision order may be dealt with by way of a fine, revocation and substation by the court with another sentence, and, if made by the Crown Court, committal to custody or released on bail to appear before the Crown Court, and when he appears the court may deal with him by substituting another sentence.[35]

3-153   Attendance centre orders may be made by a court with respect to any person aged under 21 convicted by them of a sentence punishable by imprisonment or committal to prison for default of an payment of any sum or other failure to do or abstain from doing something, if there is a place in such a centre for him. The minimum number of hours is 12, depending on the age and circumstances of the offender, and not more than 36.[36] If there is a breach of the order or the attendance centre's rules, a warrant may be issued for his arrest and he may be fined, dealt with in some other way and, if made by the Crown Court, committal to custody or released on bail to appear before the Crown Court and when he appears, the court may deal with him by substituting another sentence.[37]

Community Rehabilitation Orders

3-154   Curfew orders may be made in respect of an offender of any age. The court before which a person is convicted of an offence may order him to remain for periods specified in the order at a specified place and may include requirements for the electronic monitoring of the offender's whereabouts during the specified period.[38] Community rehabilitation orders may be imposed on offenders aged 16 and over if the court considers that supervision is desirable in the interests of securing his rehabilitation or protecting the public from harm or preventing further offending by him, requiring him to be under the supervision for a period specified but not less than six months and not more

---

[30] As prescribed by the Magistrates' Court Act 1980, s.144 as amended by s.63 of the 2000 Act.
[31] Powers of Criminal Courts (Sentencing) Act 2000, s.64(7).
[32] *ibid.*, s.63.
[33] *ibid.*, Sch.6, paras 2, 3.
[34] *ibid.*, Sch.6, paras 2 to 4.
[35] *ibid.*, Sch.7, para.2.
[36] *ibid.*, s.60(4).
[37] *ibid.*, Sch.5, para.2.
[38] *ibid.*, s.37.

than three years.[39] If the offender is under the age of 18 at the time the order is made, he must be under the supervision of a local probation officer or a member of a YOT.[40] Similarly, the court may also make a community punishment order with respect to a person aged 16 or over convicted of an offence punishable by imprisonment requiring him to perform unpaid work. The total number of hours must be not less than 40 and not more than 240.[41] The court must find that the person is a suitable person to perform work under the order and there must be provision for him to perform work in the area in which he resides or works. Where the offender is aged under 18, the order should specify the relevant local authority in whose area he resides or works and copies must be provided to a probation officer or member of a YOT. The work is to be carried out under the supervision of "the responsible officer" who, in the case of a person aged under 18, is the probation officer or member of the YOT. Provisions as to breaches of community orders are the same for persons aged under 18 as those which apply to adults.[42]

Custodial Sentences

No court may pass a sentence of imprisonment on a person aged under 21 for any reason.[43] However, as noted above, such a person may be committed to prison if remanded in custody for trial or sentence in certain circumstances. There are only three forms of custody for persons aged under 18: detention at Her Majesty's pleasure,[44] detention for a specified period,[45] and detention and training orders.[46] Detention at Her Majesty's pleasure applies to convictions for murder or any other offence for which life imprisonment is fixed by law. Detention for a specified period applies with respect to a person aged under 18 where the offence would be punishable by imprisonment for 14 years or more or an indecent assault, and the court is of the opinion that none of the other sentencing options are appropriate.[47] It may also be ordered in respect of an offender aged above 14, but under 18, who is convicted of dangerous driving causing death or careless driving causing death while under the influence.[48] The offender is detained at a such place and such conditions as the Secretary of State directs.[49] It includes a power to give directions to a local authority in a community home provided or controlled by the authority.[50]

3-155

A detention and training order may be ordered where the person is convicted of an offence punishable by imprisonment and the offence is so serious that only custody should be ordered. It may be specified that it be followed by a period of supervision by a probation officer or member of a YOT. The court may not make such an order in respect of an offender aged under 15 unless it is of the opinion that he is a persistent offender.[51] In forming an opinion as to persistence, the court may consider whether he has been reprimanded or warned.[52] Nor should the court make such an order in respect of someone aged under 12 unless it considers that only a custodial sentence

3-156

---

[39] Powers of Criminal Courts (Sentencing) Act 2000, ss.34, 35.
[40] *ibid.*, s.41(5).
[41] *ibid.*, s.46(3).
[42] *ibid.*, ss.135 to 137.
[43] *ibid.*, s.89(1).
[44] *ibid.*, s.90, 92.
[45] *ibid.*, s.91.
[46] *ibid.*, ss.100 to 104.
[47] *ibid.*, s.91(1).
[48] *ibid.*, s.91(2)(b).
[49] *ibid.*, s.92(1)(b).
[50] Children and Young Persons Act 1969, s.165(1), Sch.9, para.40.
[51] Powers of Criminal Courts (Sentencing) Act 2000, s.100(2)(a).
[52] *R.v D* (2000) Crim. L.R. 867.

would be adequate to protect the public from further offending by him.[53] The term of the orders must be 4, 6, 8, 10, 12, 18 or 24 months. It cannot exceed the amount a court would order had the offender been an adult. The detention must be served in such secure accommodation as determined by the Secretary of State.

Parental Compensation Orders
3-157   Section 144 of the Serious Organised Crime and Police Act 2005 provides magistrates with a power too make an order, following an application by a local authority,[54] requiring a parent or guardian of a child under 10 years old to pay compensation of an amount specified to the person affected by the offence. Under the new s.13A, the court must first be satisfied that: (a) that the condition mentioned in subs.(2) below is fulfilled with respect to a child under the age of 10; and (b) that it would be desirable to make the order in the interests of preventing a repetition of the behaviour in question. This condition in subs.(2) is that the child has taken, or caused loss of or damage to, property in the course of committing an act which, if he had been aged 10 or over, would have constituted an offence; or acting in a manner that caused or was likely to cause harassment, alarm or distress to one or more persons not of the same household as himself. The order, under subs.(3), requires any person specified in the order who is a parent or guardian of the child (other than a local authority) to pay compensation of an amount specified in the order to any person or persons specified in the order who is, or are, affected by the taking of the property or its loss or damage. That amount must not exceed £5,000 in all. Under s.13B, the magistrates' court shall take into account the value of the property taken or damaged, or whose loss was caused, by the child; any further loss which flowed from the taking of or damage to the property, or from its loss; whether the child, or any parent or guardian of his, has already paid any compensation for the property (and if so, how much); whether the child, or any parent or guardian of his, has already made any reparation (and if so, what it consisted of); the means of those to be specified in the order as liable to pay the compensation, so far as the court can ascertain them; whether there was any lack of care on the part of the person affected by the taking of the property or its loss or damage which made it easier for the child to take or damage the property or to cause its loss. Under subs.(7), proceedings in respect of an offence under this subsection may, despite anything in s.127(1) of the Magistrates Court Act 1980, be commenced at any time within two years from the date of the commission of the offence or within six months of its first discovery by the local authority, whichever period expires earlier. An appeal, under s.13D, lies to the Crown Court.

"Diversionary Schemes"
3-158   There are three types of diversionary schemes: some are focused on children most at risk of offending or of engaging in anti-social behaviour; others are directed towards all children which have the effect of helping to reduce anti-social behaviour which may also have the effect of reducing offending and anti-social behaviour; and those run by the voluntary sector that are reducing anti-social behaviour and offending and assisting children in need. In the first category there are:

(1) Behaviour Improvement Programmes: support for children at risk of exclusion, truancy, criminality, and anti-social behaviour;

[53] Powers of Criminal Courts (Sentencing) Act 2000, s.100(2)(b).
[54] Under subs.13A(7), "local authority" has the same meaning as in the Children Act 1989.

(2) Positive Futures: multi-agency projects that offer opportunities in sport, education, training and employment for young people in deprived areas;

(3) Positive Activities for Young People: diversionary and developmental activities for young people during school holidays and after school;

(4) Sure Start: childcare and parental support for those with children up to the age of four in areas of high deprivation;

(5) Youth Inclusion Programmes: youth work and support for 13 to 16 year olds most at risk of offending in 70 of the most deprived and high crime estates in England and Wales (to be extended to a further 30 areas);

(6) Youth Inclusion and Support Panels: targeted support for 8 to 13 year olds at risk of offending or engaging in anti-social behaviour.

Such diversionary programmes have been credited with a reduction of up to 40 to 60 per cent in arrests nationally. An evaluation of the first three years of the Youth Inclusion Programme found that arrest rates for the 50 young people considered most at risk in each programme had been reduced by 65 per cent; that of those who had offended before joining the programme, 73 per cent were arrested for fewer offences after engaging in such a programme; and of those who had not been arrested before but who were at risk, 74 per cent did not go on to be arrested after the programme. It also found the seriousness of the offending decreased. According to the Chief Executive of Crime Concern there are not enough of them. The Youth Justice Board asked for 200 such programmes and there are only about 70 with approximately another 30 to follow.[55]   **3-159**

Education

In the Anti-social Behaviour White Paper, schools are considered to have a "pivotal role in tackling anti-social behaviour" and there are direct links between poor education and offending behaviour. Hence, it is part of the Government's anti-social behaviour strategy to improve behaviour in schools, tackle truancy and reinforce parental support and responsibility for their children's education.[56] As noted earlier in this chapter, there are numerous references in national crime and disorder policy documents to the link between social exclusion and lack of education attainment and opportunities. See *A New Commitment to Urban Renewal*:   **3-160**

> "Multiple deprivation blocks the routes out of poverty, as having had a poor education or coming from an area with a bad reputation makes it harder to get a job. This deprives the economy of workers, customers, entrepreneurs and taxpayers, and costs society dear in terms of higher unemployment, poor health and high crime rates."

Poor educational and leisure opportunities for young people, and a failure to support vulnerable children, or to tackle truancy and school exclusion is described in that document as one of several threats to a community's well-being. Reforms in education are a major part of the government's "Respect Action Plan":

---

[55] Home Affairs Committee Anti-Social Behaviour Report 2004–05, para.142; see also the evidence of Professor Morgan, Chair of the Youth Justice Board.

[56] White Paper, p.29.

"The values and behaviour which support respect form the basis of good teaching and children's experiences in schools. We will legislate to tackle poor behaviour, including a new measure to ensure parents take responsibility for their child's behaviour in the classroom and when they are excluded from school. We will take targeted action on persistent truants and place a new duty on local authorities to identify children missing from school rolls and support their re-entry into mainstream education or alternative provision. We will improve provision for those who are out of school through a new regime for suspended and excluded pupils."

3-161   Lord Wilberforce, in *Thameside MBC*,[57] said that, for the past 60 years, responsibility for the education of children in England and Wales rested on "a fourfold" foundation and, while most of the legislation has changed, the basic fourfold pattern has survived. The elements are:

(1) parents of a child of compulsory school age are under a duty, under s.7 of the Education Act 1996, to cause every such child to receive efficient and suitable full-time education;

(2) the Secretary of State is required, by s.10 of the 1996 Act, to promote the education of the people of England and Wales;

(3) the local education authority (LEA) is required by s.13(1) of the 1996 Act to secure that efficient secondary education is available to meet the needs of the population of their area; and

(4) each school maintained by an LEA is subject to the control of a governing body who must, under s.38 of the School Standards and Framework Act 1998, conduct the school with a view to promoting high standards of educational achievement.

Lord Bingham, in *Ali v Head Teacher and Governors of Lord Grey School*,[58] commented that this fourfold foundation has endured because it contains certain inherent strengths. First, it recognises that the party with the keenest personal interest in securing the best education available to the child would ordinarily be the parent. Secondly, the regime recognises that, for any child attending school, it is the school through which the education provided by the state is in practice delivered. There is "a close and personal relationship" between the school and the pupil, resembling a contractual relationship. Thirdly, the regime recognises the need for a safety net or longstop to ensure that the education is not neglected of those who for any reason, including exclusion, are not being educated in the ordinary way.

Nuisances on or near school premises

3-162   The proper place to start is to consider the extent to which local authorities, as LEAs or otherwise, are able to control anti-social behaviour at or near schools. They will ordinarily own the land upon which a school for which they are responsible is based and therefore enjoy the usual range of common law powers of land owners with regard to controlling the behaviour of persons on school premises. These common law powers are fortified by the existence of statutory offences concerning nuisances caused on or near LEA premises. Under s.547 of the Education Act 1996, a person causing or permitting a nuisance or disturbance to persons who lawfully use certain school premises is guilty of a summary offence. The relevant premises are any school

---

[57] [1977] A.C. 1014 at 1046.
[58] [2006] WL 690558.

maintained by an LEA and include play grounds, playing fields and other premises for outdoor recreation. See also s.40 of the Local Government (Miscellaneous Provisions) Act 1982 where a similar offence lies as against any person causing or permitting a nuisance or disturbance on LEA further or higher education premises. In addition, under s.547(3) of the 1996 Act, if a constable or any person empowered by the LEA believes, or has reason to believe, that a person is committing or has committed an offence, he may remove them from the school premises. That power may also be exercised in relation to premises of a foundation, voluntary aided or foundation school, if so authorised by the governing body of the school. A police constable or the LEA may bring proceedings for an offence under s.547; or, in the case of a foundation, voluntary aided or foundation special school, a person so authorised by the governing body.[59] However, the LEA may not bring such proceedings regarding an offence committed in foundation, voluntary aided or foundation special schools without obtaining the consent of the governing body.

A pupil may be excluded because of the anti-social behaviour of a parent **3-163** at or near the school.[60] A head teacher may terminate that licence and ban the parent from the premises but only after giving the parent due notice and an opportunity to make representations. In *Wandsworth LBC v A*,[61] the appellant, the mother at a school for which the respondent authority was the LEA, was banned by the headmaster from entering the school beyond the school gate and from engaging in conversation with members of staff without a third party present because of her behaviour while on school grounds. The Court of Appeal found that the appellant had a licence to enter the school by reason of a practice to permit parents to do so. That licence did not mean that parents had the right to roam at will; however, the licence was more than enjoyed by a milkman or postman or other casual enquirer. The local authority has an obligation in public law to educate a parent's child and the parent has an interest in seeing the duties of authority properly performed. Therefore, a parent is a more significant figure in the public activities of a school than a casual enquirer. While a school may exclude a milkman without public law inhibitions, it is not quite the same case as regards a parent. A school was in the nature of premises which belong to an authority which are open to the public, although there is no statutory duty to permit the public to have access. The headmaster's decision deprived the appellant of access to the school and in doing so treated her differently from other parents. Therefore, she was entitled to an opportunity to make representations which, in the circumstances of this case, was denied to her. Accordingly, the decision was flawed in public law terms.

Control and Discipline of Pupils
The common law is summarised in *Fitzgerald v Northcote*: **3-164**

"The authority of the schoolmaster is, while it exists, the same as that of the parent. A parent when he places his child with a schoolmaster delegates to him all his own authority so far as it is necessary for the welfare of the child."

See also *Gateshead Union Guardians v Durham CC*:[62]

---

[59] Education Act 1996, s.547(6), (7).
[60] *R. v Board of Governors and Appeal Committee of Bryn Elian High School, Ex p. Whippe* [1999] E.L.R. 380; and *R. v Secretary of State Education and Employment, Ex p. Governors of Southlands Community Comprehensive School* [1999] Ed C.R.35.
[61] [2000] E.L.R. 257.
[62] [1918] 1 Ch. 146.

". . .a child may be refused admission on reasonable grounds. . .as for example that he is in such condition of person or health as to render contact with him offensive or dangerous to others, or he is guilty of conduct prejudicial to good discipline."

That authority and any concomitant duties do not extend to matters that occur away from the school. In *Bradford-Smart v West Sussex CC*,[63] the claimant claimed damages against the local authority for psychiatric injury resulting from bullying whilst she was a pupil at a maintained school for which the authority was responsible. She had been bullied between the ages of nine and 12, on the housing estate where she lived and on the bus whilst travelling to and from school. The court held that, although schools were under a common law duty to safeguard the well being of children on school premises and to prevent bullying, that duty did not extend to bullying that occurred outside school. A duty of care could only be inferred on the basis of foreseeability, proximity and on what was fair and reasonable in the circumstances. It would not be practical or fair to impose a greater duty on the school than to ensure that a pupil was not bullied at school. The duty was to prevent bullying on school premises. If the school chose to take an active stance against bullying outside of school, that was a matter of discretion. In the instant case, the teacher had taken steps to ensure that B was not bullied at school.

3-165   Responsibility for discipline within a school is shared between the governing body and the head teacher, the former developing policies and the latter for implementing them. The governing body of a maintained school must ensure that there are policies aimed at promoting good behaviour and discipline on the part of the pupils.[64] In particular, after consulting the head teacher and parents of registered pupils, they must make and then review a written statement of general principles to which the head teacher is to have regard in deciding on disciplinary matters. If they think he should take any particular measures or have regard to any particular matters, they are to notify him accordingly and give guidance as they think fit. The governing body are to have regard to any guidance issued by the Secretary of State. For example, guidance issued in January 2000 declared that schools should reduce the number of exclusions by one third by 2002. Otherwise, under s.61 of the School Standards and Framework Act 1998, the head teacher is responsible for disciplinary matters with the following aims in mind: promote among pupils self-discipline and proper regard for authority; encourage pupils to behave well and have respect for others; secure that the standard of behaviour of pupils is acceptable; and otherwise regulate the behaviour of pupils. He must also decide, subject to the governing body, what standard of behaviour is to be regarded as acceptable. He must publicise his disciplinary measures in writing so as to make them known within the school and to parents and draw attention to them at least annually. The disciplinary authority of the head teacher may also extend to acts that take place outside of school.[65] It is also the duty of the LEA to prepare and/or review a similar statement of arrangements made or proposed to be made by the authority in connection with children with behavioural problems.[66] The LEA has the power to intervene to prevent a breakdown of discipline if, in their opinion, the behaviour of the pupils or action taken by pupils or parents severely prejudices the education at the school, or is likely to do so, and the governing body have been informed in writing; or if a warning notice has been given, and there has been no

---

[63] [2002] E.L.R. 139.
[64] Education Act 1996, s.60(1).
[65] *Bradford-Smart v West Sussex CC* [2001] E.L.R. 138.
[66] Education Act 1996, s.527A.

compliance.[67] The LEA is liable if they have expressly or impliedly authorised any improper punishment.

Any member of staff[68] of a school may use reasonable force with regard to **3-166** a pupil at the school so as to prevent the pupil from doing or continuing to commit an offence, cause personal injury or damage to property, or engage in any behaviour prejudicial to the maintenance of good order and discipline in the school, whether or not the behaviour occurs during a teaching session or otherwise.[69] Within reasonable limits, and subject to the parent's philosophical or religious views, corporal punishment is not per se contrary to the European Convention on Human Rights,[70] nor unlawful under the common law of battery and assault. However, it is effectively banned by s.548 of the Education Act 1996 in England and Wales.

Detention
The main ways in which a pupil may be punished for disciplinary breaches are **3-167** detention, suspension or exclusion. All maintained schools have the power to detain pupils without parental consent at common law: a teacher has this authority because he is the *in loco parentis* whereby he has been delegated all parental authority by the parents when they place the child with the school.[71] However, s.550B of the 1996 Act provides that where a pupil has not attained the age of 18 and is attending a school maintained by the LEA, or college of further education, and is required on disciplinary grounds to spend a period of time in detention after school hours, his detention is not unlawful by reason of the lack of the parents' consent if certain conditions are satisfied. These are: that the head teacher has made parents, pupils and staff members aware that after-hours detention may be used; the detention is reasonable; it is imposed by the head teacher or another teacher specifically or generally authorised by him for the purpose; and the parent is given at least 24 hours notice in writing that the detention is due to take place.[72]

Cleanliness
Section 521 of the Education Act 1996 provides that the LEA may, by direc- **3-168** tions in writing, authorise one of its medical officers to have the persons and clothing of pupils in attendance at relevant schools examined whenever, in their opinion, such examinations are necessary in the interests of cleanliness. If, on such examination, the person or clothing of a pupil is found to be infested with vermin or in a foul condition, any LEA officer may serve a notice on the pupil's parent requiring him to cause the pupil's person and clothing to be cleansed. If, after a specified period, a medical officer is still not satisfied that the pupil's person or clothing have been properly cleansed, he may by order direct that they be cleansed under arrangements made by the authority. If after the person or clothing of a pupil has been cleansed under this section and they again become infested with vermin or in a foul condition, at any time while he is in attendance at a relevant school, and the condition of his person or clothing is due to neglect on the part of the parent, the parent is guilty of an offence not exceeding level 1 on the standard scale.[73]

---

[67] School Standards and Framework Act 1998, s.62(3).
[68] A teacher who works at the school and any other person who with the authority of the head teacher has lawful control or charge of pupils at the school: Education Act 1996, s.550A(4).
[69] Education Act 1996, s.551A(1).
[70] *Tyrer v UK* (1978) 2 E.H.R.R. 1; *A. v U.K.* [1998] 2 F.L.R. 959.
[71] *Fitzgerald v Northcote* (1865) 4 F.&F. 656.
[72] Education Act 1996, s.550B.
[73] *ibid.*, ss.522(4), 523.

School Exclusion

3-169   In 1996/97, there were 12,000 permanent exclusions from maintained schools and special schools in England; in 2001/02, there were around 9,000.[74] As already noted, school exclusions are a major priority of the Social Exclusion Unit. In the Anti-Social Behaviour White Paper, it was said that around two thirds of excluded pupils admitted having committed an offence in the past year and 44 per cent admitted to offending played truant.[75] Head teachers, governing bodies, LEAs and appeal panels are required to have regard to guidance on exclusion by the Secretary of State.[76] National targets were set in 1998 to reduce the number of exclusions by one third. The policy was criticised by the National Teachers Union and it was amended so as to make it easier for head teachers to exclude violent or very disruptive pupils from schools. All the same, permanent exclusions are of last resort: Lord Bingham in *Ali*:

> "The immense damage done to vulnerable children by indefinite, unnecessary or improperly-motivated exclusions from state schools is well-known and none could doubt the need for tight control over the exercise of this important power."

3-170   The power of exclusion may only be exercised on disciplinary grounds: s.64(4), School Standards and Framework Act 1998. Under the 1998 Act, the head teacher of a maintained school may exclude a pupil from the school of a fixed period or permanently.[77] Where a pupil is excluded, the head teacher must notify as soon as possible the pupil's parents, setting out his reasons and how representations may be made to the governing body.[78] If the exclusion is to be permanent, or for more than five days in any one term, or if the pupil would lose an opportunity to take a public examination, or if the head teacher decides to exclude the pupil permanently, he must inform the LEA and governing body of the period or permanence of, and the reasons for, exclusion.[79] The governing body must then consider the circumstances of the exclusion and any representations made about it, allow a parent, or the pupil if aged 18 or over, and an LEA officer to attend a meeting and consider what each has to say.[80] The governing body may order reinstatement or uphold the decision and, in the latter case, they must also give the pupil or his parents written notice of the reasons and how to appeal. An appeal lies to the Independent Appeal Panel established by the LEA.[81] For the purposes of Art.6(1) of the Convention, the appeal is a determination of civil rights.[82] No appeal against a decision not to reinstate a pupil may be made after the 15th day on which the pupil and or his parents or guardian was notified.[83]

3-171   Section 52 of the Education Act 2002 amends these provisions. Subsections (1) and (2) give head teachers of maintained schools power to exclude any pupil from the school on disciplinary grounds and gives the same power to teachers in charge of pupil referral unit. Otherwise, it re-enacts the existing provisions in s.64(1) of the 1998 Act and para.7 of Sch.1 to the Education Act

---

[74] DfES Statistical Bulletins.

[75] Page 15.

[76] School Standards and Framework Act 1998 Act, s.68. *R. (on the application of S (A Child)) v Brent LBC* [2002] E.L.R. 556.

[77] School Standards and Frameworks Act 1998, s.64(1).

[78] *ibid.*, s.65(1).

[79] *ibid.*, s.65(3).

[80] *ibid.*, s.66(2).

[81] *ibid.*, s.67(3).

[82] *R. (on the application of S.) v Brent LBC* [2002] EWCA Civ 693.

[83] Education Act 1996, Sch.18.

1996. The rest of the new section provides for the procedures relating to the exclusion of pupils, including the arrangements for reviewing exclusions and appealing against decisions not to reinstate the pupil in question, to be set out in regulations. It is intended that the existing requirement for head teachers, governing bodies, LEAs and appeal panels to have regard to the Secretary of State's guidance relating to exclusion will be continued under those regulations. Under the proposed regulations, the procedures for excluding a pupil from a maintained school, other than a pupil referral unit, will be largely unchanged. However, it is proposed that regulations may provide for altering the constitution of the appeal panel; ensuring that, when reaching a decision, panels will be required to consider the interests of the whole school community, not just those of the excluded pupil; and for ensuring that defects in prior procedure will not alone constitute grounds for reinstating a pupil. Regulations may also provide for changes to the number of days a fixed period exclusion must be before the governing body, through its discipline committee, is required to review it. In relation to pupil referral units, the section provides that the parent of a pupil permanently excluded from such a unit has a right of appeal equivalent to that available to the parents of pupils excluded from maintained schools. The right will be given retrospectively to September 1, 1994, the date when pupil referral units were first recognised in statute.

Guidance on exclusions was published by the Secretary of State for Education and Skills in 2004.[84] In most cases exclusion will be the last resort after a range of measures have been tried to improve the pupil's behaviour. In schools and LEAs a range of strategies should be in place to address the bad behaviour which may lead to exclusion. Head teachers should be able to refer pupils identified at risk of exclusion to alternative or additional provision to meet their individual needs, which could include working in partnership with other agencies. A decision to exclude a pupil should be taken only in response to serious breaches of the school's behaviour policy, and if allowing the pupil to remain in school would seriously harm the education or welfare of the pupil or others in the school. Only the head teacher, or teacher in charge of a PRU, (or, in the absence of the head teacher or teacher in charge, the acting head teacher or teacher in charge) can exclude a pupil. A decision to exclude a child permanently is a serious one. It will usually be the final step in a process for dealing with disciplinary offences following a wide range of other strategies which have been tried without success. It is an acknowledgement by the school that it has exhausted all available strategies for dealing with the child and should normally be used as a last resort. There will, however, be exceptional circumstances where, in the head teacher's judgment, it is appropriate to permanently exclude a child for a first or "one off" offence. These might include: serious actual or threatened violence against another pupil or a member of staff; sexual abuse or assault; supplying an illegal drug; or carrying an offensive weapon. Schools should consider whether or not to inform the police where such a criminal offence has taken place. They should also consider whether or not to inform other agencies, e.g. youth offending teams or social workers. These instances are not exhaustive, but indicate the severity of such offences and the fact that such behaviour can affect the discipline and well-being of the school community. In cases where a head teacher has permanently excluded a pupil for: one of the above offences; or persistent and defiant misbehaviour including bullying (which would include racist or homophobic bullying); or repeated possession and/or use of an illegal drug on school premises, the Secretary of State would not normally expect the

3-172

---

[84] *Improving Behaviour and Attendance: Guidance on Exclusion from Schools and Pupil Referral Units*, which was issued in January 2003 (Ref: DfES/0087/2003), and which replaced Chapter 6 and Annex D of Circular 10/99, issued in July 1999, and the letters subsequently amending it.

governing body or an Independent Appeal Panel to reinstate the pupil. In making a decision on whether or not to exclude for a drug-related incident the head teacher should have regard to the school's drug policy and should consult the designated senior member of staff responsible for managing drug incidents. But the decision will also depend on the precise circumstances of the case, for example, the seriousness of the incident, the circumstances and needs of those involved and the evidence available. Where legal drugs are concerned, again head teachers should conduct a careful investigation to judge the nature and seriousness of each incident before deciding what action to take. Exclusion should not be imposed in the heat of the moment, unless there is an immediate threat to the safety of others in the school or the pupil concerned. Before deciding whether to exclude a pupil, either permanently or for a fixed period, the head teacher should:

(a) ensure that a thorough investigation has been carried out;

(b) consider all the evidence available to support the allegations, taking account of the school's behaviour and equal opportunities policies, and, where applicable, the Race Relations Act 1976 as amended and the Disability Discrimination Act 1995 as amended;

(c) allow the pupil to give his or her version of events;

(d) check whether the incident may have been provoked, for example by bullying, including homophobic bullying, or by racial or sexual harassment;

(e) if necessary, consult others, but not anyone who may later have a role in reviewing the head teacher's decision, for example a member of the governing body.

The standard of proof to be applied is the balance of probabilities. However, the more serious the allegation, the more convincing the evidence substantiating the allegation needs to be: when investigating more serious allegations, head teachers will need to gather and take account of a wider range of evidence (extending in some instances to evidence of the pupil's past behaviour), in determining whether it is more probable than not that the pupil has committed the offence. Where a police investigation leading to possible criminal proceedings has been initiated, the evidence available may be very limited. However, it may still be possible for the head teacher to make a judgment on whether to exclude the pupil.[85]

3-173   In the case of a permanent exclusion the pupil remains on the roll of the school until any appeal is determined, or until the time limit for the parents to lodge an appeal has expired without an appeal being brought, or the parent has told the LEA in writing that no appeal is to be brought. Again, while the pupil is on the roll of the school it is the responsibility of the school that his or her education continues but, as in the case of longer fixed period exclusions, it may be necessary for the school to seek the help of the LEA which maintains the school. Once a permanent exclusion has been upheld by the governing body, the LEA should arrange to assess the pupil's needs and how to meet them, including any special educational needs the pupil may have. The LEA should also arrange a meeting with the parents to discuss options. Once the pupil is removed from the roll, the LEA is responsible for ensuring that suitable education is provided. This will be the pupil's home LEA in cases where the school is maintained by a different LEA. Since September 2002, all LEAs have been committed to

---

[85] However, it was this particular piece of guidance which caused so much trouble in the *Ali* case, see below at para.3–174.

ensuring that all permanently excluded pupils receive suitable full time education, either at another school or, where necessary, making use of a Pupil Referral Unit or other alternative provision. If the school or LEA considers that parenting is a factor in the behaviour of the pupil who has been excluded, they should consider whether it may be appropriate to offer a parenting contract or apply to the magistrate's court for a parenting order. In accordance with the law on admissions, a school may not require a parent to sign a parenting contract as a condition of their child being admitted following permanent exclusion.

In *Ali v Lord Grey School Governors*,[86] the appellant school appealed against **3-174** the decision that a pupil was entitled to damages on the basis that his right to education under the Human Rights Act 1998 Sch.1, Pt II, Art.2 had been affected by his exclusion from the school. The pupil had been excluded from the school in March 2001, pending the result of a police investigation following an allegation against him of arson. From the date of exclusion until June 2001, the school provided the pupil with work to do from home. In June 2001, following the discontinuance of the criminal proceedings, the head teacher invited him and his parents to attend a meeting to arrange his re-entry to the school but they failed to attend. At the same time as the criminal proceedings were discontinued the local education authority recommended that the child be provided with tuition, but the offer of tuition was never taken up. By the time the child decided that he wished to return to the school he had been removed from the school roll and his place in the school year had been filled. He brought an unsuccessful claim for damages. On appeal the Court of Appeal found that his right to education had been denied in breach of Art.2, in relation to the period from June 2001 to January 2002, and remitted the case for the assessment of damages. The school submitted that the 1998 Act did not confer on anyone a right to be educated at a particular school, but rather conferred a right not to be denied access, in a non-discriminatory manner, to the general level of educational provision available in the Member State. It further submitted that on the facts there had been no denial and it could not be said that the child had been denied access, least of all by the school, to the general level of educational provision in the United Kingdom. The child submitted that the effect of Art.2 was to give the individual pupil and parent a right, not merely to the general level of educational provision available in a Member State, but to compliance with the domestic educational regime, and thus to education in and by the school of which a child was registered as a pupil, unless and until the relationship between school and pupil was lawfully ended. The House of Lords allowed the appeal. The ECHR jurisprudence in this area was summarised in this way:

"The underlying premise of the article was that all existing member states would have an established system of education. It was intended to guarantee fair and non-discriminatory access to that system by those within the jurisdiction of the respective states. The fundamental importance of education in a modern democratic state was recognised to require no less. But the guarantee, compared with most other Convention guarantees, is a weak one and deliberately so. There is no right to education of a particular kind or quality, other than that prevailing in the state. There is no Convention guarantee of compliance with domestic law. There is no Convention guarantee of education at or by a particular institution. There is no Convention objection to the expulsion of a pupil from an educational institution on disciplinary grounds unless in the ordinary way there is no alternative source of education. The test, as always under the Convention, is a highly pragmatic one, to be applied to the specific facts of the case."

[86] [2006] WL 690558.

The question to be decided was whether between June 2001 and January 2002 the school had denied the child effective access to such educational facilities as the United Kingdom provided. The House of Lords concluded that the school had not. The school had invited his parents to collect work for him, which they had failed to do, had referred him to an education provider whose offer of tuition was declined and had arranged a meeting to discuss his re-admission, which the child and his parents failed to attend with no good reason. The LEA's attempts to secure his re-admission to the school or admission to another school were thwarted by his family's uncertainty as to what they wished to do and as soon as they made up their minds a place at another school was found. He had not therefore been excluded from school education in breach of his Convention rights. However, the school had not done all that was reasonable. After the failure of his parents to attend the re-admission meeting, the school had effectively permanently excluded the pupil, yet there were no good grounds to do so, and he had not been given any of the procedural protection afforded by the established system. This was the paradigm of a case in which it would be just and appropriate to grant a declaration that the school had acted incompatibly with the child's right to education. Yet the child had sought damages, not a declaration, and damages were not necessary in his case. If, as had been found below and agreed between the parties for the purposes of the instant appeal, the school had acted inconsistently with domestic law, the inadequacy of the law contributed to that result. The 1998 Act and the guidance issued under it seemed singularly inapt to regulate the problem that had confronted the school in the instant case, where the exclusion was on precautionary rather than penal grounds. The school wanted neither to exclude him for any particular fixed period nor to exclude him permanently. It would have been likely to want him back if he was found innocent. In these circumstances s.64 of the 1998 Act provided no way of excluding him for the necessarily indeterminate period that had to elapse until the investigation or prosecution was completed, except by the artificial method of a succession of periods fixed by references to a guess as to when the police investigation was likely to finish, continuing until the 45 day maximum was reached, or by permanent exclusion on some understanding that an application for readmission would be considered after an acquittal.

3-175   In *R v Denbigh High School Governors, Ex p. SB*,[87] the appellant was a student who appealed against a decision dismissing her application for judicial review of the refusal of the respondent school to allow her to attend the school if she was not willing to comply with school uniform requirements. She was Muslim and wished to wear a jilbab to school, rather than a shalwar kameeze as dictated by school's uniform policy. The school's complaints committee decided that the uniform policy satisfied all the requirements of the Islamic dress code and refused to allow her to attend school in a jilbab. The pupil maintained that the shalwar kameeze did not comply with the strict requirements of her religion. She lost two years' schooling before she was accepted by a different school. She contended that the school had unlawfully excluded her from school and denied her the right to manifest her religion and access to suitable and appropriate education in violation of the Human Rights Act 1998 Sch.1, Pt I, Art.9 and Sch.1, Pt II, Art.2. The Court of Appeal allowed the appeal. Contrary to the finding of the judge, the school did in fact exclude: it sent her away for disciplinary reasons because she was not willing to comply with the discipline of wearing the prescribed school uniform, and she was unable to return to school for the same reason:

"They told her, in effect: 'Go away, and do not come back unless you are wearing proper school uniform.' They sent her away for disciplinary reasons

[87] [2005] 1 W.L.R. 3372.

because she was not willing to comply with the discipline of wearing the pre-scribed school uniform, and she was unable to return to the school for the same reason. Education law does not allow a pupil of school age to con-tinue in the limbo in which the claimant found herself. It was very soon clear that she was not willing to compromise her beliefs despite the best efforts of the educational welfare officers who visited her home and the teachers at the school who tried to persuade her to return. If the statutory procedures and departmental guidance had been followed, the impasse would have been of very much shorter duration, and by one route or another her school career (at one school or another) would have been put back on track very much more quickly."

If the statutory procedures and departmental guidance had been followed, her schooling would have been put back on track much more quickly. Further, the fact that the pupil's view, that Islamic law required her to wear a jilbab was held by a minority of Muslims, was nothing to the point in considering the issue whether Art.9(1) was engaged. Her Art.9(1) freedom to manifest her reli-gion was limited and, as a matter of Convention law, it was for the school, as an emanation of the state, to justify the limitation on her freedom created by its uniform policy and the way in which it was enforced. In England and Wales provision was made for religious education and worship in schools. Schools were under a duty to secure that religious education was given to pupils and that each pupil should take part in an act of collective worship every day, unless withdrawn by their parent. The school's position was distinctive in the sense that despite its policy of inclusiveness, it permitted girls to wear a head-scarf that was likely to identify them as Muslim. The school approached the issues from an entirely wrong direction and did not attribute to the pupil's beliefs the weight they deserved:

"The decision-making structure should therefore go along the following lines:

1) Has the claimant established that she has a relevant Convention right which qualifies for protection under Article 9(1)?
2) Subject to any justification that is established under Article 9(2), has that Convention right been violated?
3) Was the interference with her Convention right prescribed by law in the Convention sense of that expression?
4) Did the interference have a legitimate arm?
5) What are the considerations that need to be balanced against each other when determining whether the interference was necessary in a demo-cratic society for the purpose of achieving that aim?
6) Was the interference justified under Article 9(2)?

The School did not approach the matter in this way at all. Nobody who con-sidered the issues on its behalf started from the premise that the claimant had a right which is recognised by English law, and that the onus lay on the School to justify its interference with that right. Instead, it started from the premise that its uniform policy was there to be obeyed: if the claimant did not like it, she could go to a different school."

It started from the premise that its uniform policy was there to be obeyed, rather than from the premises that the pupil had a right recognised by English law and that the onus lay on it to justify its interference with that right. Accordingly, the school had unlawfully denied her the right to manifest her religion in violation of Art.9(1) and had denied her access to suitable and appropriate education in violation of Sch.1, Pt II, Art.2.

3-176   Under s.19 of the Anti-Social Behaviour Act 2003, where a pupil has been excluded on disciplinary grounds for a fixed period or permanently, or where a child of compulsory school age has failed to attend regularly at a relevant school at which he is a registered pupil, an LEA or the governing body of a relevant school may enter into a parenting contract with a parent of the pupil or child. A parenting contract is a document which contains a statement by the parent that he agrees to comply with such requirements as may be specified in the document for such period as may be so specified, and a statement by the local education authority or governing body that it agrees to provide support to the parent for the purpose of complying with those requirements. These requirements may also include a counselling or guidance programme. Subsection (6) declares that the purpose of the requirements is to ensure that the child attends regularly at the relevant school at which he is a registered pupil. However, a parenting contract does not create any obligations in respect of whose breach any liability arises in contract or in tort.[88]

3-177   Further, under s.20 of the 2003 Act, where a pupil has been excluded on disciplinary grounds for a fixed period or permanently, and such conditions as may be prescribed in regulations made by the appropriate person (i.e. Secretary of State) are satisfied, an LEA may apply to a magistrates' court for a parenting order in respect of a parent of the pupil.[89] If such an application is made, the court may make a parenting order in respect of a parent of the pupil if it is satisfied that making the order would be desirable in the interests of improving the behaviour of the pupil. The duration of the order is at least 12 months. It may be a requirement of the order that the parent attend a counselling or guidance programme. That programme may include a residential course, but only if the attendance of the parent at a residential course is likely to be more effective than his attendance at a non-residential course in improving the behaviour of the pupil and any interference with family life which is likely to result from the attendance of the parent at a residential course is proportionate in all the circumstances.[90] In deciding whether to make a parenting order under s.20, the court must take into account (amongst other things) any refusal by the parent to enter into a parenting contract under this section or, if the parent has entered into such a parenting contract, any failure by the parent to comply with the requirements specified in the contract.[91] Further, in the case of a pupil under the age of 16, a court must obtain and consider information about the pupil's family circumstances and the likely effect of the order on those circumstances.[92]

3-178   Section 29(3) of the Education Act 2002 gives the governing body of a school the power to direct a pupil in attendance at that school to attend alternative provision. The Education Act 2005 amends the power of Governing Bodies to send pupils to education or training which takes place off the school premises. From September 1, 2005, governing bodies have the power to send all pupils registered at the school to off-site provision, including pupils on fixed term exclusions or permanently excluded pupils where the appeal process is not complete. The amendment was made because there was some doubt whether Governing Bodies current power to refer pupils who are "in attendance" at the school included excluded pupils.

---

[88] Anti-Social Behaviour Act 2003, s.19(8).
[89] From April 2000 to December 2002, there were 3,105 parenting orders; 2,129 for criminal offences, 538 for school attendance offences and 438 others: *HC Deb* December 18, 2002 c 846W and Home Office. For parenting orders generally see para.3–143.
[90] Anti-Social Behaviour Act 2003, s.20(6).
[91] *ibid.*, s.21.
[92] *ibid.*, s.21(2).

Truancy
On any one school day, 50,000 pupils in England are away from school without **3-179**
the school's permission; and, in a recent MORI survey undertaken on behalf
of the Youth Justice Board, more than 70 per cent of children who did not
attend school regularly committed a criminal offence. The Audit Commission
found that pupils who truant are twice as likely to offend as those in school.
In a recent three-hour truancy sweep in Portsmouth, half of the 73 truant
pupils were with a parent or guardian at the time and only 3 per cent were
authorised to be away from school.[93] The Home Office Youth Lifestyles
Survey in 1998/99 showed that 47 per cent of male persistent truants aged 12
to 16 offended, compared with 10 per cent of boys who had not truanted.[94]
Curtailing truancy is a key part of the Home Office strategy to reduce crime.[95]
In the Government's view, truancy and anti-social behaviour are directly
related.[96] Sections 18 to 23 of the Anti-Social Behaviour Act 2003 build on
provisions relating to exclusions, and truancy. The basic aim is to offer parents
support through parenting contracts and, if necessary, to compel them to take
responsibility for their children through parenting orders and penalty notices.
Government policy is that there is an inextricable link between truancy and
youth crime and anti-social behaviour. It is estimated that of 3.7 million pupils
in maintained primary schools, 15 per cent have taken a half day of unauthorised absence at least once; the average truant missed nine days of school; and
the average secondary truant missed 17 half days of school.[97] Regulations may
require, or enable the Secretary of State to require, maintained school governing bodies to set annual targets for reducing truancy.[98] In particular, the
regulations may provide for the Secretary of State to impose a target where in
the previous school year unauthorised absences exceeded the level specified for
that year. The target may be set for a specified period, but the Secretary of
State may grant exemption for any year. Following the recommendations of a
Social Exclusion Unit Report, *Truancy and School Exclusion*, the government
set targets to reduce the number of children out of school by one third by
2002. At para.1.8:

"Parents bear the primary responsibility for ensuring that their children
attend school regularly and home circumstances exert an important influence over pupils' attendance and punctuality. Poor parental supervision and
lack of commitment to education are crucial factors behind truancy."

Section 7 of the Education Act 1996 provides that it is the duty of parent of
every child of compulsory school age to cause him to receive efficient full-time
education suitable to his age, ability and aptitude and to any special educational needs he may have, either by regular attendance at school or otherwise.
This duty is simply to ensure that the child receives full-time education and
not that the child attends school so that parents may comply with the duty by
providing education at home.[99] The duty does not apply where it is not practicable for the parent to arrange for him to be admitted as a pupil at a school.[1]
Under s.14 of the 1996 Act, LEAs are under a duty to ensure that there are

---

[93] Martin and Hayden, "Truancy: Absent Without Leave" (2001) *Magistrate*, 104.
[94] Martin and Hayden, *ibid.*
[95] *Crime Reduction Strategy,* Home Office, November 1999.
[96] White Paper, paras 2.33 to 2.38.
[97] *Pupil Absence in Schools in England* 2001/2 SFR 30/2002/17, December 2002.
[98] School Standards Frameworks Act 1998, s.63. The Education (School Attendance Targets)
(England) Regulations 2005 (SI 2005/58).
[99] The possibility of a school attendance order may only arise where a local authority determines
that a child is not receiving suitable education, either at school or otherwise.
[1] Education Act 1996, s.433.

sufficient schools in the area to provide for both primary and secondary education: see also s.19, with regard to children with special needs. Note also the general duty under s.13 ". . .to contribute towards the spiritual, moral, mental and physical development of the community by securing the above provision."[2] Therefore, the LEA is potentially in breach of their (target) duties whenever a child is not receiving suitable education. If it appears to the LEA that a child of compulsory school age in their area is not receiving suitable education, either by regular attendance at school or otherwise, they must serve a notice in writing[3]—a school attendance order—on the parent, requiring them to satisfy it within the period of the notice, 15 days, that the child is receiving such education.[4] If the parent fails to satisfy the authority, within the period of the notice and in the opinion of the authority, that it is expedient that the child should attend school, then the authority must serve on the parent a school attendance order requiring him to cause the child to be registered at a school named in the order. It is an offence to fail to comply with the requirements of the order and it is a defence that the parent is causing the child to receive suitable education otherwise than at school; if so, the court may discharge the order.[5]

3-180   Under s.444 of the 1996 Act:

"If a child of compulsory school age who is a registered pupil at a school fails to attend regularly at the school, his parent is guilty of an offence."

Subsection (1A), which was subsequently added to the Act, provides for the second and more serious offence:

"If in the circumstances mentioned in subsection (1) the parent knows that his child is failing to attend regularly at the school and fails without reasonable justification to cause him to do so, he is guilty of an offence."

Section 444(6) of the 1996 Act provides that the only lawful excuses for non-attendance at school, at least as regards a non-boarding pupil, are: the school is not within walking distance of the child's home; or no suitable arrangements have been made by the LEA for his transport to and from the school or to enable him to become a registered pupil at a school near his home. Under s.444(8B), if, on the trial of an offence under subs.(1A), the court finds the defendant not guilty of that offence, but is satisfied that he is guilty of an offence under subs.(1), the court may find him guilty of that offence. However, before instituting criminal proceedings, the LEA must consider whether it would be appropriate to apply for an education supervision order instead of or in addition to the criminal proceedings.[6] The court may also direct the LEA to

---

[2] Note also s.175 of the Education Act 2002 which imposes a duty on LEAs, the governing bodies of maintained schools, and the governing bodies of FE institutions to make arrangements in regard to the welfare of children. LEAs must make arrangements to ensure that their functions in the capacity of an LEA are exercised with a view to safeguarding and promoting the welfare of children. Similarly governing bodies must make arrangements to ensure that their functions relating to the conduct of the school, or institution, are exercised with a view to safeguarding and promoting the welfare of children who are pupils at the school, or who are receiving education or training at the institution. All the bodies concerned must have regard to any guidance issued by the Secretary of State, in regard to England in deciding what arrangements they must make to comply with their duty.

[3] In a format prescribed the Education (School Attendance Order) Regulations 1995 (SI 1995/2090).

[4] Education Act 1996, s.437.

[5] *ibid.*, s.443.

[6] *ibid.*, s.447.

apply for such an order, unless the authority have already decided that the child's welfare is already safeguarded without it.[7] On application of the LEA, the court may make an education supervision order placing the child under the supervision of a designated LEA. The court must be first satisfied that the child is of compulsory school age and that he is not being educated properly.[8] The duration of the order is one year. It is the duty of the supervisor to advise, assist and befriend and give directions to the supervised child and his parents so as to secure that he is properly educated.[9] If the parent or the child fail to comply with the order, he is guilty of an offence, punishable on summary conviction by a fine up to level 3.[10] It is a defence that they took all reasonable steps to ensure that the direction was complied with or that the direction was unreasonable. If an education supervision order does not work, the LEA may apply for a supervision or care order under s.31 of the Children Act 1989.

There is comprehensive departmental guidance on legal remedies with respect to truancy.[11] Before commencing any kind of formal action, education welfare officers should make every effort to engage the parent and help them get their children to school. This may include making sure the parent is aware of the location of schools in the area, and explaining the admission or admission appeal arrangements where necessary. If it is not possible to persuade the parent to make arrangements for their child's education, then the parent should be served with a notice stating that they are failing in their duty to provide their child with education and informing them that they must satisfy the LEA that they are providing an education at school or otherwise within a specified time period (but not less than 14 days). Upon expiry of the notice, the LEA should write to the parent, referring them to the notice and informing them of the LEAs intention to serve a school attendance order. The LEA should inform the parent of schools that are suitable for the child to attend and should also inform the parent that they have the right to educate their child at home if they choose to. The parent should be told that they have 15 days in which to take action or the LEA will proceed to make a school attendance order. It is good practice to provide the parent with detailed information explaining the law. The LEA must consult the school before naming the school in any order. This consultation needs to take into account the code of practice on special educational needs and the code of practice on school admissions. If the 15 days expire without the parent taking any action then the LEA should issue a school attendance order. The order should specify which school the child should attend. The parent should be informed that they have 15 days to comply with the order. If a parent, on whom an order has been served, fails to comply with the requirements of the order, they are guilty of an offence under s.443 of the Education Act 1996, unless they prove that the child is receiving a suitable education otherwise than at school. The case should thus be taken to the Magistrates Court where a summons can be obtained. The parent will be named on the summons and will have to appear before the Court. The order continues to be in force for as long as the child is of compulsory school age. If there is a continued failure to register the child, the LEA has the option of referring to Social Services for consideration of care proceedings. Alternatively, the case may be taken to the Family Proceedings Court, instead of the Magistrates Court, where an application can be made for an Education Supervision Order under s.36(5)a of the Children Act 1989.

3-181

[7] Education Act 1996, s.447.
[8] Children Act 1989, s.36.
[9] *ibid.*, Sch.3, para.12.
[10] Education Act 1989, Sch.3, para.18.
[11] "Ensuring Regular Attendance" DfES (2003).

3-182   In *Barnfather v Islington LBC*,[12] the defendant appealed by way of case stated against her conviction for a strict liability offence under s.444(1) of the 1996 Act. Her child had been a registered pupil at a school but had failed to attend regularly. The main issues before the court were whether s.444(1) was compatible with the provisions of the European Convention on Human Rights 1950, and if not, whether the section could be reinterpreted compatibly with the Convention pursuant to the Human Rights Act 1998. The defendant argued that that the section was inconsistent with Art.6 of the Convention as it created a strict liability offence which did not require proof of any knowledge or fault on the parent's part, and the reasoning in *Salabiaku v France*[13] enabled the courts to scrutinise a strict liability offence to establish whether it was within reasonable limits on a proportionality basis. The appeal was dismissed. Although it was an offence of strict liability, it was not one which required the reversal of the burden of proof. It was for the local authority to prove that the child, (a) was a registered pupil at a relevant school, (b) was of compulsory school age, (c) had failed to attend regularly and (d) that the reason for the absence was not with leave or by reason of illness or unavoidable cause in a case where such an issue was raised. Given the restricted way in which the last requirement, (d), had been determined by the courts and the fact that no reverse burden arose, the defendant's case was not based on the most obvious concern of Art.6(2), namely the presumption of innocence. The question was whether Art.6(2) provided a criterion against which the substance of a domestic offence could be scrutinised or whether it was confined to procedural and evidential matters. The issue in *Salabiaku* was of the latter kind. Neither the decision in *Salabiaku*, nor anything else relied upon by the defendant, provided a basis for holding that s.444 was incompatible with Art.6(2). Therefore, the answer to the first question was in the affirmative and so the second did not arise. Further, given the policy of the prevention of truancy, the offence prescribed by s.444 sought to achieve a legitimate aim. While punishment under s.444(1) could be accompanied by a degree of social stigma, the strict liability offence was reasonable and proportionate given the context.

3-183   In *London Borough of Sutton v S*,[14] the local education authority appealed by way of case stated from a decision acquitting the respondent's parents of an offence under s.444(1A) and refusing to return an alternative verdict under s.444(1) of the Act. The authority had brought an information against the parent in relation to one of the parent's children who was of compulsory school age but had only attended school on 29 days in a 174-day period. The magistrates had found that the parent had made out the defence of "reasonable justification" as she had co-operated with all recommendations made by the school to persuade the child to attend. The magistrates concluded that the child had serious emotional and behavioural problems and that there was a limit to what a parent could do to force a 14-year-old to attend school if he had made up his mind not to go. The magistrates had also considered whether they should return an alternative verdict pursuant to s.444(8B) of the Act, but had decided that to do so would be inappropriate in all the circumstances. The authority submitted that as there was no guidance on what amounted to "reasonable justification" under s.444(1A) of the Act, this was an appropriate case in which to give such guidance. The Divisional Court held, dismissing the appeal, that on the evidence the magistrates had made a clear finding that the defence of reasonable justification had been made out. The appeal was misconceived and should never have been brought. Local education authorities had a responsibility to consider

[12] [2003] E.L.R. 263.
[13] (A/141-A) (1991) 13 E.H.R.R. 379.
[14] [2004] EWHC 2876.

carefully the distress that might be caused to both parents and children when contemplating a prosecution for non attendance at school or whether to appeal a decision. In bringing the appeal, the council had caused enormous distress to the parent with no reasonable prospect of success. The human factor was a very important consideration in deciding whether or not to bring an appeal. This was not a case suitable for giving guidance on the nature of the statutory defence. As to the alternative verdict, the test was whether such a verdict would be in the interests of justice. That test was also applicable to the exercise of discretion under s.444(8B). In this, due to the clear defence having being made out and taking into consideration the distress caused to the parties, it would not have been in the interests of justice to return an alternative verdict.

See also *R v Ceredigion, Ex p. Jones*[15] in which the court considered the interplay of the defence of a unreasonable distance from school and the LEAs statutory duty to provide a child with transport. A secondary school boy sought judicial review of his local authority's refusal to fund his transport to a school in the next county. He lived in the county of Ceredigion. His parents preferred for him to attend the nearest Welsh school, Preseli, in Pembrokeshire. Preseli was not within walking distance. The local authority conceded that the nearest school, an English school, was not suitable for the child since it was not a Welsh medium school. The child contended that a local authority was required under s.509(1) of the Education Act 1996 to provide free transport to a child if his parents would otherwise have a defence to a s.444 truancy prosecution, and that his parents would have a defence under s.444(4) since the nearest suitable school was Preseli. The local authority contended that it was anomalous to decide whether transport should be provided on the basis of whether there was a defence to a charge which was unlikely to be brought, s.444 having become a last resort provision for truancy, and, in any case, the suitability of the nearer school was irrelevant to s.444(4)(b)(iii) provided suitable arrangements had been made for the child's attendance at that school. The court granted the application, and held that a local authority was obliged by s.509(1) of the Act to provide a child with free transport if his parents would otherwise have a defence under s.444(4) to a s.444 truancy prosecution, should the child fail to attend school regularly. Parliament had not repealed s.444, and s.444(4)(b) clearly recognised a link between the section and the provision of transport. It would be inconsistent with the basic obligation under s.7 to arrange to register a child at a school which was known to be incapable of providing education suitable to his age, ability, aptitude and any special education needs he might have. Consequently, a local authority's arrangements for a child's registration at a school would not be "suitable" for the purposes of s.444(4)(b)(iii) if the school was not educationally suitable for the child. The local authority had accepted that the nearer school was not educationally suitable for the child, and their refusal to provide free transport to Preseli had to be quashed.

Further, where a parent knowingly and without justification condones the absence of a child from school without good cause, there is an "aggravated" version of the offence under s.444(1A) of the Education Act 1996[16] which provides that if, in the circumstances mentioned in s.444(1), the parent knows that his child is failing to attend regularly at the school and fails without reasonable justification to cause him to do so, he is guilty of an offence. The maximum fine is £2,500 and/or imprisonment for three months. The intention was to provide for a higher penalty for persistent and aggravated truancy. In May 2002, for example, one defendant parent was given a prison sentence in Oxfordshire for not ensuring that two of her daughters regularly attended

3-184

3-185

---

[15] [2004] EWHC 1376.
[16] Inserted by s.72 of the Criminal Justice and Court Service Act 2000.

school.[17] In certain areas, a "fast track" prosecution process for such parents has been piloted and there are plans for national implementation in late 2003. Under this procedure, parents are to be given 12 weeks to improve their child's attendance and, if there is no improvement, they will be fined or imprisoned. Departmental guidance on truancy prosecutions, "Ensuring Regular School Attendance", provides further information about the fast-track procedure. The "Fast-track to Prosecution Framework" is described as a "time-focused model of best practice which concentrates on early intervention in cases of persistent non-attendance and aims to ensure a faster and more effective approach to the implementation of strategies to tackle this behaviour and the underlying causes". Under this framework, in cases where parents have not cooperated with the school or LEA in ensuring their child's regular attendance at school, they should be given a specified period of time (usually 12 weeks) to engage with the Education Welfare Service and school in bringing about an improvement in their child's attendance. They should be informed at the beginning of this period about the possible consequences of non-cooperation which ultimately should be prosecution. The LEA, school and parent should sign up to an action plan at the beginning of the time period in which it is stated how they intend to work together to improve the child's school attendance. Any other agencies that may be able to make a contribution in improving the child's attendance should be engaged at this point by the LEA. If the parent does not sign up to the action plan, this should be recorded by the LEA. During the specified time period the child's attendance should be monitored closely by the LEA and the school. The parent's level of engagement should also be monitored. Progress against the action plan should be reviewed regularly during the time period, perhaps through a formal panel involving a range of different agencies. If an improvement in the child's attendance is not seen, and the LEA consider that the parent has failed in their responsibilities, they may choose to bring a prosecution. Information about the parent's cooperation during the Fast-track process should be brought to the attention of the court. The Guidance emphasises that the prosecution process itself is not affected by the Fast-track to Prosecution Framework. Fast-track is about bringing cases, where parents have failed to cooperate in carrying out their responsibilities, to court more quickly. It does not in any way extend to influencing the court proceedings.

Parenting Contracts under the 2003 Act and Education

3-186   In the Anti-Social Behaviour White Paper, it is said that parents have a legal responsibility to ensure that their children behave in an acceptable way and attend school regularly and, while the great majority of parents live up to these responsibilities, some do not. Therefore, the government proposes that LEAs and schools have formal powers to ask parents who have failed to secure their child's attendance or whose child has been excluded to sign parenting contracts.[18] Hence, under s.19 of the Anti-Social Behaviour Act 2003, where a pupil has been excluded on disciplinary grounds from a relevant school for a fixed period or permanently, or where a child of compulsory school age has failed to attend regularly at a relevant school at which he is a registered pupil, the LEA or the governing body of a relevant school may enter into a parenting contract with a parent of the pupil or child. Under this section, a parenting contract is a document which contains a statement by the parent that he agrees to comply with such requirements as may be specified in the document for such period as may be so specified, and a statement by the local education authority or governing body that it agrees to provide support to the parent for the purpose of complying with

[17] Ares, and others, *Research Paper, Anti-Social Behaviour Bill*, 3/034, April 2003, p.58.
[18] White Paper *Anti-Social Behaviour*, p.31.

those requirements. The requirements may include (in particular) a requirement to attend a counselling or guidance programme. The purpose of the requirements is to improve the behaviour of the pupil, or to ensure that the child attends regularly at the relevant school at which he is a registered pupil. The contract must be signed by the parent and signed on behalf of the LEA or governing body.

Home Office Guidance on Parenting Contracts

Guidance published in 2004 by the Home Office on parenting contracts provides that they consist of two elements.[19] Parenting contracts and orders can consist of a programme designed to meet the individual needs of parents so as to help them address their child's misbehaviour; or one which specifies particular ways in which parents are required to exercise control over their child's behaviour to address particular factors associated with offending or anti-social behaviour. Examples would be ensuring that their child goes to school every day or is home during certain hours. When parents are unwilling to engage with parenting support on a voluntary basis, and a YOT assesses that a parent could be supported to improve the child's behaviour, YOTs can apply for a free-standing parenting order or recommend a parenting order linked to a child's conviction or another order. Assessment is needed to form a picture of the child and the family circumstances. This should be informed by information from other agencies. Initially the YOT will complete an asset assessment, but where this suggests that parenting is a significant factor in the child or young person's misbehaviour a detailed assessment of the parents should be carried out. This should identify: parenting risk and protective factors; the individual needs and circumstances of the parents; whether a programme could support the parents so they can positively influence their child and if so, what form it should take and whether it should involve a parenting contract or an order; any cultural, racial, linguistic, literacy, religious or gender specific issues that may affect the kind of programme that will be effective for a particular parent; the facts relating to a particular parent or child without invalid assumptions relating to culture, race or gender; whether the parent has any disability, special educational need or mental health problem that would affect the parent's ability to participate in a programme and if so, how it can be accommodated; and any other issue that could affect a parent's ability to participate (such as transport or child care). Any intervention must be in accordance with any existing Child Protection Plan or care plan and be responsive to issues that emerge during the intervention process, such as serious mental health problems, personality disorder, domestic violence or child abuse. Practitioners should follow Area Child Protection Committee procedures. Parenting practitioners have a duty to protect children and young people. Information that emerges during the intervention or assessment process about domestic violence or abuse will need to be passed on to police and social services for action. Information about other risks may also need to be referred to the appropriate agency. Practitioners should also establish with other agencies, including the police and social services, whether they have information regarding the family about child abuse or domestic violence. If this is the case then there must be discussion with the agencies already involved with the family to establish a joint agency approach. Protocols must be drawn up to ensure that satisfactory information and data sharing is achieved in any joint working arrangements between agencies.

3-187

Parenting work can be carried out by, or on behalf of, a local education authority (under an educational parenting contract or order), social services, health services or by voluntary organisations. The YOT must identify any work with the child or parents by other agencies and coordinate any further

3-188

---

[19] *Guidance on Parenting Contracts and Parenting Orders*, Home Office, 2004.

intervention. Other agencies may also be able to provide useful information about the child or young person's behaviour or the nature and extent of parental supervision. For instance a young person may be playing truant from school and the parent might therefore already be subject to an "educational" parenting contract or order. This should be included in the YOT assessment. When a parent is taking part in a programme it is important to inform other agencies so they are able to relate to the child and family consistently. When arranging a contract or applying for, or recommending, an order, YOTs should consider whether this should also cover poor behaviour inside school and/or truancy and, if so, who should be the lead agency. Truancy and misbehaviour at school can both be risk factors associated with offending and therefore a YOT parenting intervention can address educational issues. On the other hand, educational parenting orders and contracts cannot address criminal or anti-social behaviour outside school. Therefore it will usually be appropriate for YOTs to lead in cases where the YOT and LEA both wish to work with the parents of a child or young person. However there will be cases where it will be more appropriate for the LEA to take the lead. Local protocols will need to be agreed about co-operating and supplying resources in such cases. Local co-ordination in the delivery of parenting programmes may also help target effort where it can be most effective; contracts are not intended to replace all voluntary work with parents but to provide an additional option backed by statute. As many parents want support, YOTs will often be able to work effectively with them without using a contract.

3-189   The purpose of a parenting contract is to prevent the child or young person from engaging or persisting in criminal conduct or anti-social behaviour. Whether a parenting contract will serve this purpose will be determined by the YOT in light of the assessment. A YOT worker may negotiate a parenting contract when a child or young person has been referred to the YOT and he or she has reason to believe that the child or young person has engaged, or is likely to engage, in criminal conduct or antisocial behaviour. Whether or not they accept that their child's behaviour is criminal or antisocial, the phrase "is likely to engage" allows for work with parents without giving the child or young person a reprimand or final warning or charging them with a view to court proceedings. The phrase also allows early supportive work with parents who have consented to be referred to a YOT as their child has been identified as being at risk of engaging in criminal conduct or anti-social behaviour. Where a child has not engaged in criminal conduct or anti-social behaviour, the referral to the YOT and any subsequent intervention must be on a voluntary basis. Children referred to a YOT, when a parenting contract may be suitable, will include: a child convicted of an offence; a child who is referred to the YOT in connection with a reprimand or a final warning; a child under 10 that a member of the YOT has reason to believe has committed an act, which if the child had been older, would have constituted an offence; a child identified as being at risk of offending by a Youth Inclusion Support Panel. If a YOT considers a parenting contract would be useful, the YOT worker should first consult with other agencies working with the child or young person, or with the parents or guardians, to establish both how a parenting contract would fit in with any existing interventions and whether other agencies should be involved in the work on the contract. It will be for the YOT worker to decide how best to engage the parents in discussions leading to a contract, depending on the circumstances. Usually both parents or guardians should be involved and, subject to age, maturity and understanding, the child or young person as well. The parents, and where appropriate their child, should be asked to outline their views on the misbehaviour, how they believe it should be tackled and what they think of the idea of a parenting contract. The YOT worker should outline what a parenting contract is and why one may be appropriate. The parents and YOT worker will also be able to discuss support the parents would like and what the YOT is able to provide. The aim should be to work in partnership to improve the behaviour of the child or young person. All efforts to engage the parents using a contract should be recorded, as this would be a relevant factor in any subsequent application for a parenting order. If a contract is negotiated, the specified requirements for the parents under s.25(3)(a) of the Anti-Social Behaviour Act 2003 will need to be designed to prevent criminal conduct or anti-social behaviour or further criminal conduct or anti-social behaviour. Parents should be asked about any requirements they would find helpful in addition to those the YOT suggest. Examples are: to ensure their child stays away, unless supervised, from a part of town where he or she has misbehaved; to ensure their child is effectively supervised at certain times; to ensure their child avoids contact with certain disruptive individuals; to ensure their child avoids contact with someone he or she has been harassing; to ensure their child attends school regularly; to ensure that they (the parents) attend all school meetings concerning their child. Parenting contracts are designed to be voluntary. If a parent refuses to enter into one the YOT worker should meet constructively to meet all legitimate concerns and ensure that a written record is kept of all efforts to negotiate a contract. This should include whether the parents were at least willing to meet to discuss the possibility and, if so, what was said. If the conditions of s.26(3) are met, and a parent or guardian refuses to enter into a contract or fails to agree to an appropriate contract to try to secure agreement, the YOT worker may wish to warn of the intention to apply for a free-standing parenting order and that the court will take into account the refusal to enter into a parenting contract (per s.27(1)(a) of the 2003 Act). The YOT should work with the parents to gain their co-operation and compliance with the contract, but will have to judge whether any failure to comply is reasonable and whether the contract remains useful and should continue. There is no penalty for failing to comply with a parenting contract but it would be a relevant consideration for a YOT in deciding whether to apply for, and a relevant consideration for a court in deciding whether to make, a parenting order. If no explanation is given, or the YOT worker is not satisfied with the explanation, they should serve the parents with a warning and keep a record of it. If repeated failures to comply are seriously undermining the contract's effectiveness, the YOT worker should meet the parents or guardians to discuss how the contract can be made to work. If the conditions at s.26(3) of the 2003 Act are met, the YOT worker should remind them that if the contract fails, the YOT would be able to apply for a free-standing parenting order, and that a court would take account of how far the parents had complied with the contract. In light of this meeting, the YOT worker should decide whether the non-compliance is undermining the contract to the extent that the YOT needs to apply for a parenting order, or whether to persevere with the contract. The YOT worker must record the decision and reasons. This can be used in any future application for a parenting order.

Recently published Education Department guidance[20] provides that if a pupil fails to regularly attend school or alternative provision, the LA or governing body of the school may consider whether it would be appropriate to offer a parenting contract to the parent. Parenting contracts will, however, often be a useful tool in identifying and focusing on the issues behind the non-attendance and in developing a productive relationship with parents to

3-190

[20] Guidance on Education-Related Parenting Contracts, Parenting Orders and Penalty Notices (2005).

address these issues. The LEA or governing body should be responsive to the needs of the parent in deciding what type of support they will provide. The issues behind truancy can be complex and the type of support required will depend on each individual case. The LEA or governing body may agree to provide support in the form of a parenting programme. The contract may specify that the parent is required to attend the sessions of any such programme. There is a wide range of providers of parenting programmes, including voluntary organisations, YOTs and LEAs. In assessing the nature of the counselling or guidance programme in which the parent should take part, the LEA or governing body should consider who will administer the sessions, the training and experience of the facilitators, including their ability to engage with parents, the curriculum used, whether classes will be group or individually-based and whether there are particular cultural and social factors to be considered. Under this guidance, failure to comply with the parenting contract cannot lead to action for breach of contract or for civil damages, and there is no direct sanction for a parent's failure to comply with, or refusal to sign, a parenting contract. However, if the pupil's irregular attendance continues, or escalates to such a level where a prosecution is deemed appropriate, this should be presented as evidence in the case. There is nothing to prevent an LA or school entering into an agreement (either formal or informal) with a parent in relation to their child's attendance at any time. Parenting contracts simply provide an additional option which has the backing of statute. A parenting contract may be used in cases of truancy where a pupil has failed to attend regularly at the school at which he is registered or the alternative provision made for him. The purpose of a parenting contract is to improve the pupil's attendance at school or alternative provision and to address any underlying issues. A parenting contract will be an appropriate course of action where the parent is willing to address their child's truanting behaviour, but needs support to do so effectively. In deciding whether a parenting contract might be appropriate, the LA or governing body should consider all the issues behind the non-attendance, in particular whether attendance may be improved through working with the parent and providing support to them and, if so, what form this support should take.

Parenting Orders and Education

3-191   Under s.20 of the Anti-Social Behaviour Act 2003, where a pupil has been excluded on disciplinary grounds from a relevant school for a fixed period or permanently, and such conditions as may be prescribed in regulations made by the appropriate person are satisfied, a local education authority may apply to a magistrates' court for a parenting order in respect of a parent of the pupil. If such an application is made, the court may make a parenting order in respect of a parent of the pupil if it is satisfied that making the order would be desirable in the interests of improving the behaviour of the pupil. A parenting order is an order which requires the parent to comply, for a period not exceeding 12 months, with such requirements as are specified in the order, and which may include a requirement to attend, for a concurrent period not exceeding three months, such counselling or guidance programme as may be specified in directions given by the responsible officer. A counselling or guidance programme which a parent is required to attend, by virtue of subs.(4)(b), may be, or include, a residential course, but only if the court is satisfied that the following two conditions are fulfilled. These conditions are set out in subss.(7) and (8): the first condition is that the attendance of the parent at a residential course is likely to be more effective than his attendance at a non-residential course in improving the behaviour of the pupil. The second condition is that any interference with family life, which is likely to result from the attendance of the parent at a residential course, is proportionate in all the circumstances.

Under s.21, in deciding whether to make a parenting order under s.20, a court **3-192** must take into account (amongst other things) any refusal by the parent to enter into a parenting contract under s.19 in respect of the pupil in a case or, if the parent has entered into such a parenting contract, any failure by the parent to comply with the requirements specified in the contract. Further, before making a parenting order under s.20, in the case of a pupil under the age of 16, a court must obtain and consider information about the pupil's family circumstances and the likely effect of the order on those circumstances. An appeal lies to the Crown Court against the making of a parenting order under s.20.

Penalty Notices for Truancy
As an alternative to prosecution, it was proposed in the Anti-Social Behaviour **3-193** White Paper that designated LEA and school staff and police officers are to be empowered to issue fixed penalty notices to parents who condone or ignore truancy.[21] Section 23 of the Anti-Social Behaviour Act 2003 inserts a new section into the 1996 Act, s.444A. It provides that, where an authorised officer[22] has reason to believe that a person has committed an offence under s.444(1), and that the school to which the offence relates is a relevant school in England, he may give the person a penalty notice in respect of the offence. A penalty notice is defined as a notice offering a person the opportunity of discharging any liability to conviction for the offence under s.444(1) to which the notice relates by payment of a penalty in accordance with the notice.[23] Where a person is given a penalty notice, proceedings for the offence to which the notice relates (or an offence under s.444(1A) arising out of the same circumstances) may not be instituted before the end of such period as may be prescribed. Under subs.(4), where a person is given a penalty notice, he cannot be convicted of the offence to which the notice relates (or an offence under s.444(1A) arising out of the same circumstances) if he pays a penalty in accordance with the notice.

Under the new s.444B, the Secretary of State may make regulations gov- **3-194** erning the form and content of the notices, including the amount of the penalty and the time by which it must be paid and codes of conduct. The regulations will also provide for the persons who are to be authorised by the LEA or the head teacher to give penalty notices. The Education (Penalty Notices) (England) Regulations 2004 (as amended),[24] Reg.2, sets out the matters to be contained in a penalty notice, such as the name and address of the recipient, the name and address of the child who is failing to attend school regularly or who is failing to attend alternative educational provision regularly and, as applicable, (a) the name of the school where he is a registered pupil; (b) the place where the alternative educational provision is provided for the child or at which he is required to attend; (c) the name and official particulars of the authorised officer issuing the notice; and (d) the date of the offence and of the issue of the notice. Regulations 3 and 4 prescribe the level of the penalty which is to be paid to the local education authority,[25] and what is evidence of its payment or non-payment. Regulation 5 prescribes 42 days as the period before which no proceedings can be commenced. If the penalty is not paid within that time, Reg.6 requires the local education authority either to prosecute for the offence under s.444 or to withdraw the notice on one of the grounds set out in Reg.7. Regulations 12 to 14 require the local education authority to draw up

---

[21] White Paper *Anti-Social Behaviour*, p.31.
[22] A constable or an authorised staff member or officer of an LEA: s.444B(4).
[23] Education Act 1996, s.444A(2).
[24] Education (Penalty Notices) (England) Regulations 2004 (SI 2004/181).
[25] Currently, £50 where the amount is paid within 28 days of receipt of the notice; £100 where the amount is paid within 42 days of receipt of the notice.

and consult on a code of conduct for the issuing of penalty notices. Regulations 15 and 16 provide for the Secretary of State to have power to direct a local education authority to draw up a draft code or revisions to a code and for the Secretary of State to approve the draft code or revisions. Regulations 17 to 19 require records to be kept, a copy of any penalty notice issued to be given to the local education authority, and information to be given to the Secretary of State. Regulation 20 sets out how penalty notices may be served on the recipient and makes it clear that the recipient may prove that a notice served by post was not delivered to him. It also provides that two days service is to be calculated without taking account of Saturdays, Sundays or Bank Holidays. Further, s.444B(3) extends the list of Community Service Officer powers under Pt 1 of Sch.4 to the 2002 Act so that, under para.1(2) of Sch.4 to the Police Reform Act 2002, they may now issue fixed penalty notices under s.444A of the 1996 Act.[26]

3-195   Section 116 of the Education Act 1996 adds another section to these provisions of the 1996 Act, s.444ZA. This new section applies in two situations:

(1) in the case of a child of compulsory school age who is not a registered pupil at any school, and an LEA has made arrangements under s.19 of the 1996 Act for the provision of education for him otherwise than at a school; or

(2) in the case of a child of compulsory school age excluded from a relevant school, and remains for the time being a registered pupil at the school and is required by the appropriate authority for the school to attend at a place outside the school premises for the purpose of receiving any instruction or training, and notice in writing of the requirement has been given to the child's parent.

In either of those two cases, subss.(1) to (7) of s.444 have effect as if the place he were a registered pupil is at that school. That is, the parent commits an offence under s.444 of the 1996 Act where they fail to ensure that a child for whom he is responsible attends the alternative provision that has been made for the child. This amendment does not affect Pupil Referral Units which are legally defined as schools and must register all of their pupils. Therefore, parents of pupils who fail to attend Pupil Referral Units already fell within the scope of ss.444 and 444A of the Education Act 1996.

Truancy Partnerships
3-196   On November 18, 2004 the Secretary of State outlined the expectation that all secondary schools should be working in collaboration or partnership to improve behaviour and persistent truancy by September 2007, and this was outlined in a letter to all Chief Education Officers or Directors of Children's Services. More recently the Minister sent a letter on July 4, 2005 to update them on the outcomes and design principles which emerged from joint working between practitioners, the Prime Minister's Delivery Unit and the Department. The Department expects school collaboration to improve behaviour and persistent truancy to develop very much in the context of Education Improvement Partnerships. Most areas are considered to have experience of collaborative working ranging from head teacher pupil placement panels to joint working through the Behaviour Improvement Programme (BIP), Excellence in Cities (EiC) targeted in particular areas or formal federations. The letter states:

---

[26] With equivalent amendments to Sch.5 the Police Reform Act 2002 Act as regards designated accredited persons.

"By working in collaboration, schools can share expertise and make better use of the support available from the National Strategies behaviour and attendance strand, the National Programme for Specialist Leaders of Behaviour and Attendance, the National Behaviour and Attendance Exchange, and a range of advice and guidance available from the Department. Groups of schools may join together to form a partnership that will have a specific focus on improving outcomes in behaviour, and managing persistent truants. In many areas schools will be able to build on existing collaborative arrangements perhaps by expanding a group's remit . . . The partnership might be a new Education Improvement Partnership or the development of an existing partnership such as EiC or school federations. While the focus is on secondary schools, partnerships are encouraged to include primary schools where this is appropriate."

Curfew Areas for Pupils—"Truancy Sweeps"
Under s.16 of the Crime and Disorder Act 1998, a local authority[27] may designate premises in a police area as premises to which children and young persons of compulsory school age may be removed under this section. They must also notify the chief officer of police for that area of the designation. If so, then, under s.16(2) of the 1998 Act, a police officer of or above the rank of superintendent may direct that certain powers conferred on a constable shall be exercisable as respects any area falling within the police area and specified in the direction. These powers are defined in subs.(3): if a constable has reasonable cause to believe that a child or young person, found by him in a public place[28] in a specified area during a specified period, is of compulsory school age and is absent from a school without lawful authority, the constable may remove the child or young person to designated premises, or to the school from which he is so absent. Lawful authority is defined by subs.(4) as meaning the same thing as under s.444 of the Education Act 1996.

Guidance was published in 2002 by the Home Office as to the use of s.16.[29] In order to confirm whether use of the new police power is appropriate in a given area, the LEA will need to assess the nature and extent of unauthorised absence in the locality in consultation with the police and the local YOT. Agreement as to its use must be unanimous. Particular regard should be paid to areas where schools have particularly high levels of unauthorised absence, including significant levels of post-registration truancy (children staying long enough for main registers, but avoiding lessons thereafter); and areas where schools are experiencing difficulty with high levels of parentally-condoned unjustified absence. The police may wish to have regard to local "hot spots" for juvenile crime, by children of school age in school hours, and the crime and disorder audits required under s.6 of the Crime and Disorder Act will help identify such areas. The police may also wish to be alert to areas where truants are thought to be at particular risk of becoming victims of crime or at risk of other serious harm, for example from the attentions of paedophiles, pimps or drug pushers. Once it has been decided that local circumstances warrant application of the new police power, the LEA should first hold preliminary discussions with schools in the area concerned (including independent schools) to

3-197

3-198

---

[27] That is, (a) in relation to England, a county council, a district council whose district does not form part of an area that has a county council, a London borough council or the Common Council of the City of London; (b) in relation to Wales, a county council or a county borough council: Crime and Disorder Act 1998, s.16(5).
[28] "Public place" has the same meaning as in Pt II of the Public Order Act 1986.
[29] Lengthy, comprehensive and detailed compared with that under the similar dispersal directions power in the Anti-Social Behaviour Act 2003; much of what appears in this guidance would apply to the use of the dispersal power.

agree a plan of action. LEA representatives should then meet the police to discuss the objectives and parameters of the truancy initiative and to agree operational guidelines for all concerned. During this process particular attention should be paid to ensuring that police officers are aware of categories of children who may have a justifiable cause to be out and about during school hours, especially home-educated children and excluded pupils; that clear geographical boundaries are set for the exercise; these should be kept in confidence by the partners involved; information is shared about places where truants are known to gather (e.g. shopping precincts); that the police are aware of other relevant information such as local school hours, school holidays, training days, and whether the area is frequented by children from other areas with different school holidays (e.g. is it a popular holiday destination); the police should have the names and known movement patterns of children known to be persistent non-attenders and, where appropriate, their names; the LEA provides a single reference point to cover cases where the police officers need to check the arrangements. This will need to be kept up-to-date with information not to hand at the planning meetings, for example, details of any child recently excluded from school. Consideration should be given as to how to deal with children in the company of adults. Parentally-condoned unjustified absence is said to be a significant problem for some schools and many of these children may have no good reason to be out of school; there is also a potential child protection issue. The police officer and accompanying education representative should aim therefore to establish whether the child is a registered pupil and the reason for absence. Parents should be reminded that they are legally responsible for regular school attendance. There should also be guidelines established for approaching young people. The guidance recommends that police constables operating the new power do so in uniform and, where practicable, are accompanied by an education representative such as an EWO, who will be able to check the school status of the young person concerned. Where appropriate, the British Transport Police are brought into the discussions, in respect of problems involving truants congregating on the rail network.

3-199   Before the new power is invoked, the guidance provides, the LEA will have to designate premises to which young people of compulsory school age may be taken and formally notify the chief constable in writing. These may be schools and, in most areas, it will be appropriate to return the young people direct to local schools (experience of truancy watch schemes suggests that, once intercepted, children are generally honest in identifying the school they should be attending). However, the LEA may also designate other premises which they will be responsible for staffing. These could include offices available to the education welfare service or offices within a shopping precinct maintained by the LEA for the duration of a truancy operation. The designated premises will not include police stations. Truants should not be taken to police stations in exercise of the truancy powers. In this connection, it should be borne in mind children who truant from school are not committing a crime; their parents are legally responsible for their non-attendance.

3-200   The power should only be exercisable with the authority of a police officer of superintendent rank or above. It will also be for that officer to authorise the area over which the power will be exercised and its duration. In coming to that judgment he or she will take account of the result of discussions with schools and the LEA. The superintendent should also make clear to his or her officers the locations to which truants should be taken, in line with arrangements made with the LEA. The authorisation should be recorded in writing and the record kept for a year. The power will be exercised on the basis that the constable has reasonable cause to believe that a child is a registered pupil absent from school without lawful authority. Police officers are considered to be experienced in reaching judgments of this nature in the light of the circumstances. The power is to be used in support of a multi-agency approach to the problem, which would include sharing of information which will help officers make such judgments. The police will also be assisted in this respect if they are accompanied by an education representative, such as an EWO. In exercising discretion the constable will take account of the arrangements agreed between the police, schools and the LEA, together with the individual circumstances of the case. It is said that from experience of existing truancy watch schemes children generally do co-operate when approached by the police about their absence from school. However, there may be occasional cases in which suspected truants refuse to comply. In such cases, if the constable has reasonable grounds for believing that the child or young person is absent from school without authority, the power under s.16 will enable the officer to use such reasonable force as is necessary in the circumstances. What reasonable force might be will depend on the circumstances. It must be proportionate to the nature of the power and the behaviour of the child or young person concerned. If the child or young person resists with violence, that in itself might be an offence of assault and other powers would come into play.

3-201 Once a child has been returned, it is important that there should be adequate reception arrangements. In the case of a school, this means ensuring that pastoral or other staff are ready to receive back into school registered pupils found outside school premises and return them to class or make other suitable arrangements for them. The school will also need to notify parents that their child has been picked up and returned to school. If children are being returned to other premises, the LEA needs to ensure that arrangements exist for notifying schools that their pupils are at a particular location and of the arrangements for their return. Whether truants are returned to a school or other location, formal recording procedures should be instituted. The act of returning a child to school may be helpful in identifying and resolving factors contributing to non-attendance, e.g. bullying. It is a common occurrence for a pupil living in one area to attend school in an adjacent area and truancy operations may encounter children truanting across LEA boundaries. The constable will have the discretion to take a truant back to school, or to the designated place for the LEA area in which the child is picked up, but there is no legal obligation on the police to take the child back to its own school if that school is out of the area. The LEA should therefore liaise with neighbouring LEAs about follow-up arrangements for children found out of area and ensure that an understanding is arrived at before an initiative is underway. Where a child's home area makes it impracticable for him or her to be collected by a representative of the home LEA, the LEA running the initiative should ensure that the child's details are passed to the home LEA's education welfare service or equivalent.

3-202 The Government's determination to reduce unauthorised absence and tackle truancy saw the start of national co-ordinated truancy sweeps in May 2002. Data from the previous sweeps show that, of 103,834 pupils stopped, 40 per cent of them were truanting and 42 per cent of those truants were with an adult.[30] Since then the Department has maintained the momentum of truancy sweeps by conducting national exercises twice a year. They are also regularly carried out by LEAs. According to a report by Action Rights for Children,[31] there is a question mark over their cost/effectiveness: over 16,000 hours of police time are spent annually on truancy sweeps, one truant is found for every 82 minutes of police time, one child is stopped for every 30 minutes of police time, and 63 per cent of children stopped are not truanting.

[30] www.dfes.gov.uk/schoolattendance/truancysweeps/index.cfm
[31] www.arch-ed.org/truancy/tsr05.htm

CHAPTER FOUR
Environmental Controls and Anti-social Behaviour and Disorder

Introduction

4-001 The use of environmental controls to restrain bad behaviour is not a new phenomenon. Historically, they have been used to deal with "environmental nuisances", for example, by better paving and street lighting, which were seen as "a recipe for physical and moral improvement."[1] Furthermore, the Town Police Clauses Act 1847 not only made provision for controlling such nuisances, but also extended to making inn keepers and others liable for disorderly events. The idea that improving the surrounding environment goes hand in hand with controlling general bad behaviour is, therefore, not without historical foundation on which modern governments have built upon and extended.[2]

4-002 The current government's position as to the relationship between anti-social behaviour and the environment is summarised in the Anti-social Behaviour White Paper:

> "The effects of anti-social behaviour are most visible when the results of that behaviour ruin public places such as shopping precincts, park, playgrounds, town centres or railway stations. It can also degrade local areas by allowing homes and streets to be full of litter and rubbish . . . Places that are neglected encourage more graffiti, littering and vandalism. This in turn undermines public confidence, leads people to avoid them and gives way to crime."[3]

The main theme of two government consultation papers, *Living Places—Cleaner, Safer, Greener* and *Living Places—Powers, Rights and Responsibilities*,[4] is that the current set of powers and duties was not working effectively for various reasons, including ". . . confusion and misunderstanding within and between service providers, an unawareness of the responsibilities associated with the right to have a clean and safe environment and inadequate and unmanageable powers for dealing with irresponsible and anti-social behaviour."[5] The government's solution consists of specific reforms to certain areas and, in general, a rationalisation of the current allocation of statutory responsibilities.

---

[1] D. Taylor *Policing the Victorian Town The Development of the Police in Middlesborough c.1840–1914*. Palgrove Macmillan: (Basingstoke, 2002).
[2] For example, the Environmental Protection Act 1990, the Noise Act 1996, the Environmental Protection Act 1996.
[3] White Paper (2003) p.38.
[4] Department of the Environment, Food and Rural Affairs.
[5] *Living Places – Powers, Rights and Responsibilities*, October 2002.

Town Planning Controls

Planning permission is ordinarily required with regard to any development of
land. A person who intends to carry operations on land or to change the use
of land must first obtain the permission of the local planning authority.[6]
Otherwise, an unauthorised development may well be subject to enforcement
action, such as an enforcement notice, and criminal penalties. A developer can
set down an appeal of the notice as though he were appealing the refusal of
permission and, in the meanwhile, the notice takes effect on the date specified
within it and, if an appeal is brought, it will have no effect until the final determination of the appeal. At the end of the period for the land to be restored by
the notice, if any step required by the enforcement notice has not been carried
out and/or if any activity required to be ceased is still being carried on, the
person who is then the owner of the land is guilty of an offence.[7] A stop notice
may also be served so that any activity which the local authority require to
cease is prohibited.[8] A stop notice may not be served where the enforcement
notice has taken effect. It is an offence for a person to contravene a stop notice,
with a maximum penalty of a fine of £20,000 upon summary conviction or an
unlimited fine upon a conviction on indictment. There is no appeal against a
stop notice.[9]

4-003

Under ss.215 to 219 of the Town and Country Planning Act 1990, local planning authorities may serve a notice requiring an owner or occupier of land
within 28 days to take specified steps to remedy the condition of land that
adversely affects the amenity of the neighbourhood. It is an offence to fail to
comply with the notice, attracting a fine, on summary conviction up to level 3
of the standard scale. The person served with such a notice may appeal at any
time to the magistrates' court (and subsequently on appeal for a re-hearing in
the Crown Court) during the notice period if he believes that the condition of
the land is not adverse to the amenity of the area, the steps required are excessive, or the notice period is unreasonable. The authority may also recover costs.

4-004

Authorities may also acquire compulsorily land for planning purposes under
s.226 of the 1990 Act and may also acquire listed buildings in need of repair
under ss.47 to 50 of the Planning (Listed Buildings and Conservation Areas)
Act 1990. They have powers under s.89 of the National Parks and Access to
the Countryside Act 1949 to deal with derelict, neglected and unsightly land.

4-005

Caravans and Unauthorised Encampments

We have already discussed police directions regarding trespassers and unlawful encampment directions at paras 2-109 to 2-114 and 2-117 to 2-118. In this
Chapter, we examine other powers which are available to local authorities as
regards travellers and Gypsies.

4-006

Provision of sites for Gypsies

Section 24 of the Caravan Sites and Control of Development Act 1960, as
amended by s.80 of the Criminal Justice and Public Order Act 1994, defines
Gypsies as ". . . persons of nomadic habit of life, whatever their race or origin,
but does not include members of an organised group of travelling showmen,
or of persons engaged in travelling circuses, travelling together as such."[10]

4-007

[6] Town and Country Planning Act 1990, s.192.
[7] *ibid.*, s.179(2).
[8] *ibid.*, s.183.
[9] *ibid.*, s.187.
[10] See also *R. v South Hams Ex p. Gibb* [1995] Q.B. 158.

Following the removal of the duty of local authorities to provide land for Gypsy encampments, there has been a natural decline in the amount of land set aside for such use. It is not unexpected that there has been a rise in unauthorised encampments and often in areas where there will be problems of the kind successive governments consider to fall into the category of anti-social behaviour,[11] lately ameliorated to a limited extent by the impact of the Human Rights Act 1998. It is necessary, first, to consider the powers available to local authorities and the police and, secondly, how they are to decide whether to take action. The powers enjoyed by local authorities under s.77 of the 1994 Act to direct that "unauthorised campers" leave the land is discussed at paras 2-109 to 2-114. However, in this section, we consider the particular problems for the government and local authorities raised by Gypsies and travellers and unauthorised camping.

4-008   Local authorities were under a duty to provide sites for Gypsies and control of unauthorised encampments under Pt II of the Caravan Sites Act 1968. This statutory duty was repealed by the Criminal Justice and Public Order Act 1994[12] and now local authorities have a mere power to provide sites for caravans,[13] but are not obliged to do so. The Criminal Justice and Public Order Act 1994 also gave local authorities an additional power to provide ". . . in or in connection with sites for accommodation of Gypsies, working space and facilities for carrying on of such activities as are normally carried on by them".[14] Local authorities are advised in the DoE Circular No. 18/94, Gypsy Sites Policy and Unauthorised Camping, to consider whether to provide further Gypsy sites in their area.[15]

4-009   Under s.8 of the Housing Act 1985, every local housing authority shall consider housing conditions in their district and the needs of the district with respect to the provision of further housing accommodation. By virtue of s.225 of the Housing Act 2004, that must include carrying out an assessment of the accommodation needs[16] of Gypsies and travellers[17] residing in or resorting to their district. Furthermore, where a local housing authority is required, under s.87 of the Local Government Act 2003, to prepare a strategy in respect of the meeting of such accommodation needs, they must take that strategy into account in exercising their functions.[18] The local housing authority must have regard to guidance in the carrying out of assessments and in the preparation of any strategies.[19] The ODPM issued a Circular, "Planning for Gypsy and traveller caravan sites", on February 2, 2006,[20] with the aim of helping to "promote good community relations at the local level, and avoid the conflict and controversy associated with unauthorised developments and

[11] *Managing Unauthorised Camping: A Good Practice Guide.*
[12] Section 80 of the Criminal Justice and Public Order Act 1994 repealed Pt II of the Caravan Sites Act 1968 with effect from November 3, 1994.
[13] Caravan Sites and Control of Development Act 1960, s.24.
[14] Criminal Justice and Public Order Act 1994, s.80(2).
[15] Paras 19–22 of DoE Circular No. 18/94 *Gypsy Sites Policy and Unauthorised Camping.*
[16] "Accommodation needs" includes needs with respect to the provision of sites on which caravans can be stationed: Housing Act 2004, s.225(5)(b).
[17] "Gypsies and travellers" has the meaning given by regulations made by the Secretary of State. The ODPM sought consultation on the definition for the purposes of the 2004 Act: *Definition of the term "gypsies and travellers" for the purposes of the Housing Act 2004*, ODPM, February 2006. The proposed definition is: "Persons of nomadic habit of life whatever their race or origin, including such persons who on grounds only of their own or their family's or dependant's educational or health needs or old age have ceased to travel temporarily or permanently, and all other person with a cultural tradition of nomadism and/or caravan dwelling."
[18] Housing Act 2004, s.225(2).
[19] Housing Act 2004, s.225(4) and s.226.
[20] ODPM Circular 01/ 2006.

encampments." The circular applies to the development of public sites by local authorities or registered social landlords, regardless of whether the site is for residential or transit use.[21] In the context of housing, it seeks to emphasise "the importance of assessing needs . . . and for local authorities to develop strategies to ensure that needs are dealt with fairly and effectively" and "to help to avoid Gypsies and travellers becoming homeless through eviction from unauthorised sites without an alternative to move to."

Local planning authorities need to identify suitable land for Gypsy and traveller sites through the planning system to deal with the alleged growing shortage of Gypsy sites and prevent unauthorised sites.[22] The aforementioned guidance provides guidance on the planning aspects of finding sites for Gypsies and travellers and to accommodate the increase in need for new sites.

4-010

Anti-social behaviour on unauthorised campsites

Amendments to the Department of the Environment Circular No. 1894, issued on July 26, 2000, are insistent that anti-social or criminal activity on unauthorised campsites should not be tolerated under any circumstances. Chapter five of the *Good Practice Guidance on Managing Unauthorised Camping* focuses on the problems with anti-social behaviour caused by unauthorised encampments, providing advice as to when local authorities and the police should take action and how to manage unauthorised encampments that are not being moved on so as to minimise any possibility of nuisance. The intention is that Gypsies and travellers are not to be treated any differently or more favourably in respect of their behaviour as regards anti-social behaviour than those expected of the settled community.[23] For instance, the guidance makes clear that all breaches of the law should be investigated by the police and dealt with as they would be in relation to any other person.[24] In determining whether to enforce the law, the major consideration for local authorities and the police is the degree to which any encampment is interfering with the lawful rights of others, be they local residents, farmers or businesses.[25] Prompt action is required as regards unauthorised encampments where there are problems with crime and disorder associated with the site, damage, mess and littering, and camping on unsuitable sites (e.g. school playing fields, private car parks, etc.) which cause highway hazards or deny amenities to local residents. It is suggested that local authorities should clarify their criteria as to when they will decide whether to move on unauthorised encampments, and the circumstances in which Gypsies and travellers will be permitted to stay, in policy statements which will be agreed with the police.[26] However, local authorities must consider the particular welfare issues involved in moving travellers and Gypsies away from unauthorised sites; authorities should also liaise with various statutory agencies if they decide to proceed with eviction to ensure that those agencies are not prevented from fulfilling their obligations towards those persons. The guidance suggests that the following will need to be addressed where specific welfare needs are not in issue: the nature, suitability or obtrusiveness of the encampment; the size of the group, their behaviour and the level of nuisance; and the number, validity and seriousness of complaints.[27] In making a decision on whether to evict, local authorities should apply the criteria consistently and record it carefully.

4-011

[21] ODPM Circular 01/2006, para.11.
[22] Planning Circular 01/2006 "Planning for gypsy and traveller caravan sites".
[23] *Managing Unauthorised Camping: A Good Practice Guide.*
[24] *ibid.*, para.5.3.
[25] *ibid.*, para.5.3.
[26] *ibid.*, para.5.6.
[27] *ibid.*, para.5.8.

4-012   In *Secretary of State for the Environment v Widowfield*,[28] Brooke J. upheld the decision to evict travellers from a depot which was to be sold. The court found that the decision maker had carried out a proper and careful balancing exercise and considered all the relevant issues, including the impact of the decision to evict on the occupiers and complaints regarding anti-social behaviour from local residents. The need for full explanations for their decision was emphasised by Brooke J. again, in *R. v Horsham DC Ex p. Wenman*,[29] where he stated that:

> ". . . it would be wise for all local authorities to adopt the growing practice of setting out in clear terms the criteria they will use when deciding to move Gypsies off land in their local authority area and to make it clear on the face of any resolution to take enforcement or possession action that they have had those criteria well in mind and the way in which they have applied them on the facts before them."

4-013   The guidance does not envisage that, in every case where nuisance is complained of, the local authority should move on the travellers and Gypsies. It is open for local authorities to assess whether the nuisance is serious enough to justify eviction. The amount of time the local authority is prepared to allow them to remain will depend on a number of factors, including the site itself, the educational needs of the children, and whether there have been any recent births.[30] However, local authorities are advised to monitor the situation, in particular, in relation to behaviour, environmental damage and increasing numbers of people on the site, and therefore making regular visits to the site.[31] They should also consider the provision of temporary services[32] and keep others informed, such as complainants, councillors, health and welfare agencies.[33]

Possession proceedings

4-014   According to the Good Practice Guide, the most significant problems faced by site managers on licensed sites were fly-tipping, rubbish, vandalism and damage to the site and amenities, disputes between individuals and families and "squatters".[34] Landowners may take possession proceedings against Gypsies who are guilty of anti-social behaviour. Gypsies are not protected under the Protection from Eviction Act 1977, or under any of the Housing or Rent Acts; instead, they have a particular form of statutory protection under Pt I of the Caravan Sites Act 1968. The Housing Act 2004, however, does extend the protection afforded to occupiers of such sites.

Protected sites

4-015   Part I of the 1968 Act applies in relation to any licence or contract under which a person is entitled to station a caravan on a protected site and occupy it as his residence ("residential contract"). It also applies to a person who occupies as his residence a caravan stationed on any such site and which belongs to the site owner.[35]

---

[28] Unreported, September 9, 1993.
[29] [1995] 1 W.L.R. 680 at 704.
[30] Managing Unauthorised Camping: A Good Practice Guide, para.5.10.
[31] *ibid.*, para.5.14.
[32] *ibid.*, para.5.17.
[33] *ibid.*, para.5.16.
[34] See para.2-072.
[35] Caravan Sites Act 1968, s.1(1).

"Caravan" has the same meaning as in Pt I of the Caravan Sites and Control **4-016**
of Development Act 1960.[36] It is:

". . . any structure designed or adapted for human habitation which is
capable of being moved from one place to another (whether by being towed,
of being transported on a motor vehicle or trailer) and any motor vehicle
so designed or adapted, but does not include—any railway rolling stock
which is for the time being on rails forming part of a railway system, or any
tent . . ."[37]

The Act defines "protected sites" as being "any land in respect of which a **4-017**
site licence is required under Pt I of the Caravan Sites and Control of
Development Act 1960 or would be so required if para.11 of Sch.1 to that Act
(exemption of land occupied by local authorities) were omitted".[38] Since
amendment by the Housing Act 2004, authorised county council sites are now
included within the definition of protected site, thus bringing their occupiers
into line with security of tenure provided on privately owned sites.[39] The definition specifically excludes land in respect of which the relevant planning permission or site licence is expressed to be granted for holiday use only or where
it is subject to conditions that there are times of the year when no caravan may
be stationed on the land for human habitation.[40]

Enforcement action under the Town and Country Planning Act 1990
If the site does not require planning permission, enforcement action can be **4-018**
taken by the local authority to require the removal of the caravans. The occupier will still be protected from eviction, although s.178 of the Town and
Country Planning Act 1990 enables a local authority to enter land for the purposes of ensuring compliance with an enforcement notice or seek an injunction under s.187B of the same Act.
     Where there is no planning permission and site licence, the occupier of the **4-019**
caravan does not have the benefit of protection under the 1968 Act.[41] There are
said to be public policy reasons for the Act not providing such protection to
such occupiers; Parliament has deliberately chosen to place the interests of
the community ahead of those of the individual occupier.[42] Nor does the Act
provide protection where the planning permission and site licence has lapsed.[43]

Termination of residential contract
In order to determine the residential contract,[44] the owner of a protected site[45] **4-020**
must give notice of not less than four weeks before the date on which it is to take
effect.[46] A "residential contract" is any licence or contract under which a person

---

[36] As amended by s.13 of the Caravan Sites Act 1968 to include twin unit caravans.
[37] Caravan Sites and Control of Development Act 1960.
[38] Caravan Sites Act 1968, s.1(2). The provisions relating to licensing by local authorities are set
out in ss.3–12 of Pt I of the Caravan Sites and Control of Development Act 1960. Those provisions prohibit the occupier of any land from causing or permitting any part of that land to
be used as a caravan site unless he is the holder of a site licence then in force.
[39] *ibid.*, s.1(2).
[40] 1968, s.1(2).
[41] *Balthasar v Mullane* [1985] 2 E.G.L.R. 260; and *Adams v Watkins* [1990] 2 E.G.L.R. 185.
[42] *ibid.*
[43] *Adams v Watkins, ibid.*
[44] Caravan Sites Act 1968, s.1(1).
[45] For the purposes of the Caravan Sites Act 1968, this means the person who is or would apart
from any residential contract be entitled to possession of the land: s.1(3).
[46] Caravan Sites Act 1968, s.2. This equally applies to the case where the occupier of the caravan
wishes to end the agreement.

is entitled to station a caravan on a protected site and occupy it as his residence or to occupy as his residence stationed on any such site.[47] It is also necessary to take court proceedings in order to "enforce any right to exclude the occupier[48] from the protected site or from any such caravan or to remove or exclude any such caravan from the site",[49] otherwise he will be guilty of a criminal offence.[50]

Possession proceedings

4-021 Where the owner establishes his right to exclude the occupier from the protected site, that is, the appropriate notice has been given, the court is bound to order possession. In making a possession order, the court has the power to postpone or suspend execution of the order for a period not exceeding 12 months from the date of the order as the court thinks reasonable.[51] Furthermore, where the court suspends enforcement of the order, it may impose such terms and conditions, including conditions as to the payment of rent or other periodical payments or of arrears of such rent or payments, as the court thinks reasonable.[52] On the application of either party, the court may from time to time, extend, reduce or terminate the period of suspension, or vary any terms or conditions imposed, so long as it does not extend the period of suspension for more than 12 months at a time.[53]

4-022 In considering whether or how to exercise these powers, the court must have regard to all the circumstances, and in particular:

"(a) whether the occupier of the caravan has failed, whether before or after the expiration or determination of the relevant residential contract, to observe any terms or conditions of that contract, any conditions of the site licence, or any reasonable rules made by the owner for the management and conduct of the site or the maintenance of the caravans thereon;

(b) whether the occupier has unreasonably refused an offer by the owner to renew the residential contract or make another such contract for a reasonable period and on reasonable terms;

(c) whether the occupier has failed to make reasonable efforts to obtain elsewhere other suitable accommodation for his caravan (or, as the case may be, another suitable caravan and accommodation for it)."[54]

4-023 The court can refuse to suspend the order where the occupier has breached the terms of the residential contract, particularly as regards terms concerning nuisance and annoyance. Evidence of anti-social behaviour is also relevant to the issue of costs. The general rule is that, if the order is suspended, the court may make no order as to costs. If it appears to the court, however, having regard to the conduct of the owner or the occupier, that there are special reasons for making such an order, it may do so.[55]

4-024 There are certain situations where the court has no power to suspend the enforcement of the order: where no site licence under Pt I of the Caravan Sites

[47] Caravan Sites Act 1968, s.1(1).
[48] Under s.3 of the Caravan Sites Act 1968, occupier includes the person who is an occupier under the residential contract which has expired or been determined and, in the case of the death of the occupier (whether during the subsistence or after the expiration or determination of the contract), to any person then residing with the occupier being the widow or widower of the occupier; or in default of a widow or widower so residing, any member of the occupier's family.
[49] Caravan Sites Act 1968, s.3(1).
[50] *ibid.*, s.3.
[51] *ibid.*, s.4(1).
[52] *ibid.*, s.4(2).
[53] *ibid.*, s.4(3).
[54] *ibid.*, s.4(4).
[55] *ibid.*, s.4(5).

Act 1968 is in force in respect of the site; where paragraph 11 or 11A of Sch.1 to the Caravan Sites and Control of Development Act 1960 does not apply; and where the site licence in respect of the site is expressed to expire at the end of a specified period, beyond the date set for expiration of the licence.[56]

Offences

Section 3 of the 1968 Act creates a number of offences with the purpose of protecting occupiers[57] of authorised sites from eviction and harassment. A person shall be guilty of an offence: **4-025**

(1) if, during the subsistence of a residential contract, he unlawfully deprives the occupier of his occupation on the protected site of any caravan which the occupier is entitled by the contract to station and occupy, or to occupy, as his residence;

(2) if, after the expiration or determination of a residential contract, he enforces, otherwise than by proceedings in the court, any right to exclude the occupier from the protected site or from any such caravan, or to remove or exclude any such caravan from the site;

(3) if, whether during the subsistence or after the expiration or determination of a residential contract, with intent to cause the occupier—

(a) to abandon the occupation of the caravan or remove it from the site, or

(b) to refrain from exercising any right or pursuing any remedy in respect thereof, he does acts likely to interfere with the peace or comfort of the occupier or persons residing with him, or persistently withdraws or withholds services or facilities reasonably required for the occupation of the caravan as a residence on the site.[58]

The Housing Act 2004 creates a new offence. If, whether during the subsistence or after the expiration or determination of a residential contract, the owner of a protected site or his agent[59]:   **4-026**

(1) does acts likely to interfere with the peace or comfort of the occupier or persons residing with him; or

(2) he persistently withdraws or withholds services or facilities reasonably required for the occupation of the caravan as a residence on the site,

and (in either case) he knows, or has reasonable cause to believe, that that conduct is likely to cause the occupier to abandon the occupation of the caravan or remove it from the site, or to refrain from exercising any right or pursuing any remedy in respect thereof,

he is guilty of an offence.[60]

---

[56] Caravan Sites Act 1968, s.4(6).
[57] References to the occupier include references to the person who was the occupier under a residential contract which has expired or been determined and, in the case of the death of the occupier (whether during the subsistence or after the expiration or determination of the contract), to any person then residing with the occupier being: the widow or widower of the occupier; or, in default of a widow or widower so residing, any member of the occupier's family: Caravan Sites Act 1968, s.3(2).
[58] Caravan Sites Act 1968, s.3(1).
[59] References to the owner of a protected site include references to a person with an estate or interest in the site which is superior to that of the owner: Caravan Sites Act 1968, s.3(1B).
[60] Caravan Sites Act 1968, s.3(1A).

4-027   A person guilty of an offence under s.3 is, without prejudice to any liability or remedy to which he may be subject in civil proceedings, liable on summary conviction, to a fine not exceeding the statutory maximum or to imprisonment for a term not exceeding 12 months, or both; on conviction on indictment, to a fine or to imprisonment for a term not exceeding two years, or to both.[61]

4-028   In proceedings for an offence under subs.(1), it is a defence to prove that the accused believed, and had reasonable cause to believe, that the occupier of the caravan had ceased to reside on the site. It is a defence to proceedings for an offence under subs.(1A) to prove that the accused had reasonable grounds for doing the acts or withdrawing or withholding the services or facilities in question.[62]

Injunctions to enforce planning control

4-029   Under s.187B of the Town and Country Planning Act 1990, a local planning authority, if they consider it necessary or expedient for any actual or apprehended breach of planning control to be restrained by injunction, may apply to the court, whether or not they have exercised, or are proposing to exercise, any other powers under Pt VII of the 1990 Act. Local authorities previously relied on s.222 of the Local Government Act 1972. In *Stoke on Trent CC v B & Q*,[63] the court found that the offender had deliberately and flagrantly flouted planning control and held that it was not necessary for the authority to have exhausted criminal penalties first where a prosecution would have been slow or futile and emphasised that no particular rules applied, on a case by case basis.[64] In *City of London Corp v Bovis Construction*,[65] it was held that there must be more than just an infringement of the criminal law and what mattered was not so much a flagrant breach of the law, but that breaches would continue but for the injunction. On the other hand, in *Runnymede BC v Smith*,[66] the court found that there were no deliberate or flagrant breaches of the law, but granted the injunction because the stop notices were ineffective. In *Waverley BC v Hilden*,[67] the application for the injunction was refused even though there was a clear breach of planning control as regards a caravan site; the court accepted that cause had been failure of the local authority to provide sufficient space under the Caravans Sites and Control of Development Act 1960. Following the introduction of s.187B into the 1990 Act in 1992, in *Hambleton DC v Bird*,[68] the court found not only a continuing failure to comply with an enforcement notice but also a possibility of planning permission in the future. Even so, it is not for courts to usurp planning powers of a local authority or to review whether or not it is expedient. The test under the new section was whether or not injunction would be effective to restrain a breach of the law. In *R. v Basildon DC Ex p. Clarke*,[69] the respondent sought to adjourn proceedings pending judicial review of a decision to set down proceedings for the injunction. Carnworth J. declined to do so; if there was a procedural error, or if the authority acted unreasonably, then a county court judge would dismiss the application.

4-030   In *South Buckinghamshire DC v Porter*,[70] the local authorities appealed

---

[61] Caravan Sites Act 1968, s.3(3).
[62] *ibid.*, s.3(4) and (4A).
[63] [1984] A.C. 754.
[64] See *Runnymede BC v Ball* [1986] 1 W.L.R. 353; see also *City of London Corp v Bovis Construction Ltd* [1989] J.P.L. 263.
[65] [1989] J.P.L. 263.
[66] [1986] J.P.L. 592.
[67] [1988] 1 All E.R. 807.
[68] [1995] 3 P.L.R. 8.
[69] [1995] J.P.L. 866.
[70] [2003] 3 All E.R 1.

against a decision to lift injunctions which had been granted pursuant to s.187B of the 1990 Act. The respondents in the three cases were Gypsies who were living on land in breach of planning control. In each case, the local authority applied for and obtained an injunction under s.187B to restrain the breach. The local authorities maintained that if, on an application under s.187B, a planning breach was proven, an injunction should be granted, unless it could be shown that the decision to enforce planning control was invalid on *Wednesbury* grounds. Accordingly, it was argued that the court below erred in trespassing upon issues of planning judgment by taking into account and weighing the hardship a defendant would suffer if he was forced to move from the site against pure planning considerations. The House of Lords dismissed the appeals. The jurisdiction to grant an injunction under s.187B was an original, and not a supervisory, jurisdiction. A defendant seeking to resist the grant of an injunction was not restricted to reliance on those grounds which would found an application for judicial review. The court had a discretion under s.187B which had to be exercised judicially. The courts would be strongly disposed to grant an injunction where it appeared that a breach, or apprehended breach, would continue or occur unless, and until, effectively restrained by law and that nothing short of an injunction would provide effective restraint. Issues of planning policy and judgment were matters for the local planning authorities and the Secretary of State, but the court was not precluded from entertaining issues not related to planning policy or judgment. Nor need the court refuse to consider the possibility that a pending or prospective application for planning permission might succeed. The planning authorities were entitled to consider the personal circumstances of the Gypsies. If it appeared that the local planning authority had fully considered the issues of hardship and nonetheless resolved that it was necessary, or expedient, to seek an injunction, that would ordinarily weigh heavily in favour of granting relief, since the court must accord respect to the balance which the planning authority had struck between public and private interests. Further, it was for the court to decide whether the remedy sought was just and proportionate in all the circumstances.

Human Rights

In *Harrow LBC v Qazi*[71] the House of Lords held that, while a person can occupy premises as a home for the purposes of Art.8 of the European Convention on Human Rights, even though he has no right in domestic law to do so or any such right has ended, Art.8 could not be used as a defence to resist contractual and proprietary rights which entitled the landlord to possession under domestic law. There is accordingly, no need for the court to consider an occupier's personal circumstances (or the authority's reasons for seeking possession) under Art.8(2).   **4-031**

In *Connors v United Kingdom*,[72] the European Court of Human Rights held that a Gypsy's summary eviction following termination of his licence was an unjustified interference with his rights under Art.8. The applicant, Mr Connors, was granted a licence of a plot of land. His daughter was granted a licence of an adjoining plot and resided there with her boyfriend. Following complaints of anti- social behaviour and having been given a warning about the behaviour, the local authority terminated the licences and began possession proceedings against Mr Connors. The eviction was challenged by way of judicial review; permission was refused and the county court made a possession order. A warrant for possession was obtained by the   **4-032**

---

[71] [2003] UKHL 43; 2003 H.L.R. 75.
[72] 16 B.H.R.C. 639; [2004] H.L.R. 52.

authority and duly executed. The applicant complained to the European Court claiming that his eviction was unnecessary and disproportionate, particularly as he was not given an opportunity to challenge the allegations made against him in court.

4-033   Allowing the application, the European Court held that Art.8 imposes an obligation to facilitate the Gypsy way of life because the vulnerable position of Gypsies as a minority group means that some special consideration should be given to their needs and their different lifestyle. The applicant's rights had not been attended by the necessary procedural safeguards and there was insufficient evidence to establish that it was necessary to evict the applicant using the summary possession procedure. The fact that anti-social behaviour occurs cannot, of itself, justify a summary power of eviction, because similar problems occur on housing estates where a range of powers are available and the authority may only proceed to evict subject to independent court review of the justification for the measure; judicial review does not assist a Gypsy where a licence is terminated.

4-034   In *Kay v Lambeth LBC, Price v Leeds CC*[73] upheld claims for possession by Lambeth LBC against a group of former short-life occupiers and by Leeds CC against a Gypsy family who had been trespassing on recreational land owned by the authority. Both cases relied on Art.8 of the Convention.

4-035   The appellants in *Price* were Gypsies who moved caravans onto a recreation ground owned by the authority. The land had previously been occupied, without permission, by travellers who had moved on but were replaced with others, including, eventually, the appellants. The authority issued possession proceedings two days after they had moved on to the land.

4-036   In the Court of Appeal, following *Connors*, it was held that the eviction of the Gypsies did violate their Art.8 rights and that *Connors* and *Qazi* were (despite the decision of the Court of Appeal in *Kay*) incompatible. Dismissing the appeal, however, the Court of Appeal held that it was obliged to follow *Qazi*. It accordingly granted permission to appeal to the House of Lords. An application by the occupiers in *Kay* for leave to appeal to the House of Lords was listed with *Price*.

4-037   The House of Lords unanimously dismissed the appeals. It was held that, although the enforcement of a right to possession in accordance with domestic law was capable of being incompatible with an individual's rights under Art.8(1), in the vast majority of cases domestic law would automatically supply the justification needed by Art.8(2), so as to avoid a violation of Art.8(1) in possession cases by public authorities. There was no question of a public landowner being required to plead and prove justification under Art.8(2) in every case. It was also accepted by all members of the judicial committee that there were circumstances in which the general rule that domestic law provided an automatic justification under Art.8(2) would not apply. The Committee was, however, divided as to what those circumstances were. The majority (Lords Hope, Scott, Baroness Hale and Lord Brown) held that personal circumstances could never give rise to an Art.8 issue. There could, however, be special and unusual cases, such as *Connors*, where it may be capable of being seriously argued that the law which gives rise to the right to possession is incompatible with Art.8, in which case—unless the county court can read the law compatibly in accordance with s.3 of the Human Rights Act 1998—it will be necessary for the county court to adjourn possession proceedings to enable the occupant to make a claim for a declaration of incompatibility to the High Court. The minority (Lords Bingham, Nicholls and Walker) considered that—in addition to a challenge to the compatibility of the law—an occupier may also, in "highly exceptional circumstances," be

---

[73] [2006] UKHL 10.

able to raise a seriously arguable case that an individual eviction is, on the basis of his own circumstances, in breach of Art.8; in which case it will be for the authority to adduce evidence before the county court as to the purposes of the eviction so as to establish a justification under Art.8(2). In the case of trespassers, the threshold test would "rarely, if ever" be met. Nor was it met in either of the present cases. In relation to the issue of precedent raised in *Price*, the House of Lords held that, save in very exceptional circumstances typified by *D v East Berkshire Community NHS Trust*[74], the lower courts are obliged to apply a decision of a higher domestic court, even if that decision is prima facie inconsistent with a ruling of the European Court of Human Rights.

Pollution Control

Part I of the Environmental Protection Act 1990 makes provision for two main systems of pollution control: integrated pollution control (IPC) and local authority air pollution control (LAAPC). "Pollution" means pollution of the environment due to the release, into the air, water or land[75], from any process, of substances which are capable of causing harm to man or any other living organisms supported by the environment.[76] "Process" means any activities carried on in Great Britain, whether on premises or by means of mobile plant, which are capable of causing pollution of the environment.[77] The Secretary of State may, by regulations, prescribe any process as a process which requires authorisation.[78]   **4-038**

The two regimes share the following features: the prescription of certain processes and substances; authorisations; enforcement powers; and offences. However, IPC is administered by the Environment Agency and LAAPC by local authorities.[79] Further, while both regimes have the aim of preventing or minimising environmental pollution, IPC focuses on pollution "due to the release of substances into any environmental medium"[80] while LAAPC, pollution "due to the release of substances into the air (but not any other environmental medium)."[81]   **4-039**

Authorisations under s.6 of the 1990 Act are to contain such conditions as the enforcing authority considers appropriate.[82] They are all subject to a general condition as to the use of the best available techniques not entailing excessive costs.[83] The Environment Agency and local authorities have the same range of enforcement powers: variation of authorisations, s.10; revocation of authorisations, s.12; enforcement notices, s.13;   **4-040**

---

[74] [2004] Q.B. 558, CA.
[75] Environmental Protection Act 1990, s.1(2): The "environment" consists of all, or any, of the following media, namely, the air, water and land; and the medium of air includes the air within buildings and the air within other natural or man-made structures above or below ground.
[76] Environmental Protection Act 1990, s.1(3). "Harm" means harm to the health of living organisms or other interference with the ecological systems of which they form part and, in the case of man, includes offence caused to any of his senses or harm to his property; and "harmless" has a corresponding meaning (s.1(4)).
[77] Environmental Protection Act 1990, s.1(5).
[78] Environmental Protection Act 1990, ss.2, 6; Environmental Protection (Prescribed Processes and Substances) Regulations 1991 (S.I. 1991/472).
[79] A London borough council, the Common Council of the City of London, the Sub-Treasurer of Inner Temple and the Under-Treasurer of Middle Temple, a district council and the Council of the Isles of Scilly: Environmental Protection Act 1990, s.4(11).
[80] Environmental Protection Act 1990, s.4(2).
[81] *ibid.*, s.4(3).
[82] *ibid.*, s.7(1).
[83] *ibid.*, s.7(4).

prohibition notices, s.14; powers to require information, s.19; power to take proceedings in the High Court to secure compliance with enforcement and prohibition notices, s.24; and powers to take steps to remedy harm and recover the costs of such steps, s.27. In addition, under s.108 of the Environment Act 1995, an enforcing authority, or persons authorised by that authority, may exercise powers of entry, inspection and seizure. Where a person is convicted of carrying on a prescribed process without authorisation, or in breach of conditions of an enforcement notice or prohibition notice, the court, under s.26 of the 1990 Act, may also order the offender to take steps to remedy matters which the courts considers to be within his power to remedy. Further, under s.23 of the 1990 Act, it is an offence for a person to carry on a prescribed process without due authorisation; to fail to comply with any requirement or prohibition imposed by an enforcement or prohibition notice, to fail without reasonable excuse to comply with a notice requiring information; and to fail to comply with an order of the court for the matter to be remedied. The offences are triable either way. Carrying on a prescribed process without authorisation, or without compliance of a condition, appears to be one of strict liability. Nor is there any defence of reasonable excuse.

Waste

Authorities

4-041   Part II of the Environmental Protection Act 1990 deals with the collection, recycling, deposit and disposal of waste. There are three main authorities: the Environment Agency, waste disposal authorities, and waste collection authorities.

4-042   The Environment Agency[84] is responsible for waste management licensing[85]; the supervision of the duty of care as to waste[86]; inspecting land before accepting surrender of licences[87]; supervision of licensed activities[88]; powers to remove unlawfully deposited waste[89]; and maintaining public registers.[90]

4-043   The main functions of waste disposal authorities[91] is to arrange for the disposal of the controlled waste collected in its area by the waste collection authorities and for places to be provided at which persons resident in its area may deposit their household waste and for the disposal of such waste[92]; to give directions to the waste collection authorities within its area as to the persons

---

[84] Environmental Protection Act 1990, s.30(1).
[85] *ibid.*, s.35.
[86] *ibid.*, s.34.
[87] *ibid.*, s.39.
[88] *ibid.*, s.42.
[89] *ibid.*, s.59.
[90] *ibid.*, s.64.
[91] *ibid.*, s.30(2): for the purposes of this Part the following authorities are waste disposal authorities: (a) for any non-metropolitan county in England, the county council; (b) in Greater London, the following (i) for the area of a London waste disposal authority, the authority constituted as the waste disposal authority for that area; (ii) for the City of London, the Common Council; (iii) for any other London borough, the council of the borough; (c) in the metropolitan county of Greater Manchester, the following (i) for the metropolitan district of Wigan, the district council; (ii) for all other areas in the county, the authority constituted as the Greater Manchester Waste Disposal Authority; (d) for the metropolitan county of Merseyside, the authority constituted as the Merseyside Waste Disposal Authority; (e) for any district in any other metropolitan county in England, the council of the district; (f) for any district in Wales, the council of the district; (g) in Scotland, an islands or district council.
[92] Environmental Protection Act 1990, s.51(1).

to whom, and places at which, controlled waste is to be delivered[93]; and waste recycling.[94]

Waste collection authorities[95] arrange for the collection of household waste **4-044** and, on request, arrange for the collection of commercial and industrial waste[96]; emptying privies and cesspools[97]; determine the nature and source of receptacles in which household waste is to be deposited[98]; supply receptacles for commercial and industrial waste[99]; and deliver waste as directed by the waste disposal authority.[1]

Controlled waste

Under s.33(1) of the 1990 Act, a person shall not: **4-045**

"(a) deposit controlled waste[2] or knowingly cause or knowingly permit controlled waste to be deposited in or on any land unless a waste management licence authorising the deposit is in force and the deposit is in accordance with that licence;

  (b)   treat, keep or dispose of controlled waste or knowingly cause of knowingly permit controlled waste to be treated, kept, or disposed of
        (i) in or on any land, or
        (ii) by means of any mobile plant
        except under and in accordance with a waste management licence.

  (c)   treat, keep or dispose of controlled waste in a manner likely to cause pollution or the environment or harm to human health."

Household waste which is treated, kept or disposed of, within the curtilege of **4-046** the dwelling by or with the permission of the occupier is exempt.[3] "Knowingly" means knowledge of the deposit or other act involving the waste, but not to knowledge that such deposit is outside or is not in accordance with the terms of the licence.[4] Under s.33(1)(c), it is irrelevant that the defendant has a licence if it is likely that the act nonetheless causes pollution or harms human health, even if all the conditions have been complied with.[5]

Under s.33(5), where controlled waste is carried in and deposited from a **4-047** motor vehicle, the person who controls or is in control of the vehicle shall, under subs.(1)(a), be treated as knowingly causing the waste to be deposited, whether or not he gave any instructions for this to be done. This subsection is specifically directed at fly-tipping. In the Anti-social Behaviour White Paper, fly-tipping is

---

[93] Environmental Protection Act 1990, s.51(4)(a).
[94] *ibid.*, s.55.
[95] *ibid.*, s.30(3), for the purposes of this Part the following authorities are waste collection authorities – (a) for any district in England and Wales not within Greater London, the council of the district; (b) in Greater London, the following (i) for any London borough, the council of the borough; (ii) for the City of London, the Common Council; (iii) for the Temples, the Sub-Treasurer of the Inner Temple and the Under Treasurer of the Middle Temple respectively; (c) in Scotland, an islands or district council.
[96] Environmental Protection Act 1990, s.45. See also, arrangements for separate collection of recyclable waste from December 31, 2010 (s.45A).
[97] Environmental Protection Act 1990, s.45.
[98] *ibid.*, s.46.
[99] *ibid.*, s.47.
[1] *ibid.*, s.48.
[2] Controlled waste means household, industrial and commercial waste or any such waste: Environmental Protection Act 1990, s.75(4).
[3] Environmental Protection Act1990, s.33(2).
[4] *Ashcroft v Cambro Waste Products* [1981] 1W.L.R. 1349; *Shanks and McEwan (Teeside) Ltd v Environment Agency, The Times,* January 28, 1997.
[5] *R. v Leighton and Town and Country Refuse Collections Ltd* [1997] Env. L.R. 411.

said to be a type of anti-social behaviour simply because it "seriously reduces the quality of the local environment".[6] In *Environment Agency v Melland*,[7] controlled waste had been fly-tipped from a vehicle onto land forming part of an industrial estate. The justices found that there was no case to answer as the owner of the vehicle was not the driver at the material times and was not therefore the person "who controls or is in a position to control use of the vehicle". On appeal it was held that evidence of ownership of a vehicle was prima facie evidence that the owner controls or is in a position to control it.

4-048   Breach of s.33(1) is an offence and it is also an offence to contravene any condition of a waste management licence.[8] A person who commits an offence under this section is liable, on summary conviction, to imprisonment for a term not exceeding 12 months, or a fine not exceeding £50,000, or both. On conviction on indictment, a person is liable to imprisonment for a term not exceeding five years or a fine or both.[9] The Clean Neighbourhoods and Environment Act 2005 inserts new ss.33A, B and C into the Environmental Protection Act 1990. Under s.33A[9A], on conviction of an offence under s.33(1)(a), the court may make an order requiring the defendant to pay to the Environment Agency or waste collection authority a sum which appears to the court not to exceed the costs arising from: (a) investigations of the enforcement authority which resulted in the conviction; and (b) the seizure by the enforcement authority under s.34B of a vehicle involved in the offence.[10] New s.33B[10A] makes provision for the payment of clean-up costs incurred in removing the waste deposited or disposed of in or on the land and/or the taking other steps to eliminate or reduce the consequences of the deposit or disposal. The compensation may be payable to the Environment Agency, a waste collection authority, or the occupier or owner of the land.[11] Section 33C[11A] also operates to deprive the defendant of his rights in the vehicle (including its fuel) at the time of his conviction and to vest those rights in the relevant enforcement authority. The court must be satisfied that the vehicle was used in or for the purposes of the commission of the offence and at the time of his conviction the defendant had rights in the vehicle.

4-049   It is a defence to an offence under s.33(1) that the defendant took all reasonable precautions and exercised due diligence to avoid the commission of the offence or that the acts alleged to constitute the contravention were done in an emergency in order to avoid danger to human health in a case where: (a) he took all such steps as were reasonably practicable in the circumstances for minimising pollution of the environment and harm to human health; and (b) particulars of the acts were furnished to the waste regulation authority as soon as reasonably practicable after they were done.[12]

---

[6] White Paper, para.3.27.

[7] [2002] EWHC Admin 904.

[8] Environmental Protection Act 1990, s.33(6).

[9] *ibid.*, s.33(8).

[9A] Inserted by the Clean Neighbourhoods and Environment Act 2005, s.42 which came into force on October 18, 2005 (SI 2005/2896).

[10] The power of a court to make an order under this section is in addition to its power to make an order under s.18 of the Prosecution of Offences Act 1985 (award of costs against accused): Environmental Protection Act 1990, s.33A(4). See also provisions for forfeiture of vehicle under Environmental Protection Act 1990, s.33C.

[10A] Inserted by the Clean Neighbourhoods and Environment Act 2005, s.43 which came into force on October 18, 2005 (SI 2005/2896), and amended by the Waste Management (England and Wales) Regulations 2006 (SI 2006/937, reg.2(3)).

[11] i.e. under s.130(1)(a) of the Powers of Criminal Courts (Sentencing) Act 2000.

[11A] Inserted by the Clean Neighbourhoods and Environment Act 2005, s.44 which came into force on October 18, 2005 (SI 2005/2896), and amended by the Waste Management (England and Wales) Regulations 2006 (SI 2006/937, reg.2(4)).

[12] Environmental Protection Act 1990, s.33(7).

Carrying controlled waste

Under s.1 of the Control of Pollution (Amendment) Act 1989, it is an offence for a person, who is not a registered carrier of controlled waste, in the course of any business of his or otherwise, with a view to profit, to transport any controlled waste to or from any place in Great Britain. There are three exceptions: transporting waste within the same premises; transporting waste in Great Britain which was brought in from a country outside of the UK and is not landed until it arrives at that place; and the transport by air or sea of waste from a place in Great Britain to a place outside of Great Britain.[13] It is a defence for the person transporting the waste to show that it was transported in an emergency of which notice was given as soon as practicable after it occurred to the Environment Agency or the waste disposal authority.[14] A person guilty of an offence under this section shall be liable on summary conviction to a fine not exceeding level 5 on the standard scale.[15] **4-050**

Initially, the relevant authority was the waste regulation authority. The 1989 Act was amended so as replace that term with "regulation authority" in 1990, under the Environmental Protection Act 1990, in effect to transfer these powers to the Environment Agency. This is now amended by s.62 of the Anti-Social Behaviour Act 2003, so that regulation authority also means a waste collection authority falling within s.30(3) of the 1990 Act. **4-051**

Section 2 of the 1989 Act provides for the Secretary of State to make regulations for the purpose of enabling registration of carriers with a regulation authority.[16] An authorised officer of a regulation authority or a constable may stop any person appearing to him to be engaged in transporting waste; require him to produce an authority; or they may search any vehicle that appears to be a vehicle which is being used, or has been used, to transport waste; carry out tests on anything found in any such vehicle (including by taking away samples for testing of anything so found); and seize any such vehicle and any of its contents.[17] A person who is required by virtue of s.5 to produce an authority for transporting controlled waste shall do so by producing it forthwith or at a time and place as directed by the officer.[18] **4-052**

An authority may refuse an application for registration where there has been a contravention of the requirements of the regulations, or the applicant has been convicted of a prescribed offence and, in the opinion of the authority, it is undesirable for the applicant to be authorised to transport controlled waste. They may also revoke a registration if the person has been convicted of a prescribed offence and in the opinion of the authority, it is undesirable for them to continue to be authorised to transport controlled waste.[19] There is an appeal to the Secretary of State from the authority's decision under s.4. **4-053**

---

[13] Control of Pollution (Amendment) Act 1989, s.1(2).

[14] Control of Pollution (Amendment) Act 1989, s.1(6); see also subs.(3) as to the Secretary of State's power to exempt by regulation certain categories of carrier – Controlled Waste (Registration of Carriers and Seizure of Vehicles) Regulations (SI 1991/1624).

[15] Control of Pollution (Amendment) Act 1989, s.1(5).

[16] Controlled Waste (Regulation of Carriers and Seizure of Vehicles) Regulations (SI 1991/1624), Waste Management Licensing Regulations 1994 (SI 1994/1056) and the Controlled Waste (Registration of Carriers and Seizure of Vehicles) (Amendment) Regulations 1998 (SI 1998/605).

[17] Control of Pollution (Amendment) Act 1989, s.5, as amended by the Clean Neighbourhoods and Environment Act 2005; 37 (not in force at time of writing). See also Control of Pollution (Amendment) Act 1989, s.5A in relation to seizure of vehicles.

[18] Control of Pollution (Amendment) Act 1989, s.5(3).

[19] *ibid.*, s.3.

4-054   A person is guilty of an offence if he fails without reasonable excuse to comply with a requirement to produce his authority to transport waste; to give any assistance that an authorised officer or constable may reasonably request in the exercise of his s.5 powers or that he otherwise intentionally obstructs an authorised officer or a constable in the exercise of those powers.[20] A person guilty of an offence under s.5 is liable on summary conviction to a fine not exceeding level 5 on the standard scale.[21] The regulation authority may, however, give that person a notice offering him the opportunity of discharging any liability to conviction for an offence under s.5(1)(a) (that is, a failure without reasonable excuse to comply with a requirement to produce his authority to transport waste) by payment of a fixed penalty.[22]

4-055   Section 7(3) of the 1989 Act provides that:

"(3) A person shall be guilty of an offence under this subsection if he

(a) fails, without reasonable excuse, to comply with any requirement in pursuance of regulations under this Act to provide information to the Secretary of State or a disposal authority; or
(b) in complying with any such requirement, provides information which he knows to be false in a material particular or recklessly provides information which is false in a material particular."

4-056   Subsection (4) provides that a person guilty of an offence under subs.(3) above shall be liable on summary conviction to a fine not exceeding level 5 on the standard scale. Further, under subs.(5), where the commission by any person of an offence under this Act is due to the act or default of some other person, that other person shall also be guilty of the offence; and a person may be charged with and convicted of an offence by virtue of this subsection, whether or not proceedings for the offence are taken against any other person. Section 55 of the Anti-Social Behaviour Act 2003 amends this section so that the relevant authority for the purposes of all enforcement action under this section is the waste regulation authority.

4-057   The Anti-social Behaviour White Paper states that few of the above powers were available to local authorities (until the passing of the Anti-Social Behaviour Act 2003). It was acknowledged that fly-tipping was on the increase, but it is difficult to be precise as figures are not collected centrally. New measures are proposed so that local authorities have greater powers to investigate fly-tipping and to stop and search and seize vehicles being used for this purpose.[23] These powers were transferred to the Environment Agency. It has been estimated by the Environment Agency that removing such waste costs about £500,000 per annum. However, a recent LGA survey found that the cost of clean-ups to local authorities was about £25 million per annum and that 128 of responding authorities recorded instances of fly-tipping, with 20 per cent recording more than 1000 incidents. 84 per cent of authorities believed they did not have sufficient powers to deal with the problem.[24]

4-058   Authorities were granted enhanced powers by the Environmental Protection (Duty of Care) Regulations 1991 to serve notices on businesses requiring them to produce waste transfer notes, which are the written descriptions that accompany every consignment of controlled waste and are proof that the consignment is being lawfully transported and disposed of.

---

[20] *ibid.*, s.5(7) and (10).
[21] Control of Pollution (Amendment) Act 1989, s.5(11).
[22] *ibid.*, s.5B(2). See also Control of Pollution (Amendment) Act 1989, s.5C in relation to the amounts payable.
[23] White Paper (2003), para.2.28.
[24] House of Commons Research Paper, 03/34, April 2003, p.99.

In the consultation paper, *Living Places—Powers, Rights and Responsibilities*,[25] it was proposed that enforcement bodies be granted powers to order the removal of fly-tipping and to carry out a clean-up of the land if the owner refuses to do so. There is such a power in s.59 of the Environmental Protection Act 1990 but in practice it is rarely used, and the power to recover costs only applies when the owner or occupier has caused or permitted the unlawful deposit. This, it was said in the consultation paper, was very difficult to prove and limits the use of the power to the Environment Agency rather than local authorities. Section 59 provides that if any controlled waste is deposited in or on any land in the area of a waste regulation authority or waste collection authority in contravention of s.33(1) of the 1990 Act, the authority may, by notice served on him, require the occupier to do either or both of the following: to remove the waste from the land within a specified period, not less than a period of twenty-one days, beginning with the service of the notice; and/or to take within such a period specified steps with a view to eliminating or reducing the consequences of the deposit of the waste. Subsection (2) provides that a person on whom any requirements are imposed under subs.(1) above may, within the period of twenty-one days mentioned in that subsection, appeal against the requirement to a magistrates' court. On any appeal under subs.(2) above, the court shall quash the requirement if it is satisfied that the appellant neither deposited, nor knowingly caused, nor knowingly permitted the deposit of the waste; or if there is a material defect in the notice; and in any other case shall either modify the requirement or dismiss the appeal. Under subs.(5), if a person on whom a requirement imposed under subs.(1) above fails, without reasonable excuse, to comply with the requirement, he shall be liable, on summary conviction, to a fine not exceeding level 5 on the standard scale and to a further fine of an amount equal to one-tenth of level 5 on the standard scale for each day on which the failure continues after conviction of the offence and before the authority has begun to exercise its powers under subs.(6). Subsection (6) provides that where a person, on whom a requirement has been imposed under subs.(1) above by an authority, fails to comply with the requirement, the authority may do what that person was required to do and may recover from him any expenses reasonably incurred by the authority in doing it. If it appears to a waste regulation authority or waste collection authority that waste has been deposited in or on any land in contravention of s.33(1) of the 1990 Act, above, and that: **4-059**

(1) in order to remove or prevent pollution of land, water or air or harm to human health it is necessary that the waste be forthwith removed or other steps taken to eliminate or reduce the consequences of the deposit or both; or

(2) there is no occupier of the land; or

(3) the occupier neither made nor knowingly permitted the deposit of the waste;

the authority may remove the waste from the land or take other steps to eliminate or reduce the consequences of the deposit or, as the case may require, to remove the waste and take those steps.[26] The authority may be entitled to recover the cost incurred by it in removing the waste or taking the steps or both and in disposing of the waste from the occupier of the land, unless he proves that he neither made, nor knowingly caused, nor knowingly permitted the deposit of the waste; or, in any case, from any person who deposited, or

[25] October 2002, Department of Environment, Food and Rural Affairs.
[26] Environmental Protection Act 1990, s.59(7).

knowingly caused or knowingly permitted the deposit of any of the waste; except such of the cost as the occupier or that person shows was incurred unnecessarily.

4-060   Section 55(4) of the Anti-Social Behaviour Act 2003 inserts a new section into the Environmental Protection Act 1990, s.59A. That section provides that the Secretary of State may issue directions setting out categories of waste to which a waste regulation authority or waste collection authority in England and Wales should give priority for the purposes of exercising its powers under s.59 above. Under subs.(2), priorities set out in directions under subs.(1) above may be different for different authorities or areas; but nothing in this section, or in any directions issued under it, affects any power of an authority under s.59 above.[27]

4-061   Section 55 of the 2003 Act also amends s.108(15) of the Environment Act 1995, which deals with general enforcing authorities and persons authorised by them so that an enforcing authority means not only the Secretary of State, the Environment Agency and a local enforcing authority, but also a waste collection authority, and the definition of "pollution control functions", in relation to the Agency or SEPA means, in relation to a waste collection authority, the functions conferred on it by s.59 of the Environmental Protection Act 1990.

Statutory Nuisances and the Environmental Protection Act 1990

Duty of Local Authorities

4-062   Where anti-social behaviour is in itself prejudicial to health, the Environmental Protection Act 1990 enables it to be dealt with summarily. Local authorities are under a duty to cause its area to be inspected from time to time to detect any statutory nuisances which ought to be dealt with under Part III of the Act and, where a complaint of a statutory nuisance is made to it by a person living within its area, to take such steps as are reasonably practicable to investigate the complaint.[28] The phrase "reasonably practicable" is sufficiently general to embrace considerations beyond what was physically feasible and was apt to include financial considerations.[29]

Statutory nuisance

4-063   The matters which constitute "statutory nuisances" and may be described, in certain situations, as anti-social behaviour, are as follows:

(1) any premises in such a state as to be prejudicial to health or a nuisance[30];

(2) smoke emitted from premises so as to be prejudicial to health or a nuisance[31];

(3) fumes or gas emitted from premises so as to be prejudicial to health or a nuisance[32];

---

[27] Environmental Protection Act 1990, s.59A(3).
[28] *ibid.*, s.79(1).
[29] *Jordan v Norfolk CC* [1994] 4 All E.R. 218.
[30] Environmental Protection Act 1990, s.79(1)(a).
[31] *ibid.*, s.79(1)(b). Smoke is defined in the Act as including soot, ash, grit and gritty particles emitted in smoke: Environmental Protection Act 1990, s.79(7).
[32] Environmental Protection Act 1990, s.79(1)(c). This specifically applies to fumes (airborne solid matter smaller than dust) and gas (vapour and moisture precipitated from vapour) emitted from private dwellings (s.79(7)).

(4) any accumulation or deposit which is prejudicial to health or a nuisance[33];

(5) any animal kept in such a place or manner so as to be prejudicial to health or a nuisance[34];

(6) artificial light emitted from premises so as to be prejudicial to health or a nuisance[35];

(7) noise emitted from premises so as to be prejudicial to health or a nuisance[36];

(8) noise that is prejudicial to health or a nuisance and is emitted from or caused by a vehicle, machinery or equipment in a street;[37]

(9) any other matter declared by any enactment to be a statutory nuisance.[38]

Premises

"Premises" is defined in the Act as land and any vessel.[39] Some commentators argue that "premises" may include a street.[40] In *Att-Gen v Kirk*,[41] a builder had left a trench which had filled with water across a street, and also left a footpath without proper paving, because he had quarrelled with his landlord. The court, in making a finding that there was no evidence to show that the landlord had entered into possession of the land, granted the injunction restraining the defendant from allowing the street to remain in such a state to create a nuisance or to become injurious to the public health.   **4-064**

Prejudicial to health

The Act defines "prejudicial to health" as injurious, or likely to cause injury, to health.[42] Sleeplessness has been held to fall under this definition.[43] In relation to the accumulation or deposit of rubbish, it has been held that it was prejudicial to health if it was likely to cause a threat of disease or attract vermin, but did not extend to inert matter which could cause injury to people who walked on it.[44]   **4-065**

---

[33] Environmental Protection Act 1990, s.79(1)(e). This refers to any accumulation or deposit of matter which is likely to cause a threat of disease or attract vermin, but it does not extend to inert matter (such as building materials, scrap iron, broken glass and tin cans) which may cause injury if people walk on it (*Coventry CC v Cartwright* [1975] 1 W.L.R. 845). The local authority may also be able to take action under Prevention of Damage by Pests Act 1949 if there are considerable numbers of rats and mice.

[34] Environmental Protection Act 1990, s.79(1)(f).

[35] *ibid.*, s.79(1)(f)(b), as inserted by s.102 of the Clean Neighbourhoods and Environment Act 2005, which came into force on April 6, 2006 (SI 2006/1361). It does not apply to artificial light emitted from: an airport; harbour premises; railway premises (not being relevant separate railway premises); tramway premises; a bus station and any associated facilities; a public service vehicle operating centre; a goods vehicle operating centre; a lighthouse; or a prison.

[36] Environmental Protection Act 1990, s.79(1)(g).

[37] *ibid.*, s.79(1)(ga).

[38] *ibid.*, s.79(h).

[39] *ibid.*, s.79(7) subject to s.81A (expenses recoverable from owner to be a charge on premises does not include a vessel). Furthermore, vessel does not include a vessel powered by steam reciprocating machinery (s.79(12)).

[40] See *Encyclopedia of Environmental Health*, p.2426.

[41] (1896) 12 T.L.R. See also *Brown v Eastern & Midlands Ry* (1889) 22 QBD 391.

[42] Environmental Protection Act 1990, s.79(7).

[43] *Lewisham LBC v Fenner* (1995) 248 ENDS Report 44.

[44] *Coventry CC v Cartwright* [1975] 1 W.L.R. 845.

Nuisance

4-066   "Nuisance" is not defined in the Act, but has been held to have the same meaning as public or private nuisance at common law.[45] The mere visual impact of the rubbish on overlooking householders did not constitute nuisance within the meaning of s.92(1) of the Public Health Act 1936.[46]

The test to be applied

4-067   It is not necessary for the prosecution to prove that the premises are in such a condition as to be both prejudicial to health and a nuisance. The test to be applied in determining whether premises are prejudicial to health or a nuisance is objective.[47]

4-068   In determining whether premises are prejudicial to health, the magistrates (and the local authority) should ask themselves: (a) is the state of the premises such as to be injurious or likely to cause injury to health; or (b) is it a nuisance? It is not helpful to consider the terms of fitness or otherwise for human habitation,[48] Expert evidence showing that premises are prejudicial to health may be required[49] but will not necessarily need to be given by medical professionals.[50]

Examples of matters which have been held to be prejudicial to health or a nuisance

4-069   In respect of any animal kept in such a place or manner so as to be prejudicial to health or a nuisance,[51] it has been held that the mere fact that an animal is noisy may not be prejudicial to health or a nuisance,[52] although this was doubted in *Cartwright v Coventry CC*.[53] The fact that defective premises caused the owner's large number of cats to stray and, in turn, create a nuisance, made the owner of the premises liable under the predecessor to this section. Noise emitted from premises so as to be prejudicial to health or a nuisance may be a statutory nuisance.[54] Although the 1990 Act does not define "noise" it does include vibration.[55] Some commentators suggest that this may include noise caused by groups of people in the street, although whether this could be said to be "noise emitted from the land" is still arguable.[56] It is difficult to see why premises can include a street for the purposes of premises being prejudicial to health or a nuisance,[57] but cannot be defined in such a way to include noise

---

[45] *National Coal Board v Thorn* [1976] 1 W.L.R. 543.
[46] Environmental Protection Act 1990, s.92(1)(c). Public Health Act 1936 is in the same terms as s.79 of the Environmental Protection Act 1990.
[47] *Cunningham v Birmingham CC* [1998] Env. L.R.1.
[48] *Salford CC v McNally* [1976] A.C. 379.
[49] See *Southwark LBC v Simpson* [1999] Env. L.R. 553 where the Divisional Court quashed a conviction based on hearsay evidence given by the Respondent's surveyor because he did not have the medical qualifications or adequate expertise to comment on the link between the state of the premises and the effects on the health of the occupiers.
[50] *O'Toole v Knowsley MBC* [1999] E.H.L.R. 420.
[51] Environmental Protection Act 1990, s.79(1)(f).
[52] *Galer v Morrissey* [1955] 1 All E.R. 380.
[53] [1975] 1 W.L.R. 845.
[54] Environmental Protection Act 1990, s.79(1)(g). Formerly, noise nuisance constituted a statutory nuisance under ss.58 and 59 of the Control of Pollution Act 1974. See also Noise Act 1996, below, in relation to powers of seizure and removal of equipment.
[55] Environmental Protection Act 1990, s.79(7).
[56] See p. 24271 in *Encyclopedia of Environmental Health*: *Tower Hamlets LBC v Manzoni and Walder* (1984) 148 J.P. 123, a case decided under s.58 of the Control of Pollution Act 1974. That Act did not define premises as land. See also, *Macory* [1984] J.P.L. 388.
[57] *Att-Gen v Kirk* (1896) 12 T.L.R. See also *Brown v Eastern & Midlands Ry* (1889) 22 QBD 391.

emanating from a street. In addition, the courts have given a less strict interpretation of this provision, to the extent that the noise can emanate from elsewhere but affects the premises so that it becomes a statutory nuisance itself.[58]
There is no need for the prosecution to demonstrate that the noise has occurred
above a particular decibel level or above the naturally occurring ambient
level.[59] Noise that it prejudicial to health or a nuisance and is emitted from or
caused by a vehicle, machinery or equipment in a street[60] does not apply to
noise made by traffic, any naval, military or air force of the Crown or by a visiting force or by a political demonstration or a demonstration supporting or
opposing a cause or campaign.[61]

Abatement notices

A local authority is under a duty to serve an abatement notice upon it being satisfied that a statutory nuisance exists, or is likely to occur or recur, in its area.[62]
It has been suggested, however, where there are alternative remedies, the word
"shall" does not mean that the authority are under a duty to take action under
the Environmental Protection Act 1990 in preference to any other remedy.[63] It
is notable that the Clean Neighbourhoods and Environment Act 2005 inserts a
new subs.(2A) which imposes a duty on a local authority, in the case of noise,
to take such other steps as it thinks appropriate for the purpose of persuading
the appropriate person to abate the nuisance or prohibit or restrict its occurrence or recurrence, as an alternative to an abatement notice. If the authority is
satisfied at any time before seven days that the steps taken will not be successful in persuading the appropriate person to abate the nuisance or prohibit or
restrict its occurrence or recurrence, and it is satisfied at the end of seven days
that the nuisance continues to exist, or continues to be likely to occur or recur,
the authority shall serve an abatement notice in respect of the nuisance.[64] Local
authorities are also permitted to take action where the statutory nuisance is
caused by some act or default outside their area but which affects their area.[65]

4-070

The Act does not prescribe, nor does it provide for regulations to prescribe,
the form of the abatement notice. However, the abatement notice must at least
identify clearly and precisely the nuisance complained of and impose all or any
of the requirements as set out in s.80(1) of the 1990 Act.[66] It may require that
the nuisance be abated or it may prohibit or restrict its occurrence or recurrence by requiring execution of such works, or the taking of such steps, as may
be necessary to achieve any of these purposes.[67]

4-071

If the notice specifies works or steps to be taken, then they must be specified
with some particularity.[68] Where the local authority prohibits the nuisance,
there may be no need to specify works or steps to be taken by the recipient.

4-072

[58] *Southwark LBC v Ince* (1989) 153 J.P. 597.
[59] *Godfrey v Conwy CBC* [2001] E.H.L.R. 160. See also *Cambridge CC v Douglas* [2001] E.H.L.R.
9: "There was no requirement in law upon the appellant [the local authority] to specify a permissible noise level to be measured in decibels at some particular point or positions. The effect
of noise may depend upon more factors than volume, such as pitch and the nature of the
noise."
[60] Environmental Protection Act 1990, s.79(1)(ga).
[61] *ibid.*, s.79(6A).
[62] *ibid.*, s.80(1).
[63] *Nottingham Corp v Newton* [1974] 1 W.L.R. 923.
[64] Environmental Protection Act 1990, s.80(2A)–(2E).
[65] *ibid.*, s.81(2).
[66] *Network Housing Association v Westminster*, *The Times*, November 8, 1994.
[67] Environmental Protection Act 1990, s.80(1)(a)–(b).
[68] *Salford CC v McNally* [1976] A.C. 379 at 389; *Millard v Wastall* [1898] 1 Q.B. 342; *Whatling v
Rees* (1914) 84 L.J.K.B. 1122.

In *Budd v Colchester BC*,[69] an abatement notice was served requiring the abatement of dogs barking and the prohibition of its recurrence. The recipient argued, on appeal, that the notice was defective in its failure to identify the nuisance complained of and to identify the works or steps to be taken to abate the nuisance. On appeal, it was held that the notice was effective; the nuisance complained of was sufficiently identified as dogs barking and there was no need, in the circumstances of the case, to specify how the nuisance was to be abated. On a further appeal, the Court of Appeal seemed to indicate that a local authority has a choice when serving an abatement notice as to whether to specify works or steps to be taken to abate the nuisance, depending on the circumstances of the case.[70] The notice in *Cambridge CC v Douglas*[71] required the recipient to abate the nuisance caused by the playing of amplified music by works. On appeal, the court held that the inclusion of works did not render the notice invalid through ambiguity where no works were anticipated by the local authority. By adopting a common sense approach to the notice, the recipient would know perfectly well what was required to abate the nuisance. Similarly, in *Sevenoaks DC v Brands Hatch Leisure Group*,[72] the notice referred to steps to be taken to abate the noise nuisance without specifying what those steps might be. On a true reading of the notice, it was clear that no works were required at all. Laws L.J. held, that it would "be hopelessly mechanistic to fix on the word 'steps' and then to condemn the notice for not specifying the 'steps' required".[73] In *Greenwich BC v London CC*,[74] a statutory notice was served requiring the abatement of smoke nuisance. This was duly complied with, but the problem recurred six months later. It was held that there was sufficient evidence to justify the magistrate in finding that the later nuisance was a separate and independent occurrence and not a recurrence of the earlier nuisance.

4-073   The notice must specify the time or times within which the requirements of the notice are to be complied with,[75] although the failure to insert a time limit does not render an abatement notice invalid.[76] The time for compliance must be reasonable.[77] The notice must be served in accordance with s.233 of the Local Government Act 1972. The person on whom the notice is served will generally be the person responsible[78] for the nuisance.[79] Where the nuisance arises from any defect of a structural character, the notice is to be served on the owner of the premises.[80] Of more relevance perhaps to anti–social behaviour is the situation where the person responsible for the nuisance cannot be found or the nuisance has not yet occurred. In such a case, the notice will be served on the owner or occupier of the premises.[81] Thus, notwithstanding that a notice will lie against trespassers who have caused a statutory nuisance, if the trespasser cannot be found it will lie against the occupier. If the owner continues the nuisance, the notice will lie

---

[69] [1997] Env.L.R. 128. See also *Falmouth and Truro Port Health Authority v South West Water Services* [2000] E.H.L.R. 306; *Kirklees MBC v Field* [1998] Env.L.R. 337; *Brighton & Hove Council v Ocean Coachworks (Brighton) Ltd* [2000] E.H.L.R. 279.
[70] *Budd v Colchester BC* [1999] E.H.L.R. 347.
[71] [2001] E.H.L.R. 9.
[72] [2001] E.H.L.R. 7.
[73] *ibid.* at 123.
[74] (1912) 76 J.P. 267; see also *Battersea BC v Goerg* (1906) 71 J.P. 11.
[75] Environmental Protection Act 1990, s.80(1).
[76] *R. v Tunbridge Wells JJ. Ex p. Tunbridge Wells BC* [1996] Env. L.R. D7.
[77] *Bristol Corp v Sinnott* [1918] 1 Ch. 62; *Thomas v Noakes* (1894) 58 J.P. 672.
[78] "Person responsible" is defined by s.79(7) as the person to whose act, default or sufferance the nuisance is attributable.
[79] Environmental Protection Act 1990, s.80(2)(a).
[80] *ibid.*, s.80(2)(b).
[81] *ibid.*, s.80(2)(c).

against him in any event.[82] When more than one person is responsible for a statutory nuisance, action may be taken against each such person, regardless of whether or not any of those persons is responsible for what would by itself amount to such a nuisance.[83]

There are specific provisions in relation to service of an abatement notice in the case of a statutory noise emitted from, or caused by, a vehicle, machinery or equipment in a street,[84] which has either not yet occurred or arises from unattended vehicle, machinery or equipment.[85] The notice shall be served, where the person responsible for the vehicle, machinery or equipment can be found, on that person, or where that person cannot be found, or where the local authority determines that this should apply, by fixing the notice to the vehicle, machinery or equipment.[86] If the person can be found within the hour of the notice being fixed on the machinery, then a copy of that notice must be served on that person with the necessary time extension for compliance.[87]   **4-074**

Proceedings

Proceedings brought by a local authority
It is an offence to contravene or fail to comply with any requirement or pro-   **4-075**
hibition imposed by an abatement notice, without reasonable excuse.[88] A person guilty of such an offence shall be liable on summary conviction to a fine not exceeding level 5 on the standard scale, together with a further fine of an amount equal to one-tenth of that level for each day on which the offence continues after conviction.[89] A defendant can argue in his defence that he has a reasonable excuse for not complying with the requirements or prohibition in the abatement notice.[90] The burden of proof lies with the prosecution. Once the defendant set the evidential basis for his contention of reasonable excuse, it will be up to the prosecution to prove, beyond reasonable doubt, that he did not have a reasonable excuse.[91] Personal circumstances are capable of constituting a reasonable excuse. In *Butuyuyu v Hammersmith & Fulham LBC*,[92] it was held that proper consideration should have been given to the fact that the defendant was HIV positive and that one of her children had died two days after the notice had been served. In establishing that a nuisance has occurred or recurred, there is no need for the prosecution to prove that an occupier has been caused a nuisance.[93] The defence of best practicable means to prevent or counteract the effects of the nuisance will not be applicable in the case of statutory nuisances normally associated with anti-social behaviour.[94]

Local authorities may take action themselves to abate a statutory nuisance   **4-076**
where a notice has not been complied with and do whatever may be necessary in the execution of the notice.[95] This includes a power to seize and remove any equipment which appears to the authority is being or has been used in the

---

[82] *Sedleigh-Denfield v O'Callaghan* [1940] A.C. 880.
[83] Environmental Protection Act 1990, s.81(1A).
[84] *ibid.*, s.79(1)(ga).
[85] *ibid.*, s.80A(1).
[86] *ibid.*, s.80A(2).
[87] *ibid.*, s.80A(3) and (4).
[88] *ibid.*, s.80(4).
[89] *ibid.*, s.80(5).
[90] *ibid.*, s.80(4).
[91] *Polychronakis v Richards and Jerrom Ltd*, *The Times*, November 19, 1997.
[92] CO 1184/96, October 16, 1996.
[93] *Cooke v Adatia* (1989) 153 J.P. 129.
[94] Environmental Protection Act 1990, s.80(8), as amended by s.103 of the Clean Neighbourhoods and Environment Act 2005.
[95] Environmental Protection Act, 1990, s.81(3).

emission of noise nuisance. Where a person obstructs the exercise of this power he will be liable on summary conviction to a fine not exceeding level 3 on the standard scale.[96] Local authorities are able to recover any expenses reasonably incurred by them in abating, or preventing, the recurrence of a statutory nuisance in such a situation.[97] The expenses must be reasonably incurred.[98] They can recover them from the person whose act or default has caused the statutory nuisance.[99] If that person was the owner of the premises, the local authority may recover expenses from the person for the time being who is the owner.[1] There is also provision for the court to apportion expenses between persons by whose acts or default then nuisance arose in such manner as it considers fair and reasonable.[2]

4-077　　If, in the opinion of the local authority, proceedings taken under s.80(4) of the 1990 Act will afford an inadequate remedy, they have a discretion to commence proceedings in the High Court for the purpose of securing the abatement, prohibition, or restriction of the statutory nuisance, regardless of whether the local authority has not suffered damage from the nuisance.[3] It has been suggested that this power should not be used lightly, but in cases where the nuisance is a substantial one, and the defendant is considered likely to be contumacious.[4]

Proceedings brought by persons aggrieved

4-078　　Any person may make a complaint to the magistrates' court on the ground that he is aggrieved by the existence of a statutory nuisance,[5] which will refer to a person whose own health, or that of their family, is being prejudicially affected by the nuisance or whose reasonable enjoyment of their property is being affected. "Aggrieved person" was defined in *Inland Revenue Commissioners v National Federation of Self-Employed and Small Businesses Ltd*[6]:

> "The correct approach in such a case is . . . to look at the statute under which the duty arises, and to see whether it gives any express or implied right to persons in the position of the applicant to complain of the alleged unlawful act or omission."

If the magistrates' court is satisfied that the alleged nuisance exists, or that although abated it is likely to recur on the same premises or on the same street (in the case of noise emissions from cars, etc.), the court must make an order requiring the defendant to abate the nuisance, within a time specified in the order, and to execute any works necessary for that purpose prohibiting a recurrence of the nuisance, and requiring the defendant, within a time specified in the order, to execute any works necessary to prevent the recurrence.[7] Thus, the magistrates have a wide discretion as to the steps that need to be taken in order to abate the nuisance.[8] The order should be made as specific as possible[9]and

[96] Noise Act 1996, s.10(7)(8).

[97] Environmental Protection Act 1990, s.81(4).

[98] *ibid.*

[99] *ibid.*

[1] *ibid.* See also s.81A in respect of expenses recoverable from owner to be a charge on the premises and interest and s.81B in respect of payment of expenses by instalments.

[2] *ibid.*

[3] Environmental Protection Act 1990, s.81(5).

[4] *Encyclopedia of Environmental Health*, p.24288, n. s.81(5).

[5] Environmental Protection Act 1990, s.82(1).

[6] [1981] 2 W.L.R. 722.

[7] Environmental Protection Act 1990, s.82(2).

[8] *McGillivray v Stephenson* [1950] 1 All E.R. 942.

[9] *Salford CC v McNally* [1976] A.C. 379; *R. v Secretary of State for the Environment Ex p. Watney Mann (Midlands)* [1976] J.P.L. 368; *R. v Wheatley* (1885) 16 QBD 34; *R. v Harrocks Ex p. Boustead* (1900) 69 L.J.Q.B. 688.

must look at all the circumstances having regard to the prevailing situation in making a sensible and just order.[10] The magistrates may also impose on the defendant a fine not exceeding level 5 on the standard scale.[11]

Persons against whom proceedings may be brought

Proceedings can be brought against the person responsible for the nuisance,[12]   **4-079**
save where the nuisance arises from a structural defect, when they will be brought against the owner, or, where the perpetrator cannot be found, against the owner or occupier.[13] In the case of a statutory nuisance caused by noise emitted from or caused by an unattended vehicle or unattended machinery or equipment,[14] proceedings should be brought against the person responsible for the vehicle, machinery or equipment.[15] The magistrates, on finding that an alleged nuisance existed at the date the complaint was made,[16] shall order the defendant to pay any such amount that they consider reasonably sufficient to compensate the victim for any expenses reasonably incurred by him in the proceedings.[17] It is irrelevant that at the date of the hearing the nuisance no longer exists.[18] If it appears to the magistrates that neither the person responsible for the nuisance nor the owner or occupier of the premises, or owner of machinery, etc. can be found, the court may direct the authority in whose area the nuisance has occurred, to do anything which the court would have ordered the perpetrator to do.[19] The local authority must be given an opportunity of being heard before the court makes such an order.[20]

Noise Control

Anti-Social Behaviour Act 2003 and Clean Neighbourhoods and Environment Act 2005

According to the White Paper, loud noise at night caused by inconsiderate   **4-080**
neighbours is a very real problem. Powers to deal with noise at night are ineffective and slow to implement compared to those powers which are applicable to noise during the day. The Noise Act 1996 makes provision about noise emitted from dwellings at night, the forfeiture and confiscation of equipment used to make noise unlawfully and for connected purposes. The 1996 Act has been substantially amended by the Anti-Social Behaviour Act 2003 in that:

(1) people making excessive noise at night will now be given a warning and ten minutes to stop; and if they do not, a local authority officer will be able to issue a fixed penalty notice; and,

(2) local authority offices are able to close immediately noisy premises such as clubs and bars.

---

[10] *Nottingham Corp v Newton* [1974] 2 All E.R. 760.
[11] Environmental Protection Act 1990, s.82(8).
[12] *ibid.*, s.81(4)(a).
[13] *ibid.*, s.81(4)(c).
[14] *ibid.*, s.79(1)(ga).
[15] *ibid.*, s.82(4).
[16] It is necessary to prove, beyond reasonable doubt, that the alleged nuisance existed. These proceedings are criminal in nature by virtue of the magistrates' powers to impose a fine on the perpetrator: *Lewisham LBC v Fenner* [1995] ENDS Report 44, Crown Court.
[17] Environmental Protection Act 1990, s.82(12).
[18] *ibid.*
[19] *ibid.*, s.82(13).
[20] *ibid.*

4-081   The Clean Neighbourhoods and Environment Act 2005 has also amended the Noise Act 1996, so that the same provisions will apply to premises which have been granted a premises licence or temporary event licence.

Local authority area

4-082   The Noise Act 1996 now applies to the area of every local authority in England and Wales, rather than, as was the case, only to an area of the local authority if the authority had resolved that it should do so.[21] Under a review of the take up and workings of the Noise Act 1996 commissioned by the DETR and carried out by the University of Birmingham (*Review of Implementation of the Noise Act 1996* (DETR) December 28, 2000) it was found that only 13 local authorities had adopted the Act, and of those 13 only two per cent of night noise complaints were actually dealt with under the Act.

Steps to be taken by a local authority

4-083   Where any individual present in a dwelling[22] during night hours[23] complains about excessive noise being emitted from another dwelling[24] or to the local authority,[25] they may arrange for an officer to take reasonable steps to investigate the complaint.[26] Prior to the coming into force of the Anti-Social Behaviour Act 2003, there was a duty on the local authority to take reasonable steps to investigate such a complaint. If the local authority receives a complaint about noise being emitted from a dwelling located in the area of another local authority, the first authority may still take action under ss.2 to 9 of the Noise Act 1996, as if the offending dwelling was within their area.[27] A warning notice[28] may be served by the officer if the noise is being emitted[29] from the offending dwelling during night hours, and the noise, if it were measured from within the complainant's dwelling, would, or might exceed the permitted level.[30] There is no requirement for the officer to use any device for measuring the level of noise. Rather, it is for the officer to decide whether any noise, if it were measured from within the complainant's dwelling would or might exceed the permitted level, and for the purposes of that decision, to decide whether to assess the noise from within or outside the complainant's dwelling and whether or not to use any device for measuring the noise.[31]

Warning notices

4-084   The warning notice must contain specific information:

(1) it must state that an officer of the authority considers that noise is being emitted from the offending dwelling during night hours; and

---

[21] Noise Act 1996, s.1.
[22] "Dwelling" means any building, or part of a building, used or intended to be used as a dwelling: Noise Act 1996, s.11(2).
[23] That is, the period beginning with 11pm and ending with the following 7am.
[24] Noise Act 1996, s.2(2).
[25] *ibid.*, s.2(7).
[26] *ibid.*, s.2(1).
[27] *ibid.*, s.2(7).
[28] *ibid.*, s.3.
[29] References to noise emitted from a dwelling include noise emitted from any garden, yard, outhouse or other appurtenance belonging to or enjoyed with the dwelling: Noise Act 1996, s.11(2).
[30] Noise Act 1996, s.2(4).
[31] *ibid.*, s.2(5).

(2) that the noise exceeds, or may exceed, the permitted level, as measured from within the complainant's dwelling;

(3) it must give warning that any person who is responsible for noise which is emitted from the dwelling, in the period specified in the notice, and exceeds the permitted level, as measured from within the complainant's dwelling, may be guilty of an offence[32];

(4) the period specified in the notice must be a period beginning not earlier than 10 minutes after the time when the notice is served and ending with the following 7 am[33]; and

(5) it must state the time at which it was served.[34]

The warning notice must be served by delivering it to any person present at or near the offending dwelling and appearing to the officer to be responsible for the noise.[35] This is defined as being a person to whose act, default or sufferance the emission of the noise is wholly or partly attributable.[36] If it is not reasonably practicable to identify any person present at or near the dwelling as being a person responsible for the noise on whom the notice may reasonably be served, the warning notice must be served by leaving it at the dwelling.[37]   **4-085**

Offences

A person is guilty of an offence if a warning notice has been served in respect of noise emitted from a dwelling, he is responsible for noise which is emitted from the dwelling in the period specified in the notice, and that noise exceeds the permitted level, as measured from within the complainant's dwelling.[38] The permitted level[39] means a level applicable to noise as measured from within any other dwelling in the vicinity by an approved device.[40] It is possible, however, to determine different permitted levels for different circumstances and this may be determined partly by reference to other levels of noise.[41] It is a defence for a person charged with an offence to show that there was a reasonable excuse for the act, default or sufferance in question.[42] A person guilty of an offence is liable on summary conviction to a fine not exceeding level 3 on the standard scale.[43]   **4-086**

---

[32] Noise Act 1996, s.3(1).
[33] *ibid.*, s.3(2).
[34] *ibid.*, s.3(4).
[35] *ibid.*, s.3(3)(a).
[36] *ibid.*, s.3(5).
[37] *ibid.*, s.3(3)(b).
[38] *ibid.*, s.4.
[39] The Secretary of State may by directions in writing determine the maximum level of noise referred to as "the permitted level" which may be emitted during night house from any dwelling: Noise Act 1996, s.5(1). The Secretary of State's directions are to be found in Circular 8/97 (Welsh Office 41/97). These may be varied from time to time: Noise Act 1996, s.5(4). The permitted level is likely to be 35dB where the underlying noise is 25dB or less or where the underlying level exceeds 25dB, 10dB in excess of that level.
[40] Noise Act 1996, s.5(2). The device must be used in accordance with any conditions subject to which the approval was given.
[41] *ibid.*, s.5(3).
[42] *ibid.*, s.4. see *Wellingborough DC v Gordon* [1993] Env. L.R. 218 for the requirements of "reasonable excuse".
[43] *ibid.*, s.4(3). By the Interpretation Act 1978, s.5, Sch.1 and the Criminal Justice Act 1982, s.37(3) this means the standard scale as set out in 37(2) of the 1982 Act. The scale is level 1: £200; level 2: £500; level 3: £1,000; level 4: £2,500; and level 5: £5,000. Different amounts may be substituted by order under the Magistrates' Courts Act 1980, s.143.

4-087   If an unapproved device is used to measure noise or the conditions of usage of the device are not satisfied, the evidence of the level of noise is inadmissible in proceedings under s.4 of the Noise Act 1996.[44] It is sufficient for the purposes of these proceedings that evidence of measurement of noise, the circumstances in which it was made, and that it was an approved device and conditions of usage were satisfied, may be given in a document.[45] This document is to be signed[46] by an officer of the local authority[47] and may consist partly of a record of the measurement produced automatically from the device.[48] Furthermore, it is sufficient that evidence of noise emitted from a particular dwelling is given by a document signed[49] by an officer of the local authority stating that he had identified that dwelling as the source at the time of the noise, or as the case may be, the noise of that kind.[50] There are, however, some limitations as to the admissibility of these documents. Documents are not admissible if copies of them are not served on the defendant less than seven days before the hearing or trial. Further, the section does not make these documents admissible as evidence of anything other than the matters of a record produced automatically by a device if, less than three days before the hearing or trial, the defendant serves a notice on the prosecutor requiring attendance of the signor of the documents at the hearing or trial.[51] The court may shorten or lengthen the time of three days in special circumstances.[52]

Fixed Penalty Notices

4-088   A person may be offered the opportunity of discharging any liability to conviction by payment of a fixed penalty. This may be done where an officer of a local authority[53] has reason to believe that a person is committing, or has just committed, an offence under s.4 of the 1996 Act and he serves a fixed penalty notice on that person.[54] This may be served by delivering the notice to him or, if it is not reasonably practicable to deliver it to him, by leaving the notice, addressed to him, at the offending dwelling.[55] The notice needs to contain such particulars of the circumstances alleged to constitute the offence as are necessary for giving reasonable information about the offence. There is no prescribed form for the fixed penalty notice. In particular it must state[56] the period during which proceedings will not be taken for the offence, the amount of the fixed penalty, and the person to whom and the address at which the fixed penalty may be paid.[57]

---

[44] Noise Act 1996, s.6(3) the approval of measuring devices and conditions as to their use is set out in Circular 8/97 (Welsh Office 41/97).

[45] Noise Act 1996, s.7(1).

[46] A document purporting to be signed is to be treated as being so signed unless the contrary is proved: Noise Act 1996, s.7(4).

[47] A member of a local authority or an officer or other person authorised by a local authority is not personally liable in respect of any act done by him or by the local authority or any such person if the act was done in good faith for the purpose of executing powers conferred by, or by virtue of, the Noise Act 1996: s.12(1). This does not apply to liability under the Audit Commission Act 1998, s.17 or 18 (powers of district auditor and court): Noise Act 1996, s.12(2).

[48] Noise Act 1996, s.7(2).

[49] A document purporting to be signed is to be treated as being so signed unless the contrary is proved: Noise Act 1996, s.7(4).

[50] Noise Act 1996, s.7(3).

[51] *ibid.*, s.7(6).

[52] *ibid.*

[53] Authorised for the purposes of the Noise Act 1996, s.8.

[54] Noise Act 1996, s.8(1).

[55] *ibid.*, s.8(2).

[56] *ibid.*, s.9(1).

[57] *ibid.*, s.8(4).

The Clean Neighbourhoods and Environment Act 2005 inserts a new s.8A **4-089**
specifying the amount of fixed penalty. Whereas before, the fixed penalty was
£100,[58] the amount is now that specified by the local authority.[59] If it is not so
specified, the amount of fixed penalty is £100.[60] The local authority may make
provision for treating the fixed penalty as having been paid if a lesser amount
is paid before the end of a period specified by the authority.[61] The Secretary
of State may, by regulations, substitute a different amount to £100 default,
require the fixed penalty specified by the local authority to fall within a prescribed range and restrict the circumstances in which a lesser amount may be
treated as payment of the fixed penalty.[62] The fixed penalty may (among other
methods) be paid by pre-paying and posting in cash or otherwise.[63]

Once a fixed penalty notice has been given proceedings cannot be com- **4-090**
menced before the end of 14 days following the date of the notice.[64] The
person to whom the notice has been given cannot be convicted of the offence
if he pays before the end of that period.[65] The local authority cannot serve a
further fixed penalty notice during the period specified in the notice, but the
person may be convicted of a further offence, under s.4 of the 1996 Act, in
respect of noise emitted from the dwelling after the notice is given and before
the end of the period specified in that notice.[66]

The 2005 Act also confers power on an authorised officer of a local author- **4-091**
ity to require a person to whom he proposes to give a fixed penalty notice to
give him his name and address.[67] A person commits an offence if he fails to
give his name and address when required to do so, or he gives a false or inaccurate name or address in response to a requirement under that subsection.[68]
A person guilty of either offence is liable on summary conviction to a fine not
exceeding level 3 on the standard scale.[69]

Seizure of equipment

An officer of the authority (or a person authorised by the authority for the **4-092**
purpose)[70] may seize and remove equipment from the offending dwelling
which it appears to him is being or has been used in the emission of the
noise.[71] Under s.10(7) of the 1996 Act, the power may only be exercised where
the officer has reason to believe that a warning notice has been served in
respect of noise emitted from a dwelling and, at any time in the period specified in the notice, noise emitted from the dwelling has exceeded the permitted level, as measured from within the complainant's dwelling.[72] If entry is

---

[58] Noise Act 1996, s.8(8). This has now been repealed by s.82 of the Clean Neighbourhoods and Environment Act 2005, which came into force on April 6, 2006 (SI 2006/795).
[59] Noise Act, s.8A(2)(a).
[60] *ibid.*, s.8A(2)(b).
[61] *ibid.*, s.8A(3).
[62] *ibid.*, s.8A(5).
[63] *ibid.*, s.8(6). Payment is regarded as having been made at the time at which the letter would be delivered in the ordinary course of post: Noise Act 1996, s.8(7).
[64] Noise Act 1996, s.8(3)(a).
[65] *ibid.*, s.8(3)(b).
[66] *ibid.*, s.8(2).
[67] *ibid.*, s.8B(1).
[68] *ibid.*, s.8B(2).
[69] *ibid.*, s.8B(3).
[70] Such a person must produce his authority, if he is required to do so: Noise Act 1996, s.10(3).
[71] Noise Act 1996, s.10(2) the generally held view appears to be that the seizure of equipment is best carried out the following day in the presence of police: *Review of Implementation of the Noise Act 1996* (DETR) December 28, 2000. See also the similarly expressed power set out in s.81(3) of the Environmental Protection Act 1990.
[72] Noise Act 1996, s.10(1).

refused, the local authority can obtain a warrant from a justice of the peace in order to enter the dwelling, if need be, by force. It is necessary to show to a justice of the peace on sworn information, in writing, that: a warning notice has been served in respect of noise emitted from a dwelling; at any time in the period specified in the notice, noise emitted from the dwelling has exceeded the permitted level, as measured from within the complainant's dwelling; and entry of an officer of the local authority, or of a person authorised by the authority for the purpose, to the dwelling has been refused; or such a refusal is apprehended; or a request by an officer of the authority, or of such a person, for admission would defeat the object of the entry.[73] The warrant, once issued, continues in force until the purpose for which entry is required has been satisfied.[74] The person who enters may take with him such other persons and equipment as may be necessary and if, when he leaves, the premises are unoccupied, must leave them as effectively secured against trespassers as he found them.[75] It is an offence for any person to wilfully obstruct any person entering a dwelling to seize and remove equipment either under powers conferred by s.10(2) of the Noise Act 1996, or s.81(3) the Environmental Protection Act 1990.[76]

4-093   Any seized equipment may be retained during the period of 28 days beginning with the seizure, or if it is related equipment in proceedings for a noise offence instituted within that period against any person, until he is sentenced or otherwise dealt with for the offence or acquitted of the offence, or the proceedings are discontinued.[77] This does not authorise the retention of seized equipment if a person has been given a fixed penalty notice under s.8 of the Noise Act 1996 in respect of any noise; the equipment was seized because of its use in the emission of the noise in respect of which the fixed penalty notice was given and that person has been paid the fixed penalty before the end of the period allowed for its payment.[78]

4-094   Where a person is convicted of a noise offence the court may make an order for forfeiture of any related equipment, regardless of whether or not the court also deals with the offender in any other way.[79] The court may also make the order without regard to any restrictions on forfeiture in any enactment.[80] In considering whether to make a forfeiture order, the court must have regard to the value of the equipment and to the likely financial and other effects on the offender of the making of the order (taken together with any other order that the court contemplates making).[81] A forfeiture order operates to deprive the offender of any rights in the equipment to which it relates.[82] Where equipment has been forfeited, the owner (other than the person in whose case the forfeiture has been made) can apply to have it returned to him. The circumstances in which the equipment can be returned are as follows:

(1) the application needs to be made before the expiry of six months from the date of the forfeiture order;

(2) the court has to be satisfied that the applicant appears to be the owner of the equipment; and

---

[73] Noise Act 1996, s.10(4).
[74] *ibid.*, s.10(6).
[75] *ibid.*, s.10(5).
[76] *ibid.*, s.10(8).
[77] *ibid.*, Sch. para.2(1).
[78] *ibid.*, Sch. para.2(2).
[79] *ibid.*, Sch. para.3(1).
[80] *ibid.*, Sch. para.3(2).
[81] *ibid.*, Sch. para.3(3).
[82] *ibid.*, Sch. para.3(4).

(3) the applicant had not consented to the offender having possession of the property.

Closure of noisy premises

The second main reform of the Anti-Social Behaviour Act 2003, as regards noise is the power for local authorities to close noisy premises. Under s.40(1), the chief executive officer[83] of the relevant local authority may make a closure order in relation to premises to which this section applies if he reasonably believes that: a public nuisance is being caused by noise coming from the premises; and the closure of the premises is necessary to prevent that nuisance. Subsection (2) provides that s.40 applies to premises if a premises licence has effect in respect of them, or a temporary event notice has effect in respect of them. A closure order is an order which requires the premises to be kept closed during a specified period which does not exceed 24 hours, and begins when a manager of the premises receives written notice of the order.[84] It is an offence under subs.(4) if a person, without reasonable excuse, permits premises to be open in contravention of a closure order. The penalty is comparatively steep: a person guilty of an offence under this section shall be liable on summary conviction to imprisonment for a term not exceeding three months or a fine not exceeding £20,000, or both.[85] The chief executive[86] may cancel the closure order by notice in writing to the manager[87] of the premises, and, in any event, shall cancel the order as soon as is reasonably practicable if he believes that it is no longer necessary in order to prevent a public nuisance being caused by noise coming from the premises, and give notice of the order as soon as is reasonably practicable to the licensing authority for the area in which the premises are situated.[88]

4-095

Licensed Premises

By virtue of Sch.1 to the Clean Neighbourhoods and Environmental Act 2005, the Noise Act 1996 will apply to any premises in respect of which a premises licence or a temporary event notice has effect.[89] The provisions detailed above will, subject to minor amendments, apply to such premises.[90] The responsible person of the premises is defined as follows. Where a premises licence has effect it will be: (1) the person who holds the premises licence if he is present at the premises at that time; (2) where that person is not present, the designated premises supervisor under the licence if he is present at the premises at that time; or (3) where neither of those persons are present at the

4-096

---

[83] Under s.41(2), the chief executive officer of a local authority may authorise an environmental health officer of the authority to exercise a power or duty of the chief executive officer under s.40(1) or under subs.(1) above; and (a) authority under this subsection may be general or specific, and (b) a reference in s.41(1) or subs.(1) above to a belief of the chief executive officer includes a reference to a belief of a person authorised under this subsection.

[84] Anti-Social Behaviour Act 2003, s.41(3).

[85] *ibid.*, s.41(5).

[86] The term, chief executive, means the head of the paid service of the authority designated under s.4 of the Local Government Act 1989, s.43, s.41(3).

[87] "Manager" in relation to premises means (a) a person who holds a premises licence in respect of the premises, (b) a designated premises supervisor under a premises licence in respect of the premises, (c) the premises user in relation to a temporary event notice which as effect in respect of the premises, and (d) any other person who works at the premises in a capacity (paid or unpaid) which enables him to close them: Anti-Social Behaviour Act 2003, s.41(3).

[88] Anti-Social Behaviour Act 2003, s.41(1).

[89] Premises licence and temporary event notice has the same meaning as given in the Licensing Act 2003 (1996, s.2(7A)).

[90] See Noise Act 1996, ss. 2,3,5,6,7,8,8A,9 and 10.

premises at that time, any other person present at the premises at that time who is in charge of the premises. In the case of a temporary event notice the responsible person will be: (1) the premises user in relation to that notice if he is present at the premises at that time; or (2) where the premises user is not present at the premises at that time, any other person present at the premises at that time who is in charge of the premises.

4-097   The responsible person will be guilty of an offence if a warning notice has been served under s.3 in respect of noise emitted from premises, noise is emitted from the premises in the period specified in the notice, and the noise exceeds the permitted level, as measured from within the complainant's dwelling.[91] A person guilty of an offence under this section is liable on summary conviction to a fine not exceeding level 5 on the standard scale.[92]

Intruder Alarms

4-098   The Clean Neighbourhoods and Environment Act 2005 repeals the provisions dealing with intruder alarms in the Noise and Statutory Nuisance Act 1993[93] and replaces them with new powers for local authorities. Those new powers concern: designating areas in which the local authority is to be notified of nominated key-holders; and entering premises for the purposes of silencing an alarm.

Designation of alarm notification areas

4-099   A local authority may designate all or any part of its area as an alarm notification area.[94] Section 69 of the 2005 Act explains that notice of a proposed designation is to be published in a newspaper circulating in the area and the local authority must consider any representations sent within a specified period (at least 28 days of publication of the notice). The decision of the local authority, regardless as to whether there is to be a designated area, must be published in a newspaper circulating in the area.[95] In addition, where the local authority decides to designate an alarm notification area, notice must be sent to all premises specifying the date the designation is to take effect.[96] Section 70 makes provision for the withdrawal of a designation by the local authority which must be published in the newspaper and notification sent to premises in the area.

Key-holders

Notification of nominated key- holders
4-100   Where the premises are in a designated alarm notification area and an audible intruder alarm has been installed in or on the premises, the occupier or, if there is no occupier, the owner ("the responsible person")[97] must nominate a key-holder.[98] In addition, the responsible person must notify the local authority of the key-holder's name, address and telephone number within 28 days of the coming into force of the designated area or 28 days of the installation of the intruder alarm.[99] A failure to nominate or notify is an offence

---

[91] See Noise Act 1996, s.4A(1).
[92] See Noise Act 1996, s.4A(2).
[93] Namely, s.9 and Sch.3 (2005 Act, Sch.5, Pt 7).
[94] Clean Neighbourhoods and Environment Act 2005, s.69(1).
[95] *ibid.*, s.69(6) and (9).
[96] *ibid.*, s.69(6)(b).
[97] *ibid.*, s.81(1).
[98] *ibid.*, s.71(2).
[99] *ibid.*, ss.71(2),(3) and 72(2).

punishable on summary conviction to a fine not exceeding level 3 on the standard scale.[1]

Nomination of Key-holders

A person may be nominated as a key-holder in respect of premises under this section only if—   **4-101**

(1) he holds keys sufficient to enable him to gain access to the part of the premises in which the controls for the alarm are situated;

(2) he normally resides or is situated in the vicinity of the premises;

(3) he has information sufficient to enable him to silence the alarm;

(4) he has information sufficient to enable him to silence the alarm;

(5) he agrees to be a nominated key-holder in respect of the premises;

(6) where the premises are residential premises, he is: (a) an individual who is not the occupier of the premises; or (b) a key-holding company.

(7) where the premises are non-residential premises, he is: (a) an individual who is the responsible person, or is acting on behalf of the responsible person; or (b) if the responsible person is not an individual, a key-holding company.[2]

If the responsible person becomes aware that these conditions are not satisfied then he is required to inform the local authority within 28 days of being becoming aware.[3]

Fixed penalty notices

Sections 73 to 76 of the 2005 Act make provision for fixed penalty notices similar to those provisions under the Noise Act 1996. Subject to any Regulations made by the Secretary of State, the amount will be an amount specified by the local authority or £75. A person, to whom a local authority officer is proposing to serve a fixed penalty notice, who fails to give his name and address or provides a false or inaccurate name or address, commits an offence. The offence is punishable on summary conviction by a fine not exceeding level 3 on the standard scale.   **4-102**

Powers of entry

Under s.77 of the 2005 Act, an authorised officer[4] of a local authority may enter premises for the purpose of silencing an alarm if he is satisfied: **4-103**

(1) that the alarm has been sounding continuously for more than 20 minutes or intermittently for more than one hour;

(2) that the sounding of the alarm is likely to give persons living or working in the vicinity of the premises reasonable cause for annoyance;

(3) if the premises are in an alarm notification area, that reasonable steps have been taken to get the nominated key-holder to silence the alarm.

---

[1] Clean Neighbourhoods and Environmental Act 2005, s.71(4) and (5).
[2] *ibid.*, s.72(3), (4) and (5).
[3] *ibid.*, s.72(6) and (7).
[4] *ibid.*, s.77.

The premises must be in the local authority area and if requested, the officer must show evidence of his authority to act under this section.

4-104   There is no power to use force to enter premises under s.77. Under s.78, however, a justice of the peace may, on an application of the authorised officer, issue a warrant authorising the officer to enter the premises, using reasonable force if necessary, for the purpose of silencing the alarm. Before applying for the warrant, the officer must leave a notice at the premises stating:

(1) that the officer is satisfied that the sounding of the alarm is likely to give persons living or working in the vicinity of the premises reasonable cause for annoyance; and

(2) that an application is to be made for a warrant authorising the officer to enter the premises, using reasonable force if necessary, for the purpose of silencing the alarm.

The justice of the peace needs to be satisfied that the following conditions are met:

(1) that the alarm has been sounding continuously for more than 20 minutes or intermittently for more than one hour;

(2) that the sounding of the alarm is likely to give persons living or working in the vicinity of the premises reasonable cause for annoyance;

(3) if the premises are in an alarm notification area, that reasonable steps have been taken to get the nominated key-holder to silence the alarm; and

(4) that the officer is unable to gain entry to the premises without the use of force.

The warrant continues in force until the alarm has been silenced, the premises have been secured and a notice left explaining the action which has been taken.

4-105   Section 79 applies to the exercise of the power of entry under both ss.77 or 78. The authorised officer may take any steps he thinks necessary for the purpose of silencing the alarm. Section 79 expressly provides that he take other persons and equipment as he thinks necessary to silence the alarm although they must not cause more damage to or disturbance at the premises than is necessary for the purpose of silencing the alarm. If the premises are unoccupied or, where the premises are occupied, the occupier of the premises is temporarily absent, the officer must leave a notice stating what action has been taken and leave the premises (so far as is reasonably practicable) as effectively secured against entry as he found them. This does not mean that the alarm needs to be re-set.

4-106   Nothing done by, or by a member of, a local authority or by an officer of, or another person authorised by a local authority, if done in good faith for the purposes of ss.77, 78 or 79, subjects the authority or any of those persons personally to any action, liability, claim or demand. This appears to suggest that that any damage incurred by lack of reasonable force, if done in good faith, will not be recoverable. Any expenses reasonably incurred by the local authority in connection with entering the premises, silencing the alarm and leaving the premises may be recovered by the authority from the responsible person.

Graffiti and Fly-Posting

4-107   Graffiti and fly-posting are activities identified by the Government as contributing to anti-social behaviour by reducing environmental amenity and as a barrier to re-generation. Graffiti is a criminal damage but convictions are not recorded separately. According to ENCAMS, an environmental charity responsible for the Keep Britain Tidy Campaign, generally graffiti and litter have reduced but where it does exist, it is an intense problem[5]:

"Where it does occur it is immediately and highly visible and greatly influences the public in their perception of the area. In the cases of graffiti and fly-posting, these are often in prominent locations, having a disproportionate effect on the perceptions of passers-by."

The GLA estimated that the total cost of graffiti in London is more than £100m per year. Average London borough expenditure to deal with it is about £13m.[6] In *Living Places—Power, Rights and Responsibilities*, it was proposed that the litter laws be extending to include graffiti and fly-posting; local authorities already have powers under the Environmental Protection Act 1990 and there is also the fixed penalty system for littering. However, these powers are fragmentary. Hence, in the Anti-social Behaviour White Paper, it was proposed that real reductions to graffiti could be made if it were unlawful to sell spray paints to persons under the age of 18 years and the police were given powers to stop and search for such items.

Provisions dealing with fly-posting and graffiti are found in Pt 6 of the Anti-Social Behaviour Act 2003. Part 4 of the Clean Neighbourhoods and Environment Act 2005 has made a few amendments concerning fly-posting and graffiti; fixed penalty notices; extension of graffiti removal to fly-posting; sale of aerosol paint to children; defences to the unlawful display of posters; and removal of placards and posters. **4-108**

Fixed Penalty Notices

Section 43 of the 2003 Act provides that where an authorised officer[7] of a local authority[8] has reason to believe that a person has committed a relevant offence in the area of that authority, he may give that person a notice offering him the opportunity of discharging any liability to conviction for that offence by payment of a penalty in accordance with the notice. However, in two special cases, he need not give such a notice: if he considers that the commission of the offence falls within s.44(1)(c) of the 2003 Act, or involves the commission of an offence under s.30 of the Crime and Disorder Act 1998; or, in the case of any other relevant offence, it was motivated (wholly or partly) by hostility towards a person based upon his membership (or presumed membership) of a racial or religious group, or towards members of a racial or religious group based on their membership of that group. **4-109**

---

[5] *The Environmental Quality Survey for England* 2001–2002, Sept 2002.
[6] *Graffiti in London, Report of the London Assembly Graffiti Investigative Committee*, May 2002.
[7] An officer of a local authority means: (a) an employee of the authority who is authorised in writing by the authority for the purpose of giving notices under s.43(1); (b) any person who, in pursuance of arrangements made with the authority, has the function of giving such notices and is authorised in writing by the authority to perform that function; and (c) any employee of such a person who is authorised in writing by the authority for the purpose of giving such notices: Anti-Social Behaviour Act 2003, s.47(1) as amended by the Clean Neighbourhoods and Environment Act 2005, s.30(1). The Secretary of State may by regulations prescribe conditions to be satisfied by a person before a parish or community council may authorise him in writing for the purpose of giving notices under s.43(1): Anti-Social Behaviour Act 2003, s.43(4) as inserted by The clean Neighbourhoods and Environment Act 2005, s.30(2).
[8] Local authority means an authority which is also a litter authority for the purposes of s.88 of the Environmental Protection Act 1990.

4-110   "Relevant offence" means an offence under para.10 of s.54 of the Metropolitan Police Act 1839 (affixing posters, etc.); an offence under s.20(1) of the London County Council (General Powers) Act 1954 (deface- ment of streets with slogans, etc.); an offence under s.1(1) of the Criminal Damage Act 1971, which involves only the painting or writing on, or the soiling, marking or other defacing of, any property by whatever means; an offence under s.131(2) of the Highways Act 1980 (including that provision as applied by s.27(6) of the Countryside Act 1968) which involves only an act of obliteration; an offence under s.132(1) of the Highways Act 1980 (painting or affixing things on structures on the highway etc); or an offence under s.224(3) of the Town and Country Planning Act 1990 (displaying advertisement in contravention of regulations).[9] In the case of a relevant offence falling within s.44(1)(f) of the 2003 Act, displaying an advertisement in contravention of regulations under s.224(3) of the Town and Country Planning Act 1990, an authorised officer may not give a notice to a person under s.43(1), in relation to the display of an advertisement, unless he has reason to believe that that person personally affixed or placed the advertise- ment to, against or upon the land or object on which the advertisement is or was displayed.[10]

4-111   Where a person is given a notice under s.43 in respect of an offence, no pro- ceedings may be instituted for that offence (or any other relevant offence arising out of the same circumstances) before the expiration of the period of 14 days following the date of the notice, and he may not be convicted of that offence (or any other relevant offence arising out of the same circumstances) if before the expiration of that period he pays the penalty in accordance with the notice.[11] A notice under subs.(1) must give such particulars of the circum- stances alleged to constitute the offence as are necessary for giving reasonable information of the offence. Under subs.(6), the notice must also state the period during which proceedings will not be instituted for the offence, the amount of the penalty, and the person to whom, and the address at which, the penalty may be paid. Without prejudice to payment by any other method, payment of a penalty in pursuance of a notice under subs.(1) may be made by pre-paying and posting a letter containing the amount of the penalty (in cash or otherwise) to the person mentioned in subs.(6)(c) at the address so men- tioned.[12] Where a letter is sent in accordance with subs.(7) payment is to be regarded as having been made at the time at which that letter would be deliv- ered in the ordinary course of post.[13]

4-112   The Clean Neighbourhoods and Environment Act 2005 repeals s.43(10) and (11) and inserts a new s.43A specifying the amount of fixed penalty. Previously, the fixed penalty was £50, subject to amendment by order, payable to the local authority. The amount is now that specified by a relevant local authority in relation to its area (whether or not the penalty is payable to that or another authority).[14] If it is not so specified, the amount is £75.[15]

---

[9] Anti-Social Behaviour Act 2003, s.44(2). Note that s.33 of the Clean Neighbourhoods and Environment Act 2005 provides for new defences to the unlawful display of advertisements, namely, that the advertisement was displayed without his knowledge, he took all reasonable steps to prevent the display or, after the advertisement had been displayed, to secure its removal: Town and Country Planning Act 1990, s.224(5) and (6).

[10] Anti-Social Behaviour Act 2003, s.43(3).

[11] *ibid.*, s.43(4).

[12] *ibid.*, s.43(7).

[13] *ibid.*, s.43(8).

[14] *ibid.*, s.43A(1)(a). Relevant local authority means: a district council in England; county council in England for an area for which there is no district council; London borough council; the Common Council of the City of London; the Council of the Isles of Scilly; county or county borough council in Wales: s.43A(2).

The local authority may make provision for treating the fixed penalty as having been paid if a lesser amount is paid before the end of a period specified by the authority.[16] The Secretary of State may, by regulations, substitute a different amount to the £75 default payment, require the fixed penalty specified by the local authority to fall within a prescribed range and restrict the circumstances in which a lesser amount may be treated as payment of the fixed penalty.[17]

The 2005 Act also confers power on an authorised officer of a local authority to require a person to whom he proposes to give a fixed penalty notice to give him his name and address.[18] A person commits an offence if he fails to give his name and address when required to do so, or he gives a false or inaccurate name or address in response to a requirement under that subsection.[19] A person guilty of either offence is liable on summary conviction to a fine not exceeding level 3 on the standard scale.[20]   **4-113**

In any proceedings a certificate which: (a) purports to be signed by or on behalf of the person responsible for the financial affairs of a local authority, and (b) states that payment of a penalty payable in pursuance of a notice under s.43(1) was or was not received by a date specified in the certificate, is evidence of the facts stated. A local authority may use any sums it receives in respect of penalties payable to it in pursuance of notices under subs.(1) (its "penalty receipts") only for the purposes of its functions that are qualifying functions. These are defined in s.45(4): functions under s.43 and functions of a description specified in regulations.   **4-114**

Section 46 of the Anti-Social Behaviour Act 2003 amends para.1 of Sch.4 to the Police Reform Act 2002 (powers of community support officers to issue fixed penalty notices) so that community support officers have the power of an authorised officer of a local authority to give a notice under s.49(1); and similar powers are granted to accredited persons under para. 12 of Sch.5 to the 2002 Act.   **4-115**

Removal Notices

Section 48 of the 2003 Act applies to a relevant surface which has been defaced by graffiti, poster or flyer, the display of which contravenes regulations under s.220 of the Town and Country Planning Act 1990. Graffiti is defined by s.48(12) of the 2003 Act as including painting, writing, soiling, marking, or other defacing by whatever means.   **4-116**

Under s.48 of the 2003 Act, where a local authority[21] is satisfied that a relevant surface in an area has been defaced by graffiti, and that the defacement is detrimental to the amenity of the area or is offensive, they may issue a "graffiti removal notice" upon any person who is responsible for the surface imposing the requirement mentioned in subs.(3). Subsection (3) provides that the requirement is that the defacement be removed, cleared or otherwise remedied within a period specified in the notice being not less than 28 days beginning with the day on which the notice is served. Under subs.(4), if the requirement mentioned in subs.(3) is not complied with, the authority, or any person authorised by the authority may remove, clear or otherwise   **4-117**

---

[15] Anti-Social Behaviour Act 2003, s.43A(1)(b).

[16] *ibid.*, s.43A(3).

[17] *ibid.*, s.43A(4)–(6).

[18] *ibid.*, s.43B(1).

[19] *ibid.*, s.43B(2).

[20] *ibid.*, s.43B(3).

[21] s.48(12) defines this as an authority which is also a litter authority for the purposes of s.88 of the Environmental Protection Act 1990.

remedy the defacement. In exercising the power under subs.(4) the authority, or any person authorised by the authority, may enter any land to the extent reasonably necessary for that purpose. A graffiti removal notice must explain the effect of subss.(4) and (5) and of s.49 and 51. Such notices are deemed to have the same effect as notices issued under ss.160 of the Environmental Protection Act 1990.[22]

4-118   If, after a reasonable enquiry, a local authority is unable to ascertain the name or proper address of any person who is responsible for a relevant surface, the authority may affix a graffiti removal notice to the surface, and enter any land to the extent reasonably necessary for that purpose, that notice shall be treated as having been served upon a person responsible for the surface. The provisions have effect regarding "relevant surface". Subsections (9) and (10) define this term as referring to any of the following surfaces, whether internal or external or open to the air or not: the surface of any street[23] or of any building, structure, apparatus, plant or other object in or on any street; the surface of any land owned, occupied or controlled by a statutory undertaker or of any building, structure, apparatus, plant or other object in or on any such land; or the surface of any land owned, occupied or controlled by an educational institution[24] (including its governing body) or of any building, structure, apparatus, plant or other object in or on any such land. However, a surface is not a relevant surface unless, in the case of a surface within subs.(9), the street is public land; in the case of any other surface within the meaning of subs.(9), the land is public land, the surface is visible from public land, or the surface is otherwise visible to members of the public using the services or facilities of the statutory undertaker or educational institution in question or any other statutory undertaker or educational institution.

Person Responsible

4-119   Section 48(11) of the 2003 Act provides that a person is responsible for a relevant surface if: where it is the surface of any land (including a street), he owns, leases, occupies, controls, operates or maintains the land; and where it is the surface of any other thing mentioned in subs.(9), he owns, leases, occupies, controls, operates or maintains the thing.

Recovery of Expenditure

4-120   Under s.49 of the 2003 Act, a local authority may recover from the person, on whom a graffiti removal notice was served, expenditure reasonably incurred in exercise of the power under s.48(4). They may not recover expenditure from a person unless they have served on that person a notice which sets out the amount of, and details of, the expenditure which it proposes to recover.

Guidance

4-121   Section 50 of the 2003 Act provides that the Secretary of State must issue guidance to local authorities to which they must have regard in England for the purposes of ss.48 and 49; or, in Wales, the National Assembly for Wales.

Appeals

4-122   A person on whom a graffiti removal notice is served may, under s.51 of the 2003 Act, within the period of 21 days beginning with the day on which it is served, appeal against the notice to a magistrates' court on any of the following grounds as set out in subs.(2):

---

[22] Anti-Social Behaviour Act 2003, s.48(8).
[23] As defined by s.48(1) of the New Roads and Street Works Act 1991: Anti-Social Behaviour Act 2003, s.48(12).
[24] As defined by s.98(2) of the Environmental Protection Act 1990.

(1) that the defacement is neither detrimental to the amenity of the area nor offensive,

(2) that there is a material defect or error in, or in connection with, the notice; or

(3) that the notice should be served on another person.

Where an appeal is brought under s.51(1), the graffiti removal notice shall be of no effect pending the final determination or withdrawal of the appeal.

Further, under s.51(6), a person on whom a notice under s.49(2) is served **4-123** may, within the period of 21 days beginning with the day on which it is served, appeal to a magistrates' court on the grounds that the expenditure which the authority is proposing to recover is excessive. On the determination of an appeal under subs.(6), the magistrates' court must do either of the following: confirm that the amount which the authority is proposing to recover is reasonable, or substitute a lower amount as the amount which the authority are entitled to recover.

By virtue of s.52, certain persons are exempt from liability in relation to **4-124** graffiti removal notices. They include the local authority and any employee of the authority, any person authorised by the authority under s.48(4) and the employer or any employee of that person. However, this does not apply if the act or omission is shown to have been in bad faith and/or arising out of a failure to exercise due care and attention, or so as to prevent an award of damages made in respect of an act or omission on the ground that the act or omission was unlawful under s.6(1) of the Human Rights Act 1998.

Aerosol Paint

Under s.53 of the Anti-Social Behaviour Act 2003, it is an offence to sell an **4-125** aerosol paint container to a person under the age of sixteen. Subsection (2) defines "aerosol paint container" as "a device which (a) contains paint stored under pressure, and (b) is designed to permit the release of the paint as a spray." A person guilty of an offence under this section shall be liable on summary conviction to a fine not exceeding level 4 on the standard scale.[25] It is a defence for a person charged with an offence under this section in respect of a sale to prove that he took all reasonable steps to determine the purchaser's age, and he reasonably believed that the purchaser was not under the age of sixteen[26]; and as regards a person charged with an offence under this section in respect of a sale effected by another person, it is a defence to prove that he (the defendant) took all reasonable steps to avoid the commission of an offence under this section.

The Clean Neighbourhoods and Environment Act 2005 imposes a duty **4-126** on every weights and measures authority to consider, at least once in every period of 12 months, the extent to which it is appropriate for the authority to carry out, in their area, a programme of enforcement action in relation to s.54; and to the extent that they consider it appropriate to do so, carry out such a programme.[27] A programme of enforcement action involves all or any of the following in respect of offences under s.54: the bringing of prosecutions; the investigation of complaints in respect of alleged offences; and the taking of other measures intended to reduce the incidence of offences.[28]

[25] Anti-Social Behaviour Act 2003, s.61(3).
[26] *ibid.*, s.61(4).
[27] *ibid.*, s.54A(1).
[28] *ibid.*, s.54A(1).

Litter

Offence of Leaving Litter

4-127   Under s.87 of the Environmental Protection Act 1990, if any person ". . . throws down, drops or otherwise deposits in, into or from any place to which this section applies and leaves, anything whatsoever in such circumstances as to cause or contribute to or tend to lead to, the defacement by litter of any place to which this section applies he shall subject to subsection (2), be guilty of an offence."

The place to which the offence applies

4-128   It applies to any public open space and also any highway, road or trunk road which is a special road, any place on relevant land of a principal litter authority[29]; any place on relevant Crown land[30]; any place on relevant land of any designated statutory undertaker[31] or designated educational institution[32]; and any place on relevant land within a litter control area of a local authority.[33] "Public open space" means a place in the open air to which the public are entitled or permitted to have access without payment and any covered place open to the air on at least one side and available for public use.[34]

Defences

4-129   Subsection (2) provides that no offence is committed under this section where the depositing and leaving of the thing was authorised by law or done with the consent of the owner, occupier or authority having control of the that place or thing into which the that thing was deposited. The offence is triable summarily.

Fixed Penalty Notices

4-130   An authorised officer[35] of a litter authority may give a person, whom he has reason to believe has committed an offence under s.87, a fixed penalty notice.[36] Where a person has been given a notice, no proceedings shall be set down for 14 days following the offence; and he shall not be convicted of that offence if he pays the fixed penalty before the expiry of that period.[37] Currently the penalty is £25.[38]

4-131   The scheme is based on a Westminster City Council pilot scheme. A consultation paper in 1989 stated that the government monitored the Westminster

---

[29] A county council, a county borough council, a district council, a London borough council, the City of London Common Council, and the Council of the Isles of Scilly: Environmental Protection Act 1990, s.86.

[30] Under this part of the Environmental Protection Act 1990 Act, land is Crown land if it is occupied by the Crown Estate Commissions as part of the Crown Estate or by or for the purposes of a government department or for military purposes: s.86(5).

[31] Land under the control of any statutory undertaker so designated by the Secretary of State, being land to which the public have access with or without payment: Environmental Protection Act 1990, s.86(6).

[32] Land which is open to the air and under the direct control of the governing body of the designated education institution: Environmental Protection Act 1990, s.86(7).

[33] This is land if it is included in an area designated by the local authority under s.90 of the Environmental Protection Act 1990 Act to which the public have access with or without payment: s.86(13).

[34] Environmental Protection Act 1990, s.87(4). See also s.87(13).

[35] An officer of a litter authority who is authorised in writing by that authority for the purpose of issuing notices under this section: Environmental Protection Act 1990, s.88(10).

[36] Environmental Protection Act 1990, s.88(1).

[37] *ibid.*, s.88(2).

[38] *ibid.*, s.88(6).

scheme, and concluded that it was a "helpful and workable tool" in the local authority's efforts to fight litter and improve public awareness of the problem:

"Almost all approaches made by the authorised officers resulted in the person concerned picking up the litter rather than the officer issuing a ticket. This bears out that the value of the scheme is above all one of education and persuasion and that the demand of operating the scheme on the resources of the local authority and the courts are modest."

Note that police were not given the same power as authorised officers as the additional burden ". . . would effectively detract resources from serious crime prevention and detection."

The Clean Neighbourhoods and Environment Act 2005

The 2005 Act makes a number of significant changes to the 1990 Act.[39] New s.87(1) provides that: "A person is guilty of an offence if he throws down, drops or otherwise deposits any litter in any place to which this section applies and leaves it". Litter includes the discarded ends of cigarettes, cigars and like products, and discarded chewing-gum and the discarded remains of other products designed for chewing.[40] It is immaterial whether the litter is deposited on land or in water.[41]   **4-132**

Moreover, the litter offence is extended to all open places, that is, it applies to any place in the area of a principal litter authority which is open to the air. New subs.(3), however, provides an exception to this rule. By virtue of s.86(13), it does not apply to a place which is "open to the air" if the public does not have access to it, with or without payment.   **4-133**

It is a defence if the depositing of the litter is authorised by law or done by or with the consent of the owner, occupier or other person having control of the place where it is deposited.[42] A person may only give consent in relation to the depositing of litter in a lake or pond or watercourse if he is the owner, occupier or other person having control of: all the land adjoining that lake or pond or watercourse; and all the land through or into which water in that lake or pond or watercourse directly or indirectly discharges, otherwise than by means of a public sewer.[43]   **4-134**

The 2005 Act also makes provision for the payment of fixed penalty notices, the amount of which is £75, if not otherwise specified, whether by the local authority or by regulations made by the Secretary of State. Similar provisions to those under the Noise Act 1996 and the 1990 Act are made relating to the payment of a lesser amount and as to additional offences concerning the failure to give, or giving inaccurate information as to, a name or address when required to do so by an authorised officer.[44]   **4-135**

Duties of the Secretary of State, Local Authorities and Principal Litter Authorities

Local authorities under the Environmental Protection Act 1990 are required, with regard to any highway for which they are responsible, and each principal   **4-136**

---

[39] The Clean Neighbourhoods and Environment Act 2005, s.18 replaces ss.87(1)–(4) with new ss.87(1)–(4C) although at the time of writing this section was not in force.

[40] Environmental Protection Act 1990, s.98(5A) as inserted by s.27 of the Clean Neighbourhoods and Environment Act 2005. This is not yet in force.

[41] Environmental Protection Act 1990, s.87(4)

[42] *ibid.*, s.87(4A).

[43] *ibid.*, s.87(4B). "Lake or pond", "watercourse" and "public sewer" have the same meanings as in s.104 of the Water Resources Act 1991.

[44] Environmental Protection Act 1990, s.88 as amended by the Clean Neighbourhoods and Environment Act 2005, s.19.

litter authority,[45] as regards relevant land,[46] to keep the highway and/or land clean of litter and refuse.[47] Consideration must be given to the character and use of the land and highway as to the standard of cleanliness required.[48] Furthermore, any current code of practice must be taken into account.[49] A local authority may also arrange for the cleaning of any relevant land[50] with the consent of any person who has an interest in the land or occupies it and may enter into an agreement with such a person for the payment by him of any charges.[51]

Court, yard or passages

4-137   Under the Public Health Act 1936, where a court, yard or passage is used in common by occupants of two or more buildings, but it is not a highway maintainable at the public expense, and it is not regularly swept or kept clean and free from rubbish to the satisfaction of the local authority,[52] the authority may have it cleansed and swept.[53] They may recover any expenses reasonably incurred by it under these provisions from the occupiers of buildings which front or abut the yard or to which the passage affords access.[54]

Byelaws

4-138   A local authority may also make byelaws for the prevention of nuisances occurring from snow, filth, dust, ashes and rubbish, preventing the keeping of animals so as to be prejudicial to health, and for prescribing times for the removal or carriage through the streets of any offensive or noxious matter or liquid, preventing the escape of such matter or liquid from the vehicle, and the cleansing of any place where such matter or liquid has been dropped or spilled in the course of removal or carriage.[55]

Street Litter Control Notices

4-139   In order to prevent the accumulation of litter or refuse in or around any street or open land adjacent to any street a principal litter authority, other than an English county council or joint board,[56] may issue street litter control notices containing requirements in relation to the litter or refuse on occupiers of certain

---

[45] County councils, county borough councils, district councils, London boroughs and the Common Council of the City of London and the Council of the Isles of Scilly: Environmental Protection Act 1990, s.87(3)(b).

[46] Defined as land which is open to the air and under the direct control of the authority not being a highway to which the public is entitled or permitted to have access with or without payment: Environmental Protection Act 1990, s.86(1)(4).

[47] Environmental Protection Act 1990, s.89(1).

[48] *ibid.*, s.89(3).

[49] The current code of practice is *Environmental Protection Act 1990: Code of Practice on Litter and Refuse*, Department of the Environment, Transport and the Regions, June 1999.

[50] Defined as any land to which members of the public have access to as a right or otherwise which is not a highway: Control of Pollution Act 1974, s.22(3).

[51] Control of Pollution Act 1974 Act, s.22(3).

[52] District council, London borough and Common Council of the City of London, the Sub-Treasurer of Inner Temple, the Under-Treasurer of Middle Temple and, in Wales, the county borough or county council: s.1 of the Public Health Act 1936.

[53] Public Health Act 1936, s.78(1).

[54] *ibid.*, s.78(2).

[55] *ibid.*, s.82.

[56] "Street" means a relevant highway or any other highway over which there is a right of way on foot: s.93(4), of the 1990 Act; "open land" means land in the open air: Environmental Protection Act 1990, s.93(4).

premises.[57] If they are satisfied that the premises are of the prescribed type and have a frontage on a street in their area, they may serve a street litter control notice on the occupier of the premises or, if unoccupied, the owner[58] if:

(1) there is a recurring defacement by litter or refuse of any such land in the vicinity of the premises;

(2) the condition of any part of the premises which is open land in the vicinity of the frontage is such that it is detrimental to the amenities of the locality because of the presence of litter or refuse; or,

(3) quantities of litter or refuse are the result of activities taking place on the premises which deface or are likely to deface the street or open land.

The notice must identify the premises and state the grounds upon which it is issued; specify the open land which adjoins or is in the vicinity of the frontage of the premises on the street; and specify the requirements as the authority considers reasonable in the circumstances.[59]   **4-140**

If the authority is satisfied that the person served with such a notice has failed to comply with it, they may apply to the magistrates' court for an order compelling the person to comply with it.[60] A person who, without reasonable excuse, fails to comply with such an order is guilty of an offence.[61]   **4-141**

The 2005 Act also makes provision for the payment of fixed penalty notices, the amount of which is £100, if not otherwise specified, whether by the local authority or by regulations made by the Secretary of State. Similar provisions to those under the Noise Act 1996 and the Environmental Protection Act 1990 are made relating to the payment of a lesser amount and as to additional offences concerning the failure to give, or giving inaccurate information as to, a name or address when required to do so by an authorised officer.[62]   **4-142**

The street cleansing notice system has been criticised for being slow and cumbersome, particularly when compared to s.19 of the London Local Authorities Act 2000. This provides that London boroughs may serve a cleansing notice specifying the standard and frequency with which land must be cleaned. It has advantages over the street cleansing notice system available to non-London authorities in that all that is required of the premises is simply that neighbouring land adjacent to a street does not have to be a of a specified type. Further, they allow the local authority to carry out the work and recover the costs if the notice is not complied within 42 days.   **4-143**

Litter Abatement Notices

A magistrates' court may act on complaint by any person who is aggrieved by the defacement by litter or refuse to any relevant highway, trunk road, relevant land of a principal litter authority, Crown land, land of a designated statutory undertaker or educational institution or relevant land within the litter control area of a local authority.[63] The court may also act on any complaint that a person is aggrieved by the want of cleanliness of any relevant highway or trunk road.[64] A principal litter authority cannot be a person aggrieved for   **4-144**

---

[57] Environmental Protection Act 1990, s.93(3) – essentially commercial or retail premises or large properties: see Street Litter Control Notices Order 1991 (SI 1991/1324).

[58] Environmental Protection Act 1990, s.93.

[59] *ibid.*, s.93(3).

[60] *ibid.*, s.94(8).

[61] *ibid.*, s.94(9); on conviction a fine not exceeding level 4 on the standard scale.

[62] *ibid.*, s.94A.

[63] Environmental Protection Act 1990, s.91.

[64] *ibid.*

these purposes.[65] The proceedings must be brought against the person who has the duty to keep the land clear or to keep the highway clean.[66] If satisfied that the complaint is made out, the court may order the person responsible to require the defendant to clear the litter or refuse. Where the principal litter authority, other than an English county council or joint board, is satisfied that Crown land, relevant land of a designated statutory undertaker or educational institution or relevant land within the area of the principal litter authority[67] is defaced by litter refuse, or that defacement of it in that way is likely to re-occur, they must serve a litter abatement notice requiring that the litter or refuse be cleaned within a specified time in the notice and prohibiting the land from becoming defaced by litter or refuse.[68] The person served with the notice may appeal to the magistrates' court within 21 days from the date the notice was served.[69] If the person served fails, without reasonable excuse, to comply with the notice, he is guilty of an offence.[70] The authority may also enter the land and clear and recover the reasonable expenses of doing so from the that person.[71]

Litter Clearing Notices

4-145   The Clean Neighbourhoods and Environment Act 2005 introduces a new scheme of litter clearing notices.[72] A principal litter authority must, in discharging its functions under this section, have regard to any guidance given to the authority by the appropriate person.[73]

Land

4-146   A principal litter authority[74] may in accordance with this section serve a notice (a "litter clearing notice") in relation to any land in its area which is open to the air. A litter clearing notice may, however, not be served in relation to land of any of the following descriptions:

(1) a highway maintainable at the public expense;

(2) land under the direct control of a principal litter authority;

(3) Crown land;

(4) relevant land of a designated statutory undertaker;

(5) relevant land of a designated educational institution;

(6) land which is covered (but "open to the air" for the purposes of this Part by virtue of s.86(13) above) and to which the public are not entitled or permitted to have access, with or without payment.[75]

---

[65] Environmental Protection Act 1990, s.91(3).
[66] i.e., the same authorities as under s.89 of the Environmental Protection Act 1990.
[67] i.e., the person occupying the land or, if unoccupied, the owner of the land: S.92(3) of the Environmental Protection Act 1990.
[68] Environmental Protection Act 1990, s.92.
[69] *ibid.*, s.92(4).
[70] *ibid.*, s.92(6).
[71] *ibid.*, s.92(9).
[72] The Clean Neighbourhoods and Environment Act 2005, s.22 inserts a new s.92A into the Environmental Protection Act 1990. This came into force on April 6, 2006 (SI 2006/795)
[73] Environmental Protection Act 1990, s.92A(7).
[74] *ibid.*, s.92A(1) does not apply to an English county council for an area for which there is a district council: s.92A(10).
[75] *ibid.*, s.92A(11).

Conditions of service of a litter clearing notice
Before serving a litter clearing notice in relation to any land a principal litter **4-147**
authority must be satisfied that the land is defaced by litter or refuse so as to
be detrimental to the amenity of the locality.[76]

Contents of a litter clearing notice
A litter clearing notice requires the person on whom it is served to clear the **4-148**
land of the litter or refuse; the notice may specify the time period within which
it is to be carried out (not less than 28 days) and the standards of compliance.[77]
In addition, if the principal litter authority is satisfied that the land is likely to
become defaced by litter or refuse again, the notice must require the person to
take reasonable steps to prevent it from becoming so defaced.[78] The form and
content of a litter clearing notice is to be such as the appropriate person may
by order specify.[79]

Person on whom a litter clearing notice must be served
A litter clearing notice must be served on the occupier of the land to which it **4-149**
relates or, if the land is not occupied, the owner.[80] Where a principal litter
authority is unable, after reasonable enquiry, to ascertain the name or proper
address of the occupier of the land (or, if the land is unoccupied, the owner),
it may post the notice on the land. It may also enter any land to the extent reasonably necessary for that purpose. The notice is to be treated as having been
served upon the occupier (or, if the land is unoccupied, the owner) at the time
the notice is posted.[81]

Appeals
Section 92B makes provision for appeals against litter clearing notices. The **4-150**
appeal is made to the magistrates' court within 21 days of service of the notice.
The grounds on which the notice may be appealed are as follows:

(1) there is a material defect or error in, or in connection with, the notice;

(2) the notice should have been served on another person;

(3) the land is not defaced by litter or refuse so as to be detrimental to the
amenity of the locality;

(4) the action required is unfair or unduly onerous.[82]

A notice against which an appeal under this section is made is of no effect **4-151**
pending the final determination or withdrawal of the appeal.[83] On the determination of an appeal under this section, the magistrates' court must quash
the notice, modify the notice (including modifying it by extending the period
specified in it), or dismiss the appeal.[84]

Failure to comply with a litter clearing notice
A person who fails, without reasonable excuse, to comply with a litter clear- **4-152**
ing notice is guilty of an offence and liable on summary conviction to a fine
not exceeding level 4 on the standard scale.[85]

---

[76] Environmental Protection Act 1990, s.92A(2).
[77] *ibid.*, s.92A(3)(a), (5), (6).
[78] *ibid.*, s.92A(3)(b).
[79] *ibid.*, s.92A(8).
[80] *ibid.*, s.92A(4).
[81] *ibid.*, s.92A(9).
[82] *ibid.*, s.92B(3).
[83] *ibid.*, s.92B(4).
[84] *ibid.*, s.92B(5).
[85] *ibid.*, s.92C(1) and (2).

4-153   In addition, the principal litter authority may enter the land to which the notice relates and clear it of litter and refuse and require the person to pay a reasonable charge in respect of the exercise of that power.[86]

4-154   The 2005 Act also makes provision for the payment of fixed penalty notices, the amount of which is £100 if not otherwise specified, whether by the local authority or by regulations made by the Secretary of State. Similar provisions to those under the Noise Act 1996 and the Environmental Protection Act 1990 are made relating to the payment of a lesser amount and as to additional offences concerning the failure to give, or giving inaccurate information as to, a name or address when required to do so by an authorised officer.[87]

Free Distribution of Printed Matter

4-155   Section 23 of the Clean Neighbourhoods and Environment Act 2005 creates two new offences regarding the distribution of printed matter.[88]

Offences

4-156   First, a person commits an offence if he distributes any free printed matter without the consent of a principal litter authority on any land which is designated by the authority under Sch.3A of the Environmental Protection Act 1990, where the person knows that the land is so designated.[89] Secondly, a person commits an offence if he causes another person to distribute any free printed matter without the consent of a principal litter authority on any land designated by the authority.[90]

4-157   Schedule 3A defines the meaning of "distributes printed matter" as " to give it out to, or offer or make it available to, members of the public and includes placing it on or affixing it to vehicles, but does not include putting it inside a building or letter-box." Printed matter is "free" if it is distributed without charge to the persons to whom it is distributed.[91]

4-158   Note that a person does not distribute printed matter if the distribution takes place inside a public service vehicle (within the meaning of the Public Passenger Vehicles Act 1981). Furthermore, it does not apply to the distribution of printed matter by or on behalf of a charity within the meaning of the Charities Act 1993; where the printed matter relates to or is intended for the benefit of the charity; or where the distribution is for political purposes or for the purposes of a religion or belief.[92]

4-159   A person guilty of an offence under this paragraph is liable on summary conviction to a fine not exceeding level 4 on the standard scale.[93] A person is not guilty of an offence if he causes another person to distribute any free printed matter if he took reasonable steps to ensure that the distribution did not occur on any land designated under this Schedule.[94] Provision is also made for the payment of fixed penalty payments in order to discharge liability. If no amount is specified the amount payable is £75. As with similar provisions elsewhere in

---

[86] Environmental Protection Act 1990, s.92C(3) and (4). A principal litter authority may for the purposes of subs. (4) above impose charges by reference to land of particular descriptions or categories (including categories determined by reference to surface area): s.92C(5).

[87] *ibid.*, s.94A.

[88] The Clean Neighbourhoods and Environment Act 2005, s.23 inserts a new s.94B into the Environmental Protection Act 1990. This gives effect to Sch.3A to the 1990 Act. This came into force on April 6, 2006 (SI 2006/795).

[89] Environmental Protection Act 1990, Sch.3A, para.1(1).

[90] *ibid.*, Sch.3A, para.1(2).

[91] *ibid.*, Sch.3A, para.1(6).

[92] *ibid.*, Sch.3A, paras 1(4) and (7).

[93] *ibid.*, Sch.3A, paras 1(4) and (7).

[94] *ibid.*, Sch.3A, para.1(3).

the 1990 Act, a person commits an offence where a person refuses to give his name and address or gives an inaccurate name and address.[95]

Designation of Land
Paragraph 2 of Sch.3A to the 1990 Act makes provision for the designation of land by a principal litter authority. It may only designate land where it is satisfied that the land is being defaced by the discarding of free printed matter which has been distributed there. The land designated must consist of relevant land of the authority and/or all or part of any relevant highway for which the authority is responsible. The authority must give notice of the designation, take into account any objections and give notice of any revocation.   **4-160**

Application to distribute free printed matter in designated land
Paragraph 3 of Sch.3A to the 1990 Act explains the giving of limited or unlimited consent, the revocation of consent, the payment of fees related to the application and appeals to the magistrates' court against a refusal to give consent, the imposition of conditions or revocation of consent. Consent may be refused because the person has been convicted of an offence under para.1 (or has paid a fixed penalty) or failed to comply with any conditions imposed on the giving of consent. Furthermore, a principal litter authority need not give consent to any applicant where it considers that the proposed distribution would in all the circumstances be likely to lead to defacement of the designated land.   **4-161**

Seizure of material
Where it appears to an authorised officer[96] of a principal litter authority that a person distributing any printed matter is committing an offence under para.1 above, he may seize all or any of it. Any person claiming to own any printed matter seized under this paragraph may apply to a magistrates' court for an order that the printed matter be released to him.[97]   **4-162**

Control of Refuse

Under this heading, we consider a miscellany of various powers as regards the control of refuse, other than waste and litter which are dealt with above, namely, refuse dumping; abandoned trolleys; and general rubbish. Again, the Clean Neighbourhoods and Environment Act 2005 has made a number of amendments to existing legislation.   **4-163**

Control of Refuse Dumping

Under the Refuse (Disposal) Amenity Act 1978, a local authority[98] must provide places where refuse, other than waste with a commercial origin, may be deposited at all times free of charge to any resident in the area and by   **4-164**

---

[95] Environmental Protection Act 1990, Sch.3A, para.7.
[96] "Authorised officer", in relation to a principal litter authority, means an employee of the authority who is authorised in writing by the authority for the purpose of giving notices under para.7 (fixed penalty notices); any person who, in pursuance of arrangements made with the authority, has the function of giving such notices and is authorised in writing by the authority to perform that function; and any employee of such a person who is authorised in writing by the authority for the purpose of giving such notices: Environmental Protection Act 1990, Sch.3A, para.6.
[97] Environmental Protection Act 1990, Sch.3A, para.6(2).
[98] London boroughs and the Common Council of the City of London, Greater Manchester Waste Disposal Authority, the Merseyside Waste Disposal Authority and, elsewhere, county or metropolitan district council: Refuse (Disposal) Amenity Act 1978, s.1.

other persons for a payment that the authority thinks fit. The place must be situated in the authority's area or be reasonably accessible. The authority may permit, on such terms as they think fit, deposit at such a place refuse from a business.[99] They may also provide plant and apparatus for the treatment and disposal of the deposited refuse and sell or otherwise dispose of it.[1]

Abandoned shopping and luggage trolleys

4-165   A local authority under the Environmental Protection Act 1990 may resolve that provisions in that Act regarding abandoned shopping trolleys and baggage trolleys are to apply in their area.[2] Where they apply, the authority may seize the trolley and remove it to a place they think fit.[3] If the trolley is found on land appearing to the authority to be occupied by any person, the trolley cannot be removed without the consent of the occupier, unless the authority have served on that person a notice stating that they propose to remove the trolley and 14 days pass without a notice objecting to the removal.[4] The authority must keep the trolley for a period of six weeks and may sell or otherwise dispose of it thereafter.[5] As soon as reasonably practicable, but not later than 14 days after its removal, the authority must serve a notice on the person who appears to be the owner of the trolley stating that they have removed it, where it is being kept and that if unclaimed the authority will dispose of it.[6] If the person wants it back, the authority shall deliver it to them, subject to the payment of the authority's reasonable expenses. No trolley may be disposed of unless the authority has made reasonable inquiries as to who owns it.[7]

4-166   Section 99 of the Clean Neighbourhoods and Environment Act 2005 makes a number of amendments to Sch.4 to the 1990 Act, including the power to impose a charge on the owner in respect of the removal, storage and disposal of the trolley.[7A]

Accumulations of Rubbish

4-167   Local authorities, under the Public Health Act 1961,[8] may take steps to remove rubbish on any land in the open air in their area, which they consider to be seriously detrimental to the amenities of the neighbourhood, as they may consider necessary in the interests of amenity.[9] The authority must serve a notice on the owner and occupier of the land setting out the steps they propose not less than 28 days before taking action. Any such person may, within 28 days of service of the notice, serve a counter-notice stating that he intends to take those steps himself or appeal to the magistrates' court on the

---

[99] Refuse (Disposal) Amenity Act 1978, s.1(3)(a).
[1] *ibid.*, s.1(3)(c), 1(4).
[2] White Paper (2003), p.44.
[3] A district council, London borough or Common Council of the City of London and, in Wales, a county council or county borough council.
[4] Refuse (Disposal) Amenity Act 1978, s.3(2).
[5] *ibid.*, s.3; the person responsible is the owner of the vehicle at the time when it was put in the place from which it was removed unless he can show that he was not concerned in and did not know it was placed there; or any person who put it in that place, or any person convicted of an offence under s.2(1) of the 1978 Act: s.5(4).
[6] Refuse (Disposal) Amenity Act 1978, s.2.
[7] *ibid.*, s.6(1).
[7A] Section 99 came into force on April 6, 2006 (SI 2006/795).
[8] *ibid.*, s.6.
[9] Refuse (Disposal) Amenity Act 1978, s.4A.

ground that the authority was not justified in concluding that action should be taken or that the proposed action is unreasonable.[10]

Vehicles

Many complaints relating to vehicles concern abandonment, illegal parking and repairs being carried out on the road. To a large extent, the first two problems were dealt with in the Refuse (Disposal) Amenity Act 1978 (abandonment) and the Road Traffic Regulation Act 1984 (illegal parking). In addition to giving local authorities power to offer fixed penalty notices in discharge of liability for such offences, the Clean Neighbourhoods and Environment Act 2005 also creates two new offences for exposing and repairing cars on roads.

4-168

Abandoned motor vehicles

Around 238,000 cars were abandoned in the year 2000 and it is considered to be a significant drain on local authorities and the police.[11] Under the Refuse (Disposal) Amenity Act 1978, where it appears to a local authority that a motor vehicle in its area is abandoned without lawful authority on any land in the open air or on any other land forming part of the highway, the authority[12] must remove it. If the land is occupied by a person, the authority must give him notice that they propose to remove the vehicle.[13] They may dispose of any vehicle in their custody as they think fit and seek the costs and charges of collecting and disposing of the vehicle from the person responsible.[14] The vehicles may be disposed of by the authority as they see fit. Any person who, without lawful authority, abandons on any land in the open air or on any other land forming part of a highway a motor vehicle, or anything which formed part of the motor vehicle, or abandons on any such land any other thing other than a motor vehicle being a thing brought onto the land with the intention of abandoning it, is guilty of an offence and liable on summary conviction to a fine.[15] Furthermore, the authority may, if it thinks fit, remove any property other than a motor vehicle which is abandoned without lawful authority on any land in the open air or land forming part of a highway.[16] The authority must first give notice to the person occupying the land and that person must have failed to object to its removal. The authority may seek the costs and expenses of removing and disposing of such property from the person who left it there or a person convicted of an offence under s.2(1) of the 1978 Act.[17]

4-169

The Clean Neighbourhoods and Environment Act 2005 amends s.3 of the 1978 Act, disapplying subs.(2) where the vehicle is abandoned on a road (within the meaning of the Road Traffic Regulation Act 1984).

4-170

Section 10 of the Clean Neighbourhoods and Environment Act 2005 inserts a new s.2A to the 1978 Act providing that, where on any occasion it appears to an authorised officer of a local authority that a person has committed an offence under s.2(1)(a) in the area of that authority, the officer may give that person a notice offering him the opportunity of discharging any liability to conviction for the offence by payment of a fixed penalty to the authority. The provisions are

4-171

---

[10] Local authority has the meaning given by The Road Traffic Regulation Act 1984, s.101(5) and (6).
[11] The Road Traffic Regulation Act 1984, ss.99–102.
[12] Clean Neighbourhoods and Environmental Act 2005, ss.15–17 amends 1984, ss.99, 101 and 103. These sections came into force on October 18, 2005 (SI 2005/2896).
[13] The Road Traffic Regulation Act 1984, s.103(4).
[14] "Motor vehicle" has the same meaning as in the Refuse Disposal (Amenity) Act 1978, s.3(4).
[15] "Road" has the same meaning as in the Road Traffic Regulation Act 1984, s.3(4).
[16] The Clean Neighbourhoods and Environment Act 2005, s.3(1) (not yet in force).
[17] *ibid.*, s.3(2).

similar to that found in the Environment Protection Act 1990, as amended by the 2005 Act. The fixed penalty payable to a local authority is, subject to order by the Secretary of State, £200. Section 2B creates two offences for the failure to give a name and address when requested to do so or giving an inaccurate name and address. New section 2C makes provision for the use of fixed penalty receipts by the local authority. Any authority on whom functions are conferred under ss.3 or 4 above must, in exercising those functions, have regard to any guidance given to the authority for the purpose by the appropriate person.[18]

Illegally Parked Vehicles

4-172   The Road Traffic Regulation Act 1984 gives power to a local authority[19] to remove illegally parked vehicles.[20] The 2005 Act makes some amendments to the disposal and removal of such vehicles.[21] Furthermore, a local authority must have regard to any guidance given to the authority by the Secretary of State.[22]

Exposing Vehicles for Sale on a Road

4-173   If, at any time, a person leaves two or more motor vehicles[23] parked within 500 metres of each other on a road or roads[24] where they are exposed or advertised for sale, or he causes two or more motor vehicles to be so left, he is guilty of an offence.[25] It is a defence if he proves to the satisfaction of the court that he was not acting for the purposes of a business of selling motor vehicles.[26] A person guilty of the offence is liable on summary conviction to a fine not exceeding level 4 on the standard scale.[27]

Body Corporate

4-174   Where an offence is committed by a body corporate and is proved to have been committed with the consent or connivance of or to have been attributable to any neglect on the part of any director, manager, secretary or other similar officer of the body corporate, or a person who was purporting to act in any such capacity, he, as well as the body corporate, is guilty of the offence and liable to be proceeded against and punished accordingly.[28]

Fixed Penalty Notices

4-175   Where, on any occasion, an authorised officer of a local authority[29] has reason to believe that a person has committed an offence under s.3 in the area of that authority, the officer may give that person a notice offering him the opportunity of discharging any liability to conviction by payment of a fixed penalty to the local authority. The fixed penalty payable to a local authority under this

---

[18] *ibid.*, s.3(3).
[19] *ibid.*, s.5.
[20] "Local authority" means a district council, London borough or Common Council of the City of London, the Council of the Isles of Scilly and, in Wales, a county council or county borough council: The Clean Neighbourhoods and Environment Act 2005, s.9.
[21] The Clean Neighbourhoods and Environment Act 2005, s.4(1).
[22] *ibid.*, s.4(2).
[23] *ibid.*, s.4(6).
[24] *ibid.*, s.4(3) and (4).
[25] *ibid.*, s.4(5).
[26] *ibid.*, ss.5–9.
[27] District councils, London boroughs and the Common Council of the City of London, the Council of the Isles of Scilly and, in Wales, a county or county borough: Environmental Protection Act 1990, s.95.
[28] Environmental Protection Act 1990, Sch.4.
[29] *ibid.*, Sch.4, para.2(2).

section is, subject to order of the Secretary of State, £100. Under s.7, the local authority has power to require a person's name and address and it is an offence to give a false or inaccurate name and address punishable on summary conviction to a fine not exceeding level 2 on the standard scale. Section 8 provides for the use of fixed penalty receipts by the local authority.

Repairing Vehicles on a Road

A person who carries out restricted works on a motor vehicle on a road is **4-176** guilty of an offence.[30] Restricted works are defined as: "works for the repair, maintenance, servicing, improvement or dismantling of a motor vehicle or of any part of or accessory to a motor vehicle works for the installation, replacement or renewal of any such part or accessory."[31] A person guilty of an offence under this section is liable on summary conviction to a fine not exceeding level 4 on the standard scale.[32]

Defences
Save where the carrying out of the works gave reasonable cause for annoyance **4-177** to persons in the vicinity, it is a defence if the works were not carried out in the course of, or for the purposes of, a business of carrying out restricted works or for gain or reward.[33] Furthermore, a person is not to be convicted of an offence if he proves to the satisfaction of the court that the works carried out were works of repair which arose from an accident or breakdown in circumstances where repairs on the spot, or elsewhere on the road were necessary and were carried out within 72 hours of the accident or breakdown or were within that period authorised to be carried out at a later time by the local authority for the area.[34]

Bodies corporate and fixed penalty notices
The provisions are the same as for the offence of exposing vehicles for sale on **4-178** a road.[35]

Hedge Disputes

Part 9 of the Anti-Social Behaviour Act 2003 was introduced into the Act at **4-179** a very late stage. In a press release in October 2003, Yvette Cooper, Minister for Regeneration at the Office of the Deputy Prime Minister, said that high hedges can block out the light from neighbours' homes and gardens and make their lives a misery:

> "This is anti-social behaviour, just as much as graffiti and noisy neighbours, and it isn't fair on those who have to suffer as a result. That is why we want to take action through the Anti-Social Behaviour Bill so that local authorities will have the power to sort out high hedge disputes and where necessary to chop those hedges back."

Without intending to demean the very real problems experienced by persons who suffer real distress as result of a hedge disputes, it is unclear to us how hedge disputes problems are so pressing an instance of anti-social behaviour

[30] *ibid.*, Sch.4, para.3.
[31] *ibid.*, Sch.4, para.3(2).
[32] *ibid.*, Sch.4, para.3(4).
[33] Council of a borough or urban district, the Common Council, the Inns, the Council of the Isles of Scilly.
[34] The Public Health Act 1961, s.34.
[35] *ibid.*, s.34(3).

that they required a complete exhaustive code and some 18 sections of the 2003 Act. There is no mention of hedge disputes in the White Paper as an instance of anti-social behaviour. Nor does the subject appear in any other government document in this area.[36] It is difficult to see the reason why the law, such as it once stood, relating to hedge disputes was so different to any kind of neighbour dispute that it demanded administrative resolutions, in contrast to other kinds of neighbour disputes which must still make do with courts. Hedge disputes may be bitter and hard-fought disputes; but then so can many other kinds of legal battles between neighbours. We are unable to find a reported case on the subject that is more recent than the 1970s and so it is difficult to see what it is about hedge disputes that they require law reform, particularly of such a dense and complex nature.

The complaint system

4-180   The process, under s.65 of the 2003 Act, starts with a complaint made by an owner or occupier of a domestic property[37] to the local authority that the reasonable enjoyment of his property is being adversely affected by the height of a high hedge situated on land owned or occupied by another person. A complaint may also be made by an owner of a domestic property that is for the time being unoccupied, if he alleges that the reasonable enjoyment of that property by a prospective occupier of that property would be adversely affected by the height of a high hedge. The term high hedge is defined in s.66(1): it means a hedge that causes so much of a barrier to light or access as is formed wholly or predominantly by a line of two or more evergreens and rises to a height of more than two metres above ground level.

4-181   Section 68 contains a distinct procedure for dealing with complaints about such hedges. Once the complainant[38] has made a complaint to the relevant authority[39] and paid any such fee as the authority may determine, the authority shall consider it. They cannot, under subs.(2), proceed with it if they conclude that: (a) the complainant has not taken all reasonable steps to resolve the matters complained of without proceeding by way of such a complaint to the authority; or (b) that the complaint is frivolous or vexatious. Otherwise, if they do proceed, the issues that they must consider are set out at subs.(3), namely (a) whether the height of the high hedge specified in the complaint is adversely affecting the complainant's reasonable enjoyment[40] of the domestic property

---

[36] In 2002 a review of the legislative framework for providing and maintaining a clean and safe local environment was carried out by Defra to accompany the cross-Government report *Living Places—Cleaner, Safer, Greener*. That report makes no mention of hedge disputes. Nor is it mentioned in the consultation paper *Living Places—Powers, Rights, Responsibilities* launched at the Urban Summit on October 31, 2002.

[37] Anti-Social Behaviour Act 2003, s.67. (1) In this Part "domestic property" means: (a) a dwelling; or (b) a garden or yard which is used and enjoyed wholly or mainly in connection with a dwelling; (2) In subs.(1) "dwelling" means any building or part of a building occupied, or intended to be occupied, as a separate dwelling.

[38] Anti-Social Behaviour Act 2003, s.64(5): "Complainant" means (a) a person by whom the complaint is made; or (b) if every person who made the complaint ceases to be an owner or occupier of the domestic property specified in the complaint, any other person who is for the time being an owner or occupier of that property; and references to the complainant include references to one or more of the complainants.

[39] Anti-Social Behaviour Act 2003, s.64(5) "the relevant authority" means the local authority in whose area that land is situated. Under s.89, "local authority", in relation to England, means (a) a district council; (b) a county council for a county in which there are no districts; (c) a London borough council; or (d) the Common Council of the City of London; and, in relation to Wales, means a county council or a county borough council.

[40] Anti-Social Behaviour Act 2003, s.65(3). In relation to a complaint falling within subs.(2), references in ss.65 and 66 to the effect of the height of a high hedge on the complainant's reason-

so specified; and (b) if so, what action (if any) should be taken in relation to that hedge, in pursuance of a remedial notice under s.69, with a view to remedying the adverse effect or preventing its recurrence. If the authority decide that action should be taken, they must, as soon as is reasonably practicable, issue a remedial notice under s.69 implementing their decision; send a copy of that notice to the certain persons (that is, every complainant; and every owner and every occupier of the neighbouring land)[41]; and notify each of those persons of the reasons for their decision. If the authority: decide that the complaint should not be proceeded with; or decide either or both of the issues specified in subs.(3) otherwise than in the complainant's favour, then, under subs.(5), they must, as soon as is reasonably practicable, notify the appropriate person[42] or persons of any such decision and of their reasons for it.

Remedial Notices

Section 69 deals with remedial notices. A remedial notice is a notice issued by the relevant authority in respect of a complaint and stating the matters mentioned in subs.(2). Those matters are as follows: **4-182**

(1) that a complaint has been made to the authority under this Part about a high hedge specified in the notice which is situated on land so specified;

(2) that the authority have decided that the height of that hedge is adversely affecting the complainant's reasonable enjoyment of the domestic property specified in the notice;

(3) the initial action[43] that must be taken in relation to that hedge before the end of the compliance period[44];

(4) any preventative action that they consider must be taken in relation to that hedge at times following the end of that period while the hedge remains on the land; and

(5) the consequences of a failure to comply with the notice.

The action specified in a remedial notice cannot require a reduction in the height of the hedge to less than two metres above ground level or the removal of the hedge.[45]

The notice is to take effect on "the operative date" which is the date (falling at least 28 days after that on which the notice is issued) as is specified in the notice as the date on which it is to take effect.[46] While the remedial notice has **4-183**

---

able enjoyment of a domestic property shall be read as references to the effect that it would have on the reasonable enjoyment of that property by a prospective occupier of the property.
[41] Anti-Social Behaviour Act 2003, s.65(5):"the neighbouring land" means the land on which the high hedge is situated.
[42] Anti-Social Behaviour Act 2003, s.67(6). For the purposes of subs.(5) (a) every complainant is an appropriate person in relation to a decision falling within para.(a) or (b) of that subsection; and (b) every owner and every occupier of the neighbouring land is an appropriate person in relation to a decision falling within para.(b) of that subsection.
[43] Anti-Social Behaviour Act 2003, s.69(9): "initial action" means remedial action or preventative action, or both; "remedial action" means action to remedy the adverse effect of the height of the hedge on the complainant's reasonable enjoyment of the domestic property in respect of which the complaint was made; and "preventative action" means action to prevent the recurrence of the adverse effect.
[44] s.69(6) provides that "the compliance period" in the case of a remedial notice is such reasonable period as is specified in the notice for the purposes of subs.(2)(c) as the period within which the action so specified is to be taken; and that period shall begin with the operative date of the notice.
[45] Anti-Social Behaviour Act 2003, s.69(3).
[46] *ibid.*, s.69(4), (5).

effect, it shall be a local land charge and shall be binding on every person who is for the time being an owner or occupier of the land specified in the notice as the land where the hedge in question is situated.[47]

4-184   Section 70 provides for the withdrawal or relaxation of requirements of remedial notices. Under subs.(1), the relevant authority may: (a) withdraw a remedial notice issued by them; or (b) waive or relax a requirement of a remedial notice so issued. The powers conferred by this section are exercisable both before and after a remedial notice has taken effect.[48] Where the relevant authority exercises the powers conferred by this section, they must give notice of what they have done to every complainant, owner and occupier of the neighbouring land.[49] The withdrawal of a remedial notice does not affect the power of the relevant authority to issue a further remedial notice in respect of the same hedge.

Appeals

4-185   Sections 71 to 73 provide for appeals. Those sections need to be read with the High Hedges (Appeals) (England) Regulations 2005 which came into force on June 1, 2005. Under s.71(1) where the relevant authority issues a remedial notice, withdraws such a notice, or waives or relaxes the requirements of such a notice, specified persons may appeal to the appeal authority against that decision.[50] Those specified persons are, every person who is a complainant in relation to the complaint by reference to which the notice was given, and every person who is an owner or occupier of the neighbouring land.[51] Where the relevant authority decides either or both of the issues specified in s.68(3)[52] otherwise than in the complainant's favour, the complainant may appeal to the appeal authority against the decision.[53] Where an appeal is duly made under s.71(1), the notice or (as the case may be) the withdrawal, waiver or relaxation in question shall not have effect pending the final determination or withdrawal of the appeal.[54]

Appeal authority

4-186   The appeal authority is defined in subs.(7). They are: (a) in relation to appeals relating to hedges situated in England, the Secretary of State; and (b) in relation to appeals relating to hedges situated in Wales, the National Assembly for Wales.

4-187   Under s.72(3), where an appeal is made to the Secretary of State under s.71, he may appoint a person to hear and determine the appeal on its behalf. The appeal authority may require such a person to exercise on its behalf any functions which: (a) are conferred on the appeal authority in connection with such an appeal by ss.71 or 73 or by regulations under this section; and (b) are specified in that person's appointment; and references to the appeal authority in ss.71 or 73 in any regulations under this section shall be construed accordingly. Regulations under this section may provide for any provision of Sch.20 to the Environment Act 1995 (delegation of appellate functions) to apply in relation to a person appointed under subs.(3) with such modifications (if any) as may

---

[47] Anti-Social Behaviour Act 2005, s.69(8).
[48] *ibid.*, s.70(3).
[49] *ibid.*, s.70(4).
[50] *ibid.*, s.71(1).
[51] *ibid.*, s.71(2).
[52] Namely, (a) whether the height of the high hedge specified in the complaint is adversely affecting the complainant's reasonable enjoyment[39] of the domestic property so specified; and (b) if so, what action (if any) should be taken in relation to that hedge, in pursuance of a remedial notice under section 69, with a view to remedying the adverse effect or preventing its recurrence.
[53] Anti-Social Behaviour Act 2003, s.71(3).
[54] *ibid.*, s.71(6).

be prescribed. Regulation 6 of the High Hedges (Appeals) (England) Regulations 2005 provides: "Paragraph 2(c) of Schedule 20 to the Environment Act 1995 (revocation of appointments) shall apply in relation to appointments under section 72(3) of the Act as it applies in relation to appointments under section 114 of the Environment Act 1995."

Grounds of Appeal

The grounds depend on the decision being appealed. In respect of an appeal against the issue of a remedial notice, the appeal may be made on any of the following grounds— **4-188**

   (1) that the height of the high hedge specified in the remedial notice is not adversely affecting the complainant's reasonable enjoyment of the domestic property so specified;

   (2) that the remedial action or preventative action, or both (as the case may be) specified in the remedial notice is insufficient to remedy the adverse effect of the high hedge on the complainant's reasonable enjoyment of the domestic property so specified or to prevent its recurrence;

   (3) that the remedial action or preventative action, or both (as the case may be) specified in the remedial notice exceeds what is necessary or appropriate to remedy the adverse effect of the high hedge or to prevent its recurrence;

   (4) that the period specified in the remedial notice for taking the initial action so specified falls short of what should reasonably be allowed.[55]

Where a remedial notice is withdrawn without the agreement of the complainant, and the relevant authority have not issued a further remedial notice in respect of the same high hedge, an appeal against the withdrawal of the notice may be made on the ground that there has been no material change in circumstances since the remedial notice was issued that justifies withdrawal of the notice. **4-189**

Where the relevant authority has waived or relaxed the requirements of a remedial notice, without the agreement of the complainant or the owner or occupier of the land where the high hedge is situated (as the case may be), an appeal against the waiver or relaxation may be made on any of the following grounds: **4-190**

   (1) that there has been no material change in circumstances since the notice was issued that justifies the waiver or relaxation of its requirements;

   (2) that the requirements of the remedial notice, as waived or relaxed, are insufficient to remedy the adverse effect of the high hedge on the complainant's reasonable enjoyment of the domestic property specified in the notice or to prevent its recurrence;

   (3) that the requirements of the remedial notice, as waived or relaxed, exceed what is necessary or appropriate to remedy the adverse effect of the high hedge or to prevent its recurrence.[56]

An appeal against a decision of the relevant authority, otherwise than in the complainant's favour, may be made on either of the following grounds: **4-191**

   (1) that the relevant authority could not reasonably conclude that the height of the high hedge specified in the complaint is not adversely

[55] High Hedges (Appeals) (England) Regulations 2005, Reg.3.
[56] *ibid.*, Reg.4.

affecting the complainant's reasonable enjoyment of the domestic property so specified;

(2) that, having concluded that the height of the high hedge specified in the complaint is adversely affecting the complainant's reasonable enjoyment of the domestic property so specified, the authority could not reasonably conclude that no action should be taken with a view to remedying that adverse effect or preventing its recurrence.[57]

Procedure

4-192   Under s.71(4), an appeal under this section must be made before the end of the period of 28 days, beginning with the relevant date or such later time as the appeal authority may allow. Subsection (5) defines the relevant date; in the case of an appeal against the issue of a remedial notice, it is the date on which the notice was issued; and in the case of any other appeal under this section, means the date of the notification given by the relevant authority under ss.68 or 70 of the decision in question.

4-193   Section 72(1) provides that the Secretary of State may by regulations make provision with respect to the procedure which is to be followed in connection with appeals to that authority under s.71 and other matters consequential on or connected with such appeals. Regulations under this section may, in particular, make provision:

(1) specifying the grounds on which appeals may be made;

(2) prescribing the manner in which appeals are to be made;

(3) requiring persons making appeals to send copies of such documents as may be prescribed to such persons as may be prescribed;

(4) requiring local authorities against whose decisions appeals are made to send to the appeal authority such documents as may be prescribed;

(5) specifying, where a local authority are required by virtue of para (d) to send the appeal authority a statement indicating the submissions which they propose to put forward on the appeal, the matters to be included in such a statement;

(6) prescribing the period within which a requirement imposed by the regulations is to be complied with;

(7) enabling such a period to be extended by the appeal authority;

(8) for a decision on an appeal to be binding on persons falling within s.71(2) in addition to the person by whom the appeal was made;

(9) for incidental or ancillary matters, including the awarding of costs.

4-194   Regulations 7 to 13 make a number of provisions concerning:

(1) the appeal form and a copy of any supporting documents which needs to be sent to the Secretary of State and the relevant authority;

(2) informing the Secretary of State and the appellant of the name and address of every person, other than the appellant, who is a complainant or an owner or occupier of the land where the high hedge is situated by the relevant authority forthwith;

(3) completion of a questionnaire by the relevant authority;

---

[57] High Hedges (Appeals) (England) Regulations 2005, Reg.5.

(4) request of further information by the Secretary of State; and

(5) notification to all parties of the reason for his decision.

Decision on Appeal

Under s.71 the appeal authority may allow or dismiss the appeal, either in **4-195** whole or in part. Where the appeal authority decides to allow such an appeal to any extent, it may do such of the following as it considers appropriate: (a) quash a remedial notice or decision to which the appeal relates; (b) vary the requirements of such a notice; or (c) in a case where no remedial notice has been issued, issue on behalf of the relevant authority a remedial notice that could have been issued by the relevant authority on the complaint in question. On an appeal under s.71 relating to a remedial notice, the appeal authority may also correct any defect, error or misdescription in the notice, if it is satisfied that the correction will not cause injustice to any person falling within s.71(2). Once the appeal authority has made its decision on an appeal under s.71 it must, as soon as is reasonably practicable, give a notification of the decision, and if the decision is to issue a remedial notice or to vary or correct the requirements of such a notice, send copies of the notice as issued, varied or corrected, to every person falling within s.71(2) and to the relevant authority. Where, in consequence of the appeal authority's decision on an appeal, a remedial notice is upheld or varied or corrected, the operative date of the notice shall be: (a) the date of the appeal authority's decision; or (b) such later date as may be specified in its decision. Where the person making an appeal under s.71 against a remedial notice withdraws his appeal, the operative date of the notice shall be the date on which the appeal is withdrawn. In any case falling within subss.(5) or (6), the compliance period for the notice shall accordingly run from the date which is its operative date by virtue of that subsection (and any period which may have started to run from a date preceding that on which the appeal was made shall accordingly be disregarded). Regulation 14 provides that decision of the Secretary of State or the appointed person (as the case may be) shall be binding on the appellant and every other person who is a complainant or an owner or occupier of the land where the high hedge is situated.

Powers of Entry

Section 74 provides the relevant authority with substantial powers of entry for **4-196** the purposes of complaints and appeals. Where, under this Part, a complaint has been made or a remedial notice has been issued, a person authorised by the relevant authority may enter the neighbouring land in order to obtain information required by the relevant authority for the purpose of determining whether this Part applies to the complaint; whether to issue or withdraw a remedial notice; whether to waive or relax a requirement of a remedial notice; and/or whether a requirement of a remedial notice has been complied with. Where an appeal has been made under s.71 a person authorised: (a) by the appeal authority, or (b) by a person appointed to determine appeals on its behalf, may enter the neighbouring land in order to obtain information required by the appeal authority, or by the person so appointed, for the purpose of determining an appeal under this Part. A person shall not enter land in the exercise of a power conferred by this section unless at least 24 hours' notice of the intended entry has been given to every occupier of the land. A person authorised under this section to enter land shall, if so required, produce evidence of his authority before entering and shall produce such evidence if required to do so at any time while he remains on the land. He may take with him such other persons as may be necessary, as well as equipment and materials needed in order to obtain the information required, and may take samples of any trees or shrubs that appear to him to form part of a high hedge. If, in the exercise of a power conferred by this section, a person enters land which is unoccupied or from which all of the persons occupying the land are temporarily absent, he must on his departure leave it as effectively secured against unauthorised entry as he found it. Subsection (7) provides that a person who intentionally obstructs a person acting in the exercise of the powers under this section is guilty of an offence and shall be liable, on summary conviction, to a fine not exceeding level 3 on the standard scale.

Offences

4-197   Under s.75, where: (a) a remedial notice requires the taking of any action, and (b) that action is not taken in accordance with that notice within the compliance period or (as the case may be) by the subsequent time by which it is required to be taken, every person who, at a relevant time, is an owner or occupier of the neighbouring land is guilty of an offence and shall be liable, on summary conviction, to a fine not exceeding level 3 on the standard scale. "Relevant time" means as follows: in relation to action required to be taken before the end of the compliance period, a time after the end of that period and before the action is taken; and in relation to any preventative action which is required to be taken after the end of that period, a time after that at which the action is required to be taken but before it is taken. In proceedings against a person for an offence under subs.(1) it shall be a defence for him to show that he did everything he could be expected to do to secure compliance with the notice. In any such proceedings against a person, it shall also be a defence for him to show, in a case in which he is not a person to whom a copy of the remedial notice was sent in accordance with a provision of this Part, and he is not a person assumed to have had knowledge, of the notice at the time of the alleged offence, that he was not aware of the existence of the notice at that time. Subsection (5) provides that a person shall be assumed to have had knowledge of a remedial notice at any time if at that time he was an owner of the neighbouring land; and the notice was at that time registered as a local land charge. Under subs.(7), where a person is convicted of an offence under subs.(1) and it appears to the court: (a) that a failure to comply with the remedial notice is continuing, and (b) that it is within that person's power to secure compliance with the notice, the court may, in addition to, or instead of, imposing a punishment, order him to take the steps specified in the order for securing compliance with the notice. An order under subs.(7) must require those steps to be taken within such reasonable period as may be fixed by the order. Under subs.(9), where a person fails without reasonable excuse to comply with an order under subs.(7) he is guilty of an offence and shall be liable, on summary conviction, to a fine not exceeding level 3 on the standard scale. Further, under subs.(10), where a person continues after conviction of an offence under subs.(9) (or of an offence under this subsection) to fail, without reasonable excuse, to take steps which he has been ordered to take under subs.(7), he is guilty of a further offence and shall be liable, on summary conviction, to a fine not exceeding one-twentieth of that level for each day on which the failure has so continued.

Remedial Action

4-198   Section 76 provides for a power to require an occupier to permit action to be taken by owner. Specifically, under subs.(1), s.289 of the Public Health Act 1936 (power of court to require occupier to permit work to be done by owner) shall apply with any necessary modifications for the purpose of giving an owner of land to which a remedial notice relates the right, as against all other persons interested in the land, to comply with the notice. Where a remedial notice requires the taking of any action, and that action is not taken in accordance with that notice within the compliance period, or (as the case may be) after the end of that period when it is required to be taken by the notice, then under s.76: (a) a person authorised by the relevant authority may enter the neighbouring land and take the required action; and (b) the relevant authority may recover any expenses reasonably incurred by that person in doing so from any person who is an owner or occupier of the land. Subsection (3) provides for the recovery of expenses as a local land charge and binding on successive owners of the land and on successive occupiers of it. Where expenses are recoverable under this section from two or more persons, those persons shall be jointly and severally liable for the expenses.

Section 74(5) provides that a person shall not enter land in the exercise of a **4-199** power conferred by this section, unless at least seven days' notice of the intended entry has been given to every occupier of the land. A person authorised under this section to enter land shall, if so required, produce evidence of his authority before entering; and shall produce such evidence if required to do so at any time while he remains on the land.[58] A person who enters land in the exercise of a power conferred by this section may use a vehicle to enter the land, take with him such other persons as may be necessary, and take with him equipment and materials needed for the purpose of taking the required action. If, in the exercise of a power conferred by this section, a person enters land which is unoccupied, or from which all of the persons occupying the land are temporarily absent, he must on his departure leave it as effectively secured against unauthorised entry as he found it. A person who wilfully obstructs a person acting in the exercise of powers under this section to enter land and take action on that land is guilty of an offence and shall be liable, on summary conviction, to a fine not exceeding level 3 on the standard scale.[59]

Offences by Bodies Corporate

Section 78 deals with offences committed by bodies corporate. If the offence **4-200** is proved to have been committed with the consent or connivance of, or to be attributable to any neglect on the part of: (a) a director, manager, secretary or other similar officer of the body corporate, or (b) any person who was purporting to act in any such capacity, he, as well as the body corporate, shall be guilty of that offence and be liable to be proceeded against and punished accordingly. Where the affairs of a body corporate are managed by its members, subs.(1) applies in relation to the acts and defaults of a member in connection with his functions of management as if he were a director of the body corporate.

Licensing

Reforms to the Licensing System

Reforms to the licensing system were necessary to deal with what the govern- **4-201** ment in the White Paper described as the "yob culture", which revolved around excessive drinking and associated anti-social behaviour and crime.[60]

[58] Anti-Social Behaviour Act 2003, s.84(6).
[59] *ibid.*, s.84(9).
[60] *Time for Reform: Proposals for the Modernisation of Our Licensing Laws*, Cm.4696, p.45. See Institute of Alcohol Studies occasional paper, *Crime and Disorder, Binge Drinking and the Licensing Act 2003*, January 2005.

To an extent this has been achieved through the Licensing Act 2003 which created, for the first time, an integrated licensing system covering the sale of alcohol, the provision of public entertainment and late night refreshments, and performances at theatres and cinemas.[61] One of the fundamental changes to the system has been the transfer of the functions for liquor licensing from the magistrates' and licensing justices to the licensing authority.[62]

4-202   Importantly, the licensing authority must carry out those functions with a view to promoting the following four licensing objectives:

(1) the prevention of crime and disorder;

(2) public safety;

(3) the prevention of public nuisance; and

(4) the protection of children from harm.[63]

4-203   In addition, regard must be had to its licensing policy, a statement of which must be published under s.5. The policy must be devised to deal with issues relevant to its area and involves consultation with other bodies or persons. As part of that policy and, in determining applications for a licence, the government guidance also advises that authorities should be concerned with the cumulative impact of licensed premises on the promotion of licensing objectives; for instance, where applicable, the problems of nuisance and disorder that can arise where there is a concentration of licensed premises. It is made clear, however, that licensing should not be used as the sole means of controlling anti-social behaviour, but as a complement to other powers, such as anti-social behaviour orders, CCTV, and closure powers. Furthermore, applicants for licences will be expected to seek advice from police authorities and take into account other relevant policies (planning, crime prevention strategies, etc.) when proposing operating schedules for licensed premises.

Offences

4-204   Part 7 of the 2003 Act creates the following offences:

(1) carrying on unauthorised licensable activities (s.136);

(2) exposing alcohol for unauthorised sale (s.137);

(3) keeping alcohol on premises for unauthorised sale (s.138);

(4) knowingly allows disorderly conduct on licensed premises (s.140);

(5) knowingly selling or attempting to sell alcohol to a person who is drunk (s.141);

(6) knowingly obtaining or attempting to obtain alcohol for a person who is drunk (s.142);

(7) failing to leave premises when drunk and requested to do so or entering or attempting to enter premises when drunk and has been requested not to do so (s.143);

---

[61] Licensing Act 2003, ss.1 and 2.

[62] "Licensing authority" means the council of a district in England, the council of a county in England in which there are no district councils, the council of a county or county borough in Wales, the council of a London Borough, the Common Council of the City of London, the Sub-Treasurer of the Inner Temple, the Under-treasurer of the Middle Temple, or the Council of the Isles of Scilly.

[63] Licensing Act 2003, s.4.

(8) knowingly keeping smuggled goods (s.144);

(9) selling alcohol on moving vehicles (s.156);

(10) knowingly selling alcohol in breach of an order prohibiting sales of alcohol on trains (s.157);

(11) knowingly or recklessly making false statements (s.158).

Section 139 provides a defence to the offences cited at paras (1), (2), (3) and **4-205** (9) above if his act was due to:

(1) a mistake; or

(2) to reliance on information given to him; or

(3) to an act or omission by another person; or

(4) to some other cause beyond his control,

and in all those cases, he took all reasonable precautions and exercised all due diligence to avoid committing the offence.

There is a defence of lack of knowledge (offences cited at paras (4), (5), (6), (8) and (11) above) and reasonable excuse (para.(7) above).

A person found guilty of any of the offences described at paras (1) and (2) **4-206** above is liable to a maximum of six months' imprisonment and/or a maximum fine of £20,000. In relation to the offence at para.(3), the penalty is a fine not exceeding level 2 of the standard scale; at paras (4), (5), (6), (8), a fine not exceeding level 3 of the standard scale; at para. (7), a fine not exceeding level 1 of the standard scale; and at para. (11), a fine not exceeding level 5 of the standard scale. Offences relating to the sale of alcohol on vehicles (paras (9) and (10)), attract a penalty of a maximum of three months' imprisonment and/ or a maximum fine of £20,000.

Closure of premises

Orders to close premises in area experiencing disorder
Section 160 of the Licensing Act 2003 gives the magistrates' court power to **4-207** make an order requiring all premises (in respect of which a premises licence or a temporary event notice has effect) situated at or near the place of disorder, or expected disorder, to be closed for a period of 24 hours. The power is only available on the application of a police officer who is of the rank of superintendent or above where there is, or is expected to be, disorder in any petty sessions area.

Closure order of identified premises
Under s.161, a senior police officer may make a closure order in relation to any **4-208** relevant premises if he reasonably believes that there is, or is likely imminently to be, disorder on, or in the vicinity of and related to, the premises and their closure is necessary in the interests of public safety. In addition, he may make such an order where he reasonably believes that a public nuisance is being caused by noise coming from the premises and the closure of the premises is necessary to prevent that nuisance. In determining whether to make a closure order in respect of any premises, the senior police officer must have regard, in particular, to the conduct of each appropriate person in relation to the disorder or nuisance. The order may be extended by a senior police officer for a further 24 hours under s.162, either because closure is necessary in the interests of public safety because of disorder or likely disorder on, or in the vicinity of and related to, the premises; or to ensure that no public nuisance is,

or is likely to be, caused by noise coming from the premises. Under s.163, a senior police officer may cancel a closure order or any extension of it if he does not consider that the closure order is necessary for those reasons. He may do so after the making of the order, but before a magistrates' court has determined the application under s.165.

4-209   As soon as the closure order comes into force, the responsible officer must, under s.164, make an application to the magistrates' court for it to consider the order and any extension of it and notify the relevant licensing authority. Section 165 makes provision for the matters to be considered by the magistrates' court in determining such an application, namely, closure is necessary in the interests of public safety because of disorder or likely disorder on, or in the vicinity of and related to, the premises, or to ensure that no public nuisance is, or is likely to be, caused by noise coming from the premises. The magistrates' court has power to make the following orders set out at subs.(2):

(1) revoke the closure order and any extension of it;

(2) order the premises to remain or to be closed until such time as the relevant licensing authority has made a determination on review of premises licence following the making of a closure order under s.167;

(3) order the premises to remain or to be closed until that time subject to such exceptions as may be specified in the order; or

(4) order the premises to remain or to be closed until that time unless such conditions as may be specified in the order are satisfied.

4-210   Any person aggrieved by a decision of a magistrates' court under s.165 may appeal to the Crown Court within 21 days of the making of the decision.

Offences
4-211   A person commits an offence under ss.160, 161 and 167 if he allows premises to open, without reasonable excuse, in breach of a closure order or any extension of it.

Review of decision following closure order
4-212   Section 167 imposes a duty on the licensing authority to carry out a review of the premises licence on the coming into force of a closure order and on receipt of the determination of any order made by the magistrates' court. It would appear that this includes an order revoking the closure order. The licensing authority must hold a hearing to determine the review. The Licensing Act 2003 (Hearings) Regulations 2005 (SI 2005/44) and the Licensing Act 2003 (Premises Licences and Club Premises Certificates) Regulations 2005 (SI 2005/42) make provision for notification to the parties and advertisement of the review. In determining the review, the licensing authority must take such steps as set out in subs.(7) as it considers necessary for the promotion of the licensing objectives, namely:

(1) to modify the conditions of the premises licence;

(2) to exclude a licensable activity from the scope of the licence;

(3) to remove the designated premises supervisor from the licence;

(4) to suspend the licence for a period not exceeding three months; or

(5) to revoke the licence.

Public Drunkenness

Successive licensing laws have, to an extent, attempted to curb the public nui-   **4-213**
sances associated with public drunkenness, although the full effect of the more
relaxed licensing laws is yet to be seen. Historically, however, public drunkenness has largely been a matter left to the discretion of the police. In this section
we are concerned with offences concerned with public drunkenness some of
which have been discussed at paras 2-26, 2-31, 2-38 and 2-66.

Any person who is in any public place while drunk and disorderly is guilty   **4-214**
of an offence.[64] It is limited to cases involving alcohol and not, for example,
glue-sniffing.[65] "Public place" means any highway and any other premises or
place at which at the material time the public have or are permitted to have
access, whether on payment or otherwise.[66] Such a person may be arrested
without a warrant.[67]

A person found drunk in any highway or other public place, whether a   **4-215**
building or not, or on any licensed premises commits an offence under s.12 of
the Licensing Act 1872. It is irrelevant that the person's presence on the
highway was fleeting. It is also a summary offence for a person, when found
drunk in any such place, to be in charge of a child under the age of seven
years.[68]

Drugs and Crack Houses

Government Strategy

Reforms to drug control laws are an important part of the government's anti-   **4-216**
social behaviour strategy. Drug abuse is considered in the White Paper to be a
major cause of anti-social behaviour or, at the very least, intrinsically associated with it. Areas with the higher rates of acquisitive crime, such as burglary,
are said to be the same areas that have higher drugs misuse problems and one
in three think that drug use or dealing is a very or fairly big problem in their
local area.[69] According to the Government's National Drug Strategy,[70] many
police forces estimate that around half of all recorded crime has some drug
related element to it, whether in terms of individual consumption or supply of
drugs, or the consequent impact of it on criminal behaviour; a small number
of people are responsible for huge numbers of crimes—664 addicts surveyed
committed 70,000 offences over a three month period. A random sample of
suspected offenders arrested by the police suggests that the vast majority of
arrestees have traces of illegal drugs in their urine. Emerging evidence suggests
that effective and targeted treatment for drug misusing offenders can have a
major impact on reducing subsequent offending. The general costs to the
criminal justice system of drug-related crime are, at a very conservative estimate, at least £1 billion every year.

Obvious drug use and dealing may, additionally, increase fear of crime and   **4-217**
render neighbourhoods less attractive. In a Home Office report, *Tackling Drug
Use in Rented Housing*, it was observed that drug use can force residents out of an
area, leaving empty properties prone to being vandalised, squatted or boarded up,
thus creating opportunities for the properties to be used for criminal activities

---

[64] Criminal Justice Act 1967, s.91(1).
[65] *Neale v R.M.J.E. (a minor)* (1985) 80 Cr. App. R. 20.
[66] Criminal Justice Act 1967, s.91(4).
[67] *ibid.*, s.91(1).
[68] 1902, s.2(1).
[69] White Paper, p.16.
[70] *Tackling Drugs to Build a Better Britain*, Cmnd. 3945.

such as drug dealing. As an estate or neighbourhood gains a reputation for drug-related problems, many people become reluctant to take up housing in the area. Void properties may be used to house current or ex-drug users.

4-218   In Chapter Six we also discuss the ways in which the government has sought to tackle anti-social behaviour caused, in part, by drug abuse, in the context of the court's ancillary powers when making anti-social behaviour orders.

Drug Offences

4-219   Under s.5(2) of the Misuse of Drugs Act 1971, it is an offence for any person to have a controlled drug in his possession. Possession means physically in the custody of the defendant and they must know that it was a controlled drug. A controlled drug is any substance or product which is specified in Sch.2 to the 1971 Act. It is also an offence under s.4 of the 1971 Act to produce a controlled drug, or to supply or offer to supply it to another; and, under s.5(3), it is an offence for a person to have a controlled substance in his possession with an intent to supply it to another. Section 6(2) of the 1971 Act makes it an offence to cultivate any plant of the genus cannabis.

4-220   Under s.8, a person commits an offence if, being the occupier or concerned in the management of premises, he knowingly permits or suffers any of the following activities to take place on those premises. These are: producing a controlled drug; supplying or attempting to supply it to another; preparing opium for smoking; or smoking cannabis, cannabis resin or prepared opium. The term "occupier" means simply a person in occupation, whatever his legal status as regards the premises, so long as he has the requisite degree of control over them so as to enable him to exclude people who would take drugs there. "Concerned in the management of premises" means running, organising or planning the use of the premises. In 2000, 584 people were found guilty or cautioned under the 1971 Act for permitting premises to be used for unlawful purposes.[71]

4-221   Section 23 of the 1971 Act contains extensive powers of entry, search and seizure. A constable, or other person authorised by an order of the Secretary of State, has the power to enter premises of a person carrying on business as a producer or supplier of any controlled drugs and to demand the production of and to inspect any books or documents relating to the dealings in any such drugs and to inspect stocks of such drugs. Under subs.(2), if a constable has reasonable grounds to suspect that any person is in possession of a controlled drug unlawfully, the constable may search him and detain him for that purpose. He may also search any vehicle in which he suspects such drugs may be found and seize and detain anything found in the course of the search which appears to him to be evidence of an offence under the 1971 Act.[72] If a justice of the peace is satisfied by information on oath that there is a reasonable ground for suspecting that any controlled drugs are unlawfully in the possession of a person on any premises, he may grant a warrant authorising a constable to enter and search the premises named in the warrant and any person found therein and to seize and detain any controlled drugs or documents.

Crack houses

4-222   A crack house is a property which has been taken over by drug dealers and users for the purpose of producing and consuming crack cocaine. Many of those found running crack houses are unwanted guests of the property's legitimate occupier and are able to remain there because of intimidation and

---

[71] Home Office, *Drug Seizure and Offender Statistics 2000.*
[72] Misuse Of Drugs Act 1971, s.23(4).

threats of violence. Once established, a crack house can undermine the local area by increasing the rate of acquisitive crime on the part of local drug users and other users attracted to the area. Crack houses are also well-known to local residents and their appearance and condition and the behaviour of visitors undermine the local amenity.[73]

The offence under s.8 of the 1971 Act requires proof that the defendant knew that prohibited activities were taking place. It was noted in the Runciman report that the s.8 offence was not a trafficking offence for the purposes of the Drug Trafficking Act 1994, so that a conviction did not lead to confiscation. The committee recommended amending s.8, and it was extended by the Criminal Justice and Police Act 2001 to cover all controlled drugs and not just cannabis and opium, but the amendments are not yet in force. Hence, currently, operators of crack houses are not liable to prosecution for allowing the use of crack on their premises, only for allowing the dealing or supply of the drug on their premises. However, the amendment is not popular with voluntary agencies as it would mean that those working to rehabilitate drug users are more exposed to a prosecution. The Home Affairs Select Committee in the Session 2001/02 therefore decided to wait and see the effects of the implementation of the Anti-Social Behaviour Act 2003 before deciding to bring into force the amendment.[74]   **4-223**

It was said in the White Paper that local authorities and police are said to be frustrated by their lack of powers to close down premises where Class A drugs are being sold. It was proposed that there be new powers granted to the police, after consulting the local authority to issue a notice of impending closure, ratified by a court order, to enable the property to be closed within 48 hours and sealed for a fixed period of up to six months.   **4-224**

Part 1 of the Anti-Social Behaviour Act 2003 provides for closure of premises which are believed to be crack houses by way of a closure notice issued by a police officer followed by the making of a closure order by the magistrates' court.   **4-225**

Closure Notices

Under s.1(1), a police officer not below the rank of superintendent (the authorising officer) may authorise[75] the issue of a closure notice in respect of premises if: **4-226**

(1) he has reasonable grounds for believing that at any time during the relevant period (that is, the period of three months ending with the day on which the authorising officer considers whether to authorise the issue of a closure notice in respect of the premises), the premises have been used in connection with the unlawful use, production or supply of a Class A controlled drug; and

(2) he has reasonable grounds for believing that the use of the premises is associated with the occurrence of disorder or serious nuisance to members of the public; and

(3) he is satisfied that the local authority[76] for the area in which the premises are situated has been consulted; and

[73] See Ares et al *The Anti-Social Behaviour Bill; 83 of 2002–3*, House of Commons Research Paper 3/34, April 4, 2003.
[74] *ibid.*, p.39.
[75] Which may oral or in writing and, if oral, it must be confirmed in writing as soon as possible, Anti-Social Behaviour Act 2003, s.1(3).
[76] A district council, a London borough council, a county council for an area for which there is no district council, the Common Council of the City of London, the Council of the Isles of Scilly, and, in Wales, a county council and a county borough council: Anti-Social Behaviour Act 2003, s.11(6) and (7).

(4) he is satisfied that reasonable steps have been taken to establish the identity of any person who lives on the premises or who has control of or responsibility for or an interest in the premises.[77]

4-227   The Home Office guidance refers to the police officer having a reasonable *suspicion* of Class A drug production, supply, or use occurring at the premises within the last three months. That must be incorrect since the 2003 Act states that the police officer must have reasonable grounds for *believing* that to be the case. In *R. (on the application of Errington) v Metropolitan Police Authority*,[78] Collins J. said there was a clear distinction between suspicion and belief[79] and that there must be an immediate change to the guidance. At the time of writing, the guidance is yet to be updated.

4-228   Hearsay evidence may be relied upon by the superintendent in forming his belief. For instance, the superintendent is permitted to consider information given to him by an officer of lower rank deputed to investigate the matter or complaints from anonymous witnesses fearful of reprisals.[80]

4-229   The notice itself must contain certain particulars.[81] It must:

(1) give notice that an application will be made under s.2 for the closure of the premises;

(2) state that access to the premises by any person other than a person who habitually resides in the premises or the owner of the premises is prohibited;

(3) specify the date and time when and the place at which the application will take place;

(4) explain the effects of an order made in pursuance of section;

(5) state that failure to comply with the notice amounts to an offence; and

(6) give information about relevant advice providers.

4-230   It must be served by a constable and by one of the following methods[82]:

(1) fixing a copy of the notice to at least one prominent place on the premises;

(2) fixing a copy of the notice to each normal means of access to the premises;

(3) fixing a copy of the notice to any outbuildings which appear to the constable to be used with or as part of the premises;

(4) giving a copy of the notice to at least one person who appears to the constable to have control of or responsibility for the premises; and

(5) giving a copy of the notice to the persons identified in pursuance of s.2(2)(b) and to any other person appearing to the constable to be a person of a description mentioned in that subsection.

4-231   Under s.1(7), the closure notice must also be served on any person who occupies any other part of the building or other structure in which the premises are

---

[77] Anti-Social Behaviour Act 2003, s.1(2).
[78] [2006] EWHC 1155 (Admin).
[79] See *R. v Moys* 79 Cr. App. R. 72.
[80] *R. (on the application of Errington) v Metropolitan Police Authority* [2006] EWHC 1155 (Admin).
[81] Anti-Social Behaviour Act 2003, s.1(4).
[82] *ibid.*, s.1(5), (6).

situated if the constable reasonably believes, at the time of serving the notice, that the person's access to the other part of the building or structure will be impeded if a closure order is made under s.2.

Closure Order

Once a notice has been issued a constable, under s.2, must then apply to a magistrates' court for a closure order, which must be heard not later than 48 hours after the notice was served. The magistrates' court may make a closure order if and only if it is satisfied that: **4-232**

(1) the premises in respect of which the closure notice was issued have been used in connection with the unlawful use, production or supply of a Class A controlled drug;

(2) the use of the premises is associated with the occurrence of disorder or serious nuisance to members of the public; and

(3) the making of the order is necessary to prevent the occurrence of such disorder or serious nuisance for the period specified in the order.[83]

The effect of the order is that the premises,[84] in respect of which the order is   **4-233** made are closed to all persons for such period (not exceeding three months) as the court decides[85] and the order may include such provision as the court thinks appropriate relating to access to any part of the building or structure of which the premises form part.[86]

An application for a closure order is considered to be civil, adopting the   **4-234** analogous situation with anti-social behaviour orders.[87] Accordingly, hearsay evidence is admissible; the weight to be attached to such evidence is matter for the justices. The standard of proof, however, has been held to be the civil standard of proof, namely, the balance of probabilities. In *Chief Constable of Merseyside Police v Harrison*[88] the High Court distinguished anti-social behaviour orders where the criminal standard of proof is to be applied. In contrast to closure orders, anti-social behaviour orders are regarded as being more serious, contain allegations and findings against named individuals, are of longer duration and a breach attracts a higher penalty. Reliance was also placed upon the statement of the junior minister, Mr Ainsley, who was responsible for taking the bill through this particular passage of its process through Parliament. In response to a specific question concerning the standard of proofs in making a closure order he replied:

"They are concerned to ensure that we have not set the barrier too high and that we are not rendering the powers difficult to use . . . When we say 'satisfied' we mean that the court needs to be satisfied with regard to Class A drugs. That might not be as straightforward as he might think, but we are talking about the balance of probability and not proof beyond reasonable doubt."

---

[83] Anti-Social Behaviour Act 2003, s.2(3).
[84] A order may be as regards all or part of the premises: Anti-social Behaviour Act 2003, s.2(8) "Premises" is defined to include mean any land or other place whether enclosed or not and any outbuildings which are or are used as part of the premises: s.11(3).
[85] Anti-Social Behaviour Act 2003, s.2(4).
[86] *ibid.*, s.2(5).
[87] *The Commissioner of the Metropolitan Police v Karen Hooper* [2005] EWHC 340 (Admin); *R. (on the application of Errington) v Metropolitan Police Authority* [2006] EWHC 1155 (Admin); *Chief Constable of Merseyside Police v Harrison* [2006] EWHC 1106 (Admin). See also discussion at paras 4-237 to 4-238.
[88] [2006] EWHC 1106 (Admin).

4-235   The jurisdiction of the magistrates to hear an application for a closure order is not affected by any defects in the notice, although they would make it impossible to maintain criminal proceedings in so far as they depended on the validity of the notice; s.2(3) does not depend on the validity of the closure notice.[89] If the defects are not cured, however, during the period of time allowed by the magistrates then the application for a closure order is likely to be refused.[90]

Adjournment of proceedings

4-236   The magistrates' court may adjourn the hearing of the application for a period of not more than 14 days to enable the occupier of the premises, the person who has control of or responsibility for the premises, or any other person with an interest in the premises, to show why a closure order should not be made.[91] If the magistrates' court adjourns the hearing, it may order that the closure notice continues in effect until the end of the period of the adjournment. The limited period ensures that the beneficial object of the statute is not defeated: to procure the closure of the crack house and to protect the neighbours of such premises form the severe nuisance caused by them.[92]

4-237   In *The Commissioner of the Metropolitan Police v Karen Hooper*[93], Mitting J. held that the magistrates' court had power, under s.54 of the Magistrates' Court Act 1980, to adjourn over and above the express statutory power in s.2(6).[94] This power must not, however, be exercised in a manner which undermines the statute under which the proceedings are brought, but only when no other way is available to avoid a breach of a person's Convention rights.[95] Accordingly, in determining whether to adjourn proceedings beyond the 14 day time limit, the court should have regard to the statutory purpose of closing down premises by a speedy procedure; the absence of any power to order that the closure notice continues in effect until the end of the period of the adjournment; and the option of adjourning to another bench. The court should exercise its power consistently with the Convention rights of affected persons.

4-238   In *R. (on the application of Errington) v Metropolitan Police Authority*,[96] while approving the decision in *Hooper* as to the power to adjourn under s.54, confusingly suggested that it was inappropriate for an application for a closure order to be made by way of complaint under ss.51 and 52 of the 1980 Act. If this is correct, then it cannot be the case that s.54 will apply, since this only relates to the power to adjourn the hearing of a complaint.

Powers of entry

4-239   Once the order is made, then, under s.3 of the 2003 Act, a constable or an authorised person (who may use reasonable force) may enter the premises in respect of which the order is made and do anything reasonably necessary to secure the premises against entry by any person. However, a constable or authorised person[97] seeking to enter the premises must, if required to do so by or on behalf of the owner, occupier or other person in charge of the premises,

---

[89] [2006] EWHC 1106 (Admin).
[90] *ibid.*
[91] Anti-Social Behaviour Act 2003, s.2(6).
[92] *The Commissioner of the Metroplitan Police v Karen Hooper* [2005] EWHC 340 (Admin).
[93] *ibid.*
[94] The magistrates' court does not have an inherent power to adjourn only to stay for abuse of its process: *R. (on the application of Mathialagan) v London Borough of Southwark* [2004] EWCA Civ 1689.
[95] *R. v Dudley Magistrates' Court Ex p. Hollis* [1999] 1 W.L.R. 1999 642 at 660E.
[96] [2006] EWHC 1155 (Admin).
[97] An authorised person is a person authorised by the chief officer of police for the area in which the premises are situated: Anti-Social Behaviour Act 2003, s.3(6).

produce evidence of his identity and authority before entering the premises. They may also enter the premises at any time while the order has effect for the purpose of carrying out essential maintenance of, or repairs to, the premises.

Offences

Section 4 provides that a person commits an offence if he remains on or **4-240** enters premises in contravention of a closure notice, obstruct a constable or an authorised person acting under s.5, or enters the premises. A person guilty of an offence under this section is liable on summary conviction to imprisonment for a period not exceeding six months, or to a fine not exceeding level 5 on the standard scale, or to both. There is a defence of reasonable excuse for entering or being on the premises. A constable in uniform may arrest a person he reasonably suspects of committing or having committed an offence under s.4.

Extension of closure order

Section 5(1) provides that, at any time before the end of the period for which **4-241** a closure order is made or extended, a constable may make a complaint to an appropriate justice of the peace for an extension or further extension of the period for which it has effect. However, a complaint must not be made unless it is authorised by a police officer not below the rank of superintendent, and he has reasonable grounds for believing that it is necessary to extend the period for which the closure order has effect, for the purpose of preventing the occurrence of disorder or serious nuisance to members of the public, and who is satisfied that the local authority has been consulted about the intention to make the complaint.[98] If a complaint is made to a justice of the peace under subs.(1), the justice may issue a summons directed to:

(1) the persons on whom the closure notice relating to the closed premises was served under subs.(6) or (7) of s.1; or

(2) any other person who appears to the justice to have an interest in the closed premises but on whom the closure notice was not served,

requiring such person to appear before the magistrates' court to answer to the complaint.

If the court is satisfied that the order is necessary to prevent the occurrence **4-242** of disorder or serious nuisance for a further period, it may extend the period for which the order has effect by a period not exceeding three months, but a closure order must not have effect for more than six months.[99]

Discharge of a closure order

Section 5(6) provides that any of the following persons may make a complaint **4-243** to an appropriate justice of the peace for an order that a closure order is discharged:

(1) a constable;

(2) the local authority;

(3) a person on whom the closure notice relating to the closed premises was served under subs.(6)(d) or (e) or (7) of section 1; or

(4) a person who has an interest in the closed premises but on whom the closure notice was not served.

---

[98] Anti-Social Behaviour Act 2003, s.5(2).

[99] *ibid.*, s.5(4), (5).

If a complaint is made under subs.(6) by a person other than a constable, the justice may issue a summons directed to such constable as he thinks appropriate, requiring the constable to appear before the magistrates' court to answer to the complaint.[1]

4-244   The court must not make an order discharging a closure order unless it is satisfied that the closure order is no longer necessary to prevent the occurrence of disorder or serious nuisance to members of the public. If a summons is issued in accordance with this section, a notice stating the date, time and place at which the complaint will be heard must be served on the persons to whom the summons is directed if it is issued, such constable as the justice thinks appropriate (unless he is the complainant) and the local authority (unless they are the complainant).

Appeals

4-245   Section 6 provides a right to appeal an order made under s.2 or s.5, or any decision by a court not to make an order under either of those sections. An appeal against an order or decision to which this section applies must be brought to the Crown Court before the end of the period of 21 days, beginning with the day on which the order or decision is made. The appeal may be brought by:

(1) a person on whom the closure notice relating to the closed premises was served under s.1(6); or

(2) a person who has an interest in the closed premises but on whom the closure notice was not served.

An appeal against the decision of a court not to make such an order may be brought by a constable or the local authority. On an appeal under this section the Crown Court may make such order as it thinks appropriate.

4-246   Any person who occupies or owns any part of a building or structure in which closed premises are situated, and in respect of which the closure order does not have effect, may apply to the magistrates' court, under s.7, at any time while a closure order has effect under ss.2 or 5 or the Crown Court in respect of an order made under s.6. On an application under this section the court may make such order as it thinks appropriate in relation to access to any part of a building or structure in which closed premises are situated.

Recoverable costs

4-247   Section 8 provides that a police authority or a local authority, which incurs expenditure for the purpose of clearing, securing or maintaining the premises in respect of which a closure order has effect, may apply to the court which made the order for those costs. The court may make such order as it thinks appropriate in the circumstances for the reimbursement (in full or in part) by the owner of the premises of the expenditure. An application for an order under this section must not be entertained unless it is made not later than the end of the period of three months starting with the day the closure order ceases to have effect. The application under this section must be served on:

(1) the police authority for the area in which the premises are situated if the application is made by the local authority;

(2) the local authority if the application is made by a police authority; or

(3) the owner of the premises.[2]

---

[1] Anti-Social Behaviour Act 2003, s.5(8).
[2] *ibid.*, s.8(4).

A constable is not liable for relevant damages in respect of anything done, or **4-248** omitted to be done by him, in the performance or purported performance of his functions under this Part. A chief officer of police is not liable for relevant damages in respect of anything done, or omitted to be done, by a constable under his direction or control in the performance or purported performance of the constable's functions under this Part.[3] This does not apply if the act or omission is shown to have been in bad faith or to prevent an award of damages made in respect of an act or omission on the ground that the act or omission was unlawful by virtue of s.6(1) of the Human Rights Act 1998.

Relevant damages are damages in proceedings for judicial review or for **4-249** the tort of negligence or misfeasance in public duty.[4] Further, under s.10 of the 2003 Act, any person who incurs financial loss in consequence of the issue of a closure notice, or a closure order having effect, may apply to the magistrates' court which considered the application for a closure order, or to the Crown Court if the closure order was made or extended by an order made by that Court on an appeal under s.6, for compensation out of central funds. An application under this section must not be entertained unless it is made not later than the end of the period of three months, starting with whichever is the later of the day the court decides not to make a closure order, the day the Crown Court dismisses an appeal against a decision not to make a closure order, or the day a closure order ceases to have effect. The court may order the payment of compensation out of central funds if it is satisfied:

(1) that the person had no connection with the use of the premises as mentioned in s.1;

(2) if the person is the owner[5] or occupier of the premises, that he took reasonable steps to prevent the use,

(3) that the person has incurred financial loss; and,

(4) having regard to all the circumstances it is appropriate to order payment of compensation in respect of that loss.

Nuisances and Obstructions on the Highway[6]

Nuisance

It is a nuisance at common law to obstruct a highway[7] or render it dangerous.[8] **4-250** A nuisance on a highway is any wrongful act or omission upon or near a highway, whereby the public is prevented from freely, safely and conveniently passing along it.[9] Any obstruction or hindrance may be justified as an exercise

[3] Anti-Social Behaviour Act 2003, s.9(1), (2).
[4] *ibid.*, s.9(5).
[5] A person "owns" the premises if, other than a mortgagee not in possession, they are for the time being entitled to dispose of the fee simple in the premises or they hold or are entitled to the rents and profits of the premises under a lease of three years or more: Anti-Social Behaviour Act 2003, s.11(10).
[6] For a detailed look at nuisances and obstructions on the highway see *The Encyclopaedia of Highway, Law and Practice*, Sweet & Maxwell.
[7] A highway at common law is a way over which there exists a public right of passage, at all seasons of the year freely and at their will to pass and repass without let or hindrance: *Ex p. Lewis* (1888) 21 QBD 191, 197.
[8] *Trevett v Lee* [1955] 1 All E.R. 406, 409; *Dymond v Pearce* [1972] 1 Q.B. 496.
[9] *Jacobs v LCC* [1950] A.C. 361 at 375.

of the rights of the dedicated owner[10] or as a reasonable exercise of the rights of the frontager, such as scaffolding for repairs or under statutory powers. Causing danger on a highway does not necessarily require an obstruction. It is no defence that in other respects the nuisance is beneficial to the public.[11] At common law, the owner or occupier of adjoining premises is not liable to repair objects, such as gratings or gates, which form part of the highway, as they vest in the highway authority. However, they may be liable in nuisance if the object is under his control and they fail to keep it in repair. A permanent obstruction upon a highway without lawful authority which interferes with public access is a nuisance, such as erecting a gate or a stile or placing heaps of stone or other material on the highway. It is a nuisance to dig a trench across the highway for the purpose of laying wires or cables. It is also a nuisance to use vehicles of excessive size and character in highways so as to injure the surface or obstruct other users or cause excessive noise. Using vehicles calculated to endanger passengers or damage property is a nuisance or to use it, or any part of it, for a purpose other than as a highway, such as repairing vehicles. An owner of premises adjacent to the highway may make reasonable use of it for the purpose of access to his own premises and to load and unload goods for a reasonable period of time; they may also erect scaffolding for the purpose of building or repairing a building. It may be a nuisance to race upon the highway and there is no right to organise, or to take part in, a procession which results in an obstruction or is an unreasonable use of the highway.[12] Owners or occupiers of adjacent premises may also be liable in nuisance if they allow such premises to fall into a condition where they become dangerous to users, such as building a wall which is likely to collapse or allowing trees to grow over it.

Public Nuisance

4-251   As a public nuisance, a nuisance on a highway may be a criminal offence maintainable by the Attorney-General in an action for an injunction to restrain the commission of a nuisance. Local authorities may also take similar steps under s.222 of the Local Government Act 1972. However, as highway authorities,[13] they are subject to a common law duty to prevent nuisances and remove obstructions, regardless of any express statutory duty. A member of the public may also maintain an action if he has suffered an injury beyond that suffered by the rest of the public.

Duty of Highway Authority

4-252   There is a general duty of highway authorities to protect the rights of the public to use and enjoy any highway for which it is the highway authority.[14] A local

---

[10] i.e. a way may become a highway by way of the dedication of the right of passage to the public by the owner of the soil and the acceptance of that use by the public. Dedication means that the owner has either said as much in words or conducted himself so as to lead the public to infer that he was willing that they should have this right of passage: para.65, *Halsbury, Highways* Vol. 21.

[11] *Denaby and Cadeby Main Collieries Ltd v Anson* [1911] 1 K.B 171, 205; *Att-Gen v Wilcox* [1938] Ch. 934.

[12] See also the offence of breaching an order for the route to be observed during a procession under the Town Police Clauses Act 1847, s.21.

[13] i.e, the Secretary of State as regards any highway which is a trunk roads and special roads provided by him: Highways Act 1980, s.1; for highways outside Greater London, the county council or metropolitan district council for all highways in their area which are not the Secretary of State's highways: s.1(2); in Wales, the county or county borough council,; the Council of the Isles of Scilly; in Greater London, London boroughs and Common Council.

[14] Highways Act 1980, s.130.

authority which is also the highway authority must prevent, so far as it is possible, the stopping up or obstructing of the highways for which they are the highway authority, and also any highway for which they are not the authority if in their opinion the stopping up and obstruction of it would prejudice the interests of the public.[15] Under s.130(5) of the Highways Act 1980, a local authority may commence or defend proceedings in their own name and take such steps as they deem to be expedient and without prejudice to s.222 of the 1972 Act.

Highway authorities must remove obstructions caused by snow or material **4-253** falling down banks on the side of the highway or "any other cause". The latter is construed to mean sudden and substantial obstructions.[16] If they fail to do so, then a magistrates' court on the complaint of any person may order the authority to remove it within such period not less than 24 hours.[17] The authority may take any reasonable steps including placing signs and lights and fences to warn users of the obstruction and sell anything removed in performing the duty unless claimed by the owner within seven days of its removal.[18]

Damage to the Highway

If a person without a lawful excuse causes damage to the highway, including **4-254** making a ditch or excavation in a highway, removing soil or turf, except for the purpose of improving the highway, or deposits anything on it which damages it, he is guilty of an offence under s.131(1) of the 1980 Act. It is also an offence to disturb, without lawful excuse, the surface of a footpath, bridleway or other highway which is not a made-up carriageway so as to render it inconvenient for use by the public.[19] It is an offence under the 1980 Act to pull down or obliterate a traffic sign without lawful authority.[20] If a footway or street which is a highway maintainable at public expense is damaged by excavation works or other work in land adjoining the street, the highway authority may carry out works to make good the damage and recover the expenses reasonably incurred by it from the owner of the land or the person who caused the damage.

Obstruction of the Highway

Any person who, without lawful authority or excuse in any way, wilfully **4-255** obstructs the free passage along the highway, is guilty of an offence.[21] An obstruction is unlawful if it substantially prevents the public having free access over the whole of the highway. There is a *de minimis* defence where the obstruction encroaches only slightly onto the highway. It is not necessary to show that any particular person was obstructed.

In *Nagy Weston*,[22] Lord Parker C.J. said that in order for an offence to be **4-256** committed, there must be proof that the use was an unreasonable one in the circumstances, including the length of time the obstruction existed, where it took place, the purpose of it, and whether it caused an actual, as opposed to a potential, obstruction. Lawful excuse means showing that the person causing the obstruction honestly believed on reasonable grounds that the facts were of a certain order and that had they been so, the conduct would have been

[15] Highways Act 1980, s.130(3).
[16] *Worcestershire CC v Newman* [1974] 2 All E.R. 867.
[17] Highways Act 1980, s.50(2).
[18] *ibid.*, s.150(4).
[19] *ibid.*, s.131A(1).
[20] *ibid.*, s.131(2).
[21] *ibid.*, s.137(1); liable on summary conviction to a fine not exceeding level 3 of the standard scale.
[22] [1965] 1 All E.R. 78, at 80.

lawful.[23] An offence is committed even if only part of the road is occupied, if the whole road is obstructed[24] and even where there is sufficient room for pedestrians to pass by.

4-257   Conducting a business on premises next to a highway so as to cause a crowd to form may be a relevant obstruction.[25] Picketing, even when peaceful, may amount to obstructing if it compels others to stop.[26] Distributing banners and leaflets may cause an obstruction, within the meaning of s.137 of the 1980 Act, if it causes others to leave the pavement to pass by the distributor.[27]

4-258   In order to be wilful conduct, it must be shown that the obstruction is deliberate and knowing.[28] A reasonable and honest belief that the obstructor had lawful authority is no defence as what is meant by the term "lawful authority" is a licence or permit.[29] "Lawful excuse", on the other hand, means whether or not the user was reasonable. It is a question of fact in each case. A peaceful non-obstructive assembly of more than 20 persons on the highway was held not to have be a sufficient impediment to the public's right of access.[30] Lying down outside of premises which the obstructors had said was guilty of criminal offences, for example, was not reasonable and the court was right not to receive evidence about the alleged criminal activities.[31]

4-259   "Wilfully" means that *mens rea* is not required for the act to be wilful and anyone who, by an exercise of free will, causes an obstruction is guilty of the offence.[32] Failing to remove an obstruction after notice to do so is wilful obstruction.[33] Selling ice cream from a shop window so as to cause a crowd to assemble and obstruct the highway was a wilful obstruction because the obstruction could have been avoided had the defendant sold ice cream in the usual way inside the store.[34] It is not a wilful obstruction to allow trees to grow across the highway[35] or to allow rainwater to flow onto a highway from eaves.[36]

4-260   It is also an offence for a person to obstruct a footway by leaving or placing things on it[37]; to cause or permit a vehicle or trailer to remain on a road in such circumstances that it is likely to cause a danger to other persons[38]; to erect a building, or fence; and erect a hedgeway on a highway without lawful authority.[39]

4-261   In *Westminster City Council v Haw*,[40] the Council (being the local authority responsible for the highways, including the pavements, in Parliament Square in London) applied for an injunction to restrain Mr Haw from obstructing the pavement opposite the House of Commons by displaying a

[23] *Cambridgeshire and Isle of Ely Council v Rust* [1972] 2 Q.B. 426.
[24] Hence, the presence of only one person may be an obstruction: *Scarfe v Wood* (1969) 113 S.J. 1432.
[25] *Dwyer v Mansfield* [1946] K.B. 437. In *Pugh v Pidgen and Powley* (1987) 151 J.P. 644, it was irrelevant that the respondents had done their best to control the crowds encroaching on the street.
[26] *Broome v DPP* [1947] A.C. 587; *Kavanagh v Hiscock* [1974] A.C.587.
[27] *Hirst and Agu v Chief Constable of West Yorkshire* (1987) 151 J.P. 304.
[28] *Arrowsmith v Jenkins* [1963] 2 Q.B. 561.
[29] *Arrowsmith v Jenkins, ibid.*
[30] *DPP v Jones* [1992] 2 A.C. 240.
[31] *Birch v DPP Independent*, January 13, 2000.
[32] *Arrowsmith v Jenkins* [1963] 2 Q.B. 561.
[33] *Abel v Stone* (1969) 134 J.P. 237.
[34] *Fabbri v Morris* [1947] 1 All E.R. 315. However, in *Dwyer v Mansfield* [1946] K.B. 437, queues outside a shop resulted from a scarcity of goods and not from unusual methods of sale and so was not a wilful obstruction.
[35] *Walker v Himer* (1875) 1 QBD 4.
[36] *Crossdill v Ratchff* (1862) 26 J.P. 365.
[37] Town Police Clauses Act 1847, s.28.
[38] Road Traffic Act 1988, s.22.
[39] Highways Act 1980, s.130.
[40] [2002] EWHC 2073.

considerable number of placards supporting his protest against the policies of the Government in relation to Iraq. The Defendant maintained that he had been conducting a protest from the pavement in Parliament Square ever since June 2001 on a 24-hour a day basis, every day, since then. According to his witness statement, Mr Haw slept and ate there, and he had from time to time been fasting. He also maintained that he had not obstructed the highway, but rather used it in a lawful and reasonable manner to exercise his rights of freedom of expression and assembly contained respectively in Arts 10 and 11 of the European Convention on Human Rights. The Council relied upon s.130 of the Highways Act 1980 and alternatively, s.222 of the 1972 Act. Gray J. held that the Council had established that the placards and other protest materials were a physical obstruction and that it was wilful in the sense of being deliberate. The issue was whether or not the obstruction was a lawful use of the highway. That meant considering the length of time for which the obstruction continued, the place where it occurred, its purpose and whether actual obstruction occurred. In this case, the obstruction had continued for 15 months. The duration of the obstruction would be an indication of unreasonableness except that the defendant contended that, given his objective to influence Parliament in relation to policy towards Iraq, the location opposite the Houses of Parliament was a suitable one. It was unlikely that, given the location and nature of the placards, pedestrians would be inconvenienced by it. In all the time that the defendant had been present, the police did not once consider it necessary to take action against Mr Haw or even to warn him of any possible future action. Nor was there any suggestion of violence or disorder or breach of the peace arising out of the presence of Mr Haw in Parliament Square. It was also important that Mr Haw was exercising his right to freedom of expression and on a political issue. Interference with the right was permissible where it was to do so in order to protect the rights of others. Gray J. found no pressing social need to interfere with the display of placards so as to protect the right of others to pass and re-pass. Objection may be taken to the defendant's activities on the ground that they constitute an eyesore, but that was a different matter. Therefore, it was held that the obstruction for which the defendant was responsible was not unreasonable.

Town Police Clauses Act 1847

The Town Police Clauses Act 1847 Act originally applied only to those areas **4-262** of local authorities which had expressly adopted it. Sections 21 to 29 concerning "obstructions and nuisances in the streets" were extended to the areas of all former boroughs and urban districts by s.171(1) of the Public Health Act 1875, save for those in Greater London.[41]

Under s.28 of the 1847 Act, every person who, in any street, to the obstruc- **4-263** tion, annoyance, or danger of the residents or passengers, commits any of the specified offences, shall be liable to a penalty not exceeding level 3 on the standard scale for each offence, or, in the discretion of the justice before whom he is convicted, may be committed to prison, there to remain for a period not exceeding 14 days. Those specified offences are as follows:

> "Every person who exposes for show, hire, or sale (except in a market or market place or fair lawfully appointed for that purpose) any horse or other animal, or exhibits in a caravan or otherwise any show or public entertainment, or shoes, bleeds, or farries any horse or animal (except in the cases of accident), or cleans, dresses, exercises, trains, or breaks, or turns loose any horse or animal, or makes or repairs any part

---

[41] Local Government Act 1972 , Sch.14, paras.23 and 26.

of any cart or carriage (except in cases of accident where repair on the spot is necessary);

Every person who suffers to be at large any unmuzzled ferocious dog, or sets on or urges any dog or other animal to attack, worry, or put in fear any person or animal;

Every person who slaughters or dresses any cattle, or any part thereof, except in the case of any cattle over-driven which may have met with any accident, and which for the public safety or other reasonable cause ought to be killed on the spot;

Every person having the care of any waggon, cart, or carriage who rides on the shafts thereof, or who without having reins, and holding the same, rides upon such waggon, cart, or carriage or on any animal drawing the same, or who is at such a distance from such waggon, cart, or carriage, as not to have due control over every animal drawing the same, or who does not, in meeting any other carriage, keep his waggon, cart, or carriage to the left or near side or who in passing any other carriage does not keep his waggon, cart, or carriage on the right or off side of the road, (except in cases of actual necessity, or some sufficient reason for deviation,) or who, by obstructing the street, wilfully prevents any person or carriage from passing him, or any waggon, cart, or carriage under his care;

Every person who rides or drives furiously any horse or carriage, or drives furiously any cattle;

Every person who causes any public carriage, sledge, truck, or barrow, with or without horses, or any beast of burden, to stand longer than is necessary for loading or unloading goods, or for taking up or setting down passengers, (except hackney carriages, and horses and other beasts of draught or burthen, standing for hire in any place appointed for that purpose by the commissioners or other lawful authority,) and every person who, by means of any cart, carriage, sledge, truck, or barrow or any animal, or other means wilfully interrupts any public crossing or wilfully causes any obstruction in any public footpath or other public thoroughfare;

Every person who causes any tree or timber or iron beam to be drawn in or upon any carriage, without having sufficient means of safely guiding the same;

Every person who leads or rides any horse or other animal, or draws or drives any cart or carriage, sledge, truck, or barrow, upon any footway of any street, or fastens any horse or other animal so that it stands across or upon any footway;

Every person who places or leaves any furniture, goods, wares, or merchandise, or any cask, tub, basket, pail, or bucket, or places or uses any standing-place, stool, bench, stall, or showboard, on any footway, or who places any blind, shade, covering, awning, or other projection over or along any such footway, unless such blind, shade, covering, awning, or other projection is eight feet in height at least in every part thereof from the ground;

Every person who places, hangs up, or otherwise exposes to sale any goods, wares, merchandize, matter, or thing whatsoever, so that the same project into or over any footway, or beyond the line of any house, shop, or building at which the same are so exposed, so as to obstruct or incommode the passage of any person over or along such footway;

Every person who rolls or carries any cask, tub, hoop, or wheel, or any ladder, plank, pole, timber, or log of wood, upon any footway, except for the purpose of loading or unloading any cart or carriage, or of crossing the footway;

Every person who places any line, cord, or pole across any street, or hangs or places any clothes thereon;

Every person who wilfully and indecently exposes his person;

Every person who publicly offers for sale or distribution or exhibits to public view any profane book, paper, print, drawing, painting, or representation, or sings any profane or obscene song or ballad or uses any profane or obscene language;

Every person who wantonly discharges any firearm, or throws or discharges any stone or other missile, or makes any bonfire, or throws or sets fire to any firework;

Every person who wilfully and wantonly disturbs any inhabitant, by pulling or ringing any door bell, or knocking at any door, or who wilfully and unlawfully extinguishes the light of any lamp;

Every person who flies any kite, or who makes or uses any slide upon ice or snow;

Every person who cleanses, hoops, fires, washes, or scalds any cask or tub, or hews, saws, bores, or cuts any timber or stone, or slacks, sifts, or screens any lime;

Every person who throws or lays down any stones, coals, slate, shells, lime, bricks, timber, iron, or other materials (except materials so inclosed as to prevent mischief to passengers);

Every person who beats or shakes any carpet, rug, or mat (except door mats beaten or shaken before the hour of eight in the morning);

Every person who fixes or places any flower-pot or box, or other heavy article, in any upper window, without sufficiently guarding the same against being blown down;

Every person who throws from the roof or any part of any house or other building any slate, brick, wood, rubbish, or other thing, except snow thrown so as not to fall on any passenger;

Every occupier of any house or other building, or other person, who orders or permits any person in his service to stand on the sill of any window, in order to clean, paint, or perform any other operation upon the outside of such window, or upon any house or other building within the said limits, unless such window be in the sunk or basement storey;

Every person who leaves open any vault or cellar, or the entrance from any street to any cellar or room underground, without a sufficient fence or handrail, or leaves defective the door, window, or other covering of any vault or cellar, or who does not sufficiently fence any area, pit, or sewer left open, or who leaves such open area, pit, or sewer, without a sufficient light after sunset to warn and prevent persons from falling thereinto;

Every person who throws or lays any dirt, litter, or ashes, or nightsoil, or any carrion, fish, offal, or rubbish, on any street, or causes any offensive matter to run from any manufactory, brewery, slaughterhouse, butcher's shop, or dunghill, into any street: Provided always, that it shall not be deemed an offence to lay sand or other materials in any street in time of frost, to prevent accidents, or litter or other suitable materials to prevent the freezing of water in pipes, or in case of sickness to prevent noise, if the party laying any such things causes them to be removed as soon as the occasion for them ceases;

Every person who keeps any pigstye to the front of any street, not being shut out from such street by a sufficient wall or fence, or who keeps any swine in or near any street, so as to be a common nuisance."

Proceedings are normally initiated by the local authority. It seems that if the police take proceedings they must obtain the consent of the local authority.[42]

Gating Orders

4-264   Part 8A of the Highways Act 1980 creates a new type of order, the gating order, which restricts the public right of way over the highway.[43] The council may make such an order in relation to any relevant highway[44] for which they are the highway authority.[45]

4-265   Before making a gating order in relation to a relevant highway the council must be satisfied that:

(1) premises adjoining or adjacent to the highway are affected by crime or anti-social behaviour;

(2) the existence of the highway is facilitating the persistent commission of criminal offences or anti-social behaviour; and

(3) it is in all the circumstances expedient to make the order for the purposes of reducing crime or anti-social behaviour (including the likely effect of making the order on the occupiers of premises adjoining or adjacent to the highway, on other persons in the locality, and in a case where the highway constitutes a through route, the availability of a reasonably convenient alternative route).[46]

4-266   Anti-social behaviour has the same meaning as in the Crime and Disorder Act 1998, that is, "behaviour by a person which causes or is likely to cause harassment, alarm or distress to one or more other persons not of the same household as himself."[47]

Contents of a gating order
4-267   A gating order may restrict the public right of way at all times, or in respect of such times, days or periods as may be specified, exclude persons of a description specified in the order from the effect of the restriction.[48] Furthermore, the

[42] Town and Police Clauses Act 1847, s.28 is incorporated with the Public Health Act 1875 under s.171. Therefore s.253 will apply: *Sheffield Corp v Kitson* (1929) 93 J.P. 135.
[43] Part 8A of the Highways Act 1980 was inserted by s.2 of the Clean Neighbourhoods and Environment Act 2005, which came into force on April 6, 2006 (SI 2006/795).
[44] "Relevant highway" means a highway other than a special road, a trunk road, a classified or principal road; a strategic road, within the meaning of ss.60 and 61 of the Traffic Management Act 2004 (strategic roads in London), or highway of such other description as the Secretary of State may by regulations prescribe.
[45] Highways Act 1980, s.129A(2).
[46] *ibid.*, s.129A(3) and (4).
[47] *ibid.*, s.129G.
[48] *ibid.*, s.129B(1) and (2).

order may authorise the installation, operation and maintenance of a barrier or barriers for the purpose of enforcing the restriction and such works may be carried out by the council.[49]

The gating order may not be made so as to restrict the public right of way over a highway for the occupiers of premises adjoining or adjacent to the highway or which is the only or principal means of access to any dwelling. In relation to a highway which is the only or principal means of access to any premises used for business or recreational purposes, a gating order may not be made so as to restrict the public right of way over the highway during periods when those premises are normally used for those purposes.[50]

4-268

Procedure
Before making a gating order in relation to a highway a council must notify the occupiers of premises adjacent to or adjoining the highway. The procedure regarding notification and publication of gating orders is to be prescribed in regulations.[51]

4-269

Challenging gating orders
Under section 125D, a person may challenge the validity of a gating order by application to the High Court on the grounds that the Council had no power to make the order or they failed to comply with any requirement under Part 8A. The application must be made within 6 weeks of the making of the gating order. It is only under section 129D that the order may be challenged; subsection 6 expressly states that either before or after the order has been made, it may not be questioned in any legal proceedings other than under section 129D. Presumably, this will rule out any judicial review challenges.

4-270

If the High Court is satisfied that the council had no power to make the order, or the interests of the applicant have been substantially prejudiced by any failure to comply with a requirement, it may quash the order or any of its provisions. It may also suspend the operation of the gating order, or any of its provisions, until final determination of the application under section 125D.[52]

4-271

Variation and revocation of gating orders
Section 125F makes provision for the variation and revocation of gating orders. The council may vary a gating order made by them so as further to restrict any public right of way over the highway to which the order relates if they are satisfied that in all the circumstances it is expedient to do so for the purpose of reducing crime or anti- social behaviour. A council may also vary or revoke a gating order made by them so as to reduce the restriction, or remove the restriction as the case may be, as imposed by the order, if and to the extent that they are satisfied that the restriction is no longer expedient in all the circumstances for the purpose of reducing crime or anti-social behaviour. The Secretary of State will make regulations as to the procedure to be followed regarding notification and publication of the variation or revocation.

4-272

Closed Circuit Television[53]

The rapid growth of CCTV and other electronic or automated surveillance systems as part of the criminal justice system is seen by some as a result of the increasingly punitive and actuarial style trends we discussed above and also in

4-273

---

[49] Highways Act 1980, s.129B(6) and (7).
[50] *ibid.*, s.129B(3) to (5).
[51] *ibid.*, s.129C and E.
[52] *ibid.*, s.129D(3)–(5).
[53] See also paras. 3-30 to 3-31 above regarding Regulatory Investigative Powers Act 2000.

Chapter One. Some writers see it as an electronic version of Bentham's Panopticon,[54] the guard in a central observation tower, watching the minutiae of a prisoner's behaviour. Others see it as new form of social control. Norris cites Foucault describing CCTV as having the potential "to induce in the inmate a state of conscious and permanent visibility that assures the automatic function of power."[55] Surveillance does not concern itself with particular individuals so much as places, times and categories of persons. If "penal welfarism" was concerned with the identification of individual criminals to determine liability, the new penology is concerned with techniques for classifying and managing groups assorted by levels of dangerousness and the possibility that a person in a particular high-risk category or area may be an offender. Modern surveillance is pre-emptive and interventionist, concerned with intervening in respect of pre-defined categories of deviance before they have actually taken place.

4-274   There are also doubts about its effectiveness as a crime control measure. Norris analysed CCTV systems in London. Two thirds relied on fixed rather than pan-tilt or zoom cameras, making proactive targeting difficult; less than one in 20 systems recorded data in a digital form that would allow computerized analysis of images. In 120 hours of observation, there were only 29 instances of proactive targeting, three-quarters of which were initiated by a single operator. CCTV operators interpret images in highly idiosyncratic ways, looking for people who are "out of place". The gaze of the cameras, as Norris observed, did not fall equally on all sections of the population: "it gives an electronically mediated twist to that very old-fashioned mantra of round up the usual suspects."

4-275   Under s.163 of the Criminal Justice and Public Order Act 1994, and in addition to s.111 of the Local Government Act 1972 and s.2, the well-being power, of the Local Government Act 2000, a local authority,[56] may provide and maintain closed-circuit television systems if they consider that this will, in relation to their area, promote the prevention of crime or the welfare of the victims of crime. However, they must first consult the chief officer of police for the area. Authorities also have the power to provide the media with video recordings to facilitate crime prevention.[57] However, in *Peck v UK*,[58] the applicant complained that the disclosure by a council of closed circuit television footage and photographs, which had resulted in images of himself being published and broadcast on a local and national level, was a breach of his right to respect for family and private life under Art.8 of the European Convention on Human Rights. He also argued that there was also a breach of Art.13 in that no effective domestic remedy existed in relation to the violation of his Art.8 right and he sought compensation for non-pecuniary and pecuniary damages under Art.41. He said that he had been captured on closed circuit television when he had attempted suicide by cutting his wrists on a high street. Although the images used did not show the attempted suicide, they clearly identified him brandishing a kitchen knife in a public place. The police had attended the scene but he was not charged with any criminal offence. There had been no attempt to mask the applicant's identity. The images had been used in a campaign to reflect the effectiveness of closed circuit television in combating crime. He subsequently appeared on a

---

[54] Fyfe and Bannister "City Watching: CCTV in Public Spaces" (1996) Area 28/1 37–40; Reeve, "The Panopticonisation of Shopping: CCTV and Leisure Consumption", (1998) in Norris, Moran and Armstrong (eds) *Surveillance, Closed Circuit Television and Social Control* (Ashgate Publishing, 1998).

[55] "CCTV: Beyond Penal Modernism" (2006) 46 Brit. J. Criminol. 97

[56] A county or district council in England; a county or county borough in Wales.

[57] *R. v Brentwood Borough Council, Ex p. Peck The Times*, December 18, 1997.

[58] (2003) E.M.L.R. 15; (2003) E.H.R.R. 41.

number of television broadcasts to discuss the publication of the footage and photographs. He had complained to the relevant media commissions about the disclosures and had also been unsuccessful in judicial review proceedings of the council' disclosure. The European Court upheld the complaint. There had been no relevant or sufficient reasons which justified the council's disclosure. They should have first sought the complainant's consent, masked his identity, or ensured that the media had masked his identity. Particular scrutiny and care had been required in the context of the crime prevention objective and context of disclosures. The disclosures had not been sufficiently accompanied by safeguards to prevent the disclosure of his identity. The disclosure had been a disproportionate and unjustified interference with his private life and accordingly infringed his Art.8 rights under the Convention. His later voluntary appearances on television shows did not diminish the serious nature of the interference with his right to privacy and the need for care in such disclosure. Further, there had been a violation of his right under Art.13 as he did not have an effective remedy in relation to the breach of his Art.8 rights. Judicial review was not an effective remedy and the commissions to which he had complained lacked legal power and could not award damages or prevent the publications or broadcasts. An action in breach of confidence had not been available at the time as an appropriate remedy. He was awarded 11,800 Euros for non pecuniary damage and 18,705 Euros for costs and expenses.

In *Friedl v Austria*[59] the police photographed and noted the identity of the **4-276** complainant involved in a demonstration. No prosecution was brought. The applicant complained that his Art.8 rights had been violated and that because there had been no effective remedy in the Austrian courts, there had also been a violation of Art.13. The Court held that there had been no violation of Art.8. While the taking and storing of personal data (which must also include CCTV footage) in the course of a public incident was closely related to the complainant's private affairs amounted to a violation, there was a legitimate aim in the prevention of disorder and crime. The keeping of records relating to criminal cases of the past could be regarded as necessary in a democratic society for the prevention of crime even though, in this case, an ensuing prosecution for road traffic offences was not pursued. The information in question was kept only in a general administrative file and not in a data processing system.

Animals

Dangerous species

Strict liability is imposed on any person who is a keeper of an animal which **4-277** has caused damage and belongs to a dangerous species.[60] "Animal" is not defined in the 1971 Act, although it has been suggested that it includes birds, reptiles and even insects (but not bacteria).[61] The term, "dangerous species" is as one ". . . which is not normally domesticated in the British Islands, and whose fully grown animals have such characteristics that they are likely, unless restrained, to cause severe damage or that any damage they may cause is likely to be severe."[62] A "keeper" is a person ". . . who owns the animal or has it in his possession; or he is the head of a household of which a member under the age of sixteen owns the animal or has it in his possession".[63]

---

[59] (1996) 21 E.H.R.R. 83.
[60] Animals Act 1971, s.2(1).
[61] See P. North, *Modern Law of Animals* (Butterworths, London, 1972) at p.22 n.5
[62] Animals Act 1971, s.5(2).
[63] *ibid.*, s.6(3).

Non-dangerous species

4-278   Where the animal is of a non-dangerous species, s.2(2) of the 1971 Act imposes strict liability on the keeper of the animal in these circumstances:

> "(a) the damage is of a kind which the animal, unless restrained, was likely to cause or which, if caused by the animal, was likely to be severe;
>
> (b) the likelihood of the damage or of its being severe was due to characteristics of the animal which are not normally found in animals of the same species or are not normally to be found except at particular times or in particular circumstances; and
>
> (c) those characterises were known to that keeper or were at any time known to a person who at that time had charge of the animal as that keeper's servant or, where that keeper is the head of a household, were known to another keeper of the animal who is a member of that household and under the age of sixteen."[64]

4-279   Under s.6(2), the definition of keeper is extended to include anyone "who has ceased to own or possess the animal until another person becomes a keeper thereof by virtue of those provisions."[65] Therefore, where a person was attacked by a dog which was known to be aggressive with other dogs but did not attack humans, the propensity to attack other dogs could extend to humans so as to render the owner liable.[66]

Defences

4-280   The following defences are provided under the 1971 Act as follows:

> (1) the voluntary assumption of risk; but this is not available to an employer where a person is employed as a servant by a keeper of an animal and incurs a risk incidental to his employment[67];
>
> (2) where the claimant was a trespasser[68];
>
> (3) under sections 2, 3 and 4, where the damage is "due wholly to the fault of the person suffering it" or where the damage was partly due to his fault and the court may apportion blame under the Law Reform (Contributory Negligence) Act 1945[69]; and
>
> (4) there is no defence on the basis that it was an act of God or an act of a third party.

Dogs

4-281   Section 3 provides that "where a dog causes damage by killing or injuring livestock, any person who is a keeper of the dog is liable for the damage, except

---

[64] *ibid.*, s.2(2). The court is to "consider each part of the subsection in turn and satisfy themselves that the plaintiff has made out his case on one or other of the limbs of each part" *per* Stuart-Smith L.J. in *Curtis v Betts* [1990] 1 W.L.R. 459.

[65] Animals Act 1971, s.6(4).

[66] *Smith v Ainger Times* (1990), June 5, 1990.

[67] Animals Act 1971, s.5(2) and s.6(5).

[68] *ibid.*, s.5(3).

[69] ibid., ss.5(1), 10 and 11. Fault is defined in the Law Reform (Contributory Negligence) Act 1945 under s.4 as "negligence, breach of statutory duty or other act or omission which gives rise to liability in tort, or would, apart from this Act, give rise to the defence of contributory negligence".

as otherwise provided by this Act".[70] There are three defences available to the keeper in an action under this section: it is the fault of the person suffering damage; that there was contributory negligence; or that the livestock was killed or injured on land to which the animal had strayed and either the dog belonged to the occupier or its presence on the land was authorised by the occupier.

Livestock

Section 4 provides that where livestock[71] belonging to any person[72] strays on **4-282** land in the ownership or occupation of another and damage is done by the livestock to the land or to any property on it which is in the ownership or possession of the other person; or any expenses are reasonably incurred by that other person in keeping the livestock while it cannot be restored to the person to whom it belongs or while it is detained in pursuance of s.7 of the 1971 Act in ascertaining to whom it belongs, the person to whom the livestock belongs is liable for the damage or expenses.[73] The effect of s.4 is to allow an owner of the land to sue under this section, rather than merely by one in possession of the land.

It is a defence for the possessor of the offending livestock where any damage **4-283** is wholly due to the fault of the person suffering it subject to the fencing rules, contributory negligence, straying from the highway, when the livestock was lawfully present on the highway, and failure to fence. In determining liability under s.4, the straying is not to be regarded as wholly the claimant's fault by reason only that it could have been prevented by fencing.[74] There is no defence available based on an Act of God, voluntary assumption of risk, and the act of a third party.

Straying animals

Section 8(2) provides that, where damage is caused by animals straying from **4-284** unfenced land to the highway, a person who placed them on the land shall not be regarded as having committed a breach of the duty to take care by reason only of placing them there if the land is common land, or is land situated in an area where fencing is not customary, or is a town or village green, and he had a right to place the animals on that land.[75]

Dangerous dogs

It is an offence to own or keep[76] a pit bull terrier,[77] Japanese tosa,[78] Dogo **4-285** Argentino and Fila Braziliero,[79] or any other dog identified by the Secretary of State,[80] unless it is on the Index of Exempted Dogs and is in compliance

[70] This replaces similar provisions of the Dogs Act 1906 and the Dogs Act 1928.
[71] See Animals Act 1971, s.11 which includes most ordinary farm animals but not cats and dogs.
[72] That is, belongs to the person in whose possession the livestock is: see Animals Act 1971, s.4(2).
[73] Animals Act 1971, s.4.
[74] *ibid.*, s.5(6).
[75] See also Environmental Protection Act 1990, ss.149 and 150 as amended by the Clean Neighbourhoods and Environment Act 2005, s.68.
[76] Dangerous Dogs Act 1991, s.1(3).
[77] *ibid.*, s.1(a).
[78] *ibid.*, s.1(b).
[79] *ibid.*, s.1(c).
[80] *ibid.*, s.1(c). See Dangerous Dogs (Designated Types) Order 1991 (SI 1991/1743) and Dangerous Dogs Compensation and Exemption Schemes Order 1991 (SI 1991/1744).

with certain requirements.[81] Regardless of whether it is on the Index of Exempted Dogs, it is an offence to breed, or breed from, sell or exchange, advertise or expose such a dog for sale or exchange, or give the dog as a gift, or advertise or expose the dog as such, or abandon or allow it to stray.[82] A person found guilty of any of these offences shall be liable on summary conviction to imprisonment or a term not exceeding six months or a fine not exceeding level 5 on the standard scale.[83] A person on conviction will not be liable to imprisonment if he shows that he published the advertisement to the order of someone else and did not himself devise it.[84] That person shall not be convicted if, in addition, he shows that he did not know or had no reasonable cause to suspect that it related to a prohibited dog.[85]

4-286   The owner, or the person for the time being in charge, of a dog dangerously out of control in a public place is guilty of an offence.[86] It is an aggravated offence where a dog is so out of control that it injures any person.[87] Where proceedings have been brought against the owner for such an offence (aggravated or otherwise), but the owner was not at the material time in charge of the dog, it is a defence to prove that the person in charge of the dog at that time was a person whom he reasonably believed to be a fit and proper person to be in charge of it.[88] Public place is defined as meaning any street, road or other place (whether or not enclosed) to which the public have, or are permitted to have, access, whether for payment or otherwise. It specifically includes the common parts of a building containing two or more dwellings.[89] Therefore, it will extend to those parts of a block of flats where, although there may be a secure front entry door so that the interior of the flat is not a place to which the public has unrestricted access, nevertheless the common parts are, in all other respects, a public place. There is a further offence which extends to a place which is not public; if the owner, or if different, the person for the time being in charge of a dog, allows it to enter a place which is not a public place but where it is not permitted to be and while it is there it injures any person or there are grounds for reasonable apprehension that it will do so.[90] It is an aggravated offence if a person is injured by the dog.[91] A person guilty of any of these offences, other than an aggravated offence, is liable on summary conviction to imprisonment for a term not exceeding six months or a fine not exceeding level 5 on the standard scale or both.[92] A person guilty of an aggravated offence is liable on summary conviction to imprisonment for a term not exceeding six months or a fine not exceeding the statutory minimum or both, on conviction on indictment, to imprisonment for a term not exceeding two years or a fine or both.[93] Constables and officers of local authorities authorised by it to exercise these powers may seize such dogs in certain circumstances.[94]

4-287   Under the Dogs Act 1871, a dangerous dog can be destroyed or a number of conditions imposed, in a wide range of circumstances. Compared to crim-

---

[81] Dangerous Dogs Act 1991, s.1(5).
[82] *ibid.*, s.1(2).
[83] *ibid.*, s.1(7).
[84] *ibid.*, s.1(7)(a).
[85] *ibid.*, s.1(7)(b).
[86] *ibid.*, s.3(1).
[87] *ibid.*, s.3(1)
[88] *ibid.*, s.3(2).
[89] *ibid.*, s.10(2).
[90] *ibid.*, s.3(3).
[91] *ibid.*, s.3(3).
[92] *ibid.*, s.3(4).
[93] *ibid.*, s.3(4)(a)–(b).
[94] *ibid.*, s.5.

inal proceedings, there are two main advantages: the standard of proof is lower, that is, on the balance of probabilities; and applies everywhere, even in and around a private house.

The Dangerous Dogs Act 1991 provides that an order under the Dogs Act **4-288** 1871 on complaint that a dog is dangerous and not kept under proper control may be made whether or not the dog is shown to have injured any person. Further, the court may specify the measures to be taken for keeping the dog under proper control, whether by muzzling, keeping it on a lead, excluding it from specified places or otherwise[95] and if male, neutered.[96] This is a flexible provision which can be used to deal with a number of nuisance complaints about dogs, including circumstances where dogs in one back garden cause fear of risk or injury to neighbours in another.

Anti-social behaviour is not restricted to the urban environment; there is **4-289** enough evidence of anti-social behaviour impinging on rural areas and, in particular, farmland.[97] In relation to problems caused by dogs, a dog owner is liable in trespass if he deliberately sends a dog on to another person's land in pursuit of game. It is a civil matter if the owner allows a dog to roam at large in the knowledge that it is likely to kill game. Similarly it is a civil matter for a dog to be at large, that is, not on a lead or under close control, in a field of sheep. Provision is made for criminal offences in relation to dogs worrying live-stock[98] under the Dogs (Protection of Livestock) Act 1953 and civil liability arises under the Animals Act 1971 where the dog causes damage by killing or injuring livestock.[99]

Under s.79(1)(f) of the Environmental Protection Act 1990, any animal kept **4-290** in such a place so as to be prejudicial to health or a nuisance constitutes a statutory nuisance under that Act. This section overlaps with local authority powers to make byelaws "for preventing the keeping of animals so as to be prejudicial to health".[1] Further, under s.235 of the Public Health Act 1936, local authorities have the power to make byelaws for good rule and govern-ment and for the suppression of nuisances, which may include the suppression of noisy animals.

Dog control orders

The Clean Neighbourhoods and Environment Act 2005 creates a new method, **4-291** the dog control order, as a way of tackling the nuisance caused by dogs and aims to encourage responsible dog ownership. Prior to the coming into force of the 2005 Act, and in addition to the common law and legislation cited above, the Dogs (Fouling of Land) Act 1996 created a criminal offence "if a dog defecates at any time on designated land and a person who is in charge at that time fails to remove the faeces from the land forthwith".[2] The 2005 Act

---

[95] *ibid.*, s.3(5).
[96] *ibid.*, s.3(6).
[97] *Lippiatt v South Gloucestershire CC* [1999] 3 W.L.R. 137.
[98] That is, cattle, sheep, goats, horse and poultry, but not game.
[99] The definition of livestock under the Animals Act 1971 extends to pheasants, partridges and grouse whilst in captivity.
[1] Public Health Act 1936, s.81(b). Note that authorities do not have the power to make byelaws in respect of the same subject matter covered under dog control orders (Clean Neighbourhoods and Environment Act 2005, ss.64 and 65 and see para.4-291 ff below).
[2] Dogs (Fouling of Land) Act 1996, s.3; a local authority had the power, by order, to designate for the purposes of this Act any land in their area which is land to which this Act applied. In the Act, "designated land" meant land to which this Act applied which was for the time being so designated: Dogs (Fouling of Land) Act 1996, s.2(1). See also The Dogs (Fouling of Land) Regulations (SI 1996/2762) under s.2(3) and (4) of the Dogs (Fouling of Land) Act 1996 in rela-tion to orders of designation of land.

repeals the 1996 Act and also replaces the right to make byelaws in respect of the same subject matter.[3]

4-292   A dog control order provides for one or more offences prescribed by regulations as follows:

(1) failure to remove dog faeces;

(2) not keeping a dog on a lead;

(3) not putting and keeping a dog on a lead under direction;

(4) permitting a dog on land from which it is excluded; and

(5) taking more than a specified number of dogs on land.[4]

4-293   Dog control orders may be made by a primary or secondary authority[5] in respect of any land in its area which is open to the air and to which the public are entitled or permitted to have access (with or without payment).[6] The procedure to be followed in making a dog control order is set out in the Dog Control Orders (Procedures) Regulations, that is, primary and secondary authorities need to be consulted and the public notified. Provision is also made for the revocation of such orders.[7]

4-294   The orders must specify the offences and penalties, the wording of which is prescribed.[8] A dog control order may not come into force until at least 14 days after it is made.[9]

4-295   A person guilty of an offence contained in a dog control order, save for exempted persons as specified in the regulations, is liable on summary conviction to a fine not exceeding level 3 on the standard scale.[10] Sections 59 to 62 also make provision for the issue of fixed penalty notices in the event that an offence is committed.

4-296   A number of defences are provided in the regulations. The offences of failure to remove faeces and permitting a dog on land from which it is excluded do not apply to a person who is registered as a blind person in a register compiled under s.29 of the National Assistance Act 1948, or to a person who has a disability which affects his mobility, manual dexterity, physical co-ordination or ability to lift, carry or otherwise move everyday objects, in respect of a dog trained by Dogs for the Disabled (registered charity number 700454), Support Dogs (registered charity number 1088281) or Canine Partners for Independence (registered charity number 803680) and upon which he relies for assistance. No offence is committed where a person has a reasonable excuse for failing to remove the faeces, or the owner, occupier or other person or authority having control of the land has consented (generally or specifically) to his failing to do so. It is a defence to an offence of not keeping a dog on a

---

[3] Clean Neighbourhoods and Environment Act 2005, ss.64 and 65. Section 64 explains the effect on existing byelaws. See also the guidance issued by Defra. Note that the guidance contains numerous errors.

[4] Clean Neighbourhoods and Environment Act 2005, s.55 and The Dog Control Orders (Prescribed Offences and Penalties, etc.) Regulations (SI 2006/1059), reg.3(1) and Schs 1–5.

[5] A primary authority in England is a district council, county council, London Borough Council, common council of the City of London, the Council of the Isles of Scilly and, in Wales, a county or county borough council. A secondary authority is a parish council. See Clean Neighbourhoods and Environment Act 2005, ss.58 and 63.

[6] Clean Neighbourhoods and Environment Act 2005, s.57.

[7] SI 2006/798.

[8] Dog Control Orders (Prescribed Offences and Penalties, etc.) Regulations (SI 2006/1059), reg.4 and Schs 1–5. See also Sch.6 in relation to amendments of such orders.

[9] Reg.6.

[10] Reg.3(2).

lead or failing to do so when directed that a person has a reasonable excuse for failing to keep the dog on a lead, or the owner, occupier or other person or authority having control of the land has consented (generally or specifically) to his failing to do so. Furthermore, no offence is committed where a person has a reasonable excuse for taking more than the specified maximum number of dogs onto the land, or the owner, occupier or other person or authority having control of the land has consented (generally or specifically) to his doing so.[11]

---

[11] Dog Control Orders (Prescribed Offences and Penalties, etc.) Regulations (SI 2006/1059), Sch.1, para.1(2), (3); Sch.2, para.1(2); Sch.3, para.1(2); Sch.4, para.1(3); Sch.5, para.1(2).

CHAPTER FIVE
Housing Management

Introduction

5-001 We have so far considered anti-social behaviour in the context of the criminal law, the use of statutory powers granted to local authorities to deal with it, and specific environmental controls. However, the most conspicuous area of anti-social behaviour law is housing. In Chapter One, we summarised the evidence supporting the case that it is a major contributory factor in the deterioration of the social and physical condition of estates, particularly in areas of low housing demand and its impact on tenants and landlords.[1] There is an argument that housing law reform significantly stimulated developments in other fields and the problem of "the neighbour from hell" has preoccupied the media and several national governments. It was the last Conservative Government which extended the nuisance grounds for possession in the Housing Acts and launched the introductory tenancy scheme. Given the communitarian style to the current government's social and legal policy, further wide scale developments in the area of housing law are not surprising. Furthermore, as part of its project, Ensuring Responsible Renting, the Law Commission is focusing on the anti-social behaviour of tenants and the inadequacy of the law in ensuring that tenants behave properly.[2] This chapter is concerned with the legal powers available to landlords and housing managers, in both the private and public sector, to control anti-social behaviour on or near their properties.

Public vs Private Sector Landlords

5-002 The powers available to landlords to tackle anti-social behaviour largely depend on the category of landlord in to which they fall. Parliament has granted wider powers to the public sector for the very reason that they are social landlords. In the private sector, landlords have more limited powers, but at the same time have less reason to evict a tenant who is responsible for anti-social behaviour. In this section, we compare the range of powers available to the public and private sector.

Definition of Public Sector Landlord

5-003 It is not easy to precisely define the types of landlords who fall under the public sector category. It obviously includes local authorities; however, in

---

[1] See also Law Com Paper No. 162, Part XIII, paras 13.1–13.9.
[2] See Law Commission, Ninth Programme of Law Reform, Pt. Three, paras 3.15–3.23. The Report is due to be published in April 2007.

recent years, local authorities have been disposing of their housing stock to other types of organisations namely, registered social landlords (RSLs) and housing action trusts (HATs). Hence, on the one hand, it would be over simplifying matters to describe such organisations as being in the public sector. HATs have been described as "quasi local authorities"[3] and RSLs are a hybrid of a public and private body.[4] Courts have refused to treat housing associations as public authorities, in relation to landlord and tenant disputes[5] or the management of a residential home, for the performance of a local authority's statutory duties.[6] The reason for this may be that the policy of the Housing Act 1988 is seen as bringing housing associations within the private sector regime.[7] On the other hand, it would also be over simplifying matters to describe RSLs and HATs as private sector landlords simply because their tenants enjoy roughly the same security of tenure as in the private sector.

The situation is a little clearer since the coming into force of the Human Rights Act 1998. In considering the effect of s.6(3)(c) of the 1998 Act, the Lord Chancellor said: **5-004**

"That provision is there to include bodies which are not manifestly public authorities, but some of whose functions only are of a public nature. It is relevant to cases where the courts are not sure whether they are looking at a public authority in the full bloodied Clause 6(1) sense with regard to those bodies which fall into the grey area between public and private. The Bill reflects the decision to include as 'public authorities' bodies which have some public functions and some private functions."[8]

Thus, the 1998 Act makes housing associations subject to challenge for breach of the Convention. It does not mean that every decision or action by an RSL will be treated as a public function subject to that type of challenge. In *Poplar HARCA v Donoghue*[9] the Court of Appeal held that an RSL per se is not a public body in all circumstances; nor is the act of providing accommodation for rent, without more, a public function simply because it is provided for a certain section of society. It is a feature, or combination of features, which imposes a public character on the act that makes an act public which would otherwise be private. The fact that there is statutory authority for what is done may help to mark the act as being public, as can the extent of control over the function exercised by another body which is itself a public authority. The more closely the acts that could be of a private nature are enmeshed in the activities of a public body, the more likely they are to be public. **5-005**

---

[3] Housing Act 1988, s.63.
[4] There are also unregistered housing associations which are not registered with the Housing Corporation and in particular, housing associations discharging local authority's duties, fully mutual housing corporations, charitable housing trusts, self-build housing societies and industrial housing associations. It is unlikely that they will be treated as public bodies.
[5] *Peabody Housing Association Ltd v Green* (1978) 38 P. & C.R. 644. See also *Riverside Housing Association Ltd v The Commissioners for Her Majesty's Revenue and Customs*, VAT Tribunal no. 19341 where it was held that the registered social landlord was not a public body for the purposes of Art. 4(5) of the Sixth VAT Directive (77/388/EEC). C.f. the government's acknowledgement that registered social landlords are public bodies for the purposes of directives on procurement (ODPM News release 208, September 10, 2004). This may strengthen arguments that registered social landlords should be treated as public bodies although "a body governed by public law" is closely defined in the directives.
[6] *R. v Servite Houses and Wandsworth LBC Ex p. Goldsmith and Chatting* (2000) 3 C.C.L.R. 325; (2000) 32 H.L.R. 35.
[7] Tenancies granted by housing associations fall under the Housing Act 1988 regime.
[8] *Hansard* (HL) November 24, 1997, Vol. 583, col 811; also see Home Secretary, *Hansard* (HC) June 17, 1998, Vol. 314, cols 409–10.
[9] [2001] EWCA Civ 595; [2001] 3 W.L.R. 183.

5-006   The particular circumstances in *Poplar HARCA* which led to the Court of
Appeal deciding that it was a public authority for the purposes of the 1998 Act
are as follows: *Poplar HARCA* had been created by the Council for the
purpose of taking a transfer of the housing stock, five of its members were
also members of the local authority and it was subject to local authority guidance as to how it acted towards its tenants.[10]

Local Authorities and Registered Social Landlords

5-007   The powers and remedies available to RSLs and HATs have become more
closely assimilated to those of local authorities in recent years. In its consultation paper, *Renting Homes 1: Status and Security*, the Law Commission considered that local authorities and registered social landlords should have the
same powers and duties as landlords in respect of anti-social behaviour[11] and
said that it was, ". . . anxious to maintain the principle of equality between
local authorities and registered social landlords in respect of duties relating to
anti-social behaviour".[12] The Law Commission's *Renting Homes: The Final
Report*, which was published on May 5, 2006 together with a draft Bill, continues this theme, providing for "a single social tenancy", the secure contract,
to be used by both local authorities and registered social landlords, described
as "community landlords." The current government has also pursued a continuing merger of the two types of social landlord. Prior to the coming into
force of the Anti-Social Behaviour Act 2003, the courts could only attach a
power of arrest to an injunction on an application brought by an RSL, HAT
or local authority but not by a private sector landlord.[13] Further, even where
the applicant was an HAT or RSL, the injunction could only relate to a breach
of a tenancy agreement so that a power of arrest could only be attached where
the defendant was one of their own tenants. Local authorities were in a
slighter stronger position as they were able to obtain an injunction together
with a power of arrest against anyone who was causing a nuisance in the locality.[14] The 2003 Act has replaced these injunctions with new powers: the anti-
social behaviour injunction and an injunction restraining the unlawful use of
premises, both of which may have a power of arrest attached and include an
exclusion provision where certain conditions apply. The power of arrest and
exclusion order may also apply to an injunction to restrain breaches of a
tenancy agreement if the ground for making such an application is that the
conduct is capable of causing nuisance or annoyance to any person. There is
no distinction between the power available to the local authority and that of
the RSL. The 2003 Act has also created a new form of tenancy; the demoted
tenancy, applicable to tenants of local authorities. Similarly, RSLs have been
given power to demote assured tenants who are guilty of anti-social behaviour
to assured shorthold tenants on the same grounds. Even before the 2003 Act,
local authorities and RSLs could, at their discretion, introduce a probationary tenancy regime for new tenants.[15] Local authorities and RSLs are now

[10] See also *R. (Heather and Others) v The Leonard Cheshire Foundation* [2001] EWHC Admin
429; [2001] All E.R. (D) 156 (Jun).
[11] Consultation Paper no. 162 *Renting Homes 1: Status and Security* para.13.18.
[12] Para.13.27 Law Comm. The rationale behind this is that both are social landlords as opposed
to providers of housing for commercial gain and therefore have a general obligation to the
community in which their housing is located. Furthermore, the growing number of large stock
transfers means that the registers social landlord sector is increasing.
[13] Housing Act 1996, s.153.
[14] *ibid.*, s.152.
[15] In the case of local authorities, the Housing Act 1996 created the introductory tenancy scheme.
RSLs were able to implement a system of probationary tenancies by granting assured shorthold tenancies with limited security of tenure.

both under a duty to publish anti-social behaviour policies. Furthermore, the housing management controls of an RSL are now more extensive than in the private sector, including the use of anti-social behaviour contracts, rehabilitation, mediation and liaising with other agencies to help improve behaviour, instead of merely evicting the tenant.[16]

In April 2006, the ODPM published a consultation paper seeking views on **5-008** developing a "respect standard for housing management." The consultation paper is concerned with the role of the social landlord in tackling anti-social behaviour. The proposed Respect Standard comprises of ten "commitments" social landlords should sign up to namely: (1) accountability, leadership and commitment; (2) empowering residents; (3) delivering preventative approaches and rewarding "pro-social behaviour"; (4) ensuring people are clear about how to report anti-social behaviour and are encouraged and supported to do so; (5) building procedures around the needs of the customer and providing support for victims and witnesses; (6) delivery of early interventions to nip problems in the bud; (7) taking swift enforcement action to protect communities as quickly as possible; (8) publicising action to reassure communities and encourage their engagement; (9) working to enforce breaches to ensure that communities are clear that persistent anti-social behaviour will carry penalties; and (10) delivery or facilitation of support to tackle the causes of anti-social behaviour. The purpose behind such commitments, it is said, is to make social landlords accountable to residents and "provide a clear outline of the core components of an effective response to tackling anti-social behaviour and delivering respect." These "commitments", however, seem to do no more than the policies and procedures social landlords are required to formulate and adopt under s.12 of the Anti-Social Behaviour Act 2003. The guidance on such policies and procedures has also been given by the ODPM, in respect of local authorities, and the Housing Corporation, in respect of registered social landlords. Moreover, it is recognised that there is a significant overlap with the Housing Inspectorate's (part of the Audit Commission) service inspections using published key lines of enquiry (Kloe). These include coverage of ways of dealing with anti-social behaviour. Indeed, the consultation papers admits that delivery against the Respect Standard will be broadly commensurate with the level of service required to gain a good rating against the anti- social behaviour section of the estate management Kloe. It is proposed that the sign- up will not be obligatory nor is there any provision for enforcement.

The Private Sector

In contrast, private sector landlords have limited powers to deal with anti- **5-009** social behaviour. Many private sector landlords grant assured shorthold tenancies, which provide a limited security of tenure to the tenant. In order to obtain possession, all the landlord is required to do is serve a notice requiring possession.[17] There is no need to give reasons for seeking possession and the court must order possession if the notice requirements are met. However, there is a downside if the landlord wants to evict a problem tenant as quickly as possible. The landlord is required to give at least two months notice[18] and the court will not be able to order possession until after the first six months of the tenancy.[19]

---

[16] Much of this is beyond the scope of the book which concentrates on legal powers and remedies. However, it has been referred to, albeit briefly, in the section below on housing management controls.

[17] Housing Act 1988, s.21(1) and (4).

[18] *ibid.*, s.21(1).

[19] *ibid.*, s.21(5).

5-010   One way of overcoming this problem is by seeking possession on one of
the grounds in Sch.2 to the Housing Act 1988 in the same way as a "fully
assured tenant". There are two grounds which are relevant in cases of anti-
social behaviour, namely, breach of tenancy agreement[20] and nuisance or
criminal conduct.[21] Under Ground 12, it is necessary to consider the wording
of the terms of the agreement to ascertain whether there has been a breach.
Ground 12 can be particularly useful where the tenancy agreement specifies
conduct which is considered to be anti-social, although it will not be
sufficient to include a term prohibiting the tenant from doing anything
which, in the landlord's opinion, might be or become a nuisance.[22] The usefulness of Ground 14 is that it is the tenant who will be liable, even if the nuisance was caused by a mere visitor to the property. Thus, the ground will be
applicable where family members use the dwelling-house as a gathering-
point, or catalyst, for others who actually cause the nuisance (but do not live
with the tenant). The risk in pursuing possession under these grounds is that
the court is required to consider whether it would be reasonable to order possession and, if necessary, whether it would be reasonable to suspend or postpone possession.[23] It is at this stage that the extent of personal fault becomes
more relevant to the issue of whether or not it is reasonable to make a possession order and, if so, whether to suspend it.[24] Thus, the landlord is always
at risk of only obtaining a suspended possession order and, even if an outright order is made, the tenant is entitled to make an application to suspend
the warrant for possession.[25]

5-011   In order to obtain possession, the landlord needs to serve a notice seeking
possession in the prescribed form[26] specifying the grounds and particulars of
nuisance. The benefit of going under Ground 14, unlike the assured shorthold
ground, is that proceedings can be commenced immediately on service of the
notice.

5-012   Another way in which the landlord may combat anti-social behaviour is by
way of proceedings for an injunction. It is possible to obtain an interim
injunction if the court accepts that the conduct is so serious that the landlord
should not have to wait until trial. An urgently required injunction may also
be sought without notice to the tenant if putting him on notice would defeat
the purpose of the injunction. It will be necessary to show that there is a cause
of action, the most obvious being for breach of the tenancy agreement.
Whether a court would grant an injunction against the tenant for the behaviour of visitors or other residents will very much depend on the terms of the
tenancy agreement. The court is only likely to grant an injunction for nuisance if it can be shown that the landlord's use and enjoyment of the land has
been interfered with. If perpetrators of nuisance do not have any lawful
reason for being on land belonging to the landlord, an injunction can be
sought against trespass.

5-013   In summary, the landlord should consider the seriousness of the anti-
social behaviour in order to decide on the best course of action. The most
effective way is to obtain possession under Grounds 12 and 14, although
there is always the risk that the court may suspend or delay possession. If the
anti-social conduct is so serious, it is worth considering whether to seek an

---

[20] Housing Act 1988, Sch.2, Ground 12.
[21] *ibid.*, Sch.2, Ground 14.
[22] *Camden LBC v McBride* (1999) 1 C.L. 284, CC.
[23] Housing Act 1988, s.7(4) and *West Kent Housing Association v Davies* (1999) 31 H.L.R. 415.
[24] *Portsmouth CC v Bryant* (2000) 32 H.L.R. 906, CA.
[25] Housing Act 1988, s.9.
[26] *ibid.*, s.8; Assured Tenancies and Agricultural Occupancies (Forms) Regulations 1997 (SI 1997/194).

injunction in the meantime. However, if the landlord can wait for two months (in effect, longer, by the time the possession hearing is heard) then an outright possession order is guaranteed, subject to all the requirements being met.

Private landlords supply housing for commercial and profitable reasons. It **5-014** is for this reason that the private sector is excluded from having the wide powers which are available to social landlords.[27] What is of some concern, however, is new legislation limiting the freedom of the private sector and punishing it for the conduct of their tenants. The Housing Act 2004 allows local authorities to licence landlords in areas which are considered to be of low housing demand. The idea is that properties in these areas are owned by bad landlords who encourage anti-social tenants. The evidence for this assertion is obscure; even in the consultation paper it was admitted that this "might be", rather than "is", happening. It is questionable whether such licensing would have any effect. If a landlord is not licensed to let property, or is refused a licence, the chances are that either the property will be left vacant or it will be let to tenants who may indeed be anti-social.

The government also continues to entertain proposals to sanction housing **5-015** benefit, under which housing benefit will not be payable where tenants have been found guilty of anti-social behaviour.[28] The consequences for private landlords, many of whom own no more than one or two properties as a small investment, could be dramatic. If housing benefit is not paid, tenants who rely on housing benefit, and are by their very nature on low or no income, will not be able to pay the rent. Arrears will accrue and landlords will have no choice but to seek possession either under discretionary grounds, or more likely under Ground 8 (two months of arrears), or where they are let under an assured shorthold tenancy under the mandatory s.21 of the Housing Act 1998 notice. This may indeed ultimately shift the burden on to the public sector.

As part of its project, Housing: Ensuring Responsible Renting (in the Ninth **5-016** Programme of Law Reform), the Law Commission is considering anti-social behaviour in the private sector. This will include consideration as to the extent to which the principles and procedures available in connection with anti-social behaviour by rental-occupiers should also apply to owner-occupiers.

Management Controls

The principal way in which landlords can control the behaviour of their **5-017** tenants is through the terms and conditions of the tenancy agreement. Relatively recently, landlords (predominantly in the "social sector") have devised new methods to protect other tenants under their control as well as prevent anti-social behaviour.

Tenancy Agreements

There is wide scope in controlling the behaviour of tenants by imposing **5-018** certain terms relating to unacceptable conduct of the tenant in any letting

---

[27] The Law Commission does not consider that private landlords should have the same powers and duties as landlords in the social sector. Even under the proposed reforms for security of tenure, private landlords will still have available to them, as they do now, a mandatory ground for possession. See also The Law Commission, Ensuring Responsible Renting project which will consider anti-social behaviour in the private as well as the social sector. The Report is due to be published in April 2007.

[28] See Respect Agenda.

agreement. In the event of a breach, the landlord will be entitled to seek possession[29] or seek an injunction to prevent any further breaches.[30]

5-019   The specific clauses in tenancy agreements relating to nuisance vary widely. Most landlords provide for a general clause on nuisance; others will include specific areas such as violence, racism, offensive language, drunkenness, types of noise and pets.[31] It is common for a term to be included which prohibits the tenant from taking part in any criminal activity on the premises. The tenant will be in breach if he engages in such activity, notwithstanding that he has not been convicted of a crime. It will, however, be necessary for the allegation to be made out on a higher than normal standard of proof.[32]

5-020   The terms of the tenancy agreement may limit the scope of the statutory ground for possession under which possession can be sought. Thus, where a landlord included a clause stating it would seek possession under Ground 14 of Sch.2 to the Housing Act 1988, if ". . . you [the tenant] have been convicted of using the premises for immoral or illegal purposes or of an arrestable offence carried out at or in the locality of the premises", the Court of Appeal held that the inclusion of the word "you" could only have been intended to refer to the criminal conviction of the tenant and was not to be read as "you or anyone living in or visiting the premises".[33] The clause in the tenancy agreement was not descriptive of the statutory rights but restrictive.

5-021   In contrast, where a landlord agreed under the terms of the tenancy agreement that it could seek possession under Ground 14 of Sch.2 to the Housing Act 1988, but sought to rely on the extended Ground 14 as amended by the Housing Act 1996, May L.J. held:

> "In my view, it was not the purpose of this tenancy agreement to restrict the landlord for ever to the statutory grounds for possession as they stood in 1988 as paraphrased in the tenancy agreement and irrespective of statutory amendment. On the contrary, it provided for the tenant to have security of tenure as provided by the 1988 Act and the intention must have been that, if the statutory grounds for possession (or other related provisions) were amended, neither party would be disentitled from relying on the amended provisions . . . Any other construction would fossilize the agreement when this is my view obviously not the intention."[34]

5-022   The Court of Appeal refused to substitute a shorter notice period[35] since it was an express term of the tenancy agreement that four weeks' notice would be given. Nonetheless, since the landlord had not contracted out of s.8(1)(b) of the Housing Act 1988, it was possible for the court to dispense with the requirement of the notice if it considered it just and equitable.

5-023   Where the victims of anti-social behaviour have been the landlord's employees, the terms of the tenancy agreements have been crucial in deciding whether

---

[29] For example, Ground 1 of Sch.2 to the Housing Act 1985 in the case of secure tenancies or Ground 12 of Sch.2 to the Housing Act 1988 in the case of assured tenancies.

[30] They were also important in relation to injunctions with powers of arrest under the now repealed Housing Act 1996, s.153; they continue to be relevant in relation to powers of arrest under s.153D.

[31] See Caroline Hunter, *Dealing with Anti-social Behaviour: the Tenancy Terms and Conditions*, [2000] J.H.L. 3; *The Use of Legal Remedies by Social Landlords to Deal with Neighbour Nuisance*, Centre for Regional, Economic Research (Paper no. H8), Sheffield Hallam University.

[32] *Bristol CC v Mousah* (1998) 30 H.L.R. 32 at 41, *per* Otton L.J.

[33] *Pollards Hill HA v Marsh* [2002] EWCA Civ 199.

[34] *North British Housing Association v Sheridan* [2003] EWCA Civ 1046; [2003] I.R.L.R. 885.

[35] The Housing Act 1996 amended the Housing Act 1988 so that where possession is sought under Ground 14, proceedings can be commenced as soon as the notice seeking possession has been served on the tenant: Housing Act 1988, s.8(6).

possession or an injunction can be sought. If the neighbourhood office or town hall is not in the locality of the tenant's property, it will not be possible to seek possession under the specific nuisance grounds.[36] This problem has been overcome to some extent in the case of local authorities, RSLs and HATs. The Anti-Social Behaviour Act 2003 amended the Housing Act 1996 Act so as to create a new anti-social behaviour injunction. A relevant landlord may obtain an injunction where the conduct of the defendant is capable of causing nuisance and annoyance to a person employed (whether or not by the relevant landlord) in connection with the exercise of the relevant landlord's housing management functions.[37]

Landlords will not be able to impose unfair terms on the tenant. The Unfair Terms in Consumer Contracts Regulations[38] apply to tenancy agreements which have not been individually negotiated. A term shall always be regarded as not having been individually negotiated where it has been drafted in advance and the tenant has therefore not been able to influence the substance of the term.[39] It will be regarded as unfair ". . . if, contrary to the requirement of good faith, it causes a significant imbalance in the parties' rights and obligations arising under the contract, to the detriment of the consumer".[40] The term will be unenforceable. Additionally, the Office of Fair Trading (OFT) has the power to regulate terms and apply to the court for offending terms to be struck out of tenancy agreements without reference to the tenant.[41] It also issued guidance ". . . to explain why it considers some standard contractual terms used in [assured and assured shorthold] tenancy agreements to be potentially unfair under the regulations." It objects to terms in tenancy agreements that impose obligations or restrictions which are, or can be, wholly unreasonable, or which give the landlord the power to make unreasonable conditions of that nature. Thus, where a landlord sought possession, inter alia, on the ground that the defendant had acted in breach of a contractual term of the tenancy, which provided that the tenant would not do or permit anything to be done on the premises which in the landlord's opinion might be or become a nuisance, the county court held that the term was unenforceable and unfair because the question of its breach was to be determined subjectively by the landlord.[42]

5-024

The guidance not only applies to assured and assured shorthold tenancies in the private sector but will also provide some assistance to social landlords.[43] It will also be of assistance to public sector landlords in ensuring that contract terms will comply with the Regulations. The Regulations and the recent OFT guidance is a major step forward in treating tenants as consumers and this has been developed further by the Law Commission[44] with regard to standard contractual terms.

5-025

---

[36] Housing Act 1985, Sch.2, Ground 2; 1988, Sch.2, Ground 14; *Lewisham LBC v Simba-Tola* (1992) 24 H.L.R. 644.

[37] Housing Act 1996, s.153A(4)(d).

[38] The Unfair Terms in Consumer Contracts Regulations 1999 (SI 1999/2083) made under Directive 93/13/EEC. See also Law Com No. 292 "Unfair Terms in Contracts" published in February 2005. This makes recommendations and includes a draft bill for the statutory and regulatory provisions to be unified into a single regime.

[39] SI 1999/2083, Reg.5(2).

[40] *ibid.*, Reg.5(1).

[41] Stop Now Orders (EC Directive) Regulations 2001 (SI 2001/1422).

[42] *Camden LBC v McBride* (1999) 1 C.L. 284, C.C.

[43] Social landlords are also subject to the Regulations. See Reg.3(1) which provides, that a "seller or supplier" means any natural or legal person who, in contracts covered by these Regulations, is acting for purposes relating to his trade, business or profession, whether publicly owned or privately owned.

[44] See Consultation Paper *Renting Homes 1: Status and Security* and *Renting Homes* Law Com No.284 at Pt IV.

5-026   Initially, the Law Commission recommended that tenancy agreements should have four types of term.[45] This included "special terms" which would impose obligations on occupiers for social policy reasons and, in particular, obligations relating to anti-social behaviour. They would only be capable of variation by the Secretary of State by amending the law. It was proposed that these recommendations would be translated into legislative form in 2004, although the Housing Act 2004 made no such provision. The Law Commission's *Renting Homes: The Final Report*, which was published on May 5, 2006, has since recommended that it should be a fundamental term in all contracts that contract- holders may not:

(1) use or threaten to use violence against a person lawfully living in the premises;

(2) do anything which creates a risk of significant harm to such a person;

(3) engage or threaten to engage in conduct that is capable of causing nuisance or annoyance to a person:

   (a) living in the locality of the premises; or
   (b) engaged in lawful activity in the premises or in the locality of the premises;

(4) use or threaten to use the premises, or any common parts that they are entitled to use under the contract, for criminal purposes.

Breach of this "prohibited conduct term" would give rise to a ground for possession and injunction proceedings. Additionally, in the case of local authorities and registered social landlords, "community landlords", this would also enable a power of arrest and an exclusion order to be attached to the injunction proceedings and the court to demote the tenancy to a standard contract, similar to the current assured shorthold tenancy, terminable by the court on service of a notice only ground. The standard contract would also be used for the probationary tenancy if such a scheme was adopted by the community landlord.[46]

Anti-Social Behaviour Policies

5-027   Local housing authorities, registered social landlords and housing action trusts are under a duty to prepare a policy in relation to anti-social behaviour[47] and procedures for dealing with such behaviour.[48] The purpose is to inform the public (including tenants of the landlord) about the way in which the landlord will tackle the problems of anti-social behaviour in the context of their housing stock. The Parliamentary Under-Secretary at the Home Office, explaining the reason behind this new duty when giving evidence to the Home Affairs Committee on the March 25, 2003, said:

"The publishing is not just for information about those who are likely to wind up being confronted by action, it is about trying to make local authorities and social landlords accountable to the wider community. Publish what

[45] *Renting Homes* Law Com No. 284, published on November 5, 2003. See also note 27 above.
[46] *Renting Homes: The Final Report*, Law Com No. 297, paras 2.10, 2.31 and Pt 9. See also the Draft Bill, Pt 2, Ch.3.
[47] Housing Act 1996, s.218A(8) provides that anti-social behaviour is any conduct to which s.153A or 153B applies.
[48] Housing Act 1996, 218A (2). A statement of the policy was to be published six months after the commencement of the Anti-Social Behaviour Act 2003, s.13: Housing Act 1996, s.218A(3), that is, December 31, 2004.

you are supposed to be doing, so that we can see what you are doing along-side what you are supposed to be doing. That is the motive behind obliging them to publish their policies."[49]

The Secretary of State[50] and, in the case of registered social landlords, the Housing Corporation,[51] have issued guidance on the content of the policy and procedure. It is important that policy and procedures are compatible with other legislation and strategies.[52] The policy statement should include a definition of anti- social behaviour,[53] the services available,[54] the obligations of tenants[55,] the strategic context,[56] and other policies which have been adopted by the landlord in tackling anti-social behaviour.[57] The procedure statement sets out the ways in which the landlord will operate its policy. Thus, not only will it explain the various ways in which the landlord may take enforcement action,[58] but it will also outline the procedures to be adopted when a complaint is made, what provision will be arranged for witness support, and how data will be collected and behaviour monitored.[60] **5-028**

The duty is unlikely to be particularly onerous on landlords. Local housing authorities are already required to take reasonable steps to prevent crime and disorder under the Crime and Disorder Act 1998 and to promote the well-being of their areas under the Local Government Act 2000. Furthermore, under the Homelessness Act 2002, local housing authorities are required to carry out a homelessness review for their district and formulate and publish a homeless strategy based on its results.[61] This involves looking at other groups that address the problems, including anti-social behaviour, that can lead to homelessness, such as Local Strategic Partnerships and Community Strategies, Drug Action Teams, Crime and Disorder Strategies and Youth Offending Teams (YOTs).[62] It would, therefore, appear that policy and strategies are already in **5-029**

---

[49] Uncorrected Evidence Q.80.
[50] The Housing Act 1996, s.218A(7)(a). The ODPM issued *Anti-social behaviour. Policy and Procedure, Code of Guidance for local housing authorities and housing action trusts* in August 2004. The guidance is also relevant to those managing housing stock on behalf of the local housing authority, e.g. arms length management organisations, tenant management organisations; See also Commission for Local Administration in England, *Neighbour Nuisance and Anti-social Behaviour. Special Report*, February 2005.
[51] Housing Act 1996, s.218A(7)(b). The Housing Corporation issued guidance, *Anti-social behaviour. policy and procedure, Guidance for Housing Associations*, under Circular no. 08/04. The guidance is applicable to housing associations registered under the Housing Act 1996, s.2. It may also relevant to those organisations managing social housing stock on behalf of associations and other agencies managing housing stock and tackling anti-social behaviour. In relation to Wales, the guidance is issued by the National Assembly for Wales (Housing Act 1996, s.218A(9)).
[52] ODPM Guidance, paras 1.10–1.11, in relation to local housing authorities, Children Act 1989, Crime and Disorder Act 1998, Disability Discrimination Act 1995, Homelessness Act 2002, Race Relations Act 1976 and the Human Rights Act 1998 and housing strategies under Local Government Act 2003, s.87. See also Hg. Corp. Guid. paras 1.8–1.11.
[53] ODPM Guid., paras 3.1–3.4; Hg. Corp. Guid., paras 3.1–3.3.
[54] ODPM Guid., paras 3.5–3.6; Hg. Corp. Guid., paras 2.12., 3.4–3.5.
[55] ODPM Guid., paras 3.8; Hg. Corp. Guid., paras 3.7.
[56] ODPM, Guid., paras 3.7; Hg. Corp. Guid., paras 3.6.
[57] For, e.g. policies regarding the support of complainants and witnesses, professional witness schemes, racial harassment, domestic violence, prevention of anti-social behaviour, rehabilitation of perpetrators, multi-agency partnership working, data protection and information sharing, publicity, confidentiality, tackling anti-social behaviour in the private sector, protection of staff, training (ODPM Guid., paras 3.9–3.44; Hg Corp. paras 3.2–3.37).
[58–59] ODPM Guid., paras 4.10–4.11; Hg Corp. paras 4.10.
[60] ODPM Guid., paras 4.2–4.16; Hg Corp. paras 4.1–4.16.
[61] Homelessness Act 2002, s.2(1)(a).
[62] See Annex 1 to the Homelessness Code of Guidance for Local Authorities (England).

place in relation to anti-social behaviour and the additional requirement under yet another Act of Parliament only serves to repeat what is already required of local housing authorities. In relation to registered social landlords, many already publish policies as a matter of good practice.[63]

5-030   The statements of policy and procedure will be available to the public and not just to tenants of the relevant landlord. It must be available for inspection at all reasonable hours at the landlord's principal office and must be provided on payment of a reasonable fee to any person who requests it.[64] Additionally, the landlord must prepare a summary of its current policy and procedures and provide, without charge, a copy of the summary to any person who requests it.[65] The guidance suggests that the policy and procedure statements and the summary should be reviewed annually.[66] Any review will be subject to consultation.[67]

Anti-Social Behaviour Contracts

5-031   One way in which some social landlords are attempting to curb anti-social behaviour without resorting to the courts is through "acceptable behaviour contracts",[68] or in the case of children, "parent control agreements". The aim is to stop the anti-social behaviour by discussion with the perpetrator, rather than by punishing him. While these contracts are not legally binding, they are useful in curbing behaviour where there is insufficient evidence, or the level of nuisance is not serious enough, to justify taking possession proceedings, obtaining an injunction or anti-social behaviour order or prosecuting in the criminal courts. They act as a warning to the perpetrator who, if he breaches the agreement, may find himself subject to criminal proceedings, eviction or subject to an injunction or anti-social behaviour order.

5-032   There are a variety of ways in which social landlords may wish to implement such contracts although it would appear that the aim is to involve the perpetrator in discussions at the initial stage. In most cases, the contract is formulated with the perpetrator being given the opportunity to discuss the terms. This can be achieved through an informal meeting between the perpetrator and housing officer. The aim is to discuss what is anti-social behaviour

---

[63] Since 2001, it has been a requirement in the Housing Corporation's Regulatory Code that registered social landlords tackle anti-social behaviour. Local Authorities are referred to two good practice documents: *Homelessness Strategies: A Good Practice Handbook* and *Preventing Tomorrow's Rough Sleepers: A Good Practice Handbook*.

[64] Housing Act 1996, s.218A(5).

[65] Housing Act 1996, s.218A(6). The Guidance also deals with the content of the summary at ODPM Guid., paras 5.1–5.8 and Hg. Corp. Guid., paras 5.3–5.8.

[66] ODPM Guid., para.2.9; Hg. Corp. Guid., para.2.9.

[67] Under Housing Act 1985, s.105, local housing authorities are obliged to make and maintain arrangements to secure a degree of consultation with their secure tenants on matters of housing management. Similar provisions apply in relation to introductory tenants (Housing Act 1996, s.137). The ODPM Guidance also encourages consultation with other groups (ODPM Guid., para.2.13). The Housing Corporation makes similar suggestions in respect of registered social landlords in addition to the requirement that landlords work with residents to develop, produce and agree policies and procedures in accordance with the *Charter for Housing Association Applicants and Residents* (Circular No. 08/04, para.3; Hg. Corp. Guid., para.2.11).

[68] For instance, London Borough of Islington, London Borough of Waltham Forest, Birmingham City Council, London Borough of Newham, Merthyr Tydfil, Southend on Sea, Burnley Housing Association and Padiham Community Housing. Since publication of the first edition, many other authorities and registered social landlords have begun to use acceptable behaviour contracts as the first stage in controlling anti-social behaviour. According to the Home Office, 13,000 acceptable behaviour contracts were made in 2005 (Home Office *Tacking Anti-social Behaviour in 2005: Summary of Survey Results* (2006)).

and the implications for neighbours, as well as for the perpetrator, if that behaviour persist, for instance, the threat of possession proceedings, anti-social behaviour orders or criminal action. The police are, in many cases, involved with the contract at this stage or at least at the stage when a contract is thought advisable.

The contract itself will include the actions the perpetrator has agreed not to **5-033** do and all present should sign the contract. The contract is thereafter monitored by housing officers and the police. If there is a breach, proceedings may be taken in respect of eviction from the home or, as in many cases, anti social behaviour orders. The contract can apply to children and adults.

The first anti-social behaviour contracts were introduced by the London **5-034** Borough of Islington at the end of 1999. Since then, the "scheme" has been adopted by a number of authorities around the country. In practice, the London Borough of Islington have said that the act of formulating the contract can be helpful for the family involved.[69] They also ran a pilot scheme involving contracts between neighbours as a form of mediation between neighbours, identifying the problems that each neighbour has with the other and assist in easing tension between the parties involved.

In the main, most local authorities send out warning letters to tenants who **5-035** are behaving in an anti-social manner. This assists in attempting to start resolving problems from the onset and may, if ignored, in combination with notices seeking possession, assist in showing the court that it is reasonable to make a possession order. These may be followed up by visits.

Some local authorities, as part of their strategy in tackling anti-social **5-036** behaviour, organise visits to the offender from the housing department and the police community and where the perpetrator is a juvenile in the presence of the parent. They are warned that, if they do not stop their behaviour, their tenancy (or their parents' tenancy as the case may be) is at risk and they may be subject to an anti-social behaviour order.[70]

Parenting contracts

The Police and Justice Bill proposes giving powers to local authorities and reg- **5-037** istered social landlords to enter into parenting contracts with a parent of a child or young person who has engaged, or is likely to engage, in anti-social behaviour.[71] Registered social landlords may only do so where that behaviour directly or indirectly relates to or affects their housing management functions.[72] The parenting contract will contain requirements which have been agreed by the parent, which may include attendance at a counselling or guidance programme. They are based on the same principles which underlie

---

[69] See R. Lucas and J. Whitworth, *Tackling Anti-social Behaviour: Information and Case Studies* Local Government Association, published July 2002.
[70] *ibid.*
[71] Police and Justice Bill, cl.16 proposes to insert a new s.25A and B to the Anti-Social Behaviour Act 2003.
[72] Police and Justice Bill, cl.16 inserting s.25B(1(b). Housing management functions include: (a) functions conferred by or under an enactment; (b) the powers and duties of the landlord as the holder of an estate or interest in housing accommodation (s.25B(2)). Some assistance may be drawn from the Housing Corporation Guidance, *Anti-social Behaviour: Policy and Procedure, Guidance for Housing Associations*, August 2004. It suggests that matters which directly affect the landlord's housing management functions may include tenant and community participation, maintenance and repairs, rent and rent arrears collection, neighbourhood management and dispute resolution. Matters which indirectly affect their housing management functions may include social care and housing support, environmental health and refuse collection and other services which enable a registered social landlord to operate effectively (para.2.5).

acceptable behaviour contracts; they are not legally binding[73] and work to address bad behaviour, in appropriate circumstances, without recourse to the courts. It is questionable, therefore, whether there is a need for this to be formulated in statute, other than as political window dressing.

Mediation

5-038 Anti-social behaviour may arise from disputes between neighbours. It may not always be appropriate for a landlord to seek possession against one tenant. One way in which landlords, and in particular social landlords, may seek to resolve problems is through mediation.[74]

Wardens[75]

5-039 It is considered by the government that the presence of wardens on estates and streets helps to deter anti-social behaviour and to address many of the other problems faced by deprived neighbourhoods. Under the auspices of the Neighbourhood Renewal Unit, the Neighbourhood and Streets Warden Unit manages grants for the provision of such wardens to be given to deprived areas in England and Wales.[76]

5-040 The Neighbourhood Warden Scheme provides a uniformed, semi-official presence in a residential area with the aim of improving quality of life. Their duties include promoting community safety, assisting with environmental improvements and housing management and contributing to community development. This may involve patrolling, providing concierge duties or acting as "super caretakers". Furthermore, they may act as professional witnesses in anti-social behaviour proceedings. Neighbourhood wardens who have been accredited by the chief officer of the police may be given additional powers to deal with anti-social behaviour, rather than having to call the police.[77]

5-041 Launched in August 2001, the Street Wardens Programme builds on the success of the Neighbourhood Wardens scheme and provides highly visible uniformed patrols in town and village centres, public areas and neighbourhoods. The emphasis is on them caring for the physical appearance of the area and they tackle such problems as litter, graffiti and dog fouling. In addition, they are to be used to deter anti-social behaviour, reduce the fear of crime and foster social inclusion.

5-042 More recently the government has re-iterated its attempts to introduce warden schemes in more deprived areas.[78]

---

[73] Police and Justice Bill, cl.16, inserting new Anti-Social Behaviour Act 2003, s.25A(6); s.25B(6).
[74] See R. Lucas and J. Whitworth, *Tackling Anti-social Behaviour: Information and Case Studies* Local Government Association, published July 2002.
[75] See para.2.34 above.
[76] For schemes in England, the grant is paid under s.126 of the Housing Grants, Construction and Regeneration Act 1996. For Schemes in Wales, Neighbourhood Warden grant is paid under s.169 of the Criminal Justice and Public Order Act 1994.
[77] A chief officer of Police can accredit employees of an employer who has entered into arrangements concerning community safety (Police Reform Act 2002, ss.40–43).
[78] In 2006, £155 million of the neighbourhood element of the Safer Stronger Communities Fund will, according to the "Respect Action Plan", be used to introduce neighbourhood management and warden schemes in 100 areas where they do not currently exist. Furthermore, the Plan will ensure that all government funded regeneration schemes "are accompanied by approaches which promote good [,] and tackle bad [,] behaviour" such as warden schemes. For example, Pathfinders will have to agree to a protocol for 2006–2008 which will set out the approaches—known to work—which they must adopt to tackle anti-social behaviour." Confusingly, the "Respect Action Plan" appears to suggest that they do not have the statistics to support warden schemes (p.28).

Rehabilitation

The Dundee Families project was set up to assist families who were homeless, **5-043** or at severe risk of homelessness, as a result of anti-social behaviour. The aim of the project was to deal with families who have caused difficulties to their neighbours and/or landlords. This is achieved in three main ways: first, by admissions to a core block providing accommodation for up to four families and intensive support; secondly, by support to a small number of dispersed flats mainly for families to move into from the core block; thirdly, by an outreach service provided to selected families in their existing accommodation, who are at risk of eviction by Dundee City Council by reason of their antisocial behaviour.

The project offers support and assistance in adult mental health, child and **5-044** adolescent mental health, child protection, drug issues, alcohol issues, child development, family violence, parenting skills and special needs. According to the evaluation report, the success of the project has been partly due to the inter agency co-operation: "Virtually everyone interviewed in the study—parents, children and young people, representatives of other agencies—praised the work of the Project, saw it as offering a unique service and wished it to continue. It was seen as not duplicating other services, but offering distinctive and usually more intensive help".[79]

The success of the project has led to similar schemes being set up in England **5-045** and Wales.[80] While it is notable that the Dundee project is entirely a private initiative, the Respect Action Plan proposes operating them in areas where anti-social behaviour is most acute and will require local authorities to provide intensive family support where it is needed.[81]

Others

In its Consultation Paper, *Tackling Anti-Social Tenants*, the government **5-046** advised landlords to use the opportunity of media coverage in order to enhance their reputation, raise resident's hopes and expectations of landlord engagement and make clear to perpetrators of anti-social behaviour that their landlord will take action.[82] The importance of publicity has been underpinned in guidance on ASBOs in particular.[83] Whilst this may be a useful and potentially workable option to deal with anti-social tenants, the "naming and shaming" of perpetrators and the encouragement of neighbours to assist in the "policing" of orders made against perpetrators has somewhat uncomfortable political connotations to it of the type discussed more broadly in Chapter One. In every case, a balance must be struck between ensuring the injunction is effective against creating a situation which may get out of hand[84] and rendering a community that is not at ease with itself.

Landlords are advised to have regard to the design and layout of develop- **5-047** ments in order to deter crime and enhance community safety. For instance,

---

[79] *Evaluation of the Dundee Families Project*, para.8.14.
[80] For e.g. Sheffield High Support Services, Manchester Foundations Project, Bolton Families Project, Salford ASSFAM Families Project, Oldham Families Project and Blackburn with Darwen Families Project.
[81] See "Respect Action Plan", p.22.
[82] *Tackling Anti-Social Tenants*, p.29.
[83] *Working Together, Guidance on publicising anti-social behaviour orders.*
[84] For example, the extreme and utterly misguided reaction of some members of local communities to the *News of the World*'s paedophile campaign in 2001. See also in *Moat Housing Group-South Ltd v Harris and Hartless* [2005] EWCA Civ 287; [2005] H.L.R. 33 where the housing association turned up with television cameras when serving a "without notice" anti-social behaviour injunction.

there should be high quality door and window locks, access to entrances to flats should be restricted to residents, there should be good sound insulation between dwellings and care should be taken to avoid incompatible lifestyles.[85]

Nuisance

5-048 Nuisance is an unlawful interference with the use or enjoyment of land either as a member of the public (public nuisance) or as owner or occupier of land or the use or enjoyment of some right over or in connection with it (private nuisance).

Public nuisance

5-049 A public nuisance concerns the situation where the act or omission materially affects the reasonable comfort and convenience of a class of Her Majesty's subjects who come within the sphere or neighbourhood of its operation.[86] In Chapter 2, at paras 2.119 to 2.123, we discussed public nuisance offences. Public nuisance is a criminal offence and is defined as follows: "A person is guilty of a public nuisance . . . who (a) does an act not warranted by law, or (b) omits to discharge a legal duty, if the effect of the act or omission is to endanger the life, health, property, morals, or comfort of the public, or to obstruct the public in the exercise or enjoyment of rights common to all Her Majesty's subjects."[87] It is a civil wrong where the victim has suffered damage over and above the general inconvenience and injury suffered by the public. Parliament has seen fit to make a number of matters a public nuisance which are covered elsewhere in this book. For instance, matters which are relevant to anti-social behaviour have been dealt with under the Environmental Protection Act 1990,[88] the Noise Act 1996[89] and the Animals Act 1971. In relation to the common law, holding an acid house party[90] and keeping a brothel ("the perambulations of the prostitutes and their visitors")[91] have been held to be a public nuisance.[92]

Private nuisance

5-050 In *Thompson-Schwab v Costaki*,[93] Lord Evershed M.R. categorised private nuisance in this way:

(1) causing an encroachment on his neighbour's land, when it closely resembles trespass;

(2) causing physical damage to his neighbour's land or building or works or vegetation upon it; and

(3) unduly interfering with his neighbour in the comfortable and convenient enjoyment of his land.

---

[85] *Tackling Anti-Social Tenants*, p. 32.
[86] A. Dugdale, et al. *Clerk and Lindsell on Torts* (19th edn, Sweet & Maxwell, 2005), para.20–03.
[87] J. Richardson et al, *Archbold: Criminal Pleading, Evidence and Practice* (Sweet & Maxwell, 2001), paras 31–40.
[88] As amended by the Clean Neighbourhoods and Environment Act 2005.
[89] *ibid.*
[90] *R. v Ruffell (David)* (1992) 13 Cr.App.R.(S.) 204; *R. v Shorrock (Peter)* [1994] Q.B. 279, CA.
[91] *Thompson-Schwab v Costaki* [1956] 1 W.L.R. 335 Also see *Laws v Florinplace* [1981] 1 All E.R. 659 which concerned a sex shop in a residential area.
[92] See also paras 2-119 to 2-123.
[93] *ibid.*

Although anti-social behaviour can arise under any of the above categories,[94] **5-051**
this chapter is primarily concerned with the third category. It is important to
note regarding the first and second categories of private nuisance, that the surrounding circumstances and neighbourhood are not a factor to be taken into
account and it is necessary to prove the actual encroachment or damage,
where applicable.[95]

In contrast, with nuisances of the third category, for the nuisance to be **5-052**
actionable, it will be necessary for the interference to be unreasonable "according to the ordinary usages of mankind living in society, or more correctly in a
particular society".[96] In essence, what is reasonable will depend on the facts of
the individual case. It will include consideration of the following matters: the
act of nuisance; the timing of the act; the place of its commission; the manner
of committing it; and the duration of the nuisance.[97] It is always a question of
degree whether an act or omission is an actionable nuisance. Thus, the nuisance must be substantial, on an objective basis, regardless of the victim's age,
health or position in life. It must be ". . . an inconvenience materially interfering with the ordinary comfort physically of human existence, nor merely
according to elegant or dainty modes and habits of living, but according to
plain and sober and simple notions among the English people".[98] In
Kennaway v Thompson,[99] the court held:

> "The question is whether the neighbour is using his property reasonably,
> having regard to the fact that he has a neighbour. The neighbour who is
> complaining must remember, too, that the other man can use his property
> in a reasonable way and there must be a measure of 'give and take, live and
> let live'."[1]

There must also be some right in or appertaining to the claimant's land with **5-053**
which there is an interference.[2] In *Hunter v Canary Wharf Ltd*,[3] the House of
Lords held that there was no cause of action in nuisance where television
signals were interfered with by the erection of tall buildings; the claimant as
landowner had no right to receive the television transmissions.[4]

In relation to the character of the neighbourhood, it is suggested that the **5-054**
cases appear to be concerned with a situation, for instance, where the victim
lives in an industrial town and cannot expect the same purity of air as in a
rural area,[5] rather than a victim who lives on an inner city estate; the courts
do not expect them to have to suffer harassment, verbal and physical abuse or
foul language merely because they live on undesirable estate.

The question of the duration of the nuisance is a relevant, but not a deci- **5-055**
sive, factor in determining whether it is actionable. Thus, where noise lasted
for three weeks but was substantial, it was held that this constituted an actionable nuisance.[6]

Although malicious acts may not create an actionable nuisance per se, **5-056**
it is a relevant consideration in determining reasonableness of user. In

[94] See *St Helens Smelting Co v Tipping* (1965) 11 H.L.C. 642 at 650, per Lord Westbury L.C.
[95] *ibid.*
[96] *Sedleigh-Denfield v O'Callaghan* [1940] A.C. 880 at 903, per Lord Wright.
[97] See *Stone v Bolton* [1949] 1 All ER 237 at 238–239, per Oliver J.
[98] *Walter v Selfe* (1851) 4 De G. & Sm. 315 at 322.
[99] [1980] 3 All E.R.
[1] See also *Southwark LBC v Mills* [2001] 1 A.C.1 at 20; [1994] 4 All E.R. 449 at 464.
[2] *Aldred's Case* (1610) 9 Co. Rep. 57b.
[3] [1997] A.C. 655, HL.
[4] Renting Homes: The Final Report, Law Com No.297, paras 5.31–5.42; Sch. 7 of the draft Bill.
[5] *Sturges v Bridgman* (1879) 11 Ch.D. 852 at 856.
[6] *Metropolitan Properties v Jones* [1939] 2 All E.R. 202.

Christie v Davey,[7] the defendants responded to the defendant's playing of a piano by banging cooking pans on the wall. Such malicious behaviour rendered the degree of noise they made unreasonable. North J. said:

".. . if what had taken place had occurred between two sets of persons both perfectly innocent, I should have taken an entirely different view of the case. But I am persuaded that what was done by the Defendant was only done for the purpose of annoyance, and in my opinion it was done on a legitimate use of the Defendant's house to use it for the purpose of vexing and annoying his neighbour."

Therefore, it can be seen that where the actions are malicious, it will be a significant determining factor in respect of unreasonableness of user.

5-057   Normal use of a person's land will not constitute an actionable nuisance despite it causing interference and annoyance with the victim's use of his land. In *Southwark LBC v Mills*,[8] the local authority was not liable for the serious interference caused by the everyday activities of the local authority's tenants (and as a result of poor sound-proofing) because, notwithstanding the substantial interference with the enjoyment of the premises, the acts complained of were: (a) necessary for the common and ordinary use and occupation of the defendant's land; and (b) were done with proper consideration for neighbouring occupiers.

Who may sue?

5-058   The person in possession or occupation of the land can sue in private nuisance. Thus, in *Malone v Laskey*,[9] a bare licensee was not able to maintain an action in nuisance because she had no legal right to possession of the land which she occupied.[10] However, in *Khorasandjian v Bush*,[11] the Court of Appeal held that a girl who lived with her parents was able to bring an action in nuisance for pestering telephone calls even though she was not entitled to possession of the property in which she lived. The decision was overruled in *Hunter v Canary Wharf*,[12] which restated the traditional thinking that nuisance is a tort against land and interests in land. In any event, the House of Lords saw no reason to bend the tort of nuisance to include such persons with the coming into force of the Protection from Harassment Act 1997 which would have provided a remedy for the claimant in *Khorasandijan v Bush*.

5-059   Nevertheless, de facto possession may be sufficient. In *Foster v Warblington*,[13] the claimant was the licensee of oyster beds; he was entitled to maintain an action in nuisance where sewage was discharged on those beds. In *Pemberton v Southwark LBC*,[14] a secure tenant who, on breach of the terms of the suspended possession order, became a tolerated trespasser,[15] was held to be able to maintain a cause of action in nuisance. The claimant was entitled to exclusive possession of the dwelling-house, notwithstanding the breach of the terms of the suspended possession order, by virtue of the protection

[7] [1893] 1 Ch. 316.
[8] [2001] 1 A.C. 1; [1999] 3 W.L.R. 939; [1999] 4 All E.R. 449; (2000) 32 H.L.R. 148.
[9] [1907] 2 K.B. 144.
[10] Approved by the House of Lords in *Hunter v Canary Wharf*, above; see also, *Jan de Nul (UK) v NV Royal Belge* [2000] 2 Lloyd's Rep. 700 where licences to moor boats did not confer a right to maintain an action in private nuisance.
[11] [1993] Q.B. 727.
[12] [1997] A.C. 655.
[13] [1906] 1 K.B. 648.
[14] [2000] 1 W.L.R. 1672; [2000] 3 All E.R. 924; (2000) 32 H.L.R. 784.
[15] See *Burrows v Brent LBC* [1996] 1 W.L.R. 1448 at 1455.

afforded to such persons by the Housing Act 1985.[16] Additionally, trespassers in adverse possession can sue in nuisance if their occupation is capable of defeating the owner's title by adverse possession.[17]

A freeholder owner with a right to possession is entitled to a cause of action **5-060** in nuisance for interference with his enjoyment of the premises.[18] If the free-holder is not in actual occupation of the property but can show that the nuisance is causing him problems in finding other tenants he will be entitled to damages.

In order for a landlord, as opposed to a direct victim of nuisance, to act on **5-061** the basis of behaviour amounting to a nuisance, the landlord must be able to show that its use and enjoyment of the land has been interfered with. It has been held that a landlord who had let his property could not take action where the nuisance merely annoyed his tenants.[19] The reasoning behind this is that the right to use and enjoy the premises is vested in the tenant and the nuisance might stop at any time before the end of the lease.[20]

Similarly, in *Jones v Llanrwst UDC*,[21] Parker J. said that it was reasonably **5-062** certain that a reversioner could not maintain an action in the nature of tres-pass (the context here indicates that nuisance is covered by this phrase):

". . . including, I think, actions for the infringement of natural rights arising out of ownership of land, without alleging and proving injury to the rever-sion. If the thing complained of is of such a permanent nature that the reversion may be injured, the question whether the reversion is or is not injured is a question for the jury."

Permanent was defined by Parker J. as follows: **5-063**

"I take permanent, in this connection, to mean such as will continue indef-initely unless something is done to remove it. Thus a building which infringes ancient lights is permanent within the rule, for, though it can be removed before the reversion falls into possession, still it will continue until it be removed. On the other hand, a noisy trade, and the exercise of a right of way, are not in their nature permanent within the rule, for they cease of themselves unless there be someone to continue them."

The degree of permanence here appears to relate to an inanimate object such **5-064** as buildings, and the actual cause of nuisance of persons. In any event, the reversioner does not have a cause of action unless the nuisance is permanent. Thus, it has been held that a reversioner cannot maintain a cause of action in nuisance where the use and enjoyment of the land has been interfered with by noise or smoke,[22] even if it drives the tenants away or reduces the letting value of the property.[23] Thus, a reversioner can sue for the locking of a gate across a way to which he is entitled for his tenants[24] or physical injury to the prop-erty which will be permanent.[25] However, in *Hampstead & Suburban*

[16] Housing Act 1985, s.85.
[17] *Pemberton v Southwark LBC* (2000) 32 H.L.R. 784.
[18] *Hunter v Canary Wharf* [1997] A.C. 655.
[19] *Jones v Chappell* (1875) L.R. 20 Eq. 539.
[20] *ibid.*
[21] (No. 2) [1911] 1 Ch. 393, 404, per Parker J.
[22] *Simpson v Savage* (1859) 1 C.B. N.S. 347; *Mott v Shoolbred* (1875) L.R. 20 Eq. 22; *Cooper v Crabtree* (1882) 20 Ch.D. 589, CA; *House Property and Investment Co v HP Horse Nail Co* (1885) 29 Ch.D. 190; *Mayfair Property Co v Johnston* [1894] 1 Ch. 508.
[23] *Mumford v Oxford, Worcester, etc., Ry* (1856) 1 H. & N. 34; *Simpson v Savage*, (1859) 1 CB. N.S. 347.
[24] *Kidgill v Moor* (1850) 9 C.B. 364; *Bell v Midland Ry* (1861) 10 C.B. (N.S.) 287.
[25] *Meux's Brewery Co v City of London Electric Lighting Co* [1895] 1 Ch. 287, 317.

Properties v Diomedous,[26] an argument was raised that the landlord could not have been affected by the loud music in the restaurant; only its tenants could have been affected. Megarry J., seemingly contrary to the weight of authority, rejected this contention as "absurd" and he pointed to the likely effects on the landlord of diminution in value of the property, of complaints from the tenants and difficulty in re-letting. He dismissed the assertion that it does not matter to landlords that their tenants cannot sleep because of nuisance caused by a neighbour, and by implication, could not take action to prevent the nuisance. He stated,

> "*Res ipsa loquitur.* It may be that in some remote corner of the world there is a country where it makes no difference to a landlord that such noise is emitted from one of his premises that the tenants of the other parts cannot sleep, where the market value of his reversion is increased or at least maintained by these emissions, and where his life is made sweeter by the complaints of his tenants and the prospect of difficulty in re-letting the premises which they occupy if they determine their tenancies or default. Applied to the only jurisdiction with which I am concerned, these propositions have only to be enunciated for their absurdity to appear."[27]

Human rights

5-065 It has been suggested that the common law may develop to provide further protection from nuisances for those who do not have the right to possession of their homes.[28] In *Hunter v Canary Wharf*, Lord Cooke, dissenting,[29] referred to Art.8 of the European Convention on Human Rights. He considered that this provision, inter alia,[30] was aimed, in part, at protecting the home and was to be construed to give protection against nuisances. He referred to a number of European cases, namely, *Arrondelle v United Kingdom*[31] (aircraft noise), and *Lopez Ostra v Spain*[32] (fumes and smells from waste treatment plant).[33] He asserted that the protection went beyond possession or property rights and "[wa]s a legitimate consideration in support of treating residence as an acceptable basis of standing at common law." Therefore, it may be possible to argue that even a mere licensee could sue a public body in nuisance where their rights under Art.8 are adversely affected. It is also notable under those European cases that the European Court required the public authority not merely to avoid interference with the exercise of the claimant's rights under Art.8 but to take positive steps to ensure effective respect for the Claimant's rights.[34]

Action taken on behalf of the victim

5-066 It was becoming increasingly common for social landlords to fund the legal costs of their employees in pursuing a civil action where there was no other cause of action available to the landlord or where this was used in conjunction

---

[26] [1969] 1 Ch. 248.

[27] *Hampstead & Suburban Properties Ltd v Diomedous* [1969] 1 Ch 248 at 258.

[28] See D. Elvin Q.C. and J. Karas *Unlawful Interference with Land* (2nd ed., Sweet & Maxwell, 2002).

[29] [1997] A.C. 655 at 714 A–D.

[30] Article 16 of the Convention on the Rights of the Child, Art.12 of the Universal Declaration of Human Rights.

[31] Application No. 7889/77 (1982) 26 D. & R. 5.

[32] (1994) 20 EHRR 277.

[33] Also see *Guerra v Italy* (1998) 26 E.H.R.R. 357.

[34] See below in relation to landlord liability for nuisance at para 5-074ff.

with other proceedings. This has been remedied to some extent by tenancy agreements imposing an obligation on tenants not to cause nuisance to the landlord's employees, contractors or agents. Furthermore, the anti-social behaviour injunction extends to nuisance caused to a person engaged in lawful activity in, or in the locality of, housing accommodation owned or managed by the relevant landlord or a person employed (whether or not by the relevant landlord) in connection with the exercise of the relevant landlord's management functions.[35]

5-067 If taking action on behalf of tenants, RSLs must have regard to the constitution of the organisation and any advice from the Housing Corporation. Local authorities are more constrained in their actions; there is no specific power to take action on the victim's behalf. A local authority may, however, "do anything. . .which is calculated to facilitate, or is conducive or incidental to the discharge of their functions."[36] Note also the well-being powers in the Local Government Act 2000.[37] Furthermore, they have a general power to manage their properties.[38]

5-068 It is also recommended that a formal agreement is reached between the victim and the body taking action on behalf, or paying for the legal costs, of that victim. Such terms will need to cover the naming of the parties to the litigation, the support for the litigation, potential costs of both the defendant and claimant, and various eventualities such as withdrawal and losing.

Who may be sued?

5-069 The person who will be liable is the perpetrator of the nuisance.[39] There is no requirement for such a person to have some interest in the land to be held liable for a nuisance which he causes on land.[40] In relation to agents or servants of the perpetrator of the nuisance, he will still be liable if he authorises the nuisance. Thus, in *Lippiatt v South Gloucestershire*[41] the Council were held liable for the acts of nuisance caused by Gypsies because they allowed them to camp on the land and use it as base for causing nuisance against neighbouring farmers.[42]

5-070 An occupier will not be liable for a nuisance created by a trespasser without his knowledge or consent, unless he continues or adopts the nuisance so created.

> "If he is to be liable a further condition is necessary, namely, that he had knowledge or means of knowledge or means of knowledge, that he knew or should have known of the nuisance in time to correct it and obviate its mischievous effects."[43]

Defences

5-071 There are a number of defences that can legitimately be raised in a claim for nuisance, some of which have already been discussed, namely, nuisance caused

[35] Housing Act 1996, s.153A(4); *c.f. Manchester City Council v Lee* [2003] EWCA Civ 1256; *Wigan Metropolitan Council v G (A Child)* [2004] 1 W.L.R. 349. [2003] in relation to s.152 injunctions. The Court of Appeal held that the victims of anti-social behaviour had to be in premises which were let by the local authority or RSLs in order to be able to obtain this type of injunction.
[36] Local Government Act 1972, s.111.
[37] See para.3-006.
[38] Housing Act 1985, s.21.
[39] *Southwark LBC v Mills*; *Camden LBC v Baxter* [2001] 1 A.C. 1 at 15D; [1994] 4 All E.R. 449 at 459g, per Lord Hoffman and per Lord Millett at 464c.
[40] *Southport Corporation v Esso* [1956] A.C. 218 at 224–225 obiter; [1954] 2 Q.B. 182, 204, 182, 196–197; *Clerk & on Torts, op. cit*, paras 20–51.
[41] [1999] 4 All E.R. 149; (1999) 31 H.L.R. 1114.
[42] See also *Att-Gen v Stone* (1894) 2 T.L.R.; *Page Motors v Epsom & Ewell B.C.* (1981) 125 S.J. 590.
[43] *Sedleigh-Denfield v O'Callaghan* [1940] A.C. 880 at 904.

by a trespasser and continuation or authorisation of the nuisance. In cases concerning anti-social behaviour, however, the defences will be of limited use unless there is an authorisation or adoption of the nuisance.[44] Therefore, defences to nuisance are referred to, briefly, as follows[45]:

(1) permission: if the claimant has allowed or consented to the defendant creating a nuisance[46];

(2) easements or other rights: a defendant may have a right to what would otherwise constitute a nuisance by reason of an easement or right granted over the claimant's land entitling him to do those acts;

(3) statutory authority;

(4) inevitable accident;

(5) Act of God;

(6) ignorance of the nuisance: it is a defence to prove ignorance of the facts constituting the nuisance, unless that ignorance is due to the omission to use reasonable care to discover the facts;

(7) contributory negligence[47];

(8) necessity and private defence; and

(9) *novus actus interveniens.*

5-072 There is no defence to an action in nuisance that the activity is giving rise to the nuisance is carried on at a convenient or suitable place[48] or that it is in the public interest.[49] Furthermore, it cannot be argued that the claimant has come to the nuisance[50] or that a third party has a better title than the claimant to land affected by the nuisance.[51]

Damages

5-073 Damages in nuisance are for whatever loss results to the victim as a natural consequence of the tortious act of the defendant (be it the perpetrator of the nuisance or any other person who can rightfully be sued in nuisance).[52] Clearly, where enjoyment of the property is concerned it "cannot be assessed mathematically".[53] It is useful to consider recent cases, albeit decided in the county courts, to assess the level of damages which may be awarded.[54]

Landlord Liability for Nuisance

5-074 In the absence of seemingly ineffective action being taken by landlords, the victims of anti-social behaviour have recently been directing legal action away

[44] *Lippiatt v South Gloucestershire*, above.
[45] For a detailed discussion on defences to nuisance see *Clerk & Lindsell on Torts, op. cit*, paras 20–66ff.
[46] *Gilson v Kerrier DC* [1976] 1 W.L.R. 904 at 912–914.
[47] See Law Reform (Contributory Negligence) Act 1945.
[48] *Bamford v Turnley* (1860) 3 B. & S. 62.
[49] *Miller v Jackson* [1977] Q.B. 966 at 981–982.
[50] *ibid.*
[51] See *Clerk & Lindsell on Torts, op. cit*, paras 20–92.
[52] See *Grosvenor Hotel Co v Hamilton* [1894] 2 Q.B. 836 at 840.
[53] *Hunter v Canary Wharf* [1997] AC 655 at 696.
[54] See A. Arden Q.C., D. Carter and A. Dymond, *Quiet Enjoyment*, (6th edn, LAG Books, 2002) and Legal Action Group Updates for recent cases on the level of damages.

from the impecunious perpetrator and towards the financially solvent land-lord.[55] It has also been suggested that with increasing (and highly publicised) powers being given to landlords to tackle anti-social behaviour that tenant expectations have been raised.[56] If the landlord has these powers at its dis-posal, tenants expect to have a quiet life and expect their landlord to deal with it if the case is otherwise. In this section we consider the potential causes of action that a victim of anti-social behaviour may have.

Breach of contract

It is common for social landlords to include a clause that the landlord will "take **5-075** all reasonable steps to prevent any nuisance". The courts have been reluctant to hold a landlord in breach of that term,[57] although since *Moat Housing Group South Ltd v Harris and Hartless*[58] there may be more scope for arguing other-wise. In that case, the Association expressly incorporated into the tenancy agreement any guidance issued by the Housing Corporation with the approval of the Secretary of State. In July 2004, the Housing Corporation published its regulatory circular 07/04, *Tenancy Management, Eligibility and Evictions*, which advises registered social landlords to use the full range of tools to tackle anti-social behaviour, retaining eviction as a last resort.[59] The absence of any warn-ings about the behaviour and the failure of the association to use the full range of tools available before seeking possession led the Court of Appeal to find that the association had breached its own obligations under the terms of the tenancy agreement.[60] Whether the incorporation of the guidance and a registered social landlord's own policy and procedure will expose a landlord to a potential claim for breach of contract for failing to take any action remains to be seen. It is unlikely, however, that the courts will interpret any policy as an express obliga-tion on the landlord to take action in cases of anti-social behaviour.

In its consultation paper, *Renting Homes: Status and Security*, the Law **5-076** Commission invited views about the imposition of a contractual duty on social landlords.[61] It suggested that the contractual term should specify that the land-lord would take all reasonable steps to ensure that the occupier would be able to occupy the home unaffected by anti-social behaviour by other occupants of premises owned by the landlord.[62] This would, therefore, provide a tenant with a remedy for breach of contract in damages and or injunction order for spe-cific performance. It also suggested that the term would be enforceable by not only tenants, but also members of their household under s.1 of the Contracts (Rights of Third Parties) Act 1999. The Law Commission have subsequently rejected this idea and suggested that a general target duty be placed on social landlords thereby avoiding unnecessary claims for compensation.[63]

---

[55] See Loveland, "Fixing Landlords with Liability for the Anti-Social Behaviour of their Tenants 1: Stretching the Orthodox Position", (2005) J.P.L. 273; Loveland, "Landlord Liability for a Tenant's Nuisance", (2006) J.H.L. 9(1), 4–8.

[56] See Luba, "Meeting the Tenant's Expectations of 'Quiet Enjoyment'", Law. & Tax .R. 9(6), 154–158.

[57] *Helsdon v Camden LBC* (1997) Legal Action, December, p.12.

[58] [2005] EWCA Civ 287; [2005] H.L.R. 33.

[59] Housing Corporation Circular 07/04, *Tenancy Management, Eligibility and Evictions*, para.3.2.1.

[60] Although this did not prevent the Court of Appeal from concluding that it was still reasonable for the possession order to be made; the guidance had been issued recently and the behaviour was seriousness enough to merit the making of the order.

[61] Law Com Paper No.162.

[62] Law Com Paper No 162, para.13.33–13.34.

[63] Law Com No. 284, Pt XV, paras 15.17–15.19. Note also The Law Commission, Ensuring Responsible Renting project. The Report is due to be published in April 2007.

5-077   The courts will also not imply a term that the landlord will seek to enforce a nuisance clause in the tenancy of another.[64] The reason for this is that there is no need to imply such a term when the tenant has a cause of action in nuisance against the other tenant without intervention of the landlord. The contract is neither inefficacious, futile or absurd, without such a term.[65] There are also policy reasons for this view as the effect of such a term in the agreement would be far reaching and would mean, in some cases, the court requiring the council to take possession proceedings against the anti-social tenant. This would lead to an absurd situation where a court would be interfering with the council's discretion as to whether to take action and the Council would have to make submissions regarding reasonableness of the making of a possession order when they do not believe this to be the case.

Breach of statutory duty

5-078   In *O'Leary v Islington*,[66] an attempt was made to argue that the Council's statutory duty in relation to the general management, regulation and control of houses provided by them[67] gave rise to a general duty in tort to take particular care in relation to their tenants; the duty would therefore oblige them, if a tenant did not behave properly, to bring proceedings against them. The Court of Appeal was wholly unconvinced by the argument. Breach of statutory duty was, however, revisited by the Court of Appeal in relation to anti-social behaviour, in *Hussain v Lancaster CC*.[68] That case referred to an earlier House of Lords' decision in *X (minors) v Bedfordshire CC*[69] in which Lord Browne Wilkinson held:

> "To found a cause of action flowing from the careless exercise of statutory duties the plaintiff has to show that the circumstances are such that as to raise a duty of care at common law. . .The local authority cannot be liable for doing that which Parliament has authorised [unless] the decision complained of is so unreasonable that it falls outside the ambit of such statutory discretion."

5-079   As a result, the Court of Appeal in *Hussain v Lancaster CC* said that it would not be fair, just and reasonable to hold the Council liable in negligence. In dealing with racial harassment, co-operation is required between various agencies. It was unreasonable to impose liability in negligence upon any of the agencies for failing to achieve success. Moreover, the court held that it would cut across effective multi-agency working if one of the agencies involved was required by injunction to take specific steps. At the end of the day, it was for the local authority, and not for the court, to decide matters of policy, such as how much of the council's resources should be allocated to this particular problem and what action the council should take.

5-080   The Law Commission also raised the possibility of the creation of a general duty on local authorities to deal with anti-social behaviour. It was not intended, however, that this should provide a cause of action by an aggrieved occupier for breach of a statutory tort.[70] The advantage of such a duty was to seek public renown for action taken by central and local government in their

---

[64] *O'Leary v London Borough of Islington* (1983) 9 H.L.R. 81.
[65] *ibid.* per Ackner L.J. at 85–86 and per Dillon L.J. at 89.
[66] (1983) 9 H.L.R. 81.
[67] Under the Housing Act 1957.
[68] [2000] Q.B. 1; [1999] 2 W.L.R. 1142; [1999] 4 All E.R. 125; (1999) 31 H.L.R. 164.
[69] [1995] 2 A.C. 633; 3 All E.R. 353.
[70] W. Wade and C. Forsyth, *Administrative Law* (8th edn, Oxford University Press 2000) pp. 580–581.

fight against anti-social behaviour. The Law Commission also considered that it would ". . . provide a focus for those, such as occupiers, seeking to hold local authorities democratically to account for their action (or inaction) in dealing with anti-social occupiers."[71] In relation to housing associations, it was suggested that a general duty should be imposed on registered social landlords but such a duty would not give rise to a statutory tort. The enforcement of such a duty would be achieved through the regulatory structure whereby the Housing Corporation would have regard to the duty in performing its functions.[72] Additionally, the general duty would be taken account by such bodies as the Independent Housing Ombudsman.[73]

Following concerns raised by local authorities, the Law Commission **5-081** decided to recommend the creation of a general target duty on local authority landlords to take into account, in the management of their rented property, the need to deal with anti-social behaviour.[74] A similarly worded duty would be imposed on registered social landlords, expressed so as not to take effect in tort, which the Housing Corporation would be obliged to take into account in the performance of its regulatory functions.[75] This would therefore avoid unnecessary claims for compensation.[76]

To an extent this has been achieved by the duty to prepare and publish poli- **5-082** cies and procedures to deal with anti-social behaviour and the Housing Corporation's advice to registered social landlords to use the full range of tools available.[77] Furthermore, the Respect Action Plan proposes requiring social landlords to take certain types of action in areas where anti-social behaviour is most acute. It is questionable, however, that this gives rise to any contractual obligation between the landlords and its tenants.

Nuisance

The general rule is that a landlord will not be liable for nuisance committed by **5-083** his tenant. The exception to this rule is where the nuisance has either been expressly authorised or is certain to result from the purposes for which the property has been let.[78] In *Malzy v Eichholz*,[79] Pickford L.J., quoting Lord Collins M.R. in *Jaeger v Mansions Consolidated*,[80] said:

"The acts of the persons using these flats for immoral purposes could be construed to be the acts of the defendant in the sense that they authorised them—not merely that they did not stop them but that they were in effect a party to them."

In *Sedleigh-Denfield v O'Callaghan*,[81] the House of Lords held that an owner- **5-084** occupier of land is responsible for the acts of third persons on his land if he has continued or adopted the nuisance. Lord Wright explained that the

---

[71] Law Comm Paper No. 162, para.13.26.
[72] Housing Act 1996, s.34.
[73] If the case law develops so that registered social landlords are come to be seen as public bodies, the Law Commission proposes that the general statutory duty should be imposed.
[74] Law Com No.284, para.15.18.
[75] Law Com No.284, para.15.18.
[76] Law Com No.284, para.15.19.
[77] Housing Act 1996, 218A. See paras 5.27–5.30 above.
[78] *Rich v Basterfield* (1847) 4 C.B. 783, 136 E.R. 715; *Harris v James* (1876) 45 L.J.Q.B. 545; *Ayers v Hanson, Stanley & Prince* (1912) 56 Sol. Jo. 735; *Malzy v Eichholz* [1916] 2 K.B. 308; *Hilton & Another v James Smith & Sons (Norwood) Ltd* (1979) 257 E.G. 1063.
[79] [1916] 2 K.B. 308.
[80] (1902) 87 L.T. 690.
[81] [1940] A.C. 880.

ground of responsibility of an occupier of land is the possession and control of the land from which the nuisance emanates.[82] Viscount Maugham added,

"In my opinion an occupier of land 'continues' a nuisance if with knowledge or presumed knowledge he fails to take any reasonable means to bring it to an end. . .He 'adopts' it if he makes any use of the erection, building, bank or artificial contrivance which constitutes the nuisance."

Lord Atkin went on to say in his judgment in *Sedleigh-Denfield*[83]:

"For the purposes of ascertaining whether as here the plaintiff can establish a private nuisance I think that nuisance is sufficiently defined as a wrongful interference with another's enjoyment of his land or premises by the use of land or premises either occupied or in some cases owned by oneself."

5-085 The question of authorisation and adoption specifically in relation to anti-social behaviour arose in the case of *Smith v Scott*.[84] That case concerned an elderly couple, Mr and Mrs Smith, who were owner-occupiers of a dwelling house. The council had acquired a number of properties in the same road and, in particular, a property next door to the Smiths. In 1971, the council housed a large and unruly family called the Scotts in the adjoining property to the Smiths. It was known to the council that the Scotts were the sort of people who did not appear to be good tenants and were likely to be guilty of anti-social behaviour. The Smiths sought an injunction against the council restraining them from allowing any person to be permitted by them to occupy the adjoining house to create a nuisance. One of the arguments put forward on behalf of the Smiths was that the council, in placing the Scotts in the adjoining property with the knowledge that they were likely to cause a nuisance itself, committed the wrongful act of nuisance. Dismissing this argument, Pennycuick V.C. held that:

". . .the authorisation of nuisance has been rigidly confined to circumstances in which the nuisance has either been expressly authorised or is certain to result from the purposes for which the property is let . . . The exception is squarely based in the reported cases[85] on express or implied authority. In the present case the corporation [council] let no. 25 to the Scotts as a dwelling house on conditions of tenancy which expressly prohibited the committing of a nuisance and notwithstanding that the corporation [council] knew the Scotts were likely to cause a nuisance, I do not think it is legitimate to say that the corporation [council] impliedly authorised the nuisance."[86]

5-086 The courts appeared to take a different approach in a number of subsequent cases.[87] In *Page Motors v Epsom*,[88] the plaintiffs were tenants of business

[82] *ibid.*, at 903.
[83] At p. 896.
[84] [1973] 1 Ch. 314.
[85] *Rich v Basterfield* (1847) 4 C.B. 783, 136 ER 715; *Harris v James* (1876) 45 L.J.Q.B. 545; *Ayers v Hanson, Stanley & Prince* (1912) 56 Sol. Jo. 735; *Malzy v Eichholz* [1916] 2 K.B. 308.
[86] *Smith v Scott* was approved by the Court of Appeal in *Elizabeth v Rochester-upon-Medway CC* [1993] CA Transcript 456 refusing leave to appeal. In that case the Council were being sued as landlords in comparable circumstances. *Smith v Scott* was recently approved by the House of Lords in *Southwark LBC v Tanner* [1999] 3 W.L.R. 939. Hoffman quoted the passage from Lord Pennycuick's judgment at 950. See also Lord Millett at 956.
[87] *Hilton v James Smith & Sons (Norwood) Ltd* (1979) 251 E.G. 1063; *Page Motors Ltd v Epsom and Ewell BC* (1981) 80 L.G.R. 337; *Chartered Trust v Davies* [1997] 2 E.G.L.R. 83; *Lippiatt v South Gloucestershire Council* (2000) Q.B. 2001; [1999] 3 W.L.R. 137; [1999] 4 All E.R. 149; (1999) 31 H.L.R. 1114.
[88] [1981] 80 L.G.R. 337.

premises on the council's estate. The adjoining land was owned by the council but occupied illegally by Gypsies who were generally causing a nuisance to the business tenants. It was decided, by the Court of Appeal, in that case, that the local authority had adopted and continued the nuisance by not taking steps to remove the Gypsies from the land and allowing it to be used as an unsupervised caravan site.

A similar approach was adopted in the later case of *Chartered Trust Plc v Davies*.[89] The defendant was granted a lease of a shop in a mall owned by a common landlord. An adjoining unit was let to a pawnbrokers who attracted the customers who had little money to spend in other shops and would hang around in the common parts of the mall near the defendants shop. The pawnbroker's sign was centrally placed in the High Street entrance, as agreed in the terms of the lease, and light was restricted by reason of the pawnbroker's blocked windows. The Court of Appeal decided that:

    5-087

> "Where a landlord is granting leases in his shopping mall, over which he has maintained control, and charged a service charge thereof, it is simply no answer to say that a tenant's sole protection is his own ability and willingness to bring his individual action. Litigation is too expensive, too uncertain and offers no proper protection against, say, trespassing and threatening members of the public. The duty to act lies with the landlord".[90]

Prima facie, the judgments in these two cases would appear to overtake the decision in *Smith v Scott* and introduce a less restrictive test for establishing liability in nuisance. In *Hussain v Lancaster City Council*[91] these arguments were rejected by the Court of Appeal on the basis that the adverse decisions against both landlords were attributable to the special circumstances of the relationship between the parties. In *Page Motors*, the council deliberately continued the Gypsies' possession of the land on policy grounds by providing a water supply, skips and other amenities. In *Hussain*, the landlord had done no such thing. The Court of Appeal distinguished *Chartered Trust Plc v Davies*, because of the special role of the landlord in the management of the shopping mall where both shops were situated.

    5-088

Approximately a year after *Hussain* was decided, the issue of third party liability arose again in *Lippiatt v South Gloucestershire DC*.[92] In that case, the defendant council owned a strip of land, which was occupied, for three years, by Gypsies. The council resolved to tolerate what they regarded as an unauthorised encampment and provided toilet, water and other facilities. Adjoining this strip was land farmed by tenants of the Duke of Beaufort. The tenant farmers complained about the considerable nuisance the Gypsies were causing on their land and issued proceedings against the council. The Court of Appeal held that the occupier of land could be held liable in the tort of nuisance for the activities of licensees, even though those activities took place on the plaintiff's land. Thus, the court was not precluded from holding a defendant occupier liable for nuisance consisting of repeated acts on the plaintiff's land which, to the defendant's knowledge, were committed by persons based on his land but did not occur on his land.

    5-089

The Court of Appeal in *Lippiatt* distinguished *Hussain* on the facts. In *Hussain* the scope of nuisance had been confined to acts involving the defendant's use of his own land (following the opinion of Professor Newark that the term "nuisance" is properly applied only to such actionable user of land

    5-090

[89] [1997] 2 E.G.L.R. 83.
[90] *ibid.*, at 88B–C.
[91] [2000] Q.B. 1; [1999] 2 W.L.R. 1142; [1999] 4 All E.R. 125; (1999) 31 H.L.R. 164.
[92] [2000] Q.B. 51; [1999] 3 W.L.R. 137; [1999] 4 All E.R. 149; (1999) 31 H.L.R. 1114.

as interferes with the enjoyment by the plaintiff of rights in land).[93] This was approved by Lord Goff in *Hunter v Canary Wharf*[94] and by the Court of Appeal in *Sedleigh Denfield*. The disturbance complained about was a public nuisance for which the individual perpetrators could be held liable and they were identified as individuals who lived in council property. Their conduct, however, was not in any sense linked to, nor did it emanate from, the homes where they lived. The Court of Appeal held it was arguable that where the Gypsies were allowed to congregate on the council's land and used that as a base for their unlawful activities, that this could give rise to liability.

5-091   The Court of Appeal referred to *Attorney-General v Corke*[95] where the owner of a disused brick field allowed travellers to occupy his land, who then committed various acts including trespass in the neighbourhood. In that case, Bennett J. held the landlord liable on the express basis that the acts complained of gave rise to a public nuisance under the rule in *Rylands v Fletcher*. The Court of Appeal attached weight to an obiter reference to *Corke* by Sir John Pennycuick V.C. in *Smith v Scott*, that *Corke* could at least have been equally decided on the basis that the landowner was in possession of the property and was himself liable for the acts of his licensees. Sir John Pennycuick V.C. did not, however, go on to explain why it was equally applicable and did not address the issue of liability for third party activities committed off the defendant's land.[96] In *Thompson Schwab v Costaki*,[97] the Court of Appeal held that the perambulations of prostitutes and their customers constituted a nuisance. This case was used a basis for the proposition that the defendant could be liable for nuisance off the defendant's land in *Lippiatt*, although in *Costaki* the defendants had never argued in their defence that the nuisance occurred off their land. Consequently, the issue of third party liability for nuisance off his land was not fully argued nor was it fully analysed by the court in giving judgment. Evans L.J. acknowledged that both *Scott* and *Costaki* were silent on the issue but stated that since the proposition that nuisance activities must take place on the defendant's land had been rejected in *Attorney-General v Corke* ". . . that suggests, in my mind, that the reason for not raising it in the later cases was not that it had been overlooked".[98] By suggesting that the issue had been decided by *Corke* the Court of Appeal arguably imputed a specific holding that was simply not there; this appears to have arisen from a misreading of Sir John Pennycuick's reference to *Corke* in Scott. Moreover, the Court of Appeal then drew inferences from the absence of any specific holding on the issue in *Costaki* and *Scott* to assert that the question had already been correctly decided in *Corke* and was still good law, despite clear authority to the contrary in *Hussain*.

5-092   In *Lippiatt*, the Court of Appeal also appeared to suggest that the presence of travellers on the council's land constituted nuisance. It has been argued that "by adopting this analysis. . .he omitted to address the fact that the anti-social activities complained of were committed off the defendant's land and on the claimant's land".[99] The Court in *Lippiatt* looked at the relationship between the parties rather than the landlord's control over the land as a basis for nuisance liability.

5-093   There is a possible inconsistency between the liability of landlords and licensors for activities of third persons on their land. Landlords are only liable

---

[93] *The Boundaries of Nuisance* (1949) 65 L.Q.R. 480.
[94] [1997] A.C. 655, HL.
[95] [1933] 1 Ch. 89.
[96] See Baker, "Nuisance Behaviour: Local authority liability for anti-social behaviour of tenants and licensees", (2000) 30 J.H.L. 30.
[97] [1956] 1 All E.R. 652, [1956] 1 W.L.R. 335.
[98] *Lippiatt v South Gloucestershire Council* [2000] Q.B. 51; [1999] 3 W.L.R. 137; [1999] 4 All E.R. 149; (1999) 31 H.L.R. 1114at 144H–145A.
[99] Baker, *op. cit.* n.92.

for the acts of their tenants if they authorised those acts and if the acts involve the tenant's use of his land. Owners, on the other hand, seem to be responsible if they have adopted or continued a nuisance, for the activities of licensees or trespassers wherever they occur.[1]

These apparent inconsistencies were more or less clarified in the more recent case of *Mowan v Wandsworth LBC*,[2] even more so since Sir Christopher Staughton sat in both *Lippiatt* and *Mowan*.[3] In *Mowan*, the claimant had acquired a long lease of her flat under the right to buy legislation. The flat above was occupied by a secure tenant of the local authority who suffered from a mental disorder. The claimant complained that the secure tenant's behaviour (inter alia, deliberately blocking her toilet, causing floods, and making threats to kill) affected her enjoyment of her flat. The claimant issued proceedings against the secure tenant and the council. The claim against the council was based on the argument that a landlord could authorise a nuisance simply by failing to take action to prevent it; it was no longer necessary to show consent or active participation by the landlord (as held in *Malzy v Eicholz*[4]). Sir Christopher Staughton referred to *Hilton, Page Motors, Chartered Trust* and *Lippiatt* and said, "for good or ill, those are a different kind of case".[5] They were cases where the landlords had been occupiers of the land on which, or from which, a nuisance had been created by others.

5-094

The distinction between tenant and licensee arose again in *Winch v Mid Bedfordshire DC*.[6] In this case, some Gypsies were granted a licence over land owned by the council but caused anti-social behaviour to neighbours. It was accepted by the High Court, that the council remained in occupation of the land because a licence does not confer an interest in land. The failure of the council to adopt any, or any consistent, policy to tackle the known anti-social problems emanating from the site, the internal wrangling, the lack of internal communication, the failure to instruct or properly instruct those who had responsibility for site control and management and the failures of the legal department which allowed the site to go unchecked as a seat of lawless and anti-social behaviour, constituted a nuisance to the claimants. The court held that the council were aware of the emanations and had the means to abate the nuisances, but had failed to take steps to do so in a reasonable time and was therefore liable.

5-095

It is interesting that the law of nuisance has developed in a rather different way in Queensland, Australia. In *Aussie Traveller Pty Ltd v Marklea Pty Ltd*.[7] the Queensland Court of Appeal held that a landlord may be liable for the nuisance caused by the tenant if, at the time of letting, it was reasonably foreseeable that the tenant would commit the nuisance. The Court of Appeal in *Mowan* did not consider that argument in much depth; *Smith v Scott* had not

5-096

---

[1] See Loveland, *op. cit.* n.51 where he suggests that the distinction drawn by the common law between the bases for liability of an owner qua occupier and an owner qua landlord makes no sense when looking at various scenarios. For example, the case of a secure licensee (with significantly more security than an ordinary licensee), an introductory tenant who become secure although he may have caused a nuisance, and a tolerated trespasser. If the distinction is correct, then the owner, according to his analysis, would be liable for any nuisance caused by these persons. This, however, ignores the degree of security and control given to the secure licensee and tenant unlike the true trespasser or licensee.
[2] (2001) 33 H.L.R. 56.
[3] See Loveland, *Fixing Landlords with Liability for the Anti-Social Behaviour of their Tenants 2: Challenging the Orthodox Position* (2005) J.P.L. 405 which suggests that the decision in *Mowan* is based on a misreading of *Malzy v Eicholz* (above).
[4] *ibid.*
[5] *Mowan* (2001) 33 H.L.R. 56, at para.16.
[6] [2002] WL 1876048.
[7] [1998] 1 Qd. R. 1.

been cited in *Aussie Traveller* and in any event, the law of Queensland has now diverged from English law.

Negligence

5-097   The issue is whether a landlord owes a duty of care to its tenants to protect them from nuisance created by other tenants. In *Mowan*, Sir Christopher Staughton considered that "the argument of negligence is simply nuisance by another name".[8] The claim in negligence was similarly dismissed in *Smith v Scott*,[9] *O'Leary v London Borough of Islington*[10] and *Hussain v Lancaster City Council*.[11]

Human rights

5-098   There have been attempts to impose positive obligations on States to take action to prevent nuisance and to provide a cause of action to enable persons to take effective action under Art.8 of the European Convention on Human Rights.

5-099   Article 8 provides:

"1. Everyone has the right to respect for his private and family life, his home and his correspondence.
2. There shall be no interference by a public authority with the exercise of this right except such as is in accordance with the law and is necessary in a democratic society in the interests of national security, public safety or the economic well-being of the country, for the prevention of disorder or crime, for the protection of health or morals, or for the protection of the rights and freedoms of others."

5-100   The obligations are primarily negative, but may also involve positive obligations requiring a public authority to take action if it is to comply with Art.8. The positive requirements of Art.8 were described in *Botta v Italy*[12] as follows:

"In the instant case the applicant complained in substance, not of action but of a lack of action by the State. While the essential object of Article 8 is to protect the individual against arbitrary interference by the public authorities, it does not merely compel the State to abstain from such interference; in addition to this negative undertaking, there may be positive obligations inherent in effective respect for private or family life. These obligations may involve the adoption of measures designed to secure respect for private life even in the sphere of the relations of individuals between themselves. However, the concept of respect is not precisely defined. In order to determine whether such obligations exist, regard must be had to the fair balance that has to be struck between the general interest and the interest of the individual, while the State has, in any event, a margin of appreciation."

5-101   The same approach was adopted in *Lopez Ostra v Spain*.[13] In that case the applicant complained that a waste treatment plant, which had been built close to her home, began to operate without a licence and to emit fumes and smells which caused health problems for local residents. The Court stated[14]:

[8] *Mowan* (2001) 33 H. L. R. 56, at para.20.
[9] *ibid.*
[10] (1983) 9 H.L.R. 81.
[11] *ibid.*
[12] [1998] 26 E.H.R.R. 241 at para.33.
[13] (1995) 20 E.H.R.R. 277.
[14] *ibid.* at para.51.

"Whether the question is analysed in terms of a positive duty on the State—to take reasonable and appropriate measures to secure the applicant's rights under paragraph 1 of Article 8—as the applicant wishes in her case, or in terms of an interference by a public authority to be justified in accordance with paragraph 2, the applicable principles are broadly similar. In both contexts regard must be had to the fair balance that has to be struck between the competing interests of the individual and of the community as a whole, and in any case, the State enjoys a certain margin of appreciation. Furthermore, even in relation to the positive obligations flowing from the first paragraph of Article 8, in striking the required balance the aims mentioned in the second paragraph may be of a certain relevance."[15]

In the domestic courts, private law actions for noise nuisance have been successfully brought using Art.8.[16] There have, however, been few cases specifically concerned with the failure to tackle anti-social behaviour. In *Mowan*,[17] Sir Christopher Staughton gave short shrift to the idea that common law nuisance should be extended to impose positive duties on landlords to prevent or control a nuisance by others. The common law had been stretched as far as it could go in *Chartered Trust v Davies*.[18] Furthermore, the Court of Appeal held that it was not clear that the application for an injunction against her neighbour would fail simply because she suffered from mental health problems nor was an application for judicial review of the council out of the question. It is, however, difficult to ascertain what exactly Ms Mowan would be seeking a judicial review of or what relief could be granted.   **5-102**

A rather different outcome was achieved in *Donnelly v NI Housing Executive*.[19] The appellant was a tenant of the Northern Ireland Housing Executive. He alleged that his neighbour, another tenant, Mrs Gamble and her family, persecuted and intimidated him and identified over 100 incidents. The allegations were not in dispute, but the Executive refused to commence possession proceedings against the Gamble family because of the risk to its employees if they did so. Although it had carried out a risk assessment in conjunction with the police, the Executive declined to provide any details for security reasons. Mr Donnelly applied for judicial review of the decision arguing that it was in breach of Arts 2,3,6,8 and Art.1 of Protocol 1. The Northern Ireland Court of Appeal held that Art.8 imposed a positive obligation on the Executive to take action if it is to comply with Art.8:   **5-103**

"In the present case the failure of the Executive to exercise its power to seek possession of the Gambles' house has undoubtedly given rise to a substantial detriment to the enjoyment of their private and family life on the part of the appellant and the members of his family. The issue is whether, as the judge held, that failure is to be regarded as necessary under the terms of Article 8(2) or, putting it the other way, the Executive failed to take reasonable and appropriate measures to secure the appellant's rights under Article 8(1)."[20]

---

[15] See also *Guerra v Italy* (1998) 26 E.H.R.R. 357; *Hatton v United Kingdom* (2002) 34 E.H.R.R. 1; and more recently, *Gomez v Spain* (2005) 41 E.H.R.R.40.

[16] See *Dennis v Ministry of Defence* [2003] EWHC 793 (low-flying aircraft); and *Andrews v Reading BC* [2005] EWHC 256 (road traffic).

[17] *ibid*; (2001) 33 H.L.R. 56.

[18] *ibid*; [1997] 2 E.G.L.R. 83.

[19] *NI* [2003] NICA 55.

[20] *ibid*; at para.10.

5-104   It remains to be seen whether this decision will open the floodgates to similar claims.[21] Unless there has been a flagrant disregard of policies and procedures, it is difficult to see that social landlords will be required to face genuine claims such as in the *Donnelly* case. The issue is whether the correct balance has been struck between the general interest and the interests of the individual. As discussed above, social landlords have polices and procedures in place for tackling anti-social behaviour. There is also a wide armoury available to social landlords of which eviction is to be used as a last resort. Thus, the failure to issue possession proceedings against a particular nuisance tenant is unlikely to meet with particular sympathy from the courts. On the other hand, the failure to take any type of action may lead to a potential claim and landlords need to be cautious in the way in which they handle and deal with complaints.

Local Government Ombudsman

5-105   Tenants of local authorities may complain to the Local Government Ombudsman where the authority has failed to take any, or any effective, action against perpetrators of nuisance. In February 2005, the Commission for Local Administration in England published, *Neighbour Nuisance and Anti-Social Behaviour: Special Report*, to draw attention to the complaints most commonly made concerning the way in which authorities handle nuisance complaints.

Harassment

Who may sue?

5-106   Generally, only a tenant or someone in actual possession or occupation of the land is capable of suing in nuisance. In *Maloney v Laskey*,[22] it was held that the tenant's spouse was not able to sue in nuisance as it was the tenant who had possession of the premises in question. In *Khorasandjian v Bush*,[23] the owner's daughter was allowed to sue in nuisance for harassing telephone calls. This part of the case, however, was overruled in *Hunter v Canary Wharf Ltd.*[24] Accordingly, a landlord's employee will not be able to sue in nuisance if a tenant is harassing them. Neither will a landlord be able to sue on behalf of one of its tenants in nuisance where a neighbour is causing a nuisance because it is not in possession of the property.

5-107   Moreover, a landlord may not be able to take possession proceedings and enforce the terms of the tenancy agreement where its employees are being harassed unless there is express provision in the tenancy agreement or the landlord is a relevant landlord for the purposes of obtaining an anti-social behaviour injunction.[25]

5-108   The Protection from Harassment Act 1997 is primarily directed at stalkers, but the civil remedy is useful in combating anti-social conduct (in so far as it can be described as harassment) towards persons who are not in actual possession of property. Furthermore, it provides for three criminal offences in relation to harassment.[26] We refer to Chapter Two, above, at paras 2.84 to 2.95 for definitions of harassment and course of conduct. In this Chapter, we are concerned with the civil law of harassment.

---

[21] Luba, *op. cit.* n.52.
[22] [1907] 2 K.B. 141.
[23] [1993] Q.B. 727; (1993) 25 H.L.R. 392.
[24] [1997] 2 W.L.R. 684.
[25] That is, a local authority, registered social landlord or housing action trust.
[26] See also paras 2.84–2.95.

Injunctions

The High Court and county court can grant injunctions to restrain the defen- **5-109**
dant from pursuing any conduct which amounts to harassment.[27] The standard of proof to be applied in such applications is the civil standard, that is,
on the balance of probabilities. In *Hipgrave v Jones*,[28] it was argued that the
criminal standard should apply because injunctions under the 1997 Act were
akin to anti-social behaviour orders under the Crime and Disorder Act 1998.
Distinguishing the orders,[29] Tugendhat J. held that, inter alia, injunctions
under the 1997 Act provided a remedy for individuals as opposed to public
bodies in the case of anti- social behaviour orders. Furthermore, the 1998 Act
was designed to prevent crime and disorder. The concern raised by this decision is whether the same principles may be applied to injunctions sought under
the Housing Act 1996 which provide a remedy for public and quasi-public
bodies (an extension of the same policy behind anti- social behaviour orders),
thus raising the standard of proof. It is submitted that this should not be the
case; the same principles should be applied as in the case of other civil injunctions.[30]

CPR Pt 65 makes provision for applications for injunctions under the 1997 **5-110**
Act[31] which are subject to the Pt 8 procedure.[32]

Where the claimant believes that defendant is in breach of such an injunc- **5-111**
tion, he may apply for the issue of a warrant for the arrest of the defendant.[33]
Where such an application is to be made depends on where the injunction
was granted. If it was granted by the High Court, the application will be
made to a judge of that court. If the injunction was granted by the county
court, a circuit judge can hear the application.[34] The application must be
made in accordance with CPR 23[35] and be supported by affidavit evidence.[36]
It must:

(1) set out the grounds for the application;

(2) state whether the claimant has informed the police of the conduct of the
defendant as described in the affidavit; and

(3) state whether, to the claimant's knowledge, criminal proceedings are
being pursued.[37]

The court may only issue the warrant if the application is substantiated on oath
and the court has reasonable grounds for believing that the defendant has done

---

[27] Protection from Harassment Act 1997, s.3(3)(a); CPR Pt 65.28. District Judges have jurisdiction to hear such applications (CPR PD 2B, 8.1). *c.f.* committals which must be heard by a
circuit judge in the County Court (CPR PD 2B, 8.3 and CCR O. 29 r.1).

[28] [2004] EWHC 2901 (Q.B.).

[29] Some of the distinctions were inaccurate and misleading. For example, that a threat would not
satisfy the first limb of the test for the making of an anti-social behaviour order (at para.31(ii))
and ASBOs are only sought in the magistrates' court (at para.56).

[30] See *Moat Housing Group-South Ltd v Harris and Hartless* [2005] EWCA Civ 287; [2005] H.L.R.
33. The issue of the standard of proof was not raised.

[31] CPR 65 and its Practice Direction were introduced by the Civil Procedure (Amendment) Rules
2004 (see SI 2004/1306). They came into effect on June 30, 2004.

[32] CPR 65.28. Therefore, the claim must be issued in Form N208 and is automatically allocated
to the mutli-track.

[33] The Protection from Harassment Act 1997, s.3(3)(a)–(b). See also CPR 65.29.

[34] CPR PD 2B, para.8.3 and CCR O. 29 r.1.

[35] CPR 65.29(1). The application may be made without notice.

[36] CPR 65.29(2).

[37] *ibid.*

anything which he is prohibited from doing by the injunction.[38] The judge before whom a person is brought following his arrest may deal with the matter or adjourn the proceedings. Where the proceedings are adjourned and the arrested person is released the matter must be dealt with (whether by the same or another judge) within 28 days of the date on which the arrested person appears in court and the arrested person must be given not less than two days' notice of the hearing.[39]

5-112   Anything, which the defendant does, without reasonable excuse, and which is prohibited by the injunction, is an offence under the Act,[40] but the conduct is not punishable as contempt of court.[41] If the defendant has been punished for contempt as a result of his conduct he cannot be convicted of an offence for breach of the injunction on the basis of the same conduct.[42]

5-113   A person who has breached the injunction and has not already been punished for contempt of court in respect of that same conduct, is liable on conviction on indictment, to imprisonment for a term not exceeding six months, or a fine not exceeding five years, or a fine, or both; or, on summary conviction, to imprisonment for a term not exceeding six months, or a fine not exceeding the statutory maximum, or both.[43]

Trespass [44]

5-114   Anti-social behaviour may take the form of unlawful intrusion upon land belonging to another, whether by foot or by vehicle or other means. It may also include the depositing, throwing or discharging of material on another person's land. In the case of housing management, this may be relevant where the anti-social behaviour takes place on land belonging to the landlord, for example, in vacant property which has become occupied by "squatters" or in common parts of a property owned by the landlord. In addition, owners or persons in control of animals may also be liable for animals which trespass on another's land without authorisation.[45] Since animals are regarded as chattels and as instrument of the persons owning or controlling them, such persons will be liable for the acts of the animals. The remedies available to the claimant will be damages and/or an injunction. Furthermore, where the perpetrators of anti-social behaviour are occupying property, possession proceedings may be taken.

Who may sue?

5-115   It is necessary for the claimant to be in actual possession[46] or to have an immediate entitlement to possession of the land at the time of the trespass. Since only one person can be in possession at any one time,[47] a landlord will not be able to sue where the perpetrator has trespassed onto land occupied by one of its tenants because it has parted with possession. The landlord may, however,

---

[38] Protection from Harassment Act 1997, s.3(5) and PD 65 para.14.1.
[39] CPR 65.30.
[40] Protection from Harassment Act 1997, s.6.
[41] *ibid.*, s.3(7).
[42] *ibid.*, s.3(8).
[43] *ibid.*, s.3(9).
[44] For a detailed analysis of the law of trespass see D. Elvin and J. Karas, *Unlawful Interference with Land*, (2nd edn., Sweet & Maxwell, 2002) and *Clerk & Lindsell on Torts, op. cit.* Ch. 19.
[45] *Ellis v The Loftus* (1874) L.R.C.P. 10.
[46] It would appear that exclusive possession is not required. A licensee with a right to enter and occupy land for a limited purpose was held to be able to sue in trespass: *Manchester Airport Plc v Dutton* [2000]1 Q.B. 133.
[47] *J.A. Pye (Oxford) Ltd v Graham* [2002] 3 W.L.R. 221.

be able to sue in respect of common parts retained by it or in respect of property which has been left vacant.

What amounts to trespass?

It is necessary to prove that there has been a direct interference by an unauthorised person. Furthermore, it is a requirement to show that the act of trespass is intentional, although this "may be of little practical interest, for the majority of trespasses to land are, in the nature of things, self evidently intentional".[48] What it does do, is to prevent wholly unintentional acts from constituting a trespass.[49]

5-116

Defences

The defences to trespass in the context of anti-social behaviour will be fairly limited. It is a defence to show that the defendant has permission, whether express or implied, to enter the claimant's land or place objects on that land. Conversely, it is a defence to trespass where the defendant enters on the land of another to abate a nuisance. The law, however, does not favour abatement by a private individual because of disorder[50] or the likelihood of a breach of the peace.[51] In cases where a trespasser is occupying land, adverse possession may be used as a defence if he is in factual possession and has the relevant intention to possess.[52]

5-117

Remedies

As mentioned above, the claimant will be able to sue in trespass for damages and seek an injunction to prevent the trespass.

5-118

Possession

In managing housing stock, the most common way of controlling anti-social behaviour is through possession proceedings and ultimately eviction. The way in which a landlord can take possession depends on the type of tenancy the tenant holds. Most tenants will either be secure (governed by the Housing Act 1985) or assured (governed by the Housing Act 1988). This section will, therefore, first discuss the main issues which may arise in seeking possession on nuisance grounds in the context of secure and assured tenants; to a certain extent, the issues will also be relevant to rent act and assured shorthold tenants. Thereafter, the specific requirements which must be followed to seek possession of all categories of tenancy will be considered.

5-119

Grounds for possession

Secure and assured tenants cannot be brought to an end except by the landlord obtaining an order for possession from the court.[53] Before the court will order possession, a landlord will need to prove that a ground has been made out.[54] In relation to nuisance generally, two grounds can be relied upon: the

5-120

---

[48] *Pollock* (1891) 7 L.Q.R. pp. 10–11.
[49] *Braithwaite v South Durham Steel Co Ltd* [1958] 1 W.L.R. 986.
[50] *Burton v Winters* [1993] 1 W.L.R. 1077.
[51] Or the use of force may amount to a criminal offence if the Criminal Law Act 1977 is breached.
[52] Limitation Act 1980, ss.15 and 17 and Sch.1; Land Registration Act 2002.
[53] Housing Act 1985, s.82(1) and Housing Act 1988, s.5(1).
[54] Housing Act 1985, s.84(1) and Housing Act 1988, s.7(1).

general breach of the tenancy agreement (Ground 1 of Sch.2 to Housing Act 1985 and Ground 12 to Sch.2 to the Housing Act 1988) and the specific nuisance ground (Ground 2 to Sch.2 to the Housing Act 1985 and Ground 14 to Sch.2 to the Housing Act 1988).

Breach of tenancy agreement

5-121   Ground 1 of Sch.2 to the Housing Act 1985 reads:

"Rent lawfully due from the tenant has not been paid or an obligation of the tenancy has been broken or not performed."

Ground 12 of Sch.2 to the Housing Act 1988 which provides:

"Any obligation of the tenancy (other than one related to the payment of rent) has been broken or not performed."

5-122   Landlords can include terms in the tenancy agreement relating to unacceptable conduct of the tenant. In the event of a breach, the landlord will be entitled to seek possession. Where there is a term prohibiting the tenant from taking part in any criminal activity on the premises, it will be necessary for an allegation of any breach to be made out on a higher than normal standard of proof.[55]

Specific nuisance ground

5-123   Ground 2 of Sch.2 to the Housing Act 1985/Ground 14 of Schedule 2 to the Housing Act 1988 provides for a specific nuisance ground and reads:

"The tenant or a person residing in or visiting the dwelling-house –

(a) has been guilty of conduct causing or likely to cause a nuisance or annoyance to a person residing, visiting or otherwise engaging in a lawful activity in the locality, or
(b) has been convicted of—
    (i) using the dwelling-house or allowing it to be used for immoral or illegal purposes, or
    (ii) an arrestable offence committed in, or in the locality of, the dwelling-house."

5-124   "Nuisance" does not necessarily mean nuisance in a technical legal sense, but in a natural sense. Annoyance is a term with a wider meaning, although it must be such as would annoy an ordinary occupier, not an ultra sensitive one.[56] It will include racial and sexual harassment.[57] In *Harlow DC v Sewell*,[58] the keeping of 38 cats in a terrace house in a densely residential area, where those cats wandered over the neighbourhood and defecated on neighbouring residential property, was held to be both a nuisance and annoyance.

5-125   The Housing Act 1996 extended the nuisance ground so that it will include visitors to the property in question and not just members of the same household. Thus, no personal fault on the tenant's part is required to bring a possession action based on the ground of nuisance and annoyance to neighbours, although it will be a relevant consideration in determining the reasonableness

---

[55] *Bristol CC v Mousah* (1997) 30 H.L.R. 32 at 41 per Otton L.J.
[56] *Todd-Heatly v Benham* (1888) 40 Ch. D. 80; *National Schizophrenic Fellowship v Ribble Estates S.A.* (1993) 25 H.L.R. 476; [1994] 03 E.G. 132; [1993] E.G.C.S. 39.
[57] *Woking BC v Bistram* (1995) 27 H.L.R. 1, CA; *Kensington & Chelsea RBC v Simmonds* (1997) 29 H.L.R. 507.
[58] [2000] E.H.L.R. 122.

of making a possession order.[59] In *Kensington & Chelsea RBC v Simmonds*,[60] where the conduct was on the part of the tenant's son, the Court of Appeal upheld a suspended possession order. In that case, the Court of Appeal held that it would offend common sense and the terms of Ground 2 to suggest that a degree of positive fault had to be shown on the part of the tenant, as distinct from an inability to control unruly children.[61] It will also cover situations where the tenant did not know a member of the household or a visitor was causing the nuisance or if he did know he was powerless to take action.[62] In *Northampton BC v Lovatt*,[63] the Court of Appeal confirmed that a tenant could be held responsible for the acts of a minor.

The amendment made by the 1996 Act does not differentiate between a public **5-126** or private nuisance; it is not restricted by legal definition. Instead, it is to be given its ordinary meaning and will include any conduct likely to cause an annoyance as well as nuisance.[64] Furthermore, there is no requirement for the landlord to prove that acts have caused annoyance or nuisance only that it is conduct which is likely to cause a nuisance. This has two effects. First, past conduct is sufficient to establish the ground for possession. Secondly, it avoids the need for the victim to give evidence in order to establish the ground for possession.[65] For instance, a housing officer giving evidence to the court regarding conduct of the tenant will be sufficient if it is conduct likely to cause a nuisance or annoyance.

Landlords must, however, have regard to the Civil Evidence Act 1995[66] and **5-127** CPR 33[67] when adducing hearsay evidence.[68] It is well established that hearsay evidence is admissible in a trial for a possession action.[69] Nonetheless, a party who wishes to adduce such evidence must give the other side such notice of his intention as is reasonable and practicable.[70] The inclusion of hearsay evidence in a witness statement provides adequate notice[71] but, where the witness is not being called, the party relying on that evidence must inform the other parties that that is the case and give the reason why.[72] Section 4(2) of the 1995 Act

---

[59] *Portsmouth CC v Bryant* (2000) 32 H.L.R. 906.

[60] (1997) 29 H.L.R. 507.

[61] See also *West Kent Housing Association v Davies* (1999) 31 H.L.R. 415.

[62] *Portsmouth CC v Bryant* (2000) 32 H.L.R. 906; *London & Quadrant Housing Trust v Root* [2005] EWCA Civ 43; [2005] H.L.R. 28.

[63] (1998) 30 H.L.R. 875; [1998] 07 E.G. 142; [1997] E.G.C.S. 167; *The Times*, January 3, 1998, CA.

[64] *Harlow DC v Sewell*, [2000] E.H.L.R. 122.

[65] It ". . . will enable a third party rather than the victim of the behaviour to give evidence against the perpetrator . . . the government's aim is that landlords should be able to obtain possession in some cases on evidence from third parties who are not victims . . . we have already rehearsed in Committee the extent to which fear of intimidation of potential witnesses is a problem": *Hansard*, HC, cols 382–383, February 27, 1996, Minister for Local Government, Housing and Urban Regeneration (Mr Curry).

[66] Civil Evidence Act 1995, ss.1–7.

[67] CPR 33.1–33.5.

[68] i.e. any statement by a person, whether made orally or in writing, other than one made by a witness giving oral evidence, which is offered for the truth of its contents *(R. v Sharp (Colin)* [1988] 1 W.L.R. 7).

[69] Civil Evidence Act 1995, s.1. See also *Moat Housing Group-South Ltd v Harris and Hartless* [2005] EWCA Civ 287; [2005] H.L.R. 33 *Solon South West Housing Association Limited v James* [2004] EWCA Civ 1847; [2005] H.L.R. 24 (nuisance possession proceedings); *R. (on the application of McCann) v Manchester Crown Court* [2002] UKHL 39; [2003] 1 A.C.787; [2003] 1 A.C. 787; [2002] 3 W.L.R. 1313; [2002] 1 All E.R. 593; [2003] H.L.R. 17 (anti-social behaviour orders).

[70] Civil Evidence Act 1995, s.2.

[71] CPR 33.2(1).

[72] CPR 33.2(2). Note that the failure to comply with the notice requirements under the 1995 Act and CPR 33 does not affect the admissibility of the evidence, but may be taken into account by the court in considering the exercise of its powers with respect to the course of proceedings and costs and as a matter adversely affecting the weight to be given to the evidence in accordance with s.4 (Civil Evidence Act 1995 Act, s.2(4)).

gives guidance as to the matters to be considered in determining the weight to be given to hearsay evidence. It reads as follows:

"(2) Regard may be had, in particular, to the following—

(a) whether it would have been reasonable and practicable for the party by whom the evidence was adduced to have produced the maker of the original statement as a witness;
(b) whether the original statement was made contemporaneously with the occurrence or existence of the matters stated;
(c) whether the evidence involves multiple hearsay;
(d) whether any person involved had any motive to conceal or misrepresent matters;
(e) whether the original statement was an edited account, or was made in collaboration with another or for a particular purpose;
(f) whether the circumstances in which the evidence is adduced as hearsay are such as to suggest an attempt to prevent proper evaluation of its weight."

5-128 One of the main reasons why witnesses do not wish to attend possession trials is for fear of reprisals.[73] There has been considerable sympathy expressed for such victims by the courts, although in *Moat Housing Group-South Ltd v Harris and Hartless*[74] the Court of Appeal, recognising the ease with which rumours abound on housing estates, emphasised the need for landlords,

". . .to state by convincing direct evidence why it was not reasonable and practicable to produce the original maker of the statement as a witness. If the statement involves multiple hearsay, the route by which the original statement came to the attention of the person attesting to it should be identified as far as practicable. It would also be desirable for judges to remind themselves in their judgments that they are taking into account the s.4(2) [of the Civil Evidence Act 1995] criteria. . . so far as they are relevant."[75]

5-129 "Locality" is not defined in the Housing Act 1985 or the Housing Act 1988. It is not restricted to the neighbourhood but to the locality so as:

". . . to cover as wide an area as possible, while maintaining the link between the tenant's behaviour and the fact that he lives in the area. "Locality" is our preferred replacement for that, and is designed to catch such behaviour over that larger area, *e.g.* "behaviour on a large estate towards tenants on a further part of the estate . . . our amendments, by not attempting to give a specific definition to the area we want to cover, give us. . .flexibility. . . I assure Opposition members that our amendments are intended to cover all the areas set out in their amendments—the common parts of blocks of flats, other parts of the estate and even parts of the locality that may not have the same landlord. . . We want an all embracing term that common sense people understand. . ."[76]

[73] *Solon South West Housing Association Limited v James* [2004] EWCA Civ 1847; [2005] H.L.R. 24 at para.33.
[74] [2005] EWCA Civ 287; [2005] H.L.R. 33.
[75] *Moat Housing Group-South Ltd v Harris and Hartless* (above) at para.140.
[76] *Hansard*, HC, cols 384–387, February 27, 1996, Minister for Local Government, Housing and Urban Regeneration (Mr Curry).

It is a question of fact for the judge whether the place in which the conduct **5-130** occurred was or was not within the locality.[77] In *Manchester CC v Lawler*,[78] it was held that locality may be part or the whole of the estate[79] and that neighbours had a wider meaning than adjoining occupiers. Accordingly, anti-social and criminal behaviour by the family of a secure tenant which took place on a local authority estate where the family lived, but not within 100 metres of their home, was held to be "conduct which is a nuisance or annoyance to neighbours".

In order to satisfy the first part of the second limb of the nuisance ground, **5-131** it is necessary to show that the conviction related to the use of the dwelling house. Thus, it is not sufficient that the crime merely took place at the dwelling house. In *S Schneiders & Sons v Abrahams*,[80] it was held that:

". . . for the purpose of committing the crime, the premises have been used . . . [it is] not enough that the tenant has been convicted of a crime with which the premises have nothing to do beyond merely being the scene of its commission."

It is not, however, a requirement that the offence needs to specifically refer to use of premises.[81] Using the dwelling for immoral purposes includes prostitution.[82]

The latter part of the second limb of the nuisance ground does not require **5-132** that the premises were actually used. It is necessary, however, that the arrestable offence was committed in, or in the locality of, the dwelling house. An arrestable offence is defined by ss.24 and 24A of the Police and Criminal Evidence Act 1984.[83] There are three prescribed categories where a constable may arrest without a warrant. First, he may arrest anyone who is about to commit an offence, is in the act of committing an offence or anyone whom he has reasonable grounds for suspecting to be about to commit an offence or committing an offence. Secondly, where there are reasonable grounds for suspecting that an offence has actually been committed, he may arrest anyone whom he has reasonable grounds to suspect of being guilty of it. Thirdly, where an offence has been committed, a constable may arrest anyone who is guilty of the offence and anyone whom he has reasonable grounds for suspecting to be guilty of it. These powers, however, are only exercisable if the constable has reasonable grounds for believing that it is necessary to arrest the person in question for any of the following reasons:

(1) to enable the name of the person in question to be ascertained;

(2) to enable the address of the person in question to be ascertained;

(3) to prevent the person in question causing physical injury to himself or any other person, suffering physical injury, causing loss of or damage to property, committing an offence against public decency, or causing an unlawful obstruction of the highway;

---

[77] *Manchester CC v Lawler* (1999) 31 H.L.R. 119.
[78] (1999) 31 H.L.R 119. This was decided in relation to Housing Act 1985, Sched.2, Ground 2, prior to the amendment made by the 1996 Act.
[79] See also *Northampton BC v Lovatt & Lovatt* [1996] L.G.R. 548; (1997) 30 H.L.R. 875.
[80] [1925] 1 K.B. 301, at 311.
[81] *Abrahams v Wilson* [1971] 2 Q.B. 88.
[82] Use of premises for prostitution: *Frederick Platts C. Ltd v Grigor* (1950) 66 T.L.R. 859; *Yates v Morris* [1950] 2 All E.R. 577, CA; see *Benton v Chapman* [1953] C.L.Y. 3099, Cty Ct on private immorality.
[83] As substituted by Serious Organised Crime and Police Act, Pt 3, s.110(1). These provisions came into force on January 1, 2006.

(4) to protect a child or other vulnerable person from the person in question;

(5) to allow the prompt and effective investigation of the offence or of the conduct of the person in question; and

(6) to prevent any prosecution for the offence from being hindered by the disappearance of the person in question. Any person, other than a constable, may arrest without a warrant in similar circumstances in the case of an indictable offence.[84]

5-133 Drug use and drug dealing on housing estates is strongly dealt with by the courts in cases of possession. It will only be in exceptional circumstances that an order for possession will not be made where serious offences have been committed at the premises.[85] The courts have emphasised the need to protect the public and other tenants. In the case of local housing authorities who have a duty to manage, regulate and control allocation of their houses, for the benefit of the public[86]:

". . . the public interest would be best served by [the housing authority] being able . . . to re-let the premises to someone who will not use them for peddling crack cocaine."[87]

5-134 Where a landlord is seeking to rely on a conviction, it is necessary to plead that the conviction falls under s.11 of the Civil Evidence Act 1968, the type of conviction, its date, the court which made the conviction and the issue in the claim to which it relates.[88] Under s.11 of the Civil Evidence Act 1968, in any civil proceedings, the fact that a person has been convicted of an offence shall be admissible in evidence for the purpose of proving, where to do so is relevant to any issue in those proceedings, that he committed that offence.

Reasonableness

5-135 Once the ground is established the court has to go on to consider whether it is reasonable to make a possession order.[89] In considering whether it is reasonable to make an order for possession:

". . . the duty of the judge is to take into account all relevant circumstances as they exist at the date of the hearing . . . in a broad, common- sense way as a man of the world, and come to his conclusion giving such weight as he

---

[84] A person other than a constable may arrest without a warrant: (a) anyone who is in the act of committing an indictable offence; (b) anyone whom he has reasonable grounds for suspecting to be committing an indictable offence. Where an indictable offence has been committed, a person other than a constable may arrest without a warrant: (a) anyone who is guilty of the offence; (b) anyone whom he has reasonable grounds for suspecting to be guilty of it. The power of summary arrest is exercisable only if: (a) the person making the arrest has reasonable grounds for believing that it is necessary to arrest the person in question for prescribed reasons (i.e. to prevent the person in question causing physical injury to himself or any other person, suffering physical injury, causing loss of or damage to property, making off before a constable can assume responsibility for him); and it appears to the person making the arrest that it is not reasonably practicable for a constable to make it instead (Police and Criminal Evidence Act 1984, s.24A).
[85] *Bristol CC v Mousah* (1998) 30 H.L.R. 32.
[86] Housing Act 1985, s.21.
[87] *Bristol CC v Mousah,* (1998) 30 H.L.R. 32.
[88] See the Practice Direction to CPR Pt 16, paras 8.1(1–2).
[89] Housing Act 1985, s.84(1) and Housing Act 1988, s.7(1).

thinks right to the various factors in the situation. Some factors may have little or no weight, others may be decisive, but it is quite wrong for him to exclude from his consideration matters which he ought to take into account."[90]

In *West Kent Housing Association v Davies*,[91] the Court of Appeal set out the tripartite test for obtaining a possession order (although a determination of one issue in favour of the tenant may make further issues academic):   **5-136**

(1) whether the ground for possession has been made out, which is an issue of fact;

(2) whether it is reasonable to make an order for possession, which involves the exercise of judicial discretion, but with a substantial element of judgment as to whether or not the making of an order is reasonable; and

(3) whether to postpone the date for possession or to stay or suspend execution, which involves a further exercise of judicial discretion.

Structured discretion
In the White Paper, *Tackling Anti-Social Tenants*, it was recognised that one of the main concerns expressed by social landlords was a lack of certainty regarding the outcome of trials in relation to anti-social behaviour. Despite a survey of landlords by the Joseph Rowntree Foundation (2000) finding no evidence of widespread difficulty with judges making possession orders where sufficient evidence was put before them, some social landlords have expressed concern about the certainty of claims for possession on the ground of anti-social behaviour and, in particular, the effect on witnesses and the community as a whole where the landlord has failed to secure a possession order. Furthermore, the Law Commission has expressed concern about suggestions of a lack of consistency in judicial decision making in respect of the reasonableness in making a possession order.[92] One way in which the government proposed to increase certainty was to provide for a structured discretion. This was also put forward as part of the solution by the Law Commission in its Consultation Paper, *Renting Homes 1: Status and Security*,[93] although it did not draw up a specific list of matters that ought to be taken into account.   **5-137**

The imposition of a structured discretion, however, was faced with opposition precisely because the reasonableness requirement imported a wide discretion into possession cases. The importance of having such a wide discretion may be summed up by Somervell J. in a much earlier case,   **5-138**

"I think that when Parliament gave this overriding discretion to the county court judge and said 'You must consider whether it is reasonable to make an order', it gave him a very wide discretion, which it is most undesirable to seek to limit or interfere with. I think the words of the section themselves indicate that the county court judge must look at the effect of the order on each party to it. I do not see how it is possible to consider whether it is reasonable to make an order unless you consider its effect on landlord and tenant, firstly, if you make it, and secondly, if you do not. I do not think we

---

90 Per Lord Greene M.R. in *Cumming v Danson* [1942] 2 All E.R. 653, at 655. See also *Creswell v Hodgson* [1951] 2 K.B. 92, per Somervell L.J. at 45 and per Denning L.J. at 97.
91 (1999) 31 H.L.R. 415. See also *Norwich City Council v Famuyiwa* [2004] EWCA Civ 1770, *The Times*, January 24, 2005.
92 Law Comm. Paper No. 162 para.13.70.
93 Law Comm. Paper No.162.

should say anything which restricts the circumstances which the county court judge should take into consideration."[94]

Furthermore, it should be recognised that "each case must depend on its own facts and the weight to be given to various factors will vary depending on the circumstances."[95]

5-139   It is right that the government has not introduced a structured discretion as such, but the Anti-Social Behaviour Act 2003 has amended the Housing Act 1985 and the Housing Act 1988 so as to include some additional requirements. In considering whether it is reasonable to make an order for possession under Ground 2 of Sch.2 to the Housing Act 1985, or as the case may be, Ground 14 of Sch.2 to the Housing Act 1988, the court must consider, in particular:

(1) the effect that the nuisance or annoyance has had on persons other than the person against whom the order is sought;

(2) any continuing effect the nuisance or annoyance is likely to have on such persons;

(3) the effect that the nuisance or annoyance would be likely to have on such persons if the conduct is repeated.[96]

5-140   Precisely why this is necessary is unclear as the case law shows that they are the very issues that judges take into account in any event.[97] In *Woking DC v Bistram*,[98] for instance, the Court of Appeal held that the following were factors that were plainly material on the issue of reasonableness:

(1) the claimant's obligation to the other tenants of the estate;

(2) the interest of those other tenants;

(3) the continuation of the nuisance; and,

(4) assurances as to future conduct.

5-141   On the other hand, it may be said that Parliament was emphasising the need for judges to consider the victims in nuisance possession cases.[99] The focus of these provisions, however, does not take away the need to consider the interests of the defendant tenant. In *Moat Housing Group-South Limited v Harris and Hartless*,[1] Brooke L.J. said,

"Although s.9A [of the Housing Act 1988] uses the words 'in particular', this does not mean that the court is not bound to take into account all relevant circumstances, and the interests of this family, and in particular the two relatively blameless members of it (who had a right to respect for their home under ECHR law), certainly warranted some attention."

---

[94] See *Creswell v Hodgson* [1951] 2 K.B. 92 per Somervell L.J. at 95.

[95] *Manchester City Council v Higgins* [2005] EWCA Civ 1423.

[96] Housing Act 1985, s.85A(1) and (2) as amended by s.16(1) of the Anti-Social Behaviour Act 2003; s.9A(1) and (2) of the Housing Act 1988 as amended by s.16(2) of the Anti-Social Behaviour Act 2003.

[97] *West Kent Housing Association v Davies* (above) and other cases mentioned in this section. As early as *Creswell v Hodgson* [1951] 2 K.B. 92, Denning L.J. said that he thought the word "reasonable" meant "reasonable having regard to the interests of the parties concerned and also reasonable having regard to the interests of the public.".

[98] (1995) 27 H.L.R. 1, at 3.

[99] *Moat Housing Group-South Ltd v Harris and Hartless* [2005] EWCA Civ 287; [2005] H.L.R. 33 at paras 143–144; *Manchester City Council v Higgins* [2005] EWCA Civ 1423 at paras 29 and 36.

[1] [2005] EWCA Civ 287; [2005] H.L.R. 33.

Interestingly, the Law Commission, in their Final Report, have concluded that **5-142**
the watered down version of a structured discretion in the Housing Acts
should be taken further. The draft Bill sets out provisions to structure the
court's discretion to make an order for possession when the decision is based
on the test of reasonableness and whether to adjourn or postpone possession.
The court will need to have regard to relevant circumstances divided into four
categories: general, contract-holder, the landlord, and other persons. General
relevant considerations will relate to the nature, frequency or duration of the
breach, the degree to which the tenant is responsible, the likelihood of recurrence of the breach, and any action to end the breach or prevent recurrence
by the landlord. As regards the tenant, or contract- holder as the tenant is
described, the court will be required to consider the effect of the possession
order on their private and family life including that of any permitted occupiers
and whether the tenant will be likely to comply with the terms of any postponement of the possession order. In so far as the landlord is concerned, the
court must consider the effect of the order if it is not made and in the case of
community landlords, how this will effect the fulfilment of its housing functions. Relevant circumstances regarding other persons will include those on
the housing waiting list, others living, visiting or engaging in a lawful activity
in the locality of the premises or those wishing do so, and in particular as
regards anti-social behaviour, the general public interest in restraining the
conduct. As will be seen below, these factors have been derived from the considerable case law on the subject of the exercise of the court's discretion.[2]

The interests of the landlord and neighbours
Often, the nuisance has had such a deleterious effect that neighbours are **5-143**
unwilling to come forward to give evidence.[3] Therefore, one of the factors the
court should take into account is the difficulty in proving a breach of any suspended order; witnesses may be unwilling to come forward for fear of reprisals
or those who may have given evidence at trial may be reluctant to come to
court again.[4]

In *Lambeth LBC v Howard*,[5] it was held that it was proportionate to make **5-144**
an outright order for possession where the incident was so serious and nothing
else less would achieve the purpose of protecting the victims of anti-social
behaviour.

In so far as the claimant is a social landlord, the court should take into **5-145**
account its obligations in tackling anti-social behaviour.

Serious offences
Courts are reluctant to refuse to make possession orders in cases where **5-146**
serious offences have been committed. In *Bristol CC v Mousah*,[6] under the
terms of the tenancy agreement, Mr Mousah agreed not to supply drugs from
the property and was responsible in this respect for his visitors. There were

---

[2] See also *Creswell v Hodgson* [1951] 2 K.B. 92; *Woking BC v Bistram* (1993) 27 H.L.R. 1, CA;
Darlington BC v Stirling (1996) 29 H.L.R. 309; *Kensington & Chelsea RBC v Simmonds* (1996)
29 H.L.R. 507; *West Kent Housing Association v Davies* (1998) 31 H.L.R. 415; *Newcastle CC
v Morrison* (2000) 32 H.L.R. 891; *Moat Housing Group-South Ltd v Harris and Hartless* [2005]
EWCA Civ 287, [2005] H.L.R. 33; *London & Quadrant Housing Trust v Root* [2005] EWCA Civ
43; [2005] H.L.R. 28; and *Manchester City Council v Higgins* [2005] EWCA Civ 1423.
[3] *Canterbury City Council v Lowe* (2001) 33 H.L.R. 53 and confirmed in *New Charter Housing
(North) Limited v Ashcroft* [2004] EWCA Civ 310, [2004] H.L.R. 36. *c.f. Moat Housing Group-
South Ltd v Harris and Hartless* [2005] EWCA Civ 287; [2005] H.L.R. 33 at para.140.
[4] *ibid.*
[5] [2001] EWCA Civ 468; [2001] 33 H.L.R. 58.
[6] (1998) 30 H.L.R. 32.

three police raids on the property and arrests were made for possession of crack cocaine. At trial, the judge found that Mr Mousah was not involved directly in dealing in crack cocaine and had been away at the time. But the judge did find that he was aware of the dealing. Notwithstanding this, the judge decided that it was not reasonable to making a possession order. Overturning this decision, the Court of Appeal concluded that in cases of such serious offences committed at the premises it would only be in exceptional circumstances that possession would be denied. There were no such circumstances in this case.[7]

5-147   In a more recent case, *Stonebridge Action Trust v Gabbidon*,[8] the landlord obtained a suspended possession order on the ground of rent arrears. Ms Gabbidon failed to comply with the terms of the order and a warrant for possession was obtained. She applied to stay the warrant or to further suspend the possession order. The court found that fresh rent arrears had accrued and that she had allowed the premises to be used for drug use. The judge at first instance held that the rent arrears were insufficient to justify the immediate possession order. Further, that although the allegations of drug use were serious and would have been grounds for making a possession order, there were two mitigating factors. First, the judge was not satisfied that Ms Gabbidon had been involved personally in drug dealing and secondly, no recent allegations had been proved. The judge also took into consideration the fact that Ms Gabbidon had a young child, Art.8 and the requirement of reasonableness. The further suspension of the possession order was granted. The landlord appealed submitting that an immediate possession should have been ordered.

5-148   Dismissing the appeal, Lloyd J. held that, although it had been established in *Bristol CC v Mousah*, that where premises had been used for a serious criminal offence it would be only in exceptional circumstances that the court would not make an order for possession, there was nothing in that case which addressed the question whether it was appropriate to stay an order in such circumstances. The court in *Gabbidon* was addressing the third element of the test for making a possession order. It was not the case that the court could only come to one possible answer (that is, an outright order for possession should be granted) where incidents of the kind under consideration occurred. Since, therefore, the drug incidents were not conclusive and since the judge below made a decision to suspend the possession order after considering all the relevant factors there was no error of law or misdirection.

5-149   It was contended by the landlord that this would set a precedent for its other tenants to oppose a possession order being granted. Lloyd J. disagreed and said that the present case could not be used as an analogy by other tenants to oppose a possession order. The court was not disagreeing that it would be reasonable to make a possession order because there were clearly serious breaches of the tenancy agreement, rather, on the facts of this case, it was reasonable to make a possession order but that it should be suspended (in the exercise of its discretion under s.85(2) of the Housing Act 1985).

5-150   That this overrules *Mousah* in any technical sense is not established. First, the court could not do so as *Mousah* was a Court of Appeal decision. Second, *West Kent Housing Association v Davies*, where the tripartite test was established, was decided after *Mousah*. Third, there was no disagreement in *Gabbidon* that it was only in exceptional circumstances, in a case of this kind, that a possession order should be granted; the court merely considered that it should also be suspended.

---

[7] *c.f. Stonebridge Action Trust v Gabbidon*, [2003] EWHC 2091, *The Times*, December 13, 2002, Ch.D.

[8] [2003] EWHC 2091, *The Times*, December 13, 2002, Ch.D.

Attitude of the defendant
The Court of Appeal in *Lambeth LBC Howard* was also influenced by the defen-   **5-151**
dant's attitude to his victim even though there had been only one serious incident which had occurred over a year prior to the possession trial. The defendant
in that case had shown no genuine sign of remorse for his behaviour.[9] In determining whether to suspend a possession order the court must focus on the
future; there is no point in suspending an order if the inevitable outcome is a
breach. Therefore, any factor which is relevant to whether there will be future
breaches is relevant to the question of suspension.[10] That may include whether
the defendant has shown genuine remorse,[11] whether there has been an improvement in the behaviour or what the likelihood of any improvement may be.[12]

Personal fault
It is irrelevant whether the tenant is personally to blame for the nuisance when   **5-152**
establishing the ground for possession. The question of personal fault,
however, is relevant to the issue of reasonableness.[13] In *Gallagher v Castle Vale
Action Trust*,[14] the cause of the nuisance was the tenant's daughter and her
boyfriend. The possession order was suspended on appeal because by that
time the daughter and her boyfriend had moved out of the property. It is also
relevant whether the tenant has taken any action to prevent the nuisance from
occurring.[15] In *Portsmouth CC v Bryant*,[16] the Court of Appeal, dismissing the
appeal, held inter alia:

(1) where the nuisance is at the hands of an ill-disciplined/uncontrollable child
it may often be impossible to make a finding of fault against the tenant;

(2) the Defendant had "allowed" the grandson to commit acts of nuisance
complained over a long period of time;

(3) the Defendant had failed to control her grandson and therefore it was
reasonable to make the order.

The level of support available to a parent who is making proper efforts to control   **5-153**
an errant child, however, will be relevant.[17] In *Gallagher v Castle Vale Action
Trust*,[18] the Court of Appeal emphasised the need to illustrate acquiescence or
participation in the nuisance to justify the making of an outright order.[19]

Abatement of the nuisance
In *Ottway v Jones*,[20] the court refused to make an order where the last act com-   **5-154**
plained of was some nine months before the hearing. This would not seem to

---

[9] See also, *Canterbury City Council v Lowe* (2001) 33 H.L.R. 53, at para.32 and *Solon South
West Housing Association Limited v James* [2004] EWCA Civ 1874; [2005] H.L.R. 24, at paras
74 and 78.
[10] *Canterbury City Council v Lowe* (2001) 33 H.L.R. 53, at para.24 and confirmed in *Manchester
City Council v Higgins* [2005] EWCA Civ 1423, at paras 37, 45 and 55.
[11] *Solon South West Housing Association Limited v James* [2004] EWCA Civ 1874; [2005] H.L.R.
24, at para.73.
[12] *New Charter Housing (North) Limited v Ashcroft* [2004] EWCA Civ 310; [2004] H.L.R. 36, at
paras 30–33; *Manchester City Council v Higgins* [2005] EWCA Civ 1423, at para.45.
[13] Although a degree of personal fault is not required to make it reasonable to make a possession
order.
[14] [2001] EWCA Civ 944; (2001) 33 H.L.R. 72.
[15] *Portsmouth CC v Bryant* (2000) 32 H.L.R. 906.
[16] *ibid.*, at 919.
[17] *Manchester City Council v Higgins* [2004] EWCA Civ 1423, at para.37.
[18] [2001] EWCA Civ. 944; (2001) 33 H.L.R. 72.
[19] See below for a detailed analysis of this case under Art.8.
[20] [1955] 1 W.L.R. 706.

be relevant authority under the nuisance ground as re-drafted. However, if the nuisance has been abated the issue will go to the reasonableness of making a possession order. In *Greenwich LBC v Grogan*,[21] the Court of Appeal replaced an outright order with a suspended order on the basis that the defendant was attempting to live a life free of crime. If he was evicted and left to his own devices, there was a serious possibility that his attempt to live such a life would come to an end. In the public interest generally and in the interests of the community, it seemed to the court that he was more likely to live an honest life if he remained in the flat and an opportunity for him to do so should be provided.

Alternative Remedies

5-155   In *Newcastle CC v Morrison*,[22] the Recorder refused to grant a possession, inter alia, on the ground that more appropriate remedies, such as an injunction, were available against the son, and that he would continue to cause a nuisance on the estate in any event. The Court of Appeal allowed the authority's appeal and, granting a possession order, held that the Recorder had been plainly wrong to find that it was not reasonable to make an order; the catalogue of appalling conduct, which was more like "a reign of terror", spoke for itself. It was wrong to see the question of reasonableness as turning on the notion that there was an alternative and, as the judge below thought, more appropriate remedy available.[23]

5-156   The relevance of an alternative remedy may go to the issue of reasonableness of suspending an order. As we have discussed, the court, in determining whether it is reasonable to suspend the order, will focus on the future. In *Canterbury City Council v Lowe*[24] the Court of Appeal held that the likelihood of a person observing an injunction if one was granted at the same time as a possession order would be a relevant factor (as would the improvement of behaviour following the grant of an earlier injunction). In that case, however, the authority had applied for an injunction and the court was not imposing an injunction as an alternative to making a possession order. Similarly, in *Moat Housing Group-South Limited v Harris and Hartless*,[25] the failure of the housing association to consider other steps to tackle the behaviour complained of—in compliance with its own obligations under the terms of the tenancy agreement—did not preclude the court from granting a possession order.

5-157   In *Manchester City Council v Higgins*,[26] Ward L.J., giving guidance on the exercise of the judge's discretion in nuisance possession cases, said that,

"if the misconduct of the tenant or even by a member of his household were serious and persistent enough to justify an ASBO then that will be strong but not conclusive evidence that the tenant will have forfeited his entitlement to retain possession."[27]

---

[21] (2001) 33 H.L.R. 12.
[22] (2000) 32 H.L.R. 891.
[23] See also, *Sheffield City Council v Jephson* (1993) 25 H.L.R. Ralph Gibson L.J. held that, although the authority could have obtained an injunction rather than seeking possession, he saw no reason why a council should be required or expected to take that course. It is in the public interest that necessary and reasonable conditions in tenancy agreements of occupiers of public housing should be enforced fairly and effectively. See also *Norwich City Council v Famuyiwa* [2004] EWCA Civ 1770.
[24] [2001] 33 H.L.R. 53, at para.24.
[25] [2005] EWCA Civ 287; [2005] H.L.R. 33.
[26] [2005] EWCA Civ 1423; at para.36.
[27] See also *London & Quadrant Housing Trust v Root* [2005] EWCA Civ 43; [2005] H.L.R. 28.

Mental health
The mental health of a defendant will be very relevant as to whether the court **5-158**
should make a possession order. In *Croydon LBC v Moody*,[28] it had become
apparent at trial that the defendant would be putting forward mental health
problems as a reason for his anti-social behaviour. No reference to the defendant's mental health problems was made in the pleadings, but two days before
trial the defendant produced a psychiatrist's report which diagnosed the defendant as suffering from a complex personality disorder. The Recorder, having
found that the defendant had been guilty of conduct amounting to nuisance,
went on to consider the question of reasonableness. He rejected the defendant's psychiatric evidence as he was not satisfied that there had been mental
health reasons for the defendant's behaviour. The defendant appealed on the
grounds that the judge had misdirected himself when he rejected the psychiatrist's evidence. The Court of Appeal allowed the appeal for the following
reasons:

(1) the judge at first instance had considered the medical evidence in determining whether the defendant had been guilty of the anti-social behaviour. Once it is recognised that one ground for seeking an order for
possession was a failure to observe the terms of the tenancy, any need
for guilt was removed;

(2) there was no justification for the judge's rejection of the psychiatrist's
evidence. Such evidence should have been taken into account in considering the question of reasonableness. If there was a prospect of the
defendant's mental health improving then that had to be put into the
balance; and,

(3) the judge's findings of fact were not to be disturbed, but a retrial on the
issue of reasonableness was appropriate.

Disability Discrimination Act 1995
The Disability Discrimination Act 1995 introduced a new regime of protec- **5-159**
tion for disabled persons in employment, in relation to goods and services,
and in respect of the buying and letting of land.[29] *North Devon Homes HA
v Brazier*[30] was the first case where provisions of the Act were considered in
relation to a tenant with a mental disability who was guilty of anti-social
behaviour. The result on appeal, at first glance, is surprising. The court
declined to make an order for possession, even though the allegations of
anti-social behaviour were serious and admitted by the tenant and where it
was commonly accepted that there was little chance of abatement. The decision appears to be authority for the proposition that mentally disabled
persons have a complete defence in even the strongest nuisance possession
cases. However, on a closer analysis, what the decision means is that landlords, when deciding whether or not to evict a mentally disabled tenant on
nuisance grounds, must take into account certain additional matters and
should only decide to set down proceedings when there is evidence that the
tenant's conduct endangers his or her own health and safety or that of the
neighbours.
　　Under s.1(1) a person has a disability if he or she has a physical or mental **5-160**
impairment which has a substantial and long-term adverse impact on his

[28] (1999) 31 H.L.R. 738.
[29] See Collins, "Mentally Disabled Tenants, Anti-Social Behaviour and the Disability
Discrimination Act 1995: North Devon Homes v Brazier", [2003] J.H.L. 57.
[30] [2003] EWHC 574; [2003] H.L.R. 59.

or her ability to carry out normal day-to-day activities. There are no further definitions of the term disability.[31]

5-161   By para.4(1), Sch.4, a relevant impairment affects the ability of a person to carry out day-to-day activities only if it affects one of the following: mobility; manual dexterity; physical co-ordination; continence; ability to lift and carry or otherwise move everyday objects; speech, hearing or eyesight; memory, or ability to concentrate, learn or understand; perception of the risk of physical danger.[32] A long-term impairment is defined by para.2 of Sch.1 as one which has lasted at least 12 months, or it is likely to last at least 12 months, or it is likely to last the rest of the life of the person affected. Special provision is made for the consequences of disfigurement. Where an impairment consists of a severe disfigurement it is deemed to have a substantial adverse effect on the person's ability to carry out normal day-to-day activities.

5-162   Under s.4, it is unlawful for an employer to discriminate against a disabled person in the field of employment. However, it is also unlawful to discriminate against disabled persons in other areas: under s.19, in relation to the provision of goods, facilities and services; and, under s.22, in relation to premises. Section 22(1) provides that it is unlawful for a person with power to dispose of any premises to discriminate against a disabled person as to:

"(a)   the terms on which he offers to dispose of those premises;
(b)   by refusing to dispose of those premises; or
(c)   in his treatment of the disabled person in relation to any list of persons in need of premises of that description."

5-163   Further, under s.22(2), it is unlawful for a person managing any premises to discriminate against a person occupying those premises

"(a)   in the way he permits the disabled person to make use of any benefits or facilities;
(b)   by refusing or deliberately omitting to permit the disabled person to make use of any benefits or facilities; or
(c)   by evicting the disabled person or subjecting him to any other detriment . . ."

---

[31]   However, see para.1 of Sch.1 to the Disability Discrimination Act 1995 Act: mental impairment as an impairment resulting from or consisting of a mental illness only if it is a well-recognised illness. In *Morgan v Staffordshire University*, the applicant contended that stress and anxiety caused by an incident at work was a disability. The only medical evidence was in the form of medical notes and no medical expert evidence was adduced. The tribunal found that there was no mental impairment within the meaning of the 1995 Act. At para.20, it was said that ". . . the existence or not of a mental impairment is very much a matter for qualified and informed medical opinion". Specific medical conditions may be expressly included or excluded by regulation. For example, addiction to alcohol, nicotine or any other substance is not an impairment for the purposes of the Act: Disability Discrimination (Meaning of Disability) Regulations 1996 (SI 1996/1455).

[32]   The term *substantial* adverse effect is not defined. Guidance issued under the Disability Discrimination Act 1995 states that the effect must be more than trivial, and this requirement "reflects the general understanding of disability as a limitation going beyond the normal differences in ability which may exist among people" (para.A1). The Guidance also provides that the cumulative effects of an impairment and the ability of a person to modify his behaviour to cope with the impairment are matters which must be taken into account. Hence, an impairment may exist notwithstanding a continuing ability to carry out tasks. In *Leonard v Southern Derbyshire Chamber of Commerce*, [2001] I.R.L.R. 19, EAT the applicant suffered depression and was able to accomplish many normal day-to-day activities but could not sustain an activity over a reasonable period of time because of fatigue associated with her depression. She also found it difficult to complete routine domestic tasks within normal time. The EAT found her to be disabled within the meaning of the Act.

"Premises" is defined by s.68(1) as referring to land of any description. Under s.64, the Act applies to the Crown as it does to any private person. However, under s.24, certain types of small dwellings are exempt: i.e., where the disabled person is a lodger or flat-sharer.

Discrimination in the context of s.22 is defined by s.24. Under s.24(1), a person discriminates against a disabled person if: **5-164**

"(a) for a reason which relates to the disabled person's disability, he treats him less favourably than he would treat others to whom that reason does not or would not apply; and

(b) he cannot show that the treatment is justified."

Under subs.(2), the treatment is justified only if, in the alleged discriminator's opinion, certain conditions set out subs.(3) are met; and it is reasonable in all the circumstances for him to hold that opinion. The conditions in subs.(3) are:

(a) in any case, the treatment is necessary in order not to endanger the health or safety of any person;

(b) in any case, the disabled person is incapable of entering into an enforceable agreement or of giving informed consent and for that reason the treatment is reasonable;

(c) in a case falling within s.22(3)(a) above, "the treatment is necessary in order for the disabled person or the occupiers of other premises forming part of the building to make use of the benefit or facility"; or

(d) in a case falling within s.22(3)(b) the treatment is necessary in order for the occupiers of other premises forming part of the building to make use of the benefit or facility.

A claim by a person that another person has discriminated against him in a way which is unlawful under this part of the Act may be made in the county court in ordinary civil proceedings as though it were a claim for breach of statutory duty.[33] Any damages awarded may include an element for compensation for injured feelings. Section 57 provides that a person who knowingly aids another person to do an act made unlawful by this Act is to be treated for the purposes of this Act as himself doing the same kind of unlawful act. **5-165**

In *North Devon Homes v Brazier*, the appellant defendant suffered from a paranoid psychosis and schizophrenia. From about 1999, she began to behave in what the court described as "bizarre behaviour" as a result of hallucinations in which she heard voices insulting, attacking, and threatening her. She also believed that she was under constant surveillance and that her mind and body and that also of her dog were being interfered with and contaminated. Additionally, she was severely depressed and anxious. Her neighbours complained about regular shouting and abuse, banging the walls at night, swearing, rude gestures, inside and near the premises and at all hours of the day and night. Throughout the tenancy, there was a high-level of police and social services involvement. Possession proceedings were commenced in January 2002 on nuisance grounds. **5-166**

Before the Recorder, the defendant accepted that the allegations of nuisance were made out but she contended that it would be unlawful for the court to make a possession order on the ground that it amounts to unlawful discrimination under the Act. Supported by psychiatric evidence, it was common ground that the defendant was a disabled person within the meaning of the 1995 Act, her disability arising from a mental impairment which had a substantial and long-term effect on her ability to carry out normal day-to-day **5-167**

---

[33] Disability Discrimination Act 1995, s.25(1).

activities and that it caused her to behave in a hostile, abusive and threatening way to other persons. The Recorder found that the defendant was unable to prevent herself from behaving in a way which was in breach of her tenancy agreement. The Recorder held that the landlord's behaviour was unlawful under the 1995 Act (hence, the claimant respondent's cross-appeal) but he made an outright possession order on the ground that her behaviour was unlikely to improve and her neighbours would otherwise continue to suffer (hence, the defendant appellant's appeal). To do otherwise, the Recorder said, would lead to the illogical conclusion that the 1995 Act provided disabled persons with a complete defence to actions in nuisance.

5-168   On appeal, David Steel J. allowed the appellant's appeal and dismissed the respondent's cross-appeal. It is necessary to consider the respondent's cross-appeal first. The respondent landlord had three main contentions. First, it argued that there was no question of discrimination under s.22 since it was not evicting the appellant but the court. This was rejected: the court noted that it was accepted that the whole purpose of the proceedings was to regain possession of the property by evicting the appellant and that there was no value or desire for a suspended order.

5-169   The landlord then submitted that there was no discrimination because, pursuant to s.22(1)(a), the appellant was not being treated any less favourably than others to whom the reason relating to the disabled person's impairment did not apply: if any other tenant behaved in this way, then they would also have been evicted. David Steel J. dismissed this submission. In *Clark v Novacold Ltd*,[34] the applicant was dismissed from his employment by reason of his long-term inability to work. The E.A.T. accepted the argument that, under earlier provisions of the 1995 Act similar to s.22, there had been no discrimination because any non-disabled person unable to carry out long-term work would have been dismissed. The Court of Appeal allowed the appeal because the others with whom the comparison was made were not required to be in the same circumstances as the disabled person. At p.963. Mummery L.J. said:

> "In the context of the special sense in which discrimination is defined in section 5 of the Act of 1995, it is more probable than not that Parliament meant 'that reason' to refer only to the facts constituting the reason for the treatment and not to include within that reason the added requirement of a causal link with the disability; that is more properly regarded as the cause of the reason for the treatment than as in itself a reason for the treatment."

5-170   Hence, it was simply a case if identifying others to whom the reason for the treatment does not or would not apply. The test of less favourable treatment was based on the reason for the treatment of the disabled person and not on the fact of his disability. It did not turn on a like-for-like comparison of the treatment of the disabled person and of others in similar circumstances.

5-171   In *Brazier*, David Steel J. held that the issue was one of fact: whether or not the breach of the tenancy terms was caused by the disability. If so, then the defendant, as a disabled person, could nonetheless not be treated less favourably than someone who is not similarly disabled. In this regard, he noted that that the Recorder found that the appellant was unable to prevent herself from behaving in a manner that was in breach of the tenancy agreement and agreed that the "overwhelming preponderance of her bizarre and unwelcome behaviour was attributable to her mental illness which forms her disability".

5-172   The respondent's last submission was that the discrimination was justified on the ground that the eviction was necessary in order not to endanger the

---

[34] [1999] I.C.R. 951.

health or safety of the any person including the disabled person. This too was rejected for three reasons:

(1) there was no evidence that the respondent ever formed that opinion— in fact, it appeared that the respondent did not have any of the requirements of s.24 in mind at all[35];
(2) the psychiatric report stated that eviction and homelessness would worsen the appellant's condition;
(3) the Recorder found that, although the neighbours suffered from the behaviour, there was no evidence of a danger to health and safety of any person.

Therefore, the court upheld the Recorder's finding that the respondent's **5-173** conduct was unlawful under the 1995 Act and dismissed the cross-appeal. Even so, the Recorder made a possession order; hence, the appellant's appeal. David Steel J. recited a passage in the Recorder's judgment where he held that he must make the possession order in spite of his finding that the claimant's conduct was unlawful because, otherwise every defendant in a nuisance action would never be evicted even where, as in this case, the nuisance was serious, admitted and unlikely to improve. David Steel J. disagreed and allowed the appeal. At para.23:

"Whilst I accept the fact that unlawfulness under the 1995 Act would not necessarily be determinative of the application under the Housing Act 1988, nonetheless it seems to me this passage is based upon a misconception. The Act does not bar evictions: only those which are not justified by the specific circumstances set out in section 24. The respondent, having adopted a proper review of the situation in accordance with the express terms of the Act, may conclude in the future that the health and safety of her neighbours are prejudiced and thus steps should be taken to evict the appellant. But this situation has not arisen."

Therefore, on appeal, the court held that the finding that eviction was not jus- **5-174** tified by the terms of the Act and was therefore unlawful was "a highly rele- vant consideration" of the exercise of the discretion. There were three reasons:

(1) although the degree of anti-social behaviour was significant and without much prospect of it abating, the 1995 Act "furnishes its own code for justified eviction which requires a higher threshold";
(2) against this background, the court was being invited to exercise its dis- cretion by way of promoting unlawful conduct; and,
(3) the limitations on interference with the appellant's right to respect for her home are set out in 1995 Act and, pursuant to s.3 of the Human Rights Act 1998, it was therefore appropriate for the powers of the 1988 Act to be read in a manner compatible with the 1995 Act.

North Devon Homes v Brazier is not authority for the proposition that to evict **5-175** a mentally disabled tenant guilty of nuisance is unlawful. What happened in this case is that the respondent landlord simply did not consider whether or not the Act applied when making the decision to evict the appellant.[36] Given

[35] See *Beart v HM Prison Service* [2003] I.R.L.R. 238.
[36] This view was confirmed in *Manchester City Council v Romano* [2004] EWCA Civ 834; [2005] 1 W.L.R. 2775; [2004] 4 All E.R. 21; [2004] H.L.R. 27 at para.68. "For many years the county courts had to take the health of both landlord and tenant into consideration when deter

that this was the first time the Act had been raised in any reported decision concerning anti-social behaviour, it is not surprising that it was overlooked. However, even if the landlord had considered whether or not the treatment was justified pursuant to s.22(2)(a), there was the additional hurdle in this case that there was no evidence of a danger to the health and safety of either the appellant or her neighbours. The medical evidence showed that eviction would have only worsened the appellant's condition; and there was no evidence of any neighbour's health or safety being "endangered" by the appellant's behaviour.

5-176   In *Manchester City Council v Romano*,[37] the Court of Appeal upheld the decision that to evict a person by reason of his behaviour caused by a disability was discriminatory under the 1995 Act. In order to show that there has been discrimination there needs to be a link between the disability of the defendant and the behaviour complained of.[38] Moreover, the Court of Appeal held that the landlord did not have to prove that a person's health had actually been damaged only that their health or safety would be endangered. Interpreting the 1995 Act compatibly with the European Convention on Human Rights, Art.8 rights of the neighbours, it adopted the World Health Organisation definition of health:

"A state of complete physical, mental and social well-being and not merely the absence of disease and infirmity".[39]

The definition, therefore, provides a relatively low threshold of justification.

5-177   The Court of Appeal also considered the question of when the landlord should justify eviction. It was conceded that the service of a notice seeking possession subjects a person to a detriment for the purposes of the 1995 Act. The landlord should therefore first consider whether the service of the notice is justified in accordance with s.24 of the 1995 Act.[40] A failure to hold the appropriate opinion at the time of serving the notice, will not, however, vitiate the act; the landlord may not have known of the disability and there may have been nothing to put him on inquiry. Provided the landlord can be shown reasonably to have reached the appropriate opinion—giving rise to justification—by the time of the proceedings earlier breaches will only give rise to a claim for damages.[41]

5-178   So, how should a landlord behave with regard to a mentally disabled tenant who is guilty of anti-social behaviour? It is suggested that, in addition to the usual relevant considerations in a nuisance case, the landlord should also take into account the following considerations:

(1) is the conduct the result of the mental disability? Is the medical or social services evidence such that it appears that the tenant cannot prevent himself behaving in breach of the tenancy? If the answer is no, then the eviction is not going to be discriminatory; if the answer is yes, then the authority must consider s.22(2);

[36] Footnote (*cont.*)
      mining whether it is reasonable to make an order for possession. All that the 1995 Act has done is to state that if a tenant is disabled and the reason why the landlord is seeking possession relates to the tenant's disability, then the landlord must believe that he is justified in taking this action on section 24(3) grounds and his justification must be objectively reasonable.".
[37] [2004] EWCA Civ 834; [2005] 1 W.L.R. 2775; [2004] 4 All E.R. 21; [2004] H.L.R. 27.
[38] *ibid.*, at paras 82–85; 90 and 93.
[39] *ibid.*, at para.70.
[40] *ibid.*, at para.50.
[41] *ibid.* at para.60.

(2) considering s.22(2) means expressly forming an opinion that the eviction is justified;

(3) in order to do so, the landlord must have evidence that the eviction is necessary in order not to endanger the health or safety of any person.

(4) exactly what kind of evidence should that be? Every case will be different. In some cases, the expert evidence might be that the tenant, because of his behaviour, should be in sheltered accommodation. If so, then it is likely that the landlord's opinion that the treatment is justified is reasonable and therefore not unlawful. If there is no such evidence, then it almost goes without saying that the eviction of any mentally disabled person is always likely to have adverse consequences on his or her own health and safety. This does not mean that the landlord should stop there. The landlord should also consider the health and safety of neighbours. An easy case would be where there is evidence of threats of violence against neighbours and the opinion of the experts is that the tenant is likely to carry them out. However, in another case, it might be sufficient to show that a neighbour's sleep is regularly disturbed; or that the tenant's behaviour causes a neighbour to suffer stress and depression because they are elderly or disabled themselves.

Issues not relevant to reasonableness

As we have seen, the courts have a wide discretion in determining whether it is **5-179** reasonable to make a possession order and whether to suspend that order. The question of reasonableness must, however, be determined by regard to what is relevant and by leaving out of account what is irrelevant. For instance, it is not right that a judge will grant a possession order on nuisance grounds on condition that the landlord provides suitable alternative accommodation.[42] Furthermore, it is not the function of the courts to determine whether someone is intentionally homeless; that is the function of the local housing authority.[43]

In relation to appeals, evidence of conduct post trial is irrelevant to an **5-180** appeal.[44]

Postponed possession orders

All of the decisions refer to suspended possession orders. The combined effect **5-181** of the decisions in *Harlow District Council v Hall*[45] and *Bristol City Council v Hassan & Glastonbury*[46] is that such orders (that is, in the case of secure tenancies) should more properly be described as postponed possession orders. Furthermore, although those decisions related to the use of Form N28 suspended possession orders in rent arrears cases, some guidance may be obtained as regards the drafting of postponed possession orders and the inclusion of a date with the effect of terminating the tenancy. The orders suggested in the latter decision may be found in the Appendix.

Relationship between nuisance and other grounds for possession

The Housing Act 1985 s.85 provides: **5-182**

"(2) On the making of an order for possession of such a dwelling-house on any of those grounds, or at any time before the execution of the order, the court may—

---

[42] *Darlington BC v Stirling* (1997) 29 H.L.R. 309.
[43] *Bristol City Council v Mousah* (1997) 30 H.L.R0 32.
[44] *Canterbury City Council v Lowe* (2001) 33 H.L.R. 53.
[45] [2006] EWCA Civ 156.
[46] [2006] EWCA Civ 656.

(a) stay or suspend the execution of the order, or
(b) postpone the date of possession,
for such period or periods as the court thinks fit.

(3) On such an adjournment, stay, suspension or postponement the court—

(a) shall impose conditions with respect to the payment by the tenant of arrears of rent (if any) and rent or payments in respect of occupation after the termination of the tenancy (mesne profits), unless it considers that to do so would cause exceptional hardship to the tenant or would otherwise be unreasonable, and
(b) may impose such other conditions as it thinks fit.

(4) If the conditions are complied with, the court may, if it thinks fit, discharge or rescind the order for possession."

Similar provision is made under the Housing Act 1988 s.9 for assured tenancies.

The Possession Order

5-183   Landlords may seek possession on grounds of rent arrears which result in a suspended possession order. Where the tenant has been guilty of anti-social behaviour, the landlord can seek conditions in relation to anti-social behaviour, although this ground was not originally relied upon; the court has the power to impose such conditions as it thinks fit.[47] In *Sheffield CC v Hopkins*,[48] the Court of Appeal suggested:

"It would be perfectly appropriate for a landlord to give informed notice to a tenant (and those who represent the tenant) that although certain matters were not going to be relied upon as a basis for an order for possession, if the court decided to make an order for possession, the landlord would ask the court to impose a condition to prevent the conduct referred to taking place thereafter. This would be particularly appropriate where the fear is nuisance or annoyance. The condition should be sufficiently specific and clear for the tenant to be in no doubt as to the conduct that would constitute a breach of the condition. . . There would have to be some prima facie evidence that there had been conduct on the part of the tenant which justified the imposition of the condition."

5-184   There is nothing preventing a landlord from applying to vary a possession order so as to include conditions relating to the tenant's conduct, although that order was first obtained on other grounds. In *Manchester CC v Finn*,[49] the council had obtained a possession order on the ground of rent arrears. The court suspended the order on condition that the defendant paid the current rent and an amount off the arrears. The defendant complied with the order but she was subsequently convicted of handling stolen goods. The authority applied to the court under s.85(2)(b) of the Housing Act 1985 for an order varying the suspended possession order to a forthwith order on the ground that the defendant had breached her tenancy agreement. The district judge, refusing the application, said that he was *functus officio* and had no jurisdiction to entertain the application. On appeal, the council applied for the possession order to be varied to include a condition that the defendant should not use the property for an illegal activity. The circuit judge allowed

---

[47] The Housing Act 1985, s.85(3); 1988, s.9(3).
[48] (2001) EWCA Civ 1023; [2002] H.L.R. 12.
[49] [2002] EWCACiv 1998; [2003] H.L.R. 41.

the appeal. The defendant appealed. Dismissing that appeal, the Court of Appeal held that the court could make a new order postponing the date of possession even if the existing possession order had not yet expired and even if the new order provides for possession to be given up forthwith. The tenant, however, is not to be taken by surprise by an application made under s.85(2). Nonetheless, the court is not bound to allow additional time simply because it would have taken the landlord longer if new proceedings had been commenced. It was also held that the court could impose other conditions in accordance with s.85(3)(b) and should also have regard to the guidance given by Lord Woolf in *Hopkins* for which see para.5–176ff.

Enforcing the Possession Order

Hopkins was primarily concerned with the position at warrant stage. The claimant authority had obtained a suspended possession order on the ground of rent arrears. The order was breached and a warrant was issued. The defendant applied to suspend the warrant. In opposing the application to suspend, the authority sought to rely on incidents of nuisance. Lord Woolf, with whom the other members of the Court of Appeal agreed, held[50]:

5-185

> "Under section 85(2) [Housing Act 1985] I have little doubt that the legislation did not seek to confine the discretion of the court to facts connected to the ground which was relied upon for initially seeking possession. Nor is the court restricted to the ground on which the order is made. It would be very unfortunate if the position were otherwise. There could be matters occurring subsequent to the order for possession which makes it very clear that it would be wrong to suspend or stay the execution of an order for possession. . .we are concerned with social landlords who often have to deal with the problems of large housing estates. There may be many situations where considerable inconvenience and disturbance is caused as a result of tenants not complying with the ordinary standards of those living in an urban setting."

Lord Woolf also provided guidance to district judges dealing with such applications saying[51]:

5-186

(1) the discretion should be used to further the policy of Pt IV of the Housing Act 1985 reinforced as it is by Art. 8. Accordingly, the courts should bear in mind that the policy is one which involves evicting the tenant from his or her home only after a serious breach of the tenant's obligations has been established, when it is reasonable to do so, and the tenant has been proved to have breached any condition of the order for suspension;

(2) the overriding principles contained in the Civil Procedural Rules and in particular the need for applications to be dealt with in a summary and proportionate manner; and

(3) the need for the tenant to have clear notice of the allegations being made.

As we have seen, the same purposive approach in the construction of the Housing Act 1985 was taken by the Court of Appeal in *Finn*. In that case, Arden L.J. said: "Parliament must be taken to have enacted section 85 in the knowledge that it is the practice of the court to allow applications in

5-187

[50] *ibid.*, at para.22.
[51] *ibid.*, at para.29.

proceedings at any time when orders are running without the need to start new proceedings." The same approach, in her judgment, was also to be found in *Burrows v Brent London Borough Council*[52]: "Parliament cannot have intended to penalize a landlord who acted within the spirit of the Act by granting indulgences to defaulting tenants without going through time- wasting and expensive court procedures".

5-188   The ratio of the decisions in *Hopkins* and *Finn* lend support to the argument that there is nothing in the scheme of the Housing Acts 1985 and 1988 which precludes an application asking the court to consider afresh, in the light of the circumstances prevailing at the date of the application, whether it is appropriate for the court to exercise its power to continue to suspend the warrant.

Human Rights

5-189   Since the coming into force of the Human Rights Act 1998 on October 2, 2000, a number of decisions have been made in relation to possession proceedings and, specifically, in relation to possession sought on the grounds of nuisance. Under the 1998 Act, it is unlawful for a public authority to act in a way which is incompatible with a Convention right. This is not limited to local authority landlords or registered social landlords, whose functions are public in nature.[53] The court is also a public body for these purposes.[54] Thus, the court is required to act in a way which is compatible with the Convention. Furthermore, the court, when determining a question which has arisen in connection with a Convention right, must take into account any judgment, decision, declaration or advisory opinion of the European Court on Human Rights.[55]

5-190   The most relevant of the Convention rights in relation to possession proceedings is Art.8. This reads:

"(1) Everyone has the right to respect for his private and family life, his home and his correspondence.
(2) There shall be no interference by a public authority with the exercise of this right except such as is in accordance with the law and is necessary in a democratic society in the interests of national security, public safety or the economic well-being of the country, for the prevention of disorder or crime, for the protection of health or morals, or for the protection of the rights and freedoms of others."

5-191   It is settled that possession is an interference with the right to respect of the home.[56] In *Lambeth LBC v Howard*,[57] Sedley L.J. assumed that any eviction of a tenant fell within Art.8(1). He said:

"Respect of a person's home is neither an absolute concept, nor, given Article 8(2), an unqualified right. I do find myself puzzled by the learned judge's remark that Article 8 "at first sight. . .has no application in the present circumstances". It seems to me that any attempt to evict a person, whether directly or by process of law, from his or her home would on the

---

[52] [1996] 1 W.L.R. 1448 at 1459C–F.
[53] See *Poplar Housing and Regeneration Community Association Ltd v Donoghue*, [2001] EWCA Civ 595; [2001] 3 W.L.R. 183.
[54] Human Rights Act 1998, s.6(3).
[55] *ibid.*, s.6(2)(1).
[56] *R. (on the application of Johns and McLellan) v Bracknell Forest DC* (2001) 33 H.L.R. 45; *Harrow LBC v Qazi* [2003] UKHL 43; 2003 H.L.R. 75; *Kay v Lambeth LBC; Price v Leeds City Council* [2006] UKHL; [2006] 2 W.L.R. 570.
[57] [2001] EWCA Civ 468; (2001) 33 H.L.R. 636.

face of it be a derogation from the respect, that is the integrity, to which the home is prima facie entitled."[58]

He went on to consider in detail the impact of the Human Rights Act 1998 on possession claims under the nuisance ground. He held that there was nothing in Art.8 which would lead county courts to materially different outcomes from those which they had reached for many years, when assessing whether it was reasonable to make a possession order and whether that order should be suspended. Sedley L.J. also stated that it could do no harm, and may do good, if the exercise is approached as an application of the principle of proportionality. **5-192**

In *Gallagher v Castle Vale Action Trust Ltd*,[59] the Court of Appeal restated the three stage test to be applied in possession cases: **5-193**

"The first stage is to consider whether the Claimant landlord makes out its ground of possession under Schedule 2. . . The second stage, if the Claimant landlord does make out a ground of possession, is to consider whether, in the case of the discretionary grounds, it is reasonable to order possession. . . The third stage is to consider whether. . .to exercise a discretion to stay or suspend or postpone the date for possession."

The defendant appealed against an outright possession order granted previously on the basis of noise nuisance and bad language inside and outside of the flat at all times of the day. She submitted that the nuisance complained of took place at times when her family were visiting the property; it was significant that the county court concluded that most of the grossly offensive behaviour and language was caused by her daughter's boyfriend and, to a lesser extent, her daughter.

According to Sedley L.J. on appeal, if a tenant has the power to control the acts of nuisance caused by visitors or residents yet does nothing, it would be reasonable to make an order for possession (under the second stage). However, he added in respect of the third stage of the test: **5-194**

"No outright possession order may be made without regard to the question of participation or acquiescence on the tenant's part."

In *Gallagher* it was apparent that Ms Gallagher did not carry out the relevant acts of nuisance that were complained of, nor did she acquiesce in them. Despite this the judge at first instance granted an outright order, and not a suspended order as may have been expected if Sedley's reasoning had been followed. The trial judge had ignored the fact that the offenders had moved to alternative accommodation and for that reason he should have gone on to consider the likelihood of the nuisance recurring. This failure enabled the Court of Appeal to re-visit the question of reasonableness and suspend the order (unanimously). **5-195**

The Court of Appeal applied the reasoning of Simon Brown L.J. in *Kensington & Chelsea LBC v Simmonds* and used Art.8 to justify the making **5-196**

[58] In *Poplar Housing and Regeneration Community Association Ltd v Donoghue* the court had decided that Poplar was a public body and that Art.8 was directly applicable. Waller L.J. said: "It seems to me that even if it had been a private landlord seeking to evict a tenant under an assured shorthold tenancy, the court as a public authority would have to approach section 21(4) in much the same way. It would have concluded that section 21(4) did not infringe any Art. 8 right but not because Art. 8 did not apply at all but because the eviction was in accordance with the law and it was not disproportionate to allow the tenancy to be brought to an end in accordance with the rights of the landlord." See also *Kay v Lambeth LBC; Price v Leeds City Council*, [2006] UKHL; [2006] 2 W.L.R. 570.
[59] [2001] EWCA Civ 944; [2001] 33 H.L.R. 810.

of a suspended possession order rather than an outright order. However, given the comment of Sedley L.J. above, it is unlikely that the Convention will effect a major shift in the approach of the courts to the outcomes of such cases. See also the decision in *Kay v Lambeth, LBC, Price v Leeds CC.*[60]

Appeals in Nuisance Cases

5-197 It is possible to appeal the exercise of the judge's discretion in deciding whether to suspend a possession order where he has erred (to the appropriate extent) in the exercise of its discretion.[62] Guidance may be sought from the speech of Lord Fraser in *G v G (minors: Custody Appeal)*[63] as to what constitutes a sufficient error in the exercise of discretion to warrant interference by the appeal court:

"the appellate court should only interfere when they consider that the judge of first instance has not merely preferred an imperfect solution which is different from an alternative imperfect solution which the Court of Appeal might or would have adopted, but has exceeded the generous ambit within which a reasonable disagreement is possible."[64]

5-198 In *Greenwich LBC v Grogan*,[65] Sir Christopher Staughton held that where the judge has exercised his discretion and then granted leave to appeal, that this was or might be an admission by the judge that he would like the Court of Appeal, if asked, to reconsider the exercise of his discretion.

Assured and Secure tenancies

5-199 In order to obtain possession, the landlord must serve a notice seeking possession.[66] The court does have a discretion to dispense with the requirement of such a notice if it considers that it would be just and equitable to do so,[67] although it is advisable to serve a notice in order to avoid having to overcome this hurdle. It is highly unlikely that the court will dispense with the requirement where no intimation of an intention to seek possession has been given.[68]

5-200 The notice seeking possession under s.83(2a) of the Housing Act 1985 must be in the prescribed form. The current form can be found in the Secure Tenancies (Notices) (Amendment) Regulations 1997[69] and further amended by the Secure Tenancies (Notices) (Amendment No.2) Regulations 1997.[70] The notice needs to set out the particulars of the allegations of the nuisance. In *Slough BC v Robbins*,[71] the claim was struck out because the notice was defective. The notice seeking possession merely said:

[60-61] *Kay v Lambeth LBC; Price v Leeds City Council* [2006] UKHL; 2006 2 W.L.R. 570.
[62] CPR Pt 52.11(3)(a).
[63] [1985] 1 W.L.R. 647.
[64] *ibid.* at 652.
[65] (2001) 33 H.L.R. 12.
[66] Housing Act 1985, s.83(1); Housing Act 1988, s.8(1).
[67] Housing Act 1985, s.83(1)(b); Housing Act 1988, s.8(1)(b).
[68] *Kelsey HA v King* (1995) 28 H.L.R. 270. The notice was held to be invalid because of the inadequacy of the particulars of the allegations of nuisance. The Court of Appeal, however, held that it was just and equitable to dispense with the notice because of: (a) developments since the commencement of proceedings; and (b) the fact that the point was raised at a late stage in proceedings. See also *North British HA v Sheridan* [1999] 2 E.G.L.R. 138.
[69] Secure Tenancies (Notices) (Amendment) Regulations 1997 (SI 1997/71).
[70] Secure Tenancies (Notices) (Amendment) Regulations 1997 (SI 1997/377).
[71] [1996] 12 C.L. 353, Slough County Court.

"Numerous complaints have been received over a period of time that annoyance and nuisance is being caused to your neighbours by noise and disruptive behaviour. This nuisance and annoyance has been investigated by my staff and I believe the complaints to be substantiated."

It must be obvious to tenants in default what they must do to avoid possession proceedings. The particulars in the notice should be as accurate as possible. Note Gibson L.J. in *Dudley MBC v Bailey*[72]:   **5-201**

". . . the question is whether, at the date of the notice, the landlord has in good faith stated the ground and given the particulars of that ground. The requirement of particulars is satisfied, in my judgment, if the landlord has stated in summary form the facts which he then intends to prove in support of the stated ground for possession. Error in the particulars does not, in my judgment, invalidate the notice, although it may well affect the decision of the court on the merits."

In the case of assured tenants, the notice has to be in the prescribed form[73] informing the tenant that: (a) the landlord intends to bring proceedings for possession of the dwelling-house on one or more of the grounds specified in the notice; (b) those proceedings will not begin earlier than a date specified in the notice; and (c) those proceedings will not begin later than 12 months from the date of service of the notice.   **5-202**

In order to deal with anti-social tenants swiftly, landlords can commence possession proceedings immediately upon service of the notice.[74]   **5-203**

Rent Act Tenancies

Tenancies granted before January 15, 1989, or which fall under the exceptions in s.34 of the Housing Act 1988, will, subject to certain requirements, have security of tenure under the Rent Act 1977. Thus, the tenant has a right to occupy, even after the contractual tenancy is at end, as a statutory tenant.[75] The landlord, however, may seek possession under specific grounds, which if proved, will allow the court to grant possession. Case 1 of Sch.15 to the Rent Act 1977, provides a ground for possession on the basis, inter alia, that: **5-204**

"any obligation of the protected or statutory tenancy which arises under this Act, or—

(a) in the case of a protected tenancy, any other obligation of the tenancy, in so far as is consistent with the provisions of Part VII of this Act [Rent Act 1977], or
(b) in the case of a statutory tenancy, any other obligation of the previous protected tenancy which is applicable to the statutory tenancy, has been broken or not performed".[76]

This is similar to the breach of tenancy ground under the Housing Act 1985 and Housing Act 1988.

The Rent Act 1977 also allows a landlord to seek possession under a nuisance ground. Case 2 of Sch.15 to the Rent Act 1977 provides: **5-205**

---

[72] [1991] 10 E.G. 140; (1990) 22 H.L.R. 424.
[73] Housing Act 1988, s.8(3). The form to be used is Form No. 3 of SI 1997/1194.
[74] Housing Act 1985, s.83 and Housing Act 1988, s.8(4).
[75] Rent Act 1977, s.2.
[76] *ibid.*, s.3(1) which provides that the original provisions of the contractual tenancy will bind a statutory tenant in so far as they are consistent with the Rent Act 1977.

"Where the tenant or any person residing or lodging with him or any sub-tenant of his has been guilty of conduct which is a nuisance or annoyance to adjoining occupiers, or has been convicted of using the dwelling-house or allowing the dwelling house to be used for immoral or illegal purposes."

This ground for possession is more restrictive than the grounds under the Housing Act 1985 and Housing Act 1988, as amended. First, the ground can only be established if the perpetrator of the nuisance or annoyance is the tenant, person residing with the tenant, lodger or sub-tenant. Secondly, the nuisance or annoyance is to adjoining occupiers; a more limited area than "locality". It is not necessary for the act of nuisance or annoyance to have taken place on the premises. In *Whitbread v Ward*[77] relations between the tenant and landlord's daughter took place 200 yards away from the premises. Thirdly, there has to be conduct which has caused nuisance or annoyance rather that conduct likely to cause nuisance and annoyance. The court must be satisfied that it is reasonable to make a possession order.[78]

Assured shorthold tenancies[79]

5-206 Many private sector landlords grant assured shorthold tenancies which provide a limited security of tenure to the tenant. In addition to the normal grounds for possession available under Sch.2 to the Housing Act 1988 (and in particular, breach of tenancy agreement and nuisance grounds),[80] the landlord is able to obtain possession under s.21 of the 1988 Act. All the landlord is required to do is serve a notice requiring possession. There is no need to give reasons for seeking possession and the court must order possession if the notice requirements are met. There is, however, nothing preventing landlords from serving a notice under s.8 of the 1988 Act if they wish to issue proceedings immediately, although the court will be obliged to consider whether it is reasonable to make a possession order.

Procedure

5-207 The procedure for claims for possession can be found in CPR Pt 55.[81] CPR Pt 55 must be used where a claim includes a possession claim brought by a landlord (or former landlord), mortgagee, licensor (or former licensor), a possession claim against trespassers or a claim by a tenant for relief from forfeiture.[82]

5-208 Nearly all claims have to be brought in the county court for the district in which the land is situated. It is only in exceptional circumstances that a claim may be brought in the High Court and any such claim must be filed with a certificate stating the reason for bringing the claim in the High Court, verified by a statement of truth. Exceptional circumstances include complicated disputes of fact and points of law of general importance, and, in the case of trespassers, where there is a substantial risk of public disorder and/or damage to persons or property. Although the value of the property and the amount

---

[77] (1952) 159 E.G. 494.
[78] Rent Act 1977, s.98(1).
[79] The scope of this book is not wide enough to encompass all the issues that may be raised in respect of assured shorthold tenancies. For more detail see G. Webber and D. Dovar *Residential Possession Proceedings* (7th edn, Sweet & Maxwell, 2005).
[80] See above as to the requirements for obtaining possession under these grounds.
[81] CPR Pt 55 was introduced by the Civil Procedure (Amendment) Rules 2001 (SI 2001/256). This came into force on October 15, 2001.
[82] CPR Pt 55.2.

of any financial claim may be relevant circumstances, these factors alone will not normally justify starting the claim in the High Court.[83] There is a risk of the claim being struck out if the High Court decides the claim should have been started in the county court. Otherwise, the High Court will transfer the claim to the county court and usually disallow the costs of starting the claim in the High Court and the costs of any transfer.[84]

The Particulars of Claim must be filed and served with Claim Form N5.[85]   **5-209**
The Practice Direction to CPR Pt 55 and CPR Pt 16 sets out the contents of the Particulars of Claim. Practice Direction 55/2.1 sets out the general requirements for a possession claim. In particular, the landlord needs to:

(1) identify the land to which the claim relates;

(2) state whether the claim relates to residential property;

(3) state the ground on which possession is claimed;

(4) give full details of any mortgage or tenancy agreement; and

(5) give details of every person who, to the best of the claimant's knowledge, is in possession of the property.

There are also specific requirements in the case of a residential property let on a tenancy.[86] Where the claim relates to the conduct of a tenant, the Particulars of Claim must state the details of the conduct alleged.[87]

The defendant is not required to serve an acknowledgement of service and   **5-210**
accordingly CPR Pt 10 (acknowledgment of service) does not apply. Where a defendant wishes to defend a claim, the defence should be filed within the time specified,[88] generally 14 days after service of the particulars of claim, and must be in Form N11, N11B, N11M or N11R, as appropriate.[89] Failure to file a defence, although not fatal in that the Defendant may still take part in the hearing, may result in a costs penalty. CPR Pt 12 (default judgment) does not apply.

The court will fix a hearing date on issue of the claim.[90] The basic rule is   **5-211**
that the hearing will be no fewer than 28 days from date of issue. The standard period will be not more than eight weeks between the date of issue and the hearing. The defendant must be served with the claim form and particulars not less than 21 days before the hearing date.[91] The court may extend or shorten the time periods.[92] In determining whether to shorten time, the court will give particular consideration to the following:

(1) whether there has been an assault or a threat of assault by the defendant or a person for whom the defendant is responsible, against the claimant, a member of the claimant's staff or another resident in the locality;

[83] See PD 55, para.1.4.
[84] PD 55, para.1.2.
[85] CPR Pt 55.4. The Claimant must use the appropriate claim form and particulars of claim form set out in Table 1 to PD 4 (PD 55, para.1.5). The Particulars of Claim should be in Form N119 (rented residential) and N120 (mortgaged residential).
[86] PD 55, para.2.2–2.4A.
[87] PD 55, para.2.4A.
[88] See CPR Pt 15.4.
[89] This change was effected by Update 25 contained in the December 25, 2001 supplement which, inter alia, inserted revised PD 55, para.1.5.
[90] CPR Pt 55.5(1).
[91] CPR Pt 55.3.
[92] CPR Pt 3.1(2)(a)(b); PD 55, para.3.1.

(2) whether there are reasonable grounds for fearing such an assault;

(3) whether there has been serious damage or a threat of serious damage
by the defendant or a person for whom the defendant is responsible, to
the home or property of another resident in the locality.[93]

5-212 Where the above applies but the case cannot be determined at the first fixed
hearing, the court is required to consider what steps are needed to finally determine the case as quickly as reasonably practicable.[94] At the first hearing of the
claim, or at any adjournment of that hearing, the court may decide the claim or
give case management directions.[95] Where there is a genuine dispute on grounds
which appear to be substantial, case management directions will include allocation of the claim to a track or directions as will enable it to be allocated.[96]
5-213 When allocating a claim, the court has regard to:

(1) CPR Pt 26.8 (matters relevant to allocation);

(2) arrears of rent/mortgage instalments;

(3) the importance to the defendant of retaining possession;

(4) the importance of vacant possession to the claimant.[97]

5-214 Any fact that needs to be proved by the evidence of witnesses may be proved
by evidence in writing, except where the claim is allocated to the fast track or
multi-track or the court orders otherwise.[98] Wherever possible, each party
should include within the statement of case all the evidence which is to be presented.[99] It is essential to ensure that the statement of case is verified by a statement of truth so that it may be relied on at the hearing.[1] Where witness
statements are to be used, they must be filed and served at least two days before
the hearing, other than in trespasser cases where they must be filed and served
with the claim form.
5-215 If the maker of the witness statement does not attend and the other party
disputes material evidence contained in the statement, the court will normally
adjourn the hearing so that oral evidence can be given.[2]

Accelerated possession: Housing Act 1988[3]
5-216 The claimant may only bring a possession claim under the relevant section of
CPR Pt 55 where the claim is brought under s.21 of the Housing Act 1988 and
all the conditions listed in CPR Pt 55.12 are satisfied. The conditions are:

(1) the tenancy and any agreement for the tenancy were entered into on or
after 15 January 1989;

---

[93] CPR Pt 55, PD 55, para.3.2.
[94] PD 55, para.3.3.
[95] CPR Pt 55.8(1).
[96] CPR Pt 55.8(2).
[97] CPR Pt 55.9(1).
[98] CPR Pt 55.8(3) and CPR Pt 32.2 (oral evidence at trial subject to any other provision or order).
[99] PD 55, para.5.1.
[1] PD 22, para.4.
[2] PD 55, para.5.4.
[3] In *Poplar HARCA v Donoghue* [2001] 3 W.L.R. 183, it was held that the right to possession
under the accelerated possession procedure, despite its mandatory nature, did not conflict with
Art.8 E.C.H.R. as s.21(4) was necessary in a democratic society as a procedure for recovering
possession at the end of a tenancy. The decision of Parliament to restrict the jurisdiction of
the court when ordering possession under s.21(4) was a policy decision to which the courts
should defer.

(2) the only purpose of the claim is to recover possession of the property and no other claim is made;

(3) the tenancy did not immediately follow an assured tenancy which was not an assured shorthold tenancy;

(4) the tenancy fulfilled the conditions provided by s.19A or 20(1)(a) to (c) of the 1988 Act;

(5) the tenancy—

    (i) was the subject of a written agreement;

    (ii) arises by virtue of s.5 of the 1988 Act but follows a tenancy that was the subject of a written agreement; or

    (iii) relates to the same or substantially the same property let to the same tenant and on the same terms (though not necessarily as to rent or duration) as a tenancy which was the subject of a written agreement; and

(6) a notice in accordance with ss.21(1) or 21(4) of the 1988 Act was given to the tenant in writing.

The claim must be started in the county court for the district in which the property is situated. Generally the new procedure is very similar to the old, but there is a new prescribed form.[4] An affidavit is no longer required; a claim form verified by a statement of truth is sufficient.

5-217   A defendant who wishes to oppose the claim or seek a postponement of possession on grounds of exceptional hardship[5] must, within 14 days after service of the claim form, file a defence in the prescribed Form N11B. If no defence is filed within the 14 day period, the claimant may file a written request for possession which will be referred to the judge.[6] Where the 14 day period expires with no defence being filed and the claimant has not made a request for an order for possession within three months after that period, the claim will be stayed.[7] If a defence is filed, either within the 14 day period or before any written request is filed by the claimant, the court will send a copy of the defence to the claimant and refer the claim and defence to the judge.[8]

5-218   The judge will, after considering the claim and any defence, make an order for possession unless he or she is not satisfied that the claim form was served; that the claimant is entitled to summary possession or that the claim form discloses no reasonable grounds for bringing the claim. In the latter case, the claim will be struck out, otherwise the judge will order a date to be fixed for a hearing and give any appropriate case management directions.[9] Where the claim is struck out the court will serve its reasons with the order and the claimant may apply, within 28 days of service of the order, to restore the claim.[10]

5-219   Where a defendant seeks postponement of possession the judge may direct a hearing of the issue on a date, which must be before possession is due to be given up. If satisfied at the hearing that exceptional hardship would be caused, the judge may order that possession be given up no later than six weeks after the making of the order for possession on the papers.[11]

---

[4] Form N5B.
[5] Housing Act 1980, s.89(1).
[6] CPR Pt 55.15(2).
[7] CPR Pt 55.15(4).
[8] CPR Pt 55.15(1) and (3).
[9] CPR Pt 15.16.
[10] CPR Pt 55.16(4).
[11] Housing Act 1980, s.89.

Possession will only be postponed without a hearing where the judge is satisfied that the defendant has shown exceptional hardship: considers that possession should be postponed and where the claimant has indicated on the claim form that such a hearing need not be held.[12] Where the claim has been allocated to the small claims track, it will be treated, so far as costs are concerned as if it were allocated to the fast track. Costs will be at the court's discretion, but will not exceed the amount set out under CPR Pt 46.2. If all the parties agree, the court can order that CPR Pt 27.14 applies (costs on small claims track).

Appeals

5-220 Permission to appeal will be required in all cases. Most claims will lie on appeal from the district judge to the circuit judge. Appeals from the circuit judge will be to the High Court, with permission in all cases other than multi-track (final decisions); cases referred under CPR Pt 52.14 (that is, where the appeal would raise an important point of principal or practice or there is some other compelling reason for the Court of Appeal to hear it; and where the decision of the circuit judge was itself a decision on an appeal) will be to the Court of Appeal.

Patients

5-221 A person may not, without the permission of the court, make an application against a patient before proceedings have started or take any step in proceedings save for the issue and service of the claim form and applying for the appointment of a litigation friend until the patient has a litigation friend.[13] Any step taken before child or patient has a litigation friend shall be of no effect unless the court otherwise orders.[14] Patient means a person who by reason of mental disorder within the meaning of the Mental Health Act 1983 is incapable of managing and administering his own affairs.[15]

Introductory Tenancies

5-222 The most innovative way in which Parliament attempted to combat anti-social behaviour in the Housing Act 1996 was through the optional introductory tenancy scheme, which acts as an exception to the security of tenure of secure tenants.[16] The aim of the scheme is to make it easier for the landlord to evict those tenants who persistently engage in anti-social behaviour before they achieve security of tenure[17] by providing for a trial period in which the landlord can terminate the tenancies of "the minority of tenants"[18] during the first year of the tenancy.

Election of the scheme

5-223 Under Pt V of the 1996 Act, a local housing authority[19] or housing action trust[20] may elect to operate an introductory tenancy scheme whereby all new

[12] CPR Pt 55.18 and PD 55, para.8.2.
[13] CPR Pt 21.3(2) and (3).
[14] CPR Pt 21.3(4).
[15] CPR Pt 21.1(2)(b).
[16] Housing Act 1985, Sch.1, para.1A (as amended by Housing Act 1996, Sch.14, para.5) provides that introductory tenancies cannot be secure tenancies.
[17] Circular. No. 2/97 para.4.
[18] White Paper, *Our Future Homes*, Ch.7.
[19] Housing Act 1996, s.230 and Housing Act 1985, ss.1 and 2.
[20] Housing Act 1996, s.230; Housing Act 1985, s.4; Housing Act 1988, Pt III and in particular, Housing Act 1988, s.63.

periodic tenancies[21] granted,[22] which would otherwise have been secure tenancies,[23] will be introductory tenancies.[24] This does not apply to new tenancies granted to existing secure tenants or an assured tenant of a registered social landlord[25] or to tenancies entered into or adopted[26] in pursuance of a contract made before the authority elected to operate an introductory tenancy scheme.[27] An election may be revoked at any time, without prejudice to the making of a further election.[28]

Consultation

The introduction of the scheme by a local housing authority is a matter of housing management[29] and accordingly, local authorities are required to inform their secure tenants of its proposals to implement it.[30] They must also give their secure tenants a period of time in which to make their views known to the local authority and such representations must be considered in accordance with those arrangements.[31] Any details of the arrangements must be published and a copy of the publication is: (1) to be made available at the principal office of the authority for inspection at all reasonable hours, without charge, by any member of the public – not just its secure tenants, and (2) shall be provided on demand to any member of the public who asks for a copy, on payment of a fee.[32]

5-224

The trial period

Section 125 of the 1996 Act prescribes that an introductory tenancy is subject to a trial period, usually of one year from the date of grant, at the end of which the tenancy does not come to an end but automatically becomes either a secure tenancy[33] or an ordinary contractual tenancy.[34] The trial period is the period of one year beginning with the date on which the tenancy was entered into, or if later, the date on which a tenant was first entitled to possession under the

5-225

---

[21] i.e., a tenancy which is not for a fixed term.
[22] This also applies to licences to occupy a dwelling-house with the exception of a licence granted as a temporary expedient to a person who entered the dwelling-house or any other land as a trespasser (Housing Act 1996, s.21).
[23] Housing Act 1996, s.230; Housing Act 1985, s.79, sets out those tenancies which are excluded from security and therefore, cannot be introductory tenancies but are mere contractual tenancies.
[24] This does not apply to new tenancies granted to existing secure tenants or an assured tenant of a registered social landlord (Housing Act 1996, s.124(2)) or to tenancies entered into or adopted in pursuance of a contract made before the authority elected to operate an introductory tenancy scheme (s.124(3) of the Act).
[25] Housing Act 1996, s.124(2).
[26] A periodic tenancy is adopted by a person if that person becomes the landlord under the tenancy, whether on a disposal or surrender of the interest of the former landlord: Housing Act 1996, s.124(4).
[27] Housing Act 1996, s.124(3).
[28] *ibid.*, s.124(5). Once the election is revoked existing introductory tenancies will become secure (s.125(5)(c) so long as they satisfy the conditions of becoming secure.
[29] Housing Act 1985, s.105(2).
[30] The DoE Circular considers that "while the introduction of the scheme will not directly affect the rights of existing secure tenants, for most authorities it will form part of a wider strategy for dealing with anti-social behaviour by new and existing tenants alike, and so information about the landlord's intention will be germane to secure tenants." See para.6 Circular 2/97.
[31] Housing Act 1985, s.105(1).
[32] *ibid.*, s.105(6).
[33] Housing Act 1996, s.125(5).
[34] *ibid.*, s.125(6).

tenancy.[35] If the introductory tenancy was adopted by the authority or trust, the period runs from the date of adoption.[36] Where a tenant was formerly a tenant under another introductory tenancy, or held an assured shorthold tenancy from a registered social landlord any period during which he was a tenant, will count towards the trial period.[37] If there was more than one such previous introductory tenancy or assured shorthold, then they will all be taken into account if each succeeded the other without interruption.[38] In the case of joint tenants under an introductory tenancy, then it lasts for the minimum time that any one of the joint tenants would be subject to it, i.e. the maximum previous time is deducted.[39]

5-226   The Housing Act 2004 amends Pt V of the 1996 Act so that the trial period may be extended by a further six months',[40] so long as two conditions are met. First, the landlord must have served a notice of extension on the tenant at least eight weeks before the original expiry date.[41] Secondly, the tenant has not requested a review or, if he has, the decision on the review was to confirm the landlord's decision to extend the trial period.[42] The notice of extension must set out the reasons for the landlord's decision to extend the introductory tenancy period by six months and inform the tenant of his right to request a review of the landlord's decision and of the time within which such a request must be made.[43]

5-227   The tenant may request a review of the landlord's decision to extend the trial period, although such a request must be made within 14 days of service of the notice of extension.[44] The landlord is under a duty to review its decision once the request is made.[45] It shall notify the tenant of the decision on the review and, if the decision is to confirm the original decision, the landlord shall also notify him of the reasons for the decision.[46] The review shall be carried out and the tenant notified before the original expiry date.[47] The Secretary of State may make provision by regulations as to the procedure to be followed in connection with a review including (but not limited to): (1) requiring the decision on review to be made by a person of appropriate seniority who was not involved in the original decision; and (2) the circumstances in which the person concerned is entitled to an oral hearing, and whether and by whom he may be represented at such a hearing. It is thought that the procedure to be followed will be similar to a review to seek possession.[48]

Rights of introductory tenants

5-228   Save for the lack of security (which is dealt with below), and the absence of the right to buy, introductory tenants have many of the rights enjoyed by

---

[35] Housing Act 1996, s.125(2).
[36] *ibid.*, s.125(2)(b).
[37] *ibid.*, s.125(3).
[38] *ibid.*, s.125(3).
[39] *ibid.*, s.125(4).
[40] Housing Act 2004, s.179. This provision came into force on June 6, 2005 (Housing Act 2004 (Commencement No.3) (England) Order 2005). The amendments do not apply in relation to any tenancy entered into before, or in pursuance of an agreement made before, the day on which this section came into force, that is, before June 6, 2005.
[41] Housing Act 1996, s.125A(2).
[42] *ibid.*, s.125A(3). The "original expiry date" means the last day of the period of one year that would apply as the trial period apart from this section (Housing Act 1996, s.129A(6)).
[43] Housing Act 1996, s.125A(4) and (5).
[44] *ibid.*, s.125B(1).
[45] *ibid.*, s.125B(2).
[46] *ibid.*, s.125B(5).
[47] *ibid.*, s.125B(6).
[48] *ibid.*, s.125B(3) and (4).

secure tenants: succession[49]; assignment[50]; right to repair[51]; provision of information about introductory tenancies[52]; and consultation on all relevant housing management matters.[53]

Vulnerable tenants

The DoE guidance makes it clear that introductory tenancies should not be **5-229** used as a weapon against vulnerable tenants and "it is essential that landlords are fully alive to the special needs of vulnerable tenants and their relationship with the community as a whole".[54] Vulnerable tenants have been defined by the Local Authority Association Guidance as including those under law and local policy who are: "vulnerable" as defined by s.189(c) of the 1996 Act; "in need" as defined by the Children Act 1989; people assessed as needing services under the National Health Service and Community Care Act 1990; and who do not speak English as their first language.[55] The DoE guidance recommends that where problems have arisen between a vulnerable tenant and neighbours, eviction may not necessarily be the most appropriate action to take.[56] The Race Relations Act 1976 imposes duties on local authorities to ensure they do not discriminate either directly or indirectly on the grounds of race, gender and sexual orientation in the allocation or management of housing that they own.

Cessation of an introductory tenancy

A tenancy can cease to be an introductory tenancy before the end of the pro- **5-230** bationary period in a number of situations[57]:

(1) the circumstances are such that the tenancy would not otherwise be a secure tenancy. Thus, where the tenant no longer occupies the dwelling house as his only or principal home, the introductory tenancy will cease[58] or where there has been an unlawful assignment.[59] This will not apply where there has been subletting of part of the dwelling-house until there has been a subletting of the whole[60]; or

(2) the election was in force when the tenancy was entered into or adopted is revoked; or

---

[49] Housing Act 1985, ss.131–133.
[50] *ibid.*, s.134.
[51] *ibid.*, s.135 and The Secure Tenants of Local Housing Authorities (Right to Repair) (Amendment) Regulations 1997.
[52] *ibid.*, s.136.
[53] *ibid.*, s.137.
[54] See Circular 2/97, paras 10–15 and Department of Health and the Department of the Environment's joint guidance, *Housing and Community Care—Establishing a Strategic Framework*, published on January 22, 1997.
[55] Local Authority Association Guidance, para.4.6.
[56] Also see *The Local Authority Association Guidance on Introductory Tenancies*. The Secretary of State endorsed that guidance and has said that "it should be read in conjunction with the Circular 2/97".
[57] Housing Act 1996, s.125(5).
[58] See Housing Act 1985, s.81 which provides that "The tenant condition is that the tenant is an individual and occupies the dwelling-house as his only or principal home; or, where the tenancy is a joint tenancy, that each of the joint tenants is an individual and at least one of them occupies the dwelling-house as his only or principal home."
[59] Housing Act 1985, ss.105–106.
[60] *ibid.*, s.93.

(3) the tenancy ceases to be an introductory tenancy by virtue of succession[61]; or

(4) a person or body other than a local housing authority or housing action trust becomes the landlord under the tenancy.

5-231 Although the introductory tenancy comes to an end, the tenancy itself does not automatically end and therefore, will need to be terminated by a notice to quit.[62]

Possession proceedings

5-232 The landlord may only bring an introductory tenancy to an end by obtaining an order of the court for possession and the tenancy comes to an end on the date on which the tenant is to give up possession in pursuance of the order.

Notice
5-233 In order to determine an introductory tenancy, the landlord must first serve notice on its tenant. There is no prescribed notice although the tenant must be informed of the following[63]:

(1) that the landlord will ask the court to make an order for possession;

(2) the landlord's reasons for seeking possession;

(3) the date after which possession proceedings will be started (which must not be earlier than the date on which the tenancy could be determined by notice to quit);

(4) that the tenant has the right to request a review of the landlord's decision to seek an order for possession and of the time in which such a request must be made;

(5) that if the tenant requires help or advice, he should take it immediately to a Citizen's Advice Bureau, a housing aid centre, a law centre or a solicitor.

5-234 As mentioned above the introductory tenancy scheme was devised to combat the increasing problem with anti-social behaviour. Where a tenant is in breach of his tenancy agreement (including breaches in relation to the conduct of the tenant), the landlord can serve a notice stating that they require possession of the property. However, it is recognised by the Local Authority Association Guidance that possession should not be sought immediately where there have been minor breaches. In such a case, they suggest that the landlord serves two warning notices rather than a notice pursuant to s.128 of the Housing Act 1996.[64] Minor breaches might include littering, occasional noise, upkeep of gardens or minor damage to the home.[65] More serious breaches, which would generally merit the service of a notice under s.128 of the Housing Act 1996, include violence or threats of violence, damage or threats of damage to a victim's property, minor harassment having a serious detrimental effect on the victim or members of the family and where there are a substantial number of incidents which are still continuing notwithstanding warnings to the tenant.[66]

[61] Housing Act 1985, s.133(3).
[62] Protection from Eviction Act 1977, s.5.
[63] Housing Act 1996, s.128.
[64] Local Authority Association Guidance, para.4.3.
[65] *ibid.*
[66] Local Authority Association Guidance, para.4.4.

Reasons

Where reasons are statutorily required to be given, the courts have held **5-235**
that "the reasons that are set out must be reasons which will not only be
intelligible, but which deal with the substantial points that have been
raised".[67]

On a strict reading of s.128, a new notice is required if an authority wish to **5-236**
rely on grounds additional to those already specified.[68] However, in *R. (on the*
application of Laporte) v The London Borough of Newham[69] the bringing of
possession proceedings was not rendered unlawful where the authority, in
upholding its decision to seek possession on review, relied upon reasons additional to those specified in the notice. There had been no material prejudice to
the tenant because the tenant had been provided with details of the additional
allegations which were considered on review and there was nothing to shake
the original decision to seek possession.

Jurisdiction of the court

The court must make an order for possession if it is satisfied that the require- **5-237**
ments regarding notice under s.128 of the 1996 Act have been met. It does
not have a discretion to consider the reasonableness of making the order or
to go into the reasons behind the landlord's claim for possession.[70]
Furthermore, the court is not concerned with the review process or its
outcome.[71] An authority's decision on a review may only be challenged by
way of judicial review. If the county court is satisfied that there is a real
chance of leave to apply for judicial review being granted, it has the power
to grant an adjournment of the possession action to allow an application to
be made.[72]

Unlike secure tenancies, the landlord is not required to establish a ground **5-238**
for possession; he merely has to satisfy the court that the notice has been
served in compliance with s.128.

Review of decision to seek possession[73]

A tenant is entitled to request the authority to conduct a review of this deci- **5-239**
sion[74] before the end of the period of 14 days beginning with the day on which
the notice of proceedings is served.[75] On a request being made the landlord
must review its decision.[76] The procedure to be followed in connection with a

---

[67] Per Megaw J. in *Re Poyser and Mills Arbitration* [1964] 2. Q.B. 467, approved by the House of
Lords in *Westminster CC v Great Portland Estates plc* [1985] A.C. 661.

[68] *c.f.* the situation where a further incident of nuisance of substantially the same nature occurs
after service of the notice which reinforces the authority's decision to begin possession proceedings; there is no problem in relying on the original s.128 notice: *Cardiff City Council v Stone*
[2002] EWCA 298; [2003] H.L.R. 47.

[69] [2004] EWCA 227 (Admin). See also *Forbes v London Borough of Lambeth* [2004] EWHC 222
(Admin); [2003] H.L.R. 49.

[70] The county court only has jurisdiction to review the exercise or failure to exercise its public law
duty if there is parliamentary authority for it to do so (County Courts Act 1984, s.38).

[71] *Manchester CC v Cochrane* [1999] 1 W.L.R. 809.

[72] *ibid.*

[73] See also the Local Authority Association Guidance on review procedures.

[74] Housing Act 1996, s.129. The procedures to be followed by the authority in a review of its decision are contained in the Introductory Tenants (Review) Regulations, (SI 1997/72). Guidance
1997 (SI 1997/72)has also been provided by the Secretary of State in D.o.E. Circ.2/97
Introductory Tenancies and Repossession for Secure Tenancies.

[75] Housing Act 1996, s.129.

[76] *ibid.*, s.129(2). See *R. (on the application of Chelfat) v Tower Hamlets London Borough Council*
[2006] EWHC 313 (Admin).

review is set out in regulations made by the Secretary of State[77] and is as follows:

(1) the review will not be by way of an oral hearing unless the tenant requests one by the end of the 14 day time limit[78];

(2) the review must be carried out by a person who was not involved in the decision to apply for a possession order[79];

(3) the officer reviewing the decision must be made by a more senior officer than the officer who made the original decision[80];

(4) if there is no oral hearing, the tenant may make representations in writing and such representations shall be considered by the landlord who shall inform the tenant of the date by which such representations must be received, which shall not be less than five days after the landlord received the information from the tenant.[81]

Oral hearing

5-240 The procedure to be followed at the oral hearing is determined by the person carrying out the review subject to the following.[82] If there is an oral hearing, the landlord authority must inform the tenant of the date, time and place of the hearing which shall not be less than five days after receipt of the request for a hearing.[83] Where the tenant has not been given notice, the hearing may only take place with the consent of the tenant or his representative.[84] If notice has been given, and the tenant does not attend, the reviewing officer may, having regard to all the circumstances, proceed with the hearing or give further directions with a view to the conduct of the further review as that person may think proper.[85] A tenant may make an application to the landlord to postpone the hearing; it is up to the landlord to refuse or allow the application as he sees fit.[86] The hearing may be adjourned by the person hearing the review at the request of the tenant, his representative or at the motion of the person hearing the review. Where there is more than person hearing the review then if one of them is absent, the review can proceed but only with the consent of the tenant or his representative.[87] The tenant has a right to be heard and to be accompanied by a person (legally qualified or not). For the purpose of the proceedings, the representative will have the same rights and powers which the tenant has under the regulations. The tenant has the right to call persons to give evidence and put questions to any persons giving evidence at the hearing. The tenant also has the right to make representations in writing.

5-241 If the original decision is upheld on review, the authority may commence proceedings for possession in the county court, which must make an order for possession unless the provisions of s.128 of the 1996 Act apply.

---

[77] Housing Act 1996, s.129(2) and The Introductory Tenants (Review) Regulations 1997 (SI 1997/72) which came into force on February 12, 1997.
[78] Introductory Tenants (Review) Regulations 1997 (SI 1997/72), Reg.2.
[79] *ibid.*, Reg.3(1).
[80] *ibid.*, Reg.3(2).
[81] *ibid.*, Reg.4.
[82] *ibid.*, Reg.6.
[83] *ibid.*, Reg.6.
[84] *ibid.*, Reg.6.
[85] *ibid.*, Reg.7.
[86] *ibid.*, Reg.8.
[87] *ibid.*, Reg.10.

Human rights

The Court of Appeal upheld the compatibility of the introductory tenancy **5-242** scheme contained in the Housing Act 1996 with Arts 6 (fair trial), 8 (respect for home and family life) and 14 (discrimination) of the European Convention on Human Rights (the Convention).[88] The judgment generally follows recent decisions concerning the interaction of housing legislation and the Convention, but it has also left open the suggestion that the courts may need to take a different approach to judicial review proceedings in order to make them Art.6 compliant.

Article 8: Is it engaged?

It was submitted, in the *R. v Bracknell Forest BC and the Secretary of State for* **5-243** *Transport, Local Government and the Regions Ex p. McLellan and Johns; Reigate and Banstead BC v Benfield* that Art.8 was not engaged. Since a tenant would know the basis on which he had become a tenant (i.e. under the introductory tenancy scheme), the rights of the tenant to occupy the premises were simply in accordance with the scheme. The first question would be whether the scheme had been complied with which, if answered in favour of the Council, would lead to the conclusion that Art.8(1) was not engaged and accordingly, there is no need to justify the eviction under Art.8(2).

The Court of Appeal disagreed with this approach. Previous authorities **5-244** had held that Art.8 was engaged in any attempt to evict a tenant. In *Lambeth LBC v Howard*,[89] (albeit concerning a decision made before the Human Rights Act), the Court of Appeal held that:

". . .any attempt to evict a person, whether directly or by process of law, from his or her home would on the face of it be a derogation from the respect, that is integrity, to which the home is prima facie entitled."

Further, in *Poplar HARCA Ltd v Donoghue*,[90] Lord Woolf, delivering the judgment of the court, said "to evict the defendant from her home would impact on her family life".

In addition, the court held that the approach put forward by *Reigate* was at **5-245** odds with the terms of Art.8(2). It is not a preliminary question whether the tenancy has been properly terminated in accordance with its terms: whether an eviction was in accordance with the law, and whether it was necessary for the protection of the rights and freedoms of others is a question to be considered under Art.8(2).

Article 8: Is the introductory tenancy scheme justified under Article 8(2)?
The Court of Appeal upheld Longmore J.'s decision in *McLellan and Johns* **5-246** that the introductory tenancy scheme is justified by reference to the factors under Art.8(2); it is in accordance with the law as laid down in the Housing Act 1996 and it is not in any way inevitable that the legislation will act disproportionately; it is for Parliament to make the relevant judgments in this area.[91]

---

[88] *R. v Bracknell Forest BC and the Secretary of State for Transport, Local Government and the Regions Ex p. McLellan and Johns; Reigate and Banstead BC v Benfield* [2001] EWCA Civ 1510; (2001) 33 H.L.R. 86. See further R. Cattermole, *Introductory Tenancies and the Human Rights Act: The Queen (on the application of Johns and McLellan)* [2001] J.H.L. 27; [2002] J.H.L. 7.

[89] [2001] EWCA Civ 468; (2001) 33 H.L.R. 58.

[90] [2001] EWCA Civ 595; [2001] 3 W.L.R. 183; [2001] 4 All E.R. 608; (2001) 33 H.L.R. 823.

[91] See also *Poplar HARCA. op cit.*, p.364 n.74 at para.72.

Is the tenant entitled to raise his or her particular circumstances
in the county court?

5-247 In *Poplar HARCA*, the housing association was seeking possession under
s.21(4) of the Housing Act 1988. Under s.21(4), a court is required to make an
order for possession of a periodic assured shorthold tenancy if the landlord
has properly served a notice in writing requiring possession of the property.[92]
One of the issues before the Court of Appeal was whether the mandatory
terms of the section contravened Art.8. It was further submitted that the court
should have a residual discretion to protect the defendant's basic human
rights. The Court of Appeal held:

> "We are satisfied, that not withstanding its mandatory terms, section 21(4)
> of the 1988 Act does not conflict with the defendant's right to family life.
> Section 21(4) is certainly necessary in a democratic society in so far as there
> must be a procedure for recovering possession of property at the end of a
> tenancy. The question is whether the restricted powers of the court is legit-
> imate and proportionate. This is the area of policy where the court should
> defer to the decision of Parliament. We have come to the conclusion that
> there was no contravention of Article 8 or Article 6."[93]

5-248 Although *Poplar HARCA* provides some guidance on mandatory orders for
possession, the courts must consider other factors when granting possession
in the case of introductory tenancies. Unlike s.21(4) proceedings, the circumstances of the particular tenant are brought directly into focus: the local
authority is required to provide reasons for seeking possession[94] and those
reasons can be reviewed upon an application by the tenant.[95] The question
therefore arises whether the court has jurisdiction to consider the particular
circumstances of the tenant.

5-249 In *Manchester CC v Cochrane*,[96] decided prior to the coming into force of
the Human Rights Act 1998, the Court of Appeal ruled that the court had no
discretion to refuse to make an order for possession once the requirements of
s.128 regarding notice of proceedings had been complied with.[97] The county
court's powers were limited to granting an adjournment of possession proceedings—pending determination of judicial review proceedings in the High
Court—if the county court formed the view that there was a real chance of
leave to apply for judicial review being granted.[98]

5-250 In the *Bracknell Forest BC* case, the Court of Appeal conceded that an
introductory tenant must have the right to raise the question whether it is reasonable to insist on eviction and to rely on his or her Convention rights in any
proceedings.[99] However, this does not mean that a tenant can raise—by way
of defence—his or her particular circumstances. It held:

---

[92] See further Alder, *Donoghue v Poplar HARCA: Housing Associations and the Human Rights Act 1998* [2001] J.H.L. 69.

[93] *Poplar HARCA, op cit.*, p. 364, n.74 at para.72.

[94] Housing Act 1996, s.128(3).

[95] *ibid.*, s.129.

[96] [1999] 1 W.L.R. 809; (1999) 31 H.L.R. 810.

[97] The court held that it would be a clear contravention of the mandatory terms of s.127(2) for the county court to entertain a defence based on a denial of allegations of breaches of the tenancy agreement provided for in the notice under s.128. Further, under s.38(3) of the County Courts Act 1984 a county court was prohibited from reviewing the exercise or failure to exercise a public duty in the absence of parliamentary authority to do so. Part V of the Housing Act 1996 conferred no such authority.

[98] *Manchester CC v Cochrane* [1999] 1 W.L.R. 809 at 819.

[99] Human Rights Act 1998, s.7(1)(b) provides: "A person who claims that a public authority has acted (or proposed to act) in a way which is made unlawful by section 6(1) may . . . rely on the Convention right or rights concerned in any legal proceedings . . .".

". . .because the point can be raised, it does not mean that the court is bound to do anymore than Cochrane envisaged i.e. consider the arguability of the point, and then adjourn to allow the point to be properly considered if the point is arguable. The court is making the order it considers appropriate (see section 8(1)). Section 127 does not prevent the tenant relying on a Convention right if the procedure in *Cochrane* is followed."[1]

In short, an introductory tenant can raise his or her particular circumstances in the county court but the court's jurisdiction is limited to considering whether there is an arguable case and whether, accordingly, an adjournment should be granted so that permission to seek judicial review can be sought. Moreover, since the House of Lords decision in *Kay v Lambeth London Borough Council*, there would be very limited circumstances in which the landlord would have to provide justification under Art.8(2). **5-251**

Section 89 of the Housing Act 1980
In the context of introductory tenancies, the Court of Appeal held that s.89 (which states that a court may not suspend an order for possession for longer than six weeks, even where there is exceptional hardship) was not incompatible with Art.8. The court's reasoning was as follows: **5-252**

"The court has the power to adjourn if it is arguable that a tenant's right is being infringed. If it does that, section 89 is simply not in play. Section 89 only comes into play if either the court thinks its use with its limitation will prevent an infringement of human rights, or of there is no arguable infringement of those rights."

Article 6: Is it engaged?
As regards Art.6, the Court of Appeal in the *Bracknell Forest BC* case followed the ruling in *R. (Alconbury Developments Ltd) v Secretary of State*.[2] The decision by a council to terminate an introductory tenancy engages Art.6: the decision is of an administrative nature which affects the civil rights of the individual. Waller L.J. referred to Lord Clyde's judgment in *Alconbury*, **5-253**

"It is thus clear that article 6(1) is engaged where the decision which is to be given is of an administrative character, that is to say one given in an exercise of a discretionary power, as well as a dispute in a court of law regarding the private rights of the citizen, provided that it directly affects civil rights and obligations of a genuine and serious nature."

The Court of Appeal also indicated that even if there was no express procedure for review and hearing, the decision to terminate an introductory tenancy might well bring into play an obligation to provide an opportunity to be heard, and indeed under European jurisprudence, Art.6 may well be engaged. **5-254**

Is the combination of a review panel and judicial review enough to meet the requirements of Article 6?
Under Art.6, a person is entitled to a "fair and public hearing . . . by an independent and impartial tribunal." Where a tribunal does not comply with all the requirements of Art.6, European jurisprudence has held that access to a court with full jurisdiction may remedy those failings: see *Albert and Le* **5-255**

---

[1] [2001] EWCA Civ 1510 at para.59.
[2] [2001] UKHL 23; [2001] 2 W.L.R. 1389.

Compte v Belgium.[3] It has been argued that the Administrative Court's powers of judicial review do not entitle it to make underlying determinations of fact, and therefore the court does not have full jurisdiction.

5-256   The Court of Appeal in the *Bracknell Forest BC* case identified three principles in considering whether judicial review, plus statutory review procedures, are Art.6 compliant[4]: it is relevant whether findings of fact are material to the review decision; if findings of fact are material to that decision, that will not finally determine whether judicial review provides a remedy in compliance with Art.6; and if the facts have themselves been found by "an expert tribunal" sufficiently independent to make it unnecessary for the court to have a broad jurisdiction to review those decisions of fact that is likely to lead to the conclusion that judicial review is sufficient.

5-257   It was accepted that the review panel itself would not satisfy the requirements of Art.6 by virtue of its lack of independence. The Court of Appeal did, however, take into account that Parliament had decided that a review panel was a suitable method of reviewing an authority's decision and therefore there was no reason why a decision taken by a junior council officer to terminate an introductory tenancy—taking into consideration the competing interests of other tenants and prospective tenants—cannot fairly be reviewed by a senior officer. Judicial review will, in any event, provide a check on the fairness and legality of such decisions.[5]

5-258   The Court of Appeal held that under the introductory tenancy scheme, the council are required only to be satisfied that the breaches of the tenancy agreement have in fact taken place. Accordingly, the court will not be determining issues of fact but whether it was reasonable for the council to take a decision to proceed with the termination of the introductory tenancy. It concluded:

> "That is again a matter which can be dealt with under judicial review either of the traditional kind or if it is necessary so to do intensified so as to ensure that the tenant's rights are protected."

It would appear, therefore, that the Court of Appeal is indicating that the scope of judicial review may need to be extended in order to make it Art.6 compliant.

5-259   As a final note, where a review has taken place, local authorities should be aware of the need for affidavits spelling out: (1) the procedure that was operated in the individual case; (2) the degree of independence of the tribunal from the person who took the personal decision; (3) the way the hearing was conducted; and, (4) the reason for taking the decision to continue with the proceedings.[6] Therefore, the judge will be able to take an informed view as to whether the matter should be adjourned to allow for an application to be made for permission to seek judicial review. At the same time the defendant will be

---

[3] (1983) 5 E.H.R.R. 533. It was held that where powers of adjudication are conferred on a jurisdictional organ of a professional body, this did not itself infringe the Convention provided that one of the two following systems exist: either the jurisdictional organs themselves comply with the requirements of Art.6(1), or they do not so comply but are subject to subsequent control by a judicial body that has full jurisdiction and does provide the guarantees of Art.6(1).

[4] The Court of Appeal considered *Albert and Le Compte v Belgium* (1983) 54 E.H.R.R. 533 at para.29; *Zumtobel v Austria* (1994) 17 E.H.R.R. 116; *Bryan v UK* (1996) 21 E.H.R.R. 342; *Alconbury* at paras 79; 86; 87; 88; 110; 114; and 115.

[5] See *Albert and Le Compte v Belgium* at para.29: "The Convention calls for at least one of the two following systems: either the jurisdictional organs themselves comply with the requirements of Article 6(1), or they do not so comply but are subject to subsequent control by a judicial body that has full jurisdiction and does provide the guarantees of Article 6(1).".

[6] *Bracknell Forest BC*, at para.103.

given the opportunity to rely on his or her convention rights in the possession proceedings.[7]

Demotion

The Anti-Social Behaviour Act 2003 gave a new power to local housing authorities, Housing Action Trusts (HATs) and Registered Social Landlords (RSLs) to apply for an order for the demotion of a tenancy, where a tenant or resident of, or visitor to, the dwelling is guilty of anti-social behaviour.[8] This was a proposal first put forward by the Law Commission in its Consultation Paper, *Renting Homes 1: Status and Security*. The demotion order operates so that the existing tenancy is terminated and replaced with a lesser form of security of tenure for a basic period of one year thereby allowing the landlord to recover possession quickly. Demoted tenancies have been designed to be a warning and provide a last opportunity for the tenant to change his behaviour. The government is keen to encourage landlords to use them instead of seeking suspended or outright possession orders.[9]

5-260

How to seek a demotion order

There are two steps which a landlord needs to take before obtaining a demotion order; first, a notice needs to be served on the tenant; and secondly, an application must be made to the county court.[10]

5-261

As with possession orders, the court may not grant a demotion order unless the landlord has served a notice on the tenant before commencement of proceedings or it is just and equitable for the court to dispense with that requirement.[11] In the case of a secure tenant, the landlord is required to serve a notice for a demotion order in the prescribed form[12] or one which is substantially the same.[13] The notice must specify the date after which proceedings may be begun; that it ceases to be in force twelve months after that date; and give details of the particulars of conduct. The date must not be earlier than the date on which a landlord's notice to quit might otherwise be effective to terminate the tenancy, that is, 28 days.[14]

5-262

In contrast, the notice to be served on assured tenants is not prescribed but it must contain the following information[15]:

5-263

(1) particulars of conduct;

(2) proceedings will not begin before the date specified in the notice;

(3) that date must not be before the end of the period of two weeks beginning with the date of service of the notice;

(4) proceedings will not begin after the end of twelve months beginning with the date of service of the notice.

---

[7] This will comply with s.7 of the Human Rights Act 1998: a person who claims that a local authority has acted in way which is made unlawful by virtue of being incompatible with a Convention right may rely on the Convention rights concerned in any legal proceedings.

[8] The demoted tenancy regime came into force on June 30, 2004 (Anti-Social Behaviour Act 2003 (Commencement No. 3 and Savings) Order 2004 (SI 2004/1502)).

[9] *Hansard*, HL Vol. 653, col. 1805 (October 23, 2003) Lord Bassam.

[10] Housing Act 1985, s.82A(2), s.83(1); Housing Act 1988, s.6A(2) and (5).

[11] Housing Act 1985, s.83(1) and Housing Act 1996, s.6A(5).

[12] Housing Act 1985, s.83 (2). Secure Tenancies (Notices) (Amendment) (England) Regulations 2004 (SI 2004/1627)).

[13] *ibid.*, para.2(1).

[14] Housing Act 1985, s.83(4A) and (5).

[15] Housing Act 1988, s.6A(6).

The justification for different treatment of secure and assured tenants is unclear, although registered social landlords will need to be extra vigilant in assuring that the correct notice is served in respect of their assured and secure tenants.

5-264 Where possession is sought as an alternative to a demotion order a further problem arises as to the service of notices for demotion and issue of proceedings. Ordinarily, if the landlord is simply seeking possession on nuisance grounds,[16] he may commence proceedings on the date the notice seeking possession is served. In relation to demotion, however, it is necessary to give 28 days' (in the case of secure tenants) or 2 weeks' notice (in the case of assured tenants). Therefore, unless the landlord applies to dispense with the requirement of the notice seeking demotion, or issues two sets of proceedings (and later applies to have them joined), the landlord must wait until the demotion notice has expired.

5-265 The procedure to be followed in applying to the court for a demotion order depends on whether the landlord is seeking a demotion order as an alternative to possession in which case the normal procedure under CPR 55 applies. If the landlord seeks only a demotion order, CPR 65 applies[17] and the claim must be issued using Form N6.[18] The Particulars of Claim (which may be in Form N122) must:

(1) state whether the demotion claim is made under the Housing Act 1985, s.82A(2) or the Housing Act 1988, s.6A(2);

(2) state whether the claimant is a local housing authority, a housing action trust or a registered social landlord;

(3) identify the property to which the claim relates;

(4) provide details about the tenancy, including the parties, the period of the tenancy, the rent, the dates on which the rent is payable and any statement of express terms of the tenancy served on the tenant; and

(5) state details of the conduct alleged.[19]

5-266 The provisions relating to the hearing are the same as the comparable provisions which apply to possession claims.[20] In particular, the court may abridge time between service and the hearing if:

(1) the defendant has assaulted or threatened to assault the claimant, a member of the claimant's staff or another resident in the locality;

(2) there are reasonable grounds for fearing such an assault; or

(3) the defendant has caused serious damage or threatened to cause serious damage to the property or to the home or property of another resident in the locality.[21]

The test to be applied by the court in making a demotion order

5-267 The court can only make a demotion order if it is satisfied that:

(1) the tenant or a person residing in or visiting the dwelling-house has engaged or has threatened to engage in conduct to which s.153A or s.153B of the Housing Act 1996; and

---

[16] Under Grd.2, Sch. 2 of the Housing Act 1985 or Grd.14, Sch. 2 of the Housing Act 1988.
[17] CPR Pt 65.11.
[18] CPR Pt 65.14(2).
[19] CPR Pt 65.15, PD 65, para.6.2 and para.7.1.
[20] CPR Pt 65.16–65.18.
[21] PD 65, para.8.2.

(2) that it is reasonable to make the order.[22]

Thus, the test to be applied is a combination of the tests for an anti-social **5-268** behaviour injunction (or an injunction against unlawful use of premises as the case may be) and for the making of a possession order both of which are discussed elsewhere in this Chapter.[23]

The effect of the demotion order on secure tenancies

Once a demotion order has been made, the secure tenancy is terminated with **5-269** effect from the date specified in the order. If the tenant remains in occupation of the dwelling-house after that date a new tenancy, the demoted tenancy, is created.[24] For a tenancy to be a demoted tenancy, it needs to satisfy the following conditions[25]:

(1) it is a periodic tenancy of a dwelling-house;

(2) the landlord is either a local housing authority or a housing action trust;

(3) the tenant condition under s.81 of the Housing Act 1985 is satisfied[26];

(4) the tenancy is created by virtue of an order under s.82A of the Housing Act 1985.

A tenancy ceases to be a demoted tenancy if[27]: **5-270**

(1) the landlord is neither a local housing authority or a housing action trust;

(2) the tenant condition under s.81 of the Housing Act 1985 is not satisfied;

(3) The demotion order is quashed;

(4) The tenant dies and no-one is entitled to succeed to the tenancy.

These provisions apply if at any time before the end of the demotion period the landlord serves a notice of proceedings for possession.[28]

The tenancy does not come to an end merely because it ceases to be a **5-271** demoted tenancy.[29] Thus, if the tenant condition is not satisfied because the tenant no longer occupies the dwelling-house as his only or principal home, the landlord will need to serve a notice to quit in accordance with s.5 of the Protection from Eviction Act 1977 to determine the tenancy and then obtain an order for possession from the court.[30]

Promotion of demoted tenancy to secure tenancy
The tenancy continues to be a demoted tenancy until the end of the demotion **5-272** period or (if later) until any of the following occurs:

(1) the notice of possession proceedings is withdrawn by the landlord;

[22] Housing Act 1985, 82A(4); Housing Act 1988, s.6A(4).
[23] See para.5-317ff. (conduct) and para.5-135ff (reasonableness).
[24] Housing Act 1985, s.82A(3).
[25] Housing Act 1996, s.143A(1)–(4).
[26] Housing Act 1996, s.143A(3). The tenant condition is that the tenant is an individual and occupies the dwelling-house as his only or principal home; or where the tenancy is a joint tenancy, that each of the joint tenants is an individual and at least one of them occupies the dwelling-house as his only or principal home (s.81 of the Housing Act 1985).
[27] Housing Act 1996, s.143B(2)(a).
[28] *ibid.*, s.143B(3), as amended by 2003, para.1 of Sch.1.
[29] *ibid.*, s.143B(5).
[30] Protection from Eviction Act 1977, s.3.

(2) the possession proceedings are determined in favour of the tenant;

(3) the period of six months beginning with the date on which the notice is served ends and no proceedings for possession have been brought.[31]

5-273 A demoted tenancy becomes a secure tenancy at the end of the period of one year ("the demotion period") starting on the day on which the demotion order takes effect.[32]

Rights of the demoted tenant
5-274 The tenant loses a number of rights on demotion. The demoted tenancy is incapable of being assigned save in particular circumstances.[33] Furthermore, the secure tenant loses the right to buy during the period of demotion. Although the right to buy will be regained on promotion the period of demotion will not count towards the qualifying period or discount.[34] The mere application for a demotion order will also effect the right to buy. If there is an application for a demotion order pending, the landlord is under no obligation to complete the transaction until that application has been determined in the tenant's favour[35] in addition to the power for the landlord to apply for an order suspending the right to buy under s.121A of the Housing Act 1985.[36] Furthermore, an application for a demotion order will provide a ground for refusing to give consent to a mutual exchange.[37]

Succession
5-275 On the death of the tenant, the status of the demoted tenancy depends on whether the tenant was himself a successor and if not, whether there is a person entitled to succeed to the tenancy. Where the tenant was a successor, the tenancy ceases to be a demoted tenancy but does not subsequently become a secure tenancy.[38] Thus, there can be no further succession where the tenant was a successor. The tenancy is merely contractual and is determinable by service of a notice to quit.
5-276 A person can qualify as a successor if:

(1) he occupies the dwelling-house as his only or principal home at the time of the tenant's death;

(2) he is a member of the tenant's family; and

(3) he has resided with the tenant throughout the period of 12 months ending with the tenant's death.[39]

A person is a member of another's family in relation to demoted tenancies if:

(1) he is the spouse of that person[40];

---

[31] Housing Act 1996, s.143B(4).
[32] *ibid.*, s.143B(1).
[33] *ibid.*, s.143K(1) and (2). A demoted tenancy is only capable of being assigned in pursuance of an order made under s.23A or 24 of the Matrimonial Causes Act 1973 (property adjustment orders in connection with matrimonial proceedings); s.17(1) of the Matrimonial and Family Proceedings Act 1984 (property adjustment orders after overseas divorce etc.); para.1 of Sch.1 to the Children Act 1989 (orders for financial relief against parents).
[34] Para.2(b) of Sch.1 to the Housing Act 1985 and para.9A of Sch.4 to the Housing Act 1985.
[35] Housing Act 1985, s.138(2B).
[36] See below.
[37] Housing Act 1985, Sch. 3, Ground 2A.
[38] Housing Act 1996, s.143H(2).
[39] *ibid.*, s.143H(3).
[40] *ibid.*, s.143P(1)(a).

(2) he and that person live together as a couple in an enduring family relationship, but he does not fall within (3). This includes persons who are in a homosexual relationship since the Housing Act 1996, as amended by the Anti-Social Behaviour Act 2003, provides that it is immaterial that two persons living together in an enduring family relationship are of the same sex[41];

(3) he is that person's parent, grandparent, child, grandchild, brother, sister, uncle, aunt, nephew or niece.[42]

The Housing Act 1996, as amended by the Anti-Social Behaviour Act 2003, stipulates that a relationship by marriage is to be treated as a relationship by blood; a relationship of the half-blood is to be treated as a relationship of the whole blood; and a step-child of a person must be treated as his child.[43]

If only one person qualifies to succeed, the tenancy vests in him automatically.[44] If there is more than one such person the tenancy vests in the person preferred in accordance with the following rules:

5-277

(1) the tenant's spouse or (if the tenant has no spouse) the person who lived with the tenant as a couple in an enduring family relationship[45];

(2) if there are two or more other members of the tenant's family the person preferred may be agreed between them (or if there is no such agreement) selected by the landlord.[46]

A tenancy ceases to be a demoted tenancy if the tenancy is vested or otherwise disposed of in the course of the administration of the tenant's estate, unless the vesting or other disposal is in pursuance of an order under[47]:

5-278

(1) ss.23A or 24 of the Matrimonial Causes Act 1973 (property adjustment orders in connection with matrimonial proceedings);

(2) s.17(1) of the Matrimonial and Family Proceedings Act 1984 (property adjustment orders after overseas divorce etc.);

(3) para.1 of Sch.1 to the Children Act 1989 (orders for financial relief against parents).

A tenancy also ceases to be a demoted tenancy where it is known that when the tenancy is vested or otherwise disposed of in the course of the administration of the tenant's estate it will not be in pursuance of an order under s.143I(3). In both cases, the tenancy that ceases to be demoted cannot subsequently become secure.[48]

5-279

The effect of demotion on assured tenants of RSLs

An assured tenancy which is demoted becomes an assured shorthold tenancy if the landlord is a registered social landlord regardless of whether it was originally a secure or assured tenancy.[49]

5-280

---

[41] Housing Act 1996, s.143P(2).
[42] *ibid.*, s.143P(1).
[43] *ibid.*, s.143P(3).
[44] *ibid.*, s.143H(4).
[45] *ibid.*, s.143H(5)(a).
[46] *ibid.*, s.143H(5)(b).
[47] *ibid.*, s.143I(3).
[48] *ibid.*, s.143I(5).
[49] Housing Act 1988, s.20B.

5-281   A demoted assured shorthold tenancy ceases to be an assured shorthold tenancy at the end of a period of one year starting with the day when the demotion order takes effect.[50] If, however, before the end of the period of one year, the landlord gives notice of proceedings for possession of the dwelling-house, it continues to be a demoted assured shorthold tenancy[51] until one of the following occurs:

(1) the notice of proceedings for possession is withdrawn;

(2) the proceedings are determined in favour of the tenant; or

(3) the period of six months beginning with the date on which the notice is given ends and no proceedings for possession have been brought.[52]

The effect of demotion on secure tenants of RSLs

5-282   On the making of a demotion order, a secure tenant of an RSL will become a demoted assured shorthold tenant.[53] Furthermore, the tenant will irretrievably lose its secure status so that on promotion the tenant will become an assured tenant.[54] Unlike demoted tenants, an RSL former secure tenant will not regain the preserved right to buy on promotion to an assured tenancy. Some commentators have suggested that the preserved right to buy is only lost during the period of demotion.[55] Undoubtedly, this will be a matter for the court in determining whether to make a demotion order.

Change of Landlord

5-283   If there is a change of landlord, and the new landlord is either a local housing authority or HAT, the tenancy will continue to be a demoted tenancy for the duration of the demotion period.[56] If the new landlord is not a local housing authority or HAT, but satisfies the landlord condition in s.80 of the Housing Act 1985, then the demoted tenancy will become secure.[57] If the new landlord, however, does not satisfy the landlord condition (that is, it is not a local housing authority or HAT), the tenancy becomes an assured shorthold tenancy.[58] Thus, where housing stock is transfer to a registered social landlord or a person who does not satisfy the landlord condition the tenancy will become an assured shorthold tenancy.

5-284   Where the landlord has begun proceedings for possession of a dwelling-house let under a demoted tenancy and the demotion period ends or it ceases to be a demoted tenancy (because it fails to satisfy the landlord or tenant condition, the demotion order is quashed or the tenant dies and there is no successor)[59]:

(1) the landlord (or the new landlord as the case may be) may continue the proceedings;

[50] Housing Act 1988, s.20B(2).
[51] *ibid.*, s.20B(3).
[52] *ibid.*, s.20B(4).
[53] *ibid.*, s.20B(1).
[54] *ibid.*, s.20B(2) and s.35. See also Baker, "Demoting Tenancies: Innovation or Exasperation? Part 2-The Position After Demotion", [2004] J.H.L. 85.
[55] See "Defending Demoted Tenancy Claims—Part 2" (October 2004) Legal Action 23.
[56] Housing Act 1996, s.143C(1).
[57] *ibid.*, s.143C(4).
[58] *ibid.*, s.143E(3).
[59] *ibid.*, s.143G.

(2) the tenant is not entitled to exercise the right to buy unless the proceedings are finally determined; and he is not required to give up possession of the dwelling-house;

(3) the proceedings must be treated as finally determined if they are withdrawn; any appeal is abandoned; the time for appealing expires without an appeal being brought.

Terms of the demoted tenancy or demoted assured shorthold tenancy

The following will be transferred as terms of the demoted or demoted assured shorthold tenancy[60]: **5-285**

(a) the parties to the tenancy;

(b) the period of the tenancy;

(c) the amount of the rent; and

(d) the dates on which the rent is payable.

Any arrears of rent payable at the termination of the secure tenancy will become payable under the new tenancy and will constitute a term of that. Likewise, it is also a term that any rent paid in advance or overpaid at the termination of the secure tenancy is credited to the tenant's liability to pay rent under the demoted tenancy.[61] **5-286**

The landlord must also serve on the tenant a statement of any other express terms of the secure/assured tenancy which are to apply to the tenancy which has been demoted. It is not possible, however, for additional terms to be imposed which were not also terms of the secure/assured tenancy. **5-287**

An anomaly arises as to when the express terms need to be served on the tenant. Local housing authorities and housing action trusts must supply the tenant with a written statement of the terms of the tenancy (so far as they are neither expressed in the lease or written tenancy agreement nor implied by law[63]) on the grant of the tenancy or as soon as practicable afterwards.[64] Furthermore, the landlord must from time to time publish information about the demoted tenancy in such form as it thinks best suited to explain in simple terms and so far as it considers appropriate the effect of the express terms of the demoted tenancy; the provisions of Ch.1A of Pt V of the Housing Act 1996; and the provisions of ss.11 to 16 of the Landlord and Tenant Act 1985 (landlord's repairing obligations).[65] The landlord must ensure that such published information is, as far as is reasonably practicable, kept up to date.[66] In contrast, registered social landlords are not under any obligation to serve notice of the express terms within a specified period of time so theoretically can serve the terms at any time during the life of the demoted assured shorthold tenancy. **5-288**

RSLs will need to ensure that the express terms relating to rent increases are imported to the new tenancy, otherwise they will have to comply with the statutory requirements under s.13 of the Housing Act 1988. It has also been suggested that repairing covenants implied under s.11 of the Landlord and Tenant Act 1985 will not apply if it is not expressly carried over to the new **5-289**

[60] Housing Act 1985, s.82A(5); Housing Act 1988, s.6A(8).
[61] Housing Act 1985, s.82A(3)(c)–(d); Housing Act 1988, s.6A(3)(c)–(d).
[62] Housing Act 1985, s.82A(7); Housing Act 1988, s.6A(10).
[63] Housing Act 1996. s.143M(4).
[64] *ibid.*, s.143M(5).
[65] *ibid.*, s.143M(2).
[66] *ibid.*, s.143M(3).

tenancy. That section only applies to the grant of a residential lease and since there is no grant either by the court or the landlord it may not apply. Having said that, local housing authorities and housing action trusts are required to publish material explaining the provisions of ss.11 to 16 of the Landlord and Tenant Act 1985, thus confirming an intention that these provisions will apply to tenancies which have been demoted.[67]

Proceedings for possession: demoted tenancy

5-290   In order to obtain possession of a dwelling-house[68] let under a demoted tenancy, the landlord is required to serve a notice of proceedings and obtain an order from the court. The demoted tenancy can only be brought to an end by obtaining an order of the court for possession of the dwelling-house.[69]

5-291   There is no prescribed form of notice but the notice must[70]:

(1) state that the court will be asked to make an order for the possession of the dwelling-house;

(2) set out the reasons for the landlord's decision to apply for the order[71];

(3) specify the date after which proceedings for the possession of the dwelling-house may be begun. This must not be earlier than the date on which the tenancy could (apart from Ch.1A of Pt V of the Housing Act 1996) be brought to an end by notice to quit given by the landlord on the same date as the notice of proceedings;

(4) inform the tenant of his right to request a review of the landlord's decision and of the time within which the request must be made.

(5) inform the tenant that if he needs help or advice about the notice, or about what to do about the notice, and that he must take the notice immediately to a Citizen's Advice Bureau, housing aid centre, a law centre or a solicitor.

5-292   These are similar to the provisions relating to notices for possession of premises let under an introductory tenancy. Although reasons must be given for seeking possession, as with introductory tenancies, there is no requirement that those reasons should be related to anti-social behaviour. Furthermore, the court may not dispense with the requirement of the notice.

Review of decision to seek possession

5-293   A demoted tenant may request the landlord to review its decision to seek an order for possession within 14 days of service of the notice for possession.[74] The landlord must review the decision if the request has been made on time.[75]

---

[67] See Baker, "Demoting Tenancies: Innovation or Exasperation? Part 1-The Process of Demotion", [2004] J.H.L. 72.

[68] Dwelling-house is defined in the Housing Act 1996 (as amended) as being a house or part of a house. Land let together with a dwelling-house must be treated as part of the dwelling-house (for the purposes of Chapter 1A of Sch.5 of the Housing Act 1996 in relation to demoted tenancies) unless the land is agricultural land which would not be treated as part of a dwelling-house for the purposes of Pt 4 of the Housing Act 1985: s.143O(1) and (2) of the Housing Act 1996 as amended by para.1 of Sch.1 to the Anti-Social Behaviour Act 2003.

[69] Housing Act 1996, s.143D(1).

[70] *ibid.*, s.143E(2).

[71] *ibid.*, s.143E(2)(b). See also n. 76 concerning reasons.

[72] *ibid.*, s.143E(2)(c) as amended by the Anti-Social Behaviour Act 2003, para.1 of Sch.1.

[73] See s.5 of the Protection from Eviction Act 1977.

[74] Housing Act 1996, s.143F(1).

[75] *ibid.*, s.143F(2).

The Housing Act 1996 does not specify the procedure on review but leaves **5-294** it to regulations made by the Secretary of State,[76] which may include provision requiring the decision on review to be made by a person of appropriate seniority who was not involved in the original decision; and as to the circumstances in which the tenant is entitled to an oral hearing, and whether and by whom he may be represented at the hearing.[77]

The most recent regulations came into force on July 30, 2004.[78] These reg- **5-295** ulations are similar to the review procedure under the introductory tenancy regime and, in outline, provide as follows:

(1) The review must be carried out by a person who was not involved in the original decision to recover possession and who is more senior than the original decision maker [Reg.2].

(2) The landlord must give the tenant not less than five days' notice of the date of the review [Reg.3].

(3) The landlord must consider the tenant's written submissions if they are received by the landlord two clear days before the review [Reg.5].

(4) There must be an oral hearing if the tenant requests this [Reg.4]. The tenant also has the right to be heard, to call and cross-examine witnesses and to be accompanied and/or represented by someone else, who need not be professionally qualified [Reg.6].

(5) The review may be postponed or adjourned at the instigation of the review officer or on the application of the tenant [reg.7, 8 and 9]. If neither tenant nor the representative attends the hearing, the review may proceed in their absence. Alternatively, the review officer may also give directions as appropriate [Reg.7].

The landlord must notify the tenant of the decision on review and of the **5-296** reasons for the decision.[79] The timing of the review and the notification of the decision is tight; it must be carried out and the decision notified to the tenant before the date specified in the notice of the proceedings, that is, as the date after which proceedings for possession of the dwelling-house may be begun. In many cases, the service of the notice of proceedings, request for review, review and the notification decision will have to be done in a matter of four weeks.[80]

The court is obliged to make an order for possession unless the landlord has **5-297** failed to comply with the requirements regarding notice and review. Therefore, challenges arising from the review procedure or the notice provisions may be raised as a defence to a claim for possession. Moreover, the county court has jurisdiction to determine questions arising, and entertain proceedings under, the demoted tenancy regime and to determine claims (for whatever amount) in connection with a demoted tenancy.[81] This should be contrasted with the position with introductory tenants who may only challenge a review decision by way of judicial review. Accordingly, it is questionable whether the demoted tenancy scheme is completely analogous to the introductory tenancy regime.

Commencing proceedings in the county court
Once the notice has expired but not on or before the date specified in the **5-298** notice, the landlord is able to commence proceedings in the county court. CPR

[76] Housing Act 1996, s.143F(3).
[77] *ibid.*, s.143F(4).
[78] The Demoted Tenancies (Review of Decisions) (England) Regulations 2004 (SI 2004/1079).
[79] Housing Act 1996, s.143F(5).
[80] *ibid.*, s.143E(4).
[81] *ibid.*, s.143N.

Pt 55 will apply in cases concerning possession of dwelling-houses let on demoted tenancies. If a person takes proceedings in the High Court which he could have taken in the county, he is not entitled to any costs.[82]

The order

5-299 The court must make an order for possession unless it thinks that

(1) the requirements in relation to the notice of proceedings have not been met; and/or

(2) the procedure on review has not been followed.[83]

5-300 Since the order is mandatory and there is no provision for postponement, delay or suspension of the order, the court only has a discretion to delay possession for up to 42 days under s.89 of the Housing Act 1980. Similarly, once the possession order is made, the court will not be able to then further delay possession at another hearing.[84] Furthermore, there is also no provision for any warrant for possession to be suspended.

Proceedings for possession: demoted assured shorthold

5-301 As a demoted RSL tenancy takes effect as an assured shorthold tenancy, possession may be obtained in the usual way (i.e. by serving a Housing Act 1988 s.21 notice and obtaining a court order).[85]

5-302 A demoted RSL tenancy (who was previously, assured or secure) enjoys no right to a review of a decision to recover possession. It was considered that the Housing Corporation Guidance would provide sufficient protection for demoted assured shorthold tenants,[86] although guidance specifically dealing with demoted assured shortholds has not been forthcoming. In exceptional cases, the decision to seek possession may be judicially reviewed if the RSL falls within the *Poplar HARCA v Donoghue*[87] definition of public body.

5-303 The procedure to be followed is set out in CPR Pt 55 and the landlord may use the accelerated possession procedure where applicable.

5-304 RSLs have been slow to use their powers to obtain demotion orders. On the one hand this seems surprising, not least because of the ease in which possession may be obtained once the assured tenancy is demoted. On the other hand, the lack of guidance from the Housing Corporation, and the fear of potential judicial review proceedings, may have led many RSLs to simply pursue the eviction route as being the easier option. RSLs need to be careful in adopting such a policy. The purpose of the demotion scheme was to encourage landlords to use demotion orders instead of seeking suspended or outright possession orders and to provide a real chance to work with the tenant to improve behaviour. Indeed, the willingness to use the full range of tools available to tackle anti-social behaviour should be reflected in their policies and procedure. Importantly, the Housing Corporation have also emphasised the need for eviction to be used as a last resort. This is not to say, however, that RSLs should always seek demotion as a first option nor that possession proceedings will be defeated for a failure to do so. As we have discussed in the context of nuisance possession proceedings, it may be a consideration for the court in determining

---

[82] Housing Act 1996, s.143N(4).
[83] *ibid.*, s.143D(2), as amended by 2003, para.1 of Sch.1.
[84] *Moore v Registrar of Lambeth County Court* [1969] 1 All E.R. 782.
[85] Housing Act 1988, s.20B and CPR Pt 55.
[86] *Hansard*, HL Vol. 652, cols 515–516 (September 11, 2003).
[87] [2001] EWCA Civ 595; [2001] 3 W.L.R. 183.

the reasonableness of making a possession order, but as was seen in *Moat Housing v Harris*[88] it is unlikely to be entirely successful.

Conclusion

The initial view of demotion orders was that they would be a popular weapon **5-305** in the already extensive armoury to tackle anti-social behaviour.[89] It is unfortunate that they are used so infrequently since they provide a speedy and cheap way in which to evict once the tenancy is demoted, as opposed to the suspended possession order which may lead to lengthy and expensive court proceedings. Furthermore, the circumstances in which a warrant may be suspended will be limited in the case of demoted assured shorthold tenancies in contrast to the potential problems of facing yet another trial if the defendant tenant denies the breaches of a suspended possession order. It is not right, however, to put the blame entirely at the door of the social landlord. The government has implemented the scheme through a complex set of amendments and insertions into three different Housing Acts. RSLs are also at a significant disadvantage in the lack of guidance given by the Housing Corporation. In short, the demoted tenancy scheme has not been the success story the government had hoped and has simply added to an already complicated array of powers available to tackle anti-social behaviour and contributed to the minefield of what is landlord and tenant law.

Injunctions

This section examines the use of the injunction in combating anti-social behav- **5-306** iour.[90] An injunction is a court order prohibiting a person from doing something (a prohibitory injunction) or requiring a person to do something (a mandatory injunction). An order granted at the end of trial may be described as a final or perpetual injunction. An order, other than one made as a final order, is described as an interim[91] (previously, known as interlocutory) injunction.[92]

Generally

The High Court has the power to grant an injunction (whether interim or **5-307** final) in all cases where it appears to the court to be just and convenient to do so.[93] The county court may make any order which could be made by the High Court if the proceedings were in the High Court if the action is within its jurisdiction.[94] The applicant has to satisfy a number of conditions in order to obtain an injunction. In view of the different nature of final and interim injunctions, the tests are set out separately.

Final injunctions
In relation to final injunctions: **5-308**

(1) it will not be possible to obtain an injunction if damages will provide an adequate remedy.

[88] *Hansard*, HL Vol. 652, cols 515–516 (September 11, 2003).
[89] See *Demotion or Suspension? Tackling Anti-social Behaviour through the Possession Process*, Landlord and Tenant Review Vol.9, Issue 1. January/February 2005.
[90] See also para.3-007 for local authority powers as regards injunctions.
[91] CPR Pt 25.1(1)(a).
[82] Under the CPR, "interim" is preferred to "interlocutory". See CPR Pt 25.1(a).
[93] Supreme Court Act 1981, s.37(1).
[94] County Courts Act 1984, s.38. See also CPR Pt 25, PD para.1.1–1.4 in respect of interim injunctions.

(2) the applicant must establish a cause of action; the injunction will not be granted if he has not established a right.

(3) the applicant must have sufficient interest. He "must show that he has some property, right or interest in the subject matter of his complaint".[95]

Interim injunctions

5-309 In some cases, it would be unjust for the claimant to wait until trial for relief. Therefore, the court may grant an interim injunction even though it gives the claimant the relief he would ask for at trial.[96] The general principles in obtaining an interim injunction are set out in *American Cynamid Co v Ethicon*[97] which are as follows:

(1) There is a serious question to be tried.

(2) The main issue is the balance of convenience, to which a number of other considerations will be relevant including:
  (i) whether damages would adequately compensate the applicant, if the defendant succeeds at trial;
  (ii) whether he would be adequately compensated in damages by the applicant;
  (iii) whether the applicant would be able to pay the damages;
  (iv) if in doubt whether either party would be able to pay damages, the court should consider the matters under the general balance of convenience.

(3) The court should attempt to keep the status quo. The time period relates to the period immediately before the conduct which led to the litigation.[98]

(4) The court should consider the relative strength of the case but should not embark on a trial on the issues.[99]

In essence, the decision as to whether an injunction should be granted is at the discretion of the court; that is, whether it is just and convenient.

5-310 The applicant will have to give an undertaking to the court in damages, that is, the applicant will have to pay damages to the defendant if at trial it appears that the injunction was wrongly granted. The undertaking will be to the court and not to the applicant. The undertaking cannot be enforced unless at or before the trial the injunction should not have been granted or if the defendant admits liability and pays the money into court.

5-311 There are exceptions to the rule that an applicant is required to give an undertaking. The fact that the undertaking given is of a limited value is not an absolute bar to obtaining an injunction.[1] In the case of local authorities who are seeking to enforce general law, the court may in its discretion not require undertakings.[2]

[95] *Maxwell v Hogg* (1867) 2 Ch. App. 307 at 311 per Turner L.J.
[96] *Heywood v BDC Properties Ltd* (No.1) [1963] 1 W.L.R. 975; *Woodford v Smith* [1970] 1 W.L.R. 806 at 817, 818.
[97] [1975] A.C. 396.
[98] *Garden Cottage Foods Ltd v Milk Marketing Board* [1984] A.C .130 at 140.
[99] CPR Pts 32.6 and 32.7.
[1] *Allen v Jambo Holdings Limited* [1980] 1 W.L.R. 1252.
[2] *Rochdale BC v Anders.* [1988] 3 All E.R. 490; *Kirklees BC v Wickes Building Supplies Ltd., Independent*, May 15, 1990.

Procedure

An application for an interim injunction must be made in the court where the   **5-312**
claim was started (or is likely to be started).[3] It must be made by filing an application notice and must state what order the applicant is seeking and why,[4]
together with the time date, time and place of the hearing.[5] The application
must be supported by evidence (unless the court orders otherwise)[6] which sets
out the facts on which the applicant relies for the claim being made against the
respondent.[7] The evidence may be in a witness statement, statement of case
(provided that it is verified by a statement of truth)[8] or in the body of the application notice (provided that it is verified by a statement of truth)[9] unless
the court, an Act, a rule or practice direction requires evidence by affidavit.[10]
The general rule is that a copy of the application notice must be served on the
respondent[11] as soon as practicable after issue and in any event, not less than
three days before the court is due to hear the application.[12]

"Without Notice" applications

The court may grant an interim injunction without notice if it appears to the   **5-313**
court that there are good reasons for not giving notice[13]:

> "They should, in general, only be made where there are strong grounds to
> justify such an application, where there is real urgency and impossibility of
> giving notice. It will be often preferable to abridge time and the respondent
> may attend on short notice . . ."[14]

The evidence in support of the application must state the reasons why no
notice was given.[15] The practice direction at CPR Pt 25 makes provision for
urgent applications made without notice. Where the claim has already been
issued, the application notice, evidence in support and a draft order should be
filed with the court at least two hours before the hearing.[16] The applicant
should notify the respondent of the application unless secrecy is essential.[17]
Where the application is made before the issue of the claim, the applicant must
additionally undertake to the court to issue a claim immediately or the court
will give directions for the commencement of the claim.[18] The claim form
should be served with the order for the injunction where possible.[19] If an order
is made before the issue of the claim, the order should state in the tile after the
names of the parties, "the Claimant and Defendant in an Intended Action".[20]
In extremely urgent cases, applications may be made by telephone.[21]

---

[3] CPR Pt 23.2.
[4] CPR Pt 23.3(1) and 23.6.
[5] CPR Pt 25 PD para.2.1.
[6] CPR Pt 25.3(2).
[7] CPR Pt 25, PD para.3.3.
[8] CPR Pt 22.
[9] *ibid.*
[10] CPR Pt 25, PD para.3.2.
[11] CPR Pt 23.4(1).
[12] CPR Pt 25, PD para.2.2.
[13] CPR Pt 25.3(1) and CPR Pt 25, PD para.3.4.
[14] per Butler-Sloss L.J., *Wookey v Wookey, Re. S (a minor)* [1991] Fam. 121, CA at p.131 B-D.
[15] CPR Pt 25.3(3).
[16] CPR Pt 25 PD para.4.3(1).
[17] CPR Pt 25 PD para.4.3(3).
[18] CPR Pt 25 PD para.4.4(1).
[19] CPR Pt 25 PD para.4.4(2).
[20] CPR Pt 25 PD para.4.4(3).
[21] CPR Pt 25 PD para.4.5.

Causes of action

5-314 An injunction is an available remedy for a landlord in order to restrain a tenant from breaching the tenancy agreement. It is necessary to consider the terms of the tenancy agreement very carefully. Depending on the terms of the tenancy, it may be possible to obtain an injunction restraining a tenant from allowing a person residing in or visiting the premises causing a nuisance. In relation to nuisance, there will be causes of action in trespass, common law nuisance, and powers available to a local authority under the Local Government Act 1972, s.222.[22]

Undertakings

5-315 Once an interim injunction has been granted on an ex parte basis, the court will set a date for the defendant to make representations. On the return date, it is possible that the parties may agree to an undertaking by the defendant rather than continue with the injunction. An undertaking is no admission as to the facts alleged.

Injunctions under the Housing Act 1996

5-316 The Anti-Social Behaviour Act 2003 repealed ss.152 and 153 of the Housing Act 1996[23] and made provision for three types of injunction: the anti-social behaviour injunction[24]; injunction against the unlawful use of premises[25]; and an injunction against breach of tenancy agreement.[26]

The Anti-Social Behaviour Injunction

5-317 This relates to conduct which is capable of causing nuisance or annoyance to any person, and which directly or indirectly relates to or affects the housing management functions of a relevant landlord.[27] Only a relevant landlord[28] can apply to the county or High Court[29] for an anti-social behaviour injunction. Relevant landlord is defined as a Housing Action Trust, a local authority or a registered social landlord.[30]

5-318 In order for a relevant landlord to obtain an anti-social behaviour injunction it is necessary to show first, that the defendant is engaging, has engaged or threatens to engage in conduct which is capable of causing nuisance or annoyance to any person, and which directly or indirectly relates to or affects its housing management functions.[31] The landlord is not required to prove that the conduct has caused nuisance or annoyance only that it is capable of doing so. The threshold is lower than proving the nuisance ground for possession where the conduct has to be *likely* to cause nuisance or annoyance. The Housing Act 1996 defines the housing management functions of a relevant landlord as including functions conferred by or under any enactment and the powers and duties of the landlord as the holder of an estate or interest in housing accommodation.[32] The ODPM and Housing Corporation suggests that housing management functions cover any day-to-day activities and strategic management of stock. It gives the following examples: tenant and community partici-

[22] See para.3-007ff.
[23] Anti-Social Behaviour Act 2003, s.13 came into force on June 30, 2004.
[24] Housing Act 1996, s.153A.
[25] *ibid.*, s.153B.
[26] *ibid.*, s.153D.
[27] *ibid.*, s.153A(1).
[28] *ibid.*, s.153A(2).
[29] *ibid.*, s.153E(6).
[30] *ibid.*, s.153E(7).
[31] *ibid.*, s.153A(1) and (3).
[32] *ibid.*, s.153E(11).

pation; maintenance and repairs; rent and rent arrears collection; neighbour-hood management; and dispute resolution. Matters that indirectly affect housing management functions include: social care and housing support; environmental health and refuse collection; and other services which enable the RSL to operate efficiently.[33]

Secondly, the landlord has to show that the conduct is capable of causing nuisance or annoyance to any of the following: **5-319**

(1) a person with a right (of whatever description) to reside in or occupy housing accommodation owned by or managed by the relevant land-lord;

(2) person with a right (of whatever description) to reside in or occupy other housing accommodation in the neighbourhood of housing accommodation owned by or managed by the relevant landlord;

(3) a person engaged in engaged in lawful activity in or in the locality of housing accommodation owned or managed by the relevant landlord;

(4) a person employed (whether or not by the relevant landlord) in connection with the exercise of the relevant landlord's management functions.[34]

Housing accommodation is defined as including flats, lodging-house, hostels and any yard, garden, outhouses and appurtenances belonging to the accommodation or usually enjoyed with it.[35] Ownership by a landlord of housing accommodation applies to the case where: **5-320**

(1) he is a person (other than a mortgagee not in possession) who is for the time being entitled to dispose of the fee simple in the premises, whether in possession or reversion;

(2) he is a person who holds or is entitled to the rents and profits of the premises under a lease which (when granted) was for a term not less than three years.[36]

Importantly, it is immaterial where the conduct occurs.[37] Thus, it is irrelevant if the conduct occurs outside of the locality of the housing accommodation, so long as the conduct is capable of causing a nuisance to the persons so described in the amended Housing Act 1996.   **5-321**

The anti-social behaviour injunction will only prohibit the defendant from engaging in conduct which is capable of causing nuisance or annoyance to any person, and which directly or indirectly relates to or affects its housing management functions.[38]   **5-322**

---

[33] "Anti-Social Behaviour: Policy and Procedure, Code of Guidance for Local Housing Authorities and Housing Action Trusts", August 2004, para.2.5; "Anti-Social Behaviour: Policy and Procedure, Guidance for Housing Associations", para.2.5.

[34] Housing Act 1996, s.153A(4); *c.f. Manchester CC v Lewis Lee* [2003] in relation to s.152 injunctions. The Court of Appeal held that the victims of anti-social behaviour had to be in premises which were let by the local authority in order to be able to obtain this type of injunction; it did not apply so as to protect persons simply residing in the locality of the residential premises. There had to be a nexus between the residential premises and the person who was sought to be protected by s.153(1). See also *Enfield v B* (2000) 32 H.L.R. 799 at 304.

[35] Housing Act 1996 s.153E(9).

[36] *ibid.*, s.153E(10).

[37] *ibid.*, s.153A(5).

[38] *ibid.*, s.153A(6).

Injunctions against unlawful use of premises

5-323 The injunction against unlawful use of premises is available where the conduct consists of or involves the using or threatening to use housing accommodation owned by or managed by a relevant landlord for an unlawful purpose.[39] The court has a discretion as to whether to grant an injunction on the application of the relevant landlord.[40]

5-324 "Unlawful purpose" is not defined in the Act but would appear to be wider than the similar provision under the nuisance possession ground, "immoral or illegal purpose." Moreover, it cannot be limited to merely criminal offences. Acts which constitute criminal behaviour, however, such as using the dwelling-house for drugs or as a brothel, will inevitably fall under this definition. There is no requirement for the landlord to show that the use of premises has caused or is capable of causing nuisance or annoyance to any person and will thus be useful where neighbours are reluctant to give evidence.

Exclusion Order and Power of Arrest

5-325 If the court grants an injunction under s.153A (anti-social behaviour injunction) or s.153B (injunction against unlawful use of premises), the court may prohibit the defendant from entering or being in any premises or any area specified in the injunction.[41] Additionally, a power of arrest can be attached to any provision of the injunction.[42] Before attaching either or both provisions to injunctions under s.153A and s.153B, the court has to be satisfied that either the conduct consists of, or includes, the use or threatened use of violence or there is a significant risk of harm[43] to any of the following people[44]:

(1) a person with a right (of whatever description) to reside in or occupy housing accommodation owned by or managed by the relevant landlord;

(2) a person with a right (of whatever description) to reside in or occupy other housing accommodation in the neighbourhood of housing accommodation owned by or managed by the relevant landlord;

(3) a person engaged in engaged in lawful activity in or in the locality of housing accommodation owned or managed by the relevant landlord;

(4) a person employed (whether or not by the relevant landlord) in connection with the exercise of the relevant landlord's management functions.[45]

An exclusion order can have the effect of excluding a person from his normal place of residence.[46] Thus, it is irrelevant whether the defendant has a tenancy or licence at his normal place of residence.

"Without notice" applications

5-326 "There is a primary precept governing the administration of justice, that no man is to be condemned unheard; and therefore, as a general rule, no order

[39] Housing Act 1996, s.153B.
[40] *ibid.*, s.153B(2).
[41] *ibid.*, s.153C(2).
[42] *ibid.*, s.153C(3).
[43] *ibid.*, s.153 E(12) defines "harm" as including serious ill-treatment or abuse (whether physical or not).
[44] *ibid.*, s.153C(1); 1996, s.153A(4).
[45] *ibid.*, s.153A(4); *c.f. Manchester CC v Lewis Lee* [2003] in relation to s.152 injunctions. The Court of Appeal held that the victims of anti-social behaviour had to be in premises which were let by the local authority in order to be able to obtain this type of injunction.
[46] Housing Act 1996, s.153E(2).

should be made to the prejudice of a party unless he has the opportunity of being heard on defence."[47]

As we have seen, the Civil Procedure Rules make provision for the granting of an interim remedy without notice.[48] CPR Pt 25.3(1) states that: **5-327**

"the court may grant an interim remedy on an application made without notice if it appears to the court that there are good reasons for not giving notice."

The Practice Direction to CPR Pt 23 also makes provision for the making of an application without serving an application:

"3. (1) where there is exceptional urgency,

(2) where the overriding objective is best furthered by doing so . . ."
There is little statutory guidance as to the circumstances which may lead to the granting of a Housing Act 1996 injunction without notice. Section 153E(4) says:

"If the court thinks it just and convenient it may grant or vary an injunction without the respondent having been given such notice as is otherwise required by rules of court."

The Court of Appeal, in *Moat Housing Group South Ltd v Harris and*   **5-328**
Hartless,[49] compared the granting of anti-social behaviour injunctions with similar orders under the Family Law Act 1996; the justification being that "intrusive ex parte orders" such as ouster clauses and exclusion orders had been subject to much discussion in the family courts for some time and subsequently codified in the Family Law Act 1996.[50] The more intrusive the order, the stronger must be the reasons for the departure from the general rule that notice must be given.

The facts of that case were as follows. The second defendant, Ms Hartless,   **5-329**
was the assured tenant of the housing association. She lived with her four children. The first defendant was the children's father who lived elsewhere but frequently visited the family. The association began to receive complaints about the behaviour of the children and their parents. The first defendant was not sent any warning or notice regarding their behaviour. The association, however, applied for a without notice anti-social behaviour injunction against the defendants, one of the terms of which was to exclude them from the family home starting at 6pm that day. A power of arrest was attached to the injunction. The evidence before the court consisted mainly of hearsay evidence and failed to differentiate between complaints made against the defendants and their children and the behaviour of a neighbouring family. The district judge granted the injunction at midday and it was drawn up by the court at 3.40pm The association served the injunctions at 9pm by attending the premises accompanied by police and television cameras.

The Court of Appeal said that it was difficult for the court to envisage a   **5-330**
more intrusive "without notice" order and gave guidance as to what the

---

[47] *Thomas A Edison Ltd v Bock* (1912) 15 C.L.R. 679, 681.
[48] See para.5-308.
[49] [2005] EWCA Civ 287; [2005] H.L.R.33.
[50] See *Ansah v Ansah* [1977] 138 Fam. 138; *Masich v Masich* (1977) Family Law 245; *Practice Note (Matrimonial Cause: Injunction)* 1978 1 W.L.R. 925; *G v G (Ouster: Ex p. Application)* [1990] Family Law 254.

county courts should bear in mind when granting an injunction without notice:

(1) that to make an order without notice is to depart from the normal rules as to due process and warrants the existence of exceptional circumstances;

(2) that one such exceptional circumstance is that there is a risk of significant harm to some person or persons attributable to conduct of the defendant if the order is not made immediately;

(3) that the order must not be wider than is necessary and proportionate as a means of avoiding the apprehended harm.

5-331 More controversially, the Court of Appeal went on to consider whether a power of arrest should have been attached to the "without notice" injunction. We have already discussed the test to be applied in attaching a power of arrest. The only guidance in the 1996 Act to do so on a "without notice" application is that the court must have regard to all the circumstances. This will include whether it is likely that the applicant will be deterred or prevented from seeking the exercise of the power if the power is not exercised immediately, whether there is reason to believe that the respondent is aware of the proceedings for the injunction but is deliberately evading service, and that the applicant or any person of a description mentioned in s.153A(4) (as the case may be) will be seriously prejudiced if the decision as to whether to exercise the power were delayed until substituted service is effected.[51] The Court of Appeal said that the court should only attach a power of arrest to one or more of the provisions contained in an order made without notice if it is satisfied that:

"(a) that the conduct includes the use or threatened use of violence; *and*
(b) that there is a significant risk of harm to any person."

The reason for use of the conjunctive "and" was that it was inconceivable that a court would grant an anti-social behaviour injunction without notice unless there was violence (or a threat of violence) and a risk of significant harm. Similar provision was made in the Family Law Act 1996 for the attachment of a power of arrest.[52]

5-332 Although there may have been some initial alarm at this decision it should not lead courts to consider that a power of arrest may never be attached to a provision of a "without notice" injunction; even in *Moat*, the Court of Appeal considered that the district judge had been properly entitled to attach a power of arrest to some of the terms of the injunction. Nor should it mean that the court has no power to impose an ouster or exclusion order without notice if the facts are sufficiently serious to warrant such a draconian order. If the court is satisfied that there is a risk of significant harm to some person attributable to the defendant's conduct and if such an order is made immediately and that it is necessary and proportionate to make such a drastic order as a means of avoiding the apprehended harm, then the order may be lawfully made.[53]

5-333 What landlords need to do to ensure that appropriate "without notice" applications are made is to consider:

---

[51] Housing Act 1996, s.154.
[52] See Family Law Act 1996, s.47(3).
[53] *Moat*, para.100.

(1) whether there is sufficient evidence to justify an urgent application: when did the last incident occur?

(2) whether the nature of the behaviour is so serious: are there threats of, or actual, violence? Is there is a significant risk of harm?

(3) whether the defendant has been given any warning about his behaviour;

(4) whether there is direct evidence of the incidents alleged;

(5) whether there is only hearsay evidence and if so why;

(6) if an exclusion order is sought, whether this is necessary and the likely effect. For example, whether there are dependants living at the property, when the order is to take effect;

(7) that the witness statement specifically deals with the incidents alleged rather than taking a broad brush approach and simply complaining of "anti-social behaviour"[54];

(8) that each term of the order addresses the behaviour complained of; there is no point simply using a pro forma draft for all anti-social behaviour injunctions;

(9) that the order has been drawn up properly.

Injunction against Breach of Tenancy Agreement

We have already discussed the case where a landlord can obtain an injunction **5-334** to prevent any further or anticipated breaches of the tenancy agreement. Under the Housing Act 1996, as amended by the Anti-Social Behaviour Act 2003, a new power is given to local authorities, RSLs, HATs and charitable housing trusts,[55] which allows them to apply for an exclusion order and/or a power of arrest to be attached to the terms of any injunction against a tenant in respect of a breach or anticipated breach of a tenancy agreement.[56] It applies where the injunction is sought on the grounds that the tenant is engaging or threatening to engage in conduct that is capable of causing nuisance or annoyance to any person; or is allowing, inciting, or encouraging any other person to engage or threaten to engage in such conduct.[57] The court has a discretion whether to prohibit the defendant from entering or being in any premises or any area specified in the injunction or to attach a power of arrest[58] where it is satisfied that the conduct includes the use or threatened use of violence, or that there is a significant risk of harm to any person.[59]

As with anti-social behaviour injunctions and injunctions against unlawful **5-335** use of premises, the injunction against breach of tenancy agreement with an exclusion order attached can have the effect of excluding a person from his normal place of residence.[60] Therefore, a relevant landlord could theoretically

---

[54] The Court of Appeal criticised the witness statement as being serious deficient. The evidence given by the "anti-social behaviour consultant" was "so lacking in specifics. . . that it would not have been easy for the appellants to respond to them properly. . .[it] resembled more closely the opening speech of the prosecution in a criminal trial".

[55] Housing Act 1996, s.153E(8). Charitable housing trusts which are not RSLs do not have the power to apply for anti-social behaviour injunctions or injunctions against unlawful use of premises.

[56] Tenancy agreement includes any agreement for the occupation of residential accommodation owned or managed by a relevant landlord: Housing Act 1996, s.153D(5). *c.f.* Housing Act 1996, s.153 injunctions.

[57] Housing Act 1996, s.153D(1).

[58] *ibid.*, s.153D(3) and (4).

[59] *ibid.*, s.153D(2).

[60] *ibid.*, s.153E(2)(b).

exclude persons from the home without having to go through the normal possession proceedings route.

Variation and discharge

5-336 The injunction may be made for a specified period or until varied or discharged.[61] An injunction may be varied or discharged by the court on an application by the person in respect of whom it is made or by a relevant landlord.[62] It may also grant or vary an injunction without the respondent having been given notice only if the court considers it just and convenient.[63] The court must, however, give the person against whom the injunction is made an opportunity to make representations in relation to the injunction as soon as it is practicable for him to do so.[64] It would, therefore, appear to be the case that a person can vary or have the injunction discharged without the relevant landlord being given the opportunity to make representations against a variation or discharge. Presumably, the landlord would be able to make an application to set aside any such order.

Procedure

5-337 CPR Pt 65 governs the procedure for applications for injunctions under the Housing Act 1996. The application must be:

(1) made in Form N16A which must state:

    (a) the remedy sought;
    (b) the legal basis for the claim to that remedy;
    (c) the enactment under which the remedy is sought; and
    (d) the terms of the injunction sought.[65]

(2) commenced in the court for the district in which the defendant resides or the conduct complained of occurred; and

(3) supported by a witness statement which must be filed with the claim form.[66]

5-338 In every application made on notice, the application notice must be served, together with a copy of the witness statement, by the claimant on the defendant personally[67] not less than two days before the hearing.[68]

5-339 A power of arrest should made be in Form N110A. Each provision which has attached to it a power of arrest must be set out in a separate paragraph of the injunction and the claimant must deliver a copy of the relevant provisions to any police station for the area where the conduct occurred.[69] This will also apply where the order has been varied or discharged.[70] The claimant must deliver a copy an injunction with a power of arrest to any police station for the area where the conduct occurred—but if it was granted without notice, only after service on the defendant.[71] The claimant must immediately inform the police station if an injunction containing a power of arrest is varied or discharged.

---

[61] Housing Act 1996, s.153E(2)(a).
[62] *ibid.*, s.153E(3).
[63] *ibid.*, s.153E(4).
[64] *ibid.*, s.153E(5).
[65] CPR Pt 65.2(a); 65.3; PD to CPR 65, para.8.2.
[66] CPR Pt 65.3(2).
[67] CPR Pt 65.3(5).
[68] CPR Pt 65.3(6)(a).
[69] CPR Pt 65.4(2).
[70] CPR 65.4(4).
[71] CPR, r.65.4.

In addition to the requirements for with notice applications, the witness state- **5-340**
ment must explain why the application is being made without notice. Where
an injunction has been granted without notice, and a power of arrest is
attached to one or more of its provisions, the claimant must not deliver a copy
of the relevant provisions to any police station for the area where the conduct
occurred before the defendant has been served with the injunction containing
the relevant provisions.[72]

Jurisdiction
The former position was that the jurisdiction of the court[73] could be **5-341**
exercised by district judges as well as circuit judges. District and deputy
district judges have jurisdiction to grant anti-social behaviour injunctions.[74] There is no longer any requirement that district judges and deputy
district judges have to have had appropriate training before exercising the
jurisdiction.[75]

Effect of the changes
Registered social landlords now have access to the same powers as local **5-342**
authorities in relation to injunctions. They are not limited to obtaining injunctions where there has been a breach of the tenancy agreement thereby only
having the power to take action against their own tenants. They now have the
power to be able to obtain injunctions against perpetrators of anti-social
behaviour which interferes with their housing management functions. This
also means that RSLs can seek an injunction where anti-social behaviour
takes place in the housing office, for instance, so that they can provide protection for their employees. Thus, this avoids the problem where the victim of anti
social behaviour may be an employee of the landlord, such as a housing officer,
but where the perpetrator is not a tenant. Under s.153 of the Housing Act
1996, it would not have been possible for an RSL to obtain an injunction
against such a person.

The injunctions per se have not been met with much opposition. What is **5-343**
of more concern is whether, with the extension of the power of
arrest beyond cases involving threats of, or actual violence, there are enough
resources to make it workable. When the White Paper, *Anti-social
behaviour—Respect and Responsibility*, was published on March 12, 2003,
Oliver Letwin, the Opposition Spokesman, said that he feared that in the
absence of police on the streets, and "in the absence of coherent long
term programmes to lift young people off the conveyor belt to crime, the
Home Secretary would find that the vast new range of powers would no
more than mask his failure to enforce effectively the laws that already
existed". Similar concerns have also been raised by the National Housing
Federation which, in responding to the White Paper, *Tackling Anti-social
Tenants*, said:

> "Greater powers for the courts to grant injunctions need to be matched by
> police resources to respond to potential breaches and make arrests as
> appropriate. Some of our members do not support the extension of injunc-
> tions without reassurances."[76]

---

[72] CPR Pt 65.4(3).
[73] See repealed 1996, ss.152 and 153.
[74] CPR Pt 2, PD 2B, paras 8.1(d).
[75] *c.f.* the Practice Direction made by the Lord Chancellor on August 28, 1997 which has been
revoked and not replaced.
[76] NHF's *Response to Tackling Anti-Social Tenants*, July 2002, para.2.6.1.

The Future

5-344 The government has reacted to the decision in *Moat* by proposing new legislation. Clause 19 of the Police and Justice Bill seeks to amend s.153A of the Housing Act 1996 in two ways: first, to enable courts to make injunctions to protect entire communities; and secondly, "anti-social conduct" will be defined as "conduct capable of causing nuisance or annoyance to some person who need not be a particularly identified person." This simply appears to be a politically attractive move for the current government—in line with its general policy on the criminal justice system—to redress the balance in favour of the victim. The Housing Act 1996 injunctions are already very wide in scope, particularly in the case of the people they are designed to protect. Moreover, the problems associated with case law pre-Anti-Social Behaviour Act 2003 has been addressed. In addition, the Civil Evidence Act 1995 deals with the issue of hearsay evidence which strikes a fair balance between the interests of the victim and perpetrator. As we have discussed above, the Law Commissions' paper, *Renting Homes: The Final Report*, proposes a prohibited conduct term, breach or anticipated breach of which will give rise to injunction proceedings thus superseding the s.153D injunction. Clause 214 of the Bill also provides for the repeal of s.153A(4)(d).

Children

5-345 Landlords will encounter difficulties in obtaining injunctions against children because, generally, they will be unenforceable. The method of enforcing an injunction is limited to imprisonment, fine or sequestration but, in the case of a child, only fine and sequestration are lawful. It is unlawful to imprison under-18s.[77]

5-346 In *Wookey v Wookey*,[78] the court distinguished between the "recalcitrant teenager in good employment who may be appropriately injuncted" against the vast majority of children in respect of whom recourse to the civil courts is not appropriate. Since the injunction will, in most cases, be unenforceable, applications for injunctions will be doomed to failure. In *Enfield London Borough Council v B*,[79] the Court of Appeal, although not deciding the issue, expressed the opinion that an injunction under s.152 of the Housing Act 1996 could be made against a minor.

5-347 In *G v Harrow*,[80] held that where an application is made for an injunction against a minor (in this case, under s.152), the applicant must provide the court with evidence of the personal circumstances of the minor to show that the injunction could be enforced against him, whether by way of a fine or sequestration of assets. Thus, where a landlord is considering applying for an injunction against a minor he must be prepared to show that the injunction can be enforced. In addition, it is suggested that other methods of preventing the minor's "anti-social behaviour" should be considered. For instance, it may be preferable to consider entering into an acceptable behaviour contract or applying for an ASBO in the magistrates' court.

Committals

5-348 Breach of an injunction is contempt of court and may be enforceable by committal proceedings in the county court. The procedure to be followed depends on the type of order which has been breached.

---

[77] Powers of Criminal Courts (Sentencing) Act 2000, s.89.
[78] [1991] Fam. 121.
[79] (2000) 32 H.L.R. 799.
[80] [2004] EWHC 17 QB.

Injunctions generally and undertakings
Breach of an undertaking[81]or an injunction may be enforced by committal proceedings under CPR, Sch.2, CCR O.29. The breached judgment or order must have been served been served personally on the defendant,[82] although this may be dispensed with if the judge is satisfied that, pending such service, the defendant has had notice of it by being present when the judgment or order was given or made or by being notified of the terms of the judgment or order whether by telephone or otherwise.[83] The court may also dispense with service of a copy of a judgment if it thinks it just to do so.[84] The order needs to be endorsed with a penal notice.[85] In the case of injunctions this should be done by the court.[86] The court may dispense with the requirement of the penal notice although this power should be used only in exceptional cases.[87]

5-349

Committal proceedings may be brought by way of claim form[88] or, as the case may be, an application notice.[89] In most cases it will be appropriate to use the application notice,[90] in which case it must state that the application is made in the proceedings in question and its title and reference number must correspond with the title and reference number of those proceedings. CPR Pt 23 will apply.[91] In outline, in preparing the application the following needs to be noted:

5-350

(1) the application notice together with copies of all written evidence in support must, unless the court otherwise directs, be served personally on the respondent;

(2) the written evidence must be in the form of an affidavit;

(3) the application notice must set out in full the grounds on which the committal application is made and must identify, separately and numerically, each alleged act of contempt, including, if known, the date of each of the alleged acts;

(4) the application notice must contain a prominent notice stating the possible consequences of the court making a committal order and of the respondent not attending the hearing. A form of notice, which may be used, is annexed to this practice direction;

(5) The hearing date must be specified in the claim form or application notice or in a Notice of Hearing.[92]

An amendment to the application notice can be made with the permission of the court but not otherwise.
The Practice Direction gives guidance as to dealing with the procedure to be adopted at a committal hearing. The court may not dispose of the committal application without a hearing. Unless the court otherwise directs, the hearing date will be not less than 14 days after service of the application notice. The court may, however, at any time give management decisions, including

5-351

[81] CCR O.29, r.1A applies the same provision for breach of orders with appropriate amendments.
[82] CCR O.29, r.1(2).
[83] CCR O.29, r.1(6).
[84] CCR O.29, r.1(7).
[85] For which see Form N77.
[86] CCR O.29, r.1(3).
[87] *Jolly v Jolly* [2000] 2 F.L.R. 69.
[88] See CPR Pt 7.
[89] See CPR 23 and CCR O.29, r.1(4).
[90] See Practice Direction to RSC O.52, para.2.2.
[91] Subject to the provisions of the Practice Direction above.
[92] See CCR O.29, r.1; also, Practice Direction to RSC O.52 and CCR O. 29, paras 2.1–2.6.

directions for the service of written evidence by the respondent and written evidence in reply by the applicant, or may hold a directions hearing. In dealing with any committal application, the court will have regard to the need for the respondent to have details of the alleged acts of contempt and the opportunity to respond to the committal application. The court should also have regard to the need for the respondent to be:

(1) allowed a reasonable time for responding to the committal application including, if necessary, preparing a defence;

(2) made aware of the availability of assistance from the Community Legal Service and how to contact the Service;

(3) given the opportunity, if unrepresented, to obtain legal advice; and

(4) if unable to understand English, allowed to make arrangements, seeking the assistance of the court if necessary, for an interpreter to attend the hearing.

5-352   There is provision for the court to strike out a committal application on its own motion or on the application of another party.[93] The court may, however, waive any procedural defect in the commencement or conduct of a committal application if satisfied that no injustice has been caused to the respondent by the defect.[94]

5-353   A district judge has power to commit in respect of assaults on staff and contempts in the face of the court[95] and for breach of injunctions under the Housing Act 1996, but not generally for breach of orders.

5-354   Civil contempt is not a criminal offence but the standard of proof in all forms of contempt is the criminal standard, that is, proof beyond a reasonable doubt.

5-355   There is always a risk that criminal proceedings have been taken in relation to the same incident which is the subject of the committal action. The court, however, should be reluctant to stay or adjourn the committal proceedings for that reason alone because they should be promptly determined. The first court to sentence must not allow for or anticipate a likely further sentence. It is for the second court to reflect the prior sentence to ensure that the defendant is not punished twice for the same act.[96]

Housing Act 1996 Injunctions

5-356   Where a power of arrest is attached to certain provisions of an injunction,[97] a constable may arrest without warrant a person whom he has reasonable cause for suspecting to be in breach of any such provision or otherwise in contempt of court in relation to a breach of any such provision.[98] A constable shall, after making any such arrest, forthwith inform the person on whose application the injunction was granted. The defendant must be brought before the relevant judge within the period of 24 hours beginning at the time of his arrest and if the matter is not then disposed of forthwith, the judge may remand him.[99]

---

[93] Practice Direction to RSC O.52, CCR O.29, para.5.
[94] Practice Direction to RSC O.52, CCR O.29, para.10.
[95] County Courts Act 1984, ss.14 and 118.
[96] *Lomas v Parle* [2003] EWCA Civ 1804.
[97] By virtue of Housing Act 1996, s.153C(3) or 153D(4).
[98] Housing Act 1996, s.155(1).
[99] *ibid.*, s.155(2). CPR Pt 65.6(2) provides that the judge before whom a person is brought following his arrest may) deal with the matter or adjourn the proceedings. In reckoning for the purposes of this subsection any period of 24 hours no account shall be taken of Christmas Day, Good Friday or any Sunday.

Where the proceedings are adjourned and the arrested person is released the   **5-357**
matter must be dealt with (whether by the same or another judge) within 28
days of the date on which the arrested person appears in court and the arrested
person must be given not less than two days' notice of the hearing.[1]
Nevertheless, an application may be issued for the committal in the normal
way[2] even if the matter is not dealt with in that time frame.[3]

Where a power of arrest has not been attached to a term of the injunction,   **5-358**
the applicant may apply for the issue of a warrant for the arrest. The trigger
is that the court has granted an injunction in circumstances such that a power
of arrest could have been attached[4] but: (1) has not attached a power of arrest
under the section in question to any provisions of the injunction; or (2) has
attached that power only to certain provisions of the injunction; and at any
time the applicant considers that the respondent has failed to comply with the
injunction.[5] The court has no power to issue the warrant unless the application is substantiated on oath, and has reasonable grounds for believing that
the respondent has failed to comply with the injunction.[6] CPR Pt 65.5 makes
provision for applications for a warrant of arrest under s.155(3) of the
Housing Act 1996.[7] The court has the same remand powers where a person is
brought before a court by virtue of such a warrant.[8]

Remand

There is no inherent power for the court to remand (in custody or on bail). The   **5-359**
Housing Act 1996, however, makes provision for the power to remand[9] corresponding to that applying in magistrates' courts in civil cases.[10]

The court may not remand a person for more than eight clear days unless   **5-360**
he is remanded on bail with the consent of both parties or the court is remanding for the purpose of a medical examination.[11]

Where a person is brought before the court after remand, the court may   **5-361**
further remand him[12] although the time limit will apply. So, if the person has
already been remanded in custody for eight clear days he may not be remanded
in custody for a further period of time, save where a medical examination is
being carried out, s.35 of the Mental Health Act applies, or the court is satisfied that a person who has been remanded is unable by reason of illness or
accident to appear or be brought before the court.[13]

If a person remanded under this section is granted bail, he may be required   **5-362**
by the relevant judge to comply, before release on bail or later, with such
requirements as appear to the judge to be necessary to secure that he does not
interfere with witnesses or otherwise obstruct the course of justice.[14] The court

---

[1] CPR 65.6(4).
[2] i.e. under CCR O.29 r.1: see CPR Pt 65.6(6).
[3] CPR 65.6(5).
[4] Under Housing Act 1996, s.153C(3) or s.153D(4).
[5] Housing Act 1996, s.155(3).
[6] *ibid.*, s.155(4).
[7] CPR Pt 65.5 provides: "(1) An application for a warrant of arrest under section 155(3) of the
1996 Act must be made in accordance with Part 23 and may be made without notice. (2) An
applicant for a warrant of arrest under section 155(3) of the 1996 Act must—(a) file an affidavit
setting out grounds for the application with the application notice; or (b) give oral evidence as
to the grounds for the application at the hearing."
[8] Housing Act 1996, s.155(5).
[9] *ibid.*, 155(2) and Sch.15, para.2(1).
[10] Magistrates' Courts Act 1980, ss.128 and 129.
[11] Housing Act 1996, s.155(4).
[12] *ibid.*, Sch.15, para.2(3).
[13] *ibid.*, Sch.15, para.5.
[14] *ibid.*, s.155(7).

may remand him on bail by taking from him a recognizance, with or without sureties,[15] or by fixing the amount of the recognizances with a view to their being taken subsequently, and in the meantime committing him to custody as mentioned in sub-para.(1)(a).[16]

5-363 An application for bail made by a person arrested under a power of arrest attached to an injunction or a warrant of arrest issued under s.155(3) may be made either orally or in an application notice. An application notice seeking bail must contain:

(1) the full name of the person making the application;

(2) the address of the place where the person making the application is detained;

(3) the address where s/he would reside if bail were granted;

(4) the amount of any proposed recognizance; and

(5) the grounds for the application and, where a previous application has been refused, full details of any change in circumstances which has occurred since that refusal.

A copy of the application notice must be served on the person who obtained the injunction.[17] The person arrested may apply to the county court to review a decision to refuse bail.[18]

Medical examination

5-364 If the relevant judge has reason to consider that a medical report will be required, any power to remand a person under s.155 may be exercised for the purpose of enabling a medical examination and report to be made.[19] If such a power is so exercised the adjournment shall not be for more than four weeks at a time, unless the judge remands the accused in custody.[20] If the judge so remands the accused, the adjournment shall not be for more than three weeks at a time.[21]

Remand where the defendant is suffering from mental health

5-365 If the judge has reason to suspect that a person, who has been arrested under s.155 of the 1996 Act, is suffering from mental illness or severe mental impairment, he has the same power to make an order under s.35 of the Mental Health Act 1983 as the Crown Court has under that section.[22] Furthermore, the county court has a general power to make an order under s.35 of Mental Health Act 1983.[23]

---

[15] As provided in Housing Act 1996, Sch.15 para.3: "(1) Where a person is remanded on bail, the court may direct that his recognizance be conditioned for his appearance – (a) before that court at the end of the period of remand, or (b) at every time and place to which during the course of the proceedings the hearing may from time to time be adjourned. (2) Where a recognizance is conditioned for a person's appearance as mentioned in sub-paragraph (1)(b), the fixing of any time for him next to appear shall be deemed to be a remand. (3) Nothing in this paragraph affects the power of the court at any subsequent hearing to remand him afresh."

[16] Housing Act 1996 Act, Sch.15, para.2(2); see also CPR Pt 65.7.

[17] Practice Direction to CPR Pt 65, para.3.

[18] *Newham LBC v Jones* [2002] EWCA Civ 1779.

[19] Housing Act 1996, s.155(1).

[20] *ibid.*, s.155(2).

[21] *ibid.*, s.155(3).

[22] *ibid.*, s.156.

[23] Contempt of Court Act 1981, s.14(4A).

The Crown Court's power is that it may remand an accused person to a hos- **5-366**
pital specified by the court for a report on his mental condition.[24] An accused
person is any person who is awaiting trial before the court for an offence punishable with imprisonment or who has been arraigned before the court for
such an offence and has not yet been sentenced or otherwise dealt with for the
offence on which he has been arraigned.[25]

The powers conferred by s.35 may be exercised if: **5-367**

"(1) the court is satisfied, on the written or oral evidence of a registered
medical practitioner, that there is reason to suspect that the accused person
is suffering from mental illness, psychopathic disorder, severe mental
impairment or mental impairment; and
(2) the court is of the opinion that it would be impracticable for a report on
his mental condition to be made if he were remanded on bail . . ."

Where a court has remanded an accused person under s.35 it may further **5-368**
remand him if it appears to the court, on the written or oral evidence of the
registered medical practitioner responsible for making the report, that a
further remand is necessary for completing the assessment of the accused
person's mental condition.[26]

An accused person shall not be remanded or further remanded for more **5-369**
than 28 days at a time or for more than 12 weeks in all; and the court may at
any time terminate the remand if it appears to the court that it is appropriate
to do so.[27]

Sentencing
If the breach is proved the court may impose a period of imprisonment of **5-370**
up to two years and/or an unlimited fine.[28] Comparisons between sentences
for criminal offences and those for committal to prison for contempt of
court are of limited value. When committing a person to prison for breach
of a court order, it is true that, as in a criminal case, an element in the sentencing process is punishment, but the court has to take into account the
importance of obedience to court orders and disobedience to them and
importantly, the protection of the persons in respect of whom the court
order was made.[29]

In *Leicester City Council v Lewis*[30], the Court of Appeal considered a sen- **5-371**
tence imposed for a breach of an injunction under s.152 of the Housing Act
1996.[31] The facts in *Lewis* were as follows. In 1999, the authority obtained an
injunction excluding the first and second defendants from a certain specified
area in the locality of the first defendant's flat. In May 2000, the police entered
premises in the locality of that flat to execute a search warrant issued under
the Misuse of Drugs Act 1971. They found evidence of drug dealing and consumption of illegal drugs. The second defendant was arrested for breach of
the injunction and possession of cocaine. The second defendant admitted that
he was in breach of the injunction, but claimed that he was not involved in any
illegal activity in the premises. The judge at first instance committed him to

[24] Mental Health Act 1983, s.35(1).
[25] *ibid.*, s.35(2)(a).
[26] *ibid.*, s.35(5).
[27] *ibid.*, s.35(7).
[28] Contempt of Court Act 1981, s.14.
[29] *Nottingham City Council v Cutts* (2001) 33 H.L.R. 7 at para.6.
[30] (2001) 33 H.L.R. 37.
[31] i.e. the precursor to the anti-social behaviour injunction introduced by the Anti-Social
Behaviour Act 2003.

prison for six months. The second defendant appealed the sentence on the basis it was excessive.

5-372   Dismissing the appeal, the Court of Appeal held that it was important to have the following considerations in mind:

(1) the injunction was aimed at protecting people;

(2) the evidence against the defendant before the original injunction was strong and compelling;

(3) the injunction related to a particular specified area;

(4) there had been a deliberate breach of the court's order;

(5) the second defendant was found in the premises subject to the search warrant. Although these were different premises from the flat, they were close by;

(6) within the premises, it was plain that the consumption of drugs was going on. The second defendant must have been aware of the fact, even though he arrived at the property shortly before the police officers arrived and that he was not directly involved in the consumption of drugs. He did not, however, leave the premises as soon as he appreciated that drugs were being consumed but was found sitting in a chair;

(7) the defendant was not a person of good character.

5-373   If a committal order is made, the order shall be for the issue of a warrant of committal and, unless the judge otherwise orders:

(1) a copy of the order shall be served on the person to be committed either before or at the time of the execution of the warrant; or

(2) where the warrant has been signed by the judge, the order for issue of the warrant may be served on the person to be committed at any time within 36 hours after the execution of the warrant.[32]

Hospital Orders

5-374   The county court may exercise the same power to make a hospital order or guardianship order, under s.37 of the Mental Health Act 1983, or an interim hospital order, under s.38 of that Act, in the case of a person suffering from mental illness or severe mental impairment who could otherwise be committed to prison for contempt of court as the Crown Court has under that section in the case of a person convicted of an offence.[33]

5-375   Where a person is found guilty of contempt the court may by order authorise his admission to and detention in such hospital as may be specified in the order ("hospital order") or, as the case may be, place him under a guardianship of a local social services authority as may be so specified so long as certain conditions are met ("guardianship order").[34] Those conditions are:

(1) the court is satisfied, on the written or oral evidence of two registered medical practitioners, that the defendant is suffering from mental illness or severe mental impairment and that either:

---

[32] CCR Ord.29, r.1(5).
[33] Contempt of Court Act 1981, s.14(4).
[34] Mental Health Act 1983, s.37(1).

(a) the mental disorder from which the defendant is suffering is of a nature or degree which makes it appropriate for him to be detained in a hospital for medical treatment . . .; or
(b) the mental disorder is of a nature or degree which warrants his reception into guardianship under the 1983 Act;

and:

(2) the court is of the opinion, having regard to all the circumstances including the nature of the offence and the character and antecedents of the offender, and to the other available methods of dealing with him, that the most suitable method of disposing of the case is by means of an order under s.37 of the 1983 Act.

and:

(3) the court is satisfied, on the written or oral evidence of the registered medical practitioner who would be in charge of his treatment or of some other person representing the managers of the hospital, that:

(a) arrangements have been made for his admission to that hospital; and
(b) for his admission within the period of 28 days from the beginning with the date of the making of such an order.

The hospital order shall specify the form or forms of mental disorder which the defendant is found by the court to be suffering.

Jurisdiction
District and deputy district judges have jurisdiction to commit for breaches of Housing Act 1996 injunctions.[35] **5-376**

Allocation Policies

The current government has given local authorities the power to exclude from their allocations scheme, or give less preference to, those applicants who have been guilty of anti-social behaviour. These provisions also go further in purporting to protect the victims of anti-social behaviour in giving them additional preference in the allocation of housing. This has been achieved through the Homelessness Act 2002[36] which significantly changes Pt VI of the Housing Act 1996 (allocation of housing by local authorities). **5-377**

Allocations under the Housing Act 1996

Prior to the coming into force of the Housing Act 1996, local authorities were largely free to allocate their housing stock as they wished, the only constraint being that in the selection of tenants certain groups were to be given a reasonable preference.[37] The Housing Act 1996 fundamentally limited that power in order to prevent homeless persons obtaining a secure tenancy and in effect, "jumping the queue" in front of those who had long been waiting for local authority accommodation.[38] The Housing Act 1996 therefore set up two separate schemes; Pt VII was concerned with applications made by homeless persons; Pt VI was solely concerned the allocation of permanent housing. **5-378**

---

[35] CPR Pt 2, PD 2B, para.8.3.
[36] Homelessness Act 2002 received Royal Assent on February 26, 2002.
[37] Housing Act 1985, s.22.
[38] See Minister for Local Housing and Urban Regeneration, *Hansard*, March 12, 1996, SCG, col. 614.

5-379 It was mandatory for local authorities to comply with Pt VI of the Housing Act 1996 in allocating housing accommodation.[39] Allocation was defined as being the selection of a person to be a secure[40] or introductory[41] tenant,[42] the nomination of a person to be a secure or introductory tenant of another, e.g. housing action trust, and the nomination of a person to be an assured tenant of housing accommodation held by a registered social landlord.[43] Part VI, therefore, provided a single route into social and public sector housing.[44] The exemptions from the allocation provisions were the allocation to anyone who was already a secure or introductory tenant or the assured (but not assured shorthold) of a registered social landlord, or an assured tenant of accommodation allocated by a local housing authority.[45]

Qualifying persons

5-380 Allocations of housing could only be made to "qualifying persons". The main group of persons who were disqualified were those subject to immigration control by the Asylum and Immigration Act 1996 and Immigration and Asylum Act 1999.[46] Subject to the statutory exclusions,[47] local authorities could decide what classes of persons were, or were not, qualifying persons. The Code of Guidance suggested that authorities could consider a number of factors in determining eligibility criteria, including whether there was a history of anti-social behaviour, whether the applicant had attacked housing department staff or whether there was a record of rent arrears.[48] This was confirmed by Judge L.J. in *R. v Wolverhampton MBC Ex p. Watters*,[49] who said that " 'a reasonable preference' implies the power to choose between different applicants on 'reasonable grounds' . . . it is not unreasonable to prefer good tenants to bad tenants".

Housing register

5-381 Local authorities were obliged to establish and maintain a housing register but in such form as they saw fit.[50] However, the register had to record all those details which were prescribed by regulations.[51] Local authorities could place a person on the register either upon an application being made or upon its own motion. Therefore, those whom the local authority owed the full homeless duty, under s.193 of the Housing Act 1996, would ordinarily be placed on the housing register. Provisions were made regarding notification, amendment and removal of persons from the register, including a right to, and procedure on, review of an adverse decision.[52] Persons on the register were entitled to see their entry and be given such general information as would enable him to

---

[39] Housing Act 1996, s.159(1).
[40] Housing Act 1985, s.83.
[41] Housing Act 1996, s.124.
[42] This did not include the grant of a tenancy which is exempt from security by Housing Act 1985, Sch.1.
[43] Housing Act 1996, s.159 (2)(a)–(c).
[44] Minister for Local Housing and Urban Regeneration, *Hansard*, March 12, 1996, SCG, col. 614.
[45] The Housing Act 1996, s.159(5). See s.159(6) in relation to the exemption of allocation of housing accommodation by a local housing authority to two or more persons jointly if one of them is included within s.159(5). Other exemptions can be found under s.160 of the Housing Act 1996 and Allocation of Housing Regulations 1996 (SI 1996/2753), reg.3.
[46] Housing Act, 1996, s.161(2).
[47] Housing Act 1996, s.161(3), (5)–(6).
[48] Code of guidance paras 4.25–4.28.
[49] (1997) 29 H.L.R. 931, CA or per Carnwarth J. in *R. v Newham LBC Ex p. Miah* (1996) 28 H.L.R.L. at 288.
[50] Housing Act 1996, s.162.
[51] *ibid.*, s.162(4) and Allocation of Housing Regulations 1996 (SI 1996/2753).
[52] Housing Act 1996, ss.163–165.

assess the how long it was likely to be that appropriate accommodation would be available.[53]

Allocations scheme

Each local housing authority was required to establish an allocation scheme **5-382** for determining priorities between qualifying persons and as to the procedure[54] to be followed in allocating housing accommodation.[55] It was not permissible for the local authority to allocate housing accommodation except in accordance with their scheme.[56] As regards priorities, the scheme had to be framed so as to ensure that reasonable preference was given to particular groups of persons including persons occupying unsanitary or overcrowded housing, persons occupying temporary accommodation or on insecure terms and families with dependent children. Where a person, or a member of their household, with a particular need for settled accommodation on medical or welfare grounds were not only to be given reasonable preference, but also where they could not reasonably be expected to find settled accommodation for themselves in the foreseeable future, they were to be give additional preference.[57] Local authorities were required to have regard to the Code of Guidance and a registered social landlord was obliged to co-operate to such extent as is reasonable in the circumstances in offering accommodation to people with priority on the authority's housing register.[58]

Allocations under the Homelessness Act 2002

The main changes to the Housing Act 1996 which are relevant to anti-social **5-383** behaviour are the power to assess a person as being ineligible and the power not to accord a person reasonable preference because of their conduct. Under the new provisions, local authorities are no longer required to maintain a housing register.[59]

Local authorities' allocation policies will now apply to existing secure or **5-384** introductory tenants who apply for a transfer[60] and, in the absence of any express exclusion, will also apply to assured tenants of registered social landlords.[61] Thus, transfer applications will be determined in accordance with the same criteria as those who are applying for social housing.[62] Any transfers of secure and assured tenants will not fall under the allocations policy where the local authority has had to move a tenant, e.g. because of renovation works.

Any person may be allocated housing accommodation by a local housing **5-385** authority (whether on his application or not) subject to the following statutory exceptions[63]:

(1) a person subject to immigration control within the meaning of the Asylum and Immigration Act 1996 unless he is of a class prescribed by

---

[53] Housing Act 1996, s.166.
[54] For this purpose, procedure included all aspects of the allocation process, including the persons or descriptions of persons by whom decisions were taken: Housing Act 1996, s.167(1).
[55] Housing Act 1996, s.167(1).
[56] *ibid.*, s.167(8).
[57] *ibid.*, s.167(2). See also the Code of Guidance, Allocation of Housing (Reasonable and Additional Preference) Regulations 1997, amended by the Housing Act 1996, s.167 to include homeless families amongst the other categories to whom local authorities should give reasonable preference in allocating their stock.
[58] Housing Act 1996, ss.169 and 170.
[59] Homelessness Act 2002, s.14.
[60] *ibid.*, s.13.
[61] Lord Falconer, Lords Debates, December 10, 2001, col. CWH 46.
[62] Housing Act 1996, ss.160A, 160A(3).
[63] *ibid.*, ss.160A, 160A(3).

regulations made by the Secretary of State or who is already a secure or introductory tenant or an assured tenant of accommodation allocated to him by a local housing authority.[64] No person excluded from entitlement to housing benefit by s.115 of the Immigration and Asylum Act 1999 (exclusion from benefits) can be included in such Regulations;

(2) a person excluded under Regulations made by the Secretary of State[65];

(3) a person that the local authority has decided is ineligible by virtue of their behaviour[66];

(4) two or more persons jointly if any of them is a person mentioned in the above.[67]

Local authorities may decide to that an applicant is ineligible for an allocation of housing accommodation if it is satisfied that he, or a member of his household, has been guilty of unacceptable behaviour serious enough to make him unsuitable to be a tenant of the authority; and, in the circumstances at the time his application is considered, he is unsuitable to be a tenant of the authority by reason of that behaviour.

Unacceptable behaviour
5-386   Unacceptable behaviour is defined by the Act as being:

(1) behaviour of the person concerned which would (if he were a secure tenant of the authority) entitled the authority to a possession order under s.84 of the Housing Act 1985 on any ground mentioned in Pt I of Sch.2 of the Act (other than Ground 8, temporary accommodation); or

(2) behaviour of a member of his household which would (if he were a person residing with a secure tenant of the authority) entitle the authority to such a possession order.[68]

It should be noted that the behaviour goes wider than the more commonly used nuisance or annoyance to neighbours or convictions for illegal or immoral use of the dwelling (Ground 2)[69]; it extends to: rent arrears (first limb of Ground 1); general breaches of the tenancy agreement (second limb of Ground 1); domestic violence (Ground 2A); deterioration in condition of the dwelling (Ground 3); deterioration of furniture (Ground 4); obtaining a tenancy by deception (Ground 5); payment of an illegal premium on an assignment of a tenancy (Ground 6); and inappropriate conduct in non-housing accommodation (Ground 7).

5-387   Furthermore, these "fault grounds" can be established where the culpable party is a member of the applicant's household. In the absence of any provision in the Act, it would appear that the local authority would not be able to establish these grounds relying on the behaviour of visitors to the dwelling. This may pose problems where an applicant's property, or otherwise, is used as a meeting point for drug dealers and users or as a focal point for large gatherings; precisely, the reason why the Housing Act

[64] Housing Act 1996, s.160A(3).
[65] *ibid.*, s.160A(5).
[66] *ibid.*, s.160A(7).
[67] *ibid.*, s.160A(1)(c).
[68] *ibid.*, s.160A(8).
[69] Housing Act 1985, as amended by the Housing Act 1996.

1996 was amended to include visitors. The fact that the applicant has been moved from his current place of abode will not necessarily, in turn, prevent the groups of visitors following and in effect, will transfer the nuisance to another estate or area. However, it would assist those persons who are being harassed by drug dealers and want to move on to a different area.

In order to determine whether a person is ineligible for allocation, the local **5-388** authority should follow the following steps[70]:

Step 1: Has there been unacceptable behaviour within the definition of the Act?
The local authority will have to be satisfied that there has been unacceptable behaviour[71] by the applicant or a member of his household which falls with the definition of s.160A(8) of the Homelessness Act 2002. It is for the local authority to consider all the evidence and, where there is conflict, to make its own finding of facts. The Code of Guidance makes it clear that "it is not necessary for the applicant to have actually been a tenant of the housing authority when the unacceptable behaviour occurred".[72]

Step 2: Will the local authority be entitled to a possession order?
The authority will have to consider whether the behaviour would have entitled the housing authority to a possession order, if, whether actually or notionally, the applicant had been a secure tenant.[73] In considering whether a possession order would have been granted, the local authority will have to consider not only: (a) whether the grounds would have been established (the unacceptable behaviour test) but also (b) whether the court would decide that it would be reasonable to make a possession order.[74] The "reasonableness test" includes consideration of all the circumstances and having regard to the interests of the parties and interests of the public. The Code of Guidance, "in practice, courts are unlikely to grant possession orders in cases which have not been properly considered and are supported by thorough and convincing evidence. It is acknowledged that in cases involving noise problems, domestic violence, racial harassment, intimidation and drug dealing, courts are likely to grant a possession order."

Step 3: Is the behaviour seriousness enough to make the person unsuitable to be a tenant of the authority?
The housing authority will need to be satisfied that the behaviour is serious enough to make the person unsuitable to be its tenant.[75] So that if, in the opinion of the housing authority, it is likely that the court would have suspended the order, he would be a suitable tenant of the housing authority.[76] The Code of Guidance also states that where the behaviour involved the accrual of rent arrears, "which have resulted from factors outside the applicant's control—for example, delays in housing benefit payments; or liability for a partner's debts, where the applicant was not in control of the household's finances or was unaware that arrears were accruing—should not

---

[70] The Code of Guidance helpfully sets out the steps to be followed by local authorities.
[71] See paras 6.291–6.292 above for the meaning of "unacceptable conduct"; Housing Act 1996, s.160A(8).
[72] Para.4.22 Code of Guidance.
[73] Para.4.22 Code of Guidance and s.160A(8)(b) of the Homelessness Act 2002.
[74] Grounds under Pt I of Sch.2 to the Housing Act 1985 are discretionary grounds and the court always has to consider whether it would be reasonable to make a possession: Housing Act 1985, s.84.
[75] Housing Act, 1996, s.160A(7)(a).
[76] Para.4.22(ii) Code of Guidance.

be considered serious enough to make the person unsuitable to be a tenant."[77]

Step 4: Is the behaviour seriousness enough to make the person unsuitable to be a tenant of the authority at the time the application is considered?
The housing authority will need to satisfy itself that the applicant is unsuitable to be a tenant by reason of the behaviour in question—in the circumstances at the time the application is considered.[78] Thus, where behaviour can be shown to have improved, the housing authority may not be justified in treating the applicant as ineligible.[79] The housing authority has to be satisfied on all these aspects before it can consider exercising its discretion to decide that the applicant is to be treated as ineligible for an allocation. The draft Code of Guidance states that "the housing authority will have to act reasonably, and will need to consider all the relevant matters before it. This will include all the circumstances relevant to the particular applicant, whether health, dependant or other factors. In practice, the matters before the housing authority will include the information provided on the application form."[80]

Further applications
5-389 A person whom the local authority has considered to be ineligible, may make a fresh application to the authority for an allocation of housing accommodation if he considers that he should no longer be treated as ineligible.[81] The local authority will only be under a duty to reconsider the application if there has been a change of circumstances. Unless there has been a considerable lapse of time it will be for the applicant to show that his circumstances or behaviour have changed.[82]

Notification of decision
5-390 If a local housing authority decides that an applicant is ineligible by virtue of their immigration status[83] or by reason of their behaviour,[84] then it must the notify the applicant of its decision and the grounds for it.[85] The Code of Guidance states that the notice must give clear grounds for the decision which must be based firmly on the relevant facts of the case.[86] The notice must be in writing and, if not received by the applicant, will be treated as having been given if it is made available at the authority's office for a reasonable period for collection by him or on his behalf.[87]

Review of decision
5-391 Applicants have a right to request a review of a decision as to eligibility and a right to be informed of the decision on review and the grounds for that decision.[88] There is no provision for appeal to the county court and so any challenge to the decision on review can only be made by way of judicial review.[89]

[77] Para.4.22(ii) Code of Guidance.
[78] Housing Act 1996, s.160A(7)(b) and para.4.22(iii) Code of Guidance.
[79] Para.4.22(iii) Code of Guidance.
[80] Para.4.23 Code of Guidance.
[81] Housing Act 1996, s.160A(11).
[82] Para.4.24 of Code of Guidance.
[83] Housing Act 1996, s.160A(3) or (5).
[84] *ibid.*, s.160A(7)–(8).
[85] *ibid.*, s.160A(9).
[86] Para.4.29 Code of Guidance.
[87] Housing Act 1996, s.160A(10).
[88] *ibid.*, s.167(4A)(d).
[89] *Begum v Tower Hamlets LBC* [2002] EWCA 239; [2002] 2 All E.R. 668.

Human rights and applications for housing accommodation

Local authorities are now required to secure that: **5-392**

(1) advice and information is available free of charge to persons in their district about the right to make an application for housing accommodation; and

(2) any necessary advice and assistance is making such an application is available free of charge to persons in their district who are likely to have difficulty in doing so without assistance[90]; and

(3) to ensure that an applicant is informed that he has those rights.[91]

The applicant also has a right to request such general information as will enable him to assess: (1) how his application is likely to be treated under the scheme; and (2) whether housing accommodation appropriate to his needs is likely to be made available to him and, if so, how long it will be likely to be before such accommodation will become available for allocation to him.[92] Additionally, the applicant must be notified in writing of any decision that he is a person not to be treated as a group of people whom are to be given preference.[93] The tenant has the right to request the authority to inform him of any decision about the facts of his case which is likely to be, or has been, taken into account in considering whether to allocate housing accommodation to him.[94] The applicant has a right to request a review of that decision as well as a decision regarding eligibility and preference[95] The local housing authority must be informed of the decision on review and the grounds for it.[96] The local housing authority must secure that an applicant is informed that he has those rights.[97] Every application must be considered by the local housing authority if it is made in accordance with the procedural requirements of the authority's allocation policy.[98]

Preferences in the allocation scheme

As mentioned previously, local authorities are no longer required to main-   **5-393**
tain a housing register[99] and instead are given wider powers to allocate accommodation in accordance with their own scheme. The scheme must also include a statement of the authority's policy on offering people who are to be allocated housing:(1) a choice of housing accommodation; or (2) the opportunity to express preferences.[1] There is no provision that local authorities must allocate accommodation in accordance with the choice of the applicant.[2]

[90] Housing Act 1996, s.166(1), as amended by the Homelessness Act 2002.
[91] *ibid.*, s.166(2) as amended by the Homelessness Act 2002.
[92] *ibid.*, s.167(4A)(a)(i)–(ii) as amended by the Homelessness Act 2002.
[93] *ibid.*, s.167(4A) (b) as amended by the Homelessness Act 2002.
[94] *ibid.*, s.167(4A)(c) as amended by the Homelessness Act 2002.
[95] *ibid.*, s.167(4A)(d) as amended by the Homelessness Act 2002.
[96] *ibid.*, s.167(4A)(d) as amended by the Homelessness Act 2002.
[97] *ibid.*, s.166(2) as amended by the Homelessness Act 2002.
[98] *ibid.*, s.166(3) as replaced by Homelessness Act 2002.
[99] Homelessness Act 2002, s.14(1).
[1] Housing Act 1996, s.167(1A)(a)–(b) as amended by the Homelessness Act 2002.
[2] This topic is too wide for the purposes of this book. For further information on choice based lettings scheme, see "The Green Paper Quality and Choice: a Decent Home for all" (DETR, April 2000), the draft Code of Guidance; and C. Hunter, "The good, the bad... reasonable preference, exclusion and choice in housing allocation", [2001] J.H.L. 77.

5-394   The allocations scheme, however, must be framed so as to ensure that reasonable preference is given to:

(1) people who are homeless;

(2) people who are owed a duty by any local housing authority under ss.190(2), 193(2) or s.195(2) of the Housing Act 1996[3] who are occupying any accommodation by any such authority under s.192(3) of the Housing Act 1996;

(3) people occupying insanitary or overcrowded housing or otherwise living in unsatisfactory housing conditions;

(4) people who need to move on medical or welfare grounds;

(5) people who need to move to particular locality in the district of the authority, where failure to meet that need would cause hardship (to themselves or to others).[4]

5-395   Local housing authorities may give additional preference to these classes of persons with urgent housing needs.[5] The Code of Guidance gives examples of persons to whom a housing authority should consider giving additional preference within their allocation scheme. This includes those owed a homeless duty as a result of violence or threats of violence likely to be carried out and who as a result require urgent housing such as victims of domestic violence, racial harassment, harassment on the grounds of a persons' sexuality. It suggests that local housing authorities need to have local liaison arrangements with the police to ensure that allocations can be made quickly and confidentially, when necessary.[6]

5-396   In determining priorities in the allocation of accommodation to the people mentioned above, the factors which the scheme may allow to be taken into account include:

(1) the financial resources available to a person to meet his housing costs;

(2) any behaviour of a person (or of a member of his household) which affects his suitability to be a tenant; and,

(3) any local connection (within the meaning of s.199 of the Housing Act 1996) which exists between a person and the authority's district.[7]

Thus, local housing authorities can give a lower priority to an applicant guilty of behaviour affecting his suitability as a tenant. Additionally, an applicant may be given no preference at all where the housing authority is satisfied that:

(1) that he, or a member of his household, has been guilty of unacceptable behaviour serious enough to make him unsuitable to be a tenant of the housing authority; and

(2) the housing authority is satisfied that the, in the circumstances at the time his case is considered, he deserves not to be treated as a person who should be given reasonable preference.[8]

---

[3] And the similar provisions under the Housing Act 1985 namely, ss.65(2) or 68(2) of that Act.
[4] Housing Act 1996, s.167(2)(a)–(e) as amended by the Homelessness Act 2002.
[5] Housing Act 1996, s.167(2) as amended by the Homelessness Act 2002.
[6] Para.5.18 (a) of the Code of Guidance.
[7] Housing Act 1996, s.167(2A) as amended by the Homelessness Act 2002.
[8] *ibid.*, s.167(2C), as amended by the Homelessness Act 2002.

In determining "unacceptable behaviour", local authorities will need to apply **5-397** the same test as apply to a decision on eligibility.[9] On first appearances this is rather contorted. If the local housing authority is satisfied that the applicant fits all the criteria for being ineligible why would there be a situation where the local housing authority would need to consider the exclusion from preference or a lower priority. The answer is that where local authorities are satisfied that an applicant is unsuitable to be a tenant they are not required to decide that he or she is ineligible for an allocation; they may instead proceed with the application and decide to give the applicant no preference for an allocation.

Review
The applicant has a right to be notified in writing of any decision that he is a **5-398** person to whom no preference or lower priority will be given by virtue of his behaviour[10] and has a right to request a review of that decision.[11] The applicant is entitled to be informed of the review decision and the grounds for it. Any challenges to the review decision will need to be made by judicial review, in the absence of any statutory right to appeal to the county court.

Homelessness

The use of eviction in dealing with anti-social tenants inevitably contributes to **5-399** the number of persons applying as homeless to local housing authorities. It is therefore necessary to examine the law relating to a local housing authority's duties towards such persons. The relevance of homelessness to anti-social behaviour, however, does not stop there. The Homelessness Act 2002, which amends Pt VI of the Housing Act 1996, seeks to prevent and tackle homelessness.

A strategic approach

The Homelessness Act 2002 requires local housing authorities to carry out a **5-400** homelessness review for their district and formulate and publish a homeless strategy based on its results.[12] A review may be carried out from time to time at the discretion of the local authority,[13] although the first strategy must be published by July 31, 2003[14] and be published every five years thereafter.[15] The homelessness review will involve a review of the levels, and future levels, of homelessness in the district; the activities which are carried out for preventing homelessness, or which contribute to, securing that accommodation is or will be available for people in the district who are or may become homeless, providing support for people who are or may become homeless or providing support for people who have been homeless and need support not to become homeless again[16]; and the resources available to the authority, the social services authority, other public authorities, voluntary organisations and other persons for such activities.[17] The homelessness strategy will need to be consistent with other local plans and strategies[18] and should also link with other

---

[9] Housing Act 1996, s.167(2D), as amended by the Homelessness Act 2002; and Housing Act 1996, s.160A(8), as amended by the Homelessness Act 2002.
[10] Housing Act 1996, s.267(4A)(b).
[11] *ibid.*, s.267(4A)(d).
[12] Homelessness Act 2002, s.1(1)(a).
[13] *ibid.*
[14] *ibid.*, s.1(3).
[15] *ibid.*, s.1(4).
[16] *ibid.*, s.2(2).
[17] *ibid.*, s.2(1).
[18] Homelessness Code of Guidance for Local Authorities (England), para.1.4.

programmes that address the problems that can lead to homelessness including anti-social behaviour such as Local Strategic Partnerships and Community Strategies, Supporting people, Drug Action Teams, Crime and Disorder Strategies and Youth Offending Teams.[19]

5-401   The review must take into account all forms of homelessness[20] and not just people who are unintentionally homeless and have a priority need for accommodation; that is, it will include people who are homeless with no priority need, homeless with priority need but intentionally homeless or a rough sleeper. Accordingly, the review will have to take into account those persons who have made themselves homeless as a result of their anti-social behaviour. The Code of Guidance also suggests useful data sources such as court records on possession orders, evictions by local authorities and registered social landlords and prison/probation service records of ex prisoners homeless on discharge.[21]

5-402   Homelessness strategy is defined in the Homelessness Act 2002 as being a strategy formulated by a local housing authority for:

(1) preventing homelessness in their district;

(2) securing that sufficient accommodation is and will be available for people in their district who are or may become homeless; and

(3) securing the satisfactory provision of support for people in their district who are or may become homeless or who have been homeless and need support to prevent them becoming homeless again.[22]

It is intended that a multi-agency approach will be adopted so that housing authorities will work together with other public authorities and voluntary organisations to tackle issues related to homelessness,[23] such as street drinking, begging, drug misuse and antisocial behaviour.[24] The Act states that the strategy should include the setting of specific objectives and activities for the local housing authority, the social services authority, other public authorities and voluntary organisations.[25] Furthermore, the housing authority is required to have regard to the homelessness strategy when undertaking any of its other statutory functions.[26] This approach has been recommended by the government in *More than a Roof: A Report into Tackling Homelessness*, published in March 2002.

5-403   This multi-agency approach coincides with the Supporting People Programme, which commences in April 2003. The government has recommended that "full consideration should be given to utilising the opportunities of this new programme to deliver focused packages of support" in the rehabilitation of anti-social tenants and a way in which to tackle homelessness.[27] The programme is a partnership between housing, social services, health

---

[19] See Annex 1 to the Code of Guidance. Local Authorities are referred to two good practice documents: *Homelessness Strategies: A Good Practice Handbook* and *Preventing tomorrow's rough Sleepers: a good practice handbook*.

[20] See ss.175–178 of the Housing Act 1996 for the definition of homelessness.

[21] Code of Guidance, para.1.13.

[22] Homelessness Act 2002, s.3(1).

[23] *ibid.*, s.3(3).

[24] See para.1.39 Homelessness Code of Guidance for Local Authorities (England).

[25] Homelessness Act 2002, s.3(2). see also Local Government Act 2000, s.2 which gives local authorities the power to act in relation to, and for the benefit of, any person or area outside their district if they consider that to do so is likely to promote or improve the social, economic or environmental well-being of their own district.

[26] Homelessness Act 2002, s.1(5).

[27] *Tackling Anti-Social Tenants, A Consultation Paper*, DTLR, April 2002 p.39.

and probation and will be administered by a Supporting People Team. It will transfer the funding, strategic planning, monitoring and review of housing related support to local authorities.

Intentionality

If the local housing authority have reason to believe that an applicant is homeless or may be threatened with homelessness, they must make enquiries to satisfy themselves whether he is eligible for assistance and if so, whether any duty is owed to him.[28] Under Pt VII of the Housing Act 1996, that duty would depend on whether the applicant was homeless or threatened with homelessness, in priority need and intentionally homeless. The question of whether someone was intentionally homeless was left for consideration only if the authority accepted that the person was in priority need. **5-404**

The Homelessness Act 2002 has amended that scheme so that local housing authorities now have a power to secure accommodation for persons who are unintentionally homeless but not in priority need.[29] The amendment has meant that local housing authorities are required to enquire as to whether the applicant's actual or threatened homelessness was intentional for all eligible applicants, whether or not the applicant is in priority need.[30] A person becomes homeless intentionally if he deliberately does or fails to do anything in consequence of which he ceases to occupy accommodation which is available for him and which it would have been reasonable for him to continue to occupy.[31] A person becomes threatened with homelessness intentionally if he deliberately does or fails to do anything the likely result of which is that he will be forced to leave accommodation which is available for his occupation and which it would have been reasonable for him to continue to occupy.[32] An act or omission made in good faith by someone who was unaware of any relevant fact must not be treated as deliberate.[33] **5-405**

Each case must be considered on an individual basis. Housing authorities should not adopt general policies which seek to pre-define circumstances that amount to intentional homelessness.[34] It is important to consider whose conduct has resulted in making the applicant homeless. This is important in the situation where one of the applicants, or a member of the applicant's household has been found homeless intentionally or is susceptible to such a finding.[35] It is the applicant who must have done or failed to do something which resulted in homelessness or threatened homelessness. So where an applicant is evicted as a result of anti-social behaviour of a member of the household, it could be argued that he did not do or fail to do something, which resulted in homelessness. If the applicant, however, acquiesced in the anti-social behaviour, he could be regarded as making himself intentionally homeless. Thus, where it was the conduct of the applicants' children which resulted in possession orders being granted, it was held that the applicants **5-406**

---

[28] Housing Act 1996, s.184.

[29] *ibid.*, s.192(3) as amended by the Homelessness Act 2002 s.5(1).

[30] *Crawley v B* (2000) 32 H.L.R. 636; A. Arden Q.C. and C. Hunter "The Homes Bill: The Detail and the Deep Blue Sea" [2001] J.H.L. 15.

[31] Housing Act 1996 s.191(1).

[32] *ibid.*, s.196(1).

[33] *ibid.*, s.191(2) and s.196(2).

[34] Homelessness Code of Guidance for Local Authorities (England), para.7.3.

[35] The duty to a homeless person is also owed to anyone who might reasonable be expected to reside with him which may include the intentionally homeless member of the household.

were intentionally homeless.[36] In *R. v East Hertfordshire DC Ex p. Bannon*,[37] it was held that the local housing authority was entitled, if not bound, to consider whether the applicant had acquiesced in the conduct of the family as whole, either by acquiescing in it in the sense of being a party to it, or by doing nothing to prevent it. Similarly, it was held that an applicant who was evicted because of her lodger's behaviour when she was away from the flat, had acquiesced in his conduct because she had failed to evict him.[38] The act or omission must have been deliberate and the applicant must always be given the opportunity to explain his behaviour.[39] The Code of Guidance advises that local housing authorities should not consider an act or omission to be deliberate, *inter alia*, where:

(1) the housing authority have reason to believe the applicant is incapable of managing his or her affairs for example, by reason of old age, mental illness or handicap;

(2) particular acts or omissions were the result of limited mental capacity or the result of temporary aberrations caused by mental illness or frailty;

(3) the applicant has fled his home because of violence or threats of violence likely to be carried out, and the applicant has failed to pursue all legal remedies against the perpetrator because of fear of reprisal or because he was unaware of the remedies available.[40]

5-407 This would appear to assist an applicant who has been evicted as a result of his behaviour but where it is attributable to limited mental capacity or that he is incapable of managing his affairs by reason of mental health problems. However, in *R. v Wirral MBC Ex p Bell*,[41] the applicant had been evicted from her home on the grounds of nuisance and annoyance. She was considered by the local authority to be in priority need because of the state of her mental health but intentionally homeless. She sought judicial review of the decision on the basis that the council had failed properly to take her mental state into consideration. It was held that there was a distinct difference between a finding of priority need based on vulnerability and a finding of intentionality. Having regard to the Code of Guidance,[42] it was said that it was one thing to be less able to fend for yourself and another thing to be incapable of managing your own affairs. There was no inconsistency between the findings of the council.

5-408 The Code of Guidance continues to list acts or omissions which may be regarded as deliberate which include the following[43]:

(1) where someone is evicted because of anti-social behaviour such as nuisance to neighbours, harassment, etc.; and

---

[36] *Devenport v Salford CC* (1983) 8 H.L.R. 54; and *R. v Southampton CC Ex p. Ward* (1984) 14 H.L.R. 114. It was argued in *R. v Oldham MBC Ex p. G.*; *R. v Bexley LBC* (1993) 25 H.L.R. 319, that the child applicants had not acquiesced in the conduct. This failed because the House of Lords held that they were not in priority need in their own right.
[37] (1986) 18 H.L.R. 515.
[38] *R. v Swansea CC Ex p. John* (1982) 9 H.L.R. 56. See also *Smith v Bristol CC* LAG Bulletin, December 1981 287.
[39] Homelessness Code of Guidance for Local Authorities (England), para.7.11.
[40] Homelessness Code of Guidance for Local Authorities (England), para.7.12.
[41] (1994) 27 H.L.R. 234.
[42] Issued under the Housing Act 1985, s.71.
[43] Homelessness Code of Guidance for Local Authorities (England), para.7.14.

(2) where someone is evicted because of violence or threats of violence by them towards an associated person.[44]

Nuisance and annoyance are therefore, considered "deliberate" for this purpose.[45] In *R. v Hammersmith & Fulham Ex p. LBC*,[46] a finding of intentionality was upheld in relation to alleged criminal and anti-social behaviour which had led to threats from the IRA that the applicants would be killed if they did not leave their accommodation. **5-409**

Community Care

Under the National Assistance Act 1948, s.21(1): **5-410**

"A local authority with the approval of the Secretary of State, and to such an extent as he may direct shall, make arrangements for providing—

(a) residential accommodation for persons aged eighteen or over who by reason of age, illness, disability, or any other circumstances are in need of care and attention which is not otherwise available to them."

A local authority has a duty to assess an applicant's needs under s.1(1) of the 1948 Act.[47] If the applicant's needs satisfy the criteria under s.21(1), the local authority has a duty to provide accommodation on a continuing basis so long as the needs of the applicant remains as originally assessed.[48] If, for whatever reason, the accommodation is withdrawn or otherwise becomes unavailable to the applicant, then (subject to any negative assessment of his needs) the authority are under a continuing duty to provide further accommodation. **5-411**

The duty, however, is not absolute. In *R. v Kensington & Chelsea RLBC Ex p. Kujtim*,[49] the applicant came to the UK and applied for asylum. The authority accepted a duty to house him under s.21(1)(a). He was evicted from a hotel in which he was placed by the authority because he had threatened to kill the manager. The authority said that they would re-house him, but if he was evicted again because of his violent behaviour they would consider that they had discharged their duty. They re-housed him in a different hotel. The applicant, however, caused further problems, including assaulting another resident and threats to kill hotel staff. The authority then informed the applicant that he would not be provided with any further assistance and he sought a judicial review of this decision. The Court of Appeal held that the duty to provide accommodation was not absolute. If the applicant either unreasonably refuses to accept accommodation offered to him or if, following the provision of accommodation, he manifests a persistent and unequivocal refusal to observe the authority's reasonable requirements in relation to occupation of the accommodation, the authority are entitled to treat their duty as discharged **5-412**

---

[44] Associated persons are defined under s.178 of the Housing Act 1996. A person is a associated with another if: (a) they are or have been married to each other; (2) they are cohabitants or former cohabitants; (3) they live or have lived in the same household; (4) they are relatives; (5) they have agreed to marry one another (whether or not that agreement has been terminated); and (6) in relation to a child, each of them is a parent of the child or has, or has had, parental responsibility for the child.

[45] *Devenport v Salford CC* (1983) 8 H.L.R. 54, *R. v Swansea CC Ex p. John* (1982) 9 H.L.R. 56 and *R. v East Hertfordshire DC Ex p. Bannon* (1986) 18 H.L.R. 515.

[46] (1989) 22 H.L.R. 21.

[47] By virtue of National Health Service and Community Care Act 1990, s.47(1).

[48] *R. v Kensington & Chelsea RLBC Ex p. Kujtim.* (1999) 4 All E.R. 161; (1999) L.G.R. 761.

[49] [1999] 4 All E.R. 161; 32 H.L.R. 579; (1999) 2 C.C.L.R. 340.

and to refuse to provide further accommodation. It was suggested that it was desirable that the authority write to the applicant giving him a final warning before concluding that there been such a refusal.

Regulation of Houses in Multiple Occupation

5-413 The Housing Act 2004 repealed the provisions made under the Housing Act 1985 for schemes for houses in multiple occupation (HMOs) and under Pt 2 introduces a mandatory licensing scheme for certain prescribed HMOs. It also gives local housing authorities the power to impose additional licensing for HMOs outside that scheme. The aim of the compulsory licensing, first proposed in the *Housing Green Paper: A Decent Home for All*,[50] was to ensure a healthier private rented sector providing better protection for the tenant and the good landlord alike. Its relationship with anti-social behaviour, it is argued, is that the "unscrupulous and uncaring" landlord is more than willing to let properties to anti-social tenants because he has no interest in the condition of the property or the behaviour of the tenant and fails to have regard to the law.[51]

The old system

5-414 Under the old system, there were five types of action, which a local authority could take specifically in relation to HMOs:

(1) overcrowding controls[52];

(2) registration schemes[53];

(3) execution of works[54];

(4) management regulations[55];

(5) control orders.[56]

Previously, it was at the local authority's discretion to introduce registration and devise a scheme for HMOs. In brief, there were two main types of scheme:

(1) notification scheme: this only required details of the property such as number of rooms and amenities and provides local authorities with information about HMOs in their areas.

(2) control provisions: this limited properties, which may be used as HMOs, to registered properties, and where the person having control or managing the property was considered, by the local authority, to be a fit and proper person. Other conditions related to works or management.

---

[50] Published December 13, 2002.
[51] Para.5.4 of Ch.5 of the Housing Green Paper "A Decent Home for All". See also "Licensing of Houses in Multiple Occupation—England" (1999), paras 10–11.
[52] Housing Act 1985, ss.352, 354 and 358.
[53] *ibid.*, ss.346 and 346A.
[54] *ibid.*, s.352 and s.372.
[55] *ibid.*, s.369. Local authorities are under a duty to ensure that fire safety measures are adequate in all HMOs of three storeys or above: The Housing (Fire Safety in Houses in Multiple Occupation) Order 1997.
[56] Housing Act 1985, s.3.

Licensing of HMOs

The Housing Act 2004 introduces a somewhat complex definition of HMO to **5-415**
counteract the problems posed by the definition in the Housing Act 1985.[57] An
analysis and explanation of the definition of HMO is beyond the scope of this
book, but it is defined as a building or part of a building if it satisfies certain
conditions depending on the nature of occupation and type of building in
question.[58] Certain buildings or parts of a building including those managed
or controlled by public sector bodies are excluded from the definition.[59]

An HMO is subject to mandatory licensing if: **5-416**

(a) the HMO or any part of it comprises three storeys or more;

(b) if it is occupied by five or more persons; and

(c) if it is occupied by persons living in two or more households.[60]

A local housing authority[61] may, however, designate part or all of its area to
be subject to HMO licensing in addition to the mandatory scheme subject to
confirmation or general approval by the national authority.[62] Before making
a designation, the authority must consider that a significant proportion of the
HMOs which are to be included are being managed sufficiently ineffectively as
to give rise, or to be likely to give rise, to problems either for the occupiers of
the HMOs or for members of the public.[63] Thus, this will include consideration of anti-social behaviour, the definition of which is derived from the nuisance grounds for possession in the 1985 and 1988 Housing Acts.[64] That is:

"conduct on the part of occupiers of, or visitors to, residential premises:

(a) which causes or is likely to cause a nuisance or annoyance to persons
residing, visiting or otherwise engaged in lawful activities in the vicinity of

---

[57] Housing Act 2004, ss.254–259. The previous definition of an HMO was "a house which is occupied by persons who do not form a single household" (Housing Act 1985, s.345(1)); a definition
which proved problematic in practice: *Ashbridge Investments Ltd v Ministry of Housing and
Local Government* [1965] 1 W.L.R. 1320; *R. v Hackney LBC Ex p. Evenbray Ltd* (1987) 19 H.L.R.
557, QBD; *Reed v Hastings Corp* (1964) 62 L.G.R. 588); *Living Waters Christian Centres Ltd v
Conwy CBC* (1999) 31 H.L.R. 371, CA; *R. v Camden LBC Ex p. Rowton (Camden Town) Ltd*
(1983) 10 H.L.R. 28; *Okereke v Brent LBC* [1967] 1 Q.B. 42, CA; *Norwich City Council v Billings*
(1997) 29 H.L.R. 679, CA; *Barnes v Sheffield City Council* (1995) 27 H.L.R. 719, CA.
[58] Housing Act 2004, s.77 defines HMO as follows: (a) a house in multiple occupation as defined
by sections 254 to 259; and (b) references to an HMO include (where the context permits) any
yard, garden, outhouses and appurtenances belonging to, or usually enjoyed with, it (or any
part of it).".
[59] Housing Act 2004, Sch.14.
[60] Licensing of Houses in Multiple Occupation (Prescribed Descriptions) (England) Order 2006
(S.I.2006/371), Reg.3; The Licensing and Management of Houses in Multiple Occupation and
Other Houses (Miscellaneous Provisions) (England) Regulations 2006 (SI 2006/373) Regs3 and
4; Reg.6 and Sch.1.
[61] i.e. in relation to England, a unitary authority; a district council so far as it is not a unitary
authority; a London borough council; the Common Council of the City of London (in its
capacity as a local authority); the Sub-Treasurer of the Inner Temple or the Under-Treasurer
of the Middle Temple (in his capacity as a local authority); and the Council of the Isles of Scilly
(The Housing Act s. 2004, s. 261(2)). In relation to Wales, it means a county council or a county
borough council (s.261(4)).
[62] Housing Act 2004, s.58; National authority" means in relation to England, the Secretary of
State and in relation to Wales, the National Assembly for Wales (s.261(1)). The Licensing and
Management of Houses in Multiple Occupation and Other Houses (Miscellaneous Provisions)
(England) Regulations 2006 (SI 2006/373) Regs9 and 10 concerning publication requirements.
[63] Housing Act 2004, s.56(2).
[64] *ibid.*, s.57(5).

such premises, or (b) which involves or is likely to involve the use of such premises for illegal purposes."[65]

Moreover, an authority is under a duty to ensure that any exercise of the power is consistent with its overall housing strategy[66] and to seek to adopt a co-ordinated approach in connection with dealing with homelessness,[67] empty properties and anti-social behaviour[68] affecting the private rented sector, including combining licensing with other courses of action available to them, and with measures taken by other persons.[69] The authority must not make a particular designation unless: (a) they have considered whether there are any other courses of action available to them (of whatever nature) that might provide an effective method of dealing with the problem or problems in question; and (b) they consider that making the designation will significantly assist them to deal with the problem or problems (whether or not they take any other course of action as well).[70] The designation must have a date on which it ceases to take effect and must be no longer than five years from the date it comes into force.[71]

5-417   Every HMO to which Pt 2 of the 2004 applies must have a licence[72] which includes such provisions as the local housing authority considers appropriate. In particular, inter alia,[73] they may impose conditions requiring the taking of reasonable and practicable steps to prevent or reduce anti-social behaviour by persons occupying or visiting the house.[74] If a person commits an offence because he fails, without reasonable excuse,[75] to comply with any condition of a licence,[76] he is liable on summary conviction to a fine not exceeding level 5 on the standard scale.[77] In effect, this is imposing an obligation on private landlords which Parliament has declined in relation to social landlords.[78]

5-418   The licence must be in writing, be non-transferable and not relate to more than one HMO.[79] The period for which the licence will be valid is specified although it may be brought to an end earlier if there is non-compliance with a provision of the licence.[80]

5-419   There are various provisions as to how to apply for a licence to the local housing authority.[81] The authority may grant a licence if it is satisfied of

---

[65] Ground 2 of Sch.2 to the Housing Act 1985 and Ground 14 of Sch. 2 to the Housing Act 1988.

[66] e.g. Local Government Act 2000, s.4 (strategies for promoting well-being), Local Government Act 2003, s.87 (housing strategies).

[67] Homelessness Act 2002, ss.1–4.

[68] Housing Act 1996, s.218A (tackling anti-social behaviour); Crime and Disorder Act 1998, s.5 (strategies for the reduction of crime and disorder and substance misuse).

[69] Housing Act 2004, s.57(3).

[70] *Ibid.*, s.57(4).

[71] *Ibid.*, 60(2) and s.59(2)(c).

[72] *Ibid.*, s.61(1); The Licensing and Management of Houses in Multiple Occupation and Other Houses (Miscellaneous Provisions) (England) Regulations 2006 (SI 2006/373) Regs9 and 10 concerning publication requirements.

[73] The licence must contain the conditions specified under Sch.4 (Housing Act 2004, s.67(3)) in addition to discretionary conditions which the authority may consider appropriate for regulating the management, use and occupation of the house concerned and/ or its condition and contents (Housing Act 2004, s.67(1) and (2)).

[74] Housing Act 2004, s.67(2)(b).

[75] *ibid.*, s.72(5)(c).

[76] *ibid.*, s.72(3).

[77] *ibid.*, s.72(7).

[78] See para.5-074ff.

[79] Housing Act 2004, s.68.

[80] *ibid.*, ss.68(3) and (4) and ss.70(1)(b) and 70(2).

[81] *ibid.*, s.63; The Licensing and Management of Houses in Multiple Occupation and Other Houses (Miscellaneous Provisions) (England) Regulations 2006, (SI 2006/373) Reg.7 and Sch. 2.

certain matters.[82] Importantly, the authority must be satisfied that the proposed licence holder[83] and proposed manager of the house[84] are fit and proper persons to be the licence holder and manager of the house respectively.[85]

In relation to whether a person is a fit and proper person to be a licence **5-420** holder or a manager, the authority must have regard to any evidence tending to show that the person concerned, or any person associated or formerly associated with him (whether on a personal, work or other basis), has:

(1) committed any offences involving fraud or other dishonesty, or violence or drugs or any offence listed in Sch.3 to the Sexual Offences Act 2003 (offences attracting notification requirements);

(2) practised unlawful discrimination on grounds of sex, colour, race, ethnic or national origins or disability in, or in connection with, the carrying on of any business;

(3) contravened any provision of the law relating to housing or of landlord and tenant law;

(4) acted otherwise than in accordance with any applicable code of practice approved under s.233.[86]

The authority must consider evidence if it shows that any person associated **5-421** or formerly associated with the applicant (whether on a personal, work or other basis) has done any of the things set out above *and* it appears to the authority that the evidence is relevant to the question whether he is a fit and proper person to be the licence holder or manager of the house.[87]

In deciding whether the proposed management arrangements for a house in **5-422** multiple occupation are otherwise satisfactory, the local housing authority shall, among other things, consider:

(1) whether any person proposed to be involved in the management of the house is of a sufficient level of competence to be so involved;

(2) whether any person proposed to be involved in the management of the house (other than the manager) is a fit and proper person to be so involved;

(3) whether any proposed management structures and funding arrangements are suitable.[88]

Licensing of Other Residential Accommodation

The 2004 Act also introduces selective licensing of other residential accom- **5-423** modation to combat the causes of anti-social behaviour by landlords. The Consultation Paper on the Housing Bill, published in March 2003, stated that:

"areas of low housing demand suffered from the linked problems of falling prices and rents, empty properties and, above all, crime and anti-social

---

[82] Housing Act 2004, s.64(3).
[83] The authority have to be satisfied that the proposed licence holder is, out of all the persons reasonably available to be so, the most appropriate person to be the licence holder (Housing Act 2004, s.64(3)(b)(ii)). The authority must assume, however, that the person having control of the house is a more appropriate person to be the licence holder than a person not having control of it, unless the contrary is shown (Housing Act 2004, s.66(4)).
[84] Housing Act 2004, s.64(3)(c).
[85] *ibid.*, s.64(b) and (d).
[86] *ibid.*, s.66(2).
[87] *ibid.*, s.66(3).
[88] *ibid.*, s.66(5) and (6).

behaviour. As owner occupiers flee unpopular and hard to sell properties, the private rented sector could grow by default and exploitative landlords might then seek to operate on a large scale, forcing out responsible tenants and owner-occupiers with the help of anti-social tenants, and contributing to the spiral of decline".[89]

This was also part of the wider strategy to improve the condition of properties and reduce the levels of anti-social behaviour prevalent in poor run down areas.[90] The ODPM's consultation paper, *Licensing in the Private Sector* (2004), also attempts to explains the rationale for selective licensing:

"15 . . .[T]here are problems with the management of the private and rented sector in some areas of low housing demand, particularly in some parts of the North and Midlands. The absence of owner-occupiers wishing to live in the area has sometimes led to an influx of speculative landlords. Some landlords with a shortage of good tenants have increasingly offered homes to tenants whose behaviour is unacceptable. In some cases the large-scale operation of some unscrupulous landlords have been linked to criminal activities such as Housing Benefit fraud, drug dealing and prostitution.

16. These activities contribute to the destabilisation of local communities, adding to the range of social and economic problems, and seriously hampering efforts at regeneration. Even a single anti-social household can seriously influence the condition of a neighbourhood and undermine efforts to improve the area.

17. The problem of anti-social tenants is not restricted to areas of low housing demand. In some areas of high demand, particular types of housing or housing in particular neighbourhoods can be difficult to let or sell. Letting to some types of tenant in such areas can exacerbate such problems, leading to a spiral of decline in certain neighbourhoods."

5-424   A local housing authority may designate the area of its district or an area in its district[91] as subject to selective licensing if it considers that[92]:

(1) that the area is an area of low housing demand, or is likely to become an area of low housing demand[93]and that the designation will, when considered together with other measures being taken in the area by the authority, or by other persons together with the local housing authority, contribute to the improvement of the social or economic conditions in the area[94]; or

[89] Housing Bill – Consultation on draft legislation, p.19, para.4.
[90] See *National Strategy for Neighbourhood Renewal*, Report of Policy Action Team 8: *Anti-social behaviour*, Annex D: Glossary of main government initiatives which impact on anti-social behaviour.
[91] References to the district of a local housing authority are to the area of the council concerned, that is to say: (a) in the case of a unitary authority, the area or district; (b) in the case of a district council so far as it is not a unitary authority, the district; (c) in the case of an authority within s.261(2)(c) to (f), the London borough, the City of London, the Inner or Middle Temple or the Isles of Scilly (as the case may be); and (d) in the case of a Welsh county council or a county borough council, the Welsh county or county borough (Housing Act 2004, s.261(6)).
[92] Housing Act 2004, s.80(2).
[93] In determining whether a particular area is, or is likely to become, an area of low housing demand local housing authority shall take into account, inter alia, the value of residential premises in the area, in comparison to similar premises in comparable areas; the turnover of occupiers of residential premises; the number of residential premises which are available to buy or rent and the length of time for which they remain unoccupied (Housing Act 2004, s.80(4)).
[94] Housing Act 2004, s.80(3).

(2) that the area is experiencing a significant and persistent problem caused by anti-social behaviour[95], that some or all of the private sector landlords[96] who have let premises in the area (whether under leases or licences) are failing to take action to combat the problem that it would be appropriate for them to take; and that making a designation will, when combined with other measures taken in the area by the local housing authority, or by other persons together with the local housing authority, lead to a reduction in, or the elimination of, the problem[97]; and/or

(3) any conditions imposed by order by the appropriate national authority.[98]

In effect, in order for the local housing authority to designate an area for selective licensing, it needs to be satisfied that one of the two conditions above have been satisfied in addition to any conditions which may be imposed by the Secretary of State; such persons who are likely to be affected by the designation have been consulted; it has considered any representations made in accordance with the consultation and not withdrawn[99]; in the same way as for designation of an area for HMO licensing, it has to consider other housing related strategies, other courses of action which may be available and that the designation will significantly assist them[1]; and the designation has been confirmed by the Secretary of State.[2] The properties that will be affected by such a designation will be any building or part of a building which is situated within an area which is designated as subject to selective licensing and in relation to which the designation is in force; and is occupied under a tenancy or a licence; and is occupied as a residence.[3] **5-425**

It does not include HMOs which are required to be licensed under the provisions of Pt 2 of the Housing Act 2004,[4] nor does it include a house occupied under a tenancy or licence which is exempt.[5] A tenancy or licence is an exempt tenancy or licence if it is granted by a body which is registered as a social landlord under Pt 1 of the Housing Act 1996.[6] **5-426**

Once an area is designated, the relevant house must have a licence authorising occupation under a tenancy or licence.[7] As with HMOs, that licence may be granted subject to conditions. For instance, the licence may impose conditions relating to the management of the house or steps to prevent or reduce anti-social behaviour by persons occupying or visiting the house.[8] Furthermore, the licence must include provisions about, inter alia, the demand by the licence holder of references from persons who the licence holder intends will occupy the house and the supply by the licence holder to the occupants of the house of a written statement of the terms on which they occupy the house.[9] **5-427**

[95] For the definition of anti-social behaviour see the Housing Act 2004, s.56(5).
[96] Private sector landlord does not include a registered social landlord within the meaning of Pt 1 of the Housing Act 1996, s.80(6).
[97] Housing Act 2004, s.80(6).
[98] *ibid.*, s.80(7).
[99] *ibid.*, s.80(9).
[1] *ibid.*, s.81.
[2] *ibid.*, s.82.
[3] *ibid.*, s.79.
[4] *ibid.*, s.79(1)(b) and s.85(1)(a).
[5] *ibid.*, s.79(2).
[6] *ibid.*, s.79(3).
[7] *ibid.*, s.85(1); The Selective Licensing of Houses (Specified Exemptions) (England) Order 2006 (SI 2006/370).
[8] Housing Act 2004, s.90.
[9] *ibid.*, s.90(4) and Sch.4.

5-428   A person commits an offence if he is the person having control of or managing a house which ought to be licensed but is not so licensed.[10] It is a defence to such an offence for that person to prove that he has a reasonable excuse.[11] A person who commits such an offence is liable on summary conviction to a fine not exceeding £20,000.[12]

5-429   There is a further offence where a person fails, without reasonable excuse, to comply with any condition of a licence.[13] Such a person is liable on summary conviction to a fine not exceeding level 5 on the standard scale.[14]

5-430   In a similar way to HMOs, no rent or licence fee is payable by an occupier and no other compensation is payable for use or occupation of the house during the period in which the house is unlicensed.[15] Furthermore, the Residential Property Tribunal has power to order landlords to repay rent in respect of unlicensed houses.[16] The provisions relating to applications for licences, the power to grant licences and in particular, the test for fitness and satisfactory management arrangements are more or less the same as for HMOs.[17]

5-431   As mentioned above, the link between anti-social behaviour and areas of low housing demand has been widely acknowledged. The power given to local housing authorities, however, is not limited to areas which are in low demand; the power extends to areas which *might* become areas of low housing demand. Similarly, the government, in its consultation paper predicted that, ". . .as owner occupiers fled unpopular and hard to sell properties, the private rented sector could grow by default and exploitative landlords might then seek to operate on a large scale, forcing out responsible tenants and owner-occupiers with the help of anti-social tenants, and contributing to the spiral of decline."[18] There is no statistical evidence to support this, and instead the government has granted wide powers to introduce selective licensing into areas which may, in fact, be adversely affected if private landlords realise that it is not worth their while purchasing properties to let, thereby reducing the level of private investment. When the Government published a consultation paper *Selective Licensing of Private Landlords*, in October 2001, of the 134 responses, only 24 were from private landlords, agents, landlord agents and property interest groups.

Additional control provisions in relation to residential accommodation

5-432   The scope of this book is not wide enough to discuss all the provisions relating to control provisions concerning HMOs, properties required to be licensed and, importantly, other properties in the private sector outside both of these regimes. The additional controls given to local housing authorities, in relation to properties required to be licensed, relate to interim management orders where there is no reasonable prospect that the house will be licensed in the near future or it is necessary to protect the health, safety or welfare of the occupiers or persons occupying or having an estate or interest in any premises in the vicinity.[19] In such circumstances the authority is under a duty to make an

[10] Housing Act 2004, s.95.
[11] *ibid.*, s.95(4).
[12] *ibid.*, s.95(5).
[13] *ibid.*, s.95(2).
[14] *ibid.*, s.95(6).
[15] *ibid.*, s. 96. Furthermore, there are similar restrictions placed on termination of tenancies (s.98).
[16] *ibid.*, ss.96 and 97.
[17] *ibid.*, s.87 (applications); s.94 and Sch.5 (appeals); s.88 and 89 (tests for fitness and satisfactory management arrangements).
[18] Housing Bill-Consultation on draft legislation, p.19, para.4.
[19] Housing Act 2004, s.102(2).

interim order. As the scope of the health and safety condition is not limited to protecting the occupiers of the premises but also extends to persons in the vicinity an authority's duties and powers may be triggered by anti-social behaviour caused by the occupiers. Furthermore, the duty extends to making an order in respect of a house licensed under Pts 2 and 3, but where the licence has been revoked (although not yet in force) and on revocation the same conditions concerning licensing and health and safety will apply.[20]

An authority also has the power to make interim orders in respect of properties outside the scope of the licensing regimes subject to authorisation of the Residential Property Tribunal.[21] The categories of prescribed circumstances in which special interim management orders may be made must reflect the conditions which justify the introduction of selective licensing, i.e. areas of low housing demand, areas subject to significant and persistent anti-social behaviour and any other circumstances which may be prescribed. A special interim order must be authorised by the residential property tribunal. Two conditions have to be satisfied: **5-433**

(a) The circumstances of the house must fall within circumstances prescribed by the appropriate national authority;

(b) The order be must necessary for the purpose of protecting the health, safety or welfare of persons occupying the house, or persons occupying or having an estate or interest in any premises in the vicinity of the house.

The prescribed circumstances are:

(a) the area in which the house is located is experiencing a significant and persistent problem caused by anti-social behaviour;

(b) that problem is attributable, in whole or in part, to the anti-social behaviour of an occupier of the house;

(c) the landlord of the house is a private sector landlord;

(d) the landlord of the house is failing to take action to combat that problem that it would be appropriate for him to take; and

(e) the making of an interim management order, when combined with other measures taken in the area by the local housing authority, or by other persons together with the local housing authority, will lead to a reduction in, or elimination of, that problem.[22]

Part 4 of the Housing Act 2004 also deals with final management orders which are made where, on expiry of the interim order, the house does not have to be licensed but the authority consider that making the final order is necessary on a long-term basis for the protection of the health, safety, or welfare of persons occupying the house, or persons occupying or having an estate or interest in any premises in the vicinity.[23] **5-434**

---

[20] Housing Act 2004, s.102(3).

[21] *ibid.*, s.102(4) deals with interim management orders in respect of a house which is an HMO other than one that is required to be licensed under Pt 2. The Housing Act 2004, s.102(7) is concerned with a house to which s.103 applies. The Housing Act 2004, s.103 applies to a house if the whole of it is occupied either: (a) under a single tenancy or licence that is not an exempt tenancy or licence under s.79(3) or (4); or (b) under two or more tenancies or licences in respect of different dwellings contained in it, none of which is an exempt tenancy or licence under s.79(3) or (4).

[22] Housing (Interim Management Orders) (Prescribed Circumstances) (England) Order 2006 (SI 2006/369).

[23] Housing Act 2004, s.113.

5-435   What is important in relation to management orders is that the local housing authority takes the place of the landlord or licensor or person granting the rights under the agreement although this does not amount to an interest in law of the premises.[24] In which case, it will be open to the local housing authority to deal with anti-social tenants either by injunction or possession proceedings. These additional control provisions are very similar to the "control orders" under the Housing Act 1985.

5-436   Local housing authorities have also been given power to tackle the problem of empty properties by use of empty dwelling management orders.[25] Part of the reasoning behind the introduction of such orders was that government considered that empty homes have a significant impact on community as they attract vandalism and other anti-social behaviour.[26] Although the majority of responses to the consultation paper *Empty Homes: temporary management, lasting solutions* agreed with such sentiments, only 10 of the 134 responses were from private individuals and most accepted that there had been steady decline with current initiatives working. Like management orders, there is provision for interim[27] and final orders[28]; the purpose of each is to ensure that the dwelling becomes occupied. Of concern is that whereas an interim order only allows the authority to let out the dwelling with the proprietor's consent, a final order allows them to let the dwelling without the proprietor's consent.

Housing Benefit

5-437   The Respect Action Plan, launched in January 2006, re-visited the idea of imposing housing benefit sanctions for anti-social behaviour. This time the government justifies such action as a means of "encouraging those involved in perpetrating anti-social behaviour to engage with more intensive family support". As yet, it is not known what proposals are going to be put forward and whether they will follow the Private Members' Bill put forward by Frank Field MP in 2003.[29]

5-438   The imposition of housing benefit sanctions was first raised in the White Paper, *Respect and Responsibility—Taking a Stand Against Anti-Social Behaviour*. The government indicated that that would consult on whether to give local authorities an enabling power to withhold payments of Housing Benefit to individual tenants where they believe this is the most effective way of tackling anti-social behaviour.[30] Furthermore, it was considered whether an

---

[24] In respect of interim management orders: Housing Act 2004, ss.108–110. Similar provision is made for final management orders (ss.116–118). As for agreements and legal proceedings, s.125 applies to both types of management order. See Housing (Management Orders and Empty Dwelling Management Orders) (Supplemental Provisions) (England) Regulations 2006 (SI 2006/368) concerning the situation where the authority is to be treated as a lessee under a lease.

[25] Chapter 2 of Pt 4 and Sch.7 to the Housing Act 2004. The Housing (Empty Dwelling Management Orders) (Prescribed Exceptions and Requirements) (England) Order 2006 (SI 2006/367); The Housing (Management Orders and Empty Dwelling Management Orders) (Supplemental Provisions) (England) Regulations 2006 (SI 2006/368).

[26] Empty Dwelling Management Orders: Consultation on Secondary Legislation, August 2005.

[27] Housing Act 2004, s.135.

[28] *ibid.,* s.137.

[29] Respect Action Plan, p.23. The Respect Action Plan relies on the report produced by Sheffield Hallam University, *Interim evaluation of rehabilitation projects for families at risk of losing their homes as a result of anti-social behaviour* (2006). The report, however, is very cautious about reaching any conclusions regarding those families who disengaged from projects providing intensive support; some of the families did so because of the provision of alternative forms of support and the cessation of nuisance behaviour. The final stage of the evaluation will explore in more depth the reasons for disengagement.

[30] See para.4.47 of the White Paper, *Respect and Responsibility – Taking a Stand Against Anti-Social Behaviour*.

automatic trigger for housing benefit sanctions should apply, on a wider scale, in designated areas where anti-social behaviour was a problem or in individual cases where the behaviour had reached a particular level and required enforcement.[31] Over a year later, and after the private members bill put forward by Frank Field MP fell during its passage through Parliament, proposing that benefit could be reduced because of anti-social conduct, the government finally decided to consult. Strangely enough, the government sought consultation even before the Anti-Social Behaviour Bill had become law, thereby attempting to introduce more legislation dealing with anti-social conduct without allowing time for the first provisions to work.[32]

The policy behind the introduction of housing benefit sanctions is that the **5-439** welfare state should be based on rights and responsibilities. In recent years, successive governments have looked at reducing the social security budget. There has also been concern at the "money for nothing" culture which has developed. Hence, the introduction of the job seekers allowance which forced claimants to actively seek work in order to receive payment. In a similar way, it is now proposed that housing benefit should be granted conditional on the behaviour of the claimant. Frank Field, who introduced the now lapsed Bill, said, ". . .it is increasingly accepted that the right to receive money from taxpayers depends on fulfilling the duty to behave in a way which does not damage others."[33]

The Bill not only purported to act as a sanction against anti-social behaviour but also as a preventative measure; it is hoped that the threat of a reduction in benefits will force people to behave themselves. Another effect of the scheme would be to penalise landlords who do not keep their tenants under control. It is true that the Bill targeted those who are on low incomes, but it also hit landlords and would act as a way to take action against their anti-social tenants. The Bill introduced penalties for those on housing benefit and would not affect other tenants and owner-occupiers who are guilty of anti-social behaviour. It is arguable that this ignored the use of injunctions, possession proceedings and claims in damages for nuisance against tenants and home-owners alike, the financial penalties for whom would be much higher because of the greater chances of actually recovering damages from such perpetrators. On the other hand, landlords would suffer as a result of non-receipt of housing benefit. In the case of private landlords, any arrears accruing as a result of a reduction in housing benefit would force any reasonable landlord to seek possession on one of the mandatory grounds for possession.[34] This, in effect, might simply do no more that shift the problem.

Notwithstanding the lapse of the Frank Field's Bill, many of his proposals **5-441** have been considered in the consultation paper. Indeed, the first option in the paper is based on that Bill. The main feature would be that in criminal proceedings a declaration of anti-social behaviour would have to be made where the court convicts a person of an offence involving anti-social behaviour. It would also appear that the court would have such a duty in civil proceedings, although this seems to be limited to proceedings in the criminal courts, such as under the Environmental Protection Act 1990.[35] The declaration would then be notified to the Department of Work and Pensions, who would then check whether the person was claiming housing benefit and then tell the local

---

[31] White Paper, para.4.48.
[32] See Editorial by A. Arden Q.C. and C. Hunter, *Feeding the National Obsession: Anti-Social behaviour and housing benefit* [2003] J.H.L. 67.
[33] F. Field, "First take their benefits, then their children", *Daily Telegraph* May 5, 2002.
[34] Either under the Housing Act 1988, s.21 (in the case of assured shorthold tenants) or under Sch.2, Ground 8 (in the case of assured or assured shorthold tenants and where rent arrears are over 8 weeks in arrears).
[35] See p.6 of the consultation paper.

authority administering the claim that the sanction could be applied. It expected that the housing benefit sanction would be imposed where the behaviour is that of members of the tenant's household and visitors. It is not clear how this will operate as applicants of housing benefit may not be parties to the criminal proceedings.

5-442   There is no definition of anti-social behaviour in the consultation paper. This inevitably raises questions as to how an offence will be marked out as anti-social since most offences could be described as "anti-social" in some way.[36] In the Bill, however, "anti-social manner" was as defined in the Bill. A person has behaved in such a way ". . .if his conduct caused, or was likely to cause, harassment, alarm or distress to one or more persons (not of the same household as himself) residing in, visiting, or otherwise engaged in lawful activity in the locality of the home". As with Frank Field's Bill, the proposal has been widely condemned by housing and homeless groups as targeting the poorest families and exacerbating the already growing number of homeless persons.[37] It is argued that the withdrawal of benefit is not the way to punish perpetrators of anti-social behaviour.

5-443   Under the second and government preferred option, it would be for the officer of a local authority[38] to identify and determine cases of anti-social behaviour. That authority would signal its determination to the Housing Benefit Department which could then apply the sanction. The tenant would have a right of appeal to an independent tribunal against the co-ordinator's determination and to the Appeals Service against the application of the sanction. Thus, the onus will be on the tenant to prove that his behaviour has not been anti-social. The consultation paper is extremely vague; there are many gaps as to how the system would operate and a number of things the government has failed to take into account.

5-444   On June 5, 2006, the government returned to their plan to cut housing benefit of nuisance neighbours who refuse to take part in rehabilitation courses. Under the proposals, members of a household evicted for anti-social behaviour will be offered "appropriate rehabilitation." If they refuse, the local authority will be able to issue a warning notice, advising them that their housing benefit will be reduced accordingly. with penalties rising incrementally. Yet more legislation is promised and the first pilot schemes are hoped to be introduced in 2008.

---

[36] See Editorial by A. Arden Q.C. and C. Hunter, *Feeding the national obsession: Anti-Social Behaviour and Housing Benefit*, [2003] J.H.L. 67.

[37] Although see the proposals put forward by the government in relation to penalising private sector landlords who fail to, or are in breach, of new licensing laws soon to be introduced.

[38] It is suggested that this might be the anti-social behaviour co-ordinator.

CHAPTER SIX
Anti-Social Behaviour Orders

"Pamela won her award after securing the first ever five-year ASBO in Lincolnshire. A gang of up to 50 youths were gathering at a bungalow next door, with the abuse so bad that Pamela didn't leave the house for two years. With little support from terrified neighbours, Pamela kept up her fight, reporting incidents to the police, and eventually secured an eviction for the neighbour, and ASBOs and Acceptable Behaviour contracts for several of the gang. 'It sounds stupid but the damage has done me some good. I've done the accreditation course after winning a Taking a Stand Award and I'm one of 12 on the first pilot course for accredited police volunteers to man the Local Partnership Team desk.' "[1]

6-001

"The British Institute for Brain Injured Children (BIBIC) has details of more than 15 examples where children with Asperger's, Tourette's Syndrome and Attention Deficit Hyperactivity Disorder (ADHD) were given orders, and says there are many more cases. In one case, a 12-year-old autistic boy was punished for staring over his neighbour's fence; another boy with Tourette's Syndrome was given his order for constantly swearing . . ."[2]

6-002

"The Single Judge, granting leave to appeal, commented briefly: 'For being drunk and disorderly: a year's imprisonment and termination of a community rehabilitation order? Can this be right?' "[3]

6-003

As of March 2005, 7356 anti-social behaviour orders were issued by courts in England and Wales: 1045 in Greater Manchester and 749 in Greater London; someone in Manchester is 12 times more likely to receive an ASBO than someone in Lincolnshire. Only 62 applications, less than 1 per cent of the total granted, have ever been refused.[4] During the first eight months in 1999, only 104 orders were made, but more than 2,600 orders have been made since November 2003. Fifty-six per cent of ASBOs in Manchester concerned persons under the age of 18 years and ranged from 33 per cent in Bedfordshire to 100 per cent in Dorset.[5] According to a Home Office press release, 47 per cent of anti-social behaviour orders issued during April–June 2005 were orders on application and 53 per cent were orders on conviction. Fifty-four per cent of ASBOs were issued to adults, and 43 per cent to juveniles (3 per cent are "age unknown")[6] The Home Office, in a report on ASBOs dated July 8, 2003, found that, between April 1, 1999 and March 31, 2003, 36 per cent of

6-004

---

[1] Case Study, Respect
[2] August 15, 2005.
[3] *R. v Tripp* [2005] EWCA Crim 2253.
[4] Home Office Research and Development Directorate, March 2005.
[5] *ibid.*
[6] December 21, 2005.

orders were breached within nine months of being granted, and about half of those sentenced for a breach received custodial sentences and the rate is now at about 42 per cent. In 2001, 114 persons breached by the courts following the imposition of an ASBO were jailed out of 322 issued. In 2002, 212 were jailed out of 403 issued.

6-005   ASBOs were first proposed by the Labour Party in a policy paper in 1995.[7] The main problems with the existing law were said to be a lack of criminal sanctions designed to deal with persistent anti-social criminal conduct, reliance upon expensive civil remedies which might not be available in all cases of persistent anti-social behaviour and a lack of co-ordination between the police, local authorities, social landlords and other agencies. They proposed the introduction of a "Community Safety Order" to deal with "chronic" anti-social behaviour, typified by multiple convictions by the defendant, evidence of the commission of multiple offences without a conviction, or evidence of unlawful acts by an individual or members of his household which would interfere with the peace and comfort of a residential occupiers. The unlawful acts were the criminal versions of various torts such as nuisance, trespass, or assault.

"Trigger Behaviour": Defining anti-social behaviour

6-006   The term "trigger behaviour" appears in s.1F of the Crime and Disorder Act 1998, in respect of intervention orders. It is used to describe the type of conduct which attracts the imposition of the orders of this part of the 1998 Act, the main one being the ASBO itself. Under s.1(1) of the 1998 Act, an application for ASBO may be made by a relevant person if it appears to them that the following conditions are fulfilled, with respect to any person aged 10 or over, namely:

> "1(a) that the person has acted, since the commencement date, in an anti-social manner, that is to say, in a manner that caused or was likely to cause harassment, alarm or distress to one or more persons not of the same household as himself; and
>   (b) that such an order is necessary to protect relevant persons from further anti-social acts by him."

The definition of anti-social behaviour, as discussed in Chapter One, is deliberately loose and general. In its earlier versions of the draft bill, the definition of anti-social behaviour did not contain the phrase, "caused or was likely to cause harassment, alarm or distress". Even after it was included, there was criticism that the term was still far too wide—"a dangerous catch-all"—and the powers in the act could be used against anyone who did not conform to a normal pattern of reasonable behaviour or lifestyle.[8] During the report stage of the 1998 Act in the House of Lords, Lord Goodhart suggested that the definition should cover only behaviour which would cause alarm and distress to a reasonable person and moved for an amendment to require that the acts must be motivated by an intention to harass or cause alarm or distress.[9] The Solicitor-General, in reply, argued that this was unnecessary as it was ". . . the heedless, careless anti-social actions that the order needs to target and not just those with a deliberate intent and that there would be sufficient protections to

---

[7] *A Quiet Life: Tough Action on Criminal Neighbours* (1995). Following the 1997 election, the Government released a second paper, *Community Safety Order: A Consultation Paper.*
[8] Lord Rodgers of Quarry Bank, HL Deb vol. 584, col. 544. See generally Thorp, House of Commons Research Paper 98/44, *The Crime and Disorder Bill*, April 1998.
[9] HL Deb vol. 587, col. 584

prevent applications being made where the behaviour was trivial".[10] The requirement that the victim not be of the same household was inserted so as to distinguish the new orders from domestic violence remedies contained in Pt IV of the Family Law Act 1996. Note also the term "likely to cause harassment, alarm or distress", which was said to be included so that professional witnesses, such as local authority officers, could give evidence about the behaviour; in that way, it was not necessary for any person to give evidence that they were actually distressed by the anti-social behaviour.[11] Perhaps in an effort to deal with criticism as to the possibility of arbitrary or subjective assessments by courts or authorities of what constituted the trigger behaviour, s.1(5) provides that, for the purpose of determining whether the condition mentioned in subs.(1)(a) above is fulfilled, the court shall disregard any act of the defendant which he shows was reasonable in the circumstances.

The trigger behaviour is conduct which causes "harassment, alarm or distress." We reviewed the meaning of that phrase under the Public Order Act 1986 and the Protection from Harassment Act 1997 and related acts in Chapter Two. We concluded that it had no precise legal definition. However, it has certain characteristics: it is a kind of nuisance; it need not always be criminal but it normally is; it has to have a public element to it in that it does not take place in private; or, at any rate, some other person experiences or could experience it but only outside of some kind of built environment (hence, the exclusions of members of the same household in subs.1(a)); the conduct need not be associated with an intent to cause harassment, alarm or distress because what matters is the reaction it causes or could cause in others; it can be serious conduct in itself or, if not serious, then persistent; and it must be anti-social or unreasonable (hence, subs.1(1)(a) and (5)). All the same, despite the fact that the concept it so inchoate, it is clear that is something that is regularly and routinely dealt with by the criminal courts. **6-007**

Rather than attempting to define the deliberately nebulous concept of the trigger behaviour in the context of the 1998 Act, it might be more productive to think of it in terms of what the ASBO is intended to achieve; that is, what is the problem that these new orders are intended to address? It was held in *McCann*,[12] by the House of Lords, that ASBO proceedings were civil, not criminal, proceedings. Although the proceedings for breach of an order were criminal in character, the procedure leading to the making of the order was separate and independent. The proceedings also did not constitute the bringing of a criminal charge for the purposes of Art.6(1). They were described as preventative in character, rather than punitive or disciplinary. Since the proceedings were civil in nature, hearsay evidence would be admissible. The use of such evidence would be necessary in many cases if magistrates were to be properly informed about the scale and nature of the anti-social behaviour and the prohibitions that were needed for the protection of the public. Therefore, the standard of proof to be applied to a defendant's conduct was the criminal standard. There were good reasons, in the interests of fairness, it was held, for applying that higher standard where allegations were made of criminal or quasi-criminal conduct which, if proved, would have serious consequences for the person against whom they were made. Lord Steyn at para.16 said that the new orders were aimed at an important social problem: **6-008**

> "It is well known that in some urban areas, notably urban housing estates and deprived inner city areas, young persons, and groups of young persons, cause fear, distress and misery to law-abiding and innocent people by

[10] HL Deb vol. 587, col. 584; HL Deb. vol. 587 col. 586.
[11] *Community Safety Order: Consultation Paper*, Home Office, September 1997.
[12] [2003] 1 A.C. 787.

outrageous anti-social behaviour. It takes many forms. It includes behaviour which is criminal such as assaults and threats, particularly against old people and children, criminal damage to individual property and amenities of the community, burglary, theft, and so forth. Sometimes the conduct falls short of cognisable criminal offences. The culprits are mostly, but not exclusively, male. Usually they are relatively young, ranging particularly from about 10 to 18 years of age. Often people in the neighbourhood are in fear of such young culprits. In many cases, and probably in most, people will only report matters to the police anonymously or on the strict understanding that they will not directly or indirectly be identified. In recent years this phenomenon became a serious social problem. There appeared to be a gap in the law. The criminal law offered insufficient protection to communities. Public confidence in the rule of law was undermined by a not unreasonable view in some communities that the law failed them."

6-009 See also Lord Hope, at para.42:

"On the whole we live in a law-abiding community. Most people respect the rights of others, most of the time. People usually refrain from acts which are likely to cause injury to others or to their property. On the occasions when they do not, the sanctions provided by the criminal law are available. But it is a sad fact that there are some individuals for whom respect for the law and for the rights of others has no meaning. Taken one by one, their criminal or sub-criminal acts may seem to be, and indeed often are, relatively trivial. But, taken together, the frequency and scale of their destructive and offensive conduct presents a quite different picture. So does the aggression and intimidation with which their acts are perpetrated. The social disruption which their behaviour creates is unacceptable. So too is the apparent inability of the criminal law to restrain their activities. This provides the background to the enactment of s.1 of the Crime and Disorder Act 1998 with which your Lordships are concerned in these appeals. . . . So often those who are directly affected by this conduct lack both the inclination and the resources to do anything about it. Above all, they have been intimidated and they are afraid. They know that they risk becoming targets for further anti-social behaviour if they turn to the law for their protection. It is unrealistic to expect them to seek the protection of an injunction under the civil law. Reports to the police about criminal conduct are likely to result in their having to give evidence. In this situation the opportunity which civil proceedings provide for the use of hearsay evidence is a valuable safeguard. It greatly increases the prospect of persuading those who are likely to be exposed to further anti-social behaviour to co-operate with the authorities in protecting them from such conduct."

6-010 That the ASBO has no particular penal consequences in itself was an important criterion in that determination. At paras 75 to 76 of Lord Hope's judgment:

"The defendants say that prohibitions which banish the defendant from an area of the city where he lives, or which expose him to harsher penalties than he would normally face if he commits an offence, have all the characteristics of a penalty for the anti-social acts which he is found to have committed. An anti-social behaviour order may well restrict the freedom of the defendant to do what he wants and to go where he pleases. But these restrictions are imposed for preventative reasons, not as punishment. The test that has to be applied under section 1(6) is confined to what is necessary for the purpose of protecting persons from further anti-social acts by the defendant. The court is not being required, nor indeed is it permitted, to consider what an appropriate sanction would be for his past conduct."

The key aim of prevention was referred to by Lord Steyn, at para.22: **6-011**

"The starting point is that in proceedings under the first part of section 1 [that is of the Crime and Disorder Act 1998] the Crown Prosecution Service is not involved at all. At that stage there is no formal accusation of a breach of criminal law. The proceedings are initiated by the civil process of a complaint. Under section 1(1)(a) all that has to be established is that the person has acted 'in an anti-social manner, that is to say, in a manner that caused or was likely to cause harassment, alarm or distress to one or more persons not of the same household as himself'. This is an objective inquiry, mens rea as an ingredient of particular offences need not be proved. It is unnecessary to establish crime liability. The true purpose of the proceedings is preventative."

These remarks were considered recently by the Court of Appeal. See Maurice **6-012**
Kay L.J., in *Lonergan*, at para.12[13]:

"However, when a prohibition is imposed as part of an ASBO, even though it restricts freedom of movement in the same way and possibly for a more prolonged period of time, its purpose is not to punish but is preventative and protective. It is implicit in the above passages from Lord Hope's speech that, because the content and duration of an ASBO is conditioned solely by what is necessary for the purpose of protecting members of the public from further anti-social behaviour, the court is not required to consider what sentence would have been imposed, whether by way of curfew order or otherwise, if it had been sentencing the same person for one or more of the same acts which justify the making of an ASBO."

Hooper L.J. in *Boness*,[14] at paras 28 to 29: **6-013**

"Following a finding that the offender has acted in an anti-social manner (whether or not the act constitutes a criminal offence), the test for making an order prohibiting the offender from doing something is one of necessity. Each separate order prohibiting a person from doing a specified thing must be necessary to protect persons from further anti-social acts by him. Any order should therefore be tailor-made for the individual offender, not designed on a word processor for use in every case. The court must ask itself when considering any specific order prohibiting the offender from doing something, "Is this order necessary to protect persons in any place in England and Wales from further anti-social acts by him? The purpose of an ASBO is not to punish an offender (see *Lonergan*, para.10). This principle follows from the requirement that the order must be necessary to protect persons from further anti-social acts by him. The use of an ASBO to punish an offender is thus unlawful. We were told during the course of argument that the imposition of an ASBO is sometimes sought by the defendant's advocate at the sentencing stage, hoping that the court might make an ASBO order as an alternative to prison or other sanction. A court must not allow itself to be diverted in this way—indeed it may be better to decide the appropriate sentence and then move on to consider whether an ASBO

---

[13] *Lonergan v Lewes Crown Court, Brighton & Hove City Council, Secretary of State for the Home Department* [2005] 1 W.L.R. 2570.
[14] [2005] WL 2673805.

should be made or not after sentence has been passed, albeit at the same hearing."

Procedure

The Defendant

6-014   Section 1(1) of the 1998 Act provides that an ASBO may be obtained against any person aged 10 or over.

Relevant Authorities

6-015   The 1998 Act uses the term "relevant authority" to describe those persons who can set down an application. They are set out in s.1(1A). Until it was amended in 2002, only the council of a local government area (defined in s.1(12) in relation to England, as district or London borough, the City of London, the Isle of Wight and the Isles of Scilly and, in relation to Wales, a county or county borough) and the chief officer of police could apply for an ASBO.[15] The list was extended to include the chief constable of the British Transport Police Force and any person registered under s.1 of the Housing Act 1996 as a social landlord who provides or manages any houses or hostel in a local government area. Applications by the British Transport Police and the registered social landlords must relate to the premises for which they are responsible. Registered social landlords may apply for orders against residents and non-residents; and they, and the British Transport Police, are required to consult the local authority and police before making the application. This subsection was further amended by the Anti-Social Behaviour Act 2003 so as to include a housing action trust established under s.62 of the Housing Act 1988 and county councils and county councils.[16] It is proposed that the Environment Agency and Transport for London be added to the list of relevant authorities in the Respect Action Plan.[17] By way of s.86 of the Anti-Social Behaviour Act 2003, s.1C(3)— orders on conviction of an offence to prevent anti-social acts—of the 1998 Act was amended to allow for applications to be made by the CPS. It also amends s.3(2) of the Director of Public Prosecutions Act 1986 so that the bringing of applications under section 1C is one of the Director's functions.

Relevant Persons

6-016   The term "relevant person" is defined in s.1(1B). It means:

"(a) in relation to a relevant authority falling within paragraph (a) of subsection (1A), persons within the local government area of that council;[18]
(aa) in relation to a relevant authority falling within paragraph (aa) of subsection (1A0, persons within the county council;
(b) in relation to a relevant authority falling within paragraph (b) of that subsection, persons within the police area[19];

---

[15] In *R. (on the application of Chief Constable of West Midlands) v Birmingham Magistrates' Court*, [2003] Crim. L.R. 37, it was held that it was Chief Constable was entitled to delegate to his officers his power under s.1 of the Act to consult a local authority and bring an application for an anti social behaviour order.
[16] Anti-Social Behaviour Act 2003, s.85(2).
[17] *Together—Tackling Anti-Social Behaviour* at *www.together.gov.uk/article*
[18] Local authority applicants.
[19] Police authority applicants.

(c) in relation to a relevant authority falling within paragraph (c) of that subsection—

(i) persons who are on or likely to be on policed premises in a local government area; or
(ii) persons who are in the vicinity of or likely to be in the vicinity of such premises[20];

(d) in relation to a relevant authority falling within paragraph (d) or (e) of that subsection—

(i) persons who are residing in or who are otherwise on or likely to be on premises provided or managed by that authority; or
(ii) persons who are in the vicinity of or likely to be in the vicinity of such premises."[21]

This section was amended by s.139 of the Serious Organised Crime and Police Act 2005 by way of the addition of a new subsection, subs.(2). It provides that the Secretary of State may by order:

"(a) provide that a person or body of any other description specified in the order is, in such cases and circumstances as may be prescribed by the order, to be a relevant authority for the purposes of such of sections 1 above and 1B, 1CA and 1E below as are specified in the order; and
(b) prescribe the description of persons who are to be "relevant persons" in relation to that person or body"

The Relevant Court—The Magistrates' Court

There are three courts in which an ASBO can be made: the magistrates' court, **6-017** the County Court and the Crown Court. In the magistrates' court, the application may be made by complaint to a magistrates' court whose commission area includes the local government area or police area concerned.[22] Under subs.(4) if, on such an application, it is proved that the conditions mentioned in subs.(1) above are fulfilled, the magistrates' court may make an order under this section which prohibits the defendant from doing anything described in the order. The prohibitions that may be imposed by an anti-social behaviour order are those necessary for the purpose of protecting persons (whether relevant persons or persons elsewhere in England and Wales) from further anti-social acts by the defendant.[23] The youth court has no civil jurisdiction so all applications concerning children will be heard in the magistrates' court. The application must be as a complaint in writing in a prescribed form.[24] Under s.1(3) of the 1998 Act, the application should be made in the magistrates' court whose area includes the police or local government area in which the applicant resides. The summons must be given to the defendant in person or sent by first class post to his last-known address. If the proposed defendant is a child, a person with parental responsibility should also receive a copy of the summons. Section 53 of the Magistrates' Courts Act 1980 provides that on hearing the complaint, the court will, if the respondent appears, state the substance of the complaint and, if contested, hear evidence and the parties and then either make the order or dismiss the application.

---

[20] British Transport Police applicants.
[21] Registered social landlord applicants and housing actions trusts.
[22] The Crime and Disorder Act 1998, s.1(3).
[23] *ibid.*, s.1(6).
[24] The summons forms will be set out within the Magistrates' Courts (Anti-Social Behaviour Orders) Rules 2002 (SI 2002/2784).

6-018   Home office guidance on ASBOs provides that the lead individual in charge of the case should arrange for a summons form to be completed, with a copy retained on the application file, and for the defendant to be served with the following: the summons; a copy of the completed ASBO application; documentary evidence of statutory consultation; guidance on how the defendant may obtain legal advice and representation; any notice of hearsay evidence; details of evidence in support of the application as agreed with the applicant agency's solicitor; a warning to the defendant that it is an offence to pervert the course of justice and that witness intimidation is liable to lead to prosecution. Wherever possible the lead officer in charge should ensure that service of the summons is made on the defendant in person. If personal service is not possible, the summons should be served by post as soon as possible to the last known address. Where a child or a young person is concerned, a person with parental responsibility must also receive a copy of the summons. This could be a local authority social worker in the case of a looked-after child as well as, or instead of, the parent.

6-019   Where an application was made to a magistrates' court for an antisocial behaviour order or for such an order to be varied or discharged, and the person against whom the order was sought was under 18, the magistrates constituting the court should normally be qualified to sit in the youth court. However, applications for interim orders, including those made without notice, could be listed before magistrates who were not so qualified. Further, the direction would not apply where it was not practicable to constitute a bench in accordance with the direction, particularly where to do so would result in a delayed hearing.[25]

The Relevant Court—The County Court

6-020   The Police Reform Act 2002 amended the 1998 Act in order to allow for ASBOs to be made by a county court. Under subs.(1) and (2) of s.1B of the 1998 Act, if a relevant party to proceedings in the county court considers that a party to those proceedings is a person in relation to whom it would be reasonable for it to make an application under s.1, it may make an application in those proceedings for an order under subs.(4). Even if it is not an party to such proceedings, then, under subs.(3), if it considers that a party to those proceedings is a person in relation to whom it would be reasonable for it to make an application under s.1, a relevant applicant may apply to be joined to those proceedings to enable it to apply for an order under subs.(4) and, if it is so joined, may apply for such an order. Subsection (4) provides that if, on an application for an order under this subsection, it is proved that the conditions mentioned in s.1(1) are fulfilled as respects that other party, the court may make an order which prohibits him from doing anything described in the order. It may also be subsequently varied on application.[26] The order is the same as regards content, duration and breach as in the case of an order made by the magistrates. Section 1B was further amended by s.85(5) of the Anti-Social Behaviour Act 2003. There are three new subsections, 1B(3A) to (3C). Under the new s.1B(3A), where the relevant authority is a party to the principal proceedings and considered that a person who is not a party to the proceedings has acted in an anti-social manner and their anti-social acts are material in relation to the principal proceedings, then, under the new s.1B(3B), they may make an application for that person to be joined to the principal proceedings to enable an order to be made in relation to that person and to apply

---

[25] Practice Direction (QBD: Magistrates Courts: Anti Social Behaviour Orders: Composition of Benches) [2006] 1 W.L.R. 636.
[26] The Crime and Disorder Act 1998, s.1B(5).

for order under s.1B(4). However, under s.1B(3C), a person must not be joined to proceedings under subs.(3B) unless his anti-social acts are material to the principal proceedings.

Rules of Court

CPR Pt 65.23 deals with applications by a relevant authority to join a person **6-021** to the principal proceedings. An application under s.1B(3B) of the 1998 Act, by a relevant authority which is a party to the principal proceedings, to join a person to the principal proceedings must be made in accordance with s.I of Pt 19; in the same application notice as the application for an order under s.1B(4) of the 1998 Act against the person; and as soon as possible after the relevant authority considers that the criteria in s.1B(3A) of the 1998 Act are met. The application notice must contain the relevant authority's reasons for claiming that the person's anti-social acts are material in relation to the principal proceedings; and details of the anti-social acts alleged; and should normally be made on notice to the person against whom the order is sought. Where the relevant authority is not a principal party to the proceedings, then, under CPR Pt 65.24, an application under s.1B(3) of the 1998 Act to be made a party must be made in accordance with s.I of CPR Pt 19 (substitution and addition of parties) and the application to be made a party and the application for an order under s.1B(4) of the 1998 Act must be made in the same application. Again, the applications must be made as soon as possible after the authority becomes aware of the principal proceedings; and should normally be made on notice to the person against whom the order is sought. Under CPR Pt 65.25, an application for an order under s.1B(4) of the 1998 Act must be accompanied by written evidence, which must include evidence that s.1E of the 1998 Act has been complied with. CPR 65.26 deals with interim applications: An application for an interim order under s.1D of the 1998 Act must be made in accordance with CR Pt 25. The application should normally be made in the claim form or application notice seeking the order; and on notice to the person against whom the order is sought.

Under the relevant practice direction, the order under s.1B(4) or an interim order under s.1D of the 1998 Act must be served personally on the defendant. **6-022** Except as provided in para.13.3, an application by a relevant authority under s.1B(3B) of the 1998 Act to join a person to the principal proceedings may only be made against a person aged 18 or over. However, under para.13.3, there is a pilot scheme to operate from October 1, 2004 to September 30, 2006 in the county courts specified below, under which a relevant authority may apply under s.1B(3B) of the 1998 Act to join a child to the principal proceedings; and if that child is so joined, apply for an order under s.1B(4) of the 1998 Act against him. The county courts in which the pilot scheme shall operate are: Bristol, Central London, Clerkenwell, Dewsbury, Huddersfield, Leicester, Manchester, Oxford, Tameside, Wigan and Wrexham. The Practice Direction refers to the provisions of Pt 21 and its practice direction: in particular as to the requirement for a child to have a litigation friend unless the court makes an order under r.21.2(3), and as to the procedure for appointment of a litigation friend. The Official Solicitor may be invited to act as litigation friend where there is no other willing and suitable person. Rule 21.3(2)(b) shall not apply to an application under the pilot scheme, and subpara.(6) shall apply instead. A relevant authority may not, without the permission of the court, take any step in an application to join a child to the principal proceedings, except filing and serving its application notice; and applying for the appointment of a litigation friend under r.21.6, unless the child has a litigation friend.

The Criminal Courts—Section 1C (the "CRASBO")

6-023   Section 1C(1) (introduced by the Police Reform Act 2002) applies where a person (the "offender") is convicted of a relevant offence. Under s.1C(2), if the court considers:

> "(a) that the offender has acted, at any time since the commencement date, in an anti-social manner, that is to say in a manner that caused or was likely to cause harassment, alarm or distress to one or more persons not of the same household as himself; and
>   (b) that an order under this section is necessary to protect persons in any place in England and Wales from further anti-social acts by him,"

it may make an order which prohibits the offender from doing anything described in the order. The court may make an order under this section if the prosecutor asks it to do so or if the court thinks it is appropriate to do so.[27] Section 86(2) of the Anti-Social Behaviour Act 2003 also amended this section by inserting subs.(3A) and (3B). Subsection 3A provides that, for the purpose of deciding whether to make an order under this section, the court may consider evidence led by the prosecution and the defence; and, under subs.(3B), it is immaterial whether evidence led in pursuance of subs.(3A) would have been admissible in the proceedings in which the offender was convicted. Subsection (4) provides that an order under this section shall not be made except: (a) in addition to a sentence imposed in respect of the relevant offence; or (b) in addition to an order discharging him conditionally. The order takes effect on the day on which it is made, but the court may provide in any such order that such requirements of the order as it may specify shall, during any period when the offender is detained in legal custody, be suspended until his release from that custody.[28] An offender subject to an order under this section may apply to the court which made it for it to be varied or discharged.[29] However, under subs.(8), no application may be made under subs.(6) for the discharge of an order before the end of the period of two years beginning with the day on which the order takes effect. Subsection (9) provides that subs.(7), (10) and (11) of s.1 apply for the purposes of the making and effect of orders made by virtue of this section as they apply for the purposes of the making and effect of anti-social behaviour orders. An order made on conviction of a criminal offence may be applied for by any agency which is concerned in the case and would be entitled to apply for an ASBO in the form of a request to the court that the order be imposed in addition to the sentence; alternatively, the court may make the order of its own volition. The Youth Court has no civil jurisdiction, so applications for orders for respondents under the age of 18 will be heard in the magistrates' court, except where the youth court is asked to impose an order on conviction. Section 86(3) of the Anti-Social Behaviour Act 2003 contains a further amendments to s.1C of the 1998 Act by adding a further subsections. Under subs.(9A) of s.1C, the council for the local government area in which a person in respect of whom an anti-social behaviour order has been made resides or appears to reside may bring proceedings under subsection (9) above for a breach of subs.(2) above.

6-024   In *Anti-Social Behaviour Orders: A Guide to Law and Procedure in the Magistrates' Court*,[30] guidance is offered as to the exercise of this power by magistrates. Reliance may be placed upon the current conviction without

---

[27] Amended by s.38(1) of the Anti-Social Behaviour Act 2003.
[28] The Crime and Disorder Act 1998, s.1C(5).
[29] *ibid.*, s.1C(6).
[30] Justices' Clerks' Society, April 2004.

more. An offence may be so serious and inherently anti-social that the court will consider imposing prohibitions on activities associated with the crime. The example of criminal damage or assault is offered. The primary consideration, according to the guidance, is whether an order is necessary to protect persons from further anti-social acts. For this it may require a pattern of anti-social behaviour to be established, and evidence beyond that associated with the current offence would be required. This may consist of evidence disclosed by virtue of previous convictions,[31] or other evidence properly adduced. A pattern of anti-social behaviour could be established, for example, by evidence that the offender has targeted a particular family, harassed members of the community, or targeted their behaviour in a particular area. The legislation, it is observed, does not require a 'nexus' between the evidence to be adduced in support of an order on conviction and the current offence. However, there may be circumstances where an ASBO, under s.1 of the 1998 Act, would be more appropriate, for example where there is no nexus to either the current conviction or previous convictions and no link to a wider pattern of anti-social behaviour. Where a defendant pleads guilty to an offence, but disputes the facts as presented by the prosecution, then if those facts would, if established in evidence, form the basis for a post-conviction order, a "Newton" hearing may be held to establish the facts. The court should be cautious when considering applications that relate to offenders with defined medical/mental problems that give rise to the anti-social behaviour in issue.

Procedural Fairness

Courts will expect applicants to observe elementary rules of procedural fairness, particularly when breach of such an ASBO exposed a person to potential criminal penalties. In *C v Sunderland Youth Court and Northumbria Police*,[32] the claimant, 15 at the time, had a lengthy criminal record. In January 2003, he committed further offences. He was dealt with at different times for different offences. He appeared before the court again in May 2003 and was sentenced to a 12 month supervision order with ISSP, and disqualified him from driving for a period of two years. The magistrates also made a parenting order for three months. However, while the Crown reminded the magistrates of their powers under s.1C of the 1998 Act, they declined to impose an ASBO as part of the sentence. There were residual offences dealt with at a later hearing in June, at which the Crown reminded the court again of its powers to make an ASBO. However, this time, the court were not told that the earlier court had been reminded of its powers under s.1C on 8 May, but had decided not to make such an order on that date. The second court imposed 24 hours reparation and an anti-social behaviour order for two years. The Administrative Court granted leave to apply for judicial review. It was held that there was no proper explanation as to the magistrates' reasons for making the order, and in particular, why they considered it appropriate to make an order in June when the previous court had not made such an order, and the claimant's anti-social behaviour having been fully explained to them in May. While s.1C did not prescribe any particular procedure for making an order, whether the proceedings are civil or criminal, it was common ground that, in making an order, the magistrates' court must act fairly and have regard to all relevant considerations. What fairness requires and what considerations are relevant will depend upon the circumstances of each particular case. In addition to the requirement to act fairly, there was the elementary requirement that

6-025

---

[31] In which case, the guidance notes, further and better particulars of the previous convictions will normally be required.

[32] [2003] EWHC 2385 Admin.

there should be clarity as to the basis for, and scope of, any order made by the magistrates under s.1C, particularly if breach of such an order exposed a person to potential criminal penalties. The procedure adopted by the court in the present case failed to meet these criteria and was said to be wholly unsatisfactory: the magistrates had been invited to consider whether to make an order under s.1C when the claimant was sentenced for numerous offences including causing harassment, alarm, distress and criminal damage in May. After having had matters fully explained to them by the prosecutor, the court clearly decided not to make an order under s.1C on that occasion. The court had a discretion to make such an order at the June hearing as s.1C applied if a relevant offence was committed. The offence did not itself have to be of an anti-social character and it was sufficient that it was an offence and it has been committed after December 2002. The claimant had committed an offence and therefore s.1C applied and the court could make an order if it was satisfied that the conditions in subs.(2), paras (a) and (b) were met. Paragraph (a) was met if the court was satisfied that the claimant had acted in an anti-social manner at any time since December 2, 2002. However, the discretion conferred by s.1C, although broad, was not unfettered: it must be exercised fairly, reasonably and having regard to all relevant circumstances. That it had been decided not to make an order, despite the claimant's past history of anti-social behaviour from December 2002 up to that date, was a relevant consideration. Whatever may be the extent of the general duty upon magistrates to give reasons for their decisions, in the particular circumstances of this case, fairness to the claimant required the court to give him an explanation, however brief, as to why it was now considered appropriate to make an order under s.1C. Consistency in the exercise of discretionary powers was an important aspect of fairness. If, having had the matter fully explained to them on 8 May, the magistrates decided not to make a s.1C order, then absent any further evidence justifying the making of such an order, it would not be prima facie reasonable to make one in June. The only change of circumstances since May was the two matters for which the claimant was being sentenced in June. Since the magistrates have chosen not to give any reasons for their decision, the extent to which they revisited the anti-social conduct evidenced by the offences for which the claimant was sentenced on 8 May was unclear. It may be a case where the addition of a relatively minor offence might finally tip the balance in favour of making an order, when previously the balance had been struck the other way. However, the offences committed in January 2003 were committed well before the claimant was sentenced to a 12 month supervision with 90 days ISSP on 8 May. The evidence from the Youth Offending Service was that the claimant was complying fully with that order which was an order intended to address his offending behaviour. In these circumstances, it was not clear why, no order having been thought necessary in May, it could reasonably have been concluded that an order was necessary at the June hearing to protect persons from further anti-social acts by the defendant. Elementary fairness requires a court, if it proposes to make an order of its own motion, to indicate the basis on which it provisionally considers an order may be appropriate, and the material on which it proposes to rely so that the person potentially liable can make meaningful submissions as to why the order should not be made at all or should not be made in the form provisionally proposed by the court. That did not happen in the present case.

6-026   See also *R. v P*,[33] the facts of which are set out below at para.6-044. The Court of Appeal said that, even if an ASBO was appropriate, they had grave misgivings as to the procedures adopted in the Crown Court. First, when applying for the order, counsel then appearing for the prosecution addressed

---

[33] [2004] 2 Cr. App. R. (S.) 63.

the judge for quite some time in the absence of the defendant. During that period of time, counsel asserted that the remand into custody of this defendant would indicate that the massive fall in crime in this particular area and the remanding into custody of the defendant were not matters of coincidence. The Court of Appeal commented that while it was correct that the appellant was arrested in March 2003, it was positively misleading to suggest that the reduction in the number of incidents was attributable to the appellant's arrest. Prosecuting counsel also told the judge that the claimant "liked to go to the Airport and make a thorough nuisance of himself." This was unsubstantiated by any clear evidence before the court and in any case subsequently challenged. Such an observation should plainly not have taken place in the absence of the defendant and in the absence of plain evidence to substantiate it. The totality of the proceedings should have been in the presence of the appellant. Further, it was submitted that the procedure adopted in the Crown Court was defective, in that the appellant was not given any opportunity to dispute the allegations contained in the witness statement of the police officer who had brought the application. It was plainly the duty of a court making such an order to identify matters relied upon by the party seeking the order, to give the defendant an opportunity to dispute the allegation, and to record the findings of fact in the order. Complaint was also made that the order, as signed by the judge and as served upon the appellant, differed from that pronounced in open court. The order served was without limit as to time, whereas the order made in open court was for a duration of two years post release. Further, in the order served, some conditions were expressed to be suspended until the appellant's release from custody; others were not. In open court no such distinction was made. The court order must accurately represent what is said by the judge in open court. Further, it was said that no attempt was made by the judge to explain to the appellant the requirement of the order. Again, the Court said, this submission is unanswerable. Accordingly, the Court set out some basic rules:

"In our judgment the following principles clearly emerge:

(1) The test for making an order is one of necessity to protect the public from further anti-social acts by the offender.
(2) The terms of the order must be precise and capable of being understood by the offender.
(3) The findings of fact giving rise to the making of the order must be recorded.
(4) The order must be explained to the offender.
(5) The exact terms of the order must be pronounced in open court and the written order must accurately reflect the order as pronounced."

However, the prosecution is also entitled to a fair hearing. In *R. v Manchester* **6-027**
Crown Court, Ex p. Oldham MBC,[34] the claimant local authority sought judicial review of the defendant Crown Court's decision to quash an anti social behaviour order against a convicted offender. He had appealed against the order to the Crown Court contending that it was excessive and unreasonably restrictive. Paragraph (b) of the order, prohibited him from congregating in any public place in the open air in a group of more than two individuals in addition to himself, save for waiting for a bus at a bus stop or attending any activity arranged by the Probation Service. The notice of appeal stated as a ground that the order was excessive and unreasonably restrictive and did not accurately reflect the nature of the allegations against him which gave rise to the application for an ASBO. The terms of the order, the Court of Appeal held, were extraordinarily wide and restrictive. The local authority, which had applied for

[34] [2005] WL 1185469.

the order, accepted that the magistrates' court had made it too broad. However, it argued that the order should be made less restrictive rather than be set aside. The local authority asked the Crown Court to adjourn the case because its counsel could only provide the court with part of the information it required about the offender's history. The Crown Court bench retired to consider the application to adjourn, but when the court reconvened it allowed the appeal and discharged the order. The local authority contended that the Crown Court's decision to give judgment without hearing the facts or inviting submissions constituted procedural impropriety and a breach of natural justice. The Court of Appeal held, granting the application, that, although the local authority could be criticised for not having provided the full facts of the case to its representative at the appeal, the Crown Court's refusal to allow the local authority, which was in the position of a prosecutor, to present its case on the evidence available constituted procedural impropriety and a breach of natural justice. The prosecution had a right to be heard and there was a public interest that, save in exceptional circumstances, it should be heard.

6-028 There is also a duty to give reasons or at any rate proper reasons whether granting the order or not. In *Boorman*, Calvert-Smith J. said that Art.6 of the European Convention on Human Rights placed a duty on courts to give reasons for their decisions. In general terms, however, it was desirable that when hearing an ASBO application, whichever way the decision goes, that reasons were given for it. In a criminal trial in the Crown Court the jury did not give reasons for their decision, whether it was an acquittal or a conviction, and there were good reasons for that. In the magistrates' court in a criminal trial it was more desirable, since the tribunal which convicts was also going to be the tribunal that sentences, that it gave reasons for its decision so that the appropriate sentence could be passed in view of the findings of fact that had been made. So far as an acquittal was concerned, the normal procedure was that no reasoned judgment would be given. However, even in this kind of matter, there were two parties to the case. Effectively standing behind the chief constable in this case are the members of the public. They had an entitlement to reasons in the average case if the application was refused.

Time Limits in the Magistrates Court

6-029 Section 127(1) of the Magistrates' Courts Act 1980 provides:

> "Except as otherwise expressly provided by any enactment and subject to subsection (2) below, a magistrates' court shall not try an information or hear a complaint unless the information was laid, or the complaint made, within 6 months from the time when the offence was committed, or the matter of complaint arose."

Section 127 was considered in *Stevens v South East Surrey Magistrates' Court, Surrey Police*,[35] in which permission for leave for judicial review was granted in respect of a decision of magistrates to hear evidence which concerned events which took place more than six months before the information. The judgment also contains useful comments on the nature of the evaluative process, as described by Lord Steyn in *McCann*, with respect to evidence that would, were they criminal proceedings, be completely inadmissible.

6-030 In the *Stevens* case, the Surrey Police sought to rely on documentary hearsay evidence of 30 alleged incidents of anti-social behaviour, eight of them within the six months period and 22 before it, the oldest going back to some three years before the hearing itself. The evidence took the form of police incident

---

[35] [2004] EWHC 1456 (Admin).

reports, computerised crime reports and victim statements. There was also a witness statement from a neighbourhood specialist police sergeant, responsible for policing the area, who had collated all that material and had interviewed victims and complainants of the defendant's behaviour. Many of them, he stated, were unwilling to attend court for fear of reprisals. The police indicated that they were not relying on evidence of the "out-of-time" incidents as similar fact evidence in support of the eight "within-time" incidents and that they did not put them forward as essential background evidence to those incidents; they relied on them solely to support that part of their case going to the necessity, under s.1(1)(b) of the 1998, for making an order. The defendant applicant sought to have the out of time evidence excluded, arguing that the police were wrongly putting the "out-of-time" incidents on the same basis as the eight "within-time" incidents, though none of the "out-of-time" incidents had ever been proved by, for example, certificates of conviction, civil proceedings or by way of admission. The only way in which they could have had probative value, he submitted, was for the magistrates to try each of the allegations and they had no jurisdiction to do so by virtue of s.127. He also argued that to admit such evidence, especially in hearsay form, was in any event unfair to the appellant because he was in no position to meet such stale allegations. The magistrates, rejecting these submissions, ruled that it would be a matter, of weight for them when considering the evidence and they proceeded to try the matter, taking into consideration all the documentary evidence on the 30 incidents on which the police relied. They found the eight "within-time" incidents proved and made an anti-social behaviour order in respect of them of two-and-a-half years, subject to specified prohibitions. The claim was dismissed. The Divisional Court held that s.127 was concerned with jurisdiction, not with the admissibility of evidence once magistrates have properly accepted jurisdiction, as they had done here in relation to the last eight of the 30 incidents on which the police relied when applying for the order.

Secondly, where the matter was one of a continuing nature, as that alleged here, the section appears to operate differently according to whether the proceedings are begun by information or complaint. In the case of an information the weight of authority suggested that time runs from the date of each day, charged as a separate offence. There were two basic constituents for making an anti-social behaviour order: first, harassment whether by a single incident or course of conduct; and second, and importantly in the context of this appeal, a necessity to make the order in order to protect others. It was only if the magistrates were satisfied that the total course of anti-social behaviour they had found proved brought about such necessity that the basis for making an order was complete.
6-031

Thirdly, the House of Lords held in *McCann* that an application for an anti-social behaviour order was a civil proceeding. Nevertheless, as the House also held it engaged the right to a fair trial under Art.6.1, the use of hearsay evidence, admissible in such proceedings under the Civil Evidence Act 1995, was not unfair and, therefore, did not violate that right; but given the serious nature of such proceedings, the court should not find that a defendant has acted in an anti-social manner, unless it was satisfied to the criminal standard of proof that he has acted in that way. Hearsay evidence depending on its legal probativeness might be sufficient to meet such standard of proof. There was a distinction between the first constituent under s.1(1)(a) of a finding of anti-social behaviour and the second in s.1(1)(b) as to the necessity for making an order, with the result that the latter does not involve a standard of proof but an exercise of judgment and evaluation. Lord Steyn said that the distinction between magistrates' function when determining the facts of such behaviour and what, if anything, it was necessary to do about it comes into play did not depend on proof but was an evaluative judgment. In making that judgment it
6-032

made sense for them to look at what has happened in the past, just as courts do in addition to relying on reports when considering sentence in criminal cases where it may be necessary to form a view whether the convicted man is likely to be a danger to the public. This deepened on the quality of such information, how relevant and reliable it was to the issue of the need for protection of others and, if so, the nature and range of prohibitions to secure that protection. An important factor going both to relevance, and hence admissibility, and possibly to reliability, going to its weight, was the age of the earlier "out-of-time" incidents to which magistrates are asked to have regard on this issue. If they were very old and amounted to only a single or very few incidents they might have had little relevance or weight however reliable the evidence of them may be, looking at each incident on its own. On the other hand, if, as here, they indicated a solid and consistent line of anti-social behaviour beginning possibly well out-of-time and ending within-time they would usually be highly relevant to the decision whether an order is, in the circumstances, necessary, and to what form it should take. As to reliability, it was plain that such orders are most usually sought as a result of complaints from vulnerable and or frightened neighbours who had a reasonably based fear of reprisals if they volunteer to give evidence or even provide witness statements that could identify them. In this connection, it was interesting to note from the neighbourhood police officer's witness statement that he felt it necessary to ask that the applicant should not view a CCTV camera tape of some of his behaviour which was the subject of the "in time" conduct, lest it reveal its location and lead to reprisals against the occupiers of the property where the camera had been fixed. It was clearly for this reason that documentary hearsay evidence was held to be admissible in proof of both constituents of an anti-social behaviour order. The only question was whether, in the individual circumstances of each case, it was fair to admit such evidence of "out-of-time" conduct or what, if any, weight to give to it once admitted in order to persuade magistrates of the necessity for making an order if the "within-time" anti-social behaviour is proved to the criminal standard.

6-033   The Court also observed that s.127 related only to proceedings for an anti-social behaviour order in the magistrates courts. There is provision in the 1998 Act for County and Crown courts to make an ASBO and in neither of those cases would any time limit of the sort provided for the magistrates courts by section 127 apply. Therefore, it would be curious if that section were to have an additional role as an "evidential filter" for conduct outside the six months' limit denied to the county court and crown court. In this case, the magistrates were entitled to admit the documentary hearsay evidence of the "out-of-time" incidents for the purpose of considering the necessity to make an order despite the age of many of them. They revealed a fairly regular and consistent pattern of "out-of-time" anti-social behaviour, continuing seamlessly into the several course of conduct "within-time" incidents. In the various and sometimes overlapping evidential forms they were capable of being regarded by the magistrates as relevant and as reliable indicators of what was needed by way of protection of the public.

6-034   See also *McGrath*,[36] in which the appellant appealed against a two year ASBO imposed on him following his guilty plea to theft. The appellant had been convicted of 112 offences, mainly for dishonesty, over a 10 year period. The British Transport Police had identified the geographical areas where his offending had occurred. To take this and the nature of the appellant's offending into account, the ASBO included a term preventing him from entering any car parks, a term preventing him from trespassing and a term preventing him from having any tool or implement which could be used for the

[36] [2005] 2 Cr. App. R. (S.) 85.

purposes of breaking into motor vehicles. The appellant submitted that the judge had not been entitled to take into account his behaviour prior to the commencement of the 1998 Act and that an ASBO was not applicable to an offence of dishonesty. The Court held that, allowing the appeal in part, for the purposes of determining the necessity for an ASBO, the 1998 Act required an offender to have acted anti-socially after the commencement date. However, it did not preclude the judge from considering the totality of the offender's behaviour, both before and after the commencement date. To read a limitation in the 1998 Act would be wrong and would run contrary to the purpose of the legislation. In the instant case, the judge had not erred as he had been entitled to have regard to the totality of M's conduct both before and after the commencement date. There was no restriction in principle preventing the imposition of an ASBO in relation to vehicle crime. However, an ASBO should be approached with a proper degree of caution and should not be imposed lightly. In principle, the judge had been justified in imposing the ASBO.

Notice of Hearsay

In *Wadmore*,[37] the two appellants appealed against anti-social behaviour orders made against them. They had been convicted of robbery and sentenced to 12 months' detention and training. They were 14 and 15 years old at the time of the offence. Each had also been made subject to a five year ASBO under s.1C(2) of the Crime and Disorder Act 1998, to start on release from custody. The ASBO application form was unsigned and undated, with no indications of how and when it had been served, and it stated an intention to rely on hearsay evidence without mentioning the witness statements to be relied on. The Court of Appeal, allowing the appeal, that there were no clear rules to follow in serving and adducing evidence, especially hearsay evidence, in support of applications for ASBOs in the Crown Court. Proceedings for ASBOs in magistrates' courts were civil, not criminal in nature, and governed by the Magistrates' Courts (Hearsay Evidence in Civil Proceedings) Rules 1999. Proceedings in the Crown Court under s.1C of the 1998 Act constituted civil, not criminal proceedings. However, the Magistrates' Hearsay Rules were not the correct procedural rules to follow in relation to adducing hearsay evidence in support of an ASBO in the Crown Court. Although the Criminal Procedure Rules 2005 were stated to apply to all criminal cases in the magistrates' courts and the Crown Court, as ASBOs were civil in nature it was not clear that those Rules applied to such proceedings. On the other hand, the civil procedure rules did not govern that type of application. For the purposes of the instant case, the court presumed that hearsay evidence was capable of being adduced in the Crown Court in support of such an application under s.1C of the 1998 Act because the proceedings were civil in nature and so subject to the provisions of the Civil Evidence Act 1995. Under s.1(1) and 1(2) of the 1995 Act, hearsay evidence should not be excluded on the ground that it was hearsay. Because of the significant restrictions that could be placed on liberty it was particularly important that procedural fairness was scrupulously observed. A defendant had to have a proper opportunity to consider prosecution evidence in support of the ASBO and as the Magistrates' Hearsay Rules provided for that, the court would presume that, by analogy, the principles set out in those Rules should have been followed in the instant case. It was not clear when and how the appellant's were given notice of the ASBO application and the material in support of it. There was no indication that any procedure analogous to the Magistrates' Hearsay Rules had been used, and the case summary attached to the application did not set out the particular facts

6-035

---

[37] [2006] WL 755486.

on which the CPS intended to rely. Accordingly, apart from the facts of the robbery offence, the judge was in no position to make findings of particular facts to support his general conclusion that the appellants were guilty of anti-social behaviour, and it was impossible to uphold his conclusion that the order was necessary pursuant to s.1C of the 1998 Act. It would have been wrong in principle to impose an ASBO taking effect on release if the basis for it had been merely the facts of the robbery offence. The Court stated that, in future, it was imperative that the prosecution identified the particular facts, as opposed to evidence, said to constitute anti-social behaviour. If the offender accepted those facts they should be put in writing in the same way as a basis of plea. If not accepted, the facts would have to be proved to the criminal standard before they could be acted upon. The judge should state his findings of fact expressly and record them on the order.

The Essential Nature of the ASBO Proceedings

6-036   The applicant, the relevant authority, must prove that the respondent's conduct is of the type that falls within s.1(1)(a) and (b) (and 1C): that is, that it is trigger conduct. That is the statutory test and it has two parts. Under s.1(1)(a), the person has acted in an anti-social manner: that is, in a manner that caused or was likely to cause harassment, alarm or distress to one or more persons not in his household; and under s.1(1)(b), an order is necessary to protect persons in the local government area in which the harassment, alarm or distress was caused or likely to be caused from further anti-social acts by him. It was stated in the 1997 consultation paper that ASBOs were to be civil proceedings so that the applicant only needed to prove its case to the civil standard of proof. The reason for this was that the government considered that one of the main problems with the existing criminal law was the difficulty in proving the case to the criminal standard. Where the behaviour could be proved to a criminal standard, then criminal proceedings should be set down; where it could only be proved to the civil standard, then proceedings for an ASBO are appropriate.[38] However, the Attorney-General referred to the rule that, in civil cases, the more serious the allegation, the higher the standard of proof.[39]

6-037   In *McCann*,[40] the House of Lords held that ASBO proceedings were civil proceedings with the consequence that the court does not need to make a decision on a criminal standard of proof. As Lord Steyn noted, the ASBO is modelled on well-established precedents of techniques of prohibiting by statutory injunction conduct deemed to be unacceptable and making a breach of the injunction punishable by penalties: the Company Directors Disqualification Act 1986; s.14B of the Public Law Act 1986, which created criminal offences in respect of breaches; residence orders, requiring a defendant to leave a dwelling house; or non molestation orders, requiring a defendant to abstain from threatening an associated person under s.33(3) and (4) and s.42 of the Family Law Act 1996; s.152 to 153A of the Housing Act 1996; s.3 of the Protection from Harassment Act 1997. Lord Hope refers to pre-existing statutory modes in the Scots legal system in which the distinction between criminal and civil proceedings is not important. Lord Steyn remarks that all these statutory models have the same form and they were created for the same reason:

> "In all these cases the requirements for the granting of the statutory injunction depend on the criteria specified in the particular statute. The

---

[38] *Community Safety Order Consultation Paper,* September 1997, p.4.
[39] HL. Deb. vol. 585, col. 560.
[40] [2003] 1 A.C. 787.

unifying element is, however, the use of the civil remedy of an injunction to prohibit conduct considered to be utterly unacceptable, with a remedy of criminal penalties in the event of disobedience. There is no doubt that Parliament intended to adopt the model of a civil remedy of an injunction, backed up by criminal penalties, when it enacted s. 1 of the Crime and Disorder Act 1998. The view was taken that the proceedings for an anti-social behaviour order would be civil and would not attract the rigour of the inflexible and sometimes absurdly technical hearsay rule which applies in criminal cases."

Crucially, since the ASBO is a civil proceeding, the court must apply civil evidence rules and civil standards of proof. Even so, the ASBO carries with it a stigma and it exposes a respondent to the possibility of criminal proceedings if breached. Hence, it would be wrong to apply automatically civil standards of proof; and the assessment of hearsay in civil proceedings of this very serious kind is something courts are well-used to. At para.35, Lord Steyn remarks that:

"Having concluded that the proceedings in question are civil under domestic law and Article 6, it follows that the machinery of the Civil Evidence Act 1995 and the Magistrates' Courts (Hearsay Evidence in Civil Proceedings) Rules 1999 allow the introduction of such evidence under the first part of s. 1, the weight of such evidence might be limited. On the other hand, in its cumulative effect it could be cogent. It all depends on the particular facts . . . in principle it follows that the standard of proof ordinarily applicable in civil proceedings, namely the balance of probabilities, should apply. However, I agree that, given the seriousness of matters involved, at least some reference to the heightened civil standard would usually be necessary. . . But in my view pragmatism dictates that the task of magistrates should be made more straightforward by ruling that they must in all cases under s. 1 apply the criminal standard. . . The inquiry under s. 1(1)(b), namely that such an order is necessary to protect persons from further anti-social acts by him, does not involve a standard of proof: it is an exercise of judgment or evaluation. This approach should facilitate correct decision-making and should ensure consistency and predictability in this corner of the law. In coming to this conclusion I bear in mind that the use of hearsay evidence will often be of crucial importance. For my part, hearsay evidence depending on its logical probativeness is quite capable of satisfying the requirements of s. 1(1)."

There is nothing, therefore, particularly unusual about the conduct to which the ASBO is directed; it is something, as we noted earlier, that regularly appears in the criminal courts. Nor is there anything particularly unusual about the procedure of the statutory injunction and the treatment of evidence by courts in proceedings for a statutory injunction (and generally) according to civil standards of proof, heightened or otherwise, using civil rules of evidence. What is unusual and novel about the ASBO is that it merges the concepts of harassment and public order derived from the criminal law with the civil procedures of the statutory injunction. It is an injunction, but it is the public, rather than a particular individual, who is intended to benefit from it; it deals with essentially criminal conduct, but for which there are no immediate criminal consequences, as it looks forward to controlling it rather than punishing it.[41]

6-038

---

[41] See Chapter One for a review of criticisms of the "strange hybrid", at para.1-059.

Likelihood

6-039   In *Chief Constable of Lancashire v Potter*,[42] the appellant appealed against a
decision dismissing his application for an anti-social behaviour order against
the defendant, a 22 year old street prostitute who was addicted to crack
cocaine. She had been convicted of street prostitution three times and had
been seen regularly loitering for the purpose of prostitution. The judge had
been unable to find that anyone had actually been caused harassment, alarm
or distress by her behaviour. She had been convicted three times for street
prostitution offences and had been seen regularly loitering and soliciting in the
problem areas. She was one of many women who resorted to prostitution in
that area. There was hearsay and opinion evidence before the court that, for
some time, the activities of prostitutes in a particular area had caused substantial problems for residents and lawful visitors. The case against her was
simply that, by her mere presence for the purpose of prostitution, she caused,
by way of contributing, to the problem, albeit that there were many other con-
tributors and her own contribution was small. The appeal concerned the question of whether, in order to prove that a defendant's conduct was "likely" to
cause harassment, alarm or distress, it was necessary to prove that likelihood
to the criminal standard of proof. The appellant argued that whether proved
conduct was likely to have caused harassment, alarm or distress, was not a
matter of proof to any standard, but an evaluative exercise requiring the court
to be satisfied of such likelihood. It was submitted that the meaning of the
word "likely" was the same or less than the normal civil standard of proof. The
District Judge dismissed the application. He made the following findings:

(1) her mere presence when loitering and soliciting in the problem area was
a cause of the problem because of her contribution to the presence of
prostitutes;

(2) there was no direct evidence that any individual had been actually
caused harassment, alarm or distress by the defendant's behaviour;

(3) all of the evidence he heard was police officers and hearsay evidence
from unidentified persons;

(4) therefore, he could not be sure that anyone had actually been caused
harassment, alarm or distress.

Having found that no harassment, alarm or distress had been proven, he then
held that it was not necessarily the case that this would have been likely to have
been caused to someone; to find otherwise, he said, would be unfair, as it
would mean that anyone in the defendant's situation would always be deemed
to have been likely to have caused harassment, alarm or distress to someone.
This problem could have been cured by direct evidence from an interested or
affected person.

6-040   The first question was whether or not the District Judge was right to require
proof to the criminal standard as to the likelihood of causing harassment,
alarm or distress, and the possibility of a lower standard of proof as to likelihood was considered by the House of Lords in *McCann*. Auld L.J. noted that
proof of likelihood is an evaluative exercise with which magistrates are familiar in other contexts, such as under s.4(1) of the Public Order Act 1986. There
were in fact three elements in s.1(1)(a), the first two cumulative and the third,
an alternative to the second. They are:

(1) the person acted in a certain manner; and

---

[42] [2003] EWHC 2272 (Admin).

(2) the manner was one that caused harassment, alarm or distress; or

(3) the manner of acting was likely to cause harassment, alarm or distress.

On appeal, there were three main grounds of appeal. Where the word "likelihood" was used in ASBO proceedings, it would be appropriate to give it the meaning "more probable than not", as opposed to "a real risk or possibility" as may be found in child protection cases. As to the standard of proof required, the court must be sure to the criminal standard that a defendant's conduct has caused the likelihood in the sense of more probably than not. However, in this case, the court held, the District Judge fell into error because he confused the second and third constituents of s.1(1)(a) so as to require proof to the criminal standard that the defendant's conduct actually caused someone harassment, alarm or distress. As the evidence as to any instances of harassment, alarm or distress was poor, the District Judge wrongly rejected the likelihood alternative. Further, he confused the likelihood of harassment, alarm or distress caused by the defendant's conduct, with the standard of proof required to establish that likelihood.

The second issue was whether or not it was permissible to aggregate the defendant's conduct with that of others with whom she was not acting in concert but with whom collectively caused or was likely to cause others harassment, alarm or distress. The District Judge found that prostitution in certain areas of Preston caused a "substantial problem" and that the defendant's presence as a prostitute was a cause of this problem. However, he could not find that her conduct caused or was likely to cause harassment, alarm or distress because he found that it would be wrong to aggregate her own conduct with the conduct of other prostitutes. Auld L.J. said that it was inconsistent, on the one hand, to find that to the criminal standard the defendant's conduct or had been likely to have caused the problems of prostitution in the area in the sense of contributing to it but, on the other hand, that she had not caused harassment, alarm or distress because it had not been proved that her own conduct was aggravated or that she was more responsible than any of the other prostitutes. It was a question of fact as to whether or not an individual prostitute by her contribution to that activity and its overall effect caused a problem which would be caught by s.1(1)(a). Proof of such a fact need not depend on the attribution to her of proved conduct of other prostitutes that might, on its own, be considered harassment, alarm or distress. **6-041**

Thirdly, the Court of Appeal held that the District Judge's finding that it would be wrong to find that the defendant's conduct had caused or had been the likely to cause harassment, alarm or distress, because it would mean that any prostitute who solicited in a residential area would always be deemed to have been likely to have caused harassment, alarm or distress to someone, was perverse. While not all prostitution would fall foul of the 1998 Act, the cumulative effect of street prostitutes operating in residential areas would, as a matter of common sense, have caused or have been likely to have caused harassment, alarm or distress to at least some of the broad range of nearby residents, so that that fact that any one of the prostitutes contributing to that effect was a proper and intended consequence of the provision and not a reason for not giving it effect. **6-042**

Men Rea and the Objective Standard

In *Chief Constable of West Mercia Constabulary v Boorman*, the court considered a question by way of case stated as to whether or not they should require proof of an incident or incidents within the six month time-frame **6-043** which were objectively anti-social. Calvert-Smith J. considered Lord Steyn's remarks as to the objective nature of the inquiry under s.1 of the 1998. Calvert-Smith J. said that the word "objective" in the context in which Lord Steyn used it meant that it was not necessary to consider the mens rea or the defendant:

> "In other words, it is no use the drunken lout saying that he did not mean to cause harassment, alarm or distress, that he was only having a laugh, if in fact he was causing such harassment, alarm or distress. Likewise, it is perfectly clear that the requirement cannot be based solely on the evidence of a member of the public who claims that he or she was caused harassment, alarm or distress. A reasonable view has to be taken, both as to the decision in subsection (1)(a), as well, of course, as to the eventual decision that an order is necessary to protect persons."

In that way, he said, the test is an objective one, in the sense that the court had to make its mind up as to whether the conduct complained of was such as to cause, or likely to cause, harassment, alarm or distress. It was the kind of test that magistrates' courts perform all the time in the context of the Public Order Act 1986 and related offences.

Necessity

6-044   The test is to prevent harm to the community: ss.1(1)(b), and 1C. In *R. v P.*[43] the appellant, aged 15 at the time of the offences, pleaded guilty to assault with intent to rob, theft, robbery, false imprisonment and attempted robbery. He was involved in a number of incidents in which he approached younger boys, threatened them and in one case struck the boy with a stick, and stole their mobile phones. He was sentenced to a total term of four years' detention under s.91 of the Powers of Criminal Courts (Sentencing) Act 2000, and also subject to an ASBO prohibiting him from various activities, principally excluding him from two parks in the locality and from Manchester Airport. The duration of the restraint was stated to be for a period of two years after the appellant's release from custody. As he aged 16, this meant that he would remain in custody until he was 18. Thereafter, he would remain on licence for a further year if he was convicted of any imprisonable offence committed within two years of his release from custody or 18 months on the reduced sentence which we are minded to substitute. It was submitted that these sanctions are sufficient to provide a deterrent to criminal behaviour in the period after his release from custody and accordingly it was not necessary to add a further sanction in the form of an ASBO to cover the period during which he will be liable to the revocation of his licence or to be returned to custody under s.116 of the Powers of Criminal Courts (Sentencing) Act 2000. It was also submitted that, in the case of an offender aged 15 at the time of the offences, the sentencing court should in principle assume that the term of custody will have a beneficial effect on his behaviour on release. The present ASBO carried with it the implication that the appellant was a hopeless case who would not succeed in amending his behaviour. The judge failed to address the issue that at 18 the appellant was going to be a very different individual to the 15-year-old who committed the offences; or for that matter, to the 16-year-old being sentenced. The Court of Appeal, having read the pre-sentence and psychiatric reports concluded that the appellant was by no means a lost cause; he was certainly not regarded by the Youth Offending Team as such. The Court observed that from November 2002 until February 20, 2003 he had been on bail with

[43] [2004] 2 Cr. App. R. (S.) 63.

bail support which worked well. He co-operated and had a good relationship with the bail support worker. Between 1999 and 2001 there was a gap in his offending of over two years. Offending behaviour programmes, education and training programmes would be planned within a fortnight of sentence. The appellant last saw his mother when he was five. He was brought up by a father with acute psychiatric problems, requiring frequent admissions to hospital. He has spent much time in children's homes and with foster parents. The psychiatrist recommended psychological intervention for chronic depression, and there is no indication that he considers such a course to be hopeless. On the most pessimistic prognosis, however, the court's powers under s.116 to return the appellant to custody would provide such deterrent as is appropriate in all the circumstances of this particular case. Even having regard to the reduced sentence of three years' detention, the Court held, it was not possible for a court to determine that an order is necessary to protect members of the public at some future date, having regard to the real possibility that the custodial element of the sentence imposed will prove to be effective:

> "It will be readily observed from a consideration of the Home Office 'Guide to Anti-Social Behaviour Orders' that the conduct primarily envisaged as triggering these orders was for a less grave offence than street robbery, namely graffiti, abusive and intimidating language, excessive noise, fouling the street with litter, drunken behaviour and drug dealing. Doubtless in drafting that report the Home Office had in mind that courts have considerable powers to restrain robbers. We do not go so far as to suggest that anti-social behaviour orders are necessarily inappropriate in cases with characteristics such as the present. But where custodial sentences in excess of a few months are passed, and offenders are liable to be released on licence, circumstances in which there is demonstrable necessity to make anti-social behaviour orders are likely to be limited. We endorse the suggestion properly made by Miss Dagnall that there will be cases in which geographical restraints may properly supplement licence conditions."

R. v P was considered but not applied in *Parkinson*.[44] In April 2004, in the   **6-045**
Crown Court, following a plea of guilty to one count of robbery, the appellant was sentenced to three years' detention in a young offender institution. In addition a two year ASBO was imposed to commence on the date of release. Unlike the appellant in *P*, the appellant in this case had a very considerable criminal record, described in his counsel's advice as "formidable and unenviable". He was now aged 19, having been born on June 16, 1985. He had been before courts on seventeen occasions previously since December 1999 for 28 offences. Those included burglaries, thefts, assault occasioning actual bodily harm, being drunk and disorderly, criminal damage, aggravated vehicle taking and a host of other driving offences. The Court of Appeal noted that almost every means of sentencing him had been tried with apparent lack of success. He had served custodial sentences on four occasions, although not for as long as three years. The judge also had material from the officer setting out the problems that the Council had had with the appellant's family, dating back to 1998 and culminating in an eviction order in September 2003. The Court said that it was perfectly plain that the residents of Brookfield had had to put up with a great deal from this family, including this appellant, in the preceding years. The judge considered that that material, and the oral evidence before her, entitled her to conclude that an anti-social behaviour order was necessary in this case to protect the public from further anti-social acts by the appellant. This, the Court of Appeal said, was one of those exceptional cases where the

---

[44] [2004] EWCA Crim 2757.

judge quite properly reached the conclusion that this order for two years, taking effect on this young man's release, was necessary. In addition to protecting the public, it is perhaps significant that this order may in fact protect him from succumbing to the temptation of resorting to his old ways.

6-046   If the current sentence is sufficient, then, under the test in *R. v P,* the court should not make an ASBO. For example, see *R. v M.*[45] The appellant, who had pleaded guilty to robbery, appealed against his sentence of three years' detention in a young offender institution and an anti social behaviour order lasting for two and a half years after his release. The offence was that he had snatched a mobile phone from his victim. He was 15 at the time of the offence and had appeared in court on four previous occasions, but had not received any custodial sentences. He was assessed as posing a high risk of re-offending and consequently the judge passed the three year term. The appellant contended that a detention and training order would have been a more appropriate sentence; and that the anti-social behaviour order was unnecessary. The Court of Appeal allowed the appeal. The appellant had not been in custody before, despite his criminal record, and it was inappropriate to send him to a young offender institution for three years for a single offence of robbery which did not involve violence. A detention and training order for 24 months would be imposed instead. An anti-social behaviour order should be made where it was necessary to protect the public from further anti-social acts by the offender. When he was released, he would be subject to licence for the remainder of his sentence and thus would be under supervision for a further 12 months. The detention and training order, with the licence period that it would automatically carry, was sufficient to protect the public from M's future conduct. The anti-social behaviour order was quashed.

6-047   The test in *R v P* was considered most recently by the Court of Appeal in *R. v Boness.*[46] The Court of Appeal said that in favour of making an ASBO was the fact that the appellant had consistently engaged in anti-social behaviour over a period of approximately three years. He was a persistent prolific offender and had admitted to drug misuse in the community. There were three main aspects to his anti-social behaviour: threatening behaviour (two incidents), vehicle crime (three incidents) and other offences of dishonesty such as burglary and theft (three incidents and other incidents of handling stolen goods). On the other hand, he was being sentenced to a custodial sentence of three years detention in a young offender institution and was thus subject to a period on licence and subject to recall or return to custody. Hooper L.J. said that each separate order prohibiting a person from doing a specified thing must be necessary to protect persons from further anti-social acts by him. The court must ask itself when considering any specific order prohibiting the offender from doing something, "Is this order necessary to protect persons in any place in England and Wales from further anti-social acts by him?" The use of an ASBO to punish an offender is thus unlawful. It follows from the requirement that the order must be necessary to protect persons from further anti-social acts by him, that the court should not impose an order which prohibits an offender from committing a specified criminal offence if the sentence which could be passed following conviction for the offence should be a sufficient deterrent:

"If following conviction for the offence the offender would be liable to imprisonment then an ASBO would add nothing other than to increase the sentence if the sentence for the offence is less than 5 years' imprisonment. But if the offender is not going to be deterred from committing the offence

[45] [2005] WL 816024.
[46] 2005 WL 2673805.

by a sentence of imprisonment for that offence, the ASBO is not likely (it may be thought) further to deter and is therefore not necessary. It has been held, rightly in our view, that an ASBO should not be used merely to increase the sentence of imprisonment which an offender is liable to receive."

He added that there was another reason why a court should be reluctant to impose an order which prohibits an offender from, or merely from, committing a specified criminal offence. The aim of an ASBO is to prevent anti-social behaviour. To prevent further anti-social behaviour, the police or other authorities needed to be able to take action before the anti-social behaviour it was designed to prevent takes place. If, for example, a court was faced by an offender who caused criminal damage by spraying graffiti, then the order should be aimed at facilitating action to be taken to prevent graffiti spraying by him and or his associates before it took place. An order in clear and simple terms preventing the offender from being in possession of a can of spray paint in a public place gave the police or others responsible for protecting the property an opportunity to take action in advance of the actual spraying and made it clear to the offender that he has lost the right to carry such a can for the duration of the order. The Court said that bail conditions provided a useful analogy:

"A defendant may be prohibited from contacting directly or indirectly a prosecution witness or entering a particular area near the alleged victim's home. The aim is to prevent the defendant trying to tamper with witnesses or committing a further offence. But the police do not have to wait until he has tampered or committed a further offence and thus committed a very serious offence. If he breaks the conditions even without intending to tamper, he is in breach of his bail conditions and liable to be remanded in custody. The victim has the comfort of knowing that if the defendant enters the prescribed area, the police can be called to take action. The victim does not have to wait for the offence to happen again."

Boness was followed in *Stephen*[47]: prior to 2004, the appellant lived on the Isles **6-048** of Scilly with his wife who ran a bed and breakfast. The bed and breakfast accommodation was in a loft conversion. The appellant had completed the loft conversion himself in 1999 and during the course of that had built a number of access hatches into the eaves so access could be gained to storage and the pipe work. On January 10, 2004, after the appellant had separated from his wife, her new partner had a problem with the plumbing and went into the converted loft area. He removed some flooring to see if he could find the cause of the problem. He found items of women underwear, vibrators, some pornographic magazines and photographs of various friends of the appellant's wife. She looked at the photographs and recognised her friends. The police were then contacted. Her partner found other items of women's underwear, videos, personal photographs and more vibrators over the next week and these were handed over to the police. A number of women on the island heard about the discovery and they had to go to the police station to identity their own very personal items and the photographs. The appellant was subsequently arrested. When interviewed he admitted stealing items of underwear from washing lines and using them as a sexual aid to masturbate. He said he was trying to get help and that he was deeply ashamed of his actions. The pre-sentence report recommended a community penalty. It said because of his good character there was a low risk of re-offending, but concern was expressed

[47] [2005] EWCA Crim 3429.

due to the nature of his offending because his motivation and thinking under-pinning the offending was not understood. He seemed unaware of the impact of his offending and he believed that the offences had been blown out of all proportion. This was not helpful to his understanding of the victims' issues. In July 2004, the appellant pleaded guilty to ten counts of theft and was sentenced to 150 hours community punishment on each to run concurrently and made the subject of an ASBO for 7 years. The terms of the order were as follows: the appellant was forbidden from landing on or entering the Isles of Scilly; and (ii) entering the curtilage of any dwelling house within the United Kingdom unless so invited in writing or verbally by a person authorised to give consent at that time. He appealed against sentence by leave of the judge. In sentencing, the judge noted that these offences had taken place over a four to five year period, which is what made them serious. They were offences which would be particularly upsetting to those who owned the various items he had stolen. In some instances they must have been committed in breach of specific trust vested in him by the people who were prepared to admit him in his home. They were committed in breach of general trust in the Isles of Scilly, since it was a community where people did not have to lock their doors because they trusted everyone to behave in an honourable and decent way. He had eventually pleaded guilty, so would receive some credit for that, as it meant the complainants did not have to come to court to give evidence for a second time. The original grounds of appeal are that in the circumstances of the case the order banning the appellant from the Isles of Scilly for seven years was too long. Leave was granted by the single judge, on the basis that (a) the Full Court should consider, whether in the light of *R. v Boness*, an order should have been made against a man with the appellant's good character; and (b) if appropriate, whether it is too wide and too long. On appeal, it was submitted that it was not necessary to impose such an order in this case, due to the appellant's age and his hitherto good character, saying that the deterrent factor of any further thefts of underwear in such a small community, inevitably leading to his arrest, was sufficient. The order had been imposed by way of punishment, when clearly on the authorities it is not to be used in that way. The purpose of the order, it was said, was to prevent the appellant from committing further thefts in the Isles of Scilly and anywhere else in the United Kingdom. Given that this is the only behaviour complained of and the maximum sentence for theft is seven years, then it is difficult to see what further deterrent an ASBO can have over and above the theft. The Court of Appeal held that the making of an order was right in principle. First of all, there is clear evidence that the appellant acted in an anti-social way. Secondly, that his course of conduct had, without doubt, caused alarm and distress to those women in that small community. Thirdly, given the appellant had clearly not yet fully got to the root of his behaviour, the imposition of the ASBO was necessary for the protection of those persons from any further anti-social behaviour on his part. The under-lying cause for the behaviour of that kind, without some kind of intervention, is not necessarily deterred by the fact of detection and prosecution, nor does the question of good character assist this aspect.

6-049   Applying the *R. v P* and *Boness* test, should an ASBO or CRASBO be made in respect of very trivial offences, such as shoplifting, where it is difficult to see evidence of harassment, alarm or distress? In *R. v Birmingham Magistrates' Court Ex p. Mills*,[48] the claimant applied for judicial review of a decision of the defendant magistrates' court to make her subject to an ASBO when she was caught ineptly trying to take three pairs of gloves from a shop in Birmingham without paying for them. She was seen leaving the shop by a police officer who arrested her and returned the gloves to the shop. She was cooperative and was

---

[48] [2005] WL 2493291.

not abusive. She subsequently pleaded guilty to a single count of theft. The CPS then applied for an ASBO under s.1 of the 1998 Act to prevent her from entering retail stores in Birmingham city centre without written police consent. The CPS maintained that she had numerous convictions for similar offences and that the ASBO was justified under the 1998 Act in order to prevent her causing harassment, alarm or distress. The judge held that the criteria contained in s.1 of the 1998 Act were met and granted the ASBO. Before the Administrative Court, she contended that on the facts of the case the imposition of an ASBO was unjustifiable. The Court granted the application. Whilst some thefts or acts of shoplifting could cause harassment, alarm or distress, and so would fall within the 1998 Act, all thefts or acts of shoplifting did not automatically fall within the criteria of s.1 of the 1998 Act. It was not suggested that what she did actually caused harassment, alarm or distress. No employee of Next was even aware of the theft until the police officer took the gloves back to the shop and told them. Further, it was impossible to say that by stealing the gloves unbeknown to the store the claimant had done anything that was likely to cause either harassment, alarm or distress within the meaning of the section. Whether s.1 of the 1998 Act was triggered was dependent upon the individual facts of a case. In the instant case M's behaviour had not caused harassment, alarm or distress to anyone and the ASBO was accordingly quashed. While the circumstances of some shopliftings or other thefts may very well fall within the relevant words of s.1C(2), it did not seem to the Court that harassment, alarm or distress inevitably followed or was likely to follow, especially in the circumstances of this case. There was in fact, nothing about the facts of this theft to trigger the section. Were the section to have been triggered in this case, it would be difficult to imagine any shoplifting that did not likewise trigger the section; and that was not the situation.

Similarly, in *R. v Israilov*,[49] the appellant was sentenced to 12 months' imprisonment and a two year anti social behaviour order, ordered to run from the date of release, following his pleas of guilty to two counts of theft in which, he had entered stores and had stolen goods. At the time of sentencing, he was subject to a community punishment order for a similar offence of theft. He contended that a sentence of 12 months was disproportionate and that the ASBO was not necessary and was disproportionate in terms. It prohibited entry to any store signed up to the "Shop Safe" scheme, a large area in the central shopping precinct. On appeal, the court agreed it was disproportionate. They also held that it was wrong to impose a two year ASBO in the terms stipulated by the judge and which was to be suspended until the appellant had served his sentence. The terms of the ASBO imposed were too wide and there was also omitted from it a clear specification of the period during which it was to run. Accordingly, they set aside the concurrent sentences of 12 months' imprisonment and the ASBO and to impose instead a sentence of six months' imprisonment.

6-050

R. v P has been applied in civil proceedings. In *Moat Housing Group-South Ltd v Harris*,[50] the appellants appealed against anti-social behaviour injunctions, a possession order and anti-social behaviour orders obtained by the respondent, a registered social landlord. The second appellant was the tenant of the respondent of a house where she lived with her four children. The other appellant was the children's father who lived with his parents but often visited the house. The housing association had applied without notice for an anti social behaviour injunction under s.153A of the Housing Act 1996, including provisions ousting the father from the property and excluding the appellants from the area under s.153C of the Act. The judge made the injunction sought on the basis of the alleged conduct of the appellants and their children and

6-051

---

[49] [2005] WL 607480.
[50] [2005] H.L.R. 33.

the alleged conduct of another family who lived in the same street and who were also tenants of the respondent. A power of arrest was attached to the injunction which was expressed to last for six months. The housing association then served a notice seeking possessions alleging breaches by the first appellant of her tenancy agreement and the judge made a possession order and anti-social behaviour orders against both appellants under the 1998 Act. Allowing the appeal the Court of Appeal held that no order should be made in civil or family proceedings without notice to the other side, unless there was a very good reason for departing from the general rule that notice should be given. It was hard to envisage a more intrusive without notice order, Brooke L.J. said, than one that required the mother and her four children their home immediately and banned the appellants from re-entering a large part of the area where they lived. It was neither necessary nor proportionate to the harm sought to be avoided to make an ouster order or an exclusion order without notice. Once the judge had decided that the instant case was one in which an injunction was justified on a without notice basis, for protecting named persons from harm or restraining acts of nuisance until the hearing on notice, she was entitled to attach a power of arrest to that part of the order. The extent of the injunction was much too wide and it ought to have been restricted to what was judged necessary to protect prospective witnesses and to restrain acts of nuisance. So long as the without notice order was of a non-intrusive type, and the hearing on notice took place timeously, there was no harm in that practice. There would have been nothing objectionable in the judge making a without notice injunction for an initial period of six months to restrain nuisance and or intimidation of witnesses. The judge failed to take into account the interests of the appellant and her children when making an immediate possession order, and the fact that the respondent had given her no prior warning of any kind. However, those matters could not properly outweigh the seriousness of the conduct complained of. Therefore it was reasonable to make a possession order, but the order should be suspended on terms that there were no further breaches of the tenancy agreement and no further nuisance. The judge was wrong to make anti-social behaviour orders of four years duration. It was not appropriate to make such orders at all. There was not the persistent and serious anti-social behaviour on the part of the appellants which was required before it could be held to be necessary to make such an order. Although the judgment in *R. v P* related to an order made in the Crown Court under s.1C of the 1998 Act, in contrast to the present case, which relates to an order made in a county court under s.1B, the governing principles must be the same. In particular, in the event of any breach of the order, the breach court must be able to understand the facts on which the original order was made without having to incur the heavy expense of commissioning a transcript of the judgment in the county court. This discipline would have been particularly valuable in the present case because the judge would have had to identify, to the criminal standard of proof, which of the hearsay allegations, whether anonymous or not, he found proved so as to constitute acts of either appellant committed after December 2, 2002. The agreed chronology shows that a number of the complaints against these appellants antedated December 2002. ASBOs were inappropriate on the facts of this case, and that some form of undertaking as to future conduct, backed by a penal notice, was all that the situation required in the case of each appellant. In particular, the judge never identified the conduct on the part of the father which warranted the making of an ASBO against him, and there was not the evidence of "persistent and serious anti-social behaviour" on the part of the two adults (as opposed to two of their children) which is required before it can be held to be necessary to make an ASBO. The judge's most serious explicit findings against either of them stemmed from the very unpleasant events of a single night.

The Order

Formalities

Like a civil injunction, the order should be served on the defendant in person **6-052** as soon as possible and, in the case of children and young people, a copy must be served on the parent or guardian. The order comes into effect on the day it is made, but the two year period during which no order shall be discharged, except with the consent of both parties, starts from the date of service. The Home Office advises that if an ASBO is granted it is preferable for a copy of the order to be served on the defendant in person prior to his or her departure from court. Where an individual has not been personally served with the order at the court, the court should be asked to arrange for personal service as soon as possible thereafter. The lead agency, if not the police, should ensure that a copy of the ASBO is forwarded immediately to the police. The agency should also give copies of the order to the ASB co-ordinator of the local crime and disorder reduction partnership, the other partner agencies, and to the main targets and witnesses of the anti-social behaviour, so that breaches can be reported and acted upon. The police should notify the appropriate police area command on the same working day so that details of the defendant and the conditions of the order can be recorded. A copy of the order should be provided to the lead agency's legal representative on the same day as the court hearing, and in the case of a juvenile the court will provide a further copy for the youth offending team (YOT). The YOT should arrange for action to be taken by an appropriate agency (for example, social services) to ensure that the young person understands the seriousness of the ASBO.

In *Walkling v DPP*,[51] the appellant appealed by way of case stated against **6-053** a decision that an ASBO pronounced in court was a valid order. An ASBO was made against the appellant for a period of two years. It was pronounced in court and contemporaneously recorded in the court register. The written document purporting to be the ASBO did not reflect what was pronounced in court as it recorded the appellant as being subject to an ASBO for less than two years. The appellant submitted that the ASBO was not the order that was pronounced in court, but rather the written document which came into existence as a result of the court hearing, because s.1(9) of the 1998 Act displaces the general rule that the order of the court was that pronounced by the judge in open court. He further contended that the written document did not comply with s.1(7) of the Crime and Disorder Act 1998 because it had effect for less than two years. The Divisional Court dismissed the appeal, holding that s.1(9) referred to the date of service of the ASBO as if the ASBO were a written document rather than an oral pronouncement. However, the terms of s.1(9) were an insufficient basis for the conclusion that Parliament intended to depart from the general rule applicable to orders made by magistrates' courts, namely that the order of the court was that pronounced by the judge. If such a departure had been intended, clearer wording would have been needed. It followed that the ASBO was that which was pronounced in court. Even if the ASBO had been the written document, it would not have been invalidated by a failure to comply with the requirements of s.1(7). The error was an error which favoured the appellant. It abbreviated the duration of the ASBO rather than prolonged it. There was no reason to conclude that Parliament intended any contravention of the requirements of s.1(7) to result in the nullity of the order pronounced in open court or the order signed by the magistrate as a result of the hearing before the bench.

[51] [2003] WL 22936799.

6-054   In *English*,[52] the appellant appealed against his conviction of breaching an anti-social behaviour order. The relevant document, which was signed by the chairman of the magistrates, set out his conviction of theft, stated that he had acted in an anti-social manner and that an order was necessary to protect others from further anti-social behaviour, and prohibited him from doing certain things. He argued that the order was invalid in that it failed to set out details of the anti-social behaviour which it was alleged he had been responsible for. His appeal was dismissed: the order, which was the basis for any subsequent proceedings, was the order made by the court in court. What had been said in court was purportedly set out in the paragraph which set out the prohibitions, which had been signed by the chairman of the magistrates and served on him. There was no suggestion that that was not the form of the order that was made in court. It inevitably followed that the form provided admissible evidence of the order that had been made. That was all that was necessary for the purposes of establishing the basis for the charge that was brought by the prosecution. There was no suggestion that the form of the order, as recorded in the prohibitions section, indicated that the magistrates had exceeded the limits of their jurisdiction under s.1C of the 1998 Act; nor was the form of the order defective in that it failed to identify what it was that the appellant was precluded from doing. The presumption that any document, such as the one in question here, was recording a valid order was one which should prevail in all cases, other than those in which the relevant order was "plainly invalid". The only way to challenge an order which was apparently valid was by way of an appeal under s.108 of the Magistrates' Courts Act 1980 or, if the underlying facts justified it, by an application for judicial review on the basis of some failure or defect in procedure. In the circumstances, there was no basis for the argument that the prosecution had failed to establish the underlying order which justified his conviction.

Duration

6-055   The duration of the order is any period not less than two years.[53] However, under s.(1)(8) and subject to subs.(9), the applicant or the defendant may apply by complaint to the court which made an anti-social behaviour order for it to be varied or discharged by a further order. Subsection (9) provides that, except with the consent of both parties, no anti-social behaviour order shall be discharged before the end of the period of two years beginning with the date of service of the order. Terms may be indefinite and this raises difficult issues of proportionality and necessity. In *Vittles*,[54] during the night, the applicant broke into a car parked in the driveway of a home and stole a tool. At his subsequent sentence hearing, he asked for 15 offences to be taken into consideration, all of which related to similar offences in which he had stolen over £3,500 worth of goods, of various kinds, from parked cars. In interview, he admitted these offences. He had broken into somewhere between 10 and 30 vehicles, at night, in an area he knew well. He was a heavy drug user, requiring something of the order of £900 a week to feed his habit and he had, as he admitted, deliberately targeted cars belonging to American servicemen and their dependents who lived off the air bases in the area. While on bail for the theft offences, he was caught driving while disqualified. He was committed to the Crown Court for sentence and received three and-a-half years' imprisonment for theft and four months for driving whilst disqualified. Twelve offences of theft and three of attempted theft were taken into

---

[52] [2005] WL 3048970.
[53] The Crime and Disorder Act 1998, s.1(7).
[54] [2004] WL 1959793.

consideration. The court also imposed on him an ASBO preventing the applicant from entering the Forest Heath District Council area, except to attend court, for an indefinite period. In passing sentence, the judge said that the applicant had an absolutely terrible criminal record, predominantly for theft from vehicles and, occasionally, for driving while disqualified. It was apparent that his criminal record extends back to 1987 and contains offences of dishonesty, particularly, in recent times, thefts from motor vehicles of a kind similarly targeted to those in the present case. The learned judge pointed out that community sentences had not worked in the past and therefore a substantial custodial sentence was justified to deter the applicant and to give the public, from whom he stole, the protection which they deserved. He was plundering the vehicles of American servicemen and their families in this area. It was for those reasons, also, that the learned judge made the anti-social behaviour order. The applicant submitted that, in relation to the ASBO, although an order intended to protect those working at and living in the vicinity of the two American air bases could not be criticised in principle, the lifetime disqualification imposed by the learned judge is not supportable. The Court of Appeal agreed. The transient, vulnerable nature of the American population specifically targeted by the appellant makes it appropriate that, exceptionally, an anti-social behaviour order should here be made, notwithstanding the imposition of a substantial prison sentence. It was practicable terms for a more precise geographical limitation to be imposed. While an order preventing the appellant (as he now is) from entering the Forest Heath District Council area, save for the purpose of attending court, was a proper order to make, an indefinite period was not. The new period would be five years, to run from the date on which the appellant was sentenced.

In *R. v Hall*,[55] in June 2004, the appellant, who had an "appalling" criminal record, including ten convictions for driving while disqualified, three of taking vehicles without consent, one of attempting, one of dangerous driving, one of reckless driving, one of failing to provide a specimen, one of failing to stop, one of failing to report, one of having no test certificate, pleaded guilty and was sentenced for driving whilst disqualified to five months' imprisonment concurrent to 12 months' imprisonment for dangerous driving. He was also made subject to an ASBO prohibiting him from driving any mechanically propelled vehicle on a public road in the United Kingdom without being the holder of a valid driving licence and certificate of insurance. That ASBO was ordered to run indefinitely. He submitted that the ASBO was unnecessary for this offending. In *R. v P*, the test for making an order is one of the necessity to protect the public from further anti-social acts by the offender. The Court of Appeal held that there was nothing wrong in principle in making such an order when they are driving offences of such a regularity and type and in such an area that they do constitute anti-social behaviour. It was said that the terms of the order must be precise and capable of being understood by the offender. The findings of fact giving rise to the making of the order must be recorded and the order must be explained to the offender. The exact terms of the order must be pronounced in open court and the written order must accurately reflect the order as pronounced. It was noted that the making of such an order is strictly not part of the sentencing process. However, the Court was concerned with the indefinite period of the order. Just as it is not advisable to make long periods of disqualification, because it only makes it much more difficult for somebody to comply, the specific terms of the anti-social behaviour order should have been set out, rather than an indefinite order. The length of the anti-social behaviour order was two years.

6-056

[55] [2005] 1 Cr. App. R. (S.) 118.

Orders By Consent

6-057   In *R. v Manchester Crown Court Ex p. T*,[56] the claimant sought judicial review of a decision to strike out his appeal against the imposition of an anti-social behaviour order. He was aged 14 and there had been a series of complaints about his behaviour. His behaviour culminated in an ASBO being granted against him after his mother had consented to the order. After the ASBO had been made, his mother changed her mind and an appeal was entered. The appeal was dismissed by the recorder, without considering its merits, on the ground that his previous consent to the granting of the ASBO barred the appeal. The claimant submitted that the approach of the recorder was inconsistent with the statutory provisions pursuant to which an ASBO was made. An ASBO could not be made by consent and he should not be debarred from appealing against it, even though no objection had been made at the court below. Moses J. granted the application: an ASBO could not be made merely on the basis of the consent of the claimant. Before making an order, the court had to be satisfied to the required standard of proof as to matters under s.1(1)(a) of the 1998 Act and, further, had to exercise its own judgment pursuant to s.1(1)(b) of the Act as to the necessity of making such an order. The cooperation and consent of the person who it was suggested should be made the subject of the order was welcome and relevant. If an applicant was prepared to consent, it would not only show a cooperative state of mind, but would afford considerable saving of time and money. In requiring proof of the relevant matters, it was not intended to discourage cooperation or consent. However, consent was only a factor, both in relation to the matters that were required to be proved, and as to the value judgment that the court had to exercise in deciding whether an order was necessary. An ASBO was made in the interests of the public at large after a lot of work had gone on by ASBO teams and various parties before the matter ever reached court. Therefore, the consent of a parent could not be dispositive of the issue. In the instant case, the recorder had been incorrect in his approach. Exactly the same considerations, as identified by the terms of the Act, had to govern an appellate Crown Court's consideration of an ASBO. There was no basis for saying that the Crown Court was deprived of jurisdiction in relation to an appeal, merely because there was evidence that consent was given by the parent below. Whether or not such consent was given, if a claimant sought to appeal, the appeal had to be heard. The consent did not bar the appeal, and despite the evidence that T's mother had consented, the appeal ought to have been considered on its merits. The decision was quashed and it was ordered that the case be reheard before the Crown Court.

Drafting the Terms of the Order

6-058   It is for the court to decide what prohibitions are to be imposed by the order. The basic model is the civil injunction in higher courts. Home Office guidance is that the applicant agency should propose conditions (including duration) to the court. A full order should be drawn up using the form in the court rules. In the county court the proposed order should accompany the application. Where the order is made on conviction in criminal proceedings an agency concerned in the case, such as the police, may propose prohibitions or the court may draw them up of its own volition. It should be noted that the order may not impose positive requirements, only prohibitions. The prohibitions should cover the range of anti-social acts committed by the defendant; they should be necessary for protecting persons within a defined area from the anti-social

---

[56] [2005] WL 1505135.

acts of the defendant; they should be reasonable and proportionate; they should be realistic and practical, clear, concise and easy to understand, and specific when referring to matters of time if, for example, prohibiting the offender from being outside or in particular areas at certain times and when referring to exclusion from an area, include street names and clear boundaries such as the side of the street included in the order (a map with identifiable street names should also be provided). They should also be in terms which make it easy to determine and prosecute a breach.[57]

The minimum duration of the order (other than an interim order) is for two years. Duration will depend on the age of the respondent, the nature of the anti-social behaviour and the respondent's response to previous measures to deal with the behaviour. The Home Office advises that the duration applied for should take into account the age of the recipient, the severity of his or her anti-social behaviour, the length of time it has gone on and the recipient's response to any previous measures to deal with the behaviour. A longer order will generally be appropriate in the case of more serious or persistent anti-social behaviour. **6-059**

Great care should be taken to ensure that the terms of the order are proportionate and reasonable and, at all times, with the test in *R. v P* and *Boness* in mind. This is true of any such prohibitory order. In *B v Chief Constable of Avon and Somerset*,[58] Lord Bingham C.J., speaking of a similar statutory provision, said this at para.33: **6-060**

"If anyone is the subject of a prohibitory court order for breach of which he is liable to severe punishment, that person is entitled to know, clearly and unambiguously, what conduct he must avoid to comply with the order. Such clarity is essential for him. It is scarcely less essential for any authority responsible for policing compliance with the order and for any court called upon to decide whether the terms of the order have been broken. The order should be expressed in simple terms, easily understood even by those who, like the appellant, are not very bright. If the order is wider than is necessary for the purposes of protecting the public from serious harm from the defendant, the order will not meet the requirements of section 2(4) of the 1998 Act and will fall foul of the Convention requirement that the means employed, if restrictive of guaranteed rights, should be necessary and proportionate to the legitimate ends towards which they are directed."

In *R. v P*, it was submitted that the prohibitions were redundant as they prohibited conduct which is already subject to a general prohibition by the Public Order Act 1986 and the Prevention of Crime Act 1953 respectively. The Court of Appeal was not persuaded that the inclusion of such matters was to be actively discouraged. So far as more minor offences are concerned, there was no harm in reminding offenders that certain matters do constitute criminal conduct. However, it was also submitted that the order served on the appellant in this case was defective in that it failed to set out or identify the anti-social behaviour in relation to which the order was made, notwithstanding the fact that para.2 of the order commenced in these terms: "The court found that the defendant had acted in the following anti-social manner which caused or was likely to cause harassment, alarm or distress, etc." The paragraph was not filled in when gull particulars should be included in such an order. Paragraph 1 read "it is ordered that the defendant is prohibited from either by himself or by instructing, encouraging or inciting any other person to act in any anti-social manner"; para.3 prohibited him "either by himself or by instructing, **6-061**

---

[57] 2002, pp.35–36.
[58] [2001] 1 W.L.R. 340.

encouraging or inciting any other person to engage in any conduct that tends to prevent the public from passing freely along the highway or enjoying free access to any place to which the public has access." It was argued that paras 1 and 3 of the order were too vague and general and could not be readily understood by a person of the appellant's age and educational attainment. The Court of Appeal agreed and said that plain, simple, ordinary language should be used by courts when making orders in circumstances such as this and approved of the Home Office as containing helpful instruction as to the drafting of such orders.

6-062   Following a finding that the offender has acted in an anti-social manner, the test for making an order prohibiting the offender from doing something is one of necessity and that also applies to the drafting of its terms. In *Boness*,[59] Hooper L.J. said that each separate order prohibiting a person from doing a specified thing must be necessary to protect persons from further anti-social acts by him. The court must ask itself when considering the making of the order and any specific order terms in it prohibiting the offender from doing something, "Is this order necessary to protect persons in any place in England and Wales from further anti-social acts by him?" There was, he added, another reason why a court should be reluctant to impose an order which prohibits an offender from, or merely from, committing a specified criminal offence. The aim of an ASBO was to prevent anti-social behaviour. To prevent further anti-social behaviour, the police or other authorities needed to be able to take action before the anti-social behaviour it was designed to prevent takes place. If, for example, a court was faced by an offender who caused criminal damage by spraying graffiti then the order should be aimed at facilitating action to be taken to prevent graffiti spraying by him and or his associates before it took place. An order in clear and simple terms preventing the offender from being in possession of a can of spray paint in a public place gave the police, or others responsible for protecting the property, an opportunity to take action in advance of the actual spraying and made it clear to the offender that he has lost the right to carry such a can for the duration of the order.

6-063   Therefore, in *Stephen*[60]:

> "The real questions, in our judgment therefore, are the questions of the scope and lengths of the orders. Orders of this kind have to be proportionate, that is commensurate to the risk to be guarded against. The appellant was given a community punishment order rather than a community rehabilitation order. Thus there has been no mandatory treatment or therapy programme that he has been subjected to. Time must be given therefore to allow the appellant to address and manage his problem, whilst at the same time protecting certain members of the public from him. Hooper LJ in the case of Boness at paragraph 47 in which he refers to the question of policing. This is pertinent to the second half of the order which restricts entry to any curtilage of any dwelling-house in the United Kingdom without permission. The scope of this clause is very wide. It was impracticable to police. There is not the added concern of the women in that small community on the Isles of Scilly to consider. It seems to us therefore that the scope of the second clause is too wide and should be deleted. As to duration., the appellant still has family on the island. Access to his children is restricted in any event in the light of his separation from his wife. It seems that access now takes place on the mainland, where the appellant works. The period of 7 years was too long. An appropriate period of restraint would be one of 2 years."

[59] [2005] WL 2673805.
[60] [2005] EWCA Crim 3429.

Hooper L.J.'s remarks in the case of *Boness*, in which he referred to the ques- **6-064**
tion of policing, was very pertinent, the Court in *Stephen* said, to the second
half of the order which restricted entry to any curtilage of any dwelling-house
in the United Kingdom without permission. The scope of this clause was very
wide and so was impracticable to police. As to duration, the appellant still has
family on the island. Access to his children was restricted in any event in the
light of his separation from his wife. The period of seven years was too long.
An appropriate period of restraint would be one of two years.

In *Pedder*,[61], the appellant in February 2005 pleaded guilty to a count of **6-065**
burglary and was committed to the Crown Court for sentence. When he
appeared at the Crown Court for sentence, he also asked for a total of 67
offences, of which 56 were dwelling house burglaries, to be taken into consideration. In March 2005, Crown Court sentenced him to three years' imprisonment and an ASBO was imposed on his release, for a period of five years
The conditions that were imposed were that the appellant upon his release, for
a period of five years thereafter, would be prohibited from:

(1) entering the districts of Penwith and Kerrier;
(2) entering any private area of public buildings within England and Wales
unless so invited in writing by a person authorised to give consent at that
time;
(3) entering the curtilage of any dwelling house within England and Wales
unless so invited in writing or verbally by a person authorised to give
consent at that time;
(4) acting or engaging in any behaviour which causes or is likely to cause
harassment, alarm or distress to others or to incite or encourage others to
do so.

The Court of Appeal could find nothing wrong about the sentence for the burglary. They considered the remarks of Hooper L.J. in *Boness*,[62] that the court
must ask itself when considering any specific order prohibiting the offender
from doing something, "Is this order necessary to protect persons in any place
in England and Wales from further anti-social acts by him?" The terms of the
order must be proportionate in the sense that they must be commensurate with
the risk to be guarded against. It followed that before any condition in an
ASBO can be imposed, the court has to be satisfied in respect of each restriction under consideration: (a) that it is necessary to protect people in any place
in England and Wales from further anti-social acts by the offender; (b) that it
is proportionate, in the sense that it is commensurate with the risk to be
guarded against; and (c) its terms are so clear that the offender will know precisely what he is prohibited from doing. It was held in this case that restriction
1, not to enter the districts of Penwith and Kerrier, could not be justified as
being necessary or proportionate. It was difficult to see why the appellant
should be precluded from visiting any friend or relative in the districts of
Penwith or Kerrier, or why he should be prevented from travelling through
that area. The restriction as to entering any private area of public buildings
within England and Wales unless invited so in writing by a person authorised
to give consent at that time could not be upheld because it is not necessary or
proportionate, as there is no risk apparent to us of the appellant stealing from
the private areas of public buildings. The third restriction should not have
been made because it bears no relation to any particular offence for which
the appellant was before the court and it was not necessary or proportionate;
it would preclude the appellant from visiting to see a friend or relative, or

61 [2005] WL 3299101.
62 [2005] Crim EWCA 2395, para.20.

obtaining work which entailed visiting people's homes, for instance, by making a delivery. The last restriction, dealing with public order matters, bore no relationship to any crime for which the appellant was before the court and it was not necessary. Furthermore, the court could not understand what it covered as, for example, when it uses the terms precluding the appellant from causing "distress".

6-066   General terms prohibiting the commission of a criminal offence should be avoided. In *McGrath,* the terms of the order were:

"1. Entering any car park which is owned, opened or leased by Network Rail, any train operating company or London Underground Ltd whether on payment or otherwise within the counties of Hertfordshire, Bedfordshire or Buckinghamshire.
2. Entering any other car park whether on payment or otherwise within the counties of Hertfordshire, Bedfordshire or Buckinghamshire.
3. Trespassing on any land belonging to any person whether legal or natural within those counties.
4. Having in his possession in any public place any window hammer, screwdriver, torch or any tool or implement which could be used for the purpose of breaking into motor vehicles.
5. Being found drunk in a public place in those three counties."

The Court of Appeal held that the terms preventing the appellant from entering any car parks or trespassing on any land were unjustifiably draconian and were far too wide. The term preventing him from carrying "any tool or implement" was not properly justified as the meaning of the words was impossible to ascertain. Term 2 was unjustifiably draconian; it was far too wide and would prohibit the appellant from entering, even as a passenger, any car park in a supermarket. A party at risk of a prison sentence should not be left to the discretion of the prosecution as to whether to prefer charges. The same considerations applied with equal, if not greater, force to the term prohibiting trespassing. If the appellant took a wrong turn on a walk and entered someone's property, he would be at risk of a five year prison sentence. It would be small comfort that there was a prosecutor's discretion. Term 4 was also unacceptably wide. Neither an ASBO nor even a civil injunction could be made in such terms. The meaning of the words "any tool or implement" was impossible to ascertain. In addition, insofar as the wording of term 4 was sufficiently qualified by the final wording "which could be used for the purpose of breaking into motor vehicles", effectively term 4 overlapped with the offence of going equipped. It was not properly justified.

6-067   In *R. v DPP Ex p. W*,[63] the appellant young offender appealed by way of case stated against a decision of the district judge to convict him of a breach of an ASBO. He had been made subject to an ASBO, which was of two years' duration, which restrained W from:

"1. Entering [an area defined on an attached map].
2. Causing physical harm to or intimidating anyone.
3. Damaging or attempting to damage property not belonging to himself.
4. Sitting in the driver's position of any motor vehicle save on private land with owner's permission.
5. Remaining in any public place when he is considered to be causing a nuisance and has been requested to leave by a Police Officer or any person in authority.
6. Committing any criminal offence."

---

[63] [2005] WL 1287499.

He committed an act of theft whilst subject to the ASBO. He appeared in the youth court for sentencing and was sentenced to a conditional discharge in respect of the offence and to an absolute discharge for the breach of the ASBO. The judge held that, whilst the prohibition in the ASBO against committing any criminal offence was too wide and unnecessary for the protection of the public, it was unambiguous and therefore valid. On appeal an issue arose as to the validity of the clause in the ASBO prohibiting the commission of any criminal offence. The Court, allowing the appeal, held that the clause in the ASBO was plainly too wide and was unenforceable. There was a danger that the offender, at his age, would not know what a criminal offence was and what was not. It was well established that an order had to be clear and in terms that would enable an individual to know what he could and could not do. A general restriction was not necessary where specific behaviour restrictions were in place. Had it been felt necessary, a prohibition against committing theft could have been included in the ASBO when it was drafted.

Two cases consider terms imposing a curfew as a condition of the ASBO. **6-068** In *Lonergan v Lewes Crown Court*,[64] the claimant offender sought judicial review of a prohibition contained in an ASBO made under the Crime and Disorder Act 1998, requiring him to be resident at any one of a number of specified addresses during particular times, in essence imposing a curfew. He submitted that the prohibition was unlawful because it amounted to a curfew which was mandatory in nature, whereas s.1(4) and s.1(6) of the 1998 Act only allowed for prohibitions. The test of whether a relevant part of an order was prohibitory was one of substance rather than form. The positive obligation contained in a curfew could not be circumvented by expressing it in a superficially negative formulation, as in the instant case. The definition of a curfew order in the Powers of Criminal Courts (Sentencing) Act 2000, s.37, and the imposition of a condition of residence on a grant of bail by the Bail Act 1976, s.3(6), supported the conclusion that the prohibition in the instant case was unlawfully mandatory in nature. Secondly, a curfew was tantamount to a penal sanction and, as such, was incompatible with the classification of ASBOs. The Court refused the application. While in *M v Sheffield Magistrates' Court*,[65] it was said that orders should contain negatively worded prohibitions, there was nothing wrong with imposing a condition of residence by having the claiming not live anywhere other than at a stipulated address. When a curfew order was imposed as a sentence under the Powers of the Criminal Courts (Sentencing) Act 2000, it was properly described as a penalty because that is its purpose—to punish. However, when a prohibition was imposed as part of an ASBO, even though it restricted freedom of movement in the same way and possibly for a more prolonged period of time, its purpose was not to punish but was preventative and protective. It was implicit in the above passages from Lord Hope's speech that, because the content and duration of an ASBO was conditioned solely by what is necessary for the purpose of protecting members of the public from further anti-social behaviour, the court was not required to consider what sentence would have been imposed, whether by way of curfew order or otherwise, if it had been sentencing the same person for one or more of the same acts which justify the making of an ASBO. Accordingly, there was nothing legally objectionable in the inclusion of a curfew provision in an ASBO if it is necessary for protection. However, just because the ASBO must run for a minimum of two years it does not follow that each and every prohibition within a particular order must endure for the life of the order. A curfew for two years in the life of a teenager was a very considerable restriction of freedom. It may be necessary, but in many cases it

[64] [2005] 1 W.L.R. 2570.
[65] [2004] EWHC 1830 (Admin).

was likely that either the period of curfew could properly be set at less than the full life of the order or that, in the light of behavioural progress, an application to vary the curfew under s.1(8) might well succeed.

6-069   In *Starling*,[66] the appellant appealed against a five year anti-social behaviour order imposed as part of his sentence for a charge of affray. He pleaded guilty to charges of aggravated vehicle taking and affray. In respect of the former, he had been sentenced to 12 months' imprisonment and had been disqualified from driving for two years and further disqualified until he passed a retest. In respect of the latter, a consecutive period of 12 months' imprisonment had been imposed and, upon release from custody, the ASBO was to take effect. The ASBO imposed a nightly curfew, as well as prohibitions on criminal behaviour; on the consumption of alcohol in a public place; on possession of bladed articles, and from driving a motor vehicle. He had agreed to the terms of the ASBO before sentence, but it was not in dispute that such agreement had been in the expectation that the ASBO alone was a sufficient punishment for the offence. He submitted that although the ASBO was appropriate in principle, it was too harsh in a number of respects, namely that: (1) the curfew did not specify a particular address at which he must remain; (2) the prohibition on alcohol consumption ought to exclude consumption of alcohol in licensed premises; (3) the prohibition on the use of bladed articles should be limited to use in public places; and (4) the prohibition from driving was inconsistent with the disqualification from driving, which formed part of the sentence for the offence of aggravated vehicle taking. The Court of Appeal allowed the appeal: a curfew which stated only that he was to remain indoors between specified hours was difficult to enforce effectively and ought instead to name premises at which he should reside. In any event, a five year curfew was excessive and a two year curfew was substituted. The prohibition on consuming alcohol in a public place was to be amended by adding the words "other than licensed premises" and the duration of the prohibition was reduced to two years. The additional clause prohibiting him from being under the influence of alcohol in a public place was too vague to be enforceable and was quashed. Unless the words "in a public place" were added to the prohibition on the use of bladed articles, he would be unable to use a knife to eat or prepare food at home. However, such an amendment would be a prohibition on what was already a criminal offence. The bladed articles provision was therefore set aside. The prohibition on driving in the ASBO was effectively a substitute for disqualification from driving, which was inappropriate and had to be quashed, especially as it had been open to the judge to disqualify him from driving for a longer period. An order in an ASBO prohibiting criminal behaviour was not, in most circumstances, appropriate. Taking into consideration the other elements of the ASBO, there was sufficient protection of the public and the prohibition on criminal behaviour was set aside.

6-070   In *Boness*, the ASBO contained these restrictions and almost none of them survived scrutiny on appeal:

"(1) Entering any public car park within the Basingstoke and Deane Borough Council area, except in the course of lawful employment.
(2) Entering any land or building on the land which forms a part of educational premises except as an enrolled pupil with the agreement of the head of the establishment or in the course of lawful employment.
(3) In any public place, wearing, or having with you anything which covers, or could be used to cover, the face or part of the face. This will include hooded clothing, balaclavas, masks or anything else which could be used to

---

[66] [2005] WL 2273349.

hide identity, except that a motorcycle helmet may be worn only when lawfully riding a motorcycle.

(4) Having any item with you in public which could be used in the commission of a burglary, or theft of or from vehicles except that you may carry one door key for your house and one motor vehicle or bicycle lock key. A motor vehicle key can only be carried if you are able to inform a checking officer of the registration number of the vehicle and that it can be ascertained that the vehicle is insured for you to drive it.

(5) Having possession of any article in public or carried in any vehicle, that could be used as a weapon. This will include glass bottles, drinking glasses and tools.

(6) Remaining on any shop, commercial or hospital premises if asked to leave by staff.

(7) Entering any premises from which barred.

(8) Entering upon any private land adjoining any dwelling premises or commercial premises outside of opening hours of that premises without the express permission of a person in charge of that premises. This includes front gardens, driveways and paths. Except in the course of lawful employment.

(9) Touching or entering any unattended vehicle without the express permission of the owner.

(10) Acting or inciting others to act in an anti-social manner, that is to say, a manner that causes or is likely to cause harassment, alarm or distress to one or more persons not of the same household.

(11) Congregating in groups of people in a manner causing or likely to cause any person to fear for their safety or congregating in groups of more than SIX persons in an outdoor public place.

(12) Doing anything which may cause damage.

(13) Not being anywhere but your home address as listed on this order between 2330 hours and 0700 hours or at an alternative address as agreed in advance with the prolific and priority offender officer or anti-social behaviour co-ordinator at Basingstoke Police Station.

(14) Being carried on any vehicle other than a vehicle in lawful use.

(15) Being in the company of Jason Arnold, Richard Ashman, Corrine Barlow, Mark Bicknell, Joseph (Joe) Burford, Sean Condon, Alan Dawkins, Simon Lee, Daniel (Danny) Malcolm, Michael March or Nathan Threshie."

The duration of the order was five years after release from custody. The Court **6-071** of Appeal rejected all of the terms of the orders. The first order did not state whether any of the vehicle crimes committed by the appellant took place in a public car park. However, it was submitted that it could sensibly be argued that a person intent on committing vehicle crime was likely to be attracted to car parks. The prohibition as drafted did not appear to allow the offender to park his own vehicle in a public car park or, for example, to be a passenger in a vehicle driven into a public car park in the course of a shopping trip. Thus, in the absence of evidence showing that the appellant committed vehicle crime in car parks, there would appear to be a question mark over whether the prohibition is proportional, particularly as prohibition (3) seems to be drafted with a view to allowing the appellant to ride a motorcycle. If the court contemplated the lawful use of a motorbike as an activity which the appellant could pursue, then this prohibition would significantly limit the places he might be able to park it. Even if the order was necessary to prevent anti-social behaviour by the appellant, it was not proportionate.

As to the second order prohibited the appellant from: entering any land or **6-072** building on the land which forms a part of educational premises except as an enrolled pupil with the agreement of the head of the establishment or in the course of lawful employment, it was not clear what information provided the basis for making this prohibition. There was nothing in the appellant's previous offending history which suggests that he engaged in anti-social behaviour in educational premises. The term "educational premises" arguably lacks clarity; for example, it was not clear whether or not it included teaching hospitals or premises where night classes are held. There also a danger that the appellant might unwittingly breach the terms of the order were he, for example, to play sport on playing fields associated with educational premises. The term was neither clear nor necessary.

6-073   As to the third term, it was presumed that this prohibition was based upon the assertion that the appellant is forensically aware and will use items to attempt to prevent detection. The terms were too wide, resulting in a lack of clarity and consequences which are not commensurate with the risk which the prohibition seeks to address. The phrase "having with you anything which. . .could be used to cover the face or part of the face" covered a huge number of items. For example, it was not unknown for those seeking to conceal their identity to pull up a jumper to conceal part of the face, but the prohibition could not have been intended to limit so radically the choice of clothing that the appellant can wear. The appellant would potentially be in breach of the order were he to wear a scarf or carry a newspaper in public.

6-074   The fourth term suffered from lack of clarity and was drafted too widely. There were many items that might be used in the commission of a burglary, such as a credit card, a mobile phone or a pair of gloves. Was the appellant being prohibited from carrying such items? If so, the order is neither clear nor proportionate. The fifth term was defective because the necessity for such a prohibition was not supported by the material put forward in support of the application. There is very little in the appellant's antecedent history which indicated a disposition to use a weapon. Furthermore, it was submitted that the wording of the prohibition was obviously too wide, resulting in lack of clarity and consequences which were not commensurate with the risk. Many otherwise innocent items had the capacity to be used as weapons, including anything hard or with an edge or point. This prohibition had draconian consequences. The appellant would be prohibited from doing a huge range of things, including having a drink in a public bar. However, as to the sixth term, the appellant had convictions for offences of dishonesty, including an attempted burglary of shop premises and he had been reprimanded for shoplifting. Thus, there appeared to be a foundation for such a prohibition. It was submitted that this term is capable of being understood by the appellant and was proportionate given that it hinges upon being refused permission to enter/remain on particular premises by those who have control of them.

6-075   The seventh term was too wide. In *McGrath*, the Court of Appeal held that a term which prohibited the appellant from "trespassing on any land belonging to any person whether legal or natural within those counties" was too wide and harsh. If the appellant took a wrong turn on a walk and entered someone's property, he would be at risk of a five year prison sentence. Although certain pieces of land might easily be identified as being caught by the prohibition (such as a front garden, driveway or path) it might be harder to recognise it in more rural areas. The absence of any geographical restriction reinforced the court's view. Furthermore, there was no practical way that compliance with the order could be enforced, at least outside the appellant's immediate home area. As to the eighth term, the appellant has previous convictions for aggravated vehicle taking and interfering with a motor vehicle, and has been reprimanded for theft of a motorcycle. It was sufficiently clear and precise, and is commensurate with the risk it sought to meet. However, it should have had a geographical limit so as to make it feasible to enforce the order. Local officers, aware of the prohibition, would then have a useful weapon to prevent the appellant committing vehicle crime. They would not have to wait until he had committed a particular crime relating to vehicles. As to term nine, while it was properly made, it required some geographical limit, in the absence of good reasons for having no such limit.

The first part of the tenth term, given the appellant's previous history, was **6-076** necessary. However, the final clause prohibited the appellant from attending sporting or other outdoor events. Such a prohibition was disproportionate. Although, the appellant would be able to argue that he had a reasonable excuse for attending the event, this was not a sufficient safeguard. Term eleven was far too wide. The twelfth order, a curfew order, could be properly be included in an ASBO, but it was unnecessary in this case. Although the offences of interfering with a motor vehicle and attempted burglary were both committed between 10pm and midnight on the same evening, there was nothing to suggest that other offences had been committed at night. Moreover, the author of the pre-sentence report stated that the appellant's offending behaviour did not fit a pattern which could be controlled by the use of a curfew order. Even if an ASBO was justified, a five year curfew to follow release is not, in our view, proportionate. The thirteenth term was not clear and unambiguous. The expression "lawful use" was unclear in scope; if "the carrying" was likely to constitute a specific criminal offence, it added nothing. The court would have preferred some geographical limit.

The final order appeared to be based on the assertion in a police officer's **6-077** statement that the appellant was associating with other criminals who were also nominated as persistent prolific offenders. The appellant admitted that the offending spree which recently brought him before the court was the result of being contacted by an old friend. Care had been taken to identify the individuals with whom the appellant is not to associate; however, a prohibition that prevents the appellant from associating with any of the named individuals for five years after his release, even in a private residence where one or more resides, was disproportionate to the risk of anti-social behaviour it is designed to prevent.

Boness was followed in *Dickenson*.[67] In November 2005 the applicant, **6-078** having entered a guilty plea, was sentenced for offences of theft, of two months' imprisonment concurrent to count 2; and for assault occasioning actual bodily harm, of six months' imprisonment, which was to be consecutive to the sentence imposed arising from an offence on the second indictment; for another offence of assault occasioning actual bodily harm he was sentenced to nine months' imprisonment. In addition, the judge imposed an anti-social behaviour order for four years to commence from the date of the appellant's release from prison. That order was in the following terms:

"The defendant is prohibited from:

1. Behaving in an anti-social manner so as to cause harassment, alarm or distress to any person not in the same household as himself.
2. Damaging, taking or interfering with the property of any person except with their express permission."

On January 10, 2005 the appellant, who was 26 years of age at the date of the offence and 27 years of age at the date of sentence, entered a supermarket and stole three bottles of spirits. He was apprehended by a security guard and, as he was being prevented from leaving the supermarket, he struck the security guard over the head with one of the bottles, causing a small cut which required medical attention. Charges were not laid against him in respect of these offences until July 7, 2005 as he had been serving a custodial sentence in the

---

[67] [2006] EWCA Crim 188.

meantime. On July 10, 2005 the appellant had returned to the home he had previously shared with his partner, who had offered him accommodation after his release on July 7. He had insisted that their relationship continue but she was adamant that the relationship was over and that caused friction between them. On the evening of July 10 she was at her parents' address with their young child when the appellant appeared. He had climbed on to the little roof over the front door and she told him effectively that their relationship was over. He began to cry and pleaded with her but she would not relent. He grabbed hold of her by the wrists and punched her in the mouth. As a result she suffered a bloodied and bruised nose, a cup lip and lost one tooth. In his interview he said that the injuries were caused by a window being shut. He had a poor record for dishonesty, which was entirely consistent with his long-standing drug addiction. However, there had been no previous offences of violence or public order offences. His appeal was on the basis that the terms of the anti-social behaviour order could not be shown to be necessary to protect persons in any place in England and Wales from further anti-social acts by the defendant and that therefore the order should not have been made. If following conviction for the offence the offender would be liable to imprisonment, an anti-social behaviour order would add nothing, other than to increase the sentence if the sentence for the offence was less than five years' imprisonment. However, if the offender was not going to be deterred from committing the offence by a sentence of imprisonment for that offence, the anti-social behaviour order was not likely further to deter and was therefore not necessary. The test for making the order was not whether the offender needs reminding that certain matters constitute criminal conduct but whether it was necessary. An anti-social behaviour order should not be used merely to increase the sentence of imprisonment which an offender was liable to receive. Different considerations may apply if the maximum sentence was only a fine, but the court must still go through all the steps to make sure that an anti-social behaviour order was necessary. Further, the order should be directed at conduct preparatory to the commission of such an offence. Not only must the court, before imposing an order prohibiting the offender from doing something, consider that such an order was necessary to protect persons from further anti-social acts by him, but the terms of the order must be proportionate, in the sense that they must be commensurate with the risk which must be guarded against. This was particularly important where an order may interfere with a Convention right protected by the Human Rights Act 1998. Before the trial judge, the crown sought an anti-social behaviour order comprising five limbs. The judge made an order which comprised the first and third limbs of the draft order provided by the prosecution. He expressed the view that para.1 of the order he proposed to make would in effect cover all of the behaviour which the prosecution sought to prohibit under the other four limbs. So far as the first limb of the order is concerned, his order was not necessary to protect persons from further anti-social acts. The first paragraph essentially prohibited the commission of offences contrary to s.5 of the Public Order Act. That offence attracted only a fine, not a term of imprisonment. However, there was no question that the appellant was a person who caused low level nuisance of the nature of s.5. Although the appellant had a bad criminal record, he had no previous convictions for public order offences. Moreover, the judge's intention was that the first limb of the order was intended to prohibit behaviour that the prosecution had sought to prohibit under the other four limbs of its draft order. These essentially prohibited the commission of criminal offences. For the reasons given by the court in *Boness*, this was not permissible. So far as the second limb was concerned, the effect was to prohibit the commission of criminal damage or theft. To that extent it cannot be considered to have been necessary to protect persons from further anti-social acts by the defendant for the reasons given by this court in *Boness*. To the extent that it extended beyond the commission of such offences, that was in so far as it related to interference with property which does not constitute a criminal offence, it was not necessary in order to protect members of the public from anti-social behaviour.

What is the consequence of breaching a term of an order that is rightly held to be wide and unenforceable? In *CPS v T*,[68] this is a prosecution appealed by case stated a decision of a District Judge, sitting in the Manchester City Youth Court in September 2005, when he dismissed a charge against the respondent child of a breach of an ASBO on the ground that the relevant provision of the ASBO was unenforceable and void. The ASBO was of two years duration. However, the ASBO was treated as having been made "by consent". The terms of the order were that the child was not to:

    6-079

"(1) Act in an anti-social manner in the City of Manchester.
(2) 2. Use abusive, insulting, offensive, threatening or intimidating language or behaviour in a public place or in any place to which the or to which the (sic) public has access. Approach, threaten, intimidate, or communicate directly or indirectly with . . . [there followed a list of names].
(3) Enter the area in red on the plan attached, MARKED A.
(4) Congregate in a group numbering greater than three persons in the area marked red on Map B.
(5) Associate in any way in a public place, or a place to which the public has access, with . . . [there followed a list of names] or any of them in the area marked in red on Map B."

The appeal turned the application of para.(1), that the respondent shall not "act in an anti-social manner in the City of Manchester". In June 2005, the order was quashed by Moses J. The City Council did not resist the quashing order, despite having taken the point in the court below. Moses J. ordered that the appeal be relisted before the Crown Court as soon as possible. No steps were taken to do this, and indeed the Crown Court were never informed of the order of Moses J. quashing the order of that court. Then, in July 2005 the offender committed an offence of interference with a motor vehicle, to which he pleaded guilty and for which he was sentenced by the District Judge. The offence took place within the City of Manchester local government area, but was not within the locations specified in either of the maps attached to the ASBO. The offender submitted that the prohibition in para.1 of the order was invalid and therefore unenforceable, being far too widely drawn. Nor were the terms of the order made sufficiently clear to enable him, a boy aged only 13 when it was made, to know what he may and may not do. The expression "not act in an anti-social manner" entirely failed this test. Because that definition appears in the Act, the term was easily understood by those made subject to such orders. The District Judge held that the prohibition "not to act in an anti-social manner" was too vague, lacked clarity and was therefore unenforceable and void; by committing the offence of interfering with a motor vehicle the respondent could not therefore be in breach of a prohibition not to act in an anti-social manner. Therefore, the charge of breaching the Respondent's anti-social behaviour order should be dismissed; and an appropriate sentence in this case, and having regard to all the circumstances, for the offences of interfering with a motor vehicle was a Supervision Order for 12 months, together with an electronically monitored curfew order for one month each day between the hours of 9pm and 7am.

    6-080

The Court of Appeal agreed that cl.6 of this order was unenforceable, but held it was not open to him to hold that it was not a valid order. The ASBO

    6-081

---

[68] [2006] EWHC 728.

in this case was made by a court of competent jurisdiction and is valid on its face; any challenge should have been by way of appeal against the making of the order or by application to vary it. First, the normal rule in relation to an order of the court was that it must be treated as valid and be obeyed unless and until it is set aside. Even if the order should not have been made in the first place, a person may be liable for any breach of it committed before it was set aside. Secondly, the person against whom an ASBO was made has a full opportunity to challenge that order on appeal or to apply to vary it: indeed, the respondent did appeal the order made against him in this case, though the matter was not pursued to a conclusion. Accordingly, in so far as any question does arise as to the validity of such an order, there was no obvious reason why the person against whom the order was made should be allowed to raise that issue as a defence in subsequent breach proceedings, rather than by way of appeal against the original order. Even if that were wrong, any issue as to the validity of the original order should be raised by way of an appeal against that order (or possibly by an application for judicial review, if that were an appropriate remedy despite the existence of an avenue of appeal) rather than as a defence to breach proceedings. Yet another consideration in the present case was that, although it is alleged that the relevant provision of the ASBO was unduly wide and uncertain and unnecessary for the purpose of protecting against further anti-social acts, that did not go to the validity of the order. The magistrates' court had jurisdiction under the Crime and Disorder Act 1998 to make an ASBO. If the court was in error in including a provision in these terms, that did not have the consequence of taking the order outside the court's jurisdiction; and if the order was within the court's jurisdiction, it would remain valid even if there were errors in it that were open to correction on appeal. The Divisional Court in *R(W)* was wrong to hold that because an order was "plainly too wide" it was also "plainly invalid". It did not follow that the District Judge lacked any means of giving effect to the concerns he had about the width and uncertainty of the order. It was open to him to consider whether the relevant provision lacked sufficient clarity to warrant a finding that the respondent's conduct amounted to a breach of the order; whether the lack of clarity provided a reasonable excuse for non-compliance with the order; and whether, if a breach was established, it was appropriate in the circumstances to impose any penalty for the breach. However, the term not to act in an anti-social manner, would have been struck out on appeal or on an application to vary the order, so the District Judge was right in the conclusion which he reached in relation to para.1 of the order. It did not even include the explanatory words contained in the statutory definition, namely the words "that is to say in a manner that caused or was likely to cause harassment, alarm or distress to one or more persons not of the same household of himself". It lacked the essential element of clarity as to what the respondent was and was not permitted to do. He, a boy aged 13 to 15 years during the currency of the order, could not be taken to know the ambit of the words "act in an anti-social manner". He would probably not know the geographical ambit of the City of Manchester. His case, the Court said, provided a particularly good example of the need to carefully match the prohibitions in an ASBO to the type of behaviour which it is necessary to prohibit for the purposes specified in the Crime and Disorder Act. Such a wide provision as "not to act in an anti-social manner", without further definition or limitation, should never again be included in an ASBO. The ASBO Guidance gave numerous examples of proper forms of prohibitions, and courts could not do better than to adopt and follow the guidance contained in that document. The District Judge had not been entitled to strike down the offending paragraph of the ASBO, and it remained in force until it expired in October 2005. It was in force when the respondent committed the offence of vehicle interference, and indeed it was still in force when the breach proceedings were heard. Thus, however inappropriate he considered it to be, he should have gone on to determine whether there was a breach of the order and, if so, to consider the question of penalty. It may very well be that the District Judge would have been entitled to hold that there was no breach of the order.

Interim Applications

The Police Reform Act 2002 introduced interim ASBOs. Home Office   **6-082**
Guidance provides that the benefit of the interim order is that it enables the courts to order an immediate stop to anti-social behaviour and thereby to protect the public more quickly; it reduces the scope for witness intimidation by making it unlawful for the offender to continue the behaviour whilst the ASBO application is being processed; it also removes any incentive for delaying the proceedings on the part of the perpetrator. The interim order will send a clear message to the community that swift action against anti-social behaviour is possible.[69] Under s.1D(2), if, before determining an application to which this section applies, the court considers that it is just to make an order under this section pending the determination of that application ("the main application"), it may make such an order. An order under this section is an order which prohibits the defendant from doing anything described in the order.[70] An order under this section: (a) shall be for a fixed period; (b) may be varied, renewed or discharged; or, (c) shall, if it has not previously ceased to have effect, cease to have effect on the determination of the main application.[71]

Section 1D has been amended by s.139 of the Serious Organised Crime and   **6-083**
Police Act 2005. The new version of s.1D contains new versions of s.1D(1) and (2). These are:

"(1) This section applies where-

(a) an application is made for an anti-social behaviour order;
(b) an application is made for an order under section 1B;
(c) a request is made by the prosecution for an order under section 1C; or
(d) the court is minded to make an order under section 1C of its own motion.
(2) If, before determining the application or request, or before deciding whether to make an order under section 1C of its own motion, the court considers that it is just to make an order under this section pending the determination of that application or request or before making that decision, it may make such an order."

And so, subs.(4)(c) is amended. The term "main application" is substituted now by "application or request mentioned in subsection (1), or on the court's making a decision as to whether or not to make an order under section 1C of its own motion." Accordingly, there is a new subs.(6). It provides:

"(a) subsections (6) and (10) to (12) of section 1 apply for the purposes of the making and effect of orders under this section as they apply for the purposes of the making and effect of anti-social behaviour orders; and
(b) section 1CA applies for the purposes of the variation or discharge of an order under this section as it applies for the purposes of the variation or discharge of an order under section 1C."

---

[69] The Police Reform Act 2002, p.18.
[70] The Crime and Disorder Act 1998, s.1D(3).
[71] *ibid.*, s.1D(4).

Such an order may be made ex parte: in the magistrates' court, an ex parte order would require leave of the justices or court clerk. Unlike the permanent order, an interim ASBO is for a fixed period and will cease to have effect if the application for the ASBO or county court order is withdrawn or refused. However, the consequences for breach are the same. Note also that the geographical area over which any ASBO may have effect is no longer limited to the local authority area and may extend across England and Wales.[72]

6-084	The Magistrates' Court (Anti-social Behaviour Orders) Rules 2002 make express provision for interim ASBOs. Rule 5 provides:

"(1) An application for an interim order under section 1D, may, with leave of the justices clerk, be made without notice being given to the defendant.
(2) The justices clerk shall only grant leave under paragraph (1) of this rule if he is satisfied that it is necessary for the application to be made without notice being given to the defendant.
(3) If an application made under paragraph (2) is granted, then the interim order and the application for an anti-social behaviour order under section 1 (together with a summons giving a date for the defendant to attend court) shall be served on the defendant in person as soon as practicable after the making of the interim order.
(4) An interim order which is made at the hearing of an application without notice shall not take effect until it has been served on the defendant.
(5) If such an interim order made without notice is not served upon the defendant within 7 days of being made, then it shall cease to have effect.
(6) An interim order shall cease to have effect if the application for an anti-social behaviour order is withdrawn.
(7) Where the court refuses to make an interim order without notice being given to the defendant it may direct that the application be made on notice.
(8) If an interim order is made without notice being given to the defendant, and the defendant subsequently applies to the court for the order to be discharged or varied, his application shall not be dismissed without the opportunity for him to make oral representations to the court."

6-085	Rule 6 makes provision for applications for variation or discharge of an ASBO:

"(1) This rule applies to the making of an application for the variation or discharge of an order made under section 1, 1C, or subject to rule 5(8) above, 1D.
(2) An application to which this rule applies shall be made in writing to the magistrates court which made the order, or in the case of an application under section 1C to any magistrates' court in the same petty sessions area, and shall specify the reason why the applicant for variation or discharge believes the court should vary or discharge the order as the case may be.
(3) Subject to rule 5(8) above, where the court considers there are no grounds upon which it might conclude that the order should be varied or discharged, as the case may be, it may determine the application without hearing representations from the applicant for variation or discharge or from any other person.
(4) Where the court considers that there are grounds upon which it might conclude that the order should be varied or discharged, as the case may be, the justices chief executive shall, unless the application is withdrawn, issue a summons giving not less than 14 days notice in writing of the date, time and place appointed for the hearing."

---

[72] The Crime and Disorder Act 1998, s.1(6); s.1C(2)(b) as regards orders made in criminal proceedings.

In *Kenny and M*,[73] the applicant applied for judicial review of a decision **6-086** making an interim ASBO against him. The police had been concerned to remove the drugs market from a local area. By July 2003 the West Yorkshire Police Force had become increasingly concerned at the problem of drug dealing and abuse and associated criminal behaviour in the area of Leeds known as Little London ("the area"). There was a thriving street trade in drugs, in particular heroin and crack cocaine. It was very difficult to police effectively given its geographical layout, which enabled dealers to place lookouts to warn of the approach of the police, and the numerous side streets affording escape routes for suspects. The open dealing in drugs had brought large numbers of drug users into the area with associated crime, as drug users commit acquisitive crime to fund the purchase of drugs, and may also themselves be the victims of crime. Analysis of crime statistics showed high levels of violent crime within the area. The presence of drug dealers and their customers had had a very serious impact on the neighbourhood, with complaints from residents of lawless behaviour, and of the detritus associated with drug abuse, in particular discarded used syringes. In consequence the area had deteriorated with residents seeking to move out, and potential tenants of the Leeds City Council refusing to move in. There was evidence from a detective to say that the area has been the subject of many police operations over the past two years, none of which have had a lasting effect on the core problem of drug-dealing and abuse, and associated crime. Police officers called to the area have been met by increasingly aggressive and abusive groups of young males, and information has been received that the carrying and use of firearms has become prevalent within the area. The police came to the conclusion that the problem of violent crime and general lawless behaviour associated with drug-dealing and drug abuse would remain unless the drugs market could be removed. Consideration was therefore given to addressing the problem by seeking ASBOs under s.1D of the Crime and Disorder Act 1998 as amended, and in late July the West Yorkshire Police met officials of the Home Office ASBO Department. Officers of Leeds City Council met the West Yorkshire Police with a view to commencing proceedings for ASBOs. The police were responsible for the collation of evidence from their intelligence records and for obtaining witness statements from police officers. An initial list of 132 names of those linked to the drugs trade in the area was produced, but reduced to 66 on August 22. An application for permission to hear applications for ASBOs without notice was heard and granted on August 27. The applications were heard by the District Judge in September, and ASBOs were made against 66 individuals, including Kenny and M.

The order made against M prohibited him from: **6-087**

"1. Acting in a manner which causes or is likely to cause nuisance, harassment, alarm or distress to any person in the area of West Yorkshire.
2. Abusing, insulting, harassing or threatening any person in the area of West Yorkshire.
3. Using or threatening violence towards any person in the area of West Yorkshire.
4. Entering or remaining within the area(s) marked in red on the attached map(s).
5. Being in possession of a drug or substance described as controlled by the Misuse of Drugs Act 1971.
6. Being present when controlled drugs (as defined by Misuse of Drugs Act 1971), or substances are traded, sold, supplied (commercial or otherwise) or otherwise distributed in any place to which the public have access.

---

[73] [2004] 1 All E.R. 1333.

7. Encourage or inciting others to carry out any of the prohibited acts on your behalf.
8. Having contact with, in public, whether by being in a group with, talking to or otherwise associating with any of the following – . . ."

There then followed a list of 13 names. The order stated that it would end on 15 December 2003, and further ordered the claimant to attend at the magistrates' court on September 15, 2003. He was under 18 years old when the ASBO was made. He applied unsuccessfully for the discharge of the ASBO. He argued that the judge had erred in law when making the ASBO and when refusing to discharge it. He contended that there was no basis upon which an interim ASBO could properly have been made as such relief could only be granted in exceptional circumstances and where there was compelling urgency. In considering whether it was just to make an interim ASBO, the court must have regard to the principle that the best interests of the child are a primary consideration. Owen J. granted the application for judicial review. The fact that prohibitions made under s.1(6) of that Act may have this effect was sufficient to attract the right to a fair trial which is guaranteed by Art.6(1). This meant that the court must act with scrupulous fairness at all stages within the proceedings. When it was making its assessment of the facts and circumstances that have been put before it in evidence and the prohibitions, if any, that were to be imposed, it must ensure that the defendant does not suffer any injustice. There was nothing inherently unlawful in interim injunctions made without notice. The power to make such orders was a necessary weapon in the judicial armour, enabling the court to do justice in circumstances where it was necessary to act urgently to protect the interests of a party, or where it was necessary to act without notice to a prospective defendant in order to ensure that the order of the court is effective, such as search orders and freezing orders. Nor did the fact that criminal sanctions attached to a breach of an ASBO render the r.5 procedure unlawful. Furthermore, the 2002 Rules provided important safeguards for the protection of a defendant, namely that an order does not take effect until served on the defendant (r.5(4)); if not served within seven days of being made the order would cease to have effect (r.5(5)); it was open to a defendant to apply for the discharge or variation of an order (s.1D(4)(b)); and on such an application the defendant had the right to make oral representations (r.5(8)), and finally that a defendant has a right of appeal to the Crown Court (s.4(1) as amended).

6-088   Owen J. also held that there was no determination of civil rights within the meaning of Art.6(1) on the making of an interim ASBO without notice. Article 6 was concerned with procedural fairness. An interim order was by its very nature temporary, and served to regulate behaviour until the determination of the parties' civil rights at the substantive hearing. After the making of the interim order Art.6 was engaged, as procedural fairness was necessary prior to the determination so that there could be a fair hearing at the determination. But at that stage the requirements of Art.6 were satisfied by the procedural safeguards embodied in the 2002 Rules. Secondly, the information before the District Judge was to the effect that a very serious problem existed in the area with regard to drug dealing and associated crime and disorder. Owen J. said that he was satisfied that, on the basis of that material, the judge could properly conclude that the imposition of an interim order was urgently required to provide some regulation of the anti-social behaviour, and that it was necessary for the application to be made without notice. The test for making an interim order under s.1D of the Act was whether it was just to do so pending the determination of the main application. That was to be contrasted with the test under s.1(4), whereby an order may be made by a magistrates' court if it is proved that the conditions mentioned in subs.(1) were satisfied, namely that the person had acted in an anti-social manner and secondly that such an order was necessary to protect persons in the relevant area from further anti-social acts by him. Consideration of whether it was just to make an order without notice was necessarily a balancing exercise. The court must balance the need to protect the public against the impact that the order sought will have upon the defendant. It would need to consider the seriousness of the behaviour in issue, the urgency with which it is necessary to take steps to control such behaviour, and whether it was necessary for orders to be made without notice in order for them to be effective. On the other side of the equation it would consider the degree to which the order would impede the defendant's rights as a free citizen to go where he pleased and to associate with whosoever he pleased. It was implicit in the balancing exercise that the considerations that weigh in favour of injunctive relief must be sufficiently serious to warrant what may amount to a serious interference with the civil rights of a defendant. 41 of those against whom ASBOs were made on September 2 were under the age of 18. It was submitted that, in considering whether it is just to make an interim ASBO, the court must have regard to the principle that the best interests of the child are a primary consideration, per Art.24(1) of the European Union Charter of Fundamental Rights. There was also a duty on public bodies to have regard to the principles embodied in the United Nations Convention on the Rights of the Child and the European Union Charter of Fundamental Rights.[74] These considerations applied to proceedings before a magistrates' court for an interim ASBO. Where a defendant was under 18 the court must have regard to the principle that his best interests are a primary consideration when addressing the question of whether it is just to make an order. The Court of Appeal dismissed an appeal.[75]

Although it is unusual for a court in this country to make an order against **6-089** a person who had not been given notice of the proceedings, that course was adopted when it was necessary to do so, and subject to safeguards which enabled the person affected at an early stage to have the order reviewed or discharged. The more intrusive the order the more the court would require proof that it was necessary that it should be made, and made in the particular form sought, but there was nothing intrinsically objectionable about the power to grant an interim ASBO without notice. It was important to note that an interim ASBO made without notice was ineffective until served, and when made as required in the standard form it made provision for all parties to attend at court, either on a return date or on a date fixed for the hearing of the full application. If it be the former then it would be open to the court to reconsider the order, either to vary it or discharge it, if it considered that to be the appropriate course. It was the practice at Leeds always to ask the court to fix an early return date (in this case it was 13 days after the date of the order), and that seems to the Court to be desirable. Reliance upon the date for the hearing for the full application would seem to be undesirable, unless it could be heard at a very early date. From the time that the order was served the person upon whom it was served could apply, under r.6, to have the order varied or discharged, and the requirement that the justices' chief executive give not less than 14 days notice of the hearing of the application was, in the Court of Appeal's judgment, a sensible and realistic procedural requirement, which

---

[74] Munby J. in *R. (Howard League for Penal Reform) v Secretary of State for the Home Department* in the context of those under 18 detained in Young Offender Institutions, at para.67: "Such measures (the measures taken with regard to those detained in YOIs) must strike a fair balance between the competing interests of the particular child and the general interests of the community as a whole . . . but always having regard to; (i) first, to the principle that the best interests of the child are at all times a primary consideration."

[75] [2004] 1 W.L.R. 2298.

did not undermine the right of the person affected to seek rapid relief. Nothing could be made of the fact that under r.6 it is for the parties, and not for the court, to seek a review. Because an application for an interim order without notice can only be made when the justices' clerk was satisfied that it was necessary for the application to be made without notice, and because the order can only be made for a limited period, when the court considers that it was just to make it, and in circumstances where it could be reviewed or discharged as indicated above, it would be impossible to say that it determined civil rights. Certainly for a time it restricted certain freedoms, and the restriction could be enforced by sanctions, but that was the nature of any interim order, so provided the interim order followed its normal course, Art.6 of the European Convention would not be engaged. Although Art.6 was not engaged, the procedure must be fair, and there was no apparent unfairness in the procedure. If Art.6 were engaged it would be appropriate to look at the process as a whole, bearing in mind that the application for an ASBO is a civil procedure to which an application for an interim order was ancillary, and if that approach were adopted no contravention of the requirements of Art.6 could be discerned. The test to be adopted by a Magistrates' Court when deciding whether or not to make an interim order must be the statutory test, whether it was just to make the order. That involved consideration of all relevant circumstances, including, in a case such as this, the fact that the application had been made without notice. Obviously the court must consider whether the application for the final order had been properly made, but there was no justification for requiring the Magistrates' Court, when considering whether to make an interim order, to decide whether the evidence in support of the full order discloses an extremely strong prima facie case. The correct test having been used in the present case, there was ample evidence to support the conclusion of the District Judge that in relation to M, it was just for an interim order to be made. The fact that no vulnerable witnesses were identified by name was of no significance when the available evidence and information was considered as a whole. There was therefore no substance in any of the grounds of appeal, and it is unnecessary to consider the availability of the relief sought. If the procedure had been successfully impugned it would certainly be necessary to consider the possible impact of s.3 of the Human Rights Act before deciding to quash r.5.

6-090   *M* and *Kenny* were applied in *R. v Manchester Magistrates, Ex p. Manchester CC*.[76] The claimant local authority sought judicial review of the decision of a justices clerk to the defendant court to refuse leave for an application for an interim ASBO to be made without notice. The local authority had sought the order following a complaint by one of its female tenants, who lived alone, that she had been subjected to verbal abuse and intimidation by her neighbour, a male tenant of an adjoining property, which included threats to kill her and to burn down her house. The local authority argued that the adviser had erred by carrying out the balancing exercise under s.1D of the 1998 Act, rather than that r.2 of the Magistrates' Courts (Anti-social Behaviour Orders) Rules 2002, and that her conclusion that the alleged misconduct was at the lower end of the scale of behaviours tackled by the use of ASBOs was irrational. The application was granted. The justices clerk had carried out the wrong balancing exercise. On an application for leave to make an application for an interim ASBO without notice, the role of the justices' clerk was to determine whether it was necessary for the application to be made without notice, applying the test under r.5(2). It was for the justices, and not the clerk, to decide, at a later stage, applying the more stringent test under s.1D, whether it was just to make the interim order. The evidence before the court indicated that the justices' clerk, in her delibera-

[76] [2005] WL 460720.

tions, had failed to have regards to all the relevant factors and/or made errors of fact. These included her failure to consider relevant information on the frequency of the misconduct; the likely effect the giving of notice would have upon each of the parties; and the nature of the prohibitions sought. Moreover her conclusion that the misconduct was at the lower end of the scale was irrational. The alleged threats to kill and destroy the complainant's home would, if proved, amount to serious criminal conduct. The conduct alleged, having regard to the proximity of both parties homes, should have persuaded the justices clerk that it was necessary for the interim application to be heard without notice. A mandatory order was made that leave be granted under r.5(2).

Judicial Review, Discharge, Revocation, Appeals

An order may be varied or discharged by way of an application by complaint. **6-091**
The application may be made by the police, the local authority or the defendant. An order cannot be discharged within the minimum two year period without the agreement of the police and the local authority. Variation or discharge of an order, including an interim order, may be made on application to the court that originally made it. An application to vary or discharge an order made on conviction in criminal proceedings may be made to any magistrates' court within the same petty sessions areas as the court that made the order. The application can be made either by the original applicant in the case or the defendant. An order cannot be discharged within two years of its service without the agreement of both parties. An order made on conviction cannot be discharged before the end of two years. The procedure for variation or discharge will be set out in the Magistrates' Courts (Anti-Social Behaviour Orders) Rules 2002, the Crown Court (Amendment) Rules 2002 and the Civil Procedure Rules. If the individual asks for a variation or discharge of an order, the agency that obtained the order needs to ensure that a considered response is given to the court.

Under a practice direction,[77] where an application was made to a magis- **6-092**
trates' court for an anti social behaviour order or for such an order to be varied or discharged, and the person against whom the order was sought was under 18, the magistrates constituting the court should normally be qualified to sit in the youth court. However, applications for interim orders, including those made without notice, could be listed before magistrates who were not so qualified. Further, the direction would not apply where it was not practicable to constitute a bench in accordance with the direction, particularly where to do so would result in a delayed hearing.

There is now, by virtue of s.140 of the Serious Organised Crime and Police **6-093**
Act 2005 a new section dealing with variation and discharge of orders under s.1C. It provides:

"(1) An offender subject to an order under section 1C may apply to the court which made it for it to be varied or discharged.
(2) If he does so, he must also send written notice of his application to the Director of Public Prosecutions.
(3) The Director of Public Prosecutions may apply to the court which made an order under section 1C for it to be varied or discharged.
(4) A relevant authority may also apply to the court which made an order under section 1C for it to be varied or discharged if it appears to it that—

(a) in the case of variation, the protection of relevant persons from anti-social acts by the person subject to the order would be more appropriately effected by a variation of the order;

---

[77] [2006] 1 W.L.R. 636.

(b) in the case of discharge, that it is no longer necessary to protect relevant persons from anti-social acts by him by means of such an order.

(5) If the Director of Public Prosecutions or a relevant authority applies for the variation or discharge of an order under section 1C, he or it must also send written notice of the application to the person subject to the order.
(6) In the case of an order under section 1C made by a magistrates' court, the references in subsections (1), (3) and (4) to the court by which the order was made include a reference to any magistrates' court acting in the same local justice area as that court.
(7) No order under section 1C shall be discharged on an application under this section before the end of the period of two years beginning with the day on which the order takes effect, unless—

(a) in the case of an application under subsection (1), the Director of Public Prosecutions consents, or
(b) in the case of an application under subsection (3) or (4), the offender consents."

Section 140 of the 2005 Act also amends s.3 of the Prosecution of Offences Act, so that where it appears to him appropriate to do so, the Director is to have the conduct of applications under s.1CA(3) of the Crime and Disorder Act 1998 for the variation or discharge of orders made under s.1C of that Act and, where it appears to him appropriate to do so, to appear on any application under s.1CA of that Act made by a person subject to an order under s.1C of that Act for the variation or discharge of the order. Previously an application to vary or discharge an order on conviction (a 1C order) could only be made by the defendant. Subsection 140(4) inserts s.1CA into the CDA 1998 which allows a "relevant authority", as set out in s.1(1A) of the CDA 1998, or the Crown Prosecution Service (CPS) to apply to vary or discharge the order. In addition, previously it was not possible to discharge an order on conviction within two years of it being made. Section 1CA(7) replicates the same provision that exists for s.1 and 1B orders and provides that the order on conviction may be discharged before two years, with consent of both the defendant and applicant authority, if it is deemed that the order is no longer necessary to protect others from the anti-social behaviour of the defendant

6-094   Section 4 of the Crime and Disorder Act 1998 provides the offender with the right of appeal against the making of an order. Appeal is to the Crown Court. Rules 74 and 75 of the Magistrates' Courts' Rules 1981 and 6 to 11 of the Crown Court Rules 1982 apply to appeals against orders. Both parties may provide additional evidence. By virtue of s.79(3) of the Supreme Court Act 1981, an appeal is by way of a re-hearing of the case. In determining an appeal, the Crown Court should have before it a copy of the original application for an order (if applicable), the full order and the notice of appeal. The lead agency should ensure that copies are sent to the court. Notice of appeal must be given in writing to the clerk of the court and the applicant body within 21 days of the order (Crown Court Rules, r.7). But the Crown Court has the discretion to give leave to appeal out of time (r.7(5)). The Crown Court may vary the order or make a new order. Any order made by the Crown Court on appeal shall be treated, for the purpose of any later application for variation or discharge, as if it were the original magistrates' court order, unless it is an order directing that the application be re-heard by the magistrates' court. Although, on hearing an appeal, it is open to the Crown Court to make any incidental order, for example, to suspend the operation of a prohibition pending the outcome of the appeal where this appears to the Crown Court to be just, there is no provision for automatic stay of an order pending appeal. The order remains in force pending the outcome of the appeal and breach is a criminal offence, even if the appeal subsequently succeeds. An appeal against the ruling of the Crown

Court is to the High Court by way of case stated under s.28 of the Supreme Court Act 1981, or by application for judicial review by virtue of s.29(3) of that Act. It is also open to the applying authority to seek to challenge a magistrates' decision to refuse to grant an order by way of case stated (judicial review of the decision to the Divisional Court) by virtue of s.111 of the Magistrates' Courts Act 1980. In the county court, any appeal against an ASBO made in the county court must be made in accordance with Pt 52 of the Civil Procedure Rules. Appeals against orders made by district judges will be to a circuit judge and against orders made by circuit judges to the High Court.

Section 4 of the 1998 Act provides that the respondent may appeal against **6-095** the making of the order to the Crown Court.[78] It is a rehearing of the entire case; parties are free to provide further evidence. The Crown Court may vary the order or make a new order. An appeal from the Crown Court is to the High Court by way of case stated under s.28 of the Supreme Court Act 1981 or by application for judicial review under s.29(3) of the 1981 Act. Where the magistrates have declined to make the order, the relevant authority may challenge the decision by way of cases stated under s.111 of the Magistrates' Court Act 1980. An appeal against an ASBO made in the county court is regulated by CPR 52. Appeals in other types courts will be governed by the relevant procedures in each case.

Judicial Review

In *C v Sunderland Youth Court*, the court referred to the right of appeal against **6-096** the order under s.108 of the Magistrates' Court Act 1980 and that applications for judicial review are not appropriate when there is an alternative remedy to appeal against sentence to the Crown Court. However, in *Kenny*, the respondents argued that the claimants should be refused permission to apply for judicial review as it was open to them to appeal to the Crown Court against the ASBOs. In *R. v Hereford Magistrates' Court Ex p. Rowlands*[79] it was held that:

"... having regard to the central role performed by magistrates' courts in administering the criminal justice system and to the absence of any supervisory jurisdiction by the Crown Court over their proceedings, it was the more important to retain the Divisional Court's supervisory jurisdiction to ensure the maintenance of high standards of procedural impartiality and fairness; that where a party complained of procedural irregularity or bias, he should not, by denial of leave to move for judicial review, be required to pursue such rights as he might have in the Crown Court, and that, accordingly the existence of a right of appeal to the Crown Court, particularly if unexercised, should not ordinarily weigh against the grant of leave to move or of substantive relief."

So, in *C*, it was submitted on behalf of the Claimants that the proceedings before the District Judge were flawed by procedural irregularity, and Owen J. considered that it was appropriate for the supervisory jurisdiction of this court to be invoked. The issue was considered again in *R. v Leeds Magistrates' Court, Ex p. A*.[80] The applicant sought permission to apply for judicial review of interim ASBO made against him without notice in September and December 2003. In November 2003, he was arrested for an alleged assault, which constituted a breach of the September ASBO, following which a district judge made the second interim order against him. The applicant contended

---

[78] See rr.74 and 75, Magistrates' Court Rules 1981 and rr.6 to 11 of the Crown Court Rules 1982.
[79] [1998] Q.B. 110.
[80] [2004] WL 413077.

that a judge, when deciding whether to make an interim or final ASBO against a young person, should primarily have regard to the young person's best interests. He argued that the district judge had failed to do so and had thereby applied the wrong test and made an error of law. The application was refused: there had been an unexplained four-month delay before the applicant brought judicial review proceedings which was sufficient justification for a refusal of permission to apply for judicial review. Secondly, the applicant could have applied to the magistrates' court at any time to vary or discharge the first order, but he had not done so. He had also delayed for two months before instructing his solicitors. Finally, of all the procedures available to a defendant seeking to contest the making of an interim ASBO without notice against him, judicial review was the least suitable in cases like the instant case where the applicant had conceded that there was sufficient evidence before the magistrates' court to justify an ASBO being made. The primary route should have been to apply to the magistrates' court for the ASBO to be varied or discharged, or to appeal to the Crown Court. Alternatively, he could have appeared before the court and opposed the making of a further interim ASBO or a final ASBO, or appealed to the High Court. In judicial review proceedings, the High Court could not consider the evidence which was before the district judge or substitute its discretion for that of the magistrates' court. The applicant's allegation that the judge had failed to apply the correct legal test was an allegation of a substantive error, and as such was not appropriate for judicial review when more appropriate procedures were available.

Breach of the Order

6-097   Section 1(10) provides that, if without reasonable excuse a person does anything which he is prohibited from doing by an anti-social behaviour order, is guilty of an offence and he shall be liable—

   (1) on summary conviction, to imprisonment for a term not exceeding six months or to a fine not exceeding the statutory maximum, or to both; or

   (2) on conviction on indictment, to imprisonment for a term not exceeding five years or to a fine, or to both.

When the Crime and Disorder Bill was going through Parliament, government spokesmen stated that the high maximum penalty of five years' imprisonment for the offence of breaching an ASBO was needed (in their view) because the offender should be sentenced for his "pattern of behaviour," including the conduct giving rise to the making of the anti-social behaviour order.[81]

6-098   Breach of a civil injunction is a contempt of court and may lead to penal sanctions, including a fine and imprisonment. Breach of an ASBO is a criminal offence, under s.1(10) of the 1998 Act, and, until the Anti-Social Behaviour Act 2003, the prosecution proceedings were conducted only by the CPS and subject to criminal procedures and standards of proof. Section 1(10) of the 1998 Act was amended so that a council which is a relevant authority, or the council for the local government area in which a person in respect of whom an order has been made resides or appears to reside, may also bring proceedings.[82] Breach of an ASBO is also an arrestable offence. It may be tried summarily in the magistrates' court or on indictment in the Crown Court. Cases involving children and young persons will be heard in the youth courts. The

---

[81] Ashworth "Social Control and Anti-Social behaviour: The Subversion of Human Rights (2004) L.Q.R. 120(Apr), 263–291, at 278.

[82] By s.37(4) of the Anti-Social Behaviour Act 2003 Act.

maximum penalty on summary conviction for an adult is six months in prison or a fine not exceeding the statutory maximum: s.1(10), 1998 Act. On indictment in the Crown Court, the maximum is five years or a fine or both. In the youth court, the maximum custodial sentence for a young person aged 12 to 17 is detention and a training order which has a maximum term of 24 months; a juvenile aged between 12 and 14 must be a persistent criminal offender before they can be subject to a detention and training order. Those aged 10 and 11 years may be given a community order. Proceedings in the youth courts will be subject to automatic reporting restrictions.

Sentencing Principles

The commission of a comparatively trivial offence will lead to a breach of the order and thereby expose the defendant to a far greater penalty than that which he would have received if the court were dealing with him for the trivial offence alone. In *Thomas*,[83] the appellant was an alcoholic with an appalling record of petty offending: 237 convictions for 451 offences, 263 of which are for offences of shoplifting or theft. He was subject to an ASBO made on June 17, 2003, prohibiting him from entering four local stores until further order. It was made on the basis that the appellant had stolen from those premises, had entered them when drunk, had refused to leave when asked to do so, had been abusive and threatening to staff at those premises and had loitered outside them when drunk. Six weeks later, the magistrates' court imposed a Community Rehabilitation Order for offences of theft and of common assault. That order was breached four days later. On September 1 the appellant again appeared before the magistrates for breach of the ASBO, having entered one of the stores. He was sentenced to five months' imprisonment. He was released on licence in October 2003. Eight days later, he again entered one of the other stores, in further breach of the ASBO. The store supervisor saw him in one of the aisles holding a can of beer with something under his coat. She approached him and took from him a teddy bear valued at £19.99, which he had placed under his coat. After being ejected from the store, she saw him a short distance away holding a small, cuddly toy valued at £9.99. He appeared before the magistrates in November 2003, where he admitted breach of an ASBO and pleaded guilty to an offence of theft. On December 5, 2003, he was sentenced to 18 months' imprisonment for breach of the ASBO and one month imprisonment concurrent for the offence of theft. His appeal to the Court of Appeal was dismissed. The offence of theft, for which he was also sentenced, was committed in November 2003 when he entered a Tesco store (not one of those he was prohibited from entering under the ASBO), took a joint of meat valued at £8.28 from a display counter and walked through the check-out without paying. When he was interviewed in relation to these offences he said he thought that the ASBO had expired and admitted the offence of shoplifting. Both the breach of the ASBO and the offence of theft were committed whilst the appellant was on licence. On appeal, it was submitted that the sentence of 18 months' imprisonment was manifestly excessive in that it failed adequately to reflect four matters: first, that the appellant had pleaded guilty at the earliest opportunity; second, that, although on licence, he was not on bail for any offence at the time of committing the offences; third, that there was no ancillary conviction to the breach in October; and fourth, that the appellant had not shown any hostility or resistance to the shop manager in October. The sentence imposed was disproportionate to the offence in the sense that the behaviour of the appellant in October did not, in substance, amount to the type of behaviour for which the order had been

6-099

---

[83] [2005] 1 Cr. App. R. (S.) 9.

imposed in the first place. The Court of Appeal said that, as to the plea of guilty, the appellant had little choice but to admit his breach and to plead to the shoplifting. Secondly, that he was not on bail at the time of these offences affords scant mitigation, given that he was on licence. The proposition that the breach was mitigated by the fact that he did not, in addition, commit any other offences did not weigh in his favour. Finally, the fact that he did not show any hostility or resistance when ejected from the co-operative store affords little mitigation. The sentence imposed was fully justified. The appellant had an appalling record. He persisted in his criminal and anti-social behaviour, despite every attempt by the courts to break the pattern of his offending by the deployment of the entire range of sentencing options. He showed a flagrant disregard of the ASBO, breaching it within weeks and breaching it again a matter of days after release on licence. He also showed a complete disregard of the Community Rehabilitation Order imposed in July by breaching it within four days.

6-100   *Braxton*,[84] concerned a defendant, 39 years of age, who had appeared before the courts on 37 previous occasions. On no fewer than nine occasions in the eight years prior to his release from prison in April 2003 he had been convicted of using threatening, abusive, insulting words or behaviour contrary to ss.4(1)(a) or 5(1)(a) of the Public Order Act 1986. On nine occasions he had also been convicted of an offence of violence, albeit usually assault or battery. While in custody for these matters he sent a letter to the husband of a prison officer, saying that he intended to kill her. This led to a term of four months' imprisonment. There was also a pre-sentence report in which it was noted that the applicant could present not only as an intelligent man, but also as someone who has a variety of social difficulties; however, his ability to engage with a range of agencies to resolve such difficulties was questionable and there were grave doubts whether his full co-operation would ever be forthcoming. Because of this he will continue to pose problems for anyone involved in the management or monitoring of his chosen lifestyle. In October 2001, upon the complaint of the Housing Department of Birmingham City Council, an ASBO was made by Birmingham magistrates under s.1 of the Crime and Disorder Act 1998. This order prohibited the applicant, for a period of five years, from entering Birmingham City Centre, using or engaging in any threatening, abusive, offensive, intimidating, insulting language or behaviour or threatening or engaging in violence or damage against any person or property within the city centre. Within two months of the order being made, the applicant twice breached its terms. He was prosecuted and, in June 2002, tried in the Crown Court at Birmingham. He represented himself, as he was entitled to do, but during the course of the prosecution case, he fell out with the judge and was not in fact present thereafter. He was convicted and sentenced to terms of four years' imprisonment on each count concurrent. His appeal against conviction was dismissed, but in relation to sentence, Keith J., giving the judgment of the Court, said:

"We have every sympathy with the judge's determination to protect the public for as long as possible from a man whom he regarded as posing a danger to the public. But, as the judge himself recognised, the sentence which he passed was close to the maximum for a single offence of acting in breach of an antisocial behaviour order and it made the applicant a long term prisoner. We think that a sentence close to the maximum should really be reserved for cases in which the antisocial behaviour order had itself been the subject of persistent and prolonged breaches, or where the breaches of the antisocial behaviour order had consisted of conduct more

[84] [2004] EWCA Crim 1374.

serious than abusive, offensive and insulting language or conduct, in other words, in which the behaviour was truly intimidating. It is possible that what the judge was doing in the present case was sentencing the applicant for the behaviour which had caused the antisocial behaviour order to be sought in the first place, rather than for the subsequent breaches of the antisocial behaviour order, though we recognise, of course, that the applicant's behaviour following the antisocial behaviour order had to be seen in the context of everything which had gone before. In our judgment, it was not appropriate for sentences as long as these to be passed for the first breaches of an antisocial behaviour order, especially where the behaviour which constituted the breaches was not of the worst kind. In our opinion, sentences totalling two years' imprisonment would have been appropriate."

In April 2003, he was released from prison on licence, which lasted until **6-101** December 2. In July 2003 a police officer was working as a CCTV operator, watching cameras trained on Broad Street in the City of Birmingham. At around 10 o'clock the applicant was seen to approach people. He was trying to stop them, bar their way, and he appeared to be begging. His behaviour was described by the operator as aggressive and he looked as if he was asking for money. As soon as people refused he acted in an aggressive manner and then simply went about his way and started blocking other people, again asking for money and again being aggressive in manner. The following day, also in Broad Street, the applicant was again seen by the operator of the CCTV. On this occasion a young lady was seen to refuse the applicant's advances for money, and as she walked past him he slapped her on the bottom. The police arrived and the applicant was arrested. Upon his arrest he was totally compliant. He was cuffed and placed in a police car and taken to the police station. When walking down a corridor from one custody suite to another, however, the applicant happened to cross a police officer whom he knew. He said "Fuck you, Stuart" and then spat in the constable's face. The officer described the spit going into his eyes and mouth. He recoiled and tried to wipe the spittle from his face. When arrested for that offence, the applicant replied in a nonsensical manner. He was before the Birmingham City magistrates on July 9. The court's memorandum of conviction records that, on that day, in relation to two allegations of breach of the ASBO, he intimated before venue pleas of not guilty. The matter was considered suitable for summary trial, and it is also recorded that he consented to summary trial and pleaded not guilty. He also pleaded not guilty to the allegation of assaulting the police officer. He was convicted by the magistrates for these offences in August 2003. In October 2003, he appeared before the Crown Court was sentenced to terms of three-and-a-half years' imprisonment on each of the breaches and three months' imprisonment consecutive for the assault, making three years and nine months in all. The judge noted the observations of the Court of Appeal on the previous occasion, observing in particular that he had regard to the extent to which behaviour of the kind in which the applicant indulged was menacing to members of the public, disquieting and disturbing. He took the view that he would not re-impose the sentence originally passed by the judge on the earlier occasion; neither would he specifically impose the unexpired portion of his previous sentence, amounting to just short of three months. Rather, he had regard to the total sentence commensurate with the gravity of his offending, including the fact that he was in breach of his licence and the fact that this was his second appearance for breach of the ASBO, and in that regard to the need to protect the public.

In his application to the Court of Appeal, the applicant, representing **6-102** himself, submitted that his behaviour must be considered at the lower end of nuisance activity. He observed that begging was not an imprisonable offence and that for an officer to say that what he was doing was obviously intimidating, aggressive or likely to cause alarm and distress is no more than the expression of his opinion, at best subjective and wholly devoid of objective deduction. As for slapping the bottom of the woman, this, he said, was no more than good natured, boisterous exuberance, and again led to no complaint. Turning to the offence of common assault, he argued that this was committed only in response to nine years of physical and psychological abuse from this officer. The Court of Appeal refused his application and commented that it was unfortunate that the applicant still did not appear to understand the nature or effect of the order made against him. The antisocial behaviour order was specifically designed to protect the public from frequent and distressing repeated misbehaviour of the type which is the subject of this order, and the applicant was indeed committing a serious criminal offence, even entering the City of Birmingham within the confined area set out within the map served upon him when the order was made. He acted in deliberate breach of that order not once but twice and yet again twice more within weeks of his release from that prison sentence. While he might consider his conduct as trivial the persistence of it is now treated seriously, specifically to protect the public. It was thus vital that he address this issue and his behaviour in public if he is to avoid further conflict with the law. The public were entitled to be protected from this applicant.

6-103	The more contumelious the default, the harsher the sentence, regardless of its relative triviality. However, this will also be subject to the usual rules of sentencing practice which allows for the reduction of sentence if such ameliorating factors such as cooperation, admissions and undue hardness and personal circumstances of the defendant are present. See *Bulmer*,[85] in which the appellant, a 37 year old incurable alcoholic, with a long string of drink-related convictions behind her: 115 previous court appearances for 166 offences between late 1995 and April 2005, nearly all of them drink related, including being drunk and disorderly, attempted theft, threatening behaviour, obstructing a constable, drunk in a public place, criminal damage, common assault, breach of probation orders, assault on a constable, interrupting court proceedings, drunk on a highway, theft, failing to surrender to custody and so on. The appellant was made subject to a ASBO in December 2004 for a period of two years. One of the conditions of that order was that she should not use threatening, abusive or insulting words or disorderly behaviour in public. She breached the order on a number of occasions. On April 29, 2005 she was imprisoned for 28 days for one such breach. She was released from that sentence in May 2005. Within three days of her release, a constable saw her drinking from a can of beer in the Minster grounds. He told her to leave, or to stop drinking. She replied, "Fuck off". He asked her again to leave, but again she refused. Other police officers were called and she was arrested. On arrest she appeared to be under the influence of drink. She had with her a bag full of unopened cans of strong lager. She admitted these as breaches of the ASBOs before the magistrates. The second breach occurred only days later again: at about 11.50pm paramedics found the appellant lying on the road. She had a carrier bag of beer cans with her. They helped her up from the road. She told them as they did so that she wanted to go to jail because someone called John was after her. That was a reference to the fact that she was to be a witness in a murder trial which was to take place in October of this year, and she was in fear for her safety as a result of it being known that she was to be a witness in that trial. Just after midnight on that night the paramedics were called back again to Church Street in York. They

[85] [2005] WL 3734104.

found the appellant in the same position, lying in the road and refusing to move. They moved her to a bench at the side of the road and left her. About ten minutes later they were called back again to find her yet again in the road, lying down, and asking them to call the police. She became abusive, and told one of the paramedics to "fuck off". She then threw an empty beer can at him. By this time the paramedics felt they could do nothing but call the police. They did so. The police arrived and duly arrested the appellant. In a pre-sentence report that had been prepared for the court, she explained that had been drunk at the time of the breaches and could remember very little of them. She said she had an extensive list of previous convictions and acknowledged that they, too, had on occasion caused her to breach anti-social behaviour orders. She attributed all her offending to alcohol and seemed to be aware that if she could get off alcohol she would free herself from this train of offences. There was also a psychiatric report before the court which revealed a hopeless position. She had been a heavy drinker for 14 years. During that period the only times of detoxification that she had undergone coincided with short periods of imprisonment that had been imposed upon her. The psychiatrist diagnosed her as a severe chronic alcoholic and one of limited intelligence. He said that she required long term community rehabilitation to enable her to remain abstinent from alcohol, but he was pessimistic about finding a suitable programme for her, or that, if found, she would co-operate with it. It was with that dilemma that the judge was presented when deciding the appropriate sentences to be imposed for these comparatively trivial breaches; a dilemma between proportionality in how to respond to them through whatever tools the court had available and the need, also, to protect the public, given the hopelessness of her state and her apparent inability to cope without alcohol when outside prison. He imposed a a sentence of 21 months, expressing the hope that the prison will not take the view that the time served was enough for her to be released, but time in prison should be served, at the very least to protect the public from further activities of this nature.

The appellant submitted that the overall sentence of 21 months is mani- **6-104** festly excessive and out of all proportion to the culpability represented by these two breaches of the ASBO and referred to the guilty plea, the fact that her anti-social behaviour exhibited by these breaches, although a nuisance, was not of the worst, and "the pitiful condition of this appellant as a long term and seemingly incurable alcohol addict". Aided by the detoxification, to which she was subject while in custody, she was able enough to give critical evidence in the murder trial with the result that those guilty of murder were convicted. That was a good illustration of what she can do if she kept off drink. Auld L.J. allowed the appeal. Approaching the matter in the same way as the trial judge, the Court, he said, bore in mind the need for protection of the public from this constant disorderly conduct and to try and keep the sentence in proportion to the culpability of her conduct. It was in that latter respect where the judge went wrong:

"It may be that he believed that if this woman could be kept in custody for that little bit longer, the better might be the chances for her to maintain her improvement when finally released from prison. However laudable that intention may have been, we fear that he went beyond the bounds of proportionality, as Mr Johnson has submitted, in imposing a sentence of 21 months for these two breaches."

An appropriate disposition, and a proportionate one in the circumstances, would have one of 12 months' imprisonment in respect of each breach, those sentences to be served concurrently.

6-105   In *Morrison*,[86] the appellant, who had pleaded guilty to breaching an ASBO which prohibited him from being in the front seat of a car, appealed against his sentence of 12 months' imprisonment. After the order had been imposed, he committed the offence of driving while disqualified and, thereby, also breached the order. The maximum sentences for the driving offence and breach of the order were, respectively, six months' and five years' imprisonment. He submitted that since the breach consisted of no more than driving while disqualified, the judge should not have imposed a sentence longer than six months' imprisonment. The Court of Appeal allowed the appeal; where an ASBO prohibited conduct which would in any event be a criminal offence, if the offender subsequently committed such a criminal offence and, consequently, breached the order, then the sentence should not normally exceed the statutory maximum for the criminal offence. The maximum sentence for M's breach was, therefore, six months' imprisonment. Since he had pleaded guilty, he would be sentenced to four months' imprisonment, to which would be added four months consecutive for four months' imprisonment, to which would be added four months consecutive for another offence of driving while disqualified.

6-106   However, in *Tripp*[87] a completely different outcome was reached. In May 2004, the appellant who pleaded guilty to breach of an ASBO was sentenced to 12 months' imprisonment. The offence placed him in breach also of a conditional discharge which had been imposed on March 7. No separate penalty was imposed for that. Also, he was subject at the time to a community rehabilitation order which had been imposed on April 11 for an offence of harassment, that being only 10 days before the commission of the incident which placed him in breach of the ASBO. The community rehabilitation order was also revoked by the sentencing judge. The appellant appealed against the 12 month sentence by leave of the single judge who ordered an expedited hearing. The ASBO of which he was in breach prohibited him for two years from using threatening, abusive or insulting words or behaviour or disorderly behaviour within the hearing or sight of a person. The breach consisted of conduct on the evening of April 21 when a project worker on duty at a night shelter in Hove went to close the building for the night and found the appellant in the porch. He asked the appellant to leave and the appellant replied in aggressive language: "I won't leave, fuck off." Another night worker arrived. Again the appellant was abusive. Whilst the two members of staff went to telephone the police, the appellant repeatedly said: "Fuck off, I can see you there." He pressed the buzzer at the door and kicked the door as he did so. The police arrived, found him drunk and unsteady on his feet and he was arrested. His explanation for his conduct was that he wanted to stay at the shelter but he had gone there too late. He had had a lot to drink but had been assaulted and punched in the eye shortly beforehand and was angry. He remembered being abusive to the staff and accepted he was in breach of the order. Effectively this was a man guilty of an offence of being drunk and disorderly. We have already indicated the other orders to which he was already subject. The appellant had a long history of previous convictions. In recent years his convictions were mainly for public order offences, drunk and disorderly, criminal damage and the like. There was a pre-sentence report which anticipated the imposition of a custodial sentence and the author considered there was a high risk of reoffending. His behaviour was unpredictable when he had been drinking. He had a long history of offending linked to his misuse of alcohol. He apologised for his behaviour towards the staff. There was a letter also before the court from the appellant. He explained in fuller detail that he had been homeless for

[86] [2006] 1 Cr. App. R. (S.) 85.
[87] [2005] EWCA Crim 2253.

some time, though he had spent the occasional night at that particular shelter. But he particularly needed shelter that night because he had been attacked and injured by a group of young men, who had taken his rucksack and his sleeping bag. He was therefore unable to remain on the streets. A prison report is now before us, which shows him to be generally polite in prison, though he has bouts of moroseness when he can be sullen and uncooperative. It was argued that the sentence was manifestly excessive against the background of an early guilty plea, the nature of the conduct giving rise to the breach and the efforts that the appellant had made to address his problems":

> "The Single Judge, granting leave to appeal, commented briefly: 'For being drunk about disorderly: a year's imprisonment and termination of [community rehabilitation order]. Can this be right?' The short answer to that question, as a matter of law is of course yes. Where an anti-social behaviour order has been made and is breached, the breach consisting of conduct which is itself a criminal offence, the potential sentence may be far longer than the maximum for that basic offence."

Cited Leveson J. remarked, when giving the judgment of *Braxton*, the anti-social behaviour order provisions were a response by Parliament to increasing concerns about the impact on the public of anti-social behaviour in its many forms. That concern must therefore be reflected by the courts in the sentences which it imposes for breaches. In this case, the breach followed quickly on the imposition of the community rehabilitation order and indeed the conditional discharge. It seems to the Court that a prison sentence was right, despite the arguments addressed to the sentencing judge that the community sentence should have been allowed to continue. The judge gave no particular reason for the length of the sentence which he decided was appropriate, and so, despite the aggravating features of this breach occurring so soon after the other appearances before the court, it was disproportionate in length to the nature of the breach which affected nobody except the members of staff of the night shelter, where he was already known. An eight month sentence was more appropriate for the breach with which this Court is dealing.

The conflict between the different approaches on *Morrison* and *Braxton* was considered also *Lamb*[88]: the appellant, 18 years of age at the time of the appeal, had appeared before the courts on no fewer than 25 occasions for over 50 offences. Before he was 16, in addition to many community based penalties, he had served two sentences of detention for burglary and, by the middle of 2004, he had served a further term of detention. On October 11, 2004, at the North Tyneside Youth Court, for using disorderly behaviour or threatening abusive or insulting words likely to cause harassment alarm or distress, at Whitley Bay Metro Station and for common assault, the appellant appealed against a sentence imposed for three breaches of an anti-social behaviour order. Under the order, the duration of which was two years, he was prohibited from entering Whitley Bay Town Centre as defined in the map given to him; not permitted to enter the entire Metro transport system in Tyne & Wear or any Nexus premises forming part of the Metro system; and he was not to consume alcohol in any public place nor be drunk in any place. He was prohibited from being in a certain geographical area. He was found to have deliberately and persistently flouted the order and was found in the prohibited areas on several occasions. At his sentence hearing for the breach of the ASBO, the court had before it three pre-sentence reports. The first had been prepared on April 20 in relation to the April 1 arrest and suggested specific assessment making the point that, although he was not believed to represent a direct risk

6-107

[88] [2005] WL 3157651.

to public safety, his offending and antisocial behaviour generated a high risk of his re-offending. However, his assessment did not help as he would not be able to attend community punishment in Whitley Bay (because of the ASBO) and was not prepared to travel to North Shields. His mother, in poor health with two children to cope with, could not deal with him and, in any event, had been given notice to quit; finally, there were doubts about his motivation. Later, the probation officer wrote that the situation had not changed: he was not prepared to comply with his ASBO as he considered it difficult and unfair. He entered a plea guilty to three breaches of the order and a sentence of 22 months in a young offenders institution was imposed. In imposing the sentence the judge commented that the public needed to be protected from antisocial behaviour by people like the appellant.

6-108   Before the Court of Appeal, the appellant explained why he felt that the ASBO was unfair. The reference in the order to Nexus was to the company operating the bus service in this area. An exclusion from Nexus property was an exclusion from bus shelters operated by that company that form part of the Metro system, so that not only can the appellant not enter the Metro system but he had difficulties otherwise accessing public transport. Given that he could not enter Whitley Bay town centre either, his opportunities for social interaction were particularly limited. As a result, it was submitted that compliance meant that he would become more and more isolated from mainstream society, such that rehabilitation and reintegration would be extremely difficult. The Court of Appeal allowed the appeal. Hallett L.J. observed that the court was confronted with the problem of an offender who, without committing crime, or in fact harassing or causing distress to any member of the public, repeatedly breached the order of the court. As the trial judge observed, flouting such an order is itself a serious matter. It was to be dealt with in this way. The underlying purpose and effect of ASBOs was defined in *Braxton*[89]:

> "It is undeniable that [an ASBO] represents a serious infringement upon the liberty of the applicant, not only because it represents a restriction on his right of free movement, but also because breach constitutes a criminal offence punishable with a term of up to five years' imprisonment, which is greater than the maximum penalty which could be imposed for offences which might otherwise be reflected within the terms of the order. It is, however, a response by Parliament to the increasing concern about the impact on the public of antisocial behaviour in its many constituent forms. It follows that this concern must be reflected in the sentences which the court imposes for breach of the order."

6-109   Yet, in *Morrison*,[90] it was held that if the breach of an ASBO was no more than the commission of an offence for which the maximum penalty is prescribed by statute, so that it was normally wrong in principle to pass a sentence for a breach calculated by reference to the maximum for breach of an ASBO. This ignored the impact of anti-social behaviour on the wider public, which was the purpose of the legislation in the first place; it also meant that anti-social behaviour, short of a criminal offence, could be more heavily punished than anti-social behaviour that coincidentally was also a criminal offence. The Court preferred the contrary approach of this Court in *Tripp*[91] and *Braxton*. *Braxton* demonstrated, Hallett L.J. said, that the Court of Appeal was prepared to uphold long sentences for breach of ASBOs when such are warranted. It concerned repeated, aggressive begging addressed to pedestrians in

[89] [2004] EWCA Crim 1374, [2005] 1 Cr. App. R. (S) 36.
[90] [2005] EWCA Crim 2237.
[91] [2005] EWCA Crim 2253.

Birmingham city centre which clearly caused both real concern and distress. The appellant was a man with nine convictions for public order offences and nine convictions for minor violence, who had served two years imprisonment for breach of the ASBO imposed on him. He was refused leave to appeal a sentence of three and a half years' imprisonment for two identical breaches of the ASBO, with three months' imprisonment consecutive for common assault (also on a pedestrian who would not engage with him) all committed soon after his release from prison. The Court said that the anti-social behaviour order is specifically designed to protect the public from frequent and distressing repeated misbehaviour of the type which is the subject of this order, and the applicant was indeed committing a serious criminal offence, even entering the City of Birmingham within the confines set out within the map served upon him when the order was made. He acted in deliberate breach of that order not once but twice (which led to the four year term reduced to two years) and yet again twice more within weeks of his release from that prison sentence. He must understand that what he might consider as trivial in his case, because of the persistence of his conduct, is now treated seriously, specifically to protect the public. It was thus vital that he address this issue and his behaviour in public if he is to avoid further conflict with the law.

Hallet L.J. distinguished that case, at para.8:

"The vital distinction between that case and the circumstances with which we are concerned is that albeit the deliberate and multiple flouting of the order is the same (indeed, there are more breaches of the ASBO in this case), the social impact of this appellant's offending is very much less and, indeed, did not impact on the public in any way. Save for one occasion when the appellant was drunk (without there being any suggestion that he was causing a nuisance), none of these breaches have resulted from antisocial behaviour as such. The ever longer sentences have been driven only by the determination of the court to ensure that its orders limiting the appellant's movements are not flouted. . . An order of the court must be obeyed. We do not accept, however, that being found in a place within the proscribed area without any evidence of associated antisocial behaviour deserves to be visited with a sentence as long as 22 months imprisonment. Where breaches do not involve harassment, alarm or distress, community penalties should be considered in order to help the offender learn to live within the terms of the ASBO to which he or she is subject. In those cases when there is no available community penalty (into which category we include this case given the appellant's refusal to engage with agencies prepared to help him and the frequency of his breaches), custodial sentences which are necessary to maintain the authority of the court can be kept as short as possible."

The sentence of 22 months' imprisonment was quashed and substituted for a sentence of two months' imprisonment, to run consecutively and to commence after the two month period of licence which must also be served; effectively eight months' imprisonment.

There are a series of cases which, since *Morrison*, concern driving offences **6-110** as instances of a breach of an ASBO. In *Kirby*,[92] an order under s.1C of the Crime and Disorder Act 1998, prohibiting the appellant for 10 years from driving, attempting to drive or being carried in a motor vehicle which had been taken without the consent of the owner or lawful authority, or driving or attempting to drive a motor vehicle until after the expiry of his disqualification, was quashed. The appellant pleaded guilty to dangerous driving and driving while disqualified. The appellant was seen by police officers driving a

[92] [2005] EWCA Crim 1228.

car at about 3am. When the police officers decided to follow the car, the car was driven off at speed along a number of residential streets. The appellant negotiated a roundabout the wrong way, drove along the wrong side of the road, went through a red light and reached speeds of 80mph. He collided with an island in the centre of the road, and continued, despite the bursting of two tyres. The appellant and his passengers ran away but were found hiding nearby. The appellant had numerous previous convictions for taking vehicles without consent and driving while disqualified. He was sentenced to 20 months' imprisonment for dangerous driving, with five months' consecutive for driving whilst disqualified, with an order under the 1998 Act prohibiting him for 10 years from driving, attempting to drive or being carried in a motor vehicle which had been taken without the consent of the owner or lawful authority, or driving or attempting to drive a motor vehicle until after the expiry of his disqualification. The Court of Appeal held that the order did no more than prohibit the appellant from committing further offences of the same description. The sentencing judge indicated that the effect of the order would increase the maximum penalty for the offences of driving a vehicle which had been taken without consent or driving while disqualified to five years. It was clear from the judge's sentencing remarks that his purpose in making the order was to secure the result that, if the appellant committed such offences again, the court would not be limited to the maximum penalty for the offences themselves, but would be able to impose up to five years' imprisonment for breach of the order. The question for the Court was whether this was an appropriate use of the power. The test for the use of the power to make an order was one of necessity to protect the public from further anti-social acts by the offender. There must be a demonstrable necessity for such an order. Where a substantial custodial sentence was being imposed at the same time, on release from which the defendant would be on licence, it should not generally be assumed that there was such a necessity. To make an anti-social behaviour order such as the present, where the underlying objective was to give the court higher sentencing powers in the event of future similar offences, was not a use of the power which should normally be exercised. In the Court's judgment, the making of an order of this sort should not be a normal part of the sentencing process, particularly in cases which did not in themselves specifically involve intimidation, harassment and distress. It was an exceptional course to be taken in particular circumstances and in the Court's judgment there was nothing in the case, despite the deplorable record of the appellant for offences of this sort, to justify the use of the power in the present case. Its effect was no more than to transform any such offence into a different offence, namely breach of an anti-social behaviour order, so as to increase the potential penalties. In the Court's judgment, that was unwarranted in the absence of exceptional circumstances. The Court would set aside the anti-social behaviour order. So far as the length of sentence was concerned, the sentencing judge was entirely right to make the sentences consecutive. The appeal against the length of the sentences of imprisonment would be dismissed.

6-111   And in *Williams*,[93] the appellant appealed against the ASBO. He had admitted to being in breach of a community rehabilitation order, which had been imposed, along with a disqualification from driving order, following his conviction of driving offences. The judge revoked the rehabilitation order but left the disqualification in place. He had 223 convictions for a multitude of offences, many of which were driving offences. The judge had recognised that the ASBO was unusual, but had imposed it in order to reinforce the effect of the disqualification. The issue was whether, as a matter of principle,

[93] [2006] 1 Cr. App. R. (S.) 56.

an ASBO was available in the instant case. The Court of Appeal held, allowing the appeal, that the imposition of an ASBO following conviction of a driving offence, with the underlying objective of giving the court higher sentencing powers in the event of future offending, was something which should be done only in exceptional circumstances, following *Kirby*.[94] Such circumstances did not exist in the instant case, consequently the ASBO was quashed.[95]

The conflict is now conclusively resolved in favour of the *Tripp* and **6-112** *Braxton* approach. In *Lovegrove and Stevens*,[96] the appellant appealed against a sentence of nine months' imprisonment imposed for a breach of an ASBO. Following a total of 135 previous convictions for over 200 offences, including 133 offences of theft and kindred offences and 44 offences relating to drunkenness, an ASBO had been imposed upon the appellant prohibiting him from, inter alia, being drunk in public and from urinating or defecating other than in a lavatory for a period of five years. He was found to be in breach of that order by being drunk in the street and, when arrested, urinating. The sentencing judge said that he would have imposed a nine month prison sentence, but preferred to give him another opportunity to rehabilitate, and accordingly deferred sentence but continued the ASBO. The judge ordered that in the meantime the ASBO should continue, subject to a further condition that the appellant should live at a specified address in High Wycombe and abide by the rules of the establishment. The judge had in mind that this accommodation might help to provide the appellant with a start to rehabilitation. He explained that he wished to see whether the appellant may have learned to live reasonably and responsibly in the community, or whether it was simply going to be a question of "just locking you up for increasingly lengthy periods of time." He then gave the appellant a solemn warning that he would normally have considered the appropriate sentence to have been one of 9 months' imprisonment, but because of his hope that the appellant may indeed have learned to behave himself, he would defer making his order, reserving any breach proceedings for any further offence to himself, adding: "Let me make it perfectly plain, I only give one chance". If the appellant failed to take it, the judge told him that he would protect the public by "separating you from them for as long as I can". Three days later, he stole a bottle of whiskey from a shop. The judge imposed nine months' imprisonment for the original breach of the ASBO, and three months' consecutive imprisonment for the theft. The appellant, relying upon the decision in *Morrison*,[97] argued that the sentence of nine months' imprisonment imposed for the breach of the ASBO was wrong and excessive, since, as a matter of principle, a sentence imposed for a breach of an ASBO should not exceed the maximum statutory sentence that could have been imposed for the offence that the ASBO had sought to prohibit. Accordingly, he argued that since, the statutory maximum sentence for an offence of being drunk in public was a fine of £1,000, that was the maximum sentence that could have been imposed for the breach of the ASBO.

The appeal was dismissed. If the conduct constituting the breach was also **6-113** a distinct criminal offence, and the offence had carried a statutory maximum sentence, that was a feature to be borne in mind in the interests of proportionality. The appellant relied on some observations in *R. v Morrison*,[98] where Hughes J., giving the judgment of the Court, said that the sentence should not

---

[94] The Court of Appeal in *R. v Boness* 2005 WL 2673805 also preferred *Kirby*.
[95] See also *R. v Lawson* [2006] 1 Cr. App. R. (S.) 59.
[96] [2006] WL 502929.
[97] [2005] EWCA Crim 2237.
[98] [2005] EWCA Crim 2237.

normally be exceed the statutory maximum for the criminal offence and added later:

> "If a breach of an ASBO consists of no more than commission of an offence for which a maximum penalty is prescribed by statute, it is wrong in principle to pass a sentence for that breach, calculated by reference to the five year maximum for breach of an ASBO. Rather the tariff is determined by the statutory maximum for the offence in question. . . We draw attention, however, in that last proposition, to the words 'no more than'. There may be exceptional circumstances in which it can properly be said that the vice of the breach of an ASBO although it amounts to an offence, goes beyond that offence."

The court, in this judgment, said that decision that it was court in a two judge constitution, without the advantage of counsel for the prosecution and, perhaps more important, without reference to the earlier decision of a three judge constitution in *R. v Braxton*.[99] This case was a renewed application for leave to appeal. Nevertheless Leveson J., at para.3 observed:

> "It is undeniable that this represents a serious infringement upon the liberty of the applicant, not only because it represents a restriction on his right to free movement, but also because breach constitutes a criminal offence punishable with a term of up to five years' imprisonment, which is greater than the maximum penalty which could be imposed for offences which might otherwise be reflected within the terms of the order. It is, however, a response by Parliament to the increasing concern about the impact on the public of anti-social behaviour in its many constituent forms. It follows that this concern must be reflected in the sentences which the court imposes for breach of the order."

6-114   Judgments of this Court subsequent to *Morrison* include *Tripp*,[1] another decision of a two judge constitution, and then a decision of a three judge constitution, *Lamb*.[2] The Court addressed the possible inconsistency between *Braxton* and *Morrison*. Hallett L.J. made these observations:

> "We are conscious that in *Morrison*, this Court held that if the breach of an ASBO is no more than the commission of an offence for which the maximum penalty is prescribed by statute, it is normally wrong in principle to pass a sentence for a breach calculated by reference to the maximum for breach of an ASBO. With respect, that appears to ignore the impact of anti-social behaviour on the wider public which was the purpose of the legislation in the first place; it also means that antisocial behaviour short of a criminal offence could be more heavily punished than antisocial behaviour that coincidentally was also a criminal offence. We thus prefer the contrary approach of this Court in *Tripp* which itself reflects *Braxton*."

An ASBO required specific statutory criteria to be established. The order was intended to provide protection against harassment, alarm or distress, caused by anti-social behaviour. Judge J. said that it was obvious that, when passing sentence for breach of an anti-social behaviour order, the court is sentencing for the offence of being in breach of that order. Any sentence in any court must be commensurate. Therefore, if the conduct which constitutes the breach of

---

[99] [2005] 1 Cr. App R.(S) 36.
[1] [2005] EWCA Crim 2253.
[2] [2005] EWCA Crim 2487.

the ASBO was also a distinct criminal offence, and the maximum sentence for the offence is limited to, say, six months' imprisonment, it was a feature to be borne in mind by the sentencing court in the interests of proportionality. However, it was not right that the court's power was thereupon limited to the six months maximum imprisonment for the distinct criminal offence. That would be to treat the breach as if it were a stand alone offence, which at the time when it was committed did not amount to a breach of the court order. In reality, the breach was a distinct offence on its own right, created by statute, punishable by up to five years' imprisonment. Therefore, it was not wrong, in principle, for the judge to have imposed a custodial sentence, where, for the instant offence of drunkenness, the maximum sentence would have been a fine. Therefore, *Morrison* was not followed.

Judge J. added that the court was suggesting that an ASBO should be **6-115** imposed as a kind of device to circumvent maximum penalties which are believed to be too modest. That is a distinct point which does not arise here. The principle was covered by two decisions of this Court, *Kirby*[3] and *Boness*.[4] That was a distinct principle which related to the circumstances in which it is proper to make an ASBO, not to the consequences which may follow its breach. However, the court's power was not limited to the statutory maximum sentence that the offence that gave rise to the breach of the ASBO carried with it. In the present case there was a plain breach of the ASBO by being drunk and urinating in a public place. The judge was merciful. He deferred sentence. He gave a solemn warning. The appellant left court and within a short time returned, throwing away the chance that the judge had given him. The judge had no alternative but to do what he said he would do. Given the appellant's prolonged history of offending it would not be right for this Court to interfere with his decision.

On this point see also *Boness,*[5] in which the Court of Appeal was informed **6-116** during the course of argument that the imposition of an ASBO was sometimes sought by the defendant's advocate at the sentencing stage, hoping that the court might make an ASBO order as an alternative to prison or other sanction. Hooper L.J. said that a court must not allow itself to be diverted in this way—indeed it may be better to decide the appropriate sentence and then move on to consider whether an ASBO should be made or not after sentence has been passed, albeit at the same hearing.

Publicity

All of the relevant courts, other than a youth court, are open to the public. **6-117** Hence, the court may wish to consider an order under s.39 of the Children and Young Persons Act 1933 preventing the identification of a child or young person concerned in the proceedings.[6] In *Medway Council v BBC*,[7] the council obtained an ASBO in respect of 13 year old boy, which led to him being identified in the press. Subsequently, the BBC interviewed the child and his mother, with the mother's consent, as part of an item it intended to broadcast about anti-social behaviour orders. The council then obtained an interim care order over the boy and sought permission to apply for an injunction to restrain the

---

[3] [2005] EWCA Crim 1228.
[4] [2005] EWCA Crim 2395.
[5] [2005] WL 2673805.
[6] Section 1C(9C) of the 1998 Act provides that, while s.49 of the 1933 Act does not apply in respect of proceedings in which children and young persons are concerned, s.39 of that Act does so apply. "Child" and "young person" have the same meaning as in the Children and Young Persons Act 1933.
[7] [2002] 1 F.L.R. 104.

broadcast, on the ground that allowing the broadcast to go ahead would affect the boy's upbringing under the s.1(1) of the Children Act 1989. The application was refused as it was held that publication of the material made public as a result of the anti-social behaviour order could not be restrained and the media could use material relating to the proceedings, including the identity of the person concerned. Given the nature of the orders, the restrictions on identification would be contrary to their intended effect. The interview could be restricted in relation to material that was published after the court proceedings where the order was made, however this did not involve matters of the child's upbringing, so that s.1(1) did not apply. The council had not discharged the burden of proving the need to restrict BBC's freedom of speech and any arguments regarding damage to the child's upbringing had been undermined by the immediate post trial publicity.

6-118   Until amendments made by the Serious Organised Crime and Police Act 2005, where there are proceedings in which an order under subs.1C(2) was made against a child or young person who is convicted of an offence, then under subs.1C (9B) and (9C) of the 1998 Act, s.49 of the Children and Young Persons, Act 1933 does not apply in respect of the child or young person, but s.39 of the 1933 Act does so apply. The intention was to bring reporting restrictions in the youth courts with those of other courts as regards anti-social behaviour orders made against children and young persons. Note s.34A of the Children and Young Persons Act 1933: where the defendant is under the age of 16, the court must obtain the attendance of a parent or guardian (which may include social services). In *R. v Winchester Crown Court, Ex p. B*,[8] Simon Brown L.J., identified a set of principles which should be considered when determining whether or not to make a s.39 direction:

> "The principles to be distilled from the various authorities can, I think, fairly be summarised in this way (and substantially I use the language of the earlier judgments):
>
> (i)   In deciding whether to impose or thereafter to lift reporting restrictions, the court will consider whether there are good reasons for naming the defendant.
>
> (ii) In reaching that decision, the court will give considerable weight to the age of the offender and the potential damage to any young person of public identification as a criminal before the offender has the benefit or burden of adulthood.
>
> (iii) By virtue of section 44 of the 1933 Act, the Court must 'have regard to the welfare of the child or young person'.
>
> (iv) The prospect of being named in court with the accompanying disgrace is a powerful deterrent and the naming of a defendant in the context of his punishment serves as a deterrent to others. These deterrents are proper objectives for the court to seek.
>
> (v)   There is strong public interest in open justice and in the public knowing as much as possible about what has happened in court, including the identity of those who have committed crime.
>
> (vi) The weight to be attributed to the different factors may shift at different stages of the proceedings, and, in particular, after the defendant has been found, or pleads, guilty and is sentenced. It may then be appropriate to place greater weight on the interest of the public in knowing the identity of those who have committed crimes, particularly serious and detestable crimes.

---

[8] [2001] Cr. App. R 11; overruled in part by *R. v Manchester Crown Court Ex p. Hg and D* [2000] 1 Cr. App. R. 262.

(vii) The fact that an appeal has been made may be a material consideration."

These principles were applied in *R. (on the application of T) v St Albans Crown Court and the Chief Constable of Surrey v JHG and DHG.*[9] Elias J. held: **6-119**

> "In my judgement, where an anti-social behaviour order has been imposed, that is a factor which reinforces, and in some cases may strongly reinforce, the general public interest in the public disclosure of court proceedings. There are two reasons for this. First, disclosure of the identity of the individuals may well assist in making an order efficacious. If persons in the community are aware that the order has been made against specified individuals, then it must improve the prospect of that order being effectively enforced. Any subsequent breach is more likely to be reported back to the authorities. Second, the very purpose of these orders is to protect the public from individuals who have committed conduct or behaviour which is wholly unacceptable and of an anti-social nature. The public has a particular interest in knowing who in its midst has been responsible for such outrageous behaviour. In my judgement, this latter factor does not constitute simply 'naming and shaming' which Lord Bingham in *McKerry* thought it would be difficult to justify. This is not simply publicity to satisfy a prurient public: the local community has a proper interest in knowing who has been seriously and persistently damaging its fabric. Moreover, insofar as shaming may, and often will, have a legitimate deterrent effect, it is a relevant factor to weigh against its potential adverse effects, as the judgment of Simon Brown LJ indicates. However, I do not accept that the consequence of this is that in every case it raises a presumption in favour of refusing to make a section 39 direction. It is a weighty factor to be taken into consideration against upholding any claim for anonymity, but, in my judgment, it is not helpful in a case of this kind to talk about presumptions one way or another. In each case there will be a wide variety of factors which will have to be considered, and in each case the balance has to be struck between the desirability of public disclosure on the one hand and the need to protect the welfare of the individual at trial on the other after a full appreciation of the relevant considerations."

The *Anti-Social Behaviour Orders: Guide to Law and Procedure in the Magistrates' Court* contains a useful of summary of considerations pertaining to the exercise of the discretion, at least in the Magistrates Court.[10] They are based on the Judicial Studies Board's guidance on *Publications Reporting Restrictions in the Magistrates' Court*. For orders made on complaint in the civil magistrates' court, the Court would have to have good reason, aside from age alone, to impose any discretionary order under s.39 of the Children and Young Persons Act 1933 to prevent the identification of any child or young person concerned in the proceedings. Although any request for reporting restrictions to be imposed is for the court to decide, the applicant may resist a call from the defendant's representatives for such restrictions if the effectiveness of the ASBO will largely depend on a wider community knowing the details. It is in the community interest that any order will be enforced in order to protect the community. Unless the nuisance is extremely localised, enforcement of the order will normally depend upon the general public being aware of the order and of the identity of the person against whom it is made. Effective enforcement may require the publication of photographs of the subjects, as well as their names and addresses. The magistrates dealing with a youth in ASBO proceedings may be called upon to balance the interests of the   **6-120**

---

[9] [2002] EWHC 1129 (Admin).
[10] Justices' Clerks' Association, April 2004.

community with that of a young person against whom the order has been made. No automatic restrictions upon press and public access or upon media reporting will apply to criminal proceedings before the Magistrates' Court. Breach by a juvenile is heard in the youth court where automatic reporting restrictions do apply. There would have to be good reason to impose any restrictions to prevent media reports' identification of any under 18 year old involved in the proceedings under s.39 of the Children and Young Persons Act 1933. If the defendant is under 18 and is the subject of criminal proceedings before the Youth Court for the alleged breach of an ASBO, then the automatic restrictions upon public, but not press, access to the proceedings and upon identification of the alleged offender will apply. The press will have the right to attend the proceedings under s.47 of the Children and Young Persons Act 1933 and the right to report the proceedings, subject to the automatic restrictions upon identification of the under 18 year old involved under s.49 of the 1933 Act. However, for orders made on conviction in the youth court, the Anti-Social Behaviour Act 2003 removes automatic reporting restrictions under s.49 of the Children and Young Persons Act 1933 for the order stage of proceedings. The court retains the discretion to impose reporting restrictions under s.39 of the 1933 Act where it considers this to be appropriate. Details of the criminal offence for which the individual is in court remain subject to automatic reporting restrictions. When drawing up the order it is good practice to include details of the anti-social behaviour that led to the order being made.

6-121   Some councils have a policy of broadcasting and publicising the making of anti-social behaviour orders as widely as possible. For example, like most authorities, both Manchester City Council and the London Borough of Brent will issue press releases; however, they will sometimes go further and distribute leaflets to local inhabitants.[11] On September 19, 2003, the London Borough of Brent obtained an ASBO against seven defendants, alleged to have comprised a gang, which had between them already been found guilty of more than 100 criminal offences. They were said to have terrorised a particular estate for more than two years, assaulting, intimidating and harassing neighbours. One defendant, the eldest, was banned for life from certain streets in the council's area, while the others were subjected to only five year bans. The council issued a press release, but also sent every house in the exclusion zone a glossy leaflet which set out the details of the orders and invited residents to call the police or the council if the defendants (the photographs of whom also appeared in the leaflet) were seen in the area. Copies of the leaflets were laminated and placed in local shops and public houses.

6-122   This practice was challenged in *R. v Metropolitan Police Commissioner, London or Ors, Ex p. Stanley, Marshall and Kelly*.[12] Kennedy L.J. accepted that when the question of publicity arose it should have been recognised that publicity might infringe the rights of the claimants under Art.8.1, especially if use was made of photographs taken under the powers of PACE that did not seem to have been recognised in this case. If there had been that recognition the police and the local authority should then have gone on to consider whether the publicity which they envisaged was necessary and proportionate to their legitimate aims. In fact they did not deal with the matter in that way. However, in this case it made no difference. The resident of Brent who was informed, in an attempt to restore confidence, that several ASBOs had been obtained might turn out to be invaluable in enforcing one of those orders, particularly having regard to the relatively wide terms of the orders under consideration. Whether publicity was intended to inform, to reassure, to assist in enforcing the existing

---

[11] Manchester City Council are said to have published more than 150,000 such leaflets: *Observer*, October 12, 2003, p.15.
[12-13] [2005] H.L.R. 8; 2004 WL 2246293.

orders by policing, to inhibit the behaviour of those against whom the orders had been made, or to deter others, it was unlikely to be effective unless it included photographs, names and at least partial addresses. Not only did the readers need to know against whom orders have been made, but those responsible for publicity must leave no room for misidentification. If, as here, residents had been exposed to significant criminal behaviour for years, and orders have been obtained by reference to that behaviour and to bring it to an end, he could see no reason why publicity material should not say so. It cannot, of course, assert that those against whom orders have been made have been convicted of any crime, but none of the material that the court had to consider made that assertion. The language used in some of the publicity was colourful, but having regard to the known facts already in the public arena it was entirely appropriate, and the colour was needed in order to attract the attention of the readership. As to the spread of publicity there was no case for contending that it should have been confined to the exclusion area set out in para.1 of each order. Chronologically the first publication was on the website. It was informative and it also specifically invited assistance in enforcement. Technically it could have been read by almost anyone anywhere, but in reality only local residents would be at all likely to access the website. It was maintained in position until January 2004, but these were five year orders. Then the leaflets were dropped in and around the defined exclusion area. That was clearly a properly targeted area having regard to the need both to inform and to enforce, and it could not be assumed that those who received leaflets would have seen the website. Finally there was the report in Partnership News, intended to provide information and reassurance to all of the local authority's tenants. Many may not have seen either the website or the leaflet, so the use of the third medium for publicity cannot be criticised. The applications were dismissed, but he emphasised the need for those considering post-order publicity in future to have in mind the Convention rights of those against whom orders are made, and of the wider public (including past and potential victims of anti-social behaviour). If that was done and recorded, perhaps with the assistance of further guidance from the Home Office, it should be clear that the publicity was confined to what was reasonable and proportionate, and the possibility of further proceedings for judicial review should be eliminated.

Such guidance appeared soon afterwards: *Working Together: Advice on Publicising Anti-Social Behaviour Orders*. Publicity, the guidance advises, is essential if local communities are to support agencies tackling anti-social behaviour. There is an implied power in the Crime and Disorder Act 1998 and the Local Government Act 2000 to publicise an order so that the order can be effectively enforced. ASBOs protect local communities. Obtaining the order is only part of the process; its effectiveness will normally depend on people knowing about the order. Information about ASBOs obtained should be publicised to let the community know that action has been taken in their area. However, a case by case approach should be adopted and each individual case should be judged on its merits as to whether or not to publicise the details of an individual subject to an ASBO; publicity should be expected in most cases. It is necessary to balance the human rights of individuals subject to an ASBO against those of the community as a whole when considering publicising ASBOs. Publicising should be the norm not the exception. An individual who is subject to an ASBO should understand that the community is likely to learn about it. Publicity is not intended to punish the individual. An ASBO is a civil order, which restrains future anti-social behaviour: it is not a punishment. The benefits of publicity include:

6-123

(1) enforcement: local people have the information they need to identify and report breaches;

(2) public reassurance about safety: victims and witnesses know that action has been taken to protect them, and to protect their human rights in relation to safety and/or quiet enjoyment of their property. Making local people aware of an order that is made for their own protection can make a real difference to the way in which they live their lives, especially when they have suffered from antisocial behaviour themselves or lived in fear of it;

(3) public confidence in local services: local people are reassured that if they report anti-social behaviour, action will be taken by local authorities, the police or other agencies;

(4) deterrent to the subject of the order: the perpetrator is aware that breaches are more likely to be reported because details of the order are in the public domain; and

(5) deterrent to other perpetrators: publicity spreads the message that ASBOs are being used and is a warning to others who are causing a nuisance in the area.

6-124   Each individual case should be judged on its merits as to whether or not to publicise the details of an individual subject to an ASBO. There should be a correlation between the purpose of publicity and the necessity test: that is, what is the least interference with privacy that is possible in order to promote the purpose identified. Decision-makers should ensure that the decisions to publicise ASBOs are recorded. However, decision-makers should not see this as an onerous, lengthy task, but merely a way of recording the process they go through to arrive at a published document. To ensure it is achieved, it is good practice to identify an individual, such as the Anti-social Behaviour Co-ordinator, to be in charge of the recording process. The decision-making process should aim to consider and record several key factors:

(1) the need for publicity;

(2) "A consideration of the human rights of the public";

(3) a consideration of the human rights of those against whom ASBOs are made;

(4) what the publicity should look like and whether it is proportionate to the aims of the publicity.

6-125   If the legitimate aim is enforcement of the ASBO then personal information, such as the terms of the ASBO, the identity of the individual (including a photograph) and how to report any breach of the terms should be included. Normally the consideration of the effect of publicity on family members should not deter decision makers on the stated aim of publicising the ASBO. However, consideration of the impact of publicity on vulnerable family members should be made and recorded. The defendant and his or her family should be warned of the intention to publish details. Publicity should be consistent with the character of the ASBO itself: that is, a civil injunction (rather than a criminal order) restricting anti-social behaviour (which may be criminal but need not be criminal). It would be prudent to rehearse the facts of the case and agree on appropriate language to use. Some consideration should be given to the personal circumstances of individuals named on the order when deciding whether to include them in the leaflet, particularly if they are under 18. However, any arguments for not including their names must be balanced with the need to enable those who receive the leaflet to be able to identify a breach. The age of the person against whom the ASBO was obtained should be a consideration when deciding whether or how to inform people about the order. A photograph of the subject of the ASBO will usually be required so that they can be identified. Individuals do not welcome publicity and may view the effect of publicity as a punishment. However, a subjective assessment by the individual of the effect of publicity is irrelevant in determining the purpose of the publicity.

The 2005 Act Reforms

Section 141 of the Serious Organised Crime and Police Act 2005 contains **6-126** important provisions dealing with the reporting of ASBO proceedings involving children. Section 1(10D) provides that in relation to proceedings brought against a child or a young person for an offence under subs.1(10):

"(a) section 49 of the Children and Young Persons Act 1933 (restrictions on reports of proceedings in which children and young persons are concerned) does not apply in respect of the child or young person against whom the proceedings are brought;
(b) section 45 of the Youth Justice and Criminal Evidence Act 1999 (power to restrict reporting of criminal proceedings involving persons under 18) does so apply."

There is also another new subs.(10E). It provides:

"If, in relation to any such proceedings, the court does exercise its power to give a direction under section 45 of the Youth Justice and Criminal Evidence Act 1999, it shall give its reasons for doing so."

Section 141 of the 2005 Act disapplies automatic reporting restrictions for breaches, committed by children and young persons, of anti-social behaviour orders and orders made under ss.1B and 1C of the Crime and Disorder Act 1998. Subsection (2) provides that in proceedings brought against a child or young person for breach of such an order, a court will not be bound by automatic reporting restrictions in s.49 of the Children and Young Persons Act 1933. However, the court will retain discretion to apply reporting restrictions. Subsection (3) provides that breaches of anti-social behaviour orders made on conviction will also be covered by this amendment.

Related Orders and Procedures

Individual Support Orders

Individual support orders (ISOs) were introduced by s.322 of the Criminal **6-127** Justice Act 2003 and insert a new section into the Crime and Disorder Act 1998. Under the new s.1AA, the court may impose positive conditions on young people between the ages of 10 and 17 years to address the underlying causes of the behaviour that led to the ASBO being made. From May 2004, if a magistrates' court is imposing an ASBO (stand alone only) on a young person aged between 10 and 17 years, it will be obliged to make an ISO if it takes the view that it would help prevent further anti-social behaviour. The new section, s.1AA provides that, where a court makes an anti-social behaviour order in respect of a defendant who is a child or young person, when that order is made it must consider whether the individual support conditions are fulfilled. If so, court must make an order under this section ("an individual support order") which requires the defendant to comply, for a period not exceeding six months, with such requirements as are specified in the order; and requires the defendant to comply with any directions given by the responsible officer with a view to the implementation of the requirements. In subs.(3), the individual support conditions are:

(a) that an individual support order would be desirable in the interests of preventing any repetition of the kind of behaviour which led to the making of the anti-social behaviour order;

(b) that the defendant is not already subject to an individual support order; and

(c) that the court has been notified by the Secretary of State that arrangements for implementing individual support orders are available in the area in which it appears to it that the defendant resides or will reside and the notice has not been withdrawn.

Subsection (5) provides that the requirements that may be specified under subs.(2)(a) above are those that the court considers desirable in the interests of preventing any repetition of the kind of behaviour which led to the making of the anti-social behaviour order. They include:

(a) to participate in activities specified in the requirements or directions at a time or times so specified;

(b) to present himself to a person or persons so specified at a place or places and at a time or times so specified; and

(c) to comply with any arrangements for his education so specified.

Such requirements included in, and directions given under, an individual support order shall, as far as practicable, be such as to avoid any conflict with the defendant's religious beliefs; and any interference with the times, if any, at which he normally works or attends school or any other educational establishment. Under subs.(9), before making an individual support order, the court shall obtain, from a social worker of a local authority social services department or a member of a YOT, any information which it considers necessary in order to determine whether the individual support conditions are fulfilled, or to determine what requirements should be imposed by an individual support order if made, and shall consider that information.

6-128   See also the new s.1AB. Before making an individual support order, the court shall explain to the defendant in ordinary language the effect of the order and of the requirements proposed to be included in it; the consequences which may follow if he fails to comply with any of those requirements; and that the court has power (under subs.(6) below) to review the orders on the application either of the defendant or of the responsible officer. Under subs.(3), if the person in respect of whom an individual support order is made fails without reasonable excuse to comply with any requirement included in the order, he is guilty of an offence and liable on summary conviction to a fine not exceeding, if he is aged 14 or over at the date of his conviction, £1,000; if he is aged under 14, then £250. Note that under subs.(4), no referral order under s.16(2) or (3) of the Powers of Criminal Courts (Sentencing) Act 2000 may be made in respect of an offence under subs.(3) above.

6-129   If the anti-social behaviour order, as a result of which an individual support order was made, ceases to have effect, the individual support order (if it has not previously ceased to have effect) ceases to have effect when the anti-social behaviour order does. On an application made by complaint by the person subject to an individual support order, or the responsible officer, the court which made the individual support order may vary or discharge it by a further order. If the anti-social behaviour order, as a result of which an individual support order was made, is varied, the court varying the anti-social behaviour order may by a further order vary or discharge the individual support order.

Justice Board guidance[14] is that, in order to assess the suitability and possible programme content of ISOs and Parenting Orders, the YOT will carry out assessments for both Orders. The assessments will include whether orders are needed to secure the cooperation of the child and parents or whether they are willing to co-operate voluntarily in the kind of support or programmes that would otherwise be delivered under an order. Where a child or parent will cooperate voluntarily, an order would not usually be desirable. Because findings of fact will not be made in relation to the alleged anti-social behaviour until the date of the Court hearing, it will not be possible to carry out the assessments until after the hearing. Courts can make an interim ASBO in relevant cases and then adjourn the matter for a period of 15 working days for assessments and report preparation. The full ASBO hearing will therefore take place on the same day as the Court receives the ISO/Parenting Assessments. There is a different (lesser) standard of proof required for the making of an interim, rather than a full ASBO. However the findings in relation to the interim ASBO should provide sufficient information for ISO and Parenting Assessments and the Court will make available a copy of the magistrates' findings on the interim ASBO on the day of the interim hearing. This should be made available to the YOT workers preparing ISO and Parenting Assessment reports. The relevant YOT should be aware of an application for an ASBO through the local Anti-Social Behaviour Team, which should involve the YOT in the decision making process leading up to the application for an ASBO on a young person. This should provide advance warning of the hearing date and of the possibility of an adjournment for assessment and report preparation. An ISO may last for up to six months and can require a young person to attend up to two sessions a week. This represents a maximum and the relevant proposed level of intervention will be determined by the assessment process (see below). The ISO provisions in the Criminal Justice Act limit school attendance requirements to not more than two days in any week for a maximum of six months. ISOs cannot therefore be used to compel attendance at school on more than two days a week. However, other measures exist to tackle truancy issues (the responsibility of the Local Education Authority) and ISOs are not primarily designed to tackle truancy. Each ISO will be supervised by a "Responsible Officer" (Case Manager). Although legislation allows for the Responsible Officer to be a social worker or education officer, the Responsible Officer in most cases will be a YOT staff member. The Responsible Officer will carry out the normal case management functions as for other Court orders (coordination of programme, assessment, planning, enforcement etc.) and will also ensure it is accurately recorded on the case management system. All young people being considered for an ISO will be assessed using Asset to determine both the level of intervention needed (Risk of Future ASB) and the content of the intervention (Need). Any intervention matrix will have to be based on the premise that the most intensive/prolonged intervention will be reserved for only the most serious cases with very high Asset scores—taking into account the issue of proportionality. Consideration will need to be given to resources available—discussions with Operations/Area Managers should take place.

The process for breach of ISOs will follow that for breach of Supervision Orders, although the penalties available are different. In order to maintain the

6-130

6-131

14 "Individual Support Orders (ISO) Procedure: A protocol to be used and adapted by YOTs when managing ISOs", 2006.

credibility of the ISO, breach action in the event of non-compliance must be implemented. The same justification for breach action applies as with other orders. Breach of an ISO is a criminal offence and as such is dealt with by the Youth Court. Under s.266 of the Criminal Justice Act 2003 the court is able to require the young person within the Individual Support Order to "comply, for a period not exceeding 6 months, with such requirements as are specified in the order" and to "comply with any directions given by the responsible officer" in order to implement the specified requirements. It is crucial therefore, as with all other orders where the YOT is acting as the responsible officer, that the officer is able to provide evidence of the failure to comply with these requirements or directions. This means ensuring that copies of signed appointment forms and/ or appointment letters should be kept as this evidence will in turn prove vital in any contested breach proceedings. Missed appointments related to the ISO must be recorded initially as "no explanation" on the case management system. The Case Manager must always follow up missed appointments within one working day by telephone, home visit or letter and a judgment must then be exercised as to whether the explanation is acceptable or not. Unacceptable failures to attend a contact must result in the issuing of a missed appointment letter on the first occasion by the Case Manager. Further unacceptable missed appointments will result in a warning letter on the first occasion and a final warning letter on the next occasion. Failure to attend after a final warning letter must result in breach action within five days of the most recent failure. Breach action can only be "stayed" in exceptional circumstances with the authorisation of the Operations Manager and the reason noted on the case management system. When breach action has been initiated the young person should be allowed to continue with the order until the date of the court hearing, unless it would prove disruptive for the young person or other young people on orders to do so.

6-132   The evidence of many organisations to the Home Affairs Committee on Anti-Social Behaviour in 2005 was that ISOs were potentially of great benefit. The Magistrates Association said that they should be granted as a matter of course by magistrates if satisfied that they would help prevent repetition of the behaviour. The Local Government Association "warmly welcomed" them, arguing that their approach "fits firmly with the LGA vision to reducing anti-social behaviour". However, others questioned whether ISOs were sufficient. For instance, County Durham Youth Engagement Service argued that the maximum length of ISOs of six months, with two sessions per week "may be insufficient to provide adequate measures of supervision and support." The Home Office explained why, in its view, it would not be possible significantly to extend the length of ISOs:

> "The ISO provides a means by which a 10–17 year old with an ASBO receives interventions that address the cause of their anti-social behaviour. An order lasting 6 months was considered reasonable and proportionate with human rights legislation. To compel an individual to receive support on a longer term basis would infringe on their liberty and be considered a penalty rather than a support initiative."

6-133   However, as the Committee points out, the appeal to human rights appears specious: an ASBO is also defined in legal terms as a preventative, rather than a punitive, measure; that these can limit, for instance, freedom of movement and association, and yet last for a minimum of two years without any apparent incompatibility problems. They found more convincing the Home Office's further argument that "in addition there is an expectation that the underlying causes of the anti-social behaviour—such as drugs, alcohol or anger management problems—should improve significantly over 6 months and therefore remove the requirement to continue receiving the support an ISO offers." The Committee observed that the real problem again appears to be one of resources. Officers from the Youth Offending Service said that ISOs had not been used in the West Midlands for the following reasons:

"In terms of the legislation the responsible agencies are education, youth offending service or social services. As it is we have not set up any resources or any structures for that order. There is not any new funding; initially the Youth Justice Board said there was probably going to be funding. The Home Office Anti-social Behaviour Unit said the Youth Justice Board had the money and then we were told to go to our Crime and Disorder Reduction Partnerships. I have acquired some funding and with the Home Office money for this pilot, we will be able to offer a very limited service in the future:"

Professor Morgan, Chair of the Youth Justice Board agreed that the number of ISOs has "so far been rather small and there is a funding problem". He told us that "the original understanding about funding here was that the number of ASBOs to which they might be attached was going to be much lower than is now the case". His points appear to be supported by the available figures: between May and September 2004, only five ISOs were made. On the other hand, the minister said that each order costs an estimated £1,500 and that the Youth Justice Board had agreed to absorb £500,000 for these orders within its mainstream budgets. She also backed the notion that ISOs should be linked to ASBOs, arguing that this was "a more integrated way of looking at some of these problems". More generally, Ms Blears talked about the need for local authorities and agencies to re-focus their efforts and their expenditure:

"We have never pretended that the Home Office money is going to solve the problem of anti-social behaviour because a lot of this is about local authorities and local agencies refocusing their efforts on tackling these problems: [. . .] refocusing their activities and their existing expenditure."

The committee asked the Chair of the Association of Directors of Social **6-134** Services whether the fact that social services departments had not resourced ISOs (even though their budgets are not ring fenced, and this would be an option for them) was an indication that they are not engaged with dealing with anti-social young people. They were told:

"Many YOTs are part of social services and will be engaged with them but also they have a number of other initiatives to deliver. There is a question both for the YOTs and for the mainstream social services of how you divide up your resources. Social services departments are also working with children and child protection issues and delivering a front line service. They are also in the middle of implementing the Change for Children agenda which is a huge agenda. If you look at children's services funding and the surveys done by the ADSS each year on that funding, you will see how much of that is taken by placements and associated costs of children looked after. There are real difficulties there about delivering what you might call the core functions both of the social services departments and of the YOTs that have already been set, a lot of which have been funded particularly through the Youth Justice Board with discrete streams of money for a particular preventative programme. The ISOs have not. That is the difficulty."

In response to an earlier question, Ms Hitchen also accepted the notion that in the majority of cases where an ASBO is issued to a young person, there will have been little or inconsistent prior involvement by social services.

Intervention Orders

6-135 Section 20 of the Drugs Act 2005 creates a new civil order, the Intervention Order which can be attached to ASBOs in adult cases. It creates a new section, s.1F, in the Crime and Disorder Act 1998. The relevant authority may apply for an Intervention Order when the court is considering the ASBO application if:

  (a) they make an application for an anti-social behaviour order;

  (b) they have obtained from an appropriately qualified person a report relating to the effect on the person's behaviour of the misuse of controlled drugs[15] or of such other factors as the Secretary of State by order prescribes; and

  (c) they have also engaged in consultation with such persons as the Secretary of State by order prescribes for the purpose of ascertaining that, if the report recommends that an order under this section is made, appropriate activities will be available.

Under subs.(3), if the court makes the behaviour order, and is satisfied that the relevant conditions are met, it may also make an intervention order. These are the relevant conditions:

  (a) an intervention order is desirable in the interests of preventing a repetition of the behaviour which led to the behaviour order being made (called "trigger behaviour");

  (b) appropriate activities relating to the trigger behaviour or its cause are available for the defendant;

  (c) the defendant is not (at the time the intervention order is made) subject to another intervention order or to any other treatment relating to the trigger behaviour or its cause (whether on a voluntary basis or by virtue of a requirement imposed in pursuance of any enactment);

  (d) that the court has been notified by the Secretary of State that arrangements for implementing intervention orders are available in the area in which it appears that the defendant resides or will reside and the notice has not been withdrawn.

6-136 In subs.(5), an intervention order is an order which: (a) requires the defendant to comply, for a period not exceeding six months, with such requirements as are specified in the order, and (b) requires the defendant to comply with any directions given by a person authorised to do so under the order with a view to the implementation of the requirements under para.(a) above. It may also require the defendant to participate in the activities specified in the requirement or directions at a time or times so specified and to present himself to a person or persons so specified at a time or times so specified. These requirements must avoid any conflict with the defendant's religious beliefs, and any interference with the times (if any) at which he normally works or attends an educational establishment. If the defendant fails to comply with a requirement included in or a direction given under an intervention order, the person responsible for the provision or supervision of appropriate activities under the order must inform the relevant authority of that fact.[16] Under a new section,

---

[15] "Controlled drug" has the same meaning as in the Misuse of Drugs Act 1971: The crimsoned Disorder ACT 1998, s.1F(10).
[16] The crime and Disorder ACT 1998, s.1F(8).

s.1H, before making an intervention order the court must explain to the defendant in ordinary language:

(a) the effect of the order and of the requirements proposed to be included in it,

(b) the consequences which may follow (under subs.(3) below) if he fails to comply with any of those requirements, and

(c) that the court has power (under subs.(5) below) to review the order on the application either of the defendant or of the relevant authority.

If a person in respect of whom an intervention order is made fails, without reasonable excuse, to comply with any requirement included in the order he is guilty of an offence and liable on summary conviction to a fine not exceeding level 4 on the standard scale. Section 1H(4) provided that if the behaviour order, as a result of which an intervention order is made, ceases to have effect, the intervention order (if it has not previously ceased to have effect) ceases to have effect when the behaviour order does. Hence, under subs.(5), on an application made by a person subject to an intervention order, or the relevant authority, the court which made the intervention order may vary or discharge it by a further order. An application under subs.(5) made to a magistrates' court must be made by complaint. If the ASBO as a result of which an intervention order was made is varied, the court varying the behaviour order may by a further order vary or discharge the intervention order.

Acceptable Behaviour Contracts:

Acceptable Behaviour Contracts (ABCs) are voluntary arrangements made **6-137** between those involved in anti-social behaviour and the local police, the housing department of the local authority, registered social landlord or the local education authority or school. They were first introduced by the London Borough of Islington to deal with problems on estates caused by young people aged between 10 and 17. In April 2002 there were at least 173 contract schemes in England and Wales and 39 of the 42 police forces surveyed had implemented at least one ABC scheme. It has been estimated that about 5,380 were entered into in 2004.[17] According to an evaluation of the Islington scheme and other schemes,[18] a multi-agency approach was common, usually involving the police, housing, YOTs and social services. However, contracts were typically monitored by the police and housing. The majority (79 per cent) of respondents (police and housing officers) felt that the scheme was positive, and most ABC schemes were set up because of perceived successes elsewhere. Types of antisocial behaviour targeted included harassment, verbal abuse and criminal damage. ABCs were also used to tackle crime, e.g. prostitution and joyriding. Forty-five per cent of respondents (76 of 169) who were currently running ABC schemes reported that one or more of their contracts had been breached. A total of 286 breaches were identified; 15 per cent of all contracts issued. Most breaches involved criminal damage, verbal abuse and nuisance. Overall, young people were less likely to come to the attention of police and housing officers once they had been given a contract, that even those young people who continued with anti-social behaviour did so at a reduced rate and that 57 of

---

[17] Home Affairs Committee, Anti-Social Behaviour, Fifth Report, para.175.
[18] Bullock and Jones "Acceptable Behaviour Contracts addressing antisocial behaviour in the London Borough of Islington" Home Office, 2004

contracts were not breached and 19 per cent breached only once in a six month period. Benefits of the scheme included addressing and reducing antisocial behaviour effectively. The main implementation problems were considered to be a lack of resources and time. Practice varies from area to area. At the other end is Manchester City Council, which does not use ABCs at all because they think they are unnecessary, preferring to rely upon a threat of legal proceedings. Further, they considered them to be a useless prolongation of distress to the community.[19]

Guidance on Anti-Social Behaviour Contracts

6-138   Home Office guidance provides that the contract is agreed and signed at a meeting with the individual and the lead agencies. Where the person whose behaviour is at issue is a child or young person, parents or guardians should be encouraged to attend. The contract specifies a list of anti-social acts in which the person has been involved and which they agree not to continue. Where possible the individual should be involved in drawing up the contract. This may encourage them to recognise the impact of their behaviour and take responsibility for their actions. Support to address the underlying causes of the behaviour should be offered in parallel to the contract. This may include diversionary activities (such as attendance at a youth project), counselling or support for the family. It is vital to ascertain which agencies are already involved, especially where the individual is aged between 10 and 17 years. Legal action in the form of an anti-social behaviour order or possession order (if the young person is in social housing) should be stated on the contract where this is the potential consequence of breach. The threat of legal action provides an incentive to ensure that the contract is adhered to. The flexible nature of ABCs allows for various agencies to take the lead according to the circumstances in each case, local practice and which agencies can have greatest impact on reducing unacceptable behaviour. In Islington, for example, the Anti-Social Behaviour Team running the ABC scheme is led by representatives from the local authority housing department and the local police. In other areas the lead agency is the YOT working closely with the local police. Once agencies identify a suitable candidate for a contract, checks should be made into whether the individual or family is subject to any other investigations or support. In the case of a young person, the local youth offending team should be informed and if appropriate the social services or education welfare. It is vital that consideration is given to whether an individual is really suitable for the scheme. Where there is offending behaviour which is serious and persistent an ASBO or other legal action is likely to be more effective.

6-139   The ABC meeting should be used as an opportunity for the individual involved in the anti-social behaviour and his or her family, where appropriate, to discuss the meaning of the term "anti-social behaviour" and the impact it has on others. The meeting can be used as an early intervention process to stop the inappropriate behaviour becoming worse and to outline possible repercussions should the behaviour be repeated. It can also be used as an opportunity to provide support to address underlying causes such as family problems. Further action may then be taken by the lead agencies after the meeting to ensure that other agencies become involved as necessary. It is worth thinking about where the meeting should take place. While the use of police premises may reinforce the importance attached to an ABC, it is important that care is taken to ensure that the interview is not misinterpreted as being part of a criminal investigation. Parents or guardians, housing or local police officers and any other interested party, such as a social worker or family friend, may be

---

[19] Home Affairs Committee, Anti-Social Behaviour, Fifth Report, paras 178–9.

present if it is considered appropriate. If the individual who is to become subject to an ABC does not attend, without notification or good reason, further attempts, by letter or a visit, should be made to contact them. If this fails their non-appearance can be documented and used at any future proceedings if the inappropriate behaviour is repeated. Written warning of this should be sent to the person concerned. The meeting where the contract is signed does not constitute legal proceedings.

Key points when arranging and conducting the ABC meeting are publicising the scheme prior to holding the meeting so that those concerned are aware of the scheme and its aims; making the interview less formal to avoid intimidating the family; choosing a spacious room and only invite key stakeholders; involving other agencies prior to this meeting, for example youth services and schools; and holding a pre-meeting with key stakeholders to share relevant information. Allow adequate preparation time as this will help to keep attendance at the actual interview to a minimum. An ABC normally lasts for six months, though since it is not a statutory document any reasonable period may be specified. While the terms of the contract should reflect the behaviour to be addressed, they should not be so numerous that the individual is overwhelmed. About half a dozen might be the norm. In addition, there needs to be a balance between general and specific conditions. If they are too general it may be unclear precisely what acts are covered, but if they are too specific it may be possible to evade them too easily. The contract should be written in language that the individual can easily understand. Some schemes define all criminal offences committed by the individual as breaches, irrespective of whether the behaviour is prohibited by the contract. The contract can be renewed after further discussions have been held if breaches have occurred or other forms of anti-social behaviour are continuing. Second contracts should be considered if the behaviour does not improve during the first contract or resumes soon after. However, where an ABC is not likely to tackle the problem behaviour other measures, such as an ASBO, should be pursued quickly. A copy of the original contract should be made available to all those involved in monitoring the behaviour of the individual. Other interested parties should be informed of the agreed conditions of the contract where appropriate, which may include the youth offending team and other agencies. **6-140**

Continued monitoring is vital for the contract to be effective. Information on breaches can be collected from the same sources as those from which the original anti-social behaviour was identified (see above). Accurate and systematic data collection techniques—such as standard forms and reporting systems—will assist with the monitoring and evaluation of contracts. If the contract is breached there must always be a response. Agencies and organisations involved will need to consider the circumstances and decide upon the best course of action. The action taken should be determined by the nature of the breach. A structured approach can be taken to breaches, leading to legal action if the behaviour does not cease. Such a structured approach may involve: verbal warnings; written warnings (however this assumes a good level of literacy and visits may be more appropriate); an interview to discuss and reiterate the contract terms. This will also help to identify why the breach has occurred and enable agencies to provide additional support that may be required to prevent further breaches. Agencies such as the youth offending team (in the case of a young person) should be involved to identify appropriate measures to address the continued unacceptable behaviour. However, where the community is facing on-going anti-social behaviour, legal action should be considered. **6-141**

Under the guidance, ABCs are not a substitute for ASBOs and should not be seen as a necessary precursor to an application for an order. Evidence collected for an ABC and breach of the contract may be cited in court for an **6-142** application in support of a possession order or an ASBO. Other agencies involved with ABCs—either as signatories on the contract or in providing support to the individual and family—are registered social landlords, social services, schools, environmental health and health services. This is not a prescriptive list. Providing training for staff in partner agencies involved in ABCs will enable schemes to work more effectively. In particular, training should cover the practical implications of contracts (such as the paperwork required) and how to deal with breaches.

The Relevant Authority's Obligations

Consultation

6-143   Consultation is an essential part of the decision to make an application. Section 1E of the 1998 Act provides that it applies to all applications for an anti-social behaviour order and to applications for an order under s.1B. Under subs.(2), before making an application to which this section applies, the council for a local government area shall consult the chief officer of police of the police force maintained for the police area within which that local government area lies. Further, subs.(3) provides that, before making an application to which this section applies, a chief officer of police shall consult the council for the local government area in which the person in relation to whom the application is to be made resides or appears to reside. Finally, under subs.(4), a relevant authority, other than a council for a local government area or a chief officer of police authority (i.e. the British Transport Police and registered social landlords), shall consult the council for the local government area in which the person in relation to whom the application is to be made resides or appears to reside, and the chief officer of police of the police force maintained for the police area within which that local government area lies.

6-144   The ASBO Guidance recommends that consultation take place with the agency in whose area the subject resides or appears to reside. Hence, each district or borough council and police division or command unit should have a person who is the nominated contact for the purposes of consultation.[20] The purpose of consultation is to inform the agencies of the intended application and to obtain any relevant information. However, if the partnership arrangements are satisfactory, it is likely that they will satisfy the statutory requirements. That does not mean that other agencies should have the power to veto proposed applications, but that they are told of the proposed application and given an opportunity to comment including consideration of reservations and alternative proposals. An appropriate method would be by way of a case conference. The court should be satisfied that that there has been the necessary consultation and a signed document to that effect may be sufficient.

Consultation with Respondents

6-145   While it is not a requirement, informing the proposed defendant that the partnership is considering applying for an ASBO should be considered. In *Wareham v Purbeck DC*,[21] the appellant appealed by way of case stated against the making of an anti-social behaviour order under the 1998 Act. Before the making of the order, the respondent local authority had written to him informing him that an anti-social behaviour case conference would be held to consider his behaviour and the appropriate action to be taken, includ-

[20] *A Guide to Anti-Social Behaviour Orders and Acceptable Behaviour Contracts* Home Office (2002) p.25.
[21] [2005] WL 607501; [2005] H.L.R. 39.

ing applying to the court for an ASBO. The outcome of the meeting was that it was appropriate to apply for such an order and the appellant was so informed. The application and supporting documents filed in court were also sent to the appellant. At the hearing the judge held that the fact that W had not been involved in the decision making process prior to the application did not mean that the proceedings were in breach of the Human Rights Act 1998 Sch.1Pt I Art.6 and Art.8. The local authority submitted that there was no interference with W's rights under Art.8 at the stage of considering whether to apply to the magistrates' court for an anti-social behaviour order and that any interference as a result of the order was justified under Art.8(2). The Divisional Court dismissed the appeal. Because what had occurred prior to the court proceedings was no more than a decision to apply for an order, and because when the application was heard a defendant had a full opportunity to resist it, in the context there was no infringement of any right under Art.8 by not inviting the proposed defendant to put his views before the decision to apply was made. The appellant had a full opportunity to put his case before the magistrates' court. The local authority's failure to consult him was not a breach of Art.8. The local authority's failure to consult W was not a breach of Art.6. It was for the decision making group to consider the practical sense of involving the proposed defendant but such involvement was not required by law.

Delegation

In *Chief Constable of the West Midlands Police v Birmingham Justices, Ex p.*[22] **6-146** there were five applications for anti-social behaviour orders at which it was submitted that the proceedings were null and void because of fundamental irregularities of procedure. The Chief Constable of the West Midlands Police issued an internal memorandum authorising ". . .all OCU Commanders, their Operations and Crime Managers, Operational Departmental Heads and their Deputies to apply for Anti-Social Behaviour Orders under s.(1) and (2) of the Crime and Disorder Act 1998, and to exercise all ancillary powers in connection with those applications until such authority is terminated by me". It was not controversial that the functions of the Chief Constable under subs.(1) and (2) are delegable. However, the court held that that the memo-randum was not a prescribed means of delegation, and that the particular delegations spelt out in it were not necessarily exhaustive of the Chief Constable's powers. The District Judge accepted a defence submission at the hearing that the power to make an application under subs.(1) could not law-fully be delegated to an officer lower than the rank of superintendent, and that consultation under subs.(2) must be carried out by an officer of no lower rank. Sedley L.J. said that, applying the *Carltona* principle,[23] the Chief Constable was not the employer of the officers under his or her command but is legally answerable for them. The *Carltona* principle did not depend upon on the peculiar status of civil servants as the alter ego of their minister. It was sufficiently ample to allow a Chief Constable to discharge functions of this kind through an officer for whom he or she is answerable. To fall back instead on implied delegation and sub-delegation is capable of appearing to be a rat-ification by the court of an accomplished fact and to beg the question of power to delegate. No doubt an officer of the rank or status described in the memorandum is a proper and appropriate agent; but to hold that such an officer is the proper and appropriate agent is not to interpret but to legislate. The question for a court was not how it considers that the Chief Constable

[22] [2002] EWHC 1087 (Admin).
[23] *Carltona Ltd v Commissioners of Works* [1943] 2 All E.R. 560.

should be exercising his power of delegation; it is whether the Chief Constable has exercised it within permissible limits. Sedley L.J. could see nothing in the legislation which enabled the court to set a limit of such specificity as that set by the District Judge. It was for the Chief Constable to decide who is best suited to the sensitive task of deciding whether to apply for ASBOs when they may be directed at any person from the age of 10 upwards. It was not for the court to second-guess, him unless his choice is irrational or otherwise beyond his powers. Further, the Chief Constable was not constrained as to the rank to which he may delegate either task-so there was no logical reason why they cannot be properly carried out at different levels. It was therefore open to the Chief Constable to delegate or devolve to any officer or officers judged suitable by him the respective functions set out in subss.(1) and (2). No question of sub-delegation from the Superintendent to the Sergeant arose, and so the District Judge's ancillary finding to the contrary was not justified.

Guidance

6-147 Government guidance on ASBOs recommends a fully-coordinated, multi-agency approach including the police, local authority departments such as education, social services and housing, outside bodies such as the probation service, YOTs and voluntary bodies.[24] One individual within the lead agency should take a lead role who is to manage and co-ordinate the involvement of other agencies. A multi-agency approach should be adopted so that all agencies that could hold information on the individual in question are involved in the process at an early stage. Such agencies include the probation service, social services, health services, the YOT and voluntary organisations, all of which may have come into contact with the individual or members of their family. Crime and disorder reduction partnerships, in particular, are advised to adopt the "orders group" structure developed by the Coventry partnership. Under this approach, the orders group has delegated authority from the partnership to establish and manage protocols and procedures for implementing ASBOs. The group should consist of the local authority ASB co-ordinator and designated representatives from the police and other agencies and bodies as well as the CPS and the courts. Each representative should have delegated decision-making authority from their own agencies. A comprehensive protocol for the consideration of potential ASBOs and the pursuit of applications, where appropriate, should be committed to by the relevant partner agencies. A lead officer should be identified to oversee each case. The protocol should also enable communication with agencies not directly represented on the main orders group or the CDRP (e.g. other RSLs or the fire service). A case conference approach should be established, whereby potential ASBO cases are considered by the agencies who are able to contribute to the case and have information about the individual in question. The case conference could be held by the orders group where established, but is perhaps more likely to involve staff from agencies who are directly concerned with the case in question. It should be attended by the person with lead responsibility for the case. The role of the lead officer is to manage the case. This will include instructing solicitors, witness liaison and support, co-ordinating service of summonses, communicating developments to partners and ensuring that appropriate monitoring arrangements are in place to facilitate enforcement of orders granted. Case management meetings should be action oriented and outcome focused, the primary objective being to identify and implement appropriate measures

[24-25] *A Guide to Anti-Social Behaviour Orders and Acceptable Behaviour Contracts,* Home Office (2002), p.22. See also the more recent Together pamphlet, *Anti-Social Behaviour,* 2005.

to protect communities from anti-social acts. This may be an ASBO or another form of intervention as appropriate. Any agency should be able to request a case management meeting. Case management meetings should be held within two weeks of the identification of a case. In the majority of instances a single meeting should be sufficient to establish the action plan, inclusive of monitoring and review arrangements and a publicity strategy, where relevant. The action points of each case management meeting should be recorded by the lead officer. Where the case involves a young person, case management meetings should routinely include representatives from education, social services and the YOT. An assessment of the young person should be undertaken as soon as it is deemed appropriate. This may happen in parallel with the application. The arrangements established by the CDRP should seek to combine robust procedures that comply with relevant legislative requirements (for example, for information sharing) with flexible operation—a pragmatic approach that avoids prescription and enables the agency most suitable in an individual case to fulfil the lead officer role. The protocol and operational arrangements should be subject to review and change by the orders group or, where no orders group exists, by the main CDRP, to promote effectiveness.

According to Home Office guidance on producing arrangements in the **6-148** form of protocols for cooperation between the relevant agencies, (the Protocol Guidance),[26] the core agencies are those mentioned in s.5 of the 1998 Act: local authorities, police, probation service and health authority. These agencies should organise a formal partnership. However, it is recommended that other interested agencies should be invited to attend case conferences, such as registered social landlords, neighbourhood watch organisations, social services and YOTs. In fact, where the individual is a child or young person, the relevant youth offender's team social services and the Education Department should be represented in the partnership. If the child is the subject of a care order or has significant social or healthy problems, the partnership must consult social services and the NHS Trust. If the behaviour is motivated by racism, the partnership should consult the Racial Equality Council and the relevant ethnic minority organisation. The partnership should then designate a named person in each local authority's area to be the ASBO co-ordinator. Each agency of the partnership must provide a delegate to attend meetings chaired by the ASBO co-ordinator. The group of delegates should ensure that a complaint has not been made as a result of malice or discrimination, decide which agency is in the lead (where the ASB co-ordinator has not already done so), and agree an action plan aimed at supporting victims and witness and prevent further anti-social behaviour. If the matter is urgent, the ASBO co-ordinator should appoint the police or local authority as the lead agency; otherwise, the partner agencies will be given a period of time in which to respond and the case will be considered at the next meeting of the group. The lead agency is responsible for the progress of the application. If the behaviour complained of has taken place on council land, then the lead agency should be the local authority; if it takes place in public areas, the lead agency should be the police; in other cases, it must be determined by the group. The Protocol Guidance recommends that the group should only agree to apply for an ASBO where it concludes that it is necessary to protect an individual, group of people or a community in its area and be satisfied that it is an appropriate step to take. This is arguably more onerous than simply showing that an ASBO is "desirable". The Protocol Guidance suggests that the group should have before is clear evidence that an ASBO is necessary.

---

[26] *Anti-Social Behaviour Orders: Guidance on Drawing up Local ASBO Protocols*, Home Office.

6-149 Home Office Guidance on ASBOs,[27] accepting that the court must be satisfied as to allegations of past anti-social behaviour to a criminal standard, recommends that the lead agency in an ASBO application should obtain evidence which proves that the defendant acted in a certain way at a specific place and time and that these acts caused or were likely to cause harassment alarm or distress to one or more persons not in the same household as the defendant. It is not necessary for witnesses to prove that they were in fact alarmed or distressed, merely that the behaviour they observed was likely to produce such an effect in others. Hence, there is no reason why, in an ASBO application, evidence cannot be introduced from a police officer who wishes to remain anonymous for professional reasons or from neighbours who are reluctant to disclose their names or attend court for fear of reprisals. Although it is admissible, relevance and weight are questions for the court. Where the applicant proposes to rely upon hearsay evidence, they should comply with the requirements of the Civil Evidence Act 1995 as regards notice.

Information Exchange

6-150 Consultation is not possible unless authorities are able to share information. Reference has already been made to police and local authority powers to share information under the common law, the 1998 Act and the Data Protection Act 1998. The ASBO Guidance recommends that agencies negotiate information-sharing protocols with each other. Any covert evidence should comply with the Regulation of Investigatory Powers Act 2000. While the Rehabilitation of Offenders Act 1974 prohibits evidence of spent convictions, there is no reason why evidence from failed criminal proceedings cannot be used in an ASBO application. Section 115 of the Crime and Disorder Act 1998 empowers any person to disclose information, where necessary or expedient for the purposes of the Act, to a chief officer of police, a police force, local authorities, probation service or health authority, or to a person acting on their behalf. Where the agency requesting the information clearly needs it for the purposes of reducing anti-social behaviour, the presumption should normally be that it will be supplied. A "relevant authority" (as defined by s.115 of the Crime and Disorder Act 1998) may disclose information to a registered social landlord where the RSL is acting on behalf of the relevant authority for the purposes of the provisions of the Act. In order to be "acting on behalf of" the relevant authority the person or body so acting must have authority and must have consented to do so. Such authority may be derived in writing or orally. Authority may also be implied from the conduct of the parties or from the nature of employment. Authority may be confined to a particular act or be general in its character. If authority is general then it will still be confined to acts which the relevant authority itself has power to do. Information sharing issues can also be discussed with the Office of the Data Protection Registrar. If possible the protocol should be published, so that the public can see that information is being shared in an appropriate way. The Protocol Guidance recommends that where a partner agency receives information about anti-social behaviour, it should notify the ASB co-ordinator, the police, and the local authority, and other partner agencies. Information shared between the agencies should be accurate and relevant and only exchanged between designated liaison officers of each agency. It is recommended that the partnership implement and follow a locally agreed information exchange protocol, signed by all partner agencies.[28] The protocol also contains a Code of Practice on

---

[27] *A Guide to Anti-Social Behaviour Orders and Acceptable Behaviour Contracts*, Home Office (2002).
[28] Protocol Guidance Pt 5.

Data Protection. Decisions to exchange information between the relevant parties should only be made on a case-by-case basis by the holder of the information. The information, particularly personal data, should only be disclosed in response to a written request which explains the purpose for which the information will be used. Certain officers of each agency should be designated liaison officers, responsible for dealing with requests for information between agencies. They should be fully conversant with the Data Protection Act principles. The disclosed information should be retained by the parties only for so long as it is necessary for the purpose of the exchange. It should be accurate and factually relevant and monitored regularly by the parties.

The Home Office Guidance provides useful advice as to what kind of evidence is necessary and it should be collected.[29] It is the duty of the lead agency will be required to gather evidence to prove its case beyond reasonable doubt. This evidence can include hearsay evidence. The evidence in support of an ASBO application should prove: that the defendant acted in a specific way on specific dates and at specific places and that these acts caused or were likely to cause harassment, alarm or distress to one or more persons not in the same household as the defendant. The court then needs to evaluate whether an order is necessary to protect persons from further anti-social acts by the defendant. This is not a test to which a standard of proof will be applied. Instead it is an assessment of future risk. The applicant can present evidence or argument to assist the court in making this evaluation. Witness evidence need not prove that they were alarmed or distressed themselves, but only that the behaviour they witnessed was likely to produce such an effect on others. As hearsay evidence is allowed it may be given by "professional witnesses".   **6-151**

Experience has shown that elaborate court files are not normally required or advantageous. Where the anti-social behaviour has been persistent, agencies should focus on a few well-documented cases. A large volume of evidence and/or a large number of witnesses creates its own problems. There is more material for the defence to contest and timetabling issues may increase delays in the process. Agencies applying for orders should strike a balance and focus on what is most relevant and necessary to provide sufficient evidence for the court to arrive at a clear understanding of the matter. The evidence may consist of: breach of an acceptable behaviour contract; witness statements of officers who attended incidents; witness statements of people affected by the behaviour; evidence of complaints recorded by police, housing providers or other agencies; statements from professional witnesses, for example council officials, health visitors or truancy officers; video or CCTV evidence; supporting statements or reports from other agencies, for example probation reports; previous successful civil proceedings which are relevant, such as an eviction order for similar behaviour; previous relevant convictions; copies of custody records of previous arrests relevant to the application; and information from witness diaries.   **6-152**

Considerations Pertaining to the Relevant Person—Children, Mental Illness and Disability

The Guidance states that local authorities have a duty under the NHS and Community Care Service Act 1990 to assess any person who may be in need of community care services.[30] It is advised that if there is any evidence to suggest that the person against whom the order is being sought may be suffering from drug, alcohol or mental ill health problems, social services and other agencies should provide support which, according to ASBO Guidance,   **6-153**

---

[29] 2002, pp.27–28.
[30] NHS and Community Care Services Act 1990, s.47.

may run parallel with the collection of evidence and the application for the order.[31] Councils with social services responsibilities have a duty, arising from s.17 of the Children Act 1989, to safeguard and promote the welfare of children within their areas who may be in need. The assessment of the needs of such children is expected to be carried out in accordance with the Framework for the Assessment of Children in Need and Their Families. The guidance sets out the content and timescales of the initial assessment (seven working days) and the core assessment (35 working days). A core assessment is required when an initial assessment has determined that the child is in need. The assessment will cover the child's needs, the capacities of his/her parents and wider family, and environmental factors. This enables councils to determine whether the child is a "child in need" and what services may be necessary in order to address the assessed needs. The assessment of the child's needs should run in parallel with evidence gathering and the application process. Statutory agencies, such as social services, the local education authority or the health authority, have a statutory obligation to provide services to persons under 18. They should do so irrespective of whether an ASBO application is to be made and the timing of that application. The ASBO application does not prevent such support and can proceed in parallel, or indeed prior to, that support. Local authorities have a duty under the NHS and Community Care Act 1990 to assess any person who may be in need of community care services. If there is any evidence to suggest that the person against whom the order is being sought may be suffering from drug, alcohol, or mental health problems, the necessary support should be provided by social services or other support agencies. Such support should run parallel with the collection of evidence and application for an order, where an application for an order is deemed necessary.

6-154   An ASBO can be imposed on a child. Between June 2000 and March 2004, 1,755 ASBOs were issued against children.[32] Around 48 per cent to 65 per cent of ASBOs are issued to young people.[33] Research undertaken by the Children Society shows that children and young people have no real idea about what constitutes anti-social behaviour.[34] Twenty per cent of YOTs say they are only occasionally or never involved when an ASBO is made on a young person.[35] Thirty-six per cent of ASBOs involving young people were breached between June 2000 and December 2002; of those, 41 per cent ended in custody.[36] However, compare this to the overall percentage of young people who get into trouble with the law and receive a custodial sentence: 3.8 per cent The Youth Justice Board argues that the majority of breaches are for being in the wrong place at the wrong time or with the wrong person, rather than behaving in an anti-social manner.

6-155   In *A*,[37] the best interests of the child are a primary consideration but not the primary consideration. The interests of the public are themselves the primary consideration. Even so, the Administrative Court accepted that there will be cases where it is inappropriate to make any ASBO in respect of a child by reason of his age. In *M*,[38] in the course of a judicial review application by a child for whom the local authority had shared parental responsibility resulting from a

---

[31] ASBO Guidance at p.24.
[32] Youth Justice Board written evidence to the Home Affairs Select Committee on Anti-Social Behaviour.
[33] Home Office Statistic 2003 at http:/home-office.gov.uk/crimpol/antisocialbehaviour/orders/index.html
[34] Roche, *Children in Neighbourhoods in London.*
[35] Thomas, Vuong, Renshaw "ASBOs and Young People", (2004) Association of YOT Managers.
[36] Youth Justice Board written evidence to the Home Affairs Select Committee on Anti-Social Behaviour.
[37] *R. (on the application of A (A Child)) v Leeds Magistrates' Court* [2004] EWHC 554 (Admin).
[38] *R. (on the application of M (A Child)) v Sheffield Magistrates' Court* [2004] WL 1808762.

care order, an issue arose as to whether the same authority could seek an ASBO against the child. The Administrative Court held that the authority's ability to apply for an ASBO was supported by s.22(6) of Children Act 1989, which allowed the authority to fulfil its duty toward the public, notwithstanding its pre existing duty toward the child in its care. However, before an ASBO could be obtained, local authorities in the same situation as in the instant case had to comply with s.22(4) of the 1989 Act, before the housing department, as lead department in obtaining the ASBO, could act. Therefore officers responsible for the child had to discharge their care duties by making a full report to the authority. This had to be considered by the lead department's ASBO panel before an application under s.1 of the 1998 Act was made. Further, the child's social worker should not be involved in the ASBO application procedure, as this placed the independence of social services in jeopardy. An ASBO should not be granted without social services being given the opportunity to be heard in court. If social services wanted to support an ASBO application, the solicitor responsible for the application was precluded from attending meetings with the child's solicitor and social workers, and once it was decided to apply for an ASBO, there should be no contact between the ASBO application and social services sections without consent first being obtained from the solicitor concerned. Interim orders were not to be granted without notice or in the absence of social services, and negative prohibitions should not be drafted in such a way that they amounted to mandatory requirements.

Practice from one authority to another regarding ASBOs and children varies. The Home Affairs Committee on anti-social behaviour heard about a very gradual process in the Bridgend area: there is a letter pointing out the behaviour; a visit plus a letter from either a police officer or an ASBO support worker on the YOT. So far the local authority has reached about 30 acceptable behaviour contracts and only two ASBOs. The officer commented: ". . . although ASBOs are welcomed as a tool, they are an admission of failure in the fact that everything else has failed to address those things."[39] Similarly, in Salford: **6-156**

"Our threshold test is: is there anti-social behaviour, is it continuing, what have we done, is there anything else we can do? If the answer is yes to the first two, everything in the third, and nothing in the fourth, then we go for an ASBO. It is at that stage where you say we have tried everything, now we have to protect the community."

Salford obtained only three ASBOs in the previous year and, of the 600 young people identified as being involved in anti-social behaviour, ASBOs had been used in only 8 per cent.[40] In Manchester, on the other hand, there is simply a formal warning from the Council which, if ignored or not complied with, leads immediately to the setting down of an application.

Recommendations of the Standing Committee for Youth Justice concerning children and ASBOS include[41]:   **6-157**

(1) the presumption of privacy in cases involving children;

(2) a legal requirement that any application for an order against a child should be proceeded by a Children's Service assessment to ascertain the likely impact of the order on the child and his family and to establish what alternatives might be deployed;

[39] Home Affairs Anti-Social Behaviour Committee, 2004–05, at para.105.
[40] *ibid.*, para.106
[41] Standing Committee for Youth Justice *Youth Justice: Steps in the Right Direction: A Position Paper by the Standing Committee for Youth Justice* (2005). See also Lovell, "Children and the Use of Anti-Social Behaviour Orders" (2005) Childright 217, 14–16.

(3) courts should be required to consider the child protection implications of any proposed ASBO and reject the application where the order might compromise safe-guarding arrangements;

(4) the current minimum period of two years should not apply to children;

(5) custody should be a remedy available for breaches by an ASBO by a young person.

ASBOs, Mental Health and Disability

6-158   As was noted in Chapter One, according to one survey, up to 30 per cent of the victims and perpetrators of anti-social behaviour suffer from some kind of mental illness and so a substantial minority of persons guilty of anti-social conduct are likely to come within the mental health system. People suffering from mental illness are also vulnerable to being victims. Offenders with mental health problems create a difficult problem for the government's anti-social behaviour programme. There are in fact few mentions made of it in crime and disorder policies. The Crime Reduction Toolkit issued by the Home Office with respect to persistent young offenders states:

> "In order to both prevent and tackle persistent young offending, Crime & Disorder Reduction Partnerships will need to actively assist in the development of a programme to improve the provision of high quality care and treatment of young people by building up locally-based child and adolescent mental health services."

See also the guidance in *Together—Tackling Anti-Social Behaviour*. It provides that local authorities have a duty under the NHS and Community Care Act 1990 to assess any person who may be in need of community care services. If there is evidence to suggest that a perpetrator of anti-social behaviour is suffering from a disability, learning disability, mental health problems or is vulnerable in any other way, then a practitioner with specialist knowledge should be involved in an assessment process to determine the cause of the behaviour and how it can be addressed. In the specific case of an application for an ASBO, government policy is that where an individual has a disability, a practitioner with specialist knowledge should be involved in the assessment process to help establish whether the behaviour is a result of disability and how it can be addressed, what intervention is appropriate and, if so, what form it should take. The assessment should take account of any known disability as well as uncovering undiagnosed problems. It is accepted that there will be occasions where a disabled persons' behaviour is unacceptable and should be addressed through an intervention which may involve specialist support. In such cases a specialist should be involved in the design of any intervention so it can be properly tailored to the individual needs of the individual and their carers.

6-159   The courts and practitioners are familiar with the Disability Discrimination Act 1995 which provides a general safeguard when taking court action against an individual that has a disability. There should also be a case conference, before the making of an ASBO, where agencies who are able to contribute to the case and have information about the individual in question are present, along with the person who has lead responsibility for the case. The guide expressly states that local authorities have a duty to assess any person who may be in need of community care at the start of preparing an application for an ASBO:

> "Local authorities have a duty under the NHS and Community Care Act 1990 to assess any person who may be in need of community care services. If there is any evidence to suggest that the person against whom the order

is being sought may be suffering from drug, alcohol, or mental health problems, the necessary support should be provided by social services or other support agencies. Such support should run parallel with the collection of evidence and application for an order, where an application for an order is deemed necessary."

Even so, according to the British Institute for Brain Injured Children, more than 15 examples children with Asperger's, Tourette's Syndrome and Attention Deficit Hyperactivity Disorder (ADHD) were given ASBOs. In one case a 12-year-old autistic boy was punished for staring over his neighbour's fence; another boy with Tourette's Syndrome was given his order for constantly swearing. In another case, a child who had ADHD and speech and language problems, was 12 when he was charged with minor criminal offences, including theft. He was given an eight month custodial sentence and served four months. He was then given an ASBO and, over the last two years, has been back in court four times for breaching it by breaking the curfew conditions, even though he could not tell the time. He had learning problems and the developmental age of a child half his 12 years, but it had made no difference. His mother noted that local papers even applied twice to the courts to get restrictions lifted so he could be publicly "named and shamed". The Magistrates Courts Association said they were aware of the charity's concerns and had met them and the probation union NAPO. The Home Office said their guidelines had been designed to protect vulnerable children. A spokesman reportedly said:

> "If there is evidence to suggest that a perpetrator of anti-social behaviour is suffering from a disability, learning disability, mental health problems or is vulnerable in any other way, then a practitioner with specialist knowledge should be involved in an assessment process to determine the cause of the behaviour and how it can be addressed. . . This will enable the local authority to ensure that appropriate services are provided for the young person concerned and for the court to have the necessary information about him or her."

6-160 According to a BIBIC survey of members of YOTs in April 2004 to April 2005, 35 per cent of those under 17 with ASBOs involved children who had a diagnosed mental health disorder or an accepted learning difficulty; 3 per cent had autism/Asperger's syndrome, 42 per cent attention hyperactivity disorder; 1 per cent global developmental delay and the same percentage had dyspraxia and dyslexia; and 46 per cent had other conditions such as Tourettes syndrome, conduct disorders, emotional behavioural difficulties through to depression. Of these cases, 81 per cent had previously agreed an Acceptable Behaviour Contract and 74 per cent failed to maintain the conditions of the ABC.[42]

6-161 CPS policy about prosecutions of mentally disordered youth offenders provides useful guidance which might be relevant to the consideration of imposing an ASBO on a mentally ill young offender or for prosecuting him for breach of an ASBO. Mental Health Act classifications of mental health can be unhelpful in relation to youth offenders; they fail to allow for behaviour, which falls short of a disposable condition, but which is nevertheless "disturbed" in the ordinary sense of the word, e.g. personality disorders. It follows that when considering a prosecution, reference to "mental disorder" should not be restricted to the statutory definition as this could restrict decision-making. Mentally disordered offenders will often commit offences that are more of a public nuisance than a danger to the public. However, in serious

42-43 *www.bibic.org.uk/newsite/general/asb_survey_results.htm*

cases where the offender is a danger to the public, the public interest is likely to require a prosecution. In determining where the public interest lies the prosecutor should look particularly to: the seriousness of the offence; the circumstances of any previous offending; the nature of the youth offender's mental condition; the likelihood of repetition; and the availability of suitable alternatives to prosecution. Reprimand and final warnings can be problematic. Both require sufficient evidence and full recognition of guilt by the offender. It may be that in a proportion of cases, which might otherwise have attracted such a disposal, that this is not an advisable option, either because of doubts about the truth of any admissions made (in cases where there is little or no supporting evidence), or because of the defendants level of understanding. In such cases taking no further action will usually be the only appropriate way of dealing with the matter short of prosecution. Prosecutors should try and ensure the police are alert to these difficulties and guard against the inappropriate use of the reprimand and final warning system. The file should include the opinions of the relevant welfare agencies, particularly about the offender's stage of development or understanding of the offence and the perceived likelihood of repetition, the likely effect of proceedings on his or her mental state and the available welfare options. It is particularly important in remand cases that the prosecution is furnished with as much information as possible before making representations to the court. If necessary, an application should be made for the case to be put back until information is available. A plea should not be accepted until the prosecutor has all the available information and has reviewed the file.

6-162   This raises the additional problem for an authority of discrimination under the Disability Discrimination Act 1995, particularly now that the scope of the 1995 Act has been considerably widened. Section 21A provides that it is unlawful for a public authority[43] to discriminate against a disabled person in carrying out its functions. Subsection (2) defines "public authority" as including "any person certain of whose functions are functions of a public nature"; under subs.(4), in relation to a particular act, a person is not a public authority by virtue only of subs.(2) if the nature of the act is private. It does not apply to a decision not to institute criminal proceedings and where such a decision is made, an act done for the purpose of enabling the decision to be made; or a decision not to continue criminal proceedings, or where such a decision is made an act done for the purpose of enabling the decision to be made; or an act done for the purpose of securing that the proceedings are not continued. Under s.21D, a public authority discriminates against a disabled person in the same terms as set out in s.3A of the 1995 Act except, in addition, a public authority also discriminates against a disabled person if:

(a) it fails to comply with a duty imposed on it by s.21E in circumstances in which the effect of that failure is to make it—

   (i) impossible or unreasonably difficult for the disabled person to receive any benefit that is or may be conferred, or
   (ii) unreasonably adverse for the disabled person to experience being subjected to any detriment to which a person is or may be subjected,

by the carrying-out of a function by the authority; and

(b) it cannot show that its failure to comply with that duty is justified. .

However, under subs.(3), treatment, or a failure to comply with a duty, is justified under this subsection if in the opinion of the public authority, one or more of the conditions specified in subs.(4) are satisfied; and it is reasonable, in all the circumstances of the case, for it to hold that opinion. The conditions are:

(a) that the treatment, or non-compliance with the duty, is necessary in order not to endanger the health or safety of any person (which may include that of the disabled person);

(b) that the disabled person is incapable of entering into an enforceable agreement, or of giving an informed consent, and for that reason the treatment, or non-compliance with the duty, is reasonable in the particular case;

(c) that, in the case of treatment mentioned in subs.(1), treating the disabled person equally favourably would in the particular case involve substantial extra costs and, having regard to resources, the extra costs in that particular case would be too great;

(d) that the treatment, or non-compliance with the duty, is necessary for the protection of rights and freedoms of other persons.

It is also justified, under subs.(5), if treatment, or a failure to comply with a duty, is justified under this subsection if the acts of the public authority which give rise to the treatment or failure are a proportionate means of achieving a legitimate aim.

The duties referred to above are set out in s.21E: **6-163**

"(1) Subsection (2) applies where a public authority has a practice, policy or procedure which makes it—

(a) impossible or unreasonably difficult for disabled persons to receive any benefit that is or may be conferred, or

(b) unreasonably adverse for disabled persons to experience being subjected to any detriment to which a person is or may be subjected, by the carrying-out of a function by the authority."

The authority is also under a duty to take such steps as it is reasonable, in all the circumstances of the case, for the authority to have to take in order to change that practice, policy or procedure so that it no longer has that effect. Further, there is a new section, s.49A, which provides for more duties of public authorities. Every public authority[44] shall, in carrying out its functions, have due regard to:

(a) the need to eliminate discrimination that is unlawful under this Act;

(b) the need to eliminate harassment of disabled persons that is related to their disabilities;

(c) the need to promote equality of opportunity between disabled persons and other persons;

(d) the need to take steps to take account of disabled persons' disabilities, even where that involves treating disabled persons more favourably than other persons;

(e) the need to promote positive attitudes towards disabled persons; and

(f) the need to encourage participation by disabled persons in public life.

This subsection is without prejudice to any obligation of a public authority to comply with any other provision of the 1995 Act.

---

[44] Public authority in this part has the same meaning, in England, as under s.21A: s.49C.

Crime and Disorder Act 1998

Anti-social behaviour orders

App-001   **1.**—(1) An application for an order under this section may be made by a relevant authority if it appears to the authority that the following conditions are fulfilled with respect to any person aged 10 or over, namely—

(a)   that the person has acted, since the commencement date, in an anti-social manner, that is to say, in a manner that caused or was likely to cause harassment, alarm or distress to one or more persons not of the same household as himself; and

[(b)   that such an order is necessary to protect relevant persons from further anti-social acts by him.]¹

[...]²

[(1A)   In this section and [sections 1B, 1CA and 1E]³ "relevant authority" means—

(a)   the council for a local government area;

[(aa)   in relation to England, a county council;]⁴

(b)   the chief officer of police of any police force maintained for a police area;

(c)   the chief constable of the British Transport Police Force;

(d)   any person registered under section 1 of the Housing Act 1996 (c. 52) as a social landlord who provides or manages any houses or hostel in a local government area; or

[(e)   a housing action trust established by order in pursuance of section 62 of the Housing Act 1988.]⁵

(1B)   In this section "relevant persons" means—

(a)   in relation to a relevant authority falling within paragraph (a) of subsection (1A), persons within the local government area of that council;

[(aa)   in relation to a relevant authority falling within paragraph (aa) of subsection (1A), persons within the county of the county council;]⁵

(b)   in relation to a relevant authority falling within paragraph (b) of that subsection, persons within the police area;

(c)   in relation to a relevant authority falling within paragraph (c) of that subsection—

[(i)   persons who are within or likely to be within a place specified in section 31(1)(a) to (f) of the Railways and Transport Safety Act 2003 in a local government area; or]⁶

[(ii)   persons who are within or likely to be within such a place;]⁶

(d)   in relation to a relevant authority falling within paragraph (d) [or (e)]⁵ of that subsection—

(i)   persons who are residing in or who are otherwise on or likely to be on premises provided or managed by that authority; or

(ii)   persons who are in the vicinity of or likely to be in the vicinity of such premises.]⁷

[...]⁸

(3) Such an application shall be made by complaint to [a magistrates' court][9].

(4) If, on such an application, it is proved that the conditions mentioned in subsection (1) above are fulfilled, the magistrates' court may make an order under this section (an "anti-social behaviour order") which prohibits the defendant from doing anything described in the order.

(5) For the purpose of determining whether the condition mentioned in subsection (1)(a) above is fulfilled, the court shall disregard any act of the defendant which he shows was reasonable in the circumstances.

[(6) The prohibitions that may be imposed by an anti-social behaviour order are those necessary for the purpose of protecting persons (whether relevant persons or persons elsewhere in England and Wales) from further anti-social acts by the defendant.][10]

(7) An anti-social behaviour order shall have effect for a period (not less than two years) specified in the order or until further order.

(8) Subject to subsection (9) below, the applicant or the defendant may apply by complaint to the court which made an anti-social behaviour order for it to be varied or discharged by a further order.

(9) Except with the consent of both parties, no anti-social behaviour order shall be discharged before the end of the period of two years beginning with the date of service of the order.

(10) If without reasonable excuse a person does anything which he is prohibited from doing by an anti-social behaviour order, [is guilty of an offence and][11] liable—

(a) on summary conviction, to imprisonment for a term not exceeding six months or to a fine not exceeding the statutory maximum, or to both; or
(b) on conviction on indictment, to imprisonment for a term not exceeding five years or to a fine, or to both.

[(10A) The following may bring proceedings for an offence under subsection (10)—

(a) a council which is a relevant authority;
(b) the council for the local government area in which a person in respect of whom an anti-social behaviour order has been made resides or appears to reside.][12]

[(10B) If proceedings for an offence under subsection (10) are brought in a youth court section 47(2) of the Children and Young Persons Act 1933 (c. 12) has effect as if the persons entitled to be present at a sitting for the purposes of those proceedings include one person authorised to be present by a relevant authority.][13]

[(10C) In proceedings for an offence under subsection (10), a copy of the original anti-social behaviour order, certified as such by the proper officer of the court which made it, is admissible as evidence of its having been made and of its contents to the same extent that oral evidence of those things is admissible in those proceedings.][14]

[(10D) In relation to proceedings brought against a child or a young person for an offence under subsection (10)—

(a) section 49 of the Children and Young Persons Act 1933 (restrictions on reports of proceedings in which children and young persons are concerned) does not apply in respect of the child or young person against whom the proceedings are brought;
(b) section 45 of the Youth Justice and Criminal Evidence Act 1999 (power to restrict reporting of criminal proceedings involving persons under 18) does so apply.

(10E) If, in relation to any such proceedings, the court does exercise its power to give a direction under section 45 of the Youth Justice and Criminal Evidence Act 1999, it shall give its reasons for doing so.][15]

(11) Where a person is convicted of an offence under subsection (10) above, it shall not be open to the court by or before which he is so convicted to make an order under subsection (1)(b) (conditional discharge) of [section 12 of the Powers of Criminal Courts (Sentencing) Act 2000][16] in respect of the offence.

(12) In this section—

["child" and "young person" shall have the same meaning as in the Children and Young Persons Act 1933;][15]

[...][17]

"the commencement date" means the date of the commencement of this section;
"local government area" means—
    (a) in relation to England, a district or London borough, the City of London, the Isle of Wight and the Isles of Scilly;
    (b) in relation to Wales, a county or county borough.

[...][18]

1 Substituted by Police Reform Act 2002, Pt 4, s.61(7).
2 Repealed by Police Reform Act 2002, Sch.8.
3 Inserted by Serious Organised Crime and Police Act 2005, Pt 4, s.140(2).
4 Inserted by Anti-Social Behaviour Act 2003, Pt 9, s.85(2)(a).
5 Inserted by Anti-Social Behaviour Act 2003, Pt 9, s.85(3)(a)–(c).
6 Substituted by British Transport Police (Transitional and Consequential Provisions) Order 2004 (SI 2004/1573), art.12(5)(a), (b).

7 Inserted by Police Reform Act 2002, Pt 4, s.61(4).
8 Repealed by Police Reform Act 2002, Sch.8.
9 Substituted by Courts Act 2003 (Consequential Provisions) Order 2005 (SI 2005/886), Sch.1, para.55.
10 Substituted by Police Reform Act 2002, Pt 4, s.61(7).
11 Substituted by Police Reform Act 2002, Pt 4, s.61(2).
12 Inserted by Anti-Social Behaviour Act 2003, Pt 9, s.85(4).
13 Inserted by Anti-Social Behaviour Act 2003, Pt 9, s.85(4).
14 Inserted by Serious Organised Crime and Police Act 2005, Pt 4, s.139(2).
15 Inserted by Serious Organised Crime and Police Act 2005, Pt 4, s.141(2).
16 Substituted by Powers of Criminal Courts (Sentencing) Act 2000, Sch.9, para.192.
17 Repealed by Railways and Transport Safety Act 2003, Sch.5, para.4(2)(j).
18 Repealed by British Transport Police (Transitional and Consequential Provisions) Order 2004 (SI 2004/1573), art.12(5).

Sex offender orders

App-002   **2.**—[...]¹

1 Repealed Sexual Offences Act 2003, Sch.7.

Sex offender orders: supplemental

App-003   **3.**—[...]¹

1 Repealed by Sexual Offences Act 2003, Sch.7.

Appeals against orders

App-004   **4.**—(1) An appeal shall lie to the Crown Court against the making by a magistrates' court of an anti-social behaviour order[, an individual support order]¹, [an order under section 1D above]²[...]³.
(2) On such an appeal the Crown Court—

> (a) may make such orders as may be necessary to give effect to its determination of the appeal; and
>
> (b) may also make such incidental or consequential orders as appear to it to be just.

(3) Any order of the Crown Court made on an appeal under this section (other than one directing that an application be re-heard by a magistrates' court) shall, for the purposes of [section 1(8), 1AB(6)]² [...]³, be treated as if it were an order of the magistrates' court from which the appeal was brought and not an order of the Crown Court.

Amendments
1 Inserted by Criminal Justice Act 2003, Pt 13, s.323(2)(a), (b).
2 Inserted by Police Reform Act 2002, Pt 4, s.65(2).
3 Repealed by Sexual Offences Act 2003, Sch.7.

Crime and disorder strategies

Authorities responsible for strategies

App-005   **5.**—(1) Subject to the provisions of this section, the functions conferred by section 6 below shall be exercisable in relation to each local government area by the responsible authorities, that is to say—

> (a) the council for the area and, where the area is a district and the council is not a unitary authority, the council for the county which includes the district;
>
> (b) every chief officer of police any part of whose police area lies within the area;
>
> (c) every police authority any part of whose police area so lies;
>
> (d) every [fire and rescue authority]¹ any part of whose area so lies;
>
> (e) if the local government area is in England, every Primary Care Trust the whole or any part of whose area so lies; and
>
> (f) if the local government area is in Wales, every health authority the whole or any part of whose area so lies.

(1A) The Secretary of State may by order provide in relation to any two or more local government areas in England—

(a) that the functions conferred by sections 6 to 7 below are to be carried out in relation to those areas taken together as if they constituted only one area; and
(b) that the persons who for the purposes of this Chapter are to be taken to be responsible authorities in relation to the combined area are the persons who comprise every person who (apart from the order) would be a responsible authority in relation to any one or more of the areas included in the combined area.

(1B) The Secretary of State shall not make an order under subsection (1A) above unless—

(a) an application for the order has been made jointly by all the persons who would be the responsible authorities in relation to the combined area or the Secretary of State has first consulted those persons; and
(b) he considers it would be in the interests of reducing crime and disorder, or of combatting the misuse of drugs, to make the order.

(2) In exercising those functions, the responsible authorities shall act in co-operation with the following persons and bodies, namely—

(b) every [local probation board]¹ any part of whose area lies within the area;
(c) every person or body of a description which is for the time being prescribed by order of the Secretary of State under this subsection; and
(d) where they are acting in relation to an area in Wales, every person or body which is of a description which is for the time being prescribed by an order under this subsection of the National Assembly for Wales;

and it shall be the duty of those persons and bodies to co-operate in the exercise by the responsible authorities of those functions.
(3) The responsible authorities shall also invite the participation in their exercise of those functions of at least one person or body of each description which is for the time being prescribed by order of the Secretary of State under this subsection and, in the case of the responsible authorities for an area in Wales, of any person or body of a description for the time being prescribed by an order under this subsection of the National Assembly for Wales.
(4) In this section and sections 6 and 7 below "local government area" means—

(a) in relation to England, each district or London borough, the City of London, the Isle of Wight and the Isles of Scilly;
(b) in relation to Wales, each county or county borough.

(5) In this section—

["fire and rescue authority" means—
(a) a fire and rescue authority constituted by a scheme under section 2 of the Fire and Rescue Services Act 2004 or a scheme to which section 4 of that Act applies;
(b) a metropolitan county fire and civil defence authority; or
(c) the London Fire and Emergency Planning Authority;]¹

"police authority" means—
(a) any police authority established under section 3 of the Police Act 1996 (c. 16); or
(b) the Metropolitan Police Authority.

1 Substituted by Criminal Justice and Court Services Act 2000, Sch.7, Pt II, para.151.

Formulation and implementation of strategies

6.—(1) The responsible authorities for a local government area shall, in accordance with the provisions of section 5 above and this section, formulate and implement, for each relevant period,   **App-006**

(a) in the case of an area in England—
(i) a strategy for the reduction of crime and disorder in the area; and
(ii) a strategy for combatting the misuse of drugs in the area;
and
(b) in the case of an area in Wales—
(i) a strategy for the reduction of crime and disorder in the area; and
(ii) a strategy for combatting substance misuse in the area.

(1A) In determining what matters to include or not to include in their strategy for combatting substance misuse, the responsible authorities for an area in Wales shall have regard to any guidance issued for the purposes of this section by the National Assembly for Wales.
(2) Before formulating a strategy, the responsible authorities shall—

(a) carry out, taking due account of the knowledge and experience of persons in the area, a review—
(i) in the case of an area in England, of the levels and patterns of crime and disorder in the area and of the level and patterns of the misuse of drugs in the area; and

(ii) in the case of an area in Wales, of the levels and patterns of crime and disorder in the area and of the level and patterns of substance misuse in the area;
(b) prepare an analysis of the results of that review;
(c) publish in the area a report of that analysis; and
(d) obtain the views on that report of persons or bodies in the area (including those of a description prescribed by order under section 5(3) above), whether by holding public meetings or otherwise.

(3) In formulating a strategy, the responsible authorities shall have regard to the analysis prepared under subsection (2)(b) above and the views obtained under subsection (2)(d) above.
(4) A strategy shall include—

(a) objectives to be pursued by the responsible authorities, by co-operating persons or bodies or, under agreements with the responsible authorities, by other persons or bodies; and
(b) long-term and short-term performance targets for measuring the extent to which such objectives are achieved.

(5) After formulating a strategy, the responsible authorities shall publish in the area a document which includes details of—

(a) co-operating persons and bodies;
(b) the review carried out under subsection (2)(a) above;
(c) the report published under subsection (2)(c) above; and
(d) the strategy, including in particular—
  (i) the objectives mentioned in subsection (4)(a) above and, in each case, the authorities, persons or bodies by whom they are to be pursued; and
  (ii) the performance targets mentioned in subsection (4)(b) above.

(6) While implementing a strategy, the responsible authorities shall keep it under review with a view to monitoring its effectiveness and making any changes to it that appear necessary or expedient.
[(6A) Within one month of the end of each reporting period, the responsible authorities shall submit a report on the implementation of their strategies during that period—

(a) in the case of a report relating to the strategies for an area in England, to the Secretary of State; and
(b) in the case of a report relating to the strategies for an area in Wales, to the Secretary of State and to the National Assembly for Wales.]¹

(7) In this section—

"co-operating persons or bodies" means persons or bodies co-operating in the exercise of the responsible authorities" functions under this section;
["relevant period" means—
  (a) the period of three years beginning with such day as the Secretary of State may by order appoint; and
  (b) each subsequent period of three years.
"reporting period" means every period of one year which falls within a relevant period and which begins—
  (a) in the case of the first reporting period in the relevant period, with the day on which the relevant period begins; and
  (b) in any other case, with the day after the day on which the previous reporting period ends;
"substance misuse" includes the misuse of drugs or alcohol.]²

1 Inserted by Police Reform Act 2002, Pt 6, s.97(10).
2 Inserted by Police Reform Act 2002, Pt 6, s.97(11)

Supplemental

App-007

7.—(1) The responsible authorities for a local government area shall, whenever so required by the Secretary of State, submit to the Secretary of State a report on such matters connected with the exercise of their functions under section 6 above as may be specified in the requirement.
(2) A requirement under subsection (1) above may specify the form in which a report is to be given.
(3) The Secretary of State may arrange, or require the responsible authorities to arrange, for a report under subsection (1) above to be published in such manner as appears to him to be appropriate.

Duty to consider crime and disorder implications

17.—(1) Without prejudice to any other obligation imposed on it, it shall be the duty of each authority to which this section applies to exercise its various functions with due regard to the likely **App-008** effect of the exercise of those functions on, and the need to do all that it reasonably can to prevent, crime and disorder in its area.

(2) This section applies to a local authority, a joint authority, [the London Fire and Emergency Planning Authority,][a fire and rescue authority constituted by a scheme under section 2 of the Fire and Rescue Services Act 2004 or a scheme to which section 4 of that Act applies][2], a police authority, a National Park authority and the Broads Authority.

(3) In this section—

"local authority" means a local authority within the meaning given by section 270(1) of the Local Government Act 1972 or the Common Council of the City of London;

"joint authority" has the same meaning as in the Local Government Act 1985;

"National Park authority" means an authority established under section 63 of the Environment Act 1995.

1 Inserted by Greater London Authority Act 1999, Sch.29, Pt I, para.63.
2 Substituted by Fire and Rescue Services Act 2004, Sch.1, para.89(3).

Interpretation etc. of Chapter I

18.—(1) In this Chapter—   **App-009**

"anti-social behaviour order" has the meaning given by section 1(4) above;

"chief officer of police" has the meaning given by section 101(1) of the Police Act 1996;

"child safety order" has the meaning given by section 11(1) above;

"curfew notice" has the meaning given by section 14(6) above;

["individual support order" has the meaning given by section 1AA(2) above;][1]

"local child curfew scheme" has the meaning given by section 14(1) above;

["parental compensation order" has the meaning given by section 13A(1) above;][2]

"parenting order" has the meaning given by section 8(4) above;

"police area" has the meaning given by section 1(2) of the Police Act 1996;

"police authority" has the meaning given by section 101(1) of that Act;

"responsible officer" —

[(za) in relation to an individual support order, has the meaning given by section 1AA(10) above;][1]

(a) in relation to a parenting order, has the meaning given by section 8(8) above;

(b) in relation to a child safety order, has the meaning given by section 11(8) above;

["serious harm" shall be construed in accordance with section 224 of the Criminal Justice Act 2003;][3]

"sex offender order" has the meaning given by section 2(3) above.

[...][4]

(3) Where directions under a parenting order are to be given by [an officer of a local probation board][5], [the officer of a local probation board][5] shall be an officer appointed for or assigned to the [local justice area][6] within which it appears to the court that the child or, as the case may be, the parent resides or will reside.

(4) Where the supervision under a child safety order is to be provided, or directions under [an individual support order][7] or a parenting order are to be given, by—

(a) a social worker of a local authority [...][8]; or

(b) a member of a youth offending team,

the social worker or member shall be a social worker of, or a member of a youth offending team established by, the local authority within whose area it appears to the court that [the child, defendant or parent, as the case may be,][7] resides or will reside.

(5) For the purposes of this Chapter the Inner Temple and the Middle Temple form part of the City of London [...][8].

1 Inserted by Criminal Justice Act 2003, Pt 13, s.323(3)(a), (b).
2 Inserted by Serious Organised Crime and Police Act 2005, Sch.10, Pt 1, para.4.
3 Inserted by Criminal Justice Act 2003, Sch.32, Pt 1, para.88(a).
4 Repealed by Criminal Justice Act 2003, Sch.37, Pt 7.
5 Substituted by Criminal Justice Act 2003, Sch.7., Pt 1, para.4(1).
6 Substituted by Courts Act 2003 (Consequential Provisions) Order 2005 (SI 2005/886), Sch.1, para.8.
7 Inserted by Criminal Justice Act 2003, Pt 13, s.323(4)(a), (b).
8 Repealed by Children Act 2004, Sch.5, Pt 4.

Disclosure of information

115.—(1) Any person who, apart from this subsection, would not have power to disclose information—

(a) to a relevant authority; or
(b) to a person acting on behalf of such an authority,

shall have power to do so in any case where the disclosure is necessary or expedient for the purposes of any provision of this Act.

(2) In subsection (1) above "relevant authority" means—

(a) the chief officer of police for a police area in England and Wales;
(b) the chief constable of a police force maintained under the Police (Scotland) Act 1967;
(c) a police authority within the meaning given by section 101(1) of the Police Act 1996;
(d) a local authority, that is to say—
    (i) in relation to England, a county council, a district council, a London borough council[, a parish council]¹ or the Common Council of the City of London;
    (ii) in relation to Wales, a county council[, a county borough council or a community council;]²
    (iii) in relation to Scotland, a council constituted under section 2 of the Local Government etc. (Scotland) Act 1994;
[(da) a person registered under section 1 of the Housing Act 1996 as a social landlord;]³
(e) [a local probation board]⁴ in England and Wales;
[(ea) a Strategic Health Authority;]5
(f) a health authority[;
(g) a Primary Care Trust.]⁶

1 Inserted by Police Reform Act 2002, Pt 6, s.97(14)(a).
2 Substituted by Police Reform Act 2002, Pt 6, s.97(14)(b).
3 Inserted by Housing Act 2004, Pt 6, s.219.
4 Substituted by Criminal Justice and Court Services Act 2000, Sch.7, Pt II, para.151.
5 Inserted by National Health Service Reform and Health Care Professions Act 2002 (Supplementary, Consequential etc. Provisions) Regulations (SI 2002/2469), Sch.1, Pt 1, para.25(6).
6 Inserted by Health Act 1999 (Supplementary, Consequential etc. Provisions) Order (SI 2000/90), Sch.1, para.35(7).

APPENDIX TWO

Local Government Act 2000

PROMOTION OF ECONOMIC, SOCIAL OR ENVIRONMENTAL WELL-BEING ETC

Promotion of well-being

Promotion of well-being

2.—(1) Every local authority are to have power to do anything which they consider is likely to   **App-011**
achieve any one or more of the following objects—

   (a) the promotion or improvement of the economic well-being of their area,
   (b) the promotion or improvement of the social well-being of their area, and
   (c) the promotion or improvement of the environmental well-being of their area.

  (2) The power under subsection (1) may be exercised in relation to or for the benefit of—

   (a) the whole or any part of a local authority's area, or
   (b) all or any persons resident or present in a local authority's area.

  (3) In determining whether or how to exercise the power under subsection (1), a local authority must have regard to their strategy under section 4.
  (4) The power under subsection (1) includes power for a local authority to—

   (a) incur expenditure,
   (b) give financial assistance to any person,
   (c) enter into arrangements or agreements with any person,
   (d) co-operate with, or facilitate or co-ordinate the activities of, any person,
   (e) exercise on behalf of any person any functions of that person, and
   (f) provide staff, goods, services or accommodation to any person.

  (5) The power under subsection (1) includes power for a local authority to do anything in relation to, or for the benefit of, any person or area situated outside their area if they consider that it is likely to achieve any one or more of the objects in that subsection.
  (6) Nothing in subsection (4) or (5) affects the generality of the power under subsection (1).

Limits on power to promote well-being

3.—(1) The power under section 2(1) does not enable a local authority to do anything which   **App-012**
they are unable to do by virtue of any prohibition, restriction or limitation on their powers which
is contained in any enactment (whenever passed or made).
  (2) The power under section 2(1) does not enable a local authority to raise money (whether by precepts, borrowing or otherwise).
  (3) The Secretary of State may by order make provision preventing local authorities from doing, by virtue of section 2(1), anything which is specified, or is of a description specified, in the order.
  (4) Before making an order under subsection (3), the Secretary of State must consult such representatives of local government and such other persons (if any) as he considers appropriate.
  (5) Before exercising the power under section 2(1), a local authority must have regard to any guidance for the time being issued by the Secretary of State about the exercise of that power.

(6) Before issuing any guidance under subsection (5), the Secretary of State must consult such representatives of local government and such other persons (if any) as he considers appropriate.

(7) In its application to Wales, this section has effect as if for any reference to the Secretary of State there were substituted a reference to the National Assembly for Wales.

(8) In this section "enactment" includes an enactment comprised in subordinate legislation (within the meaning of the Interpretation Act 1978).

Strategies for promoting well-being

App-013   **4.**—(1) Every local authority must prepare a strategy (referred to in this section as a community strategy) for promoting or improving the economic, social and environmental well-being of their area and contributing to the achievement of sustainable development in the United Kingdom.

(2) A local authority may from time to time modify their community strategy.

(3) In preparing or modifying their community strategy, a local authority—

(a)   must consult and seek the participation of such persons as they consider appropriate, and
(b)   must have regard to any guidance for the time being issued by the Secretary of State.

(4) Before issuing any guidance under this section, the Secretary of State must consult such representatives of local government and such other persons (if any) as he considers appropriate.

(5) In its application to Wales, this section has effect as if for any reference to the Secretary of State there were substituted a reference to the National Assembly for Wales.

Power to amend or repeal enactments

App-014   **5.**—(1) If the Secretary of State thinks that an enactment (whenever passed or made) prevents or obstructs local authorities from exercising their power under section 2(1) he may by order amend, repeal, revoke or disapply that enactment.

(2) The power under subsection (1) may be exercised in relation to—

(a)   all local authorities,
(b)   particular local authorities, or
(c)   particular descriptions of local authority.

(3) The power under subsection (1) to amend or disapply an enactment includes a power to amend or disapply an enactment for a particular period.

(4) In exercising the power under subsection (1), the Secretary of State—

(a)   must not make any provision which has effect in relation to Wales unless he has consulted the National Assembly for Wales, and
(b)   must not make any provision in relation to legislation made by the National Assembly for Wales without the consent of the Assembly.

(5) The National Assembly for Wales may submit proposals to the Secretary of State that the power under subsection (1) should be exercised in relation to Wales in accordance with those proposals.

(6) In this section "enactment" includes an enactment comprised in subordinate legislation (within the meaning of the Interpretation Act 1978).

APPENDIX THREE

Local Government Act 1972

222 Power of local authorities to prosecute or defend legal proceedings

(1) Where a local authority consider it expedient for the promotion or protection of the interests of the inhabitants of their area—   **App-015**

   (a) they may prosecute or defend or appear in any legal proceedings and, in the case of civil proceedings, may institute them in their own name, and

   (b) they may, in their own name, make representations in the interests of the inhabitants at any public inquiry held by or on behalf of any Minister or public body under any enactment.

(2) In this section "local authority" includes the Common Council[and the London Fire and Emergency Planning Authority].[1]

[1] Words added by Greater London Authority Act 1999 (c.29), Sch.29 (I), para.20.

APPENDIX FOUR

Anti-Social Behaviour Act 2003

PART 9

MISCELLANEOUS POWERS

91 Proceedings under section 222 of the Local Government Act 1972: power of arrest attached to injunction

App-016

(1) This section applies to proceedings in which a local authority is a party by virtue of section 222 of the Local Government Act 1972 (c. 70) (power of local authority to bring, defend or appear in proceedings for the promotion or protection of the interests of inhabitants of their area).

(2) If the court grants an injunction which prohibits conduct which is capable of causing nuisance or annoyance to a person it may, if subsection (3) below applies, attach a power of arrest to any provision of the injunction.

(3) This subsection applies if the local authority applies to the court to attach the power of arrest and the court thinks that either—

(a) the conduct mentioned in subsection (2) consists of or includes the use or threatened use of violence, or

(b) there is a significant risk of harm to the person mentioned in that subsection.

(4) Harm includes serious ill-treatment or abuse (whether physical or not).

(5) Local authority has the same meaning as in section 222 of the Local Government Act 1972.

APPENDIX FIVE

Acceptable Behaviour Contracts

From Anti-Social Behaviour Orders: Guidance on drafting protocols: Home Office   App-017

ACCEPTABLE BEHAVIOUR CONTRACT – EXAMPLE

THIS CONTRACT is made on   [date]
BETWEEN   [Partner Agency]
AND   [name and address of young person]

AGREES the following in respect of future conduct—

1. I will not write graffiti or damage any property *[specify where]*
2. I will not climb on rooftops or enter lift shafts or other prohibited areas.
3. I will not throw anything at residents or passers-by *[specify where]*
4. I will not threaten or abuse residents or passers-by. This includes swearing.

FURTHER, [ ] enters into a commitment with *[agency]* not to act in a manner which causes or is likely to cause harassment, alarm or distress to one or more persons not in the same household.
FURTHER, if [ ] does anything which he/she has agreed not to do under this contract which *[agency]* considers to amount to anti-social behaviour, this may result in an application to the Magistrates' Court for an Anti-Social Behaviour Order to prohibit
[ ] from acting in a manner likely to cause harassment, alarm or distress to one or more persons not of the same household
FURTHER, [ ] acknowledges that where an Anti-Social Behaviour Order is made in the Court and breached he/she will be liable on conviction to terms of imprisonment not exceeding five years or to a fine or both

DECLARATION

I confirm that I understand the meaning of this contract and that the consequences of breach of the contract have been explained to me.

Signed [ ] Young Person   Date:...............................
Signed [ ] Parent/Social Worker   Date:...............................

WITNESSED

Signed [ ] Partner Agency Official   Date:...............................
Signed [ ] Police Officer   Date:...............................

Conducting an ABC Meeting—Islington Anti-Social Behaviour Team

App-018   *(From Guide to Anti-Social Behaviour Orders and Acceptable Behaviour Contracts, Home Office, November 2002, Appendix G)*

This draws on the experience of housing and police officers but can adapted for other agencies, such as youth offending teams.

Before the meeting

DO

- Consider other measures for tackling anti-social behaviour alongside this action. A notice seeking possession may still be appropriate.
- Identify individuals likely to benefit from the ABC scheme at regular meetings involving police and housing officers. Once a person is being considered, start an Incident Record Book.
- Give reasonable notice of the meeting and hand-deliver the letter where possible.
- Seek to involve both parents or guardians if there is a joint parenting role, even if they do not live at the same address.
- Where the family are known to social services, advise them of the interview, the purpose, and if appropriate ask if they would like to be present. Where the local authority is looking after a young person (i.e. 'in care'), a representative from social services must be invited to attend.
- If the young person is known to attend a local school, encourage their involvement. The young person could be on a school sponsored scheme that could assist with tackling the unacceptable behaviour.
- Try to find out if the young person is involved in activities organised by the play and youth service. They may be able to assist with diversion activities.
- Contact the youth offending team (YOT) to establish whether they know the young person and to ensure that the action proposed does not conflict with action being pursued by them.
- Contact the police to check whether there are currently any related criminal charges being considered by the Crown Prosecution Service in relation to the young person. If there are, an interview can still go ahead but without the police and without the use of an ABC. The interview would be used simply to clarify to the young person and his parents the terms and conditions of their tenancy agreement. If the CPS find insufficient evidence to make a criminal charge then the ABC interview may be considered again.
- Pre-meet with professionals, such as social services, to clarify the procedure and purpose of the meeting/ABC. Ideally this meeting should **not** take place immediately before the interview in case there are concerns that need to be resolved. Ensure that if officers from other departments are to be present at the meeting they are clear on who is taking the lead.
- Pre-meet to agree who will take the lead and clarify the latest position on reported incidents and action against the youth or the tenancy.
- Try to establish in advance which other agencies/individuals may attend, if any.
- Consider involving other siblings within the same family in the same meeting if you think they could be vulnerable to becoming involved in anti-social behaviour, even if an ABC is not thought to be appropriate at this stage.
- Be clear in your own mind what the purpose of the meeting is. Remember the aim is not simply to come away with a signed contract, but **to stop the anti-social behaviour.** The idea of the interview is to talk with the young person and his/her parents so that they both have an understanding of what we mean by anti-social behaviour and what the implications are should further incidents take place.

- Be prepared for the fact that both young people and parents may deny all involvement and that feelings could run high.
- Give consideration to a suitable venue and seating plan so that the meeting can take place in relative comfort with enough chairs and space for everyone. Avoid setting up barriers or creating an 'us-and-them' situation.
- Give consideration to the type of activities the young person has been involved in **and** those that are particularly relevant on the estate, which you may wish to include in the contract. These should not be used to prepare the contract in advance but to include in the discussion about which activities should be included in the contract.
- Nominate a suitable officer to take notes during the interview. Although you should aim to keep the number of officers to a minimum it is recommended to have a note-taker that will not be involved in the discussion. Detailed notes are or required but the main points do need to be jotted down.
- Try to ensure that the same people are involved for the duration of the contract and monitoring period. The ABC creates an opportunity to establish rapport with young people on contracts.

DON'T

- Hold the meeting at the police station (unless necessary).
- Expect to be able to follow a script and for all interviews to be the same. They are all different. Of the interviews carried out so far a significant number of parents have been extremely positive about the meetings once they overcome their initial suspicion and concern. The attitude of the young people has ranged in extremes from total silence to hostility and abuse, but the latter is not usual and in most cases it has been possible to have a discussion about anti-social behaviour and what it means.
- Underestimate the importance of the preparation in advance of the meeting. You cannot expect to be able to turn up on the day and carry out an effective interview without being clear on the background to the case. Also, if you fail to involve other relevant departments or organisations you are potentially compromising the council's position in being able to pursue further action.
- Prepare the final version of the contract in advance of the meeting. This is defeating one of the key points of the meeting, which is to encourage the young person to list the activities he/she has been involved in or could become involved in future. A draft list of activities that you may wish to include is, however, a good idea.

During the meeting

DO

- Arrive promptly to allow for a pre-meeting, and allow enough time for the meeting so you are not rushed. Some meetings have been known to last two hours, others have been more straightforward. N.B. The attention span of a young person is about twenty minutes.
- If the young person and his or her parent/guardian fail to attend write once more with a further date for a meeting. If they fail to attend the second meeting, consider moving straight to legal action, write setting out the seriousness of the issue including details of action proposed. Monitor the case as you would had a contract been signed.
- Wear name badges.
- Use simple language that is free from council/police jargon.
- Aim to get the message across that anti-social behaviour and the signing of the contract is an extremely serious issue, however at the same time you should aim to keep the meeting informal and relaxed to encourage full participation of the young person and their parents.
- Make the young person and their parents aware of the consequences of breach.
- Support each other and be mindful of the issues relevant to both the police and the housing department e.g. possible criminal or civil action.
- Talk to the young person. Find out how they spend their time, what their understanding is of anti-social behaviour and how it may impact upon residents, the council, his/her parents, him or herself.
- Listen to what is being said about home circumstances and any other pressures or difficulties the family is experiencing. This will help to put together information for dealing with the case and involving any other relevant agencies.
- Explain the purpose of the contract, how it will be monitored and the implications of any further incidents, both in terms of civil action such as possession orders and anti-social behaviour orders or criminal action such as criminal damage, **before** the contract is signed.
- Take any concerns raised by the young person and his/her parents seriously and attempt to address them.
- Produce the final typed version of the contract as quickly as possible once those present have agreed the activities to be included. Ideally arrange for someone outside the meeting to do

this for you so that you do not leave your colleague on his/her own. Remember that any delay could be a source of irritation to those present and may result in a contract not being signed.
- Remember to get everyone present to sign the contract and to provide a copy for the young person and their parents to take away with them.
- Allow 'time out' if the meeting becomes heated. Consider the provision of tea/coffee if appropriate but remember that a hot drink could be used as a missile.
- Take notes of the meeting and any issues that are raised.
- Sum up the main points at the end of the meeting.
- Provide contact details of lead officers to parents.
- End on a positive note. If there are no further incidents there'll be no further action.
- Thank everyone for his/her attendance.

DON'T

- Behave in a confrontational manner but state any allegations calmly. Remember that the aim is not to accuse but to stop bad behaviour.
- Single out the families for all the problems in the area, if they are told that their children are one of a number of young people and others will also be interviewed, you will find that the parents more readily accept this and be prepared to work with you.
- Attempt to force the young person to sign the contract but **DO** explain why it is important and persuade them as far as possible.
- Worry if you have been unable to get a signature. This does not mean that the meeting has been a waste of time. Try to establish why there is a reluctance to sign, attempt to address their concerns and keep a record of their responses. It may be that they need time to think it over and you can suggest meeting again in a few days time. You do need to advise that we would like a signed contract as this demonstrates a commitment on their part to taking the issue seriously, and that if they still refuse to sign we can still pursue further action should the bad behaviour continue. This must be followed up in writing.
- Disclose details of complainants.

After the meeting

DO

- Complete the **Incident Record Book** straight after the interview. This is a very important document which will be used as evidence should further action be pursued.
- Copy the contract to social services, children and families team, where they know the young person. The police are responsible for sending a copy to the youth offending team.
- Notify patrolling police officers.
- Notify the estate services officers, other housing officers, housing assistants, senior caretaker and relevant caretakers that a contract has been drawn up and request assistance in monitoring further activities.
- Write to thank those present for their attendance and to confirm the outcome, attaching a further copy of the agreement. Advise who has been given copies of the contract. This will help to serve as a reminder of what the implications are should the young person carry out further anti-social acts.
- Monitor the contract for 6 months. If there is a further incident, regardless of how minor it may seem, you must bring this to the attention of the lead officer so that consideration can be given to any further action. This could range from sending a letter to reiterate the terms of the contract, to applying for a possession order or an anti-social behaviour order. **It is most important not to let a further incident pass by seemingly unnoticed.**
- Liaise with partner agencies if there is a report of a further incident or trouble on the estate. At very least monthly updates must be provided at meetings between police and housing officers. Officers should visit the young person with the contract, as part of the monitoring process, on at least two occasions within the six-month monitoring period. A written record of the outcome must be kept on file.
- Ensure that any further incidents are documented in the incident record book promptly.
- Write to the young person at the end of the 6 month period. In the letter acknowledge that the contract period has come to an end, thank them for keeping to the terms of the agreement and remind them of the implications should there be a repeat of the unacceptable behaviour in future.

DON'T

- Generally provide complainants (or others) with details of the young people with a contract, but **DO** publicise the fact that a number of young people within the area have signed a contract. This could act as a deterrent to others as well as encourage the reporting of incidents.

Housing Act 1985

CHAPTER 68

PART IV

SECURE TENANCIES AND RIGHTS OF SECURE TENANTS

82 Security of tenure

(1) A secure tenancy which is either—

App-019

(a) a weekly or other periodic tenancy, or
(b) a tenancy for a term certain but subject to termination by the landlord, cannot be brought to an end by the landlord except by obtaining an order [mentioned in subsection (1A)].[1]

[(1A) These are the orders—

(a) an order of the court for the possession of the dwelling-house;
(b) an order under subsection (3);
(c) a demotion order under section 82A.][2]

(2) Where the landlord obtains an order for the possession of the dwelling-house, the tenancy ends on the date on which the tenant is to give up possession in pursuance of the order.

(3) Where a secure tenancy is a tenancy for a term certain but with a provision for re-entry or forfeiture, the court shall not order possession of the dwelling-house in pursuance of that provision, but in a case where the court would have made such an order it shall instead make an order terminating the tenancy on a date specified in the order and section 86 (periodic tenancy arising on termination of fixed term) shall apply.

(4) Section 146 of the Law of Property Act 1925 (restriction on and relief against forfeiture), except subsection (4) (vesting in under-lessee), and any other enactment or rule of law relating to forfeiture, shall apply in relation to proceedings for an order under subsection (3) of this section as if they were proceedings to enforce a right of re-entry or forfeiture. [. . .][3]

1 Modified by Anti-social Behaviour Act 2003 (c.38), Pt 2, s.14(1).
2 Modified by Anti-social Behaviour Act 2003 (c.38), Pt 2, s.14(1).
3 Modified by Anti-social Behaviour Act 2003 (c.38), Pt 2, s.14(1).

82A Demotion because of anti-social behaviour

(1) This section applies to a secure tenancy if the landlord is—

App-020

(a) a local housing authority;
(b) a housing action trust;
(c) a registered social landlord.

(2) The landlord may apply to a county court for a demotion order.
(3) A demotion order has the following effect—

(a) the secure tenancy is terminated with effect from the date specified in the order;
(b) if the tenant remains in occupation of the dwelling-house after that date a demoted tenancy is created with effect from that date;

(c) it is a term of the demoted tenancy that any arrears of rent payable at the termination of the secure tenancy become payable under the demoted tenancy;

(d) it is also a term of the demoted tenancy that any rent paid in advance or overpaid at the termination of the secure tenancy is credited to the tenant's liability to pay rent under the demoted tenancy.

(4) The court must not make a demotion order unless it is satisfied—

(a) that the tenant or a person residing in or visiting the dwelling-house has engaged or has threatened to engage in conduct to which section 153A or 153B of the Housing Act 1996 (anti-social behaviour or use of premises for unlawful purposes) applies, and

(b) that it is reasonable to make the order.

(5) Each of the following has effect in respect of a demoted tenancy at the time it is created by virtue of an order under this section as it has effect in relation to the secure tenancy at the time it is terminated by virtue of the order—

(a) the parties to the tenancy;
(b) the period of the tenancy;
(c) the amount of the rent;
(d) the dates on which the rent is payable.

(6) Subsection (5)(b) does not apply if the secure tenancy was for a fixed term and in such a case the demoted tenancy is a weekly periodic tenancy.

(7) If the landlord of the demoted tenancy serves on the tenant a statement of any other express terms of the secure tenancy which are to apply to the demoted tenancy such terms are also terms of the demoted tenancy.

(8) For the purposes of this section a demoted tenancy is—

(a) a tenancy to which section 143A of the Housing Act 1996 applies if the landlord of the secure tenancy is a local housing authority or a housing action trust;

(b) a tenancy to which section 20B of the Housing Act 1988 applies if the landlord of the secure tenancy is a registered social landlord.[. . .]¹

1 Added by Anti-social Behaviour Act 2003 (c.38), Pt 2, s.14(2).

83 Proceedings for possession or termination: notice requirements

App-021   (1) The court shall not entertain proceedings for [an order mentioned in section 82(1A)]¹ unless—

(a) the landlord has served a notice on the tenant complying with the provisions of this section, or

(b) the court considers it just and equitable to dispense with the requirement of such a notice.

(2) A notice under this section shall—

(a) be in a form prescribed by regulations made by the Secretary of State,
(b) specify the ground on which the court will be asked to make [the order],² and
(c) give particulars of that ground.

(3) Where the tenancy is a periodic tenancy and the ground or one of the grounds specified in the notice is Ground 2 in Schedule 2 (nuisance or other anti-social behaviour), the notice—

(a) shall also—
    (i) state that proceedings for the possession of the dwelling-house may be begun immediately, and
    (ii) specify the date sought by the landlord as the date on which the tenant is to give up possession of the dwelling-house, and

(b) ceases to be in force twelve months after the date so specified.

(4) Where the tenancy is a periodic tenancy and Ground 2 in Schedule 2 is not specified in the notice, the notice—

(a) shall also specify the date after which proceedings for the possession of the dwelling-house may be begun, and

(b) ceases to be in force twelve months after the date so specified:

[(4A) If the proceedings are for a demotion order under section 82A the notice—

(a) must specify the date after which the proceedings may be begun;
(b) ceases to be in force twelve months after the date so specified.]³

(5) The date specified in accordance with subsection (3)[, (4) or (4A)]⁴ must not be earlier than the date on which the tenancy could, apart from this Part, be brought to an end by notice to quit given by the landlord on the same date as the notice under this section.

(6) Where a notice under this section is served with respect to a secure tenancy for a term certain, it has effect also with respect to any periodic tenancy arising on the termination of that tenancy by virtue of section 86; and subsections (3) to (5) of this section do not apply to the notice.

(7) Regulations under this section shall be made by statutory instrument and may make different provision with respect to different cases or descriptions of case, including different provision for different areas.[. . .]⁵

1 Modified by Anti-social Behaviour Act 2003 (c.38), Pt 2, s.14(3).
2 Modified by Anti-social Behaviour Act 2003 (c.38), Pt 2, s.14(3).
3 Modified by Anti-social Behaviour Act 2003 (c.38), Pt 2, s.14(3).
4 Modified by Anti-social Behaviour Act 2003 (c.38), Pt 2, s.14(3).
5 Modified by Anti-social Behaviour Act 2003 (c.38), Pt 2, s.14(3).

84 Grounds and orders for possession

(1) The court shall not make an order for the possession of a dwelling-house let under a secure tenancy except on one or more of the grounds set out in Schedule 2.   **App-022**

(2) The court shall not make an order for possession—

(a) on the grounds set out in Part I of that Schedule (grounds 1 to 8), unless it considers it reasonable to make the order,
(b) on the grounds set out in Part II of that Schedule (grounds 9 to 11), unless it is satisfied that suitable accommodation will be available for the tenant when the order takes effect,
(c) on the grounds set out in Part III of that Schedule (grounds 12 to 16), unless it both considers it reasonable to make the order and is satisfied that suitable accommodation will be available for the tenant when the order takes effect;

and Part IV of that Schedule has effect for determining whether suitable accommodation will be available for a tenant.

[(3) Where a notice under section 83 has been served on the tenant, the court shall not make such an order on any of those grounds above unless the ground is specified in the notice; but the grounds so specified may be altered or added to with the leave of the court.

(4) Where a date is specified in a notice under section 83 in accordance with subsection (3) of that section, the court shall not make an order which requires the tenant to give up possession of the dwelling-house in question before the date so specified.]¹

1 Substituted subject to savings specified in SI 1997/66 Sch.1 by Housing Act 1996 (c.52), Pt V, c II, s.147(2).

85 Extended discretion of court in certain

(1) Where proceedings are brought for possession of a dwelling-house let under a secure tenancy on any of the grounds set out in Part I or Part III of Schedule 2 (grounds 1 to 8 and 12 to 16: cases in which the court must be satisfied that it is reasonable to make a possession order), the court may adjourn the proceedings for such period or periods as it thinks fit.   **App-023**

(2) On the making of an order for possession of such a dwelling-house on any of those grounds, or at any time before the execution of the order, the court may—

(a) stay or suspend the execution of the order, or
(b) postpone the date of possession,

for such period or periods as the court thinks fit.

(3) On such an adjournment, stay, suspension or postponement the court—

(a) shall impose conditions with respect to the payment by the tenant of arrears of rent (if any) and rent or payments in respect of occupation after the termination of the tenancy (mesne profits), unless it considers that to do so would cause exceptional hardship to the tenant or would otherwise be unreasonable, and
(b) may impose such other conditions as it thinks fit.

(4) If the conditions are complied with, the court may, if it thinks fit, discharge or rescind the order for possession.

(5) Where proceedings are brought for possession of a dwelling-house which is let under a secure tenancy and—

(a) the tenant's spouse or former spouse, or civil partner or former civil partner, having home rights under Part IV of the Family Law Act 1996, is then in occupation of the dwelling-house, and
(b) the tenancy is terminated as a result of those proceedings,

the spouse or former spouse, or the civil partner or former civil partner, shall, so long as he or she remains in occupation, have the same rights in relation to, or in connection with, any adjournment, stay, suspension or postponement in pursuance of this section as he or she would have if those home rights were not affected by the termination of the tenancy.

(5A) If proceedings are brought for possession of a dwelling-house which is let under a secure tenancy and—

(a) an order is in force under section 35 of the Family Law Act 1996 conferring rights on the former spouse or former civil partner of the tenant or an order is in force under section 36 of that Act conferring rights on a cohabitant or former cohabitant (within the meaning of that Act) of the tenant,

(b) the former spouse, [former civil partner,]¹ cohabitant or former cohabitant is then in occupation of the dwelling-house, and

(c) the tenancy is terminated as a result of those proceedings,

the former spouse, former civil partner, cohabitant or former cohabitant shall, so long as he or she remains in occupation, have the same rights in relation to, or in connection with, any adjournment, stay, suspension or postponement in pursuance of this section as he or she would have if the rights conferred by the order referred to in paragraph (a) were not affected by the termination of the tenancy.

1 Words inserted by Civil Partnership Act 2004 (c.33), Sch.9 (2), para.18(3)(b).

85A Proceedings for possession: anti-social behaviour

App-024

(1) This section applies if the court is considering under section 84(2)(a) whether it is reasonable to make an order for possession on ground 2 set out in Part 1 of Schedule 2 (conduct of tenant or other person).

(2) The court must consider, in particular—

(a) the effect that the nuisance or annoyance has had on persons other than the person against whom the order is sought;

(b) any continuing effect the nuisance or annoyance is likely to have on such persons;

(c) the effect that the nuisance or annoyance would be likely to have on such persons if the conduct is repeated.[. . .]¹

1 Inserted subject to savings specified in SI 2004/2557, Sch.1, para.2 by Anti-social Behaviour Act 2003 (c.38), Pt 2, s.16(1).

Housing Act 1988

CHAPTER 50

PART I

RENTED ACCOMMODATION

CHAPTER I

ASSURED TENANCIES

Fixing of terms of statutory periodic tenancy

6.—(1) In this section, in relation to a statutory periodic tenancy,— **App-025**

   (a) "the former tenancy" means the fixed term tenancy on the coming to an end of which the statutory periodic tenancy arises; and

   (b) "the implied terms" means the terms of the tenancy which have effect by virtue of section 5(3)(e) above, other than terms as to the amount of the rent;

but nothing in the following provisions of this section applies to a statutory periodic tenancy at a time when, by virtue of paragraph 11 or paragraph 12 in Part 1 of Schedule 1 to this Act, it cannot be an assured tenancy.

(2) Not later than the first anniversary of the day on which the former tenancy came to an end, the landlord may serve on the tenant, or the tenant may serve on the landlord, a notice in the prescribed form proposing terms of the statutory periodic tenancy different from the implied terms and, if the landlord or the tenant considers it appropriate, proposing an adjustment of the amount of the rent to take account of the proposed terms.

(3) Where a notice has been served under subsection (2) above,—

   (a) within the period of three months beginning on the date on which the notice was served on him, the landlord or the tenant, as the case may be, may, by an application in the prescribed form, refer the notice to a rent assessment committee under subsection (4) below; and

   (b) if the notice is not so referred, then, with effect from such date, not falling within the period referred to in paragraph (a) above, as may be specified in the notice, the terms proposed in the notice shall become terms of the tenancy in substitution for any of the implied terms dealing with the same subject matter and the amount of the rent shall be varied in accordance with any adjustment so proposed.

(4) Where a notice under subsection (2) above is referred to a rent assessment committee, the committee shall consider the terms proposed in the notice and shall determine whether those terms, or some other terms (dealing with the same subject matter as the proposed terms), are such as, in the committee's opinion, might reasonably be expected to be found in an assured periodic tenancy of the dwelling-house concerned, being a tenancy—

   (a) which begins on the coming to an end of the former tenancy; and

   (b) which is granted by a willing landlord on terms which, except in so far as they relate to the subject matter of the proposed terms, are those of the statutory periodic tenancy at the time of the committee's consideration.

(5) Whether or not a notice under subsection (2) above proposes an adjustment of the amount of the rent under the statutory periodic tenancy, where a rent assessment committee determine

any terms under subsection (4) above, they shall, if they consider it appropriate, specify such an adjustment to take account of the terms so determined.

(6) In making a determination under subsection (4) above, or specifying an adjustment of an amount of rent under subsection (5) above, there shall be disregarded any effect on the terms or the amount of the rent attributable to the granting of a tenancy to a sitting tenant.

(7) Where a notice under subsection (2) above is referred to a rent assessment committee, then, unless the landlord and the tenant otherwise agree, with effect from such date as the committee may direct—

(a) the terms determined by the committee shall become terms of the statutory periodic tenancy in substitution for any of the implied terms dealing with the same subject matter; and

(b) the amount of the rent under the statutory periodic tenancy shall be altered to accord with any adjustment specified by the committee;

but for the purposes of paragraph (b) above the committee shall not direct a date earlier than the date specified, in accordance with subsection (3)(b) above, in the notice referred to them.

(8) Nothing in this section requires a rent assessment committee to continue with a determination under subsection (4) above if the landlord and tenant give notice in writing that they no longer require such a determination or if the tenancy has come to an end.

[6A Demotion because of anti-social behaviour

App-026

(1) This section applies to an assured tenancy if the landlord is a registered social landlord.

(2) The landlord may apply to a county court for a demotion order.

(3) A demotion order has the following effect—

(a) the assured tenancy is terminated with effect from the date specified in the order;

(b) if the tenant remains in occupation of the dwelling-house after that date a demoted tenancy is created with effect from that date;

(c) it is a term of the demoted tenancy that any arrears of rent payable at the termination of the assured tenancy become payable under the demoted tenancy;

(d) it is also a term of the demoted tenancy that any rent paid in advance or overpaid at the termination of the assured tenancy is credited to the tenant's liability to pay rent under the demoted tenancy.

(4) The court must not make a demotion order unless it is satisfied—

(a) that the tenant or a person residing in or visiting the dwelling-house has engaged or has threatened to engage in conduct to which section 153A or 153B of the Housing Act 1996 (anti-social behaviour or use of premises for unlawful purposes) applies, and

(b) that it is reasonable to make the order.

(5) The court must not entertain proceedings for a demotion order unless—

(a) the landlord has served on the tenant a notice under subsection (6), or

(b) the court thinks it is just and equitable to dispense with the requirement of the notice.

(6) The notice must—

(a) give particulars of the conduct in respect of which the order is sought;

(b) state that the proceedings will not begin before the date specified in the notice;

(c) state that the proceedings will not begin after the end of the period of twelve months beginning with the date of service of the notice.

(7) The date specified for the purposes of subsection (6)(b) must not be before the end of the period of two weeks beginning with the date of service of the notice.

(8) Each of the following has effect in respect of a demoted tenancy at the time it is created by virtue of an order under this section as it has effect in relation to the assured tenancy at the time it is terminated by virtue of the order—

(a) the parties to the tenancy;

(b) the period of the tenancy;

(c) the amount of the rent;

(d) the dates on which the rent is payable.

(9) Subsection (8)(b) does not apply if the assured tenancy was for a fixed term and in such a case the demoted tenancy is a weekly periodic tenancy.

(10) If the landlord of the demoted tenancy serves on the tenant a statement of any other express terms of the assured tenancy which are to apply to the demoted tenancy such terms are also terms of the demoted tenancy.

(11) For the purposes of this section a demoted tenancy is a tenancy to which section 20B of the Housing Act 1988 applies.][1]

1 Added by Anti-social Behaviour Act 2003 (c.38), Pt 2, s.14(4).

Orders for possession

7.—(1) The court shall not make an order for possession of a dwelling-house let on an assured   **App-027**
tenancy except on one or more of the grounds set out in Schedule 2 to this Act; but nothing in
this Part of this Act relates to proceedings for possession of such a dwelling-house which are
brought by a mortgagee, within the meaning of the [1925 c. 20.] Law of Property Act 1925, who
has lent money on the security of the assured tenancy.

(2) The following provisions of this section have effect, subject to section 8 below, in relation
to proceedings for the recovery of possession of a dwelling-house let on an assured tenancy.

(3) If the court is satisfied that any of the grounds in Part I of Schedule 2 to this Act is established then, subject to subsection (6) below, the court shall make an order for possession.

(4) If the court is satisfied that any of the grounds in Part II of Schedule 2 to this Act is established, then, subject to subsection (6) below, the court may make an order for possession if it considers it reasonable to do so.

(5) Part III of Schedule 2 to this Act shall have effect for supplementing Ground 9 in that
Schedule and Part IV of that Schedule shall have effect in relation to notices given as mentioned
in Grounds 1 to 5 of that Schedule.

(6) The court shall not make an order for possession of a dwelling-house to take effect at a time
when it is let on an assured fixed term tenancy unless—

 (a) the ground for possession is Ground 2 or Ground 8 in Part I of Schedule 2 to this Act or
     any of the grounds in Part II of that Schedule, other than Ground 9 or Ground 16; and
 (b) the terms of the tenancy make provision for it to be brought to an end on the ground in
     question (whether that provision takes the form of a provision for re-entry, for forfeiture,
     for determination by notice or otherwise).

(7) Subject to the preceding provisions of this section, the court may make an order for possession of a dwelling-house on grounds relating to a fixed term tenancy which has come to an end;
and where an order is made in such circumstances, any statutory periodic tenancy which has
arisen on the ending of the fixed term tenancy shall end (without any notice and regardless of the
period) on the day on which the order takes effect.

Notice of proceedings for possession

8.—(1) The court shall not entertain proceedings for possession of a dwelling-house let on an   **App-028**
assured tenancy unless—

 (a) the landlord or, in the case of joint landlords, at least one of them has served on the tenant
     a notice in accordance with this section and the proceedings are begun within the time
     limits stated in the notice in accordance with subsections (3) and (4) below; or
 (b) the court considers it just and equitable to dispense with the requirement of such a notice.

(2) The court shall not make an order for possession on any of the grounds in Schedule 2 to
this Act unless that ground and particulars of it are specified in the notice under this section; but
the grounds specified in such a notice may be altered or added to with the leave of the court.

(3) A notice under this section is one in the prescribed form informing the tenant that—

 (a) the landlord intends to begin proceedings for possession of the dwelling-house on one or
     more of the grounds specified in the notice; and
 (b) those proceedings will not begin earlier than a date specified in the notice which, without
     prejudice to any additional limitation under subsection (4) below, shall not be earlier than
     the expiry of the period of two weeks from the date of service of the notice; and
 (c) those proceedings will not begin later than twelve months from the date of service of the
     notice.

(4) If a notice under this section specifies, in accordance with subsection (3)(a) above, any of
Grounds 1, 2, 5 to 7, 9 and 16 in Schedule 2 to this Act (whether with or without other grounds),
the date specified in the notice as mentioned in subsection (3)(b) above shall not be earlier than—

 (a) two months from the date of service of the notice; and
 (b) if the tenancy is a periodic tenancy, the earliest date on which, apart from section 5(1)
     above, the tenancy could be brought to an end by a notice to quit given by the landlord
     on the same date as the date of service of the notice under this section.

(5) The court may not exercise the power conferred by subsection (1)(b) above if the landlord
seeks to recover possession on Ground 8 in Schedule 2 to this Act.

(6) Where a notice under this section—

 (a) is served at a time when the dwelling-house is let on a fixed term tenancy, or
 (b) is served after a fixed term tenancy has come to an end but relates (in whole or in part) to
     events occurring during that tenancy,

the notice shall have effect notwithstanding that the tenant becomes or has become tenant under
a statutory periodic tenancy arising on the coming to an end of the fixed term tenancy.

Extended discretion of court in possession claims

App-029   **9.**—(1) Subject to subsection (6) below, the court may adjourn for such period or periods as it thinks fit proceedings for possession of a dwelling-house let on an assured tenancy.

(2) On the making of an order for possession of a dwelling-house let on an assured tenancy or at any time before the execution of such an order, the court, subject to subsection (6) below, may—

(a)   stay or suspend execution of the order, or
(b)   postpone the date of possession,

for such period or periods as the court thinks just.

(3) On any such adjournment as is referred to in subsection (1) above or on any such stay, suspension or postponement as is referred to in subsection (2) above, the court, unless it considers that to do so would cause exceptional hardship to the tenant or would otherwise be unreasonable, shall impose conditions with regard to payment by the tenant of arrears of rent (if any) and rent or payments in respect of occupation after the termination of the tenancy (mesne profits) and may impose such other conditions as it thinks fit.

(4) If any such conditions as are referred to in subsection (3) above are complied with, the court may, if it thinks fit, discharge or rescind any such order as is referred to in subsection (2) above.

(5) In any case where—

(a)   at a time when proceedings are brought for possession of a dwelling-house let on an assured tenancy, the tenant's spouse or former spouse, having rights of occupation under the [1983 c. 19.] Matrimonial Homes Act 1983, is in occupation of the dwelling-house, and
(b)   the assured tenancy is terminated as a result of those proceedings,

the spouse or former spouse, so long as he or she remains in occupation, shall have the same rights in relation to, or in connection with, any such adjournment as is referred to in subsection (1) above or any such stay, suspension or postponement as is referred to in subsection (2) above, as he or she would have if those rights of occupation were not affected by the termination of the tenancy.

(6) This section does not apply if the court is satisfied that the landlord is entitled to possession of the dwelling-house—

(a)   on any of the grounds in Part I of Schedule 2 to this Act; or
(b)   by virtue of subsection (1) or subsection (4) of section 21 below.

[9A Proceedings for possession: anti-social behaviour
(1) This section applies if the court is considering under section 7(4) whether it is reasonable to make an order for possession on ground 14 set out in Part 2 of Schedule 2 (conduct of tenant or other person).

(2) The court must consider, in particular-

(a)   the effect that the nuisance or annoyance has had on persons other than the person against whom the order is sought;
(b)   any continuing effect the nuisance or annoyance is likely to have on such persons;
(c)   the effect that the nuisance or annoyance would be likely to have on such persons if the conduct is repeated.][1]

1   Inserted subject to savings specified in SI 2004/2557, Sch.1 para.2 by Anti-social Behaviour Act 2003 (c.38), Pt 2 s.16(2).

CHAPTER II

ASSURED SHORTHOLD TENANCIES

Assured shorthold tenancies

App-030   **20.**—(1) Subject to subsection (3) below, an assured shorthold tenancy is an assured tenancy—

(a)   which is a fixed term tenancy granted for a term certain of not less than six months; and
(b)   in respect of which there is no power for the landlord to determine the tenancy at any time earlier than six months from the beginning of the tenancy; and
(c)   in respect of which a notice is served as mentioned in subsection (2) below.

(2) The notice referred to in subsection (1)(c) above is one which—

(a)   is in such form as may be prescribed;
(b)   is served before the assured tenancy is entered into;
(c)   is served by the person who is to be the landlord under the assured tenancy on the person who is to be the tenant under that tenancy; and
(d)   states that the assured tenancy to which it relates is to be a shorthold tenancy.

(3) Notwithstanding anything in subsection (1) above, where—

(a) immediately before a tenancy (in this subsection referred to as "the new tenancy") is granted, the person to whom it is granted or, as the case may be, at least one of the persons to whom it is granted was a tenant under an assured tenancy which was not a shorthold tenancy, and

(b) the new tenancy is granted by the person who, immediately before the beginning of the tenancy, was the landlord under the assured tenancy referred to in paragraph (a) above,

the new tenancy cannot be an assured shorthold tenancy.

(4) Subject to subsection (5) below, if, on the coming to an end of an assured shorthold tenancy (including a tenancy which was an assured shorthold but ceased to be assured before it came to an end), a new tenancy of the same or substantially the same premises comes into being under which the landlord and the tenant are the same as at the coming to an end of the earlier tenancy, then, if and so long as the new tenancy is an assured tenancy, it shall be an assured shorthold tenancy, whether or not it fulfils the conditions in paragraphs (a) to (c) of subsection (1) above.

(5) Subsection (4) above does not apply if, before the new tenancy is entered into (or, in the case of a statutory periodic tenancy, takes effect in possession), the landlord serves notice on the tenant that the new tenancy is not to be a shorthold tenancy.

(6) In the case of joint landlords—

(a) the reference in subsection (2)(c) above to the person who is to be the landlord is a reference to at least one of the persons who are to be joint landlords; and

(b) the reference in subsection (5) above to the landlord is a reference to at least one of the joint landlords.

(7) Section 14 above shall apply in relation to an assured shorthold tenancy as if in subsection (1) of that section the reference to an assured tenancy were a reference to an assured shorthold tenancy.

22B Demoted assured shorthold tenancies

(1) An assured tenancy is an assured shorthold tenancy to which this section applies (a demoted assured shorthold tenancy) if—   **App-031**

(a) the tenancy is created by virtue of an order of the court under section 82A of the Housing Act 1985 or section 6A of this Act (a demotion order), and

(b) the landlord is a registered social landlord.

(2) At the end of the period of one year starting with the day when the demotion order takes effect a demoted assured shorthold tenancy ceases to be an assured shorthold tenancy unless subsection (3) applies.

(3) This subsection applies if before the end of the period mentioned in subsection (2) the landlord gives notice of proceedings for possession of the dwelling house.

(4) If subsection (3) applies the tenancy continues to be a demoted assured shorthold tenancy until the end of the period mentioned in subsection (2) or (if later) until one of the following occurs—

(a) the notice of proceedings for possession is withdrawn;

(b) the proceedings are determined in favour of the tenant;

(c) the period of six months beginning with the date on which the notice is given ends and no proceedings for possession have been brought.

(5) Registered social landlord has the same meaning as in Part 1 of the Housing Act 1996.[. . .]¹

---

1 Added by Anti-social Behaviour Act 2003 (c.38), Pt 2 s.15(1).

APPENDIX NINE

Housing Act 1996

CHAPTER 52

PART V

CONDUCT OF TENANTS CHAPTER IA
DEMOTED TENANCIES

General provisions

143A Demoted tenancies

App-032   (1) This section applies to a periodic tenancy of a dwelling-house if each of the following conditions is satisfied.

(2) The first condition is that the landlord is either a local housing authority or a housing action trust.

(3) The second condition is that the tenant condition in section 81 of the Housing Act 1985 is satisfied.

(4) The third condition is that the tenancy is created by virtue of a demotion order under section 82A of that Act.

(5) In this Chapter—

(a)   a tenancy to which this section applies is referred to as a demoted tenancy;
(b)   references to demoted tenants must be construed accordingly.[. . .]¹

1 Added by Anti-social Behaviour Act (2003 c.38), Sch.1, para.1.

143B Duration of demoted tenancy

App-033   (1) A demoted tenancy becomes a secure tenancy at the end of the period of one year (the demotion period) starting with the day the demotion order takes effect; but this is subject to subsections (2) to (5).

(2) A tenancy ceases to be a demoted tenancy if any of the following paragraphs applies—

(a)   either of the first or second conditions in section 143A ceases to be satisfied;
(b)   the demotion order is quashed;
(c)   the tenant dies and no one is entitled to succeed to the tenancy.

(3) If at any time before the end of the demotion period the landlord serves a notice of proceedings for possession of the dwelling-house subsection (4) applies.

(4) The tenancy continues as a demoted tenancy until the end of the demotion period or (if later) until any of the following occurs—

(a)   the notice of proceedings is withdrawn by the landlord;
(b)   the proceedings are determined in favour of the tenant;
(c)   the period of 6 months beginning with the date on which the notice is served ends and no proceedings for possession have been brought.

(5) A tenancy does not come to an end merely because it ceases to be a demoted tenancy.[. . .]¹

1 Added by Anti-social Behaviour Act (2003 c.38), Sch.1, para.1.

143C Change of landlord

(1) A tenancy continues to be a demoted tenancy for the duration of the demotion period if— **App-034**

(a) at the time the demoted tenancy is created the interest of the landlord belongs to a local housing authority or a housing action trust, and
(b) during the demotion period the interest of the landlord transfers to another person who is a local housing authority or a housing action trust.

(2) Subsections (3) and (4) apply if—

(a) at the time the demoted tenancy is created the interest of the landlord belongs to a local housing authority or a housing action trust, and
(b) during the demotion period the interest of the landlord transfers to a person who is not such a body.

(3) If the new landlord is a registered social landlord or a person who does not satisfy the landlord condition the tenancy becomes an assured shorthold tenancy.
(4) If the new landlord is not a registered social landlord and does satisfy the landlord condition the tenancy becomes a secure tenancy.
(5) The landlord condition must be construed in accordance with section 80 of the Housing Act 1985.[. . .]¹

1 Added by Anti-social Behaviour Act 2003 (c.38), Sch.1, para.1.

143D Proceedings for possession

(1) The landlord may only bring a demoted tenancy to an end by obtaining an order of the **App-035**
court for possession of the dwelling-house.
(2) The court must make an order for possession unless it thinks that the procedure under sections 143E and 143F has not been followed.
(3) If the court makes such an order the tenancy comes to an end on the date on which the tenant is to give up possession in pursuance of the order.[. . .]¹

1 Added by Anti-social Behaviour Act 2003 (c.38), Sch.1, para 1.

143E Notice of proceedings for possession

(1) Proceedings for possession of a dwelling-house let under a demoted tenancy must not be **App-036**
brought unless the landlord has served on the tenant a notice of proceedings under this section.
(2) The notice must—

(a) state that the court will be asked to make an order for the possession of the dwelling-house;
(b) set out the reasons for the landlord's decision to apply for the order;
(c) specify the date after which proceedings for the possession of the dwelling-house may be begun;
(d) inform the tenant of his right to request a review of the landlord's decision and of the time within which the request must be made.

(3) The date specified under subsection (2)(c) must not be earlier than the date on which the tenancy could (apart from this Chapter) be brought to an end by notice to quit given by the landlord on the same date as the notice of proceedings.
(4) The court must not entertain proceedings begun on or before the date specified under subsection (2)(c).
(5) The notice must also inform the tenant that if he needs help or advice—

(a) about the notice, or
(b) about what to do about the notice,

he must take the notice immediately to a Citizen's Advice Bureau, a housing aid centre, a law centre or a solicitor.[. . .]¹

1 Added by Anti-social Behaviour Act 2003 (c.38), Sch.1, para.1.

143F Review of decision to seek possession

(1) Before the end of the period of 14 days beginning with the date of service of a notice for **App-037**
possession of a dwelling-house let under a demoted tenancy the tenant may request the landlord to review its decision to seek an order for possession.
(2) If a request is made in accordance with subsection (1) the landlord must review the decision.

(3) The Secretary of State may by regulations make provision as to the procedure to be followed in connection with a review under this section.

(4) The regulations may include provision—

(a) requiring the decision on review to be made by a person of appropriate seniority who was not involved in the original decision;
(b) as to the circumstances in which the tenant is entitled to an oral hearing, and whether and by whom he may be represented at the hearing.

(5) The landlord must notify the tenant—

(a) of the decision on the review;
(b) of the reasons for the decision.

(6) The review must be carried out and notice given under subsection (5) before the date specified in the notice of proceedings as the date after which proceedings for possession of the dwelling-house may be begun.[. . .]¹

1 Added by Anti-social Behaviour Act 2003 (c.38), Sch.1, para.1.

143G Effect of proceedings for possession

App-038

(1) This section applies if the landlord has begun proceedings for the possession of a dwelling-house let under a demoted tenancy and—

(a) the demotion period ends, or
(b) any of paragraphs (a) to (c) of section 143B(2) applies (circumstances in which a tenancy ceases to be a demoted tenancy).

(2) If any of paragraphs (a) to (c) of section 143B(2) applies the tenancy ceases to be a demoted tenancy but the landlord (or the new landlord as the case may be) may continue the proceedings.

(3) Subsection (4) applies if in accordance with subsection (2) a tenancy ceases to be a demoted tenancy and becomes a secure tenancy.

(4) The tenant is not entitled to exercise the right to buy unless—

(a) the proceedings are finally determined, and
(b) he is not required to give up possession of the dwelling-house.

(5) The proceedings must be treated as finally determined if—

(a) they are withdrawn;
(b) any appeal is abandoned;
(c) the time for appealing expires without an appeal being brought. [. . .]¹

1 Added by Anti-social Behaviour Act 2003 (c.38), Sch.1, para.1.

143H Succession to demoted tenancy

App-039

(1) This section applies if the tenant under a demoted tenancy dies.

(2) If the tenant was a successor, the tenancy—

(a) ceases to be a demoted tenancy, but
(b) does not become a secure tenancy.

(3) In any other case a person is qualified to succeed the tenant if—

(a) he occupies the dwelling-house as his only or principal home at the time of the tenant's death,
(b) he is a member of the tenant's family, and
(c) he has resided with the tenant throughout the period of 12 months ending with the tenant's death.

(4) If only one person is qualified to succeed under subsection (3) the tenancy vests in him by virtue of this section.

(5) If there is more than one such person the tenancy vests by virtue of this section in the person preferred in accordance with the following rules—

(a) the tenant's [spouse or civil partner or (if the tenant has neither spouse nor civil partner)]¹ the person mentioned in section 143P(1)(b) is to be preferred to another member of the tenant's family;
(b) if there are two or more other members of the tenant's family the person preferred may be agreed between them or (if there is no such agreement) selected by the landlord.

1 Words substituted by Civil Partnership Act 2004 (c.33), Sch.8, para.55.

143I No successor tenant: termination

(1) This section applies if the demoted tenant dies and no person is qualified to succeed to the **App-040** tenancy as mentioned in section 143H(3).

(2) The tenancy ceases to be a demoted tenancy if either subsection (3) or (4) applies.

(3) This subsection applies if the tenancy is vested or otherwise disposed of in the course of the administration of the tenant's estate unless the vesting or other disposal is in pursuance of an order under—

  (a) section 23A or 24 of the Matrimonial Causes Act 1973 (property adjustment orders in connection with matrimonial proceedings);
  (b) section 17(1) of the Matrimonial and Family Proceedings Act 1984 (property adjustment orders after overseas divorce, etc);
  (c) paragraph 1 of Schedule 1 to the Children Act 1989 (orders for financial relief against parents)[;]¹
  [(d) Part 2 of Schedule 5, or paragraph 9(2) or (3) of Schedule 7, to the Civil Partnership Act 2004 (property adjustment orders in connection with civil partnership proceedings or after overseas dissolution of civil partnership, etc.).]1

(4) This subsection applies if it is known that when the tenancy is vested or otherwise disposed of in the course of the administration of the tenant's estate it will not be in pursuance of an order mentioned in subsection (3).

(5) A tenancy which ceases to be a demoted tenancy by virtue of this section cannot subsequently become a secure tenancy.

1 Added by Civil Partnership Act 2004 (c.33), Sch.8, para.56.

143J Successor tenants

(1) This section applies for the purpose of sections 143H and 143I. **App-041**

(2) A person is a successor to a secure tenancy which is terminated by a demotion order if any of subsections (3) to (6) applies to him.

(3) The tenancy vested in him—

  (a) by virtue of section 89 of the Housing Act 1985 or section 133 of this Act;
  (b) under the will or intestacy of the preceding tenant.

(4) The tenancy arose by virtue of section 86 of the Housing Act 1985 and the original fixed term was granted—

  (a) to another person, or
  (b) to him jointly with another person.

(5) He became the tenant on the tenancy being assigned to him unless—

  [(a) the tenancy was assigned—
     (i) in proceedings under section 24 of the Matrimonial Causes Act 1973 (property adjustment orders in connection with matrimonial proceedings) or section 17(1) of the Matrimonial and Family Proceedings Act 1984 (property adjustment orders after overseas divorce, etc.), or
     (ii) in proceedings under Part 2 of Schedule 5, or paragraph 9(2) or (3) of Schedule 7, to the Civil Partnership Act 2004 (property adjustment orders in connection with civil partnership proceedings or after overseas dissolution of civil partnership, etc.),
  (b) where the tenancy was assigned as mentioned in paragraph (a)(i), neither he nor the other party to the marriage was a successor, and
  (c) where the tenancy was assigned as mentioned in paragraph (a)(ii), neither he nor the other civil partner was a successor.]¹

(6) He became the tenant on an assignment under section 92 of the Housing Act 1985 if he himself was a successor to the tenancy which he assigned in exchange.

(7) A person is the successor to a demoted tenancy if the tenancy vested in him by virtue of section 143H(4) or (5).

(8) A person is the successor to a joint tenancy if he has become the sole tenant.

1 s.143J(5)(a)-(c) substituted for s.143J(5)(a)-(b) by Civil Partnership Act 2004 (c.33), Sch.8, para.57.

143K Restriction on assignment

(1) A demoted tenancy is not capable of being assigned except as mentioned in subsection (2). **App-042**

(2) The exceptions are assignment in pursuance of an order made under-

  (a) section 24 of the Matrimonial Causes Act 1973 (property adjustment orders in connection with matrimonial proceedings);

(b) section 17(1) of the Matrimonial and Family Proceedings Act 1984 (property adjustment orders after overseas divorce, etc.);
(c) paragraph 1 of Schedule 1 to the Children Act 1989 (orders for financial relief against parents)[;][1]
[(d) Part 2 of Schedule 5, or paragraph 9(2) or (3) of Schedule 7, to the Civil Partnership Act 2004 (property adjustment orders in connection with civil partnership proceedings or after overseas dissolution of civil partnership, etc.).]1

1 Added by Civil Partnership Act 2004 (c.33), Sch.8, para.58.

143L Right to carry out repairs

App-043   The Secretary of State may by regulations under section 96 of the Housing Act 1985 (secure tenants: right to carry out repairs) apply to demoted tenants any provision made under that section in relation to secure tenants. [. . .][1]

1 Added by Anti-social Behaviour Act 2003 (c.38), Sch.1, para.1.

143M Provision of information

App-044   (1) This section applies to a local housing authority or a housing action trust if it is the landlord of a demoted tenancy.
    (2) The landlord must from time to time publish information about the demoted tenancy in such form as it thinks best suited to explain in simple terms and so far as it considers appropriate the effect of—

(a) the express terms of the demoted tenancy;
(b) the provisions of this Chapter;
(c) the provisions of sections 11 to 16 of the Landlord and Tenant Act 1985 (landlord's repairing obligations).

    (3) The landlord must ensure that information published under subsection (2) is, so far as is reasonably practicable, kept up to date.
    (4) The landlord must supply the tenant with—

(a) a copy of the information published under subsection (2);
(b) a written statement of the terms of the tenancy, so far as they are neither expressed in the lease or written tenancy agreement (if any) nor implied by law.

    (5) The statement required by subsection (4)(b) must be supplied on the grant of the tenancy or as soon as practicable afterwards.[. . .][1]
1 Added by Anti-social Behaviour Act 2003 (c.38), Sch 1, para.1.

143N Jurisdiction of county court

App-045   (1) A county court has jurisdiction—

(a) to determine questions arising under this Chapter;
(b) to entertain proceedings brought under this Chapter;
(c) to determine claims (for whatever amount) in connection with a demoted tenancy.

    (2) The jurisdiction includes jurisdiction to entertain proceedings as to whether a statement supplied in pursuance of section 143M(4)(b) (written statement of certain terms of tenancy) is accurate.
    (3) For the purposes of subsection (2) it is immaterial that no relief other than a declaration is sought.
    (4) If a person takes proceedings in the High Court which, by virtue of this section, he could have taken in the county court he is not entitled to recover any costs. [. . .][1]

1 Repealed by Constitutional Reform Act 2005 (c.4), Sch.18(2), para.1.

143O Meaning of dwelling house

App-046   (1) For the purposes of this Chapter a dwelling-house may be a house or a part of a house.
    (2) Land let together with a dwelling-house must be treated for the purposes of this Chapter as part of the dwelling-house unless the land is agricultural land which would not be treated as part of a dwelling-house for the purposes of Part 4 of the Housing Act 1985.[. . .][1]

1 Added by Anti-social Behaviour Act 2003 (c.38), Sch.1, para.1.

143P Members of a person's family

(1) For the purposes of this Chapter a person is a member of another's family if—   App-047

(a) he is the spouse or civil partner of that person;
(b) he and that person live together as a couple in an enduring family relationship, but he does not fall within paragraph (c);
(c) he is that person's parent, grandparent, child, grandchild, brother, sister, uncle, aunt, nephew or niece.

(2) For the purposes of subsection (1)(b) it is immaterial that two persons living together in an enduring family relationship are of the same sex.
(3) For the purposes of subsection (1)(c)—

(a) a relationship by marriage[or civil partnership][1] must be treated as a relationship by blood;
(b) a relationship of the half-blood must be treated as a relationship of the whole blood;
(c) a stepchild of a person must be treated as his child.

1 Words inserted by Civil Partnership Act 2004 (c.33), Sch.8, para.59(3).

PART V

CONDUCT OF TENANTS

CHAPTER III

INJUNCTIONS AGAINST ANTI-SOCIAL BEHAVIOUR

153A Anti-social behaviour injunction

(1) This section applies to conduct—   App-048

(a) which is capable of causing nuisance or annoyance to any person, and
(b) which directly or indirectly relates to or affects the housing management functions of a relevant landlord.

(2) The court on the application of a relevant landlord may grant an injunction (an anti-social behaviour injunction) if each of the following two conditions is satisfied.
(3) The first condition is that the person against whom the injunction is sought is engaging, has engaged or threatens to engage in conduct to which this section applies.
(4) The second condition is that the conduct is capable of causing nuisance or annoyance to any of the following—

(a) a person with a right (of whatever description) to reside in or occupy housing accommodation owned or managed by the relevant landlord;
(b) a person with a right (of whatever description) to reside in or occupy other housing accommodation in the neighbourhood of housing accommodation mentioned in paragraph (a);
(c) a person engaged in lawful activity in or in the neighbourhood of housing accommodation mentioned in paragraph (a);
(d) a person employed (whether or not by the relevant landlord) in connection with the exercise of the relevant landlord's housing management functions.

(5) It is immaterial where conduct to which this section applies occurs.
(6) An anti-social behaviour injunction prohibits the person in respect of whom it is granted from engaging in conduct to which this section applies. [. . .][1]

1 Inserted subject to savings specified in SI 2004/2557, Sch.1, para.1 by Anti-social Behaviour Act 2003 (c.38), Pt 2, s.13(3).

153B Injunction against unlawful use of premises

(1) This section applies to conduct which consists of or involves using or threatening to use   App-049
housing accommodation owned or managed by a relevant landlord for an unlawful purpose.
(2) The court on the application of the relevant landlord may grant an injunction prohibiting the person in respect of whom the injunction is granted from engaging in conduct to which this section applies.[. . .][1]

1 Inserted subject to savings specified in SI 2004/2557, Sch.1, para.1 by Anti-social Behaviour Act 2003 (c.38), Pt 2, s.13(3).

153C Injunctions: exclusion order and power of arrest

App-050   (1) This section applies if the court grants an injunction under subsection (2) of section 153A or 153B and it thinks that either of the following paragraphs applies—

(a)   the conduct consists of or includes the use or threatened use of violence;
(b)   there is a significant risk of harm to a person mentioned in section 153A(4).

(2) The court may include in the injunction a provision prohibiting the person in respect of whom it is granted from entering or being in—

(a)   any premises specified in the injunction;
(b)   any area specified in the injunction.

(3) The court may attach a power of arrest to any provision of the injunction. [. . .]¹

1 Inserted subject to savings specified in SI 2004/2557 Sch.1 para.1 by Anti-social Behaviour Act 2003 (c.38), Pt 2, s.13(3).

153D Injunction against breach of tenancy agreement

App-051   (1) This section applies if a relevant landlord applies for an injunction against a tenant in respect of the breach or anticipated breach of a tenancy agreement on the grounds that the tenant—

(a)   is engaging or threatening to engage in conduct that is capable of causing nuisance or annoyance to any person, or
(b)   is allowing, inciting or encouraging any other person to engage or threaten to engage in such conduct.

(2) The court may proceed under subsection (3) or (4) if it is satisfied—

(a)   that the conduct includes the use or threatened use of violence, or
(b)   that there is a significant risk of harm to any person.

(3) The court may include in the injunction a provision prohibiting the person in respect of whom it is granted from entering or being in—

(a)   any premises specified in the injunction;
(b)   any area specified in the injunction.

(4) The court may attach a power of arrest to any provision of the injunction.
(5) Tenancy agreement includes any agreement for the occupation of residential accommodation owned or managed by a relevant landlord.[. . .]¹

1 Inserted subject to savings specified in SI 2004/2557, Sch.1, para.1 by Anti-social Behaviour Act 2003 (c.38), Pt 2, s.13(3).

153E Injunctions: supplementary

App-052   (1) This section applies for the purposes of sections 153A to 153D.
(2) An injunction may—

(a)   be made for a specified period or until varied or discharged;
(b)   have the effect of excluding a person from his normal place of residence.

(3) An injunction may be varied or discharged by the court on an application by—

(a)   the person in respect of whom it is made;
(b)   the relevant landlord.

(4) If the court thinks it just and convenient it may grant or vary an injunction without the respondent having been given such notice as is otherwise required by rules of court.
(5) If the court acts under subsection (4) it must give the person against whom the injunction is made an opportunity to make representations in relation to the injunction as soon as it is practicable for him to do so.
(6) The court is the High Court or a county court.
(7) Each of the following is a relevant landlord—

(a)   a housing action trust;
(b)   a local authority (within the meaning of the Housing Act 1985);
(c)   a registered social landlord.

(8) A charitable housing trust which is not a registered social landlord is also a relevant landlord for the purposes of section 153D.
(9) Housing accommodation includes—

(a) flats, lodging-houses and hostels;
(b) any yard, garden, outhouses and appurtenances belonging to the accommodation or usually enjoyed with it;
(c) in relation to a neighbourhood, the whole of the housing accommodation owned or managed by a relevant landlord in the neighbourhood and any common areas used in connection with the accommodation.

(10) A landlord owns housing accommodation if either of the following paragraphs applies to him—

(a) he is a person (other than a mortgagee not in possession) who is for the time being entitled to dispose of the fee simple in the premises, whether in possession or in reversion;
(b) he is a person who holds or is entitled to the rents and profits of the premises under a lease which (when granted) was for a term of not less than three years.

(11) The housing management functions of a relevant landlord include—

(a) functions conferred by or under any enactment;
(b) the powers and duties of the landlord as the holder of an estate or interest in housing accommodation.

(12) Harm includes serious ill-treatment or abuse (whether physical or not). [. . .]¹

1 Inserted subject to savings specified in SI 2004/2557, Sch.1, para.1 by Anti-social Behaviour Act 2003 (c.38), Pt 2, s.13(3).

154 Powers of arrest: ex-parte applications for injunctions

(1) In determining whether to exercise its power under section 153C(3) or 153D(4) to attach a power of arrest to an injunction which it intends to grant on an ex-parte application, the High Court or a county court shall have regard to all the circumstances including—   **App-053**

(a) whether it is likely that the applicant will be deterred or prevented from seeking the exercise of the power if the power is not exercised immediately, and
(b) whether there is reason to believe that the respondent is aware of the proceedings for the injunction but is deliberately evading service and that the applicant or any person of a description mentioned in section 153A(4) (as the case may be) will be seriously prejudiced if the decision as to whether to exercise the power were delayed until substituted service is effected.

(2) Where the court exercises its power as mentioned in subsection (1), it shall afford the respondent an opportunity to make representations relating to the exercise of the power as soon as just and convenient at a hearing of which notice has been given to all the parties in accordance with rules of court.]¹

1 Modified subject to savings specified in SI 2004/2557, Sch.1, para.1 by Anti-social Behaviour Act 2003 (c.38), Pt 2, s.13(4).

155 Arrest and remand

(1) If a power of arrest is attached to certain provisions of an injunction by virtue of [section 153C(3) or 153D(4)]¹, a constable may arrest without warrant a person whom he has reasonable cause for suspecting to be in breach of any such provision or otherwise in contempt of court in relation to a breach of any such provision.   **App-054**

A constable shall after making any such arrest forthwith inform the person on whose application the injunction was granted.

(2) Where a person is arrested under subsection (1)—

(a) he shall be brought before the relevant judge within the period of 24 hours beginning at the time of his arrest, and
(b) if the matter is not then disposed of forthwith, the judge may remand him.

In reckoning for the purposes of this subsection any period of 24 hours no account shall be taken of Christmas Day, Good Friday or any Sunday.

(3) If the court has granted an injunction in circumstances such that a power of arrest could have been attached under [section 153C(3) or 153D(4)]¹ but—

(a) has not attached a power of arrest under the section in question to any provisions of the injunction, or
(b) has attached that power only to certain provisions of the injunction,

then, if at any time the applicant considers that the respondent has failed to comply with the injunction, he may apply to the relevant judge for the issue of a warrant for the arrest of the respondent.

(4) The relevant judge shall not issue a warrant on an application under subsection (3) unless—

(a) the application is substantiated on oath, and
(b) he has reasonable grounds for believing that the respondent has failed to comply with the injunction.

(5) If a person is brought before a court by virtue of a warrant issued under subsection (4) and the court does not dispose of the matter forthwith, the court may remand him.

(6) Schedule 15 (which makes provision corresponding to that applying in magistrates' courts in civil cases under sections 128 and 129 of the Magistrates' Courts Act 1980) applies in relation to the powers of the High Court and a county court to remand a person under this section.

(7) If a person remanded under this section is granted bail by virtue of subsection (6), he may be required by the relevant judge to comply, before release on bail or later, with such requirements as appear to the judge to be necessary to secure that he does not interfere with witnesses or otherwise obstruct the course of justice.[. . .][1]

1 Modified subject to savings specified in SI 2004/2557, Sch.1, para.1 by Anti-social Behaviour Act 2003 (c.38), Pt 2, s.13(5).

156 Remand for medical examination and report

App-055   (1) If the relevant judge has reason to consider that a medical report will be required, any power to remand a person under section 155 may be exercised for the purpose of enabling a medical examination and report to be made.

(2) If such a power is so exercised the adjournment shall not be for more than 4 weeks at a time unless the judge remands the accused in custody.

(3) If the judge so remands the accused, the adjournment shall not be for more than 3 weeks at a time.

(4) If there is reason to suspect that a person who has been arrested—

(a) under section 155(1), or
(b) under a warrant issued under section 155(4),

is suffering from mental illness or severe mental impairment, the relevant judge shall have the same power to make an order under section 35 of the Mental Health Act 1983 (remand for report on accused's mental condition) as the Crown Court has under section 35 of that Act in the case of an accused person within the meaning of that section.

157 Powers of arrest: supplementary provisions

App-056   (1) If in exercise of its power under [section 153C(3) or 153D(4)][1] the High Court or a county court attaches a power of arrest to any provisions of an injunction, it may provide that the power of arrest is to have effect for a shorter period than the other provisions of the injunction.

(2) Any period specified for the purposes of subsection (1) may be extended by the court (on one or more occasions) on an application to vary or discharge the injunction.

(3) If a power of arrest has been attached to certain provisions of an injunction by virtue of [section 153C(3) or 153D(4)][1], the court may vary or discharge the injunction in so far as it confers a power of arrest (whether or not any application has been made to vary or discharge any other provision of the injunction).

(4) An injunction may be varied or discharged under subsection (3) on an application by the respondent or the person on whose application the injunction was made.[. . .][1]

1 Modified subject to savings specified in SI 2004/2557, Sch.1, para.1 by Anti-social Behaviour Act 2003 (c.38), Pt 2, s.13(6).

SCHEDULE 15

App-057   ARREST FOR ANTI-SOCIAL BEHAVIOUR: POWERS OF HIGH COURT AND COUNTY COURT TO REMAND

Introductory

1.—(1) The provisions of this Schedule apply where the court has power to remand a person under section 155(2) or (5) (arrest for breach of injunction, &c.).

(2) In this Schedule "the court" means the High Court or a county court and includes—

(a)   in relation to the High Court, a judge of that court, and
(b)   in relation to a county court, a judge or district judge of that court.

Remand in custody or on bail

2.—(1) The court may—

(a)   remand him in custody, that is, commit him to custody to be brought before the court at the end of the period of remand or at such earlier time as the court may require, or
(b)   remand him on bail, in accordance with the following provisions.

(2) The court may remand him on bail—

(a)   by taking from him a recognizance, with or without sureties, conditioned as provided in paragraph 3, or
(b)   by fixing the amount of the recognizances with a view to their being taken subsequently, and in the meantime committing him to custody as mentioned in sub-paragraph (1)(a).

(3) Where a person is brought before the court after remand, the court may further remand him.

3.—(1) Where a person is remanded on bail, the court may direct that his recognizance be conditioned for his appearance—

(a)   before that court at the end of the period of remand, or
(b)   at every time and place to which during the course of the proceedings the hearing may from time to time be adjourned.

(2) Where a recognizance is conditioned for a person's appearance as mentioned in sub-paragraph (1)(b), the fixing of any time for him next to appear shall be deemed to be a remand.

(3) Nothing in this paragraph affects the power of the court at any subsequent hearing to remand him afresh.

4.—(1) The court shall not remand a person for a period exceeding 8 clear days, except that—

(a)   if the court remands him on bail, it may remand him for a longer period if he and the other party consent, and
(b)   if the court adjourns a case under section 156(1) (remand for medical examination and report), the court may remand him for the period of the adjournment.

(2) Where the court has power to remand a person in custody it may, if the remand is for a period not exceeding 3 clear days, commit him to the custody of a constable.

Further remand

5.—(1) If the court is satisfied that a person who has been remanded is unable by reason of illness or accident to appear or be brought before the court at the expiration of the period for which he was remanded, the court may, in his absence, remand him for a further time.

This power may, in the case of a person who was remanded on bail, be exercised by enlarging his recognizance and those of any sureties for him to a later time.

(2) Where a person remanded on bail is bound to appear before the court at any time and the court has no power to remand him under sub-paragraph (1), the court may in his absence enlarge his recognizance and those of any sureties for him to a later time.

The enlargement of his recognizance shall be deemed to be a further remand.

(3) Paragraph 4(1) (limit of period of remand) does not apply to the exercise of the powers conferred by this paragraph.

Postponement of taking of recognizance

6. Where under paragraph 2(2)(b) the court fixes the amount in which the principal and his sureties, if any, are to be bound, the recognizance may afterwards be taken by such person as may be prescribed by rules of court, with the same consequences as if it had been entered into before the court.

Civil Procedure Rules
Part 65—Proceedings Relating to Anti-Social Behaviour and Harassment

Scope of this Part

App-058 65.1 This Part contains rules—

  (a) in Section I, about injunctions under the Housing Act 1996[1];
  (b) in Section II, about applications by local authorities under section 91(3) of the Anti-social Behaviour Act 2003[2] for a power of arrest to be attached to an injunction;
  (c) in Section III, about claims for demotion orders under the Housing Act 1985[3] and Housing Act 1988[4] and proceedings relating to demoted tenancies;
  (d) in Section IV, about anti-social behaviour orders under the Crime and Disorder Act 1998[5];
  (e) in Section V, about claims under section 3 of the Protection from Harassment Act 1997[6].

1 1996 c.52.
2 2003 c.38.
3 1985 c.68.
4 1988 c.50.
5 1998 c.37.
6 1997 c.40.
7 1996 c.52. These sections were inserted by section 13 of the Anti-social Behaviour Act 2003.

Scope of this Section and interpretation

App-059 65.2 (1) This Section applies to applications for an injunction and other related proceedings under Chapter III of Part V of the Housing Act 1996 (injunctions against anti-social behaviour).
  (2) In this Section 'the 1996 Act' means the Housing Act 1996.

Applications for an injunction

App-060 65.3 (1) An application for an injunction under Chapter III of Part V of the 1996 Act shall be subject to the Part 8 procedure as modified by this rule and the relevant practice direction.
  (2) The application must be—

  (a) made by a claim form in accordance with the relevant practice direction;
  (b) commenced in the court for the district in which the defendant resides or the conduct complained of occurred; and
  (c) supported by a witness statement which must be filed with the claim form.

  (3) The claim form must state—

  (a) the matters required by rule 8.2; and
  (b) the terms of the injunction applied for.

(4) An application under this rule may be made without notice and where such an application without notice is made—

    (a) the witness statement in support of the application must state the reasons why notice has not been given; and

    (b) the following rules do not apply—
        (i) 8.3;
        (ii) 8.4;
        (iii) 8.5(2) to (6);
        (iv) 8.6(1);
        (v) 8.7; and
        (vi) 8.8.

(5) In every application made on notice, the application notice must be served, together with a copy of the witness statement, by the claimant on the defendant personally.

(6) An application made on notice may be listed for hearing before the expiry of the time for the defendant to file an acknowledgement of service under rule 8.3, and in such a case—

    (a) the claimant must serve the application notice and witness statement on the defendant not less than two days before the hearing; and

    (b) the defendant may take part in the hearing whether or not he has filed an acknowledgment of service.

Injunction containing provisions to which a power of arrest is attached

65.4 (1) In this rule "relevant provision" means a provision of an injunction to which a power of arrest is attached.   **App-061**

(Sections 153C(3) and 153D(4) of the 1996 Act(7) confer powers to attach a power of arrest to an injunction)

(2) Where an injunction contains one or more relevant provisions—

    (a) each relevant provision must be set out in a separate paragraph of the injunction; and

    (b) subject to paragraph (3), the claimant must deliver a copy of the relevant provisions to any police station for the area where the conduct occurred.

(3) Where the injunction has been granted without notice, the claimant must not deliver a copy of the relevant provisions to any police station for the area where the conduct occurred before the defendant has been served with the injunction containing the relevant provisions.

(4) Where an order is made varying or discharging any relevant provision, the claimant must—

    (a) immediately inform the police station to which a copy of the relevant provisions was delivered under paragraph (2)(b); and

    (b) deliver a copy of the order to any police station so informed.

Application for warrant of arrest under section 155(3) of the 1996 Act[1]

65.5 (1) An application for a warrant of arrest under section 155(3) of the 1996 Act must be made in accordance with Part 23 and may be made without notice.   **App-062**

(2) An applicant for a warrant of arrest under section 155(3) of the 1996 Act must—

    (a) file an affidavit setting out grounds for the application with the application notice; or

    (b) give oral evidence as to the grounds for the application at the hearing.

1 1996 c.52. This section was amended by section 13 of the Anti-social Behaviour Act 2003.

Proceedings following arrest

65.6 (1) This rule applies where a person is arrested pursuant to—   **App-063**

    (a) a power of arrest attached to a provision of an injunction; or

    (b) a warrant of arrest.

(2) The judge before whom a person is brought following his arrest may—

    (a) deal with the matter; or

    (b) adjourn the proceedings.

(3) Where the proceedings are adjourned the judge may remand the arrested person in accordance with section 155(2)(b) or (5) of the 1996 Act.

(4) Where the proceedings are adjourned and the arrested person is released—

(a) the matter must be dealt with (whether by the same or another judge) within 28 days of the date on which the arrested person appears in court; and

(b) the arrested person must be given not less than 2 days' notice of the hearing.

(5) An application notice seeking the committal for contempt of court of the arrested person may be issued even if the arrested person is not dealt with within the period mentioned in paragraph (4)(a).

(6) CCR Order 29, rule 1 shall apply where an application is made in a county court to commit a person for breach of an injunction, as if references in that rule to the judge included references to a district judge.

(For applications in the High Court for the discharge of a person committed to prison for contempt of court see RSC Order 52, rule 8. For such applications in the county court see CCR Order 29, rule 3.)

Recognizance

App-064

65.7 (1) Where, in accordance with paragraph 2(2)(b) of Schedule 15 to the 1996 Act, the court fixes the amount of any recognizance with a view to it being taken subsequently, the recognizance may be taken by—

(a) a judge;

(b) a justice of the peace;

(c) a justices' clerk;

(d) a police officer of the rank of inspector or above or in charge of a police station; or

(e) where the arrested person is in his custody, the governor or keeper of a prison,

with the same consequences as if it had been entered into before the court.

(2) The person having custody of an applicant for bail must release him if satisfied that the required recognizances have been taken.

II Applications by Local Authorities for Power of Arrest to be Attached to an Injunction

Scope of this Section and interpretation

App-065

65.8 (1) This Section applies to applications by local authorities under section 91(3) of the Anti-social Behaviour Act 2003[1] for a power of arrest to be attached to an injunction.

(Section 91 of the 2003 Act applies to proceedings in which a local authority is a party by virtue of section 222 of the Local Government Act 1972[2] (power of local authority to bring, defend or appear in proceedings for the promotion or protection of the interests of inhabitants in their area)

(2) In this Section 'the 2003 Act' means the Anti-social Behaviour Act 2003.

1 2003 c.38.
2 1972 c.70.

Applications under section 91(3) of the 2003 Act for a power of arrest to be attached to any provision of an injunction

App-066

65.9 (1) An application under section 91(3) of the 2003 Act for a power of arrest to be attached to any provision of an injunction must be made in the proceedings seeking the injunction by—

(a) the claim form;

(b) the acknowledgment of service;

(c) the defence or counterclaim in a Part 7 claim; or

(d) application under Part 23.

(2) Every application must be supported by written evidence.

(3) Every application made on notice must be served personally, together with a copy of the written evidence, by the local authority on the person against whom the injunction is sought not less than 2 days before the hearing.

(Attention is drawn to rule 25.3(3)—applications without notice)

Injunction containing provisions to which a power of arrest is attached

App-067

65.10 (1) Where a power of arrest is attached to a provision of an injunction on the application of a local authority under section 91(3) of the 2003 Act, the following rules in Section I of this Part shall apply—

(a) rule 65.4; and
(b) paragraphs (1), (2), (4) and (5) of rule 65.6.

(2) CCR Order 29, rule 1 shall apply where an application is made in a county court to commit a person for breach of an injunction.

III DEMOTION CLAIMS, PROCEEDINGS RELATED TO DEMOTED TENANCIES AND APPLICATIONS TO SUSPEND THE RIGHT TO BUY

Scope of this Section and interpretation

App-068

65.11 (1) This Section applies to—

(a) claims by a landlord for an order under section 82A of the Housing Act 1985[1] or under section 6A of the Housing Act 1988[2] ('a demotion order');
(aa) claims by a landlord for an order under section 121A of the Housing Act 1985 ('a suspension order'); and
(b) proceedings relating to a tenancy created by virtue of a demotion order.

(2) In this Section—

(a) 'a demotion claim' means a claim made by a landlord for a demotion order;
(b) 'a demoted tenancy' means a tenancy created by virtue of a demotion order;
(c) 'suspension claim' means a claim made by a landlord for a suspension order; and
(d) 'suspension period' means the period during which the suspension order suspends the right to buy in relation to the dwelling house.

1 1985 c.68. This section was inserted by section 14 of the Anti-social Behaviour Act 2003.
2 1988 c.50. This section was inserted by section 14 of the Anti-social Behaviour Act 2003.

Demotion claims or suspension claims made in the alternative to possession claims

App-069

65.12 Where a demotion order or suspension order (or both) is claimed in the alternative to a possession order, the claimant must use the Part 55 procedure and Section I of Part 55 applies, except that the claim must be made in the county court for the district in which the property to which the claim relates is situated.

Other demotion or suspension claims

App-070

65.13 Where a demotion claim or suspension claim (or both) is made other than in a possession claim, rules 65.14 to 65.19 apply.

Starting a demotion or suspension claim

App-071

65.14 (1) The claim must be made in the county court for the district in which the property to which the claim relates is situated.
(2) The claim form and form of defence sent with it must be in the forms set out in the relevant practice direction.
(The relevant practice direction and Part 16 provide details about the contents of the particulars of claim)

Particulars of claim

App-072   65.15 The particulars of claim must be filed and served with the claim form.

Hearing date

App-073   65.16 (1) The court will fix a date for the hearing when it issues the claim form.
(2) The hearing date will be not less than 28 days from the date of issue of the claim form.

(3) The standard period between the issue of the claim form and the hearing will be not more than 8 weeks.
(4) The defendant must be served with the claim form and the particulars of claim not less than 21 days before the hearing date.
(Rule 3.1(2)(a) provides that the court may extend or shorten the time for compliance with any rule and rule 3.1(2)(b) provides that the court may adjourn or bring forward a hearing)

Defendant's response

App-074   65.17 (1) An acknowledgement of service is not required and Part 10 does not apply.
(2) Where the defendant does not file a defence within the time specified in rule 15.4 he may take part in any hearing but the court may take his failure to do so into account when deciding what order to make about costs.
(3) Part 12 (default judgment) does not apply.

The hearing

App-075   65.18 (1) At the hearing fixed in accordance with rule 65.16(1) or at any adjournment of that hearing the court may—

(a)   decide the claim; or
(b)   give case management directions.

(2) Where the claim is genuinely disputed on grounds which appear to be substantial, case management directions given under paragraph (1)(b) will include the allocation of the claim to a track or directions to enable it to be allocated.
(3) Except where—

(a)   the claim is allocated to the fast track or the multi-track; or
(b)   the court directs otherwise,

any fact that needs to be proved by the evidence of witnesses at a hearing referred to in paragraph (1) may be proved by evidence in writing.
(Rule 32.2(1) sets out the general rule about evidence. Rule 32.2(2) provides that rule 32.2(1) is subject to any provision to the contrary)
(4) All witness statements must be filed and served at least two days before the hearing.
(5) Where the claimant serves the claim form and particulars of claim, he must produce at the hearing a certificate of service of those documents and rule 6.14(2)(a) does not apply.

Allocation

App-076   65.19 When the court decides the track for the claim, the matters to which it shall have regard include—

(a)   the matters set out in rule 26.8; and
(b)   the nature and extent of the conduct alleged.

Proceedings relating to demoted tenancies

App-077   65.20 A practice direction may make provision about proceedings relating to demoted tenancies.

IV ANTI-SOCIAL BEHAVIOUR ORDERS UNDER THE CRIME AND DISORDER ACT 1998

Scope of this Section and interpretation

65.21 (1) This Section applies to applications in proceedings in a county court under sub-sections (2), (3) or (3B) of section 1B of the Crime and Disorder Act 1998([1]) by a relevant author-ity, and to applications for interim orders under section 1D of that Act. **App-078**

(2) In this Section—

(a) 'the 1998 Act' means the Crime and Disorder Act 1998;
(b) 'relevant authority' has the same meaning as in section 1(1A) of the 1998 Act; and
(c) 'the principal proceedings' means any proceedings in a county court.

1 1998 c.37. Sections 1(1A) and 1B were amended by section 85 of the Anti-social Behaviour Act 2003 (c.38).

Application where the relevant authority is a party in principal proceedings

65.22 (1) Subject to paragraph (2)— **App-079**

(a) where the relevant authority is the claimant in the principal proceedings, an application under section 1B(2) of the 1998 Act for an order under section 1B(4) of the 1998 Act must be made in the claim form; and
(b) where the relevant authority is a defendant in the principal proceedings, an applica-tion for an order must be made by application notice which must be filed with the defence.

(2) Where the relevant authority becomes aware of the circumstances that lead it to apply for an order after its claim is issued or its defence filed, the application must be made by application notice as soon as possible thereafter.

(3) Where the application is made by application notice, it should normally be made on notice to the person against whom the order is sought.

Application by a relevant authority to join a person to the principal proceedings

65.23 (1) An application under section 1B(3B) of the 1998 Act by a relevant authority which is a party to the principal proceedings to join a person to the principal proceedings must be made— **App-080**

(a) in accordance with Section I of Part 19;
(b) in the same application notice as the application for an order under section 1B(4) of the 1998 Act against the person; and
(c) as soon as possible after the relevant authority considers that the criteria in section 1B(3A) of the 1998 Act are met.

(2) The application notice must contain—

(a) the relevant authority's reasons for claiming that the person's anti-social acts are material in relation to the principal proceedings; and
(b) details of the anti-social acts alleged.

(3) The application should normally be made on notice to the person against whom the order is sought.

Application where the relevant authority is not party in principal proceedings

65.24 (1) Where the relevant authority is not a party to the principal proceedings— **App-081**

(a) an application under section 1B(3) of the 1998 Act to be made a party must be made in accordance with Section I of Part 19; and
(b) the application to be made a party and the application for an order under section 1B(4) of the 1998 Act must be made in the same application notice.

(2) The applications—

(a) must be made as soon as possible after the authority becomes aware of the principal pro-ceedings; and
(b) should normally be made on notice to the person against whom the order is sought.

Evidence

App-082 65.25 An application for an order under section 1B(4) of the 1998 Act must be accompanied by written evidence, which must include evidence that section 1E of the 1998 Act has been complied with.

Application for an interim order

App-083 65.26 (1) An application for an interim order under section 1D of the 1998 Act must be made in accordance with Part 25.

(2) The application should normally be made—

(a) in the claim form or application notice seeking the order; and
(b) on notice to the person against whom the order is sought.

V Proceedings Under the Protection from Harassment Act 1997

Scope of this Section

App-084 65.27 This Section applies to proceedings under section 3 of the Protection from Harassment Act 1997[1] ('the 1997 Act').

1 1997 c.40. I Housing Act 1996 Injunctions

Claims under section 3 of the 1997 Act

App-085 65.28 A claim under section 3 of the 1997 Act—

(a) shall be subject to the Part 8 procedure; and
(b) must be commenced—
   (i) if in the High Court, in the Queen's Bench Division;
   (ii) if in the county court, in the court for the district in which the defendant resides or carries on business or the court for the district in which the claimant resides or carries on business.

Applications for issue of a warrant of arrest under section 3(3) of the 1997 Act

App-086 65.29 (1) An application for a warrant of arrest under section 3(3) of the 1997 Act—

(a) must be made in accordance with Part 23; and
(b) may be made without notice.

(2) The application notice must be supported by affidavit evidence which must—

(a) set out the grounds for the application;
(b) state whether the claimant has informed the police of the conduct of the defendant as described in the affidavit; and
(c) state whether, to the claimant's knowledge, criminal proceedings are being pursued.

Proceedings following arrest

App-087 65.30 (1) The judge before whom a person is brought following his arrest may—

(a) deal with the matter; or
(b) adjourn the proceedings.

(2) Where the proceedings are adjourned and the arrested person is released—

(a) the matter must be dealt with (whether by the same or another judge) within 28 days of the date on which the arrested person appears in court; and
(b) the arrested person must be given not less than 2 days' notice of the hearing.

APPENDIX ELEVEN

The Magistrates' Courts (Anti-Social Behaviour Orders) Rules 2002[1]

SI 2002/2784

Made   *8th January 2002*
Laid before Parliament   *11th January 2002*
Coming into force   *2nd February 2002*

The Lord Chancellor, in exercise of the powers conferred upon him by section 144 of the Magistrates' Courts Act 1980[1], and after consultation with the rule committee appointed under that section, hereby makes the following Rules:

2. Citation, interpretation and commencement

—(1) These Rules may be cited as the Magistrates' Courts (Anti-Social Behaviour Orders) **App-088**
Rules 2002 and shall come into force on 2nd December 2002.

(2) In these Rules any reference to a numbered section is a reference to the section so numbered in the Crime and Disorder Act 1998[2], any reference to a "form" includes a form to like effect, and, unless otherwise stated, reference to a "Schedule" is a reference to a Schedule hereto.

3. Transitional Provisions

After these Rules come into force, rules 6 and 7 of, and Schedules 5 and 6 to the Magistrates' **App-089**
Courts (Sex Offender and Anti-Social Behaviour Orders) Rules 1998[3] shall (notwithstanding their revocation) continue to apply to proceedings commenced prior to the commencement of these Rules.

4. Forms

—(1) An application for an anti-social behaviour order shall be in the form set out in Schedule 1. **App-090**
(2) Any summons directed to the defendant requiring him to appear before a magistrates' court to answer such an application shall be in the form set out in Schedule 2.
(3) An anti-social behaviour order made under section 1 shall be in the form set out in Schedule 3.
(4) An order made under section 1C[4] on conviction in criminal proceedings shall be in the form set out in Schedule 4.
(5) An application for an interim anti-social behaviour order made under section 1D[5] shall be in the form set out in Schedule 5.
(6) An interim anti-social behaviour order made under section 1D shall be in the form set out in Schedule 6.

5. Interim Orders

—(1) An application for an interim order under section 1D, may, with leave of the justices' **App-091**
clerk, be made without notice being given to the defendant.

1 These Rules do not include amendments.

(2) The justices' clerk shall only grant leave under paragraph (1) of this rule if he is satisfied that it is necessary for the application to be made without notice being given to the defendant.

(3) If an application made under paragraph (2) is granted, then the interim order and the application for an anti-social behaviour order under section 1 (together with a summons giving a date for the defendant to attend court) shall be served on the defendant in person as soon as practicable after the making of the interim order.

(4) An interim order which is made at the hearing of an application without notice shall not take effect until it has been served on the defendant.

(5) If such an interim order made without notice is not served on the defendant within seven days of being made, then it shall cease to have effect.

(6) An interim order shall cease to have effect if the application for an anti-social behaviour order is withdrawn.

(7) Where the court refuses to make an interim order without notice being given to the defendant it may direct that the application be made on notice.

(8) If an interim order is made without notice being given to the defendant, and the defendant subsequently applies to the court for the order to be discharged or varied, his application shall not be dismissed without the opportunity for him to make oral representations to the court.

6. Application for variation or discharge

App-092
—(1) This rule applies to the making of an application for the variation or discharge of an order made under section 1, 1C or, subject to rule 5(8) above, 1D.

(2) An application to which this rule applies shall be made in writing to the magistrates' court which made the order, or in the case of an application under section 1C to any magistrates' court in the same petty sessions area, and shall specify the reason why the applicant for variation or discharge believes the court should vary or discharge the order, as the case may be.

(3) Subject to rule 5(8) above, where the court considers that there are no grounds upon which it might conclude that the order should be varied or discharged, as the case may be, it may determine the application without hearing representations from the applicant for variation or discharge or from any other person.

(4) Where the court considers that there are grounds upon which it might conclude that the order should be varied or discharged, as the case may be, the justices' chief executive shall, unless the application is withdrawn, issue a summons giving not less than 14 days' notice in writing of the date, time and place appointed for the hearing.

(5) The justices' chief executive shall send with the summons under paragraph 4 above a copy of the application for variation or discharge of the anti-social behaviour order.

7. Service

App-093
—(1) Subject to rule 5(3), any summons, or copy of an order or application required to be sent under these Rules to the defendant shall be either given to him in person or sent by post to the last known address, and, if so given or sent, shall be deemed to have been received by him unless he proves otherwise.

(2) Any summons, copy of an order or application required to be sent to the defendant under these Rules shall also be sent by the justices' chief executive to the applicant authority, and to any relevant authority whom the applicant is required by section 1E[6] to have consulted before making the application and, where appropriate, shall invite them to make observations and advise them of their right to be heard at the hearing.

8. Delegation by justices' clerk

App-094
—(1) In this rule, "employed as a clerk of the court" has the same meaning as in rule 2(1) of the Justices' Clerks (Qualifications of Assistants) Rules 1979[7].

(2) Anything authorised to be done by, to or before a justices' clerk under these Rules, may be done instead by, to or before a person employed as a clerk of the court where that person is appointed by the magistrates' courts committee to assist him and where that person has been specifically authorised by the justices' clerk for that purpose.

(3) Any authorisation by the justices' clerk under paragraph (2) shall be recorded in writing at the time the authority is given or as soon as practicable thereafter.

SCHEDULE 1

Rule 4(1)

FORM

Application for Anti-Social Behaviour Order (Crime and Disorder Act 1998, s.1(1)   **App-095**

Magistrates' Court
(Code)
Date:

Defendant:

Address:

Applicant Authority:

Relevant authorities consulted:

And it is alleged

(a)   that the defendant has acted on

[dates(s)] at [place(s)] in an anti-social manner, that is to say, in a manner that caused or was likely to cause harassment, alarm or distress to one or more persons not of the same household as himself; and

(b)   that an anti-social behaviour order is necessary to protect relevant persons from further anti-social acts by him, and accordingly application is made for an anti-social behaviour order containing the following prohibition(s): -

Short description of acts:

The complaint of:

Name of Applicant Authority:

Address of Applicant Authority:

who [upon oath] states that the defendant was responsible for the acts of which particulars are given above, in respect of which this complaint is made.

Taken [and sworn] before me
         Justice of the Peace
         [By order of the clerk of the court]

Rule 4(2)

SCHEDULE 2

FORM

App-096

Summons on Application for Anti-Social Behaviour Order (Crime and Disorder Act 1998, s.1)

Magistrates' Court
  (Code)
Date:

To the defendant:

[name]
Address:

You are hereby summoned to appear on

[date] at

before the magistrates' court at

to answer an application for an anti-social behaviour order, which application is attached to this summons.

Justice of the Peace

[By order of the clerk of the court]

NOTE: Where the court is satisfied that this summons was served on you within what appears to the court to be a reasonable time before the hearing or adjourned hearing, it may issue a warrant for your arrest or proceed in your absence.

If an anti-social behaviour order is made against you and if, without reasonable excuse, you do anything you are prohibited from doing by such an order, you shall be liable on conviction to imprisonment for a term not exceeding five years or to a fine, or to both.

Rule 4(3)

SCHEDULE 3

FORM

App-097

Anti-Social Behaviour Order (Crime and Disorder Act 1998, s.1)

Magistrates' Court
  (Code)
Date:

Defendant:

Address:

On the complaint of

Complainant: _____

Applicant Authority: _____

Address of Applicant Authority: _____

_____

The court found that:

(i) the defendant acted in the following anti-social manner, which caused or was likely to cause harassment, alarm or distress to one or more persons not of the same household as himself:

_____

And (ii) this order is necessary to protect persons

_____

from further anti-social acts by him.
And it is ordered that the defendant

_____

[NAME]
is prohibited from

_____

_____

_____

Until [_____

] [further order]
   Justice of the Peace
   [By order of the clerk of the court]

NOTE: If, without reasonable excuse, the defendant does anything which he is prohibited from doing by this order, he shall be liable on conviction to a term of imprisonment not exceeding five years or to a fine or to both.

SCHEDULE 4

Rule 4(4)

FORM

Order on Conviction (Crime and Disorder Act 1998, s.1C)

App-098

Magistrates' Court (Code)
1. On the _____

[date] the Magistrates' Court sitting at _____

convicted
Name: [defendant]
Address: _____

_____

Date of Birth:

_____

of
Offence(s)

_____

[relevant offence(s)]
and imposed the following sentence/conditional discharge

_____

_____

2. The court found that:
        (i) the defendant had acted in the following anti-social manner, which caused or was
        likely to cause harassment, alarm or distress to one or more persons not of the same
        household as himself,

_____

_____

[details of behaviour]
  and that

      (ii) an order was necessary to protect persons in England and Wales from further anti-social
acts by him.
3. It is ordered that the defendant

_____

[name] is prohibited from:

_____

_____

[Where appropriate, the court must specify whether any of the requirements of the order are suspended until the defendant's release from custody]

_____

Until [ ] [further order].
      Justice of the Peace
      [By order of the clerk of the court]

NOTE: If without reasonable excuse the defendant does anything which he is prohibited from
doing by this order, he shall be liable on conviction to a term of imprisonment not exceeding five
years or to a fine or to both.

Rule 4(5)   SCHEDULE 5

FORM

Application for an Interim Order

App-099   **(Crime and Disorder Act 1998, s.1D)**

_____

Magistrates' Court
(Code)

Date:	
Defendant:	
Address:	
Applicant Authority:	
Relevant Authorities Consulted:	
Reasons for applying for an interim order:	
Do you wish this application to be heard:	☐ without notice being given to the defendant
	☐ with notice being given to the defendant

If you wish the application to be heard without notice state reasons: -

The complaint of:

Address of Applicant Authority:

Who [upon oath] states that the information given above is correct.
Taken [and sworn] before me.
    Justice of the Peace
    [By order of the clerk of the court]
NOTE: This application must be accompanied by an application for an anti-social behaviour order (Crime and Disorder Act 1998, s.1).

SCHEDULE 6

FORM

Interim Order
(Crime and Disorder Act 1998, s.1D)

Rule 4(6)

App-100

Magistrates' Court
  (Code)

Date:	
Defendant:	
Address:	
On the complaint of	
Complainant:	
Applicant Authority	
Address of Applicant:	
Authority	

The court makes an Interim Anti-Social Behaviour Order against the defendant.
The reasons for making this order are

_____

And the court found that it is just to make this order pending the determination of the application for an anti-social behaviour order, which application is attached to this order.
This order has/has not been made without notice.
The court orders that the defendant is prohibited from

_____

_____

_____

Until [ ] [further order].
This order will end on

_____

The court also orders all parties to attend at

_____

on

_____

or/A hearing will take place in respect of the main application on
at

_____

A summons requiring your attendance at that hearing is attached.
    Justice of the Peace
    [Justices' Clerk]

NOTE: If, without reasonable excuse, the defendant does anything which he is prohibited from doing by this order, he shall be liable on conviction to a term of imprisonment not exceeding five years or to a fine or to both.

About this Order

This is an interim anti-social behaviour order. The court has made this order because it considers it just to do so pending the determination of an application for an anti-social behaviour order against you. The court believes that you have acted in an anti-social manner, and that this order is necessary to protect people from further anti-social acts by you. Anti-social behaviour is behaviour which caused or was likely to cause harassment, alarm or distress to people outside of your household.

    If, without reasonable excuse, you do anything which is prohibited by this order you will be guilty of an offence, for which you could be punished by a term of imprisonment or by a fine or by both.

    The order will end on the date specified unless a further order is made.

You may apply to the court to end or to vary this order. You should consult a solicitor or the court office to find out how to do this.

    You must attend court for the next hearing date, which is specified in the summons accompanying this order.

App-101
                                        EXPLANATORY NOTE

(This note is not part of the Rules)

These Rules provide forms in relation to anti-social behaviour orders and set out the procedure for applying for interim orders, or for variation or discharge of anti-social behaviour orders, and make provision for service.

    Section 1 of the Crime and Disorder Act 1998 enables certain "relevant authorities"—councils for local government areas, chief officers of police, British Transport Police and registered social landlords—to apply for anti-social behaviour orders. These orders can be made in relation to persons of the age of ten years or over if the court finds that they have acted in an anti-social manner and that the order is necessary to protect the public from further anti-social acts. Similar orders can be made by the court on its own initiative, under section 1C, after conviction in criminal proceedings, if it finds that the defendant has behaved in an anti-social manner.

    These Rules will come into force on 2nd December 2002.

1 1980 (c. 43).
2 1998 (c. 37). Relevant amendments were made by sections 61 to 66 of the Police Reform Act 2002 (c. 30).
3 SI 1998/2682 (L.10). Those Rules are revoked by the Magistrates' Courts (Sex Offender Orders) Rules S.I. 2002/2784 (L. 14).
4 Section 1C was inserted by section 64 of the Police Reform Act 2002.
5 Section 1D was inserted by section 65 of the Police Reform Act 2002.
6 Section 1E was inserted by section 66 of the Police Reform Act 2002.
7 SI 1979/570 as amended by SI 1998/3107, 1999/2814, and 2001/2269.

INDEX